Footprint Thailand

Andrew Spooner, Claire Boobbyer and Daemienne Sheehan

5th edition

"Arriving in Thailand is always a relief.
The taxis smell of flowers. The people are gracious.
Hedonism comes without guilt.
So what if people want your money. And if the
city is a little crass... Here the king plays jazz."

Ian Buruma, *God's Dust: a Modern Asian Journey* (1989)

❶ Chao Phraya River
Uncover the waterways and water lives of the Chao Phraya

❷ Grand Palace
Gaudy, over-blown and the heart of the nation

❸ Weekend Market
12 hectares, 8,672 stalls, 200,000 browsers – Thailand's largest market

❹ Ayutthaya
Ruins of a plundered former capital

❺ Sukhothai
Thailand's Golden Age reflected in this ancient ruined city

❻ Umphang
Some of the best trekking in Thailand

❼ Pai
Raft the Pai River for an adrenalin rush

❽ Mae Hong Son
Discover the 'other' Thailand of hill peoples and forested highlands

❾ Chiang Mai
Thailand's second city of monasteries, bazaars, great food and an anarchic Songkran festival

❿ Wat Phra That Lampang Luang
Elegant and refined, possibly the finest wat in Thailand

⓫ Nan/Wat Phumin
Century-old murals in an absorbing provincial town

Thailand Highlights

See colour maps at back of book

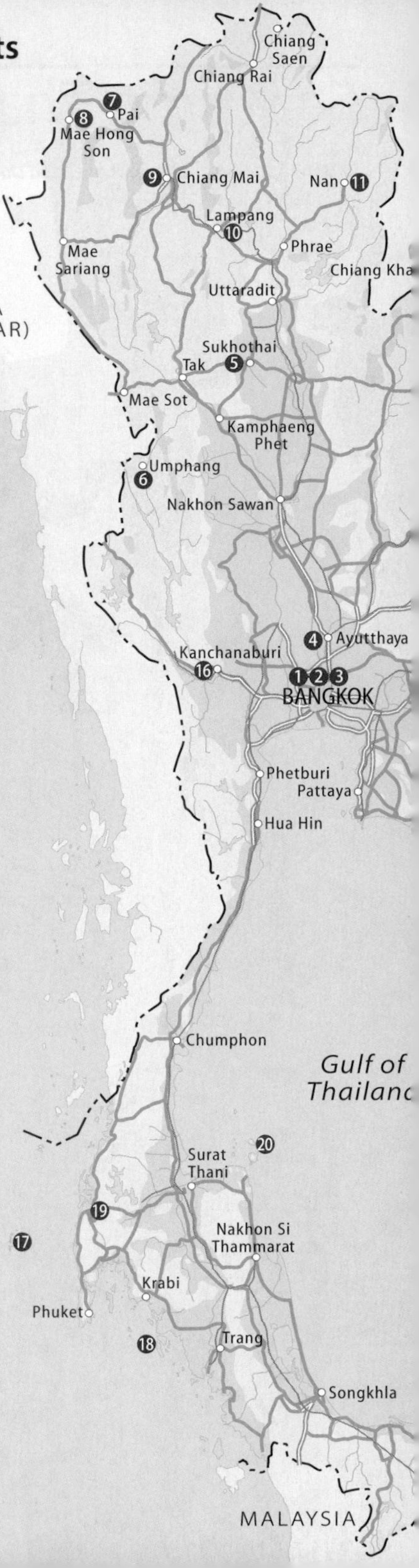

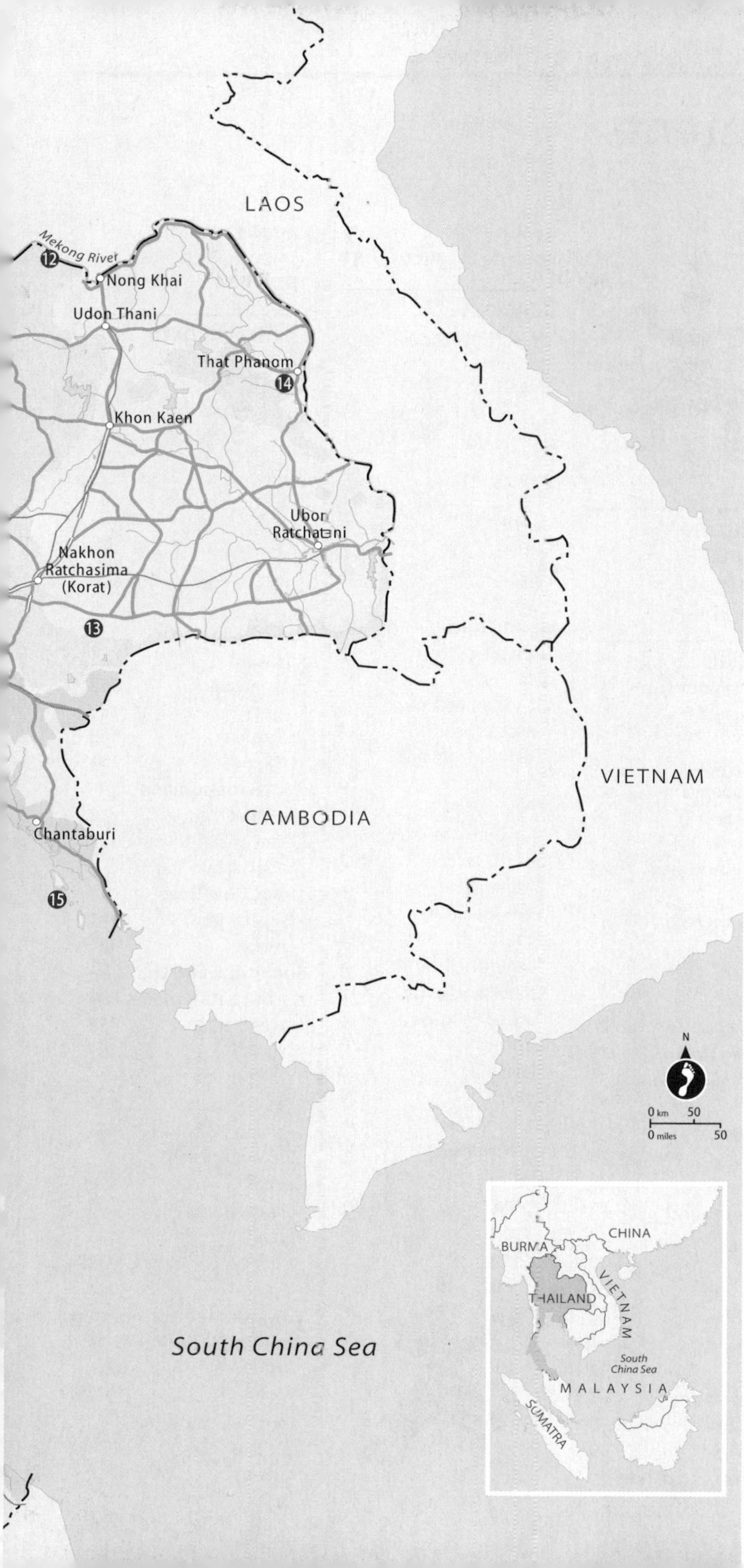

⓬ Mekong - Nong Khai/ Chiang Khan
Sip a cold beer, float on an inner tube, and imagine the enormous pla buk

⓭ Phnom Rung
Splendid 10th-13th century Khmer sanctuary

⓮ That Phanom
Visit in January or February to witness an exuberant display of Lao culture

⓯ Koh Chang
The least known of Thailand's large islands

⓰ Kanchanaburi
A dizzying combination of infamous history and marvellous natural history

⓱ Diving in the Similans
More species than a tropical rainforest – see a fraction here

⓲ Island hopping - Koh Lanta and other islands
Skip from palm-fringed to sun-dried to sea-lapped island

⓳ Khao Sok National Park
Trek, canoe and marvel in one of southern Thailand's finest parks

⓴ Samui/ Phangan/Tao
Phangan for parties, Tao for diving, Samui for everything else

Contents

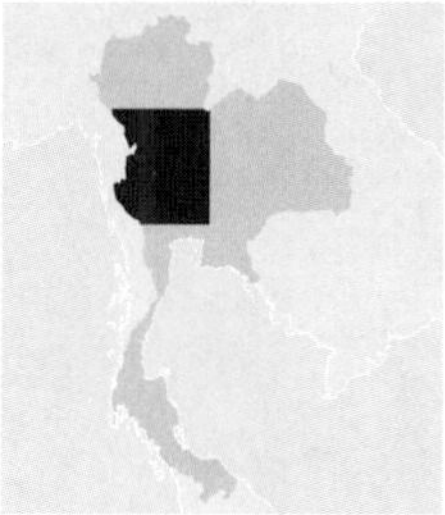

Northern Region

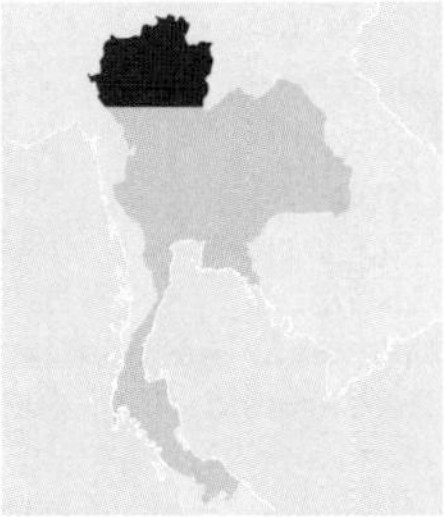

Northeastern Thailand

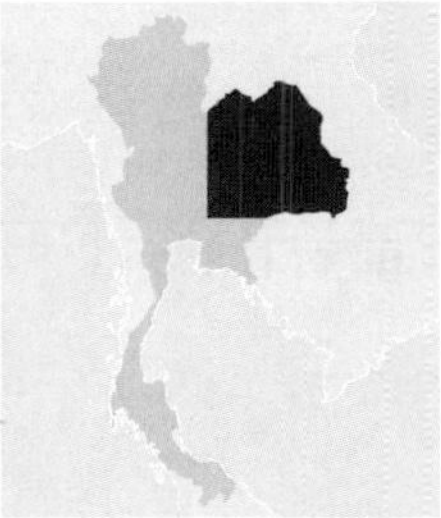

Eastern Region

Andaman Coast

Gulf of Thailand

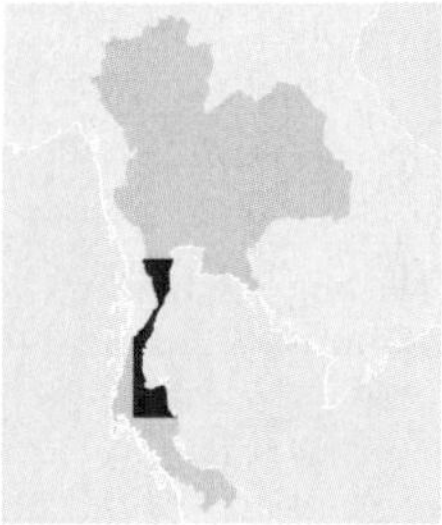

Background

Footnotes

Tropical isle
The dazzling azure waters of the Andaman Sea lap onto the shores of Maya Bay, Koh Phi Phi Le.

Contemplation
Buddha under Naga awaits deliverance in Bangkok.

A foot in the door

It doesn't take much to shatter an illusion. Take a ride in from Bangkok's airport along the Viphavadi Rangsit Highway and you'll understand why. The promise of soothing seas, ancient temples and wafting incense is replaced with an ocean of concrete, ultramodern skyscrapers and thick exhaust fumes. For many visitors, Bangkok, and its 12 million inhabitants, are too much – "we wanted monks and white sand and elephants", they probably wail. What they get is one of the most invigorating and modern cities on earth, an intense, overwhelming human hive that revels in its dynamism. Yet, if you take the time, you can find calm moments: the waft of jasmine as you walk through a back *soi*; an evening spent watching the city lights reflected in the Chao Praya River; a visit to the sanctity of one of Bangkok's stunning temples. Always remember that, whatever your expectations, you are going to be dumbfounded. The ancient Kingdom of Thailand is a proud and independent place that burns fiercely with the white heat of modernity while revering the links to its exotic past. Ancient Siam, authentic streetfood and gorgeous silks sit side by side with massive industry, a thick fug of traffic jams, fast food and seminal hi-tech. Get used to the idea that Thailand is rapidly becoming a highly advanced 21st-century society and you can then enjoy its other countless attractions with a hint of realism.

Why not start with the weird and wonderful? Grab a mouthful of cooked bugs off a street or watch *katoey* (transexual) kickboxing. If you prefer misty vistas shrouding antique temples then make for Sukhothai and Isaan. Or head for the 2500 km of coastline – the tourist fleshpots at Pattaya and Phuket or the isolated, verdant islands such as Koh Tarutao and the dive mecca of Koh Similan. There are national parks, too, hosting wild animals, deep jungles and fierce rivers, while the gentle mountainous north is home to an absorbing multi-ethnic society.

Sanuk and democracy

Buddhism is cast centre stage in Thailand. It has imbued Thai culture with compassion, continuity and genuine spiritual purpose. But that's only part of the story. Faith in Thailand is a movable feast encompassing animist spirit worship, traces of Hinduism and the consumer triumvirate of Nokia, Prada and Mercedes Benz. However, if you really want to get to the meat and potatoes of the story, the true, single faith of this extraordinary country is *sanuk*. Loosely translated as easy-going fun, *sanuk* is instilled throughout the entire circulatory system of Thai living. Everything should involve a sense of pleasure, a feeling of joy and celebration. Just try eating with the locals. Course after course of different, delicious and simultaneous flavours – spicy, sweet and succulently sour – are washed down with yards of beer. Raucous and sinful clubs, discos and karaokes, where harsh Thai whisky flows freely, are found in just about every village and town. Colour, verve and confidence are painted into the foundations of this society; the backs of buses, shrines and taxis, flower markets, bars and clothes stalls are all redolent with one of the gaudiest and most vibrant cultures on earth.

But when they're not having fun, what are the Thais doing? The struggle for democracy has been long and hard here. Numerous massacres have marked each bloody step on the route to having the right to elect

Entertainment emporium
The bright lights, bars and action of Soi Nana pull in nighttime crowds.

a government. And even when that right is enshrined, corruption, state violence and vote-buying still persist.

In 2003 several thousand 'drug dealers' were summarily executed without trial or arrest. And 2004 saw the present wave of hostilities develop in Thailand's restive and Muslim south, with a notorious massacre of prisoners at Tak Bai inflaming a volatile situation.

The present government of Thaksin Shinawatra is both authoritarian and, for the first time in Thailand's history, genuinely re-distributive. It has set up projects for the poor and attempted to establish universal health care. But Thaksin, re-elected in a massive landslide in February 2005, is seen by many commentators to trample on the hard-fought-for constitution and to sail very close to the wind of corruption. He has been lauded for his response to the December 2004 tsunami and then, in turn, criticized for focusing funds on re-starting the badly affected tourist industry while leaving poor villagers to fend for themselves.

That Thailand can be both compassionate and vengeful, fun-loving and harsh, tolerant and rigid is hard for many to grasp. That a country can house both the sanctuary of its gorgeous forests, the simple lifestyles of Isaan peasants, the pleasure of massage, sea and sand with the chaotic, wild brutality of Bangkok says all you need to know. Welcome to Thailand and, like the locals, wherever you find yourself, don't forget to smile.

Rice riches
Terraced paddy fields form the archetypal landscape in nortnern Thailand.

1

2

4

5

7

8

10

11

3

6

9

12

1 *The beautiful and fragrant frangipani is found all over Thailand. Its blossom is used for decoration and its smell often perfumes gardens and spas. ▸▸ See page 547.*

2 *The infamous Bridge over the River Kwai near Kanchanaburi was built by Allied Prisoners of War and Asians in 16 months in the 1940s. ▸▸ See page 177.*

3 *Intricately detailed shadow puppets are made from cow hide and then mounted on a bamboo stick. ▸▸ See page 608.*

4 *The monkey god Hanuman, trusted companion of Seeda, wife of Rama, King of Ayodhia, in the epic story Ramakien, supports the temple buildings of the Grand Palace and Wat Phra Kaeo compound in Bangkok. ▸▸ See page 93.*

5 *Powder blue surgeonfish colour the tropical seas around Thailand. ▸▸ See page 413.*

6 *Prayer flower beads hang in Pattaya. ▸▸ See page 377.*

7 *The dusky langur is a rare breed. It can be found in Khao Sam Roi Yod National Park and around Ao Phra Nang near Krabi. ▸▸ See page 542 and 475.*

8 *Female statues are sold at the market in Chiang Mai, one of the busiest and most popular in Thailand. ▸▸ See page 230.*

9 *The elephant is the national symbol of Thailand. Elephant treks are possible around much of the country. ▸▸ See page 68.*

10 *Koh Samui is a tropical paradise island full of great beaches, wonderful spas, chic resorts, cute beach bungalows and some very fine restaurants. ▸▸ See page 561.*

11 *The amazing-looking rhinoceros hornbill lives in Khao Yai National Park, although its natural habitat is threatened across Southeast Asia. ▸▸ See page 314.*

12 *The prehistoric man of Krabi guards the town's traffic lights in a bizarre memorial to the town's history. ▸▸ See page 458.*

The Lisu wear some of the most colourful and distinctive clothing in the north. New Year is an occasion when villagers dress up in all their finery. *See page 260.*

Paradise found

The country's beaches and islands are tempting to all, regardless of budget or lifestyle. For a quiet bungalow and hammock, framed with palms and lit with oil lamps, try one of the Tarutao islands in the Andaman Sea, or the quieter coves of Koh Phangan or Koh Tao. If you prefer your beach break to be accompanied by nightlife and good restaurants, head for Koh Samui, Phuket and Hat Rin on Koh Phangan. For an alternative to sunbathing, the country's spas, with an array of indulgent treatments, are an attraction worth seeking out. So is the vibrancy of life, colour and species of Thailand's underwater kingdom. The protected environments of Ang Thong, the Similan Islands and Koh Chang reveal a marine heaven. On land, forests, caves, wetlands and mountains teem with life; waterfalls drench the dense rainforest and rivers swerve around harsh limestone cliffs.

Hill tribes of the north

This is another Thailand and sometimes it can seem like another age too. An age when people lived distinctive, coherent lives untrammelled by the homogenizing forces of globalization. Taking the time to trek through the hills and forests of the north, rafting down its rivers and staying with the ethnic minorities are the highlights of many visitors' stay. Lives are moulded by the seasons and the demands of farming and world views have as much to do with ancient beliefs and outlooks as they have with modernity.

Reality bites

A few years ago, Thai food was tricky to track down outside Thailand. Now it's everywhere. But even if you regard yourself as something of an expert (and haven't been to Thailand before), expect to be surprised by the range, quality and sheer exuberance of the home-grown real thing. From sophisticated royal cuisine to simple noodle and rice-based dishes sold from roadside stalls for just a few baht, the Thais take their food very, very seriously. Even the simplest meals are prepared with love and commitment. The major regions of Thailand have their own distinct cuisines, and individual towns their special dishes.

Buddhism

While there may be significant populations of Muslims in the south and Christians in the north, adherence to Buddhism is viewed by many Thais as a defining characteristic of Thai-ness. The most visible sign of Buddhism in Thailand are its wats. A wat is a place of worship, refuge, meeting, healing and teaching. It is, for many villages, the heart and soul of the community. Men aspire to be ordained for at least a period in their lives and, in the past, women would be chary of marrying a man who had not been ordained, viewing him as dip or 'raw'. While some modern wats, to the western eye at least, may seem garish and gaudy, older monasteries are often beautiful with their sweeping tiled roofs, carved teak pillars, somnolent Buddha images and peaceful cloisters.

Most of the country's festivals are ostensibly Buddhist, although many are also spiced with animism and Brahmanism. Perhaps the loveliest is *loi krathong*, held during November's full moon. Model rafts fashioned from banana leaves in the shape of a lotus and carrying a candle, incense, flowers and a coin are pushed out on to rivers, canals and lakes across the kingdom. Dating from the 14th-century Sukhothai period, the boats are said to symbolize the washing away of the past year's sins and heartaches. The most exuberant festival is undoubtedly *songkran* which marks the end of the dry season. This festival began as a celebration of natural bounty; Buddha images would be bathed in lustral water and, as a mark of respect, monks and the elderly would also be sprinkled with water.

Wat Phrathat on Doi Suthep, Chiang Mai, is a popular pilgrimage spot for Thais. See page 231.

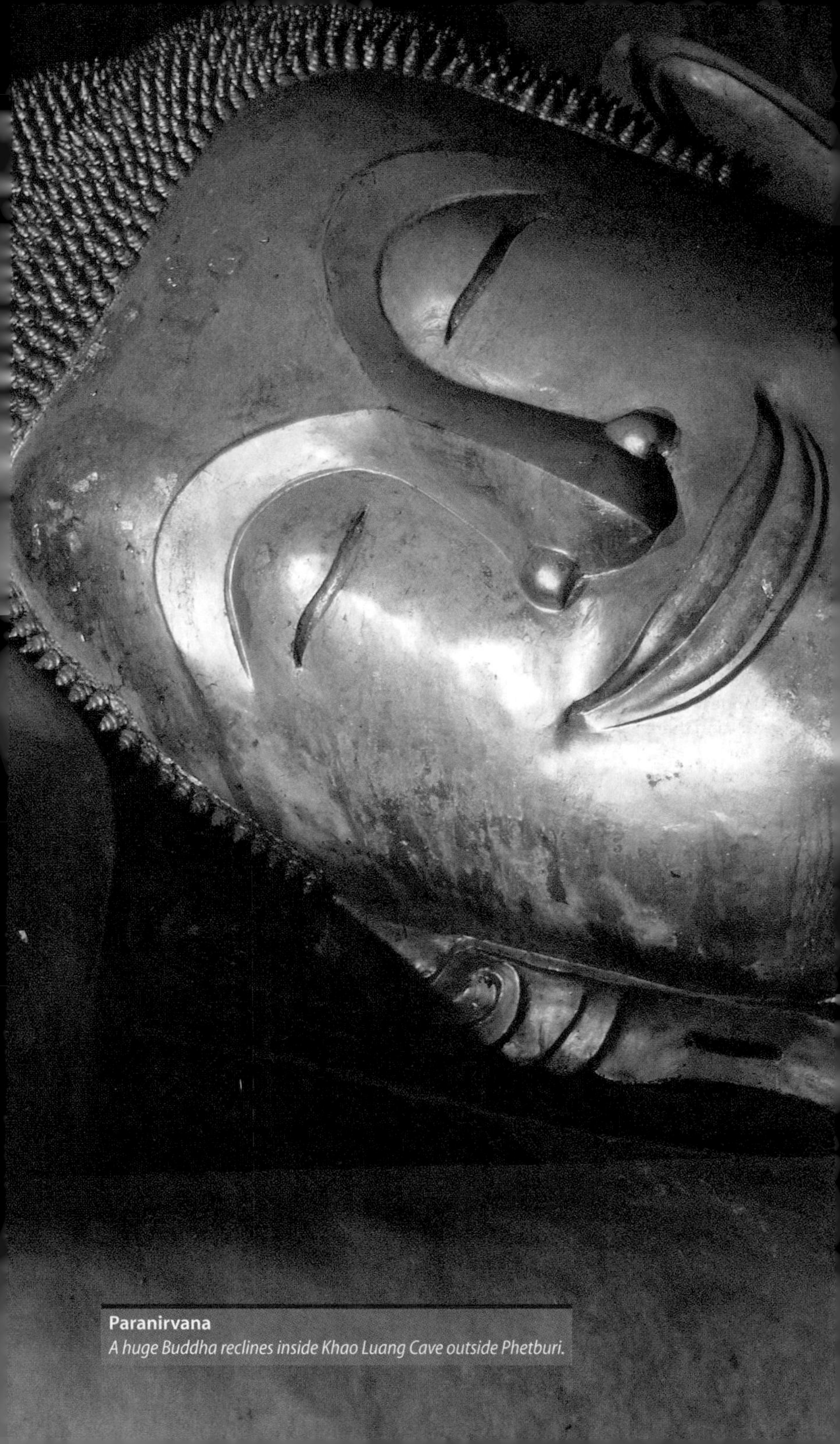

Paranirvana
A huge Buddha reclines inside Khao Luang Cave outside Phetburi.

Essentials

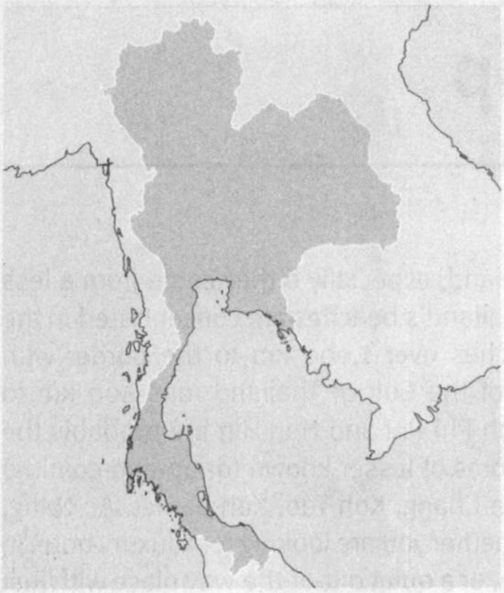

Footprint features

Planning your trip

Where to go

Top of the list for many people visiting Thailand, especially if they come from a less than tropical country, is a beach. Most of Thailand's beaches are concentrated in the south and east. The southern coast stretches over 1,000 km to the border with Malaysia while the eastern coastal fringe of the Gulf of Thailand runs 400 km to Cambodia. Pattaya, Phuket, Koh Samui, Koh Phi Phi and Hua Hin are probably the best-known beach resorts, but there are scores of lesser-known (or up-and-coming) islands and stretches of sand including Koh Chang, Koh Tao, Koh Samet, Ao Nang, Trang's Andaman Islands and Koh Lanta. Whether you are looking for a luxury hotel in a resort with nightlife and restaurants galore, or a quiet out-of-the-way place with just a handful of 'A' frame huts a few steps from the sea, it is here to be found.

Combining a stretch by the sea with a trek in the hills of the north is popular. The unofficial capital of the north is Chiang Mai. The hill peoples of this region, with their distinctive material and non-material cultures, their characteristic livelihoods and lifestyles, provide a vivid counterpoint to the lowland Thais.

The central plains are the heartland of the Thai nation. This is the site of the glorious former capitals of Sukhothai, Si Satchanalai and Ayutthaya. To the west of the central plains, en route to the border with Burma, is Kanchanaburi, site of the infamous bridge over the River Kwai. the northeast, the forgotten corner of Thailand, is the least visited region of the country. Poor and environmentally harsh, it was formerly part of the Khmer empire that built Angkor Wat in neighbouring Cambodia. In the northeast the Khmer have left their mark in the ruins of Phimai, Phnom Rung, Muang Tam and many other temples and towers. The Mekong River, which skirts the northern and eastern edges of the region and forms the border with Laos, also attracts visitors.

Most visitors begin their stay in Thailand in Bangkok. The capital has a poor reputation for pollution and congestion but it's not just an urban nightmare. The city has impressive historical sights, the canals which gave it the label (along with several other cities in Asia) 'Venice of the East', great food, a throbbing nightlife and good shopping.

Tailoring a visit

Thailand is about the size of France so don't expect to be able to see every corner in the space of a fortnight, or a month, or even a year. We have tried to highlight the 'highpoints' of many people's visits, but are mindful that two weeks in a monastery eating simple vegetarian dishes and learning to meditate will appeal to some while a sandy beach, getting a thrill from dangling from a rope half way up a cliff face, or examining some Khmer monument, appeals to others. With this in mind, while we outline what might be called the Thai Classic Tour, we have also provided a range of ideas for exploration.

See also Sport and activities, page 60.

The two-week Thai Classic The classic two-week jaunt to Thailand consists of two to four days in Bangkok, three to four days in the north and the remainder on a beach in the South. This means that the visitor gets to see the historic sights of the capital, comes face-to-face with the country's hill peoples, and then manages to catch a tan. Of course this two-week tour is endlessly expandable to three, four, five or more weeks.

The art and culture lover The historic high points must be the Khmer monuments of the northeast and the ancient capitals of the central plains (Ayutthaya, Sukhothai

Tourism Authority Thailand's overseas offices

Australia, 2nd floor, 75 Pitt Street, Sydney, NSW 2000, T9247-7549, F9251-2465, info@Thailand.net.au.
France, 90 Avenue des Champs Elysées, 75008 Paris, T5353-4700, F4563-7888, tatpar@wanadoo.fr.
Germany, Bethmannstr 58, D-6011, Frankfurt/Main 1, T69-381390, F69-13813950, info@thailandtourismus.de.
Hong Kong, 1601 Fairmont House, 8 Cotton Tree Drive, Central, T2868-0732, F2868-4585, tathkg@pacific.net.hk.net.
Italy, 4th floor, Via Barberini 68, 00187 Roma, T06-42014422, F06-4873500.
Japan, Yurakucho Denki Building, South Tower 2F, Room 259, 1-7-1, Yurakucho, Chiyoda-ku, Tokyo 100-0006, T03-218-0337, F03-218-0655, tattky@tattky.com.
Malaysia, Suite 22.01, level 22, Menara Citibank, 165 Jl Ampang, Kuala Lumpur, T216-23480, F216-23486, sawatdi@po.jaring.my.
Singapore, c/o Royal Thai Embassy, 370 Orchard Road, Singapore 238870, T2357901, F7335653, tatsin@singnet.com.sg.
UK, 3rd floor, Brook House, 98-99 Jermyn Street, London SW1Y 6EE, T020-7925 2511, F020-7925 2512, info@thaismile.co.uk.
USA, 1st floor, 611 North Larchmont Boulevard, Los Angeles, CA 90004, T461-9814, F461-9834, tatla@ix.netcom.com.

and Si Satchanalai). Bangkok has the Grand Palace and just about every town has its own monastery or wat – some very beautiful indeed. The major festivals – like **Songkran** – are celebrated across the country, others are unique to particular areas or towns like the **Skyrocket festival** of Yasothon and the northeast or Nakhon Si Thammarat's temple fair.

The shopper While Bangkok may have the greatest range of shopping – as befits Thailand's mega-city – Chiang Mai is a more amenable place to annoy the bank manager. Here, there is an abundance of crafts, sophisticated shops, great markets, and all conveniently assembled within a manageable area. Once again, areas of Thailand also have their speciality products (just about all also available in Bangkok): fine traditional silk from the northeast and leather puppets from the south, for example.

The sporty type Almost all of Thailand's beach resorts have dive companies. The larger resorts offer better introductory courses for the beginner but there is also plenty of scope for more advanced submarine experiences. Then there's rafting in the north, sea canoeing in the south, trekking in one of Thailand's many national parks, rock climbing, sea fishing and more.

The adventurer The northern hills offer trekking, rafting and elephant rides from one-day excursions to two-week explorations for the slightly firmer of frame. Treks usually include overnight stays in hill villages.

The gastronome Thai cuisine now has an international profile. Because the Thais take their food so seriously, it is possible to find good food just about anywhere, but Bangkok and large regional centres like Chiang Mai and Koh Samui have the greatest range. Tourist centres like Phuket, Pattaya and Koh Samui offer the greatest range of international cuisines, while towns like Hat Yai (Chinese), Udon Thani (Vietnamese) and Nong Khai (Vietnamese) have other cuisines on offer. For people wishing to learn more about Thai cooking, Chiang Mai has some great courses, as does Bangkok and Koh Samui.

When to go

The hottest time of year is April and May. The wet season runs from May to October in most parts of the country (as you travel south from Bangkok the seasons change). The best time to visit – for most parts of the country – is between December and February. But don't imagine that the wet season means being stuck in your room or bogged down in a tropical storm. Travel to almost all corners of the country is possible at any time of year.

For daily weather reports: www.thaimet.tmd.go.th. For more details on climate, see page 706.

During the rainy season clear skies are interspersed with heavy showers, and it is perfectly sensible to visit Thailand during the monsoon. Flooding is most likely towards the end of the rainy season in September and October. Hours of daily sunshine average five to six hours even during the rainy season. Visitors will also benefit from lower hotel room rates.

For the central (including Bangkok), northern and northeastern regions, the best time to visit is November to February when the rains have ended and temperatures are at their lowest. However, don't expect Bangkok to be cool. Note that in the south the seasons are less pronounced – and become more so the farther you travel south. Generally the best times to visit the west side of the peninsula (Phuket, Krabi, Phi Phi etc) are between November and April, while the east coast (Koh Samui, Koh Phangan etc) is drier between May and October.

In terms of festivals, it is worth planning your trip around the following: **Loi Krathong, Songkran, Chinese New Year**, the **King's Birthday, New Year's Day**, see Festivals and Events, page 58, the **Elephant Festival** in Surin, page 324, the **Rocket Festivals** in Isaan, page 335.

Most transport fares are static with the major exception being flights, which are now extremely competitive and fluid. Fluctuations in accommodation prices are becoming more sophisticated in Thailand. For example, any weekend on the island of Koh Samet, popular as a short break with Bangkok's youthful crowd, will be expensive. Mid-week prices on Koh Samet will be cheaper though only at times when it is a low season for foreign tourists. The same rule applies to Koh Chang, Koh Samui and Phuket. The busiest period is Christmas, when both Thais and farang take long holidays – though it is only the urban Thais who tend to celebrate this. The monsoon also effects the south during the months of May to October on the Andaman Sea side and during the months of November to April on the Gulf side. Prices will be lower during this period. Both the north and northeast can be cold during the winter months but this is also an extremely popular time for western tourists.

To add to a complicated picture, according to all predictions, the Chinese will soon dominate tourism numbers in Thailand. This will lead to a differing series of peak and troughs in prices but, one thing that can be guaranteed, is that when it is cold back home incoming tourist figures and prices spike.

Tour operators

UK

Asean Explorer, PO Box 82, 37 High St, Alderney, GY9 3DG, T01481-823417, www.asean-explorer.com. Holidays for adventurers and golfers in Thailand.

Exodus Travels, 9 Weir Rd, London, T020-87723822, www.exodus.co.uk. Small group travel for walking and trekking holidays, adventure tours and more.

Magic of the Orient, 14 Frederick Pl, Bristol, BS8 1AS, T0117-3116050, www.magicoftheorient.com. Specializes in tailor-made holidays to the region. Established in 1989 the company's philosophy is to deliver first-class service from knowledgeable staff at good value.

Pettitts, T01892-515966, www.pettitts.co.uk. Unusual locations.

Silk Steps, Tyndale House, 7 High St, Chipping Sodbury, Bristol, BS37 6BA, T01454-888850, www.silksteps.co.uk. Tailor-made and group travel.
Steppes Travel, 51 Castle St, Cirencester, GL7 1QD, T01285-880980, www.steppestravel.co.uk.
Symbiosis Expedition Planning, 205 St John's Hill, London, SW11 1TH, T020-79245906, www.symbiosis-travel.com, www.divingsoutheastasia.com. Specialists in tailor-made and small group adventure holidays for those concerned about the impact of tourism on environments.
Trans Indus, Northumberland House, 11 The Pavement, Popes Lane, Ealing, London, W5 4NG, T020-85662729, www.transindus.co.uk. Tours to Thailand and other Southeast Asian countries.
Travelmood, 214 Edgware Rd, London, W2 1DH; 1 Brunswick Court, Bridge St, Leeds, LS2 7QU; 16 Reform St, Dundee, DD1 1RG, T08705-001002, www.travelmood.com. 21 years' experience as a top travel specialist offering tailor-made to the Far East and adventure and activity travel in Asia.

North America
Global Spectrum, 3907 Laro Court, Fairfax, VA 22031, USA, T1800 419 4446, www.globalspectrumtravel.com.
Nine Dragons Travel & Tours, PO Box 24105, Indianapolis, IN 46224-0105, USA, T317-3290350, T0800-9099050 (toll free), www.nine-dragons.com. Guided and individually customized tours.

Adventure travel

Birdwatching
Ornitholidays, 29 Straight Mile, Romsey, Hants, SO51 9BB, T01794-519445, www.ornitholidays.co.uk.

Cycling
Bike and Travel, Thai-based tour company specializing in cycling trips, T02-9900274 (Bangkok). A useful website to check is www.cyclingthailand.com.

Cruises

Cruise Asia Ltd, 133/14 Rajthevee Rd, Rajprarop, Makkasan, Bangkok, T02-6401400, www.cruiseasia.net.

Princess Cruises, Richmond House, Terminus Terrace, Southampton, SO14 3PN, UK, T0845-3555800, www.princess.com.

Diving

See Sport and Special interest travel, page 60, for details.

Walking

Ramblers Holidays, PO Box 43, Welwyn Garden City, Herts, AL8 6PQ, T01707-331133, www.ramblersholidays.co.uk.

Finding out more

The **Tourist Authority of Thailand** (TAT) publishes a good range of glossy brochures which provide an idea of what there is, where to go and what it looks like. See page 35. www.tourismthailand.org and www.tat.or.th are a useful first stop and generally well regarded. See also the box on TAT offices overseas and Tourist information, page 19.

FCO, T0870-606-0290, www.fco.gov.uk/travel/ The UK Foreign and Commonwealth Office's travel warning section.

US State Department, www.travel.state.gov/ travel_warnings.html. The US State Department updates travel advisories on its Travel Warnings & Consular Information Sheets pages. It also has a hotline for American travellers, T202-647-5225.

www.asiasociety.org Homepage of the Asia Society with papers, reports and speeches as well as nearly 1,000 links to what they consider to be the best educational, political and cultural sites on the web.

www.asiatravelmart.com Includes deals on flights, hotels and more; especially good on cheap hotel deals in the Asian region.

www.bang-kok.com Bangkok site with information on sleeping, eating and partying.

www.bangkokpost.net Homepage for the *Bangkok Post* including back issues and main stories of the day.

www.chula.ac.th Managed by Thailand's premier university, Chulalongkorn, and introduces people to Thailand's history, culture, society, politics and economics.

www.geocities.com/~nesst/ The homepage of the Network for Environmentally & Socially Sustainable Tourism (Thailand), with information on tourism in Thailand, book reviews and a discussion page.

www.nationgroup.com Homepage for *The Nation*, one of Thailand's main English language daily newspapers.

www.nectec.or.th Homepage for Thailand in Bangkok, good links to other websites.

www.restaurantsbkk.com Website devoted to restaurants and things food related in Bangkok. Searchable directory.

www.thaifolk.com Good site for Thai culture from folk songs and handicrafts through to festivals like Loi Kratong and Thai myths and legends. Information posted in both English and Thai – although the Thai version of the site is better.

www.thaiindex.com A gateway site for a good range of Thai-oriented websites.

Language

English is reasonably widely spoken and is taught to all school children. Off the tourist trail, making yourself understood becomes more difficult. It is handy to buy a Thai/English road atlas of the country (most petrol stations sell them) – you can then point to destinations.

The Thai language is tonal and, strictly speaking, monosyllabic. There are five tones: high, low, rising, falling and mid-tone. These are used to distinguish between words which would otherwise be identical. For example: mai (low tone, new), mai (rising, silk), mai (mid-tone, burn), mai (high tone, question indicator), and mai (falling tone, negative indicator). Not surprisingly, many visitors find it hard to hear

the different tones, and it is difficult to make much progress during a short visit (unlike, say, with Malaysian or Indonesian). The tonal nature of the language also explains why so much of Thai humour is based around homonyms – and especially when farangs (foreigners) say what they do not mean. Although tones make Thai a challenge for foreign visitors, other aspects of the language are easier to grasp: there are no marked plurals in nouns, no marked tenses in verbs, no definite or indefinite articles, and no affixes or suffixes.

Visitors may well experience two oddities of the Thai language being reflected in the way that Thais speak English. An 'l' or 'r' at the end of a word in Thai becomes an 'n', while an 's' becomes a 't'. So some Thais refer to the 'Shell' Oil Company as 'Shen', a name like 'Les' becomes 'Let', while 'cheque bill' becomes 'cheque bin'. It is also impossible to have two consonants after one another in Thai. If it occurs, a Thai will automatically insert a vowel (even though it is not written). So the soft drink 'Sprite' becomes 'Sa-prite', and the English word 'start', 'sa-tart'. See also page 720.

Despite Thai being a difficult language to pick up, it is worth trying to learn a few words, even if your visit to Thailand is short. Thais generally feel honoured that a farang is bothering to learn their language, and will be patient and helpful. If they laugh at some of your pronunciations do not be put off – it is not meant to be critical.

Specialist travel

Disabled travellers

Disabled travellers will find Thailand a challenge. The difficulties that even the able bodied encounter in crossing roads when pedestrian crossings are either non-existent or ignored by most motorists are amplified many times for the disabled. And the difficulties don't end having successfully negotiated the road. The high curbs and lack of ramps will pose a challenge for even the most wheelchair savvy. Furthermore, the cracked concrete and the tendency for pavements to be littered with motorbikes, stall holders, even parked cars, will add to the challenge. Buses and taxis are not designed for disabled access and it sometimes takes alacrity for the able bodied to hop aboard a moving bus. Finally, there are relatively few hotels and restaurants that are disabled-friendly. This is particularly true of cheaper and older establishments.

This is not to suggest that travel in Thailand is impossible for the disabled, but merely to point out some of the challenges. On the plus side, you will find Thais to be extremely helpful and because taxis and tuk-tuks are cheap it is usually not necessary to rely on buses. Best of all, though, is to come to Thailand with an able bodied companion who can help in sticky situations.

Gay and lesbian travellers

On the surface, Thailand is incredibly tolerant of homosexuals and lesbians. In Bangkok and other major cities there's an openness that can even make San Francisco look tame. It is for this reason that Thailand's gay scene has flourished and, more particularly, has grown in line with international tourism. This does not mean that general norms regarding acceptable behaviour are suspended when it comes to gay relationships. In particular, overt public displays of affection are still frowned upon (see page 37). Also, when it comes to familial relationships things get more complicated; homosexuals and lesbians are still expected to raise families. Attitudes in the more traditional rural areas are far more conservative than in the cities. By exercising some cultural sensitivity any visit should be hassle free.

Several of the free tourist magazines distributed through hotels and restaurants in Bangkok, Pattaya, Phuket and Koh Samui provide information on the gay and lesbian scene, including bars and meeting points. The essential website before you get there is **www.utopia-asia.com** which provides good material on where to go,

current events, and background information on the Thai gay scene in Bangkok and beyond. **Utopia tours** at Tamtawan Palace Hotel, 119/5-10 Surawong Road, T02-2383227, www.utopia-tours.com, provides tours for gay and lesbian visitors. There's also a map of gay Bangkok. Gay clubs are listed in *Bangkok Metro* magazine (www.bkkmetro.com), and include **Icon: the Club**, Silom Road Soi 4, www.iconasia.com, and **Freeman Dance Arena**, 60/18-21 Silom Road, www.dj-station.com. The main centres of activity in Bangkok are Silom Road sois 2 and 4 and Sukhumvit soi 23. There is also a thriving gay scene in Pattaya and, to a lesser extent, on Phuket, Koh Samui and in Chiang Mai in the north.

Longstay tourism

The government has been promoting so-called 'longstay' tourism for 'aged' tourists (defined as over 55 years old) since 1998. At the end of 2001 the Cabinet set up the Thai Longstay Management Corporation to promote longstay tourism. Longstay tourists are seen as retired people who wish to make Thailand their second home. To do so they should spend between one month and six months in the country and must not earn an income. They should also be able to demonstrate a regular source of funds to support them while in Thailand.

Student travellers

Anyone in full-time education is entitled to an International Student Identity Card (ISIC). These are issued by student travel offices and travel agencies across the world and offer special rates on all forms of transport and other concessions and services. The ISIC head office is: **ISIC Association**, Box 9048, 1000 Copenhagen, Denmark, T45-33939303. Students are eligible for discounts at some museums but the use of student cards is not widespread so don't expect to save a fortune.

Travelling with children

Many people are daunted by the prospect of taking a child to Southeast Asia and there are disadvantages: travelling is slower and more expensive and there are additional health risks for the child or baby. But it can be a most rewarding experience and, with sufficient care and planning, it can also be safe. Children are excellent passports into a local culture. You will also receive the best service and help from officials and members of the public when in difficulty. A non-Asian child is still something of a novelty and parents may find their child frequently taken off their hands, even mobbed in more remote areas.

Sleeping At the hottest time of year, air conditioning may be essential for a baby or young child's comfort. This rules out many of the cheaper hotels, but air-conditioned accommodation is available in all but the most out-of-the-way spots. When the child is bathing, be aware that the water could carry parasites, so avoid letting him or her drink it.

Eating Be aware that expensive hotels may have squalid cooking conditions; the cheapest street stall is often more hygienic. Where possible, try to watch food being prepared. Stir-fried vegetables and rice or noodles are the best bet; meat and fish may be pre-cooked and then left out before being re-heated. Fruit can be bought cheaply – papaya, banana and avocado are all excellent sources of nutrition. Powdered milk is also available throughout the region, although most brands have added sugar. If taking a baby, breast-feeding is strongly recommended. Powdered food, bottled water and fizzy drinks are also sold widely.

Transport Public transport may be a problem; trains are fine, but long bus journeys are restrictive and uncomfortable. Hiring a car is undoubtedly the most convenient way to see a country with a small child. It is possible to buy child-seats in larger cities.

Health More preparation is probably necessary for babies and children than for an adult, and particularly when travelling to remote areas where health services are primitive. A travel insurance policy which has an air ambulance provision is strongly recommended. When planning a route, try to stay within 24 hours' travel of a hospital with good care and facilities. For advice about common problems, see Health, page 75. NB Never allow your child to be exposed to the harsh tropical sun without protection. A child can burn in a matter of minutes. Loose cotton clothing with long sleeves and legs and a sunhat are best. High-factor sun-protection cream is essential.

Vaccinations Children should already be properly protected against diphtheria, poliomyelitis and pertussis (whooping cough), measles and HIB, all of which can be more serious infections in Southeast Asia than at home. Measles, mumps and rubella vaccine is also given to children throughout the world, but those teenage girls who have not had rubella (German measles) should be tested and vaccinated. Hepatitis B vaccination for babies is now routine in some countries. See also Health, page 75.

Essentials Disposable nappies can be bought in Thailand but remember that you're adding to the rubbish-disposal problem. If you are staying any length of time in one place, it may be worth taking Terry's (cloth) nappies. All you need is a bucket and some double-strength nappy cleanse (simply soak and rinse). Cotton nappies dry quickly in the heat and are generally more comfortable for the baby or child. Of course, the best way for a child to be is nappy-free – like the local children. Many western baby products are available in Thailand: shampoo, talcum powder, soap and lotion. Baby wipes are expensive and not always easy to find.

Checklist Baby wipes; child paracetamol; disinfectant; first-aid kit; flannel; immersion element for boiling water; decongestant for colds; instant food for under one year olds; mug/bottle/bowl/spoons; nappy cleanse, double-strength; ORS (Oral Rehydration Salts) such as Dioralyte, widely available in Thailand, and the most effective way to alleviate diarrhoea (it is not a cure); portable baby chair, to hook onto tables – this is not essential but can be very useful; sarong or backpack for carrying child (and/or lightweight collapsible buggy); sterilizing tablets (and container for sterilizing bottles, teats, utensils); cream for nappy rash and other skin complaints, such as Sudocrem; sunblock, factor 15 or higher; sun hat; Terry's (cloth) nappies, liners, pins and plastic pants; thermometer; zip-lock bags for carrying snacks etc.

Women travellers

Compared with neighbouring East and South Asia, women in Southeast Asia enjoy relative equality of opportunity. While this is a contentious issue, scholars have pointed to the lack of pronouns in Southeast Asian languages, the role of women in trade and commerce, the important part that women play in reproductive decisions, the characteristically egalitarian patterns of inheritance and so on. This is not to suggest that there is complete equality between the sexes. Buddhism, for example – at least as it is practised in Thailand – accords women a lower position and it is notable how few women there are in positions of political power.

The implications of this for women travellers, and especially solo women travellers, is that they may face some difficulties not encountered by men – for example the possibility of some low key sexual harassment. Nonetheless, women should make sure that rooms are secure at night and if travelling in remote regions, should try to team up with other travellers.

Working in the country

Most visitors to Thailand who wish to work take up a post teaching English. Some guesthouses will provide free accommodation for guests who are willing to allot a portion of the day to English conversation classes. Those with a qualification, for example a TEFL certificate, can usually command a higher salary. There are also various NGOs/voluntary organizations that employ people. See www.thaivisa.com or www.goabroad.com. The former provides background information on getting a visa while the latter has information on language schools, volunteer work and more.

Volunteering Projects range from conservation and teaching English to looking after elephants. They vary in length from two weeks and beyond and generally need to be organized before you arrive. The application process almost always involves submitting a statement of intent, although generally no formal qualifications or experience are required; usually volunteers need to be over 18 and will pay fees upfront. Consult individual organizations about visas and lodgings – most include basic shared accommodation in the price but not travel to and from Thailand. The following international organizations run projects in Thailand:

Conservation

British Trust for Conservation Volunteers, 36 St Mary's, Wallingford, Oxfordshire, OX10 0EU, T01491-821600, www.btcv.org. Mangrove conservation and turtle monitoring from 2 weeks in duration.

Elephant Nature Park, PO Box 185, Mae Ping PO, Chiang Mai 50301, Thailand, T053-272855/818754, www.thaifocus.com. Under 1 month in duration, office work and working with elephants.

General

Cross Cultural Solutions, 47 Potter Av, New Rochelle, NY 10801, USA, T1800 3804777 (US only), T191 4632 0022, www.crosscultural solutions.org. Community work and research into local development.

Earthwatch, 267 Banbury Rd, Oxford, OX2 7HT, T01865-318838, www.earthwatch.org.

Global Services Corps, 300 Broadway, Suite 28, San Francisco, CA 94133-3312, USA, T415-788-3666, ext128, www.globalservices corps.org. Volunteers must be over 18 with an interest in international issues and sustainable development.

Involvement Volunteers, PO Box 218, Port Melbourne, Vic 3207, Australia, T613-9646 9392, www.volunteering.org.au. Australian network with international reach, organic farming, teaching and community work.

NESS Thai, PO Box 48, Amphur Muang Krabi, Thailand, T075-622377, www.nessthai.com. A network for environmentally and socially sustainable tourism offering the possibility of volunteer work while travelling in Thailand.

VSO, 317 Putney Bridge Rd, London, SW15 2PN, UK, T0208-787600, www.vso.org.uk. Worldwide voluntary organization.

Before you travel

Visas and immigration

All tourists must possess passports valid for at least six months longer than their intended stay in Thailand. Passport holders from the countries listed below do not require a visa for tourist purposes if their stay does not exceed 30 days. If you intend to stay longer, obtain a 60-day tourist visa. Visitors are fined ฿100 per day each day they exceed the 30-day limit to a maximum of ฿20,000 – or 200 days. Payment can be made at the airport before departure or at the Immigration Department (see page 28). While, in theory, visitors can be denied entry if they do not have an onward ticket and sufficient funds for their stay, in practice customs officials almost never check. The same is true of tourists who arrive via the Thai-Malaysian border by sea, rail or road.

The 30-day exemption applies to nationals of the following countries: Argentina, Australia, Austria, Bahrain, Belgium, Brazil, Brunei, Canada, Chile, Cyprus, Denmark, Djibouti, Egypt, Fiji, Finland, France, Germany, Greece, Iceland, Indonesia, Ireland, Israel, Italy, Japan, Kenya, Korea, Kuwait, Luxembourg, Malaysia, Mauritania, Mexico, Morocco, Myanmar (Burma), Netherlands, New Zealand, Norway, Oman, Papua New Guinea, Philippines, Portugal, Qatar, Saudi Arabia, Senegal, Singapore, Slovenia, South Africa, Spain, Sweden, Switzerland, Tunisia, Turkey, UAE, UK, USA, Vanuatu, Western Samoa, Yemen. Malaysian nationals arriving by road from Malaysia do not need evidence of onward journey. Visitors from Hong Kong (China) do not require a visa for visits of up to 15 days.

Visas For the latest information on visas and tourist visa exemptions see the consular information section of the **Thai Ministry of Foreign Affairs** website: www.mfa.go.th. The immigration office is at **Immigration Bureau,** Soi Suan Plu, Thanon Sathorn Tai, Bangkok 10120, T02-2873101. Open Monday-Friday 0930-1630, Saturday 0830-1200 (tourists only).

There are several types of visa, only a few of which concern visitors: transit visa, tourist visa and non-immigrant visa. 1. **Transit visa** (TS): for those who are in transit; visitors are permitted to stay 30 days. 2. **Tourist visa** (TR): for tourists; visitors are permitted to stay for 60 days. 3. **Non–immigrant visa**: for foreigners who wish to undertake official or private work, study, research or stay with family; duration 90 days.

Only tourist visa requirements are detailed below; for other visa types contact your embassy/consulate or access **www.mfa.go.th.**

Visas on arrival For tourists from 96 countries not in the list above (for a listing, see www.mfa.go.th) it is possible to have a visa issued on arrival. There is a visa booth at Don Muang (Bangkok) Airport, at customs control, and even a photo booth to provide passport snaps (one photograph required). Note that these visas are valid for 15 days only (฿300). Applicants must also have an outbound (return) ticket and possess funds to meet living expenses of ฿10,000 per person or ฿20,000 per family. Visas on arrival are issued at 12 designated international checkpoints: Don Muang International Airport, Bangkok; Chiang Mai International Airport; Phuket International Airport; Hat Yai International Airport, Songkla; U Tapao Airport, Rayong (Pattaya); Mae Sai Immigration Checkpoint, Chiang Rai; Chiang Saen Immigration Checkpoint, Chiang Rai; Chiang Khong Immigration Checkpoint, Chiang Rai; Betong Immigration Checkpoint, Yala; Sadoa Immigration Checkpoint, Songkhla; Samui Immigration Checkpoint, Surat Thani; and Sukhothai International Airport.

Tourist visas These are valid for 60 days from date of entry (single entry) and must be obtained from a Thai embassy before arrival in Thailand. They can be extended for a further 30 days. Multiple entry visas are also available.

90-day non-immigrant visas These can be obtained in the applicant's home country (about US$30 per entry). A letter from the applicant's company or organization guaranteeing their repatriation should be submitted at the same time.

Re-entry permit For those who wish to leave and then re-enter Thailand before their visa expires, it is possible to apply for a re-entry permit from the Immigration Department (see below) (฿500).

Visa extensions These are obtainable from the Immigration Department in Bangkok (see below) for ฿500. The process used to be interminable, but the system is now much improved and relatively painless, however it may be easier to leave the country

Thai embassies worldwide

Australia 131 Macquarie Street, Level 8, Sydney 2000, T02-92412542.
Austria Cottaggasse 48, 1180 Vienna, T01-4783335.
Belgium and European Community 2 Square du Val de la Cambre, Brussels, T02-6406810.
Canada 180 Island Park Drive, Ottawa, Ontario, K1Y 0A2, T613-7224444.
Germany Lepsiusstrasse 64-66, 12163 Berlin, T030-794810.
Israel 21 Shaul Hamelech Boulevard, Tel Aviv 64367, T03-695-8980.
Italy Via Nomentana132, 00162 Rome, T06-8622-051.
Japan 3-14-6, Kami-Osaki, Shinagawa-Ku, Tokyo 141, T03-34472247.
Laos Route Phonekheng, Vientiane, PO Box 128, T021-214581.
Malaysia 206 Jalan Ampang, 50450 Kuala Lumpur, T03-21488222.
Netherlands Laan Copes Van Cattenburch 123, 2585 EZ, The Hague, T3170-3450632.
New Zealand 2 Cook St, Karori, PO Box 17226, Wellington, T04-4768616.
Sweden Floragatan 3, 26220, Stockholm 100 40, T08-7917340.
Switzerland Kirchstrasse 56, 3097 Bern, T031-9703030.
UK 29-30 Queens Gate, London, SW7 5JB, T020-75892944.
USA 1024 Wisconsin Avenue, NW, Suite 401 Washington, DC 20007, T202-9443600.
Note www.thaiembassy.org is a useful resource.

and then re-enter having obtained a new tourist visa. Extensions can also be issued in other towns, such as Koh Samui and Chiang Mai. Applicants must bring two photocopies of their passport ID page and the page on which their tourist visa is stamped, together with three passport photographs. It is also advisable to dress neatly. Visas are issued by all Thai embassies and consulates. The length of time a visa is extended varies according to the office and the official. However, those on a 30-day no-visa entry can usually have their stay extended by a week, sometimes 10 days; those with a 60-day tourist visa can usually expect a 30-day extension.

Visitors who obtain a visa on arrival (see above) usually cannot file an application for extension of stay except in special cases such as an illness which prevents them from travelling. They can submit an application at the **Office of Immigration Bureau,** Immigration Division 1, Soi Suan Plu, South Sathorn Road, Bangkok 10120, T02-287-3127/287-3101-10, ext 2264-5.

Customs

Currency regulations Non-residents can bring in up to ฿2,000 per person and unlimited foreign currency although amounts exceeding US$10,000 must be declared. Maximum amount permitted to take out of Thailand is ฿50,000 per person.

Prohibited items All narcotics; obscene literature, pornography; fire arms (except with a permit from the Police Department or local registration office). Some species of plants and animals are prohibited (for more information contact the **Royal Forestry Department,** Phahonyothin Road, Bangkok, T02-5792776).

Duty free, export restrictions

Duty free 250 g of cigars/cigarettes (or 200 cigarettes) and one litre of wine or spirits. One still camera with five rolls of film or one movie camera with three rolls of 8 mm or 16 mm film.

Export restrictions No Buddha or Bodhisattva images or fragments should be taken out of Thailand, except for worshipping by Buddhists, for cultural exchanges or for research. However, it is obvious that many people do – you only have to look in the antique shops to see the abundance for sale. A licence should be obtained from the **Department of Fine Arts,** Na Prathat Road, Bangkok, T02-2241370, from **Chiang Mai National Museum,** T02-221308, or from the **Songkhla National Museum,** Songkhla, T02-311728. Five-days notice is needed; take two passport photographs of the object and photocopies of your passport.

VAT refunds Most of the major department stores have a VAT refund desk. Go to them on your day of purchase with receipts and ask them to complete VAT refund form, which you then present, with purchased goods, at appropriate desk in any international airport in Thailand. They'll give you another form that you exchange for cash in the departure lounge. You'll need to spend at least ฿4000 to qualify for a refund.

Know before you go

Consult the UK Foreign Office's Know Before You Go Campaign by clicking on its travel advisory pages to inform yourself of potentially dangerous situations (www.fco.gov.uk). It relates information on safety, natural disasters, disease risks, theft risks and any other topical facts relating to specific countries. It also advises on pre-departure planning. See also Safety, page 40.

Vaccinations

No vaccinations are required, unless coming from an infected area (if visitors have been in a yellow fever infected area in the 10 days before arrival, and do not have a vaccination certificate, they will be vaccinated and kept in quarantine for six days, or deported). See also Health, page 75.

What to take

Travellers usually tend to take too much. Almost everything is available in Thailand's main towns and cities – and often at a lower price than in the west. Even apparently remote areas will have shops that stock most things that a traveller might require from toiletries and batteries to pharmaceuticals.

Suitcases are not appropriate if you are intending to travel overland by bus. A backpack, or a travelpack (where the straps can be zipped out of sight), is recommended. Travelpacks have the advantage of being hybrid backpacks-suitcases. For serious hikers, a backpack with an internal frame is still by far the better option for longer treks.

In terms of clothing, dress in Thailand is relatively casual – even at formal functions. Jackets and ties are not necessary except in a few of the most expensive hotel restaurants. However, though formal attire may be the exception, dressing tidily is the norm. Note that if you intend to visit Buddhist monasteries or other religious sites women should cover their shoulders and knees. Sleeveless tops, shorts and flip-flops are also inappropriate in temples. In the far south visiting mosques also requires demure attire. This does not apply on beaches and islands where (almost) anything goes and sarongs, flip-flops and such like are de rigueur. Nevertheless, while dress may be casual this does not extend to undress: topless sunbathing, which does – increasingly – occur, is frowned upon by Thais who are usually too polite to say anything. This is particularly true in the Muslim areas of the south.

There is a tendency, rather than to take inappropriate articles of clothing, to pack too many of the same article. Laundry services are cheap, and the turn-around rapid. The exception to the former statement is at more upmarket hotels, where laundry services can be expensive.

Checklist Bumbag; earplugs; first-aid kit; hiking boots (if intending to visit any of the national parks); insect repellent and/or electric mosquito mats, coils; International Driving Licence; money belt; passports (valid for at least six months); photocopies of essential documents; short wave radio; spare passport photographs; sun hat; sun protection; sunglasses; Swiss Army knife; torch; umbrella; wet wipes; zip-lock bags. When travelling to out-of-the-way places, carry toilet paper, as locals don't always use it (readily available for purchase in Thailand). Those intending to stay in budget accommodation might also include: cotton sheet sleeping bag; padlock (for hotel room and pack); soap; student card; toilet paper; towel; travel wash.

Insurance

Always take out travel insurance before you set off and read the small print carefully. Check that the policy covers the activities you intend or may end up doing. Also check exactly what your medical cover includes, ie ambulance, helicopter rescue or emergency flights back home. Also check the payment protocol. You may have to cough up first (literally) before the insurance company reimburses you. It is always best to dig out all the receipts for expensive personal effects like jewellery or cameras. Take photos of these items and note down all serial numbers. You are advised to shop around. **STA Travel** and other reputable student travel organizations offer good-value policies. Young travellers from North America can try the **International Student Insurance Service** (ISIS), which is available through **STA Travel**, T1-800-7770112, www.sta-travel.com. Other recommended travel insurance companies in North America include: **Travel Guard**, T1-800-8261300, www.noelgroup.com; **Access America**, T1-800- 2848300; **Travel Insurance Services**, T1-800-9371387; and **Travel Assistance International**, T1-800-8212828. Older travellers should note that some companies will not cover people over 65 years old, or may charge higher premiums. The best policies for older travellers (UK) are offered by **Age Concern**, T01883-346964.

Money

Currency

The unit of Thai currency is the **baht** (฿), which is divided into 100 **satang**. Notes in circulation include ฿20 (green), ฿50 (blue), ฿100 (red), ฿500 (purple) and ฿1000 (orange and grey). Coins include 25 satang and 50 satang, and ฿1, ฿5, and ฿10. The two smaller coins are disappearing from circulation and the 25 satang coin, equivalent to the princely sum of US$0.003, is rarely found. The colloquial term for 25 satang is saleng.

Exchange

It is best to change money at banks or money changers which give better rates than hotels. The exchange booths at Bangkok airport have some of the best rates available. There is no black market. First-class hotels have 24-hour money changers. Indonesian rupiah, Nepalese rupees, Burmese kyat, Vietnamese dong, Lao kip and Cambodian riels cannot be exchanged for baht at Thai banks. (Money changers will sometimes exchange kyat, dong, kip and riel and it can be a good idea to buy the currencies in Bangkok before departure for these countries as the black-market rate often applies.) There is a charge of ฿23 per cheque when changing **traveller's cheques** (passport required) so it works out cheaper to travel with large denomination TCs (or avoid TCs altogether).

At the time of going to press the exchange rate was ฿41 to US$1 and ฿70 to UK£1.

Credit and **debit cards** are increasingly used in Thailand and just about every town of any size will have a bank with an ATM. Visa and MasterCard are the most

widely taken credit cards, and cash cards with the Cirrus logo can also be used to withdraw cash at many banks. Generally speaking, AMEX can be used at branches of the **Bangkok Bank**; JCB at **Siam Commercial Bank**; MasterCard at **Siam Commercial** and **Bangkok Bank**; and Visa at **Thai Farmers' Bank** and **Bangkok Bank**. Most larger hotels and more expensive restaurants take credit cards as well. Because Thailand has embraced the ATM with such exuberance, many foreign visitors no longer bother with traveller's cheques or cash and rely entirely on plastic. Even so, a small stash of US dollars cash can come in handy in a sticky situation.

Notification of credit card loss: **American Express**, IBM Building, Phahonyothin Road, T02-2730040; **Diners Club**, Dusit Thani Building, Rama IV Road, T02-2332645/2335775/2335644/2383660; **JCB**, T02-2561361/2561351; **Visa** and **MasterCard**, Thai Farmers Bank Building, Phahonyothin Road, T02-2522212/2701801-10.

Cost of living

A day's work in the fields will earn a Thai around ฿100-150, depending on the type of work and the region. The minimum daily wage in Bangkok is around ฿165 (US$4) and in most provincial areas, ฿133 (US$3). The average salary of a civil servant is around US$250 a month. Of course, Thailand's middle classes – and especially those engaged in business in Bangkok – will earn far more than this. Just look at the number of BMWs and the expensive clothes. Costs of living for Thais are much less than for expats. A simple but good meal out will cost ฿20; the rental of a modern house in a provincial city will cost perhaps ฿4000 a month.

Cost of travelling

Visitors staying in first-class hotels and eating in hotel restaurants will probably spend a minimum of ฿2000 per day and conceivably much more. Tourists staying in cheaper air- conditioned accommodation and eating in local restaurants will probably spend about ฿600-900 per day. A backpacker staying in fan-cooled guesthouses and eating cheaply, might expect to be able to live on ฿300 per day. In Bangkok, expect to pay 20-30 per cent more.

Getting there

Air

The majority of visitors arrive in Thailand through Bangkok's Don Muang airport. Chiang Mai in the north and Phuket in the south also have international airports. More than 35 airlines and charter companies fly to Bangkok. **THAI** is the national carrier. Fares inflate by 50 per cent from their low-season rate during high season. **Note** It is advisable not to fly with **Phuket Air** following a string of domestic and international incidents. The company is already banned from flying to and from the UK and France

From Europe

The approximate flight time from London to Bangkok (non-stop) is 12 hours. From London Heathrow, airlines offering non-stop flights include **Qantas, British Airways, THAI** and **Eva Air**. You can easily connect to Thailand from the UK via most other European capitals. **Finnair** flies daily from Helsinki, **KLM** via Amsterdam and **Lufthansa** via Frankfurt. **SAS** flies from Copenhagen and **Swiss Air** from Zurich. Further afield **Emirates** flies via Dubai, **Gulf Air** via Bahrain and **Qatar** via Muscat. Non-direct flights can work out much cheaper than direct so if you want a bargain

shop around – **Finnair** (www.finnair.com) often offers some of the cheapest fares. It is also possible to fly direct to Chiang Mai from Dusseldorf, Frankfurt and Munich in Germany and to Phuket from Dusseldorf and Munich.

From the USA and Canada

The approximate flight time from Los Angeles to Bangkok is 21 hours. There are one-stop flights from Los Angeles on **THAI** and two-stops on **Delta**; one-stop flights from San Francisco on **Northwest** and **United** and two-stops on **Delta**; and one-stop flights from Vancouver on **Canadian. THAI** have now started a non-stop flight from New York to Bangkok – flight time 16 hours.

From Australasia

There are flights from Sydney and Melbourne (approximately nine hours) daily with **Qantas** and **THAI**. There is also a choice of other flights with **British Airways, Alitalia, Lufthansa** and **Lauda Air** which are less frequent. There are flights from Perth with **THAI** and **Qantas**. From Auckland, **Air New Zealand, THAI** and **British Airways** fly to Bangkok.

From Asia

THAI, Air India, Indian Airlines and **Aeroflot** fly from Delhi. **Air Lanka, THAI** and **Cathay Pacific** fly from Colombo. From Dhaka, there are flights with **Biman Bangladesh Airlines** and **THAI. PIA** and **THAI** fly from Karachi. **Balkan** flies from Male. **Royal Nepal Airlines** and **THAI** fly from Kathmandu. It is also possible to fly to Chiang Mai from Kunming (China) and Singapore and to Phuket from Hong Kong, Kuala Lumpur, Penang, Singapore, Taipei and Tokyo. Numerous airlines fly from Hong Kong, Tokyo, Manila, Kuala Lumpur, Singapore and Jakarta to Bangkok. There are daily connections from Singapore and Kuala Lumpur to Hat Yai and from Singapore and Hong Kong to Koh Samui. It is also possible to fly to Phuket from Hong Kong, Kuala Lumpur, Penang, Singapore, Taipei and Tokyo.

There has been a massive proliferation of budget airlines in Southeast Asia with Bangkok becoming one of the primary hubs. There are cheap fares available to Laos, Cambodia, Singapore, China, Macau, Maldives, Hong Kong and Malaysia. The situation is changing rapidly with carriers going in and out of business – check **www.asiaoz.com/thailand_airlines.html** for a full, up to date list of budget air connections. The main players are **One Two Go** (www.fly12go.com), **Air Asia** (www.airasia.com) and **Bangkok Airways** (www.bangkokair.com). Bangkok has a concentration of tour companies specializing in Indochina and Myanmar and is a good place to arrange a visa (although most of these countries now provide visas on arrival in any case).

From the Middle and Far East

Emirates flies from Dubai, **Gulf Air** flies from Bahrain, and **Egyptair** from Cairo.

Discount travel agents

Australia and New Zealand

Flight Centres, 82 Elizabeth St, Sydney, T13- 1600; 205 Queen St, Auckland, T09-309 6171.

STA Travel, T1300-360960, www.statravelaus.com.au; 702 Harris St, Ultimo, Sydney, and 256 Flinders St, Melbourne. In NZ: 10 High St, Auckland, T09-366 6673..

Travel.com.au, 80 Clarence St, Sydney, T02-929 01500, www.travel.com.au.

North America

Air Brokers International, 323 Geary St, Suite 41⁻, San Francisco, CA 94102, T01-800-883 3273, www.airbrokers.com. Consolidator and specialist on RTW and Circle Pacific tickets.

Discount Airfares Worldwide On-Line, www.etn.nl/discount.htm. A hub of consolidator and discount agent links.

International Travel Network/Airlines of the Web, www.itn.net/airlines. Online air travel information and reservations.
STA Travel, 5900 Wilshire Blvd, Suite 2110, Los Angeles, CA 90036, T1-800-777 0112, www.sta-travel.com.
Travel CUTS, 187 College St, Toronto, ON, M5T 1P7, T1-800-667 2887, www.travelcuts.com. Specialist in student discount fares, IDs and other travel services. Branches in other Canadian cities.
Travelocity, www.travelocity.com. Online consolidator.

UK

STA Travel, 86 Old Brompton Rd, London, SW7 3LH, T020-74376262, www.statravel.co.uk. Specialists in low-cost student/youth flights and tours, also good for student IDs and insurance.
Trailfinders, 194 Kensington High St, London, W8 7RG, T020-7938 3939, www.trailfinders.co.uk.

Road

The main road access from **Malaysia**. The principal land border crossings are near Betong in Yala Province, from Sungei Golok in Narathiwat Province and at Padang Besar, where the railway line crosses the border. In April 1994 the Friendship Bridge linking Nong Khai with **Laos** opened and became the first bridge across the Mekong River. In addition to the Nong Khai/Friendship Bridge crossing, it is also possible to enter Thailand from Laos at the following places: Pakse to Chongmek (near Ubon Ratchathani); Savannakhet to Mukdahan; Thakhek to Nakhon Phanom; and Ban Houei Xai to Chiang Khong. All four require travellers to cross the Mekong by boat; in the latter three cases the river forms the border while in the first case the river is entirely within the territory of Laos.

For further details of road transport including representative fares, see pages 45.

Border crossings with **Burma** have been in a state of flux ever since the first – at Mae Sai in the north – opened in 1992. Depending on the state of relations between Burma and Thailand, and on security conditions in the borderland regions, restrictions on travel are lifted and re-imposed at a day's notice. This applies to the crossing at Mae Sai in the north, Saam Ong in the west, and at Mae Sot in the northwest. Sometimes, only Thai passport holders are permitted to cross; and usually if foreigners are permitted to enter Burma it is only for forays into the immediate vicinity and, sometimes, only for day trips.

Sea

No regular, scheduled cruise liners sail to Thailand any longer but it is sometimes possible to enter the country on a freighter, arriving at Khlong Toey Port in Bangkok. The *Bangkok Post* publishes a weekly shipping details on ships leaving the kingdom.

There are frequent passenger ferries from Pak Bara, near Satun, in southern Thailand to Perlis and Langkawi Island, both in **Malaysia** (see page 532). The passenger and car ferries at Ta Ba, near the town of Tak Bai, south of Narathiwat, make for a fast border crossing to Pengkalan Kubor in Malaysia. An alternative is to hitch a lift on a yacht from Phuket (Thailand) or from Penang (Malaysia). Check at the respective yacht clubs for information.

Train

Regular services link Singapore and Bangkok, via Kuala Lumpur, Butterworth and the major southern Thai towns. Express air-conditioned trains take two days from Singapore, 34 hours from Kuala Lumpur, 24 hours from Butterworth. The **Magic Arrow Express** leaves Singapore on Sunday, Tuesday and Thursday. An additional train from Butterworth departs at 1420, arriving Bangkok 1210 the next day. The train from Bangkok to Butterworth departs 1420, arriving Butterworth 1255, see www.ktmb.com.my for a timetable for trains between Thailand and Malaysia. All tickets should be booked in advance.

For details of the domestic train network including fares, see pages 49 and 50.

Orient-Express Hotels, which operates the *Venice Simplon Orient-Express* also runs the luxury *Eastern & Oriental Express* between Bangkok, Kuala Lumpur and Singapore. The air-conditioned train runs once a week from Singapore to Bangkok and back. This locomotive extravaganza departs from Bangkok on Wednesday and returns from Singapore every Sunday. The journey takes 41 hours (two nights, one day) to cover the 2000-km one-way trip. Passengers can disembark at Hua Hin, Butterworth (Penang) and Kuala Lumpur. Reservations can be made at **Orient-Express Hotels**, Sea Containers House, 20 Upper Ground, London, SE1 9PF, T020-78055100, www.orient-express.com; **Orient-Express Hotels** also has agents in Bangkok, Singapore and Kuala Lumpur to handle reservations – in Bangkok T02-2168661; in Singapore contact: 32-01 Shaw Towers, Beach Road, T3923500, F3923600.

Touching down

Airport information

Don Muang airport lies 25 km north of Bangkok. There are two international terminals (adjoining one another) and one domestic terminal. Terminal 1 serves Asia, and Terminal 2 the rest of the world. A 500-m long covered and air-conditioned walkway links the domestic and international terminals.

Facilities at the international terminal include: banks and currency exchange, post office, left luggage (฿90 per item per day – maximum four months, located between terminals 1 and 2), hotel booking agency, airport information, airport clinic, lost and found baggage service, duty-free shops, restaurants and bars including a whole slate of newly opened fast-food outlets. (Food is expensive here – cheap food is available across the footbridge at the railway station or in the Domestic Terminal.) The **Amari Airport Hotel** is linked to the international terminal by a walkway and provides a 'ministay' service for passengers who can take a room for up to three hours between 0800 and 1800 (T02-5661020/1). For those who can't make it to the Amari, there is now a foot massage service in the departure lounge. There is a also massage service between the two terminals. The **domestic terminal** has a hotel booking counter, post office, currency exchange counters, restaurant and bookshop. A shuttle bus is sometimes available; beware, taxis overcharge for a drive of under 1 km.

Flight information: T02-5351386 for departures, T02-5351301 for arrivals. Domestic flight information: T02-5351253.

For information on **transport from the airport into Bangkok**, see Bangkok, Transport, page 151.

Procedure for a **lost or stolen passport**: 1) File a report with the local police. 2) Take the report to your local embassy or consulate and apply for a new travel

document or passport (if there is no representation, visit the Passport Division of the Ministry of Foreign Affairs). 3) Take the new passport plus the police report to Section 4, Subdivision 4, Immigration Bureau, room 311 (third floor), Old Building, Soi Suan Plu, Sathorn Tai Road, Bangkok, T02-2873911, for a new visa stamp.

New airport plans

In 2000 a government panel finally decided that Nong Ngu Hao – or Cobra Swamp – would become Thailand's new international gateway in 2005, taking over from Don Muang. Nong Ngu Hao is in Bang Phli district, Samut Prakan province, 30 km east of Bangkok; Don Muang is north. The planned completion date was 2005 whereupon all international flights would land here and all domestic flights would depart from Don Muang (the current airport). It is now apparent that the US$2.7 billion airport will actually open in 2006.

Airport tax

Payable on departure – ฿500 for international flights. Tax on domestic departures is included in the price of the ticket. Visitors in transit for less than 12 hours are permitted to enter the country and not pay departure tax on leaving again.

Airport accommodation

A **Amari Airport Hotel**, 333 Chert Wudthakas Rd, T02-5661020, www.amari.com. A/c, restaurants, pool, fitness centre, connected to airport by a/c footbridge; 400-plus rooms look onto attractive gardens. Short-term stays for wash and rest available.

A **Asia Airport**, 99/2 Moo 8 Phahon-Yothin Road, T02-9926999. Huge and impersonal, but all the amenities if you can't face driving into town.

A-B **Quality Suites**, 99/401-486 Chaeng Wattana Rd, Soi Benjamitr, T02-9822022, F9822036. A/c, restaurant, indoor pool, 'mini' stays available (maximum 8 hrs), slightly cheaper than the Amari but 15 mins from airport, okay for a night's stopover.

Tourist information

The **Tourist Authority of Thailand** (TAT) ⓘ *head office, 10th floor, Le Concorde Building, 202 Rachadaphisek Road, towards the northeastern edge of the city centre, T02-6941222, www.tourismthailand.org, Mon-Fri 0830-1630*, is Thailand's very efficient tourism organization. There is a more convenient office at ⓘ *4 Rachdamnern Nok Av, T02-2829773, daily 0830-1630*. There is also a third minor office at the Chatuchak Weekend Market ⓘ *Kamphaeng Phet 2 Rd, T02-2724440-1, Sat-Sun 0900-1700*.

Local offices are found in most major tourist destinations in the country and their addresses are listed in the appropriate sections. TAT offices are a useful source of local information, often providing maps of the town, listings of hotels/guesthouses and information on local tourist attractions. Most open daily 0830-1630.

Local customs and laws

Bargaining

This is common, except in the large department stores – although they may give a discount on expensive items of jewellery or furniture – and on items like soap, books and most necessities. Expect to pay anything from 25-75 per cent less than the asking price, depending on the bargainer's skill and the shopkeeper's mood. Bargaining is viewed as a game, so enter into it with good humour.

Touching down

Emergency services Police: T191, T123. Tourist Police: T195. Fire: T199. Ambulance: T02-2522171-5. Tourist Assistance Centre: Rachdamnern Nok Avenue, Bangkok, T02-2828129.
Hours of business Banks: Monday-Friday 0830-1530. Exchange services: Monday-Sunday 0830-2200 in Bangkok, Pattaya, Phuket and Chiang Mai. In other towns opening hours are usually rather shorter. Government offices: Monday-Friday 0830-1200, 1300-1630. Tourist offices: daily 0830-1630. Shops: 0830-1700, larger shops: 1000-1900 or 2100.
Official time GMT plus seven hours.
Voltage 220 volts (50 cycles). Most first- and tourist-class hotels have outlets for shavers and hair dryers. Adaptors are recommended, as almost all sockets are two pronged.
Weights and measures Thailand uses the metric system, although there are some traditional measures still in use in particular the *rai*, which equals 0.16 ha. There are four ngaan in a rai. Other local measures include the *krasorp* (sack) which equals 25 kg and the *tang* which is 10-11 kg. However, for most purchases (for example fruit) the kilogram is the norm.

Clothing

In towns and at religious sights, it is courteous to avoid wearing shorts and singlets (or sleeveless tops). Visitors who are inappropriately dressed may not be allowed into temples (wats). The same is true of mosques (in the Muslim-dominated far south). Most Thais always look neat and clean. Mai rieb-roi means 'not neat' and is considered a great insult. Beach resorts are a law unto themselves – casual clothes are the norm, although nudity is still very much frowned upon by Thais. In the most expensive restaurants in Bangkok diners may well be expected to wear a jacket and tie.

Conduct

Thais are generally very understanding of the foibles and habits of foreigners (farangs) and will forgive and forget most indiscretions. However, there are a number of 'dos and don'ts' which are worth observing:

Cool and hot hearts Among Thais, the personal characteristic of jai yen is very highly regarded; literally, this means to have a 'cool heart'. It embodies calmness, having an even temper and not displaying emotion. Although foreigners generally receive special dispensation, and are not expected to conform to Thai customs (all farang are thought to have jai rawn or 'hot hearts'), it is important to keep calm in any disagreement – losing one's temper leads to loss of face and loss of respect. An associated personal trait which Thais try to develop is kreng jai; this embodies being understanding of other people's needs, desires and feelings – in short, not imposing oneself.

Greeting people Traditionally, Thais greet one another with a wai – the equivalent of a handshake. In a wai, hands are held together as if in prayer, and the higher the wai, the more respectful the greeting. By watching Thai's wai it is possible to ascertain their relative seniority where a combination of class age, wealth, power and gender all play a part. Juniors or inferiors should initiate a wai, and hold it higher and for longer than the senior or superior. Foreigners are not expected to conform to this custom – a simple wai at chest to chin height is all that is required. You should not wai to children or to waiters, waitresses and other people offering a service. When farangs and Thais do business it is common to shake hands. The respectful term of address is khun, which applies to both men and women. This is usually paired with a Thai's first

name so that, for example, Somchai Bamruang would be greeted as Khun Somchai. The closest equivalent to the English Mr and Mrs/Miss are Nai and Nang, which are also used as formal terms of address. Thais also have nicknames like Kai (Chicken), Ooy (Sugar) or Kung (Shrimp) while people from certain professions will also have respectful titles – like ajaan for a teacher or lecturer.

Heads and feet Try to not openly point your feet at anyone – feet are viewed as spiritually the lowest part of the body. At the same time, never touch anyone's (even a child's) head, which is the holiest as well as the highest part. Resting your feet on a table would be regarded as highly disrespectful while stepping over someone sitting on the floor is also frowned upon. If sitting on the floor, try to tuck your feet under your body – although westerners unused to this posture may find it uncomfortable after a short time.

The monarchy Never criticize any member of the royal family or the institution itself. The monarchy is held in very high esteem and lèse majesté remains an offence carrying a sentence of up to 15 years in prison. You should treat coins and bank notes with respect as they bear the image of the King, as well as postage stamps which are moistened with a sponge rather than the tongue. In cinemas, the National Anthem is played before the show and the audience is expected to stand. At other events, take your lead from the crowd as to how to behave. A dying custom, but one which is still adhered to in smaller towns as well as certain parts of Bangkok, like at Hualamphong railway station, is that everybody stops in their tracks at 0800 and 1800, when the National Anthem is relayed over loudspeakers.

Monastery (wat) and monk etiquette Remove shoes on entering any monastery building, do not climb over Buddha images or have your picture taken in front of one, and when sitting in a bot or viharn ensure that your feet are not pointing towards a Buddha image. Wear modest clothing – women should not expose their shoulders or wear dresses that are too short (see above, Clothing). Ideally, they should be calf length although knee-length dresses or skirts are usually acceptable. Women should never touch a monk, hand anything directly to a monk or venture into the monks' quarters. They should also avoid climbing chedis (stupas). As in any other place of worship, visitors should not disturb the peace of a wat.

Open shows of affection Visitors will soon notice that men and women rarely show open, public signs of affection. It is not uncommon, however, to see men holding hands – this is usually a sign of simple friendship, nothing more. That said, in Bangkok, traditional customs have broken down and in areas such as Siam Square it is common to see young lovers, hand-in-hand.

Sanuk A quality of sanuk, which can be roughly translated as 'fun' or joie de vivre, is important to Thais. Activities are undertaken because they are sanuk, others avoided because they are mai sanuk ('not fun'). Perhaps it is because of this apparent love of life that so many visitors returning from Thailand remark on how Thais always appear happy and smiling. However, it is worth bearing in mind that the interplay of jai yen and kreng jai means that everything may not be quite as it appears.

Smoking This is prohibited on flights, public buses in Bangkok, department stores and in cinemas. Many fast-food restaurants also ban smoking – except at outside tables.

Tips Tipping is generally unnecessary. However, a 10 per cent service charge is now expected on room, food and drinks bills in the smarter hotels as well as a tip for any personal service. Increasingly, the more expensive restaurants add a 10 per cent service charge; others expect a small tip.

Responsible tourism

"Tourism is like fire. It can either cook your food or burn your house down". This sums up the ambivalent attitude that many people have regarding the effects of tourism. It is one of Thailand's largest foreign exchange earners, and the world's largest single industry, yet many people in receiving countries would rather tourists go home. Tourism is seen to be the cause of polluted beaches, rising prices, loose morals, consumerism, and much else besides.

The Economist pointed out in a survey of the industry in 1991: "The curse of the tourist industry is that it peddles dreams: dreams of holdays where the sun always shines, the children are always occupied, and where every evening ends in the best sex you have ever had. For most of its modern life, this has been matched by a concomitant dreaminess on the part of its customers. When asked, most tourists tell whopping lies about what they did on holiday..." (*The Economist*, 1991).

Most international tourists come from a handful of wealthy countries. This is why many see tourism as the new 'imperialism', imposing alien cultures and ideals on sensitive and unmodernized peoples. The problem, however, is that discussions of the effects of tourism tend to degenerate into simplifications – culminating in the drawing up of a checklist of 'positive' and 'negative' effects. Although such tables may be useful in highlighting problem areas, they also do a disservice by reducing a complex issue to a simple set of rather one dimensional 'costs' and 'benefits'. Different destinations will be affected in different ways; these effects are likely to vary over time; and different groups living in a particular destination will feel the effects of tourism in different ways and to varying degrees. At no time or place can tourism (or any other influence) be uniformly called 'good' or 'bad'.

Some tourists are attracted to Thailand because it is seen to be 'exotic'. When cultural erosion is identified, the tendency is to blame this on tourists and tourism who become the so-styled 'suntanned destroyers of culture'. The problem with views like this is that they assume that change is bad, and that indigenous cultures are unchanging. It makes local peoples victims of change, rather than masters of their own destinies. It also assumes that tourism is an external influence, when in fact it quickly becomes part of the local landscape. Cultural change is inevitable and on-going, and 'new' and 'traditional' are only judgements, not absolutes. Thus new cultural forms can quickly become key markers of tradition. Tourists searching for an 'authentic' experience are assuming that tradition is tangible, easily identifiable and unchanging. It is none of these.

Tourist art, both material (for instance, sculpture) and non-material (like dances) is another issue where views over the impacts of tourism sharply diverge. The mass of inferior 'airport' art on sale to tourists demonstrates, to some, the corrosive effects of tourism. It leads craftsmen and women to mass-produce second-rate pieces for a market that appreciates neither their cultural or symbolic worth, nor their aesthetic value. Yet tourism can also give value to craft industries that would otherwise be undermined by cheap industrial goods. So, some people argue that the craft traditions of southern Thailand have been given a new injection of vitality by the demands that tourism creates.

The environmental deterioration that is linked to tourism is due to a destination area exceeding its 'carrying capacity' as a result of overcrowding. But carrying capacity, though an attractive concept, is notoriously difficult to pin down. A second dilemma facing those trying to encourage greater environmental consciousness is the so-called 'tragedy of the commons', better described in terms of Chinese restaurants. When a group of people go to a Chinese restaurant with the intention of sharing the bill, each customer will tend to order a more expensive dish than he or she would normally do – on the logic that everyone will be doing the same, and the

How big is your footprint?

This is taken from the Tourism Concern website which also provides further elaboration of the points noted here. The code was developed from a Young Travellers' conference in April 2001 but is not aimed only at young travellers. As they say: "It applies to everybody who loves travelling, whether on a budget holiday or staying in a luxury community run centre".

- Learn about the country you're visiting. Start enjoying your travels before you leave by tapping into as many sources of information as you can.
- Think about where your money goes – be fair and realistic about how cheaply you travel. Try and put money into local people's hands; drink local beer or fruit juice rather than imported brands, and stay in locally-owned accommodation.
- Open your mind to new cultures and traditions. It can transform your holiday experience and you'll earn respect and be more readily welcomed by local people.
- Think about what happens to your rubbish: take biodegradable products and a water filter bottle. Be sensitive to limited resources like water, fuel and electricity.
- Help preserve local wildlife and habitats by respecting rules and regulations, such as sticking to footpaths, not standing on coral and not buying products made from endangered plants or animals.
- Use your guidebook as a starting point, not the only source of information. Talk to local people, then discover your own adventure!
- Don't treat people as part of the landscape; they may not want their picture taken. Put yourself in their shoes, ask first and respect their wishes.

bill will be split. In tourism terms, it means that hotel owners will always build those few more bungalows or that extra wing, to maximize their profits, reassured in the knowledge that the environmental costs will be shared among all hotel owners. So, despite most operators appreciating that over-development may 'kill the goose that lays the golden eggs', they do so anyway. But many areas of southern Thailand have few other development opportunities and those with beautiful landscapes and/or exotic cultures find it difficult not to resist the temptation to market them and attract the tourist dollar. And why shouldn't they?

One of the ironies is that the 'traveller' or 'backpacker' finds it difficult to consider him or herself as a tourist at all. This, of course, is hubris built upon the notion that the traveller is an 'independent' explorer, somehow beyond the bounds of the industry. Anna Borzello in an article entitled 'The myth of the traveller' in the journal *Tourism in Focus* (no 19, 1994) writes that "Independent travellers cannot acknowledge – without shattering their self-image – that to many local people they are simply a good source of income. ...[not] inheritors of Livingstone, [but] bearers of urgently needed money". Although she does, in writing this, grossly underestimate the ability of travellers to see beyond their thongs and friendship bracelets, she does have a point when she suggests that it is important for travellers honestly to appraise their role as tourists, because: "Not only are independent travellers often frustrated by the gap between the way they see themselves and the way they are treated, but unless they acknowledge that they are part of the tourist industry they will not take responsibility for the damaging effects of their tourism".

Safety

In general, Thailand is a safe country to visit. Physical violence against tourists, while it does occur, is rare. There have been some widely publicized murders of foreign tourists in recent years but this should not be taken to mean that Thailand is a particularly risky place to visit. Confidence tricksters, touts, pick-pockets and other thieves are far more of a problem and all operate, particularly in more popular tourist centres. Care and common sense usually avoids them. On the whole police react efficiently to tourist complaints and the country's health infrastructure, especially in provincial capitals and popular tourist destinations, is good. For background information on staying healthy, see page 75. The UK's Foreign and Commonwealth Office's Know Before You Go campaign, www.fco.gov.uk/travel, is a useful resource.

Bribery

The way to make your way in life, for some people in Thailand, is through the strategic offering of gifts. A Chulalongkorn University report recently estimated that it 'costs' ฿10 million to become Bangkok Police Chief. Apparently this can be recouped in just two years of hard graft. Although bribing officials is by no means recommended, resident farangs report that they often resort to such gifts to avoid the time and hassle involved in filling in the forms and making the requisite visit to a police station for a minor traffic offence. As a visitor, the best first step is to play it straight.

Drugs and prostitution

Many prostitutes and drug dealers are in league with the police and may find it more profitable to report you than to take your custom (or they may try to do both). They receive a reward from the police, and the police in their turn receive a bonus for the detective work. Note that foreigners on buses may be searched for drugs. Sentences for possession of illegal drugs vary from a fine or one year's imprisonment for marijuana up to life imprisonment or execution for possession or smuggling of heroin. The death penalty is usually commuted.

Emergencies

Calling one of the emergency numbers (see box, Touching down) will not usually be very productive as few operators speak English. It is better to call the Tourist Police (see below) or have a hotel employee or other English-speaking Thai telephone for you. For more intractable problems contact your embassy or consulate.

Insurgency and security in border areas

The Communist Party of Thailand (CPT), which was influential in parts of the south, north and northeast during the late 1970s and early 1980s, is virtually moribund and does not pose a threat to visitors. Rather more problematic is the Pattani United Liberation Organization (PULO) which is agitating for an independent Muslim state in the far south. There were a handful of bombings during the 1990s and more attacks from the beginning of 2000. Around 900 have died since the beginning of 2004. Another separatist organization is the Barisan Revolusi Nasional (BRN). Tourists have died and been injured in these bombings and the UK Foreign and Commonwealth office (www.fco.gov.uk/travel) advises against all but essential travel to the four provinces of Yala, Pattani, Narathiwat and Songkhla. The US State Department (www.travel.state.gov) does the same and includes Hat Yai town in its warning. There is little doubt that more could have been done to assuage concerns in the region by considering the political demands and cultural sensitivities of the people of the far south. The lack of sensitivity represents a considerable political failure – and a long-term one. See also page 525 and Background.

Personal security

There have been some worrying attacks on tourists and a handful of murders. It must be emphasized that these are very few and far between. Most occurred when visitors became involved in local conflicts, or tried to outwit thieves. Robbery is common; it ranges from pick-pocketing to the drugging (and subsequent robbing) of bus and train passengers. Watchfulness and simple common sense should be employed. Women travelling alone should be careful. (See also Women travellers, page 25.) Always lock hotel rooms and place valuables in a safe deposit if available (or if not, take them with you).

Prisons

Thai prisons are very grim. Most foreigners are held in two Bangkok prisons – Khlong Prem and Bangkwang. One resident who visits overseas prisoners in jail recently wrote to us saying: "You cannot over-estimate the horrors! Khlong Prem has 7,000 prisoners, five to a cell, with not enough room to stretch out, no recreation, one meal a day (an egg on Sundays)...". One hundred prisoners in a dormitory is not uncommon, and prisoners on Death Row have waist chains and ankle fetters permanently welded on.

Tourist police

In 1982 the government set up a special arm of the police to deal with the demands of the tourist industry – the Tourist Police. By 1995 there were around 500 officers stationed in the main tourist destinations and now there is no important tourist destination that doesn't have a tourist police office. The Thai police have come in for a great deal of scrutiny over recent years, although most policemen are honest and only too happy to help the luckless visitor. **Tourist Police,** Bangkok, T02-2815051 or T02-2216206. Open daily 0800-2400.

Touts and confidence tricksters

Inevitably, Thailand's tourist industry has created a side-industry populated by touts and confidence tricksters. More visitors get 'stung' buying what they hope are valuable gems than in any other way (see page 145). There is also a rich tradition in card scams. Along with the scammers and confidence tricksters, there are scores of touts who make their living guiding tourists towards certain shops and hotels where they are paid a commission for their pains. Ignore touts who claim that hotels have closed, are full, or are dirty or substandard. Likewise, it is best to avoid taxi or tuk-tuk drivers who are offering to drive you to a hotel or guesthouse for free.

Traffic

Perhaps the greatest danger is from the traffic – especially if you are attempting to drive yourself. More foreign visitors are killed or injured in traffic accidents than in any other way. Thai drivers have a 'devil may care' attitude towards the highway code, and there are many quite horrific accidents. Be very careful crossing the road – just because there is a pedestrian crossing, do not expect drivers to stop. Be particularly wary when driving or riding a motorcycle (see page 48).

Getting around

Air

The budget airline boom has finally arrived in Thailand with carriers now offering cheap flights all over the country. **Air Asia, Bangkok Airways, PB Air, Phuket Air** and **One Two Go** are the present major players in this market offering dirt cheap flights – but only if you book online and in advance. **Thai Airways** (THAI) is the national flag carrier and is also by far the largest domestic airline. Although it has had a relatively turbulent few years and standards have declined since the halcyon days of the late 1980s, it is still okay.

THAI flies to several destinations in Thailand. It has a three-stop 'Amazing Thailand Air Pass' for US$169 for internal routes. The three coupons entitle you to fly economy to any of **THAI's** domestic airports for a period of three months. You can add a maximum of eight coupons for US$59 each. The pass must be bought prior to arrival in Thailand as part of an international trip to or via Thailand. **THAI** head office is found at 89 Vibhavadi Rangsit Road, T02-5130121, www.thaiair.com. It is better to book flights through a local office or travel agent displaying the **THAI** logo.

Bangkok Airways, T1771, T02-2555500, www.bangkokair.com. (Head Office 99 Mu 14, Vibhavadirangsit Rd, Chom Phon, Chatuchak, Bangkok; European Regional Office: Bethmannstrasse 58, D-60311 Frankfurt/Main, Germany, T0049 69-13377565/566, info@bangkokairways.de), flies from Bangkok to Chiang Mai via Sukhothai, Koh Samui, Phuket, Krabi, Trat and from Koh Samui to Phuket and Pattaya (U-Tapao). From Phuket it flies to Pattaya. The airline has domestic offices at all the airports it flies to and from: Dong Muang Airport, Chiang Mai, Krabi, Pattaya, Phuket, Samui, and Sukhothai airports.

Bangkok Airways also offers an **airpass** deal in conjunction with **Laos Airlines** and **Siem Reap Airways** (Cambodia). Coupons for each sector start at US$50 and a minimum of three or maximum of six must be bought. Local departure taxes are not included. See the website for full details.

PB Air, T02-2610220, www.pbair.com, flies to Nakhon Si Thammarat, Roi Et, Lampang, Sakhon Nakhon, Trang, Nan and Nakhon Phanom. **Phuket Air,** 1168/102 Lumpini Tower Building, Rama IV Road, T02-6798999, www.phuketairlines.com, flies from Bangkok to Mae Sot, Ranong and Buriram. **One Two Go,** www.fly12go.com, has no public office but a call centre, T1126, and flies from Bangkok to Chiang Rai via Chiang Mai, Hat Yai and Phuket. Malaysian-based **Air Asia,** www.airasia.com, has no public office or telephone number in Thailand. It offers routes from Bangkok to Chiang Mai, Chiang Rai, Udon Thani, Hat Yai, Phuket, Ubon Ratchathani and Narathiwat.

Note It is advisable not to fly with **Phuket Air** following a string of domestic and international incidents. The company is already banned from flying to and from the UK and France.

Boat

The waterways of Thailand are extensive. However, most people limit their water travel to trips around Bangkok or to Ayutthaya. Hang-yaaws (long- tailed boats) are a common form of water travel and are motorized, fast and fun.

Cruise holidays An alternative to the usual overland tour of Thailand is to book a berth on the *Andaman Princess*. This cruise ship sails to Koh Tao and back (three

days/two nights). Passengers can snorkel at Koh Tao and the level of service and safety is high. Large numbers of young, middle-class Thais make the journey and there is lots of entertainment. It costs around ฿5000 for a single berth. Contact **Siam Cruise**, 33/10-11 Sukhumvit Soi Chaiyod (Soi 11), T02-2554563. See also Cruises, page 22.

Domestic air routes

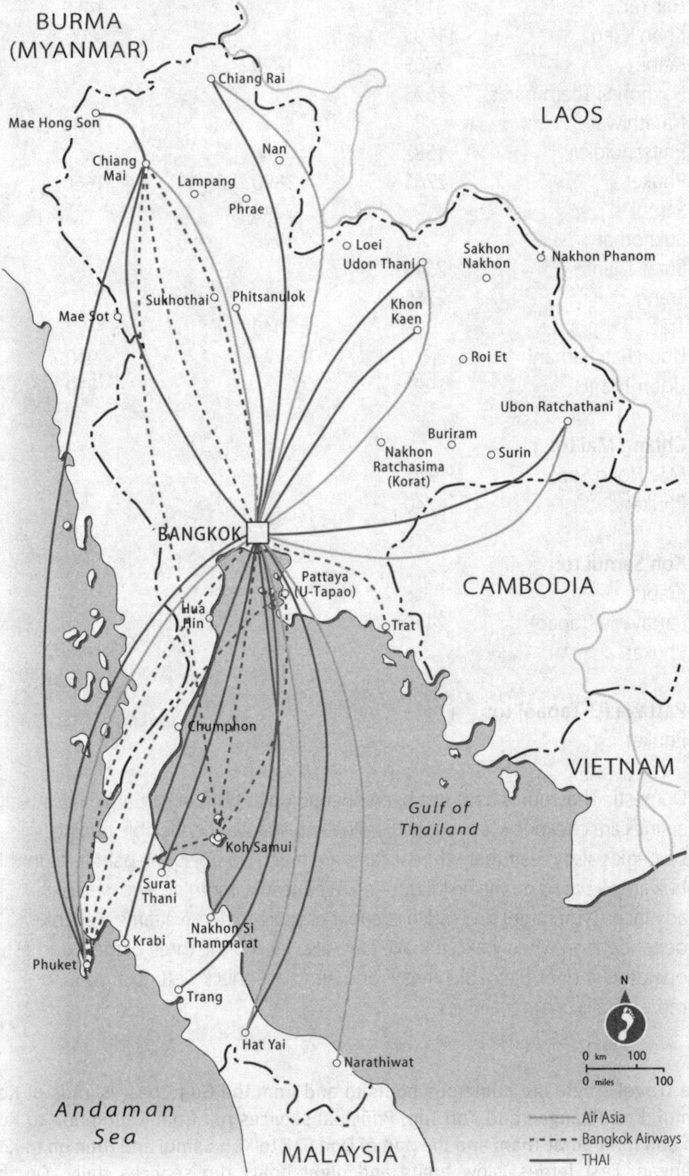

Sample domestic airfares

Route	THAI	Bangkok Airways	Air Asia
Bangkok to:	fare (baht)	fare (baht)	fare (baht)
Chiang Mai	2375	1990	1450
Chiang Rai	2745		1450
Hat Yai	3195		1450
Khon Kaen	1705		800
Krabi	2765	1890	
Nakhon Si Thammarat	2625		
Narathiwat			1980
Phitsanulok	1585		
Phuket	2765	1890	1660
Samui		2240	
Sukhothai		1940	
Surat Thani	2545		
Trang	2765		
Trat		2040	
Ubon Ratchathani	2,100		910
Udon Thani	1990		910
Chiang Mai to:			
Mae Hong Son	970		
Phuket	4740		
Koh Samui to:			
Krabi		1840	
Pattaya (U-Tapao)	2440		
Phuket		1970	
Pattaya (U-Tapao) to:			
Phuket		2740	

Domestic Thai routes have just been opened up to budget carriers. Fares for all airlines are cheaper when booked online and in advance. Flexible pricing strategies also mean that off-peak fares are much cheaper. The baht fares in this box are all based on the first flight on a Wednesday morning two weeks in advance – you might find much cheaper or more expensive fares available dependent on when you book. We have also picked the three biggest domestic operators – THAI, Bangkok Airways and Air Asia – check Getting around for more details of other airlines.

Sea travel There are numerous boats to and from the Gulf Coast Islands of Koh Samui, Koh Phangan and Koh Tao. Principal services run from Chumphon to Koh Tao and from Surat Thani and the port of Don Sak to Koh Samui and then on to Koh Phangan. Fast ferries, slow boats and night boats run services daily. On the Andaman Coast there are services to and from Phuket, Koh Phi Phi, Krabi, Koh

Lanta, the islands off Trang and from Ban Pak Bara and Koh Tarutao National Park. The islands off the eastern seaboard are also connected by regular services to the mainland. Note that services become irregular and are suspended during certain times of year because of the wet season and rough seas. Each section details information on the months that will affect regular boat services. Note also that with the return of the tourist trade to areas affected by the tsunami, such as Koh Phi Phi, more and more services will be implemented.

Road

Bus

Private and state-run buses leave Bangkok for every town in Thailand; it is an extensive network and a cheap way to travel. The government bus company is called **Bor Kor Sor**, and every town in Thailand will have a BKS terminal. There are small stop-in- every-town local buses plus the faster long-distance buses (rot duan – express – or rot air – air-conditioned). **Air-conditioned buses** come in two grades: **chan nung (first class, blue colour)** and **chan song (second class, orange colour)**. Chan song have more seats but less elbow and leg room, and will not offer hostess, food and drink services, or a toilet. Chan nung buses will have all of these as well as a maximum of 42 seats (adjustable to 70° recline). For longer/overnight journeys, air-conditioned de luxe (sometimes known as rot tour, officially Standard 1A buses, also blue like the chan rung) or VIP buses, stewardess service is provided with food and drink supplied en route and more leg room plus constant Thai music or videos. There should be no more than 24 seats (adjustable to 135° recline). Many fares include meals at roadside restaurants, so keep hold of your ticket. See also sample routes and fares box on page 46.

The **local buses** are slower and cramped but worth it for those wishing to sample local life. The seats at the very back are reserved for monks, so be ready to move if necessary.

Private tour buses Many tour companies operate bus services in Thailand; travel agents in Bangkok will supply information. These buses are normally more comfortable than the state buses but are more expensive. Overnight trips usually involve a meal stop (included in price of ticket) and stewardess service for drinks and snacks. They often leave from outside the company office which may not be located at the central bus station.

Car hire

There are two schools of thought on car hire in Thailand: one, that under no circumstances should farangs (foreigners) drive themselves; and second, that hiring a car is one of the best ways of seeing the country and reaching the more inaccessible sights. Increasing numbers of people are hiring their own cars and internationally respected car hire firms are expanding their operations (such as **Hertz** and **Avis**). Roads and service stations are generally excellent. Driving is on the left-hand side of the road.

There are a few points that should be kept in mind: accidents in Thailand are often horrific. If involved in an accident, and they occur with great frequency, you – as a foreigner – are likely to be found the guilty party and expected to meet the costs. Ensure the cost of hire includes insurance cover. Many local residents recommend that should foreigners be involved in an accident, they should not stop but drive on to the nearest police station – if possible, of course.

The average cost of hiring a car from a reputable firm is ฿1000-2000 per day, ฿6000-10,000 per week, or ฿20,000-30,000 per month. Some rentals come with insurance automatically included; for others it must be specifically requested and a

Buses in Thailand: sample routes and fares

Route	Time (hours)	Fare (baht)
Bangkok North to:		
Ayutthaya	1½	50
Sukhothai	7	210
Mae Sot	9	285
Chiang Mai	9¾	400
Chiang Rai	12	450
Chiang Khong	12¾	470
Mae Hong Son	12½	510
Bangkok Northeast to:		
Korat	4½	145
Udon Thani	9	250
Ubon Ratchathani	10	300
Khon Kaen	7	360
Nakhon Phanom	10	390
Bangkok South to:		
Hua Hin	3	99
Prachuap Khiri Khan	4	137
Chumphon	7	211
Surat Thani	11	295
Nakhon Si Thammarat	12	705
Phuket	13	755
Ranong	10	515
Phangnga	12	389
Krabi	12	710
Trang	12	750
Satun	13	865
Bangkok East to:		
Pattaya	3	75
Ban Phe	3½	100
Chantaburi	4½	120
Trat	5½	150

surcharge is added. An international driver's licence, or a UK, US, French, German, Australian, New Zealand, Singapore or Hong Kong licence is required. The lower age limit is 20 years (higher for some firms). Addresses of car hire firms are included in the sections on the main tourist destinations. If the mere thought of competing with Thai drivers is terrifying, an option is to hire a chauffeur along with the car. For this service an extra ฿300-500 per day is usually charged, more at weekends and if an overnight stay is included. Note that local car hire firms are cheaper although the cars are likely to be less well maintained and will have tens of thousands of kilometres on the clock.

Route	Time (hrs)	Fare (baht)
Phuket to:		
Bangkok	13	486
Surat Thani	5	170
Trang	5	189
Nakhon Si Thammarat	8	125
Hat Yai	6	180
Ranong	5	185
Krabi	3	117
Phangnga	2½	36
Satun	7	274
Chiang Mai to:		
Nan	6	175
Phrae	4	190
Mae Sot	6	220
Sukhothai	5	200
Khon Kaen	12	430
Chiang Rai	3	125
Mae Hong Son	7	200
Pai	4	110
Udon Thani	12	500

Fares given are standard air conditioned and are average rounded figures. These may vary by a few baht. Cheaper, non air-conditioned buses are available on nearly all routes. More expensive VIP luxury services are available on the busier routes eg Bangkok-Chiang Mai.

Cycling

The advice below is collated from travellers who have bicycled through Thailand and is meant to provide a general guideline for those intending to tour the country by bicycle (which is becoming more and more common). Bikes can be taken on trains, but check the security in the guards' van.

Bike type Touring, hybrid or mountain bikes are fine for most roads and tracks in Thailand. Spares are readily available and even small towns have bicycle repair shops where it is often possible to borrow larger tools such as vices. Mountain bikes have made an impact, so accessories for these are also widely available. What is less common are components made of unusual materials – such as titanium and rarer composites. Buses are used to taking bicycles (although the more expensive air-conditioned tour buses may prove reluctant), and most carry them free, although some drivers may ask for a surcharge. Many international airlines take bicycles free of charge, provided they are not boxed. Check your carrier's policy before checking in.

Attitudes to bicyclists It is still comparatively rare to see foreigners cycling in Thailand, so expect to be an object of interest. Cars and buses often travel along the hard shoulder, and few expect to give way to a bicycle. Be very wary, especially on main roads.

 Useful equipment Basic tool kit – although there always seems to be help near at hand, and local workshops seem to be able to improvise a solution to just about any problem – including a puncture repair kit, spare tubes, spare tyre and pump. Also take a good map of the area, bungee cords, first-aid kit and water filter.

Bicycle hire Guesthouses and specialized outlets in many places hire out touring and mountain bikes. Expect to pay between ฿80-150 per day. See above for general advice on bicycling. Take sunscreen, mosquito repellent, cover up well including a hat and avoid bicycling at night. Be aware that bicyclists give way to everything and everyone!

Hitchhiking Thai people rarely hitchhike and tourists who try could find themselves waiting a long time at the roadside. It is sometimes possible to wave down vehicles at the more popular beach resorts.

Motorbike hire

Mostly confined to holiday resorts and prices vary from place to place. ฿150-300 per day is usual for a 100-150cc machine. Often licences do not have to be shown and insurance will not be available. Off the main roads and in quieter areas it can be an enjoyable and cheap way to see the country. Riding with shorts and flip-flops is dangerous. Borrow a helmet if at all possible and expect anything larger than you to ignore your presence on the road. Be extremely wary. Thousands of Thais are killed in motorcycle accidents each year and large numbers of tourists also suffer injuries. (Koh Samui has been said to have the highest death rate anywhere in the world!) Some travellers are now not just hiring motorbikes to explore a local area, but are touring the entire country by motorcycle. It is the cheapest way to be independent of public transport, but the risks rise accordingly.

In December 1992, the Thai government introduced a new – and long overdue – law requiring motorcyclists to wear helmets on Bangkok's 240 main roads. In April 1995 this was extended to all roads and sois (lanes) in the capital. At the end of June 1995 Chiang Mai also made the wearing of helmets mandatory. However, outside Bangkok the wearing of helmets in most areas is not compulsory.

Motorbike taxi

These are becoming increasingly popular, and are the cheapest, quickest and most dangerous way to get from 'A' to 'B'. Riders wear coloured vests (sometimes numbered) and tend to congregate at key intersections or outside shopping centres for example. Agree a price before boarding – expect to pay ฿10-20.

Saamlor ('three wheels')/tuk-tuk

These come in the form of pedal or motorized machines. Fares should be bargained and agreed before setting off. It will not take long to discover what is a reasonable price, but don't expect to pay the same as a Thai. Drivers are a useful source of local information and will know most places of interest, plus hotels and restaurants (and sometimes their prices). In Bangkok, and now in some other large towns, the saamlor is a motorized, gas-powered scooter known affectionately as the tuk-tuk (because of the noise it makes). Pedal-powered saamlors were outlawed in Bangkok a few years ago and they are now gradually being replaced by the noisier motorized version throughout the country.

Songthaew ('two rows')

Songthaews are pick-up trucks fitted with two benches and can be found in many upcountry towns. They normally run fixed routes, with set fares, but can often be hired and used as a taxi service (agree a price before setting out). To let the driver know you want to stop, press the electric buzzers or tap the side of the vehicle with a coin.

Taxi

Standard taxis can be found in some Thai towns. This is the most expensive form of public motorized transport, and many now have the added luxury of air-conditioning. In Bangkok almost all taxis have meters. If un-metered, agree a price before setting off, and always bargain. In the south of Thailand, long-distance share taxis are common.

Maps of Thailand and Southeast Asia

Although maps are available locally, it is sometimes useful to buy a map prior to departure to plan routes and itineraries.

Regional maps Bartholomew *Southeast Asia* (1:5,800,000); ITM (International Travel Maps) *Southeast Asia* (1:6,000,000); Nelles *Southeast Asia* (1:4,000,000); Hildebrand *Thailand, Burma, Malaysia and Singapore* (1:2,800,000).

Country maps Bartholomew *Thailand* (1:1,500,000); ITM (International Travel Maps) *Thailand* (1:1,000,000); Nelles *Thailand* (1:1,500,000).

City maps Nelles *Bangkok*.

Road maps The best (and cheapest) road maps are available locally – easily picked up from a petrol station. They are especially handy because they often give place names in Thai and English and therefore can help when you are trying to get somewhere (but no one understands you!). Michelin also produces a good book or road maps for the country.

Other maps Tactical Pilotage Charts (TPC, US Airforce) (1:500,000); Operational Navigational Charts (ONC, US Airforce) (1:500,000). Both of these are good at showing relief features (useful for planning treks); less good on roads, towns and facilities.

Map shops in the UK The best selection is available from **Stanfords,** 12-14 Long Acre, Covent Garden, London, T020-78361321, www.stanfords.co.uk, 29 Corn Street, Bristol, and 39 Spring Gardens, Manchester. Recommended. Also recommended is **McCarta,** 15 Highbury Place, London, T020-73541616.

Train

The **State Railway of Thailand,** www.srt.or.th/httpEng/, is efficient, clean and comfortable, with five main routes to the north, northeast, west, east and south. It is safer than bus travel but can take longer. The choice is **first-class air-conditioned compartments, second-class sleepers, second-class air-conditioned sit-ups** with reclining chairs and **third-class sit-ups.** Travelling third class is often the cheapest way to travel long distance. First and second class are more expensive than the bus but infinitely more comfortable. **Express trains** are known as rot duan, **special express trains** as rot duan phiset and **rapid trains** as rot raew. Express and rapid trains are faster as they make fewer stops; there is a surcharge for the service.

For rail information T02-2237010/2237020. See also fares listings, page 50.

Reservations for sleepers should be made in advance (up to 60 days ahead) at Bangkok's Hualamphong station ⓘ *T02-2233762/2247788, the Advance Booking Office is open daily 0700-0400.* (Some travel agencies also book tickets.) A queue-by-ticket arrangement works efficiently, and travellers do not have to wait long. If you change a reservation the charge is ฿10. It is advisable to book the bottom sleeper, as lights are bright on top (in second-class compartments). It still may be difficult to get a seat at certain times of year, such as during festivals (like **Songkran** in April). Personal luggage allowance is 50 kg in first class, 40 kg in second and 30 kg in third class. Children aged three to 12 years old and under 150 cm in height pay half fare; those under three years old and less than 100 cm in height travel free, but do not get a seat. It is possible to pick up timetables at Hualamphong station (from the information booth in the main concourse). There

State railways of Thailand: sample routes and fares

Route	Time	Distance (km)	Fare (Baht) 1st class	2nd class	3rd class
Bangkok north to:					
Don Muang	45 mins	22	21	11	5
Ayutthaya	1½ hrs	71	66	35	15
Lopburi	2½ hrs	133	123	64	28
Nakhon Sawan	4 hrs	246	218	110	48
Phitsanulok	5-6 hrs	389	324	159	69
Uttaradit	8 hrs	485	394	190	82
Den Chai	8 hrs	534	431	207	90
Nakhon Lampang	11¾ hrs	642	512	244	106
Lamphun	8½ hrs	729	575	273	118
Chiang Mai	11-13 hrs	751	593	281	121
Bangkok northeast to:					
Nakhon Ratchasima	5 hrs	264	230	115	50
Surin	8 hrs	420	346	169	73
Si Saket	9½ hrs	515	416	201	87
Ubon Ratchathani	10 hrs	575	460	221	95
Bua Yai Jn	5 hrs	346	294	145	63
Ban Phai	8 hrs	408	338	165	71
Khon Kaen	8 hrs	450	368	179	77
Udon Thani	9½ hrs	569	457	219	95
Nong Khai	11 hrs	624	497	238	103
Bangkok east to:					
Chachoengsao	1½ hrs	61	57	30	13
Prachin Buri	3 hrs	122	115	59	26
Kabin Buri	3½ hrs	161	149	76	33
Aranya Prathet	4½ hrs	255	222	111	48
Chonburi	2¾ hrs	108	102	53	23
Pattaya	3¾ hrs	155	140	72	31

are two types: the 'condensed' timetable (by region) showing all rapid routes, and complete, separate timetables for all classes. Timetables are available from stations and some tourist offices. If travelling north or south during the day, try to get a seat on the side of the carriage out of the sun.

A 'bullet train' may soon transport visitors along the eastern seaboard to Pattaya. A 20-day **rail pass** costs ฿1500 for adults, ฿750 for children (blue pass), valid on all trains, second and third class, supplementary charges NOT included. A red pass includes supplementary charges, ฿3000 for adults, ฿1500 for children. For further details visit the Advance Booking Office at Hualamphong station in Bangkok, ⓣ *T02-2233762/2247788*.

Route	Time	Distance (km)	Fare (Baht)* 1st class	2nd class	3rd class
Bangkok south to:					
Nakhon Pathom	1½ hrs	64	60	31	14
Kanchanaburi	2½ hrs	133	123	64	28
Rachaburi	2 hrs	117	110	57	25
Phetburi	3 hrs	167	153	78	34
Hua Hin	4 hrs 10 mins	229	202	102	44
Prachuap Khiri Khan	5 hrs	318	272	135	58
Chumphon	7¾ hrs	485	394	190	82
Surat Thani	11 hrs	651	519	248	107
Trang	15 hrs	845	660	311	135
Nakhon Si Thammarat	15 hrs	832	652	308	133

** Mid 2005 fares quoted. Supplementary charges which apply for express trains, rapid trains, special express trains, a/c services and sleepers are not included. See www.srt.motc.go.th for the latest information.*

Sleeping

As a premier tourist destination and with an economy that has made the leap into the 'middle income' bracket, Thailand has a large selection of hotels – including some of the best in the world. However, outside the tourist centres, there is still an absence of adequate 'western-style' accommodation. Most 'Thai' hotels are lacking in character and are poorly maintained. Due to the popularity of the country with backpackers, there are also many small guesthouses, serving western food and catering to the foibles of foreigners. These are concentrated in the main beach resorts.

Hotels and guesthouses

Hotels and guesthouses are listed under eight categories, according to the average price of a double/twin room for one night. It should be noted that many hotels will have a range of rooms, some with air-conditioning (a/c) and attached bathroom facilities, others with just a fan and shared facilities. Prices can therefore vary a great deal. If a hotel entry lists 'some a/c', then these rooms are likely to be in the upper part of the range, perhaps even in the next range. Unlike, say, Indonesia, few hotels in Thailand provide breakfast in the price of the room. A service charge of 10 per cent and government tax of seven per cent will usually be added to the bill in the more expensive hotels (categories L-C). Ask whether the quoted price includes tax when checking in. Prices in Bangkok are inflated.

During the off-season, hotels and guesthouses in tourist destinations may halve their room rates so it is always worthwhile bargaining or asking whether there is a special price. Given the fierce competition among hotels, it is even worth trying during the peak season. Over-building has meant that there is a glut of rooms in some towns and hotels are desperate for business.

Hotel price codes explained

L More than ฿5,000 and **AL** ฿2,499-5,000 **International**: rooms will be air conditioned, have a minibar, in-room safe, coffee and tea making facilities and cable TV. They will have the entire range of business services, sports facilities (gym, swimming pool), possibly a spa, Asian and western restaurants and bars. It is likely they will offer tutorials on Thai cooking, flower arranging and massage for example.

A ฿1,250-2,499 **First class**: usually offer comprehensive business, sports and recreational facilities, with a range of restaurants and bars. Rooms are likely to have all or the majority of the facilities mentioned above.

B ฿750-1,249 **Tourist class**: these will probably have a swimming pool and all rooms will have air conditioning and an attached bathroom. Other services include one or more restaurants. The majority will have cable TV.

C ฿400-749 **Economy**: rooms may be air conditioned and have attached bathrooms with hot water. A restaurant and room service will probably be available. Sports facilities are unlikely.

D ฿200-399 **Budget**: rooms are likely to be fan-cooled and they should have an attached bathroom. Toilets may be either western-style or of the squat variety, depending on whether the town is on the tourist route. Many in this price range, out of tourist areas, are 'Thai' hotels. Bed linen, towels and toilet paper are usually provided, and there may be a restaurant.

E ฿100-199 **Guesthouse**: fan-cooled rooms, in some cases with shared bathroom facilities. Toilets are likely to be of the squat variety, with no toilet paper provided. Bed linen should be provided, although towels may not. Rooms are small, facilities few. Guesthouses popular with foreigners may be excellent sources of information and also sometimes offer cheap tours and services such as bicycle and motorcycle hire. Places in this category vary a great deal, and can change very rapidly. One year's best bargain becomes the following year's health hazard – or, it has been upgraded and is beyond the budget traveller's reach. Other travellers are the best source of up-to-the-minute reviews on whether standards have plummeted.

F Under ฿100 **Guesthouse**: fan-cooled rooms, usually with shared bathroom facilities. Toilets are likely to be of the squat variety with no toilet paper provided. Some of these guesthouses can be filthy, vermin-infested places. Others are superb value. As in the category above, standards change very fast and other travellers are the best source of information.

Until 10 years ago, most guesthouses offered shared facilities with cold water showers and squat toilets. Levels of cleanliness were also less than pristine. Owners have now caught on to the fact that westerners are generally weak of thigh and chary of swilling grubby toilets with a scoop-and-bucket affair. Consequently, western toilet imperialism is making inroads into Thai culture and many of the better run guesthouses will have good, clean toilets with sit-down facilities and, sometimes, hot water. Some are even quite stylish in their bathroom facilities. Fans are the norm in most guesthouses although, again, to cash in on the buying power of backpackers with more disposable income more and more offer a/c rooms as well. Check that mosquito nets are provided.

Security is a problem, particularly in beach resort areas where flimsy bungalows offer easy access to thieves. Keep valuables with the office for safekeeping (although there are regular cases of people losing valuables that have been left in 'safekeeping') or on your person when you go out. Guesthouses can be tremendous value for money. With limited overheads, family labour and using local foods they can cut their rates in a way that larger hotels with armies of staff, imported food and expensive facilities to maintain simply cannot.

Camping and national park accommodation

It is possible to camp in Thailand and **national parks** are becoming much better at providing campsites and associated facilities. Most parks will have public toilets with basic facilities. Bungalows fall into our C accommodation category but because they can often accommodate large groups their per person cost is less than this. The more popular parks will often also have privately-run accommodation including sophisticated resorts, sometimes within the park boundaries. For reservations at any of the national parks contact: Reservation Office, National Parks Division, Royal Forestry Department, Phanhonyothin Road, Bangkhen, Bangkok, T02-5794842/ 5790529/5614292; or telephone the park offices listed in the relevant sections of this guide. **Beaches** are considered public property – anybody can camp on them for free.

In terms of what to bring and wear, bear in mind that at night at high elevations, even in muggy Thailand, it can be cold. In the north and northeast it can fall to close to freezing. So make sure you have a thick coat and a warm sleeping bag. During the day, long trousers (to avoid scratches), sturdy shoes (if you are thinking of trekking any distance), and a hat are recommended. In the evening, long-sleeved shirts (to keep the mosquitoes at bay) are required. If you are camping, remember that while the more popular parks have tents for hire the rest – and this means most – do not. In addition you should bring along (in addition to the obvious things) toilet paper, torch, and a camp stove and fuel.

Eating

Thai food, for long an exotic cuisine distant from the average northerner's mind and tongue, has become an international success story. In 2002 it was said that there were 5500 Thai restaurants around the world, and even this number (intuitively) would seem to be an underestimate. The Thai government, recognizing the marketing potential of Thai food, has instituted a plan called Global Thai to boost the profile of Thai food worldwide as a means of attracting more people to visit the home of Thai food. Thai food has become, in short, one of Thailand's most effective advertisements.

Thai food is an intermingling of Tai, Chinese, and to a lesser extent, Indian cuisines. This helps to explain why restaurants produce dishes which must be some of the (spicy) hottest in the world, as well as others which are rather bland. Laap (raw – traditionally but now more frequently cooked – chopped beef mixed with rice, herbs and spices) is a traditional 'Tai' dish; pla priaw waan (whole fish with soy and ginger) is Chinese in origin; while gaeng mussaman (beef 'Muslim' curry) was brought to Thailand by Muslim immigrants. Even satay, paraded by most restaurants as a Thai dish, was introduced from Malaysia and Indonesia (which themselves adopted it from Arab traders during the Middle Ages).

Despite these various influences, Thai cooking is distinctive. Thais have managed to combine the best of each tradition, adapting elements to fit their own preferences. Remarkably, considering how ubiquitous it is in Thai cooking, the chilli

pepper is a New World fruit and was not introduced into Thailand until the late 16th century (along with the pineapple and papaya).

When a Thai asks another Thai whether he has eaten he will ask, literally, whether he has 'eaten rice' (kin khaaw). Similarly, the accompanying dishes are referred to as food 'with the rice'. A Thai meal is based around rice, and many wealthy Bangkokians own farms upcountry where they cultivate their favourite variety. There are two main types of rice – 'sticky' or glutinous (khao niaw) and non-glutinous (khao jao). Sticky rice is usually used to make sweets (desserts) although it is the staple in the northeastern region and parts of the north. Khao jao is standard white rice.

A meal usually consists (along with the rice) of a soup like tom yam kung (prawn soup), kaeng (a curry) and krueng kieng (a number of side dishes). Generally, Thai food is chilli-hot, and aromatic herbs and grasses (like lemon grass, coriander, tamarind and ginger) are used to give a distinctive flavour. Nam pla (fish sauce) and nam prik (nam pla, chillies, garlic, sugar, shrimps and lime juice) are two condiments that are taken with almost all meals. Nam pla is made from steeping fish, usually anchovies, in brine for long periods and then bottling the peatish-coloured liquor produced. Chillies deserve a special mention because most Thais like their food HOT! Some chillies are comparatively mild; others – like the tiny, red prik khii nuu (mouse shit pepper) – are fiendishly hot.

Due to Thailand's large Chinese population (or at least Thais with Chinese roots), there are also many Chinese-style restaurants whose cuisine is variously 'Thai-ified'. Many of the snacks available on the streets show this mixture of Thai and Chinese, not to mention Arab and Malay. Bah jang, for example, are small pyramids of leaves stuffed with sticky rice, Chinese sausage, salted eggs, pork and dried shrimp. They were reputedly first created for the Chinese dragon boat festival but are now available 12 months a year – for around ฿20.

To sample Thai food it is best to go in a group to a restaurant and order a range of dishes. To eat alone is regarded as slightly strange. However, there are a number of 'one-dish' meals like fried rice and phat thai (fried noodles) and restaurants will also usually provide raat khao ('over rice') which is a dish like a curry served on a bed of rice for a single person.

Strict non-fish eating **vegetarians** and **vegans** are in for a tough time. Nearly every cooked meal you will eat in Thailand will be liberally doused in nam pla (fish sauce – made from rotting fish and used as a condiment) or cooked with shrimp paste. At more expensive and upmarket international restaurants you'll probably be able to find something suitable – in the rural areas, you'll be eating fruit, fried eggs and rice, though not all at once.

Eating out

It is possible to get a tasty and nutritious meal almost anywhere – and at any time – in Thailand. Thais eat out a great deal so that most towns have a range of places. Starting at the top, in pecuniary terms at any rate, are the more sophisticated restaurants. These are usually air-conditioned, and sometimes attached to a hotel. In places like Bangkok and Chiang Mai they may be western in style and atmosphere. In towns less frequented by foreigners they are likely to be rather more functional – although the food will be just as good. In addition to these more upmarket restaurants are a whole range of places from noodle shops to curry houses and seafood restaurants. Many small restaurants have no menus. But often the speciality of the house will be clear – roasted, honeyed ducks hanging in the window, crab and fish laid out on crushed ice outside. Away from the main tourist spots, 'western' breakfasts are commonly unavailable, so be prepared to eat Thai-style (noodle or rice soup or fried rice).

Restaurant price codes explained

ΨΨΨ	Expensive	More than ฿375	Prices refer to the cost of an average main dish. They do not include drinks.
ΨΨ	Mid-range	฿125-374	
Ψ	Cheap	Less than ฿125	

Towards the bottom of the scale are stalls and food carts. These tend to congregate at particular places in town – often in the evening, from dusk – although they can be found just about anywhere: outside the local provincial offices, along a cul-de-sac, or under a conveniently placed shady tree. Stall holders will tend to specialize in either noodles, rice dishes, fruit drinks, sweets and so on. Hot meals are usually prepared to order. While stall food may be cheap – a meal costs only around ฿15-20 – they are frequented by people from all walks of life. A well-heeled businessman in a suit is just as likely to be seen bent over a bowl of noodles at a rickety table on a busy street corner as a construction worker.

A popular innovation over the last 10 years or so has been the suan a-haan or garden restaurant. These are often on the edge of towns, with tables set in gardens, sometimes with bamboo furniture and ponds. Another type of restaurant worth a mention is the Thai-style coffee shop. These are sometimes attached to hotels in provincial towns and feature hostesses dressed in Imelda-esque or skimpy spangly costumes. The hostesses, when they are not crooning to the house band, sit with customers, laugh at their jokes and assiduously make sure that their glasses are always full. They may provide other services too, but usually not at the table.

In the north, khantoke dining is de rigueur – or so one might imagine from the number of restaurants offering it. It is a northern Thai tradition, when people sit on the floor to eat at low tables, often to the accompaniment of traditional music and dance.

Tourist centres also provide good European, American and Japanese food at reasonable prices. Bangkok boasts some superb restaurants. Less expensive western fast-food restaurants can also be found – **McDonald's, Pizza Hut, Kentucky Fried Chicken** and others.

Thais love kids so are more than willing to accommodate, look after, feed, tolerate and adore your **children** should you be travelling with them. Western-style baby foods and products are widely available in good supermarkets.

The etiquette of eating

The Thai philosophy on eating is 'often', and most Thais will snack their way through the day. Eating is a relaxed, communal affair and it is not necessary to get too worked up about etiquette. Dishes are placed in the middle of the table where diners can help themselves. In a restaurant rice is usually spooned out by a waiter or waitress – and it is considered good manners to start a meal with a spoon of rice. While food is eaten with a spoon and fork, the fork is only used to manoeuvre food onto the spoon. Because most food is prepared in bite-sized pieces it is not usually necessary to use a knife. At noodle stalls chopsticks and china soup spoons are used while in the northeast most people – at least at home – use their fingers. Sticky rice is compressed into a ball using the ends of the fingers and then dipped in the other dishes. Thais will not pile their plates with food but take many small portions from the dishes arranged on a table. It is also considered good manners when invited out to leave some food on your plate, as well as on the serving dishes on the table. This demonstrates the generosity of the host.

Drink

Water in smaller restaurants can be risky, so many people recommend that visitors drink bottled water (widely available) or hot tea. Many hotels provide bottles of water gratis in their rooms.

Coffee is also now consumed throughout Thailand (usually served with Coffee-mate or creamer). In stalls and restaurants, coffee comes with a glass of Chinese tea. Soft drinks are widely available. Many roadside stalls prepare fresh fruit juices in liquidizers (bun) while hotels produce all the usual cocktails.

Major brands of **spirits** are served in most hotels and bars, although not always off the tourist path. The most popular spirit among Thais is Mekhong – local cane whisky – which can be drunk straight or with mixers such as Coca-Cola. It can seem rather sweet to the western palate but it is the cheapest form of alcohol. Red Bull may have hit the clubs and pubs of Europe but Thai truckers have been quaffing this mild stimulant drink for decades; in fact, the range of such drinks in Thailand extends beyond Red Bull to other stimulant drinks like Lipovitan and more.

Beer drinking is spreading fast. In 1987, beer consumption was 98 million litres; in 1992, 330 million litres. The most popular local beer is Singha beer brewed by Boon Rowd. The company commands 89 per cent of the beer market. It is said the beer's distinctive taste is due to the formaldehyde that it contains. When the company removed the chemical (it was no longer needed as bottling technology had been improved) there was such an outcry from Thais that they quickly reincorporated it. Whether or not the story is true, an evening drinking Singha can result in quite a hangover. Its alcohol content of six per cent must be partly to blame.

Among expatriates, the most popular Thai beer is the more expensive Kloster brand (similar to a light German beer) with an alcohol content of 5.7 per cent. Singha introduced a light beer called Singha Gold a few years back which is quite similar to Kloster. Amarit is a third, rather less widely available, brand but popular with foreigners and brewed by the same company who produce Kloster. Between them, Kloster and Amarit control about 10 per cent of the market. Two 'local' beers to enter the fray in the last 10 years are Heineken and Carlsberg. At the beginning of the 1990s Carlsberg built a brewery north of Bangkok and had clearly done their homework. The beer is sweeter and lighter than Singha and Kloster but still strong with an alcohol content of six per cent. The Carlsberg brew has made considerable inroads into the markets of the established brands – although in so doing they are said to have lost many millions of baht. A little later Carlsberg introduced a new beer specifically for the Thai market, Bier Chang or Elephant Beer, which is yet more alcoholic at seven per cent. More recently still Heineken have opened a local brewery near Sena in the central plains – again producing beer with a much higher alcohol content than the equivalent in the west. These beers have now been joined by a wave of new locally produced beers – often brewed in collaboration with overseas breweries. The cheapest is Leo beer which is brewed in Khon Kaen in the northeast. Its advertising campaign emphasizes that this is a Thai beer but Bangkok's sophisticates snigger under their breath at anyone stooping to drink the stuff. In fact, Leo Super is quite palatable – the same can't be said of Leo thammada (although a recent letter praised the delectability of Leo and fervently disagreed). Then there's Amstel (a Dutch beer) and Mittweida. The latter's advertising campaign, in contrast to Leo's, plays on the fact that, apparently, almost the entire population of Germany drinks the stuff for breakfast, lunch and tea. That few Germans seem to have heard of the brew doesn't seem to have tempered the advertising company's enthusiasm.

Beer is relatively expensive in Thai terms as it is heavily taxed by the government. But it is a high status drink so, as Thais become wealthier, more are turning to beer in preference to traditional, local whiskies. It is the burgeoning middle class, especially the young, which explains why brewers are so keen to set up shop in this traditionally non-beer drinking country. In a café, expect to pay about ฿50 for a small beer (฿80) for a large one, in a coffee shop or bar ฿70 (or ฿100-120 for a large one), and in a hotel bar or restaurant, rather more than that. Some pubs and bars also sell beer on tap – which is known as bier sot, 'fresh' beer.

Thais are fast developing a penchant for **wines**. Imported wines are expensive by international standards and Thai wines are pretty ghastly. An exception is Chateau de Loei which is produced in the northeastern province of Loei by Chaijudh Karnasuta with the expert assistance of a French winemaker. They produce a chenin blanc and a chenin rouge and they are eminently drinkable. At the 1996 Asia-Europe meeting (ASEM), Khun Chaijudh managed to get bottles placed in all the heads of state's rooms – what President Chirac thought, and whether he even tried the wine, is not known.

Entertainment

Bars and clubs

Thais are great clubbers and party-goers, although provincial nightclubs and coffee shops might not be to everyone's tastes. Karaoke is also very popular, across the country. Unsurprisingly, the most sophisticated nightlife is to be found in the largest towns and in tourist centres. Jazz and blues, nightclubs, rock, discos, wine bars, gay and lesbian bars, cabaret, straight bars, karaoke, beer gardens and more are all available. Nightclubs tend to close between 0200 and 0300 while opening hours are more variable, anywhere from 1800 to 2200. Bars tend to open earlier than nightclubs and also close slightly earlier; happy hours are usually between 1700 and 1900. For the latest offerings, including music, dance and theatre see (for Bangkok) *Bangkok Metro, Bangkok Timeout* and *BK Magazine* or, in the country's tourist centres, one of the many free newspapers and magazines.

If you want a taste of tradition, then visit one of the up-country coffee shops. Some of these are innocuous places where men gather to drink strong coffee, accompanied by Chinese tea, and chat about the price of rice and the latest political scandal. Others are really nightclubs where men drink prodigious quantities of whisky while accompanied by girls dressed in a weird assortment of dresses from figure-hugging little black numbers to Marie Antoinette extravagances. They also take it in turns to croon popular Thai ballads and rock songs to bad backing bands. Upstairs is, commonly, a brothel. An education, if nothing else.

Cinema

In Bangkok there are a range of cinemas that show films either with an English soundtrack or English subtitles (listed in the *Bangkok Post* and *The Nation*). Upcountry cinemas will often have a separate glass enclosed section where it is possible to listen to the English soundtrack of dubbed films. Generally films are screened at 1200, 1400, 1700, 1900, 2100, and at 1000 on Saturday and Sunday. In Bangkok, cultural centres such as the Alliance Française and the Goethe Institute show European films. It is also possible to rent videos and have them played in rented rooms in some towns. In the main tourist centres, bars and restaurants will often screen videos or DVDs on large-screen televisions, the night's offerings advertised in advance.

Festivals and events

Festivals where the month only is listed are movable. A booklet of holidays and festivals is available from most TAT offices. For movable festivals, check the TAT's website, www.tat.or.th/festival. Regional and local festivals are noted in appropriate sections.

January

New Year's Day (1st: public holiday).

February/March

Chinese New Year (movable, end of Jan/beginning of Feb) is celebrated by Thailand's large Chinese population. The festival extends over 15 days; spirits are appeased, and offerings are made to the ancestors and to the spirits. Good wishes and lucky money are exchanged, and Chinese- run shops and businesses shut.
Magha Puja (movable, full moon: public holiday)is Buddhist holy day and celebrates the occasion when the Buddha's disciples miraculously gathered together to hear him preach. Culminates in a candle-lit procession around the temple bot (or ordination hall). The faithful make offerings and gain merit.

April

Chakri Day (6th: public holiday) commemorates the founding of the present Chakri Dynasty.
Songkran (movable: public holiday) marks the beginning of the Buddhist New Year. The festival is particularly big in the north, much less so in the south and (understandably) the Muslim far south. It is a 3- to 5-day celebration with parades, dancing and folk entertainment. Traditionally, the first day represents the last chance for a 'spring clean'. Rubbish is burnt, in the belief that old and dirty things will cause misfortune in the coming year. The wat is the focal point of celebrations. Revered Buddha images are carried through the streets, accompanied by singers and dancers. The second day is the main water-throwing day. The water-throwing practice was originally an act of homage to ancestors and family elders. Young people pay respect by pouring scented water over the elders heads. The older generation sprinkle water over Buddha images. Gifts are given. This uninhibited water-throwing continues for all 3 days (although it is now banned in Bangkok). On the third day birds, fish and turtles are all released, to gain merit and in remembrance of departed souls.

May/June

Labour Day (1st May: public holiday).
Coronation Day (5th May: public holiday) commemorates the present King Bhumibol's crowning in 1950.
Visakha Puja (full moon: public holiday) holiest of all Buddhist days, it marks the Buddha's birth, enlightenment and death. Candlelit processions are held at most temples.
Ploughing Ceremony (movable: public holiday) is performed by the king at Sanaam Luang near the Grand Palace in Bangkok. Brahmanic in origin, it traditionally marks the auspicious date when farmers could begin preparing their rice land. Impressive bulls decorated with flowers pull a sacred gold plough.

July

Asalha Puja and **Khao Phansa** (movable, full moon: public holiday) commemorates the Buddha's first sermon to his disciples and marks the beginning of the Buddhist Lent. Monks reside in their monasteries for the 3-month Buddhist Rains Retreat to study and meditate, and young men temporarily become monks. Ordination ceremonies all over the country and villagers give white cotton robes to the monks to wear during the Lent ritual bathing.

August

The Queen's Birthday (12th: public holiday).

October

Chulalongkorn Day (23rd: public holiday) honours King Chulalongkorn (1868-1910), perhaps Thailand's most beloved and revered king.

Ok Phansa (3 lunar months after Asalha Puja) marks the end of the Buddhist Lent and the beginning of Krathin, when gifts – usually a new set of cotton robes – are offered to the monks. Particularly venerated monks are sometimes given silk robes as a sign of respect and esteem. **Krathin** itself is celebrated over 2 days. It marks the end of the monks' retreat and the re-entry of novices into secular society. Processions and fairs are held all over the country; villagers wear their best clothes, and food, money, pillows and bed linen are offered to the monks of the local wat.

November

Loi Krathong (full moon) comes at the end of the rainy season and honours the goddess of water. A krathong is a model boat made to contain a candle, incense and flowers. The little boats are pushed out onto canals, lakes and rivers. Sadly, few krathongs are now made of leaves: polystyrene has taken over and the morning after Loi Krathong lakes and river banks are littered with the wrecks of the previous night. The 'quaint' candles in pots sold in many shops at this time, are in fact large firecrackers.

December

King's Birthday (5th: public holiday). Flags and portraits of the King are erected all over Bangkok, especially down Rachdamnern Av and around the Grand Palace.

Constitution Day (10th: public holiday).

New Year's Eve (31st: public holiday).

Shopping

Bangkok and Chiang Mai are the shopping 'centres' of Thailand. Many people now prefer Chiang Mai, as the shops are concentrated in a smaller area and there is a good range of quality products, especially handicrafts. Bangkok still offers the greatest variety and choice. However, it is difficult to find bargains in Bangkok any longer; the department stores and shopping malls contain high-price, high-quality merchandise (all at a fixed price), much of which is imported.

Between shopkeepers competition is fierce. Do not be cajoled into buying something before having a chance to price it elsewhere – Thais can be very persuasive. Also, watch out for guarantees of authenticity – fake antiques abound, and even professionals find it difficult to know a 1990 Khmer sculpture from a 10th-century one.

Thailand has had a reputation as being a mecca for pirated goods: CDs and DVDs, Lacoste shirts, Gucci leather goods, Rolex watches, computer software and so on. These items are still available, but pressure from the US to protect intellectual copyright is leading to more enthusiastic crackdowns by the police. In Bangkok, genuine CDs can be bought (at what are still bargain prices compared with the west), and buying pirated DVDs requires, in many cases, a retreat to some back room. This clampdown on pirated goods is likely to continue – in 1994-1995 Thailand brought a new copyright law onto the statute books, and for fear of trade retaliation from the US, the law is being respected to a much greater degree than ever before.

The widest selection of **Thai silk** is available in Bangkok although cheaper silk, as well as good quality cotton, can be obtained in the northeast (the traditional centre of silk weaving). **Tailor-made clothing** is available although designs are sometimes rather outdated; it might be better for the tailor to copy an article of your own clothing (see page 143). However, times are changing and there are now some top designers in Bangkok. **Leather goods** include custom-made crocodile skin shoes and boots (for those who aren't squeamish after seeing the brutes in one of the crocodile farms).

Bangkok is also a good place to buy **jewellery** – gold, sapphires and rubies – as well as **antiques, bronzeware** and **celadon**. (See Tricksters below and page 40.) **Handicrafts** are best purchased up-country. In general, Bangkok has by far the best selection of goods, and by shopping around, visitors will probably be able to get just as good a price as they would further afield.

Tricksters

Tricksters, rip-off artists, fraudsters, less than honest salesmen – call them what you will – are likely to be far more of a problem than simple theft. People may well approach you in the street offering incredible one-off bargains, and giving what might seem to be very plausible reasons for your sudden good fortune. Be wary in all such cases and do not be pressed into making a hasty decision. Unfortunately, more often than not, the salesman is trying to pull a fast one. Favourite 'bargains' are precious stones, whose authenticity is 'demonstrated' before your very eyes (see page 145). Although many Thais do like to talk to farangs and practise their English, in tourist areas there are also those who offer their friendship for pecuniary rather than linguistic reasons. Sad as it is to say so, it is probably a good idea to be suspicious.

Sport and activities

Caving

The main cave systems are in the northern, western and southern regions of the country. In the most part, when open to the public, they are pretty sedate affairs and not exactly of interest to the specialist caver (but they can be enjoyable for the non-specialist). More adventurous cave expeditions are provided in Soppong (see page 261) in the north and in one or two other places.

Cultural/educational

There are several tour companies that specialize in cultural tours to Thailand. In Thailand itself, the **Siam Society**, 131 Soi Asoke, Sukhumvit Road, Bangkok, T02-6616470, www.siam-society.org, is the premier organization devoted to Thai culture and art. See also Tour operators, page 20.

Cycling

Thailand's main highways are certainly not for cycling; some would say, not even for driving. However, there is an extensive network of village roads and trails that provide excellent biking trails, particularly in the northeastern region. Several companies have exploited this potential. **Click and Travel Ltd**, www.clickandtravelonline.com, a young 'Soft Adventure Company' is based in Chiang Mai and specializes in bicycle tours in the north.

Diving

Of all Southeast Asia's countries, for divers, Thailand is perhaps one of the most blessed. As a destination it draws people like a magnet, all determined to discover the riches of her two seas. The long, thin leg of land that separates the Andaman Sea from the Gulf of Thailand is rimmed by iridescent, turquoise waters that mask rainbow coloured reefs, pristine corals and abundant marine life including the elusive, mysterious whale shark. Following the 2004 tsunami, there was localised damage to certain reefs, but this was regarded as being minimal even in the weeks immediately afterwards. Dive centres are avoiding sites that were damaged while they regenerate.

Footprint's Diving the World will be published in spring 2006.

Diving seasons and conditions With some of the richest reefs in the region, it might be hard to choose where to dive and when, until you learn that Thai diving is seasonal. At its simplest, half the year you dive on the west, the other half on the east. The western Andaman Sea is where the best and most varied diving is found. The reefs here are influenced by deep-water currents and contrasting wind patterns that sweep across the Indian Ocean. Corals are lush and marine life prolific. From November till late April, seas are mostly calm and visibility varies from good to outstanding and currents are acceptable to most divers. The east coast is a good choice for those months when the monsoon is blowing in across the Andaman Sea. The shallower waters of the Gulf of Thailand are calm from May till October. As a semi-enclosed sea, the Gulf is rarely more than 60-m deep and is heavily sedimented especially as you get closer to Bangkok. Having said that, this highly productive marine eco-system supports some good fringing reefs.

Water temperature No matter what time of year you visit Thailand and whichever coast, the water is invariably warm. The water temperature mostly hovers between 25-28°C but may drop to 23°C at its lowest. A 3 mm wetsuit is as much as you are likely to need unless you plan to do more than three dives a day.

Equipment Almost every dive centre will rent good quality equipment but bringing your own will considerably reduce costs. Prior to departure, check your baggage allowance with the airlines and try to come to some arrangement for extra weight.

Dive facilities With so much diving on the doorstep, there are more than enough operators in Thailand to meet the needs of everyone from a dedicated five-a-day diver to a never-tried-it-before rookie. In general, dive businesses are extremely professional. Many work closely with one of the international governing bodies (PADI, NAUI, CMAS, BSAC), however, some facilities in far-flung areas may be limited. It's always worth asking around if you're unsure of what you are being offered.

Recompression facilities and dive insurance As always, there are a few simple rules to avoid getting bent: don't dive too deep; don't ascend too quickly; use – and obey – your computer; drink a lot to avoid dehydration. Should you, however, become victim to a suspected decompression attack, contact one of the following facilities immediately: **Pattaya**: Apakorn Kiatiwong Naval Hospital, Sattahip, Chonburi, T038-601185, 26 km east of Pattaya. Urgent care available 24 hours. **Bangkok**: Department of Underwater & Aviation Medicine, Phra Pinklao Naval Hospital, Taksin Road, Thonburi, Bangkok, T02-4600000-19, ext 341, or T02-4601105. Open 24 hours. **Phuket**: Hyperbaric Services Thailand, 233 Raj-U-thit 200 Pee Road, Patong Beach, Phuket, T076-342518/342519. After hours emergency number: T01-7975984/ 09-8714302/ 01-9785976. **Koh Samui**: Hyperbaric Services Thailand, 34/8 Moo 4, Bo Phut, T077-427427. After hours emergency number: T01-0848485/01-0830533/ 01-0930793, www.ssnsnetwork.com.

There are no air evacuation services in Thailand and hyperbaric services can charge as much as US$800 per hour so good **dive insurance** is imperative. It is inexpensive and well worth it in case of a problem, real or perceived. Many general travel insurance policies will not cover diving. Contact **DAN** (the Divers' Alert Network) for more information, www.diversalertnetwork.org, **DAN Europe**, www.daneurope.org, or **DAN South East Asia Pacific**, www.danseap.org. You can join online.

Phuket and around Whether on land or below the waves, the island of Phuket has something for everyone. With dive centres in virtually every area, arranging a training course, a day trip or a liveaboard cruise is simplicity itself. Thousands of divers flock in to take advantage of the warm waters, diverse reefs and abundant facilities.

How big is your flipper?

As environmentally concerned visitors we should be aware of the potential threat we pose to reefs when snorkelling or diving. The following are a few simple things we can do to help to sustain this delicate ecosystem, adapted from the Marine Conservation Society's 'Coral Code':

- **Buoyancy Control** Through proper weighting and practice, do not allow yourself or any item of your equipment to touch any living organism.
- **Skills Review** If you haven't dived for a while, do a review in the pool or sandy patch before diving around the reef.
- **Control your fins** Deep fin kicks around coral can cause damage.
- **Avoid kicking up sand** Sand can smother corals and other reef life.
- **Never stand on the reef** Corals can be damaged by the slightest touch. If you need to hold on to something look for a piece of dead coral or rock.
- **Know your limits** Don't dive in conditions beyond your skills.
- **Avoid temptation** Don't disturb or move things around (eg for photography)
- **Do not collect or buy shells or any other marine curios (eg dried pufferfish)**
- **Do not feed fish**
- **Do not ride turtles or hold on to any marine animal.** It can easily cause heart attacks or severe shock to the creature.
- **Choose your operator wisely** Report irresponsible operators to relevant diving authorities (PADI, NAUI, SSI).
- **See the Marine Conservation Society** at www.mcsuk.org or contact Communications Officer, T01989-566017.

Phuket is the main departure point for the treasured Similan Islands Marine Park, as well as for cruises further north to the Burma Banks or south to the less popular regions around Krabi or Trang. More serious divers will head straight out to these areas as sites closer to Phuket shores tend to have reduced visibility, sometimes as low as 10 m. The gentle, west coast beaches are frequently used for training but the sea bed may be stirred up by other motorized watersports. All the same, there are fun dives at Freedom Beach, Paradise, Bang Tao and Koh Pu for less experienced divers. These tend to be in just 5 m or so of water and divers can spot lionfish, wrasse and occasionally rare sea robins.

An hour or so from the southern tip, there are good sites at Koh Racha Yai, Koh Racha Noi and Shark Point (see Phi Phi below). Both Racha Yai and Racha Noi can get visibility up to 25 m and are unexpectedly colourful. Octopus, cuttlefish and reef fish are plentiful and there is even a small wooden shipwreck at Racha Noi. These two islands also benefit from being protected from the winter winds and can be dived all year round.

Koh Phi Phi Phi Phi is dramatically beautiful and the rugged limestone cliffs that explode vertically from the sea are equally impressive below sea level. Long caves, fantastic overhangs and swim-throughs create some adventurous diving, but need to be approached with care. Hard coral gardens have suffered a little from inexperienced boat handlers dropping anchor but soft corals are healthy and host many small fish and crustaceans.

Shark Point is less than an hour away and equally accessible from southern Phuket. Regarded as one of South Thailand's best dives, this tiny exposed pinnacle is no indication of the large and prolific reef beneath it. The area is characterized by a mass of pink and purple corals and the almost guaranteed certainty of spotting a gentle and docile leopard shark. Currents can be strong and visibility varies from 2-25 m.

Krabi, Koh Lanta and Trang Over the last 10 years dive tourism has advanced down Thailand's southwest coast following the footsteps of intrepid travellers. Although this region has some of the most stunning beaches in the whole country, diving tends to be an hour or more offshore where visibility can reach as much as 40 m. Dive facilities across this region are not as developed as those in Phuket yet some sites are definitely world-class. Much of the diving takes place around exposed pinnacles that mask submerged marine paradises. Some even host hidden caverns where you can surface inside to admire stalactites hanging over your head. As the only light source comes from the entry channel below, this can seem a little disorientating at first but is a phenomenal natural spectacle.

Hin Daeng (red rock), Hin Muang (purple rock), Koh Ha Yai, Koh Rok and several inland islands just south and east of Koh Lanta are accessible from any of three centres. The diving here is relatively shallow, with the best corals and marine life above 18 m. The bottom is composed mostly of hard corals, with small areas of soft corals. The reefs are healthier than those further north simply because they are less dived.

Tarutao National Park Even further south, close to the Malaysian border, are the exquisite islands of the Tarutao National Park, the first marine park in Thailand. As yet fairly undiscovered, facilities are still somewhat limited but as time goes on, it's inevitable that more and more dive centres will crop up on the islands. Dives vary from shallow to 40 m and visibility can be as much as 35 m. Like everywhere in the Andaman Sea, currents can be strong at times. There is plenty of exotic marine life – lionfish, anemone fish, lobsters and stingrays are common and even snorkellers can see the occasional leopard shark snoozing on the sand. Dolphin encounters are frequent and it is said that if you're really lucky, you may even encounter a rare dugong (manatee).

Similan Islands For many people a dive trip to Thailand means just one thing – the Similans National Marine Park. This chain of nine tiny islands is ringed by perfect beaches and amazing coral reefs. The park can be reached in a long day trip but a liveaboard is best. Visibility rarely drops below 20 m and can reach mythical proportions. Currents sometimes catch divers unawares, but from November to April, conditions are usually excellent with March and April the calmest.

What makes the Similans so attractive are their two completely different sides. To the east the islands have pure white sand and hard coral gardens that slope gently to over 30 m. Colourful soft corals and sea fans are plentiful, the diving is easy and the pace is calm. The west, however, is much more dramatic, with currents that swirl around huge granite boulders creating spectacular swim throughs. It's a bit like diving between flooded skyscrapers that have been reclaimed by the sea. The variety of diving is extensive also, with more sites than you can name. On the eastern side of island No 7, East of Eden drops over a sloping reef wall to a secondary reef at 35 m. It is completely encrusted with big fans and huge soft corals. There are masses of glassy sweepers that flit and dance in the light like sparkling stars. Schooling trevally and tuna swim overhead while the upper reef hides plenty of delicate small creatures like ornate ghost pipe fish.

In comparison, sites like the western Elephants Head (Similan No 8) consist of a series of huge granite boulders all tumbling over each other with lots of crevices and swim throughs. Small fans nestle in the crevices for protection from the surge

 along with loads of colourful, schooling fish. Snappers, butterfly and surgeon appear in hundreds rather than handfuls. These sites can get strong currents on occasion as water rushes between the boulders, but the action attracts reef sharks, rays and schooling fish.

The region is not known for an abundance of wrecks but a few are worth diving. The Bonsoong Wreck, a tin mining boat, was sunk deliberately and now lies on her side at 18 m. Although not particularly big nor all that substantial a structure, the hull is covered in a mass of life. Leopard sharks patrol the sands and a wide range of nudibranchs, morays and other fish inhabit the cracks and crevices.

Surin Islands and Richelieu Rock North of the Similans, another chain of islands, was formed by enormous underwater pinnacles. Koh Bon, Koh Tachai and Koh Surin are all enveloped by excellent reefs and prolific marine life. As they're exposed to deep ocean upwellings, currents and visibility vary considerably. Sometimes, what starts as a gentle drift may end up with a fierce upwelling so care is needed. However, the rocky landscapes are very dramatic and even on a murky day there are frequent pelagic sightings. Leopard sharks seem to lurk permanently at Koh Tachai and in April and May manta rays are regular visitors to Koh Bon.

However, at the end of this string, just 20 km north of Surin, is the dive site that has it all – Richelieu Rock. Even compared with the rest of Thailand, this is the one 'do not miss' dive of your life. Completely submerged at high tide, currents and visibility around the rock can change quickly. On a single dive you can see minute harlequin shrimps, pairing ornate ghost pipefish and elegant sea horses. Down on the sand, giant grouper pose for photos while curious turtles watch over your shoulder. And that's not to mention the many different types of moray eels, nudibranchs and schooling fish. The rock's fame though is due to the enormous and endangered whale shark. The largest fish in the ocean can be seen from late February through April. Really fortunate divers will perhaps see more than one of these mammoth but elusive creatures, perhaps even a baby, as it gently swishes it's enormous tail through the blue.

The Burma Banks Still heading northwards, the next destination of note is the Burma Banks, inside Burma. Because of its political isolation, access to diving has been mostly limited to Thai liveaboards that hold special permits. As such, the reefs are regarded as virgin, with areas of pristine coral and plenty of life. Conditions are similar to the Similan and Surin Islands, with diving only from November till April. Water temperatures are over 26°C and currents vary with location and tides.

For more information on whale sharks see www.whaleshark-thai.com. For dive operations see under the Similan Islands.

The Banks are an area some 1500 km sq studded with plateaux that rise up from great depths to reasonable diving limits. They gained a reputation for sharks – including nurse, reef and silky. However, it's not guaranteed you will see them. Whether due to overfishing or the weather, the most frequently seen resident is a 'tame' nurse shark called Max. Western Rocky is a set of three pinnacles that are washed by some pretty good surges and you are likely to encounter schools of squid, seasnakes and tiny orangutan crabs. If you're really lucky a whale shark may show up too. Much of the region is still being discovered and for that alone it's worth the trip.

Closer to the Thai border is the beautiful Mergui Archipelago, a succession of tiny islands with lots of marine life, coral and numerous pelagic species hunting in the nutrient rich waters. Inshore sites suffer a little from silt run-off and boat traffic. For dive operations, see the Similan Islands.

Underwater photography

There's a saying that a boat is a hole in the ocean you throw money into.

Because light is filtered by water, taking a picture at 30 m underwater is a completely different ball game to taking one on land. The deeper you go the darker it gets, red light is filtered by the water and you're likely to end up with blue, washed out pictures. However, it's tempting to try and capture the excitement of a dive. If you're determined, buy or rent the best underwater camera you can afford. The better the quality of the camera, the better the picture. You will also need a flash to get anything worth having as it helps return the reds to your image.

There are many options for all budgets from cheap, dedicated 'point and shoot' cameras (Époque) to the mid-range Sea and Sea Motormarine with its multi-lenses. At the far end of the scale, the professional choice is a housing worth thousands of pounds made to protect SLR cameras.

However, the best option for travellers are the clear, plastic housings produced for virtually every compact camera available. You just pop your regular camera into its waterproof box and dive. If you have a digital, you even get the ability to vary exposures on the spot. Most can take an extra flash which will help improve picture quality even further.

Once you've chosen your tool, remember to get as close as possible to your subject and remember you are in an alien environment, respect both it and yourself. For more information, visit www.cameras underwater.co.uk.

Koh Samui and around Thailand's eastern side has less in the way of prolific reefs than the west and the main tourist island of Koh Samui has the least of these. Yet this island has an excellent infrastructure and good diving is within easy striking distance of her major resorts. Reefs around the island tend to be murky but the gentle, shelving beaches are popular spots for taking a course. Once training is underway, most centres take divers to the nearby Ang Thong National Marine Park where hidden lagoons and sheer limestone cliffs reflect the beauty of the underwater scenery. The diving is pleasant but not too challenging and this is also a good trip for snorkellers. Some of the most popular sites are Koh Wao and Hin Yipon, both renowned for shallow caves and colourful soft corals.

The most famous day trip from Samui, however, is Hin Bai, or Sail Rock. Jutting out of the water 18 km offshore, and rising from 30 m to the surface, it is covered in beautiful green and yellow corals and frequented by large marine animals like reef sharks and rays. Most spectacular is the journey through an underwater chimney which feels like ascending the inside of a cathedral spire. The entry point is at 19 m and the exit at 5 m surrounded by carpets of anemones and their resident clownfish.

Koh Phangan Although Phangan is often visited as a day trip from Samui, there is enough around the shores to keep most divers amused for an extended stay. Maximum depths are 24 m but generally about 14 m. With reasonable staghorn, table corals and plate corals making up the structure of the reefs, damsels, angels, snappers, stingrays, barracuda and cuttlefish are all resident. The shallow waters also make for some very easy and very fun snorkelling. Koh Ma, a small island connected to Koh Phangan by a sandbar, also has interesting scenery and nice soft corals.

Koh Tao Koh Tao (Turtle Island) and near neighbour, Koh Nang Yuan, have become the epicentre of diving in the Gulf of Thailand. The reason is simple. Unlike Samui,

 where you really need to travel for an hour or more to reach the best sites, this area has great diving just seconds from the beach. Ideal for beginners, there are more than 20 dive centres catering for them. Even in peak season visibility can be as minimal as 3 m, but will clear to an incredible 40 m in an instant. Currents away from shore can be quite strong and care is required.

There are many dive sites just a kilometre from the island where you can see large schools of barracuda, big-eyed jacks, tuna and giant trevally. The best dive in the area is undoubtedly Chumphon Pinnacle. Four massive rock pinnacles soar from 40 m to within 16 m of the surface forming an underwater mountain range. There is a huge variety of life-like giant groupers and batfish amongst colourful black coral gardens. Not only are huge schools of jacks spotted regularly, occasionally sailfish, whale sharks and even whales are too.

Koh Nang Yuan, the only place in the world where three islands are joined together by a sandbar, is ringed by a variety of shallow dive sites. There are some beautiful arches to swim through and a deep crack in its mid section mirrors the scenery above. Giant rays, morays, and even reef sharks can be found resting in it. If you are diving at White Rock, look out for a local personality, Trevor, the Terrible Trigger Fish.

Chumphon The mainland resort of Chumphon is often bypassed by divers as they board a ferry for the more idyllic Koh Tao, 75 km away. However, the area has national park status and the 40 or so Chumphon Sea Islands have some reasonable diving. Conditions are less attractive than further afield. There are some mangrove areas, good for fish breeding but often murky, and some freshwater run-off from shore. Visibility can vary from 8 to 20 m but in April it gets windy enough for an annual windsurfing competition.

For a short break, the undersea landscapes of the Chumphon isles are worth a visit. Characterized by caves, rock piles and colonies of black coral trees in shades of white, gold and yellow, the area is also a nudibranch hunters delight. There are a proliferation of sea cups – corallimorpharians – which is unusual in this region. In fact, small critters are the main interest here with the whip coral shrimp being a photographers' favourite. The region is trying to promote itself with eco-tourism as a priority.

Pattaya to Koh Chang Outside mad, crazy and magical Bangkok, the Thai coast curves southeastwards until it reaches Cambodia. This entire coastline has plenty of diving opportunities but sadly a combination of overpopulation and misuse of the environment means diving can be less than outstanding here. Pattaya has the accolade of being the birthplace of the Thai dive industry. The waters are never particularly clear so it's surprising there are so many dive centres. These specialize in courses and set good standards for elsewhere in the country. The islands just offshore from Pattaya are the most popular dive sites for beginners. The big surprise comes when you learn that this is also Thailand's best wreck diving area with several really interesting wrecks just a short sail to the southeast. *The Hardeep*, a 42-m freighter which sank in 1942 now rests on her side at 27 m, creating a good artificial reef. *The Bremen*, near Sattahip is equally popular and attracts masses of schooling snappers. She rests at 25 m and visibility is just 7-10 m.

Ko Samet, a little further around the coast, is another of the seven national marine parks in Thailand. It is a favourite with Thai visitors. Snorkelling is reasonable and diving can be arranged but a better option would be to head further towards Cambodia and Koh Chang. The largest island in Thailand after Phuket, it is becoming increasingly popular. Opinions on just how good the diving is vary considerably. Much of the shallow reefs around Koh Chang are affected by freshwater run off and silt. What can best be said about the stretch from Samet to Chang is that it remains only partly explored. The region does offer some varied diving and snorkelling experiences and the small islands around Chang have the best corals. As yet, this is not a destination for serious divers.

Dive centres

See also under each area in the text.

Phuket and around

EuroDivers, Laguna Beach Resort, Bang Tao Bay, T076-324352, and has a central reservations office in Chalong, Phuket, T076-280814, www.euro-divers.com.

Phuket Scuba Club, 5/17 Kata Noi Rd, Kata Beach, T/F076-284026, www.phuket-scuba-club.com.

Southeast Asia Divers has offices in Chalong, Kata Noi Beach and near Patong. It also teaches up to instructor level. PO Box 15, Patong Beach, T076-281299, www.phuketdive.net.

Koh Phi Phi

Phi Phi Scuba Diving Centre, Ton Sai Bay, T075-612665, www.phiphi-scuba.com. Krabi, Koh Lanta and Trang.

Lanta Diver, 197/3 Moo 1, Saladan, Koh Lanta, T075-684208, www.lantadiver.com.

Trang Scuba Dive Centre, 59/33-34 Huayyod Rd, Amphur Muang, Trang, T075-222188-90, T075-222192-3, www.thumrin.co.th.

Tarutao National Park

Adang Sea Tours, Sabye Sports, 1080 Moo. 3 Kampang, Langu, Satun, T074-734104, www.sabye-sports.com. A liveaboard, Phi Phi Harmony is scheduled to run from Phuket to Tarutao. Contact **Dive The World Thailand**, Song Roy Pee Centre, 210/26 Ratuthid Rd, Patong Beach, Phuket, T/F076-344736, www.divetheworldthailand.com.

Similan Islands

To get the best out of the Similans, you need to be on a liveaboard cruise for at least 4 days. There are boats for all tastes and budgets. The following depart from Phuket: *Ocean Rover*, a first-class boat run by **Fantasea Divers**, 43/20 Moo 5, Viset Rd, Tambon Rawai, Amphur Muang, Phuket, T076-281388, www.ocean-rover.com.

Genesis Liveaboards runs comfortable *Genesis 1* and classy *MY Anguun*, 18/18 Chaofa Road, Chalong, Phuket, T/F076-381221, www.genesis-liveaboards.com.

Jonathan Cruiser is a well-run budget boat: **Scuba Venture Co, Ltd**, 283 Patak Rd, Karon Beach, Phuket, T076-286185, www.jonathan-cruiser.com.

If you have limited time, you may want to consider a cruise departing from Khao Lak, about an hour's drive north of Phuket. Vessels departing here have less sailing time to the park.

Sea Dragon Dive Center has several: 9/1 Mu 7, T Khuk Khak, Khao Lak, T076-420420, www.seadragondivecenter.com.

Koh Samui and around

Ocean Rover now cruises around the Gulf from Jun-Oct. Contact **Fantasea Divers**, 43/20 Moo 5, Viset Rd, Tambon Rawai, Amphur Muang, Phuket, T076-281388, www.ocean-rover.com.

Pro Divers, 125/5 Moo 3 Maret, Lamai, Koh Samui, T/F077-233399, www.prodivers.nu.

Samui International Diving School, Beach Rd, Chaweng Beach, Koh Samui, T077-422386, also on Koh Tao, www.planet-scuba.net.

Koh Phangan

Chaloklum Diving, 52/1 Moo 7, Chaloklum, T077-374025, www.chaloklum-diving.com.

Phangan Divers, PO Box 4, Thong Sala, T077-375117, www.phangan divers.com.

Koh Tao

Big Blue Diving Centre, 20/1 Moo 1, Koh Tao, T/F077-456050, www.bigbluediving.com. Also on Samui.

Nangyuan Island Dive Resort, 46 Moo 1, Koh Tao (Koh Nangyuan), T077-456089-93, www.nangyuan.com.

Chumphon

Chumphon Cabana Resort & Diving Centre, 69 Moo 8, Thung Wua Laen Beach, Pathiu Chumphon, T077-560245-9, www.cabana.co.th.

Pattaya to Koh Chang

Ko Chang Divers, Bamboo Bungalows, White Sand Beach, Koh Chang, T01-8111689/01-7575172, www.winti.ch/kcd. Open Nov-Apr.

Mermaid's Dive Centre, Pattaya 75/124 Moo 12, Jomtien Beach Rd, Nongprue, Banglamung, Cholburi, T038-232219/232220, www.mermaiddive.com.

Elephant trekking

There are several elephants camps in the north of Thailand where visitors can watch elephants perform tricks and go on a short saunter. In the northern region these include the **Thai Elephant Conservation Centre** outside Lampang, see page 237, the **Elephant Training Camp** in the Mae Sa Valley outside Chiang Mai, see page 233 and the **Chiang Dao Elephant Training Centre** near Chiang Dao, also not far from Chiang Mai, see page 234. In the northeastern region there is the rather tacky **Khao Yai Elephant Camp** linked to the Khao Yai National Park and Ban Tha Klang, a village of traditional elephant tamers and trainers outside Surin, see page 314. Slightly more adventurous elephant treks are sometimes included in longer trekking programmes (see Trekking, page 71).

Environmental and social

There are now a number of 'alternative' tour companies selling ecotourism. These are of various shades of green. The **Thai Volunteer Services** (TVS) Responsible Ecological and Social Tour (REST) project allows tourists to visit and stay in rural villages, go trekking and camping, see local development projects and participate in community activities. Contact T02-6910437/6910438 and see www.ecotour.in.th.

Families and the elderly

Mae Sot Conservation Tour, 415/7 Tang Khim Chiang Road, Mae Sot, T055-532818, premat@ksc15.th.com, runs educational and soft adventure tours for families and the elderly, see page 217.

Fishing

There is little sport river fishing in Thailand. However, the main beach resorts – Pattaya, Phuket, Koh Phi Phi, Koh Samui and others – offer game fishing in both the Andaman Sea and Gulf of Thailand.

Golf

In the 1990s golf became one of Thailand's boom industries. Courses were constructed right across the country – many hoping to cash in on a wave of foreigners, particularly Japanese, enticed by the comparative cheapness of playing here. Environmental activists railed against the process, lament the use of chemicals to keep greens and fairways artificially lush and bright, the massive use of water in a country where water is a scarce and valuable resource, and the land disputes that sometimes arose as 'Big Money' leveraged land from poor farmers. Be that as it may, Thailand has an impressive network of courses, some of international standard and many attached to luxury hotels.

Historical and archaeological

In Thailand itself, the **Siam Society**, 131 Soi Asoke, Sukhumvit Road, Bangkok, T02-6616470, www.siam-society.org, is the premier organization devoted to the arts of the country and is actively involved in archaeological digs and the preservation of Thailand's artistic heritage.

Homestay

Thai Homestay is a small company based in Udon Thani arranging homestay trips to Thailand's poor northeastern region. Visitors stay with rural families and see a Thailand beyond the reach of most tourists. Contact **Thongwong & Martin Allinson**, 214 Group 2, Non Sa-At, Udon Thani 41240, Thailand, T042-391205, www.thaihomestay.co.uk.

Horse riding
Horse riding is not big business in Thailand. Most of the places that offer horse riding are pretty sedate affairs with gentle and controlled trots and canters around enclosed spaces. Chiang Mai has more opportunities than anywhere else (see page 222).

Hot-air ballooning
Hot-air balloon flying only became legal in Thailand in 1990 and the military authorities still have to be consulted about individual flights because it is such a novelty. With little in the air besides birds, going up, up and away is a wonderfully liberating experience. Thailand has good conditions for ballooning year round and flights go early in the morning before it gets too hot, particularly in the summer and even in the rainy season, as the rain usually only affects the afternoon. Wind directions and conditions are generally predictable but it can be cold at altitude in the early morning, so remember to take something warm with you. As yet there is only one company taking passenger flights, but its popularity suggests that ballooning will be taking off as a tourist trend in the next few years: **Oriental Balloon Flights**, Floraville doi Saket, 9 Moo 4 Talad Kuan, Doi Saket, Chiang Mai, T053-398609, www.orientalballoonflights.com. Daily flights run from Chiang Mai during the dry season (October to March) where you land wherever the wind takes you. Typically an hour long, the 24-hour experience includes a champagne breakfast and certificate. Flights cost ฿8500 including insurance.

Jet skiing
Wannabe action heroes will find jet skis on all major commercial beaches in Thailand, particularly around Phuket and Koh Samui. Bear in mind that jet skis can only be legally operated in certain areas and you should ensure the jet ski you hire is licensed, otherwise you risk a fine and possible imprisonment. Most beaches operate a 'swimmers only' area surrounded by a rope supported by floats which jet skis should keep well clear of; it is only deemed safe to operate a jet ski when the seas are calm ie not when there is a red flag displayed.

Language schools
Thai language schools are concentrated in Bangkok and Chiang Mai. In both cities the AUA schools are the best known: **AUA**, 179 Rachdamri, in Bangkok, T02-2528170, (see also page 158); **AUA**, 73 Rachdamnern Road, Chiang Mai, T053-278407, F211973, offers 60-hour modules (see also page 259).

Motorbike and quad bike 'trekking'
Many people hire trail bikes and make their own way into the hills of the northern region. Biking maps are available in book shops in Chiang Mai and Bangkok and there are some well-established routes. If you would rather go on a tour many trekking outfits will arrange this. Bear in mind, though, that some people object to motorbikes disturbing the peace of the hills.

Parasailing
Along with jet skiing and banana boating, parasailing is found at the more commercial beaches in Thailand like Pattaya Bay and Jomtien in Pattaya and Patong in Phuket. Perhaps one of the best places to enjoy this sport is Ko Lan, near Pattaya, where floating 'take-off and landing' platforms means that the flight occurs exclusively above the sea and you don't even have to get wet.

Rafting
There are two forms of rafting in Thailand: gentle drifting on bamboo rafts down languid rivers like the Kwai in the western region and the Kok in the north as well as the alternative high-adrenaline version. See also whitewater rafting.

Rock climbing

Most of the country's mountains are modest with 'trekking' or 'hiking' being the operative words, rather than 'climbing'. Leave the crampons at home. However, there is some excellent rock climbing, for example at Ao Nang, just outside Krabi and on Koh Phi Phi.

Sea kayaking

This has become popular over the last decade or so. Limestone areas of the south such as Phangnga Bay provide a pock-marked coast of cliffs, sea caverns and rocky islets. Specialist companies, see below, have now been joined by many other companies based in Phuket, Krabi, Ao Nang, Koh Tao and Phi Phi. Kayaks can be hired on many commercial beaches by the hour but for a comprehensive tour including a guide and organized itinerary, the following tour operators offer day trips and expeditions for all from the beginner to the advanced kayaker.

Tour operators

Discover Asia, 685/3 Ar-Karnsongkhor 3 Rd, Klongchan, Bangkapi, Bangkok T02-7331110, www.asiantraveladventures.com. Oct-Jun day trips and longer tours around south Thailand's marine parks and islands.

Paddle Asia, 53/80 Moo 5, Thambon Srisoonthon, Thalang, Phuket, T076-311222, www.seakayaking-thailand.com. Traditional kayaks taking tours around the marine parks, specifically for bird- and nature-lovers.

Sea Canoe Thailand, 367/4 Yaowarat Rd, Phuket, T076-212172, www.seacanoe.net. Established watersports company offering day trips and longer tours from Phuket.

Therapies

In addition to Thailand's growing spa industry, travellers can take advantage of opportunities for week-long fasting and alternative health programmes. Connect with your inner child, meditate on life or have a relaxing spot of self-administered colonic irrigation on Koh Samui, the country's centre for alternative healing. Programmes range from three- to 21-day courses aimed at eliminating the body's toxins and rejuvenating body and mind through a range of wince-inducing techniques. These include fasting, colonic irrigation and reflexology alongside gentler methods of iridology, meditation, reiki, massage and yoga, see **The Spa Resort**, Koh Samui, page 580. There is also the **Samui Dharma Healing Centre**, see page 578. Many Thai spas offer holistic therapy sessions, from massage to aromatherapy.

Massage Thai massage has become increasingly popular in the west and it is now possible to take courses of varying lengths and return home not just with cheap shirts and CDs but with a skill to impress your partner and friends. The best-known centre for traditional Thai massage is **Wat Pho** in Bangkok. It offers 30-hour, 15-day courses (see also page 93). Chiang Mai also has a number of centres offering courses, some up to 11 days long (see page 253). There's also a deluge of therapeutic massage places, some linked to guesthouses and hotels, where tourists can have their worries caressed away for a few bucks. Some concentrate on foot massage, but many also provide various forms of body massage, some herbal. Note that many masseuses are not trained.

Meditation **Wat Mahathat** is Bangkok's renowned meditation centre (see page 97); see page 149 for other meditation classes available in Bangkok. Beyond Bangkok, **Wat Suan Mokkh**, outside Surat Thani, offers 10-day anapanasati meditation courses (T02-4682857, see page 557), while **Wat Khao Tum** on Koh Phangan supports a **Vipassana Meditation Centre** offering 20-day courses and three-month retreats (see page 586). There are centres elsewhere too, for example on Koh Tao.

Trekking areas of the north

Centres	Trekking areas	Tribes
Around Chiang Mai	North, west and southwest of the city. Rafting on the Mae Tang.	Lisu, Akha, Karen, Lahu, Hmong and Shan.
Around Chiang Rai	Mainly along or near the Kok River and to the north in the vicinity of the Golden Triangle. Rafting on the Kok River.	Karen, Lisu, Akha, Hmong, Yao and Lahu.
Around Mae Hong Son	Most treks either run south to Mae Sariang or north and east to Pai. Rafting on the Pai River.	Karen, Lisu, Shan, Kaya, Hmong, Red Lahu and long-necked Karen' – more properly known as Padaung – as well as committee villages.
Eastern highlands	West of Nan.	Hmong, Karen, Yao, Akha, Lahu Highlands.

Spas Building upon the excellence of Thai hotels and personal service, along with a long tradition of traditional massage, the last few years has seen a flowering of spas.

Thai cooking courses

There has been an explosion of interest in Thai cuisine, and the number of Thai cookery classes has blossomed too. Bangkok (see page 147) and Chiang Mai (see page 247) offer the largest choice, but many hotels and even some guesthouses offer classes of varying length of time and intensity in many tourist centres including Koh Samui and Phuket.

Trekking and hill tribes

Hundreds of thousands of tourists each year take a trek into the hills of the northern and western regions, partly to experience Thailand's (declining) natural wealth and partly to see and stay with one or more of the country's hill tribes. Treks are often combined with elephant rides and rafting and can stretch from single day outings to two-week expeditions. The main trekking centres are Chiang Mai, Chiang Rai, Mae Hong Son, Mae Sot, Mae Sariang, Pai, Soppong, Fang, Tha Ton, Chiang Saen, Sop Ruak, Mae Sai, Nan and Umphang. Trekking companies with websites include: **The Ecotourist Center,** Umphang, www.umphanghill.com. See also Books and Background for reading material and further information.

Visiting the hill tribes There are many ways to see the hill tribes, ranging from an easy visit of a single day to a strenuous trek of a week. Although many will tell you that it is not possible to experience the 'real thing' unless you opt for the most exhausting and

Visiting the hill tribes: house rules

Etiquette and customs vary between the hill tribes. However, the following are general rules of good behaviour that should be adhered to whenever possible.

- Dress modestly and avoid undressing/changing in public.
- Ask permission before photographing anyone (old people and pregnant women often object to having their photograph taken).
  Be aware that hill people are unlikely to pose out of the kindness of their hearts – don't begrudge them the money; for many, tourism is their livelihood.
- Ask permission before entering a house.
- Do not touch or photograph village shrines.
- Do not smoke opium.
- Avoid sitting or stepping on door sills.
- Avoid excessive displays of wealth and be sensitive when giving gifts (for children, pens are better than sweets).
- Avoid introducing western medicines.

adventurous programme on offer, every encounter between a foreigner and a hill tribe community is artificial. As the Heisenberg principle has it, just by being there a visitor has a profound effect.

If you do not want to live rough, to spend five days tramping around the forests, or to spend your money on visiting the hill tribes, then opt for a half day or day trip by taxi, bus or hired motorcycle. The major towns of the north all have hill-tribe communities within easy reach. On arrival you will probably be hounded by handicraft salespeople; you may well have to pay for any photographs that you take, but at least you will get a taste of a hill-tribe village and their traditional costumes. You can also leave satisfied in the knowledge that you have not contributed too much to the process of cultural erosion.

Longer trips can either take the form of a two- or three-day excursion by bus, raft, boat and foot, or a trek of up to a week or more. The excursions are usually more comfortable, more highly organized, and do not venture far into the wilds of the north. They are easily booked through one of the many companies in Chiang Mai, Chiang Rai, Mae Hong Son and the other trekking towns of the region.

Trekking into the hills is undoubtedly the best way to see the hill tribes, however, to keep the adventure of trekking alive (or perhaps, the myth of adventure), most companies now promote 'non-touristic' trekking – if that is not a contradiction in terms. They guarantee a trek will not meet another trekking party. It is most important to try and get a knowledgeable guide who speaks good English, as well as the language(s) of the tribe(s) that are to be visited. He is your link with the hill tribes: he will warn you what not to do, tell you of their customs, rituals, economy and religion, and ensure your safety. Ask other tourists who have recently returned from treks about their experiences: a personal recommendation is hard to beat and they will also have the most up to date information. Sometimes an even better alternative is to hire a private guide, although this is obviously more expensive.

A final way to see the people of the hills is simply to set off on your own, either on foot or by motorbike DIY trekking. This can be very rewarding – and is becoming increasingly popular – but it does have its risks: parts of the north are still fairly lawless and every year there are reports of hold-ups, even murders, of tourists. Take care preparing your trip and let someone know your schedule and itinerary. It is also easy to get lost, and, unless you go fully prepared with the appropriate books, maps

Cultural extinction?

Much of the concern that has been focused upon the hill tribes dwells on their increasingly untenable position in a country where they occupy a distinctly subordinate position. Over a number of years, the government has tried culturally and economically to assimilate the hill tribes into the Thai state (read, Tai state). Projects have attempted to settle them in *nikhom* (resettlement villages) and to 'instill a strong sense of Thai citizenship, obligation and faith in the institutions of Nation, Religion and Monarchy...' (Thai Army document). This desire on the part of the government is understandable, when one considers the hill tribes occupy strategically-sensitive border areas.

There are a number of factors that have lent weight to this policy of resettlement and integration: the former strength of the Communist Party of Thailand (CPT), the narcotics problem (it has been estimated that as recently as 30 years ago, 45 per cent of hill-tribe households were engaged in the cultivation of the poppy), the more recent concern with the preservation of Thailand's few remaining forests, as well as the simple demographic reality that the population is growing. However, in many respects the most significant process encouraging change has been the commercialization of life among the hill tribes: as they have been inexorably drawn into the market economy, so their traditional subsistence systems and ethics have become increasingly obsolete. This process is voluntary, spontaneous and profound.

Although tourists may feel they are somehow more culturally aware and sensitive than the next man or woman and therefore can watch and not influence, this is of course untrue. As people, and especially monetized westerners, push their way into the last remaining remote areas of the north in an endless quest for the 'real thing', they are helping to erode that for which they search. Not that the hill tribes could ever remain, or ever have been, isolated. There has always been contact and trade between hill tribes and the lowland peoples.

Their 'westernization' or 'Thai-ization' is popularly seen as a 'bad thing'. This says more about our romantic image of the Rousseau-esque tribal peoples of the world than it does about the realities of life in the mountains. Certainly, it is impossible selectively to develop the hill-tribe communities. If they are to have the benefits of schooling and medical care, then they must also receive – or come into contact with – all those other, and perhaps less desirable, facets of modern Thai life. And if culture is functional, as anthropologists would have us believe, then in so doing they are experiencing a process of cultural erosion. To dramatize slightly, they are on the road to cultural extinction.

and other information, it is unlikely that you will gain much of an insight into hill-tribe life.

Most hill-tribe villages will offer a place to sleep – usually in the headman's house; expect to pay about ฿50. The advantage – from the hill peoples' perspective – is that the money accrues to them, and does not line the pockets of some agent or trekking company. If you are intending to venture out on your own, it is a good idea to visit the **Hilltribe Research Center** at Chiang Mai University before you leave, and to get a map of the hill-tribe areas (available from DK Books, 234 Tha Phae Road, Chiang Mai). You can also download a helpful pdf document from the website of the Tribal Research Institute at www.chmai.com/tribal.

When to trek and what to take The best time to trek is during the cool, dry season between October and February. In March and April, although it is dry, temperatures can be high and the vegetation is parched. During the wet season, paths are muddy and walking can be difficult.

Leave valuables behind in a bank safety deposit box. Trekkers who leave their credit cards for safekeeping in their guesthouses have sometimes found that a large bill awaits them on their return home. A safety deposit box hired at a bank is the safest way to leave your valuables.

Choosing a trekking company In Chiang Mai there are more than 100 trekking companies (see page 222), and many more in other trekking centres of the north. Check that the company is registered with the police and that they notify the Tourist Police before departure (as they are required to do). Shop around to get an idea of prices and try to get a personal recommendation from another tourist. Note that the best guides may move between companies or work for more than one.

Trekking companies should advise on what to take and many provide rucksacks, sleeping bags, first-aid kits and food. However, the following is a checklist of items that might be useful: good walking shoes; bed sheet (blanket/sleeping bag in the cold season November-February); raincoat (July-October); insect repellent; toiletries (soap, toothpaste, toilet paper); small first-aid kit (including antiseptic, plasters, diarrhoea pills, salt tablets); sun protection (suncream/sun hat); photocopy of passport (if venturing into border area); and water bottle (to cut down on the mountain of plastic bottles accumulating in the hills of the north).

Health precautions By living in hill-tribe villages, even if for only a few days, the health hazard is amplified significantly. Inoculation against hepatitis (gamma globulin) and protection against malaria are both strongly recommended. Particular dietary care should be exercised: do not drink unboiled or untreated water and avoid uncooked vegetables. Although the hill-tribe population may look healthy, remember that the incidence of parasitic infection in most communities is not far off 100 per cent.

Costs It does not take long to work out the going price for a trek – just ask around. For a basic walking trek, costs are ฿250-500 per day, the cheaper end of the range relating to trekking companies that specialize in the backpacking market; if rafting and elephant rides are also included, the cost rises to ฿500-1000 per day. Many trekking companies and some guesthouses take donations to help support the hill peoples, and in particular the many thousands of displaced refugees from Burma.

Opium smoking For some, one of the attractions of trekking is the chance to smoke opium. It should be remembered that opium smoking, as well as opium cultivation, is illegal in Thailand. It is also not unusual for first-time users to experience adverse physical and psychological side effects. Police regularly stop and search tourists who are motorcycle trekking. Be careful not to carry any illicit substances.

Wakeboarding and kitesurfing

Offered as an option in a few watersports centres, wakeboarding has its own specialist school in Thailand. **Air Time**, Jomtien Nivate, 152/26 Moo 10, Nong Phlue, Banglamoung, Chonburi, T01861-6736 (mobile), www.air-time.net, runs wakeboard camps near Pattaya with dedicated English, French, German, Dutch and Thai speaking coaches and the chance to try out monoboards, kneeboards, skyski and tubes. **Thailand Kitesurfing School**, Rawai, Muang Phuket, T076-288258, www.kitethailand.com, also runs courses. There are kitesurfing schools in Phuket and Hua Hin offering one- to three-day courses and instructor training.

Whitewater rafting

Whitewater rafting has become popular with tourists in the last few years and is a year-round activity. Among the popular locations are Pai (on the Pai River, see page 269) and the Mae Taeng and Mae Cham close to Chiang Mai. There is whitewater rafting in Sangkhlaburi in the western region (see page 187) and there are also opportunities on the resort island of Phuket. June to November is a particularly good time due to higher rainfall. Tour operators include: **K-Trekking**, 238/5, Chiangmai-hod Road, A Muang, Chiang Mai T053-431447, F053-431 447, day tours from US$55; **New Frontier Adventure Co**, 53/54 Onnutch 17, Suan Luang, Bangkok, T02-3003670, F9584305, rafting and whitewater rafting plus options of elephant safaris and trekking for one to three days; and **Sea Canoe Thailand**, Yaowarat Road, Phuket, T076-212172, www.seacanoe.net, full and half-day tours from Phuket for from US$65 per day.

Wildlife watching

Thailand has an extensive network of national parks and protected areas. The more popular – such as Khao Yai and Phu Kradung in the northeast, Doi Inthanon in the north, and Khao Sok in the south – have trails, camping grounds, hides, accommodation, visitors' centres and more. However, compared with other countries with a rich natural heritage, it is difficult not to feel that Thailand has not made the most of its potential. Trails are – generally – not well laid out and true nature lovers may find themselves disappointed rather than enthralled. But for those from temperate regions the sheer luxuriance and abundance of the tropical forest, and the unusual birds, insects and more, will probably make up for this. See also Land and Environment, in Background.

Health

Staying healthy in Thailand is straightforward. With the following advice and precautions you should keep as healthy as you do at home. Most visitors return home having experienced no problems at all beyond an upset stomach. However, in Thailand the health risks, especially in the tropical areas, are different from those encountered in Europe or the USA. It also depends on how you travel and where. The country has a mainly tropical climate; nevertheless the acquisition of true tropical disease by the visitor is probably conditioned as much by the rural nature and standard of hygiene of the surroundings than by the climate. There is an obvious difference in health risks between the business traveller who tends to stay in international class hotels in the large cities and the backpacker trekking through the rural areas. There are no hard and fast rules to follow; you will often have to make your own judgement on the healthiness or otherwise of your surroundings. Before you go check with your doctor on the status of Avian flu. It has been slowly spreading around Asia since early 2004 and has been contracted by some humans in the region resulting in death.

Before you go

Take out medical insurance. Make sure it covers all eventualities especially evacuation to your home country by a medically equipped plane, if necessary. You should have a dental check-up, obtain a spare glasses prescription, a spare oral contraceptive prescription (or enough pills to last) and, if you suffer from a chronic illness (such as diabetes, high blood pressure, ear or sinus troubles, cardio-pulmonary disease or nervous disorder) arrange for a check-up with your doctor, who can at the same time provide you with a letter explaining the details of your disability in English. Check the current practice for malaria prophylaxis (prevention), also see below. If you are on regular medication, make sure you have enough to cover the period of your travel.

Vaccination and immunization Ideally, you should see your GP or travel clinic at least six weeks before your departure for general advice on travel risks, malaria and vaccinations. Make sure you have travel insurance, get a dental check (especially if you are going to be away for more than a month), know your own blood group and if you suffer a long-term condition such as diabetes or epilepsy make sure someone knows or that you have a Medic Alert bracelet/necklace with this information on it.

Smallpox vaccination is no longer required anywhere in the world and cholera vaccination is no longer recognized as necessary for international travel by the World Health Organization – it is not very effective either. Yellow fever vaccination is not required either although you may be asked for a certificate if you have been in a country affected by yellow fever immediately before travelling to Southeast Asia.

Vaccination	Obligatory	Recommended
Polio		Yes if nil in last 10 years
Tetanus		Yes if nil in last 10 years
Typhoid		Yes if nil in last 3 years
Yellow fever	Not required	
Rabies		Yes if travelling to jungle and/or remote areas including islands
Hepatitis A		Yes – the disease can be caught easily from food/water

Medicines There is very little control on the sale of drugs and medicines in Thailand. You may be able to buy any and every drug in pharmacies without a prescription. Be wary of this because pharmacists can be poorly trained and might sell you drugs that are unsuitable, dangerous or old. Many drugs and medicines are manufactured under licence from American or European companies, so the trade names may be familiar to you. This means you do not have to carry a whole chest of medicines with you, but remember that the shelf life of some items, especially vaccines and antibiotics, is markedly reduced in hot conditions. Buy your supplies at the better outlets where there are more refrigerators, even though they are more expensive, and check the expiry date of all preparations you buy. Immigration officials occasionally confiscate scheduled drugs (Lomotil is an example) if they are not accompanied by a doctor's prescription.

Children More preparation is probably necessary for babies and children than for an adult and perhaps a little more care should be taken when travelling to remote areas where health services are primitive. This is because children can be become more rapidly ill than adults (on the other hand they often recover more quickly). Diarrhoea and vomiting are the most common problems, so take the usual precautions, but more intensively. Breast-feeding is the best and most convenient for babies, but powdered milk is available in the cities, as are a few baby foods. Bananas and other fruits are nutritious and can be cleanly prepared. The treatment of diarrhoea is the same for adults, except that it should start earlier and be continued with more persistence. Children get dehydrated very quickly in hot countries and can become drowsy and uncooperative unless cajoled to drink water or juice plus salts. Upper respiratory infections, such as colds, catarrh and middle ear infections, are also common and if your child suffers from these normally, take some antibiotics just in case. Outer ear infections after swimming are also common and antibiotic eardrops will help. Wet wipes are useful and can be found in the large cities, as can disposable nappies.

What to take

Anti-malarials Important to take for the key areas. Specialist advice is required as to which type to take. General principles are that all except Malarone should be continued for four weeks after leaving the malarial area. Malarone needs to be

continued for only seven days afterwards (if a tablet is missed or vomited seek specialist advice). The start times for the anti-malarials vary in that if you have never taken Lariam (Mefloquine) before it is advised to start it at least two to three weeks before the entry to a malarial zone (this is to help identify serious side effects early). Chloroquine and Paludrine are often started a week before the trip to establish a pattern but Doxycycline and Malarone can be started only one to two days before entry to the malarial area. **Note** It is risky to buy medicinal tablets abroad because the doses may differ and there may be a trade in false drugs.

Ciproxin (Ciprofloaxcin) A useful antibiotic for some forms of travellers' diarrhoea.

Immodium A great standby for those diarrhoeas that occur at awkward times. It helps stop the flow of diarrhoea and in my view is of more benefit than harm. (It was believed that letting the bacteria or viruses flow out had to be more beneficial. However, with Immodium they still come out, just in a more solid form.)

Clean needle pack, clean dental pack and **water filtration devices** For longer trips involving jungle treks taking these are common-sense measures.

MedicAlert These simple bracelets, or an equivalent, should be carried or worn by anyone with a significant medical condition.

Mosquito repellents Remember that DEET (Di-ethyltoluamide) is the gold standard. Apply the repellent every four to six hours but more often if you are sweating heavily. If a non-DEET product is used check who tested it. Validated products (tested at the London School of Hygiene and Tropical Medicine) include Mosiguard, Non-DEET Jungle formula and non-DEET Autan. If you want to use citronella remember that it must be applied very frequently (ie hourly) to be effective. If you are popular target for insect bites or develop lumps quite soon after being bitten, carry an Aspivenin kit. This syringe suction device is available from many chemists and draws out some of the allergic materials and provides quick relief.

Pain killers Paracetamol or a suitable painkiller can have multiple uses for symptoms but remember that more than eight paracetamol a day can lead to liver failure.

Pepto-Bismol Used a lot by Americans for diarrhoea. It certainly relieves symptoms but like Immodium it is not a cure for underlying disease. Be aware that it turns the stool black as well as making it more solid.

Sun block The Australians have a great campaign, which has reduced skin cancer. It is called 'Slip, Slap, Slop'. Slip on a shirt, Slap on a hat, Slop on sunscreen.

When you arrive

There are English-speaking doctors in Bangkok and other major cities who have particular experience in dealing with locally occurring diseases. Your embassy representative will often be able to give you the name of local reputable doctors and most of the better hotels have a doctor on standby. If you do fall ill and cannot find a recommended doctor, try the outpatient department of a hospital – there are excellent private hospitals in Bangkok which, although they are not cheap, offer a very acceptable standard to foreigners. The likelihood of finding good medical care diminishes very rapidly as you move away from the big cities. Especially in the rural areas there are systems and traditions of medicine wholly different from the western model and you will be confronted with less orthodox forms of treatment such as herbal medicines and acupuncture, not that these are unfamiliar to most western travellers.

An A-Z of health risks

Dengue fever

The key viral disease is Dengue fever, which is transmitted by a mosquito that bites during the day. The disease is like a very nasty form of the 'flu with two to three days of illness, followed by a short period of recovery, then a second attack of illness.

 westerners very rarely get the worst haemorrhagic form of the disease.

Symptoms This disease can be contracted throughout Thailand. In travellers this can cause a severe flu-like illness which includes symptoms of fever, lethargy, enlarged lymph glands and muscle pains. It starts suddenly, lasts for two to three days, seems to get better for two to three days and then kicks in again for another two to three days. It is usually all over in an unpleasant week. The local children are prone to the much nastier haemorrhagic form of the disease, which causes them to bleed from internal organs, mucous membranes and often leads to their death.

Cures The traveller's version of the disease is self-limiting and forces rest and recuperation on the sufferer.

Prevention The mosquitoes that carry the Dengue virus bite during the day unlike the malaria mosquitoes. Which sadly means that repellent application and covered limbs are a 24-hour issue. Check your accommodation for flower pots and shallow pools of water since these are where the dengue-carrying mosquitoes breed.

Diarrhoea and intestinal upset

This is almost inevitable. One study showed that up to 70 per cent of all travellers may suffer some form of upset during their trip.

Symptoms Diarrhoea can refer either to loose stools or an increased frequency; both of these can be a nuisance. It should be short lasting but persistence beyond two weeks, with blood or pain, require specialist medical attention.

Cures Ciproxin (Ciprofloaxcin) is a useful antibiotic for bacterial travellers' diarrhoea. It can be obtained by private prescription in the UK which is expensive, or bought over the counter in pharmacies. You need to take one 500 mg tablet when the diarrhoea starts and if you do not feel better in 24 hours, the diarrhoea is likely to have a non-bacterial cause and may be viral (in which case there is little you can do apart from keep yourself rehydrated and wait for it to settle on its own). The key treatment with all diarrhoeas is rehydration. Try to keep hydrated by taking the right mixture of salt and water. This is available as Oral Rehydration Salts (ORS) in ready-made sachets or can be made up by adding a teaspoon of sugar and a half teaspoon of salt to a litre of clean water. Drink at least one large cup of this drink for each loose stool. You can also use flat carbonated drinks as an alternative. Immodium and Pepto-Bismol provide symptomatic relief.

Prevention The standard advice is to be careful with water and ice for drinking. Ask yourself where the water came from. If you have any doubts then boil it or filter and treat it. There are many filter/treatment devices now available on the market. Food can also transmit disease. Be wary of salads (what were they washed in, who handled them), re-heated foods or food that has been left out in the sun having been cooked earlier in the day. There is a simple adage that says wash it, peel it, boil it or forget it. Also be wary of unpasteurized dairy products, these can transmit a range of diseases from brucellosis (fevers and constipation), to listeria (meningitis) and tuberculosis of the gut (obstruction, constipation, fevers and weight loss).

Hepatitis

Symptoms Hepatitis means inflammation of the liver. Viral causes of the disease can be acquired anywhere in Thailand. The most obvious symptom is a yellowing of your skin or the whites of your eyes. However, before this all you may feel is itching and tiredness.

Cures Early on, depending on the type of hepatitis, a vaccine or immunoglobulin may reduce the duration of the illness.

Prevention Pre-travel Hepatitis A vaccine is the best bet. Hepatitis B (for which there is a vaccine) is spread through blood and unprotected sexual intercourse, both of these can be avoided. Unfortunately, there is no vaccine for Hepatitis C or the increasing alphabetical list of other hepatitis viruses.

Malaria and insect bite prevention

The risk is limited to the border areas with Burma (Myanmar), Cambodia and Laos. If you are trekking to see the hill tribes most areas are safe but check what itinerary your guide actually has planned for you. The choice of malaria drug depends on where you will travel, which type of malaria you may be exposed to, and your medical/ psychological history. Always check with your doctor or travel clinic for the most up to date advice. The Royal Homeopathic Hospital in the UK does not advocate homeopathic options for malaria prevention or treatment.

Symptoms Malaria can cause death within 24 hours. It can start as something just resembling an attack of flu. You may feel tired, lethargic, headachy; or worse, develop fits, followed by coma and then death. Have a low index of suspicion because it is very easy to write off vague symptoms, which may actually be malaria. Whilst abroad and on return get tested as soon as possible, the test could save your life.

Cures Treatment is with drugs and may be oral or into a vein depending on the seriousness of the infection. Remember ABCD: Awareness (of whether the disease is present in the area you are in), Bite avoidance, Chemoprohylaxis, Diagnosis.

Prevention This is best summarized by the B and C of the ABCD: bite avoidance and chemoprophylaxis. Wear clothes that cover arms and legs and use effective insect repellents in areas with known risks of insect-spread disease. Use a mosquito net dipped in permethrin as both a physical and chemical barrier at night in the same areas. Guard against the contraction of malaria with the correct anti-malarials (see above). Some would prefer to take test kits for malaria with them and have standby treatment available. However, the field tests of the blood kits have had poor results: when you have malaria you are usually too ill to be able to do the tests correctly enough to make the right diagnosis. Standby treatment (treatment that you carry and take yourself for malaria) should still ideally be supervised by a doctor since the drugs themselves can be toxic if taken incorrectly.

Schistosomiasis

A fluke is a sort of flattened worm. Schistosomiasis can be acquired through wading through stagnant water and swimming in such waters.

Symptoms The liver fluke may cause jaundice, gall stone symptoms, right-sided abdominal pain, liver test abnormalities and changes in the white cell pattern of the blood. Schistosomiasis can cause a local skin itch at first exposure, fever after a few weeks and much later diarrhoea, abdominal pain and spleen or liver enlargement.

Cures A single drug cures Schistosomiasis. The same drug can be used for the liver fluke but this infestation is much more difficult to treat.

Prevention Avoid infected waters, be careful with unwashed vegetables check the CDC, WHO websites and a travel clinic specialist for up to date information on the whereabouts of the disease.

Severe Acute Respiratory Syndrome (SARS)

Severe Acute Respiratory Syndrome (SARS) started in Southern China back in November 2002. Since then the disease has followed geography (Hong Kong, Vietnam) and air flights (Canada and UK). The disease causes breathing problems and fever. We now know that it is caused by a virus which is different from influenza. Treatment is supportive and some patients need to be cared for on an intensive care unit. There is nothing we know that can prevent you getting it if you are exposed to someone who coughs in your presence. Travellers to Southeast Asia are at risk but to what extent and for how long is still an unknown. If you return from Southeast Asia with fever and respiratory problems ask your doctor or specialist to at least think about SARS as a possibility. There are no specific tests he/she can do but a chest X-ray may be useful.

Sexual Health

The range of visible and invisible diseases is awesome. Unprotected sex can spread HIV, Hepatitis B and C, Gonorrhea (green discharge), chlamydia (nothing to see but may cause painful urination and later female infertility), painful recurrent herpes, syphilis and warts, just to name a few. You can cut down the risk by using condoms, a femidom or avoiding sex altogether. If you do have unprotected sex, book a sexual health check on your return home.

Sun protection

Symptoms White travellers are notorious for becoming red in hot countries because they like to stay out longer than everyone else and do not use adequate sun protection. This can lead to sunburn, which is painful and followed by flaking of skin. Aloe vera gel is a good pain reliever for sunburn. Long-term sun damage leads to a loss of elasticity of skin and the development of pre-cancerous lesions. Many years later a mild or a very malignant form of cancer may develop. The milder basal cell carcinoma, if detected early, can be treated by cutting it out or freezing it. The much nastier malignant melanoma may have already spread to bone and brain at the time that it is first noticed.

Prevention Sunscreen. SPF stands for Sun Protection Facor. It is measured by determining how long a given person takes to 'burn' with and without the sunscreen product on. So, if it takes 10 times longer to burn with the sunscreen product applied, then that product has an SPF of 10. If it only takes twice as long then the SPF is 2. The higher the SPF the greater the protection. However, do not just use higher factors just to stay out in the sun longer. 'Flash frying' (desperate bursts of excessive exposure), as it is called, is known to increase the risks of skin cancer.

Underwater health

Symptoms If you go diving make sure that you are fit to do so. **British Sub-Aqua Club** (BSAC), Telford's Quay, South Pier Road, Ellesmere Port, Cheshire, CH65 4FL, UK, T01513-506200, www.bsac.com, can put you in touch with doctors who do medical examinations. Protect your feet from cuts, beach dog parasites (larva migrans) and sea urchins. The latter are almost impossible to remove but can be dissolved with lime or vinegar. Keep an eye out for secondary infection.

Cures Antibiotics for secondary infections. Serious diving injuries may need time in a decompression chamber.

Prevention Check that the dive company know what they are doing, have appropriate certification from BSAC or **Professional Association of Diving Instructors** (PADI), Unit 7, St Philips Central, Albert Road, St Philips, Bristol, BS2 0TD, T0117-3007234, www.padi.com, and that the equipment is well maintained.

Further information

Foreign and Commonwealth Office (FCO) (UK), www.fco.gov.uk. This is a key travel advice site, with useful information on the country, people, climate and lists the UK embassies/consulates. The site also promotes the concept of 'Know Before You Go' and encourages travel insurance and appropriate travel health advice.

Department of Health Travel Advice (UK), www.doh.gov.uk/traveladvice. This excellent site is also available as a free booklet, the T6, from post offices. It lists the vaccine advice requirements for each country.

Medic Alert (UK), www.medicalert.co.uk. This is the website of the foundation that produces bracelets and necklaces for those with existing medical problems. Once you have ordered your bracelet/necklace you write your key medical details on paper inside it, so that if you collapse, a medical person can identify you as someone with epilepsy or an allergy.

Blood Care Foundation (UK), www.bloodcare.org.uk. The Blood Care Foundation is a Kent-based charity "dedicated

to the provision of screened blood and resuscitation fluids in countries where these are not readily available". It will dispatch certified non-infected blood of the right type to your hospital/clinic. The blood is flown in from various centres around the world.

Public Health Laboratory Service (UK), www.phls.org.uk. This site has up to date malaria advice guidelines for travel around the world. It gives specific advice about the right drugs for each location. It also has useful information for those who are pregnant, suffering from epilepsy or planning to travel with children.

Centers for Disease Control and Prevention (USA), www.cdc.gov. This site from the US government gives excellent advice on travel health, has useful disease maps and details of disease outbreaks.

World Health Organisation, www.who.int. The WHO site has links to the WHO Blue Book (it was Yellow up to last year) on travel advice. This lists the diseases in different regions of the world. It describes vaccination schedules and makes clear which countries have Yellow Fever Vaccination certificate requirements and malarial risk.

Tropical Medicine Bureau (Ireland), www.tmb.ie. This Irish-based site has a good collection of general travel health information and disease risks.

Fit for Travel (UK), www.fitfortravel.scot.nhs.uk. This site from Scotland provides a quick A-Z of vaccine and travel health advice requirements for each country with information on various aspects of travel health and safety.

British Travel Health Association (UK), www.btha.org. This is the official website of an organization of travel health professionals.

NetDoctor (UK), www.netdoctor.co.uk. This general health advice site has a useful section on travel and has an "ask the expert", interactive chat forum.

Travel Screening Services (UK), www.travelscreening.co.uk. This is the website of the author of the health section. A private clinic dedicated to integrated travel health. The clinic gives vaccine, travel health advice, email and SMS text vaccine reminders and screens returned travellers for tropical diseases.

Keeping in touch

Communications

Internet There are internet cafés in most towns, especially in tourist areas. Rates vary but expect to pay ฿2 per minute (often with a minimum of five minutes) in tourist centres and a figure of half this or less in internet cafés frequented by locals. Some cafés in tourist destinations charge a flat fee of ฿20 for 30 minutes. In general internet access is good, with cheap rates and efficient (and improving) systems.

Post Local postal charges are ฿1.50 (postcard) and ฿2 (letter, 20 g). **International postal charges** for Europe and Australasia are ฿12-15 (postcard, varies according to dimensions), ฿17 (letter, 10 g); US ฿12-15 (postcard, varies according to dimensions), ฿19 (letter, 10 g). Airletters cost ฿15, irrespective of the destination outside Thailand. If you are buying your stamps from a shop rather than a post office, expect to pay a baht extra or two. See a listing of all costs, including for packets, at www.thaistudents.com/guidebook/postoffice/index.html. Outside Bangkok, most post offices are open from 0800-1630 Monday-Friday and only the larger ones will be open on Saturday. **Poste Restante** Correspondents should write the family name in capital letters and underline it, to avoid confusion.

Telephone and fax From Bangkok there is direct dialling to most countries. Outside Bangkok, it is best to go to a local telephone exchange for phoning outside the country. **Codes** Local area codes vary according to province. Individual area phone codes are listed through the book; the code can be found at the front of the telephone directory.

Directory inquiries Domestic long distance including Malaysia and Vientiane (Laos) T101 (free), Greater Bangkok BMA T183, international calls T02-2350030-5, although hotel operators will invariably help make the call if asked.

Callboxes Calls cost ฿1. All telephone numbers marked in the text with a prefix 'B' mean that they are Bangkok numbers.

Mobiles Mobiles are common and increasingly popular – reflecting the difficulties of getting a landline as well as a desire to be contactable at all times and places. Coverage is good except in some border areas. Mobile numbers begin '01' and '09'. Mobile phone users are charged for both receiving and making a call. A Thai mobile number is also very easy for a visitor to acquire. *Happy D Prompt* sim cards and top ups are available throughout the country, cost ฿300 with domestic call charges from ฿3 per minute and international calls from ฿8 per minute. This is a very good deal and much cheaper than either phone boxes or hotels.

Media

Newspapers and magazines Until recently there were two major English-language daily papers – the *Bangkok Post* (www.bangkokpost.net) and *The Nation* (www.nationgroup.com). They provide good international and are Thailand's best-known broadsheets. At times of social conflict they have also represented dissenting liberal voices. In the mid-1990s these two August institutions – which until then had the English-language newspaper market to them selves – were joined by three other dailies: *New Business Day*, *Asia Times* and *Thailand Times*. The latter two closed down during the economic slump of 1997 leaving *New Business Day* battling it out with the *Bangkok Post* and *The Nation*. *New Business Day* is, as the name suggests, aimed at the business market. It is jointly owned by a group of Thai investors along with *Singapore Press Holdings* and Malaysia's *New Straits Times* group (www.bday.net).

There are a number of Thai-language dailies and weeklies as well as Chinese-language newspapers. The Thai press is one of the least controlled in Southeast Asia (although controls were imposed following the coup at the beginning of 1991 and during the demonstrations of May 1992), and the local newspapers are sometimes scandalously colourful, with gruesome annotated pictures of traffic accidents and murder victims. International media are readily available in Bangkok, Chiang Mai, Pattaya, Phuket and on Koh Samui.

Television and radio CNN and BBC are available in most hotels from mid-range up and, in tourist centres, provide background noise in many restaurants and bars. As far as domestic television is concerned there are five TV channels, with English-language soundtrack available on FM Channel 3 – 105.5 MHz, Channel 7 – 103.5 MHz, Channel 9 – 107 MHz and Channel 11 – 88 MHz. The *Bangkok Post* lists programmes where English soundtrack is available on FM. Short wave radio can receive the BBC World Service, Voice of America, Radio Moscow and other foreign broadcasts. The BBC World Service's Dateline East Asia provides probably the best news and views on Asia. Also with a strong Asia focus are ABC (Australian Broadcasting Corporation) broadcasts.

Short wave radio **BBC**, London, Southeast Asian service 3915, 6195, 9570, 9740, 11750, 11955, 15360; Singapore service 88.9MHz; East Asian service 5995, 6195, 7180, 9740, 11715, 11750, 11945, 11955, 15140, 15280, 15360, 17830, 21715. **Voice of America** (VoA, Washington), Southeast Asian service 1143, 1575, 7120, 9760, 9770, 15185, 15425; Indonesian service 6110, 11760, 15425. **Radio Beijing**, Southeast Asian service (English) 11600, 11660. **Radio Japan** (Tokyo), Southeast Asian service (English) 11815, 17810, 21610. For information on Asian radio and television broadcasts. Access includes free downloadable software: www.isop.ucla.edu/eas/web/asia-web.htm.

Bangkok

Footprint features

Introduction

Dirty, dynamic, wild and sweaty, Bangkok is a heaving scrum of humanity blended with ancient beauty, booming youth culture and the rituals of a bygone age. The Thais call it the City of Angels but there's nothing angelic about Bangkok. Don't arrive expecting an exotic, languid, dreamy place trapped in some imagined, traditional past. What will hit you is the size, pace, endless olfactory/oral cacophony, friendliness of the locals and interminable gridlock traffic. The whole place resembles a giant, out of control car boot sale with pavements taken up with open-air kitchens, clothes stalls, hawkers and touts.

Some of the old King and I romanticism persists. There are the khlongs, palaces and temples but ultimately, what marks Bangkok out from the imaginings of its visitors, is its thrusting modernity in open struggle with the ancient, rural traditions of Thai culture. Neon, steel and glass, futuristic transport rubs shoulders with lumbering elephants, back soi Papaya trees, alms collecting monks, crumbling teak villas. It's all here: poverty and wealth, smog-filled thoroughfares and backstreets smothered in alluring exotic aroma, cyber cafés and fried-bug-laden barrows.

With your senses fully overloaded don't forget the sheer luxury that's on offer. Bangkok is home to some of the best, and most affordable, hotels in the world. Add the numerous spas, futuristic super-hip night life and the incredibly diverse range of markets and shops selling everything from amulets, sarongs, Prada to hi tech – and your head will be spinning. And when the urban theatre of Bangkok finally overwhelms take a day trip to the ancient summer residence of the Thai kings at Bang Pa In or drift up river to Nonthaburi for its provincial charm. Crocodile farms, wax works and other oddities will also provide Thai-style kitsch.

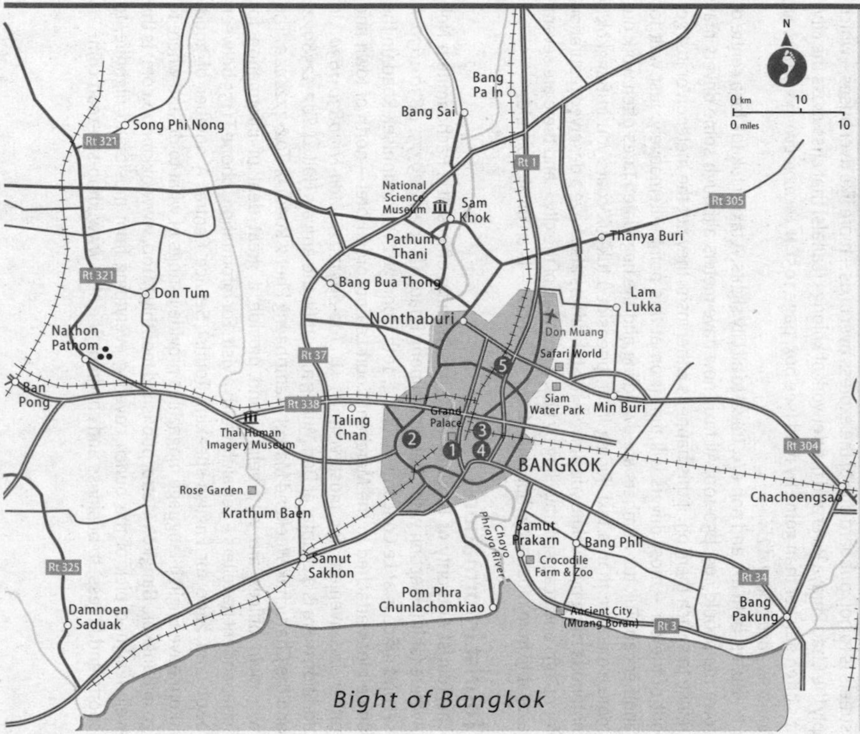

★ Don't miss...

1 **Grand Palace** Opulence, kitsch and revered religious symbolism in the form of the Emerald Buddha combine at Bangkok's Grand Palace. This place is essential, particularly in the dancing light of a sunrise, page 93.

2 **Canals and khlongs** Zoom through the remnants of the Venice of the East in a high-speed, long-tail boat. The khlongs of Bangkok provide a soothing counterpoint to the frenetic hustle and bustle, page 103.

3 **Dining** Enjoy the most mouthwateringly, incredible food – durian cheesecake at Basil or the street food at Soi Suan Plu, pages 129 and 135.

4 **Sanuk** Loosely translated as fun/party, it is essential to Thais. In Bangkok sanuk means food and nightlife. Here you'll find some of the wildest nightlife – Bed Supper Club and the Met Bar for urban sophisticates and Soi Nana and Patpong for those who like it raunchy, page 136.

5 **Shop, shop, shop** Markets, shopping centres, high-tech malls, department stores and roadside stalls. It seems that everyone in Bangkok is trying to sell you something and most of the time it is fake. The star in Bangkok's shopping firmament is the Chatuchak weekend market but there's plenty more besides – Siam Square for fashion, for example, page 141.

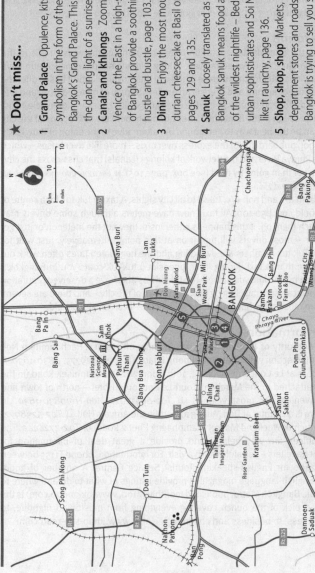

Ins and outs → *Colour map 3, grid B4.*

Getting there

Don Muang Airport is around 25 km north of the city. There are buses, trains and taxis travelling from the airport into town. On a bad day it can take an hour or more to get to the city centre by car; taking the expressway cuts the travel time down significantly. Bangkok is Thailand's domestic transport hub with flights to over 20 towns and cities; trains south to the Malaysian border (and onward to Kuala Lumpur and Singapore), north to Chiang Mai and northeast to Nong Khai and Ubon Ratchathani; and buses of every kind to all corners of the country. It is often necessary to transit through Bangkok if working your way north to south by whatever means of transport. ▸▸ *See Transport, page 151, for further details and for getting into the city from the airport. See also Essentials, page 34.*

Getting around

Bangkok has the unenviable reputation of having some of the worst traffic in the world. The Skytrain – an elevated railway – along with the sparkling new Metro have made things a lot easier for those areas of the city they cover. Plentiful buses offer the cheapest way to get around and there is an endless supply of metered taxis and lots of tuk-tuks – motorized three-wheeled taxis – and white-knuckle motorcycle taxis. Walking can be tough in the heat and fumes although there are some parts of the city where this can be the best way to get around. An alternative to the smog of Bangkok's streets is to hop onboard one of the express river taxis – more like river buses – which ply the Chao Phraya River and the network of khlongs (canals) that criss-cross the city; it's often quicker than going by road (see box, page 105). ▸▸ *For more information on boat tours, see pages 150 and 156.*

Buses, both a/c and non-a/c, travel to all city sights. A taxi or tuk-tuk for a centre of town trip should cost ฿50-100. All taxis now have meters although some drivers may refuse to switch them on. If this happens either insist they put the meter on or just get out of the car – most drivers will turn it on at this point. Alternatively, just wait for another cab. Tuk-tuk numbers are dwindling and the negotiated fares often work out more expensive than a taxi. Riding in an opensided tuk-tuk coats you in Bangkok's notorious smog by the time you arrive – tuk-tuk drivers also have a deserved reputation for rip-offs and scams. If travelling by bus, a bus map of the city – and there are several available from most bookshops and hotel gift shops – is an invaluable aid.

Tourist information

The **Tourist Authority of Thailand** (TAT) has its main offices at 4 Rachdamnern Nok Avenue (at intersection with Chakrapatdipong Road), ⓣ *T02-2829775, 0830-1630*. A second office is at Le Concorde Building, 10th Floor, 202 Rachdaphisek Road (in the office block attached to the Merchant Court Le Concorde Hotel – north of town and rather inconvenient for most visitors) ⓣ *T02-6941222, Mon-Fri 0830-1630*. In addition there is a counter at Don Muang airport (in the Arrivals Hall ⓣ *T02-5238972*) and the Chatuchak Weekend Market (Kamphaeng Phet 2 Road) ⓣ *T02-2724440*. The two main offices are very helpful and provide a great deal of information for independent travellers – certainly worth a visit. For information, phone T1155 between 0800 and 2400 for English-speaking Tourist Service Centre. A number of good, informative English-language magazines provide listings of what to do and where to go in Bangkok. **Bangkok Metro**, published monthly (฿100, www.bkkmetro.com) is the well-designed pick of the bunch covering everything from music and nightlife, to sports and fitness, to business and children. See also **www.khao-san-road.com**.

Arriving at night

All facilities at Bangkok Airport are 24 hours so you'll have no problem exchanging money, getting a massage, finding something to eat or taking a taxi or other transport into the city.

Very few buses arrive in Bangkok at night as nearly all long-distance services are timed to arrive in the morning. Bus stations are well served by taxis and if you do arrive late jump into one these.

As Bangkok is a relatively safe city it is usually okay to walk around even the most deserted streets. However, be sensible, as you would anywhere else: don't display valuables or appear lost. The best bet late at night, if you're unsure where to go, is to flag down one of the capital's ubiquitous taxis.

Background

The official name for Thailand's capital city begins Krungthep – phramaha – nakhonbawon – rathanakosin – mahinthara – yutthayaa – mahadilok – phiphobnobpharaat – raatchathaanii – buriiromudomsantisuk. It is not hard to see why Thais prefer the shortened version – Krungthep or the 'City of Angels'. The name used by the rest of the world – Bangkok – is derived from 17th-century western maps, which referred to the city (or town as it then was) as Bancok, the 'village of the wild plum'. This name was only superseded by Krungthep in 1782, and so the western name has deeper historical roots.

In 1767, Ayutthaya, then the capital of Siam, fell to the marauding Burmese for the second time and it was imperative that the remnants of the court and army find a more defensible site for a new capital. Taksin, the Lord of Tak, chose Thonburi, on the western banks of the Chao Phraya River, far from the Burmese. In three years, Taksin had established a kingdom and crowned himself king. His reign was short lived; the pressure of thwarting the Burmese over three arduous years caused him to go mad and in 1782 he was forced to abdicate. General Phraya Chakri was recalled from Cambodia and invited to accept the throne. This marked the start of the present Chakri Dynasty.

Bangkok: the new capital

In 1782, Chakri (now known as Rama I) moved his capital across the river to Bangkok (an even more defensible site) anticipating trouble from King Bodawpaya who had seized the throne of Burma. The river that flows between Thonburi and Bangkok and on which many of the luxury hotels – such as **The Oriental** – are now located, began life not as a river at all, but as a canal (khlong). The canal was dug in the 16th century to reduce the distance between Ayutthaya and the sea by shortcutting a number of bends in the river. Since then, the canal has become the main channel of the Chao Phraya River. Its original course has shrunk in size, and is now represented by two khlongs, Bangkok Yai and Bangkok Noi, see map river and khlongs, page 104.

This new capital of Siam grew in size and influence. Symbolically, many of the new buildings were constructed using bricks from the palaces and temples of the ruined former capital of Ayutthaya. However, population growth was hardly spectacular – it appears that outbreaks of cholera sometimes reduced the population by a fifth or more in a matter of a few weeks. An almanac from 1820 records that "on the seventh month of the waxing moon, a little past 2100 in the evening, a shining light was seen in the northwest and multitudes of people purged, vomited and died".

Venice of the East

Bangkok began life as a city of floating houses; in 1864 the French explorer Henri Mouhot wrote that "Bangkok is the Venice of the East (in the process making Bangkok one of several Asian cities to be landed with this sobriquet) and whether bent on

A Bangkok general

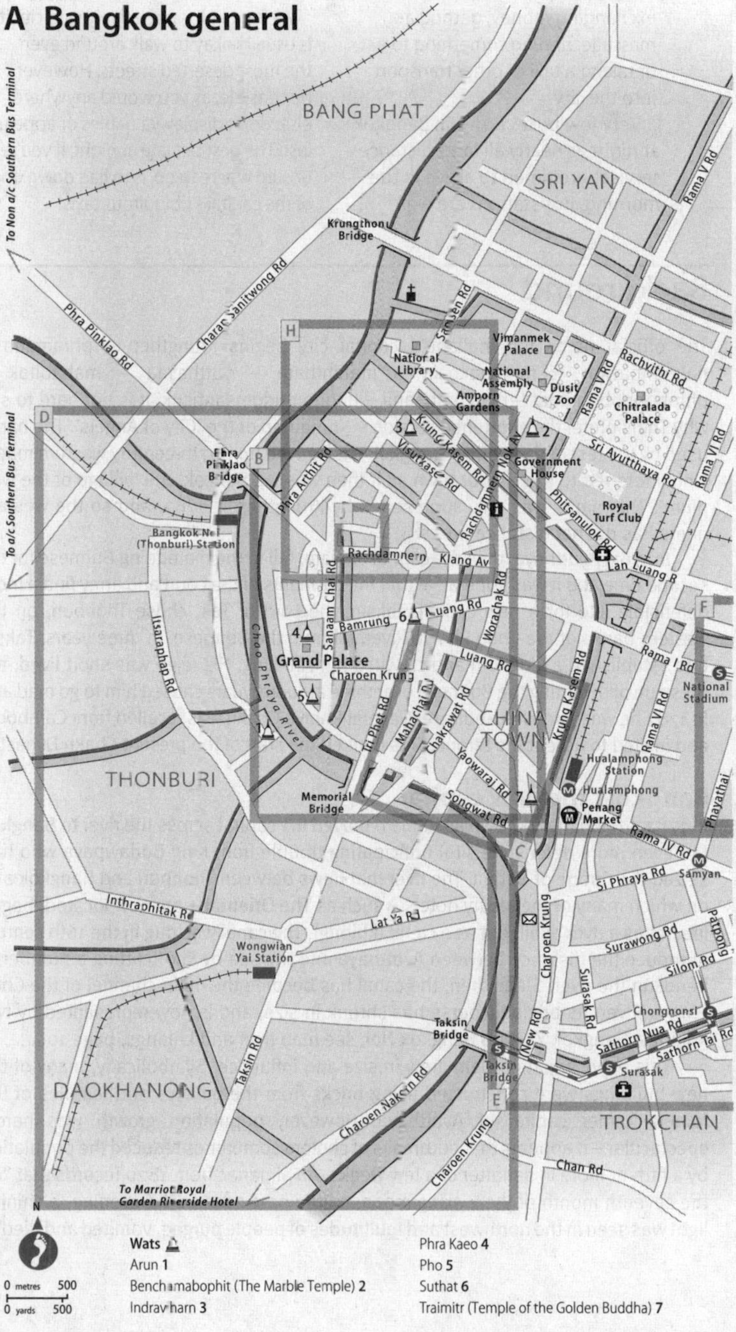

Wats

- Arun **1**
- Benchamabophit (The Marble Temple) **2**
- Indravharn **3**
- Phra Kaeo **4**
- Pho **5**
- Suthat **6**
- Traimitr (Temple of the Golden Buddha) **7**

business or pleasure you must go by water". In 1861, foreign consuls in Bangkok petitioned Rama IV and complained of ill-health due to their inability to go out riding in carriages or on horseback. The king complied with their request for roads and the first road was made running south in the 1860s – Charoen Krung ('New Road'). It was not until

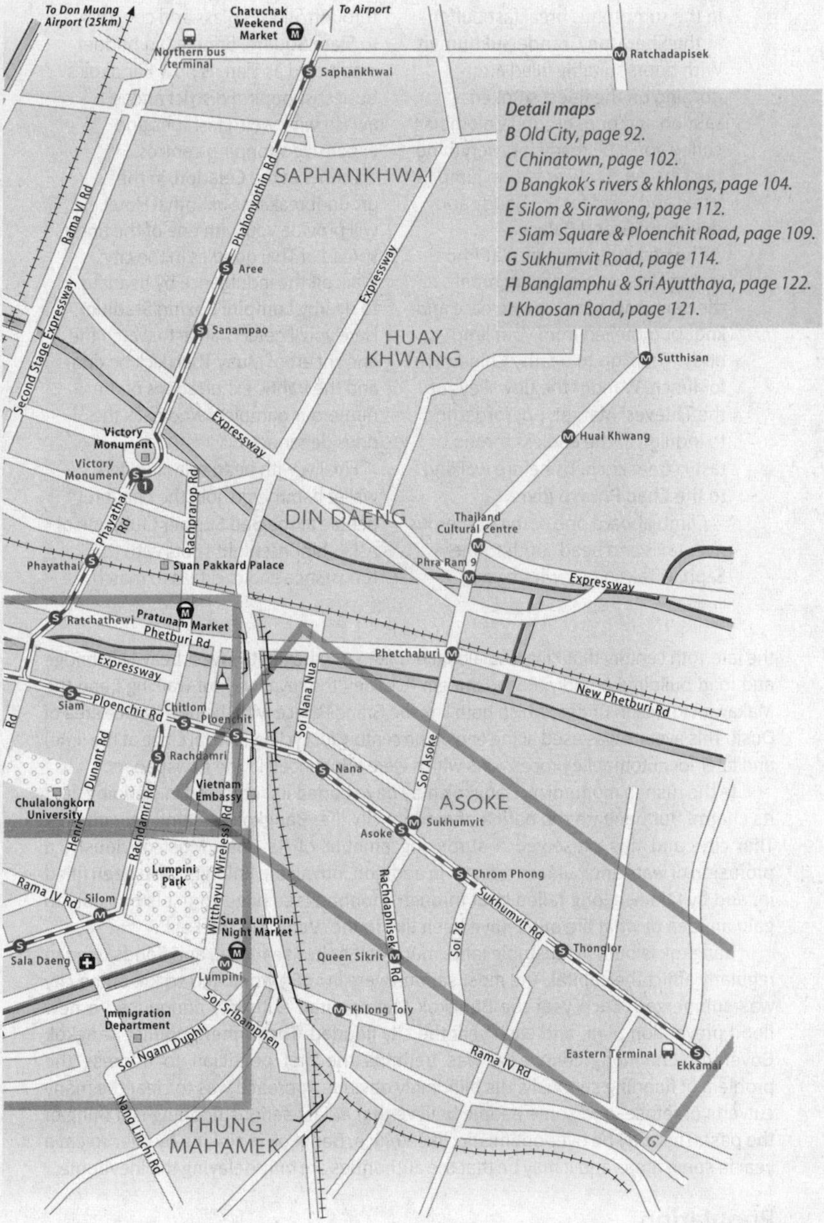

Bars & clubs

Saxophone 1

24 hours in the city

If you are lucky enough to arrive over the weekend then take in the sumptuous breakfast buffet at the **Sheraton Grande Sukhumvit.** With boots suitably filled after gorging on the finest smoked salmon and pure ground Colombian coffee you'll be ready for everything the city can throw at you so jump in a taxi and head for the gaudy and delightful **Grand Palace**.

The nearby temple of **Wat Pho** and its famous massaging monks is the next stop: have every crease and knot pummelled from your limp body. Then, go to nearby Chinatown for lunch. Wander the tiny alleys of the **Thieves' Market**, not forgetting to indulge in the endless throng of tasty street kitchens before walking to the **Chao Phrayo River**.

Climb aboard one of the numerous river taxis and head south to the Saphan Taksin pier where your carriage – Bangkok's futuristic elevated Skytrain – awaits. Zoom through Silom's glass and concrete to **Siam Square**. Bring a big budget credit card as Siam is now Bangkok's busiest shopping district and is awash with weird fashions and expensive shopping centres.

Dinner at the **Celadon**, in the groundbreaking Sukhothai Hotel, will provide you with one of the finest spread of Thai goodies in the city. Walk off the indulgence by heading to nearby **Lumpini Boxing Stadium.** Here you'll get a chance to watch the ancient art of Muay Thai (kick boxing) and the frantic exhortations of the numerous gamblers who pack the ringside terraces.

Finally, with head spinning and wallet hammered, join the beautiful people at the **Bed Supper Club**, one of Asia's hippest night spots with the tunes, style and cocktails to match.

the late 19th century that King Chulalongkorn (Rama V) began to invest heavily in bridge and road building; notably, Rachdamnern Avenue ('the royal way for walking') and the Makawan Rungsun Bridge, which both link the Grand Palace with the new palace area of Dusit. This avenue was used at the end of the century for cycling (a royal craze at the time) and later for automobile processions which were announced in the newspapers.

In the rush to modernize, Bangkok may have buried its roots and in so doing, lost its charm. But beneath the patina of modern city life, Bangkok remains very much a Thai city, and has preserved a surprising amount of its past. Most obviously, a profusion of wats and palaces remain. In addition, not all the khlongs have been filled in, and by taking a long-tailed boat through Thonburi (see page 103) it is possible to gain an idea of what life must have been like in the 'Venice of the East'.

Bangkok is built on unstable land, much of it below sea-level, and floods used to regularly afflict the capital. The most serious were in 1983 when 450 sq km of the city was submerged. Each year the Bangkok Metropolitan Authority announced a new flood prevention plan, and each year the city flooded. The former populist Bangkok Governor, Chamlong Srimuang, was perhaps the first politician to address the problem of flooding seriously. His blindingly obvious approach was to clear the many culverts of refuse, and some people believe that at last serious flooding is a thing of the past. This may be over-optimistic: like Venice, Bangkok is sinking by over 10 cm a year in some areas and it may be that the authorities are only delaying the inevitable.

Population

In 1900 Bangkok had a population of approximately 200,000. By 1950 it had surpassed one million, and by the end of 1999 it was, officially, 5,662,499. This official figure considerably understates the true population of the city – 14 million

would be more realistic. Many people who live in the capital continue to be registered as living upcountry, and the physical extent of the capital has long overrun its administrative boundaries. By 2010, analysts believe Bangkok will have a population of 20 million. As the population of the city has expanded, so has the area that it encompasses: in 1900 it covered a mere 13.3 sq km; in 1958, 96.4 sq km; while today the Bangkok Metropolitan region extends over 1,600 sq km.

Bangkok dominates Thailand in cultural, political and economic terms. All Thai civil servants have the ambition of serving in Bangkok, while many regard a posting to the poor Northeast as (almost) the kiss of death. Most of the country's industry is located in and around the city, and Bangkok supports a far wider array of services than other towns in the country.

Pollution

With the traffic comes pollution. Traffic police stationed at busy intersections have 'respite booths' with oxygen tanks wear face masks to protect them from the fumes, and are entitled to regular health checks. A study in the mid 1990s found that 34% of police officers suffered from loss of hearing, 23% had lung disease and one million of the capital's population are said to be suffering from respiratory ailments of one kind or another. It is now no longer possible to buy two-stroke motorbikes in Bangkok and the city has recently gone over to lead-free petrol.

Sights

Wats and palaces, markets and shopping, traditional dancing and Thai boxing, glorious food, tuk-tuks and water taxis fill Bangkok. Get over the pace and pollution and you'll have a ball in Bangkok. This is one of the most engaging cities on the planet and its infectious, amiable energy soon wears down even the staunchest tree-hugger. Begin your sojourn in the bejewelled beauty of the **Old City**. Here you'll find the regal heart of Bangkok at the stupendous Grand Palace. The charming **Golden Mount** is a short hop to the east, while to the south are the bewildering alleyways and gaudy temples of Bangkok's frenetic **Chinatown**. Head west over the Chao Phraya River to the magnificent spire of **Wat Arun and the khlongs of Thonburi**. To the north sits the broad, leafy avenues of **Dusit**, the home of the Thai parliament and the King's residence. Carry on east and south and you'll reach modern Bangkok. A multitude of mini-boutiques forms **Siam Square** and the Thai capital's centre of youth fashion; **Silom** and **Sukhumvit Roads** are vibrant runs of shopping centres restaurants and hotels while the **Chatuchak Weekend Market** in the northern suburbs is one of Asia's greatest markets.

Old City

Filled with palaces and temples this is the ancient heart of Bangkok. These days it is the premium destination for visitors and controversial plans are afoot to change it into a 'tourist zone'. This would strip the area of the usual chaotic charm that typifies Bangkok, moving out the remaining poor people who live in the area and creating an ersatz, gentrified feel.

Wat Phra Chetuphon (Wat Pho)

ⓘ *The entrance is on the south side of the monastery, www.watpho.com; 0900-1700. ฿20. From Tha Tien pier at the end of Thai Wang Rd, close to Wat Pho, it is possible to get boats to Wat Arun* (*see page 105*).

Wat Phra Chetuphon, or Wat Pho, is the largest and most famous temple in Bangkok. 'The Temple of the Reclining Buddha' houses one of the largest reclining Buddhas in the country – the soles of its feet are decorated with mother-of-pearl displaying the 108 auspicious signs of the Buddha – and was built in 1781.

The bustling grounds of the wat (see also box, page 688) contains more than 1,000 bronze images, mostly rescued from the ruins of Ayutthaya and Sukhothai while the bot houses the ashes of Rama I. The bot is enclosed by two galleries which house 394 seated bronze Buddha images. They were brought from the north during Rama I's reign and are of assorted periods and styles. Around the exterior base of the bot are marble reliefs telling the story of *the Ramakien* (see box, page 95) as adapted in the Thai poem the *Maxims of King Ruang*. They recount only the second section of *the Ramakien*: the abduction and recovery of Ram's wife Seeda.

There are 95 chedis of various sizes scattered across the 20-acre complex. To the left of the bot are four large chedis, memorials to the first four Bangkok kings. The library nearby is richly decorated with broken pieces of porcelain. The large top-hatted stone figures, the stone animals and the Chinese pagodas scattered throughout the

B Old City

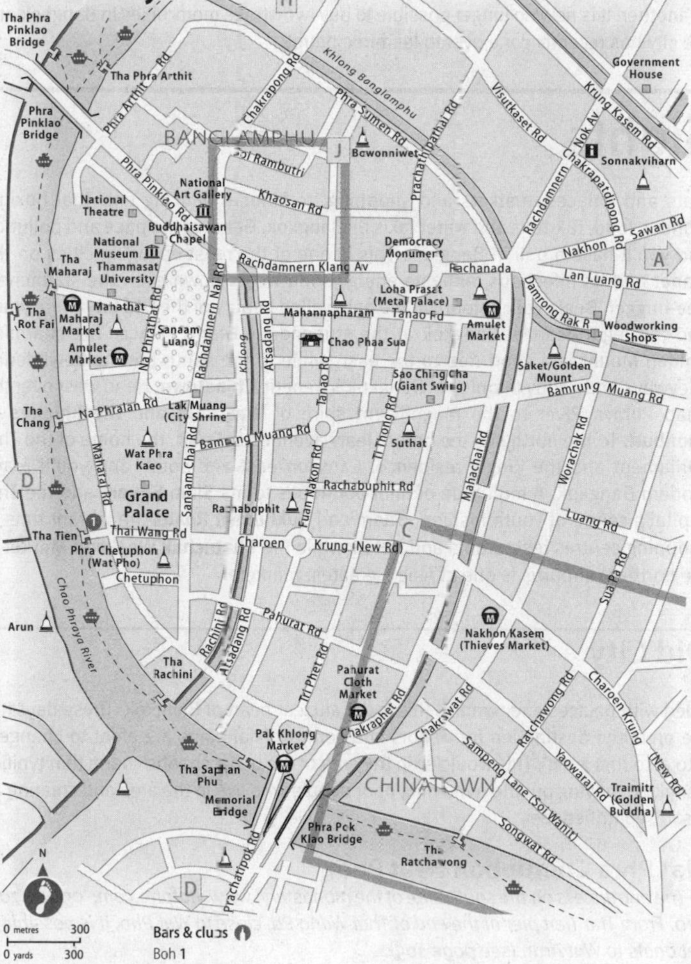

Bars & clubs
Boh 1

The Emerald Buddha

Wat Phra Kaeo was specifically built to house the Emerald Buddha, the most venerated Buddha image in Thailand. It is carved from green jade (the emerald in the name referring only to its colour), a mere 75 cm high, and seated in an attitude of meditation. It is believed to have been found in 1434 in Chiang Rai, and stylistically belongs to the Late Chiang Saen or Chiang Mai schools. Since then, it has been moved on a number of occasions – to Lampang, Chiang Mai and Laos (both Luang Prabang and Vientiane). It stayed in Vientiane for 214 years before being recaptured by the Thai army in 1778 and placed in Wat Phra Kaeo on 22 March 1784.

The image wears seasonal costumes of gold and jewellery; one each for the hot, cool and the rainy seasons. The changing ceremony occurs three times a year in the presence of the King.

Buddha images are often thought to have personalities. The Phra Kaeo is no exception. It is said that such is the antipathy between the Phra Bang image in Luang Prabang (Laos) and the Phra Kaeo that they can never reside in the same town.

compound came to Bangkok as ballast on the royal rice boats returning from China. Rama III wanted Wat Pho to become known as a place of learning, a kind of exhibition of all the knowledge of the time, and it is regarded as Thailand's first university.

One of Wat Pho's biggest attractions is its role as a respected centre of **traditional Thai massage** (see box, page 148). Thousands of tourists, powerful Thai politicians, businessmen and military officers come here to seek relief from the tensions of modern life. The Burmese destroyed most medical texts when they sacked, Ayutthaya in 1776. In 1832, to help preserve the ancient medical art, Rama III had what was known about Thai massage inscribed onto a series of stones which were then set into the walls of Wat Pho. If you want to come here for a massage then it is best to arrive in the morning; queues in the afternoon can be long. See also Activities and tours and for other centres of traditional Thai massage, see page 70.

Grand Palace and Wat Phra Kaeo

ⓘ *The main entrance is the Viseschaisri Gate on Na Phralan Road, T02-2220094, www.palaces.thai.net. Admission to the Grand Palace complex ฿250, (ticket office open daily 0830-1130, 1300-1530 except Buddhist holidays when Wat Phra Kaeo is free but the rest of the palace is closed). The cost of the admission includes a free guidebook to the palace (with plan) as well as a ticket to the Coin Pavilion, with its collection of medals and 'honours' presented to members of the Royal Family, and to the Vimanmek Palace in the Dusit area (see page 107). No photography is allowed inside the bot. The Royal Pantheon is only open to the public once a year on Chakri Day, 6 April (the anniversary of the founding of the present Royal Dynasty).*

All labels in Thai. Free guided tours in English throughout the day. There are plenty of touts offering to guide tourists around the palace. Personal audio guides, ฿100 (2 hrs), available in English, French, German and some other languages. Decorum of dress means no shorts, short skirts, no singlets, sleeveless shirts, no flip flops or sandals. There are plastic shoes and trousers for hire near the entrance. Close to the Dusit Hall is a small café selling refreshing coconut drinks and other soft drinks.

The Grand Palace is situated on the banks of the Chao Phraya River and is the most spectacular – some might say 'gaudy' – collection of buildings in Bangkok. The complex covers an area of over 1½ sq km and the architectural plan is almost identical to that of the Royal Palace in the former capital of Ayutthaya. It began life in 1782.

The buildings of greatest interest are clustered around **Wat Phra Kaeo,** or the **Temple of the Emerald Buddha** (see box, page 93). The glittering brilliance of sunlight bouncing off the coloured glass mosaic exterior of Wat Phra Kaeo creates a gobsmacking first impression for visitors to the Grand Palace. Built by Rama I in imitation of the royal chapel in Ayutthaya, Wat Phra Kaeo was the first of the buildings within the Grand Palace complex to be constructed. While it was being erected the king lived in a small wooden building in one corner of the palace compound.

The **ubosoth (1)** is raised on a marble platform with a frieze of gilded garudas holding nagas running round the base. Mighty, bronze singhas (lions) act as door guardians. The inlaid mother-of-pearl door panels date from Rama I's reign (late 18th century) while the doors are watched over by Chinese door guardians riding on lions. Inside the temple, the Emerald Buddha peers down on the gathered throng from a lofty, illuminated position above a large golden altar. Facing the Buddha on three sides are dozens of other gilded Buddha images, depicting the enlightenment of the Buddha when he subdues the evil demon Mara, the final temptation of the Buddha and the subjugation of evil spirits.

Around the walls of the shaded **cloister** which encompasses Wat Phra Kaeo, is a continuous mural depicting *the Ramakien* – the Thai version of the Indian *Ramayana* (see box, page 95). There are 178 sections in all, which were first painted during the reign of King Rama I but have since been restored on a number of occasions.

To the north of the ubosoth on a raised platform are the **Royal Pantheon (2),** the **Phra Mondop (3)** (the library), two gilt stupas, a **model of Angkor Wat (4)** and the **Golden Stupa (5).** At the entrance to the Royal Pantheon are gilded kinarees. On the same terrace there are two gilt stupas built by King Rama I in commemoration of his parents. The Mondop was also built by Rama I to house the first revised Buddhist scriptural canon. To the west of the mondop is the large Golden Stupa or chedi, with its circular base. To the north of the mondop is a model of Angkor Wat constructed during the reign of King Mongkut (1851-1868) when Cambodia was under Thai suzerainty.

Wat Phra Kaeo & Grand Palace

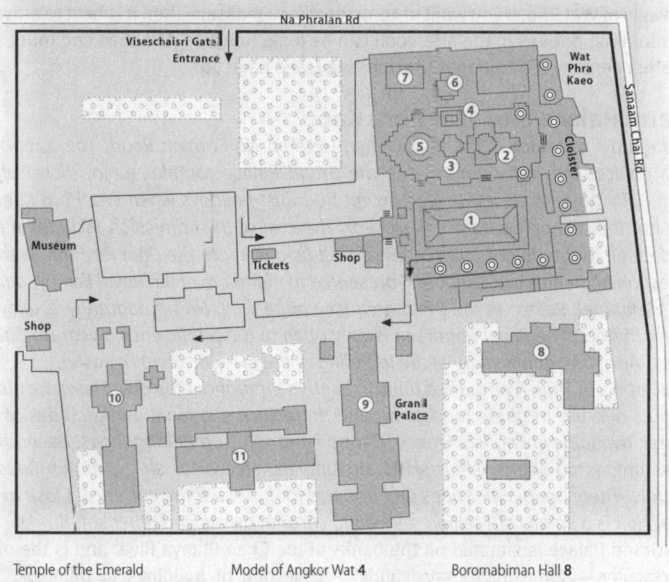

Temple of the Emerald Buddha (ubosoth) 1
Royal Pantheon 2
Phra Mondop (library) 3
Model of Angkor Wat 4
Golden Stupa 5
Viharn Yod 6
Viharn Phra Nak 7
Boromabiman Hall 8
Amarinda Hall 9
Chakri Mahaprasart 10
Dusit Hall 11

The Thai Ramayana: the Ramakien

The Ramakien – literally "The Story of Rama" – is an adaptation of the Indian Hindu classic, the *Ramayana*, which was written by the poet Valmiki about 2,000 years ago. This 48,000-line epic odyssey – often likened to the works of Homer – was introduced into mainland Southeast Asia in the early centuries of the first millennium. The heroes were simply transposed into a mythical, ancient, Southeast Asian landscape. In Thailand, *the Ramakien* quickly became highly influential, and the name of the former capital of Siam, Ayutthaya, is taken from the legendary hero's city of Ayodhia in the epic. Unfortunately, these early Thai translations of the *Ramayana* were destroyed following the sacking of Ayutthaya by the Burmese in 1767. The earliest extant version was written by King Taksin in about 1775, although Rama I's rather later rendering is usually regarded as the classic interpretation.

In many respects, King Chakri's version closely follows that of the original Indian story. It tells of the life of Ram (Rama), the King of Ayodhia. In the first part of the story, Ram renounces his throne following a long and convoluted court intrigue, and flees into exile. With his wife Seeda (Sita) and trusted companion Hanuman (the monkey god), they undertake a long and arduous journey. In the second part, his wife Seeda is abducted by the evil king Ravana, forcing Ram to wage battle against the demons of Langka Island (Sri Lanka). He defeats the demons with the help of Hanuman and his monkey army, and recovers his wife. In the third and final part of the story – and here it diverges sharply from the Indian original – Seeda and Ram are reunited and reconciled with the help of the gods (in the Indian version there is no such reconciliation). Another difference with the Indian version is the significant role played by the Thai Hanuman – here an amorous adventurer who dominates much of the third part of the epic.

There are also numerous sub-plots which are original to *the Ramakien*, many building upon events in Thai history and local myth and folklore. In tone and issues of morality, the Thai version is less puritanical than the Indian original. There are also, of course, differences in dress, ecology, location and custom.

To the north again from the Royal Pantheon is the **Supplementary Library** and two viharns – **Viharn Yod (6)** and **Phra Nak (7)**. The former is encrusted with pieces of Chinese porcelain.

To the south of Wat Phra Kaeo are the buildings of the **Grand Palace**. These are interesting for the contrast that they make with those of Wat Phra Kaeo. Walk out through the cloisters. On your left is the French style **Boromabiman Hall (8)**, which was completed during the reign of Rama VI. The **Amarinda Hall (9)** has an impressive, airy interior, with chunky pillars and gilded thrones. The **Chakri Mahaprasart** (the

Palace Reception Hall, **10**) stands in front of a carefully manicured garden with topiary. It was built and lived in by Rama V shortly after he had returned from a trip to Java and Singapore in 1876, and it shows: the building is a rather unhappy amalgam of colonial and traditional Thai styles of architecture. King Chulalongkorn (Rama V) found the overcrowded Grand Palace oppressive and after a visit to Europe in 1897 built himself a new home at Vimanmek (see page 107) in Dusit where the present King, Bhumibol, lives in the Chitralada Palace. The Grand Palace is now only used for state occasions. Next to the Chakri Mahaprasart is the raised **Dusit Hall (11)**, a cool, airy building containing mother-of-pearl thrones. Near the Dusit Hall is a museum, ⓘ *0900-1600, ฿50*, which has information on the restoration of the Grand Palace, models of the Palace and many more Buddha images. There is a collection of old cannon, mainly supplied by London gun foundries.

Turn left outside the Grand Palace and a five-minute walk leads to **Tha Chang pier and market**. The market sells fruit and food, cold drinks and the like. There is also a small amulet (lucky charm) and second-hand section. From Tha Chang pier it is possible to get a boat to Wat Arun for about ฿150 return, or a water-taxi (see page 106).

Sanaam Luang

To the north of the Grand Palace, across Na Phralan Road, lies the large open space of the Pramane Ground (the Royal Cremation Ground), better known as Sanaam Luang (see box, page). This area was originally used for the cremation of kings, queens and important princes. Later, foreigners began to use it as a race track and as a golf course. Today, Sanaam Luang is used for the annual **Royal Ploughing Ceremony**, held in May. This ancient Brahmanistic ritual, resurrected by Rama IV, signals the auspicious day on which farmers can begin to prepare their riceland, the time and date of the ceremony being set by Royal Astrologers. Bulls decorated with flowers pull a red and gold plough, while the selection of different lengths of cloth by the Ploughing Lord predicts whether the rains will be good or bad.

Kite fighting can be seen at Sanaam Luang in the late afternoons between late-Febuary and mid-April (the Kite Festival season). On Sunday, salesmen and women sell kites.

Sanaam Luang has several other claims to fame: as the place in Bangkok to eat charcoal-grilled dried squid and have your fortune told. Regarding the latter, the mor duu (seeing doctors) sit in the shade of the tamarind trees along the inner ring of the southern footpath. Each mor duu has his 'James Bond case' – a black briefcase – and having your fortune told costs around ฿30-60 or ฿100 for a full consultation. At the northeast corner of Sanaam Luang, opposite the **Royal Hotel**, is a statue of the **Goddess of the Earth** erected by King Chulalongkorn to provide drinking water for the public.

Lak Muang

ⓘ *Open daily, 24 hrs. There is no entrance charge to the Lak Muang compound; touts sometimes insist there is. Donations can be placed in the boxes within the shrine precincts.*

In the southeast corner of Sanaam Luang, opposite the Grand Palace, is Bangkok's Lak Muang, housing the City Pillar and horoscope, originally placed there by Rama I in 1782. The shrine is believed to grant people's wishes, so it is a hive of activity all day. In a small pavilion to the left of the main entrance, Thai dancers are hired by supplicants to dance for the pleasure of the resident spirits – while providing a free spectacle for everyone else.

Sanaam Luang was originally called Thung Phramane. Phramanes are funerary pyres. Cremation became the norm in the 13th century – until then corpses were left in the open to be picked clean by dogs and vultures. Members of royalty are cremated 'standing' in a large urn. The last cremation was held in 1994: that of the Queen Mother.

Wat Mahathat

Ⓘ *Daily 0900-1700.*

North along Na Phrathat Road, on the river side of Sanaam Luang, is Wat Mahathat (the Temple of the Great Relic), a temple famous as a meditation centre; walk under the archway marked 'Naradhip Centre for Research in Social Sciences' to reach the wat. For those interested in learning more about Buddhist meditation, contact monks in section five within the compound. The wat is a royal temple of the first grade and a number of Supreme Patriarchs of Bangkok have based themselves here.

At No 24 Maharaj Road a narrow soi (lane) leads down towards the river and a large daily **market** selling exotic herbal cures, amulets, clothes and food. At weekends, the market spills out onto the surrounding streets (particularly Phra Chan Road) and amulet sellers line the pavement, their magical and holy talismen carefully displayed, see box on page 100.

Thammasat University

Further north along Na Phrathat Road is Thammasat University, the site of viciously suppressed student demonstrations in 1973. Sanaam Luang and Thammasat University remain a popular focus of discontent, the last being mass demonstrations in May 1992 demanding the resignation of Prime Minister General Suchinda which led to a military crackdown. In the grounds of Thammasat, there is a new monument to the victims of 1973, 1976 and 1992.

National Museum and Buddhaisawan Chapel

Ⓘ *Wed-Sun 0900-1600, tickets on sale until 1530, ฿40, together with a skimpy leaflet outlining the galleries. Good information is lacking and it is recommended interested visitors buy the* **Guide to the National Museum**, *Bangkok or join a tour. For English, French, German, Spanish and Portuguese-speaking tour information call T02-2241333. The tours are free and start at 0930, lasting 2 hrs (usually on Wed and Thu).*

Next to Thammasat lies the National Museum, reputedly the largest museum in Southeast Asia and an excellent place to visit before visiting the ancient Thai capitals, Ayutthaya and Sukhothai. The galleries contain a vast assortment of arts and artefacts divided according to period and style.

The Buddhaisawan Chapel, to the right of the ticket office for the National Museum, contains some of the finest Bangkok period murals in Thailand. The chapel was built in 1795 to house the famous Phra Sihing Buddha. Legend has it that this image originated in Ceylon and when the boat carrying it to Thailand sank, it floated off on a plank to be washed ashore in Southern Thailand, near the town of Nakhon Si Thammarat. The chapel's magnificent murals were painted between 1795 and 1797 and depict stories from the Buddha's life.

National Theatre and National Art Gallery

Next to the National Museum, on the corner of Na Phrathat and Phra Pinklao Bridge roads, is Thailand's National Theatre Ⓘ *current programmes can be checked by calling T02-2241342, Mon-Fri 0830-1630.* Thai classical drama and music are staged here on the last Friday of each month at 1730 as well as periodically on other days.

Opposite the National Theatre is the National Art Gallery Ⓘ *Tue-Thu, Sat and Sun 0900-1600, ฿30,* on Chao Fa Road. It exhibits traditional and contemporary work by Thai artists.

Banglamphu and Khaosan Road

Northeast of the National Art Gallery is the district of Banglamphu and the legendary Khaosan Road, backpacker haunt and epicentre of Bangkok's travellers' culture. It all

 began when the **Viengtai Hotel** opened in 1962, giving the area a reputation for budget accommodation. Local families began to rent out rooms to travellers and by the mid-1970s the Khaosan Road we love/hate was firmly established. Much has been said and written about the strip. Thai purists look down their noses at it while many locals like the money it brings in but feel threatened by the loose Western culture it brings in to the capital. For some younger Thais, it's a hip, liberal hangout, a space and place apart from the constrictions of traditional Thai culture. There is no doubting Khaosan Road's sustained popularity, though the quality of food, accommodation, goods and services are easily surpassed in other parts of the city. As well as the expensive Thai food being of a very low standard, souvenirs are overpriced, while the mini-buses that take unsuspecting backpackers to the popular beaches and islands tend to be falling apart and driven by Red Bull-fuelled maniacs. Taking public buses from the respective bus stations tends to be cheaper and safer. So why stay here? If you're travelling on a budget and it's your first time in Asia there are few better places to connect with other travellers and get into the swing of things. More seasoned travellers may find Khaosan Road an homogeneous spread of banana pancake eating, tie-dyed, penny-pinching backpackers and every bit as challenging as staying in a packaged resort.

Phra Arthit Road

Running north from the National Theatre, following the river upstream, is Phra Arthit Road. The community here is recognized to be one of the most cohesive in Bangkok, and a centre for artists and intellectuals as well as traditional shop owners. The nearby addition of a park and Thai sala on the river has created a pleasant place to sit and watch the boats. Phra Arthit Road has decent pavements, interesting shops and restaurants, many of which extend out on the water. Traffic is relatively sedate and because the street is quite narrow it is a lot less busy than in other parts of the city.

Wat Indraviharn

Wat Indraviharn (See Bangkok general map) is rather isolated from the other sights, lying just off Visutkaset Road – not too far north of Phra Arthit Road and the traveller nexus of Banglamphu. It contains a 32-m standing Buddha encrusted in gold tiles that can be seen from the entrance to the wat. The image is impressive only for its size. The topknot contains a relic of the Buddha brought from Ceylon.

Golden Mount and around

This is where ancient Bangkok begins to give way to the modern thrust of this engagingly bewildering city. Apart from the obvious sights listed below there's little reason to hang around here but with its history of demonstrations and cries for democracy it beats a defining pulse in the hearts of most Thais. ▸▸ *See Old City map, page 92.*

Democracy Monument

ⓘ *Daily 0800-1800. ฿10. Refreshments available.*

The Democracy Monument is a 10-15 -minute walk from the north side of Sanaam Luang, in the middle of Rachdamnern Klang Avenue. Completed in 1940 to commemorate the establishment of Siam as a constitutional monarchy its dimensions signify, in various ways, the date of the 'revolution' – 24 June 1932. For example, the 75 buried cannon which surround the structure denote the Buddhist year (BE – or Buddhist Era) 2475 (AD 1932). In May 1992, the monument was the focus of the anti-Suchinda demonstrations, so brutally suppressed by the army. Scores of Thais died here, many others fleeing into the nearby **Royal Hotel** which also became an impromptu hospital to the many wounded.

Golden Mount

From the Democracy Monument, across Mahachai Road, at the point where Rachdamnern Klang Avenue crosses Khlong Banglamphu, the Golden Mount can be seen (also known as the Royal Mount), an impressive artificial hill nearly 80 m high. The climb to the top is exhausting but worth it for the fabulous views of Bangkok. On the way up, the path passes holy trees, memorial plaques and Chinese shrines. The construction of the mount was begun during the reign of Rama III who intended to build the greatest chedi in his kingdom. The structure collapsed before completion, and Rama IV decided merely to pile up the rubble in a heap and place a far smaller golden chedi on its summit. The chedi contains a relic of the Buddha placed there by the present king after the structure had been most recently repaired in 1966.

Wat Saket

ⓘ *Daily 0800-1800.*

Wat Saket lies at the bottom of the mount, between it and Damrong Rak Road – the mount actually lies within the wat's compound. Saket means 'washing of hair' and Rama I is reputed to have stopped here and ceremoniously washed himself before being crowned King in Thonburi (see Festivals and events, page 141). The only building of real note is the hor trai (library) which is Ayutthayan in style. The door panels and lower windows are decorated with wood carvings depicting everyday Ayutthayan life, while the window panels show Persian and French soldiers from Louis XIV's reign.

Loha Prasat

ⓘ *Daily 0830-1600.*

Also in the shadow of the Golden Mount but to the west and on the corner of Rachdamnern Klang Avenue and Mahachai Road lies Wat Rachanada and the Loha Prasat, a strange-looking 'Metal Palace' with 37 spires. Built by Rama III in 1846 as a memorial to his beloved niece, Princess Soammanas Vadhanavadi, it is said to be modelled on the first Loha Prasat built in India 2,500 years ago. The 37 spires represent the 37 Dharma of the Bodhipakya. The monks who look after the building have had problems with homeless men and woman who use the Prasat's many nooks and crannies as handy places to sleep: they are turfed out (in a suitably meritorious manner) by the monks before the place opens each morning.

Wat Rachanada

ⓘ *Daily 0600-1800.*

Next to the Loha Prasat is the much more traditional Wat Rachanada. The principal Buddha image is made of copper mined in Isaan – the ordination hall also has some fine doors. What makes the wat particularly worth visiting is the **Amulet Market** (see box, page 100) to be found close by, between the Golden Mount and the wat. The market also contains Buddha images and other religious artefacts.

Wat Mahannapharam and Chao Phaa Sua

West of the Democracy Monument on Tanao Road is Wat Mahannapharam in a large, tree-filled compound. A peaceful place to retreat to, it contains some good examples of high-walled, Bangkok-period architecture decorated with woodcarvings and mother-of-pearl inlay. Just south of here is the bustling Chao Phaa Sua, a Chinese temple with a fine tiled roof surmounted with mythological figures.

Giant Swing

A five-minute walk south of Wat Rachanada, on Bamrung Muang Road, is the Sao Ching Cha (Giant Swing), consisting of two tall red pillars linked by an elaborate cross piece, set in the centre of a square. The Giant Swing was the original centre for a festival in honour of Siva. Young men on a giant 'raft' would be swung high into the air to grab

Magic designs and tokens: tattoos and amulets

Many, if not most, Thai men wear khruang (amulets). Some Thai women do so too. In the past tattooing was equally common, although today it is usually only in the countryside that males are extensively tattooed. In the case of both tattoos and amulets the purpose is to bestow power, good luck or protection on the wearer.

Amulets have histories: those believed to have great powers sell for millions of baht and there are several magazines devoted to amulet buying and collecting. Vendors keep amulets with their takings to protect against robbery and put them into food at the beginning of the day to ensure good sales. An amulet is only to be handled by the wearer – otherwise its power is dissipated and might even be used against the owner.

Amulets can be obtained from spirit doctors and monks and come in a variety of forms. Most common are amulets of a religious nature, known as Phra khruang. These are normally images of the Buddha or of a particularly revered monk. (The most valuable are those fashioned by the 19th-century monk Phra Somdet – which are worth far more than their weight in gold).

Khruang rang are usually made from tiger's teeth, buffalo horn or elephant tusk and protect the wearer in very specific ways – for example from drowning. Khruang rang plu sek, meanwhile, are magic formulas which are written down on an amulet, usually in old Khmer script (khom), and then recited during an accident, attack or confrontation.

Tattooing is primarily talismanic: magic designs, images of powerful wild beasts, texts reproduced in ancient Khmer and religious motifs are believed to offer protection from harm and give strength. (The word tattoo is derived from the Tahitian word tattau, meaning 'to mark'. It was introduced into the English language by Captain James Cook in 1769.) Tattoos are even believed to deflect bullets, should they be sufficiently potent. One popular design is the takraw ball, a woven rattan ball used in the sport of the same name. The ball is renowned for its strength and durability, and the tattoo is believed to have the same effect on the tattooed.

The purpose of some tattoos is reflected in the use of 'invisible' ink made from sesame oil – the talismatic effects are independent of whether the tattoo can be seen. Most inks are commercial today (usually dark blue) although traditionally they were made from secret recipes incorporating such ingredients as the fat from the chin of a corpse (preferably seven corpses, taken during a full moon).

The tattooist is not just an artist and technician. He is a man of power. A master tattooist is highly respected and often given the title ajarn (teacher) or mor phi (spirit doctor). Monks can also become well known for their tattoos. These are usually religious in tone, often incorporating sentences from religious texts. The tattoos are always beneficial or protective and always on the upper part of the body (the lower parts of the body are too lowly for a monk to tattoo). Tattoos and amulets are not only used for protection, but also for attraction: men can have tattoos or amulets instilled with the power to attract women; women, alternatively, can buy amulets which protect them from the advances of men. Khruang phlad khik ('deputy penis') are phallic amulets carved from ivory, coral or rare woods, and worn around the wrist or the waist – not around the neck. Not surprisingly, they are believed to ensure sexual prowess, as well as protection from such things as snake bites.

pouches of coins, hung from bamboo poles, between their teeth. Because the swinging was from east to west, it has been said that it symbolized the rising and setting of the sun. The festival was banned in the 1930s because of the injuries that occurred; prior to its banning, thousands would congregate around the Giant Swing for two days of dancing and music.

Wat Suthat

ⓘ *0900-1700; viharn only opens on weekends and Buddhist holidays.*

The magnificent Wat Suthat faces the Giant Swing. The wat was begun by Rama I in 1807, and his intention was to build a temple that would equal the most glorious in Ayutthaya. The wat was not finished until the end of the reign of Rama III in 1851. Surrounded by Chinese pagodas, the viharn's six pairs of doors are each made from a single piece of teak, deeply carved with animals and celestial beings. Inside is the bronze Phra Sri Sakyamuni Buddha, while just behind is a very fine gilded stone carving from the Dvaravati period (second-11th centuries AD), 2½ m in height and showing the miracle at Sravasti and the Buddha preaching in the Tavatimsa heaven. The bot is the tallest in Bangkok and one of the largest in Thailand.

Wat Rachabophit

ⓘ *Daily 0800-1700. ฿10.*

The little visited Wat Rachabophit is close to the Ministry of the Interior on Rachabophit Road, a few minutes' walk south of Wat Suthat down Ti Thong Road. It is recognizable by its distinctive doors carved in high relief with jaunty looking soldiers wearing European-style uniforms and is peculiar in that it follows the ancient temple plan of placing the Phra Chedi in the centre of the complex.

The 43-m-high gilded chedi's most striking feature are the five-coloured Chinese glass tiles which encrust the lower section. The ordination hall has 10 door panels and 28 window panels each decorated with gilded black lacquer on the inside and mother-of-pearl inlay on the outside showing royal insignia.

Pahurat Indian market and Pak khlong market

From Wat Rachabophit, it is only a short distance to the Pahurat Indian textile market on Pahurat Road. To get there, walk south on Ti Thong Road which quickly becomes Tri Phet Road. After a few blocks, Pahurat Road crosses Tri Phet Road. Pak Khlong Market is to be found a little further south on Tri Phet Road at the foot of the Memorial Bridge. It is a market for fresh produce. It begins early in the morning and ends by 1000.

Chinatown

Chinatown covers the area from Charoen Krung (or New Road) down to the river and leads on from Pahurat market; cross over Chakraphet Road and immediately opposite is the entrance to Sampeng Lane. Few other places in Bangkok match Chinatown for atmosphere. The warren of alleys, lanes and tiny streets are cut through with an industrious hive of shops, temples and restaurants. Weird food, neatly arranged mountains of mechanical parts, gaudy temple architecture, gold, flowers and a constant frenetic bustle will lead to hours of happy wandering. This is an area to explore on foot, getting lost in the miasma of nooks and crannies. A trip through Chinatown can start at the Thieves' Market , or at Wat Traimitr, the Golden Buddha, to the southeast.

Nakhon Kasem (Thieves' Market)

Nakhon Kasem, strictly speaking Woeng Nakhon Kasem (Thieves' Market), lies between Charoen Krung and Yaowarat Road, to the east of the khlong that runs parallel to Mahachai Road. Its boundaries are marked by archways. As its name

suggests, this market used to be the centre for the fencing of stolen goods. It is not quite so colourful today, but there remain a number of second-hand and antique shops that are worth a browse – such as the **Good Luck Antique Shop**. Among other things, musical instruments, brass ornaments, antique coffee grinders are all on sale.

Yaowarat Road

Just to the southeast of the Thieves' Market are two roads that run parallel with one another: Yaowarat Road and Sampeng Lane. Yaowarat Road, a busy thoroughfare, is the centre of the country's gold trade. The trade is run by seven shops, the Gold Traders Association, and the price is fixed by the government. Sino-Thais often convert their cash into gold jewellery. The jewellery is bought by its 'baht weight' which fluctuates daily with the price of gold.

Sampeng Lane

The narrower Sampeng Lane, also called Soi Wanit, is just to the south of Yaowarat Road. This road's history is shrouded in murder and intrigue. It used to be populated by prostitutes and opium addicts and was fought over by Chinese gangs. Today, it remains a commercial centre, but rather less illicit. It is still interesting, but there is not much to buy here – it is primarily a wholesale centre specializing in cloth and textiles although it is a good place to go for odd lengths of material, buttons of any shape and size, costume jewellery, and such like.

Wat Traimitr (Temple of the Golden Buddha)

ⓘ *Daily 0900-1700. ฿20.*

The most celebrated example of the goldsmiths' art in Thailand sits within Wat Traimitr (Temple of the Golden Buddha) which is located at the eastern edge of

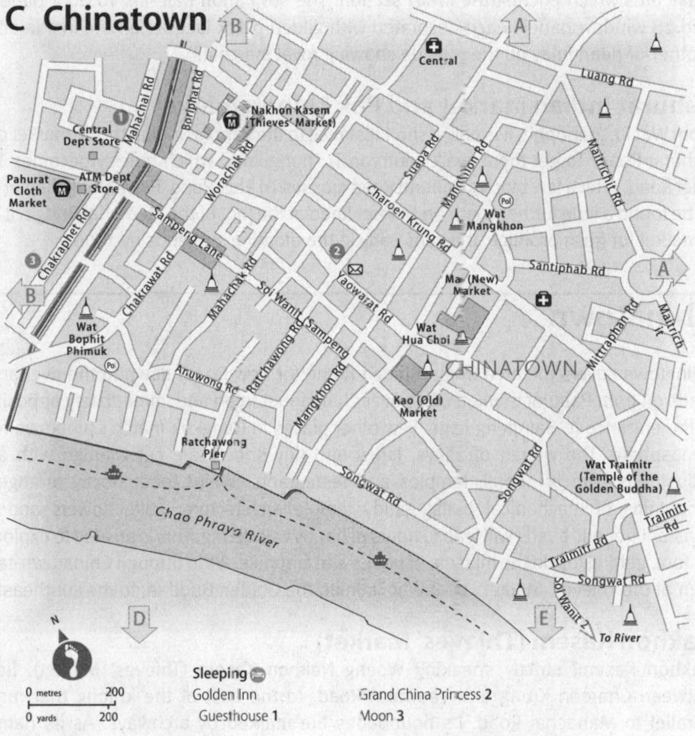

Chinatown, squashed between Charoen Krung, Yaowarat Road and Traimitr Road (just to the south of Bangkok's Hualamphong railway station). The Golden Buddha is housed in a small, rather gaudy and unimpressive room. Although the leaflet offered to visitors says the 3-m-high, 700-year-old image is 'unrivalled in beauty', be prepared for disappointment; it's featureless. What makes it special, drawing large numbers of visitors each day, is that it is made of 5½ tonnes of solid gold. Apparently, when the East Asiatic Company was extending the port of Bangkok, they came across a huge stucco Buddha image which they obtained permission to move. However, whilst being moved by crane in 1957, it fell and the stucco cracked to reveal a solid gold image. During the Ayutthayan period it was the custom to cover valuable Buddha images in plaster to protect them from the Burmese, and this particular example stayed that way for several centuries. In the grounds of the wat there is a school, crematorium, foodstalls and, inappropriately, a money changer. Gold beaters can still be seen at work behind Suksaphan store.

Between the river and Soi Wanit 2 there is a warren of lanes, too small for traffic – this is the Chinatown of old. From here it is possible to thread your way through to the River City shopping complex which is air-conditioned and a good place to cool off.

Thonburi, Wat Arun and the khlongs

Thonburi is Bangkok's little-known alter ego. Few people cross the Chao Phraya to see this side of the city, and if they do it is usually only to catch a glimpse from the seat of a speeding hang yaaw (long-tailed boat) and then climb the steps of Wat Arun. But Thonburi, during the reign of King Taksin, was once the capital of ancient Siam. King Rama I believed the other side of the river – present day Bangkok – would be more easily defended from the Burmese and so, in 1782, he switched river banks. ▸▸ *See Bangkok's river and khlongs map, page 104. See Tours, page 149, for further details on boat tours.*

Long-tailed boat tours, the Floating Market and Snake Farm

One of the most enjoyable ways to see Bangkok is by boat – and particularly by the fast and noisy hang yaaws: powerful, lean machines that roar around the river and the khlongs at breakneck speed. There are innumerable tours around the khlongs of Thonburi taking in a number of sights which include the floating market, snake farm and Wat Arun. Boats go from the various piers located along the east bank of the Chao Phraya River. The journey begins by travelling downstream along the Chao Phraya, before turning 'inland' after passing beneath Krungthep Bridge. The route skirts past laden rice-barges, squatter communities on public land and houses overhanging the canals. This is a very popular route with tourists, and boats are intercepted by salesmen and women marketing everything from cold beer to straw hats. You may also get caught in a boat jam; traffic snarl-ups are not confined to the capital's roads. Nevertheless, the trip is a fascinating insight into what Bangkok must have been like when it was still the 'Venice of the East', and around every bend there seems to be yet another stunning wat. On private tours the first stop is usually the **Floating Market** (Talaat Nam). This is now an artificial, ersatz gathering which exists purely for the tourist industry. The nearest functioning floating market is at Damnoen Saduak (see page 117).

The **Snake Farm** ⓘ ฿70, *shows every 20 mins*, is the next stop where visitors can even pose with pythons and poisonous snakes are incited to burst balloons with their fangs, 'proving' how dangerous they are. There is also a rather motley zoo with a collection of crocodiles and sad-looking animals in small cages. Refreshments available. The other snake farm in Central Bangkok (see page 114) is, appropriately, attached to the Thai Red Cross and is more professional and cheaper.

On leaving the snake farm, boats enter Khlong Bangkok Yai at the site of the large **Wat Paknam**. Just before re-entering the Chao Phraya itself, the route passes by the impressive **Wat Kalaya Nimit**.

D Bangkok's river & khlongs

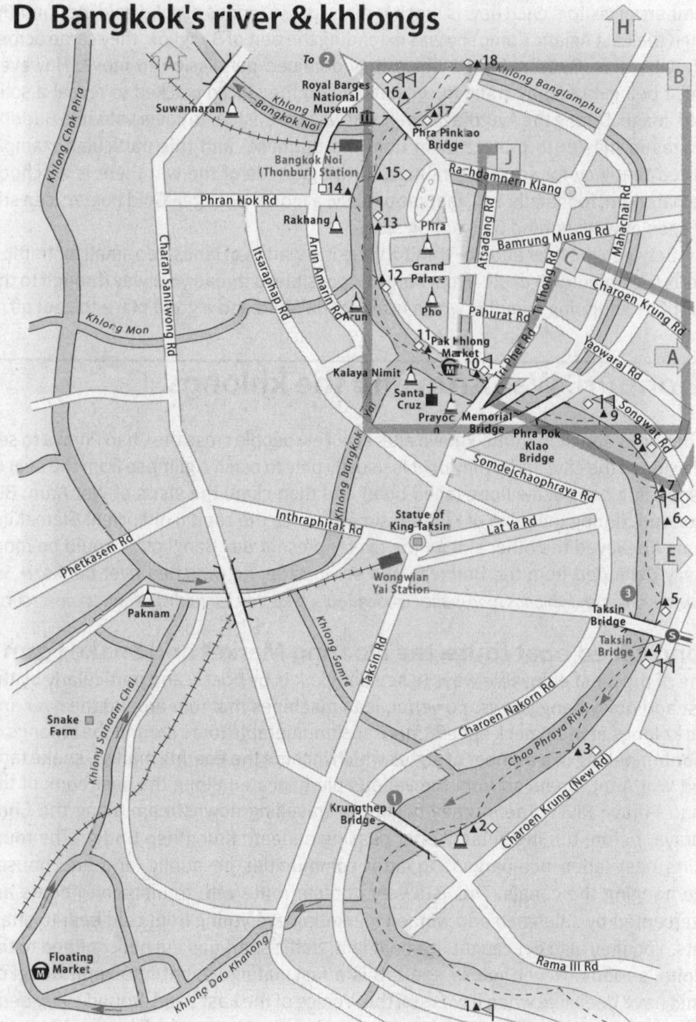

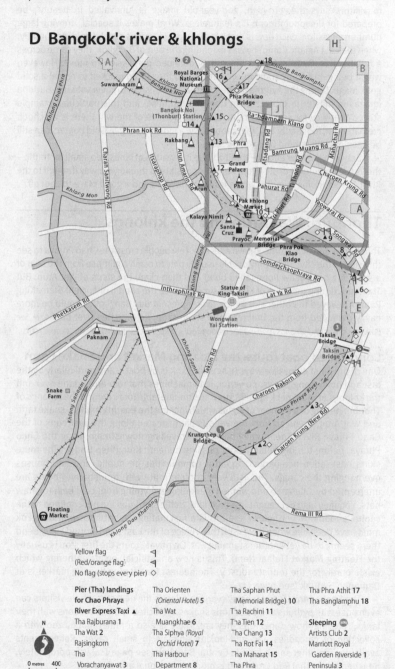

Yellow flag
(Red/orange flag)
No flag (stops every pier) ◇

Pier (Tha) landings for Chao Phraya River Express Taxi ▲
Tha Rajburana 1
Tha Wat 2
Rajsingkorn
Tha Vorachanyawat 3
Tha Sathorn 4
Tha Orienten *(Oriental Hotel)* 5
Tha Wat Muangkhae 6
Tha Siphya *(Royal Orchid Hotel)* 7
Tha Harbour Department 8
Tha Ratchawong 9
Tha Saphan Phut Memorial Bridge) 10
Tha Rachini 11
Tha Tien 12
Tha Chang 13
Tha Rot Fai 14
Tha Maharat 15
Tha Phra Pinklao Bridge 16
Tha Phra Athit 17
Tha Banglamphu 18

Sleeping
Artists Club 2
Marriott Royal Garden Riverside 1
Peninsula 3

N
0 metres 400
0 yards 400

Chao Phraya River Express

One of the most relaxing – and one of the cheapest – ways to see Bangkok is by taking the Chao Phraya River Express. Rua duan (boats) link almost 40 piers (tha) along the Chao Phraya River from Tha Rajburana (Big C) in the south to Tha Nonthaburi in the north.

The entire route entails a journey of about 1¼-1½ hours, and fares are ฿4-10. At peak periods, boats leave every 10 minutes, off-peak about every 15-25 minutes. Boats flying red/orange (downriver) or yellow (upriver) pennants are Special Express boats which only run 0600-0900, 1200-1900 and do not stop at every pier (see the map on page 104). Also, boats will only stop if passengers wish to board or alight, so make your destination known.

Selected piers and places of interest, travelling upstream:

Tha Sathorn The pier with the closest access to the Skytrain (Taksin Bridge, S6).

Tha Orienten By the Oriental Hotel; access to Silom Road.

Tha Harbour Department In the shadow of the Royal Orchid Hotel, on the south side and close to River City shopping centre.

Tha Ratchawong Rabieng Ratchawong Restaurant; access to Chinatown and Sampeng Lane.

Tha Saphan Phut Under the Memorial Bridge and close to Pahurat Indian Market.

Tha Rachini Pak Khlong Market.

Tha Tien Close to Wat Pho; Wat Arun on the opposite bank; and, just downstream from Wat Arun.

Tha Chang Just downstream is the Grand Palace peeking out above white-washed walls; Wat Rakhang with its white corn-cob prang lies opposite.

Tha Maharaj Access to Wat Mahathat and Sanaam Luang.

Tha Phra Arthit Access to Khaosan Road.

Tha Visutkasat Just upstream is the elegant central Bank of Thailand.

Tha Thewes Just upstream are boatsheds with royal barges; close to the National Library.

Tha Wat Chan Just upstream is the Singha Beer Samoson brewery.

Tha Wat Khema Wat Khema in large, tree-filled compound.

Tha Wat Khian Wat Kien, semi-submerged.

Tha Nonthaburi Last stop on the express boat route.

To the south of Wat Kalaya Nimit, on the Thonburi side of the river, is **Wat Prayoon Wong**, virtually in the shadow of Saphan Phut (a bridge). The wat is famous for its **Khao Tao** (turtle mountain) ⓘ *Khao Tao open 0830-1730; it can be reached by taking a cross-river shuttle boat from Tha Saphan Phut, ฿1*. This is a concrete fantasyland of grottoes and peaks, with miniature chedis and viharns, all set around a pond teeming with turtles. These are released to gain merit and the animals clearly thrive in the murky water. This wat is rarely visited by tourists and its large white chedi is clearly visible from Bangkok. A five-minute walk upstream from here is **Santa Cruz Church**, ⓘ *cross-river shuttles also stop at Tha Santa Cruz, running between here and Tha Rachini, close to the massive Pak Khlong fresh produce market*, facing the river. The church, washed in pastel yellow with a domed tower, was built to serve the Portuguese community.

Wat Arun

ⓘ *0830-1730. ฿20. Until the late 1990s, energetic visitors could climb up to the halfway point and view the city, however, this is no longer permitted. The men at the pier may demand ฿20 to help 'in the maintenance of the pier'. It is possible to get to*

 Wat Arun by water-taxi from Tha Tien pier (at the end of Thai Wang Rd near Wat Pho), or from Tha Chang (at the end of Na Phralan near Wat Phra Kaeo) (฿1).

Facing Wat Pho across the Chao Phraya River is the famous Wat Arun (Temple of the Dawn). Wat Arun stands 81 m high, making it the highest prang (tower) in Thailand. It was built in the early 19th century on the site of Wat Chaeng, the Royal Palace complex when Thonburi was briefly the capital of Thailand. The wat housed the Emerald Buddha before the image was transferred to Bangkok and it is said that King Taksin vowed to restore the wat after passing it one dawn. The prang is completely covered with fragments of Chinese porcelain and includes some delicate gold and black lacquered doors. The temple is really meant to be viewed from across the river; its scale and beauty can only be appreciated from a distance. The best view of Wat Arun is in the evening from the Bangkok side of the river when the sun sets behind the prang.

Royal Barges National Museum

ⓘ *0830-1630, ฿30, children free, extra for cameras and video cameras.*

After visiting Wat Arun, some tours then go further upstream to the mouth of Khlong Bangkok Noi where the Royal Barges are housed in a hangar-like boathouse. These ornately carved boats, winched out of the water in cradles, were used by the king at krathin (see **Ok Phansa festival**, page 59) to present robes to the monks in Wat Arun at the end of the rainy season. The ceremony ceased in 1967 but the Royal Thai Navy restored the barges for the revival of the spectacle, as part of the Chakri Dynasty's bicentennial celebrations in 1982. The oldest and most beautiful barge is the Sri Supannahong, built during the reign of Rama I (1782-1809) and repaired during that of Rama VI (1910-1925). It measures 45 m long and 3 m wide, weighs 15 tonnes and was created from a single piece of teak. It required a crew of 50 oarsmen and two coxwains, along with such assorted crew members as a flagman, a rhythm-keeper and singer. Its gilded prow was carved in the form of a hansa (or goose) and its stern, in the shape of a naga

Wat Rakhang

ⓘ *Daily 0500-2100. ฿2. The river ferry stops at the wat.*

Two rarely visited wats are Wat Suwannaram, see below, and Wat Rakhang. The royal Wat Rakhang is located just upstream from Wat Arun, almost opposite Tha Chang landing, and is identifiable from the river by the two plaster sailors standing to attention on either side of the jetty. Dating from the Ayutthaya period, the wat's **Phra Prang** is considered a particularly well proportioned example of early Bangkok architecture (late 18th century). The **ordination hall** (not always open – the abbot may oblige if he is available) was built during the reign of Rama III and contains a fine gilded Buddha image. The beautiful red-walled wooden **Tripitaka Hall** (originally a library built in the late 18th century), to the left of the viharn, was the residence of Rama I while he was a monk and Thonburi was still the capital of Siam. Consisting of two rooms, it is decorated with faded but nonetheless highly regarded murals of the Ramakien (painted by a monk-artist), black and gold chests, a portrait of the king, and some odd bits of old carved door.

Wat Suwannaram

Wat Suwannaram is a short distance further on from the Royal Barges National Museum on Khlong Bangkok Noi, on the other side of the canal. The main buildings date from Rama I's reign (late 18th century), although the complex was later extensively renovated by Rama III. There was a wat on this site even prior to Rama I's reign, and the original name, Wat Thong (Golden Wat) remains in popular use. On the right-hand wall, as you enter from the river-side door, is a representation of a boat foundering with the crew being eaten by sharks and sea monsters as they thrash about in the waves. Closer inspection shows that these unfortunates are wearing

white skull-caps – presumably they are Muslims returning from the haj to Mecca. The principal image in the bot is made of bronze and shows the Buddha calling the Earth Goddess to witness. Wat Suwannaram is elegant and rarely visited and is a peaceful place to escape after the bustle of Wat Arun and the Floating Market.

Almost opposite Wat Suwannaram, on the opposite bank of the river, is the home of an unusual occupational group – Chao Phraya's divers. The men use traditional diving gear – heavy bronze helmets, leaden shoes, air pumps and pipes – and search the bed of the murky river for lost precious objects, sunken boats, and the bodies of those who have drowned or been murdered.

Dusit area

Dusit, the present home of the Thai Royal family and the administration, is an area of wide tree-lined boulevards – the rationalized spaces more in keeping with a European city. It is grand but lacks the usual bustling atmosphere found in the rest of Bangkok. See Bangkok general map, for sights in the Dusit area.

Vimanmek Palace

ⓘ *T022811569, www.palaces.thai.net. 0900-1600 (last tickets sold at 1500). ฿50, ฿20 for children. Visitors are not free to wander, but must be shown around by one of the charming guides who demonstrate the continued deep reverence for King Rama V (tour approximately 1 hr). Note that tickets to the Grand Palace include entrance to Vimanmek Palace. Dance shows are held twice a day at 1030 and 1400. Visitors to the palace are required to wear long trousers or a skirt (women must wear a long skirt); sarongs available for hire (฿100, refundable). Refreshments available. Buses do go past the palace, but from the centre of town it is easier to get a tuk-tuk or taxi (฿50-60).*
The Vimanmek Palace, just off Rachvithi Road, to the north of the National Assembly, is the largest golden teakwood mansion in the world, but don't expect to see huge expanses of polished wood – the building is almost entirely painted. It was built by Rama V in 1901 who was clearly taken with western style. It seems like a large Victorian hunting lodge and is filled with china, silver and paintings from all over the world (as well as some gruesome hunting trophies). The photographs are fascinating – one shows the last time elephants were used in warfare in Thailand. Behind the palace is the Audience Hall which houses a fine exhibition of crafts made by the Support Foundation, an organization set up and funded by Queen Sirikit. Also worth seeing is the exhibition of the king's own photographs and the clock museum.

Amporn Gardens area

From Vimanmek, it is a 10-15 -minute walk to the Dusit Zoo, skirting around the **National Assembly** (which before the 1932 coup was the Marble Throne Hall and is not open to visitors). In the centre of the square in front of the National Assembly stands an equestrian statue of the venerated King Chulalongkorn. To the left lie the Amporn Gardens, the venue for royal social functions and fairs. Southwards from the square runs the impressive **Rachdamnern Nok Avenue**, a Siamese Champs Elysée. Enter the **Dusit Zoo** ⓘ *0800-1800, ฿30, ฿10 children*, through Uthong Gate, just before the square. A pleasant walk through the zoo leads to the Chitralada Palace and Wat Benchamabophit. Animal lovers might want to avoid the zoo which, like almost every other attempt to house animals in Thailand, is appaling. There is a children's playground, some restaurants and pedal-boats can be hired on the lake.

From the Dusit Zoo's Suanchit Gate, a right turn down the tree-lined Rama V Road leads to the present King Bhumibol's residence – **Chitralada Palace**. It was built by Rama VI and is not open to the public. Evidence of the King's forays into agricultural research may be visible. He has a great interest and concern for the development of the

poorer, agricultural parts of his country, and invests large sums of his own money in royal projects. To the right of the intersection of Rama V and Sri Ayutthaya roads are the gold and ochre roofs of Wat Benchamabophit – a 10-minute walk from the zoo.

Wat Benchamabophit

ⓘ *0800-1700. ฿10.*

Wat Benchamabophit (the Marble Temple) is the most modern of the royal temples and was only finished in 1911. Designed by Rama V's half brother, Prince Naris, it is an unusual display of carrara marble pillars, a marble courtyard and two large singhas guarding the entrance to the bot. The interior is magnificently decorated with crossbeams of lacquer and gold, and in shallow niches in the walls are paintings of important stupas from all over the kingdom. The door panels are faced with bronze sculptures and the windows are of stained-glass, painted with angels. The cloisters around the assembly hall house 52 figures (both original and imitation) – a display of the evolution of the Buddha image in India, China and Japan.

❢ *The best time to visit this temple complex is early morning, when monks can be heard chanting inside the chapel.*

Government House and Wat Sonnakviharn

ⓘ *Only open on Wan Dek – a once yearly holiday for children on the second Sat in Jan.*

Government House is south of here on Nakhon Pathom Road. The building is a weird mixture of cathedral Gothic and colonial Thai. The little-visited Wat Sonnakviharn, ⓘ *daily*, is on Krung Kasem Road, located behind a car park and schoolyard. Enter by the doorway in the far right-hand corner of the schoolyard, or down Soi Sommanat. It is peaceful, unkempt and rather beautiful, with fine gold lacquer doors and a large gold tile-encrusted chedi.

Siam Square area

Shop, shop and then shop some more. Head for Siam Square if you want to be at the apex of Thai youth culture and the biggest spread of shopping opportunities in the city. From the hi-tech market at Panthip Plaza, the massive MBK complex, the host of upmarket stores at Siam Discovery, pure silk at Jim Thompson's House or the warren of tiny boutiques in Siam Square you should leave with a big hole in your bank account.

Suan Pakkard Palace (Lettuce Garden Palace)

ⓘ *352-354 Sri Ayutthaya Road, south of the Victory Monument, 0900-1600. ฿100 – including a fan to ward off the heat. All receipts go to a fund for artists.*

The five raised traditional Thai houses (domestic rather than royal) were built by Princess Chumbhot, a great granddaughter of King Rama IV. They contain her collection of fine, rare but badly labelled antiquities. The rear pavilion is particularly lovely, decorated in black and gold lacquerwork panels. Prince Chumbhot discovered this temple near Ayutthaya and reassembled and restored it here for his wife's 50th birthday.

❢ *See Bangkok general map, page 88. The grounds are very peaceful.*

Jim Thompson's House

ⓘ *Soi Kasemsan Song (2), opposite the National Stadium, www.jimthompson.com, Mon-Sat 0900-1630, ฿100, children ฿25 (profits to charity). There is a sophisticated café as well as a shop. Shoes must be removed before entering; walking barefoot around the house adds to the appreciation of the cool teak floorboards. Compulsory guided tours around the house and no photography allowed. Take a bus along Rama I Rd, taxi or tuk-tuk, or take a public canal boat. To get to the jetty from Jim Thompson's, walk down to the canal, turn right and along to the jetty by the bridge. Boats travelling to the Grand Palace will be coming from the right.*

Jim Thompson's House is an assemblage of traditional teak Northern Thai houses, some more than 200 years old (these houses were designed to be transportable, consisting of five parts – the floor, posts, roof, walls and decorative elements constructed without the use of nails). Bustling Bangkok only intrudes in the form of the stench from the khlong that runs behind the house. Jim Thompson arrived in Bangkok as an intelligence officer attached to the United States' OSS (Office of Strategic Services) and then made his name by reinvigorating the Thai silk industry after the Second World War. He disappeared mysteriously in the Malaysian jungle on 27 March 1967, but his silk industry continues to thrive. Jim Thompson chose this site for his house partly because a collection of silk weavers lived nearby on Khlong Saensaep. The house contains an eclectic collection of antiques from Thailand and China, with work displayed as though it was still his home.

The head office of the Jim Thompson Silk Emporium, selling fine Thai silk, is at the northeast end of Surawong Road and there are numerous branches in the top hotels around the city. This shop is a tourist attraction in itself. Shoppers can buy high-quality bolts of silk and silk clothing here – anything from a pocket handkerchief to a silk suit. Prices are top of the scale.

Siam Square

A 10-minute walk east along Rama I Road is the biggest and busiest modern shopping area in the city. Most of it centres on a maze of tiny boutiques and covered market area known as Siam Square. Thronged with young people, Siam Square plays host to Bangkok's burgeoning youth culture – weird, experimental fashions, Thai-style fast food and dozens of urban stylists keep the kids entertained. Needless to say, it epitomizes older Thais fears about the direction their country is taking – young people aping Western mores and values. Despite this, the area is distinctly Thai, albeit with a

F Siam Square & Ploenchit Road

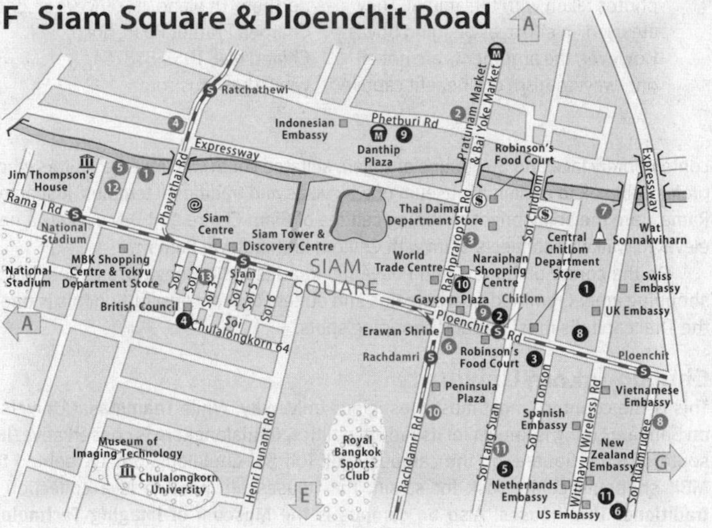

N

0 metres 100
0 yards 100

Sleeping
A1 Inn **1**
Amari Watergate **2**
Arnoma **3**
Asia **4**
Bed & Breakfast **5**
Cape House **11**
Chateau de Bangkok **8**
Four Seasons Bangkok, Spice Market & Biscotti **10**
Grand Hyatt Erawan **6**
Hilton **7**
Le Meridien President **9**
Wendy House **5**
White Lodge **12**
White Orchid Guesthouse **13**

Eating
Bali **6**
Barn Khanittha **1**
FABB Fashion Café **2**
Gianni's **3**
Hong Kong Noodles **4**
Il Paesano **5**
Kuaytiaw Rua Khuan Boke **4**
Neil's Tavern **8**
Once Upon a Time **9**
Vito's Spaghetteria **10**
Sanguan Sri **11**

Captive elephants in tourism

The Asian elephant is an endangered species, with fewer than 30,000 left in the world, and just 3,000-4,000 in Thailand (2,000 in captivity). Since the banning of logging in 1989, captive elephants have been forced to walk the streets of Thailand's major cities in order to make a living. It has been estimated that around 35% of Thailand's captive elephants are now employed in the tourist industry. Pressure groups trying to protect the interests of elephants in Thailand maintain that those animals found on the streets or in shopping malls suffer from poor diet, stress from polluted air, dehydration, loneliness, impaired hearing, and damage to their sensitive feet. They also argue that tourism is complicit in the elephants' predicament: unwitting tourists, seeing a 'cute' baby elephant, pay to have their photos taken with the animal. They are used, in effect, as begging bowls. However, the arguments are not all one-way: tourism can benefit captive elephants as they are seen to have 'value' if they are a tourist attraction. Simply put, with their former work in the forests largely a thing of the past, elephants have to pay their way. There are some elephant camps in Thailand where breeding programmes are successful and the animals are treated with respect. Two elephant welfare groups operating in Thailand are the **Elephant Help Project** (EHP) and the **Jumbo Express**. The former was founded by two companies based in Phuket. Its objective is to raise funds primarily from tourism and use these funds to support elephant welfare and conservation in Phuket and southern Thailand. Its office is at 390 Srisoontorn Road, Cherngtalay, Amphur Talang, Phuket Thailand 83110, T076-324324 ext 2147, F324174, www.elephanthelp.org. Jumbo Express operates throughout northern Thailand, its office is at 29 Charoen Prathet Road, Soi 6, Chiang Mai, T053-818754, www.tha focus.com.

contemporary face and the groups of sullen, agitated youth will unsettle visitors who'd prefer Bangkok to remain a museum of teak villas and traditional temples. Just across Rama 1 are the shiny bright shopping centres of Siam Centre and Discovery – a new, elevated walkway connects Siam with Chitlom further down Rama 1.

On the corner of Rama 1 and Phayathai Road is MBK, Bangkok's largest indoor shopping area. Crammed with bargains and outlets of every description this is one of the Thai capital's most popular shopping spots.

Chulalongkorn University

This is the country's most most prestigious university. While Thammasat University on Sanaam Luang is known for its radical politics, Chulalongkorn is conservative. Just south of Siam Square, on the campus itself (off Soi Chulalongkorn 12, behind the MBK shopping centre; ask for sa-sin, the houses are nearby) is a collection of **traditional Thai houses.** Also on campus is the **Museum of Imaging Technology** ⓘ *Mon-Fri 1000-1530, ฿100; to get to the museum, enter the campus by the main entrance on the east side of Phaya Thai Rd and walk along the south side of the playing field, turn right after the Chemistry 2 building and then right again at the entrance to the Mathematics Faculty, it is at the end of this walkway in the Dept of Photographic Science and Printing Technology*, with a few hands-on photographic displays. Occasional photographic exhibitions are also held here.

The Patpong story

On 30 September 1996, Udom Patpongsiri died at the age of 79. In 1946 his family bought a small plot of land between Silom and Surawong roads for the princely sum of US$3,000 – presumably with some advice from the young Udom who had returned from an overseas education well informed about all the latest business and management trends. (He attended the London School of Economics and the University of Minnesota.) At the time of his death half a century later the land was worth around US$100 mn and his name – or a part of it at least – had acquired an international profile: Patpong.

When they bought the land Patpong had no name; indeed there was not even a road on the plot of land to give a name. Udom's family built a track from Surawong to the canal which is now Silom Road. Later, when the canal was covered over, Udom began using his language skills and knowledge of American and British culture to entice foreigners to base their operations on his family's land. The fact that Udom joined the Free Thai Movement during the Second World War and received training from the Office of Strategic Services (OSS – the forerunner to the CIA) no doubt also introduced Udom to the predilections of US servicemen.

When the war in Indochina saw a massive influx of American servicemen into Thailand, Udom saw a market niche crying out to be filled and with his encouragement and guidance Patpong Road and the parallel Patpong 2 Road quickly made the metamorphosis from quiet business streets to a booming red-light emporium.

Erawan Shrine

East of Siam Square is the Erawan Shrine, on the corner of Ploenchit and Rachdamri roads, at the Rachprasong intersection. This is Bangkok's most popular shrine, attracting not just Thais but also large numbers of other Asian visitors. The spirit of the shrine, the Hindu god Thao Maha Brahma, is reputed to grant people's wishes. In thanks, visitors offer garlands, wooden elephants and pay to have dances performed for them accompanied by the resident Thai orchestra. The shrine is a hive of activity at most hours, incongruously set on a noisy, polluted intersection tucked into a corner, and in the shadow of the Sogo Department Store.

Panthip Plaza

Sited on Phetburi Road (it runs parallel to Rama 1, 800m to the north), Panthip Plaza is home to one of the best hi-tech computer markets in Asia. Motherboards, chips, drives and all manner and make of devices are piled high and sold cheap over its six floors. You'll be constantly hustled to buy copied software, DVD movies, games, most of which make excellent and affordable alternatives to the real thing. There's a great foodhall on the second floor while several amulet shops on the ground floor remind you that even this most contemporary of Thai-spaces is still governed by ancient beliefs. Many of the named-brand goods are cheaper back home so shop around.

Silom area

High-tech, high-rise and clad in concrete and glass, Silom is at the centre of booming Bangkok. Banks, international business and many media companies are based in this area as is the heart of Bangkok's gay community on Patpong 2, one of two

infamous sois. Patpong 1 now houses a famous night market and is largely recognized as the eponymous home of Bangkok's notorious girly shows, complete with acrobatic vaginas. Stylish, tacky and sweaty, head down the length of Silom for a slice of contemporary Bangkok life. ▸▸ *See Silom & Surawong map, below.*

Patpong

ⓘ *Catch a train to the Sala Daeng station.*

The seedier side of Bangkok life has sadly always been a crowd-puller to the Western tourist. Most people flock to the red-light district of Patpong, which runs along two lanes (Patpong 1 and 2) which link Silom to Surawong. These streets were transformed from a street of 'tea houses' (brothels serving local clients) into a high-tech lane of go-go bars in 1969 when an American made a major investment. Patpong 1 is the larger and more active of the streets, with a host of stalls down the middle at night (see box, page 111); Patpong 2 supports cocktail bars and pharmacies and clinics for STDs, as well as a few go-go bars. There are also a few restaurants and bars here. Patpong is also home to a night market infamous for its line in copied designer handbags, some of which are better made than the originals.

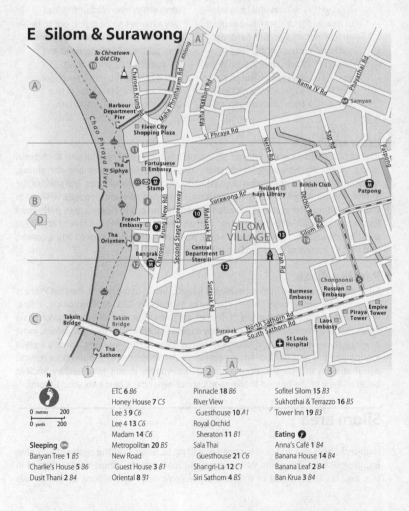

E Silom & Surawong

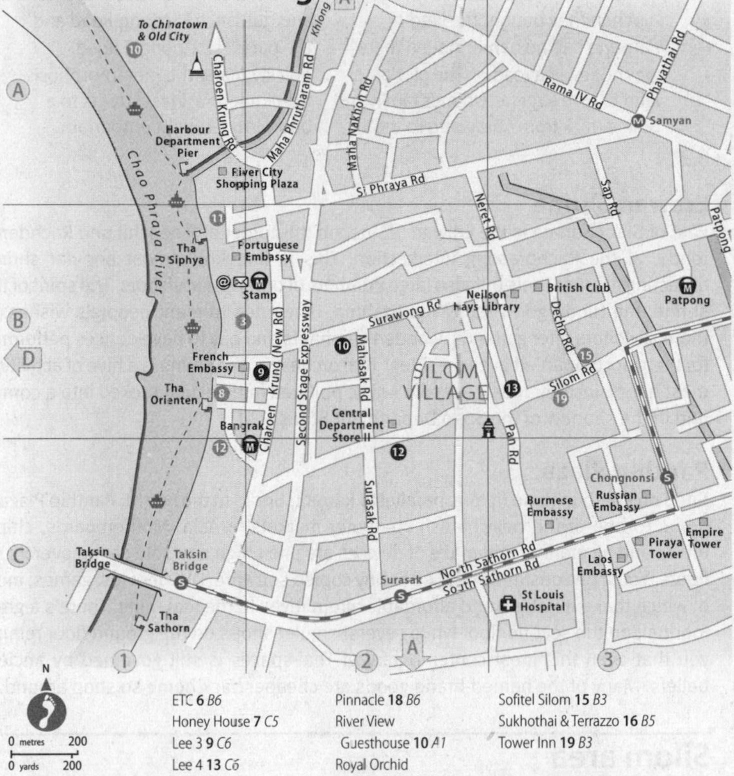

Sleeping
Banyan Tree 1 *B5*
Charlie's House 5 *B6*
Dusit Thani 2 *B4*
ETC 6 *B6*
Honey House 7 *C5*
Lee 3 9 *C6*
Lee 4 13 *C6*
Madam 14 *C6*
Metropolitan 20 *B5*
New Road Guest House 3 *B1*
Oriental 8 *B1*
Pinnacle 18 *B6*
River View Guesthouse 10 *A1*
Royal Orchid Sheraton 11 *B1*
Sala Thai Guesthouse 21 *C6*
Shangri-La 12 *C1*
Siri Sathorn 4 *B5*
Sofitel Silom 15 *B3*
Sukhothai & Terrazzo 16 *B5*
Tower Inn 19 *B3*

Eating
Anna's Café 1 *B4*
Banana House 14 *B4*
Banana Leaf 2 *B4*
Ban Krua 3 *B4*

Lumpini Park

Lumpini Park, or 'suan lum' as it is known affectionately, is Bangkok's oldest, largest and most popular public park. It lies between Wireless Road and Rachdamri Road, just across from the entrance to Silom and Sathorn Roads. Activity at the park starts early with large numbers of elderly and not so elderly Thais practising t'ai chi under the trees. At the weekend, it is a popular place for family picnics. In the evening, couples stroll along the lake and people jog or work out along the paths. Lumpini is also the site of the cool season Bangkok Symphony Orchestra concerts running from November to February. Check the Bangkok Post for performances. At night, the streets around Lumpini are filled with prostitutes and a gentle evening stroll can soon be turned into an avalanche of unwanted attention. Recently opened across the road is Bangkok's only official night bazaar, the **Suan Lumpini Night Bazaar**. Modelled on the very successful night bazaar of Chiang Mai, there is a good range of shops selling all manner of clothes, tourist trinkets, and handicrafts plus dozens of eateries and bars.

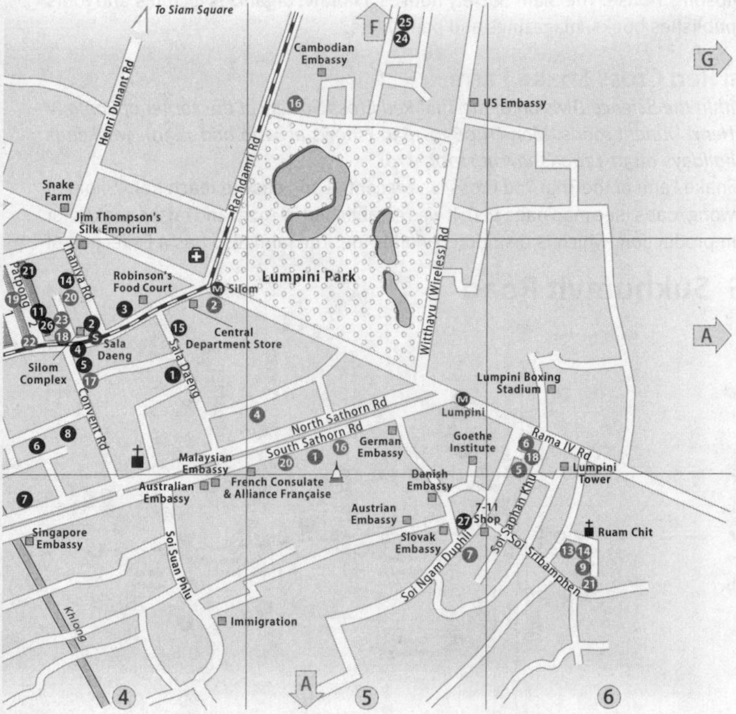

Batavia **4** *B4*
Bobby's Arms **26** *B4*
Bua **5** *B4*
Bussaracum **6** *B4*
Eat Me **8** *B4*
Himali Cha Cha **9** *B2*
Indian Hut **10** *B2*
Just One **27** *C5*
Le Basil **2** *B4*
Le Bouchon **11** *B4*
Le Café de Paris **21** *B4*
Peppers **24** *A5*
Side Walk **12** *C2*
Silom Village **13** *B3*
Sorrento **7** *C4*
Thaniya Garden **14** *B4*
Whole Earth **25** *A5*
Zanotti **15** *B4*

Bars & clubs
Brown Sugar **16** *A5*
Delaney's **17** *B4*
Music Café **19** *B4*
Noriega's **20** *B4*
Radio City **22** *B4*
Tapas **18** *B4*
White **23** *B4*

Sukhumvit Road

With the Skytrain running its length, Sukhumvit Road has developed into Bangkok's most vibrant strip. Shopping centres, girlie bars, some cf the city's best hotels and awesome places to eat have been joined by futuristic nightclubs. The grid of sois that run off the main drag are home to a variety of different communities including Arab, African and Korean as well as throngs of pasty westerners. Sordid and dynamic, there's never a dull moment on Sukhumvit Road.

Siam Society

ⓘ *131 Soi Asoke, T02-6616470 for information on lectures, info@siam-society.org, Mon-Sat 0900-1700, ฿100.*

Just off Sukhumvit Road, sited in the **Kamthieng House,** a 120-year-old northern Thai building, is the Siam Society, a learned society established in 1904. Donated to the society in 1963 the house was transported to Bangkok from Chiang Mai and then reassembled a few years later. It now serves as an ethnological museum, devoted to preserving the traditional technologies and folk arts of Northern Thailand. It makes an interesting contrast to the fine arts displayed in Suan Pakkard Palace and Jim Thompson's House. The Siam Society houses a library, organizes lectures and tours and publishes books, magazines and pamphlets.

Thai Red Cross Snake Farm

ⓘ *Within the Science Division of the Thai Red Cross Society at the corner of Rama IV and Henri Dunant roads. Mon-Fri 0830-1630 (shows at 1100 and 1430), weekends and holidays 0830-1200 (show at 1100). ฿70.*

The Snake Farm of the Thai Red Cross is very central and easy to reach from Silom or Surawong roads (see map page 112). It was established in 1923, and raises snakes for serum production, which is distributed worldwide. The farm also has a collection of

G Sukhumvit Road

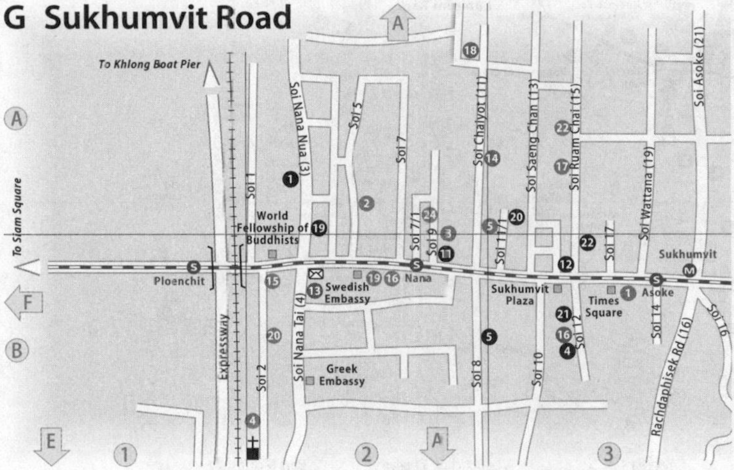

0 metres 200
0 yards 200

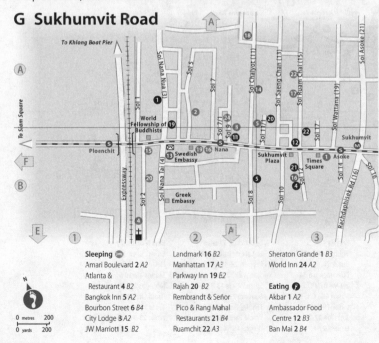

Sleeping
Amari Boulevard **2** *A2*
Atlanta & Restaurant **4** *B2*
Bangkok Inn **5** *A2*
Bourbon Street **6** *B4*
City Lodge **3** *A2*
JW Marriott **15** *B2*
Landmark **16** *B2*
Manhattan **17** *A3*
Parkway Inn **19** *B2*
Rajah **20** *B2*
Rembrandt & Señor Pico & Rang Mahal Restaurants **21** *B4*
Ruamchit **22** *A3*
Sheraton Grande **1** *B3*
World Inn **24** *A2*

Eating
Akbar **1** *A2*
Ambassador Food Centre **12** *B3*
Ban Mai **2** *B4*

non-venomous snakes. During showtime (which lasts half an hour) various snakes are exhibited, venom extracted and visitors can fondle a python. The farm is well maintained and professional.

Science Museum and Planetarium

ⓘ *Tue-Sun 0900-1600, closed public holidays, ฿40 adults, ฿20 children. Take Skytrain to Ekkamai. (There is a newer and much better science museum, the National Science Museum, see page 118).*

The Science Museum and Planetarium is just past Sukhumvit Soi 40, next to the Eastern bus terminal. It contains a planetarium, aeroplanes and other exhibits but don't expect many of them to work. As one recent report put it, there are lots of interactive buttons, but nothing much happens when you press them.

Chatuchak Weekend Market

ⓘ *At the weekend, the market is officially open from 0900-1800 (although in fact it begins earlier around 0700). It's best to go early in the day. Beware of pickpockets. There is a tourist information centre at the entrance gate off Kamphaeng Phet 2 Rd, and the clock tower serves as a good reference point should visitors become disoriented. Take a Skytrain to Mo chit station, a/c buses nos 2 (from Silom Rd), 3, 10, 13 and 29 go past the market, and non-a/c buses nos 8, 24, 26, 27, 29, 34, 39, 44, 59 and 96.*

North of Bangkok is the Chatuchak Weekend Market just off Phahonyothin Road, opposite the Northern bus terminal, near the Mo chit Skytrain and Chatuchak Park and Kampaeng Phet Metro stations. Until 1982 this market was held at Sanaam Luang in central Bangkok, but was moved after it outgrew its original home. Chatuchak is a huge conglomeration of 9,000 stallholders spread over an area of 12 ha, selling virtually everything under the sun, and an estimated 200,000 people visit the market over a weekend. There are antique stalls, basket stalls, textile sellers, shirt

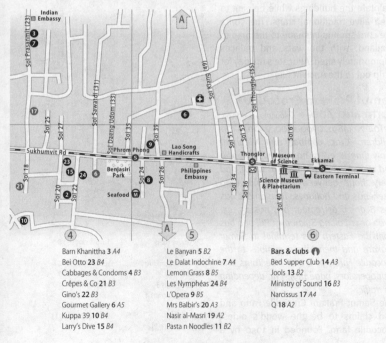

Barn Khanittha **3** *A4*
Bei Otto **23** *B4*
Cabbages & Condoms **4** *B3*
Crêpes & Co **21** *B3*
Gino's **22** *B3*
Gourmet Gallery **6** *A5*
Kuppa 39 **10** *B4*
Larry's Dive **15** *B4*
Le Banyan **5** *B2*
Le Dalat Indochine **7** *A4*
Lemon Grass **8** *B5*
Les Nymphéas **24** *B4*
L'Opera **9** *B5*
Mrs Balbir's **20** *A3*
Nasir al-Masri **19** *A2*
Pasta n Noodles **11** *B2*

Bars & clubs
Bed Supper Club **14** *A3*
Jools **13** *B2*
Ministry of Sound **16** *B3*
Narcissus **17** *A4*
Q **18** *A2*

vendors, carvers and painters along with the usual array of fish sellers, vegetable hawkers, butchers and candlestick makers. In the last couple of years a number of bars and foodstalls have also opened so it is possible to rest and recharge before foraging once more. Also here, in the north section of Chatuchak Park adjacent to Kamphaeng Phet Road, is the **Railway Museum** ⓘ *0900-1800, free,* with a small collection of steam locomotives as well as miniature and model trains.

Around Bangkok

If the heat and sprawl becomes too much then do what any self-respecting Bangkokian does and get the hell out. You don't have to travel far to see ancient palaces, dreamy rivers and bizarre museums. Travel a little further and you'll be taking in sweeping green vistas amid thick forests and dipping your toosties into warm sand.

Muang Boran (Ancient City) → *Colour map 3, grid B4.*

ⓘ *T02-2241057, 0800-1700, ฿50, ฿25 children. Take an a/c city bus nos 8 or 11, or non-a/c no 25 to Samut Prakarn and then a short songthaew ride; or by bus from the Eastern bus terminal to Samut Prakarn; or on one of the innumerable organized tours (see Tours and tour operators, page 149).*

The Ancient City lies 25 km southeast of Bangkok in the province of Samut Prakarn and is billed as the world's largest outdoor museum. It houses scaled-down constructions of Thailand's most famous wats and palaces (some of which can no longer be visited in their original locations) along with a handful of originals relocated here. Artisans maintain the buildings while helping to keep alive traditional crafts. The 50-ha site corresponds in shape to the map of Thailand, with the wats and palaces appropriately sited. Allocate a full day for a trip out to the Ancient City.

Samut Prakarn Crocodile Farm and Zoo → *Colour map 3, grid B4.*

ⓘ *T02-7034891, 0700-1800. ฿300, ฿200 children. Croc combat and elephant show-time is every hour between 0900 and 1600 Mon-Fri (no show at 1200), and every hour between 0900 and 1700 weekends and holidays. Take an a/c bus nos 8 or 11, or regular bus nos 25, 45, 1W02 or 119 along Sukhumvit Rd; or a bus from the Eastern bus terminal to Samut Prakarn and then take a minibus to the Crocodile Farm; or a tour (see Tours and tour operators, page 149), 1 hr, depending on traffic.*

The Samut Prakarn Crocodile Farm and Zoo claims to be the world's oldest crocodile farm. Founded in 1950 by a

Chatuchak Weekend Market

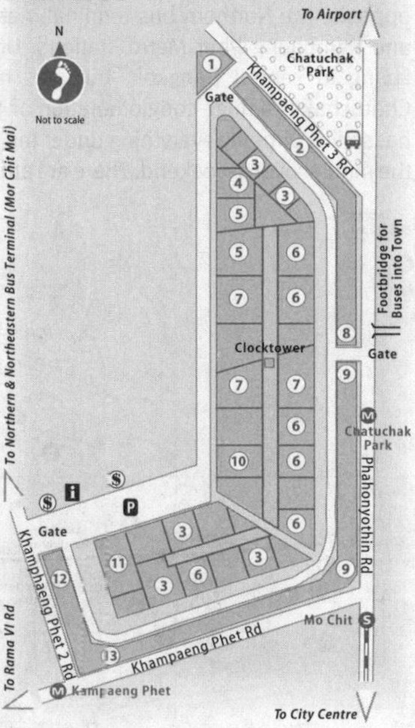

Decorative rocks & Bonsai 1
Agricultural products & clothing 2
Miscellaneous 3
Pets & handicrafts 4
Pets 5
Clothing 6
Fresh & dried fruits 7
Plants & clothing 8
Plants 9
Fresh & dried fruits & ceramic wares 10
Antiques 11
Buddha images, plants & books 12
Paintings & plants 13

My kingdom for a durian

To many Thais, durians are not just any old fruit. They are Beaujolais, grouse and Dolcellate all rolled into one stinking, prickly ball. The best durian in Thailand – the cognoscenti would say the whole world – come from Nonthaburi, north of Bangkok. The best varieties are those like the kan yao durian.

The problem is Nonthaburi has been taken over by factories and housing estates. Durian orchards are disappearing as development proceeds and many of the most famous orchards are now under concrete. In early 2000 there were just 3,000 rai of orchards left in the province (less than 500 ha). Such is the scarcity of these fruit that wealthy Thais reserve their fruit on the tree – each of which sells for ฿1,200-1,500. Nor is it just a case of land being redeveloped. Durian trees are said not to like thundering traffic and the fumes that go with Nonthaburi's gradual industrialization. The sensible things just refuse to fruit or produce second-class offerings.

certain Mr Utai Young-prapakorn, it contains over 50,000 crocs of 28 species. Thailand has become, in recent years, one of the world's largest exporters of farmed crocodile skins and meat. Never slow in seeing a new market niche, Thai entrepreneurs have invested in the farming of the beasts – in some cases in association with chicken farms. (The old battery chickens are simply fed to the crocs – no waste, no trouble.) The irony is that the wild crocodile is now, to all intents and purposes, extinct in the country – there are said to be two left alive, and unfortunately living in different areas. It is tempting to speculate that recent floods may have added to those numbers as captive crocodiles have frequently escaped from some of the less well-designed farms. While this has generated some understandable concern in the areas near the farm, most, if not all, escapees have eventually been captured or killed. The show includes the 'world famous' crocodile wrestling. In August 2002 a Thai woman committed suicide by jumping into one of the pools – home to more than 100 crocodiles – during feeding time and 'appeared to hug the first crocodile to grab her'. The keeper said "she just jumped into the pond, without a word, without a cry". The farm also has a small zoo, train and playground.

Floating market at Damnoen Saduak → *Colour map 3, grid B3.*

ⓘ *Catch an early morning bus (No 78) from the Southern bus terminal in Thonburi – aim to get to Damnoen Saduak between 0800-1000, as the market winds down after 1000, leaving only trinket stalls. The trip takes about 1½ hrs. A/c and non-a/c buses leave every 40 mins from 0600 (฿30-49) (T02-4355031 for booking). The bus travels via Nakhon Pathom (where it is possible to stop on the way back and see the Great Chedi). Ask the conductor to drop you at Thanarat Bridge in Damnoen Saduak. Then either walk down the lane (1½ km) that leads to the market and follows the canal, or take a river taxi for ฿10, or a minibus, ฿2. There are a number of floating markets in the maze of khlongs – Ton Khem, Hia Kui and Khun Phithak – and it is best to hire a hang yaaw to explore the backwaters and roam around the markets, about ฿300 per hr (agree the price before setting out). Tour companies also visit the floating market.*

It is possible to combine this trip with a visit to the Rose Garden, page 118).

Damnoen Saduak floating market, in Ratchaburi Province, 109 km west of Bangkok, is (almost) the real thing. Sadly, it is becoming increasingly like the Floating Market in Thonburi (see page 103), although it does still function as a legitimate market. It

is one of the most popular day trips from the capital. It's mostly for the tourists these days but if you take time to explore the further flung khlongs you should stumble across something more authentic. Most visitors arrive and depart on a tour bus, stopping only for a photo opportunity and the chance to buy overpriced fruit from the canny market sellers.

Rose Garden → Colour map 3, grid B3.

ⓘ Daily 0800-1800. The cultural show is at 1445 daily. ฿300. (Bangkok office: 195/15 Soi Chokchai Chongchamron Rama III Rd, T02-2953261.) Daily tour from Bangkok, half day (afternoons only).

A Thai 'cultural village' spread over 15 ha of landscaped tropical grounds, 32 km west of Bangkok. Most people go for the cultural show: elephants at work, Thai classical dancing, Thai boxing, hill tribe dancing and a Buddhist ordination ceremony. The resort also has a hotel, restaurants, a swimming pool and tennis courts, as well as a golf course close by.

Thai Human Imagery Museum

ⓘ T034-332109, Mon-Fri 0900-1730, Sat, Sun and holidays 0830-1800. ฿200. Take a bus (a/c and non-a/c) from the Southern bus terminals towards Nakhon Pathom; ask to be let off at the museum.

Situated 31 km west of Bangkok on Pinklao-Nakhon Chaisri highway, the Thai Human Imagery Museum is the Madame Tussauds of Bangkok. 'Breath-taking' sculptures include famous monks, Thai kings, and scenes from Thai life; the museum is probably more interesting to Thais than foreigners.

Nonthaburi → Colour map 3, grid B4.

ⓘ Take an express river taxi (45 mins) to Tha Nonthaburi or by Bangkok city bus (nos 32, 64, 97 and 203). A day trip, including lunch, costs ฿500. It is possible to stay here, see Sleeping.

Nonthaburi is both a province and a provincial capital immediately to the north of Bangkok. Accessible by express river taxi from the city, the town has a provincial air that contrasts sharply with the overpowering capital; there are saamlors in the streets (now banished from Bangkok) and the pace of life is tangibly less frenetic. About half an hour's walk away are rice fields and rural Thailand. A street market runs from the pier inland past the sala klang (provincial offices), selling clothes, sarong lengths and dried fish. The buildings of the sala klang are early 19th century, wooden and decayed. Note the lamp posts with their durian accessories – Nonthaburi's durians are renowned across the Kingdom. Walk through the sala klang compound (downriver) to reach an excellent riverside restaurant. Across the river and upstream (five minutes by long-tailed boat) is **Wat Chalerm Phra Kiat**, a refined wat built by Rama III as a tribute to his mother who is said to have lived in the vicinity. The gables of the bot are encrusted in ceramic tiles; the chedi behind the bot was built during the reign of King Mongkut or Rama IV (1851-1868). It is also possible to take an interesting day trip by long-tailed boat to a **traditional Thai house** here.

National Science Museum

ⓘ T02-5774172, pasopsuk@lox1.loxinfo.com, Tue-Sun 0900-1700, ฿50, ฿20 children; in Thai the museum is known as Ongkaan Phiphitiphan Withayasaat Haeng Chaat (or Or Por Wor Chor), but even if you manage to say that the chances are that the taxi driver will not know where you mean, so get someone from your hotel to make sure. Take the Chaeng Wattana-Bang Pa In expressway north and exit at Chiang Rak (for Thammasat University's new out-of-town campus). Continue west on Khlong Luang Rd, over Phahonyothin Rd, and follow your nose over khlong 1 to khlong 5 (canals) until the road ends at a T-junction. Turn right and the NSM is 4 km or so down here on the left.

The National Science Museum (NSM), north of town, past the airport, opened in Pathum Thani province in 2000. The money for the project – a cool one billion baht – was allocated before the economic crisis. Air-conditioned buildings, internet centre, and lots of hands-on exhibits to thrill children and the childlike is the result. The exhibits are labelled in English and Thai and the recorded information is also in both languages. It is very good, well designed and with charming student helpers for that human touch. The cafeteria needs some more thought though.

Bang Sai → *Colour map 3, grid B4.*

ⓘ *Take a bus from the Northern bus terminal or a boat up the Chao Phraya.*

The **Royal Folk Arts and Crafts Centre** is based north of Bangkok at Amphoe (district) Bang Sai, around 24 km from Bang Pa In, and covers an area of nearly 50 ha, ⓘ *T02-366666, bangsai@wnet.net.th, Tue-Sun 0830-1600, ฿50, ฿30 children*. Local farmers are trained in traditional arts and crafts such as basketry, weaving and wood carvings. The project is funded by the Royal Family in an attempt to keep alive Thailand's traditions. Visitors are offered a glimpse of traditional life and technologies. All products – artificial flowers, dolls, silk and cotton cloth, wood carvings, baskets and so on – are on sale. Other attractions at Bang Sai include a freshwater aquarium and a bird park.

Bang Pa In → *Colour map 3, grid B4.*

ⓘ *0830-1630, ฿50 (guidebook included). Currency exchange facilities are also available here. Regular bus connections from Bangkok's Northern terminal (1 hr) and 3 train connections each day from the capital's Hualamphong station, or long-tailed boat from Tien Pier (see map page 104).*

Bang Pa In became the summer residence of the Ayutthayan kings of the 17th century. King Prasat Thong (1630-1656) started the trend of retiring here during the hot season, and he built both a palace and a temple. The palace is located in the middle of a lake that the king had created on the island. It is said that his fondness for Bang Pa In was because he was born here.

After the Thai capital was moved to Bangkok, Bang Pa In was abandoned and left to degenerate. It was not until Rama IV stopped here that a restoration programme was begun. The only original buildings that remain are those of Wat Chumphon Nikayaram, outside the palace walls, near the bridge and close to the railway station. Start at the Varophat Phiman Hall, built by Chulalongkorn in 1876 as his private residence, and from here take the bridge that leads past the Thewarat Khanlai Gate overlooking the Isawan Thipaya-at Hall in the middle of the lake. Facing the gate and bridge is the Phra Thinang Uthayan Phumisathian, and though designed to resemble a Swiss chalet, it looks more like a New England country house. Behind the 'chalet', the Vehat Chamroon Hall, built in 1889, was a gift from Chinese traders to King Chulalongkorn. It is the only building open to the public and contains some interesting Chinese artefacts. In front stands the Hor Vithun Thasna, a tall observation tower. Another bridge leads to a pair of memorials. The second commemorates Queen Sunanda, Rama V's half-sister and favourite wife who drowned here; it is said her servants watched her drown because of the law that forbade a commoner from touching royalty. South of the palace, over the Chao Phraya River, is the Gothic-style Wat Nivet Thamaprawat, built in 1878 and resembling a Christian church.

Safari World

ⓘ *T02-5181000, www.safariworld.com. 0900-1700, ฿600, ฿360 (children). Take bus no 26 from the Victory Monument to Minburi where a minibus service runs to the park.*

Safari world is a 120-ha complex in Minburi, 9 km from the city centre, with animals and amusement park. Most of the animals are African – zebras, lions, giraffes – and visitors can either drive through in their own (closed) vehicles or take one of the park's air-conditioned coaches. There is also a marine park and a bird park.

Siam Water Park

ⓘ *101 Sukhapibarn 2 Rd, Bangkapi, T01-5170075. Mon-Fri 1000-1800, Sat-Sun 0900-1900, ฿200. Take bus nos 26 and 27 from the Victory Monument, 1 hr or 30 mins by car.*

Siam Water Park is Water World – with artificial surf, fountains, waterfalls and shute – theme park, zoo, botanical gardens and fair all rolled into one.

Chachoengsao → *Colour map 3, grid B5.*

ⓘ *Trains leaves from Hualamphong station between 0510 and 1805 and the journey takes 1 hr 40 mins. The train station is to the north of the fruit market, an easy walk to/from the chedi. Buses depart from both the Mo Chit and Ekkamai terminals but it is quickest from Ekkamai – about 2 hrs, depending on the traffic. A/c buses also stop to the north of the fruit market, and there are regular connections (every 15 mins) with Bangkok's Southern bus terminal, 1-2 hrs.*

Chachoengsao lies just 1½ hours from Bangkok by train or bus making it a nifty day excursion from the capital – and offering an insight into 'traditional' Thailand. Chachoengsao lies on the Bang Pakong River, to the east of the capital, and has almost been engulfed by fast-expanding Bangkok. Nonetheless, old-style shophouses and restaurants, as well as some evidence of a much more rustic past, remain. The old heart of the town is near the confluence of the Bang Pakong River and Khlong Ban Mai, on Supakit Road. **Ban Mai market** is worth exploring not for its wares– the main market has moved into the centre of the new town – but for its traditional architecture. A concrete footbridge over Khlong Ban Mai links the two halves of the old market. A Chinese clan house reveals the largely Chinese origin of the population of the market area; most arrived before the outbreak of the Second World War. **Wat Sothorn** Woramahavihan is the town's best known monastery and it contains one of the country's most revered images of the Buddha, Luang Por Sothorn. The monastery is a little over 2 km south of Sala Changwat (the Provincial Hall), on the banks of the Bang Prakong.

Sleeping

From humble backstreet digs through to opulent extravagance, Bangkok has an incredibly diverse range of hotels, guesthouses and serviced apartments. The best value bargains are often to be had in the luxury sector; you'll find some of the best hotels in the world here, many of which offer their rooms at knock-down prices. The guesthouses of Khaosan are cheapish but far more expensive than what you'll find in other parts of the country. Probably the biggest bargains to be had are with serviced apartments. These are lavish flats, most of which come with all the amenities (pool, gym, maid and room service) you'd expect from a 4- or 5- star hotel, but at half the price. This sector of Bangkok's accommodation market is little known a nd is becoming the choice for the city's more discerning visitors.

Many of the more expensive places to stay are on the Chao Phraya River. As well as river transport, the Skytrain provides excellent transport from here. Running eastwards from the river are Silom and Surawong roads, in the heart of Bangkok's business district and with Skytrain and Metro connections. The bars of Patpong link the two roads. Not far to the north of Silom and Surawong roads, close to Hualamphong (the central railway station and Metro stop), is Chinatown. There are a handful of hotels and guesthouses here – but it remains very much an alternative location to the better established accommodation centres. A well-established area is along Sukhumvit Rd. The Skytrain runs along Sukhumvit's length and it is intersected by the Metro at Soi Asoke. The bulk of the accommodation here is in the **A-B** range and the sois are filled with shops, bars and restaurants of every description. Note, that the profusion of go-go bars in Soi Nana [Sois 3 and 4] and Soi Cowboy [off Soi 23] can be off-putting. In the vicinity of Siam

Sq are a handful of de luxe hotels and several 'budget' establishments (especially along Rama 1 Soi Kasemsan Nung). Siam Sq is central, has a good shopping area and excellent Skytrain connections, easy bus and taxi access to Silom and Sukhumvit rds and the Old City. The main concentration of guesthouses is along and around Khaosan Rd (an area known as Banglamphu). There is a second, smaller and quieter cluster of guesthouses just north of Khaosan Rd, at the northwest end of Sri Ayutthaya Rd. A third concentration of budget accommodation is on Soi Ngam Duphli, off Rama IV Rd.

Advertisements in the *Bangkok Post* may provide some heavily discounted rates in some more upmarket hotels.

See Essentials, page 35, for hotels at or close to the airport.

Banglamphu and Khaosan Road *p97, maps p121 and p122*

The sois off the main road are often quieter, such as Soi Chana Songkhran or Soi Rambutri. Note that rooms facing on to Khaosan Rd tend to be very noisy.

AL Royal Princess, 269 Lan Luang Rd, T02-2813088, www.royalprincess.com. A/c, restaurants, pool, part of the Dusit chain of hotels, good facilities.

A Buddy Lodge, 265 Khaosan Rd, T02-6294477, www.buddylodge.com. The luxury pad of Khaosan Rd, **Buddy Lodge** dominates the far end of a smart shopping arcade. The room decor is luxurious, with fridge and TV. There is also a Japanese restaurant and coffee shop and a pool.

J Khaosan Road

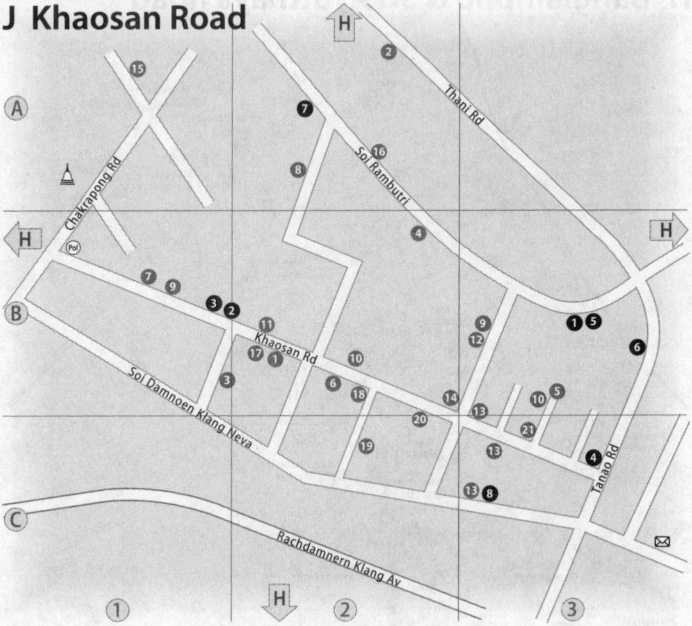

N

0 metres 50
0 yards 50

Sleeping
Bankok Guesthouse **3** *B1*
Buddy Lodge **5** *B3*
Chart Guest House **6** *B2*
D&D Inn **1** *B2*
Euro Inn Guest House **7** *B1*
Green House **8** *A2*
Hello **9** *B1*
Khao San Palace **10** *B2*
Lek **11** *B2*
Marco Polo **12** *B3*
Nana Plaza Inn **13** *C3*
Nat Guest House **14** *B2*
Orchid House **16** *A2*
Prakorb's House **17** *B2*
Sawasdee Bangkok Inn **18** *B2*
Sawasdee Krungthep Inn **19** *C2*
Siam Oriental **20** *C2*
Siri Guesthouse **21** *C3*
Tuptim B&B **4** *B2*
Viengtai **2** *A2*

Eating
Bai Bau **1** *B3*
Coffee Indeed **2** *B1*
D'Rus **3** *B1*
Khao San Thai Food **4** *C3*
Pannee Guesthouse **5** *B3*
Peter, Tony, Jimmy, Tom Fashion Café **6** *B3*
Rodeo Eat 'n' Sip **7** *A2*
Teketei **8** *C3*

Bars & clubs
Buddy Beer Lodge **10** *B3*
Lava Club **13** *B3*
Sawasdee House **15** *A1*
Susie's Pub **9** *B2*

A Viengtai, 42 Thani Rd, Banglamphu, T02-2815788. A/c, restaurant, pool. Rooms here are good, if a little worn, clean and relatively spacious, with all the advantages of its proximity to the Old City. Helpful management.

B Trang Hotel, 99/1 Visutkaset Rd, T02-28221414, www.tranghotel bangkok.com A/c, restaurant, pool. Friendly hotel and recommended by regular visitors to Bangkok. It opened way back in 1962 but is still a good establishment at this price.

C D&D Inn, 68-70 Khaosan Rd, T02-6290526, ddinn@hotmail.com. Large, purpose-built hotel with lift, tidy a/c rooms, and hot showers. The small, often deserted, swimming pool on the roof offers a fine view, and the small bar alongside makes this an excellent place to start or end the day.

C Nana Plaza Inn, Khaosan Rd, T02-2816402. Fine, well-furnished rooms (some a/c), a friendly atmosphere and charming corridors.

C Tuptim Bed and Breakfast, 82 Rambutri St, T02-629153536, info@tuptimb-b.com. Some a/c and en suite shower, but even the shared facilities are exceptionally clean, breakfast included. Very friendly staff. Highly recommended.

C-D Chart Guest House, 62 Khaosan Rd, T02-2820171. Very clean airy rooms, cosmopolitan feel, with winding staircase and retro-style bar with movies. Friendly, English-speaking staff. Recommended.

C-D Khao San Palace, near 139 Khaosan Rd, T02-2820578 Very popular with travellers, clean with some a/c and shower.

H Banglamphu & Sri Ayutthaya Road

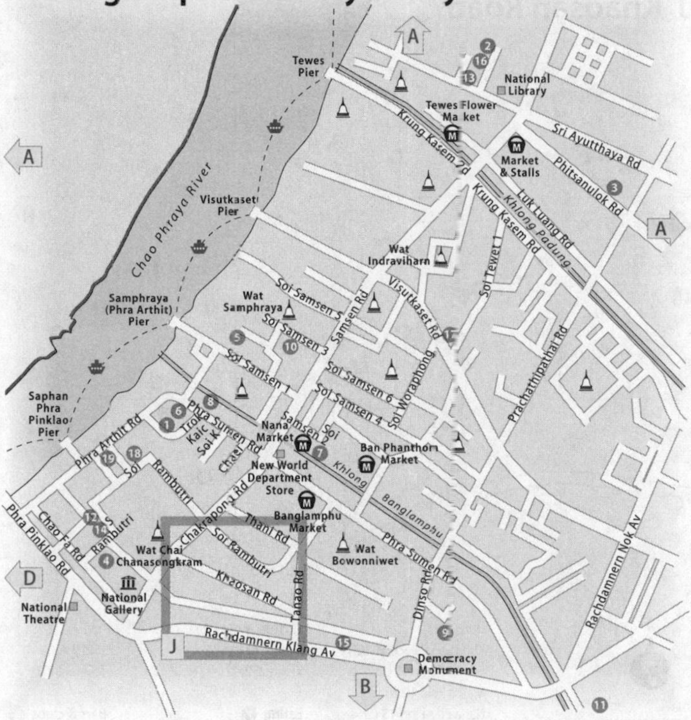

Sleeping
Apple 2 Guesthouse 1
Baan Sabai 12
Backpackers Lodge 2
Bangkok Youth Hostel 3
Chai's House 4
Clean & Calm 10
Green Guesthouse 18
Home & Garden 5
KC Guesthouse 6
Merry V 18
My House 18
New World Lodge 7
Pra Arthit Mansion 19
Pra Suri Guesthouse 9
PS Guesthouse 8
River Guesthouse 5
Royal Princess 11
Sawasdee Smile Inn 14
Sawatdee 13
Sweety 15
Tavee 16
Trang 17

0 metres 200
0 yards 200

C-D Orchid House, Rambrutri St, no a/c but some attached showers, sweet little rooms. Recommended.
C-D Siam Oriental, 190 Khaosan Rd, T02-6290312, siam_oriental@hotmail.com. Fine, clean rooms (some a/c), smart tiled corridors, and very friendly staff. Internet facilities downstairs, along with a very popular restaurant. Free safety deposit box.
C-D Top Guest House, Khaosan Rd. Good, clean, smart, newly painted rooms. Laundry facilities, left luggage (฿10 per day).
C-E New World Lodge Hotel and Guesthouse, 2 Samsen Rd, T02-2815596 (hotel), T02-2812128 (guesthouse), www.new-lodge.com. Some hotel rooms have a/c whereas the guesthouse only offers fans, good location for the Old City yet away from the hurly-burly of Khaosan Rd. Large rooms not particularly inviting or characterful and some have satellite TV for a higher price. Safety boxes are free for guests, as is the use of a small but worn-out gym.
C-E Sawasdee Bangkok Inn, 126/2 Khaosan Rd, T02-2801251, sawasdeehotel@yahoo.com. Good value, clean, fair-sized rooms with wooden floors and some with a/c. A vibrant, popular bar, and friendly staff. Free safety deposit, left luggage (฿10 per day). Highly recommended.
C-E Sawasdee Krungthep Inn, 30 Praathi Rd, T02-6290072. Recently opened, with a lively communal atmosphere. Clean and simple rooms, all with cable TV. Family rooms available with 2 double beds.
D Euro Inn Guest House, 13-15 Khaosan Rd, T02-6293822, euroinn@hotmail.com. Some a/c, clean, shared toilets.
D Green House, 88/1 Rambutri St, T02-2814293. Basic but good-value rooms, eatery and bar downstairs with widescreen television, floor cushions and book exchange, internet services available.
D Marco Polo, some a/c with shower, good value and clean although a little box-like, pleasant wood smell.
D Siri Guesthouse, 206/1 Khaosan Rd. Friendly proprietor and good value rooms.
D-E Bankok Guesthouse, bankok_cafe@hotmail.com. A tall, thin, parquet-floored guesthouse, with a herbal massage house on the 3rd floor. Clean, basic, rather warm, but pleasant.
D-E Chai's House, 49/4-8 Chao Fa Soi Rongmai, last house down Soi Rambutri, so away from the competition, T02-2814901. Some a/c, friendly atmosphere. Rooms are in traditional Thai style, with wood panelling. They vary in size but are clean and the a/c rooms are good value. Balconies and orchid-filled restaurant make it a quiet and relaxing place. Recommended.
D-E Hello, 63-65 Khaosan Rd, T02-2818579. Some a/c, most rooms without windows, outside communal areas, quite basic but internet café with free inbox-checking facility.
D-E Lek, 90/9 Khaosan Rd, T02-2812775. Up a long flight of steps off the main road. Rooms are clean but boxy. Rooms at the front can suffer from the noise of Khaosan Rd. Helpful staff and friendly atmosphere, popular. Left luggage (฿10 per day).
D-E Prakorb's House, 52 Khaosan Rd. Well-maintained, airy rooms with high ceilings. Friendly local feeling but no a/c.
D-E Pra Suri Guesthouse, 85/1 Soi Pra Suri (off Dinso Rd), T/F02-2801428. 5 mins east of Khaosan Rd, not far from the Democracy Monument, fan, restaurant, own bathrooms (no hot water), clean, spacious and quiet, very friendly and helpful family-run travellers' guesthouse with all the services to match. Recommended.
D-F Bangkok Youth Hostel, 25/2 Phitsanulok Rd (off Samsen Rd), T02-2820950. North of Khaosan Rd, away from the bustle, the dorm beds are great value (฿90) being newly furnished and with a/c. Other rooms are clean, small and basic and remain good value. If you don't have a valid YHA membership card, it will cost an extra ฿50 per night.
E KC Guesthouse, 60-64 Phra Sumen Rd Soi Khai Chae, T02-2820618, kc_guesthouse@hotmail.com. Small, friendly place with a cosy and personal ambience. Rooms and toilets are clean and well kept. Not far enough off the main road to be quiet.
E Nat Guest House, 217-219 Khaosan Rd, T02-2826401. Large, clean, cheap rooms – no a/c, but a good deal.
E PS Guesthouse, 9 Phra Sumen Rd, T02-2823932. Clean and well run, with good security. Rooms at the back have windows over the river (but it's not scenic). Some rooms have no windows. Aligns with main road, so noisy at the front. There is an airy,

open restaurant in the front downstairs that serves great filtered coffee. It offers an international and reasonably priced menu, and guests may help out in the kitchen if they want to learn a bit of Thai cooking.

E **Sweety**, 49 Thani Rd, sandwiched between 2 roads, so noisy. Rooms are large and clean, with adequately clean shared toilets.

E-F **Apple 2 Guesthouse**, 11 Phra Sumen Rd, T02-2811219. Quite hard to find: if you turn off Phra Arthit Rd, take the soi opposite Baan Chaophraya. If turning off the Phra Sumen Rd, take Trok Kaichee (soi). Not to be confused with **Apple**, which is grimy and unfriendly. Very friendly management (run by the same woman for 20 years), this place – with its homely feel and quiet, clean rooms in an old wooden house – remains a firm favourite. Dorm beds available.

E-F **Home and Garden**, 16 Samphraya Rd (Samsen 3), T02-2801475. Away from the main concentration of guesthouses, down a quiet soi (although the cocks tend to mean an early start for light sleepers), is this small house in a delightful leafy compound with a homely atmosphere. The rooms are a fair size with large windows, some face onto a balcony. Friendly owner and excellent value. Recommended.

E-F **The River Guesthouse**, 18 Samphraya Rd (Samsen 3), T02-2800876. A small, family house with a homely and friendly atmosphere. Small but clean rooms.

F **Clean and Calm Guesthouse**, 17 Samphraya Rd (Samsen 3), T02-2822093. It may be clean and calm, but this is probably due to the lack of visitors as there is no communal area.

Phra Arthit Road

B **Pra Arthit Mansion**, 22 Phra Arthit Rd, T02-2800744. Leafy though slightly dated hotel, popular with German tour operators. Rooms are good value with all the trimmings. Well-run with helpful management.

C-E **Baan Sabai**, 12 Soi Rongmai, T02-6291599, baansabai@hotmail.com. A large, colonial-style building with a green pillared entrance in front. Although it is not very expensive, it is not the typical backpacker's scene. Rooms are simple but large and airy. Storage is available at ฿10 per bag/suitcase. Occasionally local Thai bands are invited to play here.

D **My House**, 37 Phra Arthit Soi Chana Songkram, T02-2829263. Helpful and friendly management, rooms are very clean and the place maintains excellent standards of cleanliness. Popular, good travel service (minibus to airport every hour).

D-E **Sawasdee Smile Inn**, 35 Soi Rongmai, T02-6292340. Large, spacious sitting area at the front under a gaudy looking green, Thai-style roof. Restaurant and 24-hr bar, so ask for a room at the back if you want an early night. Rooms are clean and simple, all with cable TV. Free safety boxes available.

E **Merry V**, 33-35 Phra Arthit Soi Chana Songkram, T02-2829267. Clean, tidy and cheap. Some rooms with good views out over the city from the upper floor balconies, although not from the rooms (some of which have no windows), which are small and dirty around the edges. Toilets kept clean. A well-run place with good information.

E-F **Green Guesthouse**, 27 Phra Arthit Soi Chana Songkram, T02-2828994. Not to be confused with the **Green House**, rooms are very small but are clean and cheap.

Sri Ayutthaya Road

Sri Ayutthaya is emerging as an 'alternative' area for budget travellers. It is a central location with restaurants and foodstalls nearby, but does not suffer the overcrowding and sheer pandemonium of Khaosan Rd. It is also close to the Tewes Pier for the express river boats. The guesthouses are a little more expensive than those in Khaosan Rd but standards are higher. One family runs four of the guesthouses, this means that if one is full you will probably be moved on to another.

D **Taewaz Guesthouse**, Sri Ayutthaya Rd. New place with very clean rooms – a/c rooms are a bargain; internet access, highly recommended by one recent visitor.

D-F **Tavee**, 83 Sri Ayutthaya Rd, Soi 14, T02-2825983. Restaurant, a quiet, relaxed and respectable place with a small garden and a number of fish tanks. Friendly management – a world away from the chaos of Khaosan Rd. The Tavee family keep the rooms and shared bathrooms immaculately clean and are a good source of information for travellers. Dorms are also available for ฿80 per night. This place has been operating since 1985 and has managed to maintain a very high standard. Highly recommended.

E Backpackers Lodge, 85 Sri Ayutthaya Rd, Soi 14, T02-2823231. Very similar to its neighbour, Tavee (whose owner is brother of the Backpackers' manager). The rooms are a little small but the service is friendly and there is an intimate feel to the place. Quiet and recommended.

E Sawatdee, 71 Sri Ayutthaya Rd, T02-2825349. Western menu, pokey rooms, popular with German travellers, management brusque and offhand.

Thonburi, Wat Arun and the khlongs *p103, map p104*

There's presently very little accommodation on the Thonburi side of the river. This is a shame as the khlongs, particularly to the north, make it one of the most beautiful parts of the city.

L Peninsula, 333 Charoen Nakorn Rd, Klongsan, T02-2861288, bangkok.peninsula.com. Sited just across the river from Taksin Bridge, the 39-storey **Peninsula** has a commanding riverfront position providing spectacular city views. The large rooms are luxurious and a full range of leisure facilities are on offer, while 4 restaurants provide a variety of (mostly Asian) cuisine. Recommended.

AL Marriott Royal Garden Riverside Hotel, 257/1-3 Charoen Nakorn Rd, T02-4760021, www.marriot.com. A/c, restaurant, pool, spacious surroundings with over 4 ha of grounds. Free shuttle-boat service every half an hour between hotel and River City piers. Attractive, low-rise design with some attempt to create Thai-style ambience. A good place to escape from the fumes and frenzy after a day sightseeing or shopping – the soothing Mandara spa is here too. Recommended.

C-E The Artists Club, 61 Soi Tiem Boon Yang, T02-8620056. Run by an artist, this is a guesthouse cum studio-cum-gallery buried deep in the khlongs with clean rooms, some a/c. It makes a genuine alternative with concerts, drawing lessons and other cultural endeavours.

Chinatown *p101, map p102*

A Grand China Princess, 215 Yaowarat Rd, T02-2249977, www.grandchina.com. High-rise block mainly catering to the Asian market, with choice of Asian cuisine, business facilities, fitness centre (but no pool).

D Moon Hotel, Mahachai Rd, T02-2357195. A rabbit warren of cellular a/c rooms joined by damp corridors. Excellent value however.

D-E Golden Inn Guesthouse, Mahachai Rd, no telephone, excellent situation in the heart of Chinatown. Dark rooms and very noisy, but then this is Chinatown.

Siam Square area *p108 map p109*

L Grand Hyatt Erawan, 494 Rachdamri Rd, T02-2541234, www.bangkok.grand.hyatt.com. A towering structure with grandiose entrance and an artificial tree-filled atrium plus sumptuous rooms and every facility. The **Spasso Restaurant/Club** here is very popular and very pricey. On the other hand, the bakery, which has a fantastic range of really sinful and delicious cakes, and the noodle shop (**You and Mee**), which are both also on the lower ground floor are very reasonably priced. Service is excellent and friendly, and this hotel does not charge for drinking water! This makes for a good escape from the traffic and pollution for lunch or afternoon tea even if you're not staying here.

L-AL Four Seasons Bangkok, 155 Rachdamri Rd, T02-2501000, www.fourseasons.com. A/c, restaurants (including **Spice Market**, see Eating page131), pool and excellent reputation. Stylish and postmodern in atmosphere with arguably the best range of cuisine in Bangkok as well as a Swiss Perfection spa. Recommended.

L-AL Hilton, 2 Witthayu Rd, T02-2530123, www.hilton.com. A/c, restaurants, attractive pool. An excellent hotel set in lovely tropical gardens with walkways and streams. Good service, excellent restaurants, attractive rooms.

AL Arnoma, 99 Rachdamri Rd, T02-2553411, www.arnoma.com. A/c, several restaurants, pool, health club, business centre, 403 well-equipped rooms, though much like any others in this price bracket. Good location for shopping and restaurants.

AL Cape House, 43 Soi Lang Suan, T02-6587444, www.capehouse.com. Excellent serviced apartments in a great

location. Each apartment comes with DVD, stereo, free wireless broadband, cable TV, a/c and kitchenette. Has a roof top pool, library, decent Italian and Thai restaurant sauna and gym. Does monthly and nightly rates. Highly recommended.

AL Chateau de Bangkok 29 Ruamrudee Soi 1, T02-6514400. Owned by the Accor hotel chain, these serviced apartments have great amenities and are centrally located. Excellent value monthly rates.

AL Le Meridien President, 135/26 Gaysorn Rd, T02-2530444, www.lemeridien-bangkok.com. Pool, health club spa, 400 rooms in this, one of the older luxury hotels in Bangkok (it opened in 1966). Tranquil atmosphere, good service, excellent French food.

A Amari Watergate, 847 Phetburi Rd, T02-6539000, www.amari.com. A/c, restaurants (including the excellent **Thai on 4** – see Eating, page 130), fitness centre, squash court, pool. Lots of marble and plastic trees, uninspired block, good facilities and good value, great views from the upper floors on the south side of the building.

A Asia, 296 Phayathai Rd, T02-2150808, www.asiahotel.co.th. A/c, several restaurants, 2 pools. The jewellers within the hotel is one of the best in Bangkok. Entrance implies a certain degree of sophistication, but rooms are basic and the hotel is situated on a noisy thoroughfare. Good deals available when booking in advance and it is also a handy location with a Skytrain station almost outside the main door.

C-D A1 Inn, 25/13 Soi Kasemsan Nung (1), Rama I Rd, T02-2153029, aoneinn@thaimail.com. A/c, well-run, intimate hotel. Recommended.

C-D Bed and Breakfast, 36/42 Soi Kasemsan Nung (1), Rama 1 Rd, T02-2153004. A/c, efficient staff, clean but small rooms, good security, price includes basic breakfast. Recommended.

C-D Wendy House, 36/2 Soi Kasemsan Nung (1), Rama I Rd, T02-2162436. A/c, spotless but small rooms, eating area downstairs, hot water.

C White Lodge, 36/8 Soi Kasemsan Nung (1), Rama I Rd, T02-2168867, pnktour@hotmail.com. A/c, hot water, airy, light reasonably sized rooms.

C White Orchid Guesthouse, Soi 2 Siam Square, T02-2552186. 8 small rooms with pleasant atmosphere.

Silom area *p111, map p112*

Of all Bangkok, this area most resembles a western city, with its international banks, skyscrapers, first-class hotels, shopping malls, pizza parlours and pubs. It is also home to one of the world's best-known red-light districts – Patpong.

Soi Ngam Duphli to the east is much the smaller of Bangkok's two main centres of guesthouse accommodation. This area has seen better days but still makes a viable alternative for budget travellers. See below.

L Banyan Tree, 21/100 South Sathorn Rd, T02-6791200, www.banyantree.com. A/c, restaurant, pool. Famous for its luxury spa, all rooms are suites with a good location and set back from busy Sathorn Rd.

L Dusit Thani, 946 Rama IV Rd, T02-2360450, www.bangkok.dusit.com. A/c, restaurants, excellent service and attention to detail. Beautiful new spa. Recommended.

L Metropolitan, 27 South Sathorn Rd, T02-6253333, www.metropolitan.como.bz. From its funky members/guest only bar through to the beautiful, contemporary designer rooms and the awesome restaurants (**Glow** and **Cy'an** – see Eating for review) this is one of Bangkok's coolest hotels. Bargains can be had when it's quiet. Highly recommended.

L Oriental, 48 Soi Oriental, Charoen Krung, T02-2360400, www.mandarinoriental.com. A Bangkok legend, a/c, restaurants, 2 pools, considered one of the best hotels in the world though does seem to rest on its laurels, beautiful position overlooking the river, superb personal service despite its size (400 rooms). The rooms may appear a bit small, and some of the equipment and bathrooms are a little old. Recommended.

L Royal Orchid Sheraton, 2 Captain Bush Lane, Si Phraya Rd, T02-2660123, www.royalorchidsheraton.com. A/c, restaurants, pool. Lovely views over the river, and close to River City shopping centre (good for antiques). Rooms are average at this price but service is very slick.

L Shangri-La, 89 Soi Wat Suan Plu, Charoen Krung, T02-2367777, www.shangri-la.com.

A/c, restaurants, lovely pool, and great location overlooking the river. This hotel is preferred by some to the **Oriental** although others consider it dull and impersonal. Claims to be in the Top 10 World Hotels. Recommended.

L-AL Sukhothai, 13/3 South Sathorn Rd, T02-2870222, www.sukhothai.com. A/c, restaurants, pool, beautiful rooms and excellent service. The sleek design might be termed Thai postmodern and it has become a favourite place for the wealthy, hipster crowd, although it is now challenged by the nearby **Metropolitan**. Highly recommended.

AL Siri Sathorn, 27 Saladaeng Soi 1, T02-2662363, www.sirisathorn.com. Gleaming minimalist tower block with dozens of serviced apartments. Rooms are large, the upper floors have great views, amenities top rate and it has a great location. Recommended.

AL Sofitel Silom, 188 Silom Rd, T02-2381991, www.sofitel.com. A/c, restaurants, pool, stark and gleaming high-tech high-rise, all facilities. Rooms are very elegantly designed. Currently offering some good promotional offers to boost custom.

A Tower Inn, 533 Silom Rd, T02-2378300, www.towerinnbangkok.com. A/c, restaurant, pool, simple but comfortable hotel, with large rooms and an excellent roof terrace, good value.

A-D New Road Guest House, 1216/1 Charoen Krung Rd, jyskbkk@loxinfo.co.th. This Danish owned place provides a range of accommodation from de luxe rooms to hammocks on the roof. A restaurant serves inexpensive Thai dishes and there's a free fruit buffet for breakfast and tea and coffee- making facilities. A bar provides a pool table and darts and there's a small outdoor sitting area.

C River View Guesthouse, 768 Songwad Soi Panurangsri, T02-2345429, benjapak@ksc.co.th. Some a/c, the restaurant/bar is on the top floor and overlooks the river, food is mediocre. Some rooms with balconies, some with hot water, overlooking (as the name suggests) the river. This hotel is worth considering for its location away from the bulk of hotels, close to the Harbour Department boat pier and Chinatown. Recommended.

Soi Ngam Duphli

A-AL Pinnacle Hotel, 17 Soi Ngam Duphli, T02-2870111, www.pinnaclehotels.com. Clean and rooms with all mod cons, helpful staff, restaurant, nightclub.

B-C Charlie's House, Soi Saphan Khu, T02-6798330, www.charlieshouse thailand.com. Helpful owners create a friendly atmosphere and the rooms are carpeted and very clean. This is probably the best place in Soi Ngam Duphli if you are willing to pay that little bit extra. There is a restaurant and coffee corner downstairs with good food at reasonable prices. Recommended.

C-D Honey House, 35/2-4 Soi Ngam Duphli, T02-2863460. An interesting building architecturally, but set off a noisy road. Big and clean rooms with attached bathrooms, some with small balconies. Tends to cater more for those looking for a long stay.

D ETC, northern end of Soi Ngam Duphli, T02-2869424. Big, clean rooms with nice sitting area on the 4th floor, with sophorific management. Price includes breakfast.

D Sala Thai Guesthouse, Soi Saphan Khu, T02-2871436. At end of peaceful, almost leafy, soi, clean rooms have seen better days but it's family run and has a cute roof garden. Shared bathrooms. Recommended.

D-E Lee 3, 13 Soi Saphan Khu, T02-2863042. Some a/c. Wooden house with character, down quiet soi, rooms are clean, shared bathrooms. Recommended.

D-E Madam, 11 Soi Saphan Khu, T02-2869289. Wooden house, friendly atmosphere, attached bathrooms, no hot water, quiet. Recommended.

E Lee 4, 9 Soi Saphan Khu, T02-2867874. Spotless rooms and bathrooms, some with balconies and views over the city. Recommended.

Sukhumvit Road *p114,, map p114*

Sukhumvit is now one of Bangkok's premier centres of tourist accommodation and is a great place for restaurants and nightlife with several good bars and clubs. This is also a good area for shopping for furniture: antique and reproduction. Note also that the profusion of expatriate condominiums and hotels in the area between Sukhumvit Soi 18 and Sukhumvit Soi 24 attracts petty

thieves, particularly purse/bag snatchers, so hold on tight to your valuables if you are here during the evening.

L Amari Boulevard, 2 Sukhumvit Rd, Soi 5, T02-2552930, www.amari.com. Great location in the heart of Sukhumvit, good rooms, adequate fitness centre, small pool with terraced Thai restaurant. Popular place with European visitors.

L Landmark, 138 Sukhumvit Rd, T02-2540404, www.landmarkbangkok.com. Used to be one of the most glamorous hotels in the area. Excellent facilities, 12 restaurants, pool, health centre, smart shopping plaza and business facilities. Terrific views from the 31st floor. Some features need upgrading and renovating.

L Sheraton Grande Sukhumvit, 250 Sukhumvit, T02-6530333, www.sheratongrandesukhumuit.com. Superbly managed business and leisure hotel. Service, food and facilities are impeccable. The roof top garden is an exotic delight and the spa offers some of the best massage in town. **Rossini** (Italian, see Eating) and **Basil** (Thai, see Eating) are also top class. Great location and, if you can afford it, the best place to stay on Sukhumvit. Recommended.

L JW Marriott, 4 Sukhumvit Soi 2, T02-6567700, www.marriott.com. Elegant, design, 4 restaurants, pool, health club and spa. More business-like than the Marriott hotel on the river. Two weeks before the tsunami of 26 December 2004 it opened a Japanese restaurant called 'Tsunami'.

AL Rembrandt, 15-15/1 Sukhumvit Soi 20, T02-2617040, www.rembrandtbkk.com. A/c, restaurants, pool, lots of marble but limited ambience, usual facilities. The Indian **Rang Mahal** restaurant comes highly recommended (as you might expect, given the fact that an Indian family owns the hotel) although it is quite pricey.

A Manhattan, 13 Sukhumvit Soi 15, T02-2550166, www.hotelmanhattan.com. Smart hotel with 3 good, but expensive restaurants, pool. Lacks character but rooms are comfortable. Tours available and tri-weekly cabaret.

A Ruamchit, 199 Sukhumvit Soi 15, T02-2540205. A fairly well-furnished hotel with good views and pool. The staff speak little English and it mainly serves Asian clientele.

B Bangkok Inn, 12-13 Sukhumvit Soi 11/1, T02-2544884. Friendly and informative German management, clean, basic rooms, with a/c, TV and attached shower.

B Bourbon Street, 29/4-6 Sukhumvit Soi 22 (behind Washington Theatre), T02-2590328, www.bourbonstbkk.com. A/c, a handful of rooms attached to a good Cajun restaurant.

B Rajah, 18 Sukhumvit Soi 2, T02-2550040. A rather dated hotel but with an attractive pool area, good-value restaurant, travel agents and craft shop. The atrium is reminiscent of the former eastern bloc.

B-C Atlanta, 78 Sukhumvit Soi 2, T02-2521650, www.theatlanta hotel.bizland.com. Basic a/c or fan-cooled rooms. A good large pool and a children's pool are a big plus. "Oiks, lager louts and sex tourists" are requested to go elsewhere! "Those who cannot behave themselves abroad are advised to stay at home." Good restaurant (see Eating, page 136). Prides itself on its literary, peaceful atmosphere. Appears to be the cheapest and is certainly the most appealing hotel in the area at this price, particularly suited for families, writers and dreamers, 24-hr email available. Highly recommended.

B-C City Lodge, Sukhumvit Soi 9, www.amari.com/citylodge. A fairly smart, small hotel with bright rooms and a personal feel. Good room discounts at time of writing. Trendy pasta and noodle restaurant (see Eating, page 135).

B-C Parkway Inn, 132 Sukhumvit Rd, T02-2553711. Small establishment centred around the bar, which is like an English pub lounge with Thai decor, basic rooms, book exchange.

C World Inn, 131 Sukhumvit Soi 7/1, T02-2535391. Basic rooms with the standard TV, minibar and en suite bathroom. Coffee shop with Thai and western food.

Nonthaburi *p118*

A Mr Phaiboon's house. The rate includes breakfast, fan rooms, outside bathrooms and no hot water). Call Asian **Overland Adventure**, T02-2800740.

Eating

Bangkok is one of the greatest food cities on earth. You could spend an entire lifetime finding the best places to eat in this city that seems totally obsessed with its tastebuds. The locals will often eat four or five times a day, each and every one of them able to pinpoint their favourite rice, noodles, kai yang (grilled chicken), moo yang (grilled pork), som tam (spicy papaya salad), tom yam (sour, spicy soup) and Chinese eateries. Endless runs of streetfood, steak houses, ice cream parlours, Italian diners, seafood specialists and trendy nouvelle cuisine restaurants vie for your attention. In fact, if you really want to see life as the Thais do, then spend your every waking moment in Bangkok thinking about, finding and eating every conceivable gourmet delight the city has to offer. More than anything else, the Thai capital is fanatical and infatuated with eating.

Many restaurants (especially Thai ones) close early (between 2200 and 2230). Many of the more expensive restaurants listed here take credit cards. Many hotels and upmarket restaurants offer excellent lunchtime buffets. Note that while there are some old timers among Bangkok's hundreds of restaurants, many more have a short life.

Bangkok has a large selection of fine **bakeries**, many attached to hotels like the Landmark, Dusit Thani and Oriental. There are also the generic 'donut' fast-food places although few lovers of bread and pastries would want to lump the two together. Many of the bakeries also double as cafés serving coffee, sandwiches and such like. There are also increasing numbers of **coffee bars** such as Starbucks.

Streetfood can be found across the city and a rice or noodle dish, will cost ฿25-40 instead of a minimum of ฿50 in the restaurants. Service is rough and ready and there won't be menus as most **stalls** specialize in one or two dishes only. Judge quality by popularity and don't be afraid to point out what you want if your Thai is lacking. All in all, the experience is quintessential Bangkok and the street is where the majority of locals eat. Some of the best streetfood can be found on the roads between Silom and Surawong Rd, Soi Suanphlu off South Sathorn Rd, down Soi Somkid, next to Ploenchit Rd, or opposite on Soi Tonson.

Banglamphu and Khaosan Road *p97, maps p121 and p122*

Travellers' food such as banana pancakes and muesli is available in the guesthouse/travellers' hotel areas (see above). The Thai food along Khaosan Rd is some of the worst and least authentic in town, watered down to suit the tastebuds of unadventurous backpackers.

TTT **Teketei**, 202 Khaosan Rd, same entrance as Nana Plaza Inn, T02-6290173. A sushi restaurant, open 1130-0100. Excellent but pricey, daily specials.

TT **D'Rus**, Khaosan Rd, T02-2810155. It might not look like much from the outside with its bland decor punctuated by Van Gogh prints and slow-moving telly-addict waiters, but the Thai/western food is some of the best in the area.

TT **Peter, Tony, Jimmy, Tom Fashion Cafe**, Tanao Rd. Coffee, snacks and drinks, good value Thai food, excellent vegetarian range. Open 0900-2400.

TT **Rodeo eat'n'sip**, 84 Rambutri St. European and Thai food, friendly staff and spacious restaurant. Open 1030–2400.

T **Bai Bau**, 146 Rambutri St. Very tasty Thai food, good value in a quiet corner, your best bet for a relaxed authentic meal in a friendly environment. Highly recommended.

T **Coffee Indeed**, 125 Khaosan Rd. Western coffee bar, a nice little getaway if in need of a coffee or light snack. Open 0900–2100.

T **Khao San Thai food and restaurant**, eastern end of Khaosan Rd. Large range of Thai food, very popular, catfish is a house speciality. One of the better places on the street.

T **Lucky Beer**. A little quieter than some of the other restaurants on Khaosan Rd. Adequate selection of food with large eating area at rear, open till late.

T **May Kaidee**, 117/1 Tanao Rd, Banglamphu. This is a tiny, simple vegetarian restaurant tucked away down a soi at the eastern end of Khaosan Rd.

Delicious, cheap Thai vegetarian dishes served at tables on the street.

Pannee Guesthouse, 150 Rambuttri St, T02-282 5576. Small, pleasant and cheap restaurant with a good selection of Thai and Chinese food. Open 0600-2400.

Tuptim Bed and Breakfast, 82 Rambutri St. Western breakfasts and Thai main meals available, good value in a pleasant and friendly environment.

Sri Ayutthaya

Kaloang, 2 Sri Ayutthaya Rd, T02-2819228. 2 dining areas, one on a pier, the other on a boat on the Chao Phraya River, attractive atmosphere, delicious Thai food. Recommended.

Siam Square area *p108, map p109*

Siam Sq has a large number of shark's fin soup specialists. Those who are horrified by the manner by which fins are removed and the way in which fishing boats are decimating the shark populations of the world should stay clear. Siam Sq also has two great noodle shops, side-by-side on Siam Sq Soi 10.

Chinese

China, 231/3 Rachdamri Soi Sarasin. Bangkok's oldest Chinese restaurant, serving a full range of Chinese cuisine.

Hong Kong Noodles is usually packed with university students and serves stupendously good bamii muu ceang kio kung sai naam (noodle soup with red pork and stuffed pasta with shrimp).

Kuaytiaw Rua Khuan Boke is equally popular. More expensive than most noodle shops, but definitely worth the extra few baht.

French

Ma Maison, 2 Witthayu Rd, T2530123. Classic French cuisine from duck escoffier to wild mushroom soup and great soufflés, set in a traditional Thai teak house. Pricey. Open for lunch and dinner Mon-Sat and dinner only on Sun.

Indonesian

Bali, 20/11 Ruamrudee Village, Soi Ruamrudee, Ploenchit Rd, T02-2500711. Authentic Indonesian food, friendly proprietress and a charming old-style house with garden. Open Mon-Sat lunch and dinner and Sun for dinner only.

International

The Bay, 2032 New Phetburi Rd, T02-7160802. American restaurant but serving more than just the usual burgers and fries – pork, duck, seafood. Microbrewery and live music in the evening from 2130. Good atmosphere, enjoyable decor.

Wit's Oyster Bar, 20/10 Ruamrudee Village, T02-2519455. Bangkok's first and only oyster bar, run by an eccentric Thai, one of the few places where you can eat late, good salmon fishcakes, international cuisine.

FABB Fashion Cafe, Ground Floor, Mercury Tower, 540 Ploenchit Rd. Don't be put off by the clunky name, this international restaurant serves well priced Italian-meets-Thai food, good buffet lunch.

Neil's Tavern, 58/4 Soi Ruanrudee, Ploenchit Rd, T02-2566875, open Mon-Sat 1130-1400, 1730-2230. Very popular with great steaks and named after Neil Armstrong – it opened the day he stepped on the moon. There is another branch at 24 Sukhumvit Soi 21.

Italian

Biscotti, Four Seasons, 155 Rachdamri Rd, T02-2555443. Italian 'fusion', a second superb restaurant at this top-class hotel. Very popular – so book if you are sure you want to eat here.

Gianni's, Soi Tonson. The best Italian restaurant in the area with light airy decor and excellent pasta and main courses, not to mention very polished service and a good wine list.

Il Paesaro, 96/7 Soi Tonson (off Soi Langsuan), Ploenchit Rd, T02-2522834. Italian food in friendly atmosphere. This long-established restaurant has a loyal following and is very popular with farangs and westernized Thais.

Vito's Spaghetteria, Basement, Gaysorn Plaza, Ploenchit Rd (next to **Le Meridien Hotel**). Bright pasta bar, make up your own dish by combining 10 types of pasta with 12 sauces and 29 fresh condiments, smallish servings but good for quick lunches.

Food courts

If you want a cheap meal with lots of choice, then a food court is a good place to start. They are often found along with supermarkets and in shopping malls.

Buy coupons and then use these to purchase your food from one of the many stalls – any unused coupons can be redeemed. A single-dish Thai meal like fried rice or noodles should cost around ฿25-30. The more sophisticated shopping malls will have stalls servings a wider geographical range of cuisines including, for example, Japanese and Korean.

There are food courts in the following (and many more) places:

Mah Boon Krong (MBK), Phaya thai Rd (just west of Siam Square, BTS Siam station).
Panthip Plaza, Phetburi Road.
Ploenchit Centre, 2 Ploenchit Road (BTS Nana station).
Robinson, 139 Ratchadapisek Road.
Siam Discovery Centre, Rama 1 Road (BTS Siam station).
The Garden Terrace, The Emporium, 622 Sukhumvit Road (corner of Soi 24).
United Centre Building, 323 Silom Road (near intersection with Convent Road, BTS Sala Daeng station).
World Trade Centre, Ratchdamri Road (BTS Chitlom station).

Japanese

₸₸ Kobune, 3rd Floor, Mahboonkhrong (MBK) Centre, Rama 1 Rd. Japanese, sushi bar and tables, very good value. Recommended.

Thai

₸₸₸ Once Upon a Time, 32 Phetburi Soi 17 (opposite Pantip Plaza), T02-2528629. Upmarket and inventive Thai cuisine including seafood soufflé in coconut and more traditional dishes like a delectable duck curry. Open for lunch and dinner, Tue-Sun.

₸₸₸ Spice Market, Four Seasons, 155 Rachdamri Rd, T02-2516127. Westernized Thai, typical hotel decoration, some of the city's best Thai food and an excellent set menu. Open daily for lunch and dinner.

₸₸₸ Thai on 4, Amari Watergate Hotel, 847 Phetburi Rd, T02-6539000, classy, modernist restaurant on the 4th floor of this hotel. The food is excellent, pricey for Thai but good value for a hotel restaurant (the lunchtime buffet is the best value) with high standards.

₸₸ Ban Khun Phor, 458/7-9 Siam Sq Soi 8, T02-2501732. Good Thai food in stylish surroundings.

₸₸ Barn Khanittha, Ruamrudee Rd. Beautifully designed Thai restaurant particularly well known for dishes made with soft-shelled crabs.

₸ Sanguan Sri, Wireless Rd (diagonally opposite the British Embassy). Scintillating Thai food – but open only during the day.

Vegetarian

₸₸ Vegetarian House, 4/1-4/2 6th Floor, Isetan World Trade Centre, Rachdamri Rd, T02-2559898. Wide-ranging menu from Asian to western. This bright and airy vegetarian restaurant is a place where vegetables are made to look like meat: beef stroganoff, shark's fin soup and the like all cunningly crafted from soybean.

₸₸ Whole Earth, 93/3 Soi Langsuan, Ploenchit Rd, T02-2525574. Bangkok's best-known vegetarian restaurant. The lack of veggie competition in the city has led to low standards and high prices. Food, service and ambience are all ropey. Open daily for lunch and dinner.

Vietnamese

₸₸₸ Pho, 2F Alma Link Building, 25 Soi Chitlom, T02-2518900. Supporters claim this place (there are 3 other branches) serves the best Vietnamese in town even though the owner is not Vietnamese herself. Modern trendy setting, non-smoking area. Open daily f or lunch and dinner.

Cafés and bakeries

Au Bon Pain, Ground Floor, Siam Discovery Centre, Rama 1 Rd. Excellent bakery and coffee shop with French pastries, croissants, muffins, cookies and great sandwiches as well as salads and some other dishes.

Basket of Plenty, Peninsula Plaza, Rachdamri Rd (another branch at 66-67 Sukhumvit Soi 33). Bakery, deli and trendy restaurant, very good things baked and a classy (though expensive) place for lunch.

La Brioche, ground floor of **Novotel Hotel**, Siam Sq Soi 6. Good range of French patisseries.

Starbucks, Central department store Chitlom, Ploenchit Rd, Amarin Plaza, Ploenchit Rd. The Starbucks 200 m down Soi Lang Suan from Chitlom Skytrain station is a faux-Thai teak house.

Silom area *p111, map p112*

p111, map p112

French

La Normandie, Oriental Hotel, 48 Oriental Av, T02-2360400. **La Normandie** maintains extremely high standards of cuisine and service (with guest chefs from around the world), jacket and tie required in the evening but the service is still not overbearing – set lunch and dinner menus are the best value. Open Mon-Sat for lunch and dinner and Sun for dinner. Recommended.

Le Bouchon, 37/17 Patpong 2, T02-2349109, open daily 1100-0200, French country cuisine (Provence), family-run, reasonable prices and well patronized by Bangkok's expat French community.

Le Café de Paris, Patpong 2 Rd, T02-2372776. Traditional French food from steaks to pâté. Open for lunch and dinner, daily. Recommended.

Indian

There are 4 or 5 Indian restaurants in a row on Sukhumvit Soi 11.

Himali Cha Cha, 1229/11 Charoen Krung, T02-2351569. Good choice of Indian cuisine, mountainous meals for the very hungry, originally set up by Cha Cha and now run by his son – 'from generation to generation' as it is quaintly put.

Indian Hut, 311-2-5 Surawong Rd (opposite the **Manohra Hotel**), T02-2378812. Long-standing and resolutely popular North Indian restaurant; well priced and with good service.

Tamil Nadu 5/1 Silom Soi (Tambisa) 11, T02-2356336. Good, but limited South Indian menu, cheap and filling, dosas are recommended.

Indonesian

Batavia, 1/2 Convent Rd, T02-2667164. 'Imported' Indonesian chefs, good classic dishes like saté, gado-gado (vegetable with peanut sauce and rice) and ayam goreng (deep-fried chicken).

International

Peppers, 99/14 Soi Langsuan, T02-2547355. Open during the day 1000-1700, closed on Sun, small restaurant with just 20 seats serving home-cooked Italian food and international dishes, friendly atmosphere, wholesome, tasty food. Great for a lunch stop.

Isaan

Sara Jane's, 55/21 Narathiwat Ratchanakharin Rd, Sathorn, T02-6793338. Great Thai salad and good duck. The Isaan food is yummy –. excellent value. Another branch in the Sindhorn Building at 130-132 Witthaya Rd. Recommended.

International and fusion

Cy'an, Metropolitan Hotel, 27 South Sathorn Rd, T02-6253333, www.metropolitan.como.bz. With a menu concocted by one of Asia's leading chefs, Amanda Gale **Cy'an** is a scintillating dining experience, the like of which is not matched in the entire Thai capital. This is international cuisine of the highest order: the almond-fed Serrano ham and Japanese wagyu beef are highlights in a stunning menu. Strangely ignored by wealthy Thais, this is a restaurant at the cutting edge of Bangkok eating, miles ahead of the competition. Highly recommended.

Eat Me, 1/6 Phipat Soi 2 (off Convent). Newish restaurant, very well received for its fusion cuisine as much as for its stylish interior design, and clever name. Cool live music makes it even better on Sun.

Glow, **Metropolitan Hotel**, 27 South Sathorn Rd, T02-6253333, www.metropolitan.como.bz. An organic

lunch bar created by Amanda Gale. Feast on spirulina noodles and tuna sashimi, all washed down with fresh beetroot and ginger juice. Recommended.

¥¥¥ **Lord Jim's**, **Oriental Hotel**. A fine restaurant, offering great views and stunning international food.

¥¥ **The Barbican**, 9/4-5 Soi Thaniya, Thaniya Plaza, Silom Rd, T02-2343590. Chic café bistro with duck, steaks, sophisticated sandwiches, fish, DJ on Thu, Fri and Sat evenings. Open 1100-0200.

¥¥ **Bobby's Arms**, 2nd Floor, Car Park Building, Patpong 2 Rd, T02-2336828. English pub and grill, with jazz on Sun from 2000, open 1100-0100. Roast beef, fish and chips, pies and mixed grill.

Italian

¥¥¥ **Angelini**, **Shangri-La Hotel**, 89 Soi Wat Suan Plu, T02-2367777, open 1130 'till late', one of the most popular Italian restaurants in town – a lively place with open kitchens, pizza oven and the usual range of dishes. Menu could be more imaginative.

¥¥¥ **Zanotti**, 21/2 Sala Daeng Colonnade, Silom Soi Sala Daeng, T02-6360002. Wide-ranging menu including pizzas and pasta, risotto dishes, meat and poultry, all served in a renovated early 20th-century building. Open daily for lunch and dinner.

¥¥ **Papa Alfredo's**, Ground Floor, U Chu Liang Building, Rama IV Rd, T02-6324043. Italian café with Sicilian chef, recommended for its ambience, food and the size of the portions. Open for lunch and dinner.

¥¥ **Ristorante Sorrento**, 66 North Sathorn Rd (next to the **Evergreen Laural Hotel**), T02-2349841. Excellent Italian food along with imported steaks.

¥¥ **Terrazzo**. Stylish alfresco Italian restaurant overlooking the pool, wonderful Italian breads and good pasta dishes. Recommended.

Polynesian

¥¥¥ **Trader Vic's**, **Marriott Riverside Hotel**, 257/1-3 Charoen Nakorn Rd, T02-4760021. Bangkok's only restaurant serving Polynesian food which is seafood based and takes inspiration from Chinese culinary traditions. Open for lunch and dinner (1200-1400, 1800-2230).

Thai

¥¥¥ **Anna's Café**, 118 Silom Soi Sala Daeng, T02-6320619. Great Thai-cum-fusion restaurant in a villa off Silom Rd named after Anna of *King & I* fame. Some classic Thai dishes like larb, nua yaang and som tam along with fusion dishes and western desserts such as apple crumble and banoffee pie. Open daily 1100-2200.

¥¥¥ **Bua Restaurant**, Convent Rd (off Silom Rd). Classy, postmodern Thai restaurant with starched white table linen and cool, minimalist lines, refined and immaculately prepared.

¥¥¥ **Bussaracum**, 139 Pan Rd (off Silom Rd), T02-2666312. Changing menu, popular, classy Thai restaurant with prices to match. Recommended.

¥¥¥ **Thaniya Garden Restaurant**, Thaniya Plaza, 3rd Floor, Room 333-335, 52 Silom Rd, T02-2312201. Open Mon-Sat 1100-2200, excellent Thai food and enormous portions.

¥¥ **Banana Leaf**, Silom Complex, basement, Silom Rd, T02-3213124. Excellent Thai restaurant with some unusual dishes, including kai manaaw (chicken in lime sauce), nam tok muu (spicy pork salad, Isaan style) and fresh spring rolls 'Banana Leaf', along with excellent and classic larb kai (dishes such as minced chicken Isaan style), booking recommended for lunch.

¥¥ **Ban Krua**, 29/1 Saladaeng Soi 1, Silom Rd. Simple decor, friendly atmosphere, a/c room, traditional Thai food.

¥¥ **Celadon** Sukhothai Hotel, 13/3 South Sathorn Rd, T02-2870222. Scrummy contemporary Thai food in cool surroundings – one of the best upmarket places in town. Highly recommended.

¥¥ **Gallery Café**, 1293-1295 Charoen Krung Rd, T02-2340053. For reasonable Thai food in an artistic environment extending over 4 floors.

¥¥ **Side Walk**, 855/2 Silom Rd (opposite Central Dept Store). Grilled specialities, also serves French. Recommended.

¥¥ **Silom Village**. There are several excellent Thai restaurants in this shopping mall, on Silom Rd (north side, opposite Pan Rd), excellent range of food from hundreds of stalls, all cooked in front of you, enjoyable village atmosphere. Recommended.

¥ **Banana House**, Silom Rd/Thaniya Rd (2nd floor). Very good and reasonably priced Thai food; few tourists here but lots of locals.

Vegetarian

Whole Earth, 71 Sukhumvit Soi 26, T02-2584900. Slightly swisher of the two Whole Earth vegetarian restaurants (the other branch is on Soi Langsuan). Both offer the same eclectic menu from Thai to Indian dishes, live music, lassis and coffee. Open daily for lunch and dinner.

Vietnamese

Le Basil, Silom Complex, basement, Silom Rd, T02-2313114. Recommended. Favourite among Bangkok's expat population; some of the best Vietnamese food in the city.

Sweet Basil (branch at Sukhumvit also, see above), 1 Silom Soi Srivieng (opposite Bangkok Christian College), T02-2383088. Vietnamese food in an attractive 1930s era house with live music. Open daily for lunch and dinner.

Cafes and bakeries

The Authors' Lounge, Oriental Hotel, classy and relaxed atmosphere with impeccable service.

Dusit Thani Hotel library, Rama IV Rd. For afternoon tea go to sip a cuppa in the Dusit's hushed 'library'.

Harmonique, 22 Charoen Krung. Small Elegant coffee shop with good music, fruit drinks and coffee, great atmosphere.

Soi Ngam Duphli *map p112*

Thai

Just One, 58 Soi Ngam Duphli. Outside seating under a huge tree lit with fairy lights. Mix of Thai and farang customers nibbling on Thai dishes.

Cafes and bakeries

Folies, 309/3 Soi Nang Linchee (Yannawa) off southern end of Soi Ngam Duphli, T02-2869786. French expats and bake-o-philes maintain that this bakery makes the most authentic pastries and breads in town. Coffee available, a great place to sit, eat and read.

Sukhumvit Road *p114, map p114*

Arabic

Nasir al-Masri, 4-6 Sukhumvit Soi Nana Nua, T02-2535582. Reputedly the best Arabic food in Bangkok, felafel, tabhouleh, hummus, frequented by large numbers of Arabs who come to Sayed Saad Qutub Nasir for a taste of home.

Asian

Ambassador Food Centre, Ambassador Hotel, Sukhumvit Rd. A vast self-service, up-market hawkers' centre with a large selection of Asian foods at reasonable prices: Thai, Chinese, Japanese, Vietnamese, etc. Recommended.

French

Beccassine, Sukhumvit, Soi Sawatdee. English and French home cooking. Recommended.

Le Banyan, 59 Sukhumvit Soi 8, T02-2535556. Classic French food from foie gras to crêpes Suzette, expensive with tougher dress code than most places. Open only for dinner, Mon-Sat. Highly regarded food, but a shade stuffy.

Les Nymphéas, Imperial Queen's Park Hotel, Sukhumvit Soi 22, T02-2619000. An excellent restaurant (the interior theme is Monet's Waterlillies – hence the name) in an over-large and inconveniently located (unless you are staying here!) hotel – but don't be put off - creates probably the best 'modern' French cuisine in Bangkok.

Crêpes and Co, 18/1 Sukhumvit Soi 12, T02-6533990. Open 0900-2400. The name says it all, specializes in crêpes but also serves good salads. Some local culinary touches – I ke the crêpe mussaman (a Thai curry).

German

Bei Otto 1 Sukhumvit Soi 20, T02-2620892. Thailand's best-known German restaurant, sausages made on the premises, good provincial food, large helpings, attached deli next door for takeaway.

Indian

Rang Mahal, Rembrandt Hotel, Sukhumvit Soi 18, T02-2617107. Best Indian food in town, very popular with the Indian community and spectacular views from the roof top position, sophisticated, elegant and expensive.

Akbar, /4 Sukhumvit Soi 3, T02-2533479. Indian, Pakistani and Arabic. This is one of

the first Indian restaurants to open outside the Phahurat enclave; food is pretty standard. Open for lunch and dinner.

¥¥ **Mrs Balbir's**, 155/18 Sukhumvit Soi 11, T02-2532281. North Indian food orchestrated by Mrs Balbir, a Malay-Indian, serving succulent chicken dishes. Also runs cookery classes.

International

¥¥ **Gourmet Gallery**, 6/1 Soi Promsri 1 (between Sukhumvit Soi 39 and 40), T02-2600603. Interesting interior, with art work for sale, unusual menu of European and American food.

¥¥ **Larry's Dive**, 8/3 Sukhumvit Soi 22, T02-6634563. American bar which bills itself as the 'only private beach restaurant in Bangkok'. Burgers, nachos, ribs, chicken wings. Good value.

¥¥ **Longhorn**, 120/9 Sukhumvit Soi 23. Cajun and Creole food.

Italian

¥¥¥ **Hibiscus**, 31st floor, Landmark Hotel, 138 Sukhumvit Rd, T02-2540404. Italian food which extends to more than pasta and pizza. Worth it for the views. Open for lunch and dinner.

¥¥¥ **L'Opera**, 55 Sukhumvit Soi 39, T02-2585606. Italian restaurant with Italian manager, conservatory, good food (excellent salted baked fish), professional service, lively atmosphere, popular, booking essential. Recommended.

¥¥¥ **Rossini**, Sheraton Grande Sukhumvit, Sukhumvit Rd, T02-6530333. This hotel-based Italian restaurant is open for lunch and dinner. A tantalizing array of dishes and excellent bread. One of the best Italian places in town. Consistently excellent and highly recommended.

¥¥ **Gino's**, 13 Sukhumvit Soi 15. Italian food in bright and airy surroundings. The set lunch is good value.

¥ **Pasta n Noodles**, attached to City Lodge, Sukhumvit Soi 9. A trendy Italian and Thai restaurant, a/c, spotless open-plan kitchen.

Korean

¥ **New Korea**, 41/1 Soi Chuam Rewang, Sukhumvit Sois 15-19. Excellent Korean food in small restaurant. Recommended.

Laotian

¥¥ **Bane Lao**, Naphasup Ya-ak I, off Sukhumvit Soi 36 (it is number 49), T02-2586096. Laotian open-air restaurant offering haphazard but friendly service and some good food. Popular, so best to book – especially at weekends.

Mexican

¥¥ **Bourbon Street**, 29/4-6 Sukhumvit Soi 22 (behind Washington Theatre), T02-2594317. Cajun specialities including gumbo, jambalaya and red fish, along with steaks, Mexican dishes (Mexican buffet every Tue) and pecan pie, served in a/c restaurant with central bar – good for breakfast, excellent pancakes. Open 0600-2400.

¥¥ **Señor Pico**, Rembrandt Hotel, 18 Sukhumvit Rd, T02-2617100. Pseudo-Mexican decor, staff dressed Mexican style, large, rather uncosy restaurant, average cuisine, live music, open only for dinner 1700-0100 daily.

Seafood

¥¥¥ **Seafood Market**, Sukhumvit Soi 24. A deservedly famous restaurant which serves a huge range of seafood: "if it swims we have it". Choose your seafood, have it cooked to your own specifications before consuming.

Thai

¥¥¥ **Basil**, Sheraton Grande Sukhumvit, T02-6530333. One of the best Thai fine-dining experiences in town. Legendary for its Durian cheesecake – a gentle introduction to the complexities of enjoying this bizarre fruit. Recommended.

¥¥¥ **Kuppa 39**, Sukhumvit Soi 16. Closed Mon. Coffee house with blonde wood interior and an upstairs art gallery. An expensive range of Thai and international dishes.

¥¥ **Barn Khanittha**, Sukhumvit Soi 23. The original branch of this popular Thai restaurant; recently renovated and very popular with clients of all nationalities – the food is of a consistently high standard and service is excellent.

¥¥ **Lemon Grass**, 5/1 Sukhumvit Soi 24, T02-2588637. Thai food and Thai-style house. Open daily for lunch and dinner. Recommended and popular, so best to book.

¥ **Ban Mai**, 121 Sukhumvit Soi 22, Sub-Soi 2. Thai food served amongst old Thai-style

decorations in an attractive house with a friendly atmosphere, good value.

Ƴ **Cabbages and Condoms**, Sukhumvit Soi 12 (around 400 m down the soi). Population and Community Development Association (PDA) restaurant so all proceeds go to this charity, eat rice in the Condom Room, drink in the Vasectomy Room, good tom yam khung and honey-roast chicken, curries all rather similar, good value. Very attractive courtyard area decorated with fairy lights. Recommended.

Ƴ **The Restuarant**, Atlanta Hotel, 78 Sukhumvit Soi 2. Worth seeking out at the end of Soi 2 if you can be bothered with the increasingly bizarre and ad hoc set of rules governing entrance. The food is okay though its reputation is dimming. The highlight is the 1930s art-deco interior. Overrated.

Ƴ **Wannakarm**, 98 Sukhumvit Soi 23, T02-2596499. Well established, very Thai restaurant, grim decor, no English spoken, but rated food.

Vegetarian

Ƴ **Govinda**, 6/5/6 Sukhumvit Soi 22. Vegetarian restaurant serving a range of excellent pizzas and risottos.

Vietnamese

ƳƳ **Le Dalat Indochine**, 47/1 Sukhumvit Soi 23, T02-6617967. Reputed to serve the best Vietnamese food in Bangkok. Open daily for lunch and dinner. Not only is the food good, but the ambience is satisfying too.

Cafes and bakeries

The Bakery Landmark Hotel, 138 Sukhumvit Rd. Popular with expats, wide range of breads and fine cakes.

Bei Otto, Sukhumvit Soi 20. A German bakery and deli, makes very good pastries, breads and cakes.

Cheesecake House, 69/2 Ekamai Soi 22. Rather out of town for most tourists but patronized enthusiastically by the city's large Sukhumvit-based expat population. As the name suggests, cheesecakes of all descriptions are a speciality.

Chachoengsao *p120*

The best restaurants in town are along Marupong Rd which runs along the bank of the river. Specialities are prawn (this is a centre of production) and fish dishes. The **Koong Nang Restaurant** is one of the best known.

Bars and clubs

Bangkok's raunchy nightlife has taken a bit of a plunge since authoritarian PM Thaksin enforced a midnight closing time. Also in the works is a noise pollution law preventing loud nightclubs, bars and karaokes from pumping out late night sounds. Couple this with the forced urine testing that goes on at some nightspots – special police units arrive and take urine tests from all guests in the search for drug use, a process that takes all night, leads to clubs being closed and ends with arrests – and Bangkok is losing its reputation for Asia's hottest nightlife.

Don't let this put you off too much. The city still has some fantastic venues – everything from boozy pubs through to uber-trendy clubs. You can listen to decent jazz and blues or get into the latest European DJ's spinning the hippest beats.

Groovy Map's *Bangkok by Night* (฿120) includes information on bars and dance clubs, the city's gay scene, as well as music venues and drinking spots. Check the Bangkok listing magazines for the latest information on who's spinning and what's opening.

Old City *p91, map p92*

Boh, Tha Tien, Chao Phraya Express Boat Pier, Maharat Rd, open 1900-2400. A popular student hangout with good sunset views over Wat Arun.

Banglamphu and Khaosan Road *p97, maps p121 and p122*

Buddy Beer Lodge, 265 Khaosan Rd, T02-6294477, an upmarket and pleasant venue overlooking Khaosan Rd, competitve prices, worth a trip, open all day.

Lava Club, 249 Khaosan Rd, T02-2816565, open 2000-0100. Playing a mixture of hip-hop, house and funky tunes, this large and deeply cavernous venue looks not unlike a heavy metal club, decked out as it is in nothing but black with red lava running down the walls and floors.
Sawasdee House, 147 Soi Rambutree, Chakrapong Rd, T02-2818138. Seriously chilled, this is a wonderful place to relax at the end of the day with its airy atmosphere, high ceilings, spaciously arranged and enormously comfortable chairs, wooden floorboards, glowing lanterns and friendly staff.
Susie's Pub, turn right between **Lava Club** and **Lek GH**, open 2000-0200. This is the place for a more alternative Thai experience of what it is to go clubbing down Khaosan, as its always absolutely heaving more with locals than travellers. Top decibel thumping local tunes and all sorts of flashing neon outside announce its presence, but while it might be easy to find, it's not always such a simple thing to get in, as there's a seething mass of bodies to negotiate from relatively early on right up until closing.

Golden Mount and around *p98*

Saxophone, 3/8 Victory Monument, Phayathai Rd, open 1800-0300. Series of alternating house bands, including jazz, blues, ska and soul. Another place with a long-standing – and deserved – reputation for delivering the music goods.

Siam Square area *p108, map p109*

Boom Room, Novotel Siam Square, T02-2556888. Open 2100-0200. In the basement of this conveniently located hotel; music is trance, hard trance, progressive, hard house and techno.
Concept CM², T02-2556888, Novotel Siam Square. This hotel also houses this venerable (for Bangkok) bar playing pop and heavy metal. Mon and Wed are Ladies' Nights – free entrance and a free drink for those who can pass as female.
Cool Tango, 23/51 Block F, Royal City Av (between Phetburi and Rama IX roads). Open Tue-Sat 1100-0200, Sun 1800-0200. Excellent resident rock band, great atmosphere, happy hour 1800-2100.
Mingles, **Amari Atrium Hotel**, 1880 New Phetburi Rd. Open 1700-0100. Calls itself a 'Rustic Thai Fun Pub', but the vodka bar suggests otherwise. Theme nights throughout the week, some food available.

Silom area *p111, map p112*

Bamboo Bar, **Oriental Hotel**, 48 Oriental Av, T02-2360400. Open Sun-Thu 1100-0100, Fri-Sat 1100-0200. One of the best jazz venues in Bangkok, classy and cosy with good food and pricey drinks – but worth it if you like your jazz and can take the hit.
Brown Sugar, 231/20 Sarasin Rd (opposite Lumpini Park). Open Mon-Fri 1100-0100, Sat and Sun 1700-0200. Five regular bands play excellent jazz, a place for Bangkok's trendies to hang out and be cool (there are a couple of other popular bars close by too).
Met Bar, 27 South Sathorn Rd, T02-6253333, www.metropolitan.como.bz. This members and hotel guests-only bar spins great tunes, serves good cocktails and has an excellent cigar menu. The crowd can be incredibly stuck-up but this is still one of the places to be seen in Bangkok. Open daily 1800-0100.
Oriental Hotel, 48 Oriental Av. A particularly civilized place to have a beer and watch the sun go down is on the veranda here, by the banks of the Chao Phraya River, expensive, but romantic (and strict dress code of no backpacks, flip-flops or T-shirts).
Tapas, 114/17 Silom Soi 4, T02-2344737, a very popular bar with enormous variety of music and a contagious atmosphere.

Patpong *p112*

The greatest concentration of bars is to be found in the red-light districts of Patpong (between Silom and Surawong roads).
Delaney's, opposite Patpong, along Convent Rd, is an Irish pub with draft Guinness from Malaysia (where it is brewed) and a limited menu, good atmosphere and well-patronized by Bangkok's expats – sofas for lounging and reading (upstairs). Limited and predictable menu – beef and Guinness pie, etc. Open daily 1100-0200.
Derby King is one of the most popular with expats and serves what are reputed to be the best club sandwiches in Asia.

Music Café, Patpong 1. Open 2000-0200, a large open-plan, clean bar, with bags of atmosphere and frequented mainly by drinkers, rather than dancers.

Noriega's Bar, 106/108 Soi 4, Silom Rd, T02-2332814, open 1800-0200. Words like minimalist and Zen spring to mind in this relatively quiet watering hole on an otherwise bustling strip. Live acts on Sat, Sun and Mon nights help cater for the guys, gays and gals this place targets with its promise of booze, broads, bites and blues.

O'Reilly's, corner of Silom and Thaniya, is another themed Irish pub, run by a Thai (Chak) but with all the usual cultural accoutrements – Guinness and Kilkenney, rugby on the satellite, etc. Open 0800-0200.

Radio City, Patpong 1, open 2000-0100, airy and opening right onto the road, this is one of the most popular joints in the area, where locals and westerners alike come to break down the door to see Thai Tom, the local answer to international adoration of Tom Jones.

White Bar, 114/15 Silom Soi 4, T01-4823520 (mob), www.whitebarbangkok.com. Open 2000-0200. Plays contemporary dance music, with good guest DJs on Fri and Sat from the UK, New Zealand, Australia and the US. Bit of a concrete bunker, but it dishes out very generous cocktail measures.

Sukhumvit Road *p114,, map p114*

The strip of bars that run the length of Sukhumvit Rd are mostly populated by bargirls and their admirers. These watering holes usually pump out bad music and serve awful German food and tepid lager. Delve a bit further into Sukhumvit's sois and backstreets and you'll find a happening, urban nightclub scene, the match of anything in Asia. If you want to indulge in more than just alcohol, be careful of the notorious urine tests (see the introduction to the bars and clubs listings) – the nightclubs in this area are particular targets.

Bed Supper Club, 26 Sukhumvit Soi 11, T02-6513537, www.bedsupperclub.com. Open daily 2000-0200. A futuristic white-pod, filled with funky beats, awesome cocktails, superb food, gorgeous designer furniture and hordes of Bangkok's beautiful people. Can be overbearingly stuck-up and incredibly pretentious but is still one of the best spots in Asia to strut your stuff.

Cheap Charlie's, 1 Sukhumvit Soi 11. Very popular with ex-pats, backpackers and locals, open 1500 until very late. Cheap and unpretentious open-air bar.

Jools Bar, 21/3 Nana Tai, Sukhumvit Soi 4. Open 0900-0100. A favourite watering hole for Brits. Also serves classic English food.

Log Cabin, Thonglor Soi 18, Sukhumvit 55, T02-7147810. A large and vibrant bar with live music, happy hour 1730-1900.

Q Bar, 34 Sukhumvit Soi 11, T02-2523274, www.qbarbangkok.com. Housed in a modern building, it is the reincarnation of photographer David Jacobson's bar of the same name in Ho Chi Minh City. Good beats, great drinks menu and sophisticated layout. Has seen better days being surpassed by both **Bed Supper Club** and the **Met Bar** as the hippest place in town. Open 1800-0200, with live acid jazz on Sun.

Riva's, **Sheraton Grande Sukhumvit Hotel**, Sukhumvit Rd. Great jazz, often with leading US performers, makes this one of the best and most sophisticated jazz spots in town. Also serves great food.

The Londoner Brew Pub, Basement, UBC II Building, Sukhumvit 33, open 1100-0200. A large pub, now brewing its English-style ales and also sells usual lagers.

Ministry of Sound (MOS) opened a branch at 2 Sukhumvit Soi 12, T02-2295850-3, open Mon-Thu and Sun 2200-0200, Fri-Sat 2130-0200, featuring DJs from London and Hong Kong as well as local talent. Music varies through the week. Mon is vodka jelly party, Wed is 70s and '80s night and Sun is urban night.

Narcissus, 112 Sukhumvit Soi 23, T02-2582549 open 2100-0200. The classy, art deco Narcissus was awarded Metro's Best Nighclub award in 2001. The music here is trance, house and techno and the clientele are office types trying to hold on to their youth.

Zanzibar, 139 Sukhamvit Soi 11, T02-6512700 open 1730-0200. Bistro-style bar/restaurant with comfortable armchairs and a relaxing atmosphere. Plenty of glass walls, plants and trees give it that half inside, half outside feeling. Music is usually chilled jazz and blues and it regularly has live Thai bands.

Gay and lesbian bars and clubs

If you want to sample Bangkok's gay and lesbian scene you should be in for a riot of pleasure and leisure. With a highly visible, dynamic gay culture Bangkok is slowly matching San Francisco, Sydney and London as one of the great gay cities. From the famous ka-toeys (transexual Lady Boys) through to drag queens, the annual **Bangkok Pride Festival** in Lumphini Pk (mid-Nov) to the plethora of great bars and clubs, you will have a ball.

Like much else in Thailand, the tolerance that has allowed Bangkok's scene to flourish is not all that it seems. Many homosexuals have to take on the mores of 'straight' family life, getting married and having children, in order to be accepted. For a lot of Thais, homosexuality is something that should be kept quiet and hidden in the closet. And while Bangkok is largely tolerant, don't expect the same understanding in other parts of the country.

If it's your first time in Thailand, **Utopia Tours**, www.utopia-tours.com, specializes in organizing gay travel, included licensed tours of Bangkok. Its website also contains a huge amount of listings, contacts and insights for gays and lesbians.

Thai lesbians don't like using the term 'lesbian' due to its frequent use by sex clubs who put on performances of women-on-women sex for the viewing pleasure of men. The preferred term is 'tom-dee" – tom for the usually close-cropped butch girls and dee for the more glamorous la-dee. The lesbian scene is less prominent than the gay community. The **Anjaree Group** collective is an organizing body that campaigns on behalf of lesbians – it can be contacted via the **Utopia Tours** website. See also the Gay and lesbian section in Essentials, page 23.

The hub of Bangkok's gay scene can be found on Silom sois 2 and 4, with clubs, bars and restaurants.

Balcony , 86-8 Silom Soi 4, cute bar where you can hang out on the terraces watching the action below. Daily 1700-0200. **DJ Station**, Silom Soi 2, www.dj-station.com. This is the busiest and largest club on a busy soi. Three floors of pumping beats and flamboyant disco. ฿100 admission, daily 2200-0200. Essential and recommended.

The Expresso, 8/6-8 Silom Soi 2. Good place to relax, with subdued lights and a lounge atmosphere. Daily, 2200-0200.

Sphinx and Pharoah's, Silom Soi 4. Sited at the end of the soi this comfy little restaurant serves excellent food, including great larb. There's a karaoke bar upstairs. Mon-Thu 1700-0100, Fri 1700-0200, Sat and Sun, 1900-0200.

Telephone, 114/11-13 Silom Soi 4. Western style gay bar where phones at the tables allow you to call other guests. Daily 1800-0200.

The lesbian scene is a spread out thinly across the city:

Dog Days, 100/2-6 Phra Arthit Rd, Banglamphu. Cute art-bar serving a limited menu of decent food and drinks. Open daily 1000-1500, 1700-2400. A favourite of tom-dees.

Kitchenette, Duchess Plaza, Sukhumvit Soi 55. Chilled bar with an older tom-dee scene. Live folk music Fri and Sat. Mon-Sat 1700-2400.

Entertainment

International arts

Listings of current shows and exhibitions are provided in the monthly **Bangkok Metro**. For films, books and other Anglocentric entertainment, check in 'What's On' section of Sunday **Bangkok Post**'s magazine for programme of events.

About Cafe/About Studio, 402-8 Maitri Chit Rd, T02-6231742. A centre of the creative arts buried deep in the heart of Chinatown, you'll find everything from performances through to works hanging in the toilets. There are Djs, a bar, poetry readings, live music and lots of retro furniture. Daily 1900-2400. Recommended.

Alliance Française, 29 South Sathorn Rd. Great place for showcasing French culture and movies.

Bangkok University Art Gallery, 3rd floor, building 9, Kluaynam Thai Campus, Rama IV Rd. Important though tiny showcase space that mainly exhibits student work. Daily 0900-1700.

British Council, 254 Chulalongkorn Soi 64 (Siam Sq), T02-6116830, F2535311.

Chulalongkorn Art Centre, 7th floor, Central Library Building, Phayathai Rd, Chulalongkorn University. Another important university space, though you'll find more than just student work here with international artists regularly exhibiting. Mon-Fri 0800-1600.

Goethe Institute, 18/1 South Sathorn Rd, Soi Atthakan Prasit, T02-2870942, www.goethe.de/so/ban. Hosts everything from classical music through to art exhibitions. International and Thai.

Siam Society, 131 Soi 21/Asoke Sukhumvit, T02-2583494. Promotes Thai culture and organizes trips within (and beyond) Thailand. Open Tue-Sat.

Space Contemporary Art, 582/9 Ekkamai Soi 6, Sukhumvit, T02-7114427. Edgy, alternative art in a unique gallery space. Hit and miss, but you will often find some unusual work here. Mon-Sat 1000-1700.

Cinemas

Remember to stand for the National Anthem, which is played before every performance.

Most cinemas have daily showings at 1200, 1400, 1700, 1915 and 2115, with a 1300 matinee on weekends and holidays. Prices can range from ฿50-300 – so-called 'love seats' will set you back ฿200. Details of showings from English-language newspapers.

Cinemas with English soundtracks include **Central Theatre 2**, Central Plaza Lad Prao, T02-5411858. **EGV**, 6th floor, Siam Discovery Centre (Siam Tower), Rama I Rd (opposite Siam Sq), T02-6580455. Classy cinema with an added attraction of EGV gold where for ฿500 you can lounge in supreme comfort and have snacks brought to you. **Lido Multiplex**, 256 Rama I Rd, Siam Sq, T02-2526498. **Metro**, Petchaburi Rd, T02-2529764. **Pantip**, Pantip Plaza, 604/3 Petchaburi Rd, T02-2512861. **Scala**, Siam Sq Soi 1, T02-2512861. **UA Emporium**, Sukhumvit Soi 24, T02-6648711.

Sports fairs

Sanaam Luang, near the Grand Palace, is a good place to sample traditional Thai sports. From late Feb to the middle of Apr there is a traditional Thai Sports Fair held here. It is possible to watch **kite fighting** and **takraw** (the only Thai ball game – a takraw ball is made of rattan, 12-15 cm in diameter. Players hit the ball over a net, using their feet, head, knees and elbows – but not hands – and the ball should not be touched by the same team member twice in succession. Regions of Thailand tend to have their own variations; sepak takraw is the competition sport with a nationwide code of rules).

Thai boxing

Thai boxing is both a sport and a means of self-defence and was first developed during the Ayutthaya period, 1351-1767. It differs from western boxing in that contestants are allowed to use almost any part of their body. Traditional music is played during bouts. There are 2 main boxing stadiums in Bangkok – **Lumpini**, T02-2514303, on Rama IV Rd, near Lumpini Park, and **Rachdamnern Stadium**, T02-2814205, Rachdamnern Nok Av. At Lumpini, boxing nights are Tue and Fri (1830-2300) and Sat (1700), up to and over ฿1,000 for a ringside seat (depending on the card); cheaper seats cost from about ฿150 (in reality, standing) with so-called second-class seats at ฿400. At Rachdamnern Stadium, 1 Rachdamnern Rd (near the TAT office), boxing nights are Mon and Wed (1800-2200), Thu (1700 and 2100), Sun (1600 and 2000), seats from ฿160-500. Bouts can also be seen occasionally at the **National Stadium** on Rama I Rd (Pathumwan) and at Hua Mark Stadium near Ramkhamhaeng University on Khlong Ton Rd. Or you can just turn on the television – bouts are often televized live.

If you want to learn more about the sport contact the **Muai Thai Institute**, 336/932 Prachathiphat, Pathum Thani, www.muay thai.th.net.

Thai performing arts

Classical dancing and music is often performed at restaurants after a 'traditional'

Thai meal has been served. Many tour companies or travel agents organize these 'cultural evenings'.
Baan Thai Restaurant, 7 Sukhumvit Soi 32, T02-2585403, open 2100-2145.
College of Dramatic Arts, near National Theatre, T02-2241391.
College Siam Thai Classical Dance and Restaurant Theatre, 496 Sukhumvit Rd, between Soi 22 and 24, T02-2595128. Two shows per evening at 1930 and 2100.
National Theatre, Na Phrathat Rd, T02-2214885, for programme. Thai classical dramas, dancing and music on the last Fri of each month at 1730 and periodically on other days.
Thailand Cultural Centre, Rachdaphisek Rd, Huai Khwang, T02-2470028, for programme of events.

Festivals and events

January-February

Red Cross Fair (**movable**), held in Amporn Gardens next to the Parliament. Stalls, classical dancing, folk performances, etc.
Chinese New Year (**movable**), Chinatown closes down, but Chinese temples are packed.
Handicraft Fair (**mid-month**), all the handicrafts are made by Thai prisoners.

March-April

Kite Flying (**movable, for 1 month**), every afternoon/evening at Sanaam Luang there is kite fighting. An **International Kite Festival** is held in Mar at Sanaam Luang when kite fighting and demonstrations by kite-flyers take place.

May

Royal Ploughing Ceremony (**movable**), this celebrates the official start of the rice-planting season and is held at Sanaam Luang. It is an ancient Brahman ritual and is attended by the king (see page 96).

September

Swan-boat races (**movable**), on the Chao Phraya River.

November

Golden Mount Fair (**movable**), stalls and theatres set-up all around the Golden Mount and Wat Saket. Candles are carried in procession to the top of the mount.
Marathon road race, fortunately at one of the coolest times of year.

December

Trooping of the Colour (**movable**), the elite Royal Guards swear allegiance to the king and march past members of the Royal Family. It is held in the Royal Plaza near the equestrian statue of King Chulalongkorn.

Shopping

After eating the next big love for many Bangkok residents is shopping. From energetic all-night flower and fruit markets through to original – and fake – Louis Vuitton, Bangkok has the lot, though branded, western goods are often cheaper back home. It is also wise to do your shopping at the end of your trip rather than the beginning. That way you'll have had a chance to gauge the real value of things and avoid being overcharged. Most street stalls will try and fleece you, so be prepared to shop around and bargain hard. The traditional street market is now supplemented by other types of shopping. Some arcades target the wealthier shopper, and are dominated by brand-name goods and designer wear. Others are not much more than street side stalls transplanted to an arcade environment. Most department stores are fixed price, though you can still ask for a discount. Most shops do not open until 1000-1100.

Sukhumvit Rd and the sois to the north are lined with shops and stalls, especially around the **Ambassador** and **Landmark** hotels. Many tailors and made-to-measure shoe shops are to be found in this area. Higher up on Sukhumvit Rd particularly around Soi 49 are various antique and furnishing shops.

Nancy Chandler's *Map of Bangkok* is the best shopping guide. See also page 59 for further shopping information.

Antiques

Permission to take antiques out of the country must be obtained from the **Fine Arts Department** on Na Phrathat Rd, T02-2214817. Shops will often arrange export licences for their customers. Buddha images may not be taken out of the country – although many are.

In Bangkok you will find Chinese porcelain, old Thai paintings, Burmese tapestries, wooden figures, hill tribe art, Thai ceramics and Buddhist art. Be careful of fakes – go to the well-known shops only. Even they, however, have been known to sell fake Khmer sculpture which even the experts find difficult to tell apart from the real thing. For the serious, see *Brown, Robin Guide to buying antiques and arts and crafts in Thailand*, (1989) Times Books: Singapore.

Jim Thompson's, Surawong Rd, www.jimthomspon.com, for a range of antiques, wooden artefacts, furnishings and carpets.

L'Arcadia, 12/2 Sukhumvit Soi 23, Burmese antiques, beds, ceramics, doors, good quality and prices are fair. The affable owner Khun Tum is helpful and informative.

NeOld, 149 Surawong Rd, has a good selection of new and old objects, but it's pricey.

Paul's Antiques, 41 Sukhumvit Soi 19 (behind the **Grand Pacific Hotel**), mostly high quality furniture from Thailand and Burma.

Peng Seng, 942/1-3 Rama IV Rd, on the corner of Surawong Rd, has an excellent selection of antiques.

River City, a shopping complex next to the **Royal Orchid Sheraton Hotel**, houses a large number of the more expensive antique shops and is an excellent place to start. Reputable shops here include **Verandah** on the top floor, **The Tomlinson Collection Room 427-428** and **Acala Room** 312 for Tibetan and Nepalese art. More antique shops can be found in **Gaysorn Plaza** on Ploenchit Rd and at the **Jewellery Trade Centre**, 919/1 Silom Rd in the shopping mall on the ground floor called **The Galleria Plaza** or **Silom Galleria**.

Thai House Antiques, 720/6 Sukhumvit (near Soi 28).

Books

Asia Books, 3rd floor of the Emporium. Excellent for books on Asia but less comprehensive than **Kinokuniya Books**. **Asia Books** has 10 other branches including at 221 Sukhumvit Rd, between Sois 15 and 17; 2nd floor, Peninsula Plaza, Rachdamri Rd; Thaniya Plaza 3rd floor, Silom Rd; 2nd floor, Times Square, Sukhumvit Rd; and World Trade Centre 3rd floor, Rachdamri Rd.

Chatuchak Weekend Market (see page 115). Second-hand books are available in sections 22 and 25.

Chulalongkorn University Book Centre, not on campus but in a more convenient location in Siam Sq, next to the British Council; good for academic, business and travel books.

Elite Used Books, 593/5 Sukhumvit Rd, near Villa Supermarket and with a branch at 1/2 Sukhumvit Soi Nana Nua [Soi 3], offers a good range of second-hand books in several languages.

Kinokuniya Books, on the 3rd floor of the Emporium Shopping Centre on Sukhumvit Soi 24 (BTS Phrom Phong Station), has the best selection of English-language books in town (there's another branch on the 6th floor of the Isetan Department Store, World Trade Centre, Rachdamri Rd).

White Lotus, 26 Soi Attakarnprasit, Sathorn Tai Rd, for collectors' books on Southeast Asia and reprints of historical volumes under their own imprint (also available from many other bookshops).

Bronzeware

Thai or the less elaborate western designs are available in Bangkok. There are a number of shops along Charoen Krung, north from Silom Rd, eg **Siam Bronze Factory** at No

1250, also at 714/6-7 Sukhumvit Rd between Sois 26 and 28. The cutlery has become particularly popular and is now even available at the big department stores.

Celadon (Ceramicware)

Distinctive ceramic ware, originally produced during the Sukhothai period (from the late 13th century) and recently revived. **Thai Celadon House**, 8/8 Rachdapisek Rd, Sukhumvit Rd (Soi 16), also sells seconds, or from **Narayana Phand**, 127 Rachdamri Rd.

Clothes

Cheap designer wear with meaningless slogans and a surfeit of labels (on the outside) are available just about everywhere and anywhere, and especially in tourist areas like Patpong and Sukhumvit. Imitation Lacoste and other garments are less obviously on display now that the US is pressurizing Thailand to respect intellectual copyright laws but they are available. Note that the less you pay, generally, the more likely that the dyes will run, shirts will downsize after washing, and buttons will eject themselves at will.
Kai Boutique, 4th floor of Times Square. This building is worth visiting for those interested in what the best designers in Thailand are doing. Many of Bangkok's smartest ladies patronize this establishment.
Vipavee, 1st floor of the Emporium at Sukhumvit Soi 24 (there are lots of other places here as well), for unique funky designer clothes of Indian inspiration.

Tailoring services

Bangkok's tailors are skilled at copying anything; either from fashion magazines or from a piece of your own clothing. Always request a fitting, ask to see a finished garment, ask for a price in writing and pay as small a deposit as possible. Tailors are concentrated along Silom, Sukhumvit and Ploenchit roads and Gaysorn Sq. Indian tailors tend to offer the quickest service.
Ambassador & Smart Fashion, 28-28/1 Sukhumvit Soi 19, T02-253 2993, www.ambassadorfashion.com.
N and Y Boutique, 11 Chartered Bank Lane (Oriental Av), near the **Oriental Hotel** (for ladies' tailored clothes).
New Devis Custom Tailors, 179/2 Sukhumvit Rd, Soi 13, and **Rajawongse**, 130 Sukhumvit Rd (near Sukhumvit Soi 4) have both been recommended.

Department stores

Central is the largest chain of department stores in Bangkok, with a range of Thai and imported goods at fixed prices; credit cards are accepted. Main shops on Silom Rd, Ploenchit Rd and in the Central Plaza, just north of the Northern bus terminal.
Robinson's, on corner of Silom and Rama IV roads, Sukhumvit (near Soi 19) and Rachdamri roads.
Sogo in the Amarin Plaza on Ploenchit Rd.
Thai Daimaru on Rachdamri and Sukhumvit (opposite Soi 71).
Tokyu in MBK Tower on Rama I Rd.
Zen, World Trade Centre, corner of Rama I and Rajdamri roads, soon to have an ice rink.

Furniture

Between Soi 43 and Soi 45, Sukhumvit Rd, is an area where rattan furniture is sold.
Rattan House, 795-797 Sukhumvit Rd (between Soi 43 and 45). **Corner 43**, 487/1-2 Sukhumvit Rd (between Soi 25-27).
For stylish modern furniture visit the shopping mall attached to the **Hilton Hotel** on Witthayu Rd or **Home Place**, a shopping mall on Sukhumvit Soi 55 (Thonglor) at sub-soi No13.

Gold

This is considerably cheaper than in the USA or Europe; there is a concentration of shops along Yaowarat Rd (Chinatown), mostly selling the yellow 'Asian' gold. Price is determined by weight (its so-called 'baht weight').

Handicrafts

Cocoon, 3rd floor, Gaysorn Plaza. Here, traditional Thai objects have been transformed by altering the design slightly and using bright colours. Great for unusual and fun gifts.
State Handicraft Centre (**Narayana Phand**), 127 Rachdamri Rd, just north

of Gaysorn, is a good place to view the range of goods that are made around the country. Cheap but generally poor quality.

Suan Lumpini Night Bazaar, across the road from Lumpini Park (which is between Wireless and Ratchdamri roads), is rather contrived but nonetheless has a good range of shops and stalls selling clothes, tourist trinkets, and handicrafts.

The Thai Craft Museum shop is on the top 2 floors of Gaysorn Plaza and is a collection of stalls. This has a bit more style than Narayana Phand and feels less like a tour bus shopping stop.

Interior design

Siam Discovery Centre (Siam Tower) has some great interior design shops, including **Habitat**, and **Anyroom**, on the 4th floor.

Jewellery

Thailand has become the world's largest gem-cutting centre and it is an excellent place to buy both gems and jewellery. The best buy of the native precious stones is the sapphire. Modern jewellery is well designed and of a high quality. Always insist on a certificate of authenticity and a receipt.

Ban Mo, on Pahurat Rd, north of Memorial Bridge, is the centre of the gem business although there are shops in all the tourist areas particularly on Silom Rd near the intersection with Surasak Rd, eg **Rama Gems**, 987 Silom Rd.

Uthai Gems, 28/7 Soi Ruam Rudi, off Ploenchit Rd, just east of Witthayu Rd, is recommended, as is **P. Jewellery** (Chantaburi), 9/292 Ramindra Rd, Anusawaree Bangkhan, T02-5221857.

For western designs, **Living Extra** and **Yves Joaillier** are to be found on the 3rd floor of the Charn Issara Tower, 942 Rama IV Rd. **Jewellery Trade Centre** (aka Galleria Plaza), next door to the **Holiday Inn Crowne Plaza** on the corner of Silom Rd, and Surasak Rd contains a number of gem dealers and jewellery shops on the ground floor. **Tabtim Dreams** at Unit 109 is a good place to buy loose gems.

Maps

Asia Books sells a very accurate map of Bangkok called Bangkok, Central Thailand Travel Map, published by Periplus Editions, ฿85.

Nelles also publishes a good Bangkok map with an excellent detailed map of the city centre.

Markets

Nancy Chandler's Map of Bangkok, available from most bookshops, is the most useful guide to the markets of the capital.

The markets in Bangkok are an excellent place to browse, take photographs and pick up bargains. They are part of the lifeblood of the city, and the encroachment of more organized shops and the effects of the redeveloper's demolition ball are inimical to one of Bangkok's finest traditions.

Banglamphu Market is close to Khaosan Rd, the backpackers' haven, on Chakrapong and Phra Sumen roads. Stalls here sell clothing, shoes, food and household goods.

Bangrak Market, south of the General Post Office, near the river and the **Shangri-La Hotel**, sells exotic fruit, clothing, seafood and flowers.

Khaosan Rd Market (if it can be called such), close to Banglamphu Market, is much more geared to the needs and desires of the foreign tourist: CDs and cassettes, batik shirts, leather goods and so on.

Nakhon Kasem, known as the **Thieves' Market**, in the heart of Chinatown, see page 101, houses a number of 'antique' shops selling brassware, old electric fans and woodcarvings (tough bargaining is needed and don't expect everything to be genuine).

Naraiphan Shopping Centre and **Narayana Bazaar**, Rachprarop Rd, is an indoor stall/shopping centre affair (concentrated in the basement) geared to tourists and farang residents.

Pahurat Indian Market (see page 101) is a small slice of India in Thailand, with mounds of sarongs, batiks, buttons and bows.

Pak Khlong Market is a wholesale market selling fresh produce, orchids and cut flowers and is situated near the Memorial Bridge. An exciting place to visit at night when the place is a hive of activity (see page 101).

Buying gems and jewellery

More people lose their money through gem and jewellery scams in Thailand than in any other way (60% of complaints to the Tourism Authority Thailand (TAT) involve gem scams).
DO NOT fall for any story about gem sales, special holidays, tax breaks – no matter how convincing.
NEVER buy gems from people on the street (or beach) and try not to be taken to a shop by an intermediary. Any unsolicited approach is likely to be a scam. The problem is perceived to be so serious that in some countries Thai embassies are handing out warning leaflets with visas.

Rules of thumb to avoid being cheated:
Choose a specialist shop in a relatively prestigious part of town (the TAT will recommend shops). Note that no shop are authorized by the TAT or by the Thai government; if they claim as much they are lying. It is advisable to buy from shops which are members of the Thai Gem and Jewellery Traders Association.
Avoid touts.
Never be rushed into a purchase.
Do not believe stories about vast profits from reselling gems at home.
Do not agree to have items mailed ('for safety').
If buying a valuable gem, a certificate of identification is a good insurance policy. The Department of Mineral Resources (Rama VI Rd, T02-2461694) and the Asian Institute of Gemological Sciences (484 Rachadapisek Road, T02-5132112) will both examine stones and give such certificates.
Compare prices; competition is stiff among the reputable shops; be suspicious of 'bargain' prices.
Ask for a receipt detailing the stone and recording the price.

For more information (and background reading on Thailand) the *Buyer's Guide to Thai Gems and Jewellery*, by John Hoskin can be bought at Asia Books.

Patpong Market, arranged down the middle of Patpong Rd, linking Silom and Surawong roads, opens up about 1700 and is geared to tourists, selling handicrafts, T-shirts, leather goods, fake watches, cassettes and videos although some welcome additions include such items as binoculars, all-in-one pliers, etc. Bargain hard.
Penang Market, Khlong Toey, situated under the expressway close to the railway line, specializes in electronic equipment from hi-fis to computers, with a spattering of other goods as well. Watch out for pickpockets in this market!
Phahonyothin Market is Bangkok's newest, opposite the Northern bus terminal, and sells potted plants and orchids.
Pratunam Market is spread over a large area around Rachprarop and Phetburi roads, and is famous for clothing and fabric. Half of it was recently bulldozed for redevelopment, but there is still a multitude of stalls here.
Sampeng Lane (see page 102), close to the Thieves' Market, has stalls specializing in toys, stationery, clothes and household goods.
Stamp Market, next to the General Post Office on Charoen Krung operates on Sun only. Collectors come here to buy or exchange stamps.
Suan Lumpini Night Bazaar, across the road from Lumpini Park, has tried to emulate the success of Chiang Mai's night bazaar, and as a consequence is rather contrived; sells tourist trinkets, handicrafts and such like.
Tewes Market, near the National Library, is a photographers' dream; a daily market, selling flowers and plants.
Weekend Market is the largest and is at Chatuchak Park (see page 115).

West Silom/Charoen Krung (New Road). Antiques, jewellery, silk, stamps, coins and bronzeware. Stalls set up here at 2100.

Music

Tapes and CDs can be bought from many stalls in tourist areas, although the choice is limited. Cheap copies are harder to come by these days, as the genuine article is just ฿100 for a cassette or ฿500 for a CD it makes sense to buy the real McCoy.

CD Warehouse also offers a very good selection of CDs and it has branches in the Siam Centre (4th floor), as well as in the World Trade Centre.

Tower Records is on the top floor of **Siam Centre**, Rama 1 Rd, or on the 3rd floor of **The Emporium** at Sukhumvit Soi 24.

Pottery

There are several pottery 'factories' on the left-hand side of the road on the way to the Rose Garden, near Samut Sakhon (see page 118).

Silk

Beware of 'bargains' as the silk may have been interwoven with rayon. It is best to stick to the well-known shops unless you know what you are doing. Silk varies greatly in quality. Generally, the heavier the weight the more expensive the fabric. One-ply is the lightest and cheapest (about ฿200 per metre), 4-ply the heaviest and most expensive (about ฿300-400 per m). Silk also comes in 3 grades: Grade 1 is the finest and smoothest and comes from the inner part of the cocoon. Finally, there is also 'hard' and 'soft' silk, soft being rather more expensive. Handmade patterned silk, especially matmii from the northeast region, can be much more expensive than simple, single-coloured industrial silk – well over ฿10,000 per piece. There are a number of specialist silk shops at the top of Surawong Rd (near Rama IV) and a number of shops along the bottom half of Silom Rd (towards Charoen Krung) and in the Siam Centre on Rama I Rd.

Anita Thai Silk, 294/4-5 Silom Rd, slightly more expensive than some, but the extensive range makes it worth a visit.

Cabbages and Condoms (also a restaurant) on Sukhumvit Soi 12 and Raja Siam, Sukhumvit Soi 23. Village-made silks.

Chatuchak Weekend Market sells lengths from Laos and northeast Thailand.

Home Made (HM) Thai Silk, 45 Sukhumvit Soi 35, Silk made on premises, good quality matmii silk.

Jagtar, at 37 Sukhumvit Soi 11, has some lovely silk curtain fabrics as well as cushion covers in unusual shades and other accessories made from silk. Originality means prices are high.

Jim Thompson's, top of Surawong Rd, www.jimthompson.com. Famous silk shop which is expensive, but has the best selection. Open daily 0900-2100. See also Jim Thompson's House, page 108.

Khompastr, 52/10 Surawong Rd, near **Montien Hotel**, distinctive screen-printed fabric from Hua Hin.

Shinawatra on Sukhumvit Soi 31. Factory (industrial) silk available.

Shopping malls

No longer do visitors to Bangkok need to suffer the heat of the market stall, Bangkok is fast becoming another Singapore or Hong Kong with shopping malls springing up all over the place.

The Emporium, on Sukhumvit Soi 24 (directly accessible from BTS Phrom Phong Station), is an enormous place, dominated by the **Emporium Department Store** but with many other clothes outlets as well as record and book shops, designer shops and more. The ground and first floors are monopolized by the big names in fashion – Kenzo, Chanel, Versace are all there along with some expensive looking watch and jewellery shops. For the less extravagant there are a number of trendy clothes shops on the 2nd floor, namely Phalene and Soda. The 3rd floor has the more prosaic offerings in the way of shops – **Boots the Chemists** has recently opened a store here. **Exotique Thai** occupies the space between the escalators on the 4th floor. Here you can find a nice selection of decorative items for the home while the 5th floor is dedicated to household goods along with a large food hall.

Mah Boonkhrong Centre (MBK) on the corner of Phayathai and Rama 1, is long-established and downmarket and packed full of bargains with countless small shops/stalls. **Peninsula Plaza**, between the **Hyatt Erawan** and **Regent** hotels, is considered one of the smarter shopping plazas in Bangkok. **Pratunam Market**, north along Rachprasong Rd, crossing over Khlong Saensap, at the intersection with Phetburi Rd, is good for fabrics and clothing. **Siam Discovery Centre** (Siam Tower), 6 storeys of fashion across the road from Siam Sq, is more sophisticated than MBK and you are unlikely to pick up many cut-price goods. All the top designers have a presence here. **Siam Square**, at the intersection of Phayathai and Rama I roads. For teenage trendy western clothing, bags, belts, jewellery, bookshops, some antique shops and American fast-food chains. **Tokyu Department Store**, Siam Sq. Used to be great for cheap clothes, leather goods, etc, but each year it inches further upmarket. **World Trade Centre**, **Thai Daimaru**, **Robinson's**, **Gaysorn Plaza**, **Naraiphan** shopping centre (more of a market-stall affair, geared to tourists, in the basement) and **Central Chitlom** (which burnt down in a fire in 1995 but is now renovated) are a short distance to the east of the Peninsula Plaza, centred on Ploenchit/Rachprarop roads. They are shopping arcades and large department stores.

Spectacles

Glasses and contact lenses are a good buy in Bangkok and can be made up in 24 hrs. Opticians are to be found throughout the city.

Supermarkets

Central Department Store (see Department stores listing). **Isetan** (World Trade Centre), Rachdamri Rd. **Robinson's** – open until 2400 (see Department stores listing). **Villa Supermarket**, between Sois 33 and 35, Sukhumvit Rd (and branches elsewhere in town) – for everything you are unable to find anywhere else. The **Villa** supermarkets are the best place to go to for the more exotic imported foods and the branch on Sukhumvit road is open 24 hrs.

Textiles

Prayer Textile Gallery, 197 Phayathai Rd, good range and excellent quality traditional and Laotian textiles.

Wood working

Lots of woodworking shops along Worachak Rd at the point where it crosses Khlong Banglamphu. **Bua Thong** is recommended, although the sign is only in Thai. Good places to buy bracelets, curtain rings and trinkets fashioned from tropical hardwoods.

Activities and tours

Facilities for sports such as badminton, squash or tennis are either available at the 4- and 5-star hotels or are listed in Bangkok's *Yellow Pages* and the monthly publications *Metro* and Bangkok *Timeout*.

Bowling

Cosmo Bowl, Floor 7, Central Rama III, T02-6736360. Open Mon-Fri 1100-0100, Sat-Sun 1000-0200. 36 lanes, ฿45-70 per game depending on day and time. **PS Bowl**, 1191 Ramkamhaeng Rd, Huamark. Open Mon-Thu 1000-0100, Fri-Sun 1000-0200. **Sukhumvit Bowl**, 2 Sukhumvit Soi 63 (Ekamoi). Open daily 1000-0100.

Cookery courses

Mrs Balbir, 155/18 Sukhumvit Soi 11, T02-6510498, www.mrsbalbir.com. Every Fri morning, in which she instructs small classes of 10 or so, ฿450. **Oriental Hotel**, T02-4376211, organizes an intensive 4-day course, with different areas of cuisine covered each day, 0900-1200. ฿2,500 per class or ฿11,500 for 5 classes. The classes take place in an old teak house on

Traditional Thai massage

While a little less arousing than the Patpong-style massage, the traditional Thai massage (*nuat boraan*) is probably more invigorating, using methods similar to those of Shiatsu, reflexology and osteopathic manipulation. It probably has its origins in India and is a form of yoga. It aims to release blocked channels of energy and soothe tired muscles.

The thumbs are used to apply pressure on the 10 main 'lines' of muscles, so both relaxing and invigorating the muscles. Headaches, ankle and knee pains, neck and back problems can all be alleviated through this ancient art (a European visitor to the Siamese court at Ayutthaya 400 years ago noted the practice of Thai massage). Centres of massage can be found in most Thai towns – wats and tourist offices are the best sources of information. In Bangkok, Wat Pho is the best-known centre and murals on the temple buildings' walls help to guide the student. For Thais, this form of massage is as much a spiritual experience as a physical one – hence its association with monasteries and the Buddha (see page 93).

the other bank of the Chao Phraya – student gastronomes are ferried across from the hotel. For US$2,500 it is possible to combine the course with staying at the hotel, breakfast and a jet lag massage. **Wandee's Kitchen School**, 134/5-6 Silom Rd (on the 5th floor, above the Dokya Book Shop), T02-2372051. Also offers a 5-day, 40-hr course from Mon-Fri but at the slightly cheaper rate of ฿5,200. Successful students emerge with a certificate and reeking faintly of chillies and nam plaa.
UFM Baking and Cooking School, 593/29-39 Sukhumvit Soi 33, T02-2590620, www.ufmeducation.com. A variety of classes are held Mon-Sat, in groups of about 10; and politically incorrectly named **Modern Housewife Centre**, 45/6-7 Sethsiri Rd, T02-279283.

Diving

Dive Master, 110/63 Ladprao Soi 18, T02-5121664, F5124889. Organizes dive trips, NAVI and PADI courses and sells (or rents) diving equipment.

Golf

Most courses open at 0600 and play continues till dusk. Green fees start at roughly ฿500. Weekday green fees are two-thirds or less of the weekend fees. Most also have clubs for hire (as well as shoes) and players are expected to use caddies. Telephone beforehand to check on availability.
Bangpoo Country Club, Km 37 191 Mu 9, Praksa Muang, T02-324323. 18-hole course designed by Arnold Palmer; oddly set within an industrial estate on the outskirts of Bangkok.
Muang-Ake, 34 Mu 7, Phahonyothin Rd, Amphoe Muang, Pathum Thani, T02- 5359335. 40 mins from city centre. Club hire. Phone to check regulations for temporary membership.
Royal Dusit Royal Turf Club, 183 Phitsanulok Rd, T02-2811330. Small 18-hole course competing with the racetrack for space; no golf during race days (check the *Bangkok Post* or *Nation*).
There are also a number of golf practice/ driving ranges off New Phetburi and Sukhumvit roads.

Health clubs

Expensive hotels have fitness centres and health clubs.
Phillip Wain International, 8th floor, Pacific Place, 140 Sukhumvit Rd, T02-2542544. Open Mon-Sat 0700-2200.

Horse racing

At the **Royal Turf Club** and **Royal Sports Club** on alternate Sun from 1230 to 1800, each card usually consists of 10 races. Check newspapers for details.

Kite flying

Kites are sold at Sanaam Luang for ฿15-20 on Sun and public holidays during the 'season'.

Swimming

Department of Physical Education, Rama I Rd (next to Mahboonkrong Shopping Centre). Open Tue-Fri 1500-1800, Sat-Sun 0900-1800. ฿20 per hr. A reasonably priced and central pool. Good value.
SASA International House, north end of Chulalaongkorn University, 254 Soi Chulalongkorn 12, Phayathai Rd, T02-2163880.

Tennis

Many hotels have courts.
Aree Golf and Tennis, Sukhumvit Soi 26, T02-2598425. Public courts open daily 0630-2230, ฿120 per hr (0630-1730), ฿170 (1730-2230), 4 courts, racket hire, coaching, food available.
Santisuk Courts, Sukhumvit Soi 38, T02-3911830. Open daily 0700-2200, ฿80 per hr, 6 courts, racket hire, cash only.

Theme parks

Dream World, 10 mins' drive from Don Muang Airport at Km 7 on the Rangsit-Ong Kharak Rd, T02-5331152. Open Mon-Fri 1000-1700, Sat- Sun 1000-1900. ฿450. Getting there: bus nos 39, 59 and 29 to Rangsit and then local bus. Fairground fantasy land-cum-historical recreation.
Magic Land, 72 Phahonyothin Rd, T02-5131731. Amusement park with ferris wheel etc. Open Mon-Fri 1000-1700, Sat-Sun 1000-1900. ฿100, plus additional charges for rides. Getting there: near Central Plaza Hotel – ask for 'Daen Neramit'.

Therapies

Meditation

Thai Meditation Centre, World Fellowship of Buddhists building, 33 Sukhumvit Rd, (between Soi 1 and Soi 3), T02-2511188. Open Mon-Fri 0900-1630. Meditation classes at the latter are held in English on Wed at 1700-2000; lectures on Buddhism are held on the first Wed of each month at 1800-2000.
Wat Bowonniwet in Banglamphu on Phra Sumen Rd (see Old City map).
Wat Mahathat, T02-2226011, facing Sanaam Luang, is Bangkok's most renowned meditation centre (see page 97). Anyone interested is welcome to attend the daily classes – the centre is located in Khana 5 of the monastery. English instruction can be arranged. IBMC classes in English are held on the 2nd and 4th Sat of each month, 1600-1800.

Traditional Thai massage

Centres offering quality massages by trained practitioners include:
Marble House, 37/18-19 Soi Surawong Plaza (opposite Montien Hotel), T02-2353519. Open daily 0100-2400.
Vejakorn, 37/25 Surawong Plaza, Surawong Rd, T02-2375576. Open daily 1000-2400. Expect to pay around ฿200-300 for a 1-hr body massage and about the same for a 45-min foot massage. Make sure you are getting 'raksaa tang nuat' (traditional Thai massage), otherwise you'll be in for the more pornographic variety. See also box page 148.
Wat Pho. The centre is located at the back of the wat, on the opposite side from the entrance. For details, T02-211-2974, www.watpho.com. The school offers body massage, body massage with herbs and foot massage. The massage service is available from 0800-1700 and the cost of a 30-min massage is ฿150 or ฿250 for an hour-long body massage. The herbal body massage costs ฿350. A foot massage is ฿250 for 45 mins. For westerners wishing to learn the art of traditional Thai massage, special 30-hr courses can be taken for ฿7,000, stretching over either 15 days (2 hrs per day) or 10 days (3 hrs per day). There is also a foot massage course at ฿3,600 which stretches over 15 hrs during 3 days.

Yoga

Sunee Yoga Centre, 2nd floor, Pratunam Centre, 78/4 Rachprarop Rd, T02-2549768. Open Mon-Sat 1000-1200 and 1700-1900.

Tours and tour operators

Bangkok has innumerable tour companies that can take visitors virtually anywhere. If there is not a tour to fit your bill – most run

the same range of tours – many companies will produce a customized one for you, for a price. Most top hotels have their own tour desk and it is probably easiest to book through it (arrange to be picked up from your hotel as part of the deal). The tours given below are the most popular; prices per person are about ฿400-800 for a half day, ฿1,000-2,000 for a full day (including lunch).

Half-day tours

Grand Palace Tour; Temple Tour to Wat Traimitr, Wat Pho and Wat Benjamabophit; Khlong Tour around the khlongs (canals) of Bangkok and Thonburi, to Floating Market, Snake Farm and Wat Arun (mornings only); Old City Tour; Crocodile Farm Tour; Rice Barge and Khlong Tour (afternoons only); Damnoen Saduak Floating Market Tour.

Full-day tours

Damnoen Saduak and Rose Garden; Thai Dinner and Classical Dance, eat in traditional Thai surroundings and consume toned-down Thai food, ฿250-300, 1900-2200. Pattaya, the infamous beach resort; River Kwai, a chance to see the famous bridge and war cemeteries, as well as the great chedi at Nakhon Pathom; Ayutthaya and Bang Pa In.

Alternative tours

A number of so-styled 'alternative' tour companies are springing up in Bangkok. One of the best is run by the **Thai Volunteer Services**' (TVS) Responsible Ecological and Social Tour (REST) project. TVS is an NGO with links to other upcountry NGOs. People visit and stay in rural villages, go trekking and camping, are shown round local development projects and are encouraged to participate in community activities. Costs are around ฿3,000-4,000 for 3-4-day tours. Contact T02-6910437 and see www.ecotour.in.th.

Boat tours

Either book a tour at your hotel or go to one of the piers and organize your own trip. The most frequented piers are located between the **Oriental Hotel** and the **Grand Palace** or under Taksin Bridge (which marks the end of the Skytrain line. The pier just to the south of the **Royal Orchid Sheraton Hotel** is recommended. Organizing your own trip gives greater freedom to stop and start when the mood takes you. It is best to go in the morning (0700). For the trip mentioned above under half-day tours (excluding Wat Rakhang and Wat Suwannaram), the cost for a hang yaaw which can sit 10 people should be about ฿500-1,000 depending on the stops, distance and duration. If visiting Rakhang and Suwannaram as well as the other sights, expect to pay about another ฿200-300 for the hire of a boat. Be sure to settle the route and cost before setting out. There are more than 30 boats (in addition to hang yaaws and regular ferries) offering cruises on the Chao Phraya. The *Ayutthaya Princess* operates from the Shangri-La Hotel pier or the Royal Sheraton pier. The *Ayutthaya Princess* is a 2-level vessel resembling a royal barge. Leaving at 0800 daily, there are cruises to Bang Pa In, an a/c bus tour around Ayutthaya, returning to Bangkok by coach at 1730. You can also do the reverse: coach to Ayutthaya and then a boat back to Bangkok, arriving at 1730, ฿1,250, including buffet lunch on board. Kian Gwan Building, 140 Wireless Rd, T02-2559200.

Cheaper are the day boat tours to Bang Pa In via Queen Sirikit's handicraft centre at Bang Sai and the stork sanctuary at Wat Phai Lom operated by the **Chao Phraya Express Boat Company**. Tours leave on Sat and Sun only from the Maharaj and Phra Athit piers at 0800 and 0805 respectively, returning 1530, ฿180 or ฿240, T02-2225330. Another company offering a professional cruise service is **Pearl of Siam** operates 3 'yachts'. Like other companies, it offers passengers either a bus trip up to Ayutthaya and a cruise down, or vice versa (฿1,600). In the evenings the company also offers dinner cruises for ฿1,100.

Cruise Asia Ltd, 133/14 Rajthevee Rd, T02-6401400, www.cruiseasia.net runs 4 and 7 day trips on the River Kwai on the *RV Kwai*.

Dinner cruises

Chao Phraya, T02-4335453; **Loy Nava**, T02-4374932, ฿700. **Wanfah Cruise**, T02-4335453, ฿650. **Ayutthaya Princess**, T02-2559200, organizes Sunday dinner cruise for ฿850.

Train tours

State Railway of Thailand organizes day trips to Nakhon Pathom and the bridge

over the River Kwai and to Ayutthaya. Both trips run on weekends and holidays. The latter tour leaves Bangkok at 0630 and returns from Ayutthaya by boat along the Chao Phraya River.

Tour operators

Travel agents abound in the tourist and hotel areas of the city – Khaosan Rd/Banglamphu, Sukhumvit, Soi Ngam Duphli and Silom (several down Pan Rd, a soi opposite Silom Village). All major hotels will have their own in-house agent. Most will book airline, bus and train tickets, arrange tours, and book hotel rooms. Because there are so many to choose from, it is worth shopping around for the best deal. For those wishing to travel to Vietnam, Laos, Cambodia and Burma, specialist agents are recommended as they are usually able to arrange visas – for a fee. **Asian Holiday Tour**, 294/8 Phayathai Rd, T02-2155749. **Asian Lines Travel**, 755 Silom Rd, T02-2331510. **Asian Trails**, 9th floor, SG Tower, 161/1 Soi Mahadlek Luang 3, Rajdamri Rd, T02-6262000, www.asiantrails.net. **Banglamphu Tour Service**, 17 Khaosan Rd, T02-2813122. **Dee Jai Tours**, 2nd floor, 491/29 Silom Plaza Building, Silom Rd, T02-2341685, F2374231. **Diethelm Travel**, Kian Gwan Building II, 140/1, Witthayu Rd, T02-2559150, F2560248. **Dior Tours**, 146-158 Khaosan Rd, T02-2829142. **East-West**, 46/1 Sukhumvit Soi Nana Nua, T02-2530681. **Exotissimo**, 21/17 Sukhumvit Soi 4, T02-2535240, F2547683 and 755 Silom Rd, T02-2359196, F2834885. **Fortune Tours**, 9 Captain Bush Lane, Charoen Krung 30, T02-2371050. **GM Tour & Travel**, 273 Khaosan Rd, T02-2823979, F2810642. One of the more efficient operations, with impartial flight information. **Guest House and Tour**, 46/1 Khaosan Rd, T02-2823849, F2812348. **MK Ways**, 57/11 Witthayu Rd, T02-2555590, F2545583. **Patco Chiang Mai**, Hualamphong Railway Station tourist office, organizes treks in the north, recommended. **Pawana Tour and Travel**, 72/2 Khaosan Rd, T02-2678018, F2800370. **Roong Ruang Tour Travel Centre Co**, 183-185 Samsen Rd, T02-2801460. **Siam Wings**, 173/1-3 Surawong Rd, T02-2534757, F2366808. **Skyline Travel Service**, 491/39-40 Silom Plaza (2nd floor), Silom Rd, T02-2331864, F2366585. **St Louis Travel**, 18/7 Soi St Louis 3, Sathorn Tai Rd, T/F02-2121583. **Thai Travel Service**, 119/4 Surawong Rd, T02-2349360. **Top Thailand Tour**, 61 Khaosan Rd, T02-2802251, F2823337. **Tour East**, Rajapark Building (10th floor), 163 Asoke Rd, T02-2593160, F2583236. **Transindo**, Thasos Building (9th floor), 1675 Chan Rd, T02-2873241, F2873246. **Vieng Travel**, branch on the ground floor of the Trang Hotel, 99/8 Wisutkaset Rd, T02-2803537. **Vista Travel**, 244/4 Khaosan Rd, T02-2800348. **Western Union**, branch in the foyer of Atlanta Hotel, 78 Sukhumvit Soi 2, T02-2552151. Good all-round service.

Transport

Bangkok lies at the heart of Thailand's transport network. Virtually all trains and buses end up here and it is possible to reach anywhere in the country from the capital. Bangkok is also a regional transport hub, and there are flights to most international destinations. See Essentials, pages 81 and 50, for flight, train and bus fares. See also Essentials, page 31, for international transportation.

Transport to town from the airport

Bus

An a/c airport bus service operates every 15 mins, 0500-2400, ฿70 to Silom Rd (service A1), Sanaam Luang (service A2) (most convenient for Khaosan Road guesthouses) and Phra Khanong (service A3). Stops are as follows: **Silom service (A1)**: Don Muang Tollway, Din Daeng, Pratunam, Lumpini Park, Silom. This service stops at the following hotels: Century, Indra, Anoma, Grand Hyatt, Erawan, Regent, Dusit Thani and Narai hotels. **Sanaam Luang service (A2)**: Don Muang Tollway, Din Daeng, Victory Monument, Phayathai, Phetburi, Lan Luang, Democracy Monument, Sanaam Luang. This service stops at the following hotels: Victory Monument, Siam City Hotel, Soi King Phet, Saphan Khao, Majestic and Rattanakosin hotels. **Phra Khanong service (A3)**: Don

Muang Tollway, Din Daeng, Sukhumvit, Ekamai, Phra Khanong. Hotel stops are: Amari Building, Ambassador and Delta Grand Pacific hotels, Bang Chan Glass House, Novotel, Soi Ekkamai (Sukhumvit). Note that return buses have slightly different stops.

Although many visitors will see ฿70 as money well spent (but note that for 3 or 4 passengers in a taxi is as cheap or cheaper) there will still be the hardened few who will opt for the **regular bus service**. This is just as cheap and slow as it ever was, 1½-3 hrs (depending on time of day) (฿7-15). The bus stop is 50 m north of the arrivals hall. Buses are crowded during rush hours and there is little room for luggage. Bus 59 goes to Khaosan Rd, bus 29 goes to Bangkok's Hualamphong railway station, via the Northern bus terminal and Siam Sq. A/c bus 10 goes to Samsen Rd and Silom Rd via the Northern bus terminal; a/c bus 4 goes to Silom Rd, air-conditioned bus 13 goes to Sukhumvit Rd and the Eastern bus terminal, a/c bus 29 goes to the Northern bus terminal, Siam Sq and Hualamphong railway station.

Courtesy car

Many upmarket hotels will meet passengers and provide transport to town gratis. Check before arrival or contact the Thai Hotels Association desk in the terminal building.

Ferry

A civilized way to avoid the traffic – if booked in the **Oriental, Shangri-la** or **Sheraton hotels** – is to get a minibus from the airport to the ferry terminal on the river. Then take the hour-long river crossing by long-tailed boat to the appropriate hotel.

Minibus

฿100 to major hotels, ฿60 shuttle bus to the Asia Hotel on Phayathai Rd. ฿50-80 to Khaosan Rd, depending on the time of day. Direct buses to Pattaya at 0900, 1200 and 1700, ฿180.

Taxi

There is an official taxi booking service in the arrivals hall. There are three sets of taxi/limousine services. First, **airport limos** (before exiting from the restricted area), next **airport taxis** (before exiting from the terminal building), and finally, a **public taxi counter** (outside, on the slipway). The latter are the cheapest. Note that airport flunkies sometimes try to direct passengers to the more expensive 'limousine' service: walk through the barriers to the public taxi desk. A public taxi to downtown should cost roughly ฿250. Note that tolls on the expressways are paid on top of the fare on the meter (฿70, one payment of ฿30 and one of ฿40). If taking a metered taxi, the coupon from the booking desk will quote no fare – ensure that the meter is used or you may find that the trip costs ฿300 instead of ฿200. There is a ฿50 airport surcharge on top of the meter cost. Keep hold of your coupon – some taxi drivers try to pocket it – as it details the obligations of taxi drivers. Don't be surprised if your driver decides to feign that he does not know where to go: it's all part of being a new boy/girl in a new town. Some regular Don Muang visitors recommend going up to the departures floor and flagging down a taxi that has just dropped passengers off. Doing it this way will save you around ฿50 and you should be able to get into town for less than ฿200.

There have been cases of visitors being robbed in unofficial taxis. To tell whether your vehicle is a registered taxi, check the colour of the number plate. Official aiport limousines have green plates, public taxis have yellow plates – and a white plate means the vehicle is not registered as a taxi. It takes 30 mins to 1 hr to get to central Bangkok, depending on the time of day and the state of the traffic. The elevated expressway can reduce journey time to 20 min – ask the taxi driver to take this route if you wish to save time but note, again, that there is a toll fee. Also note that there have been some complaints about taxi drivers at the domestic terminal forming a cartel, refusing to use their meters and charging a fixed rate considerably above the meter rate.

Train

The station is on the other side of the north-south highway from the airport. It is well signposted in the airport. Regular trains into Bangkok's Hualamphong station, ฿5 for ordinary train, 3rd class (the cheapest option), 45 mins. There are only six ordinary trains per day. For 'rapid' and 'express' a supplementary

charge of ฿40-60 is levied. The **State Railways of Thailand** runs an 'Airport Express' 5 times a day (but not on Sat and Sun), with a/c shuttle bus from Don Muang station to airport terminal, 35 mins (฿100).

Air

Don Muang Airport is 25 km north of the city. For airport enquiries call, T02-2860190. There are regular connections on **THAI** to many of the provincial capitals. Tickets can also be bought at most travel agents. Bangkok Airways flies to **Koh Samui**, **Hua Hin**, **Phuket**, **Sukhothai**, **Chiang Mai** and **U-Tapao (Pattaya)**. It has an office in the domestic terminal at Don Muang. **Bangkok Airways** has its own check-in area and departure lounge on the ground floor of the domestic terminal (not on the 1st floor). For information on how to get to and from the airport see above. For air timetables, routes and fares, see Essentials.

A new international airport to the east of the city at Suvarnabhumi was due to be completed in 2005, though it is running far behind schedule and is unlikely to be finished until 2006 or possibly 2007. By mid 2005 even the airports website, www.suvarnabhumiairport.com, had failed to come online. Travellers are best advised to check for details at the time of travel.

Airline offices Air France, Vorawat Building, 20th floor, 849 Silom Rd, T02-6351199. **Air India**, SS Building, 10/12-13 Convent Rd, Silom, T02-2350557. **Air Lanka**, Ground Floor, Charn Issara Tower, 942 Rama IV Rd, T02-2369292. **Alitalia**, SSP Tower 3, 15th Floor, Unit 15A, 88 Silom Rd, T02-6341800. **American Airlines**, 518/5 Ploenchit Rd, T02-2511393. **Asiana Airlines**, 18th Floor, Ploenchit Centre, 2 Sukhumvit 2 Rd, T02-6568610. **Bangkok Airways**, Queen Sirikit National Convention Centre, New Rajdapisek Rd, Klongtoey, T02-2293456, www.bangkokair.com. **British Airways**, 14th floor, Abdulrahim Place, 990 Rama 1V Rd, T02-6361747. **Canadian Airlines**, 6th floor, Maneeya Building, 518/5 Ploenchit Rd, T02-2514521. **Cathay Pacific**, 11th floor, Ploenchit Tower, 898 Ploenchit Rd, T02-2630606. **Continental Airlines**, CP Tower, 313 Silom Rd, T02-2310113. **Delta Airlines**, 7th Floor, Patpong Building, Surawong Rd, T02-2376838. **Eva Airways**, Green Tower, 2nd floor, 425 Rama IV Rd, opposite Esso Head Office. **Finnair**, 6th floor, Vorawat Building, 849 Silom Rd, T02-6351234. **Gulf Air**, 12th floor, Maneeya Building, 518 Ploenchit Rd, T02-2547931. **Japan Airlines**, 254/1 Ratchadapisek Rd, T02-6925151. **KLM**, 19th floor, Thai Wah Tower 11, 21/133-134 South Sathorn Rd, T02-6791100. **Korean Air**, Ground floor, Kong Bunma Building (opposite Narai Hotel), 699 Silom Rd, T02-6350465. **Lao Airlines**, 491 17 Ground floor, Silom Plaza, Silom Rd, T02-2369822. **Lufthansa**, 18th floor, Q-House (Asoke), Sukhumvit Rd Soi 21, T02-2642400. **MAS (Malaysian Airlines)**, 20th floor, Ploenchit Tower, 898 Ploenchit Rd, T02-2630565. **Myanmar Airways**, 23rd floor, Jewellery Trade Centre, Silom Rd, T02-6300334. **PBAir**, T02-2610220, www.pbair.com. **Qantas**, 14th floor, Abdulrahim Place, 990 Rama IV Rd, T02-6361747. **SAS**, 8th Floor, Glas Haus I, Sukhumvit Rd Soi 25, T02-2600444. **Singapore Airlines**, 12th floor, Silom Centre, 2 Silom Rd, T02-2365295/6. **Swiss**, 21st floor Abdulrahim Place, 990 Rama 1V Rd, T02-6362160. **THAI**, 485 Silom Rd, T02-2343100. 89 Vibhavadi-Rangsit Rd, T02-5130121. **Vietnam Airlines**, 7th floor, Ploenchit Centre, 2 Sukhumvit 2 Rd, T02-6569056.

Bus

Local

More people have their belongings stolen on city buses than almost anywhere else. A routes map is indispensable. Good maps are available from bookshops as well as hotels and travel agents/ tour companies. Major bus stops have maps of routes in English.

This is the cheapest way to get around town. There is quite a range of buses, including a/c and non-a/c, micro, express and new improved, generally colour coded. **Standard non-a/c buses** (with blue stripe) cost ฿4.50. Beware of pickpockets on these often-crowded buses. **Red-striped express buses** are slightly more expensive, slightly less crowded, and do not stop at all bus stops. **A/c buses** cost ฿6-18 depending on distance and are coloured solid blue. Travelling all the way from Silom Rd to the

Magical mystery robbery tour

More than one traveller has been duped by the mystery rogue bus of Khao San which lures customers with offers of cheap ฿200 all-nighters to Krabi – all the way from Bangkok's notorious Khao San Rip-off Road.

According to concerned hoteliers in Krabi Town, the bus strategically breaks down – usually in the middle of the night when the passengers are at their most disorientated. The weary travellers stumble off, leaving their valuables behind on what they think is an empty bus and then re-embark only to discover money and goods missing. The trick is all in the luggage compartment where the thieves have been holded up.

In 2004, seven men were arrested in Krabi for stealing money and valuables on the bus in this manner. One Danish family lost around ฿10,000 in a single swoop.

There is, however, a way around the rogue bus. Either get the government approved VIP bus for ฿710 to Krabi or the ordinary a/c bus for ฿486 – which leaves from the bus station in Talat Kao.

airport by a/c bus, for example, costs ฿14; most inner city journeys cost ฿6. There are also smaller a/c **'micro buses'** (a bit of a misnomer as they are not micro at all, not even 'mini'), which follow the same routes but are generally faster and less crowded because officially they are only meant to let passengers aboard if a seat is vacant. They charge a flat fare of ฿20. New arrivals on Bangkok's complicated bus system are **white a/c buses** which charge a flat fare of ฿10 and **orange a/c buses** which cost ฿12.

Long distance

For bus routes and fares, see page 81.
There are 3 main bus stations in Bangkok serving the north and northeast, the east, and the south and west. Destinations in the Central Plains are also served from these terminals – places north of Bangkok from the northern and northeastern bus terminal, southwest of Bangkok from the southern terminal, and southeast from the eastern bus terminal. The **Northern bus terminal** or Mo Chit Mai (new Mo Chit), aka Mo Chit 2, is at the western side of Chatuchak Park on Kamphaeng Phet 2 Rd. It serves all destinations in the **north** and **northeast** as well as towns in the Central Plains that lie north of Bangkok like **Ayutthaya** and **Lopburi**. Non-a/c buses nos 77, 134, 136 and 145 and a/c buses nos 3, 8, 12, 134, 136 and 145 all pass the terminal. The non-a/c **Southern bus terminal** is on Phra Pinklao Rd, T02-4110061, near the intersection with Route 338. Buses for the west for places places like **Kanchanaburi** and the south leave from here. A/c town bus no 7 travels to the terminal. A/c buses to the **south and west** leave from the terminal on Charan Santiwong Rd near Bangkok Noi Train Station in Thonburi, T02-4351199. The **Eastern bus terminal**, Sukhumvit Rd (Soi Ekamai), between Soi 40 and Soi 42, T02-3912504, serves **Pattaya** and other destinations in the eastern region. To travel into Bangkok from this bus terminal by local bus, walk out of the terminal, turn left and enter the local bus terminal. Bus nos 77 and 159 will travel down to the Siam Sq area. Buses leave for most major destinations throughout the day, and often well into the night. There are overnight buses on the longer routes – **Chiang Mai**, **Hat Yai**, **Chiang Rai**, **Phuket**, **Ubon Ratchathani**. Even the smallest provincial towns such as **Mahasarakham** have de luxe a/c buses to Bangkok.

In addition to the government-operated buses there are many private companies which run **'tour' buses** to most of the major tourist destinations. Tickets bought through travel agents will normally be for these private tour buses which leave from offices all over the city as well as from the public bus terminals. Shop around as prices may vary. Note that although passengers may be picked up from their hotel/guesthouse –

therefore saving on the ride (and inconvenience) of getting out to the bus terminal – the private buses are generally less reliable and less safe. Many pick up passengers at Khaosan Rd.

Car hire

Given driving conditions in the Thai capital it's often advisable (and sometimes cheaper) to hire a car with driver. Approximate cost, ฿1,500-2,200 per day, ฿7,000-11,000 per week; Hertz and Avis charge more than the local firms, but have better insurance cover. **Avis**, 2/12 Witthayu Rd, T02-2555300. **Budget**, 19/23 Royal City Av, New Phetburi Rd, T02-9733752. **Central Car Rent**, 115/5 Soi Ton-Son, Ploenchit Rd, T02-2512778. **Hertz**, 420 Sukhumvit Soi 71, T02-3900341. **Highway Car Rent**, 1018/5 Rama IV Rd, T02-2357746. **Inter Car Rent**, 45 Sukhumvit Rd, T02-2529223. **SMT Rent-a-Car**, 931/11 Rama I Rd, T02-2168020, F2168039. See page 45 for general advice on driving in Thailand.

Metro and Skytrain (BTS)

With the opening of the new **Metro** in 2004, Bangkok is slowly developing an efficient transport system. The new line, which loops through 18 stations, connecting Hualamphong with Lumpini Park, Sukhumvit Rd and Chatuchak market and also intersects with the Skytrain, is a shining example of Thai modernity. The entire network is a/c, the comfortable trains run regularly and stations are well-lit and airy. Nonetheless, it has been beset with problems: many Thais are nervous about travelling underground and a major crash in early 2005 did little to allay these fears. Another issue is a lack of intergration with the Skytrain – separate tickets are needed and interchanges are awkward and badly planned. At present, fares for the Metro are cheap – ฿14-36. For full details go to www.bangkokmetro.co.th.

The **Skytrain** runs on an elevated track through the most developed parts of the city – it is quite a ride, veering between the skyscrapers. There are 2 lines which cross at Siam Station (Siam Sq): one runs from Mo Chit on Phahonyothin Rd (close to the Chatuchak Weekend Market, to the north of the city centre) to On Nut. The second lines runs from the National Stadium on Rama I Rd to Taksin Bridge (Saphan Taksin) at the end of Silom Rd in the heart of the business district. The Skytrain covers a large chunk of the tourist, business and shopping areas so is very useful. It is also quick and cool – although the tramp up to the stations can be a drag (10 stations have had escalators installed) and the open stations themselves are not a/c. Trains run from 0600-2400, every 3-5 mins during peak periods and every 10-15 mins out of the rush hour. Fares are steep by Thai standards but worth it for most overseas visitors: ฿10 for one stop, ฿40 for the whole route. Multi-trip tickets can also be purchased, which makes things slightly cheaper. For up to date information T02-6177300, www.bts.co.th.

Motorcycle taxi

These are usually used to run up and down the long sois that extend out of the main thoroughfares. Riders wear numbered vests and tend to congregate at the end of the busiest sois. The short-hop fare down a soi is usually ฿10 though there is usually a pricelist (in Thai) at the gathering point. Some riders will agree to take you on longer journeys across town and fares will then need to be negotiated – expect to pay anything from ฿25-100, dependent on your negotiating skills and knowledge of Thai. A ride through Bangkok's hectic traffic with a Red Bull-fuelled motorcycle taxi driver is one you are likely never to forget – if you make it back alive.

River transport

The cheapest way to travel on the river is by regular water-taxi. There are three types. The **Chao Phraya Express River Taxi** (rua duan) runs between Nonthaburi in the north and Rajburana (Big C) in the south. Fares are calculated by zone and range from ฿4-10 for the daily **Standard Express Boat and** ฿10 for the Special Express Boat. At peak hours boats leave every 10 mins, off-peak about 15-25 mins. Standard Express Boats operate daily 0600-1840, and Special Express Boats 0600-0900 and 1200-1900, Mon-Fri, to serve the commuter market (see map, page 104

for piers, and box page 105). The journey from one end of the route to the other takes 75 mins. Special Express Boats, flying either a red/orange or a yellow pennant, do not stop at all piers; boats without a flag are the Standard Express Boats and stop at all piers. Also, boats will only stop if passengers wish to board or alight, so make your destination known. Be warned that Thais trying to sell boat tours will tell you Express Boats are not running and will try to extort grossly inflated prices from you. Walk away and find the correct pier!

Ferries also ply back and forth across the river, between Bangkok and Thonburi. The fare for these slower, chunkier boats is ฿1.

There are also a number of **other boat services** linking Bangkok with stops along the khlongs which run off the main Chao Phraya River and into Thonburi. These are a good, cheap way of getting a glimpse of waterside life. Services from Tha Tien pier (by Wat Pho) to Khlong Mon, daily 0630-1800 (every 30 mins), ฿4; from Memorial Bridge pier to Khlong Bang Waek, daily 0600-2130 (every 15 mins), ฿10; from Tha Chang pier (by the Grand Palace) to Khoo Wiang floating market (market operates 0400-0700) and Khlong Bang Yai, daily 0615-2000 (every 20 mins), ฿10; and from Nonthaburi's Phibun Pier (north of the city) to Khlong Om, daily 0400-2100 (every 15 mins).

Khlong or long-tailed boats (hang yaaw) can be rented for ฿200 per hr, or more (see Tours, page 149) if you feel like splashing out in more ways than one. See the khlong trips outlined on page 103 for information on what to see on the river. A good map, 'Rivers and Khlongs', is available from the TAT office.

Taxi

Taxis are usually metered (they must have a/c to register) – look for the 'Taxi Meter' illuminated sign on the roof. Check that the meter is 'zeroed' before setting off.
Flag fall is ฿35 for the first 2 km, ฿4.50 per km up to 12 km, and ฿5 per km thereafter. Most trips in the city should cost ฿40-100. If the travel speed is less than 6 kph – always a distinct possibility in the traffic choked capital – a surcharge of ฿1.25 per min is automatically added. Passengers also pay the tolls for using the expressway. Taxi drivers sometimes refuse to use the meter despite the fact that they are required to do so by law. We have had numerous complaints about Bangkok's taxi drivers who view foreign visitors to the city as ripe for ripping-off. If they refuse to use the meter simply get out and hail another – there are usually scores around. Another popular ruse is for drivers to deny they have any change. It's best to make sure you have sufficient 20s and 100s to pay but if not just get out and get change from a nearby shop. They'll wait! Taxis should not be tipped, although it is usual to round fares up to the nearest ฿5. Remember that Bangkok's taxis are some of the cheapest in the world and their drivers some of the worst paid. For most tourists the arrival of the metered taxi has lowered prices as it has eliminated the need to bargain (assuming, of course, that the meter is being used). To call a taxi T1545 or T1661, they charge ฿20 plus the fare on the meter. Note that taxi drivers are not renowned for their knowledge of Bangkok. Many are upcountry boys and with farang visitors massacring their language it is handy to have a rough idea of where you want to go, and a map (preferably with Thai lettering too).

Train

For train timetables, routes and fares, see page 50

Bangkok has 2 main railway stations. The primary station, catering for most destinations, is **Hualamphong**, Rama IV Rd, T02-2237010/20; condensed railway timetables in English can be picked up from the information counter in the main concourse. (The Tourist Information offices at Hualamphong Railway Station are not official tourist offices and we have received a letter warning that they sometimes provide inaccurate or misleading advice.)

Trains to **Nakhon Pathom** and **Kanchanaburi** leave from the **Bangkok Noi** or Thonburi station on the other side of the Chao Phraya River. See page 49 for more information on Thailand's railways.

Tuk-tuk

The formerly ubiquitous motorized saamlor is rapidly becoming a piece of history in

Bangkok, although they can still always be found near tourist sites. Best for short journeys, they are uncomfortable and, being open to the elements, you are likely to be asphyxiated by car fumes. Bargaining is essential and the fare should be negotiated before boarding, though most tuk-tuk drivers try to rip tourists off and taking a metered taxi will be less hassle and cheaper. Expect to pay anything from ฿30-100 for a short hop across town. Tuk-tuk drivers also have a reputation for hustling in other ways and perpetrate all kinds of scams. The general advice is to try a tuk-tuk at least once for the novelty value and then avoid.

Directory

Banks

There are countless exchange booths in all the tourist areas open 7 days a week, mostly 0800-1530, some 0800-2100. Rates vary only marginally between banks, although if changing a large sum, it is worth shopping around. ATMs abound in Bangkok and can be used with all recognized credit cards and bank cards. They are open 24 hrs a day.

Embassies and consulates

Australia, 37 South Sathorn Rd, T02-2872680, F2872029. Mon-Fri 0830-1230, 1330-1630. **Cambodia**, 185 Rachdamri Rd, T02-2546630, 0900-1100, same-day visas available, ฿1000. One photo and photocopy of your passport required. **Canada**, 15th Floor Abdulrahim Place, 990 Rama 1V Rd, T02-6360541. Mon-Thu 0730-1615, Fri 0730-1300. Visas Mon-Fri 0800-1200. **France**, 35 Customs House Lane, Charoen Krung, T02-2668250. Mon-Thu 0800-1700, Fri 0800-1600. Visas Mon-Fri 0800-1200. (There is also a French consulate at 29 Sathorn Tai Rd, T02-2856104.) **Denmark**, 10 Sathorn Tai Soi Attakarnprasit, T02-2132021. Mon-Thu 0900-1530, Fri 0900-1230. **Germany**, 9 Sathorn Tai Rd, T02-2879000. Mon-Fri 0830-1200, visas 0830-1100. **Israel**, 25th Floor, Ocean Tower II, 75 Soi Wattana, Sukhumvit 19, T02-2049200. **Italy**, 399 Nang Linchi Rd, T02-2854090. **Japan**, 1674 New Phetburi Rd, T02-2526151. Mon-Fri 0830-1200, 1330-1600. **Laos**, 502/1-3 Soi Ramkhamhaeng 39, T02-5396667. Mon-Fri 0800-1200, 1300-1600. **Malaysia**, 33-35 Sathorn Tai Rd, T02-6792190. **Myanmar (Burma)**, 132 Sathorn Nua Rd, T02-2332237. **Netherlands**, 6 Wireless Rd, T02-2547701. Mon-Fri 0900-1200. **New Zealand**, 93 Wireless Rd, T02-2542530. Mon-Fri 0730-1200, 1300-1600. Visas 0900-1200, 1300-1500. **Singapore**, 129 Sathorn Tai Rd, T02-2862111. **South Africa**, 6th Floor, Park Place, 231 Soi Sarasin, Rachdamri Rd, T02-2538473. **Spain**, 7th Floor, Diethelm Building, 93 Wireless Rd, T02-2526112. Mon-Fri 0900-1430, visas 0830-1200. **Sweden**, 20th Floor, Pacific Place, 140 Sukhumvit Rd, T02-3020360. Mon-Fri 0800-1200. **Switzerland**, 35 Wireless Rd, (GPO Box 821, Bangkok 10510, T02-2546855. Mon-Fri 0900-1200. **UK**, 1031 Wireless Rd, T02-2530191/9. Mon-Thu 0800-1100, 1300-1530; Fri 0800-1200. **USA**, 95 Wireless Rd, T02-2054000. Mon-Fri 0800-1100, 1300-1500. **Vietnam**, 83/1 Wireless Rd, T02-2517202, F02-2517201. Open 0800-1130, 1330-1630, 2 photos required, same-day visas available at a price (฿2700).

Internet

There are literally thousands of internet cafés scattered around the entire city. Most offer hi- speed access and away from the tourist areas will cost from ฿15 per hr while along Khaosan and Sukhumvit prices are ฿30-60 per hr.

Bangkok Internet Café, Khaosan Rd. **Byte in @ cup**, Room 401, 4th Floor, Siam Discovery Centre, 989 Rama I Rd, www.byte-in-a-cup.com, open 1000-1900. **The Café**, Surawong Rd, corner of Soi Thaniya, ryoidii@rms.ksc.co.th. Open 1100-2200. 4 terminals and modern plugs for bringing your own laptops. **Chaiwat Tour**, Khaosan Rd. **Explorer Internet Café**, Patpong Soi 1, open 1700-0100. **Khaosan Cyber Home**, Khaosan Rd. Open 0900-2200.

Immigration

Sathorn Tai Soi Suanphlu, Silom district, T02-2873101.

Language schools

Bangkok has scores. The best known is the AUA school at 179 Rachdamri, T02-2528170. See *Metro* for information on language schools.

Libraries

British Council Library, 254 Chulalongkorn Soi 64 (Siam Sq). Open Tue-Sat 1000-1930, membership library with good selection of English-language books. **National Library**, Samsen Rd, close to Sri Ayutthaya Rd. Open daily 0930-1930. **Neilson Hays Library**, 195 Surawong Rd, T02-2331731. Open Mon-Sat 0930-1600, Sun 0930-1230. A small library of English-language books housed in an elegant building dating from 1922. It is a private membership library, but welcomes visitors who might want to see the building and browse; occasional exhibitions are held here. Open Mon-Sat 0930-1600, Sun 0930-1230. **Siam Society Library**, 131 Sukhumvit Soi 21 (Asoke). Membership library with excellent collection of Thai and foreign-language books and periodicals (especially English) on Thailand and mainland southeast Asia. Open Tue-Sat 0900-1700.

Medical services

Bangkok Adventist Hospital, 430 Phitsanulok Rd, Dusit, T02-2811422/2821100. Efficient vaccination service and 24-hr emergency unit. **Bangkok General Hospital**, New Phetburi Soi 47, T02-3180066. **Bangkok Nursing Home**, 9 Convent Rd, T02-2332610. **Dental Hospital**, 88/88 Sukhumvit 49, T02-2605000, F02-2605026. Good but expensive. **Clinic Banglamphu**, 187 Chakrapong Rd, T02-2827479. **Dental Polyclinic**, New Phetburi Rd, T02-3145070. **St Louis Hospital**, 215 Sathorn Tai Rd, T02-2120033.

Places of worship

Baptist Church, 2172/146 Phahonyothin Soi 36 (1800 Sun service). **Christ Church**, 11 Convent Rd (Anglican, Episcopalian, Ecumenical, 3 Sun services at 0730, 1000 and 1800). **Evangelical Church**, Sukhumvit Soi 10 (0930 Sun service). The **International Church** (interdenominational), 67 Sukhumvit Soi 19 (0800 Sun service). **Holy Redeemer**, 123/19 Wittayu Soi Ruam Rudee (Roman Catholic, 5 services on Sun).

Post

Central GPO (Praysani Klang for taxi drivers): 1160 Charoen Krung, opposite the Ramada Hotel. Open 0800-2000 Mon-Fri and 0800-1300 weekend and holidays. The money and postal order service is open 0800-1700, Mon-Fri, 0800-1200 Sat. Closed on Sun and holidays. 24-hr telegram and telephone service (phone rates are reduced 2100-0700) and a packing service. There is a small post office on the ground floor of the Siam Sq Car Park, behind Siam Sq.

Tourist police

Unico House, Ploenchit Soi Lang Suan, T1699 or T02-6521721. There are also dedicated tourist police offices in the main tourist areas.

Central Region

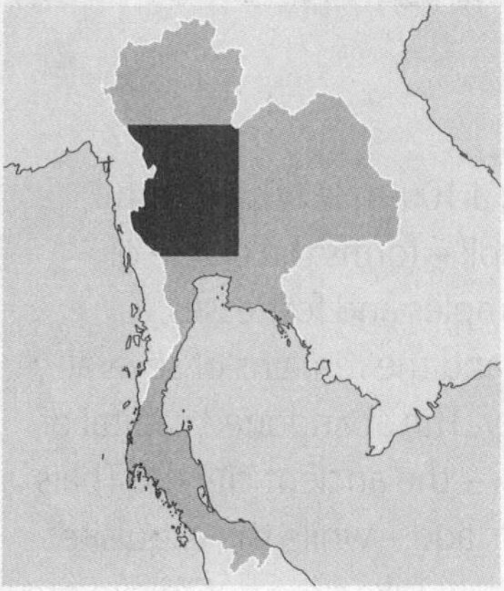

Footprint feautres

Introduction

The entire central plain – cutting a 100-mile wide swath 250 miles upcountry from Bangkok – forms the cradle of Thai civilization. Ruined cities, temples and fortresses, museums filled with antiquities, and the remains of several great civilizations await the visitor. The abandoned capital of Ayutthaya is here, as is Sukhothai – the ancient city the Thais consider represents their 'Golden' age – while the exquisite ruins of Si Satchanalai nestle nearby. Take time out to explore the forests of Sukhothai and 'Si Sat' and you'll discover revered Buddhas and chedis lost amongst thick foilage. Don't forget the diamond citadel of Kamphaeng Phet built to protect Sukhothai from attack, the assortment of monkey-colonized ruins of Lopburi and the spiritually uplifting, living temple of Wat Phra Sri Ratana Mahathat in Phitsanulok. The vast plain finally gives way to ridges of forested hills. These are relatively remote areas with trekking centres in the affable western towns of Mae Sot and Umphang.

Head north and west from Bangkok to the frontier with Burma and Thailand's history takes on a different complexion. It was through this thin slice of western Thailand that the Japanese built their infamous Death Railway. It's not only this dramatic history that attracts visitors to the region and its hub, Kanchanaburi. Add wonderful cave complexes, jungle trekking, waterfalls, river trips, elephant rides, raft houses and a host of national parks and you have an important centre of eco-tourism. Venture north of Kanchanaburi towards the Burmese border and you'll reach Sangkhlaburi and the Three Pagodas Pass. Ethnically, this is an incredibly diverse area with minority peoples, such as Karen, Mon, Burmese, Indian and Chinese all living side by side. It is a wild natural forested area with fantastic trekking and rafting and it is also possible, when the Thai and Burmese authorities are on good terms, to enter Burma.

★ Don't miss...

1 **Central Thailand** Cycle around the ruined monuments of the former capitals of Ayutthaya and Sukhothai amid the gentle mists of dawn, pages 162 and 189.

2 **Lopburi** The troupes of monkeys may look cute but try feeding them and you'll start a simian riot. Instead, take a peaceful wander around ancient palaces and engaging Khmer ruins, page 168.

3 **Kanchanaburi** Sleep on a raft, eat on a raft and dance on a raft. Then visit the infamous 'Bridge over the River Kwai', built by prisoners of war and explore the labyrinthine cave monasteries and humungous national parks, page 175.

4 **Phitsanulok** At its heart is Wat Phra Sri Ratana Mahathat – one of Thailand's holiest temples. Vibrant and stunning, you'll be lighting incense and prostrating yourself in front of Buddha before you leave, page 196.

5 **Mae Sot and Umphang** Smuggled goods – everything from cows to trees – diverse hill peoples and various Burmese insurgents have found a home here. Factor in incredible natural wealth – parks, caves and waterfalls – and you're guaranteed an adventure, pages 211 and 214.

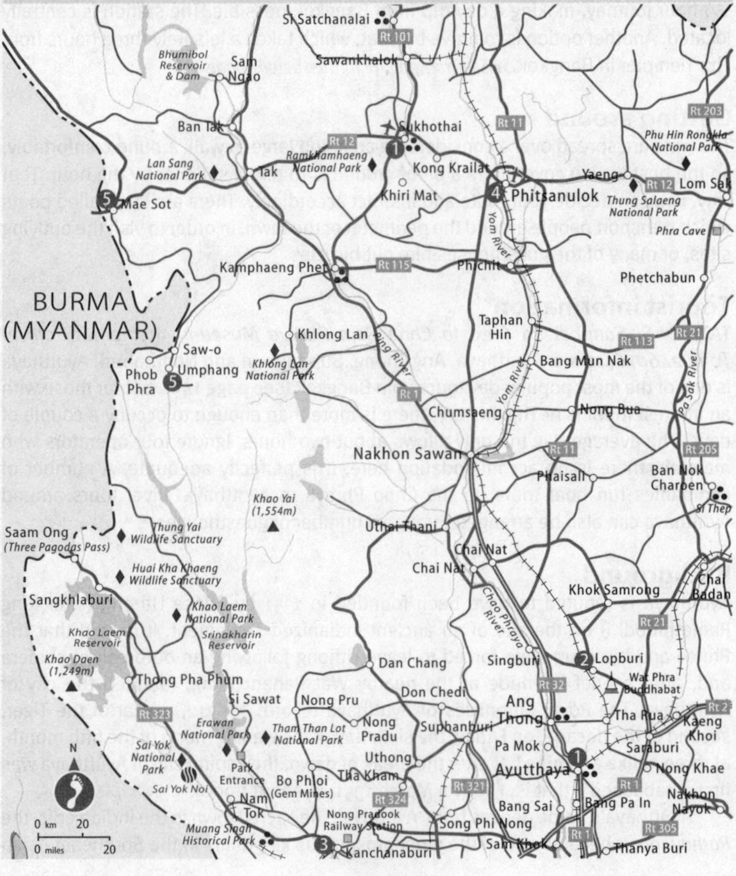

Ayutthaya and around

→ Colour map 2, grid C1.

The ancient, venerable capital of the Kingdom of Siam, Ayutthaya, had a population of 150,000 during its heyday and was the equal of any city in Europe. It was at the epicentre of an empire that controlled more than 500,000 sq km and all the wealth of this great kingdom gravitated to the capital city. Walking around the old city of Ayutthaya, with the setting sun illuminating the deep red brick ruins, it is not hard to imagine the grandeur of this place which so amazed early European visitors. Here is a stunning complex of palaces, shrines, monasteries and chedis. The historical park, which was made a UNESCO World Heritage Site in 1991, covers some 3 sq km. Rama V (1868-1910) was the first person to appreciate the value of the site, both in terms of Thailand's national identity and in terms of its artistic merit. The historic city of Lopburi, known for its kleptomaniac, monkeys lies to the north. » *For Sleeping, Eating and other listings see pages 171-174.*

Ins and outs

Getting there

Most people get here by bus from Bangkok's Northern bus terminal. It is an easy 1½-hour journey, making a day trip from Bangkok possible. The station is centrally located. Another option is to arrive by boat, which takes a leisurely three hours from Tha Tien pier in Bangkok. » *See Transport for further details, page 173.*

Getting around

The wats are spread over a considerable area, too large to walk around comfortably, so the best way to cover quite a bit of ground is to hire a saamlor by the hour. That way, you can decide your route and instruct accordingly. There are long-tailed boats which transport people around the perimeter of the town, in order to visit the outlying sites, or many of the guesthouses hire out bicycles.

Tourist information

TAT, ⓘ *Si Sanphet Rd (next to Chao Sam Phraya Museum), (temporary office) T035-246076*, covers Ayutthaya, Ang Thong, Suphanburi and Nonthaburi. Ayutthaya is one of the most popular day tours from Bangkok (see page 149), but for those with an interest in ruins or Thai history, there is more than enough to occupy a couple of days. The average day trip only allows about two hours. Ignore tour operators who maintain there is no accommodation here, it is perfectly adequate. A number of companies run boat tours up the Chao Phraya to Ayutthaya. River tours around Ayutthaya can also be arranged through a number of guesthouses.

Background

Ayutthaya is reputed to have been founded in 1351 by Prince Uthong (later King Ramathibodi I) on the site of an ancient Indianized settlement. It is said that the Prince and his court were forced to leave Uthong following an outbreak of cholera and, after a brief interlude at the nearby Wat Panancherng, founded the city of Ayutthaya. The Royal Chronicles of Ayutthaya record: "In 712, a Year of the Tiger, second of the decade, on Friday, the sixth day of the waxing moon of the fifth month, at three nalika and nine bat after the break of dawn, the capital city of Ayutthaya was first established" [that is, Friday 4 March 1351, at about 0900].

Ayutthaya's name derives from 'Ayodhya', the sacred town in the Indian epic, the *Ramayana*. It became one of the most prosperous kingdoms in the Southeast Asian

King Naresuan the Great of Ayutthaya

One of Thailand's great kings, King Naresuan of Ayutthaya (1590-1605) was one of only five who have posthumously been awarded the sobriquet 'the Great'. In 1569 the Burmese had taken Ayutthaya and placed a puppet monarch on the throne. The great kingdom appeared to be on the wane. But Naresuan, who in American historian David Wyatt's words was "one of those rare figures in Siamese history who, by virtue of dynamic leadership, personal courage, and decisive character, succeed in Herculean tasks that have daunted others before them", proceeded to challenge the Burmese. He confronted their forces in 1585, 1585-1586 and in 1586-1587, defeating armies that grew larger by turn. Finally, at the beginning of 1593, the decisive battle occurred at Nong Sarai, to the northwest of Suphanburi. The Burmese had assembled an army of monumental proportions. During the initial skirmish, Naresuan saw the Burmese crown prince mounted on his war elephant and, according to the chronicles, shouted across the battle field: "Come forth and let us fight an elephant duel for the honour of our kingdoms". When the Burmese prince lunged with his lance, Naresuan ducked beneath the blow to rake, and kill, his opponent with his sword. The battle was won and Ayutthaya was once again in a position to flourish.

region, and by 1378 the King of Sukhothai had been forced to swear his allegiance. Ultimately, the kingdom stretched from Angkor (Cambodia) in the east, to Pegu (Burma) in the west. In 1500 it was reported that the kingdom was exporting 30 junk loads (10,000 tonnes) of rice to Malacca (Melaka) each year. Ayutthaya was also an important source of animal skins, ivory, resins and other forest products.

The city is situated on an island at the confluence of three rivers: the Chao Phraya, Pasak and Lopburi. Ayutthaya's strong defensive position proved to be valuable as it was attacked by the Burmese on no less than 24 occasions. Recent research on sea-level changes indicates that in 1351 the coastline was much further north and so the city was considerably closer to the sea. Ayutthaya, therefore, would have been able to have developed as a trading port unlike the previous Thai capitals of Sukhothai and Si Satchanalai.

One of Ayutthaya's most famous kings was Boromtrailokant (1448-1488), a model of the benevolent monarch. He is best known for his love of justice and his administrative and legislative reforms. This may seem surprising in view of some of the less than enlightened legal practices employed later in the Ayutthaya period. A plaintiff and defendant might, for example, have to plunge their hands into molten tin, or their heads into water, to see which party was the guilty one.

A succession struggle in the mid-16th century led to 20 years of warfare with the Burmese, who managed to seize and occupy Ayutthaya. It wasn't long before the hero-king, Naresuan (1590-1605), recaptured the city and led his country back to independence. Under King Narai (1656-1688), Ayutthaya became a rich, cosmopolitan trading post. Merchants came to the city from Portugal, Spain, Holland, China, Arabia, Persia, Malaya, India and Japan. In the 16th century Ayutthaya was said to have 40 different nationalities living in and around the city walls, and supported a population larger than London's.

The city was strongly fortified, with ramparts 20 m high and 5 m thick, and was protected on all sides by waterways: rivers on three sides and a linking canal on the fourth creating an oriental Venice. The cosmopolitan atmosphere was evident on

It was said that the King of Ayutthaya was so wealthy that the elephants were fed from gold vessels.

the waterways where royal barges rubbed shoulders with Chinese junks, Arab dhows and ocean-going schooners. Visitors found endless sources of amusement in the city. There were elephant jousts, tiger fights, Thai boxing (Muay Thai), masked plays and puppet theatre.

It was said that the King of Ayutthaya was so wealthy that the elephants were fed from gold vessels. Indeed, early western visitors to Ayutthaya often commented on the king's elephants and the treatment they received. One of the earliest accounts is by Jacques de Countres, a merchant from Bruges who resided in the city for eight months in 1596 (during Naresuan's reign). His son later recorded his father's

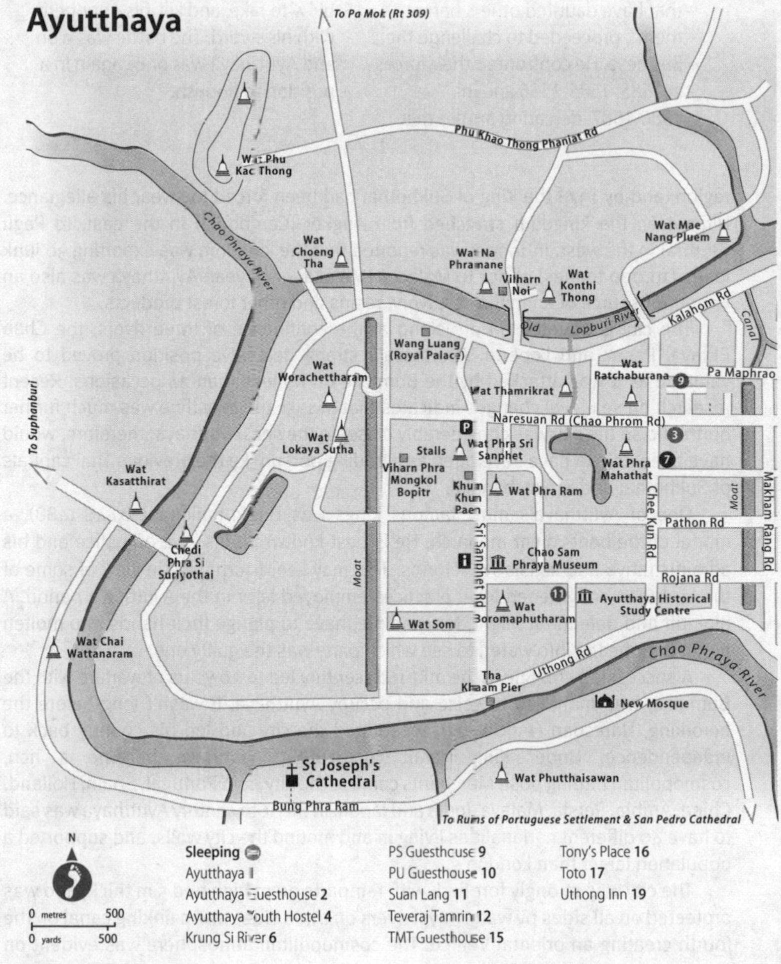

Ayutthaya
To Pa Mok (Rt 309)
Phu Khao Thong Phaniat Rd
Wat Phu Kao Thong
Chao Phraya River
Wat Mae Nang Pluem
Wat Choeng Tha
Wat Na Phramane
Vilharn Noi
Wat Konthi Thong
Old Lopburi River
Kalahom Rd
Canal
Wang Luang (Royal Palace)
Wat Worachettharam
Wat Ratchaburana
Pa Maphrao
Wat Thamrikrat
Naresuan Rd (Chao Phrom Rd)
To Suphanburi
Wat Lokaya Sutha
Wat Phra Sri Sanphet
Stalls
Viharn Phra Mongkol Bopitr
Wat Phra Mahathat
Wat Kasatthirat
Khun Khun Paen
Wat Phra Ram
Moat
Makham Rang Rd
Chee Kun Rd
Pathon Rd
Chedi Phra Si Suriyothai
Sri Sanphet Rd
Chao Sam Phraya Museum
Rojana Rd
Ayutthaya Historical Study Centre
Wat Boromaphutharam
Wat Som
Wat Chai Wattanaram
Uthong Rd
Tha Khaam Pier
New Mosque
St Joseph's Cathedral
Wat Phutthaisawan
Bung Phra Ram
To Ruins of Portuguese Settlement & San Pedro Cathedral
N
0 metres 500
0 yards 500
Sleeping
Ayutthaya 1
Ayutthaya Guesthouse 2
Ayutthaya Youth Hostel 4
Krung Si River 6
PS Guesthouse 9
PU Guesthouse 10
Suan Lang 11
Teveraj Tamrin 12
TMT Guesthouse 15
Tony's Place 16
Toto 17
Uthong Inn 19

experiences: "The palace is surrounded by stables where live the favourite elephants ridden by the king... The sumptuosity of their treatment deserves to be mentioned. Each one had its silk cushion, and they slept on it as if they were small dogs. Each one of them had six very large bowls of gold. Some contained oil to grease their skins; others were filled with water for sprinkling; others served for eating; others for drinking; others for urinating and defecating. The elephants were indeed so well trained that they got up from their beds when they felt the urge to urinate or defecate. Their attendants understood at once and handed them the bowls. And they kept their lodges always very sweet-smelling and fumigated with benzoin and other fragrant substances. "I would not have believed it if I had not actually seen it." (Smithies, Michael *Descriptions of Old Siam*, Kuala Lumpur, 1995, OUP.)

One European became particularly influential: King Narai's Greek foreign affairs officer (and later Prime Minister), Constantine Phaulcon. It was at this time the word 'farang' – to describe any white foreigner – entered the Thai vocabulary, derived from 'ferenghi', the Indian for 'French'. In 1688, Narai was taken ill and at the same time the French, who Phaulcon had been encouraging, became a serious threat, gaining control of a fortress in Bangkok. An anti-French lobby arrested the by now very unpopular Phaulcon and had him executed for suspected designs on the throne. The French troops were expelled and for the next century Europeans were kept at arm's length. It was not until the 19th century that they regained influence in the Thai court.

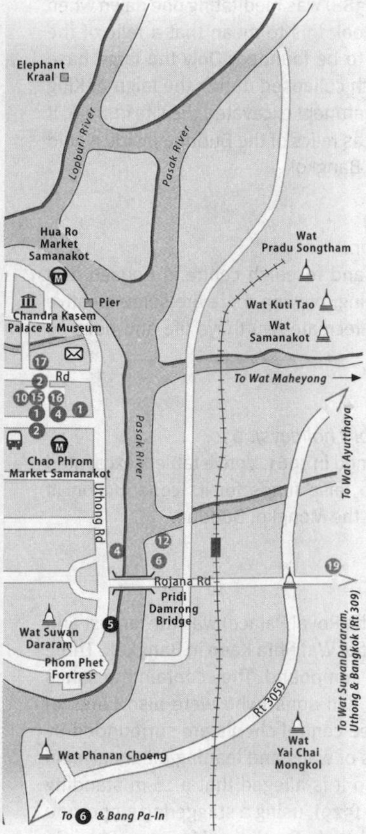
Elephant Kraal
Lopburi River
Pasak River
Hua Ro Market Samanakot
Wat Pradu Songtham
Pier
Chandra Kasem Palace & Museum
Wat Kuti Tao
Wat Samanakot
Rd
To Wat Maheyong
Chao Phrom Market Samanakot
To Wat Ayutthaya
Uthong Rd
Rojana Rd
Pridi Damrong Bridge
Wat Suwan Dararam
Phom Phet Fortress
Rt 3059
To Wat SuwanDararam, Uthong & Bangkok (Rt 309)
Wat Yai Chai Mongkol
Wat Phanan Choeng
To 6 & Bang Pa-In

Eating
Phae Krung Kao 5
Ruan Thai Mai Suay 6
Siam 7

Bars & clubs
Bohemian Bar 1
Good Luck Bar 2
Home Pub 3
Moon Café 4

In 1767 the kingdom was again invaded, by the Burmese, who, at the 24th attempt, were finally successful in vanquishing the defenders. The city was sacked and its defences destroyed, but, unable to consolidate their position, the Burmese left for home, taking with them large numbers of prisoners and leaving the city in ruins. The population was reduced from one million to 10,000. Ayutthaya never recovered from this final attack, and the magnificent temples were left to deterioriate.

Sights

Sites with an entrance fee generally open 0800-1700. For more background on Ayutthayan style, see page 686.

The modern town of Ayutthaya is concentrated in the eastern quarter of the old walled city, and beyond the walls to the east. Much of the rest of the old city is green and open, interspersed with abandoned wats and new government buildings.

The sights described below takes in the most important wats. Ayutthaya's other fine ruins are described in the

 second half of this section. The sheer size of the site means that the considerable numbers of tourists are easily dispersed among the ruins, leaving the visitor to wander in complete tranquillity among the walkways, chedis and trees.

Wat Ratchaburana

ⓘ ฿30.

This wat was built by King Boromraja II in 1424 on the cremation site of his two brothers (princes Ai and Yo), who were killed while contesting the throne. The Khmer-style prang (which has been partially restored) still stands amidst the ruins of the wat.Some of the most important treasures found in Ayutthaya were discovered here in 1958: bronze Buddha images, precious stones and golden royal regalia, belonging, it is assumed, to the two brothers.

Wat Phra Mahathat

ⓘ *฿30.*

Across the road from Wat Ratchaburana sits the Monastery of the Great Relic. It was founded in 1384, making it one of the earliest prangs in Ayutthaya, and was the largest of all Ayutthaya's monasteries, built to house holy relics of the Buddha (hence its name). It is said that King Boromraja I (1370-1388) was meditating one dawn when he saw a glow emanating from the earth; he took this to mean that a relic of the Buddha lay under the soil and ordered a wat to be founded. Only the large base remains of the original Khmer-style prang, which collapsed during the reign of King Song Tham (1610-1628). When the Fine Arts Department excavated the site in 1956, it found a number of gold Buddha images as well as relics of the Buddha inside a gold casket, now exhibited in the National Museum, Bangkok.

Ayutthaya Historical Study Centre

ⓘ *Wed-Fri 0900-1630, Sat-Sun 0900-1700. ฿100.*

Further south, on Rojana Road, this museum and research centre is housed in a surprisingly sensitively designed modern building, proving there are some creative architects in the country. The museum tries to recreate Ayutthaya life and does so with some excellent models.

Chao Sam Phraya Museum

ⓘ *Wed-Sun 0900-1200, 1300-1600 (except public holidays). ฿30.*

Located on Rojana Road, this museum was opened in 1961. Votive tablets excavated from Wat Ratchaburana were auctioned off to raise funds for its construction. It houses many of Ayutthaya's relics, in particular the Mongkol Buddha.

Wat Phra Sri Sanphet

ⓘ *฿30.*

Within the extensive grounds of Wang Luang (the Royal Palace) was the largest and most beautiful wat in Ayutthaya; the equivalent of Wat Phra Kaeo in Bangkok. Three restored Ceylonese-style chedis dominate the compound. They contain the ashes of King Boromtrailokant (1448-1488) and his two sons (who were also kings of Ayutthaya). There are no prangs here; the three central chedis are surrounded by alternate smaller chedis and viharns. Remains of walls and leaning pillars give an impression of the vastness of the wat. In 1500 it is alleged that a 16-m standing Buddha was cast by King Ramathipodi II (1491-1529), using a staggering 5,500,000 kg of bronze and covered in 340 kg of gold leaf. The image's name, Phra Sri Sanphet, later became the name of the wat. When the Burmese invaded the city in 1767 the image was set on fire in order to release the gold, in the process destroying both it and the temple.

Viharn Phra Mongkol Bopitr

South of Wat Phra Sri Sanphet stands this 'new' viharn, built in 1956 and modelled on the 15th-century original which was razed by the Burmese. It houses, at 12.5 m high, one of the largest bronze Buddhas in the world. This black image is made of sheets of copper-bronze, fastened onto a core of brick and plaster and probably dates from the 16th century.

Wat Na Phramane

ⓘ *฿20. Note the image cannot always be viewed.*

Travel back past Wang Luang to the main road, turn east and after 250 m the road crosses the Old Lopburi River. From the bridge one can see Wat Na Phramane, which dates from 1503 and is one of the most complete examples of Ayutthayan architecture. It is reputed to have been built by one of King Ramathibodi's concubines, Pra Ong, at which time it was known as Wat Pramerurachikaram. A treaty to end one of the many wars with Burma was signed here in 1549. More than two centuries later in 1767, the Burmese used the position to attack the city once again, and it is said that the King of Burma suffered a mortal blow from a cannon which backfired during the initial bombardment. Perhaps because of this, the Burmese – unusually – left the wat intact. Even without the helping hands of the Burmese, the wat still fell into disrepair and was not restored until 1838. The lovely early Ayutthayan bot is the largest in the city and contains an impressive crowned bronze Buddha image.

Wat Thamrikrat

South over the bridge that crosses a small tributary of the Old Lopburi River, again, a short distance east along Kalahom Road, is Wat Thamrikrat, the Monastery of the Pious Monarch, with singha (stucco lions) surrounding an overgrown chedi. Scholars are not sure exactly when it was built, but they are largely agreed that it predates the reign of King Boromtrailokant (1448-1488).

Wat Choeng Tha

Also on the north bank of the river, not far from the confluence of the Chao Phraya and Old Lopburi rivers, is this wat. It is not known when it was originally built – it has been restored on a number of occasions – but it is said to have been constructed by a man whose daughter ran away with her lover and never returned; it was known as Wat Koy Tha, the Monastery of Waiting. The Ayutthaya-style prang is in reasonable condition, as is the sala kan parian, although the bot and viharn are both in poor condition.

Wat Yai Chai Mongkol

ⓘ *฿30.*

Southeast of the town is Wat Yai Chai Mongkol, or simply Wat Yai ('Big' Wat), built by King Uthong, also known as King Ramathibodi I, in 1357, for a group of monks who had studied and been ordained in Ceylon. The imposing 72-m high chedi was built in the Ceylonese style (now with a rather alarming tilt) to celebrate the victory of King Naresuan over the Prince of Burma in 1592, in single-handed elephant combat. The viharn contains a massive reclining Buddha image. It is unusual as its eyes are open. Reclining images traditionally symbolize death or sleep, so the eyes are closed.

Elephant kraals

ⓘ *Take a saamlor from Chee Kun Rd northwards over the Old Lopburi River to reach the kraal. If coming from Wat Phu Kao Thong, cross the Pa Mok highway and drive for 3½ km.*

Northeast of the city, on the banks of the Old Lopburi River, are the only remaining elephant kraals in Thailand. The kraals were built in the reign of King Maha Chakrapat

in 1580 to capture wild elephants. The kraals are square-shaped enclosures with double walls. The inner walls are made of teak posts fixed to the ground at close intervals. The outer walls are made of earth, faced with brick, and are 3 m high. The kraals have two entrances: one to allow the decoy elephant to lure the herd into the enclosure, and the other to lead them out again. The outer wall on the west side is slightly wider to provide a platform from which the king, seated in a pavilion, could watch the elephant round-up. The last round-up of wild elephants occurred in May 1903, to entertain royal guests during King Chulalongkorn's reign. The kraal has been extensively restored and is rather clinical as a result.

River tours of outlying wats

The extensive waterways of Ayutthaya (more than 50 km of them) are a pleasant way to see some of the less accessible sights. Long-tailed boats can be taken from the landing pier opposite Chandra Kasem Palace, in the northeast corner of the town, see Transport, for details. During the dry season, it is not possible to circle the entire island; the Old Lopburi River becomes unnavigable. The usual route runs south down the Pasak River and round as far as Wat Chai Wattanaram on the Chao Phraya River. The following wats can also be visited by road.

Situated close to the junction of the Pasak and Chao Phraya rivers, **Wat Phanan Choeng** is the first wat to be reached by boat, travelling clockwise from the Chandra Kasem pier. The 19-m high seated Buddha image in the viharn (immediately behind the bot) is mentioned in a chronicle as having been made in 1324, some 26 years before Ayutthaya became the capital. It is likely that the wat was founded at the same time, making it the oldest in Ayutthaya. The Buddha is made of brick, plaster and is gilded. This image is said to have wept tears when Ayutthaya was sacked by the Burmese in 1767.

Wat Chai Wattanaram ⓘ *฿30*, sits on the west bank of the Chao Phraya River, to the west of the city. A decapitated Buddha sits overlooking the river in front of the ruins, while the large central prang is surrounded by two rows of smaller chedis and prang-like chedis, arranged on the cardinal and sub-cardinal points of the cloister that surrounds the central structure. The wat was built by King Prasat Thong (1630-1656) in honour of his mother and the complex has a Khmer quality about it. Relatively few tours of Ayutthaya include Wat Chai Wattanaram on their itineraries, which is a great shame as this is a marvellous site. It is also possibly the best restored of all the monasteries, avoiding the rather cack-handed over-restoration that mars some of the other sites.

North of here is **Wat Kasatthirat**. This wat represents the end of a river tour unless the Old Lopburi River is navigable in which case Wat Na Phramane (see page 167) can also be reached, returning, full circle, to the Chandra Kasem pier.

San Pedro Cathedral

Lying 11 km south outside the city, this was the site of the original Portuguese settlement in Ayutthaya, dating from 1511. At one point as many as 3,000 Portuguese and their mixed-blood offspring were living here, although with the sacking of Ayutthaya by the Burmese in 1767 the community was abandoned. Since the mid-1980s the Fine Arts Department, with financial support from Portugal, has been excavating the site and the cathedral itself is now fully renovated. It was opened to the public in 1995.

Lopburi

→ *Colour map 2, grid C1.*

To the west of Lopburi is the old city with its historical sights. To the east is the new town with its major military base. Inevitably, most visitors will be attracted to the palace, museum, monasteries and prangs of the old city. This part of town is also teeming with Lopburi's famous monkeys that clamber from one telegraph pole to

Constantine Phaulcon: Greek adventurer, Siamese minister, Roman Catholic zealot

Constantine Phaulcon (1647-1688) was a Greek adventurer who became, for a short time, the most influential man in Siam barring the king. He arrived in Ayutthaya in 1678 with the English East India Company, learnt Thai and became an interpreter in the court. By 1682 he had worked his way up through the bureaucracy to become the Mahatthai, the most senior position. But it was also at this time that, in retrospect, he sealed his fate. Phaulcon acted as interpreter for a French mission led by Mgr Pallu. An avid Roman Catholic, having recently been converted by Jesuit priests, Phaulcon was enthralled by the idea of converting King Narai and his subjects to Christianity. He discussed with Narai – who was the King's most trusted adviser – the superiority of Roman Catholicism versus Buddhism, and seemed to be representing the interests of the French in negotiations, rather than those of Siam. Phaulcon made many enemies among powerful Siamese, who doubted his integrity and his intentions. By 1688, Phaulcon's activities were becoming increasingly unacceptable, and he was also linked by association with the excesses of French and British troops, with the proselytizing of priests, and with the effect that foreign traders were having upon the interests of local businessmen. A plot was hatched to kill the foreigner on the king's death. In March 1688, when Narai fell seriously ill, Phra Phetracha – a claimant for the throne – had Phaulcon arrested, tried and convicted for treason, and then executed on 5 June.

another, laze around the temples – particularly Sam Phra Karn – feast on the offerings left by worshippers, and grasp playfully at the hair of unwitting tourists. They have a penchant for stealing sunglasses or spectacles: be warned. Don't try and feed them as you are likely to provoke a monkey riot.

Background

Lopburi has been seemingly caught between competing powers for more than 1,000 years. The discovery of Neolithic and Bronze Age remains indicate that the site on the left bank of the Lopburi River was in use in prehistoric times. The town became a major centre during the Dvaravati period (sixth-11th century), when it was known as Lavo (the original settlers were the 'Lavah', related to the Mon). In AD 950 Lopburi fell to the expanding Khmers who made it a provincial capital; in Thailand, the Khmer period of art and architecture is known as 'Lopburi' because of their artistic impact evident in the town and surrounding area (see page 684). By the 14th century, Khmer influence had waned and the Thais reclaimed Lopburi. In 1351 King Uthong of Ayutthaya gave his son – Prince Ramesuan – governorship of the town, indicating its continued importance. It fell into obscurity during the 16th century, but was resuscitated when King Narai (1656-1688) restored the city with the assistance of European architects. With Narai's death in Lopburi, the town entered another period of obscurity but was again restored to glory during Rama IV's reign.

Sights

The **Narai Ratchaniwet Palace** ⓘ *Wed-Sun 0830-1200, 1300-1630, ฿30*, represents the historical heart of Lopburi, encased by massive walls and bordered to the west by the Lopburi River. King Narai declared Lopburi his second capital in the 17th century, and built his palace between 1665 and 1677, which became his 'summer' retreat. The

main gate is on Sorasak Road opposite the **Asia Lopburi Hotel**. The well-kept palace grounds are divided into three sections: an outer, a middle and an inner courtyard.

The outer courtyard, now in ruins, contained the 'functional' buildings: (a) a tank to supply water to the palace (transported down terracotta pipes from a lake some distance away), (b) storage warehouses for hides and spices, and (c) elephant and horse stables. There was also a (d) Banquet Hall for royal visitors, and, on the south wall, (e) an Audience Hall (Tuk Phrachao Hao). The niches that line the inner side of the walls by the main gates would have contained oil lamps, lit during festivals and important functions.

An archway leads to the middle courtyard. On the left are the tall ruins of the (f) Dusitsawan Thanya Mahaprasat Hall, built in 1685 for audiences with visiting dignitaries. Next to this is the (g) Phiman Mongkut Pavilion, now the King Narai Museum, housing a fine collection spanning all periods of Thai art, but concentrating, not surprisingly, on Lopburi period sculpture. To the north, the (h) Chantra Paisan Pavilion, looking like a wat, was one of the first structures built by King Narai and served as his audience hall until the Suttha Sawan Pavilion was completed. Behind these buildings were the (i) women's quarters, again built by Rama IV. One of them has been turned into a Farmer's Museum displaying traditional Central Plains farming technology and other implements used in rural life, for pottery and iron production, weaving and fishing. The other buildings in the women's quarters are in the process of being restored.

Lopburi & Narai Ratchaniwet Palace

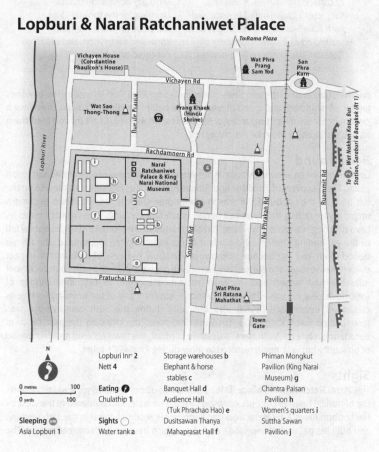

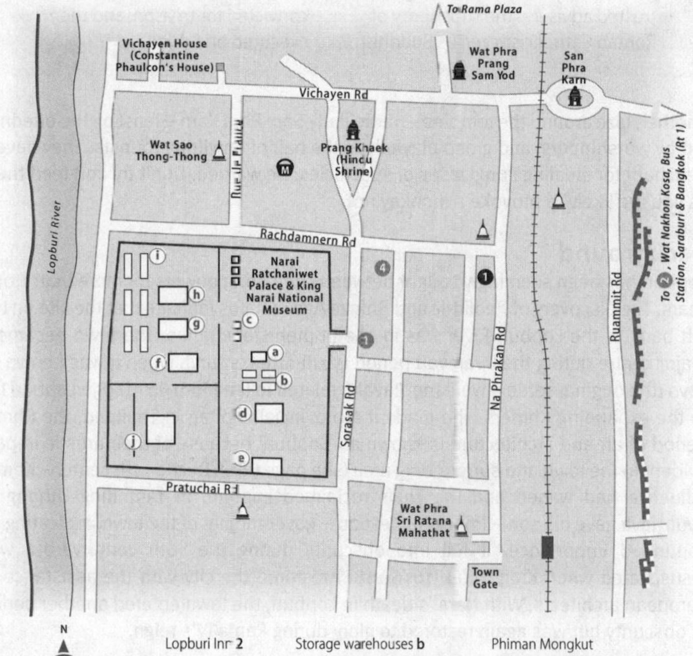

Sleeping
Asia Lopburi 1
Lopburi Inn 2
Nett 4

Eating
Chulathip 1

Sights
Water tank a
Storage warehouses b
Elephant & horse stables c
Banquet Hall d
Audience Hall (Tuk Phrachao Hao) e
Dusitsawan Thanya Mahaprasat Hall f
Phiman Mongkut Pavilion (King Narai Museum) g
Chantra Paisan Pavilion h
Women's quarters i
Suttha Sawan Pavilion j

The inner courtyard contains the ruins of King Narai's own residence, the (L) Suttha Sawan Pavilion. It is isolated from the rest of the complex and was surrounded by gardens, ponds (where the king took his bath under huge canopies) and fountains. King Narai died in this pavilion on 11 July 1688 while his opponents plotted against him.

North of Vichayen Road, next to the railway line, is **Wat Phra Prang Sam Yod** (Wat of Three Prangs), a laterite and sandstone shrine whose three spires originally represented the three Hindu deities: Brahma, Vishnu and Siva. The south prang has remnants of some fine stucco friezes and naga heads; also note how the stone door-frames are carved to resemble their wooden antecedents. The temple is also home to a large troupe of cute, vicious monkeys who are best left well alone. It's also here where the locals hold, in late November, an annual feast to honour the monkeys. Tables filled with fruit, nuts and various monkey treats are laid out. A giant monkey food-fight is the result with nasty spats breaking out over monkey favourites – thousands of Thais turn out to watch.

West along Vichayen Road is the Khmer **Prang Khaek**. Built in the late eighth century, this, like Prang Sam Yod, was also originally a Hindu shrine. The three brick spires represent the oldest Khmer prangs found in the Central region of Thailand. It was restored in the 17th century, but today lies in ruins.

Further along Vichayen Road are the remains of **Vichayen House** ⓘ *฿30*, better known as Constantine Phaulcon's House, the influential adviser to King Narai (see box page 169). The house, European in style, was constructed for Chevalier de Chaumont, the first French ambassador to Thailand who lived here in 1685. Later, it was used by the Greek Prime Minister, Phaulcon, as his residence.

Opposite the railway station is the entrance to **Wat Phra Sri Ratana Mahathat,** ⓘ *฿30*, the oldest and tallest wat in Lopburi. The laterite prang is slender and elegant and thought to be contemporary with Angkor Wat in Cambodia (12th century).

Wat Phra Buddhabat

ⓘ *24 km south of the old city in the town of Phra Buddhabat, take Route 1 south and after 23 km turn onto Route 310, or catch a Saraburi bus from the bus station; passengers are let off on the main road, from where it's 1 km to the shrine.*

This wat is founded on the site of a large footprint of the Buddha – the most renowned in the country. A short stairway, flanked by two well-wrought many headed nagas, leads up to a cluster of shrines, salas, chedis and pavilions set at different levels. The ornate tile-encrusted mondop, built to cover the footprint, was constructed during Rama I's reign. It has four pairs of exquisite mother-of-pearl doors. The footprint itself, which is a natural impression made in the limestone rock (depending on one's beliefs), was first discovered in the reign of King Song Tham (1610-1628). It is 150 cm long, edged in gold and set down below floor level. The print must be special: pilgrims not only rub gold leaf onto it, but also rain down coins and banknotes, hence the protective grill. It is said that King Song Tham ordered officials to search for the footprint, having been told by Ceylonese monks that one might be found in Thailand. A hunter stumbled across it while trailing a wounded deer – which was miraculously healed of its injury – and the site was declared a shrine.

Sleeping

Ayutthaya *p162, map p164*

L-B Uthong Inn, 210 Rojana Rd, Amphoe Phra Nakhon Si, T035-242236, www.uthonginn.com. Inconvenient location 2 km or so east of town, but a strikingly attractive 100-room hotel, primarily aimed at the business market. Some a/c. Japanese restaurant and pool.

A Krung Si River Hotel, 7/2 Rojana Rd, to the east of town, T035-244333, F243777. A 200 room-plus hotel with all facilities including restaurant, pool, sauna and fitness

centre; a/c, situated on the banks of the Pasak River. Impersonal, a major road spoils the views and it is too far out of town to explore the old city on foot.

A-B Ayutthaya Hotel, Naresuan Rd (Chao Phrom Rd), T035-232855, F251018. This is probably the best hotel on the riverine island on which the historic city of Ayutthaya was centred. Good pool, attractive decor, although now feeling a little run-down, restaurant. There is a cheaper guesthouse wing.

B Teveraj Tamrin Hotel, 91 Mu 10, Tambon Ka Mung, T035-243139, F244139. Close to the train station (turn left), with views over the River Pasak. Pleasant rooms with good western bathrooms. Floating restaurant (see Eating).

C Suan Lang Hotel, 96 Rojana Rd, T035-245537. Rooms with a/c and shower, good value, clean rooms, restaurant.

C-E PU Guesthouse, 20/1 Soi Thor Kor Sor, Naresuan Rd, T035-251213. This is undoubtedly the most delightful place to stay in Ayutthaya in this price category. Recently renovated, some a/c and en suite facilities, some fan rooms, all well maintained. Very helpful Thai owner with excellent English. Good food in a new a/c restaurant, dorms for ฿60, satellite TV, internet and information services, bicycle (฿50) and motorbike hire (฿250). Veranda for relaxation and drinks. Highly recommended.

C-E Toto, Soi Thor Kor Sor, Naresuan Rd (Chao Phrom Rd), next door to **Ayutthaya Guesthouse**. Clean rooms, some a/c and TV. Family run and friendly. Excellent dormitory, rooms are open in high season for ฿80.

D-E Ayutthaya Guesthouse, 12/34 Soi Thor Kor Sor, Naresuan Rd (Chao Phrom Rd), T035-232658. Some a/c, some fan-cooled rooms. Communal facilities in this attractive teak house are kept spotless. Dorm beds also available. Restaurant, international payphone, helpful staff and very popular. Organized tours available (but bikes no longer available for rent). Recommended.

D-E Tony's Place, 12/18 Soi Thor Kor Sor, T035-252578. Stylish wooden house, clean and smart, some rooms with fan, some with en suite showers. Very popular, with friendly English-speaking staff. Superb restaurant attached.

E Ayutthaya Youth Hostel, 48/2 Uthong Rd, T035-241978. Interesting house, clean rooms, friendly people.

E-F PS Guesthouse, 23/1 Maharaj Rd (moved from Soi Thor Kor Sor), no phone. Run by teacher Phatsaphorn, with an English manager and a Japanese receptionist. Very friendly and quiet place, with a large garden in front. Bicycles and motorbikes can be rented from here.

E-F TMT Guesthouse, 14/9 Soi Thor Kor Sor, Naresuan Rd. T035-251474. Good clean, fan-cooled rooms, with good service, basic showers and squat toilets, cheap dorm rooms. Restaurant and minibar in front.

Lopburi *p168, map p170*

Most people only stop off in Lopburi for a few hours and the standard of accommodation bears this out – those listed below are rarely full.

A Lopburi Inn, Phahonyothin Rd, T036-411625, F412010. Slightly overpowering monkey theme employed in this hotel's decor and it is also a long way out of town. Nevertheless, the smartest in the area with good facilities including a gym and a large pool.

D Asia Lopburi, 28/9 Narai Maharat Rd, T036-411625, F412010. Fairly clean rooms, friendly and great location. Good option.

E Nett, 17/1-2 Rachdamnern Soi 2, T036-411738. Clean, central and quiet, with attached shower rooms, the best of the cheaper hotels.

Eating

Ayutthaya *p162, map p164*

Restaurants in Ayutthaya are good places to sample Chao Phraya river fish like *plaa chon*, *plaa nam ngen* and snake head.

TTT Ku-Choeng Chinese Restaurant, at the Krung Si River Hotel. The flashiest restaurant in town, serving a wide choice of good but expensive Chinese food.

TT Floating Restaurant, at the Teveraj Tamrin, on the Pasak River. This pleasing restaurant is divided into a/c and open air sections. It serves sushi and a very large choice of Thai and Western food.

TT Phae Krung Kao, 4 Uthong Rd. Floating restaurant to the south of Pridi Damrong bridge, excellent Chao Phraya river fish – try

the *plaa chon* and the tasty deep-fried snake head (a fish!) with chillies.

Ruan Thai Mai Suay (Thai House), Route 3059 (south of the city). This restaurant is 2 km or so to the south, on Route 3059, but getting here is worth the effort: good Thai food in an open, wooden traditional Central Plains house, very popular with wealthier locals.

Siam Restaurant, Chee Kun Rd, T035-211070. A smart a/c restaurant. Tables upstairs in the open air have a terrific view of Wat Phra Mahathat. Good value Thai and Vietnamese food offered. Recommended.

Foodstalls

There is a night market with cheap foodstalls in the parking area in front of Chandra Kasem Palace; stalls are also concentrated at the west end of Chao Phrom Rd and in the market at the northeast corner of the city on Uthong Rd. The covered Chao Phrom Market is also an excellent place for cheap food.

Lopburi *p168, map p170*

The orchards around Lopburi are reputed to produce the finest noi naa (custard apples). Lopburi has a good selection of Chinese-Thai restaurants, especially along Na Phrakan Rd and Sorasak Rd. The market between Rachdamnern Rd and Rue de France provides the usual range of stall foods, as do the stalls along Sorasak Rd. The best places to eat in the evening are at the stalls along Na Phrakan Rd in the Old City.

Chulathip, corner of Na Phrakan and Rachdamnern rds. Nothing to do with the hotel, this 24-hr open-air restaurant is good value. Recommended.

Bars and clubs

Ayutthaya *p162, map p164*

Bohemian Bar, just opposite the Moon Café on Soi Thor Kor Sor. Cheap food and drinks. Chilled out seating area on logs and straw mats with chairs and tables extending out onto the road, and a range of music from techno to jazz. Opening times vary depending on how lively it is, but generally from around 1600 to 0300. Recommended.

Good Luck Bar and Restaurant, Soi Thor Sor Khor. Also does cheap food and drinks.

Home Pub, 51/1 Naresuan Rd, opposite BJ Guesthouse. Open daily 1900-0200. Live music every night, country pub style.

Moon Café, Soi Thor Kor Sor, Naresuan Rd (Chao Phrom Rd). More of a bar than a café. This immensely stylish, but small, venue offers a limited Thai and Western menu. Recommended.

Festivals and events

Ayutthaya *p162, map p164*

Nov Loi Krathong, festival of lights (see page 59).

Transport

Ayutthaya *p162, map p164*

Bicycle

Hired from guesthouses for about ฿50 per day.

Boat

Long-tailed boats can be hired at the jetty opposite the Chandra Kasem Palace in the northeast corner of town. Expect to pay ฿250 for 1 hr (boats can take 10 people). The **Ayutthaya Guesthouse** and several other guesthouses also arrange boats.

Private boats can also be hired from the pier opposite Chandra Kasem Palace in Ayutthaya, the most popular destination being the Summer Palace at **Bang Pa In** (see page 119). ฿250-300 one-way, ฿400 return (3 hrs).

From **Bangkok**, see Bangkok Tours, page 149. From Tha Tien pier in Bangkok daily at 1000. Boat trips around the river from the pier cost ฿600 per trip for up to 12 people. The Benjarang boat does a tour south along the Chao Phraya River, stopping at Wat Chai Wattanaram, Wat Phutthaisawan and Wat Phanam Choeng for ฿180 per person.

Bus

The station is on Chao Phrom Rd. Regular a/c and non-a/c connections with **Bangkok**'s Northern bus terminal (1½ hrs) and stops north including **Lopburi** (2 hrs), **Phitsanulok**, **Chiang Mai** and **Sukhothai** (5 hrs).

Saamlor

Around town should not cost more than ฿20-30; they can be hired by the hour.

Songthaew
From the train station into town expect to pay ฿5. They run about the old town for a flat fare of ฿3. They can also be chartered for about ฿300 per day.

Train
The station is just off Rojana Rd, across the Pasak River. Nine connections daily with **Bangkok**'s Hualamphong station (1½ hrs), and with all stops north to **Chiang Mai** (12 hrs). It is possible to catch a train from Don Muang Airport, making it unnecessary to enter Bangkok. The easiest way to get from the station in Ayutthaya to the old city is to take the small track facing the station down to the river; from the jetty here ferries cross over to the other side every 5 mins or so (฿2).

Tuk-tuk
Around town for ฿30-50.

Lopburi *p168, map p170*
Frequent buses and songthaews ferry passengers between the old and new towns.

Bus
The bus station for both a/c and non-a/c buses is in the new town, 2 km from the old town, close to the roundabout where Routes 311 and 3016 cross (Wongwian Sra Kaeo). Regular connections with **Bangkok**'s Northern bus terminal (2-3 hrs) and with **Ayutthaya** (1 hr). Buses from **Kanchanaburi** via **Suphanburi** and **Singburi** (6 hrs), and destinations north.

Train
Regular connections with **Bangkok**'s Hualamphong station (2¾ hrs), **Ayutthaya** (1 hr) and destinations to the north.

Directory

Ayutthaya *p162, map p164*
Banks Most of the banks are either on Uthong Rd or Naresuan Rd (Chao Phrom Rd) and change TCs and have ATMs. Bangkok, Uthong Rd (next to Cathay Hotel). **Siam City**, Uthong Rd (close to Uthong Hotel). **Thai** Military, Chao Phrom Rd. **Thai Farmers**, Chao Phrom Rd. **Internet** A number of internet cafés have opened up on Naresuan Rd and Soi Thor Kor Sor. **Post office** Uthong Rd (south from the Chandra Kasem Palace). International calls available here. **Useful addresses** Tourist Police, across the street from TAT office, Si Sanphet Rd, T035-242352.

Lopburi *p168, map p170*
Banks Krung Thai, 74 Vichayen Rd. Thai Military, corner of Sorasak and Rachdamnern roads. **Medical services** Hospital: Phahonyothin Rd. **Post office** On road to Singburi, not far from Prang Sam Yod. A second post office is to be found near the bus station.

Kanchanaburi and the west

The wonderful forests, hills and melange of different peoples of this western tract of Thailand are overshadowed by a terrible history – during the Second World War thousands of prisoners of war and local labourers died at the hands of their Japanese captors building a railway line through almost impassable terrain. This piece of history was made famous in David Lean's 1957 Oscar winning epic, Bridge on the River Kwai. *Today, the bridge, sited at the town of Kanchanaburi, and the war museums and memorials associated with it, has helped turn the region into a tourist mecca. Most come not only to visit the famous bridge but also to relax by Kanchanaburi's elegant Kwai Noi River.*

The more adventurous head into the national parks and hills further west. Here, the evocatively named Three Pagodas Pass (Saam Ong), miscellaneous indigenous groups, the resort town of Sangkhlaburi and the Burmese border awaits. ▸▸ *For Sleeping, Eating and other listings, see pages 184-188.*

Kanchanaburi and around

→ *Colour map 3, grid B3.*

Famous for the *Bridge over the River Kwai*, Kanchanaburi is surrounded by a vast area of great natural beauty making it a good base to visit national parks, sail down the Kwai River or travel to one of a number of waterfalls and caves. The province's wealth is derived from gems mined at the Bo-Phloi mines, teak trading with Burma, sugar cane plantations and tourism. It was from here that the Japanese set Allied prisoners of war to work on the construction of the notorious 'death railway', linking Thailand with Burma during the Second World War (see box, page 178).

Ins and outs

Getting there There are regular connections by train and bus with Bangkok. The journey from Bangkok takes around 2½ hours by train while any of the numerous buses take two hours. There are also bus connections with Nakhon Pathom (1½ hours), Suphanburi and onwards to Sangkhlaburi. ►► *See Transport, page 187, for further details.*

Getting around Bicycles, motorbikes and jeeps can all be hired in Kanchanaburi and offer the most flexible way to explore the surrounding countryside. Alternatively, saamlors provide short-distance trips around town while tuk-tuks are handy for longer journeys. Rafts and long-tail boats are available for charter on the river.

Tourist information TAT ① *Saengchuto Rd, T034-511200 (walk south, towards Bangkok, from the market and bus station)*. A good first stop as it supplies up to date information on accommodation. Covers Kanchanaburi, Nakhon Pathom, Samut Sakhon and Samut Songkhram. Most tour operators offer similar excursions: jungle trekking, elephant rides, bamboo rafting, visits to Hellfire Pass and various waterfalls. In Bangkok, virtually every hotel or tour office will be able to offer a day tour (or longer) to Kanchanaburi and surrounding sights.

Background

Kanchanaburi was established in the 1830s, although the ruins of Muang Singh (see page 179) to the west date from the Khmer period. On entering the town (called Muang Kan by most locals), visitors may notice the fish-shaped street signs. The fish in question is the yisok, a small freshwater fish and the symbol of Kanchanaburi. Another slice of Thai fauna for which this area of Thailand is known is Kitti's hog-nosed bat. As with so many tourist success stories, Kanchanaburi has its downside. In this case, it is pollution from the 900-odd raft-based guesthouse and restaurant operations. Almost none of the rafts has water treatment or waste disposal systems. This was fine when there were just a handful of rafts and a few thousand tourists a year. Now the numbers are far greater and public health officials have detected a significant rise in water pollution.

Town sights

The **JEATH War Museum** ① *0830-1800: ฿30 (no photographs)*, (its name denotes the countries involved – Japan, England, America, Australia, Thailand and Holland), can be found by the river, at the end of Wisuttharangsi Road. The museum, which holds an interesting and harrowing display of prisoners working on the railway was established in 1977 by the monks of Wat Chanasongkhram.

The **Kanchanaburi War Cemetery (Don Rak)** ① *Saengchuto Rd, 1½ km out of town, 0800-1700, or you can always look over the gates, walk, hire a bicycle* (*฿20 a day) or take a saamlor*, is immaculately maintained by the Commonwealth Cemeteries Commission. Some 6,982 Allied servicemen are buried here, most of whom died as prisoners of war whilst they built the Burma railway.

Kanchanaburi

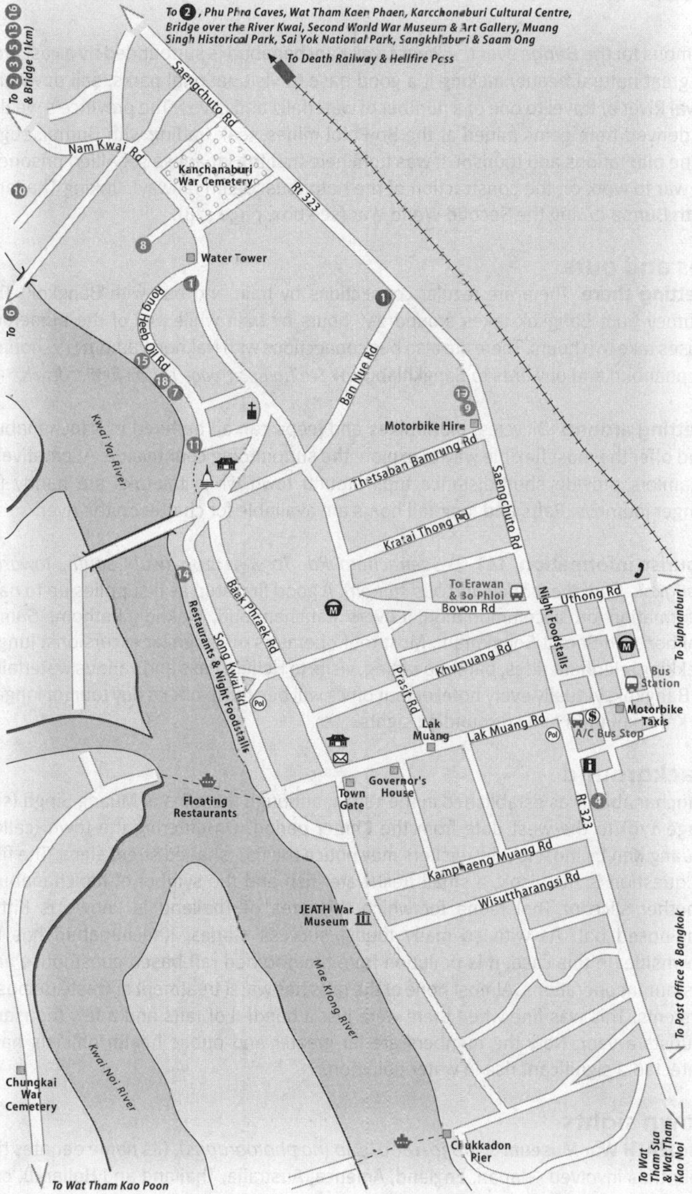

To 2, Phu Phra Caves, Wat Tham Kaen Phaen, Karcchonaburi Cultural Centre, Bridge over the River Kwai, Second World War Museum & Art Gallery, Muang Singh Historical Park, Sai Yok National Park, Sangkhlaburi & Saam Ong
To Death Railway & Hellfire Pass
To 2 3 5 13 16 & Bridge (1km)
Saengchuto Rd
Nam Kwai Rd
Kanchanaburi War Cemetery
Rt 323
Water Tower
To 6
Rong Heeb Oil Rd
Ban Nue Rd
Motorbike Hire
Kwai Yai River
Thetsaban Bamrung Rd
Saengchuto Rd
Kratai Thong Rd
To Erawan & Bo Phloi
Bovon Rd
Night Foodstalls
Uthong Rd
To Suphanburi
Baak Phraek Rd
Song Kwai Rd
Restaurants & Night Foodstalls
Khumuang Rd
Prasit Rd
Bus Station
Motorbike Taxis
Lak Muang
Lak Muang Rd
A/C Bus Stop
Town Gate
Governor's House
Floating Restaurants
Rt 323
Kamphaeng Muang Rd
Wisuttharangsi Rd
JEATH War Museum
Mae Klong River
To Post Office & Bangkok
Chungkai War Cemetery
Kwai Noi River
Chukkadon Pier
To Wat Tham Sua & Wat Tham Kao Noi
To Wat Tham Kao Poon
N
0 metres 100
0 yards 100

Sleeping
Apple's Guesthouse 1
Bamboo House 2
Blue Star 3
Canaan 4
C & C 5
Felix River Kwai 6
Prasopsuk & Restaurant 7
Jolly Frog Backpackers 8
MK 9
Mr Tee 10
River Guesthouse 11
Sam's House 13
Sam's Place 14
Sam's River Rafthouse 15
Sugar Cane 1 16
Vimol Guesthouse 18
VL 19

Eating
River Kwai Floating Restaurant 2

Bars & clubs
Apache Saloon 1

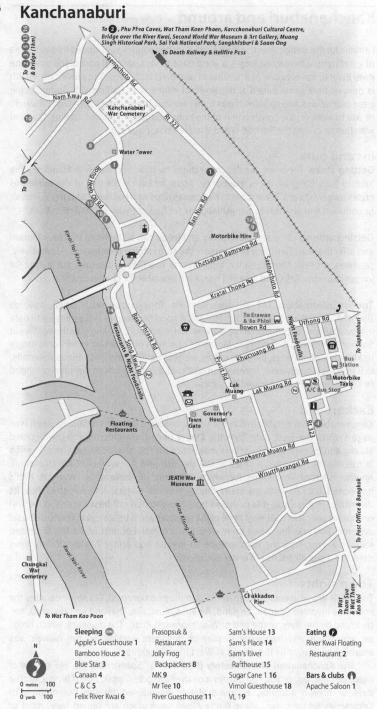

Situated 2 km south of town, the **Chungkai (UK) War Cemetery** ⓘ *take a boat from in front of the town gates, or by tuk-tuk or bicycle,* is small, peaceful and well kept, with the graves of 1,750 prisoners of war.

Kanchanaburi's **lak muang** (city pillar), encrusted in gold leaf and draped with flowers, can be seen in the middle of Lak Muang Road. Close by are the gates to Kanchanaburi town. Walking through the gates and turning right (north) is the old and most attractive part of town with wooden shops and houses.

Bridge over the River Kwai

ⓘ *Take a saamlor, hire a bicycle, catch a songthaew or board the train, which travels from the town's station to the bridge. Boats can be rented at the bridge.*

Situated 3-4 km north of the town on Saengchuto Road, the Bridge over the River Kwai (pronounced Kway in Thai, not Kwai) is architecturally unexciting and is of purely historical interest. The central span was destroyed by Allied bombing towards the end of the war, and has been rebuilt in a different style. Visitors can walk over the bridge, visit the **Second World War Museum and Art Gallery** ⓘ *0900-1630, ฿30,* or browse in the many souvenir stalls. The museum is an odd affair with some displays relating to the bridge and the prisoners of war who worked and died here, along with a collection of Thai weaponry and amulets, and a collection of astonishingly bad portraits of Thai kings.

Death Railway and Hellfire Pass

ⓘ *No admission fee, but donations requested (most visitors leave ฿100). Two trains each way daily, leaving Kanchanaburi at 1045 and 1637, with return trains at 0525 and 1300, approximately 2 hrs. From the Nam Tok station, it is another 14 km to the Hellfire Pass and Museum, for which you need a songthaew (฿400 return, 20 mins one way. To reach the pass by road take a northbound bus about 80 km on Route 323 to a Royal Thai Army farm at the Km 66 marker. A track here leads through the farm to a steep path to the pass. There are numerous organized tours to Hellfire Pass.*

Only 130 km of the Death Railway remain, from Nong Pradook station in the neighbouring province of Ratchaburi through to the small town of Nam Tok. From Kanchanaburi to Nam Tok the railway sweeps through a tranche of dramatic scenery stopping at the ancient Khmer site of Muang Singh en route (see below). The name for the pass was bestowed by one of the prisoners of war who, looking down on his comrades working below at night by the glow of numerous open fires, remarked that the sight was like 'the jaws of hell'. Australian Rod Beattie, with the support of the Australian government, has developed the pass as a memorial cutting a path through to the pass and building a museum. Clear, well-written wall panels surrounded by photographs, along with some reproduction objects, provide a very moving account of the cutting of the pass. From here it is possible to walk a fair distance of the railway route (the rails no longer exist); stout shoes recommended. There are two routes: the full circuit is 4½ km-long and ends at Hellfire Pass itself; or the Konyu Cutting.

Wat Tham Kao Poon

ⓘ *No entrance fee to the caves, but visitors are encouraged to make a contribution to the maintenance of the monastery (฿10-20). Hire a bicycle or tuk-tuk or charter a boat from in front of the town gates. Situated 5 km southwest of town, this wat is a few kilometres on from the Chungkai Cemetery.*

Wat Tham Kao Poon is a rather gaudy temple with caves attached. Follow the arrows through the cave system. There is a large Buddha image at the bottom of the system

Kitti's hog-nosed bat is the smallest in the world, with a body the size of a bumble-bee. It was discovered in 1973 by Doctor Kitti Thonglongya in limestone caves near the River Kwai Bridge.

The death railway

The River Kwai will be forever associated with a small bridge and a bloody railway.

For the Japanese high command during the Second World War, the logic of building a rail link between Siam and Burma was clear - it would cut almost 2,000 km off the sea journey from Japan to Rangoon making it easier to supply their fast-expanding empire. The problem was that the Japanese lacked the labour to construct the line through some of the wettest and most inhospitable land in the region. They estimated that it would take five to six years to finish. The solution to their dilemma was simple: employ some of the 300,000 POWs who were being unproductively incarcerated in Singapore.

Work began in June 1942. More than 3,000,000 cu m of rock were shifted, 15 km of bridges built and 415 km of track laid. The workforce, at its peak, numbered 61,000 Allied POWs and an estimated 250,000 Asians. Work was hard; a prisoner, Naylor wrote: "We started work the day after we arrived, carrying huge baulks of timber. It was the heaviest work I have ever known; the Japs drove us on and by nightfall I was so tired and sore that I could not eat my dinner and just crawled on to the bed and fell asleep. The next day was spent carrying stretchers of earth, also heavy work and incredibly monotonous. The hours were 0830 to 1930 with an hour for lunch."

The Japanese, but particularly the Korean overseers, adopted a harsh code of discipline – face slapping, blows with rifle butts, standing erect for hours on end, and solitary confinement for weeks in small cells made of mud and bamboo. By 1943, after years of torturous work combined with poor diet, most of the men were in an appalling state.

(and smaller ones elsewhere), as well as cells (kutis) in which monks can meditate. Intrepid explorers will find they emerge at the back of the hill. Early in 1996 this cave wat was the site of the murder of British tourist, Johanne Masheder (the cave where the murder took place is permanently closed), by a drug addicted Thai monk. The crime shook Thailand's religious establishment and the abbot of the monastery was suspended for neglect.

Wat Tham Sua and Wat Tham Kao Noi

ⓘ *Hire a motorbike or charter a tuk-tuk/songthaew.*

Wat Tham Sua and Wat Tham Kao Noi lie 20 km southeast of Kanchanaburi. The main temple is a strange, pagoda-like affair perched on a hilly outcrop, and can be seen from afar. At the base of the hill is a Chinese temple, and a short walk further is the steep dragon-lined staircase that leads up the hill to the wat itself. The pagoda is a weird amalgam of Chinese and Thai, new and old.

Phu Phra Caves, Wat Tham Kun Phaen and Kanchanaburi Cultural Centre

ⓘ *Take bus 8203 (tell the bus conductor where you want to get off), or hire a motorbike or songthaew/tuk-tuk.*

Phu Phra Caves and Wat Tham Kun Phaen are about 20 km north of town, just off Route 323 to Sangkhlaburi. The wat and its associated caves nestle in foothills which rise up towards Burma. Back on Route 323 is the Kanchanaburi Cultural Centre, with a collection of handicrafts, artefacts and historical exhibits

In Colonel Toosey's report of October 1945, he wrote: "On one occasion a party of 60, mostly stretcher cases, were dumped off a train in a paddy field some two miles from the Camp in the pouring rain at 0300 hours. As a typical example I can remember one man who was so thin that he could be lifted easily in one arm. His hair was growing down his back and was full of maggots; his clothing consisted of a ragged pair of shorts soaked with dysentery excreta; he was lousy and covered with flies all the time. He was so weak that he was unable to lift his head to brush away the flies which were clustered on his eyes and on the sore places of his body. I forced the Japanese Staff to come and look at these parties, which could be smelt for some hundreds of yards, but with the exception of the Camp Comdt. they showed no signs of sympathy, and sometimes merely laughed." (Quoted in Peter Davies, *The man behind the Bridge*, 1991:116).

The railway was finished in late 1943, the line from Nong Pladuk being linked with that from Burma on 17 October. For the POWs it was not the end, however; even after the Japanese capitulated on 10 August 1945, the men had to wait for some while before they were liberated. During this period of limbo, Allied officers were worried most about venereal disease, and Colonel Toosey radioed to Delhi for 10,000 condoms to be dropped by air - an incredible thought given the physical condition of the former POWs. In all, 16,000 Allied prisoners lost their lives and Kanchanaburi contains the graves of 7,000 of the victims in two war cemeteries. Less well known are the 75,000 Asian forced labourers who also died constructing the railway. Their sufferings are not celebrated.

Muang Singh Historical Park

ⓘ *0800-1700. ฿4. Hire a tuk-tuk/songthaew or motorbike, or take the train to Thakilen station – it is about a 1½ km walk.*

This ancient Khmer town, the 'city of lions', is situated on the banks of the Kwai Noi River – about 45 km west of Kanchanaburi. Built of deep red laterite, Muang Singh reached its apogee during the 12th-13th centuries when it flourished as a trading post linking Siam with the Indian Ocean. The city represents an artistic and strategic outlier of the great Cambodian Empire, and it is mentioned in inscriptions from the reign of the Khmer King Jayavarman VII.

Khao Phang and Sai Yok Noi waterfall

ⓘ *Take bus 8203 from Kanchanaburi town (1 hr). Buses leave every 30 mins between 0645 and 1800. It is 1 km to the falls and 2 km to the caves (the sign for the falls is in Thai only, so follow signs to the cave which are in English).*

Some 60 km northwest of Kanchanaburi on Route 323, Khao Phang and Sai Yok Noi waterfall are only impressive in the wet season (July-September), and swimming in the pools below the waterfall is also best during this season. Close by are the **Vang Ba Dalh caves.**

Sai Yok National Park

ⓘ *Boats can be hired from Pak Saeng pier in Tambon Tha Saaw, about 50 km north of Kanchanaburi town. A boat (maximum 10 people) to the park (including the Lawa caves and Sai Yok Yai waterfall), should cost ฿1,200 per boat (seating 10-12 people) (or go on a tour) and the trip will take 2½ hrs upstream and 1½*

Tigers and elephants still inhabit this wild region of stunning scenery, stretching to the Burmese border.

hrs down. There are also buses from Kanchanaburi to the park, 1 hr. See also Sleeping. The best time to visit: May-Dec.

Sai Yok National Park lies 104 km northwest of Kanchanaburi. The park's main attraction is the **Sai Yok Yai waterfall**. Also near Sai Yok Yai are the **Daowadung Caves** (30 minutes north by boat from the falls and then a 3-km walk).

Erawan National Park

ⓘ *0600-1800. ฿200 entrance fee to the park. Regular buses (No 8170) every 50 mins from 0800 onwards from Kanchanaburi (1½-2 hrs, ฿26). The last bus back to Kanchanaburi leaves Erawan at 1600. See also Sleeping. The best time to visit the falls is during the rainy season. It's a 35-min walk from the bus station to the first of the series of 7 falls.*

This area of great natural beauty, 65 km north of Kanchanaburi, covering 550 sq km, contains the impressive Erawan Falls. Split into seven levels the first is popular with swimmers and picnickers. Level three is very beautiful, and level seven is well worth the steep climb with refreshing pools awaiting any intrepid trekker who makes the precarious climb up. The impressive **Phrathat Caves**, with huge and stupendous stalagtites and stalagmites, are located about 10 km northwest of headquarters, a good hike or easy drive.

Arguably the most striking waterfalls are those at **Huay Khamin**, some 108 km northwest of town. The falls are awkward to reach independently but tour companies will provide arranged trips. The **Thung Yai** and **Huai Kha Khaeng wildlife sanctuaries**, where the falls are based, were once threatened by a proposed dam that would have destroyed rare stands of riverine tropical forest that exist here. Public pressure ensured that the plans were shelved, representing the first significant victory for environmentalists in Thailand. In 1992 the two sanctuaries were declared Southeast Asia's first Natural World Heritage Site by UNESCO, vindicating the environmentalists' stand.

Bo Phloi

ⓘ *Take bus 325 from Kanchanaburi bus station, 1½ hrs.*

Bo Phloi, 50 km north of town, is one of Thailand's main gem-mining areas. Here are eight open-cast mines, extracting sapphires, onyx and semi-precious stones, and a number of polishing plants. Displays of local production techniques are given.

Tham Than Lot National Park

ⓘ *There are regular connections between Kanchanaburi and Nong Pru. The road to the park cuts off left from Route 3086 shortly before entering Nong Pru; the park entrance is 22 km from this turn-off. During the week it is usually necessary to charter a motorcycle or songthaew to the park, but at weekends there is a public service from Nong Pru. See also Sleeping.*

The park encompasses a portion of the Tenasserim range of mountains that form the border between Thailand and Burma and includes small populations of **Asiatic black bear, white-handed gibbon** and **elephant**. There is even talk that there may be tigers here. The highest peak is Khao Khampaeng, which rises to 1,260 m. Within easy walking of park headquarters (where there is a visitors' centre) is **Than Lot Noi Cave**, after which the park was named. The cave reaches around 300 m into the mountain side. A trail leads from here for around 2 km to another cave, **Than Lot Yai**, where there is a small Buddhist shrine.

Sangkhlaburi and Saam Ong (Three Pagodas Pass)

→ *Colour map 3, grid A2.*

The route to Sangkhlaburi, or 'Sangkhla', and Saam Ong (Three Pagodas Pass) from Kanchanaburi, a total of some 240 km, follows the valley of the Kwai. The scenery soon becomes increasingly rugged with the road passing through remnant forests and expanses of deep red tropical soils used to grow cassava, tamarind, mango and cotton. Roughly 3 hours from Kanchanburi sits the market town of Thong Pha Phum and the eastern edge of the massive Khao Laem reservoir. From here, the road begins to wind through a steep hills and dense forest. Just before Sangkhlaburi the road skirts the reservoir; a strange landscape of submerged (now dead) trees and what appear to be raft-houses. This upland area is also home to several different ethnic groups: Karen, Mon and Burmese.

Towards Sangkhlaburi

Thong Pha Phum ⓘ *regular bus connections with Kanchanaburi's bus terminal (3 hrs) and onwards north to Sangkhlaburi*, is a small, peaceful market town situated in a beautiful position on the southern shores of the Khao Laem Reservoir, 74 km south of Sangkhlaburi. Many of the inhabitants of the town are Mon and Karen. Around Thong Pha Phum are a large number of lakeside resort hotels and raft operations, mainly geared to Thai weekenders from Bangkok. Comparatively few farang tourists make it up here but this is changing as more and more people decide to explore further west. The Khao Laem Reservoir was created in 1983 when the Electricity Generating Authority of Thailand built the Khao Laem Dam and flooded the valley. About a dozen villages were inundated as a result and submerged tree-trunks still make navigation hazardous in the lake's shallows. It's still possible to hire expensive long-tailed boats or go fishing and swimming. There are also numerous walks and trails to explore, and various waterfalls and caves.

Although the 1,500 sq km **Khao Laem National Park** ⓘ *park headquarters are close to the main road (Route 323) to Sangkhlaburi; Thong Pha Phum has regular bus connections with Kanchanaburi's bus terminal (3 hrs) and onwards north to Sangkhlaburi*, has been heavily logged, parts of it still play host to small populations of leopard, gibbon and macaque, as well as lesser mammals such as civets and mongoose. The best habitats can be found towards the northeast and the small Thung Yai wildlife sanctuary which abuts the park.

Sangkhlaburi

Sangkhlaburi is situated on the edge of the huge Khao Laem Reservoir, which was created in 1983 with the damming of three rivers which used to feed the Khwae Noi River. The village is interesting for its diverse nationalities of Karen, Mon, Burmese, Indians, Pakistanis and Chinese. It is also a centre for wood and drugs smuggling and other illicit trading.

The morning market here provides a range of textiles and various Burmese goods. A 400-m wooden bridge across the lake, largely built by the Mon people, is said to be the longest in Thailand. It leads to a Mon village (Waeng Kha), which is interesting to walk around. There are also stunning views of the surrounding hills from the bridge. The 8,000 inhabitants are mainly displaced Burmese who cannot get a Thai passport and can only work around Sangkhla.

From 1948 onwards refugees have fled Burma for the relative safety of Thailand. Most of them will never be allowed a visa or resident's permit. In 1982 the old town of Sangkhlaburi was flooded by the dam and these refugees were again left with no homes or land. The abbot of the flooded Wat Sam Prasop, the spires of which can be seen – so it is said – protruding above the lake waters during the dry season, was able to acquire land for a new wat and helped 500 households to re-establish themselves.

 However, these people are not wanted by the Thai government and there have been several raids by the army to round up Mon people without identity cards. Over the years they have been protected by the monks living here, but there is no guarantee this will continue and their existence in Thailand is uncertain to say the least.

Wat Wang Wiwekaram is situated across the lake from Sangkhlaburi on a hill. It was built in 1982 to replace the revered temple (Wat Sam Prasop), which was submerged by the reservoir. The chedi is said to be modelled on the Mahabodhi stupa in Bodhgaya, India, with the viharn, allegedly constructed with black market profits, providing a fine example of nouveau gauche temple architecture. To the east of the wat is a **Burmese handicraft market**, where sarongs, silk, cloth, lacquerware, silver jewellery are all for sale. Avoid the 'gems' since they are almost certain fakes.

Around Sangkhlaburi

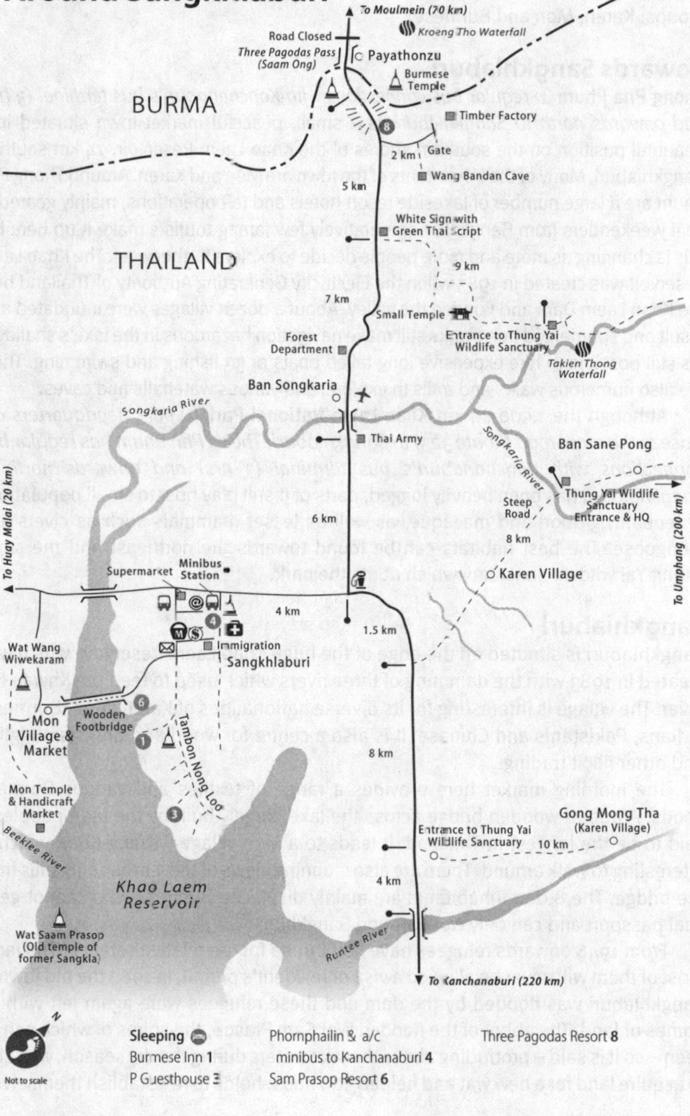

Saam Ong (Three Pagodas Pass) → *Colour map 3, grid A2.*

This is an unexciting spot with a tacky market in a makeshift shelter, which sells a few Burmese goods (teak, umghi, seed pearls) and a lot of Chinese imports. Avoid the 'gems', they will be fake. The pagodas, wrapped in red, saffron and white cloth, are truly unremarkable. This was the traditional invasion route for Burmese soldiers during the Ayutthayan period (see pages 163 and 625).

The border ⓘ *open 0600-1800*, between Burma and Thailand is periodically closed due to political conflict. It is therefore well worth checking the situation at the border before arrival. There is a tourist police office at the pass if you encounter problems.

At the border, 20 km northwest of Sangkhlaburi, where posters declare 'Love your Motherland' and 'Respect the Law', visitors can pay a US$10 immigration fee to enter Burma and the village of **Payathonzu** (meaning Three Pagodas) ⓘ *motorbike taxis can transport you to the market area of Payathonzu (฿10 from the songthaew drop-off point), which is more market than village; this fee, however, changes regularly, so you may find it to be anywhere between US$5-18*. At the time of writing it was no longer possible to pay in baht and you must also apply for an entrance permit (one passport photo needed) from the immigration office in Sangkhlaburi (see map). You will be required to leave your passport with the Sangklaburi immigration office. On the border lie the remains of the Burmese/Thai/Japanese railway. The market here is marginally more interesting than at Saam Ong, with a range of handicrafts, jewellery, jade, amulets, Burmese blankets, and an alarming amount of teak furniture. There is also a handful of Thai restaurants and noodle stalls and an Indian-run bakery.

Beyond the village, there is another border post, beyond which visitors are forbidden to go. Sometimes this area opens up to tourists and certainly the Thai and Burmese tourist organizations have plans on jointly developing the border area. Burmese restrictions may vary between 2 km and 20 km. Note that it is illegal to cross the border anywhere other than at a checkpoint. Similarly, do not go beyond Payathonzu without permission of the Burmese army.

Control of this area has vacillated between the Burmese army and Mon and Karen rebels. At present it is firmly in the hands of the Burmese authorities. Some visitors may also be put off by the fact that the immigration fees go directly to the SPDC, the Burmese regime, and therefore helps to support the military dictatorship which has made Burma one of the poorest economies and most repressed societies in the world. The democratically elected leader of Burma, Aung San Suu Kyi, continues to request that tourists do not visit her country until the political situation has changed for the better. The only place to stay at Saam Ong is the **Three Pagodas Pass Resort**, see Sleeping.

Around Saam Ong

The Mon village of **Ban Songkaria** lies 6 km north from the turn-off to Three Pagodas Pass. It was once the headquarters for the Mon army. The airstrip on the right-hand side of the road, opposite the village, was originally used by the Thai Air Force. There has been talk of flights to Kanchanaburi and Bangkok, but nothing seems to have materialized.

One of the three local entrances to **Thung Yai Wildlife Sanctuary** lies 15 km northeast of Sangkhla, in the Karen village of Ban Sane Pong. Within the park is the Takien Thong Waterfall, with big pools for swimming. The falls lie 26 km from Sangkhla, north of Ban Sane Pong, but are only accessible by taking the main road north for 13 km from the turn-off to Three Pagodas Pass, and then taking a right turn down a dirt road for 9 km, which is possible to drive down on motorbikes. Until recently this route was only negotiable during the dry season, but with the completion of a new all-weather road access should be year-round.

Malaria is common in this area, particularly in the jungle, so take precautions and try to avoid being bitten.

Wang Bandan Cave ⓘ *no entrance fee, but the monks may try to charge ฿50 to guide visitors through the cave*, lies 18 km north from the turn off to Three Pagodas Pass, 2 km down a track to the right of the road. Monks used to live in the cave until just a few years ago, but (it is said) due to the effects of increasing tourism in the area, from both Thais and foreigners, they have moved to small houses at the bottom of the hill. The entrance and exit are different.

Huay Kha Khaeng Wildlife Sanctuary ⓘ *0800-1700, ฿200, which includes accommodation in one of the 3 very basic fan huts; larger groups should seek prior approval from the Wildlife Conservation Division of the Royal Forest Department, Royal Forest Department, 61 Phaholyathin Ladyao Jatujck, Bangkok, T02-5614292, webmaster@forest.go.th; take the Uthai Thani route to Lan Sak, and turn off about 30 km before you get to Lan Sak, follow this turn-off 14 km to Huay Kha Khaeng; there is public transport available*, is a World Heritage Site and one of the largest wildlife sanctuaries in Southeast Asia. If you're looking for the best of Thailand's free ranging wildlife species – including an enormous range of birdlife – it is unmissable. It borders the Tak and Kanchanaburi Provinces and is a haven for animals with its virgin deciduous forests, prairies, mountains and many streams. Hidden among the fronds are some of Thailand's largest remaining **wild elephant herds**, the last remaining herds of **wild water buffalo, rare gibbons,** three **otter species** and the **large gaur** and **banteng wild cattle** species. Also watch out for tigers, clouded leopards and sun bears. The sanctuary is, as yet, underdeveloped and it is advised not to stray too far from the bungalows both because of the danger of the resident animals, and that of getting lost. If the staff have enough time on their hands, they will lead short walks around the area, but their command of foreign languages presents a problem for those wanting to understand more of the indigenous flora, fauna and wildlife. There is a nature trail for small groups of visitors but additional services are limited.

Sleeping

Kanchanaburi and around *p175, map p176*

Disco boats on the river can cause noise pollution but they are only really active at weekends and usually stop at 2000. There are a large number of 'back to nature' resorts around Kanchanaburi which mostly cater for Thai tourists: the Legacy, Jungle House and Kasem.

AL-B Felix River Kwai Hotel, 9/1 Moo 3 Thamakhom, T034-515061, F515086. North of the bridge on the west bank of Kwai Yai River is this hotel, the most luxurious in town. With 255 rooms it is rather rambling, but it has all the facilities you'd expect from a first-class establishment.

A Legacy River Kwai Resort, 129 Moo 2, Tambon Klandoe, T034-2139872-6, www.stcgroup-th.com/thlegacy. 154 log cabins and attractive position. A/c, TV, en suite etc. All facilities and interesting courses on macrobiotic diets, yoga, ayurvedic massage and so on.

A-B River Kwai Jungle House, 96/1 Mu 3, Amphoe Sai Yok, 40 km from Kanchanaburi, near Muang Singh Historical Park, T034-561052. Rattan bungalows float on the river.

B Kasem Island Resort, 27 Chaichumphon Rd, T034-513359, F2556303. On an island on the Mae Klong, close to town centre and thus accessible, restaurant, attractive, clean rafts.

B-E Vimol Guesthouse, 48/5 Rong Heeb Oil 2 Rd, T034-514831, F514831. Unusual split-level A-frame huts – also some new raft accommodation available for slightly more. Some rooms have river views, a/c and hot showers. Recommended.

C-D Canaan Guesthouse, 53 Paopoon Soi, T09-9198C07 (mob), canaan@hotmail.com. Situated conveniently behind the bus station, this guesthouse opened in 2002 and offers a wonderful family atmosphere which makes up for the bland rooms. Great home-cooked food. Recommended.

C-E Blue Star 241 Meanumkwai Rd, T034-512161. This extremely friendly place, which offers guests a free cookery course, boasts a variety of rooms in various styles, notably the 'tarzan stilt houses' which are on the expensive side.

C-E **Sam's House**, 14/1 Mae Nam Kwai Rd, T034-515956, sams_guesthouse@hotmail.com. Good wooden huts with toilets, and balconies on the mangrovesque edge of the Kwai – good value. Good restaurant attached (see Eating below).

C-E **Sugar Cane 1**, 22 Soi Pakstan, Mae Nam Kwai Rd, T034-624520. This secluded spot provides a pleasant retreat in a good location. Spotlessly clean with friendly staff. Restaurant commands fantastic views over the river. Tours organized. Recommended.

D **Bamboo House**, 3-5 Soi Vietnam, Tha Makham, T034-512532. A quiet, secluded and attractive spot with a/c wooden bungalows and floating bamboo huts.

D **MK**, Saengchuto Rd, T034-511184, F511269. Clean, a/c motel-style rooms with good mosquito screens, TV and shower room. Beauty salon, golf shop and laundry.

D **VL**, 18/11 Saengchuto Rd, T034-513546. Some a/c, small restaurant, 3-storey block. Quiet, cool, spacious and secluded rooms (with bathrooms) set back from the busy road. Tasteful decor and breakfast is served in an attractive shady area.

D-E **Apple's Guesthouse (Krathom Thai)**, 293 Mae Nam Kwai Rd, T034-512017. An extremely good guesthouse, with very clean, comfortable mattresses and private showers. Very good restaurant (see Eating below).

D-E **Prasopsuk**, 677 Saengchuto Rd, T034-511777. Clean rooms with shower, TV and some with a/c. Good restaurant (see Eating below below).

D-E **Sam's Place** 7/3 Song Kwai Rd, T034-513971, sams_guesthouse@hotmail.com. Convenient central location next to the river. Large bamboo huts, some with a/c and some with good attached bathrooms. Can be noisy.

D-F **Jolly Frog Backpackers**, 28 Mae Nam Kwai Rd, T034-514579. Popular, well-established guesthouse, with attractive garden overlooking the river and local tour information. Wide range of vegetarian, Thai and European food in an affordable restaurant.

D-F **Sam's River Raft House**, Soi Rong Heeb Oil, Mae Nam Kwai Rd, T034-624231, www.samsguesthouse.com. Friendly and attractive, basic guesthouse. Offers great views of the river and mountains.

E **Mr Tee**, 12 Soi Laos, River Kwai Rd, north of town. Good, cleanish rooms in a 2-storey wooden block. Expensive restaurant, attractive river location. Recommended.

E-F **C&C Guesthouse**, 265/2 Mae Nam Kwai Rd, Soi England, T034-624527-8, cctrekking@yahoo.com. Pleasant accommodation, the cheapest rooms are in bamboo rafthouses. Camping plots available for ฿20.

F **River Guesthouse**, 42 Rong Heeb Oil Rd, T034-512491. Well laid out river complex with small bamboo huts, very popular travellers' hangout, some recent visitors have complained about the state of the toilet facilities, videos nightly.

Sai Yok National Park *p179*

The following places to stay are all near the waterfall.

A-D **Rom Suk Saiyok Yai Raft**, 231/3 Moo 7, T516130, has a wide range of rooms and camping facilities.

A Panthawee Raft, T034-512572, and B See Pee Nong Raft, T034-2156224, have a few rafts in the upmarket category.

B-C Ranthawee Raft, only has 4 rooms.

B-E Kwai Noi Rafthouse, T034-591075, has a small collection of floating rooms.

Erawan National Park *p180*

Park bungalows, designed for groups, can be rented, and it's possible to pitch a tent. There are two bungalow operations outside the park boundaries, before the entrance gates: the Erawan Resort Guesthouse and the Phu Daeng Resort.

Tham Than Lot National Park *p180*

There are bungalows in the park and it is also possible to camp. Alternatively, stay a night at the only hotel in the neighbouring town of Nong Pru (฿100 for fan and attached bathroom) – cheaper than staying in the park.

Thong Pha Phum *p181*

C-E **Somjaineuk**, T034-599067. New wing with a/c rooms and en suite hot water bathrooms; older part of hotel with basic, but clean, rooms.

D-E **Boonyong Bungalows**, T034-599049. The best of the cheaper places to stay in Thong Pha Phum; set away from the road, some reasonable peaceful, clean a/c and fan rooms.

D-E **Si Thong Pha Phum Bungalows**, T034-599058. Spacious bungalows, some with a/c.

Khao Laem Reservoir *p181*
AL-A Sam Anong Raft, 438 Moo 1 Thongphaphum-Pilok Rd, T034-4039496.
A-C Ungkhana Raft, 458 Moo 1 Thongphaphum-Pilok Rd, T034-599018.
A-C **Wang Pai Chalet**, Thongphaphum-Pilok Rd, T02-2796189. Raft houses as well as terrestrial bungalows, basic and not very clean, possible to camp here too.

Khao Laem National Park *p181*
Camping possible on a site 2-3 km from park headquarters.

Sangkhlaburi *p181*
B **Three Pagodas Resort**, 1½ km before pass on right-hand side, T034-124159. Reasonably attractive wooden bungalows in a peaceful setting, restaurant, overpriced weekend resort for Thais.
B-D **Phornphailin** (formerly the Sri Daeng), in town, T034-595039, F595026. A/c and hot water, extremely clean and adequate rooms although the location is not as picturesque as the lakeside guesthouses. Lively karaoke bar.
C **Sam Prasop Resort**, overlooking lake, by the wooden bridge, T034-595050. A/c, restaurant, individual bungalows, small rooms with bathroom, no English spoken.
C-F **Burmese Inn**, 52/3 Tambon Nong Loo, T034-595556, burmese_inn@access.inet.co.th. Decent restaurant, great service and friendly atmosphere. Most rooms are basic and ensuite. Boat and motorbikes available for hire. Tours can also be booked from here. Recommended.
F **P Guesthouse**, 81/1 Tambon Nong Loo, T034-595061, F595139. Good restaurant (with honesty system), very basic huts with wafer-thin walls, mattresses on the floor, mandis outside, attractive position overlooking lake, well set up for travellers, helpful owner will organize tours and trekking (see Tour operators below), motorbikes (฿150 per day) and mountain bikes (฿100 per day), motorbike taxis to town, boat for hire ฿350 for up to 5 people for 2 hrs. A new restaurant has just been completed and, ultimately, more upmarket bungalows. Recommended.

Eating

Kanchanaburi and around *p175, map p176*
The Brew House, outstanding value for money. Tasty Thai food and cheap beer served at this friendly wood and thatch open-air establishment. Recommended.
Jolly Frogs Restaurant, 28 Mae Nam Kwai Rd. A wide range of western and Thai grub with plenty of tourist information plastered on the walls.
Kala Kala, Song Khwae Rd, excellent Thai food at very good prices.
Krathom Thais Restaurant, 293 Mai Nam Kwai Rd (attached to **Apple's Guesthouse**), delicious Thai food here. Also caters for vegetarians.
Prasopsuk Restaurant, 677 Saengchuto Rd. A large, clean restaurant serving a wide range of dishes attached to the hotel of the same name.
The River Kwai Floating Restaurant, right next to the famed bridge. This restaurant has a wide menu of mainly Thai and Chinese food.
Sam's, all of Sam's establishments have restaurants producing delectable Thai food and some of the best western food available in town.
Sugar Canes Restaurant, 22 Soi Pakistan, Mae Nam Kwai Rd. Although the menu is limited, this restaurant has a beautiful view of the river.
Woof, Mae Nam Kwai Rd. An exclusively vegetarian restaurant serving mainly Thai food at reasonable prices.

Foodstalls and bakeries
Numerous stalls set up along the river in the evening, and there is also an excellent night market with a great range of food available in the vicinity of the bus station. Recommended.
Aree Bakery, Baak Phraek Rd. Delicious ice creams and breakfasts.
Sii Fa Bakery, by bus terminal, good range of pastries.

Sangkhlaburi *p181*
There are many inexpensive restaurants around the Central Market, some serving good Burmese food.

Bars and clubs

Kanchanaburi and around *p175, map p176*

There are several karaoke joints along the riverfront.

Apache Saloon, Saengchuto Rd, the hottest nightspot in town, decorated surprisingly enough like a kitsch Wild West effort, complete with wagon wheels and Stetsons.

Bar (no name), round the corner from the **Sugar Cane guesthouse** (Mae Nam Kwai Rd). Run by friendly British expats, frequented by tourists, serving huge portions of chips and good Thai food.

Brew House, Mae Nam Kwai Rd (Soi India Corner, near the King Naresuan statue), good value beer in a place run by a UK-educated Thai.

Festivals and events

Kanchanaburi and around *p175, map p176*

Nov/Dec River Kwai Bridge Week (movable). The festival starts with an evening ceremony conducted by dozens of monks followed by a procession from the city Pillar Shrine to the bridge. There's also a very realistic re-enactment of the destruction of bridge by the Allies in 1945. Other events include longboat races, exhibitions, steam train rides and cultural shows.

Shopping

Kanchanaburi and around *p175, map p176*

Baak Phraek Rd is a pleasant shopping street. Blue sapphires, onyx and topaz are all mined at Bo Phloi, 50 km from Kanchanaburi. Good prices for them at shops near the bridge or in the market area of town.

Activities and tours

Kanchanaburi and around *p175, map p176*

Fishing

On the Kwai River, Khao Laem and Srinakharin reservoirs. Travel agents will help organize expeditions.

Tours and tour operators

Raft and boat trips are not very easily organized by oneself; it is probably better to go through a tour operator. The River Kwai Village Hotel organizes river tours to the Lawa Caves and Sai Yok Yai Falls.

BT Travel Co Ltd, T034-624630, bttravel_centre@hotmail.com, organizes raft trips to the Chungkai Cemetery, together with fishing and swimming on the River Kwai Noi. It also arranges a/c minibus tours to Muang Singh Historical Park, Ban Kao, Sai Yok Noi and elsewhere.

Good Times Travel Service, T034-624441, good_times_travel@hotmail.com, is also recommended, offering similar excursions as **BT Travel Co Ltd**, and notably the opportunity to bathe with elephants!

State Railways of Thailand offers a all-day tour from Bangkok to Kanchanaburi on weekends and holidays leaving Thonburi station at 0615, stopping at Nakhon Pathom, the River Kwai Bridge, arriving at Nam Tok at 1130. A minibus connects Khao Pang/Sai Yok Noi waterfall and the train leaves Nam Tok at 1430, arriving in Kanchanaburi at 1605 for a brief stop, arriving in Bangkok at 1930. The State Railways also offers a number of other tours, with overnight stays, rafting and fishing. Contact the Railway Advance Book Office at Hualamphong Station in Bangkok, T02-2256964, or Kanchanaburi Train Station, T034-511285. Advance booking recommended.

Toi's Tours, T034-514209, toistours@yahoo.com, offers a wide range of excursions ranging from half-day excursions to 2-day tours, all at reasonable prices.

Sangkhlaburi *p181*

Tour operators

P Guesthouse and **Burmese Inn** both organize trips around Sangkhlaburi. They include visits to Karen village by boat, a 2-hr elephant ride through the jungle, swimming and bamboo whitewater rafting. The **Burmese Inn** may be able to organize a visit to a Karen camp.

Transport

Kanchanaburi and around *p175, map p176*

Bicycle

A good way to get around town and out to the bridge. Reliable bikes at ฿30-40 per day

can be hired from **Green Bamboo** on the Mae Nam Kwai Rd, or ask at guesthouses.

Boat
Noisy, long-tailed boats roar up and down the river, tickets available at guesthouses. A more peaceful option is to hire canoes. **Safarino**, on the Mae Nam Kwai Rd, hires out canoes for ฿280 per 3 hrs.
Cruise Asia Ltd, www.cruiseasia.net runs 4 and 7 day trips on the River Kwai

Bus
Beware of overcharging songthaews from the bus station to guesthouse area (should cost ฿60). Non-a/c buses leave from the station in the market area, behind Saengchuto Rd. A/c buses leave from the corner of Saengchuto Rd, opposite Lak Muang Rd. Regular twice hourly connections with **Bangkok**'s Southern bus terminal (a/c bus No 81), 2 hrs, or non-a/c bus, 3-4 hrs. Also connections with **Nakhon Pathom** (1½ hrs, ฿15) from where there are buses to the floating market at Damnoen Saduak (see page 117).

Jeep
Can be hired on Saengchuto Rd, beside TAT office and on Song Kwai Rd.

Motorbikes/scooters
Can be hired from **The Cash Shop** on Mae Nam Kwai Rd, ฿150 per day.

Saamlor
Charter for 2-3 hrs should cost about ฿100 for a trip to the Kwai bridge, JEATH museum and the cemetery.

Songthaew/tuk-tuk
Most useful for out-of-town trips.

Train
The station is 2 km northwest of town on Saengchuto Rd, not far from the cemetery, T034-511285. Regular connections with **Nakhon Pathom** and on to Hualampong Station. Weekends and holidays, special service (see Tours above). It is possible to take a local train between Kanchanaburi and **Nam Tok**, getting off along the way. There is a left luggage office at the station.

Sangkhlaburi *p181*
Bus
Regular connections on non-a/c bus with **Kanchanaburi** (5-6 hrs, ฿90). A/c minibus: runs 3 times a day (3½ hrs, ฿130). Larger, more comfortable buses with a/c depart 3 times a day (฿151). At time of writing there is still no way of getting north directly to **Umpang**; to get there you must go from Sangklaburi to Suphanburi and then north via Mae Sot.

Motorbike taxis
฿10 to almost everywhere, but ฿30 to the Mon monastery and market.

Saam Ong (Three Pagodas Pass) *p183*
Songthaews leave every 40 mins from the bus station in Sangkhlaburi, 30 mins (฿30). The last songthaew back to Sangkhlaburi leaves at about 1630; check on arrival.

Directory

Kanchanaburi and around *p175, map p176*
Banks A number near the bus station, most with ATMs. Bangkok, 2 Uthong Rd. Thai Farmers, 160/80-2 Saengchuto Rd. Thai Military, 160/34 Saengchuto Rd. **Internet** Close to the main centres of accommodation. **Medical services** Hospital Saengchuto Rd, close to Saengchuto Soi 20. **Post office** Corner of Lak Muang Rd and Baak Phraek Rd (not far from Sathani Rot Fai Rd) – some distance out of town towards Bangkok. **Useful addresses** Police, corner of Saengchuto and Lak Muang roads.

Sangkhlaburi *p181*
Banks Sam Commercial Bank offers exchange services but no ATM. **Internet** 2 facilities in town centre. **Medical services** Hospital and malaria centre in town. **Post office** Opposite 7-Eleven store.

Sukhothai and the north central plains

→ *Colour map 1, grid C3. Population 28,000.*

The modern conurbation of Sukhothai reveals little of Thailand's ancient capital. Head west about 12 km, keeping an eye on the surrounding landscape, and the ruined brick foundations of ancient religious structures appear in the rice fields, interspersed between wooden shophouses until the road pierces the ramparts of old Sukhothai. Officially, the old city and its surroundings are a national historical park covering 640 ha, opening in 1988 after a total of 192 wats were restored. The metal lamp-posts, concrete lined ponds and horrible hedge rows of the central area evince overbearing sterility. Head out beyond the city walls and you'll discover dozens of crumbling wats, Buddhas and chedis among the surrounding woodlands. There is some excellent accommodation in the old city but choice is limited. Staying here gives you a chance to explore the atmospheric outer ruins in the fresh early morning mist. There's more accommodation available in the new town, a pleasant enough spot to stay while exploring the glories of Old Sukhothai. Guesthouses here are generally of a high standard, there is good stall food at the night market on Ramkhamhaeng Road, a fresh day market off Charodwithithong Road and a useful range of tourist amenities.

Phitsanulok, to the east, houses one of the most important Buddhist and striking shrines in Thailand – Wat Phra Sri Ratana Mahathat (Wat Yai) and Si Satchanalai, north of Sukhothai, now an historical park and once linked to Sukhothai by a 50-km highway, is full of Ceylonese-style bell-shaped chedis, Khmer prangs and Sukhothai-era buildings.

The region to the west of Sukhothai is little-visited though all the better for it. Just 80 km southwest of the ancient Thai capital sits Kamphaeng Phet. This antiquated city is also an historical park and UNESCO World Heritage Site. ⏩ *For Sleeping, Eating and other listings pages 204-210.*

Ins and outs

Getting there

Sukhothai airport is owned by Bangkok Airways which flies to Bangkok and Chiang Mai. THAI fly to Phitsanulok an hour away. Most people arrive by bus and there are regular connections with Bangkok, Chiang Mai, Phitsanulok and Khon Kaen, as well as other major towns in the North and Central Plains. There are also two buses a day from Bangkok's northern bus terminal direct to Old Sukhothai. ⏩ *See Transport, page 209, for further details.*

Getting around

Most people come to Sukhothai to see the ruins of the former capital. Regular buses (every 10 minutes) and songthaews ply the route between old and new and it is also easy to hire a motorcycle. The ruins themselves are spread over a considerable area. ⏩ *See page 192 for details on getting around the park.*

Best time to visit

Sukhothai old city is spread over a large area and this part of Thailand is one of the hottest. If visiting the site during the hot or rainy seasons (roughly March-October), it is best to explore either early in the morning or at the end of the day. The best time to visit is November-February.

Background

If you ask a Thai about the history of Sukhothai, he or she will say that King Intradit ('Glorious Sun-King') founded the Sukhothai Kingdom in 1240, after driving off the Khmers following a single-handed elephant duel with the Khmer commander. King Intradit then founded Wat Mahathat, the geographical and symbolic heart of the new kingdom. Revisionist historians and archaeologists reject this view, regarding it as myth-making on a grand scale (see page 193). They maintain that Sukhothai evolved into a great kingdom over a long period and find the big bang theory ultimately unconvincing.

Like Angkor Wat in Cambodia, until comparatively recently Sukhothai was a 'lost city in the jungle'. It was only in 1833 that the future King Mongkut discovered the famous inscription No 1 and not until 1895 that the French scholar Lucien Fournereau published an incomplete description of the site. The key date though is 1907 when crown Prince Maha Vajiravudh made an eight-day visit to Sukhothai. It was his account that laid the foundations for the Sukhothai 'myth': a proud, glorious and civilized past for a country which was on the verge of being submerged by an alien culture. What is remarkable is that Prince Vajiravudh's account, based on a cursory visit, was accepted for so long and by so many. It has only been since the mid-1980s that people have begun to question the conventional history.

Sukhothai became the first capital of Siam and the following 200 years (until the early 15th century) are considered the pinnacle of Thai civilization. There were nine kings during the Sukhothai Dynasty, the most famous being Ramkhamhaeng, whose reign is believed to have been 1275-1317. He was the first ruler to leave accounts of the state inscribed in stone (now displayed in the National Museum in Bangkok). These provide a wealth of information on conquests, taxation and political philosophy. Ramkhamhaeng created the Thai script, derived from Mon and Khmer, and the inscription No 1 of 1292 is regarded by many as the first work of Thai literature (see page 622).

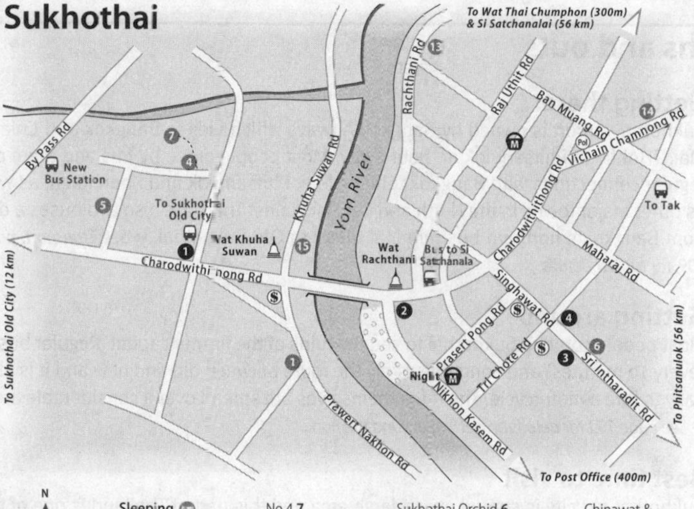

Sleeping
Ban Thai 1
J & J Guesthouse 4
Ninety Nine Guesthouse 5
No 4 7
Sukhothai Guesthouse 14
Sukhothai Lotus Village 13
Sukhothai Orchid 6
River House 15

Eating
Art's Fresh Coffee & Beer 1
Chinawat & Rainbow Café 2
Dream Café 3
Leaf Bakery 4

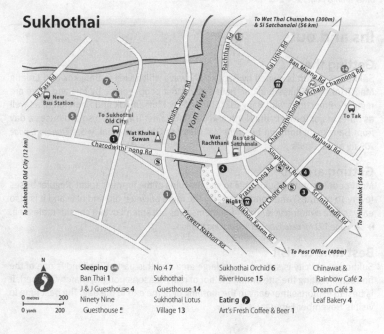

At its peak Ramkhamhaeng's kingdom encompassed much of present-day Thailand, south down the Malay Peninsula and west into Lower Burma though the northern kingdom of Lanna Thai, Lopburi and the Khorat Plateau were still controlled by the waning Khmer Empire.

Ramkhamhaeng was an absolute monarch, but one who governed his people with justice and magnanimity. If anyone wanted to lodge a complaint, he or she would ring a bell at the gate and the king would grant them an audience. King Ramkhamhaeng was responsible for the introduction of Theravada Buddhism, when he brought Ceylonese monks to his kingdom – partly intended to displace the influence of the Khmers. He displayed considerable diplomatic powers and cultivated good relations with his northern neighbours in order to form an alliance against the Khmers. In addition, he opened relations with China, establishing both economic and cultural links. The fine pottery produced at Sukhothai and Si Satchanalai is thought by some scholars to have developed only after the arrival of expert Chinese potters, with their knowledge of advanced glazing techniques.

The Sukhothai period saw a flowering not just of ceramic arts, but of art in general (see page 685). The Buddha images are regarded as the most beautiful and original to have ever been produced in Thailand with the walking Buddha image being the first free-standing Buddha the country produced.

King Ramkhamhaeng's son, Lo Thai (1327-1346), was an ineffectual leader, overshadowed even in death by his father, and much of the territories gained by the previous reign were lost. By the sixth reign of the Sukhothai Dynasty, the kingdom was in decline, and by the seventh, Sukhothai paid homage to Ayutthaya. In 1438 Ayutthaya officially incorporated Sukhothai into its realm, and the first Thai kingdom had succumbed to its younger and more vigorous neighbour.

Old City

The Old City is 1,800 m long and 1,400 m wide, and originally it was encompassed by triple earthen ramparts and two moats, pierced by four gates. Within the city there are 21 historical sites; outside the walls are another 70 or so places of historical interest. At one time the city may have been home to as many as 300,000 people, with an efficient tunnel system to bring water from the mountains and a network of roads. It was an urban centre to rival any in Europe. Within the city are monuments of many different styles – as if the architects were attempting to imbue the centre with the magical power of other Buddhist sites: there are Mon chedis, Khmer prangs and Ceylonese chedis, as well as monuments of clearly Sukhothai inspiration.

The letters after the place names in bold relate to the Old City map, page 192.

Park essentials

The park is open daily 0600-1800. It is divided into five zones, each with an admission charge: ฿40 for the central section, and ฿30 for each of the north, south, east and west sections. If you intend to visit all the zones, then it makes sense to purchase the so-called 'Total' ticket which costs ฿150, thus saving ฿10. However, as this 'all in' ticket also includes entrance to the Si Satchanalai Historical Park, the Ramkhamhaeng National Museum, the Sangkaloke Kiln Education & Preservation Center (45 km outside Sukhothai) and the Sawankha Woranayok National Museum (at Sawankhalok), you could end up saving more than ฿100. The Total ticket is valid for 30 days (each site can only be visited once within this time). There are also some additional charges: ฿50 per car, ฿10 per bike, ฿20 per motorcycle. Food and souvenir stalls are to be found just north of Wat Trapang Ngoen.

Getting around Travelling the 12 km between the new and old cities is easy enough – take one of the opensided buses that leave every 10 minutes (0600-1730, ฿10) from the station on Charodwithithong Road or from the main bus station (note that buses from the Old City to Sukhothai stop operating at 1800). Tuk-tuks cost no more than ฿100 (they congregate on Nikhon Kasem Road). Alternatively, either go on a tour (see Tour operators, page 209), hire a motorbike (฿250), or charter a tuk-tuk for the trip there and back, along with trips around the site (฿200-250 for three hours). When you arrive in the Old City hire a bicycle (฿20 per day) or moped (฿250 per day) from the entrance gate close to the museum, or take the little yellow trolley bus which tours the major sights (฿20). Don't forget a bottle of water if you're cycling.

If you cycle to the historical park on a bike rented in the new city, beware: the old city cycle shops don't like encroachment on their turf and may steal it.

Kamphanghek Gate (a) and Ramkhamhaeng National Museum (b)

T055-612167, 0900-1600, ฿30.

Situated just inside the Kamphanghek (Broken wall) Gate – the entrance gate – is the Ramkhamhaeng National Museum – a good place to begin a tour. The museum contains a copy of some wonderful Buddha images, along with explanatory information. It also houses a range of household goods giving an indication of the sophistication of Sukhothai society.

Wat Mahathat (c)

The centre of the Sukhothai Kingdom was Wat Mahathat and the royal palace – the earliest example in Thailand. This was both the religious and the political centre of the

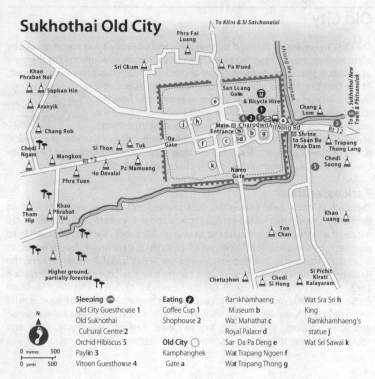

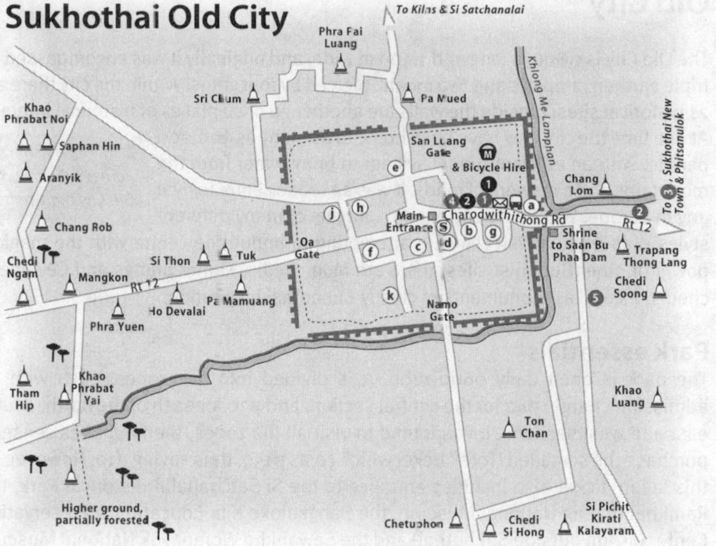

Sleeping
Old City Guesthouse 1
Old Sukhothai Cultural Centre 2
Orchid Hibiscus 5
Paylin 3
Vitoon Guesthouse 4

Eating
Coffee Cup 1
Shophouse 2

Old City
Kamphanghek Gate a
Ramkhamhaeng Museum b
Wat Mahathat c
Royal Palace d
San Da Pa Deng e
Wat Trapang Ngoen f
Wat Trapang Thong g
Wat Sra Sri h
King Ramkhamhaeng's statue j
Wat Sri Sawai k

Sukhothai: a 'Golden Age' or mother of invention?

At the beginning of March 1989, several hundred people assembled at the Bangkok Bank's headquarters on Silom Road to debate an issue that threatened to undermine the very identity of the Thai people. Some archaeologists had begun to argue that famous inscription No 1, on which the interpretation of King Ramkhamhaeng's reign is based (see page 622), was a forgery. They maintained that the then Prince Mongkut's remarkably timely 'discovery' of the inscription in 1833 served Siam's political purposes – it showed to the expansionist British and French that the country was a 'civilized' kingdom that could govern itself without outside interference. Along with certain literary and artistic anomalies, this led some commentators to maintain that King Mongkut created King Ramkhamhaeng – or at least his popular image – to protect his kingdom from the colonial powers.

Before Mongkut stumbled upon inscription No 1, knowledge of Sukhothai's history was based upon myth and legend. The great king Phra Ruang – who was believed to have hatched from the egg of a naga (serpent) and to be so powerful that he could make trees flower – was clearly the stuff of imagination. And some scholars also argued the same was true of King Ramkhamhaeng.

Since the meeting of 1989, academic opinion has swung back to viewing Mongkut's discovery as genuine. For most Thais, of course, who have been raised to believe that Sukhothai was Thailand's Golden Age and Ramkhamhaeng its chief architect, this is beyond reproach. However, this does not detract from the fact that inscription No 1 – and the other inscriptions – are fanciful portrayals of history carved to serve the interests of an elite, not to reflect 'reality'. As Betty Gosling writes in *Sukhothai: its history, culture and art* (1991) "... the controversy emphasizes the need to consider Sukhothai inscriptions ... not in the golden afterglow of Thai mythology, but in the harsh daylight of objective research".

kingdom and is usually regarded as the first truly 'Sukhothai' monument. The complex was begun by King Intradit, expanded by King Ramkhamhaeng and finally completed by King Lo Thai in 1345, or thereabouts.

The principal building is the central sanctuary, which King Lo Thai is said to have rebuilt in the 1340s to house the hair and neckbone relics of the Buddha which had been brought back from Ceylon. The central tower is surrounded by four smaller chedis in Srivijaya-Ceylonese style, alternating with four Khmer prangs. The entire ensemble is raised up on a two-tiered base with a stucco frieze of walking monks in relief.

Some original Buddha images still sit among the ruins. Particularly unusual are the two monumental standing Buddhas, in an attitude of forgiveness, either side of the central sanctuary, enclosed by brick walls, with their heads protruding over the top.

Royal Palace (Phra Ruang Palace) (d)

Little remains of the original Royal Palace. It was here that King Mongkut, while he was still the Crown Prince, found the famous inscription No 1 of King Ramkhamhaeng, the Manangsilabat stone throne, and the stone inscription of King Lithai in 1833. All three objects – which became talismen for the Thai people – were carted off to Bangkok. Whether the Royal Palace really was a palace is a subject for conjecture. The site appears rather too small and, although it has revealed a mass of objects, some scholars believe it was the site of a royal pavilion rather than a

 royal palace. To the north of Wat Mahathat is **San Da Pa Deng** (e), the oldest existing structure from the Sukhothai era. It is a small Khmer laterite prang built during the first half of the 12th century.

Wat Trapang Ngoen (f) and Wat Trapang Thong (g)

Wat Trapang Ngoen – Temple of the Silver Pond – contains a large lotus-bud chedi, similar to that at Wat Mahathat. One passage from inscription No 1 refers to this wat: "In the middle of this city of Sukhothai the water of the Pho Si Pond is as clear and as good to drink as the river of the Khong [Mekong] in the dry season." Wat Trapang Thong sits on an island, after which the monastery is named. It is approached along a rickety bridge. Particularly fine are the stucco reliefs, of which perhaps the most beautiful is that on the south side of the mondop. It shows the Buddha descending from the Tavatimsa Heaven with the attendant Brahma on his left and Indra on his right and is considered the finest piece of stucco work from the Sukhothai period.

Wat Sra Sri (h) and King Ramkhamhaeng's statue (j)

Wat Sra Sri, to the north of Wat Trapang Ngoen, is a popular photo-spot, as the bot is reflected in a pond. A Ceylonese-style chedi dominates the complex, which also contains a fine, large seated Buddha image enclosed by columns. To the east of here is King Ramkhamhaeng's statue, seated on a copy of the stone throne (the Phra Thaen Manang Silabat) that was found on the site of the Royal Palace and which is now in the Wat Phra Kaeo Museum in Bangkok. The statue was erected in 1969 and the high relief carvings depict famous episodes from the life of the illustrious king.

Wat Sri Sawai (k)

To the southwest of Wat Mahathat is Wat Sri Sawai, enclosed within laterite walls. It was built during the time that Sukhothai was under Khmer domination. The prang is in the three-tower style, with the largest central prang (rather badly restored) being 20 m tall. The stucco decoration was added to the towers in the 15th century, as were their upper brick portions. The lower laterite levels are the original sections, built under Khmer influence. It must originally have been a Hindu shrine, as carvings of Vishnu and other Hindu divinities have been found on the site.

Wats outside the Old City walls

The main reason to see the monasteries outside the Old City walls is to get a better idea of what Sukhothai was like before it became a historical park and was cleared of undergrowth. Some of the lesser known monasteries still sit in the forest. **Note** Try cycling to these wats during the morning when it is cooler as they are far apart. Alternatively hire a tuk-tuk.

Wat Sri Chum

Take the northwest gate out of the city to visit the impressive Wat Sri Chum. A large mondop, with a narrow vaulted entrance, encloses an enormous brick and stucco seated Buddha image. The temple was probably built during the seventh reign of the Sukhothai Kingdom (mid-14th century) and is said to have caused a Burmese army to flee in terror, such is the power of its withering gaze. The large Buddha seems almost suffocated by the surrounding walls which must have been added at a later stage. There is a stairway in the mondop which leads up to a space behind the head of the image (closed since 1988). Here, there are line carvings recounting the Jataka tales, covering the slate slab ceiling. Each slab depicts one story, skilfully carved with free-flowing lines – which originally would have been enlivened with paint. These are the finest and earliest (circa 1350) to be found in Thailand (there are examples from

Wat Sri Chum in the National Museum, Bangkok). The image here is said to have talked on a number of occasions – although the back stairs provide a useful hiding place for someone to play a practical joke.

Wat Phra Pai Luang

East of Wat Sri Chum is Wat Phra Pai Luang, the Monastery of the Great Wind, interesting for the remains of three laterite prangs. Built during the reign of King Jayavarman VII (a Khmer king who ruled 1181-1217) it dates from the Khmer period that preceded the rise of Sukhothai. Its Khmer inspiration is clearly evident in the square base and indented tiers. To the east of the prang is a later stupa, with niches on all four sides containing damaged Buddha images. Further east still is a ruined mondop with the remains of large stucco Buddha images, standing, walking and reclining. In total Wat Phra Pai Luang contains over 30 stupas of assorted styles. It is thought that not only was it originally a Hindu shrine, but that it was also the site of an earlier Khmer town.

Wat Saphan Hin

Take the northwest road 3 km beyond the city walls where a large standing Buddha image a hill

Wat Khao Phrabat Noi

Not far away from Wat Saphan Hin are the remains of two other monasteries. Wat Khao Phrabat Noi lies about 2½ km northwest of the city walls and it is approached along a stone lined footpath. The chedi here is unusual in that it is not really Sukhothai in style and it is presumed that it was remodelled during the Ayutthaya period. Four Buddha footprints were found here, but these have been removed to the National Museum in Bangkok.

Wat Chang Rob

South from this group of three monasteries is the better-known Wat Chang Rob, the Monastery Encircled by Elephants. In Buddhist mythology, elephants – the holiest of beasts – support Mount Meru, the centre of the universe.

Wat Chedi Ngam

Continuing south to Route 12 is the impressive, at least in size, Wat Chedi Ngam, the Monastery of the Beautiful Chedi. The large chedi, pure and simple in its form, has been well preserved. Also here are the remains of a large viharn with some standing columns, and what is thought to have been a kuti (monks' quarters) or place for bathing.

Wat Mangkon and Wat Phra Yuen

On the north side of Route 12 is Wat Mangkon, the Dragon Monastery. A relatively large complex, the bot, surrounded by large leaf-shaped boundary stones, has an unusual slate-tiled brick base. To the west of the bot is the base of a pavilion or sala, and to the north the remains of a Ceylonese-style bell-shaped phra chedi. Wat Phra Yuen is around 200 m from Wat Mangkon and 1,500 m from the city walls, just to the south of Route 12. The remains of a bot can be identified by the bai sema that surround it and a mondop houses a large standing Buddha image.

Wat Ton Chan (Sandalwood Tree Monastery) and Wat Chetuphon

There are also a series of monasteries to the south and east of the city. Travel 1 km from the city by the south gate and you'll find Wat Ton Chan. Although large, the monastery is nothing very special, although it is moated and has a bathing pool along with the usual array of viharn and chedi. Far more impressive is Wat Chetuphon, one

of Sukhothai's more important monasteries. The building materials are more varied than the usual brick and stucco; stone, slate and brick have also been used in its construction. However, archaeologists and art historians suspect that the monastery was renovated and expanded on a number of occasions, so how much of the structure is Sukhothai, is a source of conjecture.

Wat Chedi Si Hong

About 500 m from Wat Chetuphon, is Wat Chedi Si Hong. The most notable feature of this wat is the fine stucco work depicting *devas* (heavenly beings), humans and garudas riding elephants on the base of the viharn and chedi.

Around Sukhothai

Ramkhamhaeng National Park

ⓘ *Public transport is limited – take a local bus along Route 101 towards Kamphaeng Phet, getting off at the road to the national park (Uthayaan Haeng Chart Ramkhamhaeng); it's 16 km from here and we have had reports that motorcycle taxis are sometimes available at the turn-off.*

Ramkhamhaeng National Park is 30 km southwest of New Sukhothai in Amphoe Khiri Mat and covers 341 sq km. The highest peak here, Khao Luang – after which the park is also sometimes known – rises to nearly 1,200 m. Highlights of the park include the 100 m-high Sai Rung Waterfall, several caves, and an ancient dam which fed the canals of Sukhothai city.

Phitsanulok and around

→ *Colour map 2, grid B1.*

Phitsanulok, attractively positioned on the banks of the River Nan, with houseboats lining the steep banks, is home to one of the most important Buddhist and striking shrines in Thailand – Wat Phra Sri Ratana Mahathat (Wat Yai). The rest of this friendly, bustling city is non-descript with most of its old wooden buildings destroyed in a disastrous fire in the 1960s. Phitsanulok is also an important transport hub, linking the Central Plains with the north and northeast and it is a convenient base from which to visit nearby Sukhothai and Si Satchanalai.

Ins and outs

Getting there The bus terminal is not central, but bus no 10 travels between the local bus station and the terminal every 10 minutes (and takes 30 minutes). The journey from Bangkok takes five-six hours. It is possible to fly, with plenty of daily connections to Bangkok and also with other northern towns. ▸▸ *See also Transport, page 209.*

Getting around Phitsanulok is a good walking city with the main site of interest, Wat Yai, being in the northern part of town while an evening stroll along the river allows you to take in the night market at full swing.

Tourist information TAT ⓘ *209/7-8 Surasi Shopping Centre, Boromtrailokant Rd, T055-252742, tatphs@loxinfo.co.th; 0830-1630*. Helpful and informative, with good maps of the town and surrounding area. There's also a small office next to **Wat Yai** ⓘ *0900-1600*, who will furnish you with a photocopied map and little else.

Background

Phitsanulok was the birthplace of one of the heroes of Thai history: King Naresuan the Great of Ayutthaya (reigned 1590-1605) (there is a shrine to the king on the west side

of the river facing Wat Mahathat). Shortly after his birth, the young Naresuan was bundled off to Burma as a guarantor of his father's – King Thammaracha – good behaviour. He did not return to Phitsanulok until he was 16, when he was awarded the principality by his father. Here he developed the military and political skills which were to stand him in good stead when he assumed the throne of Ayutthaya 19 years later in 1590 (see box, page 163). For the short period of 25 years, during the reign of King Boromtrailokant (1448-88) of Ayutthaya, Phitsanulok was actually the capital of Siam, and over the four centuries prior to the fall of Ayutthaya to the Burmese in 1767 it was effectively the Kingdom's second city.

Wat Phra Sri Ratana Mahathat

ⓘ 0800-1700, donation of ฿50 is recommended.

The Monastery of the Great Relic, known as Wat Yai, 'Big Wat' – is to be found on the east bank of the Nan River, close to the Naresuan Bridge. It was built in the reign of King Lithai (1347-1368) of Sukhothai, in 1357. The viharn contains one of the most highly regarded and venerated Buddha images in Thailand – the Phra Buddha Chinaraj. Through the centuries, successive Thai kings have come to Phitsanulok to pay homage to the bronze image and to make offerings of gifts. The Buddha is a superlative example

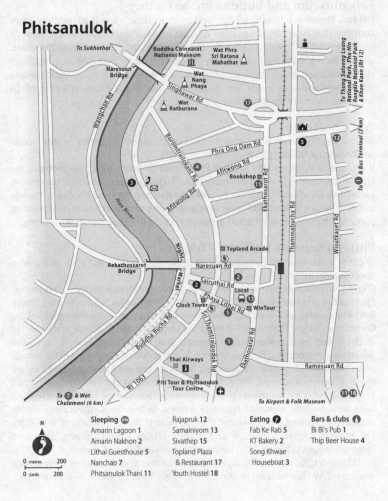

Phitsanulok

Sleeping
Amarin Lagoon 1
Amarin Nakhon 2
Lithai Guesthouse 5
Nanchao 7
Phitsanulok Thani 11
Rajapruk 12
Samainiyom 13
Sivathep 15
Topland Plaza & Restaurant 17
Youth Hostel 18

Eating
Fab Ke Rab 5
KT Bakery 2
Song Khwae Houseboat 3

Bars & clubs
Bi Bi's Pub 1
Thip Beer House 4

 of late Sukhothai style and is said to have wept tears of blood when the city was captured by the Ayutthayan army in the early 14th century. The three-tiered viharn was built during the Ayutthaya period and shows a fusion of Ayutthayan and Lanna (Northern) Thai architectural styles. The low sweeping roofs, supported by black and gold pillars, accentuate the massive gilded bronze Buddha image seated at the end of the nave. The entrance is through inlaid mother-of-pearl doors, made in 1756 in the reign of King Boromkot to replace the original ones of carved wood. The small viharn in front of the main building houses another significant Buddha image, known as the 'Remnant Buddha' because it was cast from the bronze remaining after the main image had been produced. The 36-m-high prang in the centre of the complex has stairs leading up to a niche containing relics of the Buddha but access is often locked. Also in the wat compound is the **Buddha Chinnarat National Museum**, with a small collection of Sukhothai Buddhas and assorted ceramics. Wat Yai is a very popular site for Thai tourists/Buddhists. Most buy lotuses and incense from a stall at the gate to offer to the Buddhas. There's also a large antique, food and trinket market next door to the compound plus rows of lottery ticket sellers; the trick is you gain favour by supplicating yourself to the Buddha and then get lucky.

Folk museum and Buddha image factory

The **Folk Museum** ⓘ *Wisutkaset Rd, Tue-Sun 0830-1200, 1300-1630*, exhibits items from everyday rural life, in particular agricultural implements and tools, children's games, festival and ceremonial items, and other bits and pieces. Across the street, and run by the same man, is a **factory** ⓘ *Mon-Sat 0800-1700 (the door is always shut: open it and go in)*, casting Buddha images. These are produced using the lost wax method and range in size from diminutive to monstrous. It is usually possible to see at least some of the production processes.

Wat Chulamani

ⓘ *catch bus No 5 which leaves from the City bus (local) centre, near the railway station on Ekathosarot Rd, every 10 mins (takes 20 mins).*

Wat Chulamani, 6 km to the south of Phitsanulok on Route 1063, was probably the original town centre. During the Khmer period Phitsanulok was known as Muang Song Kwae ('Two River Town'), as it lies between the Nan and the Kwae Noi rivers. The wat was built by King Boromtrailokant in 1464 and houses the remains of an ornate Khmer prang which pre-dates the Sukhothai period: note the fine stucco work of the prang.

Phu Hin Rongkla National Park

ⓘ *Catch a bus towards Loei and get off at Nakhon Thai (3 hrs, ฿35), and then a songthaew to the park (฿15-25).*

Phu Hin Rongkla National Park covers 5,000 sq km over three provinces: Phitsanulok, Phetchabun and Loei. The park, 120 km east of Phitsanulok, off Route 2113, which links Phitsanulok with Loei, has been partly deforested. It was a stronghold of the Communist Party of Thailand (CPT) until the early 1980s, and hundreds of disaffected students fled here following the Thammasat University massacre of 1976. The government encouraged farmers to settle in the park to deny the guerrillas refuge; now that the CPT has been vanquished, the same farmers have been told they are illegal squatters and must move. The buildings used by the CPT for training and indoctrination (3 km southwest of the park headquarters) have been preserved and have now become sights of historical interest to the Thais, particularly former students who joined the movement after the student demonstrations of 1973-1976. The base supported a political and military school – with printing press and communications centre, a small hospital, cafeteria and air raid shelter.

Rising to 1,780 m, the park has a pine forest on the upper slopes and many orchids and lichens. Wildlife includes small numbers of tiger, bear, sambar deer and hornbills.

Thung Salaeng National Park

On the road between Phitsanulok and Lomsak, Highway 12, is the Thung Salaeng National Park and a number of waterfalls and resort hotels. The **Sakunothayon Botanical Gardens** ⓘ *take one of the regular buses running between Phitsanulok and Lomsak*, is located off the road at the Km 33 marker. A 500-m-long access road leads to the gardens, which are best known for the picturesque, 10-m-high Waeng Nok Aen Waterfall.

The Thung Salaeng Luang National Park ⓘ *the park office is located at Km 80 on the Phitsanulok-Lomsak Highway (Highway 12); Regular buses run between Phitsanulok and Lomsak*, consisting of forest and grasslands, covers more than 1,250 sq km of Phitsanulok and Phetchabun provinces, rising from 300 m to more than 1,000 m. There's a huge variety of birdlife (190 recorded species), including hornbills, the Siamese fireback pheasants eagles and owls. Of the park's 17 mammal species the most notable is the park's small population of elephants; tigers are also said to inhabit the park, but are rarely seen. The best time for trekking is between November and March.

Si Satchanalai and around → *Colour map 1, grid B3.*

Si Sat nestles languidly on the west bank of the Yom River about 50 km to the north of Sukhothai. It remained undiscovered by tourists until 1987, when a grant was provided to prepare the town for 'Visit Thailand Year'. The site has been 'cleaned up', though not to the extent of Sukhothai and still retains a lot of charm. Si Satchanalai makes a fascinating side trip from Sukhothai with examples of Ceylonese-style bell-shaped chedis, Khmer prangs and Sukhothai-era buildings. There is no modern town here; the whole area has become a 'Historical Park'.

Si Satchanalai is littered with monuments; only major ones are included here. Most hotels in Sukhothai run day tours here, see Activities and tours, page 209.

Ins and outs

Getting around Si Satchanalai is compact and the main monuments can be seen on foot. To reach Chaliang and the sights outside the city walls it is best to hire a bicycle (฿30 per day) at the admission gate.

Tourist information The Si Satchanalai Historical Park Information Centre is just outside Ram Narong Gate, to the southeast. There's not much information here, just a scale model and map of the park and a few books for sale. Admission fee to Si Satchanalai: ฿40, ฿50 for a car, ฿30 for a motorbike and ฿10 for a bicycle. See the admission information under the entry for Sukhothai for details on the 'Total' ticket which provides entry to both Si Sat and Sukhothai.

Background

During the fourth reign of Sukhothai, Si Sat became the seat of the king's son and the two cities were linked by a 50-km long road, the Phra Ruang Highway. Bounded by a moat 10 m wide and by thick town walls during its heyday it was the equal of Sukhothai in splendour, and probably superior in terms of its defences. Protected by rapids, swamp and mountains, not to mention a triple moat filled with barbed spikes, Si Sat must have seemed immensely daunting to any prospective attacker.

Critical to Si Sat's vitality was the ceramic industry based at Ban Pha Yang and Ban Ko-noi, to the north of the city. With the technical assistance of Chinese potters these villages produced probably the finest of all Thai ceramics. These were not just for local consumption; Sangkhalok ware has been found as far afield as Java, Borneo and the Philippines.

Sights

Wat Chang Lom lies in the heart of the old city and is the most sacred wat in Si Satchanalai. The principal chedi was built between 1285 and 1291 to contain sacred relics of the Buddha, which King Ramkhamhaeng dug up, worshipped for a month and six days, buried and then had a chedi built over them which took three years to complete. The Ceylonese-style chedi is the earliest example of its kind in Thailand and became the prototype for many others. Stairs take the pilgrim from the lower, earthly levels, upwards towards the more spiritual realm of the Buddha. The chedi is enclosed by 50-m long laterite walls, and in front of it are the ruins of a large viharn, together with another smaller stupa and viharn.

Wat Chedi Jet Thaew (30 m south of Wat Chang Lom) stands within a ditch and two rows of laterite walls pierced by four gates. The wat contains the remnants of seven rows of lotus-bud chedis, some 34 in total, which house the ashes of members of the Si Satchanalai ruling family.

South of here is **Wat Suan Kaeo Utthayanyai** and the southernmost wat within the walls, **Wat Nang Phaya** (Monastery of the Queen). The latter is enclosed by single walls of laterite, with four gateways. A Ceylonese-style chedi dominates the compound. The fine stucco floral motifs (now protected by a shed) on the west wall of the large laterite viharn are early Ayutthayan in style (15th century), and are the best preserved of any such decoration in either Sukhothai or Si Sat.

Wat Khao Phanom Phloeng lies on a 20-m high hillock on the north side of the town and is reached by a laterite staircase of 144 steps. It comprises a Ceylonese-style chedi, a large seated Buddha and some stone columns. Recent excavations at this site have revealed an early animist shrine, the **Sala Chao Mae Laong Samli**, which predates both the Khmer and Tai periods here, showing that Si Sat was occupied – and important – long before the rise of the Sukhothai Kingdom. To the west of Wat Khao Phanom Phloeng and linked by a path and staircase, on a higher hillock, are the remains of **Wat Khao Suwan Khiri**.

Si Satchanalai & Chaliang

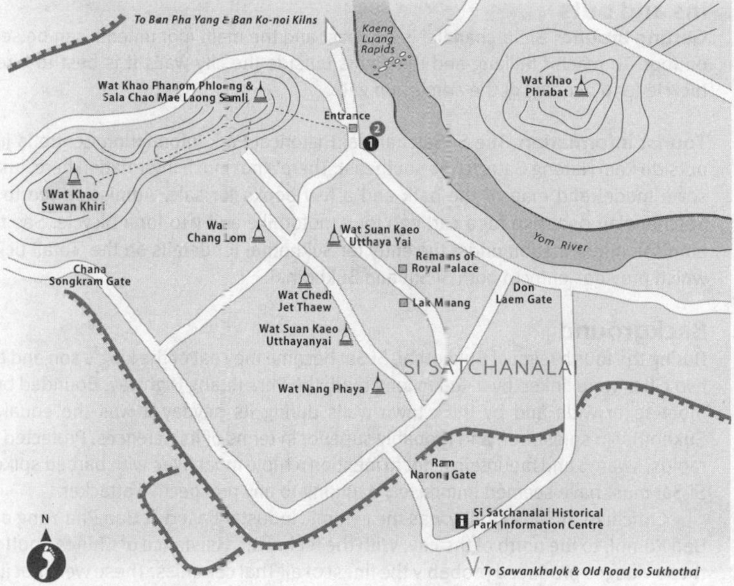

0 metres 100
0 yards 100

Sleeping
Tents & Campsite 2
Wang Yom Resort 1

Eating
Noodle Stalls 1

Chaliang

To the southeast, 2 km outside the Si Satchanalai city walls, is the area known as Chaliang. The first wat you come to along the road to Chaliang is **Wat Kok Singh Karam**, on the right-hand side, which includes three chedis on the same base. In front of these stupas a viharn and bot are to be found.

Wat Chom Chuen – the Monastery of Prince Chan – contains a prang built in the time of the Khmer King Jayavarman VII (1181-1217). It seems that Chaliang was chosen by the Khmer as the site for one of its outposts at the far extremity of the Khmer Empire because of its defensive position. Next to this wat is an **Archaeological Site Museum** ⓘ *free, a great building set into the riverbank with a grass roof. The excavations revealed 15 inhumation burials. The bodies were buried during the Dvaravati period (sixth-11th centuries). Grave goods devoted to the dead comprise glass beads, iron tools and clay paddles. Head orientation is to the west.*

Positioned on the banks of the Yom River is **Wat Phra Sri Ratana Mahathat Chaliang** (or Wat Phra Prang), an impressive laterite prang originally built in the mid-15th century. Its origins are older still, as the prang is thought to have been built on top of an earlier Khmer prasat. In front of the prang are the ruins of a viharn which houses a large seated Sukhothai Buddha image, with long, graceful fingers 'touching ground'. Even more beautiful is the smaller walking Buddha of brick and stucco to the left. It is thought to be one of the finest from the Sukhothai period displaying that enigmatic 'Sukhothai smile'. The wat also contains a number of other interesting Buddha images.

Ban Pha Yang and Kan Ko-noi

North of the city, at Ban Pha Yang and Ban Ko-noi, remains of ceramic kilns have been discovered, dating from the 1350s. The pottery produced from here is known as 'Sangkhalok', after the early Ayutthaya name for the district (there is a town of the same name to the south). The kilns of Ban Pha Yang lie 500 m north of the old city

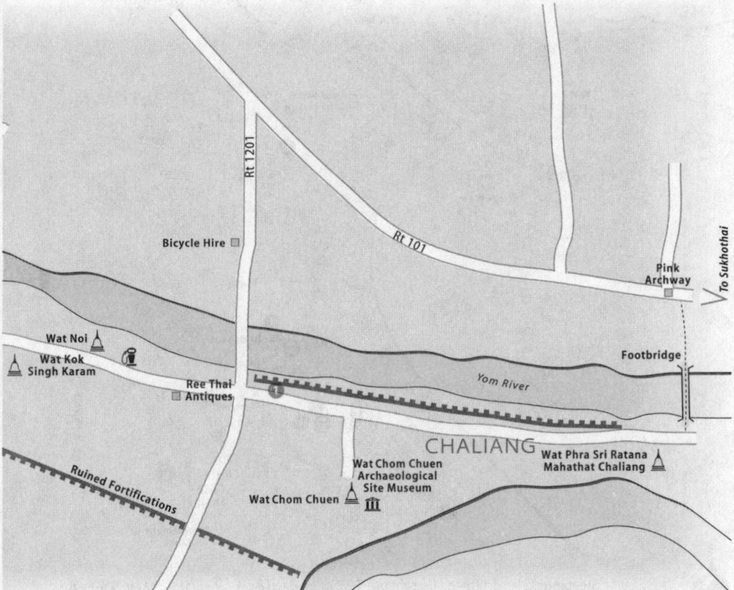

 walls, and so far 21 kilns have been found, all of the closed-kiln variety. It is thought that they produced architectural and high quality ceramics.

Kamphaeng Phet → *Colour map 1, grid C3.*

It is possible to wander through the ruined monasteries and forts of Kamphaeng Phet, many overgrown with verdant trees, without meeting a single person. The town was originally built by King Lithai in the 14th century as a garrison to protect and

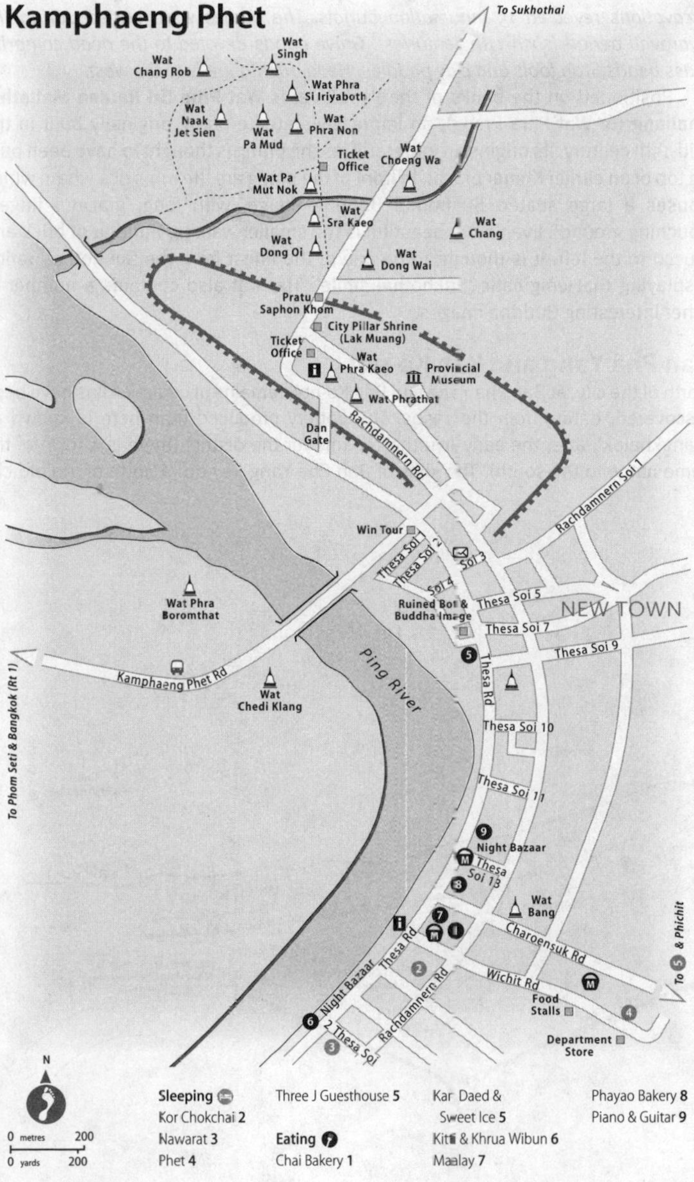

consolidate the power of the Sukhothai Kingdom (Kampheng Phet translates as 'Diamond Wall') at a time when surrounding states were growing in threat. In total, the old city, now an historical park, encompasses an area of more than 400 ha. Modern Kamphaeng Phet is sleepy and easygoing with a proportion of its older, wooden, shuttered and tiled buildings still surviving.

Ins and outs

Getting around and tourist information Open daily 0800-1630. The ticket office is next to Wat Phra Kaeo and north of the river. It costs ฿40 to visit both the area within the ancient city walls and the forested area to the north, known as Aranyik. It is possible to walk within the city walls, but vehicles are useful for the Aranyik area, for which the following charges are levied: ฿10 for a bike, ฿20 for a motorbike, ฿30 for a tuk-tuk and ฿50 for a car. It's possible to walk around the site though you can charter a saamlor or tuk-tuk for roughly ฿150 for one hour. There's a badly run **Tourist Information Office** in the Kamphaeng Phet Local Handicraft Centre, Thesa Road (near Soi 13), which should open between 0800-2000 and a second **Tourist Information Centre** next to Wat Phra Kaeo.

Sights

The massive 6-m-high defensive walls still stand – earthen ramparts topped with laterite – beyond which is a moat to further deter attackers. Within the walls, encompassing an area of 2½ km by 500 m, lie two old wats, Wat Phra Kaeo and Wat Phrathat, as well as the **Provincial Museum** ① *Wed-Sun 0900-1600,* ฿30. The museum contains, in the entrance hall, what is commonly regarded as one of the finest bronzes of Siva in Thailand. Cast in 1510, in the Khmer 'Bayon' style, its head and hands were removed by an overzealous German visitor in 1886. Fortunately, he was intercepted, and the limbs and head were reunited with the torso. The museum contains some good examples of Buddha images found in the locality.

From the museum, walk west to **Wat Phrathat**, the Monastery of the Great Relic. Not much remains except a chedi and a well-weathered seated Buddha (of laterite) sitting in the viharn. Immediately north, **Wat Phra Kaeo** was probably the largest and most important wat in Kamphaeng Phet. It was initially built during the Sukhothai period and then extensively remodelled in the Ayutthaya period. Just beyond the ticket office is Kamphaeng Phet's **Lak Muang** or City Pillar Shrine. Many saamlor drivers ring their bells when passing the shrine in recognition of the power of the spirits that reside here.

Ruins outside the old city's ramparts

Most of the more interesting ruins lie outside the ramparts, to the north of town. Start with the outer ruins, returning to view Wat Phra Kaeo, Wat Phrathat and the museum. The first wat of significance to be reached travelling north from the New Town to the Old City is **Wat Phra Non** which, like many of the structures here, dates from the 15th to 16th centuries. The monastery is surrounded by laterite walls and walking through the complex from the road the buildings are, in turn, the bot, viharn, the main chedi, and then a secondary viharn. There are also the remains of monks quarters, wells and washing areas.

The ruins are best seen early morning, when it is cooler and the deep red laterite is bathed in golden light.

North from here, there is the slightly better preserved **Wat Phra Si Iriyaboth**, locally known as Wat Yuen or the Monastery of the Standing Buddha. This wat derives its name from the large Buddha images that were to be found in the mondop at the end of the viharn. The name of the wat literally means 'four postures' – standing, reclining, sitting and walking. They were all in high stucco relief, one on each side of the mondop. The impressive standing image is the only one in reasonable repair and is a good example of Sukhothai sculpture, dating from the 14th to 15th centuries. The remains of the

 walking image give the impression of grace, so typical of the Sukhothai period. The viharn was built on a raised platform so that it is higher than the bot. It is thought that this was done to show the greater religious significance of the images in the viharn.

Adjacent to Wat Phra Si Iriyaboth is **Wat Singh**, again built in the 15th, possibly the 16th, century. The most important structure here is the stupa at the back of the compound, with porches for Buddha images on each side. In front is the bot, with its bai sema or boundary stone still evident.

Walking through the forest behind Wat Singh is **Wat Chang Rob** (the Shrine of the Elephants), probably the most impressive structure outside the city walls. The forested position of this monastery is appropriate for it was built for the use of forest-dwelling monks of a meditational sect. This consists of a huge Ceylonese-style laterite chedi with its base surrounded by 68 elephants. Only one row of elephants, on the south side, are preserved. Numerous other minor wats are scattered around the area, some in thick undergrowth, others amidst paddy fields – particularly to the northeast and southwest.

On the right-hand side of the approach road to Kamphaeng Phet (Route 1) are the remains of a laterite fort, **Phom Seti**. This walled and moated settlement had similar dimensions to Khamphaeng Phet. It seems that the location of the city was switched to the other bank of the Ping after successive attacks by Ayutthaya from 1373.

Past the bus terminal and on the left before the bridge is **Wat Phra Boromthat.** Just before the bridge, on the right-hand side, is the unusually shaped, square, restored chedi of **Wat Chedi Klang**.

New Town sights

A **ruined bot** in the heart of the city is on Thesa Road between Sois 6 and 8. The abandoned brick structure has fallen into ruin; within the 'building' is a Buddha revered by some local residents.

As with any Thai town, Kamphaeng Phet has its share of markets. On Thesa Road, opposite the tourist information centre, is a small **fresh market**; a little further south, also on Thesa Road, is a **night bazaar**, a good place to eat stall food in the evening (near Soi 13). But the main **day market** occupies a large area sandwiched between Wichit and Charoensuk roads.

Sleeping

Sukhothai Old City *p191, map p192*

AL-B Paylin, Charodwithithong Rd, about 4 km from the Old City on the road leading to Sukhothai, T055-613310, F613317. A monster of a hotel stuck out on the road between the old and new cities. This is the most luxurious place to stay, but lacks character and the restaurant has an awful reputation.

B-C Orchid Hibiscus, T/F055-633284, orchid_hibiscus_guest_house@hotmail.com Gorgeous a/c bungalows, some family size houses, a swimming pool, wonderful breakfasts and friendly management – highly recommended.

C Old Sukhothai Cultural Centre (aka Thai Village House), 214 Charodwithithong Rd, Muang Kao, T055-612275, F055-612583. A/c, rundown, ensuite teak bungalows set on a semi-island, almost surrounded by water. Large, clean and simply decorated rooms.

C-D Vitoon Guesthouse, 49/3 Jarodvithithong Rd, T055-697045, near the entrance to the park, at the bend in the road. Not as peaceful as the Old City Guesthouse, but rooms are spotless, 8 with a/c and hot showers, and 12 with fan, and immaculate western toilets attached. Bicycle hire. Good value, despite noise pollution.

D-E Old City Guesthouse, 28/7 Jarodvithithong Rd, T055-697515, in front of the National Museum, near the entrance to the park. Offers a range of rooms from tiny to enormous, from fan and shared bathroom to en suite, a/c and cable TV, all spotless. Friendly management. Outstandingly good value and highly recommended.

Sukhothai New City *p190, map p190*
There are some excellent guesthouses in Sukhothai's newer city. Beware: the tuk-tuk drivers at the bus station who are on commission with certain guesthouses/hotels may refuse to take you or try and charge exhorbitant rates (it should cost ฿ 30-40).

Call your guesthouse if in doubt – many offer a free pick-up.

B Sukhothai Orchid, 43 Singhawat Rd, T055-611193, F612038. A/c, hot shower, en suite, TV (Thai). Large and airy hotel with spacious, cool reception area and restaurant. Rooms are clean, smart with a/c and cable TV; an excellent base.

B-E Sukhothai Lotus Village, 170 Rachthani Rd, T055-621484, www.lotus-village.com. The large, leafy compound is scattered with several ponds, has a number of attractive teak houses and several spotless bungalows, some with a/c. Tastefully decorated, clean, peaceful, and managed by an informative Thai/French couple. It also serves tasty western breakfasts of toast, yoghurt, fresh juice and fresh coffee. Beds are very hard. Highly recommended.

C-D Sukhothai Guesthouse, 68 Vichien Chamnong Rd, T055-610453, www.thai.net/sukhothaiguesthouse, some a/c rooms, hot water showers, restaurant.. A well-maintained establishment, with attractive teak balconies. Friendly and informative owners. Also runs informal cookery classes and offers a range of tours, free bikes, free pick-up at the bus station and internet. Highly recommended.

D-E Ban Thai, 38 Prawert Nakhon Rd, T055-610163, www.geocities.com/guesthouse_banthai. Overlooking the Yom River, an assortment of clean, well-kept rustic bungalows and rooms in a large natural-style house. Excellent en suite bungalows and small rooms and clean shared toilets. The friendly English-speaking management offers lots of free maps to surrounding area, recycle as much plastic and paper as possible and offers delightful bicycle tours through surrounding villages – from ฿150.

D-E J&J Guesthouse, just before you come to No 4, T055-620095, jjguest@hotmail.com. Attractive bungalows, some with a/c and en suite hot showers, all spotless. Small pleasant restaurant attached, well-kept gardens. Friendly, informative English speaking management. Has bakery and bar attached.

D-E No 4, 140/4 Soi Maerampan Jarodwitheethong Rd, T055-610165, no.4guesthouse@thaimail.com. Very friendly English speaking lady owner rents out spotless bamboo bungalows, tucked into a small compound in a wonderfully secluded location. Well kept, clean, cute en suite rooms. Excellent Thai food in the restaurant. She also runs cookery classes. Tours organized from here. Good value. Highly recommended.

E Ninety Nine Guest House, 234/6 Soi Panichsan, off Charodwithithong Rd, T055-611315, ninetynine_gh@yahoo.com. A very clean family run guesthouse in a wooden house with a friendly sitting room area for relaxation. Very helpful owner who runs cooking courses. Other services include local information and history, tour guide and traditional Thai massage. Recommended.

E River House, Khuha Suwan Rd. Peaceful location by river, rooms with fan and shared shower. Friendly and helpful management. Recommended.

Ramkhamhaeng National Park *p196*
B-C There are bungalows near the park headquarters and tents for hire. Reservations can be made by contacting either Ramkhamhaeng National Park, PO Box 1, Amphoe Kirimas, Sukhothai, 64160 or by phoning the Royal Forest Department on T0-2579-4842. Some guesthouses in the new city (for example **Ban Thai**) are beginning to organize trips here.

Phitsanulok *p196, map p197*
AL-B Amarin Lagoon Hotel, 52/299 Phra Ong Khao Rd, out of town centre, T055-220999, amarin@psnulok.loxinfo.co.th. A/c, restaurant, pool, this soulless 305-room hotel on a 10-ha site is really a business hotel. However, the management provide a shuttle service, and a long time resident of Thailand reports that the hotel is well run, with courteous and efficient staff, superb views from the back over the lagoon and open countryside to the far hills.

A Topland Plaza Hotel, 68/33 Akathodsarod St, T055-247800, F247815. A/c, restaurant, well-run multi-storey hotel, with good views over the city from the

upper floors. A real bargain but it has a very noisy disco at weekends that will keep even the deepest sleeper awake.

A-B Phitsanulok Thani Hotel, 39 Sanambin Rd, T055-211065, www.phitsanulokthani.th.com. A/c, restaurant, pub, pool, luxury hotel, one of the Dusit chain, so standards are high. The room rate includes breakfast and there are a few pleasant garden restaurants just across the road. A little out of town, but within walking distance.

A-C Rajapruk, 99/9 Phra Ong Dam Rd, T055-258788, F251395. A/c, restaurant, inviting pool. Comfortable and clean with helpful and friendly staff. Recommended.

C Amarin Nakhon, 3/1 Chaophraya Rd, T055-219069, F055-219500. A/c, restaurant. Ideal central town location. All first-class facilities, and good value buffet lunches in the restaurant.

C Nanchao, 242 Boromtrailokant Rd, T055-252510. A/c, modern hotel with views from the upper floors, good value. Recommended.

D Samainiyom Hotel, 175 Ekathosarot Rd, T055-247527. All rooms a/c, satellite TV and clean en suite bathrooms for those willing to pay a little bit more. Reasonable prices.

D Sivathep Hotel, 110/21 Ekathosarot Rd, T055-244933, F219148. Some fan, some a/c, all rooms en suite with satellite TV.

D-E Lithai Guesthouse, 73/1 Phaya Lithai Rd, T055-219626, maka@loxinfo.co.th. Some fan, some a/c, satellite TV, en suite rooms. Views of either dirty rooftops or busy streets below. Still, good value for money.

D-E Youth Hostel, 38 Sanambin Rd, T055-242060. Southeast of the railway, slightly out of town. This has become the travellers' hangout, so it is very popular. Relaxing atmosphere in an attractive wooden building, large, clean rooms with some a/c and some style, helpful owner, dorm beds available, breakfast included, bicycles for rent. Outdoor sitting area for relaxing with bamboo hammocks. Possibly the only place in Thailand where you'll wake up to classical music. The best option in town for those on a budget. Highly recommended.

Phu Hin Rongkla National Park *p198*

B-C Bungalows are available at park headquarters (book in advance, T055-579573**4**). Two restaurants (take own food if self-catering) and money changer.

Camping

Camping ground (tents for hire, ฿40).

Thung Salaeng National Park *p199*

There are guesthouses and a dormitory block at the headquarters and 4 campsites. Tents are available for hire. A more comfortable alternative is to stay in one of the resort hotels along Highway 12.

B-C Rainforest Resort, at Km 44, T055-241185. Overlooks the Khek River and offers wooden bungalows with a/c, recommended.

Si Satchanalai *p199, map p200*

B Wang Yom Resort, off Route 101 to Sawankha ok, T055-611179. It has overpriced, tatty bungalows. Attached restaurant serves Thai food (mid-range).

Camping

You can rent tents (฿80) at the main gate into the park – there's a small campsite in a nice spot overlooking the river, a toilet/shower block and 24-hr security.

Kamphaeng Phet *p202, map p202*

All hotels are situated in the new town. There is a distinct lack of budget accommodation.

A-C Phet Hotel, 189 Bumrungraj Rd, T055-712810, phethtl@phethotel.com. Definitely the most comfortable hotel in town. A/c, small pool (open to non-residents), restaurant serving Thai and international food, snooker club. Good value for money with breakfast included.

B-C Nawarat, 2 Soi 15, Thesa 1 Rd, T055-711106, F711961. A/c, TV (Thai only), restaurant. Reasonable, clean rooms have thin walls, making it potentially noisy. The upper floors have good views.

D Kor Chokchai, 7-31 Rachdamnern Soi 6, T055-711247. Some a/c, some fan. Large, clean rooms and bathrooms, western toilets, though aimed at Thai businessmen.

D Three J Guesthouse, 79 Rachavitee Rd, T055-720384, charin.sri@chaiyo.com. Chintzy, clean bungalows, some a/c, some fan. The cutesy decor might leave you feeling dizzy but one of the friendliest places in town – recommended.

Eating

Sukhothai Old City *p191, map 192*

There are a number of stalls and small restaurants selling simple Thai dishes in the Old City.

¥ **The Coffee Cup**, a small, friendly café with drinks, snacks and internet facilities, just opposite the National Museum.

¥ **Vitoon Guesthouse**, 49/3 Jarodvithithong Rd (near the entrance to the park), T055-697045, provides excellent breakfasts and coffee for early risers arriving from Sukhothai. There's a great little shophouse selling tasty noodle soups and other Thai dishes on the corner of the lane that leads to Old City Guesthouse and, during the evening, dozens of stalls spring up along the main road selling everything from spicy papaya salad through to freshly roasted chicken.

Sukhothai *p189, map p190*

¥ **Art's Fresh Coffee and Beer**, by the bus station for the Old City on Charodwithithong Rd, is a good place for a mug of early morning coffee while waiting in the chill for the bus.

¥ **Chinnawat**, 1-3 Nikhon Kasem Rd. A/c restaurant with satellite TV and reasonable food, it offers the rather novel option of small and large portions – the latter are for the very hungry.

¥ **Dream Café**, near Sawatdipong Hotel, Singhawat Rd. Thai and international dishes in cool interior, with a great collection of bric-a-brac, good for breakfasts.

¥ **Leaf Bakery**, 23/6 Singhawat Rd.

¥ **Rainbow Café**, off Nikhon Kasem Rd (near night market). Good breakfasts and sometimes patrons can watch CNN or BBC World News (when it isn't set on Thai TV), although the road is a bit noisy. Also serves international food.

¥ **Sukhothai Coca**, 56/2-5 Singhawat Rd. Thai food and sandwiches.

Foodstalls

The night market (talaat to rung), on Ramkhamhaeng Rd, off Nikhon Kasem Rd, opposite the cinema, for good stalls. Open 1800-0600. Other stalls open up at about the same time along the walls of Wat Rachthani.

Coffee shops

Good coffee is available from **DK Coffee**, opposite the River View Hotel, attached to DK Books.

Phitsanulok *p196, map p197*

There is a good choice of excellent restaurants, mostly concentrated in the centre of town around Naresuan, Sairuthai and Phaya Lithai roads. Check out Phitsanulok's 2 famed specialities: kluay thaak or sweet bananas and thao mai luai or morning glory. This vegetable is flash-fried in a wok with a great burst of flame and then tossed onto the plate (the dish is usually known as phak bung loi fan). 'Flying Vegetable' artistes can be seen at work in the night market and at a few restaurants. Not to be missed! Several houseboat restaurants are to be found along Buddha Bucha Rd, near Naresuan Bridge.

Thai

¥¥ **Song Khwae Houseboat**, Buddha Bucha Rd. Nice place to hang out on the river. Serves Chinese food.

¥ **Poon Sri**, Phaya Lithai Rd. A great little Thai restaurant where you can get a good meal for ฿50 a head. Recommended.

¥ **Sor Lert Rod**, 4/5 Boromtrailokant Rd, near Phailyn Hotel. Great location for this good Thai eatery. Recommended.

¥ **Tiparot**, 9 Soi Lue Thai Rd. In the heart of town, serves up authentic and scrummy Chinese food.

¥ **Viroys**, 99/18-19 Phra Ong Dam Rd. Excellent Chinese food, with morning glory frying for the uninitiated.

Muslim

There are 2 Muslim restaurants on Phra Ong Dam Rd. The following is recommended. The other (adjacent to the level crossing) hasn't had a very good press.

¥ **Fab Ke Rab** (80 m east of the level crossing) is recommended – friendly staff, good food and very well priced.

Bakeries

KT, Phaya Lithai Rd. Excellent range of cakes and pastries.

Foodstalls

The riverside night market is open from 1800-2400, selling Thai and Chinese food.

Thai sweets (desserts) like khao niaw sangkayaa (sticky rice and custard) can be bought from the foodstalls on Phaya Lithai Rd in the evening. Basement of Topland Arcade, Boromtrailokant Rd, has a good selection of clean, well-presented foodstalls.

Si Satchanalai *p199, map p200*
Several bus loads of tourists arrive each day at Si Sat and most of them eat at the run of overpriced, though decent enough, Thai restaurants on the same stretch of road as the **Wang Yom Resort**. By the main gate (next door to the campsite) is a whole heave of cheap Thai stalls selling the usual fried rice, noodles, ice cream and drinks.

Kamphange Phet *p202, map p202*
TT **Piano and Guitar**, Tesa Rd. This restaurant, serving Thai food, has a charming interior.
T **Kitti** and **Khrua Wibun**, at 101 and 102 Thesa Rd (near Thesa Soi 2) are excellent, cheap Thai restaurants. They serve khao muu daeng (red pork and rice), khao man kai (chicken and rice) and most simple rice and noodle dishes. Recommended.
T **Maalay**, 77 Thesa Rd, look out for the rice baskets hanging outside – serves excellent Isaan (Lao) food, very traditional. Recommended.

Bakeries, coffee shops and ice cream parlours
Chai Bakery, Rachdamnern Rd (near intersection with Charoensuk Rd). Phayao Bakery, Thesa Rd (near Charoensuk Rd).
Kan Daed, Thesa Rd, coffee house inside an attractive wooden shophouse.
Two a/c ice cream parlours on Thesa Rd are Tasty (sign in Thai only) near Thesa Soi 2, and Sweet Ice near Thesa Soi 7.

Foodstalls
In the evening the best selection of foodstalls can be found at the night bazaar on Thesa Rd. A second group of stalls can be found on Wichit Rd.

Bars and clubs

Sukhothai *p189, map p190*
Several pubs are scattered along the bypass such as **Focus Bar** and **Top Country Pub**; rather out of the way for an evening drink unless you have your own transport. There is also the **Chopper Beer Bar** on Charodwithithong Rd, about 20 m after the bridge, on the left.

Phitsanulok *p196, map p197*
Most bars are near expensive hotels.
Bi Bi's Pub, Sithamtripidok Rd (down soi near Thep Nakhon Hotel). Cocktails and a wide range of drinks in an a/c 'chalet'.
Thip Beer House (opposite Phailyn Hotel), Boromtrailokant Rd. Ice-cold beer in open bar.

Festivals and events

Sukhothai *p189*
Oct/Nov Loi Krathong is very special and Sukhothai is reputed to be the 'home' of this most beautiful of Thai festivals. It is said that one of the king's mistresses carved the first krathong from a piece of fruit and floated it down the river to her king. Today, the festival symbolizes the floating away of the previous year's sins, although traditionally it was linked to the gift of water. The Thai word for irrigation, chonprathaan, literally means the 'gift of water', and the festival comes at the end of the rainy season when the rice is maturing in the paddy fields.

Shopping

Phitsanulok *p196, map p197*
Gold shops line the streets throughout town. Some jewellery and ornaments are handmade locally, with their designs taken from ruins and remains in the Sri Satchanalai area.
Mondok Thai, 10 Sithamtripidok Rd, for antiques and handicrafts.
Hat Tim, 1/7 Sithamtripidok Rd, also for antiques and handicrafts.
The **night market** on Buddha Bucha Rd, on the river, sells everything from handicrafts, clothes and toys to amulets (see page 100); something Phitsanulok has a reputation for.
Topland Arcade is a large a/c shopping centre on Boromtrailokant Rd, while the **Topland Plaza** is a similar affair on Singhawat Rd, near the **Topland Plaza Hotel**.

Si Satchanalai *p199, map p200*
Antiques
Ree Thai Antiques, a small quaint Walt Disney-style house.

Activities and tours

Sukhothai *p189, map p190*

Tours and tour operators

Many hotels and guesthouses arrange tours to the Old City, Kamphaeng Phet and Si Satchanalai. Expect to pay ฿300 for a tour to the Old City and ฿500 for Si Satchanalai.

Phitsanulok *p196, map p197*

Tour operators

Able Group Company Ltd, 55/45 Sri Thammatripidok Rd, T055-243851, F242206. Runs sightseeing and trekking tours and rents out cars.

Piti Tour and Phitsanulok Tour Centre, 55/45 Surasri Trade Centre, 43/11 Boromtrailokant Rd, T055-242206. Organizes city tours and tours to Sukhothai and Si Satchanalai by private car.

Transport

Sukhothai *p189, map p190*

For transport to the Old City, see page 192.

Air

Bangkok Airways, T055-633266/T612167, provides daily connections with **Bangkok** and **Chiang Mai**. Sukhothai Airport, T055-647224 – in fact closer to Phetchabun than Sukhothai – is privately owned by Bangkok Airways and opened in 1994.

Airline offices **Bangkok Airways**, 10 Moo 1, Jarodvithithong Rd, T055-613310.

Bicycle

฿50 per day from many guesthouses.

Bus

For regular connections with **Bangkok** (7 hrs), **Phitsanulok** (1 hr), **Chiang Mai** (6 hrs) and **Lampang** (5 hrs), the station is about 2 km west of town on the bypass road. There are two direct buses a day from the Old City to Bangkok's northern terminal – at 0900 and 2100, ฿256. You can buy tickets from the **Coffee Cup** (see Eating). Buses for other parts of the kingdom leave from offices at assorted points. For **Tak** and **Mae Sot**, buses leave from Ban Muang Rd; for **Si Satchanalai** from the corner of Raj Uthit and Charodwithithong roads.

Motorbike hire

฿250-300 per day from many guesthouses.

Tuk-tuk

For town trips and for excursions further afield; they congregate on Nikhon Kasem Rd, opposite the Chinnawat Hotel.

Phitsanulok *p196, map p197*

Air

Airport is just out of town on Sanambin Rd, T055-258029. THAI has multiple daily connections with **Bangkok**. There are also connections with **Loei, Tak, Lampang, Chiang Mai** (daily), **Mae Hong Son, Mae Sot** and **Nan**. From the airport, take a songthaew into town or buses run to/from the city bus centre near the railway station every 10 mins (฿4-6).

Airline offices THAI, 209/26-28 Boromtrailokant Rd, T055-2800060.

Bus

Terminal on the road east to Lom Sak (Route 12), 2 km out of town, T055-242430. If the bus travels through town en route to the bus terminal, ask the driver to let you off at the more convenient train station. Bus no 7 leaves the local bus station for the bus terminal every 10 mins (30-min journey). Regular connections with **Bangkok** from the Northern bus terminal (5-6 hrs), **Kamphaeng Phet** (2 hrs), **Uttaradit** (2 hrs), **Nan** (5 hrs, via Uttaradit), **Phrae** (3 hrs), **Udon Thani**, **Sukhothai** (every 30 mins), **Pattaya, Tak** (3 hrs), **Mae Sot** (5 hrs), **Chiang Mai** (5-6 hrs), **Lampang** (4 hrs), **Korat** (6 hrs) and **Chiang Rai** (6-7 hrs).

Car hire

Able Group Company Ltd, see Tour operators above.

Songthaew, tuk-tuk, saamlor and local bus

Both a/c and non-a/c (฿10-20).

Train

Swiss 'chalet' style station, with steam locomotive parked outside, Ekathosarot Rd, T055-258005. A copy of the train timetable in English is available from the TAT office, see page 196. Regular connections with **Bangkok**'s Hualamphong station, (6 hrs), **Lopburi** (5 hrs), **Ayutthaya** (5 hrs) and **Chiang Mai** (6-7 hrs). For those travelling straight on to Sukhothai, take a tuk-tuk the 4 km to the bus station.

Si Satchanalai *p199, map p200*

Bus

Regular connections 0600-1800 with **Sukhothai** from Raj Uthit Rd, 54 km, 1 hr. Ask to be dropped off at the muang kao (old city). For **Chaliang**, get off at the pink archway on Route 101, 2 km before Route 1201, which leads to a suspension footbridge crossing the Yom River to Chaliang.

Motorbike

For hire in Sukhothai, see page 209.

Kamphaeng Phet *p202, map p202*

Bus

Terminal is 2 km from the bridge, some way out of town. Regular connections with **Bangkok**'s Northern terminal (5 hrs) and with **Phitsanulok**, **Chiang Mai**, **Tak** (2 hrs), **Nan**, **Phrae** and **Chiang Rai**. **Win Tour**, Kamphaeng Phet Rd, and corner of Thesa Rd, operates a/c tour buses to Bangkok.

Songthaew

To local destinations depart from the main market (the municipal or Thetsabarn) for the bus station. Songthaews run from the bus terminal to the market in town (฿5); and from Kamphaeng Phet Rd, at the roundabout by the bridge.

Directory

Sukhothai *p189, map p190*

Banks Bangkok, 49 Singhawat Rd. Bangkok Bank of Commerce, 15 Singhawat Rd. Thai Farmers, 134 Charoen Withi Rd. There is also a currency exchange booth by the Ramkhamhaeng Museum in the old city – open daily 0830-1200. **Internet** A number of cafés have opened up in both the Old City and Sukhothai; some guesthouses provide internet services. **Medical services** Sukhothai Hospital, Charodwithithong Rd, T055-611782, about 4 km out of town on the road towards the Old City. **Post office** Nikhon Kasem Rd. There is also a sub post office and overseas telephone service in the Old City. **Useful addresses** Police Nikhon Kasem Rd, T055-611010.

Phitsanulok *p196, map p197*

Banks Bangkok, 35 Naresuan Rd. Krung Thai, 31/1 Naresuan Rd. Thai Farmers, 144/1 Boromtrailokant Rd, TCs and ATM. **Internet** A couple of places just over the Aekathossarot Bridge. More internet cafés are opening around to **Medical services** Hospital Sithamtripidok Rd, T055-258812. **Post office and telephone centre** Buddha Bucha Rd. **Useful addresses** Tourist Police Boromtrailokant Rd, next to TAT office, T055-251179.

Kamphaeng Phet *p202, map p202*

Banks Thai Farmers, 233 Charoensuk Rd, and Bangkok Bank both have ATMs. **Internet** There are an increasing number of internet cafés in town, mainly situatued along Tesa Rd. **Post office** corner of Thesa Rd and Thesa Soi 3. Also fax and overseas telephone facilities.

Towards Mae Sot and the Burmese border

West of Sukhothai is Tak – a town built on the trade of various nefarious goods that pass through from nearby Burma. Pressed right up against the Burmese border Mae Sot, Tak has a reputation for bandits and smuggling though the town authorities are eager to build on its burgeoning reputation as a trekking centre. From Mae Sot it's possible to cross the Moei River for a day trip into the Burmese town of Myawadi. Follow the Burmese border further north from Mae Sot to reach Mae Sariang and Mae Hong Son or south to the rugged forests of Umphang. » *For Sleeping, Eating and other listings, pages 215-218.*

Tak → *Colour map 1, grid C1.*

Sprawling along the east bank of the Ping River, Tak was once a junction in the river trade but is now better known as a smuggling centre; drugs, teak and gems from Burma are exchanged for guns and consumer goods from Thailand. The Phahonyothin Highway is often lined with logging lorries carrying timber from Burma; a trade which has the political and commercial support of the Thai Army. Still small and distinctly provincial, Tak has managed to retain some of its traditional architecture; wooden houses with tiled roofs are scattered amongst the ubiquitous concrete shophouses. Like a number of other areas in the more peripheral areas of Thailand, Christian missionaries have been active in Tak Province and there is a large Roman Catholic Church on the Phahonyothin Highway.

Ins and outs

TAT tourist office is situated on Thaksin Road, T055-514341.

Sights

A source of local pride is the long, slender and rather unusual suspension bridge for motorcycles and pedestrians north of the **Viang Tak 2 Hotel**. As in any other town, Tak has its share of markets and wats. There is a large general market between Chompon and Rimping roads, and a smaller food market opposite the **Viang Tak Hotel** on Mahatthai Bamrung Road.

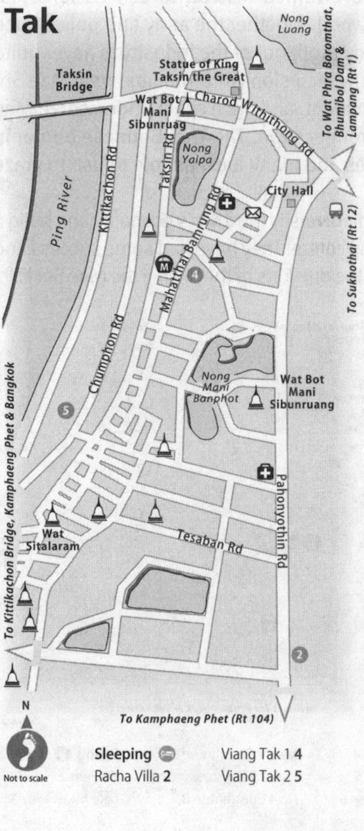

Lan Sang National Park

ⓘ *฿3, ฿20 (car); the park lies 3 km off the Tak-Mae Sot highway (No105) between Km 12 and Km 13, it is easy enough to alight from one of the many buses that make this journey and either walk the final 3 km or hitch a lift on a motorbike.* The National Park supports small populations of leopard, various deer and bear; much of the wildlife has been denuded through years of (usually illegal) hunting. There are a number of trails leading to waterfalls, together with the Doi Musur Hilltribe Development and Welfare Centre. It covers just over 100 sq km. Hilltribe products are for sale at Km 29 on the Tak-Mae Sot highway.

Mae Sot → *Colour map 1, grid C2.*

Mae Sot lies 5 km from the Burmese border, near the end of Route 105 which swoops its way through hills and forest from Tak to Mae Sot and the Moei River Valley. The town has developed into an important trading centre and just about every ethnic group can be seen wandering the streets: Thais, Chinese, Burmese, Karen, Hmong and other

Shophouses: combining domestic and working worlds

The shophouse is one of Asia's great architectural innovations, at least functionally, if not artistically. It combines domestic life and work in a single building. The family live upstairs; work is carried out on the ground floor. Mothers with children can work and meet their 'reproductive' demands at the same time, whereas in the west the spatial separation of the domestic world and the world of work means that either women cannot work or they must send (and pay for) their children to attend a crêche.

Today, shophouses continue to be built, although architecturally they may be inferior, illustrating their functional beauty and flexibility even in rapidly developing, and westernizing, Thailand. Today, it is common to see the family pick-up parked next to the refrigerator, while children play among sacks of produce. The Romanesque shophouse may have arrived, replacing the far more aesthetically pleasing wooden shophouse, but their functional logic remains the same.

hilltribes. Although Mae Sot has quietened down over the last few years, it still has a reputation as being one of the more lawless towns in Thailand. With a flourishing, and sometimes illicit, trade in drugs, teak and gems, this is perhaps unsurprising.

The importance of teak has grown since the Thai government imposed a ban on all logging in Thailand, and companies have turned instead to concessions just across the border in Burma to secure their wood. Whether the army and police force are protecting the forests or are making a tidy profit out of the industry is never quite clear. At the beginning of 1992, Burmese army incursions into Thailand near Mae Sot pursuing Karen rebels led to a diplomatic incident, and once again underscored Mae Sot's reputation as a slightly 'dangerous' frontier town. The Thai-Burmese border in this area is strewn with anti-personnel mines and many local people refuse to graze their cattle because of the danger.

The authorities in Mae Sot are now trying to diversify the town's economy and build a reputation as a tourist destination and trekking centre. They have had some success and there is now a modern, western-style hotel on the outskirts of the town – the Mae Sot Hill.

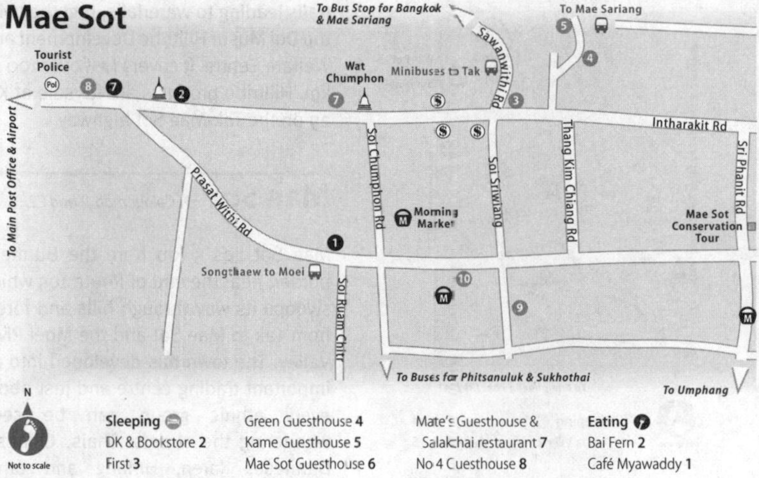

Sights

Wat Moni Phraison, on Intharakit Road, has an unusual chedi in which a golden central spire is surrounded by numerous smaller chedis rising in tiers, behind each of which is a small image of the Buddha. **Wat Chumphon**, also on Intharakit Road but on the western side of town, is worth visiting. Many of Mae Sot's older wooden shophouses are still standing, especially on Intharakit Road. There is a busy morning market between Prasat Withi and Intharakit roads in the town centre that attracts many Burmese eager to sell their produce. Burmese day migrants can be identified by their dress (many wear lungyis or sarongs), language and their finely featured and powdered faces.

Trekking and tours

Mae Sot offers some of the best trekking in northern and western Thailand. However, its potential as another Mae Hong Son or Pai has not gone unnoticed. Its popularity is increasing and in the immediate future there are likely to be new or improved bus services, as well as more guesthouses, trekking companies and associated services. It's also possible to cross the border into Burma, for an immigration fee of approximately US$10. Treks tend to either go south to Umphang or north towards Mae Sariang, and incorporate visits to caves, waterfalls, hilltribe villages and Karen refugee camps. The usual array of raft trips and elephant rides are available, in addition to straightforward trekking. See trek operators, page 217.

> *The Thai-Burmese border in this area is heavily mined and visitors should not hike without a guide. This applies particularly to Pang Ma Pha and Pai districts.*

Around Mae Sot

The Burmese border lies 5 km west of Mae Sot, and runs down the middle of the Moei River. The construction of the 420-m Friendship Bridge across the river, directly linking Mae Sot with the Burmese town of **Myawady**, was formally completed in 1997. Thai and Burmese nationals can cross the **border** ⓘ *regular blue songthaews to the Moei River and the Burmese border leave from the west end of Prasat Withi Rd, not far from the THAI office (฿10)*, here though overseas visitors are limited to one-day visas, which can be purchased at the border. It is also possible to extend your Thai visa at the immigration office here. Thai and Burmese relations are such that border crossings close and reopen with regularity. As the situation at the border is subject to frequent change it is a good idea to check on the status of the border at your hotel/guesthouse or at the Mae Sot Travel Centre before making your journey. A visit to the frontier, even if you don't cross into Burma, still makes for an interesting day trip.

There is a modern, covered market at the border selling Burmese goods (hats, blankets, gems, silver, baskets and agricultural produce like dried mushrooms), with gun-toting Thai rangers, powder-covered Burmese girls and a few restaurants.

Around 1 km from the bridge, back along the road to Mae Sot, is **Wat Thai Wattanaram**. This monastery is notable mainly for the massive, recently built, Burmese-style reclining Buddha in the rear courtyard. Also here is a gallery of over 25 smaller sitting Buddhas.

Hi Fi Forever **3**
Krua Canadian **4**
Neung Nuk **5**
Seafood **7**

Umphang and around → Colour map 3, grid A2.

Umphang lies 169 km south of Mae Sot. This district is one of the least developed in Western Thailand with its rugged terrain and large expanses of forest, including the Khlong Lan National Park making it ideal for trekking. Although an organized trek is the best way to see and experience the area's beauty (see Trekking, page 213, or take a trek arranged by one of the guesthouses in Umphang), it is possible to explore the area to a limited extent on one's own. Umphang is not much more than an oversized village and the majority of its population are Karen.

> *Malaria is a problem, not so much in Umphang itself, but in the surrounding countryside. Precautions should be taken if trekking outside the town.*

There is some excellent trekking around Umphang. Many of the trekking companies in Mae Sot head this way, with the guesthouses, tour companies and resorts in Umphang also offering similar packages. See tour operators. (Treks arranged from Umphang rather than Mae Sot can usually work out considerably cheaper though you'll have to suffer the five-hour journey from Mae Sot in a songthaew rather than the comfy four-wheel drive usually provided.)

If travelling to Umphang by your own transport, leave early in the morning as there are quite a number of worthwhile stops en route, including waterfalls and Karen villages. The Thara Rak waterfall is just over 25 km from Mae Sot. Turn off the road after the Km 24 marker.

Khlong Lan National Park

The park covers around 300 sq km with its highest point at 1,440-m-high Khun Klong Lan. Wildlife includes sambar deer, wild pig and macaques. There are also a number of waterfalls, including the Khlong Lan Waterfall which cascades over a 100-m-high rock face. Khlong Nam Lai Waterfall is good for swimming.

Mae Sot to Mae Sariang

On most maps this road – Route 105 – appears indistinct, as if it is no more than a track. In fact, the entire 230-km road, due to its proximity to the Burmese and its military and strategic significance, is in excellent shape. Police checkpoints are interspersed along its length; you might be asked to produce your passport. Travelling south to north, the road is fast to the district town of Tha Song Yang. It then follows the Moei River and the Burmese border. The landscape becomes wilder, less populated, more mountainous and the road slower with each kilometre making for a beautiful, if uncomfortable, six-hour journey.

Umphang

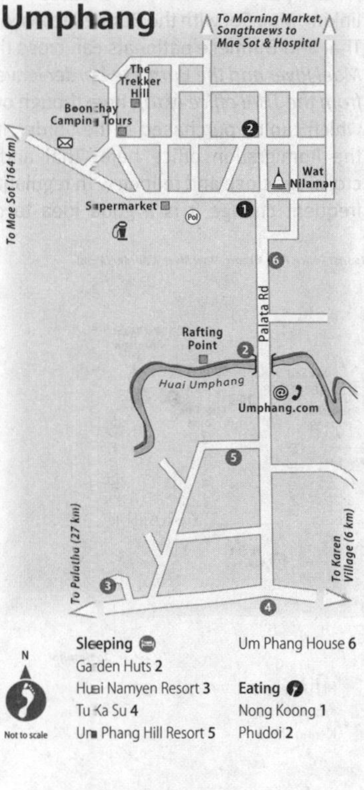
To Morning Market, Songthaews to Mae Sot & Hospital
The Trekker Hill
Boonchay Camping Tours
Wat Nilaman
Supermarket
Pol
To Mae Sot (164 km)
Palata Rd
Rafting Point
Huai Umphang
Umphang.com
To Pulathu (27 km)
To Karen Village (6 km)
N
Not to scale
Sleeping
Garden Huts 2
Huai Namyen Resort 3
Tu Ka Su 4
Um Phang Hill Resort 5
Um Phang House 6
Eating
Nong Koong 1
Phudoi 2

Sleeping

Tak *p211, map p211*
Hotels are limited here, with no guesthouses that can be recommended for budget travellers.
B **Viang Tak 2**, 236 Chumphon Rd, T055-512507, www.viangtak.com. A/c, overlooking the Ping River, the best hotel in Tak – well-run, well-maintained and clean. Pool, coffee shop, snooker, nightclub, shopping plaza with 24-hr supermarket. Significant discounts available during low season. Recommended.
C **Viang Tak 1**, 25/3 Mahatthai Bamrung Rd, T055-512507, F512687. Comfortable a/c hotel with 'western' bar and restaurant out the front. Breakfast included in room price. Spacious rooms with optional TV. Good value.
C-D **Racha Villa**, 307/1 Pahonyothin Rd, T055-512361. On the outskirts of town, this hotel is more like a motel. Facilities include a/c, TV and western toilet. The rooms are large and clean if a little tatty.

Around Tak *p213*
Limited accommodation is available in Lan Sang National Park (T02-5790529 to book) and camping is permitted.

Mae Sot *p211, map p212*
A **Mae Sot Hill**, 100 Asia Rd, T055-532601, F532600. Restaurant, bar, 2 pools, tennis courts, the only luxury place to stay. Rooms are spacious, elegant, clean and well-maintained.
C-D **DK Hotel**, 298/2 Intharakit Rd, T055-542648, F542651. Built by the Duang Kamol publishing group, the lower floor is a large Thai language bookshop. A/c and fan rooms available. The quality of the rooms differs dramatically between fan and a/c and the hotel is only good value if you get an a/c room. No double beds available. Friendliness of the staff is variable.
D **Ban Maie Guesthouse**, 59/11 Asia Rd, next to SP Guesthouse, T055-533091. Pleasant rooms on the upper storey of a large wooden house boasting a sizeable roof terrace. A/c or fan options, attached western toilets, TV, fridge, free drinking water and coffee. A nice option if you want to head slightly out of town for relatively little cost.
D **First Hotel**, 444 Sawat Withi Rd, T055-531233. Some a/c, large, clean rooms, some character. Friendly staff.
D **Fortune Guest House**, 738/1 Intarakeeree RD, T055-536392. "Be fortunate" is the motto here and its selling point, aside from reasonable rates, clean a/c and fan rooms and decent beds is the wonderfully helpful staff. Moses is Burmese and full of information about Mae Sot and his Thai wife is equally kind and hospitable. No wonder guests return. Highly recommended.
D **Mae Sot Guesthouse**, 208/4 Intharakit Rd, T055-532745, F532745. Teak house in largish garden compound. Small simple rooms in main house, bigger rooms with attached cold-water bathrooms and a/c in 'motelesque' bungalow (dorm beds available). It's full of grime and not great value. Situated opposite a karaoke bar, and it can be very noisy. Attractive dining and seating area in a large airy teak barn on the side of the house, with satellite TV and lots of information. Extremely friendly owner speaks fantastic English – but he's not always around. The guesthouse organizes trekking tours and collects unwanted clothing and medicines to distribute to Burmese refugees in the area.
E **Green Guesthouse**, 460/8 Intharakit Rd, T055-533207. The delightful smell of jasmine as you enter goes some way to combating the fact that this place is situated directly opposite the Burmese holding prison. Clean and comfortable with spotless rooms, all with attached western bathrooms and mozzie guards on the windows.
E **Mate's Guesthouse**, 630/1 Intharakit Rd, T055-531016. Only 4 rooms here, all with fans and mozzie guards over the windows. 'Mate,' who runs the place, speaks good English and is very friendly – hence the nickname. Attached is the **Salakthai Steakhouse**.
E-F **Kame Guesthouse**, 119/22 Chitwana Rd, near the Bangkok and Mae Sariang bus station and old farmers' market (still very much in evidence on Sun and Wed), T055-535868. A gem of a place, with both normal and dorm fan rooms, all as clean as can be, and very simple, with just the mattress laid down on the floor. Shared facilities, with one toilet and shower on the

roof, amid the racks ready for clothes drying. There's also a laundry service, on-site internet connection, printer, scanner and bikes for hire at ฿30 per day. Very friendly. Recommended.

E-F No 4 Guesthouse, 736 Intharakit Rd, T/F055-544976, no4guesthouse@yahoo.com. This large teak building is set back on a big plot to the west of town on the road to the Moei River (about 10-15 mins' walk from the bus station). Wooden floors, rooms are large, airy and basic with mattresses on the floor and rather dirty shared toilets, but hot showers. Seating area with Thai TV, and a few books and magazines. Eco-trekking is run from here (see Trekking and tours).

Umphang and around *p214, map p214*

For the budget traveller the accommodation here is good value for money, but if you are looking for the minibar and executive lounge experience, expect to be disappointed. In fact, hardly any of the guesthouses have a/c, although the cool weather usually makes this unnecessary.

B Huai Namyen Resort, on the road to Palatha, T055-561092. This place is hard to find despite being signposted from the road: just keep bearing left after the turnoff and you'll get to 3 houses, each made up of 2 rooms and sizeable veranda, overlooking nearby cornfields. Advance booking is essential. A peaceful and rustic choice.

B-E Um Phang Hill Resort, Palata Rd, T055-561063, www.umphang hill.com. Grubby but friendly, this guesthouse has wooden bungalows on a small hill with attractive gardens, ranging from dorm to large rooms with hot showers TV (Thai plus MTV) and fridge. Friendly management with excellent English. Recommended.

C-E Garden Huts, 106 Palata Rd, T055-561093, www.boonyaporn.com Cramped bamboo and wooden bungalows some with beds on raised platforms and some with western toilets. More expensive rooms have a river view and a small sitting area. Very friendly management with a little English.

C-E Tu Ka Su, Palata Rd, T/F055-561295, T01-8258238 (mob). Attractive setting, wooden and bamboo en suite bungalows. Very clean and pleasant atmosphere. Bicycles for rent (฿200 per day). Recommended.

D-E Um Phang House, T055-561073. Range of rooms with attached facilities, some separate bungalows. Basic, with mattresses on raised wooden platforms. Cheaper rooms have squat toilets, bungalows (2-3 people) have western toilets.

Khlong Lan National Park *p214*

B-C There are 9 bungalows sleeping between 5 and 12 people and a campsite near park HQ.

Mae Sot to Mae Sariang *p214*

There are a few places to stay en route.

E Mae Sali Guesthouse (121 km from Mae Sariang, 109 km from Mae Sot). Almost where the road stops following the river and climbs into the hills is this relaxing place to stay with a welcoming Burmese host. Further on still, about two-thirds of the way to Mae Sariang, is the **C Pa Pa Valley Resort**.

Eating

Tak *p211, map p211*

There is a limited number of restaurants, although simple Thai eateries are scattered throughout the town, particularly along Phahonyothin Rd. For even cheaper options there is stall food available from the market on Mahatthai Bamrung Rd.

Mae Sot *p211, map p212*

Several small restaurants have recently opened along the western part of Intharakit Rd; notable are the Burmese restaurants at the southern end of Tang Khim Chiang Rd.

TT Sea Food Restaurant, Intharakit Rd. Attractive teak sitting area with a good range of lobster, crab, squid, seabass and prawns served in a variety of ways.

T Bai Fern Restaurant, 660/2 Intharakit Rd, serves Thai, Western and Burmese food, with a range of pizzas and vegetarian options. The yogurt with fruit and museli is good with a selection of fruits and it is the best place in town for coffee. Pleasant indoor sitting area with wonderful decor. Popular with travellers and medical interns.

T Café Myawaddy, Prasat Withi Rd (opposite the songthaew stop for the Moei River), 0700-2100. Run by a Burmese, spotlessly maintained a/c restaurant.

Canton (Kwangtung), 2/1 Soi Sriphanich. Locals say that this place serves the best Chinese food in town.

Hi Fi Forever, Intharakit Rd, 1600-0100. Good Thai food served on this 1st-floor balcony of a restaurant, overlooking Intharakit Rd.

Krua Canadian, 3 Sri Phanit Rd, T055-534659, 0700-2100/2200. Smallish café with Canadian owner, Dave, serving good value Thai and Western dishes with a menu in English. The North American breakfast is the best in town. Truly mouth-watering steaks, excellent curries. Takeaway service. Hill tribe coffee sold (also packaged as gifts). Dave is also an excellent source of information and highly entertaining. Recommended.

Neung Nuk, Intharakit Rd. Garden restaurant serving up great Thai grub.

Foodstalls

There are 2 excellent stall restaurants by the Chiang Mai bus stop on Intharakit Rd. One specializes in superb phat thai (fried noodles), the other in seafood. The night market, just off Prasat Withi Rd, is a good place to eat cheaply in the evening.

Umphang and around *p214, map p214*

Almost all guesthouses and resorts have their own restaurants selling cheap Thai food.

Nong Koong, on the corner of Palata Rd, opposite BL Tours, is a local place serving simple Thai dishes (you'll need your phrasebook to order).

Phudoi Restaurant has an extensive menu in English and a nice wooden interior. Good food at reasonable prices.

Shopping

Mae Sot *p211, map p212*

Books

DK Bookstore, under the DK Hotel, has a large range of English-language Penguin classics. There is also a second-hand bookshop with a small selection of English books on Intharakit Rd.

Burmese goods

On sale in the market on the Moei River and in the market behind the **Siam Hotel**. For better quality objects, try the Burmese lacquerware shop on Prasat Withi Rd, almost opposite the songthaew stop for the Moei River.

Gems

A good buy; most of the jewellery shops are concentrated on Prasat Withi Rd around the Siam Hotel.

Activities and tours

Mae Sot *p211, map p212*

Tour operators

Approximate rates are ฿3,500 for a 3-day/2-night trek, ฿4,500 for 4-days/3-nights, dependent upon whether raft trips and elephant rides are part of the deal. With all tours it's worthwhile confirming precisely what's included in the price.

Eco-trekking is run from **No 4 Guesthouse**. It does 7-day tours at special request for US$400, though it's a truly unique experience. Popular.

Mae Sot Conservation Tour, 415/7 Tang Khim Chiang Rd, T055-532818, premat@ksc15.th.com, runs educational and soft adventure tours for families and the elderly (contact **Pim Hut Restaurant**).

Mae Sot Travel Centre (aka **SP Tours**), 14/21 Asia Rd, T055-531409, F532279. The main office is out of town, but they can be contacted at the Mae Sot Hill and the **Siam Hotel**.

Trek operators

Max One Tours (opposite DK Hotel), T055-542941, www.maxonetours.com, runs day trips around Mae Sot (waterfall, gibbon sanctuary, hot spring, temple and Thai-Burmese border market, ฿1,500 per person) as well as longer treks.

Umphang and around *p214, map p214*

Most of the tour companies (aside from those arranged by guesthouses) are on Palata Rd. Be aware that only a handful of outfits have English-speaking guides. These more advanced operations include the following:

The Ecotourist Center, T055-561063, F561065, **Boonchay Camping Tour**, 360 M.1 Tambol, T055-561020.

BL Tours, T055-561021, F561322. Guides are Burmese and speak English, although their local knowledge isn't perhaps quite equal to that of the guides from Umphang Hill Resort or The Trekker Hill.

Umphang Hill Resort, Palata Rd, T055-561063-4, www.umphanghill.com. Guides speak English, French, German, Japanese and Chinese.

The Trekker Hill, 620 Prawesphywan Rd, T055-561090, F561328, run by Mr T whose guides speak English and Danish, and who offers a 'service guarantee' whereby if clients aren't satisfied he'll return a portion of the cost.

Transport

Tak *p211, map p211*

Tuk-tuks, saamlors and motorcycle taxis are available. Local songthaews also leave from this station.

Bus

Non-a/c and a/c buses leave from the station on Route 12 near crossroads of Phahonyothin Rd. There are connections with **Bangkok**'s Northern bus terminal (7 hrs), **Chiang Mai** (4 hrs), **Mae Sot** (1½ hrs), **Kamphaeng Phet** (1 hr, departures hourly), **Sukhotha** (1-1½ hrs, departures hourly), **Chiang Rai, Mae Sai, Lampang** and elsewhere in the Northern and Central Plains regions.

Mae Sot *p211, map p212*

Bus

Mae Sot does not have a single bus terminal; buses and songthaews depart from various places around town (see map). A/c and non-a/c bus connections with **Bangkok**'s Northern bus terminal (8-10 hrs), from the stop out of town near Asia Rd at 0800, 0830, 1900, 1930, 2000, 2030, 2100 (and VIP buses at 2115, 2130, 2145 and 2200). A/c and non-a/c buses for **Chiang Mai** (6½ hrs) leave at 0600 and 0800. **Tak** (1½ hrs), **Lampang** and **Mae Sai** (12 hrs) leave from the bus stop on Intharakit Rd. Songthaews for **Mae Sariang** leave in the morning from the road running past the police station, off Intharakit Rd (6 hrs from 0600-1200). Songthaews for **Umphang** leave every hour from about 0700-1400 (5 hrs).

Motorbike hire

Prasat Withi Rd (close to the Bangkok Bank), ฿160 per day.

Umphang and around *p214, map p214*

Songthaew

Several songthaews a day connect Umphang with **Mae Sot**. The first leaves Mae Sot around 0700, the last at about 1400 (4-5 hrs, ฿100). For the return journey they leave Umphang for Mae Sot at 0700, 0800, 0900, 1300, 1400 and 1500, although the number of departures per day seem to be subject to demand. It is also possible to go by motorbike – but a scooter will not be powerful enough due to the steep inclines.

Directory

Tak *p211, map p211*

Banks Krung Thai, Taksin Rd (corner of Soi 9). Siam City, 125 Mahatthai Bamrung Rd. Thai Military, 77/2 Mahatthai Bamrung Rd. **Internet** There are now several internet access facilities in town, mostly concentrated on Mahatthai Bamrung Rd. **Post office** Off Mahatthai Bamrung Rd in the north of town.

Mae Sot *p211, map p212*

Banks Siam Commercial, 544/1-5 Intharakit Rd. Thai Farmers, 84/9 Prasat Withi Rd. **Internet** A few internet cafés have opened up at the western end of Prasat Withi Rd. **Telephone** Overseas service at post office on Intharakit Rd. **Post office** Intharakit Rd (opposite DK Hotel). The main post office is also on Intharakit Rd, but past the No 4 Guesthouse about 1 km out of town on the road to the Moei River. **Useful addresses** Tourist Police on Intharakit Rd (next to No 4 Guesthouse), T055-533523.

Umphang and around *p214, map p214*

Banks No banks in Umphang – make sure you bring plenty of money! **Internet and telephone** Umphang.com on Palata Rd (though there's only 1 computer and usually a handful of children glued to it). **Useful Addresses** Police T055-561112.

Northern Region

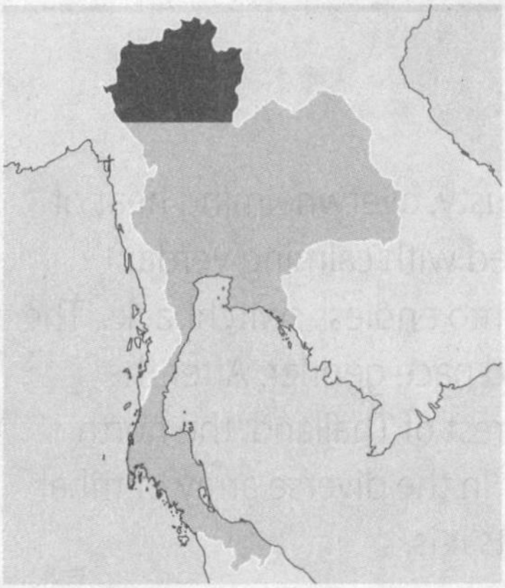

Footprint features

Introduction

It begins with an easing of the dusty, overwhelming heat of the plains. Limestone hillls, draped with calming verdant forest, roads and rivers twisting into endless switchbacks. The air seems cleaner, the people and pace gentler. After the raucous intensity of most of the rest of Thailand, the north feels like another country. Factor in the diverse array of tribal hill peoples, and in many respects it is.

The north wasn't incorporated into the Thai nation until the beginning of the 20th century. For centuries local lords held sway over shifting principalities, the most significant being centred on Chiang Mai. This city remains the largest in the north, and a magnet for thousands of tourists. With its walled centre, serene and ancient temples, bustling markets and excellent accommodation it's easy to understand why.

Travel to the west of Chiang Mai and you'll find beautiful Mae Hong Son, encircled by hills and often cloaked in mist. En route take in Pai; set in a stunning location this is a travellers hangout with all the banana pancakes you could ever consume. Head up country and you'll reach the venerable city of Chiang Rai, an important trekking centre. Most of its history has been lost but Chiang Rai is still a friendly and proud place. Further north is Mae Sai, which offers the opportunity for excursions into Burma while Chiang Khong, on the Mekong, is a crossing point into Laos. To the north east is Chiang Saen, an early 14th-century fortified wiang (walled city) and the infamous Golden Triangle, where Laos, Burma and Thailand meet. Finally, some of Thailand's most beautiful and peaceful monasteries are found in the north. Wat Phra Singh in Chiang Mai, Wat Phumin in Nan, and, perhaps the finest of them all is in Lampang - Wat Phra That Lampang Luang – an extraordinary display of temple craft.

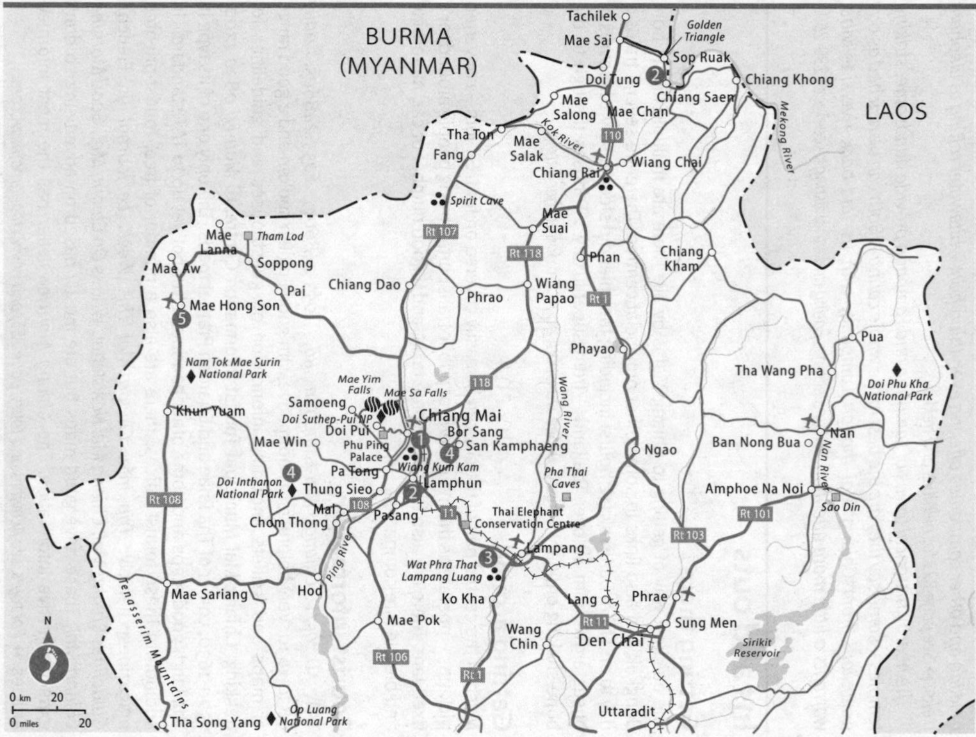

★ Don't miss...

1 **Chiang Mai** The cultural capital of the north offers great shopping, good food and beautiful monasteries, page 222.

2 **The north's small citadels** Once citadels at the heart of minute kingdoms and principalities, the towns of Lamphun and Chiang Saen are intriguing, authentic places to visit, pages 235 and 286.

3 **Wat Phra That Lampang Luang** The beauty of Lampang's stunning wat has to be seen to be appreciated. Make sure you take in Thailand's most alluring temple, page 236.

4 **Walk on the wildside** Trek out into the rolling hills and visit the northern villages' incredible array of indigenous peoples, page 254.

5 **Mae Hong Son** Deep in the highlands, surrounded by an arc of verdant hills, Mae Hong Son is a remote outpost of Thailand that ~is filled with Burmese-style monasteries and a large tribal population, page 262.

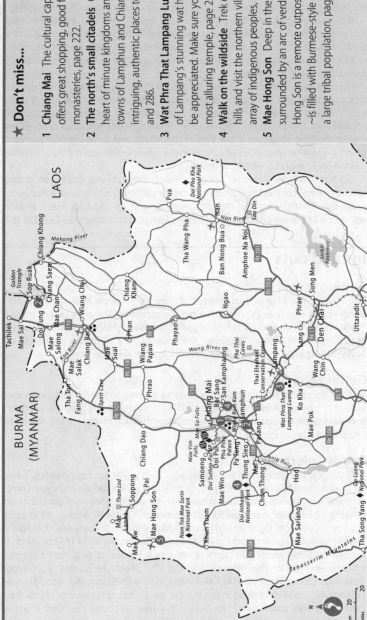

Chiang Mai and around

➔ *Colour map 1, grid B2.*

When Reginald Le May wrote about Chiang Mai back in 1938, this was, in his view, one of the loveliest cities imaginable. Life, as they say, has moved on since then. But while old Thailand hands may worry about lost innocence, Chiang Mai is still worth visiting.

While in Chiang Mai don't forget to climb Doi Suthep, the city's revered mountain that rises 1000 m above the city and is crowned with an important temple. A visit to the tribal museum, just to the north of the city centre, is essential to understanding the region's indigenous peoples while to the south rests the handsome remains of a ruined city, Wiang Kum Kam.

The city's monasteries are the most beautiful in the North; there is a rich tradition of arts and crafts, and the moated old city still gives a flavour of the past. It is the unofficial 'capital of the North', there are also some good practical reasons to base yourself here. It is an important transport hub, there is an excellent range of hotels and restaurants, the shopping is the best in the North, and there are also scores of trekking and other companies offering everything from whitewater rafting to elephant treks. ⏩ *See page 223 for hilltribes and trekking.*

The nearby historical towns of Lamphun and Lampang provide handsome, striking temples – some say they are the best in the whole country. Both can be reached as day excursions from Chiang Mai though Lampang, with its laid-back riverside vibe, warrants a little more attention. ⏩ *For Sleeping, Eating and other listings, see pages 239-259.*

Ins and outs

Getting there

The quickest way of getting to Chiang Mai is by air. There are multiple flights from Bangkok and also links to some other provincial centres. There are several trains a day to and from Bangkok (12 hours) including the splendid sleeper service. Scores of buses arrive from all over Thailand – from super-luxury VIP buses through to the bone-shaking ordinary variety. ⏩ *See Transport, page 256, for further details.*

Getting around

Much of the central part of the city can be easily covered on foot. Sii-lors – converted pick-ups – operate as the main mode of public transport, ferrying people around for a fixed fare. There are also tuk-tuks, some taxis, and a good number of car, motorbike and bicycle hire companies.

Tourist information

TAT, ⓘ *105/1 Chiang Mai-Lamphun Rd, T053-248604, F053-248605, daily 0830-1630*. Very helpful and informative with good English spoken and a good range of maps and leaflets, including information on guesthouses and guidelines for trekking. **Chiang Mai Municipal Tourist Information Centre,** ⓘ *Mon-Fri 0830-1200, 1300-1630*, corner of Tha Phae and Charoen Prathet roads. The only one of its type in Thailand, good maps and some other handouts, but not yet up to TAT standard. In addition to these tourist offices, there are also a number of free, tourist-oriented magazines, namely: *Trip Info*, *Chiang Mai This Week*, *Le Journal* (in French), *Guidelines Chiang Mai*, *Chiang Mai Newsletter*, *What's On Chiang Mai*, *Good Morning Chiang Mai*. These have good maps but are mostly based on advertising so don't expect objective information. The *Chiang Mai Newsletter* has the most informed articles. ⏩ *For tours, see Activities and tours, page 255, and www.chiangmainews.com.*

Hilltribes

A visit to a hilltribe village is one of the main reasons why people travel to the north of Thailand. The hilltribe population (Chao Khao in Thai – literally 'Mountain People') numbers about 800,000, or a little over 1% of the total population of the country.

These 800,000 people are far from homogenous: each hilltribe (there are nine recognized by the government), has a different language, dress, religion, artistic heritage and culture. They meet their subsistence needs in different ways and often occupy different ecological niches. In some respects they are as far removed from one another as they are from the lowland Thais.

As their name suggests, the hilltribes occupy the highland areas that fringe the Northern region, with the largest populations in the provinces of Chiang Mai (143,000), Chiang Rai (98,000), Mae Hong Son (83,000) and Tak (69,000). These figures are a few years old, but the relative balance between the provinces has not changed significantly. Although this guide follows the tradition of using the term 'hilltribe' to describe these diverse peoples, it is in many regards an unfortunate one. They are not tribes in the anthropological sense, derived as it is from the study of the peoples of Africa. For information on all the people, see Background page 664. For information on trekking and choosing a trek operator, see Activities and tours, page 71.

Background

Around 1290 King Mengrai annexed the last of the Mon kingdoms at Lamphun and moved his capital from Chiang Rai to a site on the banks of the Ping River called Nopburi Sri Nakawan Ping Chiang Mai. It is said he chose the site after seeing a big mouse accompanied by four smaller mice scurry down a hole beneath a holy Bodhi tree. He made this site the heart of his Lanna kingdom.

Mengrai was a great patron of Theravada Buddhism and he brought monks from Ceylon to unify the country. Up until the 15th century, Chiang Mai flourished. As this century ended, relations with up-and-coming Ayutthaya became strained and the two kingdoms engaged in a series of wars with few gains on either side.

While Chiang Mai and Ayutthaya were busy fighting, the Burmese eventually captured the city of Chiang Mai in 1556. King Bayinnaung, who had unified Burma, took Chiang Mai after a three-day battle and the city remained a Burmese regency for 220 years. There was constant conflict during these years and by the time the Burmese succeeded in overthrowing Ayutthaya in 1767, the city of Chiang Mai was decimated and depopulated. In 1775, General Taksin united the kingdom of Thailand and a semi-autonomous prince of the Lampang Dynasty was appointed to rule the North. Chiang Mai lost its semi-independence in 1938 and came under direct rule from Bangkok.

Modern Chiang Mai

Today, Chiang Mai is the second largest city in Thailand, with a population of roughly 500,000; a thriving commercial centre as well as a favourite tourist destination. The TAT estimates that 12% of Thailand's tourists travel to Chiang Mai. Its attractions to the visitor are obvious: the city has a rich and colourful history, still evident in the architecture of the city which includes over 300 wats; it is manageable and still relatively 'user friendly' (unlike Bangkok); it has perhaps the greatest concentration of handicraft industries in the country; and it is also an excellent base from which to go trekking and visit the famous hilltribe villages in the surrounding highlands. Chiang Mai has developed into a major tourist centre with a good infrastructure,

 including excellent hotels and restaurants in all price categories. Some long-term visitors argue that the city has lost some of its charm in the process: traffic congestion, pollution and frantic property development are now much in evidence.

On a clear day at the start of the cold season, or after the rains have begun towards the end of the hot season, Chiang Mai's strategic location becomes clear. Mountains surround the city to the north, west and east, enclosing a large and rich bowl of rice fields drained by the Ping River. With Doi Suthep to the west clothed in trees and the golden chedi of Wat Phrathat Doi Suthep glittering on its slopes, it is a magical place.

Chiang Mai

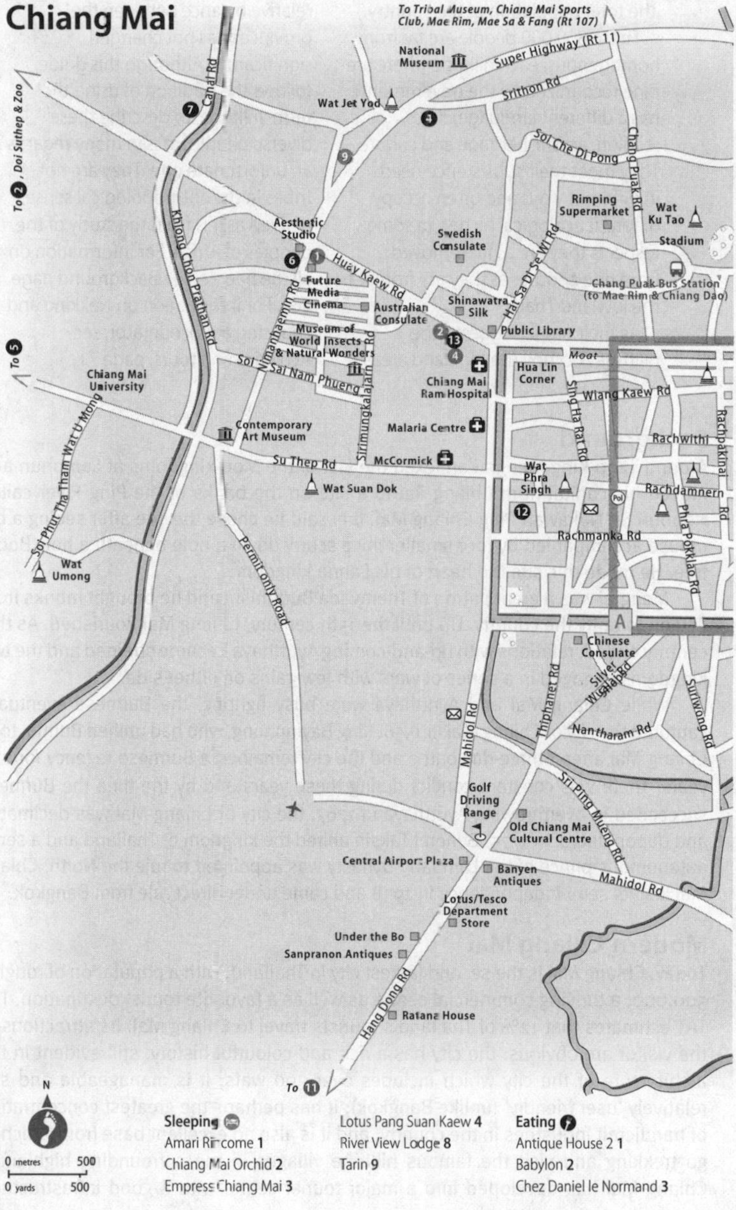

Sleeping
Amari Rincome 1
Chiang Mai Orchid 2
Empress Chiang Mai 3
Lotus Pang Suan Kaew 4
River View Lodge 8
Tarin 9

Eating
Antique House 2 1
Babylon 2
Chez Daniel le Normand 3

Sights

Chiang Mai is centred on a square moat and defensive wall built during the 19th century. The four corner bastions are reasonably preserved and are a useful reference point when roaming the city. Much of the rest of the town's walls were demolished during the Second World War and the bricks used for road construction. Not surprisingly, given Chiang Mai's

See Within the Old City map, page 227.

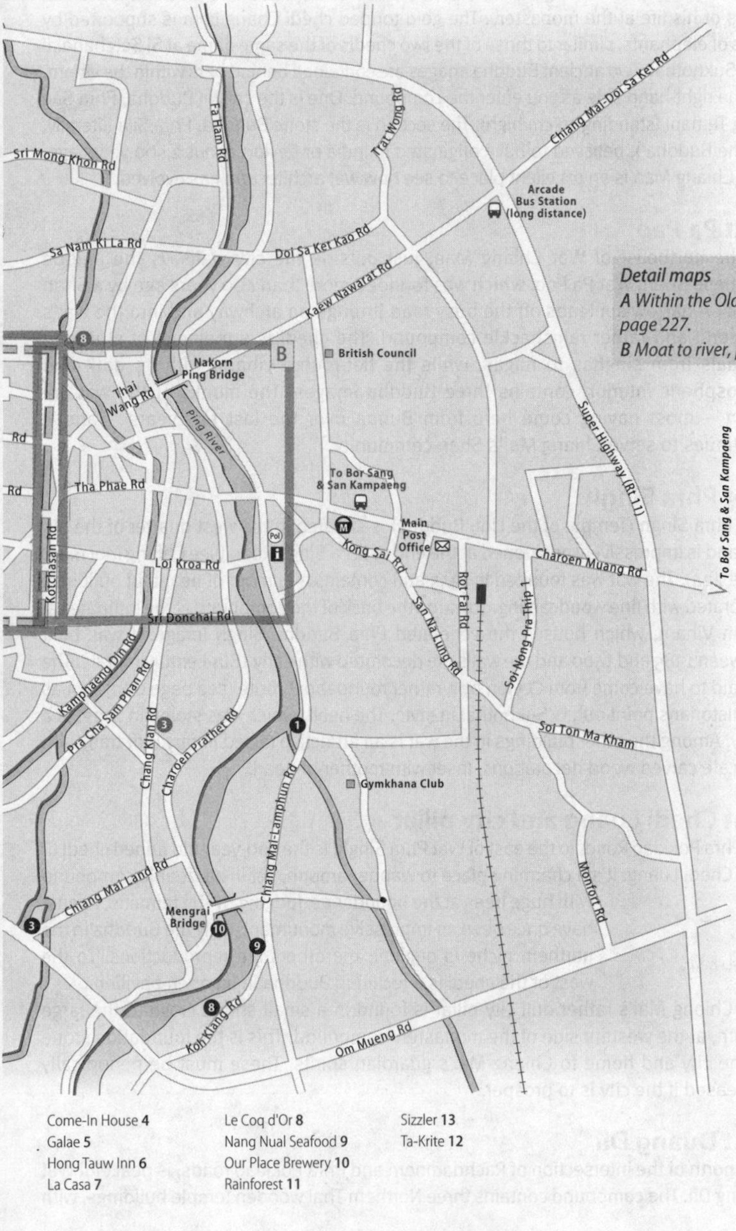

Come-In House 4
Galae 5
Hong Tauw Inn 6
La Casa 7
Le Coq d'Or 8
Nang Nual Seafood 9
Our Place Brewery 10
Rainforest 11
Sizzler 13
Ta-Krite 12

Detail maps
A Within the Old City, page 227.
B Moat to river, page 228.

 turbulent history, many of the more important and interesting wats are within the city walls which is – surprisingly – the least built-up part. Modern commercial development has been concentrated to the east of the city and now well beyong the Ping River.

Wat Chiang Man

Situated in the northeast of the walled town, Wat Chiang Man is on Rachpakinai Road within a peaceful compound. The wat is the oldest in the city and was built by King Mengrai soon after he had chosen the site for his new capital in 1296. It is said that he resided here while waiting for his new city to be constructed and also spent the last years of his life at the monastery. The gold-topped chedi Chang Lom is supported by rows of elephants, similar to those of the two chedis of the same name at Si Satchanalai and Sukhothai. Two ancient Buddha images are contained behind bars within the viharn, on the right-hand side as you enter the compound. One is the crystal Buddha, Phra Sae Tang Tamani (standing 10 cm high). The second is the stone Buddha, Phra Sila (literally, 'Stone Buddha'), believed to have originated in India or Ceylon about 2,500 years ago. Wat Chiang Man is an excellent place to see how wat architecture has evolved.

Wat Pa Pao

To the northeast of Wat Chiang Man, just outside the city walls, is the unique Burmese Shan, Wat Pa Pao, which was founded more than 400 years ago by a Shan monk. A narrow soi leads off the busy road through an archway and into the wat's peaceful and rather ramshackle compound. The chedi is a melange of stuccoed animals from singhas to nagas, while the flat-roofed viharn, with its dark and atmospheric interior, contains three Buddha images. The monks at the wat are Shan – most having come here from Burma over the last few years – and it continues to serve Chiang Mai's Shan community.

Wat Phra Singh

Wat Phra Singh (Temple of the Lion Buddha) is situated in the west quarter of the old city and is impressively positioned at the end of Phra Singh Road (see Chiang Mai map, page 224). The wat was founded in 1345 and contains a number of beautiful buildings decorated with fine woodcarving. Towards the back of the compound is the intimate Lai Kham Viharn, which houses the venerated Phra Buddha Singh image. It was built between 1385 and 1400 and the walls are decorated with early 18th-century murals. The is said to have come from Ceylon by a rather roundabout route (see page 609), but as art historians point out, is Sukhothai in style. The head, which was stolen in 1922, is a copy. Among the other buildings in the wat is an attractive raised library (hor trai), with intricate carved wood decorations, inset with mother-of-pearl.

Wat Chedi Luang and city pillar

On Phra Pokklao Road, to the east of Wat Phra Singh, is the 500-year-old ruined chedi or Wat Chedi Luang. It's a charming place to wander around, set in a sizeable compound with huge trees at the boundaries. Judging by the remains, it must have once been an impressive monument. Only the Buddha in the northern niche is original; the others are reproductions. To the west of the chedi is a reclining Buddha in an open pavilion.

Women are not permitted to climb the steps of the chedi.

Chiang Mai's rather dull city pillar is found in a small shrine close to the large viharn, at the western side of the monastery compound. This is the foundation stone of the city and home to Chiang Mai's guardian spirits. These must be periodically appeased if the city is to prosper.

Wat Duang Dii

Just north of the intersection of Rachdamnern and Phra Pokklao roads, is peaceful Wat Duang Dii. The compound contains three Northern Thai wooden temple buildings, with

Within the Old City

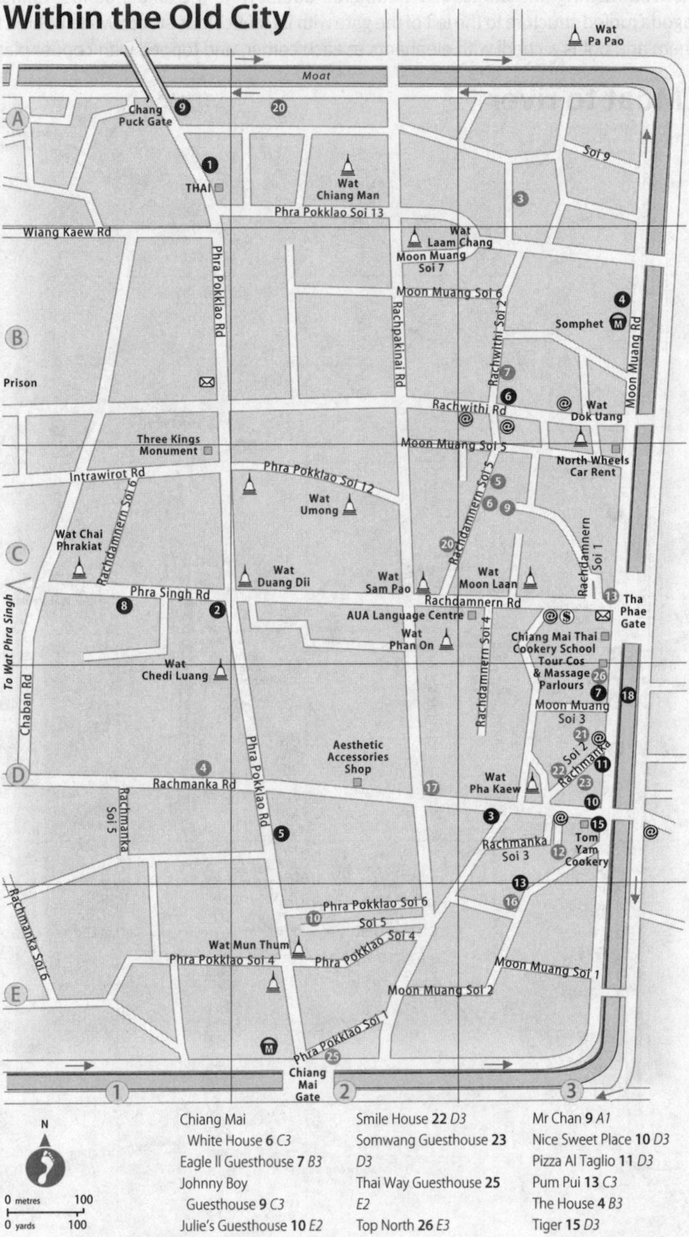

Sleeping
Blue Diamond Breakfast Club **3** *B2*
Chiang Mai Garden Guesthouse **4** *D1*
Chiang Mai Kristi House **5** *C3*
Chiang Mai White House **6** *C3*
Eagle II Guesthouse **7** *B3*
Johnny Boy Guesthouse **9** *C3*
Julie's Guesthouse **10** *E2*
Kent Guesthouse **12** *D3*
Montri's **13** *C3*
New Saitom **21** *D3*
North Star House **16** *E3*
Panda Tour Guesthouse **17** *D2*
Rendezvous Guesthouse **20** *C2*
Smile House **22** *D3*
Somwang Guesthouse **23** *D3*
Thai Way Guesthouse **25** *E2*
Top North **26** *E3*

Eating
Amazing Sandwich **1** *A1*
Café Chic **2** *C1*
Corner **3** *D3*
Il Forno **5** *D2*
UN Irish Pub **6** *B3*
Jerusalem Falafel **7** *D3*
Mr Chan **9** *A1*
Nice Sweet Place **10** *D3*
Pizza Al Taglio **11** *D3*
Pum Pui **13** *C3*
The House **4** *B3*
Tiger **15** *D3*
Zest **18** *D3*

Bars & clubs
Easy Life **20** *A2*

 fine woodcarving and attractively weathered doors. Note the small, almost Chinese-pagoda roofed structure to the left of the gate with its meticulous stucco work. Behind the viharn and bot is a chedi with elephants at each corner, and topped with copper plate.

Moat to river

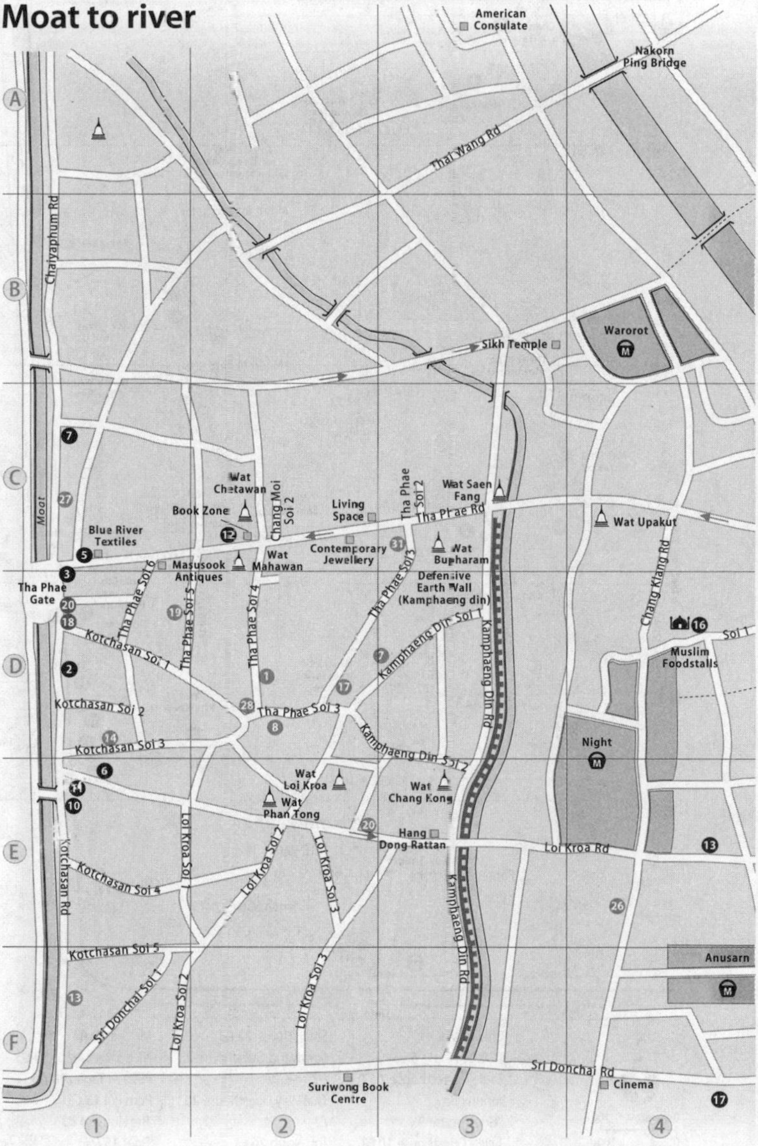

Sleeping
Bang Jong Come Guesthouse 1 *D2*
Fang Guesthouse 7 *D3*
Flamingo Guesthouse 8 *D2*
Galare 9 *D5*
Kim House 12 *E5*
Lai Thai 13 *F1*
Little Home Guesthouse 14 *D1*
Namkhong Guesthouse 17 *D2*
Orchid Guesthouse 19 *D1*
Oriental Guesthouse, Garden Restaurant & Coffee Shop 20 *E2*
River View Lodge 23 *D5*
Royal Princess 26 *E4*
Rydges Tapae 27 *C1*
Sarah's Guesthouse 28 *D2*
Tapae Place 31 *C3*

Eating
Antique House 1 1 *E5*
Aroon Rai 2 *D1*
Art Café 3 *D1*
Rot Nung 4 *E5*

N
Not to scale

Wat Suan Dok

Outside the walls, Wat Suan Dok lies to the west of town on Suthep Road (Chiang Mai map, page 224). Originally built in 1371 but subsequently restored and enlarged, the wat contains the ashes of Chiang Mai's royal family, housed in many white, variously shaped, mini-chedis. Much of the monastery was erected during the reign of King Kawila (1782-1813). Not content with just one relic, the large central chedi is said to house eight relics of the Lord Buddha.

> *The wat is also a centre of Thai traditional massage – ask one of the monks for information.*

The bot is usually open to the public and has a large, brightly lit, gilded bronze Buddha image in the Chiang Saen style. The walls are decorated with lively, rather gaudy, scenes from the Jataka stories. Above the entrance is a mural showing the Buddha's mother being impregnated by a white elephant (highly auspicious), while on the left-hand wall is depicted (along with several other episodes from the Buddha's life) the moment when, as a prince (note the fine clothes and jewellery), he renounces his wealth and position and symbolically cuts his hair.

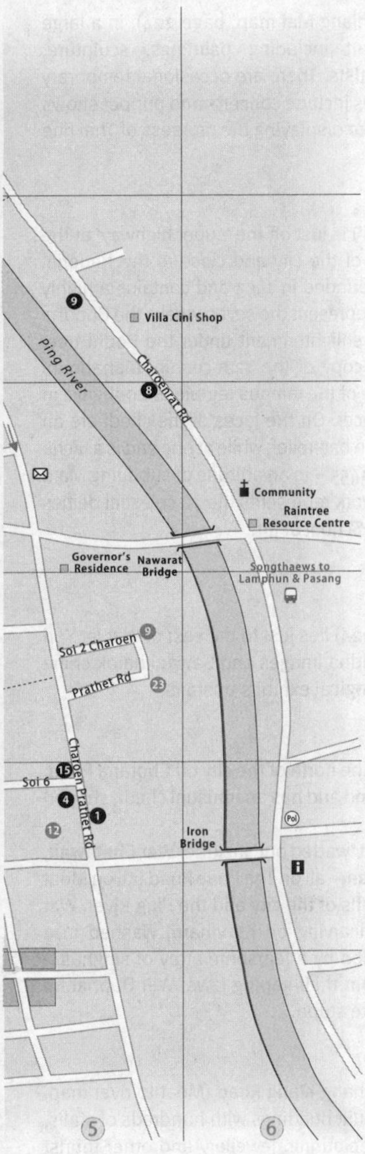
Villa Cini Shop
Ping River
Charoenrat Rd
Community
Raintree Resource Centre
Governor's Residence
Nawarat Bridge
Songthaews to Lamphun & Pasang
Soi 2 Charoen Prathet Rd
Soi 6
Charoen Prathet Rd
Iron Bridge
Pol
5
6

Da Stefani **5** *C1*
Fillmore East **6** *E1*
Gallery **9** *B5*
Good View **8** *C5*
Kruo Duangkamol **10** *E1*
Mango Tree Café **11** *E1*
Mike's **7** *C1*
Ratana's Kitchen **12** *C2*
Red Lion **13** *E4*
Shere Shiraz **15** *E5*
Sophia **16** *D4*
Whole Earth **17** *F4*

Bars & clubs
Full Monty **18** *D1*
Roof Top **20** *D1*

Wat Umong

ⓘ *Take a songthaew or bus (Nos 1 and 4) along Suthep Rd and ask to be let off at the turning for Wat Umong. It is about a 1 km walk from here (turn left almost opposite the gates to CMU, just past a market travelling west).*

The wat was founded in 1371 by King Ku Na (1355-1385) who promoted the establishment of a new, ascetic school of forest-dwelling monks. In 1369 he brought a leading Sukhothai monk to Chiang Mai – the Venerable Sumana – and built Wat Umong for him and his followers. Sumana studied here until his death in 1389. Although the wat is at the edge of the city, set in areas of woodland, it feels much more distant. There are tunnels which house several Buddha images. The wat was abandoned in the 19th century and the chedi pillaged for its treasures some years later. It became a functioning wat again in 1948. From the trees hang Thai proverbs and sayings from the Buddhist texts, extolling pilgrims to lead good and productive lives.

Chiang Mai Contemporary Art Museum

ⓘ Tue-Sun 0930-1700. ฿50, corner of Nimmahaemin and Suthep rds. The small but chic attached Art Café and shop (selling books and ceramics) is classier than the works displayed.

The Chiang Mai Contemporary Art Museum (Chiang Mai map, page 224), in a large modern structure, displays modern fine art including paintings, sculpture, installation works and prints by mostly Thai artists. There are occasional temporary exhibitions of work by non-Thais. Other activities include concerts and puppet shows (T053-933833 for information). It is interesting for displaying the progress of Thai fine art, but hardly world class.

Wat Jed Yod

The beautiful Wat Jet Yod (literally, 'seven spires') is just off the 'super highway' at the intersection with Ladda Land Road, northwest of the city and close to the National Museum (Chiang Mai map, page 224). It was founded in 1453 and contains a highly unusual square chedi with seven spires. These represent the seven weeks the Buddha resided in the gardens at Bodhgaya, after his enlightenment under the Bodhi tree. According to the chronicles the structure is a copy of the 13th-century Mahabodhi temple in Pagan, Burma, which itself was a copy of the famous temple at Bodhgaya in Bihar (although it is hard to see the resemblance). On the faces of the chedi are an assortment of superbly modelled stucco figures in bas-relief, while at one end is a niche containing a large Buddha image – dating from 1455 – in an attitude of subduing Mara (now protected behind steel bars). The stucco work represents the 70 celestial deities and are among the finest works from the Lanna School of art.

National Museum

ⓘ Wed-Sun 0900-1600. ฿30. Take bus no 6.

The National Museum (Chiang Mai map, page 224) lies just to the east of Wat Jet Yod on Highway 11 and has a fine collection of Buddha images and Sawankhalok china downstairs, as well as some impressive ethnological exhibits upstairs.

Other wats

Wat Ku Tao (on Chiang Mai map, page 224), to the north of the city off Chotana Road, dates from 1613. It is situated in a leafy compound and has an unusual chedi, shaped like a pile of inverted alms bowls.

Others worth a fleeting visit for those not yet 'watted out' include: **Wat Chetawan, Wat Mahawan, Wat Saen Fang** and **Wat Bupharam**– all on Tha Phae Road (all on Moat to River map, page 228) – between the east walls of the city and the Ping River. Wat Mahawan displays some accomplished woodcarving on its viharn, washed in a delicate yellow, while the white stupa is guarded by a fearsome array of singhas – mythical lions – some with bodies hanging from their gaping jaws. Wat Bupharam has two, fine old viharns a small bot and a white stupa.

Markets and Chinatown

The night market dominates the west side of Chang Klang Road (Moat to river map, page 228). It consists of a number of purpose-built buildings with hundreds of stalls, selling a huge array of tribal goods as well as clothing, jewellery and other tourist goodies (see page 251). For a completely different atmosphere, walk through Chiang Mai's Chinatown which lies to the north of Tha Phae Road, between the moat and the river. Small workshops run by entrepreneurial Sino-Thais jostle between excellent small restaurants serving reasonably priced Thai and Chinese food. Near the river, and running two or three streets in from the river, is the **Warorot Market** (on Moat to river map, page 228), Chiang Mai's largest. It starts on Praisani Road, close to the river, as a flower market, but transforms into a mixed market with fruit, vegetables,

dried fish, pigs' heads and trotters, great dollops of buffalo flesh, crabs, dried beans and deep fried pork skin. There are several large covered market areas with clothes, textiles, shoes, leather goods, Chinese funeral accessories, stationery and baskets.

Museum of World Insects and Natural Wonders

ⓘ *West of town at 72 Nimanhaemin Soi 13 (near Sirimungkalajarn 3), T053-211891, insects_museum@hotmail.com; 0900-1630. ฿100, ฿50 children.*

Established in 1999 by Manop and Rampa Rattanarithikul, this eccentric couple take pleasure in showing you around their house which has become a mausoleum for thousands of insectoid beasties (Chiang Mai map, page 228). Rampa's specialism is mosquitoes; there are 420 species of mosquito in Thailand (all on show here, not that they make for particularly scintillating viewing), 18 of which she personally identified and categorized, travelling to London to check the type specimens in the Natural History Museum. Interesting collection of shells, fossils, petrified wood and, of course, case after case of bugs including beetles, moths, roaches and butterflies.

Around Chiang Mai

Doi Suthep

ⓘ *Songthaew from Mani Noparat Rd, by Chang Puak Gate (฿30 up, ฿20 down), or take bus No 3 to the zoo and then change onto a minibus. A taxi should cost about ฿200 return. The temple is closed after 1630.*

Overlooking Chiang Mai, 16 km to the northwest, is Doi Suthep (Suthep mountain) a very popular pilgrimage spot for Thais, perched on the hillside and offering spectacular views of the city and plain below. A steep, winding road climbs 1,000 m to the base of a 300-step naga staircase, which in turn leads up to Wat Phrathat. If you arrive on a Sunday it's a lively occasion as hundreds of Thais come here to worship; it's much quieter during the week. If you don't fancy the climb take the cable car. A white elephant is alleged to have collapsed here, after King Ku Na (1355-1385) gave it the task of finding an auspicious site for a shrine to house a holy relic of the Lord Buddha.

The 24-m-high chedi has a number of Buddha images in both Sukhothai and Chiang Saen styles, arrayed in the gallery surrounding it. The whole compound is surrounded by bells (which visitors can ring).

Phu Ping Palace

ⓘ *Fri-Sun and public holidays 0830-1630 when the Royal Family is not in residence. Songthaews from Doi Suthep to Phu Ping, ฿20.*

The winter residence of the King, Phu Ping Palace, is 5 km past Wat Phrathat. The immaculate gardens are open to the public when the family is not in residence.

Doi Pui

ⓘ *Charter a songthaew or take a minibus from Mani Noparat Rd, by Chang Puak Gate, and then charter a songthaew from Doi Suthep, A50 one way.*

Rather commercialized, Meo village, 4 km past Phu Ping Palace, is only worth a visit for those unable to get to other villages. There are two second-rate museum huts, one focusing on opium production, the other on the different hilltribes. On the hillside above the village is an **English flower garden** ⓘ *฿8*, which is in full bloom in January.

Tribal Museum

ⓘ *T053-221933, www.chmai.com/tribal/museum/index.html, Mon-Fri 0900-1600. A slide and video show is screened at 1000 and 1400. An informative book on the hilltribes can be bought here for ฿35. Take a songthaew from the city ฿50. It takes about 15-20 mins to walk to the museum.*

The Tribal Museum, attached to the Tribal Research Institute, overlooks a lake in Rachamangkhla Park, 5 km north of town off Chotana Road. The building itself looks like a cross between a rocket and a chedi and it houses the fine collection of tribal pieces that were formerly held at Chiang Mai University's Tribal Research Centre. Carefully and professionally presented, the pieces on show include textiles, agricultural implements, musical instruments, jewellery and weapons. The museum is particularly worth visiting for those intending to go trekking (see page 223).

Wiang Kum Kam

ⓘ *Accessible by bicycle, motorbike or tuk-tuk. Take Route 106 south towards Lamphun; the ruins are signposted off to the right about 5 km from Chiang Mai – but only in Thai – from where it is another 2 km. Look out for a ruined chedi on the right and ask along the way for confirmation. To get to Wat Kan Thom, take the yellow sign to the left about 800 m from the main road. It's about a 10-15 min walk from the main road. For Wat Chedi Liam, follow the land all the way to the river road (Koh Klang Rd), about 2 km or so, and turn left. The Wat is about 200 m down here, on the left – impossible to miss.*

Wiang Kum Kam is a ruined city, 5 km south of Chiang Mai, which was established by the Mon in the 12th or 13th centuries and abandoned in the 18th century. The gardens and ruins are beautiful and peaceful, dotted with bodhi trees. Today, archaeologists are beginning to uncover a site of about 9 sq km which contains the remains of at least 20 wats. It was discovered in 1984 when rumours surfaced that a hoard of valuable amulets were found. Treasure seekers began to dig up the grounds of the Wat Chang Kham monastery until the Fine Arts Department intervened and began a systematic survey of the site to reveal Wiang Kum Kam. The most complete monument is Wat Wat Chang Kham, which has a marvellous bronze naga outside. In front of the wat is the spirit chamber of Chiang Mai's founder, King Mengrai. Nearby are the ruins of Wat Noi and two dilapidated chedis. Perhaps the most impressive single structure is the renovated chedi at Wat Chedi Liam. This takes the form of a stepped pyramid – a unique Mon architectural style of which there are only a handful of examples in Thailand.

Bor Sang and San Kamphaeng circuit

A pleasant 75-km day trip takes you east of the city, visiting craft centres a couple of interesting wats, some incredible caves and a hot spring. Almost immediately after leaving the city along Route 1006 (Charoen Muang Road), kilns, paper factories and lacquerware stalls start to appear, and continue for a full 15 km all the way to Bor Sang.

❢ *This circuit can only be undertaken by private transport.*

Bor Sang is famous for its handmade, painted paper umbrella. The shaft is crafted from local softwood, the ribs from bamboo, and the covering from oiled ricepaper. The **Umbrella Festival** in January is a colourful affair. Beyond Bor Sang is San Kamphaeng, another craft village which has expanded and diversified so that it has effectively merged with Bor Sang – at least in terms of shopping. If you make it as far as San Kamphaeng, there is a good Muslim restaurant at the intersection with the main road (left hand, near side) serving chicken biryani, other Indian dishes, ice creams and cappuccino.

For **Wat Pa Tung**, which is 10 km on from San Kamphaeng, take a right-hand fork onto Route 1147. At the junction with Route 1317, cross over the road (signposted towards the Chiang Mai-Lamphun Golf Club). Where the road takes a sharp right (with another signpost for the Golf Club), continue straight ahead on the minor road. About 3 km on is Wat Pa Tung. This wat is a lively and popular modern wat, set amongst sugar palms and rice fields. Its popularity rests on the fact that the revered Luang Phu La Chaiya Janto (an influential thinker and preacher and highly regarded for his asceticism) lived here to the ripe old age of 96. When he died in 1993 his rather diminutive body was entombed in a sealed glass coffin, which was then placed in a specially built stilted modern kuti where it still resides today.

From Wat Pa Tung, return to Route 1317 and turn right. After about 10 km, on the left, you will see a rocky outcrop with flags fluttering from the top; this is the only marker for the **Muang On Caves** ⓘ *daily during daylight hours. ฿10, drink stalls at the car park*, take a left turning (no sign in English) and wind up a lane, past a forest of ordained (buat) trees, to the car park. From here there are around 170 steps up a naga staircase to the entrance to the caves, with great views over the valley. The entrance to the caves is tricky and the steps very steep, with low overhangs of rock. But it is worth the sweating and bending; the cave opens up into a series of impressive caverns with a large stalagmite wrapped with sacred cloth and a number of images of the Buddha.

At the foot of the hill (before returning to the main road), take a left turn for the back route to the **Roong Arun Hot Springs** (2½ km) ⓘ *฿20, ฿10 children*. Here, sulphur springs bubble up into an artificial pond, where visitors can buy chicken or quail eggs to boil in wicker baskets hung from bamboo rods. The springs reach boiling point here; if you want a dip head for the public baths, where the water is cooled (ⓘ *฿60*). A full range of massages, mud baths, saunas and herbal treatments are also also available. Return to Chiang Mai by way of Route 118 – about a 20 minutes' drive.

Mae Sa Valley – Samoeng circuit

ⓘ *There are buses and songthaews along this route, but it would be much more convenient to do the round trip by hire car or motorbike.*

The 100 km loop from Chiang Mai along the Mae Sa Valley to Samoeng and then back along Route 1269 is an attractive drive that can easily be accomplished in a day. Travel north on Route 107 out of town and then turn west onto Route 1096, in the district town of Mae Rim. From here the road follows the course of the Mae Sa River. Just past Mae Rim are a couple of exclusive shops selling 'antiques': **Lanna House** and the **TiTa art gallery** (see Shopping).

Sai Nam Phung Orchid and Butterfly Farm ⓘ *0800-1600*, is to be found here too. It has the best selection of orchids in the area as well as a small butterfly enclosure (unusual jewellery for sale). At the Km 5 marker is the sign for the **Tad Mok Waterfalls**, which lie 9 km off the main road to the right. These are less popular than the Mae Sa Falls a couple of kilometres on from here (see below), but worthwhile.

Continuing west on the main road, there are two more orchid gardens: **Suan Bua Mae Sa Orchid** ⓘ *between the Km 5 and Km 6 markers; 0800-1600*, and **Mae Rim Orchid and Butterfly Farm** ⓘ *0800-1600, ฿20*, at the Km 6 marker. The orchids are beautiful, the butterflies even more so (watch them emerge from their chrysalises), and the food average and overpriced.

Mae Sa Waterfall ⓘ *0800-1800, ฿3, ฿20 per car*, is located in the **Doi Suthep-Pui National Park**, 1 km off Route 1096 (to the left) and about 1 km beyond the orchid farm. The waterfall is in fact a succession of mini-falls – relatively peaceful, with a visitors' centre and a number of stalls.

But the most popular destination of all in the valley is the **Elephant Training Camp** ⓘ *T053-297060, elephant rides available between 0700 and 1400, ฿80; two shows a day at 0800 and 0940 and an additional show at 1330 during peak periods*, 3 km further on from the waterfall. Around 100 elephants are well cared for here (with a number of babies, which must be a good indicator of their happiness). Visitors can see the elephants bathing, feed them bananas and sugarcane and then watch an elephant show.

Queen Sirikit Botanical Gardens ⓘ *www.welcome-to.chiangmai-chiangrai.com/queensirikitgarden.htm, 0800-1700; ฿20 adult, ฿10 child, ฿50 car*, was established in 1993 on the edge of the Doi Suthep-Pui National Park, 12 km from the Mae Rim turn off. The great bulk of the gardens was designated a conservation area before 1993, and there are a number of large trees. It is Thailand's first botanical gardens and a truly impressive enterprise. There are three marked trails (rock garden and nursery plus waterfall, arboreta and climber trail), a museum and an information centre. But

the highlight of the gardens is the glasshouse complex. The largest features a waterfall and elevated boardwalk, and there are also glasshouses for desert flora, savanna flora and wetland plants. What is surprising is how few people make it here.

Mae Sa Craft Village ⓘ *T053-290052, www.maesa.th.com, small entrance fee for those who just want to wander; for their activity programme,* is a leafy resort spread over a hillside, with immaculately kept gardens of brightly coloured annual flowers. There are dozens of great activities to get involved in, see Sleeping and Activities and tours.

Continuing further on along Route 1096 there are, in turn, the **Mae Yim Falls** (17 km), **Doi Sang** – a Meo village (25 km) – and the **Nang Koi Falls** (34 km). At the furthest point in this loop is **Samoeng**, the district capital. There's little to do here unless you arrive for Samoeng's annual **strawberry festival** held in January or February.

Continuing on from Samoeng, the road skirts around the heavily forested **Doi Suthep-Pui National Park**. The winding road finally descends from the hills and comes out by the north-south irrigation canal at the village of Ban Ton Khwen. Just before you reach the canal is a turning to the right and, a little further along, the bare brick walls of **Wat Inthrawat**. The entrance at the back is by a cluster of sugar palms. This spectacular viharn was built in 1858 in Lanna style. Its graceful roofs and detailed woodcarving are a fine sight. Return to Chiang Mai by way of the canal road (turn left at the junction) or on Route 108 (the Hang Dong road), which is a little further to the east of the canal road.

Chiang Dao Elephant Training Centre

ⓘ *฿60, ฿30 children. Numerous companies offer tours to the centre from Chiang Mai, although it is easy enough to get here by public transport as it is on the main road. Catch a bus or songthaew from the Chang Puak bus station.*

This elephant training centre at Chiang Dao is 56 km from Chiang Mai on the route north to Fang, about 15 km south of Chiang Dao. Elephant riding and rafting is available. There is a second elephant camp 17 km south of Chiang Dao, the Mae Ping Elephant Camp. This is not as good.

Chiang Dao

ⓘ *As Chiang Dao is on the main Chiang Mai-Fang road, there are numerous buses and songthaews from the Chang Puak bus station.*

Chiang Dao, a district town 70 km north of Chiang Mai, is a useful stopping-off point for visitors to the Chiang Dao caves (see below). The surfaced road running east from the town leads to a series of hilltribe villages: Palong, Mussur, Lahu and Karen. Most of these are situated on public Forest Reserve land and many of the inhabitants do not have Thai citizenship. They have built simple huts where tourists can stay (฿20 a night) and a number of trekking companies in Chiang Mai begin or end their treks in the villages here. The town has a number of good restaurants; of particular note is the locally renowned **Bun Thong Phanit** (on the left-hand side, travelling north, in a wooden shophouse), which serves excellent khao kha muu (baked pork with rice).

Chiang Dao Caves

ⓘ *฿5 to go as far as the electric light system extends. ฿60 to hire a guide with lamp for a 40-min tour deeper into the caves (the guides congregate 100 m or so into the caves where a rota system ensures an equal share of business). Catch a bus to Fang from the Chang Puak bus station on Chotana Rd and get off at Chiang Dao. Songthaews take visitors the final 6 km from the main road to the caves. A taxi to the caves and back should cost about ฿1,000 (1½ hrs each way). It is also possible to hire motorbikes and bicycles in Chiang Dao itself – from the 'Tourist Corner' on the left-hand side of the main road, shortly before reaching the turn-off for the caves (turn left in the town of Chiang Dao, just after the Km 72 marker, it is clearly signposted).*

These caves, located 78 km north of Chiang Mai on Route 107, penetrate deep into the limestone hills and are associated with Wat Chiang Dao. They are among the most extensive in Thailand and are a popular pilgrimage spot for monks and ordinary Thais. There is a profusion of stalls here, many selling herbal remedies said to cure most ailments. The caverns contain Buddha and hermit images, as well as impressive natural rock formations. Electric lights have been installed, but only as far as the Tham Phra Non (Cave of the Reclining Buddha), where a royal coat of arms on the cave wall records Queen Sirikit's visit to the caves. To explore further it is necessary to hire a guides.

Lamphun

ⓘ *Most people visit Lamphun from Chiang Mai and regular (blue) songthaews run along the Old Lamphun-Chiang Mai Rd, leaving Chiang Mai just over the Nawarat Bridge, near the TAT office (30-40 mins, ฿7). They pass through the middle of Lamphun town, down Inthayong Yot Rd, and can be picked up by the National Museum too. The train station is 2 km north off Charoenrat Rd, 5 daily connections with Bangkok and Chiang Mai. If travelling to Lamphun from Chiang Mai it is worth taking the old road, which is lined over a 10 km-stretch with an avenue of Yang trees. Only the action of activist monks, who ordained the trees, saved them from felling.*

This quiet, historic city lies 26 km south of Chiang Mai, and is famous for its longans – there's a **Longan Fair** every August with a contest to judge both the best fruit and to select the year's Miss Lamyai (longan). It is also a venerated place of Buddhist teaching at **Wat Phra That Haripunjaya**. This famous temple has a 50-m tall chedi crowned by a solid gold nine-tiered honorific umbrella (weighing, apparently, 6,498.75 g). Another renowned temple is **Wat Chama Devi**, which lies 1 km west of the moat on Chama Devi Road. It is said that Princess Chama Devi selected the spot by having an archer shoot an arrow to the north from town – her ashes are contained within the main chedi. Built in 1218, this square-based chedi of brick and stucco has five tiers of niches, each containing a beautiful standing Buddha.

Lamphun, which was founded in AD 600, is sited on the banks of the Ping River and was formerly the capital of the Haripunjaya Kingdom. The moat and parts of the old defensive walls are still present and it was a powerful centre of the Mon culture until King Mengrai succeeded in taking the city in 1281.

Lampang → *Phone code: 054. Colour map 1, grid B3.*

ⓘ *Regular buses from Nawarat Bridge or from the Arcade terminal and trains connect with Chiang Mai (2 hrs) while local transport is provided by the town's unique horse-drawn carriages, see page 258 for details.*

An atmospheric provincial capital complete with horse-drawn carriages, soothing riverside hangouts and the sumptious temple of Wat Phra That Lampang Luang, Lampang makes a great day or overnight trip from Chiang Mai. There's some decent accommodation and a chance to indulge in a leisurely lunch at one of the great riverside restaurants. A tourist office is at Boonyawat Rd, in the front of the police station, 1st floor, T054-218823. Good maps and brochures.

The easiest way to visit wats here is by saamlor or horse-drawn carriage.

Established in the seventh-century Dvaravati period, Lampang prospered as a trading centre, with a wealth of ornate and well-endowed wats. Re-built in the 19th century as a fortified wiang (a walled city), it became an important centre for the teak industry with British loggers making this one of their key centres. The influence of the Burmese is reflected in the architecture of some of the more important wats – a number still have Burmese abbots.

Wat Phra Kaeo Don Tao ⓘ *฿10*, and its 'sister' **Wat Chadaram** are to be found on Phra Kaeo Road, north across the Rachada Phisek Bridge. Wat Phra Kaeo housed the renowned Emerald Buddha (the Phra Kaeo – now in Wat Phra Kaeo, Bangkok) for 32 years during the 15th century. This royal temple is said to be imbued with particular

spiritual power and significance, largely because of its association with the Phra Kaeo. The ceilings and columns of the 18th-century viharn are carved in wood and are intricately inlaid with porcelain and enamel. In the compound, there is also a Burmese-style chapel (probably late 18th century) and a golden chedi. Next door, Wat Chadaram contains the most attractive building in the whole complex: a small, intimate, well-proportioned, wooden viharn.

Wat Chedi Sao ⓘ *0800-1700; walk over the bridge to the junction of Jhamatawee and Wangkhon roads and hail a saamlor there for ฿5*, the 'temple of the 20 chedis', is 3 km northeast of the town, 1 km off the Lampang-Jae Hom road at Ban Wang Moh. A large white chedi is surrounded by 19 smaller ones and a strange assortment of concrete animals and monks. The most important Buddha image here is a gold, seated image cast in the 15th century. Its importance stems both from its miraculous discovery – by a local farmer in his rice field in 1983 – and from the fact that it is said to contain a piece of the Lord Buddha's skull in its head.

Wat Sri Chum ⓘ *0700-1830, ฿10*, a beautiful wat, on Tippowan Road (also known as Sri Chum Road), was constructed 200 years ago and is regarded as one of the finest Burmese-style wats in Thailand. Tragically, the richly carved and painted viharn, was destroyed by fire in 1993. The compound exudes an ambience of peaceful meditation, although it is in urgent need of funds to complete restoration.

Wat Phra That Lampang Luang

ⓘ *It can only be viewed 0900-1200, 1300-1700. Donation. There are drinks and foodstalls in the car park area across the road from the wat. Take a songthaew to Ko Kha and then by motorbike taxi the last 2½ km to the wat. Songthaews for Ko Kha run regularly along Phahonyothin Rd. Alternatively, charter a songthaew from Lampang (฿150-200). If travelling by private transport from Lampang, drive along Route 1 towards Ko Kha. In Ko Kha pass through the town, over the bridge, and then turn right at the T-junction onto Route 1034. The wat is 2½ km away – just off Route 1034 (the chedi can be seen rising up behind some sugar palms). From Chiang Mai, turn right off Route 11 just past the Km 80 marker, signposted to Ko Kha.*

The monastery stands on a slight hill, surrounded by a brick wall – all that remains of the original fortressed city which was sited here more than 1,000 years ago. Sand and tiles, rather than concrete, surround the monuments. While the buildings have been restored on a number of occasions over the years, it remains beautifully complete and authentic.

One of the finest and most beautiful wats in Thailand. The letters in the text correspond to the plan, see below.

Originally this wat was a fortified site, protected by walls, moats and ramparts. Approached by a staircase flanked by guardian lions and nagas, the visitor enters through an archway of intricate 15th-century stone carving. The large, open central viharn, **Viharn Luang** (a), houses a ku – a brick, stucco and gilded pyramid peculiar to Northern wats – containing a Buddha image (dating from 1563), a collection of thrones and some wall paintings. The building, with its intricate woodcarving and fine pattern work on the pillars and ceiling, is dazzling.

Behind the viharn is the principal **chedi** (b), 45 m high it contains three relics of the Buddha: a hair and the ashes of the Buddha's right forehead and neck bone. Made of beaten copper and brass plates over a brick core, it is typically Lanna Thai in style and was erected in the late 15th century. The **Buddha Viharn** (c) to the left of the chedi is thought to date from the 13th century and was restored in 1802. Beautifully carved and painted, it contains a seated Buddha image. Immediately behind this viharn is a small, raised building housing a **footprint of the Buddha** (d) ① *only men are permitted*. This building houses a camera obscura at certain times of day (from late morning through to early afternoon) the sun's rays pass through a small hole in each building's walls projecting an inverted image of the chedi and the surrounding buildings onto a sheet.

To the right of the main viharn are two more small, but equally beautiful, viharns: the **Viharn Nam Taem** (e) and the **Viharn Ton Kaew** (f). The former is thought to date from the early 16th century, and may be the oldest wooden building in Thailand. It also contains some old wall paintings, although these are difficult to see in the gloom. Finally within the walls are the **Viharn Phra Chao Sila** (g), built to enshrine a stone image of the Buddha

Outside the walls, through the southern doorway, is an enormous and ancient **bodhi tree** (h), supported by a veritable army of crutches. Close by is a small, musty and rather unexciting **museum** (j). Next to this is a fine raised scripture library and a viharn, within which is another revered **Emerald Buddha** (k) – heavily obscured by two rows of steel bars. It is rumoured to have been made from the same block of jasper as the famous Emerald Buddha in Bangkok.

Wat Phra That Lampang Luang

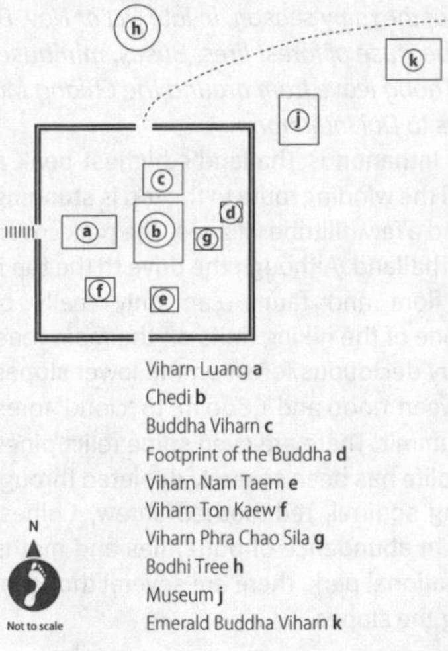
h
k
j
c
a
b
d
g
f
e
Viharn Luang a
Chedi b
Buddha Viharn c
Footprint of the Buddha d
Viharn Nam Taem e
Viharn Ton Kaew f
Viharn Phra Chao Sila g
Bodhi Tree h
Museum j
Emerald Buddha Viharn k
N
Not to scale

Thai Elephant Conservation Centre

① *Bathing sessions at 0945 daily, 'shows' at 1000 and 1100 daily, with an additional show at 1330 at weekends and holidays, ฿150. Elephant rides ฿150 for 10 mins, ฿400 for 30 mins, ฿800 for 1 hr, T054-227051. There is also a small restaurant, souvenir shop and toilets. The ECC also runs English language mahout training courses – contact them directly for details. Take an early morning bus towards Chiang Mai; get off at the Km 37 marker (ask the bus driver to let you off at the Conservation Centre). From*

the road it is a 1,800-m walk by road or take a short cut through the forest, or charter a songthaew from town for ฿350 return. It is possible to stay at the camp; check out further information at www.thaielephant.com.

The recent fate of the Thai elephant has been a slow inexorable decline. Numbers are dwindling and the few that do remain are mainly used as tourist attractions (see page 110). Many of the places that offer chances to interact with elephants are poorly run, treating their charges with contempt. Not so the excellent Thai Elephant Conservation Centre which lies 33 km northwest of Lampang near Thung Kwian, on the road to Chiang Mai (Highway 11). Here elephants are trained for forest work, others are released back into the wild, there's elephant musicians, elephant artists and elephant dung paper. There's even an elephant hospital and rescue centre. All in all there are about 100 animals here.

Pha Thai caves

ⓘ *The first 400 m of the cave is open to the public but the great majority of the system is off-limits. Refreshments are available. Take Route 1 from Lampang towards Ngao and 19 km before Ngao turn left for the caves.*

The Pha Thai caves are some of the most spectacular caves in Thailand, found on the road to Ngao. These are associated with a wat and are located about 20 km before Ngao. The cave system is one of the deepest in Thailand, extending to more than 1,200 m. The caves are renowned not only for their length but also for the quantity of snakes that have taken up residence here. From the arrival point to the cave entrance visitors have to climb 283 steps. As with many caves, it has acquired religious significance. A white chedi stands like a sentinel just outside the mouth of the cave and a large gilded Buddha fills the entrance itself.

Jai Sorn (Chae Sorn) National Park

ⓘ *Take the road from Lampang towards Wak Nua and then turn left at the Km 58-59 marker. Continue along this road for another 17 km.*

The park, Lampang's only protected area, has hot volcanic springs in the waterfall pools – the Chae Son Waterfall and Chae Son Hot Spa Park which are just 1 km apart. The waterfall tumbles down seven levels and during the wet season is particularly spectacular. The hot springs bubble out at 75-80°C, are mixed with cold water from the waterfall and channelled into 11 bathrooms.

Doi Inthanon National Park → *Colour map 1, grid B2.*

ⓘ *0600-1800. ฿200, ฿100 children. ฿30 car, ฿10 motorbike, ฿50 songthaew and minibus. Best time to visit: just after the end of the rainy season, in late Oct or Nov. By Jan and Feb the air becomes hazy, not least because of forest fires. Buses, minibuses and songthaews for Hang Dong and Chom Thong leave from around the Chiang Mai Gate. From Hang Dong there are songthaews to Doi Inthanon.*

Located off Route 108, on Route 1009, Doi Inthanon is Thailand's highest peak at 2,595 m. The mountain is a national park and the winding route to the top is stunning, with terraced rice fields, cultivated valleys and a few hilltribe villages. The park covers 482 sq km and is one of the most visited in Thailand. Although the drive to the top is dramatic, the park's flora and fauna can only really be appreciated by taking one of the hiking trails off the main road. The flora ranges from dry deciduous forest on the lower slopes, to moist evergreen between 1,000 and 1,800 m, to 'cloud' forest and a sphagnum (moss) bog towards the summit. There are even some relict pines. Once the habitat of bears and tigers, the wildlife has been severely depleted through overhunting. It is still possible to see flying squirrel, red-toothed shrew, Chinese pangolin and Pere David's vole, as well as an abundance of butterflies and moths. Although the mountain, in its entirety, is a national park, there are several thousand Hmong and Karen living here and cultivating the slopes.

The radar station on the peak must not be photographed.

Just beneath the summit, in a spectacular position, are a pair of bronze and gold-tiled chedis, one dedicated to the King in 1989 and the other dedicated to Queen Sirikit at the end of 1992. Both chedis contain intricate symbolism and have been built to reaffirm the unity of the Thai nation. The ashes of Chiang Mai's last king, Inthawichayanon, are contained in a small white chedi on the summit – the ultimate reflection of the idea that no one should be higher than the king, in life or in death.

There are a number of waterfalls on the slopes: the **Mae Klang Falls** (near the Km 8 marker and not far from the visitors' centre), **Wachiratan Falls** (26 km down from summit and near the Km 21 marker, restaurant here) and **Siriphum Falls** (3-4 km off the road near the Km 31 marker and not far from the park headquarters), as well as the large **Borichinda Cave** (a 2-km hike off the main road near the visitors' centre at the Km 9 marker). Note that it is a tiring climb up steep steps to the Mae Klang and Wachiratan falls. The **Mae Ya Falls** in the south of the park are the most spectacular, plunging more than 250 m (they lie 15 km from park headquarters and are accessible from Chom Thong town). Ask for details at the visitors' centre a few kilometres on from the park's entrance.

Sleeping

Chiang Mai *p222, maps p224, p227 and p228*

Chiang Mai has a huge range of accommodation to choose from, mostly concentrated to the east of the old walled city, although there is a significant group of guesthouses to be found west of Moon Muang Rd, south of Tha Phae Gate. It is rare for visitors to have to pay the set room (rack) rate. Booking online is one way to get a bargain - try www.chiangmai-online.com. We've had reports that the backpacker places are now putting heavy pressure on their guests to book tours through them – something you need to be aware of before checking in. Of course, a guesthouse may run very good trekking tours, but it does limit your options.

Old City

Within the old city walls and the moat is the greatest concentration of guesthouses, plus one or two small(ish) mid-range places. Most are to be found in the eastern half. The old city is relatively quiet and tree-filled and away from the main centre of commercial activity. It is about a 15-min walk to the night market, although there are bars, restaurants, tour operators, laundries, and motorbike and jeep rental outfits.

L-AL Rachamankha, 9 Phra Singh Rd, T053-904114, www.rachamankha.com (on Chiang Mai map, page 224). This oasis of calm is an inspired boutique hotel with a designers eye for detail, all built using traditional techniques. The a/c rooms can be a bit small and dark but are filled with sumptuous antiques. Service is a definitely bit ropey for the price range. Also has pool, decent library (free internet) and restaurant.

B-C Montri's, 2-6 Rachdamnern Rd, T053-211070, www.norththaihotel.com/montri.html. Some a/c, restaurant, clean, good central position near Tha Phae Gate, large rooms sparsely furnished, the restaurant here (**Zest**) is one of Chiang Mai's more popular places – but rooms tend to be very noisy due to hotel's position on an intersection.

B-C Top North, 48 Moon Muang Rd, T053-278900. Good location for this modern hotel. Has a pool and decent food. Over priced – you pay for the location.

C-D Chiang Mai White House, 12 Rachdamnern Soi 5, T053-357130, www.chiangmaiwhitehouse.com. A 3-storey block with 18 cozy rooms (some a/c), an immaculate garden and very high standard of cleanliness.

C-D Smile House, 5 Rachmanka Soi 2, T053-208661, smile208@mail.cscoms.com. In a quiet compound with 32 spotless, but rather bare, spacious rooms, some with a/c and hot water showers. Breakfast available, bikes for rent, tours and trekking organized. Small sauna in the garden.

D Chiangmai Kristi House, 14/2 Rachdamnern Soi 5, T053-418165. A largish place with over 30 rooms, down quiet soi. Rooms are well kept, very clean and a good

size, with very clean attached bathrooms, hot water. Great views from the rooms at the back.

D-E Chiang Mai Garden Guesthouse, 82/86 Rachmanka Rd, T053-278881. Good food, very clean large rooms with bathroom. The owner, Pissamorn, is exceptionally knowledgeable about the area, speaks excellent English, German and French. Popular and offers some of the best trekking packages available in the whole of Chiang Mai. Highly recommended.

D-E Eagle II Guesthouse, 26 Rachwithi Rd, Soi 2, T053-210620, www.eaglehouse.com Dorms for ฿70. Run by an Irish woman and her Thai husband. Friendly staff, rooms are clean but a little worn with a/c and some attached bathrooms. Excellent food (it is also possible to take cookery courses here). Also organizes treks. Attractive area to sit, efficient and friendly set up. Recommended.

D-E Johnny Boy Guesthouse (JB House), 7/3 Rachdamnern Soi 1, T053-213329. Small restaurant, hot water, clean, quiet and friendly – runs good treks.

D-E Kent Guesthouse, 5 Rachmanka Soi 1, T053-217578. One of the more peaceful guesthouses in this area, house in large, leafy compound down a quiet dead-end soi, the rooms are well maintained with attached bathrooms.

D-E North Star House, 38 Moon Muang Soi 2, T053-278190. Some a/c, much like the **Thailand Guesthouse** over the road, though perhaps with a touch more character.

D-E Rendezvous Guesthouse, 3/1 Rachdamnern Soi 5, T053-213763, F217229. Some a/c, situated down a quiet soi, good rooms with clean bathrooms, hot showers, cable TV and some rooms with fridge. Attractive atmosphere with relaxing plant-filled lobby, satellite TV, books and comfy chairs, good value. Very popular with travellers so worth booking in advance.

E Blue Diamond Breakfast Club, 35/1 Moon Muang Soi 7, T053-217120. Enormously warm and welcoming family run establishment with 3 spotless rooms, with fans and shared hot-water bathroom. On offer in the downstairs dining area is great home-made Thai food and plenty of herbal teas and hilltribe coffee.

E New Saitum, 21 Moon Muang Soi 2, T053-278575. Rooms in a group of traditional wooden houses in large compound, peaceful and a refreshing absence of concrete – although the bathrooms could be cleaner.

E Panda Tour Guesthouse, 130/1 Ratchamanka Rd, T053-206420. This wonderfully friendly, family run business of over 12 years' standing is a gem of a place. The usual stable-like block has meticulously clean, well-equipped rooms with fans, tiled floors and white-washed walls. Buzzing little restaurant with exceptional food. Also runs one of the best tour companies in Chiang Mai, boasting long-standing guides whose knowledge of the surrounding area is phenomenal. Recommended.

E Somwang Guesthouse, Rachmanka Soi 2, T053-278505. Large clean rooms in a rather basic setting, but still excellent value for the level of facilities provided. Very friendly and informative owner who speaks good English. Recommended.

E-F Julie's Guesthouse, 7/1 Phra Pokklao Soi 5, T053-274355, wwww.julieguesthouse.com Run by a Swiss guy, Steff. Basic fan rooms, some with own bathroom and hot water. Friendly atmosphere and plenty of communal space for chilling out, including a rooftop. Thai and western food offered and treks organized. Recommended.

E- F Thai Way Guesthouse, 63A Bamrungburi Rd (by Chiang Mai Gate), T053-206316. A new place which used to be the **Chiang Mai Youth Hostel**. Friendly woman owner provides good value accommodation. Garden and restaurant are a little scruffy, but the place is busy and is frequently fully booked.

Between the eastern city wall and Chang Klang Rd

This area of town includes two sections of hotels and guesthouses. On Chang Klang Rd and close by are a number of large, upmarket hotels. It is busy and noisy (although the hotels need not be), with a good range of restaurants. West of here, down the sois or lanes between Loi Kroa and Tha Phae roads, are a number of guesthouses and small mid-range hotels. This area, though quiet and peaceful (usually), is still close to many restaurants and the shops and stalls of Chiang Klan Rd.

L-AL Royal Princess (formerly Dusit Inn), 112 Chang Klang Rd, T053-281033, www.dusit.com. A/c, restaurant, small pool and gym. Service is to a high standard. Central location and quite noisy (on the main road). With 200 rooms, the hotel makes an effort to be more Thai than western in image and style. Of the top-range hotels in town, this is recommended.

AL Rydges Tapae Hotel, 22 Chaiyaphun Rd, T053-251531, www.rydges.com. All the facilities you'd expect from a top range place, but not quite up to the standard of other hotels in this price bracket. Staff are friendly enough, small pool, pleasant lobby.

B-D Lai Thai, 111/4-5 Kotchasan Rd, T053-271725, www.laithai.com. Some a/c, restaurant, good clean pool (but noisy, being close to the main road), free baby cots, spotless rooms, cross between a North Thai house and Swiss chalet. Popular and professional set-up, good facilities, attractive surroundings, tours, trekking and motorbike rental. Note that the cheaper rooms at the back are noisy, so expect an early wake-up. Nonetheless, recommended.

C Tapae Place Hotel, 2 Tha Phae Soi 3, T053-270159, F271982. A/c, restaurant next to Wat Bupharam, small hotel in the mid-range bracket, refined for a place in this price category and surprisingly stylish. Good central location but set off the busy Tha Phae Rd. Room rate includes breakfast.

C-D Bang Jong Come Guesthouse, 47 Tha Phae Soi 4, T053-274823. This is larger than most guesthouses, almost like a small hotel. Good rooms: light and airy with attached hot water showers and some with a/c. Attached restaurant and trekking available.

C-D Fang Guesthouse, 46-48 Kamphaeng Din Soi 1, T053-282940. Some a/c, quiet place in good central location, attached restaurant, rooms are very clean although a little dark, good attached bathrooms (some with hot water), a/c rooms are an especially good deal.

D Little Home Guesthouse, 1/1 Kotchasarn Soi 3, T/F053-206939. Not a little guesthouse at all, but a large place more like a small hotel. Don't be put off: it is peaceful, down a quiet soi within a leafy compound. The rooms are clean and well maintained and the management has insisted on no TV, videos or music – professionally run and popular, with cheaper package tours. Recommended.

D Oriental Guesthouse, Garden Restaurant and Coffee Shop, 69 Loi Kroa Rd, T053-276742. Simple, but clean and well-proportioned stable-block rooms, set in leafy gardens – excellent food.

D Sarah's, 20 Tha Phae Soi 4, T053-208271, www.sarahguesthouse.com. Run by an English woman married to a Thai. 12 basic but clean rooms, with attached bathrooms and shared hot water showers. Trekking, tour services and cookery courses available. This well-established guesthouse in the heart of the guesthouse area remains very popular. Recommended.

D-E Flamingo Guesthouse, 71 Tha Phae Soi 3, T053-273133. Small guesthouse in a converted private residence. Basic but colourful rooms with mosquito nets, quiet, simple, restaurant and bar attached.

D-E Namkhong Guesthouse, 55 Tha Phae Soi 3, T053-215556. Friendly guesthouse. All 44 rooms are a little small and can be hot, but they are clean with reasonable attached bathrooms. Treks arranged, restaurant attached, well run and popular.

D-E Orchid Guest House, 4 Tha Phae Soi 5, T053-275370. Some a/c, hot water, rooms with bathrooms, clean and quiet. Lots of travellers' information here.

On the west bank of the river and off Charoen Prathet Rd

This area includes a number of mid- and upper-range hotels on the river that are within easy walking distance of many restaurants and the shops of Chang Klang Rd.

L-AL Empress Chiang Mai, 199/42 Chang Klang Rd, T053-270240, www.empresshotels.com (on Chiang Mai map, page 224). Several restaurants, pool and fitness centre, 375 spacious, attractive rooms with silk wall panelling, carved teakwood furniture and decorated with local products. Recommended.

A River View Lodge (Chiang Mai map, page 224), 25 Soi 2 Charoen Prathet Rd, T053-271109, www.riverviewlodgch.com. Tucked away down a narrow soi. A/c, small, family run, riverside hotel with wonderful gardens, a pool and a friendly vibe. Rooms are overpriced, there's a noisy bar just across the river and service can sometimes be snooty.

B Galare Guesthouse, 7 Soi 2 Charoen Prathet Rd, T053-818887, www.galare.com. A/c, restaurant, small hotel in leafy compound, lovely position on the river. Rooms are run-down though service is good and the open-air restaurant, overlooking the Ping, serves simple, tasty food.

C- D Kim House, 62 Charoen Prathet Rd, T/F053-282441. Small hotel in leafy compound down a secluded soi, with clean rooms (some a/c) and hot showers. Friendly, welcoming atmosphere. Recommended.

Huay Kaew Rd (West of city)

There are a number of large hotels on Huay Kaew Rd, some distance from the shops and markets of the town centre – too far to walk with any ease – but some people prefer to be away from the bustle of the commercial heart of the city in any case.

L-A Amari Rincome, 1 Nimmanhaeminda Rd, T053-221130, www.amari.com. West of town, a/c, restaurant (Italian), pool, tennis court and 158 rooms. Located out of the town centre, this hotel remains popular with tour groups. Friendly and professional service puts it ahead of some of the glitzier newer places.

L-A Chiang Mai Orchid, 23 Huay Kaew Rd, T053-222099, www.chiangmaiorchid.com Situated right next to the large Pang Suan Kaew shopping complex. Attractive hotel recently expanded, a/c, restaurants, pool, health club, efficient service, relatively peaceful, very good Chinese restaurant. Low season discounts of up to 50%.

L-A Lotus Pang Suan Kaew Hotel, 99/4 Huay Kaew Rd, T053-224333, F224493., Massive hotel which is ugly from the outside but makes up for it with competitive rates and large, luxurious rooms. A/c, restaurants, pool, gym, recommended.

Bor Sang and San Kamphaeng circuit *p232*

A-B Roong Arun Hot Springs Resort, T053-248475. A/c bungalows with pleasant sitting rooms (which have open fires for the cool season) and access to the resort's swimming pool, jacuzzi, sauna etc.

Mae Sa Valley-Samoeng circuit *p233*

B Mae Sa Craft Village, T053-290052, www.maesa.th.com. Non a/c accommodation is available with an average restaurant (avoid non-Thai food) and a smallish swimming pool. There are dozens of great activities to get involved in, from ceramic painting to batik dyeing and sa paper-making (made from mulberry). There is also a working farm where visitors can help with the rice cultivation, a Thai cookery school or, for people who find all this activity just too exhausting, there's a health centre for massage and relaxation.

B Samoeng Resort, northwest of Samoeng town, T053-487074, F487075, with restaurant, pool, hot water showers, in spacious gardens set in an isolated spot.

A number of resorts (**B**) have been established along the road around the Doi Suthep-Pui National Park. Most cater for Thais. The largest and most luxurious are **Suan Bua** in the village of Ban Don, 22 km from Samoeng, set in attractively landscaped gardens and **Belle Villa,** 19 km from Samoeng, where there are cottages for longer term rental as well as some hotel accommodation, T053-365318, belle_villa@hotmail.com.

Chiang Dao Caves *p234*

F (dorm), **D** (bungalow) Malee's Nature Lovers Bungalows, 144/2 Mu 5, Chiang Dao, T01-9618387 mob). These bungalows are about 1 km from the caves, it can be cold at between November and February, restaurant, good for trekking and walking.

Lamphun *p235*

D Suphamit Hotel, Chama Devi Rd (opposite Wat Chama Devi), T053-534865, F053-534355. The one decent place to stay with simple rooms in a good location.

Lampang *p235, map p236*

Because Lampang is only 2 hrs from Chiang Mai, few tourists stay here.

A Lampang Wiengthong Hotel, 138/109 Phahonyothin Rd, T054-225801, F054-225803. A/c, restaurant, pool, 250 rooms in this, the smartest and largest of Lampang's hotels, and easily the most luxurious place to stay in town.

A-B Lampang River Lodge, 330 Moo 11 Tambon Chomrpoo, T054-2241173; 6 km south of Lampang on the banks of the Wang River. A/c, restaurant, 60 individual Thai-style bungalows on stilts, in an attractive position.

B-C Pin, 8 Suan Dok Rd, T054-221509, F054-322286. A/c, fridge, satellite TV, some rooms with attached bathrooms, squeaky clean and quiet.

C-D Asia Lampang, 229 Boonyawat Rd, T054-227844, T054-224436. A/c, restaurant, large, clean rooms with TV. Good value. Friendly staff and with the added bonus of the 'Sweety Room' for 'the romantic of your ambience moods'. Recommended.

D Siam, 260/29 Chatchai Rd, T054-217472. Some a/c, 4-storey block, bare rooms. Friendly management, restaurant has live music and dancing.

Jai Sorn (Chae Sorn) National Park *p238*

B-C Bungalows are available at the park. Contact the Chae Son National Park at T054-229000.

Doi Inthanon *p238*

There are bungalows (**A-C**, sleeping 4-30 people) at the Km 31 outstation on the route up the mountain. To book, T02-5790529 or write to the Superintendent, Doi Inthanon National Park, Chom Thong District, Chiang Mai 50160. Advance reservation recommended as this is a very popular park. A relatively new Karen eco-resort has been set up by 4 villages with support from the National Parks Authorities. The bungalows have been built in the traditional style and the location is fantastic. The resort organizes treks, teaches about medicinal plants, introduces visitors to Karen dance etc. To find the resort, it is on the road to the summit, before the second checkpoint. There is a camping ground at the Km 31 mark (฿5 per person). Small tents (฿50 per night) and blankets are available for hire.

Eating

For listings of where to go for a Northern Khantoke meal plus cultural show, see Entertainment. Some of the best Thai food, particularly seafood, is served from numerous small and large restaurants, and countless stalls, in the **Anusarn market** area (on map Moat to river, page 228. This is the best place to see what is on offer in a small area; food available all day, but best at night when there is a cacophony of talking, frying and chopping. Note that some bars and pubs also serve food. They are listed under Bars and clubs.

Chiang Mai *p222, maps p224, p227 and p228*

Old City

ΨΨΨ The House, 199 Moonmuang Rd, T053-419011. Set in a funky 1930s colonial house, this is an attempt to serve upmarket international cuisine. It largely succeeds though it is a bit hit and miss. Cute bar. Open 1200-2400.

ΨΨ Café Chic, 105/5 Phra Pokklao Rd, T053-814651. A great little place serving a limited menu of Thai and western food, its strength lies in its great range of cakes, coffees and teas. A small shop here sells a range of products, artfully displayed and therefore probably overpriced. Recommended. Open 1000-2000, closed Wed.

ΨΨ Jerusalem Falafel, 35/3 Moon Muang Rd, T053-270208. Operated by a Thai-Israeli couple, this place doesn't look much from the outside, but don't be put off – it's a cracking little eaterie, and the only one of its kind serving a wide variety of very freshly prepared Middle Eastern food. Recommended. Open daily 0900-2200, closed Fri.

ΨΨ UN Irish Pub, 24/1 Rachwithi Rd. Lamb chops, Irish stew, steaks, pasta, lasagne etc. Pretty good fare in a pub atmosphere. See Bars.

Ψ The Amazing Sandwich, 252/3 Phra Pokklao Rd, T053-218846. Only 4 tables in this sandwich bar (and a couple more outside), which makes it feel a little cramped. However, the sandwiches are to a very high quality (good bread too). Also serves a typical English breakfast. Takeaway and limited delivery service available. Open 0900-2030, closed Sun.

Ψ Il Forno, Phra Pokklao Rd. Range of pastas and pizzas, ice cream and cappuccino.

Ψ Mr Chan, 16/1 Huay Kaew, T053-400018, This unusual restaurant serves a great selection of pizzas (including calzone), Thai food and Swedish food (excellent meatballs and good fish baked on a board). Great atmosphere and great food at very reasonable prices.

🍴 **The Corner**, Rachmanka/Moon Muang Rd. Range of classics and some vegetarian dishes. Also a popular place for breakfast. Sa paper products sold here.

🍴 **Nice Sweet Place**, 27/1 Moon Muang Rd. A/c restaurant with attached bakery, good pastries, serves breakfast.

🍴 **Pizza Al Taglio**, Rachmanka Soi 2. Very good value pizzas cooked by the friendly Italian owner and his Thai wife.

🍴 **Pum Pui Restaurant and Bar**, 24/1 Moon Muang Soi 2. Traditional Thai house with large garden converted into an Italian restaurant – reasonable Italian, good value and pleasant location.

🍴 **Tiger Restaurant and Steakhouse**, 1 Rachmanka Rd. Good breakfast stop with yoghurts and lassis.

🍴 **Zest** (Montri Hotel), Tha Phae Gate and in the Chiang Inn Plaza, Chang Klang Rd. Good breakfasts and sandwiches – nice hang-out spot.

Between the eastern city wall and Chang Klang Rd

🍴🍴 **Antique House 1**, 71 Charoen Prathet Rd (next to the **Diamond Riverside Hotel**). Well prepared Thai and Chinese food in wonderful garden with antiques and an old teak house, built in 1870s (and listed as a National Heritage Site), very nice candlelit ambience, tasty but small servings and rather slow service, live music. Busy road can be intrusive. Open 1100-2400.

🍴🍴 **Antique House 2**, 154/1 Chiang Mai/Lamphun Rd, T053-240270. A terraced restaurant overlooking the River Ping, live music. Open 1600-0200. (On Chiang Mai map, page 224).

🍴🍴 **Aroon Rai**, 43-45 Kotchasan Rd. Very big restaurant, good value Thai food. North Thai specialities, very popular – try and get a table on the quieter open-air upper floor. Open 0900-2200.

🍴🍴 **Art Café**, 291 Tha Phae Rd (on the corner facing Tha Phae Gate) T053-206365. In a great position for trade, this place serves Italian specialities including pizzas and pasta, as well as Thai and Mexican favourites. Fairly expensive. Open 0700-2300.

🍴🍴 **The Fillmore East**, 15/7 Loi Kroa Rd. Super Angus beef, imported from the US, served up to DVD 'concerts'. Excellent burgers, kebabs and salads. A popular house dish is the homemade mashed potato. Pool table, friendly staff, happy customers. Recommended.

🍴🍴 **The Gallery**, 25-29 Charoenrat Rd, T053-248601. Quiet and refined Thai restaurant on the River Ping, in a century-old traditional Thai house, superb food, highly recommended for a special night out, art gallery attached, either sit in a leafy veranda (under an ancient makiang tree) overlooking the river, or inside. Particularly recommended are the fish dishes, including steamed sea bass with lime and deep-fried plaa chon.

🍴🍴 **The Good View Bar and Restaurant**, 13 Charoenrat Rd, T053-249029. Situated on the Ping River, outdoor or a/c dining available. Good live music and bar and very reasonably priced. The atmosphere is more modern than its long-established neighbour, the **Riverside Restaurant**, and it is frequented by Chiang Mai's yuppies. Not open for lunch.

🍴🍴 **Mango Tree Café**, 8/2-3 Loi Kroa Rd, T053-208292. Popular with ex-pats for its famed roast lamb Sunday lunches and northern Thai, international and fusion cuisine. Open 0700-2230.

🍴🍴 **Mike's**, corner of Chang Moi and Chaiyapoom Rd. Created by an American ex-pat, Mike's serves up the best homemade burgers, fries and shakes you'll find this side of Brooklyn. You can sit at the retro road-side bar or take away. Highly recommended. Open daily 1200-2400.

🍴🍴 **Whole Earth** , 88 Sri Donchai Rd. Also serves Indian, set in a traditional Thai house in a lovely garden, very civilized, with unobtrusive live Thai classical music. Open 1100-2200. Recommended.

🍴 **Da Stefani**, Tha Phae Rd. Good Italian food at competitive prices.

🍴 **Ratana's Kitchen**, Tha Phae Rd. Serves really good cheap Thai food and a large variety of Western food at reasonable prices in a cosy café atmosphere.

🍴 **Red Lion**,123 Loi Kroa Rd. Not a bad imitation of an English pub, with pub grub to match – sausages and mash, beans on toast, fish and chips, as well as a range of salads and sandwiches.

🍴 **Rot Nung**, Charoen Prathet Rd (opposite the **Diamond Riverside Hotel**). Excellent Thai noodle soup (kway tiaw) in a restaurant almost entirely frequented by Thais.

On the west bank of the river and off Charoen Prathet Rd

T **Shere Shiraz**, 23-25 Charoen Prathet Soi 6, T053-276132. Popular Indian restaurant with good tandoori. International.

T **Sophia**, Charoen Prathet Soi 1 (down narrow soi between the night market and the river road). Cheap and very popular Muslim restaurant, this soi also usually supports a number of stalls, serving Malay/Muslim dishes from roti to mutton curry.

Elsewhere in the city

TTT **Chez Daniel Le Normand**, 255/18 Mahidol Rd, near Ormuang Superhighway, T053-204600. Normandy-style food – home-made charcuterie, wide choice of French wine, French music in the background. Daniel has cooked for the Queen of Thailand and members of the Royal Family.

TTT **Le Coq d'Or**, 68/1 Koh Klang Rd, T053-282024. A long-established international restaurant, set in a pleasant house. Overzealous waiters anticipate your every need. High standard of cuisine (including mouth-watering steaks), choice of wines, not heavily patronized, pricey.

TT **Come-In House**, 79/3 Srithon Rd, T053-212516, Chang Puak, down a soi opposite Wat Jet Yod, set in traditional teak house and pleasant garden, not easy to locate.

TT **Our Place Brewery and Restaurant**, 411 Charoen Prathet Rd. Large and popular open-air bar and restaurant, with a long menu covering European, Thai and Chinese and dishes. Live music in the evenings from a revolving stage, range of cocktails.

TT **Ta-Krite Thai Restaurant**, Samlarn Rd Soi 1 (down the road which runs along the southern wall of Wat Phra Singh). Excellent Thai restaurant in an attractive, plant-filled house, with tablecloths and amenable atmosphere.

T **Nang Nual Seafood**, 27/2-5 Koh Klang Rd. On the east bank of the Ping River, just south of **Westin Hotel**, also serves Chinese and international food, popular with tour groups.

Huay Kaew Rd (West of city)

TTT **La Casa**, Chonlapratan Rd T053-215802, just north of Huay Kaew Rd, set in an attractive wooden house, good range of authentic Italian cuisine (heavy on the garlic), apparently a popular restaurant with the Queen of Thailand. Fairly pricey.

TT **Babylon**, Huay Kaew Rd (about 100 m past the entrance to the university, on the right travelling out of town). Open lunch and dinner. Long-established Italian restaurant with an Italian owner. Pasta, pizza, salads, steaks, veal – unpretentious and reasonable food.

TT **Hong Tauw Inn**, 95/16-17 Nimanhaemin Rd (opposite **Amari Rincome Hotel**), T053-400039. Elegant restaurant with an antique clock collection, relaxed, friendly service, northern Thai specialities from regional sausage to crispy catfish, plus ice-cold beer. Slightly more expensive than the average Thai restaurant. Recommended.

TT **Sizzler**, Pang Suan Kaew, Huay Kaew Rd. For slap-up steaks, this place is pretty good. Its 'all you can eat' salad bar is extremely good value but you might feel the restaurant is just a bit too generic.

Outside the city *p231*

TT **Rainforest**, 181 Chiang Mai-Hot Rd, T053-441908. Rather out-of-the-way Thai restaurant, only really worth considering for those with own transport. Set around a lake about 8 km out of town running south, east off the Hang Dong road. Good food; seafood and northern specialities.

T **Galae**, 65 Suthep Rd, T053-278655. In the foothills of Doi Suthep on the edge of a reservoir, west of the city, Thai and northern Thai dishes in garden setting.

T **The Tea Shop**, Huay Kaew Rd, on south side, near Chiang Mai University. A tiny little place, easy to miss, just beyond the Black Canyon Coffee Shop. Delightful place for a cappuccino. Also serves a good range of desserts. Limited menu of spaghetti and lasagne. Recommended.

Foodstalls

Anusarn Market, southeast of the night market. Stalls mostly at night, but also smaller number throughout the day, cheap (฿10-15 single-dish meals), lively and fun. Recommended. Stalls along Chang Klang Rd sell delicious pancakes, ฿3-7.

Somphet Market (page 227), on Moon Muang Rd, for takeaway curries, fresh fish, meat and fruit.

North of **Chang Phuak Gate**, outside the moat, is another congregation of good foodstalls.

Warorot Market, north of Chang Klang and Tha Phae roads, is a great place for foodstalls at night. If you need a/c comfort, then there are some excellent food courts in the basement of both the **Airport Plaza** and **Pang Suan Kaew** (aka Central) on Huay Kaew Rd. The former is better – quieter and slightly less frenetic than Pang Suan Kaew, which is a bit like eating in a crowd of pedestrians. Buy coupons (they can be redeemed if you don't spend them all) and then browse the stalls: wide range of noodle and rice dishes, drinks, kanom, Korean, Japanese and some other Asian cuisines, along with cold drinks including bottled and draft beer.

Lamphun *p235*

There are some reasonable food stalls around Wat Phra That Haripunjaya while on the road running down the south wall of the monastery is **Lamphun Ice**, an a/c place good for ice cream, coffee and a 16 page menu with such delicacies as pig's knuckle and chicken tendon. For Kuaytiaw fans, there is a tremendous **Duck Noodle Soup Shop** on Inthayongyot Rd, just south of Wat Phra That Haripunjaya.

Lampang *p235, map p236*

For a cheap meal, try one of the Thai pavement cafés along Ropwiang Rd between the clock tower and the Lampang Guesthouse.

ƬƬ **Krua Thai**, Phahonyothin Rd (near Lampang Wiengthong Hotel). Good Thai food in an immaculate a/c restaurant or in the adjoining garden.

ƬƬ **Terrace Restaurant**, Tipchang Rd. Reasonable food in open-air wooden house overlooking the river; a great place for a drink and/or a meal.

Ƭ **Cha-ba Pub and Restaurant**, off Tipchang Rd. Pleasant open-air seating area and while the food is nothing remarkable, the ambience just about makes up for it.

Ƭ **Riverside** (Baan Rim Nam), 328 Tipchang Rd. Wooden house overlooking the river, attractive ambience, reasonable Thai and international food. Recommended

Ƭ **Oey Thong Café**, Tipchang Rd (near the bridge), good Thai food in cosy surroundings.

Foodstalls

Near the railway station and around the market (see map, page 236).

Doi Inthanon *p238*

A small park shop at the Km 31 mark will serve meals. There are no stalls on the summit, although there is a restaurant near the chedis close to the summit.

Bars and clubs

Chiang Mai *p222, maps p224, p227 and p228*

Chiang Mai has a reasonable bar scene but is fairly subdued compared to Bangkok - there is the usual run of go-go bars along Loi Kroa road. If nothing grabs you from the list below there is a smattering of usually short-lived hip bohemian hang-outs scattered throughout the old city particularly along Rachdamnern and Rachwithi roads. The area around Tae Pae gate also has a high concentration of watering holes. There are quite a few pubs at the western end of Loi Kroa Rd. See Music, page 246, for more bars with live music.

Apocalypse Mexican Cantina, 80/2 Loi Kroa Rd, T053-284288, located on a busy street, this place usually pulls in a bit of a crowd, and boasts a pool table, lots of wooden, picnic tables and large swivel stools around the bar.

Baritone, 96 Fraisani Rd, live jazz from 2100.

Bubble, Pornping Tower Hotel, 46048 Charoen Prathet Rd, T053-270099, very popular disco.

Cheers Pub is down a narrow soi and serves cheap pub food like pork pies and pea and ham soup.

Early Times, Kotchasan Rd, open air with live heavy metal music.

Easy Life, 65 Seepoom Rd, east of Chang Puck Gate. Showing sport, movies and world news. The friendly owner, Noi, speaks reasonable English, and this place is never that busy, so it's worth knowing that if you buy a drink or food you get free use of the internet – when it works, that is.

The Full Monty, 29/3 Kotchasarn Rd, T09-1670879 (mob). A small but popular stop with good happy hour deals and the latest popular music.

Golden Triangle Bar serves reasonable, cheap food and is set within a teak house and has outdoor space.
The Hill, 122 Bumrungburi Rd, Thai rock and heavy metal – more of a venue than a bar.
Kazoo, 68/2 Lamphun Rd, T053-240880, 300 m from TAT office, open daily, very popular disco.
The Pub, 198 Huay Kaew Rd, bar and restaurant in a traditional wooden Thai house in a large leafy compound. Serves overpriced food. Pleasant enough spot. Open 1730-2400.
Rasta Café, off Rachpakinai Rd, near the intersection with Rachwithi Rd. Hang-out of choice for the toking traveller set. Lots of Bob Marley and interesting garden but hardly original.
The Red Lion, 123 Loi Kroa Rd, near McDonald's, an English pub (and restaurant, see under Eating) with satellite sports TV. Open 1200-0100.
Riverside Bar and Restaurant, 9-11 Charoenrat Rd, assorted music from blues to Thai rock, owner is a big Beatles fan.
Roof Top, Kotchasan Rd, just down from Tha Phae Gate, and accessed through the Tribal Hemp Connection shop – a seriously laid-back setting, the roof pulls back to create a breezy atmosphere, where countless mats, cushions, low tables play host to a merry band of travellers. Very popular.
Swiss Wine-Pub, 95/10 Nimanhaemin Rd, opposite **Amari Rincome Hotel**, also acts as a wine shop, open 1700-0200.
True Blue Pub and Restaurant, Moon Muang Rd. Australian owned, serves a wide variety of western food, including Vegemite on toast. Happy hour 1700-1900. Recommended for its relaxed atmosphere.
UN Irish Pub, Rachwithi Rd, good atmosphere and cheap food available (see Eating above). The name speaks for itself – management (which is Australian) help to organize the (small) annual St Patrick's Day parade. Has quiz nights, live music and occasionally shows English Premiership football. Open 0900-2400.

Lampang *p235, map p236*
Relax, Tipchang Rd (next to **Riverside Restaurant**), modern style bar in wooden building overlooking the river. Cold beer and more, open-air veranda.
Riverside (see Eating), live music most nights, ranging from rock and roll to romantic Thai ballad groups.

Entertainment

Chiang Mai *p222, maps p224, p227 and p228*

Boat trips
Evening departures from the **Riverside Restaurant** on Charoenrat Rd for trips along the Ping River. ฿50 a head, minimum 2 people.

Cinema
Future Media, Nimanhaemin Rd, south of **Amari Rincome** hotel on same side of road. Possible to rent a room to watch movies on big TV screens. ฿200. Good choice.
Lotus Pang Suan Kaew, Huay Kaew Rd, top floor of this shopping centre, 3 screens, latest blockbusters, changes every Fri. ฿70. Call 'Movie line' for information, T053-262661. Across the road at 12 Huay Kaew, also shows English language movies. ฿90.

Cookery classes
Baan Thai, 11 Rachdamnern Rd. T053-357339, info@CookInThai.com. All day, hands-on lesson for ฿700. Provides free transportation to and from your guesthouse.
Chiang Mai Thai Cookery School, booking at 1-3 Moon Muang Rd (by Tha Phae Gate), T053-206388, www.thaicookeryschool.com. The courses run over 1-5 days between 1000 and 1600. One of the best. Contact Samphon and Elizabeth Nabnian. The location of the course is at **The Wok**, 44 Rachmanka Rd, although some sessions take place in a charming rural location outside town.
Siam Kitchen, Rachdamnern Soi 4, beside Gap House, T053-213415, siam-kitchen@bangkok.com. Attractively laid out with pleasant seating areas to relax in after slaving over a hot stove.
Thai Kitchen Cookery School, 25 Moon Muang Rd, Soi 9, T053-219896. Run by Prathuang (Tim) Impraphai, who speaks good English (having worked as a chef in Canada for 3 years), a full days course with a recipe book costs ฿700 – a good deal.
Tom Yam Cookery School, Lake View Park II, Maejo Rd, T053-844877, 15 mins from Chiang Mai (free pick-up, swimming pool

available at lunchtime), but bookable (and more information) at 2 Rachmanka Rd. Finally, recommended cookery courses are also run at the **Eagle II Guesthouse**, 26 Rachwithi Rd, Soi 2 (see Sleeping).

Cultural centres

Alliance Française, 138 Charoen Prathet Rd, T053-275277. Presents French cultural (and some northern Thai) activities. French films with English subtitles are screened on Tue (1630) and Fri (2000). Entrance to non-members, students ฿10, public ฿20.

AUA (American University Alumni), 24 Rachdamnern Rd, T053-278407, F211973. Library open Mon-Fri 1200-1800, Sat 0900-1200. English and Thai classes; films and other shows.

British Council, 198 Bumrungrat Rd, T053-242103, F053-244781.

Cultural shows and Khantoke dinners

These traditional northern Thai meals get a lot of coverage. Average food is served at low tables by traditionally dressed women while diners sit on the floor.

Khun Kaew Palace, 252 Phra Pokklao Rd (north end), next to **Vista Hotel**, T053-210663. Admission ฿180 (book in advance), open daily 1900-2200.

Old Chiang Mai Cultural Centre, 185/3 Wualai Rd, T053-275097. Admission ฿180 (book in advance), Khantoke dinner, followed by hilltribe show, daily 1900-2200.

Diamond Riverside Hotel on Charoen Prathet Rd and the **Galare Food Centre** in the night bazaar, Chang Klang Rd, also organize Khantoke dinners, 1900, ฿180.

Festivals and events

Chiang Mai *p222*

Jan (movable) Chiang Mai Winter Fair, a 10-day festival held late Dec/early Jan, based in the Municipal Stadium. Exhibitions, Miss Beauty Contest, musical performances.

Bor Sang Umbrella Fair (outside Chiang Mai, mid-month) celebrates traditional skills of umbrella making, and features contests, exhibitions and stalls selling umbrellas and other handicrafts. Miss Bor Sang, a beauty contest, is also held.

Feb (first Fri, Sat and Sun of month) Flower Festival. This is a great festival and is centred on the inner moat road, at the southwest corner of the Old City. Small displays of flowers and plants arranged by schools, colleges and professional gardeners and garden shops from across the North. There are also, as you would expect in Thailand, lots of foodstalls as well as handicrafts. If you have ever felt the urge to grow a papaya tree then this is the place to get your seeds. The highlight is a parade of floral floats along with the requisite beauty contest. If you want to avoid the crowds, come on the Fri evening.

Apr (13-16, public holiday) Songkran, traditional Thai New Year celebrated with more enthusiasm in Chiang Mai than elsewhere. Boisterous water-throwing, particularly directed at farangs; expect to be soaked to the skin for the entire 4 days.

Nov (mid-month) Yi Peng Loi Krathong, a popular Buddhist holiday when boats (krathong) filled with flowers and lit candles are floated down the river. Fireworks at night – small hot-air balloons are launched into the sky.

Lampang *p235*

Feb (movable) Luang Wiang Lakon, 5 important Buddha images are carried through the streets in procession. Traditional dancing and a light show at Wat Lampang Luang.

Shopping

Chiang Mai *p222, maps p224, p227 and p228*

Chiang Mai is a shoppers' paradise. It provides many of the treasures of Bangkok, in a compact area. The craft 'villages' on the San Kamphaeng and Hang Dong (Ban Tawai) roads are a popular jaunt of the coach tour, whilst the night market, with its array of handicrafts, antique shops and fake designer shirts, continues to pack the tourists in night after night. A quieter, less frequented spot, is the group of sophisticated shops that have opened up near the **Amari Rincome** hotel. Tha Phae Rd is an old favourite and is smartening up its act, with the likes of **Living Space** and **Contemporary Jewellery** opening up. Two department stores at Pang

Suan Kaew on Huay Kaew Rd and the Airport Plaza, south of town near the airport, provide focal points for a vast array of shops, including plenty of cheap clothes outlets. The area around Tha Phae Gate becomes pedestrianized on a Sun afternoon and evening to make way for hundreds of food and souvenir stalls and buskers. If you want to ship your goodies back home **UPS** has a walk-in office at **S & M Parcel Express**, 9 Soi 7 Rajdamnoen Rd T053-416351 Mon-Fri 0830-1730 and 1900-2200 and Sat 0830-1730.

Antiques

There are a number of shops on Tha Phae Rd. Another good road to wander along is Loi Kroa, which supports a large number of antique and hilltribe handicraft shops. Hang Dong Rd has several places worth a browse, as does the San Kamphaeng Rd, towards Bor Sang (to get there, take a tuk-tuk or a bus from the north side of Charoen Mang Rd). Beware of fakes.

Ancient Crafts, 11/3 Rachmanka Rd. Small antique shop selling mostly Burmese lacquerware and northern Thai artefacts with some Chinese pieces.

Masusook Antiques, 263/2-3 Tha Phae Rd, T053-275135. Good range of antique ceramics, some textiles and some metalwork (opium weights and figurines from Burma).

Sanpranon Antiques, west side of Hang Dong Rd, about 4 km from Airport Plaza. Set off the road in a traditional Thai house, this is well worth a visit, just to rummage about in this huge place. There's an overwhelming amount of stock (from lacquerware to ceramics to woodcarvings), much of which is clearly not antique, but it's fun to nose.

Art

TiTa Gallery, opposite Regent Chiang Mai Hotel, on Samoeng Rd, Mae Rim, T053-298373, tita@cm.ksc.co.th. Chiang Mai is short on really good local art and this is one of the few places where you will be able to find anything of quality.

Bookshops

Book Exchange, 21/1 Soi 2 Rachmanka. Books bought and sold, probably has the largest range of English second-hand novels.

Book Zone, 318 Tha Phae Rd, part of Asia Books. This small store sells a range of Thai coffee-table books, a good range of guidebooks, some English language novels, children's books, magazines and maps. Open 0900-2130.

Bookazine, basement of Chiang Inn Plaza, Chang Klang Rd. Good range of coffee-table books, children's books and magazines.

DK Bookstore, Kotchasarn Rd, just south of Loi Kroa Rd. This big store has a good range of English-language books and magazines, plus stationery, maps and cards.

Suriwong Book Centre, 54/1-5 Sri Donchai Rd. Most extensive collection of books in English on Thailand in Chiang Mai.

Ceramics

Beautiful celadon-glazed ceramics can be found in proliferation in Chiang Mai. San Kamphaeng Rd is as good a place as any to see a number of set-ups. Several of the establishments on this road are selling outlets for small factories on the same site, which are open to visitors. One such place is **Baan Celadon**, 7 Moo 3, Chiangmai-Sankamphaeng Rd, T053-338288, F338940. A good range of ceramics for sale from simple everyday bowls to elaborate vases.

Mengrai Kilns, 79/2 Arak Rd, T053-272063. A showroom only, with a good range of celadonware – range of seconds at reasonable prices.

Siam Celadon, 38 Moo 10, Sankampaeng Rd, T053-331526, award-winning designs though it is a little far from town.

Clothing

Huge assortment of T-shirts, cotton clothing and tribal clothing in the 3 night markets on Chang Klang Rd. See Hilltribe section, on page 678, for more detailed information on the various styles of clothing. Other shops along Tha Phae Rd or for more contemporary styles, the 2 shopping centres (Pang Suan Kaew on Huay Kaew Rd and Airport Plaza) have a good range. The former has some bargains on both the top and basement floors. Also see textiles and silk entries below.

Pang Suan Kaew, Huay Kaew Rd. This is the place to come for cheap clothes – lots of small shops and stalls mostly concentrated on the top floor, with a few more in the basement and scattered through the complex.

Computers, software and IT

Panthip Plaza, 152/1 Changklan Rd, is the Chiang Mai version of the Bangkok classic. Everything any computer could ever want – mounds of hardware and mountains of software. Pick up the latest PC and Mac programme copies at a fraction of the published cost.

Cotton products

Fai Ngam, Nimanhaemin Soi 1, opposite Amari Rincome hotel. An attractive range of cotton products – some clothing, scarves, tableware and soft toys.

Furniture

If you are prepared to ship furniture home, Chiang Mai is an excellent place to rummage around for it. For locally made products, Hang Dong Rd is your best bet, with plenty of choice (and they can make furniture to order too). As well as there being several shops on the main north-south road, the best area to look is immediately to the east of Hang Dong – turn left at the junction. There is a strip of shops along here selling an excellent range of furniture, both old and new. The road to Bor Sang (the San Kamphaeng Rd, to northeast of town) is also worth a visit. There are also quite a few shops selling furniture imported from the region.

Chiangmai Sudaluck, 99/9 Chiang Mai-San Kamphaeng Rd. Custom-made pieces.

Under the Bo, 22-23 Night Bazaar, also has a shop on the west side of Hang Dong Rd, about 4 km south of the Airport Plaza. Fascinating mixture of Indonesian, Bhutanese, Afghan and Pakistani pieces. Worth a visit.

Handicrafts

Chiang Mai is the centre for hilltribe handicrafts. There is a bewildering array of goods, much of which is of poor quality (Tha Phae Rd seems to specialize in a poorer range of products). Bargain for everything. The **night market** on Chang Klang Rd also has a lot on offer, although generally of poor quality; better pieces can be found at the more exclusive shops on Loi Kroa Rd.

Co-op Handicraft, next to Thai Farmer's Bank on Tha Phae Rd.

Hilltribe Products Foundation, T053-277743, next to Wat Suan Dok on Suthep Rd.

Thai Tribal Crafts, 208 Bumrungrat Rd, near McCormick Hospital – run by Karen and Lahu church organizations on a non-profit basis, good selection, quality and prices.

Honey

Bees Knees, 7 Chang Klang Rd, sells a good range of local honeys.

Interior design

Chiang Mai is undoubtedly the best place outside Bangkok to find good quality 'decorative items' and contemporary furniture for your home. Probably the best concentration of shops of this kind are on Nimanhaemin Rd, west of town, opposite the **Amari Rincome** hotel, but Charoenrat Rd is also well worth a visit.

Aesthetic Accessories, 50-60 Rachmanka Rd, opposite **Anodard Hotel**, T053-278659. Not to be confused with the other Aesthetic opposite **Amari Rincome** hotel, this is a great little place selling beautiful small-scale 'accessories'. It's quite expensive by Thai standards.

Aesthetic Studio, 95/12 Nimanhaemin Rd, opposite **Amari Rincome** hotel, T053-222026. shop@aesthetic-studio.com Fabulous little place with some really interesting pieces from clocks to lamps to glass and ceramics.

Beau Siam, 41 Loi Kroa Rd, T053-209111. Very sophisticated range of contemporary furniture, decorative items and modern ceramics.

Gong Dee Gallery, soi just south of **Amari Rincome** hotel and factory on San Kamphaeng Rd, T053-225032. Great range of mangowood boxes, vases, bowls and frames and other beautiful decorative items – sells to John Lewis Partnership in the UK.

The Good View, 13 Charoenrat Rd, T053-241866, goodview@chmai.loxinfo.co.th. A tiny shop attached to the restaurant of the same name with an eclectic mix, ranging from dining equipment (attractive ceramics) to photo frames to T-shirts to food products. High quality products at reasonable prices.

Villa Cini, 30, 32 and 34 Charoenrat Rd, T053-244025, F244867. Beautiful range of

textiles and antiques, high quality products displayed in sophisticated surroundings makes for inflated prices, but it's fun to browse here. Also has a small restaurant in the courtyard.

Jewellery and silverwork

Chiang Mai now offers not only a proliferation of hilltribe jewellery, but also some better quality, contemporary designed jewellery. A good starting point is Tha Phae Rd, where there is a strip of about 5 shops near the Thai Farmers Bank.

CM Silver Jewellery Co, Tha Phae Rd, just to west of Book Zone. Good cheap range of jewellery.

Old Silver, 59/3 Loi Kroa Rd, and **Sipsong Panna Silver**, 95/19 Nimanhaemin Rd. Both sell traditional and modern silver jewellery.

Shiraz Jewelry, 170 Tha Phae Rd, T053-252382, a long-established gem shop. For more traditional, Thai-style silverwork, make your way to Wualai Rd which runs off the southern moat road. There are quite a number of shops and workshops down here on both sides of the road.

Lacework

Sarapee Handmade Lace, 2 Rachwithi Rd. Claims to be the only workshop in Southeast Asia using silk thread.

Lacquerware

Masusook Antiques, 263/2-3 Tha Phae Rd. Also cheaper stuff available from the night bazaar.

Night markets

Situated on the west and east sides of Chang Klang Rd, Chiang Mai's multiple night markets are now a major tourist attraction and consist of 2 or 3-storey purpose-built structures containing countless stalls. It is an excellent place to browse and, along with a wide range of tribal handicrafts, it is possible to buy T-shirts, watches, cheap CDs, leather goods, children's clothes and Burmese 'antiques'. In addition, there are some better quality shops selling jewellery, antiques and silks (both ready-made and lengths) on the 1st floor of the Viang Ping Building. Most stalls and shops open at about 1800 and close around 2300.

Warorot Market, north of Tha Phae Rd, for clothing, fabric, sportswear, hilltribe handicrafts. Open 0700-1600.

Fruit stalls and market on both sides of moat north of Tha Phae Gate. Some tuk-tuk drivers are subsidized by factories, so will take you to see silver, silk, enamel factories for about ฿20 each, with no obligation to buy.

Mae Jo, 287 Chiang Mai-Mae Jo Rd, sells fresh food, plants and household items.

Paper products

There is now a proliferation of shops selling handmade paper products. The best place to find paper is along San Kamphaeng Rd, where there are many small-scale operations making paper. Take the lane to the west just before Chiang Mai Sudaluck, and before the Bor Sang junction, signposted to Preservation House. If you are stuck in town, then try **HQ Paper Maker**, 3/31 Samlarn Rd, behind Wat Phra Singh.

Rattanware

Hang Dong Rattan, Loi Kroa Rd (near intersection with Kamphaeng Din Rd). High quality rattan products. There is also a good range of cheaper stalls strung out along Route 108 towards Hang Dong, about 10 km south of town.

Silk

Blue River, Tha Phae Rd, west end. Good range of silk and loose-weave cotton. Some interesting ready-made clothing too.

Capital Silk, 35/4 Moon Muang Rd. Similar to City Silk and Shinawatra Silk, lots of choice for silk on the roll, as well as ready-mades and some small silk items like frames.

City Silk, 360 Tha Phae Rd. Extensive range of colours and some ready-made garments.

Classic Lanna Thai, night bazaar, upper floor, far right-hand corner. Fabulous range of well-designed jackets, dresses and blouses. Also sells antique silk. Will make to measure.

Shinawatra Silk, Huay Kaew Rd (opposite Chiang Mai Orchid Hotel). For the usual array of silk products: specs cases, silk frames, ties, scarves, and endless bolts of fabric. Hardly funky, but a good stop for stocking fillers for the grandparents/parents.

Supermarkets and department stores

Lotus/Tesco, Hang Dong Rd, about 3 km south of Airport Plaza. Enormous place selling household goods, clothing, electrical goods and a big supermarket, with a good range of fresh fruit and vegetables and some western foods.

Rimping Supermarket, 171 Chotana Rd, by Novotel Hotel. One of the better small central supermarkets for Western foods (including good cheeses, salads, cold meats and pâtés). The largest department store is the ugly **Central Department Store**, in the **Pang Suan Kaew** shopping complex on Huay Kaew Rd; there is a **Tops** supermarket in the basement where a good range of food is available.

Robinsons department store and **Tops** supermarket provide good selection of clothing, household goods and Western food.

Tailors

Big Boss, 99/8 Loi Kroh Rd, T053-818953. Friendly staff and a fantastic range of silks.

Far Mee, 66 Square U Pakut, Tha Phae Rd. Many of the stalls in and around Warorot Market will make up clothes. Walk north along Vichayanon Rd from Tha Phae Rd.

Terracotta

Ban Phor Liang Muen, 36 Phra Pokdao Rd. Huge range of plaques, murals, statues, pots at in outdoor display garden.

Textiles

For a good range of textiles, it is worth walking down Loi Kroa Rd, east of the city wall.

Chatraporn, 194 Tha Phae Rd. For silks, cotton and made-up garments.

Folk Art, 326 Tha Phae Rd. For textiles, matmii, handwoven cotton.

Le Bombyx, 3 km out of town on the San Kamphaeng Rd. Ready-to-wear and made-to-measure silk and cotton clothing.

The Loom Textile Gallery, 90 Rajchiang Sean Rd, T053-278892. Attractive wooden Thai house with a good range of textiles, old and new.

Nandakwang, 6/1-3 Nimanhaemin Rd, opposite Amari Rincome hotel, T053-222261 or 3rd floor, Chiang Inn Plaza, Chiang Klan Rd, T053-281356. Loose-weave cotton 'homespun creations', ranging from napkins to cushion covers to bedspreads to made-up clothing. Attractive range of colours. Also sells some ceramics (brightly coloured coffee cups).

Pothong House, 4 Moon Muang Soi 5. For Khmer, Lao and hilltribe fabrics.

Studio Naenna, 138/8 Soi Changkhian, Huay Kaew Rd, T053-226042. Handwoven cloth, made up.

Woodcarving

Western tastes accommodated for along Tha Phae Rd, with many outlets selling woodcarved trinkets.

Ban Tawai is a woodcarving centre about 3 km east of Hang Dong (itself 15 km south of town). This place began life as a woodcarving village, and has been colonized and now overgrown by shops and stalls selling everything from cheap and cheerful frogs to grandiose sculptures. Packing services available.

Banyen, 201/1 Wualai Rd, on the junction of the Super highway and the Hang Dong Rd, opposite Airport Plaza. This long-established shop still sells a range of wooden products.

Ratana House, 284 Chiang Mai-Hang Dong Rd, east side, T053-271734. Huge range of goods from Burmese lacquerware to wood products of all descriptions – both large (chests and cupboards) and small (candlesticks and wooden frogs). Also sells china.

Silver Birch, 40 Soi 1, Nimanhaemin Rd, behind Amari Rincome hotel. Quirky collection of wooden products from mobiles to toilet-roll holders to giant frogs.

Lampang *p235, map p236*

Ceramics

Lampang is famous for its ceramics. There are more than 50 factories in and around the town; a number are to be found to the west along Phahonyothin Rd (eg, **Chao Lampang** and **Ceramic Art** at 246/1) and Route 1 towards Ko Kha (eg, **Art Lampang**). International outlets selling seconds very cheaply can also be found near Lampang – ask at the TAT office in Chiang Mai for details.

Handicrafts

Lampang Plaza, on Ropwiang Rd near the clock tower, sells an assortment of

knick-knacks like wind chimes, shells and ceramics from a series of stalls.
Northern Handicraft Hilltribe Shopping Centre, a small teak house and, unfortunately, not as grand as it sounds.

Department stores
Texas Department Store, in the centre of town, Boonyawat Rd.

Activities and tours

Chiang Mai *p222, maps p224, p227 and p228*
Latest information on sports listed in most free newspapers and newsletters, available from many shops, hotels and guesthouses. See the Mae Sa Craft Village under Sleeping for its activites.

Bungee jumping
Jungle Bungey Jump, T053-298442. Go-kart racing.
Chiang Mai Speedway, 8 km out of town on Route 108, T053-430059. Racing every Sat and Sun afternoon, open daily 0930-1900.
Chiang Mai Gokart, San Kamphaeng Rd, near Bor Sang intersection.

Cookery courses
Chiang Mai Thai Cookery, 47/2 Moon Muang Rd, T053-206388, www.thaicookeryschool.com/ Runs a variety of courses from ฿990 for one day.

Fitness and sports centres
Club House Inn, Chiang Mai Sports Club, Km 10 Mae Rim Rd, Route 107. Large pool, tennis, squash, badminton, gym, aerobics, horse riding.
Huay Kaew Fitness Park, Huay Kaew Rd at the bottom of Doi Suthep, near the zoo.
Hillside Fitness Centre, 4th floor, Hillside Plaza 4, Huay Kaew Rd, T053-225984. Fitness centre, sauna and herbal steam rooms, beauty treatment.

Golf
Information on golf in Thailand can be found at www.thailandamazinggolf.com.
Lanna Public Golf Course, Chotana Rd (at Nong Bua, 4 km north of the city). A woodland course, part of the Chiang Mai Sports Club. Green fee ฿500, ฿700 at weekends, club hire ฿300. Open 0600-1930. There is also a driving range here.
Gymkhana Club, Chiangmai-Lamphun Rd, 9-hole course, green fees ฿100 weekdays, ฿400 weekends.

Hash House Harriers
Hashes are fortnightly, Sat evening for men and women, Mon evening for men. Contact either David or Martin on T053-278503, or John on T053-271950, or the **Domino Bar**, T053-278503.

Horse racing
Next to the Lanna Public Golf Course, Chotana Rd (4 km north of the city). Races every Sun, 1200-1730.

Horse riding
Lanna Sports Centre, Chotana Rd (north of town), ฿250 per hr, call Janet on T053-217956 for details.

Squash
Gymkana Club, Chiang Mai-Lamphun Rd, T053-247352, every Thu 1730.

Swimming
Chiang Mai University, west of town, see Chiang Mai map. For serious swimmers, try the pool within this sports complex.
Padungsilpa Sports Club, Rasada Rd, large pool, clean with snack bar, open 0830-2030.

Tennis
Fees are about ฿100 per hr; rackets for hire.
Amari Rincome Hotel, Anantasiri Courts, Super highway (near the National Museum).
Padungsilpa Sports Club, Rasada Rd (฿40 per hr, ฿80 per hr under floodlights).

Thai boxing
Dechanukrau boxing ring, south of San Pakoi market, on Bumrungrat Rd. Matches every weekend at 2000 (฿20/70).

Therapies
For a traditional Thai massage, it is best to avoid the places geared to tourists around Tha Phae Gate.

Massage There are umpteen places in town offering massage. They tend to charge around the same amount (฿200 per hr).

Note that many masseuses seem to have had rudimentary training and the massage rooms consist of mattresses laid on the floors of upper rooms. The experience may be pleasant enough, but don't expect your sinuses to clear or your lower colon to sort itself out. The greatest concentration of massage outfits is to be found around Tha Phae Gate.

Let's Relax, Chiang Mai Plaza (basement), Chang Klang Rd, T053-818498, and **Chiang Mai Pavilion Plaza** (2nd floor, above McDonald's), both branches, in the night market, offer a more upmarket experience: foot, hand and back massage in clean, comfortable, a/c surroundings, and the masseuses seem to know a little bit more about what they are doing. More expensive at around ฿250 for 45 mins.

Massage courses For those who want to find out more about Thai massage, a number of courses are available: **ITM** (Institute of Thai Massage), 17/7 Morokot Rd, T053-218632, F224197, 5-10 day courses in basic, intermediate and advanced Thai massage, 0900-1600; courses begin on Mon and cost ฿1,500 – the 'Master Teacher' Chongkol Setthakorn is well qualified.
Moh Shivagakomarpaj Foundation, Old Chiang Mai Traditional Hospital, 238/8 Wuolai Rd (opposite Old Chiang Mai Cultural Centre, Chiang Mai-Hod Rd), T053-275085, www.thaimassageschool.ac.th Courses last 11 days (fee ฿2,770) and run from the beginning and middle of each month.

Meditation Holstic Self-Empowerment Center, 46 Tewan Rd, T053-406007, h_s_empower@hotmail.com. Programmes for people of all ages.
T'ai Chi T01-7067406 (mob), www.taichithailand.com. Classes start on the 1st and 16th day of each month.
Yoga Khun Wai, Huay Kaew Rd, Mon-Sat, 0800-1800. ฿100 per hr.
Raja Yoga Meditation Centre, 218/6 Chotana Rd, T053-214904.

Trekking
There are scores of trekking companies in Chiang Mai and hundreds of places selling trekking tours. Competition is stiff and most companies provide roughly the same assortment of treks, ranging from one night to over a week. Not many places actually organize the trek themselves and it is rare to meet the guide – or other people in the group – before leaving for the trek. The quality of the guide rather than the organizing company usually makes the trip successful or not and the happiest trekkers are often those who have done their homework and found a company with long-term, permanent staff who they can meet beforehand.

For further information, see Hilltribes and trekking, Essentials page 71 and Background, page 664. See also Tour operators, page 255.

Like many other areas of tourism, trekking is suffering from its own success. Companies organizing treks are finding it increasingly difficult to present their products as authentic get-away-from-it-all adventures when there is such a high probability of bumping into another group of tourists. As numbers increase so travellers are demanding more authenticity in their trekking experiences. The answer is to avoid the environs of Chiang Mai and trek in less pressured areas like Mae Hong Son, Nan and Pai. Many trek operators – like those along Moon Muang Road – are advertising special non-tourist routes, although these so-called special routes are virtually indistinguishable from established routes. Some companies even claim to offer a money-back guarantee should they come into contact with other trekkers.

The TAT office distributes a list of recommended trekking operators and a leaflet on what to look out for when choosing your trip. The Tribal Research Institute (see page 232), situated at the back of the Chiang Mai University campus on Huay Kaew Road, provides information on the various hilltribes, maps of the trekking areas, and a library of books on these fascinating people. You can also download a useful pdf file from their website, www.chmai.com/tribal/content.html .

Remember to take protection against mosquitoes; long trousers and long-sleeved shirts are essential for the night-time. When choosing a guide for the trip, ensure

that he or she can speak the hilltribe dialect as well as good English (or French, German etc). Guides must hold a 'Professional Guide Licence'. Treks must be registered with the Tourist Police; to do this the guide must supply the Tourist Police with a photocopy of the Identity page of your passport and your date of entry stamp. You can check on a company's reputation by contacting the police department. Beware of leaving valuables in guesthouses in Chiang Mai; however reliable the owner may appear, it is always safer to deposit valuables such as passport, jewellery and money in a bank (banks on Tha Phae Rd have safety deposits and charge about ฿200 per month).

Many of the companies are concentrated along Tha Phae, Chaiyaphum, Moon Muang and Kotchasan roads. Standards change so very rapidly that recommending companies is a dangerous business, but the safest bet is to find somewhere with permanent, long-term staff. Two such outfits are: **Chiang Mai Garden Guesthouse**, 82-86 Ratchamanka Rd, T053-278881, and **Panda Tour Guesthouse**, 130/1 Rachmanka Rd, T053-206420.

Prices for treks are highly variable with 2-day trips costing somewhere between ฿1,600-1,800, 3-day treks ฿1,700-2,000 and 4-days ฿2,000-2,400. Be aware that the better trips do usually cost more, either because they're more off the beaten track and therefore further away, or because the company is paying for one of the better guides, who are worth their weight in gold. If you find a trek for a price that seems too good to be true, it probably is, and will end up being a waste of both money and time.

Tours and tour operators

See also Trekking, page 254.

A range of day tours run from Chiang Mai. Prices seem to vary between companies; examples of day tours include: Wat Phrathat Doi Suthep, the Phu Ping Palace and a Meo village (฿600-800); the Mae Sa Valley to visit a waterfall, orchid farm and elephants at work (฿800); Doi Inthanon National Park (฿900-1,300); Bor Sang (the Umbrella village) and San Kamphaeng (฿100-200); Chiang Rai and the Golden Triangle (฿750); even the Sukhothai Historical Park over 200 km south (฿1,500). A ride on an elephant, some bamboo rafting and a visit to an orchid farm cost about ฿800.

Make sure you know exactly what is included in the price: some travellers have complained of hidden costs such as road tolls, tips for guides, entrance fees etc. It is advisable to shop around to secure the best deal. Most tour operators are concentrated around Tha Phae Gate, Chang Klang and Moon Muang (in the vicinity of Tha Phae Gate), so this process is not as time consuming as it may seem. Most operators will also book air, train and bus tickets out of Chiang Mai.

The TAT recommends that services should only be bought from companies that register with the tourist Business and Guide Registration Office. It provides a list of all such companies. As noted in the trekking section (see page 254), we have decided not to list or recommend companies because standards vary between tours (and guides) within individual outfits, and because these standards can change rapidly. Word of mouth is the best guarantee. Three exceptions are:

Chiang Mai Green Tour and Trekking, 29-31 Chiang Mai-Lamphun Rd, A. Muang, Chiang Mai 50000, F247374, cmgreent@chiangmai.a-net.net.th. Another notable operator, which tries to provide eco-friendly and culturally sensitive tours. However, it also runs motorbike treks which can hardly be said to be the former.

Click and Travel Ltd, www.clickandtravel online.com, is a young 'Soft Adventure Company' specializing in bicycle tours.

North Pearl Travel, 332/334 Tha Phae Rd, T/F053-232976.

Many of the larger tour companies and travel agents will also arrange visas and tours to Burma, Cambodia, Laos and Vietnam. Going rates are: Laos, US$30 on arrival or US$20 pre-arranged (30 days); Burma, ฿1,500 (30 days); Vietnam, ฿2,600 (30 days). Visas take between 3 and 7 days to arrange.

Lampang *p235, map p236*

Therapies

Northern Herbal Medicine Society. Traditional Thai massage - good value at ฿150 per hr, 108 herbs available for the full treatment. Opposite Wat Prakaew Don Tao.

Transport

Chiang Mai *p222, maps p224, p227 and p228*

Air
The airport is 3 km southwest of town. It contains a bank (currency exchange vans also park outside the terminal building), hotel booking counter, post office, Avis rent-a-car counter, tourist information counter, Pizza Hut and snack bar.
Transport to town: taxis to town cost ฿90 (fixed price from the taxi booking counter). THAI operates a shuttle bus service between the airport and its office in town (but you can get off anywhere in town), ฿40. Airport information: T053-270222.

Regular connections on THAI with **Bangkok** (1 hr). Also flights to **Chiang Rai** (40 mins), **Mae Hong Son** (30 mins), **Nan** (45 mins), **Mae Sot** (50 mins), **Phuket** (2 hrs), **Phitsanulok** (35 mins) and **Khon Kaen** (1 hr 25 mins). Bangkok Airways also operates a daily service to **Bangkok** and **Sukhothai**, with connections on to **Koh Samui**.

International air connections with **Singapore**, **Kunming** in South China, **Vientiane**, (twice a week), **Kuala Lumpur**, **Dusseldorf** and **Munich**. Lao Airlines, LTU International and Malaysian Airlines all serve Chiang Mai. International Passenger Service Charge of ฿500.

Airline offices Air Mandalay (Skybird Tour), 92/3 Sri Donchai Rd, T053-818049. Bangkok Airways, Chiang Mai International Airport, T053-922258, F281520. Lao Airlines, 840 Phra Pokklao Rd, T053-418258. Malaysian Airlines (MAS), Mae Ping Hotel, 153 Sri Donchai Rd, T053-276523. PB Air, Chiang Mai International Airport, T053-279172.

Bicycle
From Chang Phuak Gate and at the southern end of Moon Muang Rd, ฿50 per day, or on Nakhon Ping Bridge, plus some guesthouses. **The Wild Planet Adventure**, Charoen Prathet Rd, next to SK Money Changer, T053-277178. **Bike & Bite**, 23/1 Sri Phum Rd, T053-418534. A deposit or your passport will probably be required. Mountain bikes should be locked up and always tie your bag to the basket.

Bus
The long-distance bus station is at the Chiang Mai Arcade, on the corner of the super highway and Kaew Nawarat roads, northeast of town, T053-242664. Most companies will provide a transfer service to the station: pick-up points are Anusarn Market, Narawat Bridge, Sang Tawan Cinema and Chiang Inn Hotel Lane. Tuk-tuks and sii-lors wait at the station to take passengers into town. There is an information desk within the main terminal building, with information on all departure times and prices. The tourist police also have a desk here. Regular connections with **Bangkok**'s Northern bus terminal (9-12 hrs), **Phitsanulok** (6 hrs), **Sukhothai** (5 hrs), **Chiang Rai** (3-4 hrs), **Mae Sariang** (4-5 hrs), **Mae Hong Son** (8-9 hrs), **Pai** (4 hrs), **Nan** (6 hrs) and other northern towns. A number of tour companies organize coaches to the capital; these are concentrated in the Anusarn Market area and usually provide transport to the Arcade terminal, from where the buses depart. Buses to closer destinations (such as **Mae Rim, Phrao, Chiang Dao, Fang, Tha Ton** and **Lamphun**) go from Chotana Rd, north of Chang Puak Gate. For **Pasang**, there are direct buses from the Arcade Bus Station, or catch a bus to Lamphun (1 hr, ฿12) and then a connecting bus to Pasang (45 mins, ฿15). For **Bor Sang** and **San Kamphaeng** take a red bus running along the north side of Charoen Muang Rd, opposite the San Pa Khoi Market east of the Narawat Bridge, or take a bus from Chiang Puak Gate.

Car or jeep hire
Rates start at ฿800-1800 per day, ฿6,000 per week. Many guesthouses will arrange rental or there are outfits along Chaiyaphum and Moon Muang roads. National and Avis are slightly more expensive, but are more reliable.
Avis, Royal Princess Hotel, T053-281033, or the airport, T053-201574. **North Wheels**, 127/2 Moon Muang Rd, T053-216189, www.northwheels.com. Some of the cars have seen better days, but rates are competitive here and they are a local operator who have been established for at

From Chiang Mai Arcade Bus Station

Bus No & Company	Destination	Length (hours)	Distance (km)	Prices (Baht) Non A/c	A/c Std	A/c Lux	VIP
99/Orange	Bangkok	10	726	190	287	369	570
166/Green	Chiang Rai (new route)	3	194	66	92	119	
148/Green	Chiang Rai (old route)	6	337	79			
166/Green	Chiang Saen & Golden Triangle	5	265	83			
619/Green	Mae Sai	4	256	83	116	149	
170/Orange	Mae Hong Son (Via Mae Sariang)	8	359	115	206	239	
612/Orange	Pai	4	137	45	93		
617/Green	Chiang Khong	6	337	108	151	194	
169/Green	Phrae	4	216	65	91	117	
169/Green	Nan	6	338	114	160	205	
152/Green	Lampang	2	97	29			
672/Green	Mae Sot (via Tak)	6	393	115		207	
155/Orange	Pitsanulok (old route)	6	428	126	176	227	
623/Orange	Pitsanulok (new route)	6	352	104			
155/Orange	Sukhothai	5	373	109	153	196	
636/Orange	Udon Thani (via Loei)	12	712	205		369	
635/Blue	Nakhon Ratchasima/Korat	12	756	218		392	
587/Blue	Ubon Ratchathani	15	1055	300		540	
659/Blue	Rayong (via Pattaya)	15	990	282		575	

least a decade. **SMT Rent-a-car** (aka National), Amari Rincome hotel, smtcar@samart.co.th.

Motorbike

The wearing of helmets in Chiang Mai city is compulsory (but you wouldn't know it). Hire along Chaiyuphum and Moon Muang roads and at many guesthouses. Rates start at around ฿150-200 for a Honda Dream and rise up to ฿1,200 for a choppers and sports bikes. Insurance is not available for small motorbikes and most policies only protect you from 50% of the repair costs.

Ladda Motorcycle Rental, Moon Muang Soi 2 (at the Panda Guest House). **POP**, 51 Kotchasan Rd, T053-276014, ฿250 for 24 hrs.

Saamlor, sii-lor and tuk-tuk

Saamlor: ฿8-10 within city, ฿20 for longer distances.

Sii-lor ('4 wheels'): these converted red pick-ups are known as songthaews ('2 rows') in most other towns, but in Chiang Mai they are referred to as sii-lors. They are the most common means of transport around town. Travelling on regular routes costs ฿10, ฿20-30 if you want them to take you somewhere off their route. Before boarding, tell the driver where you want to go and they will either say

'yes' or, if it's not on the route, they will quote you a price for the trip. Use landmarks (such as hotels, bridges, gates etc) rather than street names as a guide for where you want to go. Tuk-tuk: minimum ฿20 per trip, ฿40-60 for longer journeys.

Train

The station is in the east of the town, on Charoen Muang Rd, across the Ping River. Ticket office open 0500-2100. Train information, T053-244795; reservations T053-242094. For more information on trains from Bangkok, see page 50.

Left luggage 0600-1800, ฿5 per bag for first 5 days, ฿10 per bag from then on.

Transport into town: frequent songthaews and tuk-tuks, or take city bus no 1, 3 or 6 which stop outside the station. Regular connections with **Bangkok**'s Hualamphong station and towns along the route (11-15 hrs). The overnight Special Express train (1st- and 2nd-class sleepers only, fan or a/c, T02-4911193) leaves Bangkok at 1800 and arrives in Chiang Mai at 0710, whilst the Sprinter (2nd-class a/c carriage only) leaves at 1925 and arrives at 0720, the Nakornping Special Express (1st and 2nd class sleeper only, T02-6111193) leaves at 1940, arriving at 0905, and the Rapid Train (2nd- and 3rd-class only, T02-161471) leaves at 2200 and arrives in Chiang Mai at 1305.

Lampang *p235, map p236*

Air

The airport is on the south edge of town, off Prabhat Rd. Daily flights to **Bangkok** via **Phitsanulok**.

Airline offices THAI, 314 Sanambin Rd, T054-217078.

Bus

Station is on Route 1, just east of the railway line (15-min walk to town centre). It is possible to leave luggage at the information counter in the terminal. Regular connections with **Bangkok**'s Northern bus terminal (9 hrs), **Chiang Mai** (2 hrs), **Chiang Rai**, **Sukhothai**, **Tak** and **Phitsanulok**. Buses from Chiang Mai leave from the Old Chiang Mai-Lamphun Rd, near the tourist office. Buses also go east to **Phrae** (2½ hrs) and on to **Nan**; these leave throughout the day, about one every hour.

Horse-drawn carriages

฿80/120 for a tour around town. They generally take 2 routes, the cheaper one takes about 20 mins, the more expensive 45 mins or ฿120 per hr.

Saamlor

฿10 around town, ฿50 per hr to hire.

Songthaew

Run routes around town (although these are flexibly interpreted); the rop muang or rop wiang ('around town') are the most useful (฿10 anywhere in town).

Train

Station is on the west side of town, at the end of Surain Rd. Regular connections with **Bangkok** (12 hrs) and **Chiang Mai** (2 hrs).

Doi Inthanon *p238*

Take a yellow songthaew for the 58 km from Chiang Mai Gate to **Chom Thong** (฿10). From Chom Thong market, take another yellow songthaew to the **Mae Klang Falls** (฿5) or the **Wachiratan Falls** (฿10). To reach **Mae Ya Falls** and Doi Inthanon **summit**, a songthaew must be chartered (this will seat 10 people); ฿350 and ฿500 respectively.

Directory

Chiang Mai *p222, maps p224, p227 and p228*

Banks Several banks on Tha Phae Rd and plenty of exchange services along Chang Klang and Tha Phae roads. Many exchange booths open daily 0800-2000. Most banks offer a safety deposit service (useful for leaving valuables when embarking on a trek), expect to pay about ฿200 per month. Good rates at SK, 73/8 Charoen Prathet Rd. **Dentists** Have excellent reputations. Two recommended clinics are **Seventh Day Adventist Clinic**, Doi Saket Rd, T053-491813, and **Dr Pramote's Clinic**, 206 Vichayanon Rd, T053-234453. Ram Hospital also has a good clinic. **Embassies and consulates** Australia, 165 Sirimungklajarn Rd, T053-213473, F219726. **French Honorary Consulate**, 138 Charoen Prathet Rd, T053-281466, F215719. **India**, 113 Bamrungrat Rd, T053-243066. **Japan**, Suite 104-107, Airport Business Park, 90 Mahidol

Rd, T053-203367. **People's Republic of China**, 111 Changlor Rd, T053-200525, F274614. **Sweden**, The International Hotel, 11 Sermsute Rd, T053-220844, F210877. **UK**,198 Bumrungrat Rd, T053-263015, F203408. **USA**, 387 Vichayanon Rd, T053-252629, F252633.

Internet There are dozens of internet places all around town, ฿1-2 per min in tourist areas.

Language schools AUA, 73 Rachdamnern Rd, T053-278407, F211973. For a more serious look at the Thai language, AUA teaches in 60-hr modules, it also offers some conversation classes. **CEC**, Nimanhaemin Rd, west side, T053-895202. Open 0800-2100, private tuition possible here for around ฿200 per hr. **Watana Language Centre**, Phra Pokklao Rd, T053-278464, 0900-2000, ฿20 per hr and learn about Thai culture. **Libraries** 21/1 Rachmanka Rd, Soi 2. Open Mon-Sat 0800-1700. Advice on routes, books on Thailand and novels available. Chiang Mai University's **Tribal Research Institute** is a useful information source for people going trekking – see page 254. **Raintree Resource Centre**, Charoenrat Rd (by Nawarat Bridge). Small English-language lending library, daily 1000-1200.

Medical services Chiang Mai's medical services have a good reputation. The most popular expat hospital is **Ram**, where there is 24-hr service available and good English-speaking doctors. **Chiang Mai Ram Hospital**, Boonruangrit Rd, T053-224851/224881. **McCormick Hospital**, Kaew Nawarat Rd, T053-241010, **Malaria Centre**, Boonruangrit Rd, north of Suan Dok Gate. Outpatient fees around ฿100-140, emergency fees are not exorbitant either.

Places of worship Chiang Mai **Community Church**, Charoen Rasada Rd. Services on Sun at 1600 and 1800 (children of all ages cared for) in English. **Christian Church of Thailand**, Kaew Nawarat Rd. English service on Sun 1700. **Seven Fountains Catholic Chapel**, 97 Huay Kaew Rd. English service on Sun 0930.

Post office General Post Office, Charoen Muang Rd (west of the railway station), telegram counter open daily 24 hrs, T053-241056. Chiang Mai's other main post office is the **Mae Ping Post Office** on Praisani Rd, near the Nawarat Bridge. This post office has a packing service and is more conveniently situated than the GPO out near the train station. It also offers an international telephone facility. Other post offices include: **Phra Singh Post Office**, near Wat Phra Singh, **Sriphum Post Office**, on Phra Pokklao Rd, **Night Bazaar Post Office**, in the basement of the bazaar, Chang Klang Rd, open until 2300, **Rachdamnern Post Office** (opposite JJ's, by Tha Phae Gate), convenient for many guesthouses on Moon Muang Rd, packing service available, open daily 0830-2200. Post office at the airport offers international telephone services. Many travel agents in town offer overseas call and fax services.

Telephone International calls can be made from many tour companies; the post offices on Charoen Muang and Praisani roads also have international telephone services.

Useful addresses Customs Office, T053-277510, F053-277510. **Fire Emergency**: T199. **Immigration**: Fang Rd, 300 m before the entrance to the airport, T053-277510. Open Mon-Fri 0830-1200, 1300-1630 (visa extensions possible, see page 27). **Police** corner of Phra Singh and Jhaban roads. **Police Emergency**: T191. **Samaritans** T053-274150, hotline counselling centre. **Tourist Police**: in the same building as the TAT office on the Chiang Mai-Lamphon Rd, T248974, at the Arcade Bus Station, the night market and at the airport.

Lampang *p235, map p236*

Banks Siam Commercial, Chatchai Rd. **Thai Farmers**, 284/8 Chatchai Rd. **Thai Military**, 173-75 Chatchai Rd. **Medical services** **Khelang Nakom Hospital**, Phahonyothin Rd (near Lampang Wiengthong Hotel), T054-217045. **Post office** Surain Rd (opposite the railway station).

Western loop: Pai, Mae Hong Son and Mae Sariang

Some of the most spectacular scenery in Thailand lies to the west of Chiang Mai, where the Tenasserim range divides Burma from Thailand. Travelling northwest from Chiang Mai on Route 107, then Route 108, the road passes through the Mae Sa Valley to the popular backpacker and trekking town of Pai, a distance of 140 km. From Pai to Soppong is more stunning scenery, then onto the hill town of Mae Hong Son, a centre for trekking and home to fine Burmese-style wats. Due south to Mae Sariang (160 km from Mae Hong Son), close to the Burmese border, there is some excellent trekking, then the road follows narrow river valleys to Doi Inthanon, one of the country's most famous peaks and national parks. *»» For Sleeping, Eating and other listings, pages 265-272.*

Pai

→ Colour map 1, grid A2.

The road from Chiang Mai winds its way through scintilating landscapes and thick forest until the view unfolds into a broad valley. In the middle, encircled by handsome, high ridges, sits Pai – a travellers' oasis. This is a de-facto backpacker town, though hip young city dwellers from Bangkok are slowly catching onto the areas' beauty, facilities, hot springs and diversity – Lisu, Karen, Shan, Red Lahu,

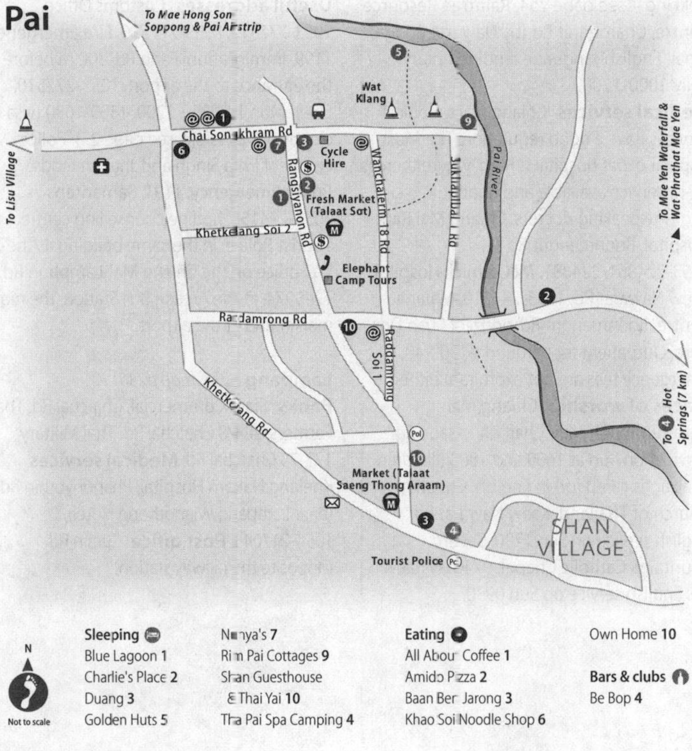

Kuomintang-Chinese are all represented. There's some excellent trekking, superb rafting, a plethora of places to get massaged and pummelled, some great food and the town still manages to retain a sense of charm. The range of accommodation is huge – everything from boutique spa resorts through to cheap and nasty huts populated with wasted travellers. All this makes Pai seductive to the visitor who likes to consume their experience rather create it. Don't come here thinking you're going to get an authentic slice of Thai life. This is a generic Khao San Road-style experience, though, admittedly, in very pleasant surroundings.

The Thai-Burmese border is heavily mined and visitors should not hike without a guide. This applies particularly to Pang Ma Pha and Pai districts.

There are two markets in town – the talaat sot (fresh market) on Rangsiyanon Road and the talaat saeng thong araam on Khetkelang Road. The finest monastery in town is Thai Yai-style **Wat Klang** near the bus station. There's another monastery, **Wat Phrathat Mae Yen**, about 1½ km east of town, on a hill. Head another 3 km east and you'll arrive at Pai's famous **hot springs**. The hot sulphurous water bubbles up through a systems of streams – bring a towel and jump in. There's also a campsite here.

Lisu, **Shan**, **Red Lahu** and **Kuomintang-Chinese villages** are all in the vicinity. Most guesthouses provide rough maps detailing hilltribe villages, **hot springs**, **caves**, **waterfalls** and other sights. See Hilltribes and trekking, Essentials page 71 and Background page 664, see also activities and tours for information on **trekking**, **rafting**, **elephant safaris**, **cookery** and **aromatherapy classes**.

Soppong

→ *Colour map 1, grid A2.*

Soppong, or Phang Ma Pha, is a small way station between Pai and Mae Hong Son. It is slowly metamorphising into an alternative to Pai – there's no real backpacker 'scene' here though there a few great guesthouses offering a decent array of trekking services. Many people come here to trek and explore the surrounding countryside. Most of the guesthouses organize treks and this is one of the best bases hereabouts. Local villages include Lisu, Black and Red Lahu, and Shan. This is also a good place to escape to if what you want to do is nothing. The journey from Pai to Soppong is stunning with magnificent views. The road winds through beautiful cultivated valleys and forest.

Around Soppong

Guesthouses provide maps of the surrounding countryside and villages, with tracks marked. The main 'sight' hereabouts is **Lod Cave** (**Tham Lod**) ⓘ *0800-1700; to explore the accessible areas of the cave system takes around 2 hrs; guides hire out their services – and their lamps – to take visitors through the cave, which has a large stream running through it, rafts are available to traverse the stream; there is also a rather poor restaurant here*, about 10 km from town. The cave (in fact a series of three accessible caves) has been used for habitation since prehistoric times and is a small part of what is presumed to be one of the largest cave systems in northern Thailand.

Mae Lanna is 6 km off the Soppong-Mae Hong Son Road, about 10 km along Route 1095 towards Mae Hong Son (after Phangmapha), ⓘ *take a bus towards Mae Hong Son and get off at the turn-off for Mae Lanna (after Phongmapha); pick-ups run the 6 km (steeply) up to the village – or walk.* The area offers limestone caves, good forest walks and stunning limestone scenery. There are hiking trails between Soppong and Mae Lanna, a quiet, highland Shan village/town – guesthouses in Soppong provide sketch maps of the area.

Mae Hong Son → *Colour map 1, grid A1.*

Mae Hong Son lies in a forested valley, surrounded by soaring verdant hills and just about lives up to its claim to being the 'Switzerland of Thailand'. The road from Pai is continuous switchback, cutting through spectacular scenery and passing by the diverse ethnicities that populate the area. On a clear day, the short flight from Chiang Mai is breathtaking – the plane crosses a range of high hills before spiralling down into a tight series of continuous banks, depositing its passengers almost in the middle of the town.

An excellent centre for trekking, the town is changing rapidly (some would say has changed) from a backpackers' hideaway to a tour centre, with the construction of two major hotels and a proliferation of 'resort'-style hotels. Despite this, Mae Hong Son still manages to retain peaceful, upland vibe.

Ins and outs

Getting there There are regular flights to/from Chiang Mai. You can easily walk from the airport to the town. The bus station is at the northern end of town; there are plenty of connections with Chiang Mai, other destinations in this area of western Thailand and Bangkok's Northern bus terminal. ▸▸ *See Transport, page 271, for further details.*

Getting around Mae Hong Son is small enough to walk around. It is a friendly, accessible and amenable place.

Best time to visit During the cool season (December-February), when the days are warm and clear and the nights are fresh, you'll need a sweater as evening temperatures can get as low as 2°C.

Tourist information There is a poor tourist information booth at the night market.

Background

Mae Hong Son Province is about as far removed from 'Thailand' as you are likely to get, with only an estimated 2% of the population here being ethnic Thais. The great majority belong to one of the various hilltribes: mostly Karen, but also Lisu, Hmong and Lahu.

Mae Hong Son has always been caught between the competing powers of Burma and Siam/Thailand. For much of recent history the area has been under the (loose) control of various Burmese kingdoms. The influence of Burmese culture is also clearly reflected in the architecture of the town's many monasteries.

Mae Hong Son also has a murky reputation for illegal logging; this area has some of the richest forests in the country. At the beginning of 1998, revelations about an alleged ฿5,000 mn bribe to officials of the Royal Forestry Department, to overlook logging in the Salween conservation area, surfaced.

Sights

Most postcards of the town picture the lake, with **Wat Jong Klang**, a Burmese wat, in the background. It is particularly beautiful in the early morning, when mist rises off the lake. Wat Jong Klang started life as a rest pavilion for monks on pilgrimage, with a wat being built by the Shans living in the area between 1867 and 1871. The monastery contains some 50 carved Burmese wooden dolls (or tukata) depicting characters from the Jataka stories (as well as a series of mediocre painted glass panels. In the same compound, is **Wat Jong Kham**, which contains a large seated Buddha. **Wat Hua Wiang**, next to the market (see below), contains an important Burmese-style brass Buddha image – the Phra Chao Phla La Khaeng. It is said that the image was cast in nine pieces in Burma and transported to Mae Hong Son along the Pai River.

Doi Kong Mu, the hill overlooking the town, provides superb views of the valley and is home to the Burmese-style **Wat Phrathat Doi Kong Mu**, constructed by the first King of Mae Hong Son in the mid-19th century. At the foot of Doi Kung Mu Hill is **Wat Phra Non**, which contains a 12-m-long Burmese-style reclining Buddha. The main fresh market in town is on Phanit Watana Road, next to Wat Hua Wiang. The usual commodities from slippery catfish to synthetic clothing are sold here, together with some produce from Burma. » *For tours and trekking see page 269.*

Around Mae Hong Son

Mae Aw ⓘ *take a songthaew (2 hrs) (from Singhanat Bamrung Rd at about 0800), or arrange a trek*, officially known in Thailand as Ban Rak Thai, is an Hmong and KMT (Kuomintang – the remnants of Chiang Kai Shek's army) village in the mountains, 22 km north of Mae Hong Son, on the border with Burma. (Chiang Kai Shek was the Chinese Republican leader who fought the Communists and then fled to Taiwan when the latter were victorious. Remnants of his army and supporters also took refuge in Thailand.) There are stunning views over Burma and the trip here is almost as worthwhile as the arriving.

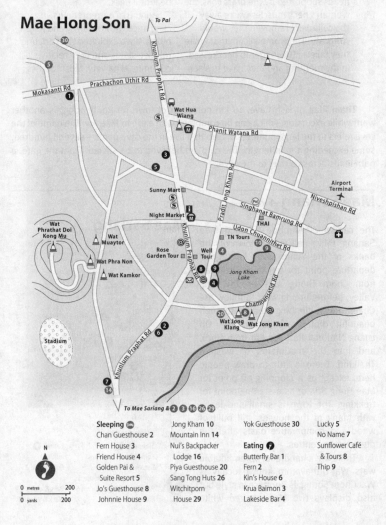

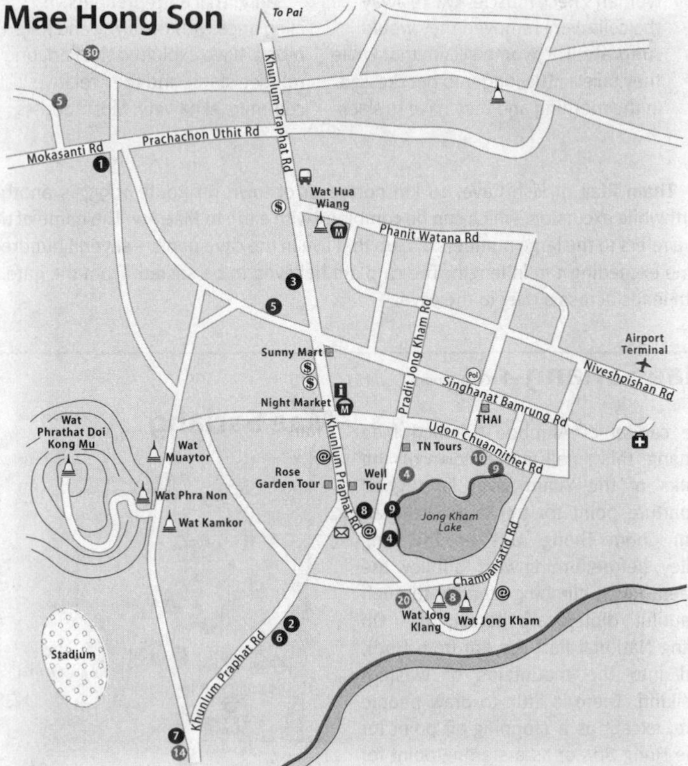

Sleeping
Chan Guesthouse 2
Fern House 3
Friend House 4
Golden Pai & Suite Resort 5
Jo's Guesthouse 8
Johnnie House 9
Jong Kham 10
Mountain Inn 14
Nui's Backpacker Lodge 16
Piya Guesthouse 20
Sang Tong Huts 26
Witchitporn House 29
Yok Guesthouse 30

Eating
Butterfly Bar 1
Fern 2
Kin's House 6
Krua Baimon 3
Lakeside Bar 4
Lucky 5
No Name 7
Sunflower Café & Tours 8
Thip 9

N
0 metres 200
0 yards 200

The Selling of the Padaung or 'Long-Necked Karen'

The Padaung, a Burmese people from the state of Kayah, are better known as the 'Long-Necked Karen' or, derogatorily, as the 'giraffe people'. Forced out of Burma, they have become refugees in Thailand and objects of tourist fascination. Their name says it all: female Padaung 'lengthen' their necks using brass rings, which they add from the age of five. An adult Padaung can have a neck 30 cm long and be weighed down with 5 kg, or more, of brass. Their heads supported by the brass coils, the women's neck muscles waste away – if the coils were removed they would suffocate. The women claim that while they take a little longer to get dressed in the morning and they have to sleep with a supportive bamboo pillow, they are otherwise able to lead full and productive lives.

Some Padaung claim that the brass rings arose from the need to protect from tiger attack. Another explanation is that the practice deliberately disfigured Padaung women so they would not be taken to the Burmese court as concubines or prostitutes. A third reason relates to a mythical Padaung dragon; the lengthening mimics the dragon's long and beautiful neck.

Sadly, Thai entrepreneurs, in allegiance with the army and Karen rebels, have exploited the Padaung's refugee status and their relative commercial naivety. Most tourists

Tham Plaa or Fish Cave, 16 km northeast of town off Route 1095, is another worthwhile excursion, which can be combined with a trip to Mae Aw. The name of the cave refers to the large numbers of carp that live in the cave pools – several hundred, some exceeding 1 m in length. The carp are believed to be sacred. From the gate, a path leads across a river to the cave.

Mae Sariang → *Colour map 1, grid B1.*

The capital of Amphoe (District) Mae Sariang, this small market town on the banks of the Yuam River is a good departure point for trekking. The road from Chom Thong runs up the Ping Valley, before turning west to follow the Chaem River, climbing steadily through beautiful dipterocarp forest, the Op Luang National Park (17 km from Hod), and into the mountains of western Thailand. There is little to draw people here, except as a stopping-off point for Mae Hong Son or as a starting point for trekking. The town is small and leafy, with many of the houses still built of wood – a comparative oasis after the dusty urban centres.

There are a handful of unremarkable wats. Wat Utthayarom, known locally as Wat Chom Soong, is Burmese in style but also displays two Mon-inspired white

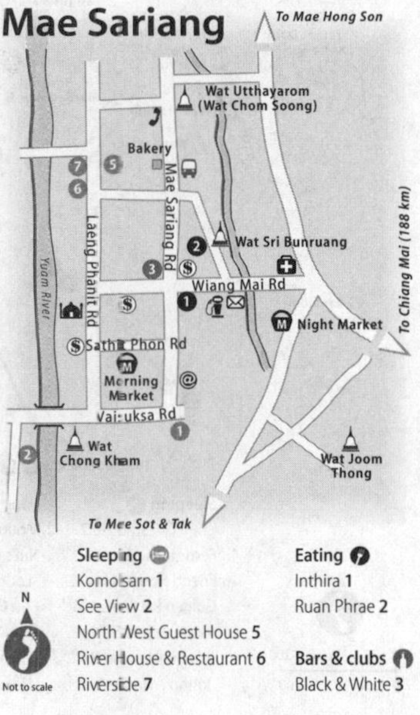
Mae Sariang
To Mae Hong Son
Wat Utthayarom (Wat Chom Soong)
Bakery
Mae Sariang Rd
Laeng Phanit Rd
Yuam River
Wat Sri Bunruang
Wiang Mai Rd
Night Market
To Chiang Mai (188 km)
Sathit Phon Rd
Morning Market
Vaisuksa Rd
Wat Chong Kham
Wat Joom Thong
To Mae Sot & Tak
N
Not to scale

Sleeping
Komolsarn 1
See View 2
North West Guest House 5
River House & Restaurant 6
Riverside 7

Eating
Inthira 1
Ruan Phrae 2

Bars & clubs
Black & White 3

who take tours to the two refugee camps (paying ฿250 to enter the villages) in Mae Hong Son Province leave disgusted at the 'selling' of these people in what can only be called a human display.

Even more tragic and contemptible is the case of a village near Tha Ton, where a small group of Padaung were held against their wishes on land controlled by the Thai army. At the end of 1997, journalist Andrew Drummond quoted from a tape smuggled out by these kidnapped people: "Please come now. Things cannot be any worse. ..I feel so sorry when foreigners come and ask about our children's schooling. They won't let us take our children to school. We cannot eat the food they give us. They shout and scream if we do not make the foreigners [tourists] happy." (Bangkok Post, 8.11.98).

Notwithstanding this particularly tragic and repugnant case, the hard fact is that the Padaung have little else to sell. Most are paid the paltry figure of ฿1,000 a month simply to pose for tourist photographs. Like so many other indigenous peoples in Southeast Asia, the Padaung find themselves caught in a web of poverty, oppression, exploitation and powerlessness. The great irony is that a custom, which had almost died out, has been revived. Every young girl is now bedecked with coils, parents hoping to cash in as unscrupulous tourists search for the exotic.

chedis. Other monasteries include Wat Sri Bunruang (in town) and Wat Joom Thong (on a hill, overlooking town). The latter has a large and recently constructed white seated Buddha image surveying the valley below. The town also has a better stock of wooden shophouses than most Thai towns – that is on Laeng Phanit Road (the river road). The morning market operates from a plot on Sathit Phon Road and there is also an evening market – good for stall food – at the end of Wiang Mai Road.

Trekking, rafting, cave and waterfall visits and elephants rides are also possible, see Activities and tours. See also Hilltribes and trekking, Essentials, page 71 and Background, page 664.

Sleeping

Pai *p260, map p260*
There are about 70 places to stay and accommodation is constantly changing and evolving. The selection here is a cross section of what's available.

B Tha Pai Spa Camping, 2 Mai Hee Rd, T053-693267, www.thapaispa.com. Outside of town near the hot springs, decent bungalows with their own hot springs though it is aimed more at Thai guests.

C Blue Lagoon T053-699824 Well-run place in centre of town. Swimming pool, clean, decent rooms, excellent disabled facilities.

C-D Rim Pai Cottages, 3 Wiang Tai Rd, T053-699133. Good position on the river, small A-frame huts which are clean and cosy. Spotless western toilets, a little overpriced but discounts available in the low season.

D-E Charlie's Place, 3 Winag Pai Rd, T053-699039. One of the larger places in town, with a range of accommodation from dormitory beds to more expensive and less rundown brick bungalows with attached bathrooms, all set in largish garden. Good trekking organized from here.

E Nunya's, Rangsiyanon Rd, T053-699051. 7 clean rooms in 2-storey building set back from the road, upstairs rooms share hot water showers, those on the ground floor have attached clean Thai-style bathrooms, rather overgrown small garden, well run. Treks organized through **Perm Chais Trekking**.

D-F Duang, 3 Rangsiyanon Rd, T053-699101. Opposite bus station, so noisy through the night. Clean and quiet,

friendly English-speaking family run guesthouse. Cheap, clean rooms with shared hot-water showers, good restaurant (excellent coffee and French bread), trekking organized. Changes cash, bicycles for hire and maps provided.

E Shan Guesthouse, Rangsiyanon Rd. Located on the edge of town in a rather exposed position (but with great views), bungalows set in quiet location around a pond, with a Burmese pagoda-esque restaurant in the middle. Bungalows are raised off the ground and made of wood with 'leaf' roofs, good balconies

F Golden Huts, T053-699949. Very quiet, beautiful out of the way location on the riverbank. Quiet and relaxing atmosphere, French owner provides a friendly service. Small but adequate restaurant with good food and great views. Recommended.

Soppong *p261*

B-C Baan Cafe Resort, T053-617081. Sited next to main road, nicely laid-out rooms and bungalows, some with terraces overlooking a river, which can be used to bathe in – cute gardens, friendly, good food. Small shop selling local produce. Recommended.

B-E Soppong River Inn, T053-617107, www.soppong.com. Sited 500 m from village centre towards Mae Hong Son, has a range of great huts, some with verandas overlooking a small gorge. Also offers trekking service, massage and fresh coffee. Friendly and recommended.

C Lemon Hill Guesthouse T053-617039, Centre of village. Adequate huts – good option if everywhere else is full.

E Jungle House, 500 m out of Soppong towards Mae Hong Son, T053-617099. Attractive restaurant, a sprawling place with simple huts, hot water, garden. It also organizes treks.

F Kemarin Garden, a short way down a lane 200 m up the hill towards Pai. Four simple A-frame bungalows, peaceful rural position with views over the hills, hot water showers. Huts and showers are surprisingly clean. Friendly management (but no English spoken). Recommended.

Around Soppong *p261*

If you want to sleep in Mae Lanna there's a selection of guesthouses.

E Mae Lanna Guesthouse (closed Jul-Aug) is a good base from which to explore the surrounding countryside in Mae Lanna itself; the guesthouse is run by a French woman who is an excellent source of information and advice.

F Wilderness Lodge. Remote and basic. This place is west of Phangmapha: get off the bus at Ban Nam Khong, turn off after Nam Khong Bridge.

Mae Hong Son *p262, map p263*

A Golden Pai and Suite Resort, 285/1 Ban Pang Moo, T053-612265. 33 modern yet traditional Shan- style chalets, well furnished, a/c, private terrace and 30 de luxe rooms. Set in landscaped gardens with 2 swimming pools, open-air restaurant overlooking Pai River. Tours organized.

B Fern House, 2 km from Highway 108 at the turn off for Ban Nua Hum Mae Sakut Village (5 km from town), T053-611374, ferngroup@softhome.net. Wooden bungalows built on rice paddies, Shan style. Simple yet comfortable and tasteful. Set in lovely grounds, friendly and helpful staff; a good eco-friendly place, with good walks from here.

B Mountain Inn, 112 Khunlum Praphat Rd, T053-611502, F612284. A/c, well thought out rooms surround an atmospheric garden. Friendly management and also serves good food (see Eating). Recommended.

B-D Sang Tong Huts, T053-620680, sangtonghuts@hotmail.com. Secluded for a range of huts northwest of town (near **Yok** Guesthouse), with great views. Dining area with great food and hilltribe coffee. Friendly and helpful owners. Recommended.

C Piya Guesthouse, 1 Soi 3 Khunlum Praphat Rd, T053-611260. In a garden setting, 14 clean rooms next to the lake, all with a/c and TV. Some with double beds, and others twin bedded. Restaurant at front has a great view of the lake – a nice place to sit and relax.

D Wichitporn House, on main road parallel to and north of airstrip, T053-612163. 10 clean twin rooms, with hot shower in 2 longhouses set around nice garden.

D-E Friend House, 20 Pradit Jong Kham Rd, T053-620119, F620060. Set back from the road, 10 rooms in this teak house are very clean with solid wooden floors, the shared showers are even cleaner, upstairs rooms

have a view of the lake, well managed and carefully maintained, small café downstairs for breakfast, laundry service. Recommended.

D-E Johnnie House, 5/2 Udon Chuannithet Rd, T053-611667. Peaceful position on the lakeside, 7 spotlessly clean and simple rooms, shared hot water showers. Breakfast menu, laundry facilities. Friendly and quiet.

D-F Jo's Guesthouse, 3 Chamnansatid Rd, T053-612417. Small personal place, 6 small clean rooms with mattresses on the floor and fans in an old teak house. More expensive rooms have own hot shower.

E Chan Guesthouse, first left after a bridge on Khunlum Prapaht Rd, heading north towards Pai, T053-620432. Clean but small fan rooms, 3 upstairs and 3 down in a traditional wooden family house. Communal showers, nice atmosphere.

E Jong Kham, on Udon Chuannithet Rd, T053-611420, lakeside, run-down bamboo bungalows with 'leaf' roofs (good for softening the sound of the rain) and some cheaper rooms in the main house, largish garden, very popular.

E Mae Hong Son Hotel, up a quiet street just north and parallel to the airstrip, T053-612510. 8 clean, good sized rooms, all with 2 single beds, with fan and shower, balcony upstairs. Small restaurant, friendly owner.

E Yok Guesthouse, 14 Sri Mongkol Rd, T053-611532. Tucked away behind a wat, this is a great place. Very clean, comfortable and has a peaceful little garden. Small restaurant with good food. Free transport to and from the bus station and airport.

F Nui's Backpacker Lodge, on corner before **Mae Hong Son Guest House**. 5 concrete and bamboo huts with shower and double bed. Laundry service and some food. Nui speaks English.

Mae Sariang *p264, map p264*

There are several reasonable guesthouses in Mae Sariang – most are a 5- to 15-min walk from the bus station.

C Komolsarn Hotel, Mae Sariang Rd, T053-681524, F681204. South of the centre, this reasonably priced hotel has good facilities and several en suite rooms.

C River House Hotel, Laeng Phanit Rd (next to **Riverside**, see below). New hotel, clean and inviting rooms with great views from the balconies and good facilities. There is an excellent restaurant with riverside seating.

D- E Riverside, 85/1 Laeng Phanit Rd, T053-681188. A 5-min stroll from the bus station, on the riverfront, this attractive building has large, clean rooms by the river. Wonderful views from breakfast/seating area. This remains a popular choice for travellers and as a result is a good source of information. The owner has plans to expand across the river, building a swing bridge and long-stay bungalows.

E North West Guest House, 87/1 Laeng Phanit Rd, T053-332464, info@faz.co.th. A new spick-and-span guesthouse under the same management as **River House hotel** across the road. Recommended.

E See View, 70 Wiang Mai Rd (across the river – and overlooking it – on the edge of town), T053-681556. Good sized rooms in stone bungalows, smaller wooden rooms also available, with shared facilities. The place is quiet and peaceful but shabby. It is a good source of information, partly because the owner speaks good English and is very helpful.

Eating

Pai *p260, map p260*

International

Amido Pizza, Ratdamrong Rd. Awesome pizza, pasta and lasagne made with love. Just over bridge on way to hot springs.

Own Home Restaurant, Ratdamrong Rd. Some Thai dishes, along with travellers' fare including tortillas, banana porridge, shakes, pizzas, moussaka and sandwiches.

Thai Yai, Rangsiyanon Rd, northern end, not far from the **Shan Guesthouse**. Thai and international, good quiche, wholemeal bread etc.

Thai

Baan Ben Jarong, edge of town, on the way to Chiang Mai, high-class Thai cuisine – exceptional and one of the best places to eat in the area. Highly recommended.

There are some very good noodle places in town. By the post office on Khetkelang Rd is an excellent restaurant specializing in duck noodle soup. At the corner of Khetkelang and Chai Songkhram roads, one serves superb Khao Soi - spicy Northern noodles.

Bakeries

All About Coffee is an arty café, with huge open chicken and cashew sandwiches and a large range of filter coffees and herbal teas.

Oy Bakery. In front of day market, good bread, cheese and other provisions.

Night market

Hardly a market as there is only a handful of stalls, but good pancakes and other food available.

Mae Hong Son *p262, map p263*

The largest concentration of restaurants is on Khunlum Praphat Rd. The cheapest place to eat is in the night market, also on Khunlum Praphat Rd. Internet cafés are proliferating on the main street among the coffee shops, see Directory below.

International

KK Bakery, near Pen Porn House. Fresh-baked cakes and bread, small selection of Thai dishes, set breakfasts, snacks and drinks.

Reaun Pap Restaurant, Singhanat Bamrung Rd. Good atmosphere, decor and music. Real coffee and good orange juice.

Sunflower Café and Tours, 2/1 Khunlum Phraphat Soi 3, T053-620549, sunctmhs@cscoms.com. Cosy café run by an Australian/Thai couple, popular with farangs. Good spot for breakfast and the best bread in town (it has its own bakery), good coffee, internet access, organizes tours and a great source of information.

Thai/Chinese

99 Restaurant, on the road out of town near the stadium. Thai dishes at reasonable prices, set breakfast, barbecue, curries and salads. Open-air roadside place.

Baby Corn Restaurant, Khunlum Praphat Rd (at the traffic lights), Thai rice and noodles, small menu but very cheap. Good shakes.

Fern Restaurant, 87 Khunlum Praphat Rd. Large restaurant on road towards Mae Sariang. Smart, unpretentious and affordable, mostly Thai dishes including good frog, spicy salads and crispy fish, also ice creams.

Kin's House, 89 Khunlum Praphat Rd (past Fern Restaurant). Selection of traditional and local Thai cuisine and western food. Nice decor, café/bar atmosphere.

Krua Baimon, Khunlun Praphat Rd. Good value Thai food, often shows Western films. Friendly owner.

Lakeside Bar, 2/3 Khunlum Praphat Rd. Bar and restaurant with tables overlooking the lake, excellent place to eat and drink in the evening.

Lucky Restaurant, 5 Singhanat Bamrung Rd. Excellent restaurant in wooden house. Good atmosphere and decor and choice of Thai and Western dishes, specialities include deep-fried catfish and steaks, also serves breakfast.

Mountain Inn, 112 Khunlum Praphat Rd, (see Sleeping) serves great Thai grub in its romantic garden.

Paa Dim, Khunlum Praphat Rd (near the 7-Eleven), popular with locals, varied but small selection of Thai dishes, good portions and cheap.

Restaurant (with no name), next to the Mountain Inn, sells a range of very authentic hilltribe dishes that are extremely popular with locals. The owner will let you taste before you buy.

Thip Restaurant, Pradit Jong Klang Rd (next to the lake). A newer touristy restaurant with upstairs balcony overlooking lake. Reasonable prices and reasonable food.

Ton Restaurant, Pradit Jong Klang Rd (near the lake). Great little local roadside restaurant run by Ton. Good Thai dishes (especially red and green curries), sticky rice, salads and soups. Menu is in French and English. Extensive, cheap and tasty.

Foodstalls

Night market, also on Khunlum Praphat Rd.

Mae Sariang *p264, map p264*

Inthira Restaurant, Wiang Mai Rd. Tasty dishes and good prices, probably the best Chinese/Thai restaurant in town. Open for breakfast, frog specialities.

River House Restaurant, Laeng Phanit Rd, excellent range of food at reasonable prices in superb surroundings.

Ruan Phrae, down soi to Wat Sri Bunruang, off Wiang Mai Rd. Thai and Chinese. Recommended.

Foodstalls

At the night market on Wiang Mai Rd (about 1 km from the centre of town).

Bars and clubs

Pai *p260, map p260*
Be Bop, Rangsiyanon Rd. Live music most nights, extremely popular with travellers. Great atmosphere, serves most western spirits.
Satang Bar, next to the bus stop. Sells Thai herbal whiskey (฿8 a shot), which is allegedly medicinal, claiming to increase blood circulation, improve your health, increase bodily strength, relieve backache, aid sleep and also act as a poor man's Viagra.

Mae Hong Son *p262, map p263*
Butterfly, at the crossroads on the way to Mae Kong Son Guesthouse, the best bar in town. A swanky Thai Lounging bar with karaoke, big 1970s style kitsch chairs, live music and open as long as you care to drink.
Lakeside Bar, 2/3 Khunlum Praphat Rd. See Eating above for details.

Mae Sariang *p264, map p264*
Black and White Bar, al fresco ambience and some live music.

Festivals and events

Mae Hong Son *p262*
Apr (movable, beginning of month) Poi Sang Long, young novices (10-16 years old) are ordained into the monkhood. Beforehand, they are dressed up as princes and on the following day there is a colourful procession through town starting from Wat Kham Ko.

Shopping

Pai *p260*
Books
Back Trax Tour and Trekking, 67/1 Rungsiyanon Rd, rents, sells and exchanges English language books.

Mae Hong Son *p262*
Books
Asia Books, Khunlum Praphat Rd (next to Panorama Hotel), for English-language novels and magazines.

Handicrafts
Chokeadradet, 645 Khunlum Praphat Rd, for antiques, tribal handicrafts and junk. Recommended. Also a number of places on Singhanat Bamrung Rd. **Thai Handicraft Centre**, Khunlum Praphat Rd.

Supermarkets
A 24-hr **7-Eleven** and 2 good supermarkets, both near the crossroads in the centre of town.

Activities and tours

Pai *p260*
Rafting
Thai Adventure Rafting, just past the bus station, T053-699111, www.activethailand.com/rafting. The oldest white-water rafting company in Thailand. It runs unforgettable, professional 2-day expeditions down the Pai River and beyond. It is run by Guy, a friendly Frenchman who has lived in Pai for 17 years. The river is only high enough between Jul and end of Jan, trips start at ฿2200 and include everything from insurance through to food/drinks. There are other companies organizing similar (and cheaper) rafting trips in the area though none match Thai Adventure. Can also organise treks. Avoid nearby Pai Adventure Rafting who are a poor copy of the real thing.

Therapies
Traditional massage Opposite the Rim Pai Cottages, 68 Rachdamrong Rd, excellent massage (฿100-150 per hr) and friendly people. Massage also available at several other places including the **Foundation of Shivaga Kommapaj**.

Tours and trekking
See also Tour operators below.
Many of the guesthouses run treks and there are plenty of companies offering a choice of treks and rafting trips.
Duang Trekking (at Duang Guesthouse) offers basic trekking with all-inclusive prices ranging from ฿1,000-2,000; **PermChais** insists it offers non-tourist treks and will organize rafting and elephant safaris; **Back-Trax Tour and Trekking** organizes treks with Khun Chao, a TAT-registered guide, and also offers Thai cookery courses and lessons in aromatherapy massage; **Lisu Tours and Trekking** has also been

recommended. Average prices are in the region of ฿800-1,000 per day. One- to four-day treks are available. Shop around and talk to people who have recently returned.

Elephant rides (they could hardly be described as 'treks') are also available from various companies, including **Pai Elephant Camp Tours**, 5/3 Rungsiyanon Rd, T053-699286. Khun Thom, the owner, runs a professional set-up and treats her animals with respect. Her elephant camp is out of town towards the hot springs. Recommended – you can even swim with the elephants in the river or ride bare-back.

Tour operators

Back-Trax Tour and Trekking, 67/1 Rungsiyanon Rd.
Duang Trekking, at the Duang Guesthouse.
Karen Tours and Trekking, Rangsiyanon Rd, opposite the market.
Lisu Tours and Trekking, Rangsiyanon Rd, next to the market.
Perm Chais Trekking, contact Nunyas or the office along Raddamrong Rd.

Mae Hong Son *p262*

Therapies

Traditional massage and herbal steam bath is a Mae Hong Son speciality; particularly welcome for those just back from strenuous treks. Available at several places.
Tubtim Thai Massage, next door to the Lakeside Bar, T053-620553, and above Sunny Supermarket (Khunlum Praphat Rd), has been recommended (฿100-150 per hr).

Tours and trekking

See Hilltribes and trekking, Essentials, page 71 and Background, page 665.
There are assorted day tours to such sights as Pha Sua Waterfall, Pang Tong Summer Palace, the KMT village of Mae Aw, Tham Plaa (Fish Cave) and Tham Nam Lot (Water Cave). A number of companies also advertise trips to the 'long-necked' Padaung, which involves a bumpy 1-hr trip to their two villages. Many people deplore this type of tourism: see box page 264. Most guesthouses will organize treks, ranging from trips down the Salween River to the Burmese border to Mae Sot, elephant treks and rafting on the Pai River. Treks can be organized from 1 day to 1 week; the average price is ฿800 per day for a group of at least 4 people (this does not include rafting and elephant rides). There are both dedicated trekking companies, and trekking outfits attached to guesthouses. The former include: **TN Tours**, Pradit Jong Kham Rd; **Rose Garden Tour**, 86/4 Kunlum Praphat, T/F053-611577; **Well Tour**, Khunlum Praphat Rd (near the post office); **Sawasdee Tour**, Khunlum Praphat Rd (by bus station).

Tour operators

The following have been recommended by a long-term resident of Mae Hong Son: **Friend Tour** at Friend Guesthouse, T053-620119. Trekking, bamboo rafting, elephant rides, boat trips.
Rose Garden Tours, 86/4 Khunlum Prapaht Rd, T053-611577. Cultural and ecological tours. French also spoken.
Sunflower Tours, Sunflower Café, eco-conscious birdwatching and nature treks.
TN Tour, 10 Udom Chuannithet Rd, T053-620059. Trekking, jeep adventure, rafting, licensed guides.

Mae Sariang *p264*

Tour operators

Baan Nam Ngao, T053-3110314, www.faz.co.th. Treks, specialist birdwatching and star-gazing trips.
Chan trekking company operates through the Roj Thip Restaurant at 661 Wiang Mai Rd.
The owners of the Riverside Guesthouse organize treks through **Salawin Tours**. Treks include rafting, elephant rides, or visits to caves, waterfalls, Karen villages within the area or to the Burmese border.
The Sea View Resort also organizes treks.

Transport

Pai *p260*

Air

There's a small airstrip just to the north of Pai and several operators are keen to set up regular flights. Something should be up and running by mid-2005, though destinations remain a mystery.

Bicycle

Hire ฿50 per day (mountain bikes) from the shop adjoining the Duang Guesthouse, or

from Nunya's. **Pai Tai Bike Society**, opposite the bus station, has information on routes and surrounding attractions.

Bus

The bus stop is on Chai Songkhram Rd, near the centre of town. Four buses run to **Mae Hong Son** daily (3 hrs) and 4 to **Chiang Mai** (4 hrs) for ฿80. A songthaew is also available and provides a slightly quicker (3 hrs), if more uncomfortable, journey to Chiang Mai. There are 5 connections a day to **Fang** (2½ hrs) via **Mae Ma Lai**. Some Fang buses continue to **Tha Ton**.

Motorbike

Hire ฿80-250 per day from several guesthouses and shops in town. Pick of the bunch is next door to Thai Adventure Rafting with gearless scooters through to dirt bikes – it also offers daily insurance.

Soppong *p261*

Bus

6-7 buses each day (1 a/c) in each direction – west to **Mae Hong Son** (2 hrs), east to **Pai** (1 hr) and **Chiang Mai** (5 hrs).

Motorbike/scooter hire

From shop close to the bus stop though most guesthouses can arrange.

Mae Hong Son *p262*

Air

The airport is to the north of town on Niveshpishan Rd. The airport has an information counter and currency exchange booth, and songthaews are also available for hire. Regular daily connections on THAI with **Chiang Mai** (35 mins).

Airline offices THAI, Singhanat Bamrung Rd, T053-611297.

Bus

Station on Khunlum Praphat Rd, a short walk from town and most guesthouses. There are 2 routes from **Chiang Mai**: the northern, more gruelling route via Pai, or the route from the south, via Mae Sariang. Buses leave through the day in both directions (in total, 7 a day each way, most non-a/c, the first via **Pai** at 0700 (฿48-100 to Pai, ฿94-180 to Chiang Mai) and the first via **Mae Sariang** at 0600 (฿69-124 to Mae Sariang, ฿133-240 to Chiang Mai). The trip to Pai takes 3-3½ hrs; to Mae Sariang, 4 hrs. For the journey all the way to Chiang Mai, the route via Pai takes 8 hrs, via Mae Sariang 9½ hrs. Regular connections with **Bangkok**, 12½ hrs.

Car

Avis, airport, T053-620457, prices from ฿1,400 per day.

Motorbike and jeep

Many places hire out jeeps, motorbikes and scooters. Prices for motorbikes/scooters from ฿150-180 per day (there are a couple of places at the southern end of Khunlum Praphat Rd), jeeps about ฿800-1,000 per day.

Mountain bike

22 Singhanat Bamrun Rd, ฿100 per day (motorbikes also available here).

Tuk-tuk

฿10-20 around town.

Mae Sariang *p264*

Bus

Station is on Mae Sariang Rd in the centre of town, 5 mins' walk from the **Riverside** Guesthouse, next to Wat Jong Sung. 7 buses daily each way to **Chiang Mai** and **Mae Hong Son** (both 4 hrs) and several a/c and non-a/c connections a day with **Bangkok**. The road south to **Mae Sot**, following the Burmese border, though slow (6 hrs), is mainly in good repair although there are 1 or 2 places where it has been allowed to deteriorate. See page 214 for a description. Songthaews depart 4 times a day from the bus station for Mae Sot (6 hrs, ฿150).

Songthaew

To local destinations, congregate at the morning market on Sathit Phon Rd.

Directory

Pai *p260*

Banks Krung Thai Bank, Rangsiyanon Rd (the largest building in town and hard to miss). Open Mon-Fri 0830-1530 (in theory). **Internet** Many internet cafés, mainly concentrated along Chi Songkhram Rd.

Post office Khetkelang Rd. Overseas calls can be made from the office on Rangsiyanon Rd, not far from the fresh market. **Medical services** Pai Hospital, Chai Songkhram Rd (about 500 m from the town centre).

Soppong *p261*
Banks The nearest bank with exchange facilities is 1 hr away in Pai. **Post office** By the Lemon Hill Guesthouse, towards Pai. **Telephone** Domestic calls can be made from the restaurant at the bus stop.

Mae Hong Son *p262*
Banks Five in town, 3 with ATMs. Bank of Ayodhya, 61 Khunlum Praphat Rd. Thai Farmers, 78 Khunlum Praphat Rd. Thai Military Bank, Khunlum Praphat (at intersection with Panit Wattana Rd). Bangkok, Khunlum Praphat Rd (0830-1900). **Medical services** Clinic, Khunlum Praphat Rd. **Hospital** at the eastern end of Singhanat Bamrung Rd. **Internet** Sunflower Café, Mae Hong Son Computer (80 Khunlum Praphat Rd), Reaun Pap Restaurant and in an office over the bridge near the immigration office (the cheapest place). **Post office** Southern end of town, corner of Khunlum Praphat Rd and Soi 3, open Mon-Fri 0830-1630 and Sat-Sun 0900-1200. **Telephone** In new building behind Paa Dim Restaurant, Mon-Sat 0830-1630. **Useful addresses** Immigration Khunlum Praphat Rd (northern end of town, towards Pai). Tourist Police, 1 Rachathampitak Rd, T053-611812 (claim 24 hrs service).

Mae Sariang *p264*
Banks Thai Farmers, 150/1 Wiang Mai Rd. Krung Thai Bank, Laeng Phanit Rd. Thai Military Bank, Wiang Mai Rd (ATM). **Internet** Large internet access point on Mae Sariang Rd. **Post office and telephone** 31/1 Wiang Mai Rd.

Chiang Rai and around

Given the ancient roots of Chiang Rai, the capital of Thailand's most northerly province, there's little here in the way of historical interest, with modern shophouse architecture predominating. There's a lot of accommodation here and most visitors use it as a trekking base and for visiting the towns of the Golden Triangle.

West of Chiang Rai are Tha Thon, a centre for rafting down to Chiang Rai and a good base for trekking.Fang, with some good examples of shophouses, is an opium trafficking centre. ▸▸ *For Sleeping, Eating and other listings, see pages 278-285.*

Ins and outs

Getting there Chiang Rai's airport is 8 km north of the city. There are daily connections with Bangkok and Chiang Mai, and some talk of flights to international destinations in the region. The bus station is in the centre of town (but a fair walk from most of the guesthouses), and there are regular connections with Bangkok, most northern towns including Chiang Mai, and with assorted destinations in the Northeast and Central Plains. Scheduled boats ply the Kok River, upstream to Tha Ton and downstream to Chiang Khong. ▸▸ *See Transport, page 284, for further details.*

Getting around Chiang Rai is a sprawling town and, while walking is fine in the morning and evening, during the day many locals choose to travel by saamlor or songthaew. Most of the area's attractions lie in the surrounding countryside, and there are ample vehicle hire shops offering bicycles, cars, motorbikes and jeeps. **Tourist information** TAT ⓘ *448/16 Singhaklai Rd (near the river, opposite Wat Phra Singh), T053-744674, F717434*. Well-run office, useful town maps and information on trekking and accommodation. Areas of responsibility are Chiang Rai, Phayao, Uttaradit, Phrae and Nan.

Towards Chiang Rai

The new route to Chiang Rai from Chiang Mai cuts through forests and is fast and scenic. There are rather novel European-style country cottages along the way and some good resort-style hotels. See Sleeping. **Mae Suai**, with a hilltop monastery, is at the junction where roads lead south to Chiang Mai, north to Chiang Rai, west to Fang and southeast to Phayao.

Chiang Rai

Background

Chiang Rai was founded in 1268 by King Mengrai, who later moved his capital here. The city became one of the key muang (city states), within the Lanna Kingdom's sphere of control – until Lanna began to disintegrate in the 16th century. Although it is now Thailand's most northerly town, at the time of its foundation Chiang Rai represented the most southerly bulwark against the Mons. It was later conquered by the Burmese and only became part of Thailand again in 1786.

Today, Chiang Rai has ambitious plans for the future. Lying close to what has been termed the 'Golden Rectangle', linking Thailand with Laos, Myanmar and southern China, the city's politicians and businessmen hope to cash in on the opening up of the latter three countries. Always searching for catchy phrases to talk up a nascent idea, they even talk of the 'Five Chiangs strategy' – referring to the five towns of Chiang Tung (or Kengtung in Burma), Chiang Rung (in China), Chiang Thong (in Laos), and Chiang Mai and Chiang Rai (both in Thailand). Roads linking the five are being planned and an EU-style free trade area discussed. Talk, as they say, is cheap; a mini-EU in this peripheral part of Asia seems a distant dream, despite a noticeable increase in cross-border activity.

Sights

The city's finest monastery is **Wat Phra Kaeo**, at the north end of Trairat Road. The wat was probably founded in the 13th century when it was known as Wat Pa-Year. Its change of name came about following divine intervention in 1434 when, local legend recounts, the stupa was struck by lightning to reveal the famous Emerald Buddha or Phra Kaeo, now in residence in Bangkok's Temple of the Emerald Buddha. With this momentos discovery, the wat was renamed Wat Phra Kaeo and was elevated to the status of a royal wat in 1987.

The finest structure here is the bot (straight ahead as you pass through the main gates on Trairat Road) featuring accomplished woodcarving, a pair of fine nagas flanking the entrance way and, inside, a 13th-century image of the Buddha calling the earth goddess to witness. Presumably slightly peeved that the Phra Kaeo itself had been carted off to Bangkok, a rich local Chinese businessman – a Mr Lo – commissioned a Chinese artist to carve a replica image from Canadian jade. The work was undertaken in Beijing to mark the 90th birthday of the Princess Mother and she gave it the gargantuan name Phraphuttaratanakorn Nawutiwatsanusornmong-khon, or The Lord Buddha is the source of the Three Gems of Buddhism. The image was kept in the monastery's bot until a new building, specially designed to house it, had been completed and the image installed in a consecration ceremony held in 1991. The Chiang Rai Phra Kaeo Shrine is behind the bot, with two ponds filled with turtles (set free by people to gain merit) in front of it.

Above Wat Phra Kaeo, perched at the top of a small hill, is **Wat Ngam Muang**, unremarkable save for the views it offers of the city and surrounding countryside. However, historically it is important, as the stupa here contains the ashes of the great King Mengrai (1259-1317). The edifice is currently being renovated and will have a statue of the king placed in front of his ku.

Chiang Rai

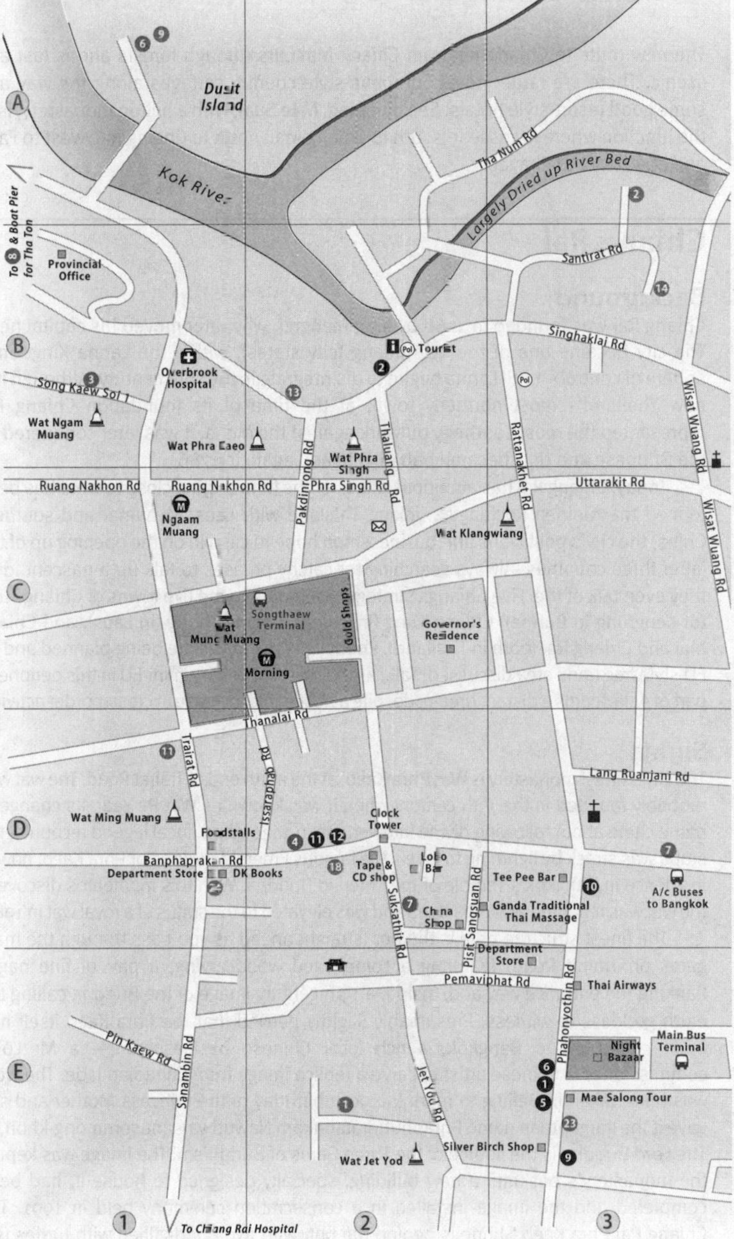

Sleeping

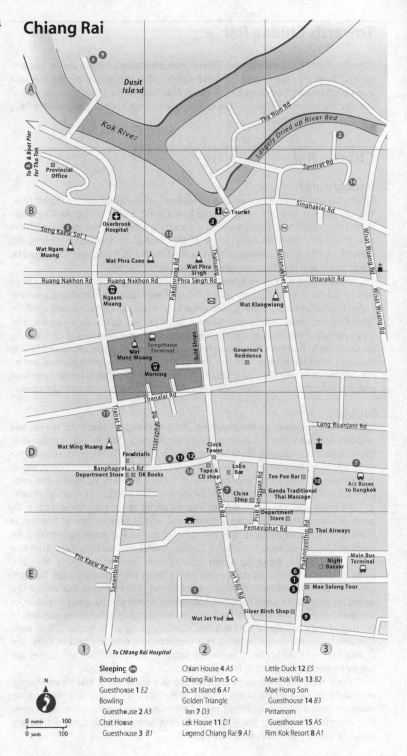

Boonbundan Guesthouse 1 *E2*
Bowling Guesthouse 2 *A3*
Chat House Guesthouse 3 *B1*
Chian House 4 *A5*
Chiang Rai Inn 5 *C4*
Dusit Island 6 *A1*
Golden Triangle Inn 7 *D3*
Lek House 11 *D1*
Legend Chiang Rai 9 *A1*
Little Duck 12 *E5*
Mae Kok Villa 13 *B2*
Mae Hong Son Guesthouse 14 *B3*
Pintamorn Guesthouse 15 *A5*
Rim Kok Resort 8 *A1*

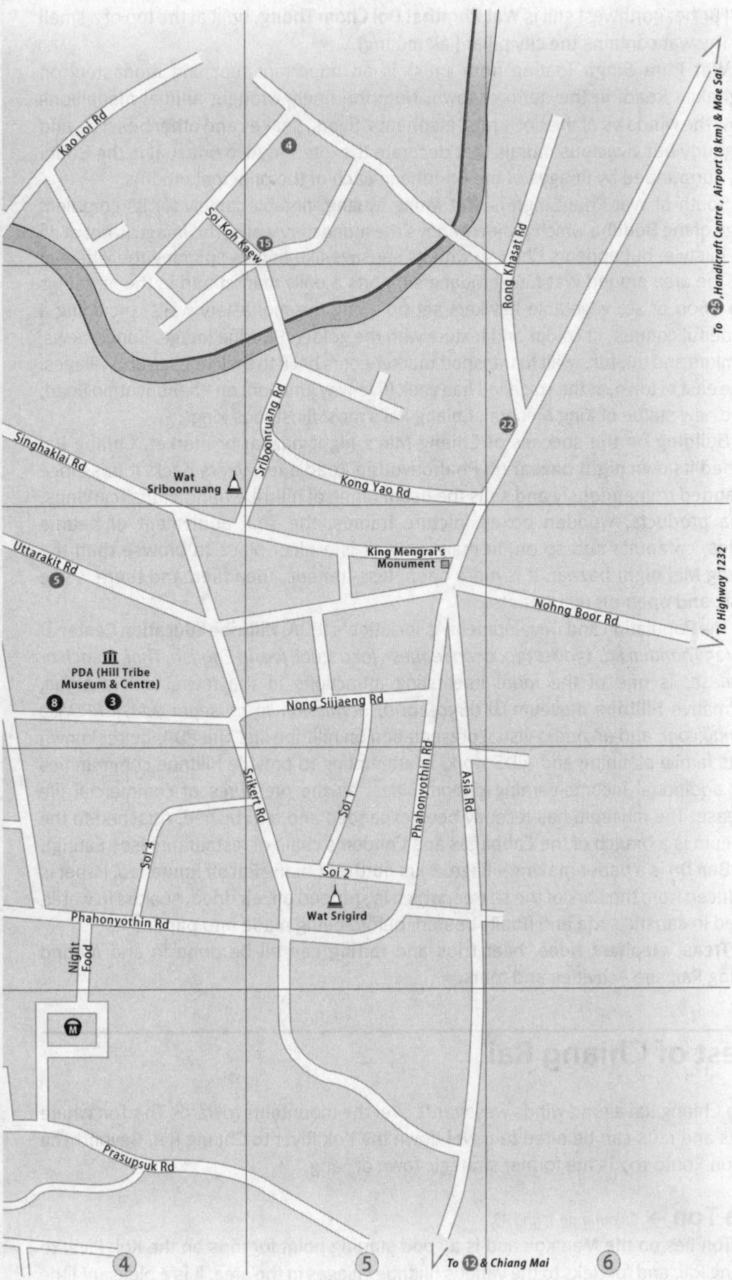

Sukniran **18** *D2*
White House **22** *B6*
Wiang Inn **23** *E3*
Ya House **24** *D1*
YMCA **25** *A6*

Eating
Aye's Place **1** *E3*
Chum Cha **2** *B2*
Cabbages & Condoms **3** *C4*
Funny House Café **5** *E3*
Hawnaliga **4** *D2*
Hungry Duck **6** *E3*
La Cantina **7** *D2*
Marco Polo Pizza **8** *C4*
Muang Thong **9** *E3*
Napoli Pizza **10** *D3*
Phetburi **11** *D2*
Ratburi **12** *D2*

Further northwest still is **Wat Phrathat Doi Chom Thong**, built at the top of a small hill. The wat contains the city pillar (lak muang).

Wat Phra Singh (dating from 1385) is an important teaching monastery on Singhaklai Road, in the north of town. Note the finely wrought animal medallions below the windows of the bot – rats, elephants, tigers, snakes and other beasts – and the gaudy but vivacious murals that decorate the interior. Also unusual is the Bodhi tree, surrounded by images of the Buddha in each of the principal mudras.

South of Wat Phra Singh is **Wat Mung Muang**, notable largely for its corpulent image of the Buddha which projects above the monastery walls. The image is not at all Thai in style, but appears Chinese with its sausage-like fingers spinning the wheel of law. The area around Wat Mung Muang supports a daily **market** and in the mornings from 0600 or so, vegetable hawkers set up along the monastery walls, providing a wonderful contrast in colour and texture with the golden Buddha image. Songthaews, saamlors and tuk-tuks wait to transport market-goers back to their houses and villages. In the east of town, at the so-called haa yaek (five-way junction) on Phahonyothin Road, is the new statue of King Mengrai, Chiang Rai's most illustrious king.

Building on the success of Chiang Mai's night bazaar or market, Chiang Rai opened its own **night bazaar** off Phahonyothin Road a few years back. It has since expanded tremendously and sells the usual range of hilltribe handicrafts, carvings, china products, wooden boxes, picture frames, the Thai equivalent of beanie babies, catapults and so on. In many ways it is a nicer place to browse than the Chiang Mai night bazaar. It is more open, less frenetic, friendlier, and there is live music and open-air restaurants.

The Population and Development Association's (PDA) **Hilltribe Education Center** ⓘ *620/25 Thanalai Rd, 1300-1330, or on request, for a small fee, in English, Thai, French or Japanese*, is one of the more interesting attractions in the town, with a small, informative **hilltribe museum** ⓘ *0830-2000; admission to museum ฿20, CRPDA@hotmail.com*, and an audio-visual presentation on hilltribe life. The PDA, better known for its family planning and AIDS work, is attempting to provide hilltribe communities with additional income-earning opportunities, as the pressures of commercial life increase. The museum has recently been expanded and refurbished. Attached to the museum is a branch of the **Cabbages and Condoms** chain of restaurants (see Eating).

Ban Du is a paper-making village, 8 km north of Chiang Rai off Route 110. Paper is produced from the bark of the sa tree, which is stripped off, air dried, soaked in water, boiled in caustic soda and finally beaten, before being made into paper.

Treks, elephant rides, boat trips and **rafting** can all be done in and around Chiang Rai, see Activities and tours.

West of Chiang Rai

From Chiang Rai a road winds westwards over the mountains towards Tha Ton where boats and rafts can be hired to travel down the Kok River to Chiang Rai. Beyond Tha Ton on Route 107 is the former strategic town of Fang.

Tha Ton → *Colour map 1, grid A3.*

Tha Ton lies on the Mae Kok and is a good starting point for trips on the Kok River to Chiang Rai, and for treks to the various hilltribe villages in the area. It is a pleasant little town with good accommodation and a friendly atmosphere. It also makes a good base for exploring this area of the north. Rafts travel downstream to Chiang Rai, while by road it is possible to head towards Doi Mae Salong, Mae Sai and Chiang Saen.

Wat Tha Ton overlooks the river, not far from the bridge. A stairway leads up to this schizophrenic monastery. On the hillside is a rather ersatz Chinese grotto, with gods, goddesses and fantastic animals including Kuan Yin, the monkey god and

entwined dragons. From this little piece of China, the stairway emerges in the compound of a classic, but rather ugly, modern Theravada Buddhist monastery. There is a restaurant, souvenir stall and more to show that Wat Tha Ton has truly embraced the pilgrim's dollar (or baht).

The boat trip to and from Chiang Rai takes four to five hours on a long-tailed boat, which is noisy and uncomfortable (฿200). A more relaxing form of transport is a gentle drift (at least in the dry season) on a bamboo raft. Most guesthouses will arrange raft trips and many will also combine the raft trip with a trek and/or elephant ride in various combinations, plus stops at hot springs, hilltribe villages and elephant camps. The rafts dock in Chiang Rai and the trip takes two days and a night, although motorized rafts complete the journey in a single day. It costs around ฿6,000 for a two-day tour on a motorized raft. The long-tail boat leaves at 1230, but they can be chartered at any time (maximum eight passengers, ฿1,700). The return boat from Chiang Rai departs at 1030.

In the past, trekkers have been robbed in this area. The TAT in Chiang Rai says the police presence in the area has been bolstered with additional checkpoints along the route making it safer.

The regular boat down the Kok River stops at riverside villages, from where it is possible to trek to hilltribe communities. (See also Hilltribes and trekking, Essentials, page 71 and Background, page 665) **Louta**, 14 km east of Tha Ton and 1½ km off the main road between Tha Ton and Doi Mae Salong/Chiang Rai, is a well-off, developed Lisu village. It's also possible to get here by yellow pick-up (14 km), then take a motorbike taxi the remaining 1,500 m uphill.

Other villages include **Tahamakeng** – one hour from Tha Ton (Lahu and Lisu villages within easy reach); **Ban Mai** – 45 minutes on from Tahamakeng (Lahu, Karen and Akha villages); and Mae Salak – further on still (Lahu, Lisu and Yao villages). See also Activities and tours.

Fang → *Colour map 1, grid A3.*

Fang is a centre for the trafficking of opium and is not a major tourist destination. It has a smattering of attractions that are worth stopping by for if you have the time.

It was founded by King Mengrai in the 13th century, although its strategic location at the head of a valley means it has probably been an important trading settlement for centuries. The government has had some success in encouraging the predominantly Yao hilltribes to switch from opium production to other cash crops such as cabbages and potatoes. These efforts haven't prevented Fang from remaining one of Thailand's key drug entrepôts. Opium, or refined heroin, passes from Burma into Thailand and to Fang, before being shipped on to other parts of the world. The valley land surrounding Fang is particularly fertile and is used for rice, fruit and vegetable cultivation. The Fang Oil Refinery, not far from the town on Route 109, also provides employment.

There are a good smattering of traditional wooden shophouses in town. Wat Jong Paen, on Tha Phae Road at the northern edge of town, is Burmese in style. The best day to be in

Tha Ton

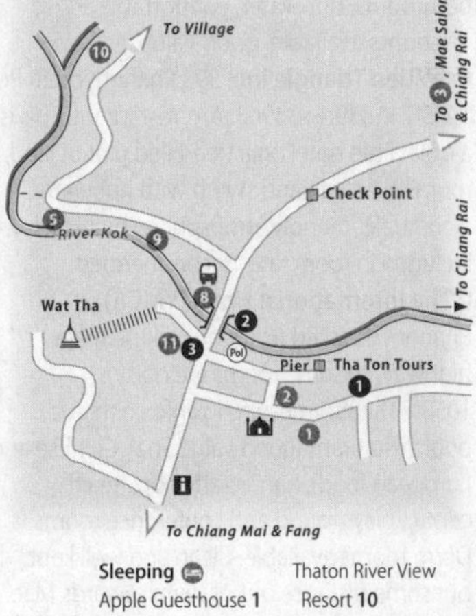
To Village
To 3. Mae Salong & Chiang Rai
Check Point
River Kok
To Chiang Rai
Wat Tha
Pier
Tha Ton Tours
To Chiang Mai & Fang
N
Not to scale

Sleeping
Apple Guesthouse 1
Apple Restaurant & Guesthouse 2
Asa's Guesthouse 3
Garden Home 5
Thaton Chalet & Restaurant 8
Tha Ton Garden 9
Thaton River View Resort 10
Thip's Travellers House & Thip Travel 11

Eating
Khao Soi 3
Riverside Thai 1
Sonay Chainam 2

 Fang is Wednesday – market day – when colourful hill peoples come to town to sell crops, textiles and more. The market winds down from 1300.

Chiang Dao Caves ⓘ *take a bus to Chiang Mai and get off at the town of Chiang Dao. Songthaews take passengers the final 6 km to the caves*, is a large cave complex, 90 km south of Fang off Route 107 towards Chiang Mai (see page 235).

Hot springs ⓘ *turn left shortly after leaving the town on the road north to Tha Ton*, (bor nam rawn) can be found 12 km west of Fang, near Ban Muang Chom.

Treks can be organized through guesthouses in town, although there is a much wider choice in Tha Ton.

Sleeping

Towards Chiang Rai *p273*

A Felix Resort, Suanthip Vana Resort, 49 Chiang Mai-Chiang Rai Rd (74 km from Chiang Rai, 12 km from Wiang Pa Pao), T053-2246984, www.felixhotels.com. This is in a lovely location with spacious villas and a good pool; a great place to relax but not near anywhere.

B-C Harin Garden Resort. Slightly more upmarket and a little further out of town is the Harin Garden with its own bakery, restaurant and reasonable villas.

D-E Karen Guesthouse, about 1 km north of Mae Suai on the road to Chiang Rai. A reasonable guesthouse 8 km north of Mai Suai.

Chiang Rai *p273, map p274*

Accommodation in Chiang Rai is of a high standard. Guesthouses, particularly, are quiet, with large and generally clean rooms – a welcome change from some of the places in Chiang Mai. Most are concentrated in the quieter northern part of the city, some on the 'island' between both branches of the Kok River.

L-AL The Legend Chiang Rai 124/15 Kohloy Rd, T053-910400, www.thelegend-chiangrai.com. A boutique hotel on the banks of the Mae Kok River.

AL Dusit Island, 1129 Kraisorasit Rd, T053-715777, chiangrai@dusit.com. A/c, restaurant, pool, overblown, fairly ostentatious hotel, just north of town on an 'island' in the river, set in lavish grounds. 271 rooms and suites, and every facility including fitness centre, tennis courts and spa.

A Little Duck, 4 Phahonyothin Rd, 2 km south of town, off main road to Chiang Mai, T053-715637, F715639. Price includes breakfast. A/c, restaurant, pool and its own department store. Large and impersonal but professionally run, with all amenities.

A Rim Kok Resort, 6 Mu 4 Chiang Rai-Thaton Rd, 5 km from town, north of the river, T053-716445, F715859. A/c, restaurant, pool, lavish hotel in modern northern Thai style. Over 500 rooms, sports complex.

A Wiang Inn, 893 Phahonyothin Rd, T053-711533, F711877. A/c, restaurant, small pool, the original 'luxury' hotel in town, renovated in 1992/93 and still holding its own. Fairly standard, but perfectly adequate rooms (with satellite TV), stylish lobby, competitively priced, central location but set back from the main road so comparatively peaceful. The buffet breakfast and lunch (with dim sum) are very good value. Recommended.

C Chiang Rai Inn, 661 Uttarakit Rd, T053-712673. A/c hotel in modern interpretation of northern Thai architecture, large, spotless but plain rooms, immaculate bathrooms, hot water, comfortable, discounts available, good value.

C Golden Triangle Inn, 590 Phahonyothin Rd, T053-711339, F713963. A/c, restaurant. This is a great little hotel on a tree-filled plot of land, rooms are clean and stylish with hot water. Good treks, friendly atmosphere, breakfast included in room rate. Recommended.

C The International Hotel (YMCA), 70 Phahonyothin Rd (6 km out on the main highway, so some rooms are noisy), T053-713785, ymcawf@loxinfo.co.th. A/c, pool, restaurant (good value Thai, Chinese and European food), handicraft shop, health centre, playground and conference rooms. Dorm rooms available. Clean and well kept, but some distance out of town towards Mae Sai, past the handicraft centre. As with YMCA Chiang Mai, all profits go to support rural development projects.

C Sukniran, 424/1 Banphaprakan Rd, T053-711955, F714701. Some a/c, good position close to clock tower, airy lobby and

rooms facing a courtyard away from the main road, so not too noisy.

C-E Boonbundan Guesthouse, 1005/13 Jet Yod Rd, T053-717040, F712914. Some a/c, outdoor eating area, quiet leafy compound near centre of town. Professionally managed, good range of services, clean rooms with hot water although becoming shabby, wide range of rates. Recommended – including the tours run from here.

D-E Chat House, 3/2 Trairat Soi Songkaew (near Wat Phra Kaeo), T053-711481. In a quiet, leafy compound down a narrow soi, and away from the main concentration of guesthouses. Reasonably clean but basic rooms and attached bathrooms with hot showers. A run-down feel about the place, although friendly people and great potential. Dorm beds available, good food and satellite TV. Trekking and motorbike hire available.

D-F Chian House, 172 Sriboonruang Rd (on the island), T053-713388. Pool, the cheapest place with a pool in town (fed by groundwater). Clean and friendly - the large bungalows are especially good value. Peaceful atmosphere and good food. Also organizes treks and tours and has an email service.

D-F Mae Kok Villa (Chiang Rai Youth Hostel), 445 Singhaklai Rd, T053-711786. This former secondary school makes for an unusual hotel, the elegant though rather ramshackle main wooden building has dorm beds, while the bungalows in the big, leafy, riverside compound are large, if slightly murky, more expensive rooms with hot water (10% discount for ISIC cardholders).

D-F Pintamorn Guesthouse, 199/1-3 Mu 21 Singhaklai Rd, T053-714161, F713317. Some a/c, a quiet and friendly guesthouse in a peaceful area of town. Rooms are large and well maintained, the 'VIP' room is a real bargain. Trekking and motorbike and jeep rental can be arranged. A friendly place with lots of atmosphere and good value. Recommended.

E-F Mae Hong Son, 126 Singhaklai Rd, T053-715367. Run by a farang (Hans, a Dutchman), this friendly guesthouse is situated at the end of a very quiet soi. The traditional wooden house has clean rooms with shared bathrooms, also available are some newer, more expensive rooms with attached bathrooms but no a/c. Treks (recommended, with a great guide), jeep and motorbike hire, good source of information, peaceful, tasty food, good value. Recommended.

E-F The White House, 789 Phahonyothin Rd, T053-713427. Set back off Chiang Rai's main road in a leafy compound. A recent coat of paint has rendered rooms bright and clean. A pool and jacuzzi have also been added which is pretty good for a place this cheap (for use by non-residents, ฿20).

F Bowling Guest House, 399 Singhaklai Rd, T053-712704. Small, quiet guesthouse, rooms are basic but clean, friendly management.

F Lek House, 95 Thanalai Rd, T053-713337. Well organized, friendly place, with a bar and food and satellite TV. Hires motorbikes.

F Ya House, down a soi at the western end of Banphaprakan Rd, T053-717090. Attractive wooden building with a quiet garden and reading library makes this a good place for backpackers to chill out. Clean rooms, some with hot water shower, breakfast and evening food provided.

Tha Ton *p276, map p277*

There is a good range of accommodation here, from basic guesthouses through to comfortable small hotels.

A Thaton River View Resort (member of Comfort Inn group), T053-459289/373173, F459288. (Rates negotiable.) River view, a/c, good restaurant with great location. Small bungalows scattered along the riverbank. This is probably the most attractively positioned of all the places to stay in Tha Ton, on the river, at a confluence of the Mae Kok and a tributary, away from town and overlooking fields and mountains. Well run with friendly atmosphere. Rooms are comfortable and clean with satellite TV. Airy restaurant (cheap) with extensive Thai menu and a smattering of Western dishes, small library. Room rate includes buffet breakfast.

B Thaton Chalet, 192/1 Mu 14, T053-373155, F373158. A/c, restaurant, 4 storeys, right by the bridge and overlooking the river with, chalets of sorts. Rooms are clean and very comfortable with hot water showers (baths in the de luxe rooms), minibar and satellite TV. Riverside bar.

B-E Garden Home, T053-373015. Away from the main bustle, this peaceful resort has good bungalows set in a large tree-filled orchard garden on the river's edge. Fan rooms are very clean, with spotless squat

toilets (western toilets, a/c and hot water showers cost more), quiet and friendly, no restaurant. Note that the bungalows here range widely in price from guesthouse level up to hotel quality. Recommended.

D Tha Ton Garden. Easily confused with the nearby **Garden Home**. Riverside location, garden compound, well maintained, hot water and a/c.

D-E Apple Restaurant and Guesthouse. There are 2 Apples. One, reminiscent of an Austrian ski chalet, has quite good clean fan rooms with bath, hot water and western toilets. The airy restaurant downstairs has an extensive menu of western and Thai dishes, but management are unhelpful. The second Apple is the guesthouse about 100 m away. Peaceful, in large garden compound, but no river view.

E Asa's Guesthouse, Louta, T01-9670268 (mob), a charming family run house, attentive service, good food. Recommended.

E Thip's Travellers House, T053-459312, in front of police box, next to the bridge on the main road so traffic noise can be disturbing. Basic, small but clean rooms with squat toilets, in a compact garden courtyard, restaurant. Mosquitoes are a problem, friendly and very popular place, rafting and trekking organized here. The manageress settled here when her policeman husband was transferred to Fang from Bangkok.

Fang *p277, map p280*

A-B Angkhang Nature Resort, 1/1 Moo 5 Baan Koom, Tambon Mae Ngon, T053-450110, www.amari.com. This place is around 40 km west of Fang, on Route 1249. The resort, which was developed under the auspices of the Royal Project Foundation, is situated high in the cool mountains, very close to the border with Burma. It consists of 72 well-appointed rooms with all mod-cons.

B Chiang Dao Hill Resort, on the main road north to Fang, 24 km from Chiang Dao and 52 km south of Fang. Another place which is only really worth visiting for those with their own transport (or on a tour). Bavarian-style building with comfortable rooms, hot water, overlooked by limestone pinnacles.

D Cheap Cheap Guesthouse, 500 m off the main road towards the southern edge of the town (road to Chiang Mai), T053-453265. Its real name is Fang Academic Centre (FAC). Dorms for rent, though it isn't cheap – ฿200 for a dorm bed with fridge, TV and fan and cold water shower. Free laundry available. Food available if ordered in advance. Quiet location overlooking rice fields.

D Magic Home, situated outside the town centre off Route 107 towards Chiang Mai. Dorm beds expensive (฿200), although dorms are clean and large. There are also more expensive rooms above the restaurant along the main road, with fan and toilet.

D-E Chok Thani, 425 Chotana Rd, just off the main road. T053-451252, F451355. Some a/c, 'best' in town with clean if bare rooms. Functional, little more.

E New Poo Guesthouse, off main road, just past **Chok Thani Hotel** down a dirt rack, T053-453210. Very small block with only 4 clean rooms, with fan and cold water shower and Thai toilet. Restaurant and snooker table, friendly management and quiet place.

E Uang Kham (Ueng Khum), 227 Tha Phae Rd Soi 3, T053-451268. Clean bungalows, hot water. Recommended.

Fang

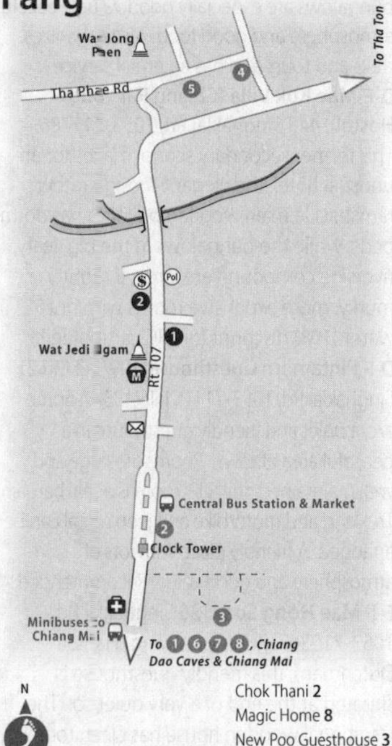

Sleeping
Angkhang Nature Resort 6
Cheap Cheap Guesthouse 1
Chiang Dao Hill Resort 7
Chok Thani 2
Magic Home 8
New Poo Guesthouse 3
Uang Kham 4
Wiang Kaew 5

Eating
JJ's Bakery 1
Muang Fang 2

E Wiang Kaew, just off Tha Phae Rd (over the bridge, north of the town centre). Simple but clean rooms, hot water, friendly place which has kept up standards long-term.

Eating

Chiang Rai *p273, map p274*

The greatest variety of restaurants is to be found in the streets around the **Wangcome Hotel**, from Mexican to French to cheap Thai and Chinese. For some reason, many of the tourist-oriented restaurants in Chiang Rai serve the same range of dishes: wiener schnitzel, lasagne, pizza, burgers, fried rice. Having said that, the food is quite good. In the evenings, the night bazaar off Phahonyothin Rd is good for stall food; there is an excellent range of places here where you can choose from spring rolls, wonton, pancakes, kebabs, noodles, rice dishes, even deep-fried beetles and grubs – and then sit at a table and listen to live music – great atmosphere.

International

La Cantina, Soi Punyodyana (near **Wangcome Hotel**, off Phahonyothin Rd by the clock tower). The manager and cook is Italian so the food is pretty authentic, including some unusual regional dishes.

Napoli Pizza, Phahonyothin Rd, reasonable pizzas, some average pasta dishes, friendly manager.

Aye's Place, Phahonyothin Rd, T053-752535, opposite entrance to **Wiang Inn**. Spacious restaurant open for breakfast (though not very early), lunch and dinner, extensive Thai and international menu. The baguettes are particularly good, the lasagne is only average.

Funny House Café, Phahonyothin Rd, opposite **Wiang Inn**. German run, this diminutive place seems to be popular and has the same menu as many of the other 'international' restaurants on this strip.

Hungry Duck, Phahonyothin Rd (opposite entrance to night market). Bar and restaurant serving burgers, lasagne and fish and chips.

Thai and Chinese

Chiangrai Island Restaurant, 1129/1 Kraisorasit Rd (part of **Dusit Island hotel**). Northern Thai specialities, also serves international food.

Haw Naliga, 401/1-2 Banphaprakan Rd (west of **Ratburi** and **Phetburi** restaurants). Country setting, rather expensive but (usually) good food, although quality is highly variable – on a good day, excellent, and on a bad day execrable!

Ratanakosin, T053-740012. Comes highly recommended for quality of food and atmospheric decor. Faces onto night bazaar, so you can feel part of the action, and dine from the upstairs balcony, whilst watching the Thai dancing down in the bazaar, 1600-2400.

Cabbages and Condoms, 620/25 Thanalai Rd (attached to the Hilltribe Museum). Run by the PDA, a non-governmental organization, all proceeds go to charity. Good northern food including larb (spicy minced meat – really a northeastern delicacy), northern spicy sausage, duck curry and chicken in banana leaves. Eat inside or outdoors (rather noisy on the road), reasonably priced – free condoms.

Chum Cha, Singhaklai Rd (next to TAT office). Clean, new place for coffee and ice cream, with some simple noodle and rice dishes.

Golden Triangle Café (at **Golden Triangle Inn**), 590 Phahonyothin Rd. Serves international food. Recommended.

Muang Man Café and Cocktail Lounge, opposite Caltex station on Phahonyothin Rd. Serves international food.

Muang Thong, Phahonyothin Rd (just south from the Wiang Inn). A serious restaurant where Chinese/Thai food is served, with little pretence, on plastic plates. Especially good vegetable dishes, recommended by locals who make up the bulk of the clientele.

Phetburi, Banphaprakan Rd, opposite **Sukniran Hotel**. Large selection of curries, eat in or takeaway, ฿15 per dish.

Ratburi, Banphaprakan Rd, opposite **Sukniran Hotel**. Large selection of curries, eat in or takeaway, ฿15 per dish.

Foodstalls

There are dozens of stalls at night around the night market off Phahonyothin Rd (by the bus terminal). There is a great roti man, who does stupendous banana, strawberry, orange and other pancakes – he usually sets up near the entrance to the night market. Other stalls

on the alley leading from Phahonyothin Rd into the night market. Another group of stalls is to be found near Wat Ming Muang, at the intersection of Trairat and Banphaprakan roads.

Tha Ton *p276, map p277*
There are a number of attractive riverside restaurants.
🍴 **Khao Soi Restaurant**, friendly place right by the river and bridge, and next to Thip's Travellers House serving khao soi (of course) and the usual rice and noodle dishes.
🍴 **Riverside Thai Restaurant**, a nice place to eat, open for breakfast, lunch and dinner. Thatched riverside affair with good fish dishes – watch out for mosis in the evening
🍴 **Sonay Chainam Restaurant**, on the north side of the bridge by the riverside, serving Thai and European food. Long wait for average food.
🍴 **Thaton Chalet Restaurant** is a riverside restaurant on the veranda of this hotel, serving Thai and Chinese food.

Fang *p277, map p280*
🍴 **JJ's Bakery**, opposite Wat Chedi Ngam on the main road. Cakes, Thai and international.
🍴 **Muang Fang**, on the main road, next to the Bangkok Bank. Thai food.

Bars and clubs

Chiang Rai *p273, map p274*
There are not many bars in Chiang Rai. On Phahonyothin Rd, near the crossroads with Banphaprakan Rd.
Easy House Bar and Restaurant, Permaviphat Rd (opposite Wangcome Hotel), cocktails, beers, live music, self-consciously hip.
Lobo Bar, a lively place is down a narrow private soi off Phahonyothin Rd, near the clock tower.

Entertainment

Chiang Rai *p273, map p274*
Music
Live music shows held periodically at the **Night Market**, close to the bus terminal off Phahonyothin Rd.

Shopping

Chiang Rai *p273, map p274*
Books
DK Book Store, along Barnphaprakan Rd, sells guidebooks of the region in English.
Pho Thong Book Store, Thanalai Rd (close to intersection with Trairat Rd). Mostly Thai language, but also some English books and magazines.

China
China shop, Pisit Sangsuan Rd, Thai-decorated seconds for US and UK shops (Whittards), on sale here at rock-bottom prices. Mugs, bowls, plates and teapots.

Department stores
Corner of Banphraprakan and Sanambin rds. Also an a/c department store near the Wangcome Hotel, on the corner of Phahonyothin and Pemavipat rds.

Handicraft centres
Chiang Rai Handicrafts Centre, 3 km out on road to Chiang Saen.
Ego, 869/81-82 (adjacent Wangcome Hotel), for Burmese and hilltribe antiques, beads, jewellery, carvings, textiles, reasonable prices. Recommended.
Silver Birch 891 Phahonyothin Rd, near Wiang Inn. For more unusual woodcarvings and silverware, more expensive but finely crafted.

Hill tribe goods, silver, textiles, woodcarvings
Many shops in town around the Wangcome Hotel plaza area and on Phahonyothin Rd.
Hilltribe Education Center, 620/25 Thanalai Rd, sells real hill tribe textiles and other goods, all profits being returned to the communities.

Night market
There is a night bazaar just off Phahonyothin Rd, close to the bus terminal. The stalls and shops sell a range of goods, including hill tribe handicrafts, silverware, woodcarvings, T-shirts, clothes, pincushions, Burmese bags and leatherware. Foodstalls and bars also open in the evening.

Tapes and CDs
There is a great little music shop near the clock tower at the northern end of Jet Yod Rd.

Activities and tours

Chiang Rai *p273, map p274*

Sports clubs

Pintamorn Sportsclub, 115/1-8 Wat Sriboonruang Rd. Sauna, exercise room, pool table.

Therapies

There are several places in the network of streets near the Wangcome Hotel.
Ganda Traditional Thai Massage, 869/59-63 Pisit Sangsuan Rd, is recommended.
Mue Thong Thai Massage, Inn Come Hotel, 172/6 Ratbamrung Rd, T053-717850.
Yogi massage and sauna centre, at the Royal Princess hotel, is the most luxurious place for a Thai Massage. (฿900 for 2-hr massage and 30-min sauna).

Tours and trekking

A 2- day/1- night **raft trip** should cost about ฿800-1,100 per person, 4- day/3-night **trek** about ฿1,500-2,000. Most treks are cheaper if organized through guesthouses and they are usually also more adventurous. The usual range of **elephant rides** and **boat trips** as part of a trek are also offered. Before embarking on a trek, it is worthwhile visiting the Hilltribe Education Center. Tribes in the area include Karen, Lisu, Lahu and Akha. Trekking companies are concentrated around the Wangcome Hotel plaza area; most guesthouses also offer trekking services. See Tour operators, below. The TAT office produces a list of companies with average prices and other useful advice. See also Hill tribes and trekking, Essentials, page 71 and Background, page 664.

Day tours to visit hill tribe villages, Sop Ruak and the Golden Triangle, Mae Sai, Mae Salong and Chiang Saen are organized by most of the tour/trekking companies listed below (฿600). Tours which include an elephant ride and boat trip, plus visits to hilltribe villages, cost about ฿700.

Mae Salong Tour, 882 Phahonyothin Rd, T053-712515, F711011, runs various **cruises** on the Mekong that include Laos, China and Thailand. Motorcycle tours are becoming increasingly popular, and many guesthouses provide rental services and information on routes to take for a day's excursion.

Tour operators

A number along Phahonyothin and Premwipak roads (a soi off Phahonyothin, near the Wangcome Hotel). **Chiangrai Agency Centre**, 428/10 Banphaprakan Rd, T053-717274, F712211. **Chiangrai Travel and Tour**, 869/95 Premwipak Rd, T053-713314, F713967. **Far East North Tours Chiang Rai**, 402/1 Moo 13, Phahonyothin Rd, T053-715690, F715691. **Golden Triangle Tours**, 590 Phahonyothin Rd, T053-711339 (attached to the Golden Triangle Hotel). Recommended. **Maesalong Tour**, 882/4 Phahonyothin Rd, T053-712515. Treks come recommended, also organizes river cruises and China and Lao tours. **PDA**, 620/25 Thanalai Rd, T053-719167, F718869. Primarily a charity, working to improve the lot of the hill tribes, but they also have a trekking 'arm', guides tend to be more knowledgeable of hill tribe ways. Note that all profits from treks are ploughed back into the PDA's charity work. Treks also introduce clients to the PDA's community development projects, advance notice is recommended. **PD Tour**, 834/6 Phahonyothin Rd, T053-712829, F719041. Guesthouses which organize treks include: Boonbundan, Bowling Guesthouse, Chat House, Chian House, Golden Triangle Inn, Mae Hong Son (recommended), Mae Kok Villa, and Pintamorn (see Sleeping above for addresses).

Ta Thon *p276, map p277*

Activities and tours

Most guesthouses in Tha Ton will help you to organize trekking or raft/boat trips, or take the scheduled daily boat from the pier. Examples of pricing for treks are as follows: ฿1,500 for 1- night/2- days including rafting. A 1-day trip on an elephant will set you back ฿950, and a trip to Mae Sai and across the border into Burma costs ฿1,250 (including visa, car and guide).
Tha Ton Tours, T/F053-373143, and **Thip Travel** (attached to Thip's Travellers House), T053-459312. Both arrange raft trips although we have received negative comment on Thip Travel – poor camping equipment and lack of care. For more imaginative but expensive tours, visit **Track of the Tiger**, based at the Mae Kok River Village Resort (see Sleeping, above).

Transport

Chiang Rai *p273, map p274*

Air

The international airport is 8 km north of the city, just off the main Chiang Rai–Mae Sai highway. Regular connections with **Chiang Mai** (40 mins) and **Bangkok** (1 hr 25 mins). The runway has been lengthened to take wide-bodied jets, and there is some talk of the possibility of international connections in the near future with other Asian destinations.

Airline offices THAI, 870 Phahonyothin Rd, T053-711179.

Bicycle

฿20-40 per day, from guesthouses.

Boat

Long-tailed boats leave from the new pier to the northwest of town, around 2 km from the city centre. Follow Trairat Rd north, past the entrance to the **Dusit Island Resort**, to the T-junction with Winitchakun Rd. Turn right and continue past the golf course to the bridge over the Kok River. The pier is on the far side of the river. Boats for **Tha Ton** depart daily at 1030 (฿200). Boats can be chartered for ฿300 per hr or for ฿1,600 to Tha Ton, ฿500 to Rim Kok, ฿1,500 to Chiang Khong. A boat takes a maximum of 8 passengers, the pier is open 0700-1600 daily (see page 277).

Bus

Central bus station is just off Phahonyothin Rd, T053-711224. Regular connections with **Chiang Saen** every 15 mins (1 hr 30 mins) and **Mae Sai** every 15 mins (1 hr 40 mins), **Chiang Mai** (3 hrs), **Phayao** (1 hr 40 mins), **Phrae** (4 hrs), **Nan** (6 hrs), **Chiang Kham** (2 hrs), **Chiang Khong** (3 hrs), **Lampang** (5 hrs), **Phitsanulok** (via Sukhothai) (6 hrs), **Khon Kaen** (12 hrs), **Nakhon Ratchasima** (13 hrs), **Bangkok** (12 hrs), **Fang**, **Mae Suai**, **Nakhon Sawan**, **Sukhothai**, **Nakhon Phanom**, **Udon Thani** and **Pattaya**. From Chiang Mai, buses taking the old route (sai kao) leave from the Old Lamphun Rd, near the Narawat Bridge; those on the new route (sai mai) leave from the Arcade bus station, northeast of the city on the 'Super highway'. The old route goes via Lampang and Phayao (6 hrs); the new route takes Route 1019, via Doi Saket and Wiang Papao (hot springs) (4 hrs). A/c and VIP buses to **Bangkok** leave from the office on Phahonyothin Rd, opposite the Golden Triangle Inn.

Car

Hire from one of the many tour and travel companies around the **Wangcome Hotel**, or from **Budget**, based at the Golden Triangle Inn.

Jeep hire is ฿800 per day from many guesthouses, eg Bowling Guesthouse, Chian House, Pintamorn, Mae Hong Son Guesthouse and from many tour companies.

Motorbike

฿150-200 per day, from most guesthouses and tour companies.

Saamlor, tuk-tuk and songthaew

The local songthaew stand is near the morning market on Uttarakit Rd. Songthaews also run on set routes around the city (฿2).

Tha Ton *p276, map p277*

Boat

The boat to **Chiang Rai** departs at 1230 and takes 2½-3½ hrs, depending on the state of the river (฿250). **Tha Ton Boat Office** is open 0900-1500, T053-459427. Or hire the whole boat (seating up to 8 people, ฿1,700, or ฿1,400 if hired through one of the tour operators, see previous page). See page 283 for details on organizing a raft trip to Chiang Rai. The pier in Chiang Rai has moved from close to the centre of town to a site around 2 km northwest, beyond the **Dusit Island Resort**. Before leaving Tha Ton by boat, travellers must sign out at the tourist police box next to the pier.

Bicycle

Hire from Apple Guesthouse and from Thaton River View Resort.

Bus

Connections with **Chiang Mai** (4 hrs), or a minibus to **Fang** which connects with more frequent buses to Chiang Mai (40 mins). Regular connections with **Chiang Rai** (2½ hrs), **Mae Sai** (1½ hrs), **Chiang Saen** (1½ hrs), **Chiang Khong** (2½ hrs) and **Mae**

Salong (2½ hrs). It is also possible to get to and from **Pai/Mae Hong Son** without going through Chiang Mai: from Tha Ton, catch a bus through Fang heading for Chiang Mai and get off at Ban Mae Malai, at the junction with Route 1095. Then, pick up a bus heading for Pai/Mae Hong Son. Travelling in the other direction, simply remember to alight at the junction of routes 1095 and 107 and then catch one of the regular buses heading north to Fang. Finally, there are also regular connections with **Bangkok**, most leaving in the evening.

Songthaew
Regular connections with **Fang** every 15 mins.

Fang *p277, map p280*
Bus
Station is on the main road in the centre of town. Regular connections with **Chiang Mai** from the Chang Puak bus station on Chotana Road, 3 hrs. Minibuses run on the hour through the week from next to the hospital to Chiang Mai (฿80).

Songthaew
Regular connections with **Tha Ton** (40 mins). There are 2 routes to Chiang Rai: either take the songthaew from Fang to Mae Suai (40 mins), then catch a bus to **Chiang Rai** (95 km), or take a songthaew from Tha Ton up to Doi Mae Salong, then to Mae Chan, then on to Chiang Rai (114 km).

Directory

Chiang Rai *p273, map p274*
Banks Profusion of exchange booths and banks on Thanalai and Phahonyothin rds. Many are open 7 days a week and often into the evening. **Internet** An abundance of internet cafés in the area around the Wangcome Hotel, about ฿30 per hr. **Medical services** Hospitals: Overbrook, opposite Chat House, Trairat Rd, T053-711366. **Provincial**, on Sanambin Rd. **Chiang Rai Hospital**, Sathorn Payabarn Rd, T053-711403/711119. **Post office** On Uttarakit Rd at the northern end of Suksathit Rd. **Useful addresses** Tourist Police, Singhaklai Rd (below the TAT office, opposite Wat Phra Singh), T053-717779, and a booth at the night market. Or in an emergency call T1155 (24 hrs). Police Station, Rattanakhat Rd, T053-711444.

Tha Ton *p276, map p277*
Telephone Ngam Muang Rd, near Wat Phra Kaeo. **Useful addresses** Tourist Police emergency telephone number, T1155 (24 hrs).

Fang *p277, map p280*
Banks A number on the main road close to the clock tower. **Post office** Past the bus station, not far from the Bangkok Bank on the main road.

Chiang Saen and the Golden Triangle

→ *Colour map 1, grid A3.*

Chiang Saen, northeast of Chiang Rai, situated on the banks of the mighty Mekong River, was once the evocative capital of an ancient kingdom. Follow the meandering Mekong downstream and the road reaches the small outpost of Chiang Khong, home of the giant Cat Fish and a crossing point into Laos. Meanwhile, 11 km upstream from Chiang Saen, is the infamous Golden Triangle, the meeting point of Laos, Thailand and Burma. This was once a lawless area filled with smugglers and drug lords. These days it's home to the tourist village of Sop Ruak and the compelling Opium Museum. Mae Sai, upstream still further and 61 km north of Chiang Rai, is Thailand's most northerly town and a busy border trading post with Burma. A new road runs off Route 110 to the hill town of Mae Salong, from where a poor track continues west to Tha Ton.

» *For Sleeping, Eating and other listings, see pages 294-299.*

Chiang Saen

Chiang Saen is an ancient capital on the banks of the Mekong River, the last village before the famed 'Golden Triangle'. Today, with the impressive town ramparts still very much in evidence, it is a charming one-street market town.

Ins and outs

Tourist information TAT ⓘ *Phahonyothin Rd, opposite the National Museum, 0830-1630*, is attached to the sensitively designed Bureau for the Restoration and Conservation of the Historic City of Chiang Mai.

Background

Chiang Saen was probably established during the early years of the last millennium and became the capital of the Chiang Saen Kingdom, founded in 1328 by King Saen Phu, the grandson of King Mengrai. Captured in the 16th century by the Burmese, the town became a Burmese stronghold in their constant wars with the Thais. It was not recaptured until Rama I sent an army here in 1803. Fearing that the Burmese might use the town to mount raids against his kingdom in the future, Rama I ordered it to be destroyed. Chiang Saen remained deserted for nearly 100 years. King Mongkut ordered the town to be repopulated, but it still feels as though it is only part-filled, its inhabitants rattling around in the area's illustrious history. The ancient city is a gazetted historic monument managed by the Thai Fine Arts Department, and in total there are 75 monasteries and other monuments inside the city walls and another 66 outside.

Sights

The city walls run along three sides of the town and are pierced by five gates. The fourth 'wall' is formed by the Mekong River. Quiet, with wooden shophouses and a scattering of ruins lying haphazardly and untended in the undergrowth, it has so far managed to escape the uncontrolled tourist development of other towns in Northern Thailand.

In September 1992, a 120-tonne ship, with 60 Chinese delegates aboard, made the 385-km trip down the Mekong from Yunnan. Since then, links with China – as well as Laos – have developed apace. Cargo boats unload apples and other produce from China, and the market in Chiang Saen is stocked with low quality manufactured goods from the neighbouring countries. Anticipating a trade boom, the local authorities began constructing two new piers – one which was promptly partly washed away – and the grandly titled Lan Chang International Development Company shares an office with the Yunnan Water Transportation Joint Operations Development Company on Rim Khong Road. The local big businessman has constructed a luxurious edifice for himself on the Mekong, a couple of kilometres south of town – demonstrating how much money there is around as people try to cash in on the 'Golden Quadrangle' (Thailand, Burma, Laos and China).

The economic crisis in Thailand changed things. Before mid-1997 Thai tourists were rushing upriver to visit their ethnic brethren in Yunnan. With the crash of the baht in July 1997, the flow reversed; Thais stayed at home, no longer able to travel abroad, while Chinese tourists from Yunnan suddenly found a trip to Thailand within their financial grasp. With the recovery in Thailand's economy from 1999, the traditional flow began to reassert itself.

Entering the town from Chiang Rai, the ruins of **Wat Phrathat Chedi Luang** can be seen on the right-hand side shortly after passing through the city's ancient ramparts. Built by King Saen Phu in 1331, this wat was established as the main monastery in the city. The chedi, resting on an octagonal base, is 60 m tall, but has fallen into disrepair over the centuries and is now clothed in long grass. The viharn is in a similar state of decrepitude and is protected by a jury-rigged corrugated-iron roof.

Just to the west of Wat Phrathat Chedi Luang is a small branch of the **National Museum** ⓘ *Wed-Sun 0900-1200, 1300-1600, ฿10*. It contains various Buddha images and other artefacts unearthed in the area, as well as a small display of hill tribe handicrafts including clothing and musical instruments. Among the Buddha

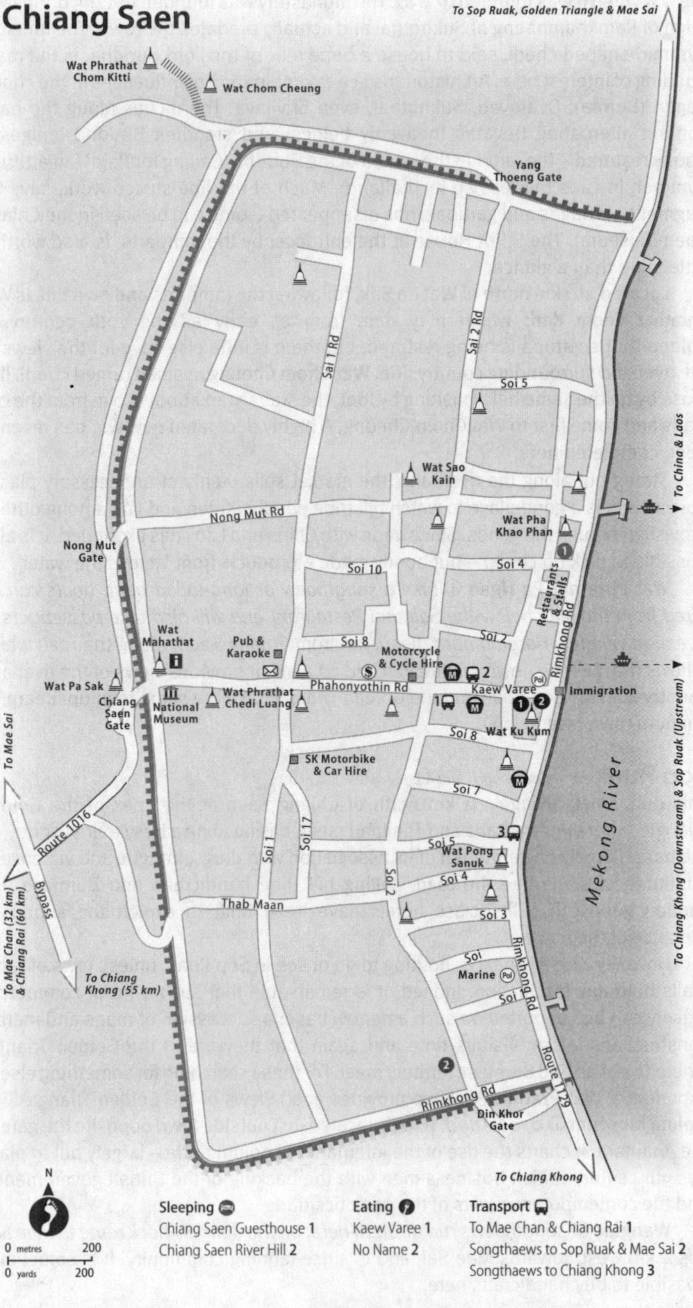
Chiang Saen
To Sop Ruak, Golden Triangle & Mae Sai
Wat Phrathat Chom Kitti
Wat Chom Cheung
Yang Thoeng Gate
Sai 1 Rd
Sai 2 Rd
Soi 5
Wat Sao Kain
To China & Laos
Nong Mut Rd
Wat Pha Khao Phan
Nong Mut Gate
Soi 10
Soi 4
Restaurants & Stalls
Rimkhong Rd
Wat Mahathat
Pub & Karaoke
Soi 8
Soi 2
Motorcycle & Cycle Hire
Wat Pa Sak
Wat Phrathat Chedi Luang
Phahonyothin Rd
Kaew Varee
Immigration
Chiang Saen Gate
National Museum
Soi 8
Wat Ku Kum
To Mae Sai
SK Motorbike & Car Hire
Soi 7
Mekong River
To Chiang Khong (Downstream) & Sop Ruak (Upstream)
Route 1016
Soi 17
Soi 1
Soi 5
Wat Pong Sanuk
Soi 2
Soi 4
Bypass
Thab Maan
Soi 3
To Mae Chan (32 km) & Chiang Rai (60 km)
Soi
Rimkhong Rd
To Chiang Khong (55 km)
Marine
Soi 1
Route 1129
Rimkhong Rd
Din Khor Gate
To Chiang Khong
N
0 metres 200
0 yards 200
Sleeping
Chiang Saen Guesthouse 1
Chiang Saen River Hill 2
Eating
Kaew Varee 1
No Name 2
Transport
To Mae Chan & Chiang Rai 1
Songthaews to Sop Ruak & Mae Sai 2
Songthaews to Chiang Khong 3

 images, the most significant are those in the so-called Chiang Saen style, with their oval faces and slender bodies. They are regarded by art historians as being among the first true 'Thai' works of art.

West of the town, just outside the city ramparts, is the beautiful **Wat Pa Sak** or 'Forest of Teak Wat' – so-called because of a wall of 300 teak trees, planted around the wat when it was founded ⓘ *฿30*. The monastery was founded in 1295 during the reign of Ramkhamhaeng of Sukhothai and actually predates the town. The unusual pyramid-shaped chedi, said to house a bone relic of the Lord Buddha, is the main building of interest here. Art historians see a combination of influences in the chedi: Pagan (Burma), Dvaravati, Sukhothai, even Srivijaya. The niches along the base contain alternating Devatas (heavenly beings) and standing Buddha images – poorly restored – the latter in the mudra of the Buddha 'Calling for Rain' (an attitude common in Laos but less so in Thailand). Much of the fine stucco work, save for fragments of nagas and garudas, has disappeared (some can be seen in the Chiang Saen Museum). The Spirit House at the entrance, by the ramparts, is also worth a little more than a glance.

Located 2½ km north of Wat Pa Sak, following the ramparts and on a hill, is **Wat Phrathat Chom Kitti**, which may date from as early as the 10th century. A golden-topped stupa is being restored, but there is little else save for the views of the river and surrounding countryside. **Wat Chom Cheung**, a small ruined chedi, lies close by on the same hill. If visiting by foot, the stairs start about 150 m from the city walls and come first to Wat Chom Cheung. A highly decorated new wat has recently been completed here.

Strung out along the riverbank, the market sells plenty of unnecessary plastic objects and is a good place to watch hill tribe people (Karen and Lua among others) browsing through the goods. Since trade with China and Laos has expanded, it is also possible to pick up cheap – but poorly made – products from 'across the water'.

Wat Phrathat Pa Ngao ⓘ *take a songthaew or long-tailed boat, boats can be hired from the jetty below the Salathai Restaurant and will also take passengers to riverside villages. Bargain hard*, lies 4 km from Chiang Saen, along the road which follows the Mekong downstream. Perched on a hill, it provides views of the river and countryside. For Sop Ruak and the Golden Triangle take the same road upstream, 11 km from town (see below).

Sop Ruak → *Colour map 1, grid A3.*

This dull, small 'village', 11 km north of Chiang Saen at the apex of the Golden Triangle, where Burma, Laos and Thailand meet, has become a busy tourist spot – on the basis (largely unwarranted) of its association with drugs, intrigue and violence. A multitude of stalls line the road, selling hill tribe handicrafts and Burmese and Laotian goods. Two first-class hotels have been built to exploit the supposed romance of the place.

However, there is next to nothing to do or see in Sop Ruak, unless rows of tacky stalls hold any fascination. Indeed, it is remarkable that such a lot of commercial activity can be supported on such a narrow base: a succession of maps and marble constructions inform visitors time and again that they are at the Golden Triangle where Thai, Lao and Burmese territory meet. For those searching for something else to experience, **Wat Prathat Phukaeo** provides good views of the Golden Triangle. The **Opium Museum** ⓘ *0700-1800, ฿20*, is located just outside town opposite the gate to the Anantara. It charts the rise of the international opium trade – largely put in place by 19th-century British business men with the backing of the British government – and the contemporary effects of the narcotics trade.

Wanglao ⓘ *songthaews run through here, on the (longer) back route to Mae Sai*, lies 4 km west, towards Mae Sai, and is a rice-farming community. It is sometimes possible to buy handicrafts here.

Boats can be chartered from the riverbank opposite the Opium Museum for trips downstream to Chiang Saen (฿400 for five people, 30 minutes), or further on still to Chiang Khong (around ฿1,500-1,700, 1½ hours). Or they can be chartered just to pootle around the Golden Triangle area. Boats are also available from the riverbank opposite the **Delta Golden Triangle Hotel**.

Chiang Khong

→ *Colour map 1, grid A4.*

This border settlement, situated on the south bank of the Mekong, is really more a collection of villages than a town: Ban Haad Khrai, Ban Sobsom and Ban Hua Wiang were all originally individual communities – and still keep their village monasteries. For such a small town, it has had a relatively high profile in Thai history. In the 1260s, King Mengrai extended control over the area and Chiang Khong became one of the Lanna Thai Kingdom's major principalities. Later, the town was captured by the Burmese.

The area is growing in popularity and becoming increasingly more tourism-orientated, due mainly to the opening of a border crossing into Laos – just the other side of the river. Boats from the Laos town of Huay Xai, the Laos settlement on the opposite side, travel down river to the ancient Laos city of Luang Prabang. Chiang Khong does have a relaxed atmosphere making it an attractive spot to unwind.

Sights

Wat Luang, in the centre of town, dates from the 13th century. An engraved plaque maintains that two hairs of the Buddha were interred in the chedi in AD 704 – a date which would seem to owe more to poor maths or over-optimism than to historical veracity. But it was reputedly restored by the ruler of Chiang Khong in 1881. The viharn

Sop Ruak & the Golden Triangle

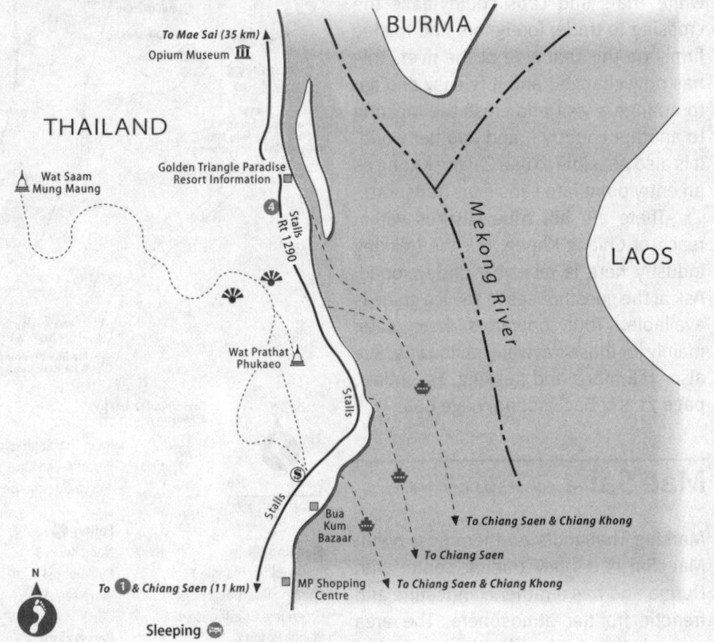

Sleeping
Anantara Golden Triangle 4
Bamboo Hut Guesthouse 1

sports some rather lurid murals. **Wat Phra Kaew**, a little further north, has two fine, red guardian lions at its entrance. Otherwise it is very ordinary, save for the kutis (monks' quarters – small huts) along the inside of the front wall, which look like a row of assorted Wendy houses, and the nagas which curl their way up the entrance to the viharn, on the far side of the building.

Further south, at the track leading to the **Pla Buk Resort** at the Economic Quadrangle Joint Development Corporation, is the town's **lak muang** (foundation pillar). Like Nong Khai and the other towns that line the Mekong in the Northeastern region, the rare – and delicious – pla buk catfish is caught here. It is sometimes possible to watch the fishermen catching a giant catfish on the riverbank to the south of town. If that is a no go, there are some pictures of stupendous pla buk in the restaurant of the **Ruan Thai Sophaphan Resort**.

The town's illegal traffic can be seen in action either at the pier end of Soi 5 or, to a greater degree, at Tha Rua Bak – 1 km or so north of town. For some years, while Thais and Laos could make the crossing to trade, foreigners had to stay firmly on the Thai side of the river. This has now changed and it is easy enough to arrange a visa and cross the Mekong to another country – and another world. It is also possible to use Chiang Khong as an entry point into Laos (see Transport).

There are **hill tribe villages** within reach of Chiang Khong, but the trekking industry here is relatively undeveloped. Ask at the guesthouses to see if a guide is available. Tour operators here cater mainly for those travelling on to Laos. See also Hill tribes and trekking, Essentials, page 71 and Background, page 664.

Mae Sai → *Colour map 1, grid A3.*

Marking Thailand's northernmost point, Mae Sai is a busy trading centre with Burma and has a rather clandestine and frenetic frontier atmosphere. The area around the bridge is the centre of activity, with stalls and shops selling

Chiang Khong

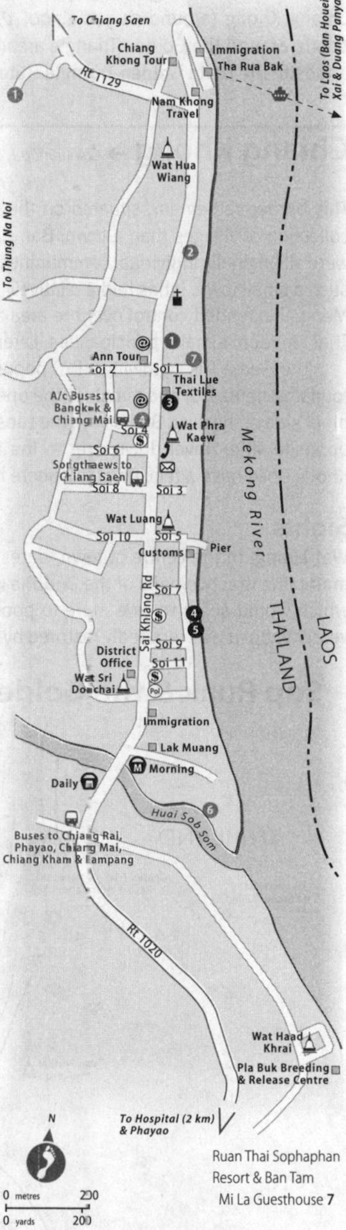
To Chiang Saen
Chiang Khong Tour
Immigration
Tha Rua Bak
Rt 1129
Nam Khong Travel
To Laos (Ban Houei Xai & Duang Panya)
Wat Hua Wiang
To Thung Na Noi
Ann Tour
Soi 2
Soi 1
Thai Lue Textiles
A/c Buses to Bangkok & Chiang Mai
Soi 4
Wat Phra Kaew
Soi 6
Songthaews to Chiang Saen
Soi 8
Soi 3
Mekong River
Wat Luang
Soi 10
Soi 5
Customs
Pier
Sai Khlang Rd
Soi 7
Soi 9
Soi 11
District Office
Wat Sri Donchai
THAILAND
LAOS
Immigration
Lak Muang
Morning
Daily
Huai Sob Som
Buses to Chiang Rai, Phayao, Chiang Mai, Chiang Kham & Lampang
Rt 1020
Wat Haad Khrai
Pla Buk Breeding & Release Centre
To Hospital (2 km) & Phayao
N
0 metres 200
0 yards 200

Sleeping
Baan Golden Triangle 1
Bamboo Riverside 2
Green Tree Guesthouse 4
Plabuk Resort & Restaurant 6
Ruan Thai Sophaphan Resort & Ban Tam Mi La Guesthouse 7

Eating
Nong Kwan 3
Rimkhong 4
Rim Naam 5

Bars & clubs
999 1

gems and Burmese and Chinese goods from knitted hats and Burmese marionettes to antiques and animal skulls. There is also an abundance of Burmese hawkers (selling Burmese coins and postage stamps) and beggars (particularly children) stretching about 1 km down the road, away from the border and towards Mae Chan.

The town of Mae Sai is rather drab, but the movement of myriad peoples across the border makes this an interesting place to visit. **Wat Phrathat Doi Wao** sits on a hill overlooking the town, off Phahonyothin Road, not far from the **Top North Hotel.** It is neither old nor beautiful and was reputedly built in the mid-1960s, in commemoration of a platoon of Burmese soldiers killed in action against a KMT (Kuomintang – the Chinese Republican Army) force.

Around Mae Sai

The border with Burma opens and closes periodically depending on the state of Thai-Burmese relations. When open, tourists, as well as Burmese and Thais, are permitted to cross the bridge that spans the River Sai and leads to the quiet Burmese town of **Tachilek**. Here, foreigners are free to roam for the day within a 5-km radius of the town, but not to stay overnight. Border open daily 0800-1800, border fee US$5, passports to be lodged with Thai customs, two photocopies of passports required. Take a photocopy of your passport and Thai visa (there are photocopy shops close to the border). Only US dollars are accepted at the border. The border has periodically closed during periods of instability and tension in Burma. Tour companies, understandably, have been keen to encourage the Burmese government to loosen their regulations and allow foreigners to venture further afield – and to stay longer. It has been suggested that tourists may also be given 'visas on arrival' to visit Mandalay. See Tour operators, below, for contacts, and Dits Travel, page 297. The market is rather disappointing. The goods on sale are of poor quality and many of the stallholders appear to be Thai rather than Burmese in any case.

The Burmese will also allow individuals and tour groups to travel the 167 km along a haphazardly upgraded road (six to eight hours) to **Kengtung**, known in Thailand as

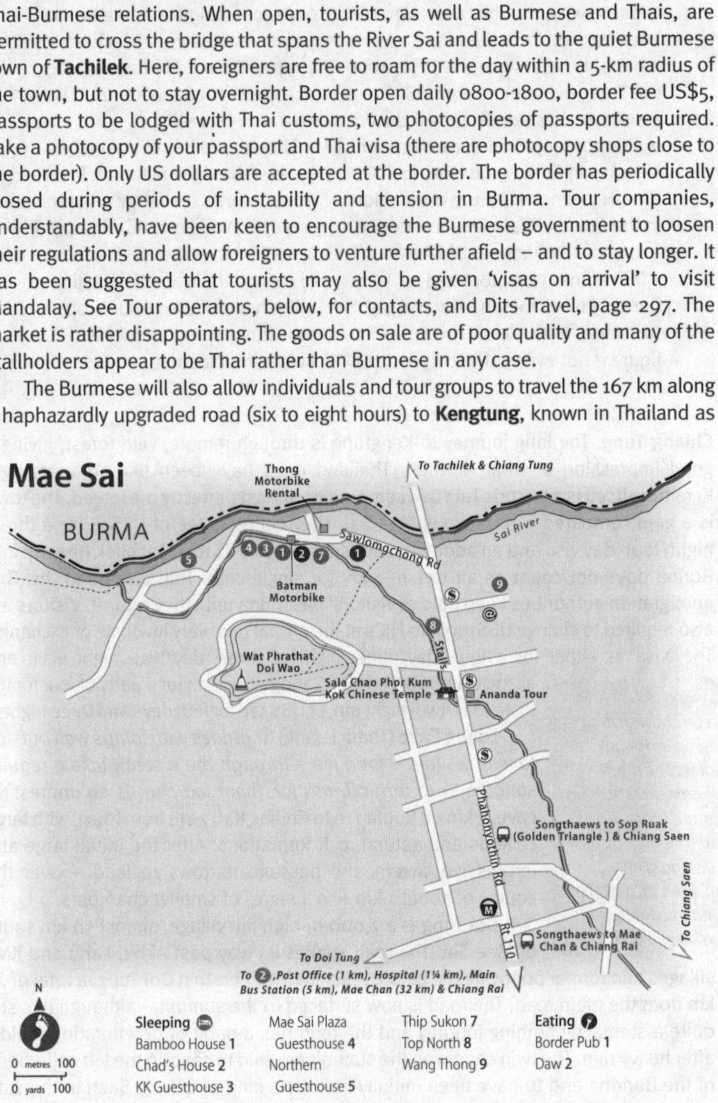
Mae Sai
BURMA
To Tachilek & Chiang Tung
Thong Motorbike Rental
Sai River
Sawlomgchong Rd
Batman Motorbike
Wat Phrathat Doi Wao
Stalls
Sala Chao Phor Kum Kok Chinese Temple
Ananda Tour
Phahonyothin Rd
Songthaews to Sop Ruak (Golden Triangle) & Chiang Saen
To Chiang Saen
Rt 110
Songthaews to Mae Chan & Chiang Rai
To Doi Tung
To 2, Post Office (1 km), Hospital (1¼ km), Main Bus Station (5 km), Mae Chan (32 km) & Chiang Rai
N
0 metres 100
0 yards 100
Sleeping
Bamboo House 1
Chad's House 2
KK Guesthouse 3
Mae Sai Plaza Guesthouse 4
Northern Guesthouse 5
Thip Sukon 7
Top North 8
Wang Thong 9
Eating
Border Pub 1
Daw 2

Opium of the people

The Golden Triangle is synonymous with the cultivation of the opium poppy. It is a favourite cash crop of the Lahu, Lisu, Mien and Hmong (the Karen and Akha only rarely grow it) and the attractions are clear: it is profitable, can be grown at high altitudes (above 1,500 m), has low bulk (important when there is no transport) and does not rot. This explains why, though cultivation has been banned in Thailand since 1959, it has only been since the 1980s that the Thai government, with US assistance, has significantly reduced the poppy crop. Today, most opium is grown in Burma and Laos. In 2001 the UN estimated opium production in the Golden Triangle amounted to a total of 1,260 tonnes of which 1,087 tonnes was produced in Burma, 167 tonnes in Laos and just six tonnes in Thailand. This latter figure is not even sufficient for opium consumption by the hill peoples themselves.

The opium poppy is sown in September/October (the end of the wet season) and 'harvesting' stretches from the beginning of January through to the end of March. The petals then drop off and the remaining 'pod' is then carefully scoured with a sharp knife. The sap oozes out, oxidizes into a brown gum – raw opium – which is scraped off, rolled into balls and wrapped in banana leaves. It is now ready for sale.

Though profitable, opium has not benefited the hilltribes. In the government's eyes they are criminals, and opium addiction is widespread - up to 30% in some areas. Efforts to change the ways of the hill tribes have focused upon crop substitution programmes and simple intimidation.

Chiang Tung. The long journey to Kengtung is through remote, wild forest, giving a good impression of what Northern Thailand must have been like 50 years ago. Kengtung itself is a historic Tai Yüan community, almost perfectly preserved. The town is a gem compared with raucous Mae Sai. They charge a fee of US$18 for a three-night/four- day visa and an additional transport fee of US$10 at Tachilek (the trip into Burma does not count as an exit/re-entry for single-entry Thai visas and the Thai immigration authorities keep hold of visitors' passports until they return). Visitors are also required to change US$100 into FECs at the official (and very low) rate of exchange. The 'visa' is either for a four- day/three- night or three- day/two- night visit, and all-inclusive tours cost US$260 per person for a party of four for the three- day/two- night trip, or US$320 for four days and three nights.

This was a violent area until recently, with drug dealers, opium poppy cultivators and drug suppression units battling for control. Today, almost all opium cultivation has been displaced into Burma. Even so, it still has a reputation as being relatively lawless.

Luang Cave (Tham Luang) ⓘ *guides with lamps wait outside to lead visitors – for a fee – through the system; take a regular songthaew to turn-off; ask for Tham loo-ang*, is an impressive cave, 3 km off Route 110 to Chiang Rai, 7 km from town, with large caverns and natural rock formations. After the initial large and impressive cavern, the passage narrows to lead – over the course of about 1 km – to a series of smaller chambers.

Doi Tung is a 2,000-m-high hill village, almost 50 km south of Mae Sai. The road snakes its way past Akha, Lahu and KMT villages and former poppy fields, before reaching Wat Phrathat Doi Tung, a total of 24 km from the main road. The road is now surfaced to the summit – although it is still quite a stomach-churning journey and the road has a habit of deteriorating rapidly after heavy rain. The twin chedis on the summit are said to contain the left collarbone of the Buddha and to have been initially built by a king of Chiang Saen in the 10th

century. The views from the wat are breathtaking. A few years ago the King's mother built a palace here, a vast Austrian/Thai chalet with fantastic views over what was, at the time of construction, a devastated and deforested landscape. (Depending on who you talk to, the culprits were either shifting cultivators growing opium or big business interests logging protected land.) With the King's mother's influence, the hills around the palace were reforested. Travel south on Route 110 from Mae Sai for 22 km to Huai Klai and then turn off onto Route 1149. Or take a bus heading for Chiang Rai and ask to be let off in Ban Huai Klai, at the turn-off for Doi Tung. From there, songthaews run to Doi Tung. Now that the road is upgraded the songthaew service is rather more regular – but check on return journeys if you intend to make it back the same day; it is easiest to explore the area by rented motorbike.

Some tour operators do **treks and tours** to hilltribe areas of this region of Thailand. Few trek from here, however, but see Tour operators.

Mae Salong (Santikhiri) → *Colour map 1, grid A3.*

Mae Salong is situated at an altitude of over 1,200 m, close to the border with Burma. It is like a small pocket of China.

After the Communist victory in China in 1949, remnants of the nationalist KMT (Kuomintang) sought refuge here and developed it as a base from which they would mount an invasion of China. This wish has long since faded into fantasy and the Thai authorities have attempted to integrate the exiled Chinese into the Thai mainstream. A paved road now leads to the town which is easily accessible. It is also an alternative place to trek from.

Despite the attempts to Thai-ify Mae Salong, it still feels Chinese. The hillsides are scattered with Japanese sakura trees, with beautiful pink blossom, whilst Chinese herbs and vegetables are grown in the surrounding countryside and sold at the morning market. Many of the inhabitants still speak Chinese, Yunnanese food is sold on the streets, and there are glimpses of China everywhere. One of the reasons why Mae Salong has remained so distinctive is because a significant proportion of the KMT refugees who settled here became involved in opium production and trade. This put the inhabitants in conflict with the Thai authorities and created the conditions whereby they were excluded from mainstream Thai society. Mae Salong's remoteness – at least until recently – also isolated the town from intensive interaction with other areas of the country.

Mae Salong

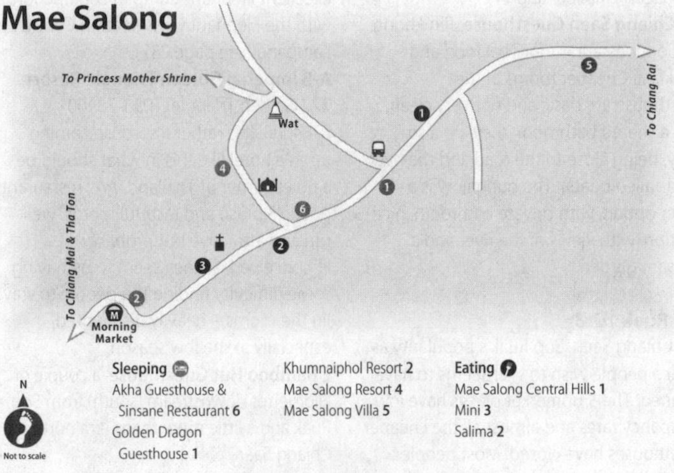

Sleeping
Akha Guesthouse & Sinsane Restaurant 6
Golden Dragon Guesthouse 1
Khumnaiphol Resort 2
Mae Salong Resort 4
Mae Salong Villa 5

Eating
Mae Salong Central Hills 1
Mini 3
Salima 2

The **Morning Market** is worth a visit for early risers (0530-0800), as this is where hill tribe people come to sell their produce. **Wat Santakhiri** is situated in a great position, with views of the hills on the road up to the impressive shrine to the Princess mother. It is a Mahayana Buddhist monastery with images of Kuan Yin and Chinese-style salas.

Around Mae Salong

Pha Dua is a Yao village, 15 km from Mae Salong. It was founded by Yao tribespeople escaping from the Communist Pathet Lao 45 years ago, and during the 1960s it became a centre for the trade in opium. With the opium trade curtailed by the government, the inhabitants have turned to food crops such as cabbages and strawberries, and to tourism, to earn a living. Handicrafts from Burma, Nan (in the eastern highlands) and even Nepal are sold from stalls, while women and children parade the streets in their traditional indigo costumes. If you wish to spend the night here, ask the village headmen if there is anyone who will accommodate you.

Treks to **Akha, Hmong, Shan** and **other hilltribe villages** are arranged by the **Shinsane Guest House,** among others (see Sleeping). It also organizes pony trekking to local hill tribe villages. See also Hill tribes and trekking, Essentials, page 71 and Background, page 664.

Sleeping

Chiang Saen *p286, map p287*

Accommodation is poor; many of the guesthouses have closed and only the Chiang Saen Guesthouse seems to be doing a reasonable trade. Most people visit the city as a day trip from Mae Sai or Chiang Rai.

B Chiang Saen River Hill Hotel, Phahonyothin Soi 2 (just inside the southern city walls), T053-650826, chiangsaen_office @cheerful.com. A/c, restaurant. Best hotel in town with 60 rooms and 4 storeys. Nothing flash, but friendly management and comfortable rooms with attached showers (very clean), minibar and TV.

D-F Chiang Saen Guesthouse, Rimkhong Rd. Good restaurant for Thai food and breakfast. Cheaper rooms in the guesthouse are basic and not very clean, with a shared bathroom; they are also noisy, being close to the road and the river (long-tailed boats). The bungalow is a better option, with private bathroom, nice position, with views of the river and a pleasant garden.

Sop Ruak *p288*

Like Chiang Saen, Sop Ruak's popularity as a place people wish to visit seems to have declined. The 3 upmarket places have low occupancy rates and almost all the cheaper guesthouses have closed. Most people come here on a day trip from Mae Sai or Chiang Rai. The Golden Triangle Paradise Resort (the casino on the island) has an office on the main road through the town.

AL Anantara Golden Triangle, north of Sop Ruak, T053-784084, F784090. Pool, 'traditional' architecture taken to the limit, good service, wonderful evening views, a bit of a blot on the landscape for this timeless area of Thailand, but very well run and good facilities (including tennis and squash courts, gymnasium, pétanque and sauna). It is situated 1 km or so north of Sop Ruak, so is relatively peaceful. Also runs an excellent Elephant Camp in conjunction with the Elephant Conservation Centre near Lampang (see page 237).

A-B Imperial Golden Triangle Resort, 222 Golden Triangle, T053-784001, F784006. It is rather a surprise coming upon a hotel like this in what should be a quiet corner of Thailand. A/c, restaurant, pool, 73 plush and tasteful rooms, well run and attractive but probably ill-conceived, as they seem to be having some difficulty finding the people to stay in the rooms – heavily discounted, especially in the low season.

E Bamboo Hut Guesthouse, a couple of kilometres downstream (south) from Sop Ruak and a little more than 6 km north of Chiang Saen.

Chiang Khong *p289, map p290*
There are now about 30 guesthouses in Chiang Khong; we've listed the pick of the bunch.

C Plabuk Resort, Tambon 122/1 Wiang Rd, T/F053-791281. A/c, restaurant open in the high season, hot water, rooms are bare, but clean and large, with small verandas and attached bathrooms.

C-D Baan Golden Triangle, T053-791350. Positioned on top of a hill to the north of town, this is a stab at a 'back-to-nature' resort: wooden bungalows, garden, cart wheels. The rooms are fine, with attached bathrooms and hot water, great views too, over a tiny rice valley to the Mekong and Laos.

C-D Ruan Thai Sophaphan Resort, Tambon Wiang Rd, T053-791023. Restaurant, big clean rooms with own bathroom and hot water, in a big wooden house with a large raised veranda. The upstairs rooms are better – down below is a little dark. There are also bungalows for 2-4 people, good river views, very friendly, self-service drinks, price negotiable out of season. Recommended.

D-E Ban Tam Mi La, 8/1 Sai Klang Rd. Down a side street (northern end of town), T053-791234. Restaurant, cheaper rooms are very basic with mosquito net and shared bathroom, more expensive rooms have own a private bathroom, bungalows with river views. Attractive rambling garden along the riverside, good food, friendly and helpful, although some recent visitors have said that it is overpriced.

D-F Bamboo Riverside, Sai Khlang Rd. Balconies on riverbank, clean, hot showers, friendly owners with good English and full of information. Generally higher standard of huts to the rest of the places in this category. Restaurant, with superb views over the river to Laos, serves great Mexican food and freshly baked bread.

E-F Green Tree Guesthouse, Sai Khlang Rd. Extremely friendly owner with exceptional English. Pleasant yet basic rooms with shared hot-water showers. Nice shady restaurant. Lots of information on tap and tours available. Recommended.

Mae Sai *p290, map p291*
Most of Mae Sai's guesthouses are concentrated along Sawlongchong Rd which follows the Sai River and the Burmese border upstream (west). The exception is **Chad's House**. Sawlongchong Rd used to be quiet and relatively peaceful but there has been a good deal of new development and it is now rather dusty, noisy and busy. The guesthouses here are ramshackle affairs.

A-B Wang Thong, 299 Phahonyothin Rd, T053-733388, F733399. A/c, restaurant (overrun by tour groups), pool, large new high-rise hotel with 150 rooms, rather over-the-top in terms of decor, small rooms. Low-season discounts are available. Set back from the road in the centre of town. Also a disco available for those (to quote their brochure) "who prefer more turmultuous jollity". Non-guests can use the pool for ฿50.

C-D Top North, 306 Phahonyothin Rd, T053-731955, F732331. Some a/c, from the outside this place doesn't look very promising, but in fact it is well run with large, cleanish rooms. They are reasonably quiet, too as the rooms are some way back from the main road over a river. Restaurant in the lobby serves relatively cheap Thai food.

C-F Northern Guesthouse, 402 Tumphachom Rd, T053-731537, F2121122. Range of rooms on a large plot of land right by the Sai River. The best deals are the raised A-frame huts which are simple but have some charm, the more upmarket rooms – some with a/c, hot water, baths and views over to Burma – are not so competitively priced.

D Thip Sukon, Sawlomgching Rd. New guesthouse with exceptionally clean and spacious rooms. Also offers rooms with cable TV. All with attached bathrooms, though some have squat toilets.

D-E Bamboo House, Sawlomgchong Rd. Good value for money, this place offers rooms with a shared veranda from which there is a fantastic view of Burma. Rooms are clean with attached hot-water bathrooms and novelty bamboo beds. Recommended.

E KK (King Kobra) Guesthouse, 35/5 Sawlomchong Rd, next door to **Mae Sai Plaza Guesthouse** restaurant, T/F053-733055. Rooms are a bit tatty, and attached bathrooms leave a lot to be desired despite hot water. Pleasant eating area with videos screened most evenings. 'Kobra Joe' speaks very good English and runs trekking tours to the area west of Mae Chan. He also organizes trips to Burma and can arrange visas for Laos.

E Mae Sai Plaza Guesthouse, 386/3 Sawlomchong Rd, T053-732230. Good position overlooking river, with views to Burma from the verandas of the huts, but rooms are liable to get damp during the wet season. Shared showers and outside sinks give the place a 'back-to-nature' feel which may not be to everybody's liking. Also available are rooms with attached bathroom and hot water, very popular, good source of local information.

E-F Chad's House, 52/1 Phahonyothin Rd (1½ km from the bridge back towards Mae Chan and Chiang Rai, and about 50 m off the road). A friendly guesthouse run by a Shan family, dorm beds available, good source of information on surrounding countryside.

Around Mae Sai *p291*

Limited accommodation available.

D-E Khwan Guesthouse, Doi Tung, A-frame huts, 2 km along Route 1149.

F Akha Guesthouse (in the Akha village of Ban Pakha), 7 km along the road.

Both are good sources of information on the surrounding area. We have been told that the Akha Guesthouse is officially closed but, unofficially, rooms are still available.

Mae Salong *p293, map p293*

Prices can be bargained down in the low season.

B Khumnaiphol Resort, 58 Moo 1, about 1 km south of town, T053-765000, F765004. Cheap restaurant (Nai Phol Tuan), Thai-style bungalows with mattresses on the floor, attached bathrooms with hot water. Perched on the hillside with great views out west and of Phra Borom That Chedi. Discounts for tours (minimum 10 people), friendly but overpriced.

B-C Mae Salong Villa, just before Mae Salong, on road in from Chiang Rai, T053-765114, F765039. Hot water, good views, some bungalows. Better value than the Mae Salong Resort. Large, barn-like Chinese restaurant attached, with views from the balcony.

C-D Mae Salong Resort, set in a small village of its own, T053-765014, F765132. This is probably the best place to stay here, set up on the hill, with individual though basic bungalows set in a pine forest. Chinese/Thai restaurant and several stalls and shops sell trinkets and Chinese products (such as tea).

D-E Golden Dragon Guesthouse, T053-765009. Own bathroom with hot water and western toilets, clean and quiet rooms, no English spoken.

E Akha Guesthouse, next door to Sinsane. Clean, basic, big rooms with shared bathrooms. A bit noisy but friendly management. Trekking organized by Dan Hill Tribe Tours from here. The restaurant outside is concrete, but the interior is all wood.

E-F Sinsane Basic, grubby and noisy. This is probably the cheapest accommodation in Mae Salong. There is a friendly atmosphere and the food is good.

Eating

Chiang Saen *p286, map p287*

🍴🍴 The areas out of town towards Sop Ruak and the Golden Triangle have better riverside restaurants selling good Thai food, eg **Rim Khong** (2 km north of the city walls) and the **Mekong River Banks** (3 km).

🍴 **Chiang Saen Guesthouse** also does good breakfasts: pancakes, fruit, yoghurt and muesli.

🍴 **Riverside**, close to the **Chiang Saen Guesthouse** is probably the best restaurant. Another clean and well-run place, although it is currently nameless, is on the corner of Rob Wiang and Phahonyothin rds. It serves simple dishes, coffee, ice cream etc.

🍴 There are a number of cheap kwaytio stalls along the riverbank and on Phahonyothin Rd.

Chiang Khong *p289, map p290*

Riverside restaurants compensate for the suprising lack of decent fish. In town, along the main road, there are a number of noodle and rice stalls. The more interesting places are along the river road, or down one of the sois leading to the Mekong.

🍴🍴 **Bamboo Riverside** guesthouse restaurant on Sai Khlang Rd (see above) is recommended – great views over the Mekong to Laos and excellent Mexican food.

🍴🍴 **Nong Kwan**, Sai Khlang Rd, serves great Thai food at reasonable prices. The chicken and cashew dishes are recommended.

Ruan Thai Sophaphan Resort is also worth considering: very comfortable with wicker chairs, cold beer, a great view and good food.
Rimkhong, in the centre, and **Rim Naam**, next door, are good value but the fish dishes are rather limited and hardly memorable.

Mae Sai *p290, map p291*
Restaurants in Mae Sai tend to be serious eating establishments with little character. There are numerous places along Phahonyothin Rd and the market area is good for cheaper stall food. Most guesthouses have restaurants serving Thai food.
Border Pub, which caters for Muslims, has a friendly vibe and good food.
Daw Restaurant, next door to **Thip Sukon** Guesthouse, comes highly recommended serving up delicious Thai grub.

Mae Salong *p293, map p293*
Mae Salong is a good place to eat Yunnanese food. There are expensive restaurants at the **Mae Salong Villa** and **Mae Salong Resort**, and there is also a restaurant housed in a conservatory-type shelter on the roof of the **Mae Salong Central Hills Hotel**, next to the bus stop (fairly priced and great views). It is also worth sampling the excellent Chinese-style chicken noodle soup, which is sold from numerous roadside stalls.
Mini, 300 m past **Sinsane** in direction of Tha Ton, friendly and good.
Salima Restaurant, 100 m past Sinsane Guesthouse, same side of the road. Recommended Muslim restaurant.

Bars and clubs

Chiang Saen *p286, map p287*
Pub and Karaoke, Sai 1 Rd (off Phahonyothin Rd, not far from the post office). Reasonable place for a cold beer.

Chiang Khong *p289, map p290*
If you're looking for a place for an evening drink most of the riverside restaurants are worth contemplating. For dedicated bars try either the **Bam-Boo bar** (which has the added advantage of a free pool) or **999 Bar**. Both are popular.

Shopping

Sop Ruak *p288*
Most people come to Sop Ruak for the shopping which is interesting, but hardly spectacular. Goods from China, Laos and Burma, as well as hill tribe handicrafts, are on sale from countless stalls. The range of goods – and what vendors have decided people would wish to buy – is sometimes perplexing: crocheted hats, nylon hammocks, animal skulls, weaver bird nests. There are also some more expected items: gems, traditional textiles and T-shirts, for example.

Chiang Khong *p289, map p290*
Chiang Khong is not the obvious place to come shopping, but there is one decent place selling traditional textiles, woodcarvings, handicrafts and other items: **Thai Lue Textiles**, on the main road, just north of Wat Phra Kaew.

Mae Sai *p290, map p291*
Most people who come to Mae Sai, come for the shopping. There are scores of stalls and shops selling Burmese, Chinese, Lao and Thai goods. The Burmese products are the most diverse and the best buys: puppets, cheroots, gemstones, 'antiques', lacquerware.
Mandalay Shop, 381/1-4 Phahonyothin Rd, for Burmese jade, sapphires and rubies (see box, page 145).

Activities and tours

Sop Ruak *p288*
Tour operators
Dits Travel, Baanboran Hotel, T053-716678, F716680. Organizes tours to Burma.

Chiang Khong *p289, map p290*
Tour operators
There is a growing number of tour companies in Chiang Khong.
Ann Tour, 6/1 Sai Klang Rd, T/F053-791218, is recommended.

North of town, by the pier, there is **Chiang Khong Tour** and **Nam Khong Travel**. They get most of their business arranging **visas for Laos** (a photocopy of your passport is needed). The process

normally takes from 24-48 hrs, although visas cannot be arranged at weekends – travellers' passports are bused to the Laos embassy in Bangkok. Note that the visa situation for Laos is fluid. It is now possible to get a visa on arrival in Laos when crossing the Friendship Bridge, near Nong Khai, in Northeast Thailand (see page 357) but for entry from Chiang Khong, advance visas are still necessary. Most people opt for a 30-day visa which can be purchased from most guesthouses, ฿1,200. Guesthouses can also provide transport and organize boat trips.

Mae Sai *p290, map p291*

Tour operators

The Mae Sai Plaza Guesthouse, Mae Sai Riverside and the Northern Guesthouse all organize treks for about ฿300 per day. See also Hill tribes and trekking, Essentials, page 71 and Background, page 664.

Ananda Tour, 22 Phahonyothin Rd, T053-731038, F731749.

Mandalay Tour, 382-83 Phahonyothin Rd (next to Mandalay Shop). Or book in Bangkok with **Diethelm Travel**, Kian Gwan Building, 140/1 Wittayu Rd, T053-2559150, F2560248. A 3- day/2- night tour to Burma costs around ฿6,500 or ฿8,000 for a 4-day/3- night tour (minimum 4 people).

Visas for Laos These can be arranged in town either through one of the tour companies or through 'Kobra Joe' at the KK Guesthouse, Kkmaesai@chmai.loxinfo.co.th.

Transport

Chiang Saen *p286, map p287*

Boat

Long-tailed boats can be hired from the riverbank at the end of Phahonyothin Rd. A boat downstream to **Chiang Khong** should cost around ฿1,200-1,500 and can take 8 people (1 hr 20 mins). To **Sop Ruak**, upstream (30 mins), should cost ฿400 for a boat.

Bus

Regular connections with **Chiang Rai** (1 hr 20 mins), **Mae Sai** (1 hr) and **Chiang Khong** (2 hrs).

Motorbike and bicycle

Hire from SK Hire on Soi 1 Rd and from a shop on Phahonyothin Rd close to Soi 2, ฿150 per day for a Honda Dream. **SK Hire** also has vehicles for hire.

Motorized saamlors

By the bus stop for trips around the sights.

Sop Ruak *p288*

Boat

From the pier, for trips to **Chiang Saen** for ฿400 per boat and on to **Chiang Khong** (see below for details).

Car

Avis, from Golden Triangle Hotel.

Songthaew

Regular connections with **Mae Sai** (40 mins) and **Chiang Saen** (10 mins, ฿10). Just flag one down on the road – they run through Sop Ruak about every 40 mins.

Chiang Khong *p289, map p290*

Chiang Khong is small enough to explore on foot, but the town does have a rather quaint line in underpowered motorized rickshaws, which struggle gamely up anything which is not billiard-table flat. Tour companies provide cars with drivers for around ฿1,200 per day. Bicycles and motorbikes are available for hire from guesthouses.

Boat

These can be chartered to make the journey to/from **Chiang Saen** (about ฿150 per head or ฿1,200-1,500 to charter an entire boat).

International connections to Laos It is possible for foreigners to cross into Laos from Chiang Khong, across the Mekong to Ban Houei Xai. Visas can be obtained in Chiang Khong from one of the tour operators that are mushrooming as travel to Laos becomes easier. Long-tailed boats ferry passengers across the Mekong to Ban Houei Xai, from Tha Rua Bak (฿20).

Visas for Laos Any tour company will organize visas; see Tour operators above. The pier and Thai immigration are 1 km or so north of town, and long-tailed boats take people across for ฿20.

Bus

Hourly connections with **Chiang Rai** (3 hrs). A/c and non-a/c connections with **Bangkok** and **Chiang Mai** (6½ hrs), as well as

Lampang and **Phayao**. A/c buses leave from the office on the main road near Wat Phra Kaew. Non-a/c buses depart from the bus station, just over the Huai Sob Som on the south edge of town. Non-a/c buses for **Chiang Saen** leave from 0600, and take the attractive river road following the Mekong and the Thai-Lao border (2 hrs).

Songthaew
Regular connections with **Chiang Saen** and from there on to **Sop Ruak**, **Mae Sai** and **Chiang Rai**. Songthaews leave from opposite the army post next to the post office, but can be flagged down as they make their way north through Chiang Khong.

Mae Sai *p290, map p291*
Bus
The main bus station is 5 km out of town, just off the main road running to Mae Chan and Chiang Rai. Songthaews and motorcycle taxis take passengers from town to the terminal and vice versa. Regular connections with **Bangkok**'s Northern bus terminal (13-15 hrs), **Chiang Mai** (5 hrs), **Chiang Rai** (1 hr 20 mins), and **Mae Chan**.

Motorbike
Many of the guesthouses that used to rent out motorbikes have stopped because of the number of accidents. However, there are still a couple of places hiring out bikes, and most guesthouses will find a machine if required. Prices start at ฿150 per day for a Honda Dream. Thong Motorbike Rental, Sawlongchong Rd. Batman Motorbike, Sawlongchong Rd.

Songthaew
Connections with **Chiang Saen**, **Sop Ruak** and the Golden Triangle, every 30-40 mins. Songthaews leave from Phahonyothin Rd, near the centre of town. Songthaews for **Mae Chan** and **Chiang Rai** also leave from town, saving a journey out to the bus terminal.

Mae Salong *p293, map p293*
Regular songthaew connections with **Chiang Rai** (1½ hrs). Also morning songthaew connections along a rough road with **Tha Ton** (2 hrs); during the rainy season the road is sometimes closed. To get from **Chiang Rai** to Mae Salong, take the Mae Sai bus and get off at **Ban Pasang** (40 mins); from there catch a songthaew up the mountain to Mae Salong (1 hr). The last songthaew leaving from Mae Salong down to **Ban Pasang** is at 1700; buses on the Chiang Rai-Ban Pasang route run every 15 mins, 0600-1800.

Directory

Chiang Saen *p286, map p287*
Banks Siam Commercial, 116 Phahonyothin Rd (exchange service). ATM on Phahonyothin Rd. **Post office** Phahonyothin Rd.

Sop Ruak *p288*
Banks Two money changers by the Opium Museum, a Thai Farmers Bank and a small branch of the Siam Commercial Bank. Open daily 0900-1600.

Chiang Khong *p289, map p290*
Banks Siam Commercial, Sai Khlang Rd, opposite the district office, has a currency exchange service. Thai Farmers, 416 Sai Khlang Rd. **Internet** There are several places with internet access at the northern end of Sai Khlang Rd. **Post office** On main road next to the army post. **Telephone** In post office for international calls.

Mae Sai *p290, map p291*
Banks A number of banks with money-changing facilities, some open daily 0830-1700. Bangkok Metropolitan Bank, Phahonyothin Rd. Krung Thai, Phahonyothin Rd. Thai Farmers, 122/1 Phahonyothin Rd. **Internet** Internet access can be found next door to the Wang Thong Hotel. **Post office** Phahonyothin Rd (2 km from bridge towards Mae Chan). **Telephone** Next door to the post office.

Phrae, Nan and the Eastern highlands

The Eastern highlands, an area of outstanding natural beauty, friendly relaxed vibes and intriguing histories, is still off the main tourist and backpacker routes. This adds to its charm: the area's burgeoning tourist industry is easily integrated into a genuine slice of Thai rural life. Phrae is an attractive and friendly provincial capital with good restaurants and accommodation. The town is situated in a narrow rice valley on the banks of the Mae Yom River, flanked by mountains to the east and west. Nan is a province to be explored for its natural beauty. Fertile valleys are chequered with paddy fields, teak plantations, hill tribes and fast-running rivers. It was not until 1931 that the central authorities managed to overcome the area's inaccessibility and bring Nan under Bangkok's direct control. Ever since then, there have been periods – most recently in the 1970s when Communist insurgency was a problem – when the army and the police have treated the province as a no-go area virtually. It still exudes an atmosphere of other-worldliness and isolation. In addition there are rarely visited national parks, some of the finest forestry in the country, weaving villages and treks to see the hill peoples of the area. ▸▸ *For Sleeping, Eating and other listings see pages 304-306.*

Phrae → *Colour map 1, grid B3.*

Phrae was founded in the 12th century – when it was known as Wiang Kosai or Silk Cloth City – and is one of the oldest cities in Thailand. It still has its own 'royal' family and was an independent Thai muang (city state) until the early 16th century, when it was captured by an army from Ayutthaya. When Ayutthaya's power began to wane in the 18th century, Phrae – like many other northern principalities – came under the sway of the Burmese. It was finally incorporated into the Siamese state in the 19th century.

Phrae's ancient roots can still be seen in the city walls and which moat the separate the old city from the new commercial centre. On Charoen Muang Road, there are also a handful of attractive wooden Chinese shophouses, although the scourge of uncontrolled development is gradually gnawing away at the remnants of old Phrae.

Ins and outs

Phrae is not a large place. The main bus terminal is a 15-minute walk from much of the accommodation and the town is pleasant enough to stroll around.

Sights

The Burmese-style **Wat Chom Sawan** ⓘ *admission by donation*, is on the edge of town, about 1 km northeast of the centre, on the road to Nan. It was commissioned by Rama V (1868-1910) and designed by a Burmese architect. Like most Burmese (Thai Yai) wats, the bot and viharn are consolidated in one elaborate, multi-roofed towering structure, with verandas and side rooms. It has survived relatively unscathed; the wooden roof tiles have not been replaced by corrugated iron, and the rich original interior decoration of mirror tiles upon a deep red ground is also intact. Ask one of the monks to point out the rare Buddhist texts carved on sheets of ivory, and the bamboo and gold Buddha 'basket'.

Wat Luang ⓘ *admission by donation*, is a few minutes' walk from Wat Sri Chum, near the city wall and moat. The wat was founded in the 12th century, although continuous renovation and expansion has obscured its ancient origins.

The wat also supports an impressive museum which houses valuable Buddha images, swords, coins, burial caskets, Buddhist texts, old photographs (one of a decapitation), betel boxes and jewellery. An old northern house, with all the accessories of traditional life, is also part of the collection. Finally, the wat is also notable for its fine well pavilion on the west wall and the individual monk's kutis, or cells, like small bungalows, along the south wall.

Around Phrae

Wat Phrathat Chor Hae ⓘ *take a songthaew from Charoen Muang Rd, near the intersection with Yantarakitkoson Rd, ฿10; there are few return songthaews in the afternoon, so it is best to make the trip in the morning, a hilltop wat, 8 km southeast of town*, probably dates from the 12th to 13th centuries. Its 28 m-high-chedi is said to contain a hair of the Lord Buddha, brought here by the Indian Emperor Asoka. The chedi is surrounded by a small cloister and linked to this is an ornate, high-ceilinged viharn, with bold murals depicting episodes from the Buddha's life. The name of the wat is the same as that of a particularly fine cloth woven by the people of the area and in which the chedi is shrouded each year. Also here, at the foot of the hill, are a number of souvenir stalls.

Muang Phi, the City of Ghosts, is an area of strange, eroded rock formations, about 15 km northeast of town. Turn right after 9 km off Route 101 to Nan, and onto Route 1134; the turning for the canyon is 6 km along Route 1134 and lies about 2 km off the road. It is easiest by chartered songthaew (about ฿200). Alternatively, take a bus towards Nan and get off at the intersection with Route 1134, which is signposted to Muang Phi. From here, catch another songthaew (not regular) and get off after 6 km to walk the final 2 km or so to Muang Phi.

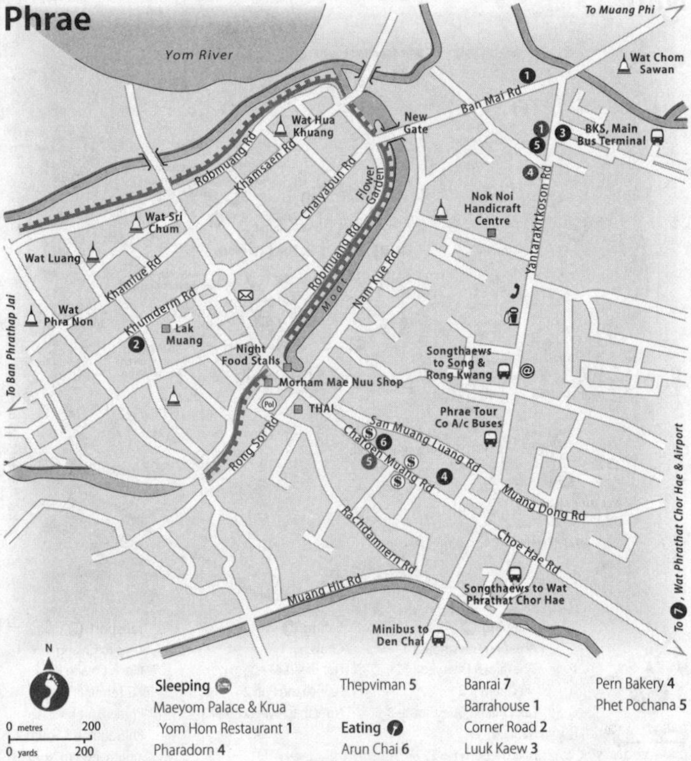

Nan → *Colour map 1, grid B4.*

A cute, friendly town with an historical ambience, Nan occupies a small valley in the far eastern highlands of the north – about 50 km from the border with Laos. It is thought the earliest settlers arrived from Laos in 1282, establishing a town 70 km north of Nan. According to legend the Buddha himself was trekking here, picking out auspicious sites for wats, over 2,500 years ago. The 13th-century inscriptions of King Ramkhamhaeng of Sukhothai named Nan as one of the muang whose 'submission he received', although it would be more accurate to view the royal house of Nan ruling autonomously until the 15th century, when Lanna established suzerainty over Nan. Even then, the turbulent politics of the area, with the Burmese, Lao, Siamese and the muang of the area all vying with one another, coupled with Nan's location, afforded it considerable independence.

Sights

The **National Museum** ⓘ *Phakong Rd, daily 0900-1200, 1300-1600, ฿30*, once the home of the Nan royal family, houses an impressive collection, including beautiful wood and bronze Buddha images, ceramics, textiles, jewellery and musical instruments. There's a decent ethnographic display offering an insight into the lives of the local ethnic groups and a collection of stone-age tools. On the second floor, protected in a steel cage is a 97-cm-long black elephant tusk which once belonged to the Nan royal family and is reputed to have magical powers. This is a great little museum and well worth a visit; exhibits are well displayed with English explanations throughout.

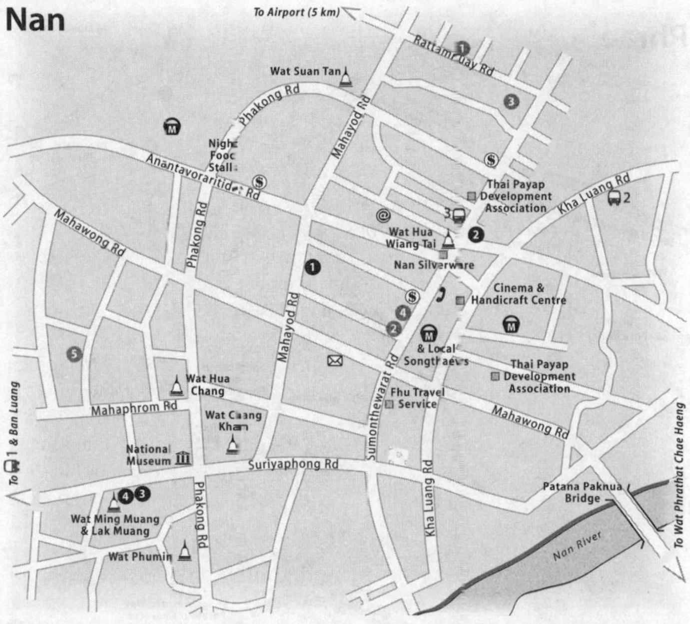

N

0 metres 100
0 yards 100

Sleeping
Amazing Guesthouse 1
Dhevaraj & Dhevee Restaurant 2
Doi Phukha Guesthouse 3
Nanfa 4
Nan Guesthouse 5

Eating
Chokchai 1
Hot Bread 4
Laanchang Pub 2
No Name Kwaytio Stall 3

Transport
Buses to Chiang Mai & Chiang Rai 1
BKS Terminal for Phrae, Bangkok, Phitsanulok & South 2
Songthaews to North 3

Just opposite the National Museum on Phakong Road is **Wat Phumin**. Built in 1596 it was restored between 1865 and 1873. The cruciform bot-cum-viharn is supported by the coils of two magnificent nagas (mythical serpents). The head forms the buttress of the north entrance, and the tail the south. Inside, there are some of the finest murals to be found in the north. Painted at the end of the 19th century – probably in 1894 – they depict the tale of the Sihanadajataka, but also illustrate aspects of northern Thai life: hunting, weaving, lovers, musicians, elephants, courtiers, a starving farang clasping a tool for premasticating food (eastern wall, top) and people with over-large testicles. The naive style of the murals – large areas of empty space, figures of various sizes – distinguish them from the sophisticated art of Bangkok.

Wat Chang Kham, on the diagonally opposite corner to Wat Phumin, features a chedi supported by elephant buttresses (caryatids), similar to those at Sukhothai. The viharn was built in 1547 and contains three Sukhothai-style Buddha images, two walking and one standing. There's a large seminary here and the temple compound is often filled with dozens of friendly, shaven-headed novices.

Wat Ming Muang, on Suriyaphong Road, contains the city of Nan's **lak muang** (city pillar), liberally draped in garlands. Wat Hua Chang, on the corner of Phakong and Mahaphrom roads, features a two-storey stone and wood tripitaka, or scripture, library, a square-based chedi with four Buddhas in raised niches and a fine bot (with bai sema). Gaudy **Wat Hua Wiang Tai** is on Sumonthewarat Road, just north of Anantavoraritdet Road and has nagas running along the top of the surrounding wall and bright murals painted on the exterior of the viharn. Other wats in the town include **Wat Suan Tan**, in Tambon Nai Wiang, which has a prang – unusual for the area – and a 15th-century bronze Buddha image named Phra Chao Thong Thit. A fireworks display takes place at the wat during **Songkran**.

Around Nan

Wat Phrathat Chae Haeng ⓘ *30-min walk across the Nan River and then east, or rent a bicycle/motorbike*, 3 km southeast of town, was built in 1355. The 55-m-high, gold-sheeted chedi is Lao in style, and the bot has an interesting multi-tiered roof (a fair with fireworks and processions is held here on the full moon day of the first lunar month). Also notable are the fine pair of nagas that form the balustrade of the approach stairway to the monastery.

Sao Din ⓘ *either catch a local bus to Amphoe Na Noi and then charter a motorcycle taxi, or charter a songthaew from town*, in Amphoe Na Noi lies about 30 km south of Nan, off Route 1026. It is a heavily eroded canyon with tall earth pillars and deeply eroded earth, reminiscent of Muang Phi outside Phrae. It's also the site of some of the prehistoric finds in Nan's museum.

Tha Wang Pha ⓘ *amphoe (district) capital 40 km to the north of Nan on Route 1080. Regular local bus or songthaew from the stand on Sumonthewarat Rd, just north of Anantavoraritdet Rd. For Ban Nong Bua, get off at the fork before Tha Wang Pha and walk about 2 km (tell the conductor where you are going)*, is famous for its Tai Lue weaving. The Tai Lue were forced out of Yunnan in southern China by King Rama I (1782-1809), settled in Nan province, turned to farming and are now peacefully assimilated into the Thai population. They've not lost all their cultural distinctiveness: these skilled weavers still wear a tubular pha sin of bright stripes and a black jacket, decorated with multicoloured embroidered stripes and silver jewellery. Tai Lue textiles and jewellery are available in town. En route to Tha Wang Pha, about 35 km north of Nan, is the turn-off for Ban Nong Bua and the fine **Wat Nong Bua**. The monastery is Tai Lue in design and features fine murals, executed by the same Tai Lue artists who are thought to have decorated Wat Phumin in Nan (see above). Tai Lue textiles are also available in this small town.

Doi Phu Kha National Park ⓘ *check at Park HQ (PO.Box 8, Tambol Phu Ka, Amphur Pua, Nan Province 55120, T01-2240789 (mob) for details on trekking. The*

 best time to visit is between Nov-Feb, but it is cold so take warm clothes. The rainy season here is May-Oct; catch a bus to Pua (1 hr from Nan); from Pua, songthaews run from 0800 to 1200 up to the Park HQ (฿20);outside those times they have to be chartered (฿350), 70 km North of Nan, is one of Northern Thailands largest and newest protected areas and offers good trekking. The mountainous park covers more than 1,700 sq km and is named after a 1,980-m peak, which provides good views. The limestone mountain ranges also offer an abundance of waterfalls, caves, crags and grottoes. A variety of deciduous and evergreen forest types provide a home for a range of hill tribes and for a number of rare and near extinct flora; particularly the pink flowered Chomphu Phukha (*bretschneidera ninensis hems 1*).

The park is in the mountains, so it can get cold at night.

Sleeping

Phrae *p300, map p301*

B-C Maeyom Palace, 181/6 Yantarakitkoson Rd, T054-521028, F522904. A/c, restaurant, pool. Best hotel in town, situated 1 km from the town centre, large rooms and professional service, organizes tours to hill tribe villages and home industries, discounts available, especially in the low season, bikes for hire (฿100 per day). Pool can be used by non-guests for ฿45.

D Pharadorn, 177 Yantarakitkoson Rd, T054-511177. Some a/c, restaurant, karaoke bar. Rooms are spacious and clean, a/c rooms benefit from carpets and hot water, good value.

F Thepviman, 226-228 Charoen Muang Rd, T054-511003. Typical Chinese hotel, friendly.

Nan *p302, map p302*

A-B City Park, 99 Moo 4 Yantarakitkoson Rd, Tambon Tuu Tai, T054-710376. A/c, restaurant, large pool. Motel/resort-style hotel on a 4-ha plot outside town, all rooms have TV and minibar, peaceful, but inconvenient for exploring the city.

B-D Dhevaraj (pronounced – thewarat), 466 Sumonthewarat Rd, T054-710094. Range of good, if bland, hotel rooms, some a/c, some fan, all en suite. Clean and well run, pool, spa and excellent restaurant. Recommended.

C-D Nanfa, 438-440 Sumonthewarat Rd, T054-710284. A 100-year-old teak building. The run-down rooms are large, en suite and have a TV.

D-E Amazing Guesthouse, 25/7 Rattamnuay Rd, T054-710893. Homely atmosphere with simple rooms and shared bathrooms with hot showers. English spoken, friendly and clean. The owner will pick you up from the bus station if you phone upon arrival. Recommended.

D-E Doi Phukha Guesthouse, 94/5 Sumonthewarat Soi 1, T054-771422. An old teak house set in leafy compound. Quiet, clean rooms with shared western toilets, dorm beds also available (**F**), lots of trekking and excursion information, sells books and a good map of Nan, very friendly, good atmosphere.

D-E Nan Guesthouse, 57/16 Mahaphrom Rd, T054-771849. Nice guesthouse in quiet, rural backstreets. More expensive rooms are en suite. Clean, friendly. Recommended.

Around Nan *p303*

Two government houses rent out rooms in Doi Phu Kha National Park when officials are not staying. Pay by donation. There also 14 bungalows with shared toilets (฿200 per night) and two campsites (one at headquarters and one at the Star Gazing Area (฿100 per night). The cook at headquarters will prepare meals for you if you call (T054-6029844) ahead of arrival; breakfast (฿60), lunch (฿80), dinner (฿120).

Eating

Phrae *p300, map p301*

There is a series of good little restaurants and foodstalls stretching along Charoen Muang and Robmuang roads and there are several bars on Rachdamnern Rd.

Krua Yom Hom (Maeyom Palace Hotel), Yantarakitkoson Rd. Expensive Thai, Chinese and European food, but live band and seafood barbecue in evening makes it worth it.

Arun Chai, Charoen Muang Rd (opposite Ho Faa Hotel). Good food.

Ban Rai, Yantarakitkoson Rd, large outdoor garden restaurant, 2 km out of town on road south.

Barrahouse, 45 Ban Mai Rd (1 km from town on road to Nan). Friendly owners, good

food, clean and welcoming, coffee and ice cream, along with usual Thai/Chinese dishes.

Corner Road, corner of Lak Muang and Khumderm roads. Serves ice cream, clean, friendly and pleasant atmosphere.

Luuk Kaew, Yantarakitkoson Rd (opposite Maeyom Palace Hotel). Excellent Thai and Chinese food, succulent satay. Highly recommended. Only open in evening.

Phet Pochana, Yantarakitkoson Rd (next to Maeyom Palace Hotel). Open-air restaurant, also serves Chinese dishes.

Bakeries

Pern Bakery, 347 Charoen Muang Rd. Cakes, pastries, coffee and ice cream.

Nan *p302, map p302*

Chokchai, Mahayot Rd. Good food and friendly.

Dhervee, found in the **Dhevaraj hotel**, serves up a large range of excellent Thai food. It also has a tasty lunchtime buffet (daily 1100-1400) for ฿59, including coffee, soft drinks and dessert – a great deal for the quality. Recommended.

Hot Bread, 38/2 Suriyaphong Rd, good veggie menu, freshly baked pitta bread, great coffee and friendly English speaking owner.

Restaurant (no name) 38/1 Suriyaphong Rd (next to Wat Ming Muang/opposite museum). Excellent spicy kwaytio khao soi (egg noodles in curry broth).

Foodstalls

There is a small night market at the intersection of Phakong and Anantavoraritidet roads, lots of decent noodle shops along Sumonthewarat Rd and an excellent daytime food market just opposite the **Dhevaraj hotel**.

Bars and clubs

Nan *p302, map p302*

62 Bar and Restaurant, Sumonthewarat Rd. Serves excellent coffee, especially espresso.

Laanchang Pub, Sumonthewarat Rd. Wild ornamentation including leopard skins and hanging vines. Good place for an evening drink, occasional live music.

Pin Pub, Nanfa Hotel, plays live country music (which adds to the Wild West ambience) most nights and cheap Thai food.

Festivals and events

Nan *p302, map p302*

Mid Oct-mid Nov Boat races, at the end of the Buddhist Lent. These races are thought to have started about a century ago, when they were part of the Songkran celebrations. The boats are hollowed-out logs, painted in bright designs. There is a lively fair in the weeks before (and during) the races.

Shopping

Phrae *p300, map p301*

Clothes

Phrae is a centre of morhom production – the traditional blue garb of the northern farmer. A simple tunic costs ฿60-100. Available all over town, but recommended is **Morhom Mae Nuu**, 60-62 Charoen Muang Rd.

Handicrafts

Nok Noi Handicraft Centre, 6/3 Yantarakitkoson Trok [Soi] 2. Woodcarvings, some clothing, baskets and hats.

Nan *p302, map p302*

Department stores

Nara Department store, Sumonthewarat Rd (north of intersection with Anantaroraritdet Rd).

Handicrafts

Ban Fai, Kha Luang Rd. Basketry, textiles and woodcarving.

Thai Payap Development Association, a co-op selling hilltribes' handicrafts.

Jewellery

Nan Silverware, corner of Sumonthewarat and Anantavoraritidet roads, for locally produced jewellery.

Supermarkets

Big D Supermarket, along the Sumonthewarat Rd (opposite the Thai Payap Development Association).

Activities and tours

Nan *p302, map p302*

Fhu Travel Service, 453/4 Sumonthewarat Rd, T054-710636, is the best tour company. Mr Fhu rents out bicycles and motorbikes

and arranges treks to see local hill tribes, the Doi Phu Kha National Park, provincial sites and boat tours up the Nan River. Prices from ฿600 per day upwards – given the quality of the service provided this isgood value for money.
The **Dhevaraj**, **Nan Guesthouse**, **Doi Phukha** and **Nan Fah** also organize tours. See also Hilltribes and trekking, Essentials, page 71 and Background, page 664.

Transport

Phrae *p300, map p301*

Air

The airport is 7 km southeast of town. Daily connections on THAI with **Bangkok** (1 hr 20 mins). THAI lays on transport from town to the airport.

Airline offices **THAI**, Rachdamnern Rd, T054-511123.

Bus

The terminal is 1 km northeast of the city centre off Yantarakitkoson Rd, opposite the Maeyom Palace Hotel. Regular connections with **Bangkok**'s Northern bus terminal (8¼ hrs), **Uttaradit**, **Chiang Mai** and other towns in the north (hourly connections with Nan, 2-2½ hrs). A/c tour buses for **Bangkok** leave from Phrae Tour's offices at 141/6 Yantarakitkoson Rd at 2030 and 2100.

Songthaew

Songthaew is the main form of local transport. Songthaews running north to Song and Rong Kwang leave from outside the Piriyalai School on Yantarakitkoson Rd; those running south to Den Chai (for the nearest train station) depart from Yantarakitkoson Rd near the intersection with Muang Hit Rd (by the petrol station).

Train

The nearest train station to Phrae is at Den Chai, 24 km southwest of town. Connections south to **Bangkok** (8½ hrs) and north to **Chiang Mai** (4½ hrs). Regular buses and songthaews from the train station to town; to get to Den Chai, pick up a bus on Yantarakitkoson Rd near the intersection with Muang Hit Rd (by the petrol station).

Nan *p302, map p302*

Air

The airport is on the northern edge of town (5 km from the centre). Connections on PB Air with **Bangkok** (2 hrs 10 mins). For ticket information contact **Fahthanin Travel** Agency, T054-711223.

Airline offices PB has an office at the airport

Bicycle and motorbike

Hire from Fhu Travel Service, Oversea Shop, Nan and Rob Muang guesthouses and Laanchang Pub.

Bus

Nan has 2 bus terminals. Buses for towns to the north and west, including **Chiang Rai**, **Chiang Mai** (5½ hrs, ฿117), **Lamphun**, **Lampang**, **Phrae** and **Den Chai**, leave from the station off Anantavoraritdet Rd about 1 km west of the town centre. Buses running north to **Chiang Rai** take 2 routes: either a trip west and northwest on routes 1091 and 1251 to Phayao and then north to Chiang Rai, or by first running south to Phrae and then north to Phayao and Chiang Rai.

Buses serving destinations to the south, including **Bangkok**'s Northern bus terminal (9½-10 hrs), **Phitsanulok**, **Uttaradit**, **Nakhon Sawan**, **Kamphaeng Phet** and **Sukhothai**, leave from the BKS terminal, 500 m to the north of the city centre on Kha Luang Rd. VIP and a/c buses go to major destinations. Bus times and costs displayed on boards at the **Nan** and **Doi Phukha** Guesthouses. The information officers at the terminals speak English.

Directory

Phrae *p300, map p301*

Banks Several on Charoen Muang Rd. **Internet** Internet café on Yantarakitkoson Rd. **Post office** Charoen Muang Rd (in the old city), with telephone. **Telephone** 163/2 Yantarakitkoson Rd.

Nan *p302, map p302*

Banks Thai Farmers and Bangkok on Sumonthewarat Rd. **Internet** Internet café on Anantavoraritdet Rd. **Post office** Mahawong Rd (with international telephone, fax facilities). **Telephone** 345/7 Sumonthewarat Rd.

Northeast Thailand

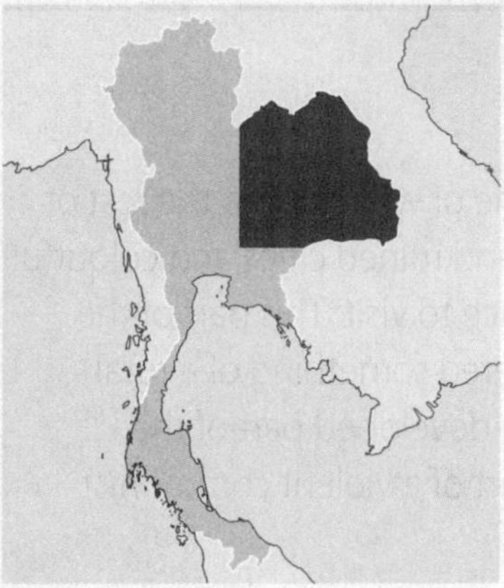

Footprint features

Introduction

The Northeastern region has none of what makes the rest of Thailand appealing: beaches, grand ruined cities and colourful hill tribes; it is not an obvious place to visit. This part of the country has always been considered something of a rural backwater. It is the poorest, least developed part of the country and was once at the heart of a violent communist insurgency in the 1970s.

So, what's the attraction? Partly it is the welcome; this is the friendliest region of a friendly country. The locals, tired of being labelled country bumpkins by the sophisticates of Bangkok, are delighted to see visitors taking an interest in their region. However, there's more than this. At Ban Chiang, a village east of Udon Thani, some of the world's earliest evidence of agriculture has been uncovered, dating back 5,000-7,000 years. The region once formed an integral part of the magnificent Khmer Empire based at Angkor. The impressive ruins at Phimai, Phnom Rung, Muang Tham and Prasat Khao Phra Viharn clearly show that Isaan – the Thai name for the Northeast – has not always been devoid of 'civilized' life, whatever those in Bangkok might like to think. There's a rich, contemporary Isaan culture too: check out the exotic temple fairs and wild rocket festivals; the fine hand-woven textiles and unique celebrations of Buddhist lent; aromatic *kai yang* (grilled chicken) and fiery *som tam* (papaya salads); while Isaan pop musicians, nasal to the max, are among the highest sellers in the country. And don't forget national parks, mountain walks, elephant treks, tubing on the Mekong and the best bicycling in the country.

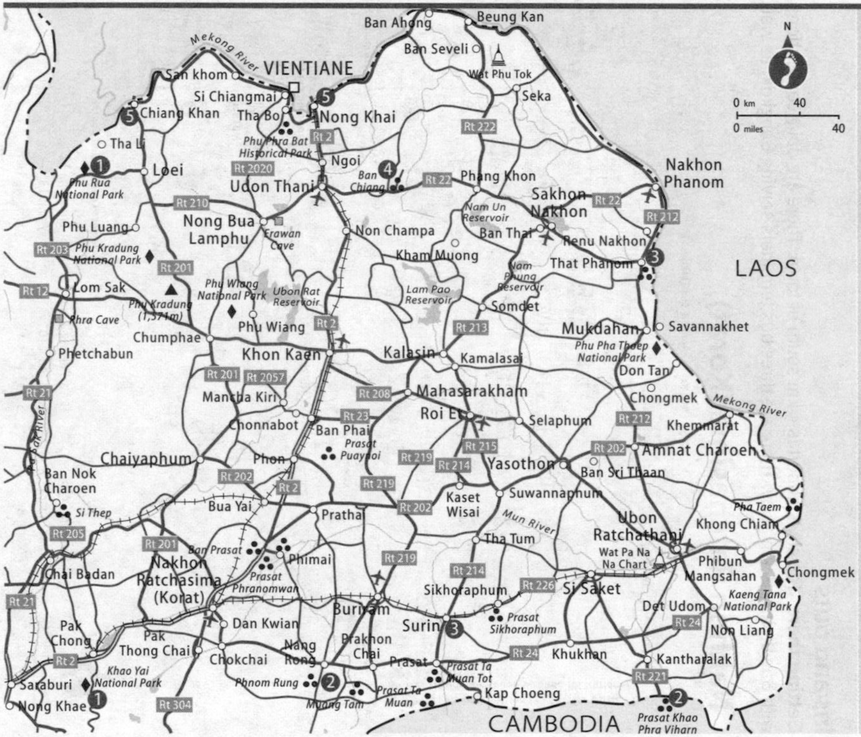

★ Don't miss...

1 **The northeast's national parks** Meander around the gorgeous rivers and forests of divine Khao Yai. Other notable national parks in the area include Phu Rua, page 314 and 351.

2 **The finest Khmer monuments outside Cambodia** Take in an unforgettable sunset at Phnom Rung and find the energy to climb up to spectacular Prasat Khao Phra Viharn, just inside the Cambodian border, pages 317 and 328.

3 **The Northeast's best-known festivals** In November, witness a spectacular elephant round-up near Surin while the That Phanom temple fair in January or February is one of Thailand's brashest, pages 324 and 368.

4 **Ban Chiang** Northeast Thailand is one of the cradles of Asian civilization – find out more by visiting the inspiring prehistoric archaeological site here, page 349.

5 **Mekong towns** Escape life, the universe and everything, particularly other travellers, by spending some languid time at a string of Mekong towns such as Chiang Khan, where lazing by the riverside is one of the chief occupations, and Nong Khai, where you can admire the French colonial architecture, pages 351 and 357.

Nakhon Ratchasima (Korat) and around

Most visitors to the Northeast only travel as far as Nakhon Ratchasima more commonly known as Korat, the largest town in the Northeast and an important provincial capital. It's the main base for visiting the magnificent Khmer monuments of Phimai, Phnom Rung and Muang Tham.

Korat was established when the older settlements of Sema and Khorakpura were merged under King Narai in the 17th century. During the Vietnamese War, Korat provided an important US airbase. The warplanes that set out from here bombed the Ho Chi Minh Trail – the infamous Vietcong supply.

The ancient sanctuary of Phimai lies to the northeast of Korat, Ban Khwao famed for its silk weaving lies to the northwest, the popular Khao Yai National Park is situated to the southwest and the remarkable Phnom Rung, the finest Khmer Temple in Thailand, lies to the southeast. » *For Sleeping, Eating and other listings, pages 319-323.*

Nakhon Ratchasima → *Colour map 2, grid C2.*

Ins and outs

Getting there The city's airport is 5 km south of town. There are daily connections with Bangkok, 256 km away. There are three bus terminals serving Bangkok, as well

Nakhon Ratchasima (Korat)

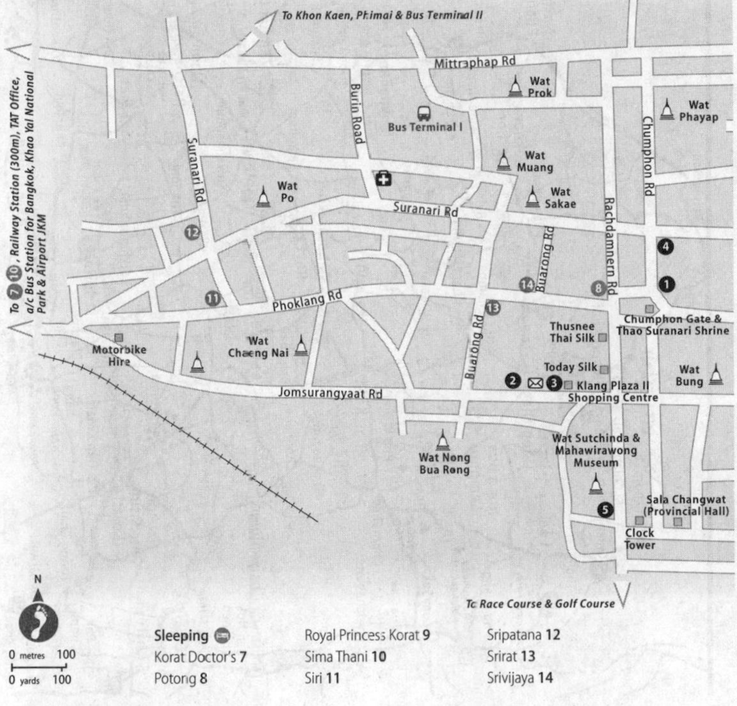

as many other destinations in the North, Northeast and Central Plains. The railway station is west of the town centre and provides links with Bangkok and other destinations in the Northeast. » *See also Transport, page 322.*

Getting around Korat is a large town. A city bus system (bus maps available from the tourist office), along with a plentiful supply of tuk-tuks and saamlors, provide transportation.

Tourist information TAT ⓘ *2102-2104 Mittraphap Rd, T044-213666, 0830-1630*, on the western edge of town, is inconveniently located – although town bus No 2 runs out here – next door to the **Sima Thani Hotel**. Good town maps available, along with a fair amount of other information of Korat and the Northeastern region. It is worth coming out here if you can find the time.

Sights

The older part of the town lies to the west, while the newer section is within the moat, to the east. The remains of the town walls, and the moat that still embraces the city, date from the eighth to 10th centuries. More obvious are the town gates which have been rebuilt and make useful points of reference while exploring this large and rapidly expanding city.

Mahawirawong Museum ⓘ *Wed-Sun 0930-1530, ฿10, a ฿100 combination ticket gives access to the museum as well as Prasat Phranomwan, Phimai and Muang Khaek, saving A40 if all are visited*, in the grounds of Wat Sutchinda just outside the city moat, on Rachdamnern Road, is an informative museum housing a small collection of Khmer art.

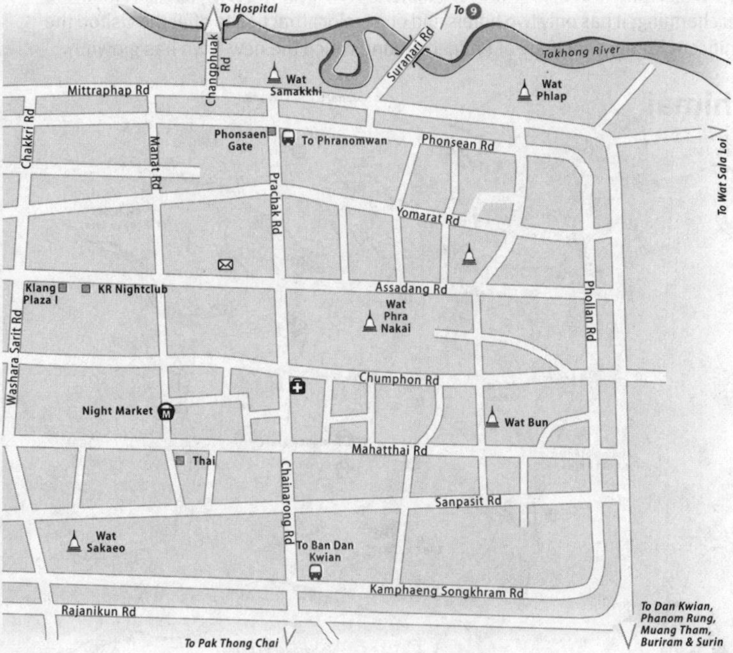

Eating 🅟
Dok Som **1**
Green House Garden **2**
MD **3**
Pizza Hut **5**
SPK (Suan Phak) **4**

Thao Suranari Shrine is in the centre of town, by the Chumphon Gate. This bronze monument erected in 1934 commemorates the revered wife of a provincial governor, popularly known as Khunying Mo, who in 1826 saved the town from an invading Lao army. Legend has it that she and some fellow prisoners plied the over confident Lao soldiers with alcohol and then, having lulled them into a drunken stupor, slaughtered them. Traditional Isaan folk songs are performed at the shrine and in late March and early April a 10-day-long festival honours the heroine (see Festivals page 322),

Just outside the northeast corner of the city moat is **Wat Sala Loi** ⓘ *walk or take bus No 5*, a modern wat, with an ubosoth resembling a Chinese junk. It was built in 1973 and is meant to symbolize a boat taking the faithful to nirvana. It is one of the few modern wats with any originality of design in Thailand (the majority repeat the same visual themes) and it has won numerous architectural awards. The ashes of the local heroine Thao Suranari are interred here.

The **night market** ⓘ *daily from 1800*, is to on Manat Road, between Chumphon and Mahatthai roads. There are lots of foodstalls here, as well as some clothes and handicraft stalls. The **general market** is opposite Wat Sakae, on Suranari Road.

Around Nakhon Ratchasima

Phimai → *Colour map 2, grid C3.*

ⓘ *Regular services to Korat. The last bus from Phimai back to Korat leaves at 1800. For buses north it is necessary to travel to Talat Khae, 10 km away. Phimai is a very small town. Saamlors are available and there are bicycles for hire from guesthouses. The Bai Teiy Restaurant, see Eating, acts as an informal tourist information centre.*

The ancient town of Phimai, northeast of Korat, lies on the Mun River – a tributary of the Mekong and one of the Northeast's major waterways. The town itself is small and rather charming; it has only two hotels and one major attraction to offer the visitor: the magnificent Khmer sanctuary of Phimai, around which the new town has grown.

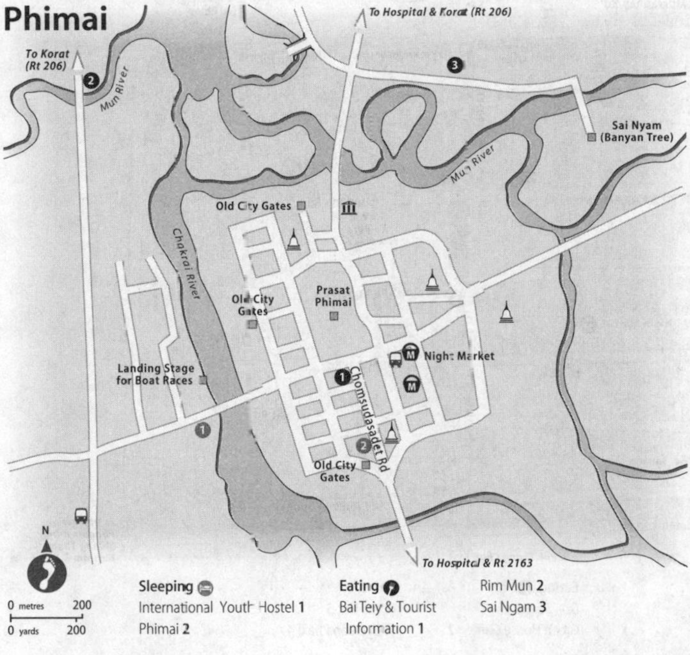

The Phimai sanctuary was important even prior to the arrival of the Khmers; excavations have revealed burnished blackware pottery from as early as AD 500. The Mun River formed a natural defensive position and the site also benefited from an extensive area of rich, arable land. These twin advantages of security and nutrition meant this area was occupied almost continuously for more than seven centuries up to the establishment of the Khmer sanctuary, for which Phimai is known.

Dating from the reign of the Cambodian King Jayavarman VII (1181-1201), Phimai was built at the western edge of his Khmer Kingdom, on a Hindu site. A road ran the 240 km from his capital at Angkor to Phimai, via Muang Tham and Phnom Rung. Unlike other Khmer monuments which face east (to face the rising sun), Phimai faces southeast; probably so that it would face Angkor, although some scholars have postulated it was due to the influence of Funan – the earliest so-called 'Indianised' state of Southeast Asia which existed in Cambodia from the first to the sixth centuries AD.

The **original complex** ⓘ *0730-1800, ฿40*, lay within a walled rectangle 1,000 m by 560 m, set on an artificial island. There are four gopuras, which have been placed in such a way that their entrances coincide with the sanctuary entrances. The **Pratu Chai (Victory Gate)** faces southeast and was built with the purpose of accommodating elephants. Shortly before the gate is the **Khlang Ngoen (Treasury)**, where important pilgrims were lodged. Within the compound are three prangs: the largest, **Prang Prathan**, is made of white sandstone; those on either side are of laterite (**Prang Phromathat**) and red sandstone (**Prang Hin Daeng**). The central and largest prang is a major departure for Khmer architecture. Though similar to Phnom Rung in plan, the elegant curving prang probably became the model for the famous towers at Angkor.

Another unusual feature of Phimai is the predominance of Buddhist motifs in the carvings that adorn the temple. The lintel over the south gateway to the main sanctuary shows the Buddha meditating under a protective naga, the naga's coiled body lifting the Buddha above the swirling flood waters. Another scene, magnificently carved on the corridor leading into the south antechamber, depicts the Buddha vanquishing the evil forces of Mara. On the west side of the building is a lintel showing the Buddha preaching – both hands raised.

To the right of the gateway is a 'homeless lintels' park where the Khmer artistry can be examined at close quarters. The temple was dedicated to Mahayana Buddhism, yet Hindu motifs are clearly discernible – the main entrance shows Siva dancing. On the lintel over the east porch of the central prang is a carving showing the final victory of Krishna over the evil Kamsa.

Of particular interest to art historians is the design of the gateways with their petal-like decorations, similar to those at Angkor itself. As Phimai predates Angkor, there is speculation that it served as the prototype for Angkor Wat. The site has been restored by the Fine Arts Department and was officially opened in 1989.

An **open-air museum**, ⓘ *0900-1600, guidebook available, ฿60*, on the edge of the town, just before the bridge, displays carved lintels and statues found in the area. An exhibition hall has recently opened with a well-displayed and labelled (in English) collection.

On Route 206, just over the bridge on the edge of town at spot known as **Sai Ngam** ⓘ *a 2-km walk northwest of town or catch a saamlor from Phimai (฿40 return)*, is Thailand's largest banyan tree. There's a couple of crusty looking fortune-tellers and a gaggle of decent foodstalls.

Prasat Phranomwan

ⓘ *฿40. See under Mahawirawong Museum, above, for combination entry ticket. Direct buses leave from Phonsaen Gate at 0700, 1000 and 1200 (฿7). Buses running towards Phimai pass the turn-off for Phranomwan; ask to be let off at Ban Saen Muang and either walk the 4 km to the monument or catch one of the irregular local songthaews.*

 This wat can be found between Korat and Phimai, next to a new monastery. It began life as a Hindu temple. The central prang and adjoining pavilion are enclosed within a galleried wall. When it was built is not certain: the carving on the lintels is early 11th century in style, yet the inscriptions refer to the Khmer King Yasovarman who ruled in AD 889.

Ban Prasat

ⓘ *Take a bus towards Phimai. The site is 2 km off the main road and 45 km from Korat city, on the left-hand side, before the turning for Phimai. Ask for Ban Prasat.*

This is a prehistoric site dating back about 5,000 years. The dig has been converted into an open-air museum, much like Ban Chiang outside Udon Thani (see page 349). Indeed, there seem to be close cultural links between Ban Prasat and Ban Chiang. Similar high quality, red slipped and burnished trumpet-rimmed pots have been discovered at both sites. Rice was eaten as the subsistence crop, domestic animals raised, and the technology of bronze casting understood. The examination of skeletons unearthed at the site reveals a high infant mortality rate, and a relatively short lifespan of only 34-36 years.

Chaiyaphum → *Colour map 4, grid B4.*

The few people who do stop off at this small provincial capital are mainly here for the famed silk-weaving at the nearby village of Ban Khwao. However, Chaiyaphum offers an authentic slice of Isaan life, away from other tourists, that can be sampled in a couple of nights.

The name Chaiyaphum means site of victory, a reference to Pho Khun Lae's – the town's first governor – success in thwarting an attack from an invading Lao army during the reign of Rama III. A statue and shrine to his memory are situated 3 km west of town and a festival is held in his honour each January.

The only real point of interest is **Prang Ku**, a 12th-century Khmer sanctuary tower built entirely of laterite blocks, 2 km east of the town centre on Bannakaan Road. Though scarcely matching the Khmer monuments to be found elsewhere on the Khorat Plateau the local people consider it an important holy site. Within the prang is a Dvaravati Buddha, highly revered by the townspeople. The statue is ritually bathed on the day of the full moon in April.

Ban Khwao ⓘ *guesthouses will help arrange tours to silk-weaving villages or simply catch a songthaew from Nornmuang Road (near the intersection with Tantawan Road), close to the centre of town, to Ban Khwao, 14 km west of Chaiyaphum (on Route 225)*, is well known for the quality of its silk. Like Surin, Chaiyaphum is a centre for silk production and weaving.

Khao Yai National Park → *Colour map 2, grid C2.*

ⓘ *฿200, ฿100 for children and ฿30 for a car. The tourist office and visitors' centre at Khao Yai provide maps and organize guides on an intermittent basis. The centre is also probably the closest you will get to rare wildlife, but it is pickled or stuffed. If you intend to trek tell someone before you leave and let them know your intentions. During the wet season, liberally apply insect repellent and take along water and food. The best time to see wildlife is weekday mornings and late afternoons – at weekends the park is inundated with visitors. Spotlight safaris can be organized up until 2100, ฿300-600 although recent visitors have suggested that these are a 'waste of time' because of the number of noisy pick-ups with searchlights keeping the animals, sensibly, out of sight. See also Sleeping and Activities and tours.*

Khao Yai National Park, one of the country's finest, covering an area of 2,168 sq km, encompasses the limestone Dangrek mountain range, a large area of rainforest, waterfalls and a surprisingly wide selection of wildlife. Visitors may be lucky enough to see **Asiatic black bear**, **Javan mongoose**, **slow loris** and **tiger**. Two notable species

One-way traffic

Isolated from the rest of the country by a string mountains, the Northeast has always been at the periphery of the Thai kingdom. The epic poem, *Nirat Nongkhai*, written during a military campaign of the 1870s, recounts the two months, 170 elephants and 500 oxen it took to proceed up a thickly forested trail from Bangkok to Korat (Nakhon Ratchasima). With his men dying all around him from malaria and food poisoning, and finding it difficult to procure supplies, the army's commander managed to miss the vital battle and returned to Bangkok having never confronted the enemy.

Isaan's marginalization is further compounded by the harshest environment anywhere in Thailand. Sparse, intermittent rainfall and some of the poorest soils in Southeast Asia completes the picture.

The inhabitants of the area are also distinct from the rest of the country and are culturally more closely affiliated with the people of Laos. They speak a thick dialect that has as much in common with Lao as it does Thai; they dress differently and eat different food. This distinctiveness, coupled with the poverty of the area, played a part in making the Northeast one of the strongholds of the Communist Party of Thailand.

Most of the population of the Northeast are farmers. They grow glutinous or 'sticky' rice (khao niaw) to meet their subsistence needs and cash crops such as cassava and kenaf (an inferior jute substitute) to earn a crust. They also migrate to Bangkok in their thousands: most of the capitals' servants and labourers, tuk-tuk and taxi drivers, prostitutes and bar girls are poor Isaan folk. Some villages are so depopulated that they seem to consist of only the very old and the very young. It is easy to see why they leave. In the Northeast the daily rate for back-breaking agricultural work is only ฿50; in Bangkok the official minimum wage is more than ฿150 per day.

With the heat, the poverty, the perceived threat of communism, and the general backwardness of the Northeast, most other Thais steer well clear of the area. But, historically, the Khorat Plateau has played a very important role in the development not just of Thailand but of the whole of Southeast Asia. The remarkable finds of the earliest forms of agriculture found at Ban Chiang (see page 347) and the grand Khmer ruins at Phimai, Phnom Rung and Muang Tham bear witness to Isaan's claim to this role.

Travelling around the Northeast is relatively easy. During the Vietnam War the Thai government, with support from the US, built an impressive network of roads, in an attempt to keep communism at bay. The opening of the Friendship Bridge in early 1994, linking Nong Khai with Vientiane, the capital of Laos, is bringing more tourists and trade. As Laos tentatively opens its doors to tourists, so the attraction of using the Northeast as a stepping-stone will increase.

are the **white-handed (or lar) gibbon** and the **pileated gibbon**. There may be as many as 200 **elephants** in the park. Having said this, recent reports have indicated a distinct lack of any wildlife, and you may travel long distances for little reward and unfortunately, because of the park's easy accessibility from Bangkok, it is overrun with visitors and its environmental integrity is at risk.

Short trails are marked in the park; for longer hikes, a guide is usually needed. The 50 km of trails are the most extensive and best marked of any national park; it was the first park to be founded in Thailand in 1962. **Kong Kaeo Waterfall** is a short walk from the visitors' centre. Six kilometres east is the **Haew Suwat Waterfall** (three to four hours' walk). There are 'rest areas' near Haew Suwat and Haew Narok waterfalls, providing drink and simple Thai food. Waterfalls are at their best between June and November, wildlife is best seen during April and May, although August and September are good months to see the **hornbills** (of which there are four species here). Night-time is good for animal observation, when you might be able to see sambar and barking deer, porcupine, gibbon, pig-tailed macaques, mongoose, civet cats and elephants.

The closest town to the national park is **Pak Chong**. While there is some accommodation in the park itself, most of the commercial hotels and guesthouses are situated here and it is a good place to base yourself. There is little to see here, apart from the markets on the north side of Mittraphap Road. The main road through town is the Bangkok-Korat (Friendship Highway).

Ban Dan Kwian

ⓘ *Take a songthaew towards Chokchai from the south city gates on Kamphaeng Songkhram and Chainarong roads, 30 mins, ฿6.*

Ban Dan Kwian, 15 km to the southeast of Korat on Route 224, is famous for producing rust-coloured clay ceramics.The ruddy clay – taking its reddish hue from its high iron content – is drawn from the local river and is used to make vases, pots, wind chimes, water jars, ceramic fish and other objects. Countless stalls and shops line the main road. Unfortunately, most of the items are too big to transport home though, some local producers are beginning to branch out into new products, designed to appeal to foreigners.

Khao Yai National Park

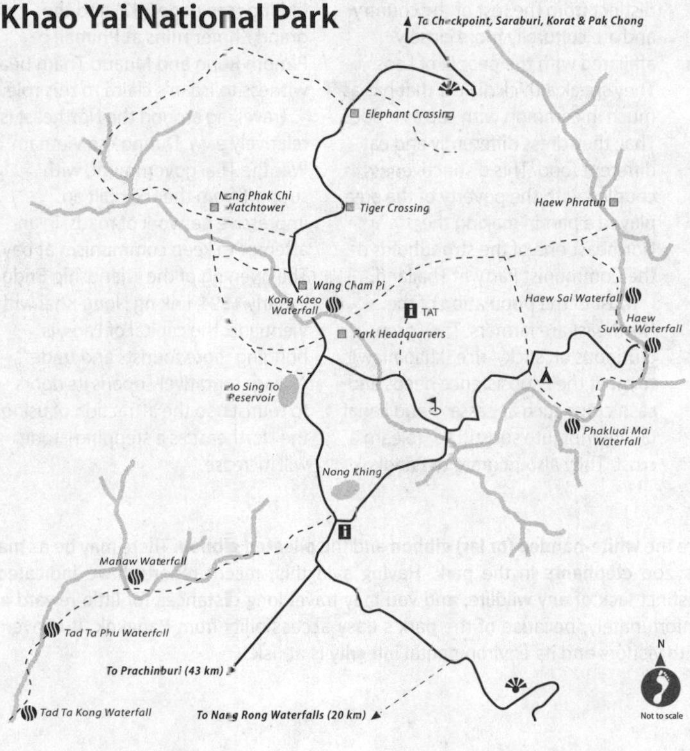
To Checkpoint, Saraburi, Korat & Pak Chong
Elephant Crossing
Nong Phak Chi Watchtower
Tiger Crossing
Haew Phratun
Wang Cham Pi
Kong Kaeo Waterfall
TAT
Haew Sai Waterfall
Haew Suwat Waterfall
Park Headquarters
Mo Sing To Reservoir
Phakluai Mai Waterfall
Nong Khing
Manaw Waterfall
Tad Ta Phu Waterfall
To Prachinburi (43 km)
Tad Ta Kong Waterfall
To Nang Rong Waterfalls (20 km)
N
Not to scale

Trails in Khao Yai

Trail 1: Kong Kaew to Haew Suwat Starts behind visitors' centre, marked in red, 6 km, 3-4 hours walking – transport back to headquarters should be arranged. One of the most popular trails, offering opportunities to observe gibbons.

Trail 2: Kong Kaew to Elephant Salt Lick 2 Starts behind visitors' centre, marked in blue, 6 km, 3-4 hours. Not well marked, over grassland to salt lick – guide advisable. Frequented by elephants.

Trail 3: Kong Kaew to Pha Kluai Mai Starts behind visitors' centre, marked in yellow.

Trail 4: Pha Kluai Mai to Haew Suwat Starts on far side of campsite, marked in red, 3 km. Popular trail along Lam Takhong riverbank. Good trail for orchids and birdlife (blue-eared kingfishers, scarlet minivets, cormorant, hornbills – both wreathed and great). Probable sightings of gibbon, macaques and elephants.

Trail 5: Haew Suwat to Khao Laem grassland Starts across the Lam Takhong River from the parking area. Difficult trail to follow, not much wildlife but good views of Khao Laem mountain.

Trail 6: HQ to Nong Phak Chi Watchtower Starts across road from Wang Kong Kaew restaurant, south of Park Office, marked in red, 6-km round-trip. Popular and easy to follow until last 500 m. The tower makes a good viewing spot at dawn or dusk. White-headed gibbon frequently seen. Clouded leopard has been seen occasionally, herds of wild pig, and even tiger.

Trail 7: HQ to Wang Cham Pi Starts in the same place as 6, marked in blue, 4½-km round-trip, 2-3 hours, good for ornithologists, gibbons and macaques easily seen.

Trail 8: Headquarters Looping Trail Marked in yellow, 2½ km.

Trail 9: Headquarters to Mo Singto Marked in blue, starts in the same place as 6, ends at a reservoir close to headquarters, 2 km. A favourite haunt for tigers.

Phnom Rung

ⓘ *0730-1800. ฿40. Take a Surin-bound bus from Terminal 2 and get off at Ban Tako. From Ban Tako motorcycle taxis wait at the bus stop and charge A250 to visit Phnom Rung and Muang Tam. From Phnom Rung it is a short trip – 8 km – on to Muang Tam (see below). The route to the site is well signposted. See also Transport, Buriram, page 337. The best way to visit Phnom Rung and Muang Tam is to go on a tour (see Activities and tours).*

Phnom Rung, the finest Khmer temple in Thailand, was built in sandstone and laterite over a period of 200 years between the 10th and early 13th centuries. It stands majestically at the top of Rainbow Hill, an inactive volcano overlooking the Thai-Cambodian border. The name Phnom Rung means 'Large Hill'. It was built on a grand scale – the approach is along a 160-m avenue of pink sandstone pillars (nang riang). Lying 112 km southeast of Korat and 64 km south of Buriram, Phnom Rung is similar in layout to Phimai and both monuments are believed to have been prototypes for Angkor Wat.

The monumental staircase is reached via a five-headed naga bridge; this 'bridge' is one of Thailand's Khmer treasures. The style is 12th century and the detail is superb: crowned heads studded with jewels, carefully carved scales and backbones

“” The naga bridge represented a symbolic division between the worlds of mortals and gods. From here the pilgrim climbed upwards to the sanctuary, a divine place of beauty and power...

and magnificent rearing bodies. The naga bridge represented a symbolic division between the worlds of mortals and gods. From here the pilgrim climbed upwards to the sanctuary, a divine place of beauty and power.

The Prasat Phnom Rung (central Hindu sanctuary) is of typical Khmer design, being symmetrical, of cruciform plan, with four gopuras leading to antechambers. It was probably built between 1050 and 1150, most likely by the Khmer King Suryavarman II. The outstanding stone carvings on the central prang illustrate scenes from the Hindu epics, the *Ramayana* and the *Mahabharata*. The Reclining Vishnu Lintel on the main east porch was discovered in the Art Institute of Chicago in 1973, and after repeated requests from the Fine Arts Department in Bangkok, it was returned to Thailand in 1988. It can now be seen in its original position. The pediment of this same eastern face portrays Siva cavorting in his dance of creation and destruction. The central hall of the shrine would probably have had a wooden floor – visitors now have to step down below ground level. The quality of the carving at Phnom Rung is regarded by some as being the finest of the Angkor period. Lunet de Lajonquiere, who first surveyed the site in 1907, wrote “in plan, execution and decoration it is among the most perfect of its kind”.

Phnom Rung

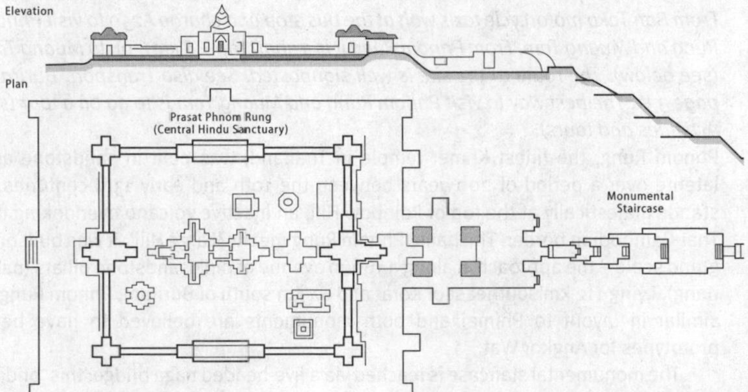

The Busabong Festival is held here every April. The only place to eat near the site is at the Phnom Rung Park, an assemblage of small restaurants and stalls serving cold drinks and good Isaan food, including kai yang (grilled chicken), som tam (spicy papaya salad) and khao niaw (sticky rice).

Muang Tam

ⓘ *Daily 0730-1800. ฿40. Catch a Surin bus to Prakhon Chai on Route 24. From there, songthaews leave for Muang Tham. If the trip is to be combined with a visit to Phnom Rung, it is necessary to charter a motorcycle taxi or hitch from Phnom Rung – there is no public transport yet (see Phnom Rung, above, for details). See also Transport, Buriram, for access from there, page 337.*

The smaller, intimate Muang Tam, or 'Temple of the Lower city', is found 8 km from Phnom Rung and dates from the 10th-11th century. It is thought to have been the palace of the regional governor of the area. It is surrounded by colossal laterite walls pierced by four gopuras, at the four points of the compass. Three still retain their sculpted lintels. Nagas decorate the L-shaped ponds which lie within the walls and are stylistically different from those at Phnom Rung: they are smooth-headed rather than adorned with crowns. Historians believe this prasat pre-dates Phnom Rung by some 100-200 years. Many regard these nagas as unparalleled in their beauty: lotuses are carved on some of their chests, jewels stream from their mouths and garlands adorn them.

Sleeping

Nakhon Ratchasima *p310, map p310*
Most hotels are geared to Thais, not farangs.
AL Royal Princess Korat, T044-256629, F256601. A/c, restaurant, pool, 200-room hotel and the best in the city, tennis courts, situated north of town across the Takhong River off Suranari Rd and about 2 km from the town centre.
A Sima Thani Hotel, 2112/2 Mittraphap Rd, T044-213100, www.simathani.co.th. West of town next to the TAT office. A/c, restaurants (food recommended at the Nai-Ruen), pool, health club, early 1990s hotel with over 130 rooms. Very good value (price negotiable), the only drawback is the out-of-town location.
C Sripatana, 346 Suranari Rd, T044-255349, http://members.xroom.com/Sripatana. A/c, hot water, sparkling, well-furnished rooms, restaurant, pool and excellent 24-hr coffee shop.
C-D Srivijaya, 9-11 Buarong Rd, T044-241284. Some a/c, breakfast and drinks

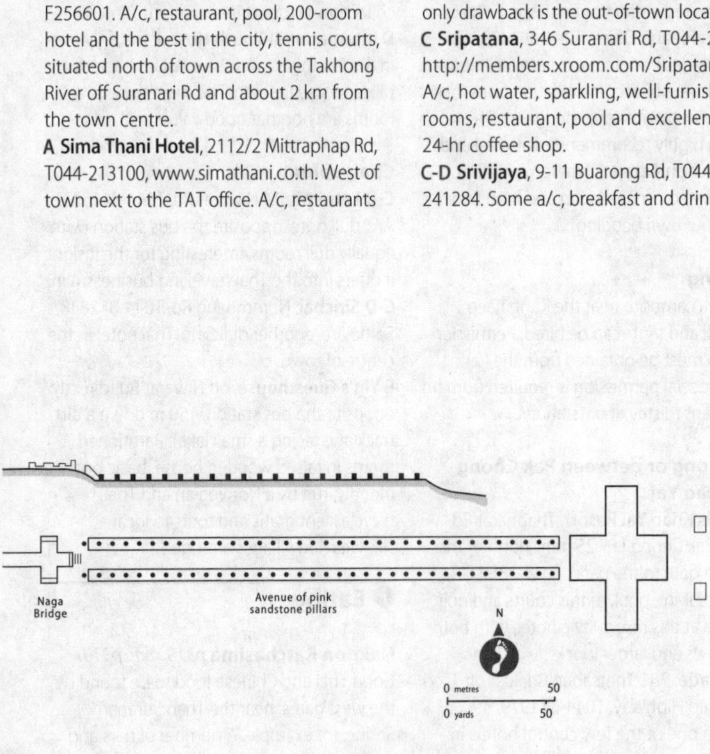
Naga Bridge
Avenue of pink sandstone pillars
N
0 metres 50
0 yards 50

available, friendly place with pleasant rooms and a good central location. Recommended.

D-E Potong, 652-8 Rachdamnern Rd, T044-242084. Near the Thao Suranari Shrine, some a/c, attached bathrooms, drab but clean rooms, those on the street are noisy, benefits from a very central location.

D-E Siri, 167-8 Phoklang Rd, T044-242831. Some a/c, centrally located, bare but clean rooms and friendly staff. The **Veterans of Foreign Wars Café** – a legacy of the years when Korat was a US airforce base during the Vietnam War – is based here.

D-E Srirat, 7 Suranari Rd, T044-243116. Pleasant tiled rooms, some a/c, but those on the front street are a bit noisy.

E-F Korat Doctor's Guesthouse, 78 Suebsiri Rd Soi 4, T044-255846. West of centre, towards TAT. Some a/c, mosquitoes can be a problem, rooms do not always have nets, clean, good value and an excellent source of information. Quiet and welcoming. Recommended.

Khao Yai National Park *p314*

B-D National Park Lodges, T044-7223579. To be booked at the National Park Accommodation Office, T044-5614292-3. Price includes bedding and bath facilities. Diverse range of accommodation from dormitories to individual bungalows. Booking highly recommended at weekends.

F Ya Wachon Camp, 2 km from park HQ. Dormitory accommodation and hard floors (bring your own bedding).

Camping

There is a campsite near the Kong Kaeo Waterfall and tents can be hired. Permission to camp must be obtained from the Park Office. Special permission is required from hq if you want to stay at outstations.

Pak Chong or between Pak Chong and Khao Yai

AL Juldis Khao Yai Resort, Thannarat Rd, Km 17, Pak Chong (15-25 mins north of the northern gate to the park), T044-2352414. A/c, restaurant, pool, tennis courts and golf available at this resort-style hotel, with both bungalows and larger blocks.

D Phubade, 781 Thetsaban Rd, just off Friendship Highway, T044-311979. 49 rooms in one of the few central hotels in town, otherwise known as Phubet, most mod cons but no frills.

E Happy Trails Tour and Guesthouse, facing the train station in Pak Chong. Run by a Thai with good English who has returned from the US. Simple rooms that could do with some sprucing up but the owner is also a guide in the park so has a good knowledge of the area.

E Jungle Guest House, 752/11 Kongwaksin Rd (off Soi 3), south of the Friendship Highway, T044-312877. A backpackers' haunt with enthusiastic staff and basic, overpriced rooms. Also over-enthusiastic in pressing guests to use their tours. Popular.

Phimai *p312, map p312*

C-D Lamai Homestay, 23/1 Moo 3, Ban Ko Phet, Bua Yai, T06-2585894, www.thailandhomestay.com. Lakeside accommodation in an Isaan rice village. Silk-weaving and basket-making tours offered.

C-D Phimai Hotel, 305/1-2 Haruethairome Rd, T044-471306, www.korat.in.th/phimaihotel/index.htm. Some a/c, comfortable but plain rooms. Front rooms are noisy, but it's good value and has a good collection of tourist information.

D International Youth Hostel, the only one in the Northeast and the most characterful place to stay in town. The more expensive rooms are not that good value.

Chaiyaphum *p314*

C-D Letnimit, 14 Niwarat Rd, T044-811522. A/c, dull hotel opposite the bus station, with equally dull rooms, interesting for the insight it offers into the Thai travelling businessman.

C-D Sirichai, Nornmuang Rd, T044-812848. Some a/c, another dull Sino-Thai hotel in the centre of town.

E Yin's Guesthouse, off Niwarat Rd (directly opposite the bus station, 150 m down a dirt track and facing a small lake). Partitioned rooms in raised wooden house, basic but friendly, run by a Norwegian and Thai, bicycles lent gratis and tours to local silk-weaving villages arranged.

Eating

Nakhon Ratchasima *p310, map p310*

Good Thai and Chinese food to be found by the west gates, near the Thao Suranari Shrine, for example. A number of bars and

restaurants are to be found on Jomsurangyaat Rd. Good kwaytio restaurant, close to the corner of Buarong and Jomsurangyaat roads. The night market on Manat Rd, open from 1800, has a good range of cheap Thai/Chinese cafés and excellent foodstalls.

Nai-Ruen, Sima Thani Hotel, 2112/2 Mittraphap Rd (slightly out of town near the TAT office). Only just in the 'expensive' bracket and an 'all you can eat and drink' experience to boot, wonderful Thai/Chinese fresh food. Recommended.

Dok Som Restaurant, 130-142 Chumphon Rd, across the street from the **Potong Hotel**. Very pleasant restaurant with covered terrace area, Thai and Western food. Recommended.

The Emperor (in the Sima Thani), Mittraphap Rd. Good Chinese restaurant, but eclipsed by the **Seow Seow** in terms of quality; prices to match.

Green House Garden, 50-52 Jomsurangyaat Rd (next to the post office). Delicious Thai and Isaan grub set in a sheltered 'garden'.

MD Restaurant, Klang Plaza, Jomsurangyaat Rd. Lots of choice, good, clean restaurant.

Pizza Hut, next to the museum on Rachdamnern Rd.

Seow Seow (pronounced She She), just off Mahathai Rd. Inexpensive Chinese restaurant that serves better food than **The Emperor** and is considerably cheaper. Huge menu, excellent service, seats 250 diners. Recommended.

SPK (Suan Phak), 196 Chumphon Rd. Hang-out for the Korat trendies, good food, also serves cakes. Recommended.

Veterans of Foreign Wars Café, Siri Hotel, 167-8 Phoklang Rd. Restaurants serving a range of Western dishes along with simple Thai food, a good place for breakfast.

Khao Yai National Park *p314*

The best place to eat in Pak Chong is at the night market, which begins operation around 1700 and continues through to shortly before midnight. There are also a fair number of restaurants in town – this, after all, is on the main Bangkok-Korat highway.

Party House Restaurant, quality food and also a good place for a cosy beer.

Another recommended small restaurant – unnamed but run by Mr Die – is 200 m up the road from the **Garden Lodge** next to a blue 'Bonanza' sign: good food, and Mr Die is also an excellent source of information, being an ex-guide.

Phimai *p312, map p312*

The best food is served at the night market near the southeast corner of the prasat, open 1800-2400.

Bai Teiy, off Chomsudasadet Rd. Open 0800-2200. Has a good range of Isaan and Chinese/Thai food and ice cream. Recommended.

Rim Mun, north of the city overlooking the river (as the name suggests). For Isaan food eaten aboard a floating raft, reported to be safe as long as the irrigation canals are not flooded.

🍴 **Rot Niyom**, off Chomsudasadet Rd, serves good Isaan food.

🍴 **Sai Ngam** is a 'garden restaurant' serving tasty Isaan food further north still, near the banyan tree (hence the name).

Chaiyaphum *p314*
The best food in town is to be had at the night market on Taksin Rd. During the day, a good place for Isaan specialities like kai yaang (grilled chicken) and somtam (spicy papaya salad) is the group of stalls on Bannakaan Rd, opposite the hospital.

Bars and clubs

Nakhon Ratchasima *p310, map p310*
KR Nightclub, (described as 'The One American Dance Club') T044-248944, opposite the **Korat Hotel** on Assadang Rd.
London Tavern, 176 Mahatthai Rd. UK-style pub where local football fans congregate.

Chaiyaphum *p314*
Relax Beerhouse, Nonthanakorn Rd (near the intersection with Bannakaan Rd), ice-cold beer, relaxing as the name suggests.

Festivals and events

Nakhon Ratchasima *p310, map p310*
Mar-Apr (end of month) Thao Suranari Fair, a 10-day fair commemorating the local heroine Thao Suranari who helped defeat an invading Lao army. Exhibitions, parades, bazaars, beauty contests and likay performances, along with thousands of participants and onlookers, make this one of Thailand's most vibrant festivals.

Phimai *p312, map p312*
Nov (second weekend) Phimai Boat races held on the Phlaimat River, competition of decorated boats, various stalls.

Shopping

Nakhon Ratchasima *p310, map p310*
Books
DK Books, Chumphon Rd (east of lak muang).

Handicrafts
Korat Craft Centre is located behind the Sala Changwat (Provincial Hall). Matmii (hand-woven cloth): Korat is the centre for matmii, both silk and cotton. There are a number of shops around the central square: **Thusnee Thai Silk**, 680 Rachdamnern Rd (opposite Thao Suranari Shrine); **Today Silk**, Rachdamnern Rd; **Klang Plaza I**, Assadang Rd, and **Klang Plaza II** on Jomsurangyaat Rd.

Activities and tours

Nakhon Ratchasima *p310, map p310*
Hill Top Tour, 516/4 Friendship Rd, Pak Chong, T044-311671.
Prayurakit, 40-44 Suranari Rd, T044-252114.

Khao Yai National Park *p314*
Pak Chong guesthouse representatives meeting visitors off the bus sometimes give the impression that theirs are the only tours to the park; there are many on offer.
KH Tours, on the Frienship Highway, T044-515709, promises to show you 'bird with ear – mouse with wings', in their two-day tour and slightly cheaper programme (฿650). Bikes for rent, ฿300 per day.
Khao Yai National Park and Wildlife Tours, which operates out of Khao Yai Garden Lodge (see Sleeping below), is another outfit that has been recommended. A 1½-day tour is charged at ฿950 per person, but it also operates tours up to 7 days long.

Phimai *p312, map p312*
See under **Lamai Homestay**, Sleeping.

Transport

Nakhon Ratchasima *p310, map p310*
Tuk-tuks (฿40-60) and saamlors.

Air
The airport is 5 km south of town on Route 304. Daily connections with **Bangkok** (30 mins).
Airline offices THAI, 14 Manat Rd, T044-257211.

Bus
The TAT office supplies a map with bus routes marked. Local buses cost ฿4-6 and are infrequent during rush hours. The a/c bus terminal for **Bangkok** is on Mittraphap Rd, west of the town centre. Connections with

Bangkok's Northeastern bus terminal (4-5 hrs). There are two more long-distance bus terminals for other destinations in Thailand. Terminal 2, which lies 2 km northwest of town on Route 2 to **Khon Kaen** and serves most Northeastern destinations, as well as places in the east, such as **Rayong** (useful for Koh Samet), **Chantaburi** and **Pattaya**. Terminal 1, off Burin Rd, closer to the centre of town, serves **Khon Kaen, Chiang Mai** and **Chiang Rai**.

Motorbike hire
From **Virojyarnyon**, 554-556 Phoklang Rd, ฿150-200 per day.

Train
The station is on Mukamontri Rd, in the west of town (T044-242044). Connections with **Bangkok**'s Hualamphong station (5-6 hrs) and also with **Ubon**, close to the border with Laos.

Khao Yai National Park *p314*
The park turning is at the Km 165 marker on Route 2, 200 km from Bangkok, 2-3 hrs by car. There are 2 entrances to the park. One from the north, near Pak Chong, the other from the south, near Prachinburi. Access from the south is mostly by hired or private vehicle; all buses go to the north entrance.

Bus
Four buses leave Korat for **Pak Chong** in the morning (฿20), or it is possible to catch a Bangkok-bound bus and get off in Pak Chong. From **Bangkok**, take a bus (2½ hrs) or train to Pak Chong. There are numerous songthaews from Pak Chong to the park itself. Cars can also be hired – or there are tours available.

Train
There are trains from **Bangkok** (3½-4 hrs) and **Ayutthaya** to Pak Chong, and onward to Ubon Ratchathani.

Phimai *p312, map p312*
Bicycle hire
฿25 per day from the **Bai Teiy Restaurant**.

Bus
Regular connections with **Korat**'s main bus station on Suranari Rd (1½ hrs), last bus leaves Korat at 2000 and leaves Phimai at 1800. Hourly service to **Bangkok** between 0830 and 2300 (5 hrs). To travel north, take a local bus to **Thalat Khae** and then catch a bus travelling north.

Chaiyaphum *p314*
Bus
The bus station is on the northeast edge of town about 1 km from the centre. Regular bus connections with **Bangkok**'s Northeastern bus terminal (7 hrs), and with **Phitsanulok, Chiang Mai** and towns in the Northeast. A/c buses (VIP and standard) to Bangkok leave from the offices of Air Chaiyaphum at 202/8-9 Nornmuang Rd, just to the north of the Sirichai Hotel in the town centre. For a/c buses to Chiang Mai and **Ubon Ratchathani**, the terminal is on Nornmuang Rd, south of the post office.

Directory

Nakhon Ratchasima *p310, map p310*
Banks There are a number of banks offering foreign exchange services on Mittraphap and Chumphon roads. Bangkok, Jomsurangyaat Rd, close to the post office. **Internet** At the internet café next to Klang Plaza II. **Medical services** Maharaj Hospital, near the bus station on Suranari Rd, T044-254990. **Post office** Main office on Assadang Rd, between Prachak and Manat roads; a more convenient branch is at 48 Jomsurangyaat Rd, next to Klang Plaza II. **Telephone** Telecom centre, Jomsurangyaat Rd, next to the post office. **Useful addresses** Police Sanpasit Rd, T044-242010. Tourist Police 2102-2104 Mittraphap Rd (on western edge of town, next to the TAT office), T044-213333.

Phimai *p312, map p312*
Banks Currency exchange service opposite the entrance to the Phimai Historical Park. Thai Farmers Bank, Chomsudasadet Rd.

Chaiyaphum *p314*
Banks Banks with exchange facilities are located on Uthittham Rd (eg **Krung Thai**) and Hot Thai Rd (eg **Thai Farmers Bank**). **Post office** Intersection of Bannakaan Rd and Nornmuang Rd (telephone and fax facilities available).

Ubon Ratchathani and around

Head into the far eastern corner of Isaan and you'll find one of the regions most important cities – Ubon Ratchathani. An important administrative capital and transport hub, it is a friendly stop off point while investigating the more impressive sights of this far-flung corner of Thailand.

Surin is famous for its annual Elephant round-up and the nearby tribal people, the Suay, who have a unique relationship with these huge beasts. If you want the spectacular, Yasothon hosts a yearly skyrocket festival. Some of these mammoth fireworks weigh hundreds of kilos and are suitably blessed by Buddhists monks before being fired into the heavens. Elsewhere there are the rapids of Tana and Kaen Sapu, the obscure river cliffs of Pha Taem while Phra Viharn – one of the most spectacular Khmer temples ever built – nestles invitingly just across the Cambodian border. ▸▸ *For Sleeping, Eating and other listings, see pages 331-339.*

Towards Ubon Ratchathani

Buriram → *Colour map 2, grid C4.*

Buriram is small, unassuming and, in all senses, provincial. It makes a good base to visit the Khmer ruins at Phnom Rung and Muang Tam yet few people stay here, preferring to travel from the larger city of Korat.

There's not much to see though the **Isaan Cultural Centre** ⓘ *opening hours are sporadic*, at the Buriram teachers' college on Jira Road supports a museum, stages dance, music and drama performances, and hosts exhibitions of folk art. The small collection is labelled in Thai. The town's fresh market is off Soonthonthep Road, not far north of Buriram's largest wat, the peaceful but otherwise plain **Wat Klang**.

Khao Krudong ⓘ *take a songthaew in the morning from the station near the market, off Sriphet Rd*, is a 300-m volcanic cinder cone 8 km southeast of town. The hill, rising up from the surrounding rice plain, is a holy place and is crowned by a white 20-m-high statue of the Buddha. The views from the summit are best at sunset (although public transport is limited in the afternoon).

Surin → *Colour map 2, grid C4.*

Surin is a silk-producing town, best known for its **Elephant Round-Up** ⓘ *contact the TAT in Bangkok for full information on the festival*, held in the third week of November at the Surin Sports Park. The forested Thai/Cambodian border has long been the domain of a tribe of elephant catchers called the Suay. At the beginning of the 20th century there were 100,000 domesticated elephants in Thailand. The Suay were much in demand to look after the working population and catch wild elephants. With the advent of other transport the need for elephants fell; today, there are about 4,000 working elephants.

During the festival, 40,000 people come to watch the Suay practise their skills with at least 200 elephants. They take part in parades and mock battles. There are also demonstrations of Thai dance and an unusual game of soccer played by elephants and their mahouts. For the rest of the year Surin becomes a backwater: the only reason to stay here is to visit the numerous Khmer temples that are to be found in this southern part of the Northeast.

The **Surin Museum** ⓘ *Wed-Sun*, on Chitbamrung Road, displays many of the accessories used by the Suay to capture wild elephants, including the magical talismans that are worn to protect men from injury. A bustling morning market lies between Thetsabarn and Krungsi-Nai roads and a very small museum ⓘ *Mon-Fri 0830-1630*, at the south edge of town on Chitbamrung Road.

Ban Tha Klang ⓘ *hourly bus from the terminal in town, 2 hrs*, is a Suay settlement, 58 km north of town, near the town of Tha Tum. The Suay are said to have filtered into Thailand from central Asia during the ninth and 10th centuries, becoming the first people of the area to tame elephants for human use. The village is sometimes called Elephant Village because of the close association the population has with the art and science of capturing and training pachyderms. Out of the official Elephant Round-Up festival period, it is sometimes possible to see training in progress here. It is best to come here in the weeks just prior to the round-up (see Festivals and events), when the villagers are intensively preparing for the festival, or try to coincide your visit with the elephant feeding schedule. Even if you don't see any elephants, the village is worth a visit.

Prasat Ta Muan Tot and **Prasat Ta Muan** lie just 100 m apart in Kab Choeng District, Surin Province, about 60 km due south of town on the Thai-Cambodian border. It's not possible to get there on public transport. However, the site is close to Phnom Rung and Muang Tam and could be included in a tour of these better known Khmer sites. Alternatively, hire a car or songthaew. Built in the 11th century during the reign of Khmer King Jayavarman VII, the prasats are situated on the road that linked Angkor Wat with Phimai. These were once fine complexes, although they have been extensively damaged in recent years – largely during a period of occupation by Khmer Rouge troops. Prasat Ta Muan Tot was built as a hospital to minister to weary and sick travellers while Prasat Ta Muan was a chapel. There is an impressive 30-m-long staircase leading down into Cambodian territory, a central sanctuary, and associated minor prangs and buildings.

Surin

To Bon Tha Klong
To Bangkok
To Ubon Ratchathani
Rt 214
Nong Toom Rd
Mit Ari Rd
S Nikhomrat Rd
Surin Phakdii Rd
Night Market
Surin Plaza
A/c Tour Buses to Bangkok
Thetsabarn Anusarn Rd
Thetsabarn 1 Rd
Bus Station
Krungsi-Nai Rd
CHINATOWN
Phetkasem Department Store
Silk, Silver & Handicrafts Shop
Tat Mai Lang Rd
Sirirat Rd
Morning Market & Local Songthaews
Wat Nong Bua
Lak Muang Rd
Thetsabarn 3 Rd
Chitbamrung Rd
Thetsabarn 2 Rd
Moonsart Rd
Thetsabarn 1 Rd
Bungalow Runrom Rd
Wat Klang
Wat Burapharam
Wat Sala Loi
Tanasarn Rd
Saren House
To Rim Khong Golf Driving Range (2 km)
Thetsabarn 2 Rd
Lak Muang Rd
Rt 2077
Canal
To Airport
N
0 metres 50
0 yards 50
Sleeping
Amarin 1
Krung Sri 2
Memorial 3
New 4
Phetkasem 5
Pirom's Guesthouse 6
Sang Thong 7
Thong Tarin 8
Eating
Big Bite 1
Chantong Thai Food 3
Phailin 5
Somboon 6
Spey Royal Karaoke Bar 7
Sumrub Tornkruang 8
Bars & clubs
Caesar's Nightclub & Café 2
Cowboy Beer Corner 4
Swing Club 9

Prasat Sikhoraphum (aka Prasat Ban Ra-ngaeng) ⓘ *฿20*, can be found at the Km 34 marker from Surin to Si Saket, Route 226. Four small prangs sit on a laterite base, surrounding a larger central prang. A 12th-century Khmer temple, Sikhoraphum began life as a Hindu shrine. The central prang retains some beautiful carvings on the lintels (dancing Siva) and door jambs (door guardians and floral designs).

Si Saket → *Colour map 2, grid C5.*

Si Saket is a good base from which to visit the lesser-known Khmer sites in the lower Northeast such as Prasat Sikhoraphum (see page 326) which is located on Route 266, 34 km before reaching Surin and 69 km from Si Saket. The town is a small provincial capital with few sights – the daily market off Khukhan Road can be entertaining – though it is an enjoyable place to absorb authentic Isaan culture.

Prasat, Phra Viham is also reachable, see page 328 for details on the site and Transport, Si Saket Khao.

Ubon Ratchathani → *Colour map 2, grid C5.*

The 'Royal city of the Lotus' is an important provincial capital on the Mun River. Like a number of other towns in the Northeast, Ubon was a US airbase during the Vietnam War and as a result houses a good selection of Western-style hotels, as well as bars and massage parlours. The money that filtered into the town during the war meant that it became one of the richest in the region: this can still be seen reflected in the impressive, although slowly decaying, public buildings. Like Udon Thani and Korat, there is still a small community of ex-GIs who have married local women and are living out their days here.

Ins and outs

Getting there The airport is a longish walk from the city centre. There are daily connections with Bangkok. Most people arrive in Ubon by bus. There are frequent buses to Bangkok, taking around eight hours. The main bus terminal is north of town (too far to walk), but many tour buses drop off in the city centre. Ubon's train station is south of town in Warin Chamrap. Connections with Bangkok and stops along the southern northeastern track. It is also possible to enter Laos from Ubon, via Chongmek. » *See also Transport, page 338, for further details.*

Getting around Ubon is a large town. The TAT provides a map marking city bus routes. There are also lots of saamlors and tuk-tuks, as well as cars and motorbikes for hire.

Tourist information TAT ⓘ *264/1 Khuan Thani Rd (facing the Srikamol Hotel), T045-243770. 0830-1630*. Provides a map of Ubon with bus routes and other handouts; a useful first stop, though not particularly efficient. Areas of responsibility are Ubon Ratchathani, Si Saket and Yasothon.

Sights

There is a good archaeological, historical and cultural **museum** ⓘ *Wed-Sun 0900-1600, ฿30* (the Ubon branch of the National Museum in Bangkok) on Khuan Thani Road. It is housed in a panya-style (southern Thai architectural style) building, erected in 1918 as a palace for King Vajiravudh (Rama VI). The collection includes prehistoric artefacts collected in the province, as well as pieces from the historic period, including Khmer artefacts, and cultural pieces such as local textiles and musical instruments. The star of the collection is a large, bronze Dong-son drum.

Wat Phrathat Nong Bua ⓘ *town bus No 2 or 3, or go by tuk-tuk*, is 500 m west off Chayangkun Road travelling north to Nakhon Phanom, not far past the army base. It is

a large, white angular chedi built in 1957 to celebrate the 2,500th anniversary of the death of the Lord Buddha. It is said to be a copy of the Mahabodhi stupa in Bodhgaya, India. It is certainly unusual in the Thai context. Jataka reliefs and cloaked standing Buddhas in various stances are depicted on the outside of the chedi.

Wat Thungsrimuang, on Luang Road, and named after the thung (field) by the provincial hall, is a short walk from the TAT office. It is notable for its red-stained

Ubon Ratchathani

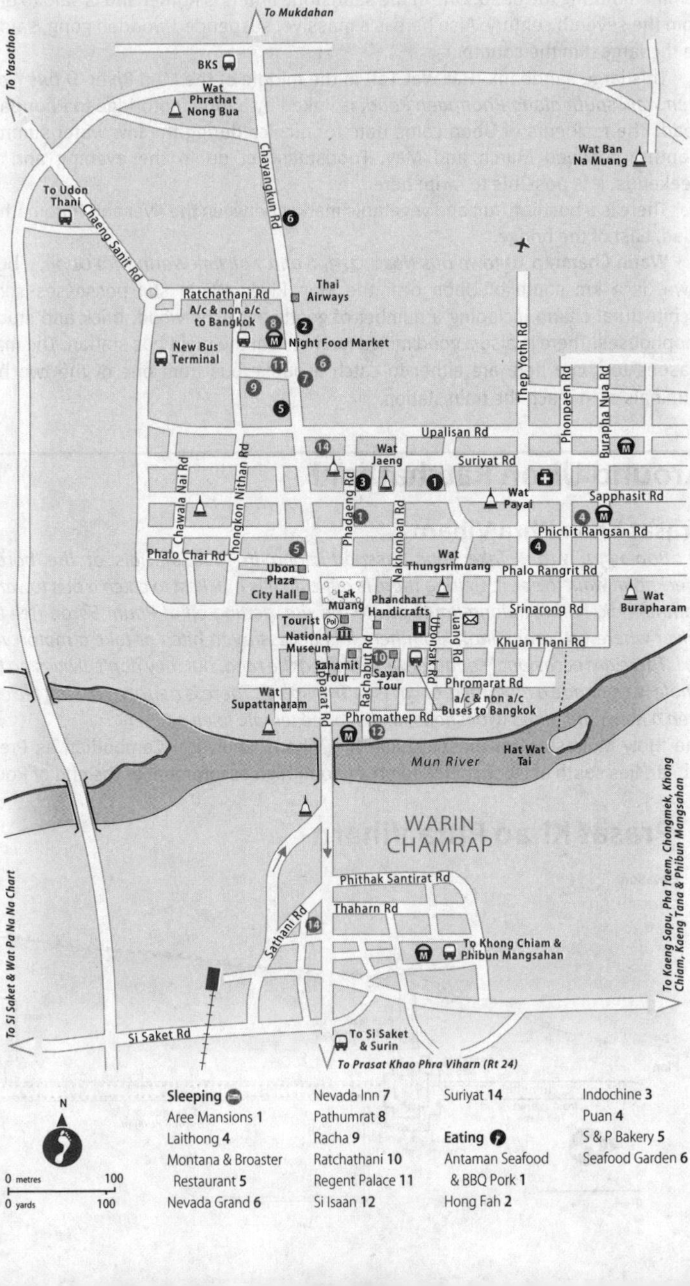

Sleeping
- Aree Mansions 1
- Laithong 4
- Montana & Broaster Restaurant 5
- Nevada Grand 6
- Nevada Inn 7
- Pathumrat 8
- Racha 9
- Ratchathani 10
- Regent Palace 11
- Si Isaan 12
- Suriyat 14

Eating
- Antaman Seafood & BBQ Pork 1
- Hong Fah 2
- Indochine 3
- Puan 4
- S & P Bakery 5
- Seafood Garden 6

wooden hor trai (library) on stilts, in the middle of a stagnant pond. The library contains Buddhist texts and rare examples of Isaan literature, but is usually locked. The monastery was built during the reign of Rama III (1824-1851) and there is a fine late Ayutthayan-style bot, graciously decaying.

At the west end of Phromathep Road, **Wat Supattanaram** is pleasantly situated overlooking the Mun River. It was built in 1853 and supports monks of the Dharmayuthi sect (a Theravada Buddhist sect best known for its meditation practises). It is significant for its collection of lintels which surround the bot, commemorating the dead. One of the sandstone lintels is Khmer and is said to date from the seventh century. Also here is a massive, suspended wooden gong, said to be the largest in the country.

This large sandbank (**Hat Wat Tai**) in the middle of the Mun River ⓘ *bus No 1, then walk south along Phonpaen Road*, is linked by a rope footbridge to Phonpaen Road. The residents of Ubon come here for picnics during the low water summer months, between March and May. Foodstalls set up in the evening and on weekends. It is possible to swim here.

There is a bustling fruit and vegetable market between the river and Phromathep Road, east of the bridge.

Warin Chamrap ⓘ *town bus Nos 1, 2, 3, 6 and 7 all link Warin with Ubon*, a busy town, is 3 km south of Ubon over the Mun River. Warin still possesses some architectural charm including a number of gently decaying wood, brick and stucco shophouses. There is also a good mixed market near the main bus station. The main reasons to come here are either to catch a public bus from one of the two bus terminals or to reach the train station.

Around Ubon Ratchathani

Prasat Khao Phra Viharn

ⓘ *0800-1530. ฿100. Take your passport along in case officials at the border checkpoint want to see it. Getting there is difficult; it is quickest to catch a bus towards Kantharalak, halfway along Route 221 to the site, getting off at Phum Saron (tell the driver where you are going). From here it is necessary to hitch or take a motorcycle taxi. There are occasional songthaews travelling the road, but they don't always go the whole way, or hire a motorbike or car (see Transport). There is a ฿100 crossing fee and then a new road, lined with shops, leads to the temple itself.*

The 'Holy Monastery' of Prasat Khao Phra Viharn, known in Cambodian as Preah Vihear, lies south of Ubon, perched on a 500-m-high escarpment at the end of Route

Prasat Khao Phra Viharn

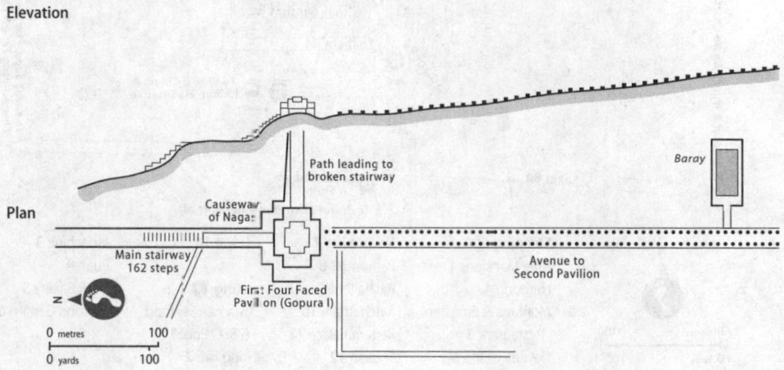

221. It is a magnificent Khmer sanctuary, in one of the most spectacular positions of any monument in Southeast Asia.

It lies close to a disputed section of the Cambodian border; 30 years ago the international court in The Hague ruled that it lay inside Cambodian territory. The Thai authorities occasionally challenge this ruling and Thai maps often mark the sanctuary as lying within Thai territory. The Cambodian side of the area was controlled by the Khmer Rouge until the end of December 1998. With the demise of the Khmer Rouge, Prasat Phra Viharn re-opened and it is well on its way to become a required stop on any tour of the Northeast.

Built about 100 years before Angkor, it occupies a truly magnificent position at the top of a steep escarpment overlooking jungle that was formerly a stronghold of the Khmer Rouge. The temple is orientated north-south along the escarpment, with a sheer drop on one side of 500 m to the Cambodian jungle below. In total, the walkways, courtyards and gates stretch 850 m along the escarpment, climbing 120 m in the process. In places the stairs are cut from the rock itself; elsewhere, they have been assembled from rock quarried and then carted to the site. In total, there are five gopuras, numbered I to V from the sanctuary outwards. Multiple nagas, kalas and kirtamukhas decorate these gateways and the balustrades, pediments and pillars that link them. At the final gateway, Gopura I, the pathway enters into a courtyard with a ruined prang within. The courtyard was encircled by a gallery, still intact on the east and west sides. Doors from here lead to two annexes – probably used for ritual purposes.

When Prasat Phra Viharn was built is not certain. Much seems to be linked to King Suryavarman I (1002-1050), and it has been hypothesized that this was his personal temple. But there are also inscriptions from the reign of King Suryavarman II (1113-1150), and he certainly seems to have commissioned parts of the second courtyard (between Gopuras I and II). With the death of Suryavarman II, Prasat Phra Viharn appears to have been abandoned and fell into disrepair.

Kaeng Sapu

ⓘ *Take town bus Nos 1, 3 or 6 to Warin Chamrap. From here buses run regularly to Phibun Mangsahan, 1 hr. The rapids are 1 km from town; walk or take a saamlor.*
A series of rapids on the Mun River, 1 km outside the district town of Phibun Mangsahan and about 45 km from Ubon, Kaeng Sapu do not compare with the rapids at Kaeng Tana National Park (see below), but are much easier to reach. Inner tubes can be hired to float downriver and there is a small market with foodstalls and poor quality handicrafts. **Wat Sarakaew** is close by, with a viharn showing some colonial influences.

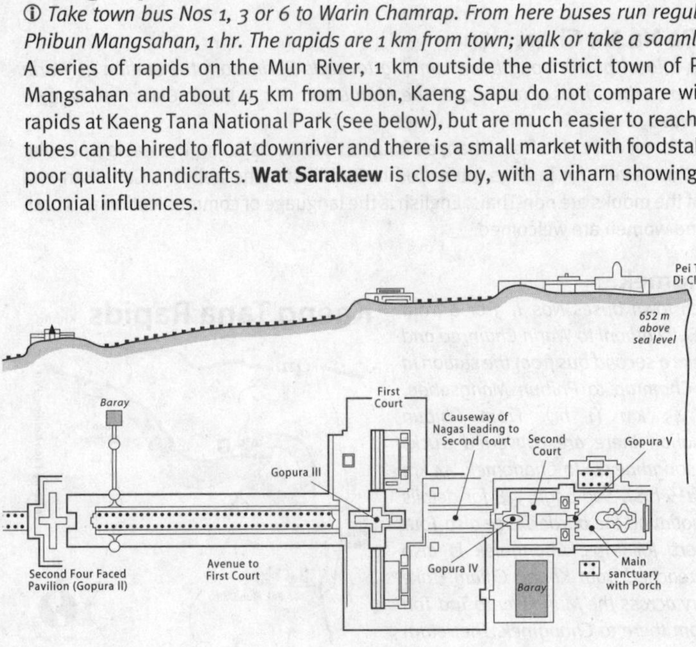
Pei Ta
Di Cliff
652 m
above
sea level
Baray
First
Court
Causeway of
Nagas leading to
Second Court
Second
Court
Gopura V
Gopura III
Second Four Faced
Pavilion (Gopura II)
Avenue to
First Court
Gopura IV
Baray
Main
sanctuary
with Porch

Pha Taem

ⓘ *It's quite difficult to reach on public transport. First take an Ubon town bus to Warin Chamrap (No 1, 3 or 6), and from there to Khong Chiam via Phibun Mangsahan (where accommodation is available, see below). There are also some direct buses to Khong Chiam from Ubon. From Khong Chiam charter a tuk-tuk for the last 20 km to the cliff (฿150 return). Chongmek Travellers and Takerng Tour organize boat trips there (see Tour operators), or hire a motorbike or car.*

In Khong Chiam district, 94 km northeast of Ubon, is a sandstone cliff overlooking a wide, deep gorge that cuts through the Mekong. Views from this clifftop across the Mekong to Laos are spectacular. Ochre prehistoric paintings, about 3,000 years old, of figures, turtles, elephants, fish and geometric forms stretch for some 400 m along a cliff set high above the Mekong. A trail leads down and then along the face of the cliff, past three groups of paintings now protected by unsightly barbed wire. Two viewing towers allow the images to be viewed at eye level.

Two kilometres before the turn off for Pha Taem is **Sao Chaliang**, an area of strange, heavily eroded sandstone rock formations.

Kaeng Tana National Park

ⓘ *The park is about 75 km to the east of Ubon off Route 217, where the park office is located. It is easiest to visit on a tour (see Tour operators) or by private car/motorcycle. There is no easy way to reach the rapids on public transport. The nearest town is Khong Chiam, which is reached by changing bus at Warin Chamrap.*

The Kaeng Tana – the Tana rapids – after which the park is named, are found at a point where the Mun River squeezes through a rocky outcrop before flowing into the Mekong. In the dry season the rocks present an almost lunar landscape of giant ossified bones, jumbled together into a heap of eroded boulders. It is possible to chicken leap across the river to midstream. The controversial Pak Mun Dam, completed in 1994 and designed to generate hydropower and irrigate land, can be seen from the rapids. Bungalow accommodation is available here or in Khong Chiam (see Sleeping, page 331).

Wat Pa Na Na Chart

ⓘ *Take a local bus or songthaew running towards Surin from the station in Warin Chamrap to the south of town, over the Mun River. Get to Warin Chamrap by town buses Nos 1, 2 or 6.*

This is a forest wat 14 km from Ubon, on Route 226 towards Surin. The wat is a popular meditation retreat for farangs interested in Buddhism. The abbot is Canadian and most of the monks are non-Thais. English is the language of communication and both men and women are welcomed

Chongmek

ⓘ *Catch town buses Nos 1, 3 or 6 from Ubon Ratchathani to Warin Chamrap and then take a second bus from the station in Warin Chamrap to Phibun Mangsahan, about 45 km (1 hr). From Phibun Mangsahan there are converted trucks (large songthaews) to Chongmek, 44 km away (1½ hrs). See page 338 for details on negotiating the border. See also Tour operators for trips. Chongmek is also easily reached from Khong Chiam. Take the ferry across the Mun River to Tad Ton and from there to Chongmek. The return*

trip costs ฿200 per 10-seater boat, so the more people you have the cheaper it is. Chongmek is an interesting border town east of Ubon. There is a large Thai-Lao market selling food (including baguettes), baskets, clothes and basic manufactured goods, as well as some 'antiques' and wild animal products from Laos. It is also an important trans-shipment point for logs from Laos; a timber yard faces the market. Even those without entry visas for Laos are allowed to cross the Thai border and mosey around the market.

Khong Chiam → *Colour map 2, grid C6.*

This attractive district town at Thailand's easternmost point is situated on the Mekong, close to the confluence of the Mun and Mekong, the so-called two-coloured river or Maenam Song Sii, because of the meeting of the red-brown Mekong and the deep blue Mun. Boats take visitors out to the point of confluence to view the ripple effect at close hand, which is best towards the end of the dry season in March to May. There is accommodation here and some excellent restaurants. Inner tubes can be hired to swim in the Mekong and it makes an alternative and much quieter place to stay than Ubon. It has also been reported that visitors can cross the Mekong to visit the town on the other bank for the day, although this cannot be used as an entry point to Laos. In addition, Khong Chiam can be used as a base to visit the other sights in this easternmost area of Thailand, eg Pha Taem, Kaeng Sapu and Kaeng Tana National Park. In the town, a morning market operates between 0600 and 0830. Boats can be hired anywhere along the riverbank. See also Sleeping.

Yasothon → *Colour map 2, grid B5. Population: 34,000.*

This small provincial capital is situated northwest of Ubon and there is really only one reason to visit: to see the famous **bun bang fai (skyrocket festival)**, which is held annually over the second weekend in May. Once a regionwide festival, Yasothon has made it its own (see box, page 335).

In the centre of Yasothon, on Withdamrong Road, is a daily market which, though not geared to tourists, does sell functional handicrafts: Isaan pillows and cushions, and baskets and woven sticky-rice containers. Wat Mahathat Yasothon, just off the main road, is said to date from the foundation of the city. The Phra That Phra Anon chedi, within the monastery's precincts, is said to date from the seventh century and contains the ashes of the Lord Buddha's first disciple, Phra Anon (better known outside Thailand as Ananda). See also Sleeping.

Sleeping

Buriram *p324*

B-C Wongthong Hotel, on the road towards the bus station off Jira Rd. A/c rooms have fridge and TV and there are hot-water bathrooms; the best place to stay at present, and good value too.

C Thepnakorn, Mu 3, Isan Rd (on edge of town, off continuation of Jira Rd), T044-613400, F613400. Reasonable, mid-range hotel.

C-D Thai, 38/1 Romburi Rd, T044-611112, F612461. Some a/c, the best of the hotels in the town centre (which isn't, admittedly, saying much), all rooms with hot water, clean but plain and a safe bet given the limited competition in this category. Note that some rooms have no windows.

E-F Chai Charoen, 114-116 Niwat Rd, T044-611559. No English sign identifies this place, directly outside railway station on the right, fan rooms with attached bath. Basic, but good value.

Surin *p324, map p325*

During the Round-up, hotels in Surin become booked up and expensive.

B-C Phetkasem, 104 Chitbamrung Rd, T045-511274, pkhotel@cscoms.com. A/c, restaurant, pool, coffee shop snooker and nightclubs. 162 smart, new-looking rooms, 30% discounts available during the off-season.

B-C Thong Tarin, 60 Sirirat Rd, T045-514281, hotel@thongtarin.co.th. A/c, restaurant, pool.

The 200 plus rooms look a bit worn and need renovating. Close to bus station.

C-D **New Hotel**, 22 Tanasarn Rd, T045-511341, F511971. Some a/c, large hotel of 100 rooms with worn and dirty prison-like corridors, but rooms are suprisingly clean, no hot water and bolshy management, close to train station, hardly 'new'.

D **Krung Sri**, 185 Krungsi-Nai Rd, T045-511037, just off the market. Basic, clean, light rooms, some with a/c, squat toilets, en suite showers.

D-E **Amarin**, 103 Thetsabarn 1 Rd, T045-511112. Large, basic hotel, friendly but no hot water, no character, rooms can be grubby.

D-E **Sang Thong**, 279-281 Tanasarn Rd, T045-512099. Some a/c, 125 fair-sized rooms, good value.

E-F **Pirom's Guesthouse**, 242 Krungsi-Nai Rd. Basic rooms in a wooden house backing onto a small lake (mosquitoes a problem), but Mr Pirom is a mine of information and very friendly, and the guesthouse is clean and well run. Mr Pirom will organize trips to Khmer sites and elsewhere at the weekends, the food is perhaps not as good value as the rooms, but nonetheless it is recommended. Mr Pirom has also constructed a guesthouse, 1 km north of the railway line. It is a mock-Scandinavian affair.

Si Saket *p326*

A-B **Kessiri Hotel**, 1102-5 Khukhan Rd, T045-614007, F614008. A/c restaurant, pool, surprisingly luxurious for a small town with 11th-floor rooftop pool, satellite TV in lobby (not in rooms), coffee shop serving excellent food, with starched linen, marble foyer, spotless, cooperative and very friendly staff. A good place to base yourself.

C-E **Kuatier Mansion**, T045-612033-4, F611596, off Khukhan Rd. the 2nd road down from the **Kessiri Hotel**. A/c, hot water, en suite facilities. Rooms are clean and spacious, and the Thai management is helpful and friendly.

D-E **Si Saket Hotel**, 384/5 Si Saket Rd, T045-611846. Some a/c, the best budget hotel within easy reach of the railway station, although that is not much of a recommendation given the competition.

Ubon Ratchathani *p326, map p327*

Discounts of 20-30% at many hotels. There are limited good budget places here, so backpackers tend to bypass the city or stay in Khong Chiam; see page 333.

AL **Laithong Hotel**, Phichit Rangsan Rd. T045-264271. Very attractive hotel with all facilities including pool, restaurant, karaoke, night club and bars. The newest and most luxurious place to stay in town.

AL-A **Pathumrat**, 337 Chayangkun Rd, T045-241501, F242313. North of town centre, near the market bus station, a/c, restaurant, pool, built during the Vietnam War to meet US military demand, it still exudes 1970s kitsch, some rooms have been modernized and there is also a rather sterile new wing, but the hong kao (old rooms), have character and atmosphere.

B **Nevada Grand Hotel**, Chayagkul Rd, T045-280999. A/c, TV, pleasant, spacious rooms, a more de luxe version of the **Nevada Inn** (see below) which is located next door.

B-C **Nevada Inn**, 436/1 Chayagkul Rd, T045-313351, F313350. A/c, TV, some rooms with good views. Divides its karaoke goers into 'very' VIPs, VIPs and the normal karaoke rooms for riff-raff. Featureless restaurant. attached to a cinema complex with internet upstairs.

B-C **Ratchathani**, 229 Khuan Thani Rd, T045-244388 F243561. Some a/c, all rooms with TV and hot water, clean and generally well run, comfortable beds in spacious rooms, competitively priced. C **Montana Hotel**, 179/1 Uparat Rd, T045-261752. A/c, 40 comfortable rooms and friendly staff, central location close to town square, room rate includes breakfast. Very popular. Recommended.

C **Regent Palace**, 265-71 Chayangkun Rd, T045-255529, F255489. A/c, restaurant, with attached snocker club. Poorly maintained and dirty rooms.

C **Si Isaan 1 and 2**, 62 Rachabut Rd, T045-261011, service@sriisanhotel.com. Some a/c, open airy and clean hotel with very friendly management. Rooms have tea and coffee making facilities and room service at very reasonable prices. A delightful place to stay, free transport to train and bus stations. Highly recommended.

C-D Aree Mansions, junction of Pha Daeng and Sapphasit rds (accessed through what looks like a covered car park). But the rooms are clean and spacious, good value although management speak no English.

C-D Suriyat, 47/1-4 Suriyat Rd, T045-241144. Some a/c, TV. Clean, simple, pleasant rooms.

D Pathumrat, 337 Chayangkun (attached to the more lavish Pathumrat). A/c, stuck away round the back of the hotel, clean but dark rooms.

D-E Racha, 149/21 Chayangkun Rd, T045-254155. Some a/c, hot water in a/c rooms, plain and basic, fairly clean and friendly people. Very tatty, but the only budget place with any character in town.

Khong Chiam *p331*

A-C Khiang Nam Resort (Ban Kiang Nam), Klaepradit Rd, T045-351374-5. Beautiful bungalows in neat little gardens. A/c, hot water, TV, and peaceful surroundings. Recommended.

B Rimkhong Resort, Klaepradit Rd, T045-351101, close to Mekong River. Luxurious, big timber bungalows, some with balconies overlooking the river. A/c, TV, fridge, and wonderful garden-like private bathrooms. There is also a restaurant, and you can take day trips to Pha Taem from here. Recommended.

B-C Araya Resort, Pukumchai Rd, T045-351191. A/c, TV, hot water, fridge, large, attractive bungalows situated in a beautiful spot on a landscaped rocky hill-garden above the river. The associated restaurant, **Araya Raft**, floats down below on the Mekong, and is justly known for its fish dishes.

B-C Khong Chiam Marina Resort, T045-361011. Range of bungalows some with a/c, good restaurant.

D-E Khong Chiam Hotel, Pukumchai Rd, T045-351160, F351074. Some a/c and hot water, private bathrooms, quiet location, good source of information.

D-E Mongkhon Guesthouse, 595 Klaepradit Rd, T01-7183182 (mob). On edge of town, close to the bus stop, large, spacious, clean rooms, some with a/c, mini-market geared to farang tastes close by.

D-E Sibae Guesthouse, 380 Ratsadonbumrung Rd, T045-351068. This is a wonderfully clean and friendly guesthouse. Rooms with fan and en suite shower. Recommended.

E Apple Guesthouse, 267 Klaepradit Rd, T045-351160. Clean, some with attached showers, fans, a bit small.

Yasothon *p331, map p333*

C-D Yot Nakhon, 143 Uthairamrit Rd, T045-711481, F711476. Some a/c, large,

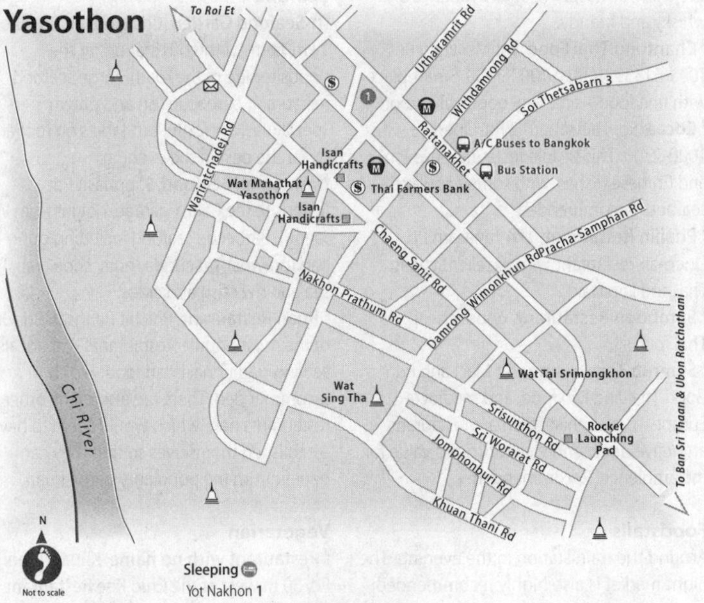
Yasothon
To Roi Et
Uthairamrit Rd
Withdamrong Rd
Soi Thetsabarn 3
Rattanakhet
A/C Buses to Bangkok
Bus Station
Isan Handicrafts
Thai Farmers Bank
Wat Mahathat Yasothon
Isan Handicrafts
Wariratchadei Rd
Chaeng Sanit Rd
Pracha-Samphan Rd
Nakhon Prathum Rd
Damrong Wimonkhun Rd
Wat Tai Srimongkhon
Wat Sing Tha
Srisunthon Rd
Sri Worarat Rd
Jomphonburi Rd
Khuan Thani Rd
Rocket Launching Pad
To Ban Sri Thaan & Ubon Ratchathani
Chi River
N
Not to scale
Sleeping
Yot Nakhon 1

featureless but comfortable enough, with, so it is claimed, a 24-hr coffee shop, a/c rooms have TV but no hot water.

D-F Surawit Watthana, 128/1 Chaeng Sanit Rd, T045-711690. Fan rooms with attached bathrooms.

Eating

Buriram *p324*

Buriram is famous for its fiery papaya pok pok salad, similar to the more widely available Isaan dish, somtam.

Phim Phit, Thani Rd. A/c, seafood restaurant selling freshwater and seawater fish, crabs and prawns; the freshwater fish is excellent.

Beer House, Romburi Rd. Open-air bar and restaurant specializing in ice-cold beer and chargrilled seafood. Recommended.

Lung Chaan Restaurant, Romburi Rd (near Thai Hotel). Excellent cheap Thai/Chinese food, with superb kwaytio and other simple dishes.

Nong Kai Restaurant, Romburi Rd (south end). Pleasant shady open-air noodle house with excellent noodle soup specialities.

Surin *p324, map p325*

Big Bite, on the side road up to the Thong Tarin Hotel. Open 1000-0200. Serves a vast range of Thai, Chinese and European food in a relaxing atmosphere. Many varieties of whisky and brandy.

Chantong Thai Food, Tat Mai Lang Rd, T045-515599. Open 1000-2400. Smart place with fine food – and very good value too.

Cocaa, Soi Thetsabarn 2 Rd. Open 1000-2300. This simple restaurant has Thai and Chinese dishes, with some excellent seafood. Recommended.

Phailin Restaurant, 174 Tanasarn Rd. Open-air restaurant with excellent cheap Thai and Lao food.

Somboon Restaurant, good, cheap Thai food.

Sumrub Tornkruang, Tat Mai Lang Rd. Good Thai and Lao food, and mediocre European, in sophisticated a/c restaurant, attractive decor and well run, good value for the ambience. Recommended.

Foodstalls

Around the train station in the evening. The night market is also highly recommended; it has a wide range of food, good prices, great atmosphere.

Si Saket *p326*

There is a collection of good Lao/Chinese/Thai restaurants strung out along Khukhan Rd.

Mr Hagen Ubon Rd. Small a/c restaurant serving a range of Western dishes; a pleasant stop-off and foot-rest.

Foodstalls

The night market off Ratchakan Rotfai 3 Rd is the best place for stall food.

Ubon Ratchathani *p326, map p327*

Chinese/Thai

Hong Fah Restaurant, Chayangkun Rd (opposite Pathumrat Hotel). Expensive but great Chinese in sophisticated a/c restaurant.

Khai Di Restaurant, 24/20 Sapphasit Rd (not far from Wat Jaeng). A rather grubby looking place serving delicious muhan or barbecue suckling pig.

Phon, Yutthaphan Rd, opposite fire station. Thai and Chinese. Recommended.

International

Broaster Chicken and Pizza, Upparat Rd. The name says it all; brash a/c restaurant selling fried chicken, pizzas and fries etc.

Seafood

Seafood Garden, Chayangkun Rd (about 1 km north of the bus station on the opposite side of the road). Large seafood restaurant, barbecue fish and prawn specialities, a/c room, but tables on roof are by far the best in the evening.

Antaman Seafood, Sapphasit Rd (opposite the Caltex garage, not far from Wat Jaeng). Barbecue seafood including gung pao (prawns), maengda (horseshoe crabs), sea and river fish and crabs.

Puan Restaurant, Phichit Rangsan Rd. One of the most popular restaurants with locals serving traditional Isaan food. Highly recommended. There are also many other restaurants here which would seem to have established themselves so that they can benefit from the popularity of the Puan.

Vegetarian

Restaurant with no name, Khuan Thani Rd, 30 m west of the Chio Kee Restaurant.

Bun bang fai: the Northeast's skyrocket festival

Perhaps the Northeast's best known festival is the bun bang fai or skyrocket festival. This is celebrated across the region between May and June, at the end of the dry season, though it is most fervently in the town of Yasothon. The festival was originally linked to animist beliefs, but became closely associated with Buddhism. The climax of the festival involves the firing of massive rockets into the air to ensure bountiful rain by invoking the rain god Vassakarn (or, as some people maintain, Phya Thaen), who also has a penchant for fire.

The rockets can be over 4 m long and contain as much as 500 kg of gunpowder. As well as these bang jut rockets, there are also elaborately constructed bang eh rockets which are just for show. Traditionally, the rockets were made of bamboo; now steel and plastic storm pipes are used while specialist rocket-makers, commissioned months beforehand, have taken over from the amateurs of the past.

The rockets are mounted on a bamboo scaffold and fired into the air with much cheering, shouting and exchanging of money. Gambling has become part and parcel of the event with bets laid on which rocket reaches the greatest height. The festival is preceded by a procession of monks, dancing troupes and musicians. There is even a beauty contest, Thida bang fai ko, or the Sparkling daughters of the skyrockets.

In the past, bun bang fai was a lewd and wild festival more akin to Rio de Janeiro than Isaan. Men wearing phallic symbols would parade through the village, drunken groups would dance wildly imitating sexual intercourse. At the same time, young boys would be ordained and monks blessed. The governor of Yasothon has banned the use of phallic symbols, regarding them as unfitting for a national event, although he has had a more difficult time trying to outlaw drunkenness.

Clean and friendly cafeteria-style vegetarian restaurant, eat all you like.

Vietnamese

Indochine Restaurant, 168-170 Sapphasit Rd (not far from Wat Jaeng). Vietnamese food in basic but attractive restaurant, good value and great food, closes at 1800.

Bakeries

Jiaw Kii, Khuan Thani Rd, a good place for breakfast with bacon and eggs, coffee and toast, as well as more usual Thai morning dishes.

S & P Bakery Shoppe, 207 Chayangkun Rd. Pastries, ice cream and pizzas in pristine a/c western-style surroundings; a little piece of Bangkok in Ubon.

Foodstalls

Ubon has a profusion of foodstalls. A good range can be found on Chayangkun Rd, just south of the **Pathumrat Hotel**, including stalls selling kanom (sweets and pastries), seafood dishes and fruit drinks.

Khong Chiam *p331*

Araya Raft, below **Araya Resort**, Santirat Rd, T045-351015. Overlooking the Mekong, a beautiful and breezy place to eat, with Mekong River fish specialities including yisok. There are 4 karaoke restaurants. There are also several floating barges that double up as restaurants moored around the peninsula, which can hold hundreds of people. All serve similar Thai dishes (cheap) and there is little to choose between them – they make a pleasant place to sit and watch the sun go down.

Bars and clubs

Surin *p324, map p325*

There is a good number of clubs and bars in Surin, although none is really geared to

overseas visitors: karaoke, Thai crooners in overblown dresses, and heavy drinking.

Caesar Nightclub and cafe, below the Thong Tarin Hotel, open 2100-0200.

Cowboy Beer Corner, Siritat Rd, which reflects this part of Thailand's enthusiasm for all things Western.

Swing Club, Sirirat Rd, open 1730-0130. Food, bar and karaoke.

Festivals and events

Buriram *p324*

Nov Annual boat races at Satuk, 40 km north of Buriram on the Mun River, with contestants coming from all over Thailand to compete. The event opens with an elephant parade and festivities, beauty pageants and dancing fill the evenings.

Dec Kite festival, held early in the month at Huai Chorakee Mak Reservoir, just south of Buriram. Processions of vehicles decorated with kites and a beauty pageant.

Surin *p324, map p325*

Nov (third week) Elephant Round-up, see page 324.

Ubon Ratchathani *p326, map p327*

Jul (movable, for 5 days from the first day of the Buddhist Lent or Khao Phansa) **Candle Festival**. Enormous sculpted beeswax candles, made by villagers from all over the province, are ceremoniously paraded through the streets before being presented to the monks. The festival seems to have been introduced during the reign of Rama I. The Buddha is said to have remarked that the monk Anurudha, in one of his previous lives, led his people out of darkness using a candle – the festival celebrates the feat and is also associated with learning and enlightenment. Candles are given to the monks so that they have light to read the sacred texts during the Buddhist Lent.

Yasothon *p331, map p333*

May Bun bang fai (skyrocket) festival, celebrated most fervently here in Yasothon (see box, page 335).

Shopping

Surin *p324, map p325*

Silk

Surin province is one of the centres of silk production in the Northeast, with villages in the area producing fine matmii silk and cotton ikat cloth. There are a number of shops on Chitbamrung Rd, near the bus station: **Surinat**, 361-363 Chitbamrung Rd, and Nong Ying (close to Phetkasem Hotel).

In the same area are numerous tailors. There are also 2 shops selling silk and cotton cloth near the **Phetkasem Hotel**: **Net Craft** and **Mai Surin**.

Saren Handicrafts and Travel Ltd, Saren House, 202/1-4 Thetsaban 2 Rd, T045-540176, F513599. This place offers a good range of silk and other handicrafts and also organizes tours of the area (see Tour operators).

Silverware

Silverware is also a traditional product of the area and many shops selling cloth also have small displays of local silverware.

Si Saket *p326*

Crafts

There is a reasonable craft shop on a lane running off Khukhan Rd to the southeast of the **Kessiri Hotel**, selling a range of products including Isaan axe pillows.

Ubon Ratchathani *p326, map p327*

Baskets

On Luang Rd, near the intersection with Khuan Thai Rd, is a short strip of shops specializing in basketwork.

Department stores

Ubon Plaza, Uparat Rd. A/c department store and supermarket selling all necessities.

Handicrafts

Peaceland, Luang Rd. Provides a wide range of cultural artefacts and a few trinkets.

Phanchart, 158 Rachabut Rd. Selection of antiques and northeastern handicrafts, including an excellent range of matmii silk.

Yasothon *p331, map p333*
Handicrafts
Baskets from the market in the centre of town. Near the market on the main road, Chaeng Sanit Rd, is a handicraft shop selling axe pillows, Northeastern textiles and some baskets. Yasothon is renowned in Thailand for the quality of its triangular, colourful, axe pillows or mon khit.

Activities and tours

Surin *p324, map p325*
Tour operators
Mr Pirom (see Sleeping above) organizes tours to the temples at weekends, as well as tours of silk-weaving villages in the area. Highly recommended.
Phetkasem Hotel also organizes day trips and overnight tours.
Saren Handicrafts and Travel Ltd, Saren House, 202/1-4 Thetsaban 2 Rd, T045-540176, sarentour@yahoo.com. Located opposite the police station on Lak Muang Rd, the friendly staff provide good information on excursions and overnight tours of the area, starting at ฿600 per person.

Ubon Ratchathani *p326, map p327*
Tour operators
Chongmek Travellers, Srikamol Hotel, 26 Ubonsak Rd, T045-255804, organizes tours along the Mekong River, taking in a Blu Meo village and the Pha Taem cave paintings, with a night in a fishing village. ฿1,340 per person, minimum 3 people for trip. Tours to Prasat Phra Viharn are also now available from companies in Ubon, see above for information.
State Railways of Thailand, T045-2256964, or visit the advance booking office at Hualamphong Station, Bangkok. Offers a weekend trip to Prasat Phra Viharn leaving at 0925 on Sat and returning 0535 on Mon, including accommodation in Ubon and all transport.
Takerng Tour, 425 Phromathep Rd, T045-255777, organizes tours to the Kaeng Tana Rapids and Pha Taem (approximately ฿1,000 per person).
Other operators include **Chi Chi Tour**, Chayangkun Rd, T045-241464. **Sakda Travel**, 150/1 Kartharalak, Warin, T045-323048. Thai agent. **Ubonsak Travel**, Chayangkun Rd, T045-311028.

Transport

Buriram *p324*
Air
A new airport has recently opened in Buriram, 30 km northeast of town.

Bus
Pink town buses criss-cross the town; ฿5 any distance. The bus station is on the west side of town off Bulamduan and Thani rds. Regular a/c and non-a/c connections with **Bangkok**'s Northeastern bus terminal (6½ hrs) and with **Pattaya**, **Chantaburi** and **Trat**, as well as many towns in the Northeast including **Khon Kaen**, **Mahasarakham**, **Ubon**, **Si Saket** and **Surin**.

Songthaew
The terminal is near the market off Sriphet Rd.

Train
The station is at the end of Romburi Rd, near the centre of town, connections with **Bangkok**'s Hualamphong station and all stops between Bangkok and **Ubon Ratchathani**. It's better to take the train as the rail route is much more direct between Buriram and either Korat or Ubon.
To get to **Phnom Rung** and **Muang Tham** from Buriram by bus from the station off Thani Rd towards Prakhon Chai. Get off at Ban Tako, before Prakhon Chai, for details thereafter, see page 317. There are also several morning songthaews from Buriram's central market to **Dong Nong Nae**, which meet up with local songthaews that run direct to both sets of ruins.

Tuk-tuk
฿10-20 around town.

Surin *p324, map p325*
Bicycle
For hire from Pirom's Guesthouse (see Sleeping above), ฿30 per day.

Bus
The station is off Chitbamrung Rd. Regular a/c and non-a/c connections with **Bangkok**'s Northeastern bus terminal (6-7 hrs). Special a/c buses are laid on by tour companies and major hotels for the Elephant

Round-up. Connections with **Korat**, **Ubon** and from other Northeastern towns, and also with **Chiang Mai**. A/c tour buses to **Bangkok** leave from the offices of Kitikarn Ratchasima near the Surin Plaza.

Songthaew

To surrounding villages leave from the market area off Thetsabarn 3 Rd (near the clock tower), mostly in the morning. Drivers will also charter their vehicles out – expect to pay about ฿500 per day. Vehicles can be rented through the Tharin Hotel.

Train

The station is at the north end of Tanasarn Rd, with a statue of 3 elephants outside. Connections with **Bangkok**'s Hualamphong station (8 hrs), stops en route between Ubon and Bangkok. The overnight a/c express leaves Bangkok at 2100 and arrives in Surin at 0424. Tickets must be booked 2 weeks in advance for travel during Nov when the Elephant Round-up is under way. The TAT organizes a special train during this period.

Si Saket *p326*

Bus

The terminal is on the south side of town off Khukhan Rd. Regular connections with **Bangkok**'s Northeastern bus terminal (8-9 hrs) and with other Northeastern centres. To **Prasat Khao Phra Viharn**. From the bus station, take an early local bus to Kantharalak, and make it known you wish to go to Prasat Khao Phra Viharn. The driver should drop you off at the intersection a few kilometres before reaching Phum Saron. From here it is necessary to hitch or take a motorcycle taxi. Alternatively, hire a car for the day (ask at the Kessiri Hotel).

Train

The station is in the centre of town on Kaanrotfai Rd. Regular connections with **Bangkok**'s Hualamphong station and stations en route between Bangkok and Ubon.

Ubon Ratchathani *p326, map p327*

Air

Airport on the north side of town. It is just about possible to walk into town with cool weather, a following breeze and light bags. A taxi service is available: ฿70 to the town centre, ฿120 to the railway station at Warin Chamrap. Bigger hotels pick up guests gratis. Regular daily connections with **Bangkok** (1 hr).

Airline offices THAI, 292/9 Chayangkun Rd, T045-254431.

Bus

Thirteen routes across town; pick up a useful map from the TAT office.

The recently renovated BKS station for non-a/c buses is some distance north of town, not far from Wat Nong Bua at the end of Chayangkun Rd. Get there by town bus no 2 or 3. The station for a/c and non-a/c buses to **Bangkok** is at the back of the market on Chayangkun Rd, south of the Pathumrat Hotel. Regular connections with Bangkok's Northeastern bus terminal (8 hrs), **Nakhon Phanom** (5½-7 hrs), and less frequently with other Northeastern towns – eg there are 2 bus companies who service **Surin** regularly (4 hrs); a/c and non-a/c tour buses to Bangkok also leave from Khuan Thani Rd, opposite the TAT Office; **Sahamit Tour**, on Khuan Thani Rd near the National Museum, runs buses to **Udon Thani** via **Mukdahan**, **That Phanom** and **Nakhon Phanom**; Sayan Tour, near the Ratchathani Hotel, runs buses to **Udon Thani** via **Yasothon**, **Roi Et**, **Mahasarakham** and **Khon Kaen**. VIP buses to Bangkok leave from the station on the south side of the Mun River, north of Warin Chamrap on the left-hand side of the road, heading north. Night bus leaves at 2130, arriving in Bangkok at 0600. Reservations recommended.

International connections with Laos: it is possible to enter Laos east of Ubon at Chongmek (for details on Chongmek, see page 330). To get to Chongmek, take a bus from the station in Warin Chamrap to Phibun Mangsahan (1 hr, about 45 km). From Phibun Mangsahan there are converted trucks (large songthaews) to the border town of Chongmek, 44 km away (1½ hrs). The border customs posts are pretty relaxed and are open 0600-1800. After passing through the Lao border post (exchange facilities available for Thai baht and US dollars cash), there are trucks and share

taxis waiting to whisk passengers to Muang Kao, along a recently upgraded road (1 hr). In mid-2000 a new bridge across the Mekong was completed, making the journey from the border to Pakse faster still.

Car and motorbike hire
Car drivers often wait on Rachabut Rd and near the TAT office. A car and driver for the day, including petrol, will cost about ฿1,000. **Chaw Watana**, 39/8 Suriyat Rd, T045-242202 (฿250 for a motorbike, ฿1,000-1,200 for a car). Chaw Watana seems to hire out anything with wheels. Saamlors and tuk-tuks also available (at break-neck speed), map from the TAT office (fare ฿3).

There are several other car/motorbike rental places on Chayangkun Rd.

Train
The station is south of the river in Warin Chamrap. Town buses Nos 2 and 6 run into town. Regular connections with **Bangkok**'s Hualamphong station (10 hrs) and all stations in between.

Khong Chiam *p331*
Bus
Catch town bus Nos 1, 3 or 6 from **Ubon Ratchathani** to **Warin Chamrap**; and from there to Khong Chiam via Phibun Mangsahan. There are also a/c bus connections with **Bangkok**'s Northeastern bus terminal.

Yasothon *p331, map p333*
Bus
The bus station is at the northeastern edge of town, an easy walk from the centre. Non-a/c buses to **Ubon**, **Udon**, **Roi Et**, Mahasarakham and **Khon Kaen**, as well as with **Bangkok**'s Northeastern bus terminal (10 hrs). A/c buses leave from offices close to the station for Bangkok (10 hrs) and Ubon.

Directory

Buriram *p324*
Banks Bangkok Bank of Commerce, corner of Thani and Romburi rds. **Thai Farmers**, 132 Soonthouthep Rd. **Post office** Intersection of Romburi and Niwat rds, by the railway station. Card phones available.

Surin *p324, map p325*
Banks Thai Farmers, 353 Tanasarn Rd. **Post office** Corner of Tanasarn and Thetsabarn 1 rds. **Medical services** Hospital, T045-511757. **Useful addresses** Police, Lak Muang Rd, T045-511007.

Si Saket *p326*
Banks Thai Farmers Bank, 1492/4 Khukhan Rd. **Post office** Chaisawat Rd.

Ubon Ratchathani *p326, map p327*
Banks Bangkok, 88 Chayangkun Rd. Thai Farmers Bank, 356/9 Phromathep Rd. Thai Military, 130 Chayangkun Rd. Siam Commercial, Chayangkun Rd. All have ATMs. **Internet** Cafés at 322 Suriyat Rd and on Uparat Chayangkun and Srinarong rds. **Medical services** Rom Kao Hospital, Upparat Rd (close to the Mun River), is said to be the best in the city. There is another hospital on Sapphasit Rd, T045-254906. **Post office** Corner of Srinarong and Luang Rd; telephone office at the back of the post office. Email next door and above the Nevada Hotel. **Useful addresses** Immigration. Phibun Mangsahan Rd, T045-441108 (in Phibun Mangsahan). **Tourist Police** Corner of Srinarong and Upparat roads, T045-243770.

Khong Chiam *p331*
Banks Krung Thai Bank, Santirat Rd (exchange facilities available). **Post office** Store opposite the Apple Guesthouse. An international phone and fax is available here and also next door.

Yasothon *p331, map p333*
Banks Thai Farmers Bank, 289 Chaeng Sanit Rd.

Khon Kaen and the Isaan Heartland

The centre of the Khorat Plateau provides the heartland of Northeast culture. Here, you'll find the dusty provincial towns of Mahasarakham and Roi Et. This is an agricultural area far off the tourist trail yet it encapsulates completely the ambience of Isaan. The larger, booming city of Khon Kaen marks a return to modernity and is an excellent transport hub for the whole region. » *For Sleeping, Eating and other listings, see pages 344-347.*

Khon Kaen → *Colour map 2, grid B3.*

Khon Kaen is a large commercial centre which houses the largest university in the Northeast and functions as an important administrative centre. Selected by the government as a 'growth pole' during the 1960s to help facilitate the development of the region, Khon Kaen was also home to a US airforce base during the Vietnam War. It has a good selection of hotels, cinemas, restaurants and bars. Because Khon Kaen is one of the principal transport hubs of the Northeast, tourists may find that they need to spend a night here en route elsewhere.

Ins and outs

Getting there The airport is 6 km from town, with multiple daily connections to Bangkok. The railway station is a 15-20-minute walk from the centre and connects to

Khon Kaen

To Udon Thani & Nong Khai
Lung Sun Rachakhan Rd
National Museum
Bung Sri Tan
Khon Kaen University Campus
Soonrachakhan Rd
Sala Klang Changwat (Provincial Hall)
Kasikhon Thungsang Rd
Thung Sang Lake
Na Soonratchakaan Rd
Tapalak Rd
Maliwan Rd
Thai Airways
Non A/c Bus Terminal
Prachasamosorn Rd
Phimphasut Rd
To Airport & Loei (Rt 12)
Ronmuang Rd
Na Muang Rd
Klang Muang Rd
Anamat Rd
A/c Bus Terminal
To Hospital & Vietnamese Consulate
Sri Chand Rd
Fairy Plaza
Mittraphap Rd
Lang Muang Rd
Chetakhon Rd
Chonchuan Rd
Ruanrom Rd
To Lao Consulate
To Mahasarakham, Roi Et, Korat & Bangkok (Rt 2)
To Bung Kaen Nakhon (500m)
N
0 metres 300
0 yards 300

Sleeping
Charoen Thani
Royal Princess 1
Kaen Inn 2
Kaen Nakorn 3
Khon Kaen 4
Kosa 5
Roma 6
Sawatdi 7
Sofitel Raja Orchid 8
Suksawad 9

Eating
Best Place 1
Diamond Garden 4
Pizza & Bake 2
Rachada 3

The story of Quan Am

Quan Am was turned onto the streets by her husband for some unspecified wrongdoing and, dressed as a monk, took refuge in a monastery. There, a woman accused her of fathering, and then abandoning, her child. Accepting the blame (why, no one knows), she was again turned out onto the streets, only to return to the monastery much later when she was on the point of death to confess her true identity. When the Emperor of China heard the tale, he made Quan Am the Guardian Spirit of Mother and Child, and couples without a son now pray to her. Quan Am's husband is sometimes depicted as a parakeet, with the Goddess usually holding her adopted son in one arm and standing on a lotus leaf (the symbol of purity).

Bangkok and Nong Khai. The a/c and non-a/c bus terminals are both reasonably central, with bus services to Bangkok. Chiang Mai and many other destinations in the Northeast, North and Central Plains. ▸▸ *See also Transport, page 346.*

Getting around Khon Kaen is a large town. Songthaews provide the main mode of public transport and run along 12 fixed routes (maps available from tourist office). There are also saamlors and tuk-tuks and local buses to out of town destinations.

Tourist information TAT ⓘ *Prachasamoson Rd, T043-244498, F244497*. New and helpful branch of the TAT, with good maps and details on accommodation and attractions in and around Khon Kaen (with a heavy emphasis on the dinosaurs; see below for more information).

Sights

Khon Kaen supports an excellent branch of the **National Museum** ⓘ *Wed-Sun 0900-1200, 1300-1600, ฿30*, at the intersection of Kasikhon Thungsang and Lungsun Rachakhan roads, at the northeast edge of the city. It contains, among other things, a good collection of Ban Chiang artefacts and beautiful Dvaravati boundary stones. Also worthy of note is the **Bung Kaen Nakhon** at the southern edge of the city, reaching a maximum extent at the peak of the rainy season of nearly 100 ha. On the northern shore of the bung (pond) is the Lao-style **Wat That**, with the characteristic lotus bud-shaped chedi of the Lao. The lake is used by local residents for walks and picnics and there are also a number of open-air restaurants.

Around Khon Kaen

Phu Wiang National Park

ⓘ *It is easiest to get here on a tour. By road, take the route from Khon Kaen towards Chumphae and turn right at the Km 48 marker onto Route 2038. Continue along this road for 38 km to the national park. It is also possible to get here by public transport: take a bus from the public bus terminal to Phu Wiang district town. From the town take a songthaew or tuk-tuk to the national park, about ฿200.*

This park, which consists of a central plain encircled by low hills, sprung to modest fame in the mid-1990s when it was discovered that the area had one of the world's largest **dinosaur graveyards**. The first dinosaur fossils were unearthed here in 1978 and by 1991 nine sites had been uncovered. In 1996 the remains of a new family of carnivorous thunder lizards were unearthed here and were appropriately called

 Siamotyrannus isaanensis. The importance of the find is that while the animals are considerably smaller than their well-known North American and Chinese cousins, the Thai tyrannosaur is much older: 120-130 million years as opposed to 65-80 million years. The dinosaur remains are concentrated in the northern part of the park and it is possible to walk from site to site.

Ban Kok

ⓘ *Ban Kok is 50 km from Khon Kaen. Take the Khon Kaen-Chumpae road past the airport and turn left at Ban Thum Then onto Route 2062. Continue along this road to the Km 40 marker and turn onto a road by the Shell petrol station. The village is a short way from main road. By public transport, take a bus to Mancha Kiri district town (there is said to be a bus at 0600 and a return bus at 1830); from here it is just another 4 km to Ban Kok.*

Also known as Tortoise Village, Ban Kok harbours a rather confusing tale about tortoises that means that these creatures are regarded as sacred by the inhabitants of Ban Kok and surrounding villages. There are 2,000 of the animals wandering about, unmolested, eating every piece of greenery in sight. Be warned: anyone hurting the tortoises has been afflicted with all sorts of strange maladies.

Chonnabot

ⓘ *Take a local bus from the station on Prachasamosan Rd (1 hr). Note that the last songthaew back to town leaves Chonnabot around 1600.*

The villages around here are well known for the quality and variety of their matmii silk and cotton cloth. This is both a small town and a district near Khon Kaen. Much of the silk and cotton cloth from here is sent to Bangkok. There is a handicraft centre where local cloth is sold, or lengths can be bought direct from weaving households – just wander through the village; looms can be seen under the houses. Note that cloth is bought by the phun. A normal sarong length will be about two phun, so prices will rarely relate to the whole piece of cloth. However, English is not widely spoken, so it either takes modest Thai or skilful hand signals to secure a deal. Chonnabot town, the capital of the district, lies 12 km off Route 2, travelling south towards Korat (turn-off near Km 399 marker onto Route 2057).

Prasat Puaynoi

ⓘ *Take the main Khon Kaen-Korat highway (Route 2) and turn off at Ban Phai onto Route 23. After 23 km, turn off again onto Route 2297. This leads to the temple, which is situated at the entrance to a village.*

This is a recently renovated 10th-century Khmer temple, about 80 km southeast of Khon Kaen. The four buildings that comprise the structure make it similar to the far better known Pimai – but smaller in scale. There is some sculpture.

Phu Wiang National Park

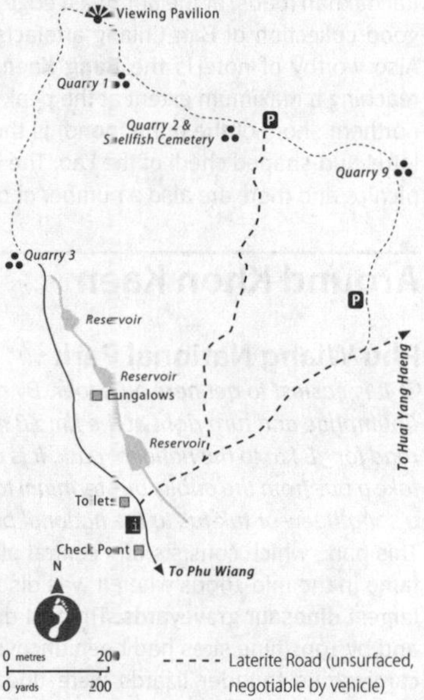

Viewing Pavilion
Quarry 1
Quarry 2 &
Shellfish Cemetery
P
Quarry 9
Quarry 3
P
Reservoir
Reservoir
Bungalows
Reservoir
To Huai Yang Haeng
Toilets
Check Point
To Phu Wiang
N
0 metres 200
0 yards 200
Laterite Road (unsurfaced, negotiable by vehicle)

Isaan Heartland

Mahasarakham → *Colour map 2, grid B4.*

Known locally as Sarakham, Mahasarakham is a quiet, provincial capital, situated right in the centre of the Khorat Plateau known as a centre for Northeastern handicrafts.

The **Research Institute of Northeastern Art and Culture** ⓘ *Mon-Fri, half day on Sat*, has a small permanent exhibition of textiles, metal casting, music, basketry and other handicrafts. It is located behind the main lecture building of the university, 2 km west of town on the road to Khon Kaen. The **Isaan Cultural & Art Centre** has an exhibition of Isaan history and handicrafts and arts including textiles and palm-leaf manuscripts. The centre is situated in the Rajabhat Institute Mahasarakham. There is a daily fresh market on the corner of Nakhon Sawan and Worayut roads, in the centre of town.

Tambon Kwao ⓘ *take one of the regular local buses from the station on Somtawin Rd*, 5 km from Mahasarakham, is a centre of pottery production. Around 100 households here produce simple, traditional pottery products including water pots and various food containers. East of Mahasarakham off Route 208 towards Roi Et, the turn-off for the village is 4 km along Route 208 and then 1 km down a laterite track.

Roi Et → *Colour map 2, grid B4.*

Roi Et is the capital of a province encompassing one of the poorest agricultural areas in Thailand. The **Tung Kula Rong Hai** is a large, dry, salty and infertile plain that covers much of the province. The name means the 'Weeping Plain of the Kula', and millions of baht have been invested in projects to improve the land and productivity of agriculture. Although there have been some successes, the incidence of circular migration – the movement of young men and women to Bangkok and elsewhere in a seasonal search for work – illustrates the inability of the land to support rapidly rising needs and expectations.

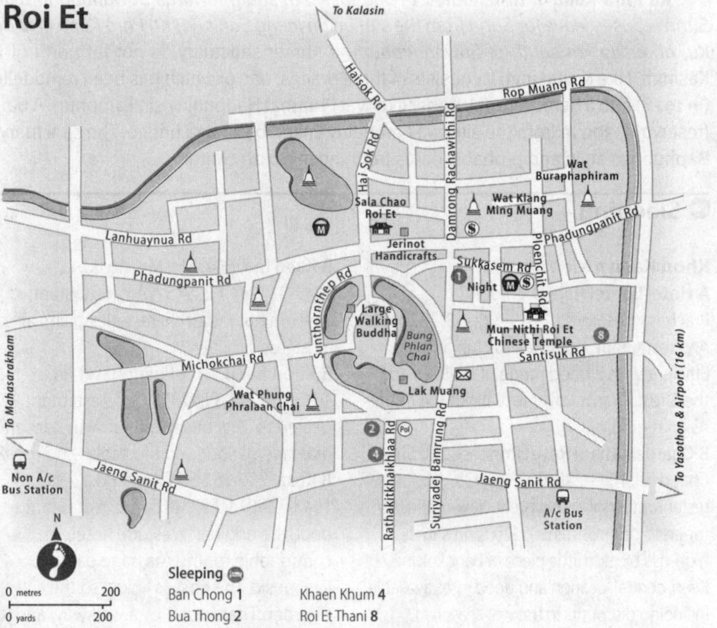

Roi Et is built around an artificial lake – the Bung Phlan Chai. The island in the centre, linked by footbridges, contains the town's **lak muang** (foundation pillar) and a large Sukhothai-style walking Buddha. This, the moat which surrounds the city and several well-stocked gardens, creates an airy, well-planned town; something of a novelty in Thailand. Paddle boats can be hired on the lake, and the island is a popular spot with locals for walking and feeding the fish.

Wat Phung Phralaan Chai, at the southwest corner of the lake, is ancient but vigorous rebuilding has obliterated the old, with the exception of the bai sema (boundary stones) which surround the new bot. The concrete high-relief morality tales which surround the three-storeyed, moated mondop are enjoyable. Roi Et's most obvious 'sight' (if size is anything to go by) is the massive 59-m (sometimes 68 m, but who's counting?) **standing Buddha of Wat Buraphaphiram**, on the east side of town near Rop Muang Road. The Buddha is known as Phra Phutta Ratana Mongkhon Maha Mani. It is possible to climb up the side of the statue for a view over the town.

On Ploenchit Road is the **Mun Nithi Roi Et Chinese Temple**. In classic Chinese style, the ground floor is a trading business; the temple is on the first floor. Three altars face the room: to the left, one dedicated to the corpulent 'laughing' Buddha; in the centre, to the historic Buddha and various future Buddhas (or Bodhisattvas); to the right, to Kuan Yin or Quan Am, the Chinese Goddess of Mercy (see box). The pagoda pragmatically combines Theravada and Mahayana Buddhism (see page 697), and Daoism and Confucianism. Despite Thailand's large Chinese population – around 15% – it is relatively rare to see Chinese pagodas and temples. This is partly because the Chinese have assimilated so seamlessly into Thai society and become good Theravada Buddhists. Another reason is a wish to blend in, in order to reduce any chance of persecution. At times of economic nationalism – 'Thailand for the Thais' – the Chinese have been discriminated against. Another, smaller, Chinese pagoda is the **Sala Chao Roi Et** on Phadungphanit Road, not far from the lake.

The market on and between Phadungphanit and Hai Sok roads sells Isaan handicrafts and fresh foods, including insects. On the roadside, women market the ingredients for betel 'nut'.

Ku Phra Kona ⓘ *take Route 215 and then 214 south towards Suwannaphum and Surin – buses leave for Surin from the station on Jaeng Sanit Rd; Ku Phra Kona is at Ban Ku, about 12 km south of Suwannaphum*, a Khmer sanctuary, is not far north of Ku Kasingh. Like Ku Kasingh it consists of three prangs, one of which has been remodelled (in 1928) into a tiered 'stupa', rather like Wat Phrathat Haripunjaya in Lamphun. A baray (reservoir), 300 m from the site, was probably linked by a naga bridge. The sanctuary is Baphuon in style and probably dates from the mid-11th century.

Sleeping

Khon Kaen *p340, map p340*
A Hotel Sofitel Raja Orchid, 9/9 Prachasamosorn Rd, T043-322155, F322150. A/c, restaurant, pool, health club and gym. Efficient with a good range of facilities and the 3 restaurants cover just about the entire Asian region.

B Charoen Thani Royal Princess, 260 Sri Chand Rd, T043-220400, F220438. A/c, restaurant, pool with a great view of the city (open to non-residents), 320 rooms in high-rise block, a little piece of Bangkok in Khon Kaen, central location and good rates available, including discounts in the wet season.

B Kaen Inn, 56 Klang Muang Rd, T043-237744, F239457. A/c, restaurant, well run but rather characterless, with all 'business' facilities.

B Khon Kaen, 43/2 Phimphasut Rd, T043-237711, F242458. A/c, restaurant, geared to Thai businessmen with bars and massage parlours, comfortable – no more.

B Kosa, 250-252 Sri Chand Rd, T043-225014, F225013. A/c, restaurant, pool, the original 'Western' hotel, comfortable rooms, massage parlour, live music. The **Kosa** is linked to the Charoen Thani hotel by a walkway, and

they share an entertainment complex. This place is often full. Recommended.

C Roma, 50/2 Klang Muang Rd, T236276. Some a/c, the poor cousin to the Khon Kaen. Bare, functional rooms in bare functional block which looks as though it has been made out of Lego – but very reasonable for a/c and hot water and the best value place in town. Recommended.

D Kaen Nakorn, 690 Sri Chand Rd, T043-224268. A/c, clean.

E Suksawad, 2/2 Klang Muang Rd, T043-236472. Wooden building down soi off main road, so relatively quiet, rooms are shabby but clean, friendly, attached bathrooms, 3-min walk from the tourist office.

Mahasarakham *p343*

D Wasu, 1096/4 Damnoen Nat Rd, T043-723075, F721290. Clean a/c rooms and excellent value. Part of a complex of pubs and clubs.

E Suthorn Hotel, 1157/1 Worayut Rd, T043-711201. Some a/c, small hotel in town centre with 30 rooms, a/c rooms have attached bathrooms, basic.

Roi Et *p343, map p343*

A Roi Et Thani Hotel, Santisuk Rd, T043-520387, F520401. Part of the Dusit group with 167 rooms on 6 floors, a good pool, gym and business centre. It is undoubtedly the most luxurious place in the area and is also professionally run.

D Khaen Khum, 50-62 Rathakitkhaikhlaa, T043-511508. Some a/c with hot water, well managed and maintained, the best of the Chinese-style hotels in Roi Et.

D-E Bua Thong, 40-46 Rathakitkhaikhlaa, T043-511142. Some a/c, best rooms on top floor where windows allow a breeze in, squat loos, no hot water, no frills but friendly.

E Ban Chong, 99-101 Suriyadej Bamrung Rd, T043-511235. Simple but good value and reasonably clean rooms with attached facilities.

Eating

Khon Kaen *p340, map p340*

The best selection of cheaper Chinese/Thai restaurants is on Klang Muang Rd, between the Kaen Inn and Suksawad Hotel

Thai/Chinese

Diamond Garden (Beer Garden), Srichand Rd, near the Fairy Plaza. Thai.

Nong Lek, 54/1-3 Klang Muang Rd. Well patronized Chinese restaurant, specialities including khaaw na pet (rice and duck) and seafood dishes. Recommended.

Western

Best Place, Klang Muang Rd (near Kaen Inn). Rather sanitized a/c restaurant, serving pizzas, burgers and other similar dishes.

Pizza and Bake, Klang Muang Rd. Pizzas, burgers and various Thai dishes, good place for breakfast and Western food if needed.

Bakeries and ice cream

Rachadaa, corner of Na Muang and Prachasamoson roads. Ice creams served at tables set in a small garden.

Sweet Home, 79 Fairy Plaza, Srichand Rd. Ice cream and bakery.

Foodstalls

Usual array of foodstalls to be found on the streets. A good selection near the a/c bus terminal, off Sri Chand Rd.

Mahasarakham *p343*

There is a row of good restaurants, bars and bakeries on Nakhon Sawan Rd, about 1 km from the town centre near the Mahasarakham University. Night market or **Talaat tor rung**, south of town behind the bus station, best place to eat (0600-2100), selling Isaan specialities like kai yang (barbecue chicken), somtam (hot papaya salad) and larb (minced meat with herbs), as well as rice and noodle dishes.

M and Y, Nakhon Sawan Rd (about 1 km from town centre). Seafood restaurant, tables in garden, excellent chargrilled prawns. Recommended.

Maeng Khian, behind the bus station. A/c restaurant in ranch house style with live music, Thai food, with good Isaan specialities.

Somphort Pochana, Somthawin Rd (near intersection with Warayut Rd). Good Chinese and Thai dishes, excellent value.

Roi Et *p343, map p343*

Excellent evening food market by the post office, from dusk until 2100, best choice of

food in town including Isaan specialities. There are also a collection of pleasant open-air garden restaurants situated around the central lake.

Entertainment

Khon Kaen *p340, map p340*
Along with the high density of karaoke bars and massage parlours, there is also a cinema on Sri Chand Rd not far from the **Kosa Hotel**.

Festivals and events

Khon Kaen *p340, map p340*
Late Nov to early Dec (movable) Silk Fair and Phuk Siao (friendship) Festival. Wide variety of silks on sale and production processes demonstrated. People tie threads around each other's wrists to symbolize their friendship, known as phuk siao (siao means 'friend' in Lao). Folk culture performances. The festival is centred on the Sala Klang Changwat or Provincial Hall on the north side of town.

Roi Et *p343, map p343*
May Bun bang fai (skyrocket) festival, celebrated most fervently in Yasothon (see page 336), but a more traditional example is held in the district town of Suwannaphum, south of Roi Et. Get there by regular bus from the station on Jaeng Sanit Rd.

Shopping

Khon Kaen *p340, map p340*
There is a general market area, opposite the bus station on Prachasamosorn Rd, and a larger market on Klang Muang Rd. Villagers hawk textiles on the street.

Books
Smart Books, Klang Muang Rd. Some English books and a good range of stationery.

Silk
Good quality matmii silk and other traditional cloth can be found in Khon Kaen.
Heng Hguan Hiang, 54/1-2 Klang Muang Rd (near intersection with Srichand Rd). Sells textiles, axe pillows, Isaan food and other handicrafts.
Prathamakant, 79/2-3 Ruanrom Rd. Silk, cotton and handicrafts.
Rin Thai, 412 Na Muang Rd, T043-221042. A long-established silk shop selling silk, cotton, local handicrafts, souvenirs and ready-to-wear clothes. Other local products include spicy pork sausages, which can be seen hanging in many shops.

Roi Et *p343, map p343*
Handicrafts
Roi Et is a centre for production of silk and cotton ikat cloth. It is sold by the phun and can range from ฿100 per phun for simple cotton cloth to ฿3,000 for a piece of finest quality silk. Go to **Jerinot**, 383 Phadungphanit Rd, or **Phaw Kaan Khaa**, 377-379 Phadungphanit Rd, to see a wide selection and to gauge prices. Also sold along this road and in market stalls are axe cushions, baskets, khaens (a Northeastern reed pipe) and other handicrafts.

Activities and tours

Khon Kaen *p340, map p340*
Tour operators
Air Booking and Travel Centre Co, 4 Srichand Rd, T043-244482.
Northeast Travel Service, 87/56 Klang Muang Rd, T043-244792, F243238. At the a/c bus terminal.

Transport

Khon Kaen *p340, map p340*
Air
The airport is 6 km from town.
Several flights a day to **Bangkok** (55 mins) on THAI.
Airline offices THAI, 183/6 Maliwan Rd, T043-236523

Bus
The vast non-a/c bus station is on Prachasamoson Rd; a/c buses leave from the terminal just off Klang Muang Rd. Regular connections with **Bangkok**'s Northeastern bus terminal. Buses, both a/c and non-a/c, run to most other Northeastern towns and to **Chiang Mai**, **Chiang Rai**, **Rayong** (for Pattaya).

Car hire
R Rent Service T043-243543, ฿1500 per day.

Songthaew
The cheapest way around town is by songthaew, which run along 12 routes, fare ฿4. A list of the routes and stops can be picked up from the TAT office.

Train
Station on Station Rd in the southwest quarter of town. Regular connections with **Bangkok**'s Hualamphong station (8 hrs), **Korat** and other stops en route north to **Nong Khai** (3 hrs on the morning stopping train).

Mahasarakham *p343*
Bus
The non-a/c bus station is just south of the town centre on Somtawin Rd with regular departures for **Bangkok**'s Northeastern bus terminal (7 hrs) and other Northeastern towns. A/c buses leave from various offices around town.

Roi Et *p343, map p343*
Air
PB Air, flies 3 times a week to Bangkok.

Bus
The main bus station is to the west of town, off Jaeng Sanit Rd (Route 23 towards Mahasarakham). Non-a/c buses to **Bangkok** (8 hrs), **Khon Kaen**, **Ubon**, **Udon**, **Nong Khai**, **Mahasarakham**, **Buriram**, **Surin** and **Korat**. A/c bus connections with **Bangkok**'s Northeastern terminal (8 hrs). The a/c bus terminal in Roi Et is at the southeast corner of town.

Directory

Khon Kaen *p340, map p340*
Banks Bangkok, Sri Chand Rd (near the Kosa Hotel). Krung Thai, 457-461 Srichand Rd. Siam Commercial, 491 Sri Chand Rd. Thai Farmers, 145 Prachasamoson Rd. **Embassies and consulates** Lao PDR Consulate, 123 Photisan Rd, T043-223698. Tourist visas available for US$40, 1-hr service. Also provides leaflets detailing 'How to enter Laos/Vietnam'. Vietnamese Consulate, 65/6 Chatapadung Rd, T043-241586. **Post office** Klang Muang Rd (near the intersection with Sri Chand Rd), T043-221147. **Medical services** Hospital: Sri Chand Rd, T043-236005. **Useful addresses** Police. Klang Muang Rd, T043-211162 (near post office).

Mahasarakam *p343*
Banks Thai Farmers Bank, Worayut Rd. Thai Military Bank, Padongwithi Rd. Both with currency exchange. **Internet** KK Internet, just south of the river. **Post office** Facing the clock tower on Nakhon Sawan Rd.

Roi Et *p343, map p343*
Banks Thai Farmers Bank, 431 Phadungphanit Rd. Thai Military Bank, Ploenchit Rd (near intersection with Sukkasem Rd). **Post office** Suriyadejbamrung Rd (at intersection with Santisuk Rd). **Telephone** Overseas calls can be made from the post office.

Udon Thani and the northern Mekong route

Udon is a frenetic place, or as close to frenetic as it is possible to get in this part of Thailand. The palm-fringed roundabouts provide a tropical Riviera feel amidst the bustle and the city has a reputation of being one of Thailand's cleanest provincial capitals. Most tourists only stay here because of its proximity to the outstanding prehistoric site at Ban Chiang. Like Khon Kaen, Udon was a boom-town during the Vietnam War, so it retains reminders of that time: massage parlours, bars, coffee shops and fully air-conditioned hotels. It is said that about 60 former US servicemen have married Thais and settled here. There is even an Udon branch of the US Veterans of Foreign Wars Association, along with a relay station of Voice of America Radio.

The Mekong forms the border between Thailand and Laos for several hundred kilometres in the Northeastern region. A good starting point is Loei, a provincial capital 50 km south of the Mekong and within easy reach of a number of fine national parks in the Phetchabun hills, including the popular Phu Kradung National Park. The nearby riverside town of Chiang Khan provides a peaceful base with atmospheric accommodation. Travelling downstream, the beautiful river road passes through, in turn, Pak Chom, Sangkhom and Si Chiangmai, before reaching the provincial capital of Nong Khai. ▸▸ *For Sleeping, Eating and other listings, pages 353-356.*

Udon Thani → *Colour map 2, grid A3.*

Ins and outs

Getting there The airport is 2 km south out of town, with multiple daily flights to Bangkok. The train station is just to the east of the town centre, and there are services south to Bangkok and a stop further north to Nong Khai. Udon's two bus terminals,

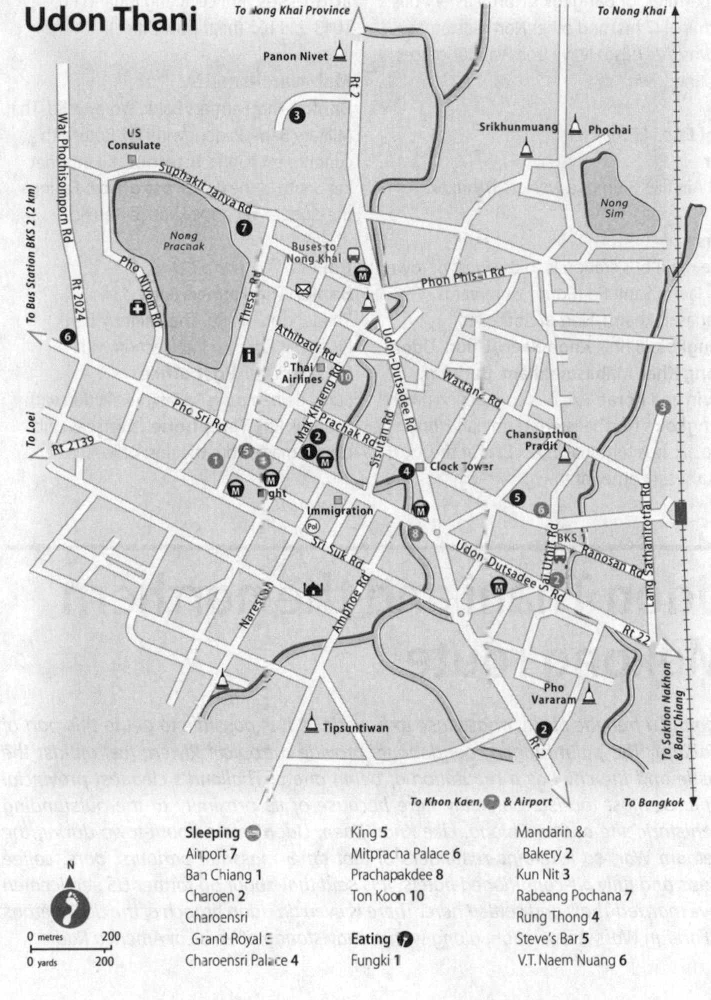

Sleeping
Airport 7
Ban Chiang 1
Charoen 2
Charoensri
Grand Royal 3
Charoensri Palace 4
King 5
Mitpracha Palace 6
Prachapakdee 8
Ton Koon 10

Eating
Fungki 1
Mandarin & Bakery 2
Kun Nit 3
Rabeang Pochana 7
Rung Thong 4
Steve's Bar 5
V.T. Naem Nuang 6

one centrally placed and the second slightly out of town, provide connections with Bangkok, Chiang Mai, Chiang Rai and most destinations in the Northeast. » *See Transport, page 355, for further details.*

Getting around A profusion of saamlors provide the main mode of city transport, with buses and songthaews linking the town with local out of town destinations. Car hire is possible.

Tourist information TAT ⓘ *Thesa Rd, facing Nong Prachak Silpakhorn, T042-325406, F325408. 0830-1630.* Limited resources but maps of Udon available.

Sights

In the northwestern quarter of town is **Nong Prachak Park**, a municipal park set around a large lake. There are a number of reasonable garden restaurants here and it is one of the more attractive places to come for an evening meal.

Ban Chiang

ⓘ *The site is open Wed-Sun 1000-1600. ฿20. Buses run direct to the village from the Udon bus station. Alternatively, take a bus going along Route 22 to Sakhon Nakhon and ask to be let off at Ban Chiang (just after the Km 50 marker). Tuk-tuk drivers hang around the junction to take visitors to the site.*

Ban Chiang, one of the most important archaeological sites to be uncovered in Southeast Asia since the Second World War, was accidentally discovered by an American anthropology student, Stephen Young, in 1966. While walking in the village he fell over the root of a kapok tree and noticed dozens of pieces of broken ancient pottery protruding from the ground. Appreciating that his find might be significant, he sent the pottery pieces for analysis to the Fine Arts Department in Bangkok and then later to the University of Pennsylvania. Rumours of his finds spread and much of the area was then ransacked by the villagers, who sold the pieces they unearthed to collectors in Bangkok and abroad. Organized excavations only really commenced during the 1970s, when a Thai archaeologist, Pisit Charoenwongsa and an American, Chester Gorman, arrived to investigate the site. Even though their task was compromised by the random digging of villagers, they still managed to unearth 18 tonnes of material in two years, including 5,000 bags of sherds and 123 burials. The site spans a time period of over 5,000 years. Perhaps the greatest discovery is the **bronzeware** which has been dated to 3600 BC, thus pre-dating bronzeware found in the Middle East by 500 years. This shattered the belief that bronze metallurgy had developed in the Tigris and Euphrates basin about 3000 BC, and from there diffused to other parts of the world. The finds also indicated to archaeologists that bronze technology may well have gone from Thailand to China instead of vice versa as the oldest known Chinese bronzes only go back to 2000 BC. The site at Ban Chiang also provides evidence of an early development of agriculture.

Little is known of the agricultural society which inhabited the site and which produced the beautiful pots of burnt ochre 'swirl' design, sophisticated metalwork and jewellery. There are two burial pits at Wat Pho Si Nai, on the edge of the village of Ban Chiang. At the other side of the village is an excellent **museum** where the Ban Chiang story is retold with clarity, exceptional displays and many of the finds.

To cash in on the visitors to the site, the villagers of Ban Chiang, prevented from selling any artefacts openly, instead market a range of their handicrafts in shops around the museum.

The large number of infant burials (in jars) found at Ban Chiang has led archaeologists to speculate that the inhabitants led a precarious existence and possibly practised infanticide to stabilize population.

Erawan Cave

ⓘ *Take a bus en route to Loei.*

Tham Erawan – 'Elephant Cave' – is 40 km west of Udon, about 2 km off Route 210, on the left-hand side of the road. The cave (as usual, linked to a wat, Wat Tham Erawan) is larger and more impressive than the usual selection of holes in the ground that pass as caves in Thailand; it is a vast cavern with very fine stalactites and stalacmites. There's a route through, with steps that emerge near the mountain top, providing spectacular views of the surrounding countryside.

Sixty kilometres north of the Erawan Cave, **Phu Phra Bat Historical Park** has been almost continuously inhabited since prehistoric times (see page 359 for further details).

Northern Mekong route

Loei → *Colour map 2, grid A2.*

This frontier settlement, known as Muang Loei, has dusty streets and seedy-looking shophouses, and is situated on the Loei River. Most tourists visit Loei either as a stop-off on the way to Chiang Khan (see below) or to sample the remarkable scenery of the area; there are no city sights as such. An important cotton growing area, it is known for its warm cotton quilts, available in many shops around town.

Of all the provinces of the Northeast, Loei has managed to preserve the greatest proportion of its forests and the surrounding area was a haven for the Communist guerrillas until the early 1980s. There are a number of national parks in the province, of which the most famous is the Phu Kradung National Park. Also accessible is the Phu Hin Rongkla National Park, an area formerly used as a sanctuary by the Communists, and the Phu Rua National Park.

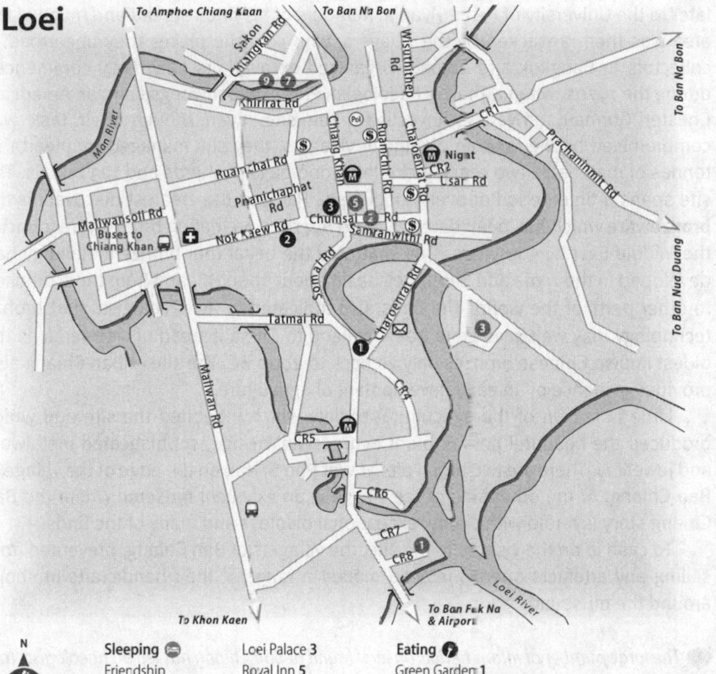

Sleeping
Friendship Guesthouse 1
King 2
Loei Palace 3
Royal Inn 5
Sor Apartments 7
TV Guesthouse 9

Eating
Green Garden 1
Luuk Chao Bu 3
Saw Ahaan 2

CR Charoen Rat

Tham Paa Phu ⓘ *take a bus towards Tha Li or by tuk-tuk*, a Buddhist meditation cave, is 11 km from town on the road to Tha Li. Kutis (monks' cells) are arranged along a steep cliff. It is a peaceful place.

Phu Kradung National Park

ⓘ *Gates open 0700-1400. ฿25. The park is closed during the rainy season June-August. The best time to visit is February-April to see wild flowers, Nov-Dec to see the waterfalls at their best. It is a very popular spot with Thais, so can be quite crowded at the weekends during the dry season, especially Dec- to mid-Jan. The park station at Sithan (at the foot of the mountain) has an Information Centre, restaurants and porters. Porters will carry luggage for ฿10 per kg. Trekking maps are available. There is also a cable car – the source of considerable friction between environmentalists and the park authorities – for those who want the easy option. The park is 82 km south of Loei, 8 km off Route 201 on Route 2019. Bus from Loei to Phu Kradung town, 1½ hrs (the Khon Kaen bus, leaving every 30 mins); from here there are motorcycles, songthaews and tuk-tuks to cover the final 8 km to the park office. From the south, catch a bus via Chumphae to Pa Nok Kao. From there, local buses leave for Phu Kradung town (8 km) and then motorcycles or charter cars are available for the trip to the park.*

Phu Kradung National Park is named after Phu Kradung ('Bell Mountain'), the highest point in the province of Loei at 1,571 m and is one of the most beautiful parks in the country. The mountain is in fact a plateau, which lies between 1,200 m and 1,500 m. There are three explanations of origin of its name: the first is that it refers to the shape of the peak; the second is that it refers to the wild bulls which used to inhabit the area; and the third is that on Buddhist holy days the noise of a bell can be heard issuing from the mountain. It is one of the coolest areas in Thailand; temperatures sometimes fall to near freezing point from November to January, so come prepared.

The park covers 348 sq km and supports a range of vegetation types: tropical evergreen forest, savanna forest and even some trees typical of temperate locations, for example oak and beech. Wild flowers are particularly prolific in the park – especially orchids. Mammals found in the park include **wild pig**, **Asian wild dog** and the **white-handed gibbon**, along with rarer elephants, **Asiatic black bears** and **sambar barking deer**. There are at least 130 species of bird in the park. Residents include the **brown hornbill**, **maroon oriole**, **large scimitar babbler** and the **snowy-browed flycatcher**.

There are nearly 50 km of marked trails for the keen trekker and naturalist, though be warned that this is a strenuous climb, with the last third being up near-vertical metal ladders (three hours each way).

Phu Rua National Park

ⓘ *Regular buses from Loei to Nakhon Thai (Route 203), 1 hr. The turn-off for the park is at the Km 48 marker. A laterite road leads for 4 km to the park entrance.*

Phu Rua National Park, literally 'Boat Mountain' National Park because of a cliff shaped like the bow of a junk, lies 1½ km outside the district town of Phu Rua, 50 km southwest of Loei. The highest point here approaches 1,500 m and temperatures can fall below freezing. There is a good network of marked trails and some fantastic views over the lowlands from the higher ground and north to Laos. Eroded sandstone boulders perched on cliff edges give the park added natural presence.

Chiang Khan and around → *Colour map 2, grid A2.*

This is a place to visit for people who enjoy slow, lazy days watching a river, in this case the mighty Mekong, drifting by. There are no bars or discos here, few obvious sights, and basic, characterful accommodation. The town marks the beginning (or end) of the Mekong River route. Chiang Khan is strung out for 2 km along the river and consists of just two parallel streets, linked by some 20 sois. The riverfront road, Chai Khong Road,

is quieter, with much of the original wooden shophouse architecture still standing; the inland road is the relatively busy Route 2186, linking Loei and Nong Khai.

The monasteries in town, like several settlements along the Mekong in this part of Thailand, show a French influence in their shuttered and colonnaded buildings. An example is **Wat Tha Khok** at the east edge of town near Soi 20 and overlooking the Mekong. The interior of the viharn displays some attractive murals. On the west edge of town, is **Wat Sri Khun Muang**. It is notable for its Lao-style chedi and the gaudy, vibrant murals on the exterior of the viharn. Other wats in town, all dating from the late-19th century, are **Wat Santi** and **Wat Pa Klang**. The oldest monastery is **Wat Mahathat**, where the bot is thought to date from the mid-17th century.

The rapids can be an anticlimax, more so in the wet season when the water is like a fast flowing river.

Kaeng Kut Kou, a series of rapids, lie 4 km downstream from Chiang Khan. There is a park here with restaurants, souvenir shops and vendors selling spicy Isaan food. It is very popular; coachloads of Thai tourists stop off here. In the dry season it is possible to walk down to the river and eat at the riverside. Most hotels and guesthouses will arrange boat trips to the rapids, ฿150-250 for the journey, depending on the number of people. Most people visit the rapids as a day trip; however, there is accommodation available. See Sleeping for more information.

Sangkhom → *Colour map 2, grid A3.*

This place is little more than a village, but with four riverside guesthouses and attractive surrounding countryside, it has become something of a laid-back backpackers refuge. As one visitor recently put it, "the only thing to worry about is finding something to worry about".

Two kilometres west of Sangkhom, is **Wat Ha Sok**, beautifully positioned overlooking the Mekong. The bananas grown in the surrounding countryside are highly regarded, and are cured, sweetened and then sold across the country as kluay khai.

There are several good walks in the vicinity of Sangkhom. One of the most interesting is to the hilltop monastery on **Patakseua Cliffs** ⓘ *walk east to the Km 81 marker (about 4 km) and then climb up to the monastery*, which offers superb views over the Mekong to Laos.

Guesthouses arrange **boat and fishing trips** on the Mekong (฿50-60 per person). Inner tubes are available free of charge from most guesthouses to languidly float down the Mekong (out of the rainy season). Guesthouses have suggested itineraries for those intending to explore the surrounding countryside; best by bicycle or motorcycle.

One recent visitor has recommended the **Than Thip Falls**. The turn-off is a short distance east of Sangkhom between the Km 97 and 98 markers, and 3 km off the main road. The falls are enclosed by forest and there are a series of pools good for swimming. Another set of falls are the **Tharn Tong Falls**, 15 km from Sangkhom. For detailed information on directions to these two places, ask at one of the guesthouses.

Wat Hin Mak Peng is about 30 km east of Sangkhom and is superbly positioned on the Mekong with great views up and downstream. The former abbot of this monastery was the highly revered Phra Thute, so much so that the King of Thailand came to the cremation when he died in 1998. The audience hall is one of Thailand's finest. There is a museum devoted to Phra Thute's life. A peaceful, clean and beautiful place.

Si Chiangmai → *Colour map 2, grid A3.*

ⓘ *It is 40 km from Sangkhom. There are regular bus connections with Nong Khai (45 mins) and Udon Thani. Less regular connections west along the river road to Loei, via Sangkhom and Chiang Khan.*

A small, rather dusty town, Si Chiangmai is best known as a centre of spring roll wrapper production and not a lot else seems to take place. Spring roll wrappers are

made from rice flour and can be seen drying on racks in the sun in villages all around the town. The main road is noisy and unattractive, but the riverside road is quiet and peaceful with restaurants built over the Mekong. The town's proximity to Laos is reflected in the availability of baguettes, which are freshly baked each day. There is also a large Lao and Vietnamese population in town; the latter are said to control the spring roll wrapper industry. Boat trips and cookery classes can be taken. See Sleeping.

Sleeping

Udon Thani *p348, map p348*

A Charoensri Grand Royal, Prachak Rd, next to the main shopping complex, T042-343555, F3435502. A/c, a decent, popular 250-room high-rise hotel with all the usual amenities.

B Ban Chiang, Mukhamontri Rd, T042-327911, F042-223200. Attractive, centrally located with 149 rooms and friendly staff. The hotel offers a luxurious spa, gym and pool complex as well as an in-house bakery, coffee shop, restaurant and karaoke bar.

B Charoen, 549 Pho Sri Rd, T042-248155, F241093. A/c, restaurant, bar and nightclub, pool, good value.

B Airport Hotel, 14 Moo 1, Udon-Nongbualamphu Rd, T042-346223, F346514. 114 rooms, set in a garden plot with all mod cons, but really only useful for those looking for a place to stay before or after catching a flight.

D Charoensri Palace, 60 Pho Sri Rd, T042-242611, F222601. A/c, clean spacious rooms with fridge and TV. Although a little dated, a good value option. Recommended.

D Mitpracha Palace, 271/2-3 Prajak Rd, T042-344184. Just 46 a/c rooms in this pleasant little hotel, good value.

D Prachapakdee, 156/8 Sulpakorn Rd, T042-221804. Functional rooms with clean attached bathrooms. Receptive staff, reasonable rates, in a convenient central location.

D Ton Koon Hotel, 50/1 Mak Khaeng Rd, T042-326336, F326349-50. A/c, restaurant, 115 rooms. A very comfortable western-style hotel with polite and friendly staff.

D-E King Hotel, 57 Phosri Rd, T042-241444. Some a/c, TV, clean and serviceable rooms much as you would expect for the price.

Ban Chiang *p349*

E Lakeside Sunrise Guesthouse, T042-208167, with simple but clean rooms close to the museum.

Loei *p350, map p350*

AL-A Loei Palace Hotel, 167/4 Charoenrat Rd, T042-815668, F815875. A/c, 2 excellent restaurants, karaoke bar, pool, gym, sauna, Thai massage and acupuncture available. Palatial and elegantly designed hotel set in attractive gardens, with friendly staff and comfortable rooms.

A-C King Hotel, 11/9-12 Chunsai Rd, T042-811701, F811235. Comfortable hotel, central location, good value. Restaurant with excellent range of food available, popular with both locals, open 0700-2300. The hotel also has the **Queen Bar**, open 1000-2400.

C-D Royal Inn, off Chumsai Rd, T042-812563. Plush renovation of average buildings, large rooms, all amenities and comfortable although the rooms at the front of the hotel can be a little noisy: a good value option.

D Sor Apartments, also located in the northern part of the city, T042-833644. Some a/c and en suite facilities, good-sized rooms, clean and airy, no English spoken.

D TV Guesthouse, in the north of town across the river, a/c, en suite shower, no English spoken.

E-F Friendship Guesthouse, 257/41 Soi Bunchareon Rd, T042-832408, north of wat, 200 m left off main road. Large rooms, shared facilities and huts on riverside.

Phu Kradung National Park *p351*

Tents can be hired (฿50) and camping is permitted at the summit (฿5). There are also cabins of various sizes and prices (**E**), T02-5790529, and stalls selling food and basic necessities.

Outside the national park are a number of guesthouses (a couple of kilometres from the entrance): **B Phu Krudung House**, T042-811449, a large number of bungalows with hot water, **B Pu Kra Dueng Resort**, with very friendly management.

Phu Rua National Park *p351*
B-C There are 8 bungalows at the visitors' centre and a camping ground part way up the mountain. It is necessary to book: T042-5790529. In addition, there are 2 'back-to-nature' resorts, 2 km north of Phu Rua town, on the road to Loei: **B Phu Rua Resort**, T042-899048, and the **B Phu Rua Chalet**, T042-899012.

Chiang Khan *p351*
Chiang Khan has a good selection of atmospheric guesthouses; hardly luxurious, but they make a change from the usual dull Thai hotels.
D-E Ton Khong Guesthouse, 299/3 Chai Khong Rd, T042-821547, tonkhong@hotmail.com. Attractive location with clean rooms and excellent food. A good choice if you can put up with the rather unwelcoming style of management. A bit noisy. Like all other guesthouses here the guesthouse can organize Thai massage and boat trips on the Mekong. Email also available.
E Friendship Guesthouse (URO), Soi 9/10, very clean rooms with friendly and informative management with a specially prepared 'Things to do in Chiang Khan' book – very useful!
E Nong Sam, 1¼ km west of town, T042-821457. English-run, quiet and atmospheric, with floral surroundings, spacious rooms, good home-cooked food and river views. Motorbikes for hire, ฿200, 0600-1800.
E-F Chiang Khan, 282 Chai Khong Rd, T042-821023, pimchiang@hotmail.com. Opposite end of town from the Loei bus stop, very clean and attractive rooms, with friendly management. Attractive riverside position and excellent cheap restaurant.
F Poonsawat, 251/2 Chai Khong Rd, Soi 9, T042-821114. Attractive wooden hotel, clean rooms, friendly management, shared bathrooms, small book collection to help while away the hours. Recommended.

Chiang Khan and around *p351*
C-D Chiang Khan Hill Resort, T042-821285, which has bungalows near the rapids, but is overrun by tourists visiting the rapids.
E Cootcoo Resort, T042-821248, Kaeng Kut Kou, has quiet huts on offer during the dry season only, but reports are that the **D See View Huts** are even better and more attractively positioned.

Sangkhom *p352*
E Mama's (aka TXK), Rim Khong Rd. T042-441462. Basic bamboo huts overlooking the river with 2 new villas with wooden floors and shutters. 'Mama', the maternal owner, has – as ever – big plans and is very proud of her Thai and Lao food.
E River Huts, pleasant open area with well-kept gardens, some of the buildings have been renovated. Friendly owners, a good choice.
F Bouy, Rim Khong Rd, 1 km west of the centre, T/F042-441065. Nice bungalows overlooking the river. The attached restaurant serves good food in large portions. Probably the best choice here.

Si Changmai *p352*
C-D Maneerat Resort, T042-451311. Very swish but under occupied, Thai cookery courses run if there is demand. Nice restaurant with good views.
E-F Tim Guesthouse, some dorm beds, attractive, quiet huts on the riverfront, the front rooms are brighter and have better views. Swiss management, good source of information, motorcycles, bicycles and boats for hire. Western, Isaan and Thai food available, as well as French liqueurs and custard in various flavours! Boat trips organized.

Eating

Udon Thani *p348, map p348*
Fresh-baked 'baguettes' are available in Udon Thani; the bakeries here are excellent. Local specialities include muu yong (shredded pork) and preserved meats.
TT **Mayfair**, Charoen Hotel, 549 Pho Sri Rd. Perhaps the best Thai/Chinese restaurant in town, pricey for Northeast Thailand but worth splashing out on.
T **Fungki Restaurant**, Pho Sri Rd. Excellent range of Thai/Indochinese food at a range of prices.
T **Kun Nit**, Udon Dutsadee Rd, T042-246128. Delicious and good value traditional, Isaan food such as chargrilled chicken and spicy salads.
T **Mandarin Restaurant and Bakery**, 225-7 Mark Kheng Rd. Specializes in fish dishes,

quiet with touches of contemporary design, attached bakery. Recommended.

Rabeang Pochana, 53 Saphakit Janya Rd, T042-241515 (beside the lake). Locals continue to recommend this restaurant as the best in town. Highly recommended.

Rung Thong, Hor Nalikaa. A simple place facing onto the clock tower, which serves good, wholesome Thai and Chinese food at reasonable prices (not open in the evening).

Steve's Bar and Restaurant, 254/26 Prajak Rd, T042-244523. Open 0900-2300. Full Thai and English menu, friendly place recently opened with an extensive spirit and wine selection, wide-screen TV and golf, bridge, cribbage and darts club! Also has a book exchange – worth a visit.

V.T. Naem Nuang, Phosri Rd, T042-348740 (next to the market). A little out of town but worth the trip, open 0600-2100 for Vietnamese food and drink.

Loei *p350, map p350*

Green Garden Restaurant. Vegetarian Thai/Chinese food.

Luuk Chao Bu, Sathorn Chiang Khan (near the clock tower). Good Thai dishes with generous portions.

Nang Nuan, 68 Sathorn Chiang Khan Rd. Attractive, well-run outdoor restaurant with nua yaang speciality – cook-it-yourself barbecue. Recommended.

Saw Ahaan, Nok Kaew Rd. Extensive Thai menu, attentive staff and pleasant open-air setting.

Bakeries

King Hotel Coffee Shop, 11/9-12 Chumsai Rd. Good for ice cream sundaes in a/c splendour.

Foodstalls

The best place for stall food is at the night market on the corner of Ruamjai and Charoenrat rds.

Chiang Khan *p351*

Isaan food is excellent in Chiang Khan; a local speciality is live shrimps, fished straight from the Mekong River, served squirming in a spicy marinade of lemon and chilli (kung ten) – not for the faint-hearted. There are several riverside restaurants – the best places to eat – with views over to Laos.

Mekong Riverside, Chai Khong Rd (opposite Soi 10). Quiet veranda, views over the Mekong, good food, especially fish dishes.

No Name, Chai Khong Soi 9 (opposite Poonsawat Hotel). Very popular restaurant serving large portions of freshly wokked rice and noodle dishes.

Prachamit, 263/2 Si Chiang Khan Rd (near Soi 9). Frequented by locals, no riverside position but good food.

Rabiang Rim Khong, Chai Khong Rd (opposite Soi 10). Small restaurant overlooking the Mekong, good food, generous portions.

Sook Somboon Hotel, 243/3 Chai Khong Rd. Wonderful position overhanging the Mekong, excellent fish dishes, including succulent sweet and sour fish.

Shopping

Udon Thani *p348, map p348*

Robinson's Plaza, off Pho Sri Rd. Shops, cafés and western-style eating places.

Activities and tours

Udon Thani *p348, map p348*

Tour operators

Most tour companies can arrange visas for Laos, but they are more expensive than in Bangkok.

Aranya Tour, 105 Mak Khaeng Rd, T042-243182. Also arranges visas for Indo-China.

Kannika Tour, 36/9 Srisatha Rd, T042-241378, F241378. Tours in the Northeast and to Laos, Cambodia and Vietnam.

Toy Ting, 55/1-5 Thahaan Rd, T042-244771.

Transport

Udon Thani *p348, map p348*

Air

The airport 2 km out of town off Route 2, south to Khon Kaen. Regular connections with **Bangkok** (1 hr), 4 times daily, on THAI.

Airline offices THAI, 60 Mak Khaeng Rd, T042-246697.

Bus

Udon has 2 main bus stations. BKS 2 is on the northwestern edge of town, about 2 km from the centre along Pho Sri Rd. Buses leave here

for **Chiang Mai** and **Chiang Rai** in the North, **Nakhon Phanom** and **Nong Khai** in the Northeast, **Phitsanulok**, and **Bangkok**. Bangkok passengers can get to/from BKS 2 by yellow town buses (No 23) which run into the centre. Buses also run from the more central BKS 1 on Sai Uthit Rd, just off Pho Sri Rd to **Korat**, **Nakhon Phanom**, **Ubon**, **Khon Kaen**, **Roi Et**, **Sakhon Nakhon** and **Nong Khai**.

Car hire

Parada Car Rent, 78/1 Mak Khaeng Rd, T042-244147. VIP Car Rent, 824 Pho Sri Rd, T042-223758.

Train

The station is off Lang Sathanirotfai Rd. Regular connections with **Bangkok**'s Hualamphong station (10 hrs) and all stops en route – **Ayutthaya**, **Saraburi**, **Korat**, **Khon Kaen** and on to **Nong Khai**.

Loei *p350, map p350*

Air

There is an airport 5 km south of town.

Airline offices THAI, next to Royal Inn Hotel, T042-812344.

Bus

The bus terminal is on Maliwan Rd, about 1 km south of town with regular connections to **Bangkok**'s Northeastern bus terminal (10 hrs), **Udon Thani** (4 hrs) **Khon Kaen** and **Phitsanulok** (4 hrs). Note that some buses travel via Lom Sak to Phitsanulok and others via Nathon Thai. For **Chiang Khan** (1 hr, ฿18) and other stops along the Mekong River route downstream (east), buses leave from the junction of Maliwan and Ruamchai roads.

Saamlor and sonthaew

Motorized saamlors cost ฿10-20 around town; songthaews for out of town trips.

Chiang Khan *p351*

Bus

Buses from Loei stop at the western end of town; a 10-min walk to the main area of hotels and guesthouses, or take a tuk-tuk. Rather unreliable buses (in fact, converted trucks) travel to **Loei** (1 hr) and east towards **Pak Chom**, **Sangkhom**, **Si Chiangmai** and on to **Nong Khai**. For Pak Chom, it may be quicker to join up with other travellers and hire a songthaew. A/c bus connections with **Bangkok** from the station on Soi 9 (inland from Si Chiang Khan Rd).

Sangkhom *p352*

Bicycle

Hire is ฿50 per day.

Bus

Connections west to **Loei** via Chiang Khan, and east to **Nong Khai** via Si Chiangmai. To travel from Chiang Khan, take the bus to Pak Chom (1½ hrs) from opposite the Shell petrol station and from there change to the bus to Nong Khai (2 hrs).

Motorcycle

฿250 per day for hire from **River Huts guesthouse**; the best way to explore the backroads.

Directory

Udon Thani *p348, map p348*

Banks Bangkok Bank, Pho Sri Rd. Krung Thai, 216 Mak Khaeng Rd. Thai Farmers, 236 Pho Sri Rd. **Embassies and consulates** US Consulate, 35/6 Suphakit Janya Rd (northern section of town), T042-244270. **Medical services** Pho Niyom Rd, T042-222572. **Post office** Wattananuvong Rd (near the Provincial Governor's Office). **Useful addresses** Police. Sri Suk Rd, T042-222285.

Loei *p350, map p350*

Banks Siam Commercial, 3/8 Ruamchai Rd. Thai Farmers, Ruamchai Rd – both banks have exchange facilities. **Post office** Charoenrat Rd (southern end), telecom office on top floor. **Medical services** Hospital: corner of Nok Kaew and Maliwan roads, T042-811806. **Useful addresses** Police: Phiphatmongkhon Rd, T042-811254.

Chiang Khan *p351*

Banks Thai Farmers (exchange facilities), 444 Si Chiang Khan Rd. **Post office** Chai Khong Rd (eastern edge of town). **Useful addresses** Immigration office: next to post office. Visa extension possible.

Nong Khai and the southern Mekong route

The last stop before the Friendship Bridge and communist Laos, Nong Khai is a charming laid-back riverside town: the sort of place where jaded travellers get 'stuck' for several days, doing nothing but enjoying the romantic atmosphere of the place. There are a number of wats to visit and from here, while supping on a cold beer, you can look across to Tha Dua in Laos and imagine the enormous and rare pla buk catfish – weighing up to 340 kg – foraging on the riverbed.

From Nong Khai, Route 212 follows the Mekong River 137 km to the riverside town of Beung Kan and from there another 175 km to the provincial capital, Nakhon Phanom. Swing 75 km westwards away from Nakhon Phanom and the Mekong and you'll reach Sakhon Nakhon and the sacred stupa, Phrathat Cheong Chum. Continuing southwards from Nakhon Phanom on the river road for another 50 km, Route 212 reaches That Phanom, the site of one of the most revered chedis in Thailand: Wat That Phanom. This area is also a centre of traditional textile production, particularly around the town of Renu Nakhon. From That Phanom, Route 212 heads 50 km south to the newly created provincial capital of Mukdahan finishing its journey 170 km away at Ubon Ratchathani. ▸▸ *For Sleeping, Eating and other listings, see pages 364-370.*

Nong Khai → *Colour map 2, grid A3.*

Nong Khai, with ferry and bridge access to Laos and the capital Vientiane, has become increasingly popular and two large hotels have recently opened. The town is one of the most attractive in the region, with French-style colonial architecture.

Ins and outs

Getting there Nong Khai is situated at the end of Route 2, the Friendship Highway, and on the banks of the mighty Mekong. Currently, visitors to Laos have to cross the Mekong by road; visas are available on arrival in the country. The bus station is on the east side of town and there are connections with Bangkok and destinations in the Northeast. This is as far as it is possible to travel on the Northeastern rail line from Bangkok. Nong Khai also happens to be the logical place to start or end a tour of the Thai towns which line the Mekong River. ▸▸ *See Transport, page 369 for further details.*

Getting around Saamlors provide the main means of local transport; the town is strung out along the river, so it is quite a hike getting from one end to the other. Some guesthouses hire out bicycles and motorbikes. Local buses link Nong Khai with out of town destinations.

Background

Nong Khai, as the flow of tourists and trade into Laos increases, is slowly transforming itself from a sleepy provincial backwater into a bustling border town. The Australian-financed Friendship Bridge at Tambon Meechai, 2 km from town, the first bridge across the lower reaches of the Mekong River, was officially opened on 8 April 1994. To cope with the expected surge in arrivals, three new hotels opened: the **Nong Khai Holiday Inn**, the **Nong Khai Grand Thani** and the **Jommanee**. Check with the Lao Embassy in Bangkok for visas and whether the border is open. Fortunately for the preservation of Nong Khai's charming core, many of the ugliest developments are

concentrated along Highway 2 which leads to the bridge. But even the formerly quiet river front road, Rim Khong Road, has been redeveloped into a 'promenade' for visiting tourists.

Sights

The influence of the French in Indochina is clearly reflected in the architecture of Meechai Road, which runs parallel with the river. Notable among the wats are the important teaching wat, **Wat Sisaket**, and, towards the east of town past the bus station, **Wat Pho Chai** – with its Lao-style viharn and venerated solid gold-headed Buddha (the body is bronze), looted from Vientiane by the future Rama I. The bot contains murals showing how the image is reputed to have got to Nong Khai: Rama I loaded the image onto a raft to cross the Mekong, but while negotiating the river the raft capsized and the image was lost. It then resurfaced (this is a common theme in the lost Buddha image genre), to be retrieved and placed in Wat Pho Chai. (Or, less miraculously, it was dredged from the river 25 years later.)

A third religious building, or rather what remains of it, is **Phrathat Nong Khai**, better known as **Phrathat Klang Nam** (Phrathat in the Middle of the River) ⓘ *to see it, walk (or take a saamlor) east along Meechai Road (downriver) for about 2 km from the town centre, and turn off, left, down Soi Paa Phrao 3*. In Henri Mouhot's account of his trip up the Mekong in 1860, the 'discoverer' of Angkor Wat, described upon arrival in 'Nong Kay' a "Buddhist tat or pyramidal landmark...that has been washed away from the shore, and now lies half submerged, like a wrecked ship". The phrathat is only visible during the dry season, when it emerges from the muddy river and is promptly bedecked with pennants.

On the riverfront road, Rim Khong Road, there is a daily market where goods from Laos and beyond are on sale.

Nong Khai

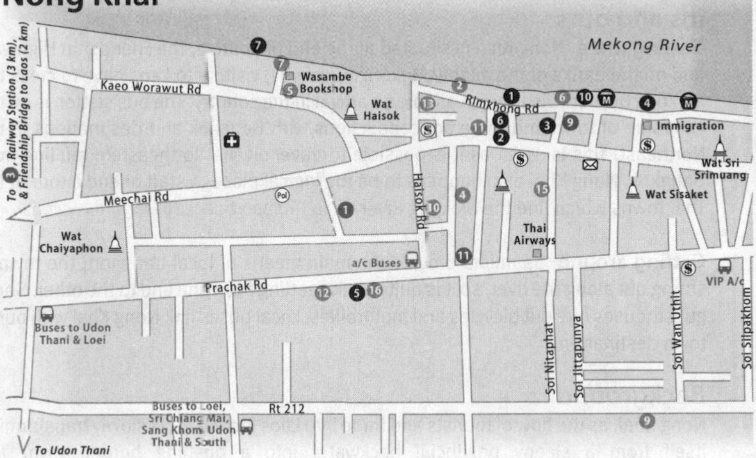

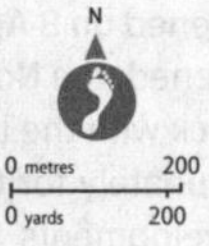

Sleeping
Chez Kaï 1
Chong Konh Guesthouse 2
Holiday Inn 3
International Meeting Place 4
KC Guesthouse 5
Mekhong Guesthouse 6
Mut Mee Guesthouse 7
Nongkhai Grand Thani 9
Panthawee 10
Poolsup 11
Prajak Bungalows 12
Rimkhong 13
Sawasdee 14
Sukhaphon 15
Suksant 16

Eating
Boat 1
Danish Baker 2

Around Nong Khai

Wat Phrathat Bang Phuan

ⓘ *Most Sangkhom bound buses stop at Phrathat Bang Phuan or at the nearby village of Ban Bang Phuan.*

The wat contains an Indian-style stupa, similar (it is presumed) to the original Phra Pathom Chedi in Nakhon Pathom. Its exact date of construction is unknown, but it is believed to date from the early centuries AD. A newer chedi was built on the sight in 1559, which toppled over in 1970. In 1978 it was restored. As a result, the unrestored Lao chedis in this same compound are now of greater historical interest. The site is really only worth visiting en route to/from Udon or Nong Khai. **Wat Phrathat Bang Phuan** is 22 km southwest of Nong Khai.

Phu Phra Bat Historical Park

ⓘ *0830-1700. A new reception centre has been built, with a historical exhibition and a small café for drinks and simple food. Guides are also available here. To see all the main sites allow at least 3 hrs. The park is just about equidistant from Nong Khai and Udon Thani, almost 70 km. Catch a bus to Ban Phu (there is a very simple hotel here should visitors need to sleep over), the town where Routes 2020 and 2021 meet, a journey of about 2½ hrs. From there (it is signposted), the park is another 15 km by songthaew towards Ban Tiu (quicker to take a motorcycle taxi from here).*

Encompassing an area of 650 ha in the Phu Phan hills, the Phu Phra Bat Historical Park has been a site of almost continuous human habitation since prehistoric times. There are prehistoric cave paintings, Dvaravati boundary stones (seventh-10th centuries), Lopburi Bodhisattvas (10th-13th centuries), Lang Chan Buddha images (14th-18th centuries), and a stupa built in 1920 to shelter a Buddha footprint. The terrain consists of rocky outcrops, bare sandy soil and savanna forest, and it is easy to imagine why people, for thousands of years, have regarded the area as a magical place.

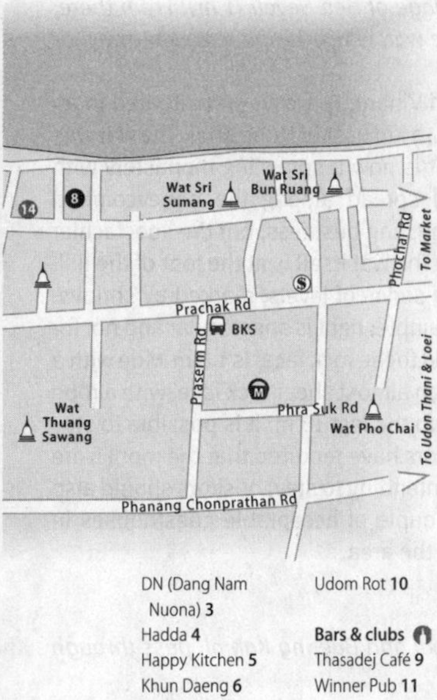

DN (Dang Nam Nuona) 3
Hadda 4
Happy Kitchen 5
Khun Daeng 6
Steakhouse 8
The Fish 7
Udom Rot 10

Bars & clubs
Thasadej Café 9
Winner Pub 11

Wat Phutthamamaka-samakhom

ⓘ *0830-1800, ฿20. Take a songthaew heading towards Beung Kan (Route 212) or by tuk-tuk. Turn right after the Km 4 marker where there is signpost to Sala Kaew Ku. To cycle from town, it is best to take the riverside road as far as Wat Sirimahakatcha, then turn right and travel south. Note that as this is not a Buddhist monastery most tuk-tuk drivers do not know it as a 'wat'; ask for Sala Kaew Ku.*

Also known as Wat Khaek ('Indian' Wat) and Sala Kaew Ku, the clumsily named Wat Phutthamamaka-samakhom, which houses bizarre sculptures too weird to miss, was established in the late 1970s and lies 4½ km east of Nong Khai on Route 212 to Beung Kan. The sculpture park – now crumbling – was set up by a Laotian artist named Luang Poo Boun Leua Sourirat, who died in 1996 at the

age of 72. Luang Poo saw himself as part holy man part artist and part sage. He studied under a Hindu rishi in Vietnam and formed his own synthesis of Buddhist and Hindu philosophy, which is displayed in his work here. He established a similar bizarre concoction of concrete figurines near Tha Deua in Laos (not far from Vientiane), but was ejected from the country shortly after it became communist in 1975, probably on the grounds that he was simply too weird. A wealthy man, he bought a small slice of Thailand and started again.

Reflecting Luang Poo's beliefs, the wat promotes a strange mixture of Buddhist and Hindu beliefs and is dominated by a vast array of strange brick and cement statues. Some are clearly of Buddhist and Hindu insp ration; others are rather harder to interpret: for example, a life-size elephant being attacked by a large pack of dogs, four in a jeep, and some wearing sunglasses. The 'Life and Death' grouping is especially interesting. An assortment of figures: a baby, a business woman, soldier and beggar. The series concludes with two couples holding hands, one pair skeletonized and standing next to a coffin on a pyre. The figures are arranged in a garden and music blares out from a large concrete-encrusted PA system. Even tour buses visit the wat.

Southern Mekong route

Beung Kan → *Colour map 2, grid A4.*

A much more scenic and adventurous way to reach Nakhon Phanom is by taking the river road east from Nong Khai. This road follows the Mekong for nearly 320 km. The only logical place to break the journey is in the small district town of Beung Kan, 137 km from Nong Khai and 175 km from Nakhon Phanom. There are regular connections with both places. Beung Kan is one of the more difficult Thai town names to pronounce: it's best to hold your nose to get the required nasal inflexion.

Wat Phu Tok

ⓘ *Take an early morning songthaew to the village of Ben Seveli (1 hr). From there, either charter a tuk-tuk or motorcycle taxi to the wat, which is about 20 km away, or there are a few public songthaews.*

Wat Phu Tok, also known as Wat Chedi Ya Khiri Viharn, is a cave wat situated in an area of breathtaking limestone scenery, about 140 km east of Nong Khai. The wat was established by Phra Acaan Juen in 1968, and it is now a sprawling monastery with meditation grottoes and kutis (monks' cells) spread among the honeycombed mountain. Climbing up the mountain is an exhausting business, but the spectacular views of the plain below make it all worthwhile. The wat itself is at the foot of the hill. From here, vertiginous steps lead up through a series of levels, marked by shrines. Part way up the path divides: left is a bit of a scramble; right is spectacular and not for the faint-hearted, because the stairway (attached to the rock face) is 1.8 m wide with a fall of several hundred feet! At the end of this is an almost sheer rock face, with a rope to help the adrenaline junkies who want to climb the last 18 m. It is possible to stay the night at the wat, although some recent visitors have reported that the monks are not terribly welcoming (take some donations if intending to stay). Visitors should also expect only very basic facilities. There are a couple of acceptable guesthouses in Seveli village and it is also possible to camp in the area.

Ban Ahong

ⓘ *Buses making the journey between Nong Khai and Bueung Kan all pass through Ban Ahong.*

Ban Ahong is around 25 km west of Beung Kan on Route 212 (at the Km 115 marker) to Nong Khai. Close by is Wat Paa Ahong and its abbot and lone monk, Luang Phor

Phraeng. The monastery is a strange oasis of shrubbery and plants. Luang Phor is renowned for his medicinal skills and is reputed to have magical powers of healing. It is possible to swim in the Mekong at this stretch of the river's course during the dry season.

Nakhon Phanom → *Colour map 3, grid B3.*

There is little to do in Nakhon Phanom except admire the view of the majestic Mekong River as it sweeps its way past the distant mountains of Laos. Like Nong Khai, sipping a beer or eating catfish curry overlooking the river does have a certain romantic appeal but most people only visit Nakhon Phanom en route to Phra That Phanom Chedi – the Northeast's most revered religious shrine – 50 km to the south. Nakhon Phanom is the closest town with adequate hotels to the wat.

The TAT tourist office is housed in an attractive building on the corner of Salaklang and Suthorn Vichit roads.

Nakhon Phanom's limited sights include **Wat Sri Thep** on Srithep Road (which boasts a statue of Luang Pu Chan, a revered Northeastern holy man) and **Wat Mahathat** (with a lotus-bud chedi), at the southern end of Sunthon Vichit Road. The former monastery has some exuberant murals depicting episodes from the Buddha's life (the Jataka tales); or simply wander along the riverfront, past handicraft shops and a Chinese temple. There is a morning market on the river. Just south of the **Grand View Hotel**, south of town, is an area of beach, Hat Sai Tai Muang, which local people use to lounge on in the evening while stalls sell Thai snacks. During the dry season the exposed area of sand expands considerably. Across the river is the Lao town of Thakhek and foreigners with visas are allowed to cross the border here.

Nakhon Phanom

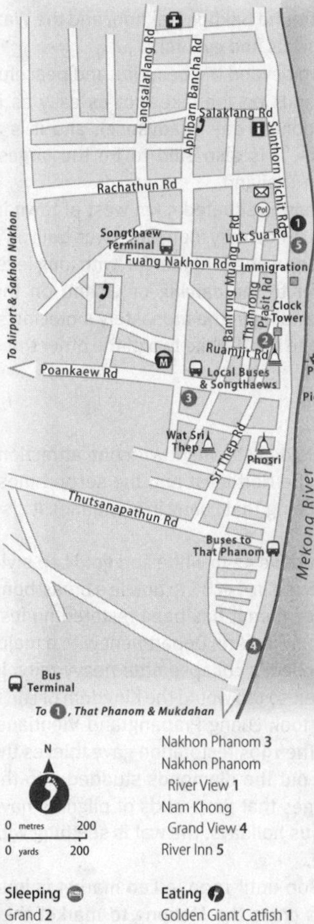

Wat Phrathat Narai Chengweng (Phrathat Naweng) ⓘ *88 km west of Nakhon Phanom on Route 22, at the junction with Route 223 (it is signposted); walk through a green archway, and the wat is 500 m along a dirt track; there is a good, cheap Thai restaurant on the other side of the road from the wat, beyond the intersection on the way to Udon Thani (about 200 m); take a bus travelling towards Sakhon Nakhon from the bus station near the market*, is a Khmer prang dating from the 11th or 12th century. Despite being reconstructed in what appears to be a remarkably haphazard fashion, this small sanctuary is very satisfying and displays finely carved lintels: the east lintel above the entrance to the sanctuary shows Siva dancing; the north face, Vishnu reclining on a naga.

Sakhon Nakhon → *Colour map 2, grid A5.*

This ancient town was one of the Khmer Empire's more important provincial centres in the Northeast, it's now one of the region's smaller provincial capitals. Along with a revered monastery, Sakhon Nakhon also has a reputation in Thailand as a centre of dog-meat consumption. Most famously though, Sakhon Nakhon is home to the second most sacred Lao-style stupa in Thailand: the Phrathat Choeng Chum (the most sacred is That Phanom).

Phrathat Choeng Chum, a 24-m-tall, white, angular, lotus-bud chedi has become an important pilgrimage spot for Thais. The chedi is built over a laterite Khmer prang dating from the 11th or 12th century, and to reach the chedi it is necessary to walk through the viharn. The chedi is surrounded by ancient images of the Buddha captured during raids into Laos and Cambodia. Behind the stupa is an entrance through which pilgrims walk to make offerings to two revered Buddha images. The older, and finer, image is set behind a newer one, and is easy to miss. The wat next to Wat Prathat Choeng Chum is a popular teaching monastery.

Another important religious site in town is **Wat Pa Suthawat** ⓘ *0800-1800*, opposite the town hall. This is important not for any artistic merit, but because one of Thailand's most revered monks lived and died here: Phra Acaan Man Bhuritatto, better known as Luang Pho Man (1871-1949). A chapel in his memory has been constructed and his (few) possessions kept on display.

The Phu Thai ethnic group inhabit the area around Sakhon Nakhon, and the **Wax Castle festival** is associated with them (see Festivals and events).

The 32-sq km **Nong Han Lake** is close to town beyond the beautiful and peaceful Royal Park. Boats can be hired to visit the islands on the lake (not as easy as it sounds, and needs to be done a day in advance), and it is a popular place at weekends. It is also said to be the largest natural inland water body in Thailand.

❢ Do not swim in the lake or eat the snails the locals do – both are infected with liver flukes that cause a nasty liver disease called opisthorchiasis.

Phrathat Narai Chenweng is situated 5 km west of town in the village of Ban Thai. The 11th-century monastery was built as a Hindu shrine. The name cheng weng is Khmer for 'with long legs' and this is thought to refer to the carving of Vishnu on the northern pediment of the laterite prasat, still standing in the monastery's precincts. The four-armed Vishnu holds his head up with one hand while two of the other three hands hold a lotus and a baton.

That Phanom → *Colour map 2, grid B5.*

The small town of That Phanom is a quaint riverside settlement with one attraction: Wat That Phanom, the most revered temple in the Northeast and the second most revered by the people of Laos (the most revered being That Luang in Vientiane). It also holds an annual temple festival.

Wat That Phanom is dominated by an impressive 52-m white and gold Lao-style chedi. Legend has it that it was originally constructed in 535 BC to house a breastbone of the Buddha, eight years after his death. Since then it has been restored no less than eight times, most recently in 1995 by the Thai Fine Arts Department with a major restoration taking place in 1977, following the chedi's collapse after heavy rains in 1975. A legend said that should the chedi fall, then so too would the Kingdom of Laos; shortly afterwards, the Communist Pathet Lao took Luang Prabang and Vientiane, and ousted the American-backed government. The 1995 restoration gave thieves the opportunity to climb the scaffolding and prise out the diamonds studded into the finial. The chedi is surrounded by Buddha images that thousands of pilgrims have covered in gold leaf. During festivals and religious holidays, the wat is seething with people making offerings of flowers and incense.

On Monday and Thursday from around 0800 until 1200, a Lao market is held upstream from town when hoards of Laotians cross the Mekong to market their

wares. They arrive laden with pigs, wild forest products and herbal remedies, returning home with cash and Thai consumer goods. The market winds down soon after midday, although the shops near the ferry pier sell excellent quality goods very cheaply every day of the week. Laotians and Thais spend the day being ferried back and forth across the river to trade, and the border here is now open for non-Thai and Laotian nationals too.

Renu Nakhon ⓘ *8 km north on Route 212, and then left onto Route 2031 for another 6½ km; by bus from That Phanom (or Nakhon Phanom) to Renu Nakhon; if the bus drops you off at the junction of routes 212 and 2031, there are songthaews for the final 6½ km*, a traditional weaving and embroidery centre, is almost 15 km northwest of That Phanom. On Wednesdays and fair days, the central wat of the village is home to hundreds of market stalls selling a wide selection of local and Lao textiles, as well as Isaan axe pillows. Outside the wat compound, there are permanent shops selling a similar selection of cloth and local handicrafts throughout the week. Cloth is sold by the phun and there are about two phun in a sarong length. Prices quoted therefore do not usually relate to the piece. For simple cotton cloth, expect to pay ฿100-200 per phun; for the best silk, up to ฿3,000.

That Phanom

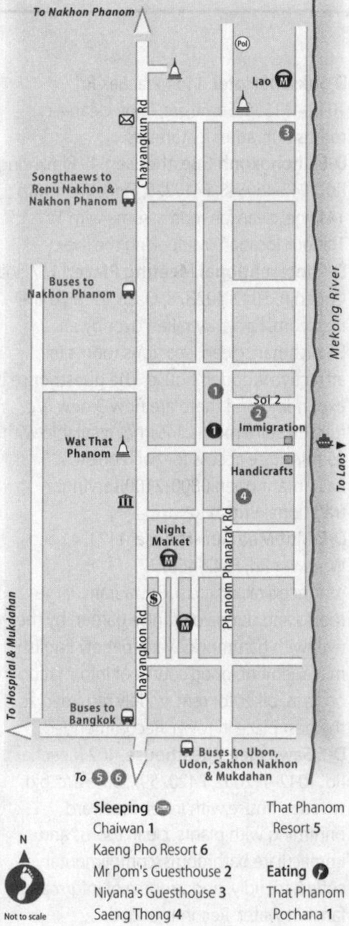

Sleeping
Chaiwan 1
Kaeng Pho Resort 6
Mr Pom's Guesthouse 2
Niyana's Guesthouse 3
Saeng Thong 4
That Phanom Resort 5

Eating
That Phanom Pochana 1

Mukdahan → *Colour map 2, grid B5.*

The capital of one of Thailand's newer provinces, Mukdahan's greatest claim to fame is as the home town of one of Thailand's best-known leaders, General Sarit Thanarat (see page 634). As one of the gateways to an emerging Laos, Mukdahan is changing fast. However, until recently many of the villages hereabouts were cut off from the outside world during the wet season. There are still a few old-style wooden houses, but they are fast disappearing. The town is situated on the Mekong River and lies directly opposite the important Lao town of Savannakhet.

Because of its location, Mukdahan has become an important trading centre with goods from Laos, like gems, timber, cattle and agricultural commodities, being exchanged for Thai consumer goods. There is a Lao and Thai market, the so-called **Talaat Indochine**, held daily opposite the pier where boats from Laos land. It is best to get to the market in the morning. Along with Thai consumer goods, Lao silk and cotton cloth (see Shopping), good French bread, china, axe cushions, khaens (a local, bamboo pan pipe) and baskets are also sold. Near the pier and opposite Wat Si Mongkhon Tai is a Bodhi tree where numerous traditional soothsayers ply their trade.

Wat Sri Sumong, on Samran Chai Khong Road, the river road, is interesting for the colonial architectural elements –

arches over the windows and veranda – reflected in the bot. A little further north on the river road, **Wat Yod Kaew Sriwichai** also has Lao lotus-bud chedis and a large, gold Buddha spinning the Wheel of Law.

The **Space Needle** (Hor Kaew Mukdahan) ⓘ *0800-1800, ฿20*, is 2 km south of town. Looking rather like an air traffic control tower, the building houses a costume museum, a display of local artefacts, a gallery of Buddha images and a viewing gallery with exceptional views of Laos.

For good views of the river and surrounding countryside, climb **Phu Manorom**, a small hill 5 km south of town. Take Route 2034 south towards Don Tan and after 2 km turn right. The summit is another 3 km from the turn-off.

Phu Pha Thoep National Park (also known as Mukdahan National Park) ⓘ *catch a songthaew travelling south towards Don Tan; the turning for the park is between the Km 14 and 15 markers and it is a 2-km walk from there to the park headquarters; camping is permitted*, covering a modest 54 sq km, lies 15 km south of Mukdahan, off Route 2034. The principal forest type here is dry dipterocarp savanna forest and there is a succession of oddly-shaped rock outcrops, easily accessible from park headquarters. The environment almost feels prehistoric, and fossils and finger paintings have been found amidst the boulders. Cut into the cliff face that rises above the headquarters, is an interesting cave packed with Buddha images.

Sleeping

Nong Khai *p357, map p358*
With the opening of the bridge into Laos, large hotels opened in Nong Khai, providing (almost) Bangkok-level opulence. Guesthouses in Nong Khai are also of a high standard. What are missing are adequate mid-range places to stay.

AL Holiday Inn Mekong Royal Nongkhai, 222 Jomanee Rd, west of railway station out of town, T042-420024, www.holidayinnhotels.co.th A/c, restaurant, pool, tennis, 8-storey block, with nearly 200 rooms overlooking Mekong with all facilities, best in town.

C-D Panthawee (and across the road the **Panthawee Bungalows**, T042-411008), 1241 Haisok Rd, T042-411568. Some a/c, newish management, run by 2 women who speak good English and German, great source of information, two grades of room available. More expensive rooms have river views.

C-D Prajak Bungalows, 1178 Prachak Rd, T042-412644. A quiet place with good facilities for the price. Clean and well run, surprisingly underutilized.

C-E Mekhong Guesthouse, 519 Rim Khong, T042-412320, naga_tour@hotmail.com. Clean, basic wooden rooms, on the river with a good veranda for sundowners and information. Restaurant next door and internet café attached (฿30 per hr). But noisy from the road.

D Suksant Hotel, 1164 Prachak Rd, T042-411585. Some a/c, large clean airy rooms but rather featureless.

D-E Chongkonh Guesthouse, 649 Rimkhong Rd, T042-460548, F412229. French run with 14 large, clean fan rooms, some with TV. Tranquil location overlooking the river.

D-E International Meeting Place, 1117 Soi Chuanjit, F042-422878, Oasis_nongkhai@msn.com. Recently taken over by an Englishman, clean, spacious rooms in attractive wooden house. The guesthouse is expanding and there are now 3 new a/c fully en suite rooms. Internet available with 15 mins free access for each guest. Restaurant open 0800-2100 serving traditional British food.

D-E Mut Mee Guesthouse, 1111/4 Kaeo Worawut Rd, F042-460717, mutmee@nk.ksc.co.th. Restaurant, large rooms and bungalows, nice garden by the river with hammocks, very friendly English management, good source of information on Laos, bikes for rent, widely regarded as the best place in town. Recommended.

D-E Sawasdee Guesthouse, 402 Meechai Rd, T042-412602, F420259. Some a/c, old wooden house with inner courtyard brimming with plants, clean rooms and immaculate bathrooms, complimentary coffee, friendly, good source of information, fan, hot water. Recommended.

E Chez Kai, 1160 Soi Samosorn, T042-460968. Clean airy rooms, some with balcony, restaurant downstairs with lots of vegetarian food all very cheap.
E KC Guesthouse, same entrance as Mut Mee Guesthouse, Kaeo Worawut Rd. Shared bathrooms, friendly place which is constantly passed by those bound for the popular Mut Mee.
E Poolsup, 843 Meechai Rd, T042-2202031. Chinese-style hotel with OK rooms and charming proprietress – try her cool rainwater.
E Rimkhong Guesthouse, Rimkhong Rd. Shared bathrooms, clean rooms with fans, friendly staff, wooden house with river views. Small bar/restaurant providing drinks and breakfast.
E-F Sukhaphon, 823 Bamtoengjit Rd, T042-2202894. Old wooden hotel, worth staying here if the more popular guesthouses are full, rooms at the back are quieter.

Beung Kan *p360*

Only basic accommodation available, but all are centrally located and have a certain provincial charm.
F Neramit, Prasatchai Rd, north of the bus station, towards the river, and opposite the Santisuk, with the only international phone in town.
F Santisuk, Prasatchai Rd. Some a/c, reasonable rooms at reasonable prices.

Ban Ahong *p360*

There is 1 guesthouse in Ban Ahong.
F Hideaway Guesthouse, a welcoming and peaceful place on the Mekong.

Nakhon Phanom *p361, map p361*

Because few travellers stop here, cheap accommodation is poor. Few places cater to travellers' needs.
A Nam Khong Grand View, 527 Sunthorn Vichit Rd, T042-513564, F511037. A/c, restaurant, pool, newish hotel with 114 impressive rooms, best in town with great views over the Mekong to Laos.
A-B Nakhon Phanom River View, 9 Nakhon Phanom-That Phanom Rd, T042-522333. A/c, restaurant, pool, fitness centre. This is a new 120-room hotel, situated on the river, out of town towards That Phanom.
B-C Nakhon Phanom, 403 Aphibarn Bancha Rd, T042-511455, F511071. A/c, restaurant, pool, rather shabby, best rooms in the newer wing.
C-D River Inn, 137 Sunthorn Vichit Rd, T042-511305. Some a/c, restaurant, nice position overlooking river, but overpriced, noisy rooms on the road side.
E Grand Hotel, 210 Sri Thep Rd, T042-511526, F513788. Some a/c, very clean and the best of the bunch in this category.

Sakhon Nakhon *p362*

A Srisakol Thani Hotel, T02-2384790. A/c, restaurant, part of Dusit chain, the most comfortable place in town.
A-C MJ Hotel, Kumuang Rd, located slightly outside town. The newest hotel in town, big and brash and certainly not beautiful, but the rooms are spacious, immaculate and good value.
C Imperial, 1892 Suk Khasem Rd, T042-713320. Some a/c, 180 rooms and a snooker parlour, rooms in the newer wing are considerably smarter, although the a/c rooms in the old wing are a good deal.
E Araya 1, 1432 Prempreeda Rd, T042-711224. Some a/c, 50 simple rooms.
E Araya 11, cheapest in town and it shows – run down, but sufficient for a night's stopover. Some rooms with bathrooms attached.

That Phanom *p362, map p363*

When the temple fair is on during the February full moon (see Festivals and events), it is often impossible to find a room. There are no upmarket hotels here. There are 2 guesthouses in That Phanom mainly serving the needs of farang visitors, and 3 Thai-style hotels.
C That Phanom Resort, south of the town, T042-541047. Some a/c, basic and boring rooms with the only plus that they are clean.
C-D Kaeng Pho Resort, Highway 212 (3 km south of town), T042-541412. Some a/c, the better of Nakhon Phanom's 2 resort-style hotels, but even so this is hardly an example of rustic splendour – attractive gardens.
E-F Chaiwan, 34 Phanom Phanarak Rd. Another small hotel, marginally cleaner than the Saeng Thong and also quite characterful.

E-F Mr Pom's Guesthouse, Soi 2, pale green building. Clean and friendly place, keen to attract business away from other more popular places. Peaceful.

E-F Saeng Thong, 34 Phanom Phanarak Rd. Small hotel with just 17 rooms, shabby, but at least it has some character.

F Niyana's Guesthouse, 288 Moo 2, Rimkhong Rd, T042-540588, upstream from town. Rooms in traditional country house, in peaceful leafy compound. Roof garden, large rooms with fans and nets, helpful and friendly owner, tours and motorbikes and bicycles for rent. Recommended.

Mukdahan *p363*

A Mukdahan Grand, 78 Song Nang Sathit, T042-630958, F612021. A/c, restaurant, comparatively plush but in a distinctly provincial manner, as evidenced in the local crooners, **Zubano Karaoke Bar** and **MG Snooker Club** – and some people would say all the more charming for it. Arguably the best hotel in town.

C-D Mukdahan, 8/8 Samut Sakdarak Rd, T042-611619, 500 m south of the town centre. Some a/c with hot water and TV, but no ambience, 4-storey hotel, quite new but already dilapidated at the edges, coffee shop with live music, friendly.

C-E Hua Nam, 36 Samut Sakdarak Rd, T042-611137. Central location on corner with Song Nang Sathit Rd, looks from the outside like a cross between an American diner and a Chinese-style hotel, but rooms are large, clean and well maintained. Some a/c with TV and hot water. Set around a courtyard, so relatively quiet despite central crossroads location. Recommended.

D-E Hong Kong, 161/1-2 Phithak Santirat Rd, T042-611123. Some a/c, Chinese-style hotel, quite well maintained, a/c rooms have hot water, central.

D-E Sansuk Bungalow, 2 Phithak Santirat Rd, T042-611294. Some a/c, near the centre of town, clean rooms with friendly management, the best of a poor selection of cheaper accommodation.

Eating

Nong Khai *p357, map p358*

DN (Dang Nam Nuong), Soi Thepbanterng opposite **Thasadej Café**, near the river. Open 0800-1900. Serves good Vietnamese food including delicious Vietnamese-style spring rolls. Eat in or takeaway. Recommended.

Banya Pochana, 295 Rim Khong Rd. Chinese, Thai and Lao food, fish dishes particularly good.

The Boat, western end of Rim Khong Rd. Nice position on the river, but the ice creams, sundaes and milkshakes are a little pricey.

Chez Kai, 1160 Soi Samosorn T042-460968. This guesthouse has a restaurant downstairs specializing in vegetarian food.

The Danish Baker, 434 Mee Chai Rd, T042-460840, www.danishbaker.dk. Mixed menu, good for a quick snack and the buffet meals are also excellent value (breakfast/brunch 0800-1200, dinner 1800-).

The Fish, vegetarian floating restaurant near to the **Mut Mee Guesthouse**. Good range of dishes at reasonable prices.

German restaurant serving fantastic food and very cheap tasty wine. Run by a friendly German/Thai couple. Open 0800 till late. Recommended.

Hadda, Rimkhong Rd, just in between the immigration office and the market, T042-411543. Wide-ranging menu including a selection of fish dishes. Fantastic setting with river views and very popular with locals. Recommended.

Happy Kitchen 1164 Prachak Rd. Restaurant attached to the **Suksant Hotel** (no English sign for the restaurant). Excellent fish dishes, recommended.

Khun Daeng, 521 Rim Khong Rd (just west from Udom Rot and the immigration office). Views over the Mekong River, seafood and superb Isaan specialities.

Mut Mee, Kaeo Worawut Rd. Wide range of Thai and western food, with delicious specialities such as pla shiu shii (fish with coconut and hot sauce).

Steak House, Meechai Rd (next to **Sawasdee Guesthouse**), predictably selling steaks, very tasty and good value.

Udom Rot, 193 Rim Khong Rd. Views over the Mekong River, great seafood as well as some Lao and Vietnamese dishes. Recommended.

Coffee shops

The Coffee Shop, Rim Khong Rd. Attractive rustic design.

Beung Kan *p360*
Santisuk guesthouse has a good and cheap restaurant; there is also a night market situated near the a/c bus terminal on Bumrungrad Rd, plus the usual street-side Thai eating houses.

Nakhon Phanom *p361, map p361*
There are numerous restaurants along the river road and they all serve the same broad range of dishes. Mekong catfish cooked in a variety of ways – curried, stir fried, deep fried, in soups – is a local speciality.
Golden Giant Catfish, Sunthorn Vichit Rd, serves pla buk, the famed giant Mekong catfish, in a variety of guises. Recommended.
Nawt Laap Phet, 464 Aphibarn Bancha Rd, an Isaan restaurant serving Lao specialities including the usual grilled chicken and spicy salad, along with great larb.

Sakhon Nakhon *p362*
Just north of Sakhon Nakhon is a dog market which sells, slaughters and serves dog meat.
Best House Suki, Prem Prida Rd. Excellent Isaan food served here, seafood specialities.
Sook Kasen, Kamchatpai Rd. Thai food.

Bakeries
Greencorner, Ratphattana Rd, pleasant a/c bakery with good breakfast and usual food selection.

Foodstalls
There are 2 night markets in town. One is close to the **Charoensuk Hotel**, at the roundabout at the junction of Charoenmuang and Jaiphasuk rds. The other is at the intersection of Charoenmuang and Suk Khasem rds.

That Phanom *p362, map p363*
Foodstalls and restaurants can be found on the riverfront and along Rachdamnern Rd; try the **That Phanom Pochana** or **Somkhane**, both fish restaurants close to the triumphal arch. Lao-style French fare is also available including good, strong fresh coffee and baguettes. The night market sells Thai dishes.

Mukdahan *p363*
The best places to eat are along the river.
Enjoy Restaurant, 7/1 Samut Sakdarak Rd. Bright and cheerful restaurant with Lao specialities, a few Vietnamese dishes and river fish and prawns.
Phai Rim Khong (Riverside), Samran Chai Khong Rd. To the south of town, serving good Thai dishes in attractive location with good views.
River View, Samran Chai Khong Rd. Chalet-style restaurant with tables overlooking Mekong, average Thai and Lao food, spectacular setting.

Bakeries
Bakery, opposite **Ploy Palace Hotel**, good cakes, coffee and ice cream.
Phit Bakery, 709 Phithak Santirat. Good breakfasts, coffee, cakes and ice creams, friendly. Recommended.

Foodstalls
Night market, Song Nang Sathit Rd (western end, near the bus station). The best place for cheap Isaan dishes and also for Vietnamese stall food.

Bars and clubs

Nong Khai *p357, map p358*
Thasadej Cafe, 387/3 Soi Thepbanterng, T042-412075. Open 0830-0100, food all day till 2300. A fun place to go, very clean with a good selection of spirits and draft beer. Free coffee refills, under friendly German management.
Winner Pub, Prachak Rd. Live easy listening/pop music, the place to go if you want a night out, also serves a selection of traditional Thai food. Open 2100-0100.

Festivals and events

Nong Khai *p357, map p358*
Mar (2nd week) Nong Khai Show.
May Rocket Festival (ngarn bang fai) (2nd week) (see page 335).
Jul Candle Festival (the beginning of the Buddhist Lent or Khao Phansa) (see page 336).
Oct (movable) Boat races on the Mekong. Naga-powered canoes with up to 40 oarsmen race along the river, with a great deal of cheering and drinking from the onlookers that line the bank.

Nakhon Phanom *p361, map p361*

Oct (9-13th, end of Buddhist Lent) Ok Phansa, 4-day celebrations with long-boat races, and the launching of illuminated boats onto the Mekong.

Sakhon Nakhon *p362*

Oct Wax Castle Ceremony, celebrated at Ok Phansa (the end of the Buddhist lent), when elaborate and intricately detailed models of wats are moulded out of beeswax in order to gain merit. Images of the Buddha are placed inside these temporary edifices and they are paraded through town accompanied by Northeastern music, singing and dancing. Boat races take place at Nong Han Lake at the same time.

That Phanom *p362*

Jan/Feb (full moon) Phra That Phanom Chedi Homage-paying Fair, the Northeast's largest temple fair, when thousands of pilgrims converge on the wat and walk around the chedi in homage. Dancing, bands and other entertainments; perhaps the most vivid display of Northeastern regional identity. The entire town is engulfed by market stalls, selling a vast array of goods for the week of the festival, day and night.

Shopping

Nong Khai *p357, map p358*

The best area to browse is down Rim Khong Rd, which runs along the riverbank. Here, Northeastern and Lao handicrafts are sold together with Chinese, Soviet and East European goods. It is possible to come away with a (former) Soviet military watch, an Isaan axe pillow, and 'French' sandalwood soap made in Laos.

Village Weaver Handicrafts, 1151 Soi Chitapanya, Prachak Rd, T042-41 1236, village@udon.ksc.co.th. This outlet sells cloth, in particular mut mee, produced by a self-help project which aims to provide women with an income-earning activity and so prevent the city-ward drift of young people. Better quality than those along the riverbank.

Wasambe Bookshop, near the Mut Mee Guesthouse, is an excellent bookshop and book exchange. It also has email and fax facilities.

Mukdahan *p363*

Antiques

Sa-aat, 77 Samut Sakdarak Rd. Small collection of antiques for sale including Chinese ceramics, old irons, Buddhist alms bowls and amulets.

Handicrafts

Mukdahan is a good place to buy Lao/Isaan handicrafts like baskets, axe cushions and textiles. Cloth is sold in phuns; a sarong length is normally 2 phuns with cotton cloth costing ฿100 per phun and silk several times more. The textiles with the elephant motif are distinctively Lao, although much of the cloth is now woven in Thailand. Textiles and other handicrafts can be bought in the daily riverside market (see Sights above). There are also permanent shops on Samut Sakdarak Rd.

Activities and tours

Nong Khai *p357, map p358*

River tours with dinner

Boats board at 1715 close to Wat Haisok with dinner provided before sailing, then a gentle saunter to take in the lights of Nong Khai – and the dark of Laos.

Therapies

Alternative Centre, next to the Mut Mee Guesthouse on Kaeo Worawut Rd. Daily yoga sessions; reiki, t'ai chi and astrology readings are some of the courses on offer.

Tour operators

With the opening of the Friendship Bridge, tour operators have multiplied and there are now more than 10, most of whom – along with many guesthouses – will arrange 30-day visas for Laos on the spot. It is worth shopping around for the best deal.

Pam Tour, 1112/1 Haisok Rd. Udorn Business Travel (Nong Khai branch), 447/10 Haisok Rd, T042-2202393.

Currently it is not necessary to pre-arrange a visa before entering Laos. 15-day visas are provided on arrival when crossing over the Friendship Bridge. See also page 151.

Mukdahan *p363*

Tour operators

There are 4 small tour offices opposite Wat Si Mongkhon Tai, at the north end of

Samran Chai Khong Road: **TAR Tour**, **Mukdahan Tour** (Thailand), **Sompong Tour** and **Sakonpasa Department Store**. They are mainly oriented towards Thai tourists travelling to Laos and Vietnam. However, now that non-Thais can cross the border into Laos at this point, they have branched into providing services for farangs. Visa services and tours to Laos available.

Transport

Nong Khai *p357, map p358*

Air

The nearest airport is in Udon Thani and a shuttle bus takes passengers there.

Airline offices THAI, 453 Prachak Rd, T042-2202530.

Bicycle

Hire from **Mut Mee Guesthouse**, ฿40 per day.

Bus

The terminal is on the east side of town on Praserm Rd, off Prachak Rd. Regular connections with **Bangkok**'s Northeastern bus terminal (9-11 hrs) and **Khon Kaen**, **Udon Thani** and other Northeastern towns. There is also a service to **Rayong** on the eastern seaboard. Note that tuk-tuk drivers have taken to hounding farangs and charging exorbitant rates. Don't pay more than ฿20. VIP buses for Bangkok leave from 745 Prachak Rd. A/c buses from the corner of Haisok and Prachak roads. A/c buses also depart from the BKS station. There are lots of sharks about.

Motorcycle

Hire from the **International Meeting Place**, 1117 Soi Chuanjit (฿200 per day), and from the **Mut Mee Guesthouse**.

Train

The station is 3 km from town, west on Kaeo Worawut Rd. Regular connections with **Bangkok**'s Hualamphong station (11 hrs) and all stops northeast: **Ayutthaya**, **Saraburi**, **Korat**, **Khon Kaen** and **Udon**.

International connections with Laos

The Friendship Bridge, over the Mekong River at Tambon Meechai, 2 km from town, offers the first road link across the Mekong. The bridge is open daily 0800-1800. Visas are now available upon entry to Laos. The price has dropped to US$30 (payable in US dollars cash only). One passport photograph is required. To get to the Friendship Bridge, take a tuk-tuk to the last bus stop before the bridge and from there catch a bus to Thai immigration.

Nakhon Phanom *p361, map p361*

Air

There are daily connections on THAI with **Bangkok**.

Boat

Foreigners can cross the Mekong to Laos using a ferry service.

Bus

The station for local buses and songthaews is near the market, opposite the **Nakhon Phanom Hotel**. There is another bus terminal 2 km southwest of town. Buses to **That Phanom** come back into town at the southern clock tower and then head south. Connections with **Nong Khai** and **Sakhon Nakhon**. Tour buses running south to **Ubon** leave every 2 hrs during the day from near the **Windsor Hotel** (4½ hrs).

Songthaew

Songthaews to **That Phanom** leave from the local bus station.

Sakhon Nakhon *p362*

Air

One flight a day on THAI to and from **Bangkok**.

Airline offices THAI, 1446 Yuwa Phattana Rd, T042-712259.

Bus

Regular connections with **Bangkok**'s Northeastern bus terminal (11 hrs) and with other Northeastern centres.

That Phanom *p362, map p363*

Bus

There is no bus terminal as such. Buses stop on Chaiyangkun Rd (the main Route 212, north to Nakhon Phanom and south to Ubon), an easy walk to the river and guesthouses. Regular connections with

Nakhon Phanom, **Mukdahan**, **Sakhon Nakhon**, **Udon Thani** and **Ubon Ratchatani**. Buses for **Bangkok** leave from the southern end of Chayangkun Rd.

Mukdahan *p363*

Boat

Ferries to Savannakhet and Laos leave from the pier near Wat Si Mongkhon Tai. Foreigners can cross from Thailand to Laos here.

Bus

The bus terminal for non-a/c and some a/c buses to **Ubon**, **Nakhon Phanom**, **That Phanom**, other Northeastern towns, and **Bangkok** is at the western end of Song Nang Sathit Rd, about 2 km from the centre (a ฿20 motor saamlor ride). You may be dropped off at the junction of Muang Mai Rd and Route 212. Tuk-tuks wait here and ฿20 is the usual rate into town. A/c buses leave from close to Bangkok Bank on Song Nang Sathit Rd.

Directory

Nong Khai *p357, map p358*

Banks Bangkok, 374 Sisaket Rd. Krung Thai, 102 Meechai Rd. Thai Farmers, 929 Meechai Rd are but a few.

Internet Wasambe Bookshop has email (wasambe@loxinfo.co.th), international phone and fax (F042-460717) available.

Embassies and consulates The closest Lao consulate is in Khon Kaen, although travel agents in Nong Khai will also arrange visas, for a fee (see Tour operators above).

Medical services Hospital Meechai Rd, T042-2202504. **Post office** Meechai Rd (opposite Soi Prisnee); there is an international telephone office upstairs.

Useful addresses Immigration Sisaket Rd, T042-2202154. Police Meechai Rd, T042-2202020.

Beung Kan *p360*

There is a Thai Farmers Bank here.

Nakhon Phanom *p361, map p361*

Banks Bangkok, Srithep Rd. Thai Farmers, 439 Aphibarn Bancha Rd. **Medical services** Sunthorn Vichit Rd, T042-511422. **Post office** Sunthorn Vichit Rd (northern end). **Telephone** Off Fuang Nakhon Rd. **Useful addresses** Immigration:. Sunthorn Vichit Rd, T042-51147. Police:. Sunthorn Vichit Rd (northern end).

That Phanom *p362, map p363*

Banks Thai Military, on the main road into town (Route 212), north of Wat That Phanom (amongst others). **Post office** North of the Thai Military Bank. No English spoken here, there is a phone available if you can make yourself understood. **Useful addresses** Immigration Rachdamnern Rd, by the river, T042-541090.

Mukdahan *p363*

Banks Bangkok Bank, Song Nang Sathit Rd. Thai Farmers, Song Nang Sathit Rd. **Post office** Phithak Santirat Rd (on the roundabout), be prepared for a steep ascent to the front desk. **Useful addresses** Immigration Samran Chai Khong Rd, T042-611074.

Eastern Region

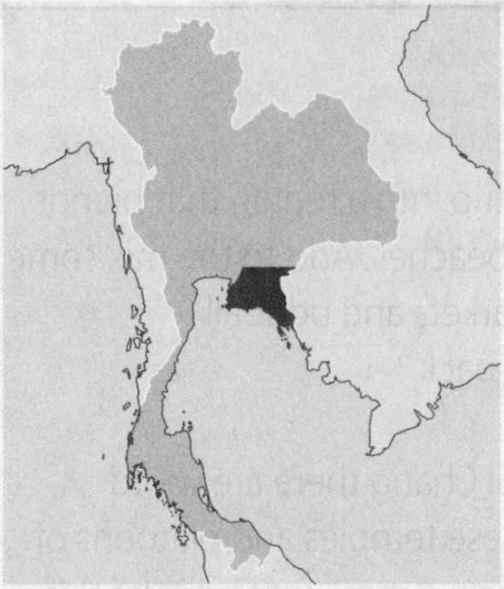

Footprint features

Introduction

Heading east from Bangkok is a trip into a region that blends trashy gaudiness and gorgeous beaches. Add to the mix some remote forested islands, gem markets and oddball idiosyncrasy and you won't look back.

On the enigmatic island of Koh Si Chang there are weird abandoned palaces, sacred Chinese temples and platoons of monkeys. Next stop is Pattaya. Even a mere utterance of this name sends tourism activists apoplectic. Polluted waters, bad planning, and an endless supply of worn-out bargirls clutching, fifty-something farang men, has done little to endear Pattaya to the more discerning traveller but amid the neon and fleshpots, it has some of the best hotels in the country and there is no better place in Southeast Asia to dig ironic kitsch. A little further east is Koh Samet, a national marine park. Here, azure seas lap crystalline beaches and a whole range of accommodation, from simple rustic bungalows through to well-designed resorts, await the visitor. Koh Samet is a popular and nifty get-away for Bangkok's younger, trendier crowd, giving it a sophisticated, chilled vibe. Chantaburi is worth a stopover for its gem market, traditional architecture and cathedral. As for Koh Chang: the traveller's idyll of isolated, white-sand beaches secreted away from the machinations of contemporary consumer society is quickly disappearing. Parts of the coast are slowly turning into a run of homogenous resorts. Girlie bars and sex tourists are proliferating and prices are rocketing. However, if you look hard enough, there are still some wonderful spots to lounge about in, losing yourself in the alluring sunsets, swimming in the calm, clear waters. Koh Chang's interior is also largely untouched, filled with waterfalls, jungle tracks and a colourful, noisy population of tropical birds and forest beasties.

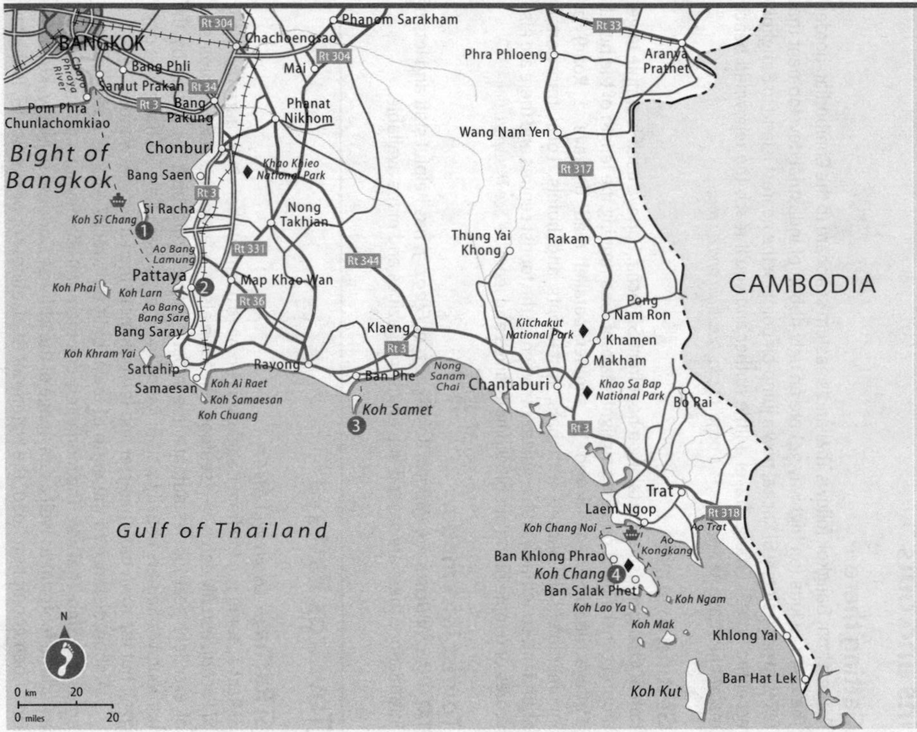

★ Don't miss...

1 **Koh Si Chang** A long-time haven for sailors, smugglers and other assorted ne'er do wells. Awesome seafood, monkeys, weird ruins and an elaborate enigmatic Chinese temple provide the colour, page 375.

2 **Pattaya** Many people head to brazen Pattaya for one thing – sex. Get beyond that and you find a dynamic, effervescent and kitsch resort town with 'ladyboy' cabaret, gun ranges, some of the best international food in the country and some surprisingly good diving, page 375.

3 **Koh Samet** Funky resorts, cheap bungalows and gorgeous beaches create a pleasant mix that soothes away the city stress, page 384.

4 **Koh Chang** Koh Chang used to be the quintessential lost Thai island – a remote place, thick with mysterious forest and edged by soft white beaches. This exotic charm still persists but, with an airport opened in nearby Trat and generic resorts endlessly replicating themselves, you better catch it while you can, page 393.

Pattaya and around

→ Colour map 3, grid C4

Brash and brazen, Pattaya ('Southwest wind') is argued by some to be Thailand's premier beach resort, yet only 35 years ago it was a little-known coastal village frequented by fishermen, farmers and a handful of weekenders. There are now two schools of thought: School 1 – it is the type of tourist resort Thailand should be thinking of bulldozing: environmentally unsound, crass, criminals and encourages sex tourism. School 2 – it is a great commercial success: the hotels are well run and very competitive, there is an enormous variety of excellent restaurants, and the sea sports are diverse and professionally managed.

Si Racha, with its excellent seafood restaurants, is a stepping stone for Koh Si Chang, an easy weekend getaway for Bangkok residents. The coast after Pattaya – running past the town of Rayong – has been developed into an elongated run of resorts that are aimed at the mass domestic tourist market. The beaches and hotels are decent enough: think of the Costa del Sol and give it an Asian twist. » For Sleeping, Eating and other listings see pages 378-383.

Ins and outs

Getting there

Route 3 from Bangkok follows Thailand's eastern seaboard to the Cambodian border. The first 130 kms (on Highway 34) are an ugly ribbon of industrial development that takes in once sleepy Si Racha, now a jump-off point for the nearest island to Bangkok, eccentric Koh Si Chang. Travel a little further and you'll reach the renowned beach resort of Pattaya. » See Transport, page 382, for bus, train and air routes.

Getting around

Koh Si Chang is visited by taking a boat from Si Racha. Pattaya itself is simple to get around consisting of one long straight seafront road running the length of the beach (Pattaya Beach Road), linked to another parallel road (Pattaya 2 Road) by innumerable sois packed with bars, restaurants and hotels. Local transport is abundant; songthaews run regularly between all the tourist centres and there are also scores of people hiring out bikes, motorbikes and jeeps. » See Transport, page 382.

Tourist information

TAT ⓘ *382/1 Beach Rd, Pattaya, T038-428750, F429113*, has helpful staff and lots of information. There are several free tourist magazines and maps available.

Towards Pattaya

Si Racha

→ Colour map 3, grid C4.

Si Racha, some 100 km from Bangkok, is home to a famous hot chilli sauce (*nam prik Si Racha*), usually eaten with seafood. The town also has a reputation for its profusion of excellent seafood restaurants; the most enjoyable are built on jetties by the harbour. Westerners usually visit Si Racha in order to reach Koh Si Chang (see page 375), but the town has character and is worth more than a cursory wander.

A short distance to the north of town, built on a rocky islet, is the gaudy and enjoyable **Sino-Thai wat**. The monastery commemorates a devout monk and boasts a Buddha footprint as well as an image of the Chinese Goddess of Mercy, Kuan Yin. On Choemchomphon Road, the waterfront road, almost opposite Soi 16, is the **Jaw**

Phor Samut Dam Chinese temple. Up the road towards the clock tower at the southern end is a large covered **market**. Keep an eye out for Si Racha's overpowered, chariot-like motorized saamlors.

Koh Si Chang → *Colour map 3, grid C4.*

Koh Si Chang is one of those places that had a moment in the spotlight – King Rama V built a palace here – and then history moved on. It does make for an entertaining, idiosyncratic short break and is relatively easy to reach from Bangkok, making it a popular spot for weekenders from the capital. There's Rama V's ruined palace, a popular Chinese temple, a handful of reasonable beaches and some truly stupendous motorized saamlors.

Koh Si Chang used to be the transshipment point for both cargo and passenger vessels before the Chao Phraya River was dredged sufficiently to allow ships to reach Bangkok. Even though many vessels now bypass Si Racha, the surrounding water is still chock-a-block with ships at anchor (normally about 50, but sometimes as many as 100 ships), their cargoes being unloaded into smaller lighters and barges. The island's main trade is now as a service base for the freighter crews. Their visas often do not allow them to disembark, so all R & R is taken to them by the varied residents of Koh Si Chang. The island also has a reputation as a sanctuary for criminals. The drugs trade is reportedly rife and corruption within the police force endemic. This activity shouldn't impact on travellers.

At the northern edge of the town, set up on a hill overlooking the town, is a **Chinese temple – Chaw Por Khaw Yai**. From its assortment of decorated shrines and caves there are great views of the island and town. It's a very important temple for Thailand's Chinese community and particularly popular at Chinese New Year when over 5,000 people visit the shrine each evening, doubling the island's population. Not far away to the south, and overlooking the town, is a **Buddhist retreat** set among limestone caves. A large, yellow seated Buddha image looks out over the bay. On the east coast, south of the retreat, are the **ruins of a palace** built by Rama V. It was abandoned in 1893 when the French took control of the island during a confrontation with the Thais. Not much remains – most of the structure was dismantled and rebuilt in Bangkok. Rather eerie stairways, balustrades and an empty reservoir remain scattered across the rocky hillside. The only remaining building of any size is **Wat Atsadangnimit** ⓘ *0800-1800,* a revered monastery that still attracts a surprising number of pilgrims largely because King Chulalongkorn used to meditate here.

The island also has a number of **beaches** with reasonable swimming and snorkelling. The quietest beach with the best coral and swimming is **Tham Phang** on the western side of the island; easier to reach are **Tha Wang** (next to the palace) – a rocky beach and not suitable for swimming – and **Hat Sai Kaew** (over the hill from the palace). While it is possible to swim, note that at certain times of year the currents can wash all sorts of rubbish onto the beach. There are plans to build a nature trail from Tham Phang to **Si Phitsanu Bungalows**.

Pattaya

Background

Pattaya began to metamorphose when the US navy set up shop at the nearby port of Sattahip (40 km further down the coast). As the war in Vietnam escalated, so the influx of GIs on 'rest and relaxation' grew and Pattaya responded enthusiastically. Today, it provides around 36,000 hotel rooms and supplies everything you could ever need from a beach holiday – except, arguably, peace and quiet. Given its origins in the Vietnam War, it is hardly surprising that Pattaya's stock in trade is sex tourism and at any one time, about 4,000 girls are touting for work around the many bars and restaurants.

While Pattaya's official population is 60,000, there are between 200,000 and 300,000 staying in town at any one time, whether international tourists or migrant workers. This has inevitably led to environmental problems. Lack of treatment of polluted water has meant that the beaches are not as clean as they once were – and the waters offshore can have a coliform count that should make most people stick to their hotel swimming pools or bathtubs.

Pattaya – according to official statements at least – is going out of its way to play down its go-go bar image and promote a 'family' resort profile. This emphasis on wholesome family fun is hard to reconcile with reality. But still the effort continues. The busiest and noisiest area is at the southern end of town (South Pattaya or 'The Village'); from about Soi 11 to Soi Post Office (with Pattayaland 1, 2 and 3 being the gay areas of town). There must be one of the highest concentration of bars, discos, massage parlours, prostitutes and transvestites of any place in the world. Many people find this aspect of Pattaya repugnant. However, there is no pretence here – either on the part of the hosts or their guests. This is a beach resort of the most lurid kind.

Pattaya

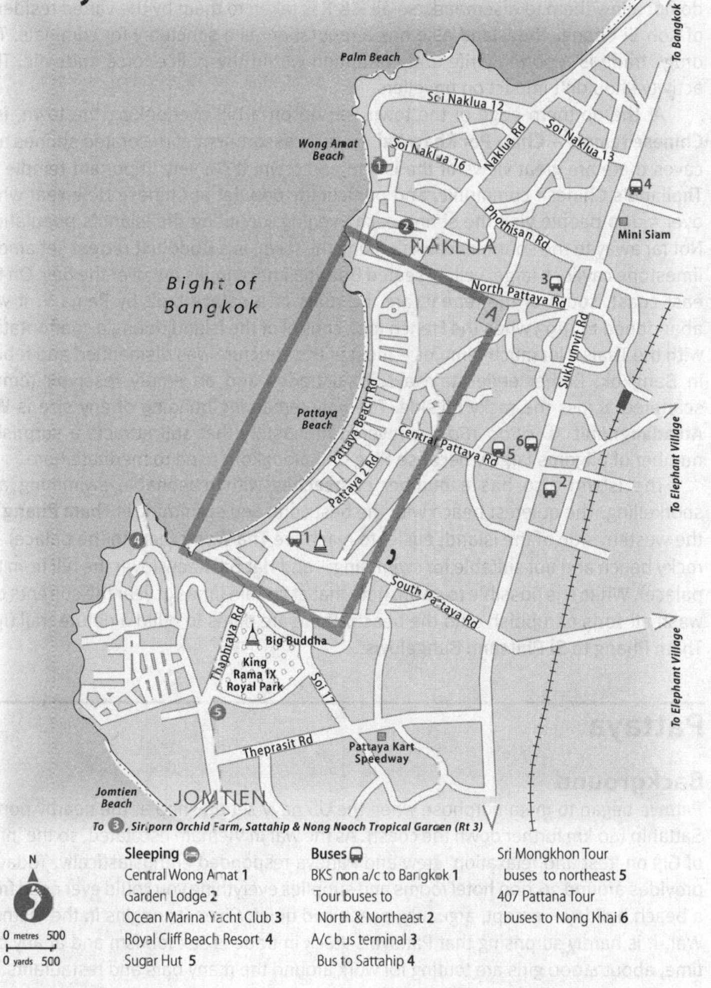
Palm Beach
To Bangkok
Soi Naklua 12
Soi Naklua 13
Wong Amat Beach
Soi Naklua 16
Naklua Rd
Phothisan Rd
Mini Siam
NAKLUA
Bight of Bangkok
North Pattaya Rd
A
Sukhumvit Rd
Pattaya Beach
Pattaya Beach Rd
Central Pattaya Rd
Pattaya 2 Rd
To Elephant Village
South Pattaya Rd
To Elephant Village
Thaphraya Rd
Big Buddha
King Rama IX Royal Park
Soi 17
Theprasit Rd
Pattaya Kart Speedway
Jomtien Beach
JOMTIEN
To 3, Siriporn Orchid Farm, Sattahip & Nong Nooch Tropical Garden (Rt 3)
N
0 metres 500
0 yards 500
Sleeping
Central Wong Amat 1
Garden Lodge 2
Ocean Marina Yacht Club 3
Royal Cliff Beach Resort 4
Sugar Hut 5
Buses
BKS non a/c to Bangkok 1
Tour buses to North & Northeast 2
A/c bus terminal 3
Bus to Sattahip 4
Sri Mongkhon Tour buses to northeast 5
407 Pattana Tour buses to Nong Khai 6

Pattaya may be infamous in the west as a city of sin, but there is more to the resort than this perception might indicate. It is also popular with watersports lovers: there is sailing, parasailing, windsurfing, ski-boating, snorkelling, deep-sea fishing and scuba-diving.

Sights

There are few sights in Pattaya though most visitors do make their way to the **Big Buddha** on the hill at the southern end of the beach. There are good views over the resort from the vantage point and the monks based here are usually willing to talk to interested visitors. The main Buddha image is surrounded by smaller images representing each day of the week.

South of Pattaya Bay, past the Big Buddha, is **Jomtien Beach**. Here, there are sports facilities and a cleaner beach. One highlight is a trip up the 240-m **Pattaya Park Tower** ⓘ *T038-251201, ฿200*, sited on the headland at Jomtien and providing spectacular views of the surrounding area.

Pattaya Beach is the central sweep on the main seafront. **Naklua** is further north. This is the quieter end of town, although it still has its fair share of clubs and bars. Both Pattaya Beach and Naklua are pretty similar - a long run of high-rise concrete, interspersed with go go bars, and eateries. Both beaches are identical - long narrow run of sand, backing onto a promenade and main road and overrun with beach brollies.

The **Siriporn Orchid Farm** ⓘ *235/14 Moo 5, Tambon Nong Prue, T038-429013, 0800-1700, ฿10*, displays an array of orchids (some are for sale).

Mini Siam ⓘ *T038-421628, 0700-2200; the park lies 3 km north of Pattaya Beach, on the Sukhumvit highway (Route 3) at the Km 143 marker*, is a cultural and historical park where 80 of Thailand's most famous 'sights' – including Wat Phra Kaeo and the Bridge over the River Kwai – are recreated at a scale of 1:25.

The **Nong Nooch Tropical Garden** ⓘ *T038-42932, 0900-1800, ฿20, ฿200 for the cultural show, or take a tour from Pattaya for ฿250, T038-238063; most people arrive on a tour; the garden is 15 mins from Pattaya town 3 km off the main road at the Km 163 marker*, is a 200-ha park containing immaculate gardens with lakes (and boating), an orchid farm, family zoo, Thai handicraft demonstrations and a thrice-daily (1015, 1500 and 1545) 'cultural spectacular' with Thai dancing, Thai boxing and an elephant show. In 2000 a British tourist was gored and killed by an enraged elephant.

Around Pattaya

Koh Larn

ⓘ *Tickets can be purchased from the booth next to the Sailing Club. Boats depart at 0930 and 1130, returning at 1600 (45 mins, ฿250). Boats can be chartered for ฿1,500 per day. A shared sailing junk ฿250 (inclusive of lunch and coral reef viewing), or a chartered sailing junk costs ฿3,000 per day.*

When Pattaya gets too much, many people retire to one of the offshore islands for rest and recreation. The largest island (and the only one with accommodation) is Koh Larn which has good snorkelling and scuba diving. Glass-bottomed boats are available for touring the reef and the island even has an 18-hole golf course.

Rayong

→ *Colour map 3, grid C5.*

Rayong makes an alternative stop-off point to Pattaya if you want a rest while travelling to the eastern reaches of Thailand. Apart from a passable beach and some decent seafood there's little to keep you occupied.

Sleeping

Si Racha *p374*

Like Si Racha's restaurants, the town's most atmospheric hotels are built on extended jetties on the waterfront – many are well run and clean with attached restaurants.

B-C Grand Bungalow, 9 Choemchomphon Soi 18, T038-312537. South end of town, range of bungalows built off a jetty. Better for larger groups or families rather than couples.

B-C Laemthong Residence Hotel, Sukhumvit Rd, T038-322888, F312651. A/c, restaurant, pool, tennis. Modern hotel lacking the character of the others listed here, but the closest thing to a starred establishment. Central location.

C-D Srivichai, Choemchomphon Rd, Soi 8, T038-311212. Wooden hotel, much like the Sri Wattana, just a shade pricier, friendly, good attached restaurant, clean and classy. Recommended.

D-E Bungalow Sri Wattana, Choemchomphon Rd, Soi 8, T038-311037. Wooden hotel constructed on a jetty, friendly and clean with great atmosphere and enthusiastic service. Good restaurant attached. Recommended.

D-E Samchai, Choemchomphon Rd, Soi 10, T038-311134. Some a/c, wooden hotel, clean rooms, good atmosphere, great food. Recommended.

Koh Si Chang *p375*

A-B Si Chang Palace, Atsadang Rd, T038-216276. A/c, restaurant, pool. Hideous building seems very out of place and is overpriced. Its redeeming feature is that is has great views (and a pool).

B-D Sripitsanu Bungalows, Hat Tham, T038-216024. Quiet and well run by English speaking management. Built into the cliff-face overlooking the sea with a range of rooms and bungalows available not far from Hat Tham. Recommended.

B-D Tew Phai, T038-216084, T01-9470573 (mob). Some a/c, restaurant (pricey), welcoming management.

C-D Benz, T038-216091. Some a/c, unusual stone bungalows, clean and well kept, close to the sea.

Camping This is possible, but bring your own equipment; at weekends Thais from the mainland camp in large numbers.

Pattaya *p375, maps p376 and p379*

The high season is Nov-Mar. Pattaya has the biggest selection of hotels in Thailand outside Bangkok and while there is little for the budget traveller (rooms start at ฿350), there are some excellent value mid-range places.

There are 3 distinct areas of accommodation. At the northern end of the beach is Naklua. Pattaya Beach, busier and noisier with the bulk of the cheaper accommodation, is at the southern end of the beach. Jomtien has a better beach but less nightlife.

All **A** accommodation has a/c, restaurant, pool, and prices are exclusive of tax. Except at weekends and high season there rates should be reduced. Check out hotels on www.hotelthailand.com/pattaya/.

Naklua

AL Central Wong Amat, 277-8 Moo 5, T038-426990, www.centralgroup.com. Set in 10 ha, choice of 100 or so de luxe rooms or 65 chalet and bungalow rooms, business facilities, 2 pools, watersports.

A Woodlands Resort, 164/1 Pattaya-Naklua Rd, T038-421707, F425663. On the edge of Pattaya and Naklua. Has tried to recreate a colonial lodge-type atmosphere. Quiet, leafy and airy with pool and landscaped gardens.

B Garden Lodge, 170 Mu 5 Naklua Rd, T038-429109, F421221. A/c, pool, bungalow rooms looking onto gardens, quiet and excellent value. Recommended.

Pattaya Beach

L-AL Royal Cliff Beach Resort, 353 Moo 12 Pratamnak Rd, South Pattaya, T038-250421, www.royalcliffco.th. A/c, restaurants, pool, every imaginable facility. A favourite with conference and incentive groups. Set high up on the the south end of the beach.

L-AL Dusit Resort, 240/2 Beach Rd (north end), T038-425611, www.pattaya.dusit.com/index.html. Excellent hotel with 474 rooms, good service and all facilities. Health club, tennis, squash courts, children's pools, table tennis and a games room, watersports, shopping arcade, disco.

AL Montien Pattaya, 369 Mu 9 Beach Rd, T038-428155, www.sawadee.com/pattaya/montien/. Central location, extensive gardens, excellent hotel, despite its age and size.

Pattaya Beach

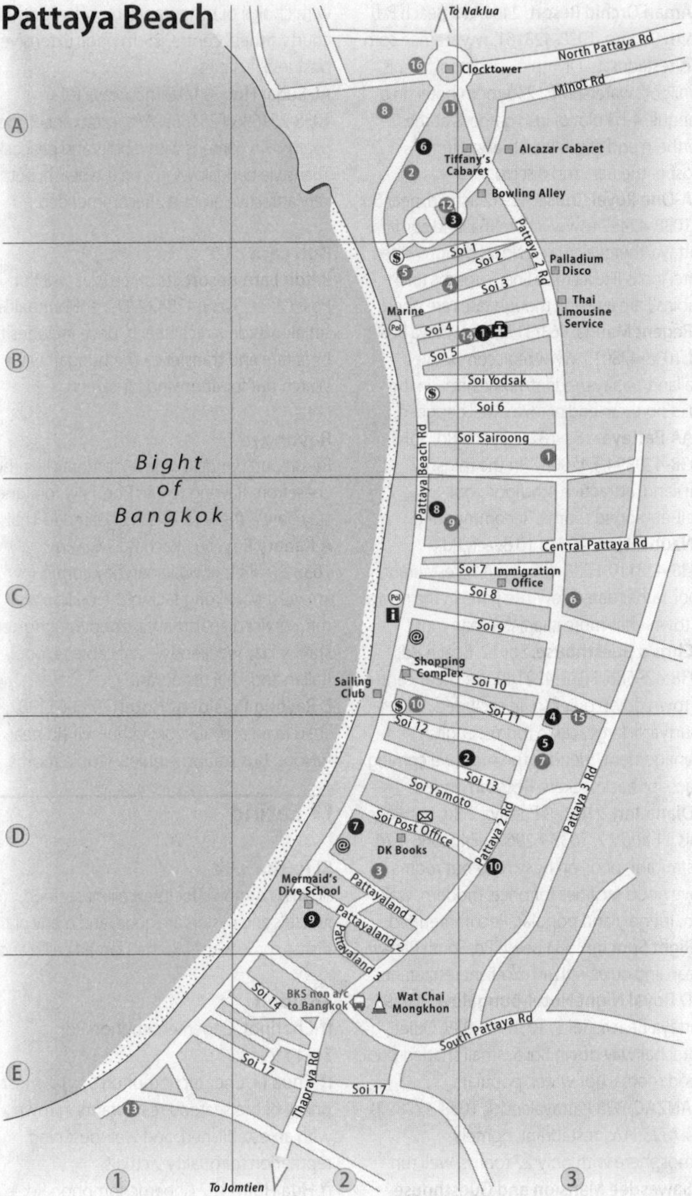
To Naklua
Clocktower
North Pattaya Rd
Minot Rd
Alcazar Cabaret
Tiffany's Cabaret
Bowling Alley
Pattaya 2 Rd
Palladium Disco
Thai Limousine Service
Soi 1
Soi 2
Soi 3
Marine
Soi 4
Soi 5
Soi Yodsak
Soi 6
Soi Sairoong
Pattaya Beach Rd
Bight of Bangkok
Central Pattaya Rd
Soi 7
Immigration Office
Soi 8
Soi 9
Shopping Complex
Soi 10
Sailing Club
Soi 11
Soi 12
Soi 13
Soi Yamoto
Pattaya 3 Rd
Soi Post Office
DK Books
Mermaid's Dive School
Pattayaland 1
Pattayaland 2
Pattayaland 3
BKS non a/c to Bangkok
Wat Chai Mongkhon
Soi 14
South Pattaya Rd
Soi 17
Thapraya Rd
To Jomtien
A
B
C
D
E
1
2
3

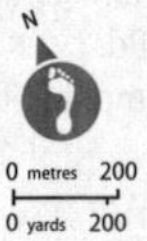
N
0 metres 200
0 yards 200

Sleeping
AA Pattaya **1** *B3*
Amari Orchid Resort **2** *A2*
ANZAC **3** *D2*
A-One Royal Cruise **4** *B2*
Beach View **5** *B2*
Chris' Guesthouse **6** *C3*
Diana Inn **7** *D3*
Dusit Resort **8** *A2*
Montien Pattaya **9** *C2*
Nautical Inn **10** *C2*
Regent Marina **12** *A2*
Right Spot Inn **13** *E1*
Royal Night **14** *B3*
Sawasdee Mansion & Guesthouse **15** *C3*
Woodlands Resort **16** *A2*

Eating
Dolf Riks **3** *A2*
Green Bottle **4** *D3*
Kiss **5** *D3*
La Gritta **6** *A2*
Peppermill **7** *D2*
Pic Kitchen **1** *B3*
Ruen Thai **10** *D3*
Yamato **2** *D3*

A Amari Orchid Resort, 240 Mu 5 Beach Rd, North Pattaya, T038-428161, www.amari.com. A/c, restaurants, Olympic-sized pool, tennis, mini golf, watersports. 230-room hotel on a tranquil, 4-ha plot of lush gardens at the northern end of the beach, away from most of the bars and discos.

A A-One Royal Cruise, 499 Beach Rd, near Soi 2, T038-424874, www.hotelthailand.com/pattaya/theroyalcruise/. Novel design – the hotel looks like a cruise liner – rooms (or 'cabins') are average though rates are good.

A Regent Marina, 463/31 North Pattaya Beach Rd, T038-428015, www.regit.com/regitel/thailand/pattaya/regent/home.htm. In the quiet northern end of town, well designed.

B AA Pattaya, 182-182/2 Beach Rd, Soi 3, T038-420894, F429057. In the midst of bar-land, attractive 4th-floor pool, well-equipped rooms. Recommended.

B Nautical Inn, 10 Mu 10 Beach Rd, T038-428110, F038-428116. A/c, restaurant, pool, rather dated, low-rise hotel in the centre of town - has more character than most.

C Chris's Guesthouse, Soi 12, Beach Rd, T038-429586, F038-422140. A/c, near centre of town down quiet soi in secluded courtyard, large, clean rooms, English management, friendly, the most welcoming place for backpackers. Recommended.

C Diana Inn, 216/6-9 Pattaya 2 Rd, between Sois 11 and 12, T038-429675, F424566. A/c, restaurant, pool, on busy road but rooms have good facilities for price, modern, well run, friendly and popular. Recommended.

C Right Spot Inn, 583 Beach Rd, South Pattaya. Clean and quiet with an excellent restaurant.

C-D Royal Night Hotel-bungalow, 362/9 Pattaya Beach, Soi 5, T038-428038. Quiet hotel halfway down Soi 5, small shaded pool, good rooms, hot water, popular.

D ANZAC, 325 Pattayaland 1, T038-427822, F427823. A/c, restaurant, homely atmosphere with only 22 rooms, well run.

D Sawasdee Mansion and Guesthouse, 502/1 Pattaya 2 Rd, Soi 10, T038-425360. Some a/c, one of the cheapest places in town in a high-rise block down a built-up soi, but the decent rooms are clean.

Jomtien

L Ocean Marina Yacht Club, 274/1-9 Moo 4, Sukhumvit Highway, T038-237310, F237325. Massive high-rise hotel linked to the marina with choice of restaurants, tennis and squash courts, fitness centre, 25-m pool. Extensive business facilities.

AL Sugar Hut, 391/18 Thaphraya Rd, T038-251686, F251689. A/c, restaurant, 2 pools, overgrown gardens with rabbits and peacocks. Thai-style bungalows not on the beach, but very attractive grounds. Recommended.

Koh Larn *p377*

B Koh Larn Resort, its office is at 183 Soi Post Office, T038-428422. Decent bungalows set alongside a nice beach, price includes the boat fare and transfer to the bungalows. Watch out for annoying jet-skiers.

Rayong *p377*

Resort and bungalow developments line the coast from Rayong to Ban Phe. Few foreigners stay here – these resorts are geared to Thais.

A Kanary Bay, 50 Beach Rd, Muang T038-804844, www.kanarybay.com A few km west of Rayong facing the beach. Well run, serviced apartments, good for long-term stay or lazy weekends – a/c cable tv, pool, Italian and Thai restaurant.

B Rayong President Hotel, T038-611307, sited in an alley just of Sukhumvit Rd near Rayong bus station – quiet, simple rooms.

Eating

Si Racha *p374*

Si Racha is known for its excellent seafood. Mussels and oysters are good, and many of the dishes come with Si Racha's famed chilli sauce.

Seafood

Cherinct, Choemchomphon Rd, Soi 14 (pier).

Chua Li Choemchomphon Soi 10, most pricey of the seafood restaurants in town with an established, and well-deserved reputation for quality victuals.

Hua Huat, 102 Choemchomphon Rd.

Jaw Sii, 98 Choemchomphon Rd.

Si Racha Seafood, Choemchomphon Rd (near the bus stop).

Koh Si Chang *p375*

Lek Naa Wang and **Noi** are famed for serving up the island's best seafood – find them just beside the road to the palace, a 10-min walk out of town.

🍴 **Si Chang Palace Coffee Shop**, an a/c refuge offering a range of coffee and cakes.

Pattaya *p375, maps p376 and p379*

Pattaya has the greatest choice of international cuisine outside Bangkok. By Thai standards prices tend to be high.

Thai

🍴🍴🍴 **PIC Kitchen**, Soi 5. Four traditional Thai pavilions, Thai classical dancing in garden compound, good food. Recommended.

🍴🍴🍴 **Ruen Thai**, Pattaya 2 Rd, opposite Soi Post Office. Very good Thai food and not excessively overpriced. Recommended.

🍴🍴 **Kiss**, Pattaya 2 Rd, between sois 11 and 12, next to **Diana Inn**. Good range of western and Thai food at low prices. An excellent place to watch the world go by.

Japanese

🍴🍴🍴 **Akamon**, 468/19 Pattaya 2 Rd. Best-known Japanese restaurant in town.

🍴🍴🍴 **Yamato**, Pattaya Beach Soi 13. Sushi bar (฿100) and sukiyaki, sashimi and tempura, all excellent.

Chinese

🍴🍴🍴 **Empress**, Dusit Resort, large Chinese restaurant overlooking Pattaya Bay. Good dim sum lunches.

International

🍴🍴🍴 **Buccaneer**, Beach Rd. Seafood and steaks in rooftop restaurant above the Nipa Lodge.

🍴🍴🍴 **Dolf Riks**, Regent Marina Complex. Speciality Indonesian, some international, one of the original Pattaya restaurants.

🍴🍴🍴 **Green Bottle**, Pattaya 2 Rd. Ersatz English pub with exposed 'beams', grills, seafood.

🍴🍴🍴 **La Gritta**, Beach Rd. Some people maintain this restaurant serves the best Italian in town. Pizzas, pasta dishes and seafood specialities.

🍴🍴🍴 **Peppermill**, 16 Beach Rd, near Soi Post Office. First-class French food.

🍴🍴 **Dream Bakery**, 485/3 Pattaya 2 Rd. English breakfasts, Thai.

🍴🍴 **Italiano Espresso**, 325/1 Beach Rd, South Pattaya. Traditional Italian food, and some Thai dishes.

🍴 **Aussie Ken's Toast Shop**, 205/31 Pattaya 2 Rd. Fish and chips, sandwiches, cheap beer.

Seafood

The best seafood is on Jomtien Beach or at the southern end of Pattaya Beach.

🍴🍴🍴 **Lobster Pot**, 228 Beach Rd, South Pattaya. On a pier, known for very fresh seafood.

🍴🍴 **Nang Nual**, 214/10 Beach Rd, South Pattaya, on the waterfront. Recommended (there is another **Nang Nual** restaurant in Jomtien).

Bars and clubs

Pattaya *p375, maps p376 and p379*

The majority of Pattaya's bars are concentrated at the south end of the beach, between Beach Rd and Pattaya 2 Rd. They are mostly open-air and lined with stools. The men-only bars are around Pattayaland Soi 3, and the karaoke bars are along Pattaya 2 Rd.

Entertainment

Pattaya *p375, maps p376 and p379*

Pattaya comes to life as dusk approaches – it is a beach version of Bangkok's Patpong. Music blares out from the bars, discos and massage parlours which are concentrated in South Pattaya, referred to as 'The Strip'.

Cabaret

Mostly performed by members of Pattaya's legendary 'ka-toey' (transvestite) population, a night at the cabaret is essential. The biggest and best are **Alcazar** and **Tiffany's**, both found on the northern end of Pattaya 2 Rd. Shows at **Tiffany's** are daily at 1900, 2030 and 2200, T038-429642 for reservations – prices starts at ฿400. There's also a gun range in the basement at Tiffany's – from ฿200 – should you want to arm yourself after the show.

Traditional Thai dance

PIC Kitchen, Soi 5. Wed 1930, ฿100.

Ruen Thai, Pattaya 2 Rd, opposite Soi PO. Recommended. ฿120.

Shopping

Pattaya *p375, maps p376 and p379*

There are hundreds of stalls and shops on Pattaya 2 Rd selling jewellery, fashion, handicrafts, leather goods, silk, and a good selection of shopping plazas where most western goods can be purchased. In the evenings South Pattaya Rd is closed to traffic.

Activities and tours

Pattaya *p375, maps p376 and p379*
Prices, times and locations of sport activities in and around Pattaya are listed in the free magazines that are available all over the city. In addition to the watersports listed in more detail below, the following are on offer: badminton, bowling, bungee jumping, fishing, fitness, golf, go-karting, helicopter rides, jet skiing, motor racing, paintball, parasailing, horseback riding, sailing, shooting, snooker, speedboat hire, squash, swimming, tennis, waterskiing and windsurfing.

Diving and snorkelling
A lot of work has been done to revitalize Pattaya's diving – dynamite fishing has been outlawed and coral beds protected. Marine life, after years of degrading, is slowly returning to normal with stunning coral, seaturtles, rays and angelfish all making an appearance. There's even a couple of wrecks within easy reach and all this, along with the best dive schools in the country. This makes Pattaya an excellent place to learn to dive. There are more than 10 dive shops here. Recommended is the 5-star PADI resort **Seafari**, Soi 5, T038-429060, www.seafari.co.th. A PADI Open Water course costs ฿13,500, including all equipment, dives and boat fees. Certified divers can do a day's diving (all equipment, two dives, boat fees, lunch and soft drinks) to the nearby islands and wrecks for ฿3200. Other dive shops include **Mermaid's Dive School**, Soi Mermaid, Jomtien Beach, T038-232219 and **Dave's Divers Den**, Pattaya-Naklua Rd, T038-420411 (NAUI). **Aquanauts**, T038-361724, aquanautsdive.com, 437/17 Soi Yodsak. Snorkelling day trips to the offshore islands can be organized through the dive shops.

Game fishing
There are 4 or 5 game-fishing operators in Pattaya. Commonly caught fish include shark, king mackerel, garoupa and marlin. **Martin Henniker**, at Jenny's Hotel, Soi Pattayaland 1, is recommended. **The Fisherman's Club**, Soi Yodsak (Soi 6) takes groups of 4-10 anglers and offer 3 different packages (including an overnight trip). Angling equipment is available from Alan Ross at the **Pattaya Sports Supply shop**, opposite the Regent Marina Hotel (North Pattaya).

Tours and tour operators
There are countless tours organized by travel agents in town: the standard long-distance trips are to Koh Samet, the sapphire mines near Chantaburi, Ayutthaya, Bangkok, the floating market, Kanchanaburi and the River Kwai Bridge (2 days). Prices for day tours (meal included) range from ฿600-1,200.

Transport

Si Racha *p374*
Boat
Ferries for **Koh Si Chang** depart from the pier at the end Jermjomphon Rd, Soi 14 (see below, for details).

Bus
Connections every 30 mins or so with **Bangkok**'s Eastern bus terminal (2-3 hrs), as well as with **Pattaya**, 29 km south, 45 mins.

Train
While just about everyone arrives here by bus, there are a handful of trains each day from Hualamphong station in **Bangkok**. Cheap, slow but considerably more attractive than the bus journey (3 hrs 15 mins, around ฿100 1st class).

Koh Si Chang *p375*
Bicycle/motorbike
Sripitsanu Bungalows can organize mountain bike hire (฿50 per day), motorbikes (฿250 per day) and boat trips to nearby islands.

Boat
Regular daytime ferry service from Jermjomphon Rd, Soi 14 in **Si Racha**, every 2 hrs from 0700-1900 (40 mins, ฿30).

Saamlor
There are a number of massive motorized saamlors and, given the state of the roads, they must be among the most overpowered taxis in the world. A tour of all the sights should be no more than ฿200 – and in chariot-like splendour (the owner of No 38, Nerng, speaks reasonable English and distributes free maps).

Pattaya *p375, maps p376 and p379*

Air

There is an airport at U-Tapao, not far from Pattaya. This is gradually expanding and is now receiving some international scheduled arrivals. There are daily connections on Bangkok Airways with **Koh Samui**, 1 hr.

Airline offices Bangkok Airways, 75/8 Moo 9, Pattaya 2nd Rd, T038-412382. Kuwait Airways, 218 Beach Rd, T038-410493. Thai, T038-602192.

Bicycle/motorbike/jeep/car hire

Along Beach Rd (bargaining required), bicycles ฿100 per day or ฿20 per hr, jeeps ฿500-700 per day (jeeps are rarely insured), motorbikes from ฿150 per day. Avis at Dusit Resort (T038-425611) and the Royal Cliff Beach Resort (T038-250421).

Limousine service THAI operates a service from Don Muang airport. T038-423140 for bookings from Pattaya. A chauffeur-driven car from travel agencies in Bangkok should cost about ฿1,600.

Boat

Charter from along Beach Rd. ฿700-1500 per day (seats 12 people).

Bus

A/c buses stop at the a/c bus terminal on North Pattaya Rd, near to the intersection with the Sukhumvit Highway. Regular connections with **Bangkok**'s Eastern bus terminal, next to Ekamai Skytrain station. There are bus connections direct with Don Muang Airport. THAI runs a service from the airport to the Royal Cliff Beach Resort, ฿250 (pre-flight check-in available at Royal Cliff) and there is also a public bus leaving every 2 hrs, 0700-1700.

Non-a/c buses to **Bangkok** leave from the BKS stop in front of Wat Chai Mongkhon, near the intersection of Pattaya 2 and South Pattaya roads. The main terminal (non-a/c) for buses to other Eastern region destinations is in Jomtien, near the intersection of Beach and Chaiyapruk Rds. If staying in Pattaya City, it is possible to stand on the Sukhumvit Highway and wave down a bus. Tour buses to the north (**Chiang Mai**, **Mae Hong Son**, **Mae Sai**, **Phitsanulok**, etc) leave from the station on the Sukhumvit Highway, near the intersection with Central Pattaya Rd. Nearby, buses also leave for **Ubon** and **Nong Khai**.

Songthaew

Songthaews are in abundance along Beach Rd (for travelling south) and on Pattaya 2 Rd (for travelling north), ฿5 for short trips around Pattaya Bay (although it is not uncommon for visitors to be charged ฿10), ฿10 between Naklua and Pattaya Beach, ฿20 to Jomtien. To avoid being charged more than the standard fare, present the driver with the correct fare – do not try to negotiate the price, as the driver will expect you to hire the vehicle as a taxi.

Train

The station is off the Sukhumvit Highway, 200 m north of the intersection with Central Pattaya Rd. The Bangkok-Pattaya train leaves at 0700, and the Pattaya-Bangkok at 1330 (3½ hrs).

Rayong *p377*

Bus

Regular connections direct from **Bangkok**'s Eastern bus terminal and from **Pattaya** (1 hr). From Rayong to **Ban Phe** songthaews stop outside Tesco Lotus on Sukhumvit Rd, ฿20.

Directory

Si Racha *p374*

Banks Bangkok Bank of Commerce, Surasak Rd.

Koh Si Chang *p375*

Banks Thai Farmers, 9-9/1-2 Coast Rd.

Pattaya *p375, maps p376 and p379*

Banks There are countless exchange facilities both on the beach road and on the many sois running east-west, many stay open until 2200. **Internet** There are many around town. **Medical services** Pattaya International Clinic, Soi 4, Beach Rd, T038-428374. Pattaya Memorial Hospital, 328/1 Central Pattaya Rd, T038-429422, 24-hr service. Dr Olivier Clinic, 20/23 Moo 10, South Pattaya Rd (opposite the Day-Night Hotel), T038-72352. There are plenty of drug stores on South Pattaya Rd. **Useful numbers** Tourist police T038-429371 or T1699 for 24-hr service. Sea rescue T038-433752 are to be found on Beach Rd, next to the TAT office.

Rayong *p377*

Banks There are several ATMs and banks on Sukhumvit Rd.

Koh Samet

→ Colour map 3, grid C5.

Koh Samet, a 6-km-long, lozenge-shaped island, just a short boat trip from the mainland, comes as a relief after brash Pattaya. Rimmed by superb beaches, Koh Samet has national park status, small-scale bungalow resorts, good restaurants, snorkelling, swimming and a laid-back atmosphere (except at weekends). It is the closest tropical island idyll to Bangkok, just four hours away.

Until the early 1980s it was home to a small community of fishermen and was visited by a few intrepid travellers. The famous 19th-century Thai romantic poet Sunthorn Phu retired to this beautiful island and, suitably inspired, proceeded to write his finest work, the epic Phra Aphaimani. *The poem recounts the story of a prince, banished by his father to live with a sea-dwelling, broken-hearted giantess. Escaping to Koh Samet with the help of a mermaid, the prince kills the pursuing giant with his magic flute and marries the mermaid.* *▸▸ For Sleeping, Eating and other listings, see pages 385-389.*

Ins and outs

Getting there

Take a bus to Ban Phe, see page 385, about 3½ hours from Bangkok, and then one of the regular boats, another 40 minutes or so. All visitors pay an entrance fee (฿200 for adults, ฿100 for children). Many visitors land at the main Na Dan Pier in the northeast of the island (it is becoming commonplace for bungalow operators to run boats directly to their beaches from Ban Phe).

Getting around

It is possible to explore on foot. Songthaews travel between the main beaches and there are tracks negotiable by motorbike (฿300-400 a day). *▸▸ See also Transport, page 388.*

Best time to visit

Samet is a dry island (1,350 mm rain per year – Chantaburi 50 km away has rainfall of 3,164 mm per year) and a good place to pitch up during the rainy season. However, between May and October there can be strong winds and rough seas, while heavy rains can be a problem between July and September. During this period rates are cut and the island is less crowded. It is best to visit during the week; at weekends and public holidays it is popular with Thais and can be full with visitors camped out every square foot.

Background

It is unlikely Sunthorn Phu would find the necessary quiet today; over the past decade, Koh Samet has become very popular with young Thai holiday makers and foreign visitors.

In 1981 Samet became part of the Khao Laem Ya National Park (hence the admission fee). Authorities have ostensibly insisted that all accommodation remains limited to bungalows set back behind the tree line of the beach. This is difficult to reconcile with the scale and pattern of development that has occurred. The park authorities have threatened to shut the island down on the basis that every bungalow owner is breaking the law. Indeed, they have closed the island to tourists on a couple of occasions, only to reopen it after protests from bungalow owners, many of whom were making a living on the island prior to 1981 when it was declared a national park.

Rubbish created by tourism is becoming an environmental threat on the island. It seems that however hard the park authorities, the TAT and the environmentalist pressure groups try to protect Samet, they are fighting a losing battle; people continue to visit the island in their thousands and yet more bungalows are being built.

Towards Koh Samet

Ban Phe → *Colour map 3, grid C5.*

A further 25 km along the coast from Raylong is Ban Phe, once a small fishing village with a national reputation for its fish sauce and now a way station for visitors heading for Koh Samet. It has many food and handicraft stalls, but few people stay any longer than it takes to catch the boat. Around the village are a number of mediocre beaches lined with bungalows and resorts – **Hat Ban Phe, Hat Mae Ram Phung** (to the west), **Laem Mae Phim, Suan Son** and **Wang Kaew** (all to the east) which are largely used by Thai tourists.

The island

There has been a settlement on Koh Samet for many years; while it is now a fishing settlement-cum-tourist service centre, junks from China used to anchor here to be checked before the authorities would allow them to sail over the sandbar at the mouth of the Chao Phraya River and north to Bangkok.

Ao Klong is a stretch of sand that runs to the west of the Na Dan pier. Apart from watching the boats moving around the island there's little else to do here though there are a few 'floating' guesthouses/seafood restaurants built on wooden stilts in the bay.

Hat Sai Kaew (Diamond or White Sand Beach) is a 10-minute walk southeast from Na Dan Pier, and remains the most popular place to stay. This is still a beautiful spot, even if it has been disfigured by uncontrolled development. Bars, restaurants, and shops all vie for attention and during the evening sound systems blare out a continual cacophony of thumping beats. Despite the crowded, bustling atmosphere, the beach remains clean and it has a sandy bottom. Just south along the coast from Hat Sai Kaew is **Ao Hin Khok** where Koh Samet's one and only sight is to be found: a rather tatty statue depicting the tale of *Phra Aphaimani* (see page 384). A short distance further south still is **Ao Phai**, which is less developed and more peaceful.

About 2½ km from Ao Phai, past the smaller **Ao Tubtim, Ao Nuan** and **Ao Cho**, is **Ao Wong Duan**. This crescent-shaped bay has a number of more upmarket resort developments and a good range of facilities: water-skiing, diving, boat trips, and windsurfing. Continuing south from Ao Wong Duan is **Ao Thian, Ao Wai** and **Ao Kiu Na Nok**. These are the most peaceful locations on Koh Samet, and the island's finest coral is also found off the southern tip of the island. **Ao Phrao**, (Paradise Beach), 2 km from Sai Kaew, is the only beach to have been developed (so far) on the west side of the island. There is a dive shop here. Hire a fishing boat (or go on a tour), take a picnic, and explore the **Kuti** and **Thalu islands**.

Sleeping

Ban Phe *p385*

B Diamond Phe, 286/12 Ban Phe Rd, T038-615826. A/c, east of Ban Phe near the pier for Koh Samet, plain and rather kitsch but comfortable and convenient.

Koh Samet *p385, map p387*

Koh Samet mostly offers bungalow accommodation, although there is an increasing number of more sophisticated 'resorts' (at Wong Duan, Hat Sai Kaew and Ao Phrao). Running costs and prices are higher than in other Thai beach resorts, particularly in the high season when a very basic bungalow with attached bathroom may cost ฿450. At low season, particularly Aug-Sep, prices can be bargained down. Prices vary enormously between high and low season.

Ao Klong

A Ploy Samed, T038-644188, www.ploytalaygroup.com. Set on wooden stilts in the middle of the bay (ring the bell by the road and a winched dinghy is sent

over to pick you up) Ploy Samed offers a quiet and well-designed spot to rest your head. Rooms are a/c, with cable TV and balconies. The seafood restaurant is superb.

B Mook Samed T038-644165. Nearer to Na Dan, and similarly laid out to Samed – you have to cross a precarious tangle of planks to reach. Rooms with a/c, all en-suite and TV.

Hat Sai Kaew

If you like to be where the action is, then this is the place to head for. All bungalows have attached restaurants.

AL Sai Kaew Beach Resort. Wide range of neat bungalows, some facing onto the beach. It also has a set of beautiful, de luxe bungalows, set just over the headland in a tranquil spot. All a/c, cable TV.

C Lost Resort is a little further inland.

C Sinsamut, T038-616858, 24-hr electricity, minibus service, boat trips, laundry.

C-D Ploy Thalay, T01-3025223 (mob), 24-hr electricity, some a/c, restaurant, email, minibus, boat trips, PADI-standard diving courses.

D-E Guesthouse, T09-2012365 (mob), offers some of the cheapest rooms and food on the island.

Ao Hin Khok

C-D Jep's Bungalow and Restaurant, T01-8533121 (mob), www.jepbungalow.com. Good value rooms, the restaurant has a large range of tasty dishes.

D Naga, T01-3532575 (mob). English-run and friendly, offers home-baked cakes, bread and pastries. The only post office on Koh Samet is located here. Basic huts, some with fans, cheaper without, all have shared, if rather smelly, bathrooms. **Naga** competes with **Silver Sand** for the title of most popular nightspot on the island – both have dance floors and cut-price alcohol in the evening.

D Tok's Little Hut, T038-644072. Very popular, good value rooms, good restaurant and films in the evening.

Ao Phai

B-C Ao Phai Hut, T01-3532644 (mob). Some a/c, friendly, clean operation, wooden huts higher up behind the tree line, mosquitoes prevalent. This place has a library and organizes minibuses to Pattaya.

B-C Samet Villa, T038-644094, F644093. This clean and friendly Swiss-run establishment offers some of the best value accommodation on Samet, all rooms have fans and attached bathrooms and electricity is on round the clock. It organizes a number of trips and excursions to neighbouring islands and rents out snorkelling equipment. Recommended.

B-D Silver Sand, T01-9965720 (mob). Good value bungalows, popular restaurant (open 0930-2200) offering a wide range of dishes, large selection of recent videos, discos at the weekends.

C-D Sea Breeze, T038-644124, F038-644125. Bungalows (some with a/c) are fairly cheap but are located facing the back wall of the restaurant and are fairly grotty inside and out, restaurant also poorly located set back from the sea beside the path. On the plus side, the seafood is good and the staff friendly and helpful.

Ao Tubtim/Ao Phutsa

B-C Tubtim, T038-644025, tubtimresort@yahoo.com, more expensive huts have their own showers, some a/c. We have received reports of dirty rooms.

Ao Nuan

C Nuan, very peaceful and friendly, fan, shared bathroom. There are lots of mosquitoes since the huts are higher up behind the tree line, but nets are provided, the food is very good.

Ao Wong Duan

This beach is becoming a close second to Hat Sai Kaew in terms of action, though it is not as cramped. Several of the guesthouses run boats to Ban Phe.

AL-B Vongduern Villa, T038-652300, F651741. One of the more pricey resorts on the island. Restaurant has its tables on rocks just beside the sea (or even in the sea at very high tides).

A-B Malibu Garden Resort, T038-651057, samet@loxinfo.co.th. Offers a range of fairly solid and characterless bungalows, some with a/c. Friendly staff.

B Seahorse T01-3230049 (mob). Some a/c, friendly and popular with 2 restaurants and a travel agency but cheaper rooms in a longhouse aren't up to much.

B Vong Duern Resort, T038-651777, F651819. Offers slightly nicer bungalows in the same price range in an attractive setting behind the tree line, restaurant offers a vast range of Thai and western dishes to suit all budgets.

Koh Samet

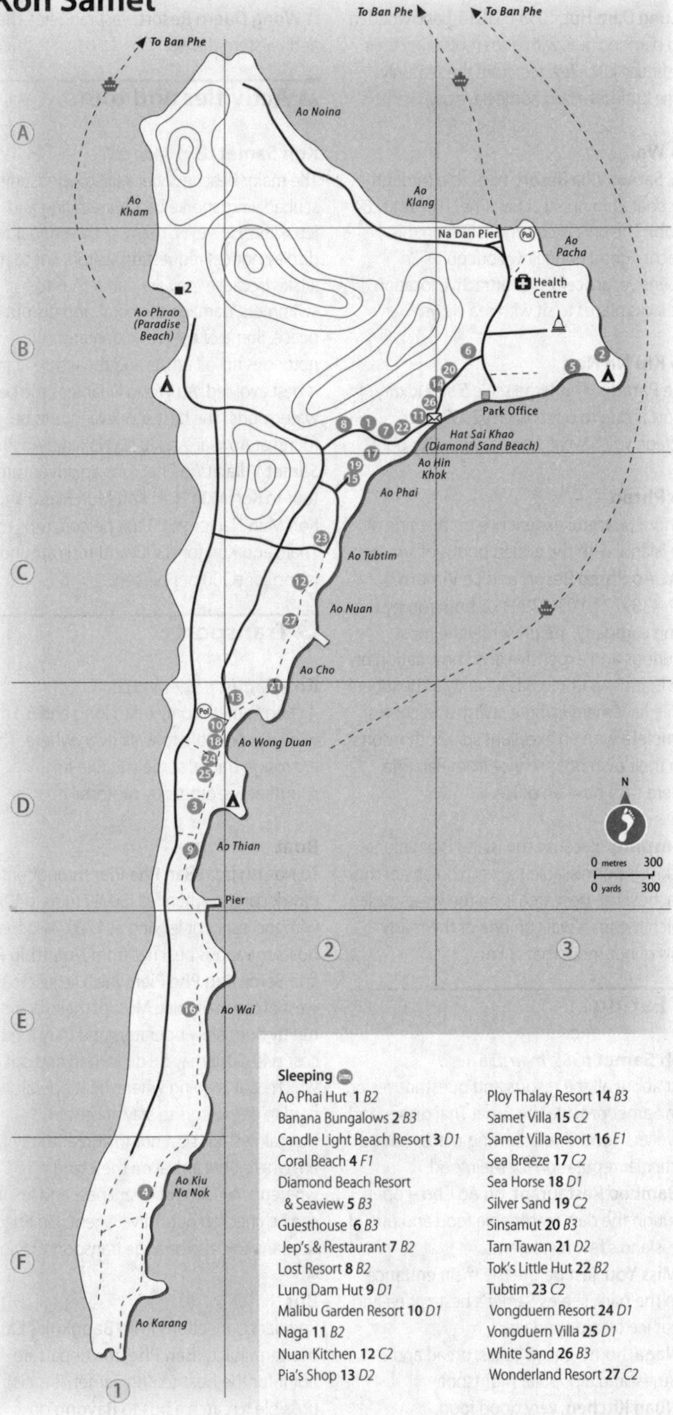

Sleeping

Ao Phai Hut 1 *B2*
Banana Bungalows 2 *B3*
Candle Light Beach Resort 3 *D1*
Coral Beach 4 *F1*
Diamond Beach Resort & Seaview 5 *B3*
Guesthouse 6 *B3*
Jep's & Restaurant 7 *B2*
Lost Resort 8 *B2*
Lung Dam Hut 9 *D1*
Malibu Garden Resort 10 *D1*
Naga 11 *B2*
Nuan Kitchen 12 *C2*
Pia's Shop 13 *D2*
Ploy Thalay Resort 14 *B3*
Samet Villa 15 *C2*
Samet Villa Resort 16 *E1*
Sea Breeze 17 *C2*
Sea Horse 18 *D1*
Silver Sand 19 *C2*
Sinsamut 20 *B3*
Tarn Tawan 21 *D2*
Tok's Little Hut 22 *B2*
Tubtim 23 *C2*
Vongduern Resort 24 *D1*
Vongduern Villa 25 *D1*
White Sand 26 *B3*
Wonderland Resort 27 *C2*

Ao Thian (Candlelight Beach)

D Lung Dam Hut, T038-651810. Basic wooden and bamboo huts with grass roofs or try their treehouse just a few feet from the sea, only some huts have fans, some have own bath.

Ao Wai

A-C Samet Villa Resort, bookable through the boat Phra Aphai at Ban Phe, T01-3211284 (mob). The only accommodation on this beach – good bungalows but quite expensive, peaceful and attractive location, but lacks places to sit with sea views.

Ao Kiu Na Nok

L Le Paradis. This large scale 5 star luxury resort is due to open in Oct 2005. Each cottage will have it's own swimming pool.

Ao Phrao

A more peaceful experience on this side of the island, with the added bonus of sunsets. **L-AL Ao Phrao Resort** and **Le Vimarn**, T02-4389771, F02-4390352, both run by the same company, are presently the most luxurious and expensive accommodation on the island. Ao Phrao has a family atmosphere while Le Vimarn is more stylish and comes complete with an excellent spa. Both resorts run their own boat service from Ban Phe, where they have an office.

Camping Because the island is a national park, it is permissable to camp on any of the beaches. The best area is on the west coast, which means a walk on one of the many trails of not more than 3 km.

Eating

Koh Samet *p385, map p387*

Just about all the resorts and guesthouses on Koh Samet provide the usual Thai dishes and travellers' food. The following places have a particular reputation for their food.

Bamboo Restaurant, on Ao Cho – open through the day, reasonable food and one of the island's few restaurants.

Miss You, just before the main entrance into the park, serves Samet's best coffee and great ice cream sundaes.

Naga, home-baked cakes, bread and pastries, and a popular nightspot.

Nuan Kitchen, very good food.

Sea Breeze, good seafood.

Wong Duern Resort, vast range of Thai and western dishes.

Activities and tours

Koh Samet *p385, map p387*

The major beaches offer sailing, windsurfing, scubadiving, snorkelling, waterskiing and jet-skiing. However, many of the bungalows display notices requesting visitors not to hire jetskis because they are dangerous to swimmers, damage the coral, and disrupt the peace. Some of the jet ski operators are notorious rip-off artists and the whole activity is best avoided. Ao Wong Duan has the best watersports. The best snorkelling is to be found at Ao Wai, Ao Kiu Na Nok and Ao Phrao. **Samet Villa** at Ao Phai runs an adventure tour to Koh Mun Nok, Koh Mun Klang and Koh Mun Nai for ฿500 per person, trips to Thalu and Kuti for ฿300, and trips around the island for ฿200 per person.

Transport

Koh Samet *p385, map p387*

As Koh Samet is only 6-km long and 3-km wide it is possible to walk everywhere. There are rough tracks, some suitable for songthaews, others by motorbike.

Boat

To Na Dan from **Ban Phe Pier** throughout the day departing when full (30-40 mins, ฿40), with the last boat leaving at 1700. Also many boats to various beaches from **Nuanthip Pier** and **Seree Ban Phe Pier** which lie just to the west of the main pier. Most of these boats are run by bungalow operators and they tend to cost ฿40-50. It may be difficult to find out which boat is going where; boat operators try hard to get visitors to stay at certain bungalows. It is best not to agree to stay anywhere until arrival on the island whereupon claims of cleanliness and luxury can be checked out. Travel agents on Khaosan Rd, Bangkok, also arrange transport to Samet.

Bus

Regular connections from **Bangkok**'s Eastern bus terminal to **Ban Phe**, the departure point for the boat to Koh Samet. It is also possible to catch a bus to **Rayong** or

Pattaya and then a connecting songthaew to **Ban Phe**. There is also a daily bus from Ban Phe to Koh Chang ฿250 with tickets on sale at several places on Samet.

Car
A private car from Bangkok to Ban Phe should cost around ฿1,600 and take 3 hrs.

Motorbike hire
Motorbikes can be hired all over the island – A300-400 per day.

Songthaew
These are the main form of public transport. Rates are fairly expensive – from Na Dan it costs ฿15 per person to Hat Sai Kaew, ฿20 to Ao Phai, ฿30 to Wong Duan or Ao Phrao, ฿40 to Ao Thian, and ฿50 to Ao Kiu Na Kok. It is also possible to charter songthaews; in fact, if a songthaew is not full the drivers may insist that the passengers make up the fares to a full load.

Directory

Ban Phe *p385*

Banks Krung Thai is a short distance west of the pier.

Koh Samet *p385, map p387*

Banks The island has no banks but a couple of ATMs near Hat Sai Kaew. So for the best rates, change money on the mainland. Many of the bungalows and travel agents do offer a money changing service but take a 5% fee. **Medical services** Koh Samet Health Centre, a small, public health unit, is situated on the road south from Na Dan to Hat Sai Kaew. **Post office** Situated inside **Naga Bungalows** at Hin Khok between Hat Sai Kaew and Ao Phai (Poste Restante). Mon-Fri 0830-1500, Sat 0830-1200. **Telephone and internet** Many places offer international calls for about ฿30 per min while internet charges should be ฿2 per min – the **Miss You** coffee shop by the National Park office at Hat Sai Kaew has new machines and a fast connection.

Chantaburi to Koh Chang

Head east from Koh Samet and you'll soon reach Chantaburi, famed for its trade in precious stones. Unless you fancy your chances on picking up a bargain in the gemstone market – most farang fair badly against the hard-nosed sapphire and ruby traders – travel down the coast to Trat and the increasingly popular island of Koh Chang. This is Thailand's second largest island and is part of a national marine park which includes 50-odd islands and islets covering 650 sq km. Despite the 'protection' that its national park status should offer, Koh Chang is developing rapidly, with resorts and bungalows springing up along its shores. It is Thailand's last tropical island idyll – at least of any size – to be developed and it supports excellent beaches, sea, coral and diving. There are treks, waterfalls, rivers and pools, villages, mangroves, three peaks of over 700 m, and a rich variety of wildlife.

The healing waters of Nam Tok Kratang waterfall are 30 km northwest of town. The border market at Aranya Prathet is the chief attraction here. *» For Sleeping, Eating and other listings, see pages 396-402.*

Chantaburi and around → *Colour map 3, grid C6.*

Chantaburi is not a popular destination for international visitors to Thailand; most pass it by en route to Trat and the island of Koh Chang. But it deserves more attention, if only because it is an unusual town with its large population of ethnic Vietnamese, a strong Catholic presence, well-preserved traditional shophouses, excellent restaurants, and some of the finest durian in Thailand. Chantaburi has built its wealth on rubies and sapphires with many of the gem mines being developed during the 19th century by Shan people from Burma, who are thought to be among the best miners in the world.

Sights

Muang Chan – as it is locally known – has a large Chinese and Vietnamese population, lending the town an atmospheric run of narrower streets, shuttered wooden shophouses, Chinese temples and an air of industriousness. This atmosphere is most palpable along Rim Nam or Sukhaphiban Road. The French-style **Catholic Cathedral** of the Immaculate Conception was built in 1880 and is the largest church in Thailand. Architecturally uninspiring, it is significant for its presence. The cathedral was built to serve the many Vietnamese Catholics who fled their homeland and settled here. The Vietnamese part of town is north of the cathedral, on the opposite side of the river.

Apart from gems, Chantaburi is also highly regarded as a source of some of the best durians in Thailand, which flourish in the lush climate. The finest cost several hundred baht (more than a week's wages for an agricultural labourer), a fact which can seem astonishing to visitors who regard the fruit as repulsive.

Nam Tok Krating

ⓘ *Regular public songthaews run past the entrance to the park on Route 3249; from here it is a 15-min walk to the park headquarters. There is accommodation available in the park, see Sleeping.*

The waterfall of Nam Tok Krating can be found within the **Kitchakut National Park** (along with a few caves), and is about 30 km northwest of town. The water is believed

Chantaburi

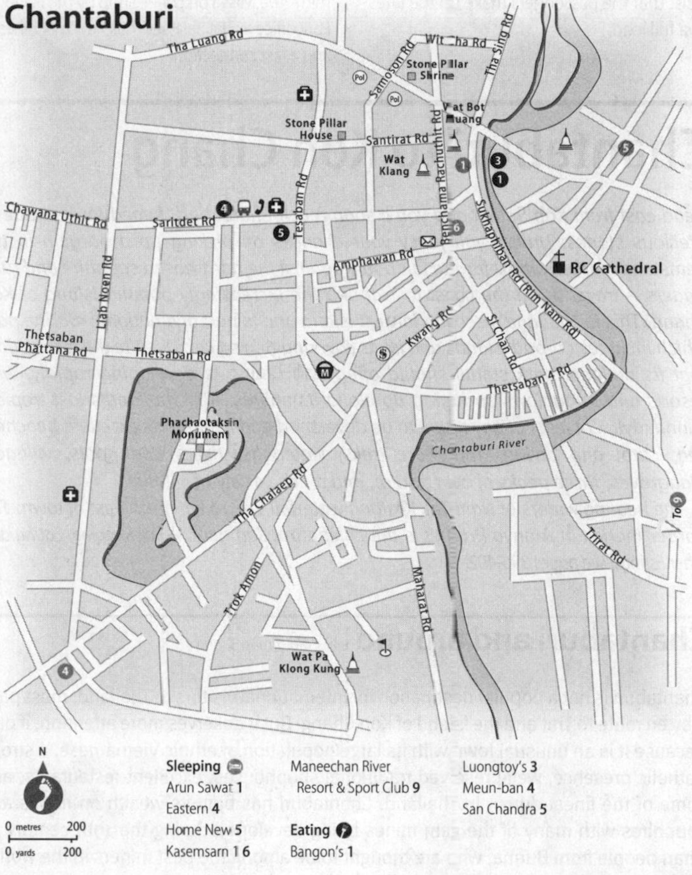

Tha Luang Rd
Wit Cha Rd
Tha Sing Rd
Samoson Rd
Stone Pillar Shrine
Wat Bot Muang
Stone Pillar House
Santirat Rd
Wat Klang
Benchama Rachuthit Rd
Chawana Uthit Rd
Saritdet Rd
Tesaban Rd
Amphawan Rd
Sukhaphiban Rd (Rim Nam Rd)
RC Cathedral
Llab Noen Rd
Thetsaban Phattana Rd
Thetsaban Rd
Kwang Rd
St Chan Rd
Thetsaban 4 Rd
Phachaotaksin Monument
Chantaburi River
Tha Chalaep Rd
To 9
Trirat Rd
Trok Amon
Maharat Rd
Wat Pa Klong Kung
N
0 metres 200
0 yards 200
Sleeping
Arun Sawat 1
Eastern 4
Home New 5
Kasemsarn 1 6
Maneechan River Resort & Sport Club 9
Luongtoy's 3
Meun-ban 4
San Chandra 5
Eating
Bangon's 1

Tears of the gods: rubies and sapphires

Major deposits of two of the world's most precious stones are found distributed right across mainland Southeast Asia: rubies and sapphires. They are mined in Thailand, Burma, Vietnam, Cambodia and Laos. The finest of all come from Burma, and especially from the renowned Mogok Stone Tract, which supports a town of 100,000 almost entirely upon the proceeds of the gem industry. Here, peerless examples are unearthed, including the rare 'pigeon's blood' ruby. One Thai trader was reported to say that "Asking to see the pigeon's blood is like asking to see the face of God".

Although the Burmese government tries to keep a tight grip on the industry, many of the gems pass into the hands of Thai gem dealers, often with the connivance of the Thai army. Corruption, violence, murder, arson and blackmail are all part and parcel of the trade. Through fair means and foul, Bangkok has become the centre of the world's gem business and Thailand is the largest exporter of cut stones – indeed, it has a virtual monopoly of the sapphire trade. Those who try to buck the system and bypass Bangkok risk having a contract taken out on their lives.

Rubies and sapphires are different colours of corundum, the crystalline form of aluminium oxide. Small quantities of various trace elements give the gems their colour; in the case of rubies, chromium and for blue sapphires, titanium. Sapphires are also found in a spectrum of other colours including green and yellow. Rubies are among the rarest of gems, and command prices four times higher than equivalent sized diamonds. The Burmese call the ruby ma naw ma ya or 'desire-fulfilling stones'.

The colour of sapphires can be changed through heat treatment (the most advanced form is called diffusion treatment) to 1,500-1,600°C (sapphires melt at 2,050°C). For example, relatively valueless colourless geuda sapphires from Sri Lanka, turn a brilliant blue or yellow after heating. The technique is an ancient one: Pliny the Elder described the heating of agate by Romans nearly 2,000 years ago, while the Arabs had developed heat treatment into almost a science by the 13th century. Today, almost all sapphires and rubies are heat treated. The most valued colour for sapphires is cornflower blue – dark, almost black, sapphires command a lower price. The value of a stone is based on the four 'C's: Colour, Clarity, Cut and Carat (1 carat = 200 milligrammes). Note that almost all stones are heat treated to improve their colour. For more on buying gems in Thailand, see page 145.

to have healing powers. The park is one of the smallest in the country, covering under 60 sq km, and was established in 1977. The falls are within hiking distance of the park headquarters. It is also possible to walk to the summit of the Phrabat Mountain, so-called because there is an impression of a footprint of the Buddha. Allow four hours to reach the top.

Aranya Prathet and the Cambodian border

ⓘ The border is open daily 0700-1800. Visas for can be obtained here (US$20 or ฿1000, 1 photo). Sometimes tourists are asked for an International Vaccination Certificate; this is a means by which local immigration officers boost their income (if you don't have one they demand US$5). The certificate is not required and most people who insist seem to get through. A moto to the border (7 km from town) should cost around ฿40-50; there is also a public truck to the border for ฿5 (10 mins). See also Transport.

A little bit more than a day trip is Aranya Prathet which has gained some measure of notoriety because of its location close to the border with Cambodia and its growing use as an alternative route to Siem Reap. The journey to Siem Reap takes around six hours by truck – a bone-jarring experience – sometimes much longer in the wet season. It is best to cross the border early so that you do not have to stay overnight in the cross-border town of Poipet. There have been reports of bandit attacks on trucks. The highlight of Aranyaprathet itself is the **Talat Rong Klua** (border market) ⓘ *around 7 km from town – a moto costs around ฿40-50*, a melee of frantic activity selling textiles, shoes, leather goods, handicrafts, fish, wickerwork, electronics, sunglasses, wild animals and agricultural products.

Trat and Khlong Yai

Trat is the provincial capital and the closest Thai town of any size to Cambodia. Like Chantaburi, Trat is a gem centre and with peace in Cambodia it has flourished as a centre of cross-border commerce. Most people visit Trat en route to beautiful Koh Chang, not staying any longer than they need to catch a bus or boat out of the place. Tourist offices are found on Soi Sukhumvit, not far from the market; helpful and informative.

If you do decide to stay longer in Trat you'll have the chance to sample the diverse selection of excellent guesthouses. There's also a bustling **covered market** on Sukhumvit Road offering a good selection of food and drink stalls. On the same road, north of the shopping mall, there is a busy **night market**. **Wat Buppharam**, also known as **Wat Plai Klong**, dates from the late Ayutthaya period. It is notable for its wooden viharn and monk's kutis, and is 2 km west of town, down the road opposite the shopping mall.

Khlong Yai ⓘ *take a songthaew from the back of the municipal market, ฿25 or shared taxi from the front of the market, ฿35 each*, is the southernmost town on this eastern arm of Thailand and an important fishing port. The journey there is worthwhile for the dramatic scenery with the mountains of Cambodia rising to the east and the sea to the west. Khlong Yai is also a pretty and bustling little port, well worth the trip. There are several Cambodian markets and the seafood is excellent.

Laem Ngop → *Colour map 3, grid C6.*

ⓘ *The TAT office is at 100 Mu 1 Trat, Laem Ngop Rd, T039-597255, Mon-Fri 0830-1630.*

This sleepy fishing village – in fact the district capital – has a long pier lined with boats, along with good seafood and

Trat

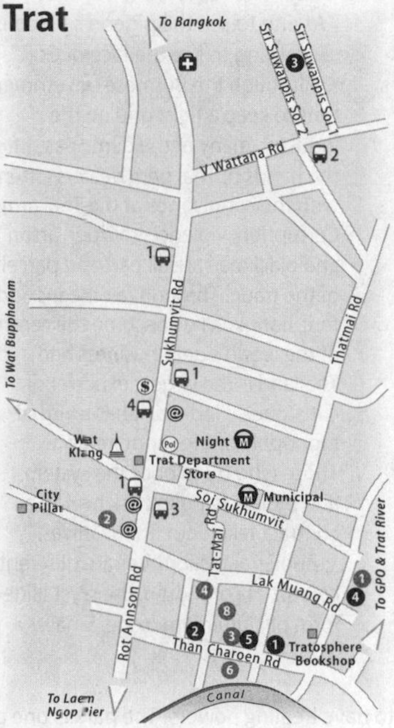
To Bangkok
Sri Suwanpis Soi 1
Sri Suwanpis Soi 2
V Wattana Rd
Sukhumvit Rd
Thatmai Rd
To Wat Buppharam
Wat Klang
Night
Trat Department Store
City Pillar
Municipal
Soi Sukhumvit
Tat-Mai Rd
Lak Muang Rd
To GPO & Trat River
Rot Annson Rd
Than Charoen Rd
Tratosphere Bookshop
Canal
To Laem Ngop Pier

N

0 metres 100

0 yards 100

Sleeping
Ban Jai Dee 1
Foremost Guesthouse 3
Friendly Guesthouse 4
Guy Guesthouse 6
NP Guesthouse 8

Eating
Cool Corner 2
Isaan 4
Joys 5
Krua Rim Klong 1
Nam Chok 3

Transport
A/c buses to Bangkok 1
Non a/c Bus Station 2
Minibus & taxis to Laem Ngop 3
Buses to Chantaburi 4

a relaxed atmosphere. As Koh Chang becomes Thailand's next island beach resort to hit the big time, expect things to get busier – at present there's a handful of guesthouses and a few waterside restaurants.

Koh Chang National Park

→ *Colour map 3, grid C6. www.ko-chang.info/index.htm.*

As you set sail from the mainland across the glittering seas, Koh Chang (Elephant Island), covered in thick, verdant forest and with a vivid, sweeping skyline, rises up to meet you. This 40-km-long and 16-km wide island is Thailand's second biggest (after Phuket) and the teeming wildlife, rustic appeal and wonderful beaches have long attracted the more adventurous traveller.

Things are changing. Koh Chang has now been earmarked as Thailand's next big destination. Hotel chains and tour operators are moving in and the beaches are now almost entirely colonized by Thai and European package tourists.

The island also forms the fulcrum of the Koh Chang National Park – an archipelago of dozens of smaller islands that stretch to the south. Many of these are also being taken over by mass tourism/backpackers and the recently pristine

Koh Chang

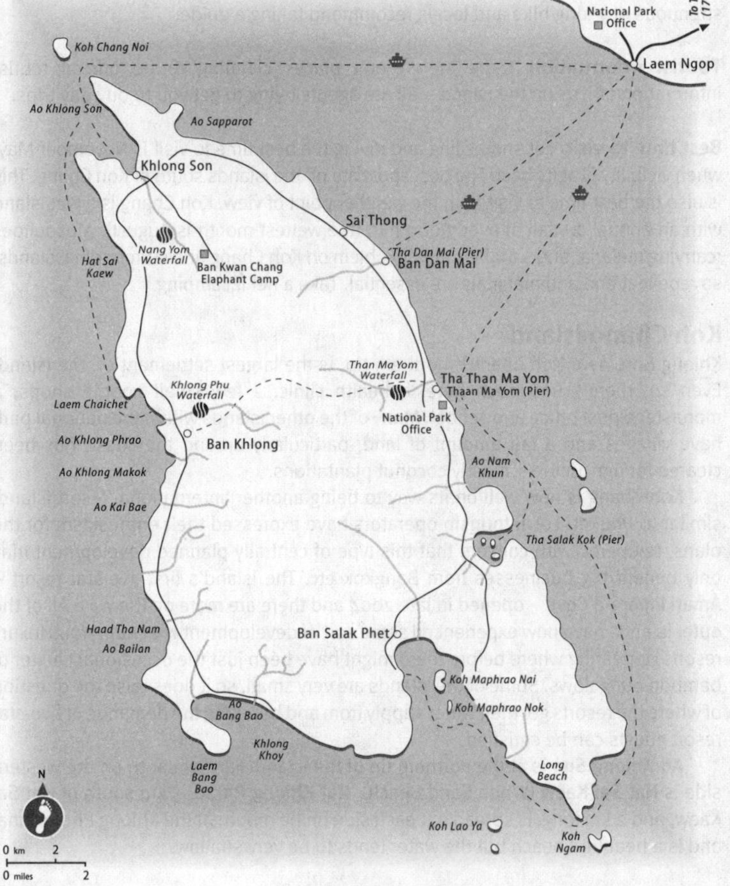

 environment is suffering – at the end of 2004 the Thai Navy cleared developers off one or two of the outlying islands. ▸▸ *For Sleeping, Eating and other listings, see pages 396-402.*

Ins and outs

Getting there With regular flights to nearby Trat (see above) getting to Koh Chang is getting easier. From Bangkok catch a bus from the Eastern bus terminal to Trat or fly (see page 401); from Trat, there are regular songthaews to Laem Ngop. During the high season (November-May) boats leave every hour or so from Laem Ngop for Koh Chang. But during the low season departures are much more intermittent. ▸▸ *See Transport, page 401 for further information.*

Getting around Koh Chang's best beaches are on the western side of the island – Hat Sai Kaew (White Sand), Hat Khlong Phrao and, on the southern coast, Hat Bang Bao. These can be reached either by jeep taxi from Ao Sapparot (price ranging from ฿20-40, depending upon destination, if you manage to fill up the taxi) or by boat from Laem Ngop. There is a paved road up the east coast and down the west coast as far south as Bang Bao. (If you need to travel later in the day there are lots of pick-up trucks that you can catch a lift with. However, it is still not possible to travel between Bang Boa and Salak Phet. In addition to songthaews there are also motorbikes (around ฿200 per day) and mountain bikes for hire. For walkers, there is a path crossing the middle of the island from Ban Khlong Phrao to Than Ma Yom but it is a strenuous day-long hike and locals recommend taking a guide.

Tourist information There are several places claiming to be official tourist information offices on the island – all are agents trying to get you to buy day trips.

Best time to visit For snorkelling and diving the best time to visit is November-May, when visibility is at its best. The best spots are off the islands south of Koh Chang. This is also the best time to visit from the weather point of view. Koh Chang is a wet island with an annual rainfall of over 3,000 mm (the wettest month is August). Mosquitoes (carrying malaria) and sandflies are a problem on Koh Chang and surrounding islands, so repellent and anti-malarials are essential. Take a net if camping.

Koh Chang Island

Khlong Son, near Koh Chang's northern tip, is the largest settlement on the island. Even so, there's not much here: a health clinic, a few small noodle shops, a monastery, post office and school. Many of the other islands within the national park have villages and a fair amount of land, particularly around the coast, has been cleared for agriculture – mostly coconut plantations.

Koh Chang is now well on its way to being another 'international resort island' similar to Phuket. Local tourism operators have expressed their enthusiasm for the plans, tempered with concern that this type of centrally planned development may only benefit big businesses from Bangkok etc. The island's first five-star resort – **Amari Emerald Cove** – opened in late 2004 and there are more on the way. All of the outer islands have now experienced some sort of development with numerous luxury resorts appearing where before there might have been just the occasional cluster of bamboo bungalows. Some of the islands are very small, so it does raise the question of where the resorts get their water supply from and how long the demands of five-star resort guests can be satisfied.

Ao Khlong Son is at the northern tip of the island. Further south on the western side is **Hat Sai Kaew** (White Sand Beach). **Hat Khlong Phrao**, 5 km south of Hat Sai Kaew, and 2 km long, is spread out each side of the mouth of the Khlong Phrao canal and is a beautiful beach but the water tends to be very shallow.

At **Ao Khlong Makok** there is almost no beach at high tide and just a couple of bungalow operations which are virtually deserted in the low season, see Sleeping. **Ao Kai Bae** is the southernmost beach on the west coast. It is beautiful but swimming is tricky as the water is very shallow and covered with rocks with dead coral in places.

Haad Tha Nam (Lonely beach) is an attractive stretch of coastline and much more quiet and relaxed than the more accessible northern stretches. Most of the well-run, cheap operations have been pushed out to be replaced with awful bungalows or generic resorts – it is best to pass this beach by.

Ao Bang Bao and Ao Bai Bin is a lovely beach on the south coast of the island. The bay dries out at low tide and it is virtually inaccessible in the low season when the accommodation tends to shut down.

Although there is a scattering of bungalow operations on the east coast, very few people choose to stay here even in the high season. The only beach is at **Sai Thong.**

Than Ma Yom Waterfall ⓘ *accessible from either Ban Dan Mai or Thaan Ma Yom, both on the east coast and getting to the first of the cascades involves a walk of around 1 hr; it is around 4 km to the furthest of the three falls*, is on the east side of the island. King Chulalongkorn (Rama V) visited this waterfall on no less than six occasions at the end of the 19th century, so even given the Thai predilection for waterfalls of any size, it counts as an impressive one (in fact there are three falls). To prove the point, the king carved his initials (or had them carved), on a stone to mark one of his visits. Rama VI and VII also visited the falls, although it seems that they didn't get quite so far – they left their initials inscribed on stones at the nearest of the falls.

Khlong Phu Falls ⓘ *taxi or motorbike in 10 mins from Hat Sai Kaew; you can also travel to it from the road by elephant for ฿200 or for free by walking just 3 km*, at Ao Khlong Phrao, are perhaps even more beautiful than Than Ma Yom waterfall. There is a good pool here for swimming as well as a restaurant and some bungalows. Because this is a national park it is also possible to camp.

Koh Chang's forest is one of the most species-rich in the country and while the island's coast may be undergoing development the rugged, mountainous interior is still largely inaccessible and covered with virgin rainforest (around 70% is said to be forested). There is a good population of birds, including **parrots**, **sunbirds**, **hornbills** and **trogons**, as well as Koh Chang's well-known population of **wild boar**, although the chances of seeing any are slim. It is advisable, however, to take a guide for exploring – Jungle Way bungalows (see page 397) organizes guided hikes for ฿450 including lunch.

Around Koh Chang Island

While the waters around Koh Chang are clear there have been some reports of a deterioration in water quality connected with coastal gem mining on the mainland. Nonetheless, hard and especially soft corals are abundant. Fish are less numerous and varied than on the other side of the Gulf of Thailand or in the Andaman Sea. During the wet season visibility is very poor, due to high seas, which also makes diving dangerous. The months between November and March are best for diving. Generally, diving is better in the waters to the south of the island. Notable are the wrecks of two Thai warships, the *Thonburi* and *Chonburi*, sunk here in an engagement with seven French ships and the loss of 36 lives on 17 January 1941. One Thai ship escaped unharmed, the *Songkhla*. A memorial tablet (in Thai) has been erected on the beach and the wrecks and marked with buoys off the southeasternmost point of Koh Chang. The raised coral reefs seen around parts of the island extends out into the sea, where soft and hard corals, including massive, columnar and stags' horn varieties can be seen. The best diving is between 5 and 25 m where blue tipped rays, moray eels, trigger fish, grouper and batfish can be seen. There is a fantastic vertical dive but even more adventourous dive sites are found off Koh Man Nok and Hun Sarn Soa. If you are lucky it is possible to spot turtles and whale sharks.

Koh Chang is not the best place for snorkelling; the best places are at the surrounding islands.

Islands off Koh Chang

Koh Kut ⓘ *two, sometimes more, boats per week leave from the pier on the Trat River in Trat (not Laem Ngop) for Koh Kut (1 hr); during the high season (Nov-May) they leave on Mon at 1100 and Fri at 1400; day visitors from Koh Mak (see below) can make the trip on regular boats linking the two islands*, is the next largest island after Koh Chang itself is Koh Kut. This island has lovely beaches, especially on the west side, and a number of small fishing villages linked by dirt roads. There is an impressive waterfall and the coral is also said to be good. However, mosquitoes are a problem. Koh Kut is not part of the national park and so there are almost no controls on development; the forest is being encroached upon by agriculture and developers are claiming the best pieces of shoreline.

Koh Mak ⓘ *Boats leave daily from Laem Ngop for Koh Mak during the high season (Nov-May); departures may be suspended during the low season*, is the third largest island in the archipelago after Koh Chang and Koh Kut. It is privately owned by a few wealthy local families and a little over half of the island has been cleared for coconut plantations. But there is still a reasonable area of forest and the coral is also good. The best beach is on the northwest shore. It is said that many of the prime pieces of shorefront have been sold to Bangkok-based developers, so it remains to be seen what happens to Koh Mak.

Koh Kham ⓘ *boats leave from Laem Ngop (3½ hrs, Α150); Koh Kham resort offers a boat service from Laem Ngop Pier to Koh Kham, departs at 1500 and arrives at 1800*, a tiny island, is well known for its swallows, nests and turtle eggs, as well as good coral and rock formations for divers.

Koh Ngam ⓘ *2 hrs from Laem Ngop by boat*, is a very small island with lush vegetation and beautiful beaches. It has two upmarket resorts. See Sleeping.

Koh Whai ⓘ *daily ferry from Laem Ngop once a day at 0800 returning at 1500 (Α130)*. Koh Whai has two resorts but these are better value than those at Koh Ngam.

Many of the more sophisticated bungalow operations on Koh Chang organize day trips to **Koh Lao Ya, Koh Phrao, Koh Khlum, Koh Kra Dad** and **Koh Rayang Nok** during the high season (when the seas are calmer, the visibility greater and there is generally more demand). In the low season few boats go between these islands and either Koh Chang or the mainland and most of the accommodation closes down. Koh Kra Dad has exceptionally beautiful beaches and lush vegetation.

Sleeping

Chantaburi *p389, map p390*

AL-A Maneechan River Resort and Sport Club, 110 Moo 11 Plubpla Rd, T039-343777, www.maneechanresort.com. Usual high quality hotel with a good range of amenities including mod cons and sports facilities.

B-C Eastern, 899 Tha Chalaep Rd, T039-312218. Pool, all rooms have a/c, TV and bath tub. Larger rooms have fridges and are almost twice the price, smaller rooms are good value.

D Home New, 99/19-26 Chanthanimit Rd, T039-354557. Pleasant and friendly with good attached restaurant, but inconveniently situated some distance from the town centre.

D Kasemsarn 1, 98/1 Benchama Rachuthit Rd, T039-312340. Some a/c, large, clean rooms in big hotel, well run, but some rooms can be noisy.

E Arun Sawat, 239 Sukha Phibal Rd, T039-311082. Situated in the most attractive part of town, though rooms are dark and small.

Nam Tok Krating *p390*

B-C Accommodation near park headquarters, T02-5790529/5794842 (Bangkok).

Aranya Prathet *p391*

B Mermaid Hotel, 33 Tanavitee Rd, T039-223655. Some a/c. Close to the bus and train stations in the northwest part of town. Comfortable with clean rooms.

D Thupthongkum Hotel, T039-231550. The best place to stay in this price bracket, clean rooms. Just over 1 km from the bus station; turn left on exiting the bus station.

Trat *p392, map p392*

C-E Foremost Guesthouse, 49 Thoncharoen Rd, by the canal, last turn on the left off Sukhumvit Rd, towards Laem Ngop, T039-511923. First-floor rooms, shared bathrooms, hot water, clean and friendly with lots of local information. Recommended.

D-F Guy Guesthouse, Than Charoen Rd. Range of rooms from very basic through to en suite with TV and a/c. Recommended.

E Ban Jai Dee, Chaimongkon Rd. The best of the bunch, very friendly English-speaking owners. Rooms have fan, shared bathrooms.

E Friendly Guesthouse, Lak Muang Rd. A small, family-run place, that lives up to its name. The owners also run the nearby and excellent **Tratosphere bookshop**, 23 Rimklong Soi – the French owner keeps up to date traveller reviews of all accommodation on Koh Chang, Koh Kut and Koh Mak. Anybody wanting to spend some time on these islands would be advised to visit here first. Basic fan rooms, breakfast available.

E NP Guesthouse, 1-3 Soi Luang Aet, Lak Muang Rd, T039-512564. Clean, friendly, well-run, converted shophouse, with a bright little restaurant, shared bathroom, hot showers, dorm beds, internet facilities. Recommended.

Laem Ngop *p392*

There are a number of guesthouses on the main road into the village.

D-E Laem Ngop Inn, T039-597044. Some a/c.

D-E Paradise Inn, T039-512831. Some a/c.

E PI, clean rooms, only open high season.

F Chut Kaew, good source of information.

Koh Chang *p393, map p393*

There are many thefts on Koh Chang. If you're staying in a basic bamboo hut be sure not to leave valuables in it when you are not, or near open windows when you are asleep. Rapid development means the accommodation below may date very quickly. The best source of information is at the **Tratosphere bookshop** in Trat. Almost all the budget accommodation consists of simple wood slat bungalows. Some of the accommodation closes during the low season so check before you travel.

As Koh Chang's popularity increases prices are rising and particularly during the very busy months (Dec and Jan).

Ao Khlong Son

Few budget travellers choose to stay here anymore but head instead for the beaches on the west or south coasts. There is a new luxury and very expensive development:

L Aiya Pura Resort & Spa, www.koh-chang.com/Aiyapura/index.htm#accom. Huge villas built into the hillside and nicely shaded with trees. Good views. The villas are well furnished but not particularly elegant. Pool and all the other facilities you'd expect for the price.

B-D Premvadee, some single rooms, and some larger bungalows with bathrooms.

E Jungle Way, about 2 km from the coastal road into the interior – there's a big sign in Khlong Son pointing the way. Simple bungalows in cute jungle location, next to bubbling stream. Run by an Englishwoman and her Thai husband. Closed Jun-Sep.

Hat Sai Kaew (White Sand Beach)

The most developed stretch on the island with lots of mid-range resorts, shops, bars and burgeoning sex tourism. There are about 40 different places to stay on this stretch of beach.

AL-B Banpu Koh Chang Hotel, T01-8637314 (mob), T039-542355, www.koh-chang.com/banpuhotel/index.htm. Large a/c but not particularly stylish bungalows, swimming pool, restaurant.

A Lagoon Resort, T01-8631530 (mob), T02-9530432, F02-9530433. Newly built seafront resort with restaurant, bar, internet. Hotel rooms and luxury bungalows. All are en suite with a/c. This is a very comfortable resort and has a fantastic seafood beach barbecue.

A-B Grand View, T01-8637802 (mob). Quite a large resort with 50 rooms, some a/c and all with en suite facilities. Set a little way down the beach in a more peaceful location than most other resorts.

A-C Cookie, efficiently run bungalows all with shower/WC in 3 rows at varying prices. Popular and cheap with long-stay discount, restaurant/bar attached serving a selection of coffees. Hotel building on main road.

A-C KC Bungalow, clean huts arranged along the seafront in a very good location, quiet but not too secluded. Friendly restaurant and staff. Recommended.

A-C Plaloma Cliff Resort, www.koh-chang.com/plalomacliffresort/index.htm, T01-8631305 (mob). German-Swiss-run

operation on the southern tip of the bay, some bungalows with a view over the sea. No beach here, but the restaurant is very good, small library.

B-C Palm Garden Hotel, T09-9398971 (mob). A newly built and very friendly place. Set back from the road, lovely rooms with a/c, fridge and satellite TV. Excellent food. Recommended.

B-D White Sand Beach Resort, T01-6837737 (mob), ko_changtour@hotmail.com. Out of the way up at the northern end of the beach, very quiet cliffside location with friendly staff. No a/c, shared and en suite rooms. Great views from the restaurant/bar.

B-E 15 Palms, very popular bamboo hut resort with some en suite rooms, great restaurant. Recommended.

C Apple Bungalow, T01-8633398 (mob), slightly smarter huts than other places in this price category.

C Mac Bungalow, a very popular centrally located resort with some hotel rooms available in addition to the bungalows, the latter are very well priced. Some a/c and all en suite. The restaurant is probably the best on the beach and has fantastic barbecues and breakfasts. Highly recommended.

C Rock Sand/Independent Bungalow, T01-8637611 (mob). A great design with huts hidden away in the cliff like a cliff treehouse! Some a/c and en suite. Friendly management with great plans for future developments.

Hat Khlong Phrao

L Amari Emerald Cove, T039-552000, T02-2552588 (central reservations), www.amari.com. The island's first 5-star resort has wonderful rooms, great restaurants (the best veggie selection on the island) and all the amenities you'd expect. The layout, though, is very dull – a uniform arc of hotel rooms facing onto the pool.

A Boutique Resort and Spa, T09-9386404 (mob), boutique_resort@hotmail.com. Brilliant pixie-like huts with beautiful interiors. A health spa is attached where you you can fine-tune your yoga positions.

A Koh Chang Resort, T039-538054-9. A/c, expensive and not particularly spacious bungalows with bamboo interiors but clunky furniture. The garden setting houses a pool and spa and is quite pleasant with shading coconut palms.

A Royal Coconut Resort, T01-7817078 (mob). Newly built hotel with a/c, friendly staff and fantastic views down the beach, lovely individual floating dining areas.

B-D Chai-chet Bungalow, T01-29911129 (mob), www.koh-chang.com/chaichet bungalows/index.htm. Bungalows set in an attractive garden at the top end of the bay, 1½-km walk to the beach.

B-D Magic Resort, 34 Moo 4, T01-8019675 (mob), www.koh-chang.com/magicresort/ index.htm. Some a/c. Mostly fairly simple bungalows in a garden setting. Well spaced but expensive at the top end for the facilities on offer. Better value are the fan bungalows.

C-E Coconut Beach Bungalow, 17/2 Moo 4, www.koh-chang.com/coconutbeachbungalows. Wooden huts with shared bath, well built, mosquito nets provided, set above the beach. Rather unfriendly management.

E Hobby Hut, quite far back from the beach, attractive wooden bungalows and restaurant in pleasant setting in wood on bank of canal.

Ao Khlong Makok

D-F Chok Dee and **Mejic** both offer huts with attached and shared bathrooms and have restaurants attractively located on stilts above the sea.

Ao Kai Bae

L-A Sea View Resort, T039-597143, T01-8307529 (mob). Very comfortable bungalows set on a steep hill in a landscaped garden, very good value for the quality (particularly in the low season when prices tend to halve), there are also a number of cheap basic huts right on the beach.

AL Koh Chang Cliff Beach, T039-6920122, www.kohchangcliffbeach.com. Strangely designed resort resembling a caravan park. A wide range of rooms are available, pleasant grounds and attractive pool, although still overpriced.

B-C Kai Bae Hut Resort, T039-21930452, T01-8628426 (mob). Some a/c, good bungalows, restaurant, good food, small shop. Recommended.

C-D Coral Bungalow, T09-9112284 (mob), coralresort@hotmail.com. This place has mountain bikes for hire for ฿30 per hr, telephone service, flight reconfirmation and has a TV and video selection.

C-E Kai Bae Beach, T09-409420 (mob). Rather tatty huts with grass roofs but the friendly management offers good organized trips.
E Porn Bungalows and **E Comfortable Resort**, both offer huts on the beach, basic and rather rundown, but cheap.
E-F Kai Bae Garden, located 500 m up from the beach and hence the huts are cheaper, there is also a shop here.

Haad Tha Nam (Lonely beach)
E Siam Hut, T09-5476364 (mob). Basic cheap and cheerful huts. Great if you fancy undisturbed peace and quiet.

Ao Bang Bao and Ao Bai Bin
C-D Nice Beach Bang Bao, situated directly on the beach, concrete bungalows with attached bathroom placed quite far apart, attractive restaurant.
D-F Bang Bao Blue Wave, 15 wooden bungalows situated in a small, shady wood (with and without bathroom), friendly vibe.
D-F Bang Bao Laguna, located at the eastern end of the bay, wooden huts, friendly management.

Tha Than Ma Yom
D-E Tha Than Ma Yom Bungalow, overpriced, grotty huts on the opposite side of the road above the beach.
D-F Tha Than Ma Yom, bungalows set above the sea in the woods.

Islands off Koh Chang *p396*
Koh Kut
There are 4 resorts – the exclusive and by far the most beautiful is:
AL Koh Kut Island Resort, T039-511824, www.sawadee.com/thai/koodisland/, which has two styles of rooms – one resembling traditional southern-style houses constructed on stilts over the water, the other in among the hills. Both are very tastefully decorated making maximum use of natural materials.
A Koh Kud Sai Khao Resort, www.sawadee.com/thai/kudsaikao/, has low bungalow buildings with rather boring rooms.

Koh Mak
A-B Ban Laem Chan, T01-9142593 (mob), F02-3982844. 7 wooden cottages with seaview, attached bathrooms and 'club house'.
A-C Koh Maak Resort & Cabana, reservations from Bangkok on T02-3196714.
B-C Ao Khao Resort, T01-9454162 (mob).
B-C T.K. Hut Bungalow, T039-521133.
C Sunshine Resort, T01-9165585 (mob).
D Alternative House, good bungalows in a pleasant location.
E-F Lazy Days, basic huts.

Koh Kham
Koh Kham has 2 bungalows (**F**), tents and the **E** Koh Kham Resort.

Koh Ngam
A Royal Paradise Koh-Ngam Resort, simple bungalows on stilts arranged in a row, simply furnished. Pricey, paying for the location.
A Twin Island Resort, similar to Royal Paradise. Both resorts have restaurants.

Koh Whai
B-D Koh Wai Coral Resort, has recently upgraded but not to good effect.
D-F Koh Wai Paradise Beach Resort, T039-597031, much friendlier, cheaper and in a beautiful location.

Koh Lao Ya, Koh Phrao, Koh Khlum, Koh Kra Dad and Koh Rayang Nok
A Lao Ya Resort, Koh Lao Ya, T039-512552. A/c, hot water, half board compulsory, excellent restaurant; the ultimate place for getting away from it all.
A Koh Sai Khao Resort, Koh Phrao, T039-511429. **A Koh Kradad Resort**, Koh Kra Dad, T01-4328027 (mob).
B Sam Marine Resort, Koh Rayang Nok, T01-2193289 (mob).

Eating

Chantaburi *p389, map p390*
Most restaurants are on Tha Chalaep Rd. Where the road runs along the eastern side of King Taksin Lake, there is a profusion of pubs, bars and ice cream parlours. Good places to eat seafood on Tha Chalaep Rd include: ¥¥ **Phikul Phochana Thalchaleb** (53 Moo 9), ¥¥ **Suan Poo Thachaleb** (134 Moo 9), and ¥¥ **Thachaleb Seafood**.
¥¥ **Bangon's**, next door, is smaller in size and also has a more limited menu, but is equally cheerful. Open 0800-2200.

Luongtoy's. Open 1200-2200. For a relaxed and friendly riverside restaurant, try Luongtoy's which has a great range of Thai food served in an attractive location under thatched roofs (free rice and fruit). Traditional music in the evenings on Tue, Thu and Fri.

Meun-ban ('Homely' restaurant) is located directly next to the bus terminal and is probably the best low-budget restaurant in town offering a multitude of Thai dishes (including a huge vegetarian selection and ice creams), at very low prices. The owners speak good English and are a helpful source of local information, it is also in an ideal location if you arrive tired and hungry after a long bus journey and need some refreshment. Recommended.

San Chandra (Chantaburi Rice and Noodle House), Saritdet Rd, is another sparklingly clean and friendly restaurant offering delicious Thai food and ice creams. Recommended.

Aranya Prathet *p391*

Steak and Bakery, situated in the centre of town in a redeveloped shopping precinct. Not much steak but recommended for its Thai food.

There are several night markets scattered around town selling the usual dishes.

Trat *p392, map p392*

Cool Corner, 21-23 Tan Charoen Rd. Serves excellent coffee, cake, Thai and veggie food – recommended.

Joys, just opposite Guy's guesthouse, is a French-run pizzeria, that does yummy thin-bases.

Krua Rim Klong, 44 Soi Rimklong, T039-524919. Just before the **Residang Guesthouse** on Than Charoen Rd. This cheerful restaurant/bar serves a superb range of food and drink. If your tastebuds are crying out for som tam, larb moo and sticky rice there's an excellent **Isaan shophouse restaurant** next door to Ban Jai Dee.

Nam Chok, corner of Soi Butnoi and Wiwatthana roads (off Thatmai Rd). Good local food served outdoors.

The **municipal market** has a good range of stalls to choose from – good value and delicious. Other markets which sell food include the night market next to the a/c bus station.

Koh Chang *p393, map p393*

Hat Sai Kaew (White Sand Beach)

15 Palms offers a wide range of delicious Thai and western food.

The Fisherman's, between Patthai and Cookie, good fresh fish.

Mac Bungalows. For barbecues Mac Bungalows is a must.

The Taxi Stop is recommended for a really munchable steak sandwich with cheese and decent bread.

Thor's Palace, excellent restaurant of the variety where you sit on the floor at low, lamp-lit tables, very friendly management, popular, library – and good Thai curries.

Cookie, south of **Patthai**, good selection of Thai and travellers' food, popular and cheap.

Bars and clubs

Koh Chang *p393, map p393*

White Sands Cat Bar, Hat Sai Kaew, opposite Best Garden Resort is a friendly little well-stocked bar and an excellent source of information as well as a good place to hire motorbikes.

Sabay Bar, Hat Sai Kaew, just next to the Sabay Resort is a night-time location where you can either relax on cushions on the beach or dance the night away inside – the buckets are a must try!

No Name Bar, next to **Kai Bae Hut Resort**, Ao Kai Be, is another good place to spend an evening

Shopping

Chantaburi *p389, map p390*

Si Chan Rd, or 'Gem Street', has the best selection of jewellery shops and gem stores. However, you are unlikely to pick up a bargain. On Fri, Sat and Sun a gem street market operates along Krachang Lane. Chantaburi is regarded as one of the centres of fine rattan work in Thailand. Available from numerous shops in town.

Activities and tours

Koh Chang *p393, map p393*

Diving

Dolphin Divers, T070281627, www.dolphinkohchang.com. British-owned, Dolphin Divers has its main office on Khlong

Phrao and offers all PADI courses from Open Water (฿11,000) through to Instructor. It runs dive trips (2 dives) around the Koh Chang archipelago starting at ฿2300 inclusive of equipment and food.

Koh Chang Divers, Hat Sai Kaew, a Swiss-run diving school, which offers PADI and snorkelling; no credit cards accepted.

Elephant trekking

Ban Kwan Chang elephant camp, near Khlong Son, was set up to look after elephants that were no longer working in Northern Thailand, rescuing them from a lifetime of walking the streets of Bangkok. It is a project set up in conjunction with the Asian Elephant Foundation to provide a natural environment for elephants and their keepers (!) To fund the project it runs elephant treks ranging from ฿450-900. The price includes transport, food and drink, and a trek. If you are wanting to go elephant trekking this is a great place to do it as the keepers are very friendly and the elephants are well looked after. To book on to a trek go to the stand next to **Jinda Bungalows** a day in advance.

Transport

Chantaburi *p389, map p390*

Bus

Regular connections with **Bangkok**'s Eastern bus terminal. Also buses from **Pattaya**, **Rayong**, **Ban Phe** and other eastern seaboard towns. If coming from **Koh Samet**, get a boat to **Ban Phe**, songthaew to **Rayong** (฿20) and then a bus to **Chantaburi** – buses leave every hr, the journey takes 2 hrs and costs ฿30. There are less regular bus connections with destinations in the northeast including **Korat**.

Aranya Prathet and the Cambodian border *p391*

Bus

There are roughly 8 buses a day from Chantburi (3 hrs) to Aranya Prathet's bus terminal (1.5 km northwest of the town centre) from where there are connections with **Korat** (Nakhon Ratchasima) and **Bangkok** (4 hrs).

Train

Trains also link Aranya Prathet with **Bangkok**: just 2 trains a day in each direction with 3rd-class/non-a/c trains only.

Trat *p392, map p392*

Air

Bangkok Airways runs twice daily flights in each direction from Bangkok to Trat, fares start at ฿1600.

Boat

From near the **Foremost Guesthouse**, boats leave very irregularly to Koh Kut and Koh Mak, see page 396.

Bus

A/c station is on Sukhumvit Rd, just north of the night market. Non-a/c buses leave from Wiwattana Rd, north, off Sukhumvit Rd. Regular connections with **Bangkok**'s Eastern bus terminal (5½ hrs), **Pattaya** (3½ hrs), and with **Chantaburi** (1 hr 40 mins). There are also a couple of daily connections to Bangkok's Northern bus terminal.

Songthaew

To **Laem Ngop** from outside the municipal market on Sukhumvit Rd (฿15).

Laem Ngop *p392*

Boat

Regular boat departures for **Koh Chang** and other islands from the main pier in town.

Songthaew

From the stand outside the shopping mall, Sukhumvit Rd, in Trat (30 mins). Regular departures during daylight hours. After dark, songthaews must be chartered.

Koh Chang *p393, map p393*

It is only possible to reach Koh Chang in a day from Bangkok by taking an early morning bus (first a/c bus 0700, non-a/c 0420). Beware of **Sea Horse**, who reputedly run minibuses to Laem Ngop and allegedly drive deliberately slowly to miss the last ferry, so they get to choose where you stay (and take a commission).

To get to Koh Chang, take a bus to **Trat** then a songthaew to **Laem Ngop** and then take a boat to the island. When leaving the island it is advisable to get immediately into a songthaew to Trat (if that is where you want to go) rather than hanging around because if you miss the one which meets the boat you may have to wait hours for the next one or have to charter one.

See page 396 for details on getting to the smaller islands of Koh Mak and Koh Kut.

Bike
Some of the guesthouses now have mountain bikes for hire (around ฿100 per day).

Boat
In bad weather ring the Laem Ngop tourist office, see page 392, or the national parks office on Koh Chang (T039-586056/ T01-7582145), open Mon-Fri 0800-1700, for information on ferry schedules.

Boats leave daily for the various beaches from one of the 3 piers in Laem Ngop hourly between 0630-1700. This service is reduced to every 2 hrs in the wet season. The ferry costs about ฿50 and takes an hour; on arrival share taxis wait to take passengers to different beaches. It costs about ฿70 to travel to the south of the island. The main pier is right at the end of the road from Trat, before you fall into the sea. The other 2 piers are several kilometres west of Laem Ngop and service the more expensive resorts. Boats to Khlong Son Beach take 1 hr, to Than Ma Yom Pier, 50 mins, to Dan Mai Pier, 35 mins. During peak season (Nov-May) there are almost hourly departures, some to Than Ma Yom Pier (east coast), others to the west coast. From the island, there are boats from 0730 from Than Ma Yom Pier (pick-ups leave from Hat Sai Kaew). Between Jun-Oct – the low season – boats are more irregular and some routes do not operate at all because of rough seas combined with limited demand. **Car ferry** Car ferries leave from Koh Chang Centrepoint Pier, northwest of Laem Ngop, 10 times daily. Another vehicular ferry leaves from Laem Ngop's third pier, at Ao Thammachat on Route 3156 – 5 departures daily.

Motorbike
Hire from many of the guesthouses – can be a much cheaper option if you intend on travelling around the island. ฿200 for 24 hrs.

Taxi
There are no cars, but there are motorbike and jeep taxis. These are pretty expensive (about ฿20-40 per 5 km). The usual rule of not getting into an empty one without checking the price first applies of course. The high prices date back to the days when the roads were poor and the machines had a very short lifespan but there is really no excuse for it now that the roads have been improved.

Directory

Chantaburi *p389, map p390*
Banks **Thai Farmers**, 103 Sirong Muang Rd. **Bangkok**, 50 Tha Chalaep Rd. **Post office** At the intersection of Amphawan and Si Chan roads.

Aranya Prathet *p391*
Banks There are a few banks including the Siam City Bank, with ATM facilities. **Internet and post office** There are a few internet cafés and a post office.

Trat *p392, map p392*
Banks On Sukhumvit Rd. **Post office** Tha Reua Jang Rd on northeast side of town.

Laem Ngop *p392*
Banks Mobile exchange service at the pier. 0900-1600. Exchange rates on Koh Chang are poor. **Medical services** Malaria Centre on main road, opposite Laem Ngop Inn. It gives the latest information on malaria and can help with treatment.

Koh Chang *p393, map p393*
Banks Koh Chang now has several ATMs located at Hat Sai Kaew and Khlong Phrao – there is also a Siam Bank branch at Khlong Phrao – opposite Boutique Resort offering an exchange service 1000-1800. **Internet, post office and telephone** There are now dozens of phoneboxes and internet cafés (฿2 a min) throughout the island and a post office at the southern end of Sai Kaew beach. **Medical services** Doctors in Ao Khlong Son and in Ao Khlong Phrao near Hobby Hut. For more serious injuries patients are transferred to Laem Ngop. **Useful addresses** Police There are 6 policemen permanently at the station in Khlong Son. Thefts should be reported immediately so that if there are suspects the next boat to the mainland can be intercepted by the mainland police.

Andaman Coast

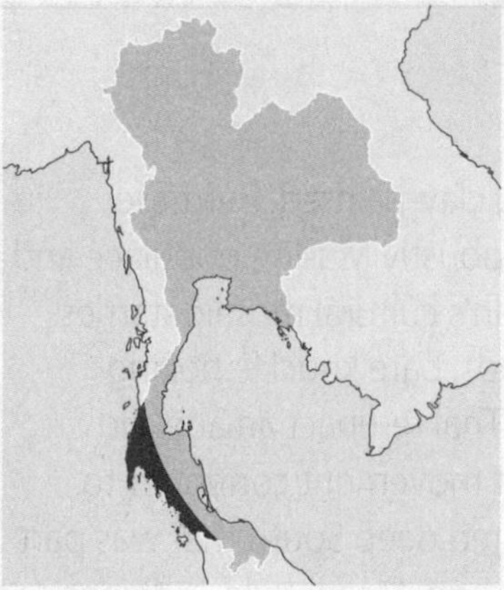

Footprint features

Introduction

From Ranong's cheroot-smoking clay-painted Burmese hilltribe diaspora to the south's robustly Muslim populace and Chao Le sea gypsies the Andaman's cultural mosaic startles. On Ranong's rain-drenched islands, bare knuckle boxing matches between Burmese and Thai re-enact an age-old rivalry while a growing separatist movement continues to spread through the hotly contested deep South that was part of Malaysia a little over a century ago. Meanwhile, indigenous sea gypsies who escaped the tsunami persist in animist practices including offerings of human hair to the spirits of the treacherous Andaman. Travellers will find many pleasures along this coast, from the Similan islands' world-famous diving sites including Richelieu Rock to Phuket's beaches including katoey paradise Patong and jetset Pansea.

Further down the coast are Phangnga's sea cave paintings and the magical floating fishing village of Koh Panyi. Off Krabi - where giant prehistoric human skulls were found - are eerie towering limestone karsts revered by climbers. Deeper south reveals Koh Lanta's white sand coral-rimmed beaches while the brooding ex-prison island of Tarutao, reputed to be haunted, offers dense and terrifying untouched jungle populated by wild boar, barking deer and poisonous snakes. And the Adang-Rawi archipelago's tiny islands - unreachable during the monsoon - prove cozy homes for pythons and hornbills while only yards off shore snorkellers can find untouched sea life including shoals of barracuda. Finally, the whole of the coast is dotted with island retreats sans electricity or cars, among them Koh Muk with the nearby Emerald Cave and the tropical idyll Koh Bulon-Leh. For every traveller from spa lovers to Robinson Crusoes, the Andaman proves a perfect host.

★ Don't miss...

1 **Rai Leh** Climb the limestone karsts of Rai Leh where a perfect harmony of sea, sunset and rock lure climbers from all over the world, page 475.

2 **Koh Lanta's Old Town** Learn the traditional fishing life when you stay at a fishermen's dwelling – the site of the original Chinese and Arabrian routes, page 495.

3 **The Emerald Cave** Swim into the cave in the pitch black and find an inland beach only large enough for 20 people, page 510.

4 **Vegetarian Festival** In Trang participants pierce their cheeks with spikes and forgo meat for five days, page 515.

5 **Koh Lipe** Snorkel off Lipe where, only yards off shore, live coral reefs feature shoals of barracuda, clown anemones, angel fish and trumpet fish, page 521.

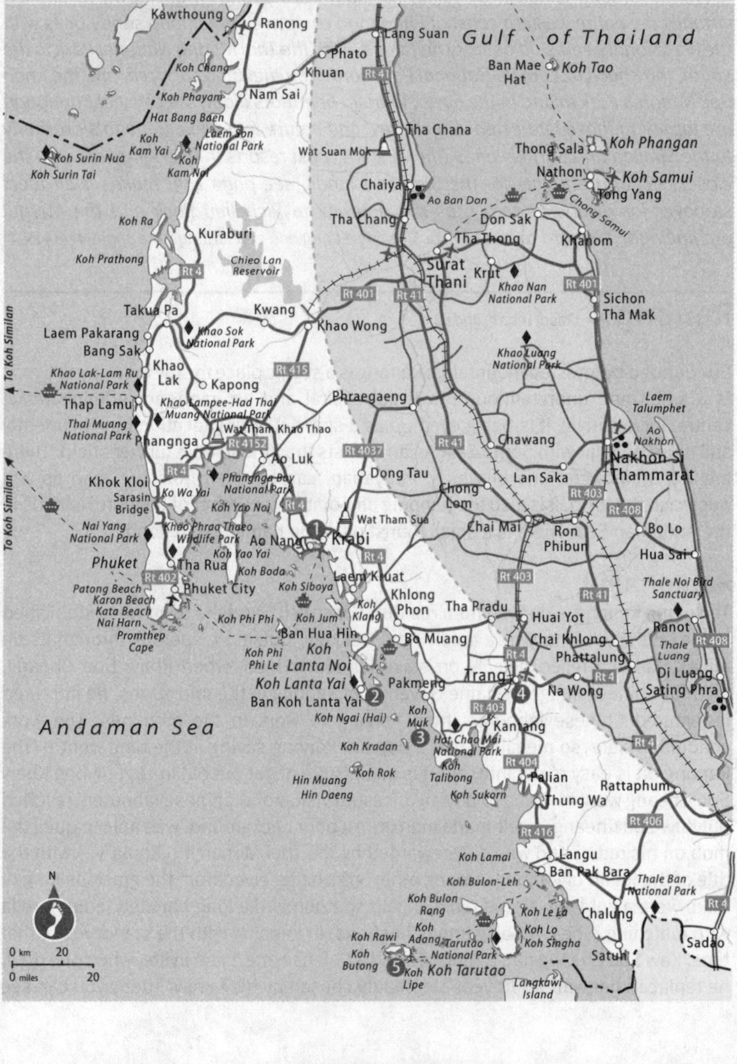

Ranong to Khao Lak

A wilder untouched landscape begins to unfold with waterfalls, lush rainforest and dense mountains all home to fantastical species like the largest flower in the world and insects the size of a man's hand. Ranong, on Route 4, is famous for both its hot springs and visa runs by expats and travellers who can cross the border into Burma by boat to renew their visas in a day. Like Mae Sot, its proximity to Burma fosters a border diaspora as Burmese workers – many illegal – hasten across, desperately searching for work in a country which traditionally has fought bitterly with the Burmese. In Ranong and the surrounding islands, the tribal Burmese clearly stand out with the men wearing sarongs and the women daubed in clay face paint smoking cheroots. There are often boxing competitions between the two nationalities which dramatically display another difference – one of fighting styles – that of the highly ritualistic Thai Muay and the frenzied freeform Burmese style.

From Prathong Island near Takua Pa (south of Ranong), right down to Phuket, virtually the entire western coast of Phangnga comprises great long sandy bays with the occasional peninsula or rocky headland. With the Thai Muang National Park to the south, the Khao Lak Lam Ru National Park bordering the Khao Lak area, and the Khao Sok National Park inland to the north, tourism operators along the coast of Phangnga are targeting those interested in 'getaway' and nature tour while Ranong's proximity to the Similan and Surin islands (the western coast resorts in Phangnga are also the closest departure points for the Similan Islands, see page 413) makes it an ideal stopover for divers. Certainly, as the gateway to Richelieu Rock and the Mergul archipelago, it is hard to beat. ▸▸ *For Sleeping, Eating and other listings, see pages 414-419.*

Ranong → *Colour map 4, grid B2.*

Surrounded by forested mountains, Ranong is a scenic place to stay for a day or two. It is a small and unpretentious provincial capital and an important administrative centre. Increasingly, it is being eyed up as a spa/hot spring location but is currently still more popular with South East Asian tourists than those from further afield. There are waterfalls here, one of which, Punyaban, can be seen from the road as you approach the town. It is also the jumping off point for a number of beautiful islands in the Andaman Sea. There is a small tourist office on Kamlungsab Road.

Background

The name Ranong is derived from *rae* (tin) *nong* (rich), and the town was established in the late 18th century by a family from Hokkien, China. Prosperous through its tin mines, Ranong relied heavily on slave labour. Indeed, when Khaw Soo Cheang, another Chinese émigré became Governor of Ranong in the mid-1800s, he imported indentured Chinese labourers from Penang to work in the tin-mines. The work conditions were so merciless that a popular Ranong saying at the time went – 'The Ranong pit is easy to get into, but it is impossible ot get out of.' In 1876, when Khaw Soo Cheang went to China to pay an ancestral visit, 2000 Chinese labourers revolted but Kaw Soo Cheang, a self-made man from a poor background, was able to quell the mob on his return and was duly rewarded by the Thai Monarch – Rama V – with the title of the Rajah of Ranong. Among other gifts he received from the gracious King of Siam were a gold jug, a gold table, a gold spittoon and a long-handled red umbrella with matching robes. A polygamous husband, in keeping with the standards of that time, Kaw Soo Cheang had a Thai wife and a Chinese one. Later in life, when one died, he replaced her with an 18-year-old beauty chosen by his family. Today you can see

1941 Japanese invasion of Burma

On 8 December 1941, the Japanese military landed at Parkham Chumpon, to seize Burma. However, young Thais – mainly students and villagers – resisted the Japanese and many were killed on both sides. Following collaboration with the Thai government, the Imperial Army were able to halt any further resisters and by the end of December had captured Victoria Point in Burma. But when the infantry discovered that the terrain along Highway 4 – which followed Chumpon, Kraburi, the La-un canal and Petchakasem – was virtually impassable, they decided to construct a railway parallel to the highway instead and set up headquarters at Khao Fachi village. Here they surveyed enemy approaches from the tops of two trees on the mountain while down below soldiers quarters were rapidly erected and underground prisons created to hold POWs – mainly Malaysian Indians and some Thai.

Used as slave labour, the POWs built roads and a complex of hospitals, kitchens, dining halls and a railway station along with a graveyard for fellow POWs. The Japanese needed more POWs in order to fulfill their obligations having signed an agreement to build the railway.

Consequently, in 1943, further POWs were brought by train from Chumpon Railway Station and marched the many arduous miles to the site, many dying en route or escaping to Petchaburi where they begged for food from villagers or were caught only to be returned and tortured.

The Japanese used the Chumpon-Kra Buri-La-un Railway for 11 months until allied forces heavily bombed the railway and base at Khao Fachi on 19 March 1945. On 10 August 1945, the Japanese surrendered. Today all that remains of the camp and railway are relics of guns, mortar bombs, samurai swords, tunnels, trenches and underground shelters while the railway is overgrown with jungle foliage and filled with defunct and rusty sleepers. The well, built and used by the POWs and the guards at the death camp, is now used by the villagers of Khao Fachi.

the legacy of Kaw Soo Cheang with Ranong still boasting a predominantly Sino-Thai population and a number of attractive 19th-century Chinese-style houses in town.

Ranong province is the first southern province bordering the Indian Ocean and it is Thailand's rainiest (often in excess of 5,000 mm per year), narrowest and least populated province. Kra Buri, 58 km north of Ranong, is the point where the Kra Isthmus is also at its narrowest, and there has been debate for centuries about the benefits of digging a canal across the isthmus, so linking the Gulf of Thailand with the Andaman Sea and short-cutting the long hike down the peninsula to Singapore and then north again through the Melaka Strait.

Sights

The town contains **geo-thermal mineral water springs** (65°C) at **Wat Tapotharam** ⓘ *2 km east of the town and behind the* **Jansom Thara Hotel**, *take a songthaew along Route 2; ask for 'bor naam rawn' (hot water well)*, the hot water bubbles up into concrete tubs named *bor mae*, *bor por* and *bor luuk saaw* – mother, father and daughter pools respectively. The springs provide the **Jansom Thara Hotel** with thermal water for hot baths and a giant jacuzzi. There is a small park with a cable bridge over the river and a number of bathing pools (sometimes empty of water). The wat is rather dull, containing a footprint of the Buddha. Continuing along Route 2 for another 6 km

or so, the road reaches the old tin-mining village of **Hat Som Paen**. The tin that brought wealth to the area was worked out long ago, but **Wat Som Paen** is worth a visit to see the giant carp which reside here, protected because of their supposed magical qualities: catch and eat them – and regret it.

Port of Ranong lies 3 km from town. Each morning the dock seethes with activity as Thai and Burmese fishing boats unload their catches. Boats can be hired, at a pontoon next to the dock, to tour the bustling harbour and look across the Kra River estuary to the Burmese border (approximately ฿300). Border officials can be touchy; carry your passport with you. Ranong is an important point of contact between Burma and Thailand. Like Mae Sot, there are more intensive searches and check-points as you leave the area. Do not be surprised if military police come onto your bus randomly up to three or four times on the way out to check passports. This intensifies in line with the guerrilla operations in Burma and the drug wars.

Laem Son National Park (Ranong's Islands) → *Colour map 4, grid B1.*

ⓘ *Laem Son National Park, T077-824224, is 45 km south of Ranong and includes islands in the Andaman Sea, ฿200. Travel agents can organize day trips taking in a couple of the islands, but to get the most out of your money it's possible to take a songthaew (฿25) 43 km south of Ranong along Route 4. On the right, there's a 10-km turn off that leads straight to the park (฿30 by motorbike taxi from the roadside). Long-tailed boats run from Ranong Port out to Koh Chang 4 times a day in the morning, no fixed fare – it depends how many people are travelling. Return boats leave Koh Chang in the afternoon. For Koh Phayam boats leave Ranong at 0900 and 1400 (2½ hrs, ฿100), returning 0800 and 1500. But these boats rarely operate to schedule and can be an hour out. The quickest and cheapest way to explore the smaller islands closer to Laem Son is to charter a long-tailed boat once almost in the national park. Negotiating directly with the fishermen operating from Hat Bang Baen (turn off left just before the park entrance) should cost about ฿1000, while* Wasana Resort *offers its guests a very worthwhile day trip including food, frisbee, badminton and snorkelling for ฿1500 per boat. Trips can also be arranged from within the park, but these tend to be costlier and without the fringe benefits of recreational equipment and food. For trips to to Koh Surin and Koh Similan, see page 413.*

The only time to visit is between November and April; outside this period the guesthouses shut and the long-tailed boats stop operating.

There are a number of notable **beaches** and **islands** in the neighbourhood of Ranong, many within the limits of the **Laem Son National Park**, such as Hat Bang Baen, Koh Khang Khao, Koh Khao Khwai, Koh Nam Noi, Koh Kam Yai, Koh Kam Tok, Koh Chang and Koh Phayam. The water here is warm and a pleasure to swim in, especially around the reefs. The park and the islands effectively lie at the outer limits of the Kra River estuary – so don't expect coral on all islands or excellent visibility. Mangroves fringe many of the islands and because of the high rainfall in the area the natural vegetation is tropical rainforest. (This park did receive a cruel blow from the tsunami, with considerable damage to the mangrove forests.) While the islands may not have the very best snorkelling and water, they hide some wonderfully white sand and secluded beaches and they do have good birdlife (there are around 138 bird species in the park). The best birdwatching months are December-February with many migrating birds in situ and optimum weather conditions. Everything conspires to generate a peaceful and relaxed stopping place.

Unlike the larger **Koh Chang** on Thailand's east coast, Ranong's tiny Koh Chang has more to offer birdwatchers than beach-lovers. Commonly sighted birds are kites, sea eagles and the endearingly clumsy hornbill. And, in the forest along the coast, monkeys and deer can be spied - and heard- through the slumbering days and nights. The beaches here are mediocre at best and grim at worst with streaks of black and

dubious grey yellow sand. The island also hibernates from June to mid-October when the monsoon rains lash down with even locals shifting to the mainland, leaving Koh Chang with its 45 houses, almost empty. But what this island lacks in beach bounty, it makes up for in the chill-out stakes. While there is a burgeoning backpacker tourist industry replete with a recent bike rally, the economy still depends on fishing and plantations of rubber, palm and cashew nut. Self-generated electricity remains sporadic and there are no sign of cars with most people getting around on motorbikes through tracks to the beaches. But, while the beaches are never going to be used in an ice cream advert, the swimmable Ao Yai on the west coast is well worth a visit. Split in two by a strip of a lagoon, from Ao Yai you can see the thuggish silhouette of Burma's mountainous jungle-covered St Matthew's island which seems to take up most of the horizon. It is intriguing to know that St Matthew's remains a military hotspot because of a massive radar site with a direct satellite link to China. Cool Koh Chang also sports a radar site - for the Thai Navy. In the days following the tsunami, the Thai Navy kept people on the island until the all-safe went out although Koh Chang fared remarkably well. Only its market was destroyed along with a few bungalows due to other islands acting as a breaker for the waves. Post-tsunami, the island is firmly back into its pleasant lazing and gazing groove.

Buffered by Koh Similan, **Koh Phayam**, along with Koh Chang, were the only islands on the Ranong coastline not to suffer any deaths from the tsunami. Only on Koh Phayam would there be both full-moon parties – albeit low-key ones – and a Miss Cashew Nut Beauty Competition (held during the Cashew Nut Festival). Koh Phayam does not have cars and boasts only narrow roads that are more like big lanes which run through the nut plantations. There is, however, a small track around the island for walking, cycling or motorbiking to break up lounging on the beaches at either Ao Yai – sunset bay – or Ao Khao Yai, both of which are long and curving with white sand. These days, Koh Phayam has become a quiet hit for the laid-back diving and snorkelling set, see Activities and tours. This is partly because Koh Phayam, often called the 'muck divers playground,' offers such offshore delights as flat worms, ascidians, sponges, soft corals, nudibranchs and a variety of sea horses. If you are not the diving sort, the island is also home to wonderfully diverse wildlife with hornbills overhead, while further inland away from the white sandy beaches are prehistoric monitor lizards, boar, deer, monkeys and snakes. There is also a tiny fishing village on the east coast of the island. As for locals, Koh Phayam is populated by Burmese and Thai, 200 and 300 respectively and there are even four full-time farang but come May, this hardy bunch dribbles down to half. And, like Koh Chang only a few miles away, Koh Phayam has a scattering of bungalows – over 20 now – but is expected to see a flourishing as the Koh Surin Islands, which are easily accessible from Koh Phayam, become ever more popular. This could easily cause the island to lose its idyll status in the near future as already, there are serious problems with sewage and rubbish as ferries crossing between the islands and the mainland throw their discards into the sea. It is possible to hire motorbikes (฿200 per day) but be warned that the roads are unpaved and sometimes treacherous, with lots of low-hanging branches and sometimes even falling fruit providing additional driving hazards.

There is limited electricity and communications on some of the islands.

Hat Bang Baen is a delightful length of beach with lovely shells and fine sand. You can also organize boat trips here to nearby islands.

Koh Khang Khao (25 minutes from Hat Bang Baen) is the stuff of dreams – it has a relatively small but white sand beach for sunbathing on and rocks to picnic on, sheltered by trees that continue to grow thick, fast and jungle-like up the steep mountainous slopes. A sandy shelf means there's about 7 m of shallow swimming – ideal for families – before the bed falls away to deeper, rockier territory with some reefs providing good snorkelling. The more adventurous can try to circumnavigate the island by clambering over the countless rocks that fringe the rest of the coastline.

Koh Khao Khwai (30 minutes from Khang Khao) is another beautiful island boasting a long stretch of beach and azure water, with lots of tiny crabs scuttling over the sand and the parched skeletons of long-dead trees lying further up the beach. The longer of the two beaches sweeps from the west along the southerly curve of the island. It's easy to walk from the west to the east side, or take a short path from the very southern tip of the beach through the rich vegetation and out into the most dreamy cove, with white sands, set against the impressive back drop of another mountainous rainforest. The water is bath-like in temperature, but beware of the stony bottom. This cove is, however, overlooked by some national park bungalows, where it's possible to pick up the odd information leaflet.

On **Koh Kam Yai** (15 minutes from Khao Khwai), the western coastline is all rocks and mountains, with just one short, quiet stretch of sand. Most of the beaches are along the northeast coast, with the biggest and most beautiful being at the very northeasterly tip. Although fairly small, the beaches are secluded and there's enough space for plenty of people to feel they have the island to themselves. Near the shore there are some good reefs suitable for snorkelling.

On **Koh Kam Noi** (10 minutes from Kam Yai), there's only one, smallish beach here, with the seabed shelving sharply away after only a couple of metres. The sand is soft and white, but considerably covered with washed-up driftwood, and the trees don't afford much cover from the sun.

Kuraburi

If travelling south from Ranong to Takua Pa, the small town of Kuraburi is worth a stop off. There is one resort here, see Sleeping. It provides a good base from which to explore the local forests, or makes for a good stopover for longer North-South routes via Ranong. The pier in Kuraburi is the jumping-off point for boats to Prathong Island (see page 410), including speedboats, if you just want a day trip there.

Prathong Island

ⓘ *Accessible via Takua Pa on the mainland.*

Prathong Island had one resort situated on the 11 km of beach and was well known for its environmental focus: the **Golden Buddha Beach Resort**. The Chelon Institute carried out research on sea turtles at Prathong Island with the help of this resort, and also accepted volunteers. However, this internationally respected resort and yoga retreat did not escape the tsunami. Three successive waves obliterated the clubhouse, offices and all other buildings. The three villages on Koh Prathong of Bak Jok, Tapa Yoi and Tung Dap were also devastated while the villages of Hat Praphat and Baan Tale Nok have endured terrific damage. The **Golden Buddha Resort** is being rebuilt in time for Christmas 2005 and work continues on the island's villages. See Sleeping.

Khao Sok National Park → *Colour map 4, grid B1.*

ⓘ *www.khaosok.com*. The closest town to Khao Sok National Park is Takua Pa but companies from Phuket, Phangnga, Krabi and Surat operate day and overnight tours. An overnight tour is the best way to explore the park. If you really want to get into the forest, take an overnight tour into the park with an experienced guide. Overnight stays by the lake, although spartan, are recommended, as the scenery is spectacular and the early morning calm is hard to beat. Tours are available from virtually all the various bungalows near the park (see Sleeping). Park rangers will also act as guides. Have a chat with your guide before you make up your mind to go so you can be sure you feel

The Rafflesia, that has mystified botanists internationally, blooms but once a year, the rest of the time lying invisible as a microscopic thread inside the root of another plant – the Liana vine. Known in Thai as 'bun putt,' this particular Rafflesia exists only in and around Khao Sok National Park.

comfortable about the level of English (or other languages) they speak, familiarity with the park and knowledge of the environment and wildlife. A park guide is a sensible idea as the treks really do take longer than a day and can be very daunting, even for the more experienced. Expect to pay from ฿300 per person for a guide to take you on a day trek, and around ฿2,000 per person for an overnight trip to the reservoir (this includes accommodation and all meals). Prices will vary depending on how many people are in the group. For further information *Waterfalls and gibbon calls: exploring Khao Sok National Park*, by Thom Henley, is available in various outlets in Southern Thailand, from the visitors' centre at Khao Sok National Park, and from many of the bungalow operators at Khao Sok.

Khao Sok National Park has limestone karst mountains (the tallest reaches more than 900 m), low mountains covered with evergreen forest, streams and waterfalls, and a large reservoir and dam. The impressive scenery alone would be a good enough reason to visit, but Khao Sok also has a high degree of endemism and an exceptionally large number of **mammals**, **birds**, **reptiles** and other fauna.

The list of 48 confirmed species of mammals include: wild elephants, tigers, barking deer, langur, macaques, civets, bears, gibbons and cloud leopards. Of the 184 confirmed bird species, perhaps the most dramatic include: the rhinoceros hornbill, the great hornbill, the Malayan peacock pheasant and the crested serpent-eagle. The plants to be found here are also of interest. The orchids are best seen from late February to April. If you visit between December and February, the **Rafflesia Kerri Meijer** is in flower. This parasitic flower (it depends on low-lying lianas) has an 80-cm bloom – the largest in the world – with a phenomenally pungent odour so that it can attract the highest number of pollinating insects. It also has no chlorophyll. Besides the astounding Rafflesia, there are also at least two palms endemic to the Khao Sok area.

In the centre of the park is the **Rachabrapah Reservoir**. Near the dam there is a longhouse of sorts, and several houseboats. The best location for animal spotting is near the reservoir where grassland at the edge of the reservoir attracts animals.

In addition to **camping**, **canoeing** and **walking tours**, you can take **elephant treks** at Khao Sok. The routes taken must be outside the park, however, as elephant trekking is not permitted within the confines of the national park.

Like many of the great wonders of nature in Thailand, Khao Sok does not come without a giant technological blot. In this case, it's a hydroelectric dam right next to Khao Sok that has formed a vast artifical lake that now comprises one border of the national park. This dam began in the 1980s and has since become the bane of the park, as it transformed hills and valleys into small islands, trapping the wildlife with rising tides. While there have been attempts to rescue the beleagured wildlife, nothing has proved successful as of yet. But Khao Sok is successfully capitalizing on its assets, including its association with the famous Canadian naturalist Thom Henley who has written about the park.

Khao Lak

In the shock aftermath of the tsunami, Khao Lak passed from being a burgeoning tourist spot particularly for the Scandinavians to a vast morgue as photographs were beamed across the world of its beaches filled with corpses. Of all the beaches along the west coast of Thailand Khao Lak suffered the most, its wide flat expanse ensuring that there was no sanctuary from the merciless waves. More than 5,000 people perished in the 10-mile strip between Khao Lak and Baan Nem Khem, the worst-hit seaside village on Phangna. Thousands are still missing, among them illegal workers from Burma and poor Thai villagers. No one, it seemed, was spared – even the King's grandson who was discovered a quarter of a mile inland and who had been on a jetski when the tsunami struck. At Laem Pakarang, between Baan Nam Khem and Laem

Hotels operating in Khao Lak include Le Meridien Khao Lak Beach and Spa, Ban Krating Khao Lak Resort, Briza Beach Resort and Spa, and Hot Spring Resort and Spa.

Wave thriller

Three months after the December 2004 tsunami, the families of victims were up in arms over rumours that a tsunami theme museum was planned – complete with a simulated wave in Khao Lak similar to a Universal Studios panorama.

In March 2005, the Tourism Authority of Thailand governor Juthamas Siriwan held an international conference about plans to regenerate the tourist market of Khao Lak.

"A museum would firstly educate everyone who comes to Phuket to make them aware of how these kinds of things happen," Siriwan began, continuing, "We would also like to use technology to make the museum more attractive and interesting by making a simulation of a tidal wave. I talked to the architect and they say they are going to make something like that so maybe this will be the next Universal Studios of the tsunamis in Khao Lak."

Siriwam later denied the rumour that the country was eyeing a "tsunami theme park, " but TAT admitted that the Thai government would still "establish a museum that would have exhibitions as well as use interactive technology to educate people" TAT did not, however, detail what the spin-off souvenirs, if any, would be at the museum.

Khao Lak, several five-star hotels were obliterated. The vast majority of hotels in Khao Lak, Bang Niang and Khuk Khuk, if they were not washed away completely, have since been bulldozed while only a few of the more expensive resorts have managed to re-open. And, in the land-grab frenzy that followed the tsunami, villagers came forth with tales of armed men hired by nai toons (money barons) to intimidate them into moving off the beach-fronts despite Thai law which says that squatters can apply for legal title to a plot of land. Such horror stories came out of particularly vulnerable spots like the Laem Pom part of Ban Nam Khem, a seaside settlement of ex-labourers who originally came to work in the tin mines. Months on from the disaster, deprived of their livelihoods, the local families of tsunami victims still found themselves waiting for vital compensation as Khao Lak was being levelled to create a new tourist market. The future of Khao Lak remains highly contentious and while well-meaning returnee visitors may feel compelled to visit the tragic region, they should also be made aware that it will not be the Khao Lak they remember. Saline deposits from the sea have left the land parched while once familiar landmarks have disappeared forever. Even the coastline has shifted in especially hard-hit areas. Despite the clear dilemmas of visiting such a region, however, tourism is needed to provide employment to a desperate populace and there are still places to visit like the world-famous off-shore dive sites and the national parks with their rare and endangered species. But, at this stage, it is wise to do a little research first before heading out to make sure that you will get the best out of your journey and perhaps manage to help out the smaller businesses which are most in need.

Khao Lak-Lam Ru and Khao Lampee-Had Thai Muang national parks

Khao Lak-Lam Ru National Park stretches from a small bay just south of the main Khao Lak tourism area inland up into the hills. There is a tiered waterfall with walks from the main path at the top of the hill, and forest rangers can take trekkers through the hills. However, the level of English spoken leaves rather a lot to be desired and the trails are less trail and more trudge through seriously thick and scratchy jungle foliage. This can be intensely rewarding but you do need to dress properly for it.

Khao Lampee-Had Thai Muang National Park, ⓘ *Park Visitor Centre, Thai Muang District, Phang-Nga Province 8210 (along the coast past Ban Thai Muang along 14 kms of beach, 6kms from Thai Muang town), T077-395025*, ฿200 for entry for three days, children ฿100. is a relatively small national park, 72 sq km, comprising two distinct geographical zones: the Thai Muang Beach and the Khao Lampee area. The western portion, Thai Muang Beach, has 14 km of undisturbed beach lined with casuarina trees. The park continues inland for about 1 km and includes mangrove forest along the edge of the sea inlet, some swamp forest (*pa samet*) and freshwater lagoons from the old mine works from which Thai Muang derives its name (Muang in this case means mine). The inland eastern portion covers several waterfalls and surrounding forested hills. **Turtle Beach** ⓘ *entrance fee ฿20*, is a 20-km-long stretch of beach where turtles, including the giant leatherback, come ashore at night to nest from November to February . Young turtles can be seen hatching from March to July. Hawksbill and Olive Ridley turtles are currently being raised in ponds near the park headquarters. There is an office in the Khao Lampee area, but the park headquarters are based in the Thai Muang area near the entrance.

Turtle releases are held every March as the highlight of an annual district festival.

Koh Surin → *Colour map 4, grid B1.*

ⓘ *The national park office is at Ao Mae Yai, on the southwest side of Koh Surin Nua. Best time to visit: Dec-Mar. Koh Surin Tai may close to visitors during the full moon each Mar, when the Chao Le hold a festival.*

Five islands make up this marine national park, just south of the Burmese border, and 53 km off the mainland. The two main islands, **Koh Surin Tai** and **Koh Surin Nua** (South and North Surin respectively), are separated by a narrow strait which can be waded at low tide. Both islands are hilly, with few inhabitants; a small community of Chao Le fishermen live on Koh Surin Tai. The diving and snorkelling is good here and the coral reefs are said to be the most diverse in Thailand. However, overfishing has led some people to maintain that diving is now better around the Similan Islands. Novices will still find the experience both exhilarating and enchanting.

There have been concerns expressed regarding the detrimental effects of tourism on several marine national parks, including the Surin Islands Marine National Park. In 1991 the national parks department closed Mae Yai Bay to tourism to allow the coral the time and opportunity to recover. In 2003 marine biologist Thon Thamrongnawasawat said there was evidence that this 12-year closure had had the desired result but called for the bay to remain closed for another five years.

Koh Similan → *Colour map 4, grid A1.*

ⓘ *The best time to visit is Dec-Apr. The west monsoon makes the islands virtually inaccessible during the rest of the year; be warned that boats have been known to capsize at this time. Also, be warned that transport away from the islands is unpredictable and you might find yourself stranded here, rapidly running out of money. At the end of Mar/beginning of Apr underwater visibility is not good, but this is the best time to see manta rays and whale sharks.*

The Similan Islands lying 80 km northwest of Phuket and 65 km west of Khao Lak are some of the most beautiful, unspoilt tropical idylls to be found in Southeast Asia. The national park consists of nine islands (named by Malay fishermen, who refered to them as 'The Nine Islands' – *sembilan* is Malay for nine). The water surrounding the archipelago supports a wealth of marine life and is considered one of the best diving locations in the world as well as a good place for anglers. A particular feature of the islands is the huge granite boulders. These same boulders litter the seabed and make for interesting peaks and caves for scuba-divers.

Avoid taking too much luggage as visitors must transfer from ferry to precarious long-tailed boat mid-ocean. Each island is identified by a number as well as a name. *See also Diving, page 60.*

Marine madness

Fish fingers took on a new meaning when a Brit lost his thumb to a giant moray eel who gobbled the digit and swam away.

Matt Butcher, of Stanstead, Essex, UK, was diving at the famous East of Eden site in the Similan Islands and had regularly fed the nearly two and half metre eel, known locally as a friendly fish, for a year and a half.

"She often swam between your legs or curled herself around your arms," said Butcher, "she liked sausages and even fruit. But, in April 2005, the eel, in a reverse sashimi move, snaffled his thumb which was still holding onto a plastic bag containing a sausage.

Butcher recalled: "I tried pushing the fingers of my right hand into her mouth to try and force her mouth open but she did not let go; she could taste blood. She was shaking her head from side to side, biting harder all the time. Five seconds later, my thumb just came off. She ate it and swam away."

Fortunately, the Royal Thai Navy on Similan 9 Island were there to give Butcher first aid before transferring him to Phuket then Bangkok, where he was told that Thai surgeons might just be able to transplant one of his big toes for his thumb.

On the west side of the islands the currents have kept the boulders 'clean', while on the east, they have been buried by sand. The contrast between the west and east dive locations is defined by the boulders. On the west, currents sweep around these massive granite structures, some as large as houses, which can be swum around and through and many have fantastic colourful soft coral growing on them. A guide is essential on the west, as navigation can be tricky. The east is calmer, with hard coral gardens sloping from the surface down to 30-40 m. Navigation is straightforward here and can be done with a buddy, without the need for a guide.

Koh Miang (colour map 4, no 4), named after the King's daughter, houses the park office and some dormitory and camping accommodation. While water did sweep over Koh Miang, it is largely recovered and was the first place that Thailand's Navy established a tsunami warning system. Koh Hu Yong (1), the southernmost island, is the most popular diving location. From some 16,000 tourists in 1994, the numbers visiting the Similan Islands has risen to more than 25,000. Anchor damage and the dumping of rubbish is a big problem here, although buoys have now been moored. The dearth of tourists following the tsunami has meant that the visibility is better than it has been for years.

Sleeping

Ranong *p406*

A Jansom Beach Resort, 135 Moo 5, T077-821611. Set in jungle foliage on Charn Damri Beach about 10 km from Ranong Town. 30 rooms bungalow style with private balconies overlooking the Andaman Sea and Victoria Point of Burma. Pool and restaurant. Rooms have rather low ceilings and are somewhat cramped by furniture. Still great location and service. Popular during Chinese New year and Songkran. Recommended.

A-B Royal Princess Ranong, 41/144 Tamuang Rd, T077-835240-44, www.ranong.royalprincess.com. A 4-star hotel with excellent service, good facilities including a mineral spa, and comfortable – one of the best hotels in Ranong. Has a pool and offers babysitting. It also pumps mineral water into the jacuzzi. Still very corporate with a suburban feeling to the rooms.

B-C Spa Inn, 1/15 Chonrau Rd, T077-821091/01-811715. All rooms have hot water, bath tub, a/c and are comfortable

with wall-to-wall carpeting. Slightly more expensive ones come with TV and fridge.

D The Asia Hotel, near the market, T077-811113/3. Large, clean rooms with fan and bath. A/c rooms a little overpriced.

E The Springs Guesthouse, 1/2 Chon Rao Rd, T077-834369. A popular place on the road to the hot springs, a/c and fan rooms available, clean, bright and big rooms with shared bathroom facilities. Restaurant serves good food at reasonable prices. Motorbikes for hire and tours to Burma organized.

E Suriyanan, 281 Ruangrat Rd, T077-811240. Gloomy but super-cheap – basic room with fan. Staff take the hard-line on bargirls. No flop-house then.

Laem Son National Park (Ranong's Islands) *p408*

There are around 14 bungalow operations on Koh Chang. Most are budget range, but some are built and owned by expats as holiday homes and leased to visitors. As Koh Chang is covered by rainforest with the resorts in Ao Yai beach on the west, it is difficult to see these from the boat because they are camoflouged in the foliage. If you have a fear of wild boars, you may want to know that there are many in the forest here. Ao Yai is roughly 2 km wide and 5 km long. Many shut down during the monsoon season so you do need to check. Prices run around ฿100-150 per night for fan bungalow with shared bathroom. There is limited electricity in most resorts. For your own bathroom, the price goes up to around ฿150-200 per night. Some can be booked through **Ranong Travel**, see Tour operators.

D Eden Bistro Café, T077-820172. Seven small bungalows. Good standard fare at restaurant. On northern end of beach.

D Full Moon, T077-820130. This resort shares the boat from **Cashew**. It is very clean and popular with Germans and Scandinavians. There are 11 bungalows. Also does German food. Recommended.

D-E Cashew Resort, T077-820116/01-4856002. This is the grandaddy of the resorts and the largest operation. 25 bungalows that need repairs. The resort has its own boat for fishing and trawling.

D-E Lae Tawan, T077-820179. 8 bungalows here in slightly out-of-way spot. But all nice. Restaurant with Thai food. Recommended.

E Horn Hill Bungalow, contact Khun Jib 66, T077-820134. 8 bungalows with bathrooms built in different styles. Small 'private' beach but a long walk to get there. There is a private boat for transport, fishing and travelling.

E Koh Chang Contex, T07782 0118/09-7252187. Run by a Thai family – 7 bungalows. Own boat. They will also cook for you on an ad hoc basis.

E Koh Chang Resort offers wooden huts, some with attached bathroom and has a restaurant. Snorkelling and fishing can be organized from here.

E Rasta Baby, T077-694563/833077. Seven bungalows on north side of island. Operated by a Thai man and his American wife. Typical backpacker reggae vibe.

E Sunset, T077-820171. This small operation offers 10 clean bungalows and a friendly atmosphere. Airy but slightly dark. It shares its boat with **Cashew Resort**.

F Sabai Jai, probably the best value and one of the best-run places on the island. Clean and with good western food, dorm beds available as well as range of bungalows. It also bakes its own bread. Owned by Swedish and Thai.

Koh Phayam

Koh Phayam offers around 20 different bungalow operations, and more will only follow as tourism develops. Most have cheap restaurants attached, but 3 others to bear in mind include **Pom's Restaurant**, in the village by the pier. It's sign, "Thai food, cheap and delicious" just about sums it up. **Richard's Bar**, also in the village, but on the beach road. Run by an Englishman, this place serves up great western and Thai dishes, and plenty of information about the island. **Banana Bar**, on the road to Aow Yai. Opened in 2003, this is a worthwhile stop. The bar is studded with countless shells and is surrounded by purple-topped tree trunks to sit on. The back wall is just a sea of beer bottles. Funky ambience – a hang-out for the party heads.

C-D Aow Yai Bungalows, 31 Moo 1 Koh Phayam, T077-821753, www.r24.org/travelsmart.net/nst/aowyai/. This operation is run by a French-Thai couple and offers both small and large bungalows on stilts, reasonably priced and well run. Variable – some are surrounding by lovely landscaping and are set among pine and coconut trees. West facing, they make for an ideal spot to

watch the wildlife and the sunsets although there are a lot of mozzies here. Tasty food served up in the attached restaurant.

C-E Bamboo Bungalows, Aow Yai, T077-820012/01-2733437. Another idyllic place to relax, this joint certainly understands the allure of hammocks and has strapped up quite a few in its large chill-out area. The restful theme is continued in the bedrooms, where all beds have sprung mattresses – a bit of a luxury for many budget travellers normally. There's a good range of bungalow styles, from the A-frame 'shell' bungalows prettily decorated with hundreds of shells and offering cool ceramic floors, attached outdoor toilets to afford the experience of showering under either the sun or the stars. There are cheaper bamboo huts. Free use of boogie boards and snorkelling equipment is offered, and there are laundry and telephone services, a safe. Also exchanges Tcs and cash. The excellent attached restaurant attracts people from neighbouring bungalows.

D-E Sai Thong Bungalows, just off the road to Aow Kao Kwai, T077-820466/01-3670438. A set up with 4 clean, lovely wood and bamboo bungalows, each with attached western toilet, veranda and requisite hammock. They're set in a lovingly tended garden that ingeniously uses empty beer bottles as ornamentation. Slap bang on the golden sandy beach, with attached restaurant offering a wide variety of dishes. The friendly owner, Mr Plai, speaks good English. Recommended.

E Anan Bungalows, on the beach road leading north from the pier, near the temple. 5 quiet wooden bungalows with western toilets. Its proximity to the village makes it one of the cheaper options available, as eating in the village can't be bettered for those on a shoestring.

E Smile Huts, Aow Yai, T077-820335, www.thaismilehut.com. 16 romantic bamboo huts sparsely decorated with shells, attached western toilets, some plots even boast gardens, up a wooden ladder within the hut is a small room on a higher level that's perfect for children old enough not to fall down the trap door in the middle of the night. Very Swiss Family Robinson. Set in well-maintained gardens, and with a restaurant attached. Electricity from 1800-2230. Very helpful staff as well.

Hat Bang Baen

C Andaman Peace Bungalows, 10 bungalows built on an idyllic spot overlooking the sea, although the beach isn't made of white sand. They come with fan and fridge and are well maintained. Mainly Thai clientele. the attached restaurant has tables outside and in.

C-D Wasana Resort, this Dutch-Thai operation is on the left before the main park entrance, T092-908423. It offers 4 small bungalows of woven bamboo and wood, and 4 larger concrete options, all simply and tastefully decorated with western toilets and verandas arranged around a pleasant garden boasting a badminton net, ping-pong table, small (children's) pool and good restaurant. The proprietors are helpful and friendly, and dab hands at arranging day trips.

D Komain Villa, 10 charming little bungalows, painted a refreshing blue and arranged in a line, with attached toilets. There's no restaurant, but food can be bought in the shop across the road.

Kuraburi *p410*

The one resort here that has traditionally proved a good base from which to explore the local forests and do a bit of trekking, has recently re-opened following the tsunami.

A-B Kuraburi Greenview Resort, 129 Moo 5 Bangwan, 7 km south of Kuraburi, offers a pool and a golf driving range as well as free pick-ups from the airport in Phuket or Ranong. The resort also offers tours to the Similan and Surin Islands and to Khao Sok.

Prathong Island *p410*

AL Golden Buddha Beach Resort, T01-922203, www.goldenbuddhabeach.com. A full-board rate of an additional ฿650 is also available. Located on Prathong Island off the Phangnga coast, the resort supports a turtle conservation project run by the Chelon Institute on the same beach as the resort. Volunteers for the project are accommodated at the resort. Most work through the British Trust for Conservation Volunteers (see page 26). To re-open in Dec 2005.

Khao Sok National Park *p410*

Tourism is well developed around Khao Sok, and visitors have a considerable

degree of choice in how they travel to the park and where they stay. There are several bungalow operations near the park headquarters and new operations are sprouting up every year in the general area. Prices range from ฿200-800.

A-B Khao Sok Riverside Cottages, Km 106.5 (Highway 401), T01-2293750, www.khao-sok.com. A simple but stylish alternative. About 2½ km down a dirt road off the main Takua Pa-Phun Phin road, east of the national park headquarters, there are several wooden and bamboo cottages dispersed through an area of forest on a small hill beside a bend in the river. The restaurant, right beside the river, serves unimpressive Thai food. The cottages are delightful, built using traditional materials, with lots of windows, spacious balconies and clean bright bathrooms. The manager and designer of the resort, Khun Daycho, is the president of the local conservation group. **Khao Sok Riverside Cottages** runs walking tours and elephant trekking to forest adjacent to the resort (not actually in the national park) and also offers overnight camping and day visits to the lake.

B-C Our Jungle House, T01-8939583, our_jungle_house@hotmail.com, is also right on a river bend with several styles of accommodation. The Thai managers are friendly and helpful and the setting is peaceful and inviting with the central Thai-style house and restaurant set in a large park-like garden.

B-D Art's Riverview Lodge, F076-421614, artsriverviewlodge@yahoo.co.uk, or write to Art's Riverview Jungle Lodge, PO Box 28, Takua Pa, Phangnga 82110, Thailand). Has a range of rooms some built like Thai houses with several rooms together, all have simple bathrooms, mosquito nets, etc. The only lighting provided is by candles. The reception area and restaurant is right beside the river near a swimming hole.

B-D Khao Sok Rainforest Resort, the first resort on the left as you go down the entrance to the park, is located right next to the forest (most other bungalows are off to the right as you go towards the entrance and are near orchards and fields). The location provides opportunities to see birds and other wildlife from your room. Excellent reports from guests although the food is bland.

E Khao Sok Homestay, khaosok_homestay@hotmail.com, www.welcome.to/khaosok, 2 km down a side road after the main Khao Sok turn off, is a much quieter option. A sign on the gate says "Happiness is here." The owner's wife speaks good English.

Khao Lak *p411*

C-D Poseidon Bungalows, 1/6 Tambon Lam Kaen, Mu 2, Amphoe Thai Muang, T076-443258, www.similantour.nu. Up and running since the tsunami and used mainly by volunteers this estabishment 5 km south of main Khao Lak area has a range of rooms, some with bathrooms and beachfronts. Restaurant built out over the sea on stilts, Thai and European food. The bungalows are situated in a bay. The owners are very friendly and are a mine of local information, they can organize day and longer trips to local places of interest, boat trips and snorkelling, including a liveaboard to the Similans dedicated to snorkellers. Closes from May-Oct. Recommended.

Khao Lak-Lam Ru and Khao Lampee-Had Thai Muang national parks *p412*

Accommodation is available in 4 fan-cooled bungalows in the Thai Muang part of Khao Lampee-Had Thai Muang National Park. Prices range from ฿800 for a bungalow which can accommodate 6 people, to ฿1,000 for a bungalow which can accommodate 10 people. Bookings can be made at the central **Forestry Department** office in Bangkok (Reservations office, Marine National Parks Division, Royal Forest Department, Chatuchak, Bangkok, 10900 – T02-5797047-8) or at the park headquarters in Thai Muang. Call ahead to see if the bungalows are in operation. Camping is allowed and food and drinks can be purchased at the canteen.

Koh Similan *p413*

E-F Bungalows may be available on Koh Ba Ngu (9) by the time of publication. Reservations can be made at the **Similan National Park Office**, Thai Muang, or at Tap Lamu Pier (T076-411914). Camping may also be possible on Koh Ba Ngu (9). Bring your own tent.

Eating

Ranong *p406*

¥¥ J&T Food and Ice, in the centre of town on Ruangrat Rd, is excellent and serves a range of delicious but very reasonably priced Thai food and ice creams, very popular place with locals and farangs alike, friendly owners. Recommended.

¥¥ Somboon Restaurant, opposite the Jansom Thara Hotel, serves delicious Thai and Chinese seafood much of which is displayed in tanks in front.

Shopping

Ranong *p406*

Batik Shop on Thawi Sinkha Rd.

Activities and tours

Ranong *p406*

Tour operators

Ranong Travel, 37 Ruangrat Rd, is probably a better source of information than the tourist information office. It can book bungalows on Koh Chang, arrange fishing trips and advise on visiting Burma.

Ranong's Islands *p408*

Diving

A-One-Diving has opened a dive school on Koh Phayam, organizing trips all over the Andaman Sea, T077-820086/01-8915510, www.a-one-diving.com.

Khao Lak *p411*

Diving

Diving operations, including liveaboard boats, day trips and courses, are still widely available from various operators including Sea Dragon and Seal-Asia, see Diving, Phuket. Dive sites along the coast, including the Similan Islands, Ko Bon, Ko Tachai, Ko Surin and Richelieu Rock as well as the Mergui Archipelago, received minimal damage during the tsunami although there has been some changes around Island Number Nine in the Similans that you will need to check. You cannot, however, stay on the damaged Surin Islands which can still be visited daily on dive trips from coastal towns. The Similan Islands accommodation is also closed. The dive sites in the Mergui Archipelago were left unscathed while the islands escaped topside damage or destruction. Contrary to reports there are still Moken sea gypsies still living in the Mergui Archipelago.

Sea Dragon, 9/1 Moo 7, T. Khuk Kak, Khao Lak, T076-420420, www.seadragondivecenter.com, is up and running again in Khao Lak. A well-established operation running day trips or liveaboards to Richelieu Rock, Similan and Surin Islands. Teaches PADI dive courses. European-managed.

Koh Similan *p413*

Hotels and tour operators (see page 472) organize boat and dive trips and most dive companies in Phuket offer tours to the Similan Islands (see page 445). See also Tour operators, Bangkok, page 149 and Diving, Essentials, page 60. Although it is possible to visit the Similan Islands independently, it can be an expensive and/or time-consuming business; it is far easier to book onto a tour. See also under Khao Lak, above, for further information.

Transport

Ranong *p406*

Air

The airport is 20 km south of town. Bangkok Airways operates between **Bangkok** and Ranong several times a week.

Airline offices **Bangkok Airways**, 50/18 Moo 1, Phetkasem Highway, T077-835096.

Bus

The road journey from the north is arduous – 8 hrs – the last half of which is through mountains; not good for travel sickness sufferers. Consider taking the train from Bangkok to **Chumphon** and the bus from there (which takes the same amount of time). The bus terminal is on the edge of town, Highway 4, near the **Jansom Thara Hotel**. However, the buses stop in town on Ruangrat before the terminal. Songthaew number 2 passes the terminal. From Bangkok, the ordinary buses are around ฿160-180 while 2nd class a/c are ฿260. VIP costs ฿515. The a/c bus departs only twice in the morning and three times in the evening. Regular a/c and non-a/c connections with

Bangkok's Southern bus terminal near the Thonburi railway station. Also connections with **Chumphon**, **Surat Thani** and **Phuket** (304 km south).

Prathong Island *p410*
Some a/c and non-a/c connections between the Southern terminal in **Bangkok** and Takua Pa (12 hrs), the jumping off point for the island. From Krabi and Phangnga, take a bus towards Phuket and change at Kochloi to a bus running north to Takua Pa. From Phuket take a local bus to Takua Pa. Local buses and songthaews provide transport between smaller communities.

Khao Sok National Park *p410*
If visiting the park independently, take a local bus from Takua Pa to Phun Phin near Surat Thani town, or vice versa, and ask the driver to stop at the Khao Sok National Park (*oo-tayaan-haeng-chart-khao-sok*). When you arrive at the stop there will usually be a number of bungalow operators waiting to whisk you off to their establishment; you can otherwise walk or take transport into the park. If you decide to walk take a small pack as it's quite a hike to some bungalows. The drive from Takua Pa to Panom (about halfway between Takua Pa and Surat) is very scenic with views of dramatic limestone karst, forested mountains and valleys.

Khao Lak *p411*
Many buses now travel on a new road which bypasses Khao Lak and goes straight to Phangnga town, and then on to Phuket. Check that your bus passes through Khao Lak/Takua Pa/Ranong if you want to get off here. Different bus companies have different routes. There are some a/c and non-a/c connections with the Southern terminal in **Bangkok**.

Koh Surin *p413*
Boats leave from Patong or Rawai on **Phuket** (10 hrs), from **Ranong** (through the **Jansom Thara Resort**), see page 406, or from the pier at Ban Hin Lat, 1 km west of Kuraburi (4-5 hrs, ฿500). Long-tailed boats can be hired around Koh Surin, ฿400 for 4 hrs.

Koh Similan *p413*
Vessels depart from **Thap Lamu** pier, 20 km north of Thai Muang (3-5 hrs) to the Similans, 40 km offshore. Boats also leave from Ao Chalong and Patong Beach, **Phuket** (**Songserm Travel**, T076-222570 every Sat, Thu and Tue from Dec-Apr, 6-10 hrs. Finally, boats leave from **Ranong**, a busy deep-sea fishing port, see page 406. See also Activities and tours above.

Directory

Ranong *p406*
Banks On Tha Muang Rd there are branches of **Bank of Ayudya**, **Siam Commercial Bank**, **Thai Farmers Bank** and **Thai Military Bank**, all with ATMs and/or exchange facilities. **Medical services** Hospital situated at the junction of Permphon and Kamlungsab roads. **Post office** Chon Rao Rd, near the junction with Dap Khadi Rd. There is also a Poste Restante service. **Telephone** Office on Ruangrat Rd.

Phuket Island

→ *Colour map 4, grid C1.*

Known as 'the Pearl of Thailand' because of its shape, Phuket lies on the west coast of the Kra Isthmus in the warm Andaman Sea and is connected to the mainland by the 700-m-long Sarasin causeway. It is a fully developed resort island with hundreds of hotels including some that are world-renowned. The name Phuket is derived from the Malay word bukit, meaning crystal mountain, and it is Thailand's only island to have provincial status. It is about the same size as Singapore (550 sq km) – making it Thailand's largest island. While its wild monkeys, rhinos, elephants and tigers disappeared around the beginning of the 19th century, there is still tropical rainforest to be found on Phuket at Kaho Phrao Thaeo National Park.

Phuket did suffer considerably following the 2004 tsunami, see Background below, for further information. ▸▸ *For Sleeping, Eating and other listings, see pages 432-449.*

Ins and outs

Getting there

Phuket is nearly 900 km south of Bangkok. Getting to the island is easy. Phuket International Airport is in the north of the island, about 30 km from Phuket City, but rather closer to many of the main beaches and hotels. There are international connections and multiple daily connections with Bangkok as well as with Koh Samui, Chiang Mai and Hat Yai and daily connections to Krabi. The main bus terminal is in Phuket City and there are regular connections with Bangkok (14 hours) as well as destinations in the south. The southern railway line doesn't come to the island. However, it is possible to take a train to Phun Phin near Surat Thani and then catch a connecting bus. ▸▸ *See Transport, page 447, for further details.*

Getting around

Songthaew buses run from Phuket City to all the beaches at regular intervals from 0600-1800 for ฿15-25. There are also numerous places to hire cars/jeeps, ฿900 a day and motorbikes, ฿150 a day as well as minivans that can be used as meterless taxis. Local buses stop around 1800; meterless taxis take advantage of this so it is essential to know what constitutes a reasonable fare. Beware and insist on the meter being used whenever possible. For a final option, an air-conditioned micro-bus service operates around Phuket City for ฿10.

Best time to visit

The driest and sunniest months are November-April. May-October are wetter with more chance of overcast conditions, although daily sunshine still averages five-eight hours. August is when the monsoon begins and red flags appear to warn swimmers not to venture out because of powerful and fatal currents.

Tourist information

TAT ⓘ *73-75 Phuket Rd, T076-212213, www.phukettourism.org/phuket/index.html, 0830-1630*, is good for specific local questions and problems relating to Phuket and Phangnga. It provides useful town maps and transport details. Two sources of free information are **The Greater Phuket Magazine**, a glossy 92-page magazine which comes out nine times a year and is available in resorts, bars and restaurants, and the **Phuket Gazette**, www.phuketgazette.com (฿20), a newspaper/magazine format which has quirky local human interest stories and scandals among the standard community updates. There are many tour companies offering a range of excursions and tours, see Activities and tours, page 444.

Background

Phuket was first 'discovered' by Arab and Indian navigators around the end of the ninth century, although it is rumoured that the island appears on charts as early as the first century. The first Europeans (Dutch pearl traders) arrived in the 16th century. Always a rich island – known for its pearls, fish and fruits – Phuket proved irresistible to the Burmese who carried out a surprise attack in 1785 after having already captured Ayutthaya, the ancient capital of Thailand. But, while the governor of Phuket had just died, he had left behind his wily young widow Chan and her equally clever sister Mook. The resourceful pair immediately disguised all the women of the town as men and had them pose as soldiers along the walls of Thalang – then capital of Phuket. Fearing the worst from the fierce-looking ranks, the Burmese retreated. Chan and Mook were honoured for their bravery and today, on the road to the airport, may be

Phuket Island

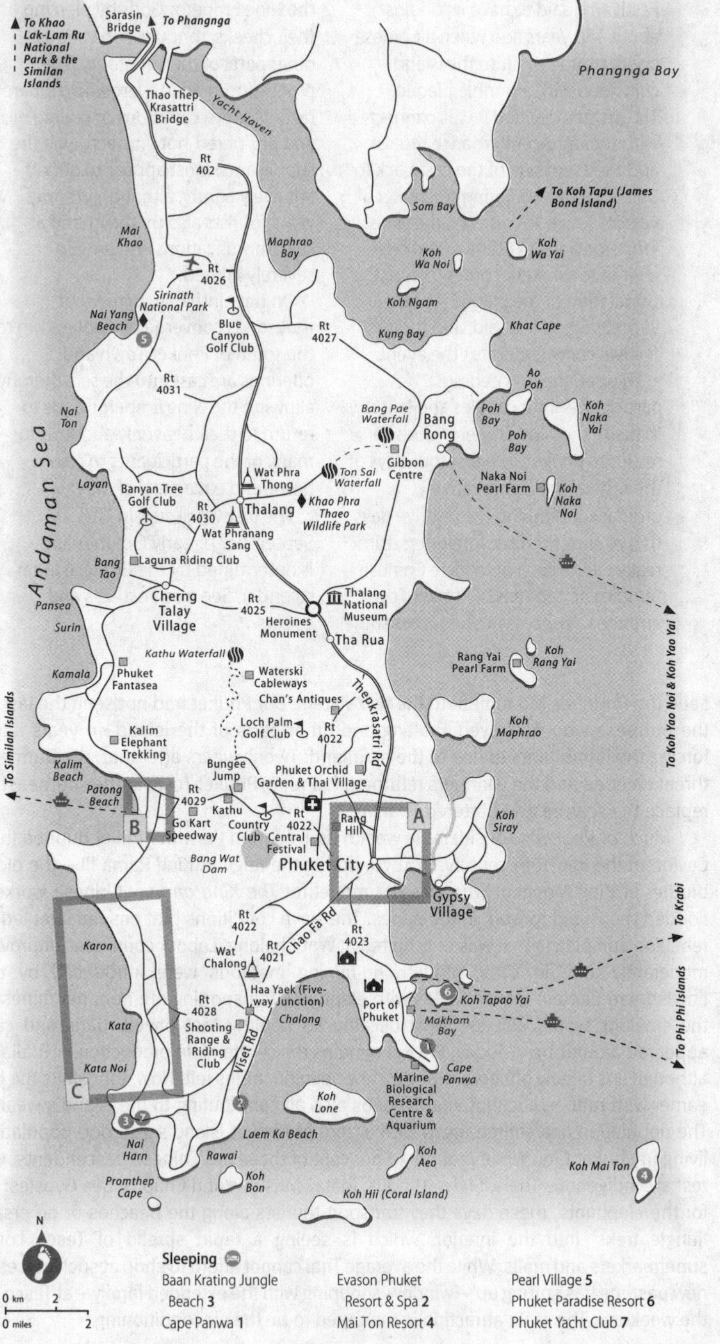
To Khao Lak-Lam Ru National Park & the Similan Islands
Sarasin Bridge
To Phangnga
Phangnga Bay
Thao Thep Krasattri Bridge
Yacht Haven
Rt 402
To Koh Tapu (James Bond Island)
Som Bay
Mai Khao
Maphrao Bay
Koh Wa Yai
Koh Wa Noi
Rt 4026
Koh Ngam
Sirinath National Park
Nai Yang Beach
Blue Canyon Golf Club
Rt 4027
Kung Bay
Khat Cape
Rt 4031
Ao Poh
Nai Ton
Bang Pae Waterfall
Bang Rong
Poh Bay
Poh Bay
Koh Naka Yai
Andaman Sea
Gibbon Centre
Wat Phra Thong
Ton Sai Waterfall
Naka Noi Pearl Farm
Koh Naka Noi
Layan
Banyan Tree Golf Club
Rt 4030
Thalang
Khao Phra Thaeo Wildlife Park
Wat Phranang Sang
Bang Tao
Laguna Riding Club
Thalang National Museum
Pansea
Cherng Talay Village
Rt 4025
Heroines Monument
Surin
Tha Rua
To Koh Yao Noi & Koh Yao Yai
Kathu Waterfall
Rang Yai Pearl Farm
Koh Rang Yai
Kamala
Phuket Fantasea
Waterski Cableways
Chan's Antiques
Thepkrasatri Rd
To Similan Islands
Koh Maphrao
Loch Palm Golf Club
Rt 4022
Kalim Elephant Trekking
Kalim Beach
Bungee Jump
Phuket Orchid Garden & Thai Village
Patong Beach
Rt 4029
Kathu
Koh Siray
B
Go Kart Speedway
Kathu Country Club
Rt 4022
Central Festival
Rang Hill
A
Bang Wat Dam
Phuket City
Gypsy Village
Rt 4022
Chao Fa Rd
Rt 4023
To Krabi
Karon
Wat Chalong
Rt 4021
Haa Yaek (Five-way Junction)
Koh Tapao Yai
Rt 4028
Chalong
Port of Phuket
To Phi Phi Islands
Makham Bay
Kata
Shooting Range & Riding Club
Viset Rd
Kata Noi
Cape Panwa
Marine Biological Research Centre & Aquarium
C
Koh Lone
Laem Ka Beach
Nai Harn
Rawai
Koh Aeo
Koh Mai Ton
Promthep Cape
Koh Bon
Koh Hii (Coral Island)
N
0 km 2
0 miles 2
Sleeping
Baan Krating Jungle Beach 3
Cape Panwa 1
Evason Phuket Resort & Spa 2
Mai Ton Resort 4
Pearl Village 5
Phuket Paradise Resort 6
Phuket Yacht Club 7

Phuket's festival of mortification

The Ngan Kin Jeh (Chinese Vegetarian Festival) is said to have its origins about 150 years ago when a Chinese opera troupe's visit to the island coincided with a terrible plague. The artistes decided it was connected with their pre-performance rituals and they sent one of the cast back to China to light and bring to Phuket a vast joss stick. In this way, the Nine Emperor Gods of China might be invited to Phuket in order to cure the population of the plague. They succeeded, so it is said and today's festival commemorates the event.

To open the proceedings, participants light candles and lanterns to invite the Nine Emperor Gods to return to Phuket. The first four days of the festival are comparatively ordinary. It is during the last five days that events, for most foreigners, turn really weird. Each of the five Chinese temples or pagodas of Phuket Town arranges a procession. Devotees show their commitment and the power of the Nine Emperor Gods by piercing their cheeks, tongues and various other parts of their anatomy. The processions end in a large field where razor ladders, cauldrons of boiling oil, and pits of red-hot embers await the supplicants. Most appear to get off relatively lightly, although in some years tourists also try their hand at such mortifications and end up severely injured.

On the ninth day, a crowd of thousands converge on Saphan Hin to the south of Phuket Town and offerings are cast into the sea, thereby allowing the Nine Emperor Gods to return to their heavenly abode, and many of the participants to return home and eat a meal of meat.

The festival occurs in late September or early October and is determined by the Chinese lunar calendar. See also Festivals and events.

seen the Heroines Monument to the two sisters. But Phuket had not seen the last of the Burmese who destroyed Thalang and other parts of the island 40 years later, forcing the inhabitants to flee to the mainland. Twenty years after that, the Burmese threat receded and the islanders returned, founding Phuket Town in the southeast to replace the scarred and battered Thalang.

Much of Phuket's considerable wealth derived from tin with Phuket dubbed Junk Ceylon in the mid-16th century. In 1876, during the reign of King Rama III – the older brother of King Mongkut who was the model for *The King and I* – Chinese workers flooded the island to work in the mines. The slave conditions that ensued later led to rebellion and pillage that was only halted at Wat Chalong. Labour conditions improved moderately and, in 1907, modern tin-mining methods were introduced by the Englishman Captain Edward Miles with elephants transporting ore from the mines to the smelting works. Phuket Town became so wealthy that paved roads and cars appeared around 1910. Today, Phuket remains the centre of tin production in Thailand although it is largely offshore with very few open tin mines left. Now, tourism is the big earner with rubber, coconut and fisheries also all contributing to the island's wealth. The population has shifted again with a third of Phuket Island's 200,000 population living in Phuket City. While around 30 per cent of these are Chinese descendents, the rest are indigenous Thais, Sikhs, Hindus, Malay Muslims and Chao Le Sea Gypsies. As for the elephants, these days they transport tourists along the beaches or on ersatz 'jungle treks' into the interior, which is seeing a rapid spread of Tesco Lotus supermarkets and malls. While the average Thai cannot afford to shop at such places, a new pastime has sprung up – window-shopping with the extended family – at Tesco on the weekend. The main attraction is rumoured to be the air-conditioning.

The tsunami of 26 December 2004 hit Phuket at a peak time for tourism, with the infamously raucous Patong Beach suffering tremendous loss of life. Indeed, much of the televised footage came from Patong which had provided nearly 40 per cent of Thailand's $10 billion annual income from tourism. The economic tsunami had begun with hand-written pleas appearing throughout devastated streets. Some signs promised "I give you low price. Victim of tsunami." Others simply read – "Phuket okay, Thailand need you." Loyal tourists who had been coming to Thailand for years, did return, fearing that a lack of travellers would prove the final blow for Thailand's formerly premier resort island. Joining them were opportunist travellers lured by the lowest prices in years and relief workers. And, since that fateful Boxing Day, Phuket's beaches have largely recovered with Patong touted as a minor miracle. The grand sweep of Patong is still enviable and the smaller beaches – amiable. Of Phuket's other beaches, Bang Tao, Kamala, Kata, Karon, Nai Harn and Phuket Fantasea all suffered damage. While it was superficial at some, like Karon, others like Kamala and Bang Tao still need time to recover fully. Even on Patong, however, the small businesses are smarting and some have had to close for good as vital compensation never appeared. Land grabs by developers in the wake of the disaster also forced out the little guy. But other grassroots businesses have cropped up. It is now possible to take home your very own tsunami souvenir DVD, home pics of piles of bloated corpses or a customized T-shirt.

Phuket City → *Colour map 4, grid C1.*

Phuket Town has recently been upgraded to Phuket City. This has come as a surprise to many who still regard it as a sleepy provincial hub, hardly big or bustling enough to merit the city crown. Treated largely as a stopover by divers en route to the Similan or Surin Islands and beach junkies headed further up the coast, Phuket City is now anxious to revamp its image and pull in a more sophisticated crowd. So, in addition to its Sino-Portugese architectural heritage – a leftover of the wealthy Chinese tin barons of the 19th century – there is a burgeoning arts and literary scene and even a foreign film festival once a year. It seems to be working as, increasingly, the city's incomers include weary Bangkok urbanites hankering for a business by the sea and expat foodies attracted by the city's excellent restaurant reputation. But, at this stage, Phuket City is still small enough and swamped enough by the glory of the beaches, to be down the pecking order. Not that this matters to the old-timers who can still remember when the town was surrounded by virgin forest and who could care less because Phuket City has always been prosperous enough. This is, perhaps, the card up Phuket City's sleeve – a subtle confidence underneath the tourist glitter, especially in the Old Town, and a feeling that another chapter is unravelling in this prosperous settlement. A cooler, hipper Phuket could easily emerge if the arts scene gets beyond the cottage industry feeling and allows itself to be injected by that incoming Bangkok and expat buzz. But they will need to ward off the High Street Anywhere effect that has taken over so many of the beaches west of Phuket City. What will aid Phuket City is that there are still some old and grand buildings left, rare in Thailand and a magnet for those with an eye for architecture.

At the end of the 19th century, Phuket Town, one of the richest settlements in the country, saw a flowering of **Sino-Portugese mansions** built by tin-barons revelling in their wealth. Old Phuket Town is the place to go to check out these jewels in the crown – houses and shops in styles similar to that of Penang and Macao and dating back 100-130 years. Featuring complex latticework, Mediterranean coloured ceramic tiles, high ceilings and gleaming wooden interiors, these architectural dreams, remain cool in the summer and free of damp during the monsoon. While the style is commonly called Sino-Portugese, many of these were actually built by Italian workers who imported materials straight from Italy. Once a year at the end of the Old Phuket Town

Festival in mid-December, these houses are open to the public. The best examples are along Thalang, Yaowarat, Ranong, Phangnga, Krabi, Dibuk, Rassada, Soi Romanee and Damrong roads.

A particularly notable example of one of Phuket's finer older buildings is the **Government House** which stood in as the 'American Embassy' in Phnom Penh in the classic film – *The Killing Fields*. Preservation orders have been placed on all buildings in Old Phuket Town. Among the finer buildings are the **Chartered Bank THAI office** on Ranong Road opposite the market, and the **Sala Phuket** on Damrong Road. You will notice that there is a police station right opposite the bank. Apparently the expatriate community involved in the lucrative tin trade demanded a police station to tackle raiders after they had a bank built. Less grand, but quietly elegant, are the turn-of-the-century **shophouses** on, for example, Thalang Road. There has been considerable renovation of buildings on Dibuk and Thalang and Krabi roads but

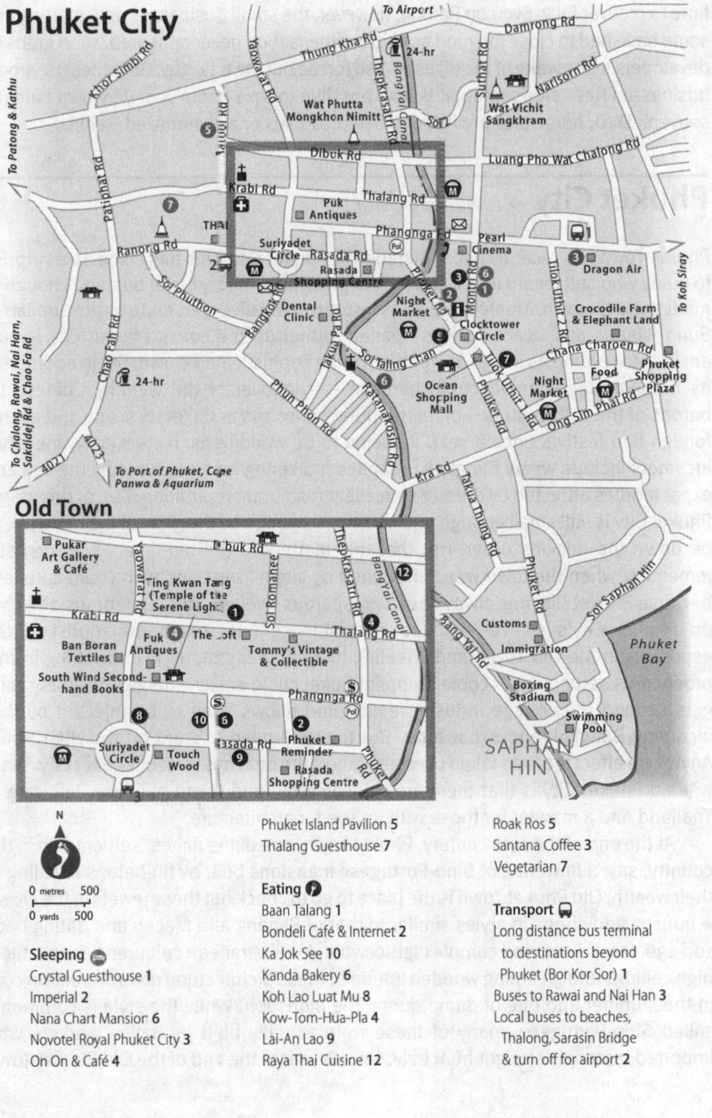

Post-pregnancy pampering

First there was Thai massage, tamarind body scrubs and herbal baths. Now the latest thing to hit the spa set is 'u fai' touted as traditional post-natal care. 'U fai' sessions can either take place at 'u fai' spa centers or in your very own space. Among the delights of 'u fai' are sitting over heated coals to reshape the vagina and wrapping the tummy with a heating brick to reduce fluid retention. This is followed by using hot compresses to refirm the slacking uterus. Perhaps more familiar to the west – and less daunting - are the herbal steam baths, bust massage (to keep those breasts from drooping) and the good old-fashioned facial and body massage.

nearby there are still side streets with some lovely examples of traditional shophouses. Soi Romanee in particular is such a street with traditional merchant houses on both sides of the road, a few with fading paintwork on the walls. Some of the renovation has introduced smart new restaurants, cafés, art galleries and antique shops. Notably, **The Loft** which sells expensive Southeast Asian antiques and Chinese porcelains and who received an award for its efforts in conserving traditional architecture. At the same time there are still plenty of more traditional hardware stores, small tailors, stationery shops and the like that clearly cater to the locals. Another sight worth visiting in the Old Town is the **Temple of the Serene Light**. This is on Phangnga road and the entrance is marked in English and Thai. Although it feels a little strange to take the narrow alleyway and to go into the temple, there are signs telling the story of the place in English, reassuring for Western visitors. Believed to be 110 years old, this is a small Taoist temple filled with paintings and religious artefacts that was rebuilt following a fire. It is the oldest Taoist temple in Phuket and is dedicated to the Goddess of Mercy, see page 341.

There are **night markets** on Ong Sim Phai and Tilok Uthit 1 roads. The night markets are excellent places to purchase spicy rolls and other street-foods suitable for nibbling on a nocturnal prowl through the Old Town.

Phuket's beaches

The gorgeous 3-km long sweep of sand and coconut palms of Patpong Beach that attracted backpackers in the 1970s is now a dim memory. While the towering palms went down with the buildings when the waves came in, new ones have been planted but the beach still looks somewhat devoid of shade and balance. The beach road is also not where returnee tourists expect it to be but then, the smaller side roads or soi, have been praised for being much cleaner than usual. Initially, there were hopes that Phuket would go for less development the second time around but this proved a fantasy. But, for less hedonistic, smaller beaches that still have charm, you can go south of Patong. Here you will find the twin, horseshoe-shaped **Karon** and **Kata beaches**. Karon is around half the size, less densely developed than Patong and the general atmosphere is more laid-back and family friendly. Kata Beach is like a mini-Patong with hotels, restaurants and shops chaotically jostling for space. The presence of surfers, their wild and crazy ladies and backpackers is a fair indication of the kind of nightlife.

At Phuket's southern end is **Nai Harn**, a pretty white beach favoured by locals with a small number of more expensive hotels and limited amenities. This was hit hard by the wave which covered it with detritus but has since been cleaned up. While

the bamboo restaurants at the back of the beach received only water damage, the restaurants at the entrance to the main hotel here – the luxury **Royal Meridien Phuket Yacht Club** – were completely wiped out. However, the hotel itself received only superficial damage and is fully operational. Not much is expected to change on this charming beach with an unexpected bodyguard against big developers proving to be Samnak Song Monastery smack dab in the middle of the beach.

The east coast of Phuket is only thinly developed from a tourist point of view. Much of it is rocky and the beaches that are to be found here do not compare with those on the west coast. There are some excellent hotels, but these are largely stand-alone establishments; don't expect a great wealth of activities and facilities.

Kamala Beach, north of Patong, was deeply affected by the tsunami, with much of the landscape left distraught and a harsh death toll. At the time of the first wave, Thai locals and tourists, who saw the tide go out over 300 metres, rushed onto the beach with buckets to collect fish that has been left stranded on the sand. When the second wave returned over 15 minutes later, it took away many more. The waters destroyed nearly everything, reaching right up to the main coast road and even flooding **Phuket Fantasea**. The local school, restuarants and shops were flattened while **Kamala Bay Terrace Resort** and **Kamala Dreams** resort received significant damage and may not reopen. The next beach north is **Surin**. Surin was home to Phuket's first golf course more than 60 years ago during the reign of King Rama V I. The course is largely in disuse now except as a park and the beach is patronized mostly by Thais – especially on Sundays when they picnic here. Choppy water – particularly during the monsoon – and a steep incline keep the beach from being too developed. While there are a few exclusive resorts close by, the guests here only rarely feel the need to venture beyond the confines of their hotels. You can camp on the beach for free.

Surin and **Bang Tao**, further north still, are similar in that the resorts are widely spaced and there is no core area of facilities and amenities. Bang Tao was formerly used for extensive tin-mining which turned the landscape into a Dune/Star Wars desert scape. **Nai Ton** and **Layan** are small bays developed with exclusive resorts. The limited development proved a saving grace at Layan as the seawater surged back some 400 metres from the more or less empty beachfront. Finally, at the northernmost end of the island, is **Nai Yang Beach** and the **Nai Yang National Park**, a 9-km-long stretch of casuarina-lined beach with a small number of resorts and some park bungalows. See under each area for further details.

Patong Beach

Patong began to metamorphose from a hippy paradise into a commercial centre during the 1970s. It is now a mass of neon signs advertising hotels, massage parlours, restaurants, straight bars, gay bars, nightclubs and the plain peculiar. Moralistic despair set firmly to one side, it is a haven of 'short-time' hotel stays of an hour, yabba and E-dealing katoeys (lady boys) (see box page 668) and bog-eyed dissolutes. But, at the same time, while families may not be able to avoid vulgarity by the bucketload and may even add to it, they will be able to bypass psychotic lady boys and devious side-street deals by choosing from a range of excellent tailored family hotels. In general, the tourists of Patong are a mixed lot – a Butlins overspill, utterly shameless Jack-the-lads and plump retirees. Increasingly, Russians are also turning up – both for business and as revellers.

On the watersport front, Patong also offers the widest selection on Phuket and in spite of the hotel development, it is still possible to snorkel on the reef at the southern end of the bay.

Karon and Kata beaches

The horseshoe-shaped Karon and Kata beaches south of Patong are divided by a narrow rocky outcrop. Karon started tourist life as a haven for backpackers; it is now

Shake, Rattle and Roll

A sure sign of recovery from the tsunami in certain rock and roll venues in Patong was the re-appearance of Thai Elvis singing Wooden Heart.

Clad in the usual shimmering array of enough rhinestones to sink the Titanic, the King can be fawned over, once again, at theme nights and even while noshing on BBQ ribs at the Karon Sea Sands Resort in Karon Road.

The enduring popularity in Thailand of the former trucker from Memphis, Tennessee, is all down to a chance meeting in 1960 between the King of Siam and Elvis in 1960. Captured in a tinted photograph, on the set of G.I. Blues in Hollywood, are the two Kings - Elvis in freshly pressed army fatigues.

Consequently, the King of rock and roll , who never visited Thailand, became an enduring icon on cigarette packets, telly adverts and clothes brands. But the best time to catch the King is either on Elvis' birthday or the anniversary of his death. That's when bands like "The President Band" and Elvises named "Lek (little) Elvis" or Yaowarat Elvis come out to croon. For the truly Elvis obsessed, there's even Elvis conferences, the last one in Bangkok attracting 200 imitators of the immortal rocker.

well developed, with a range of hotels and bungalows and a wide selection of restaurants. Although there is a tiny hippy/alternative corner at the southern end of the beach, tipped off by a reggae bar, on the whole, prosperous Scandinavians dominate now. Some places bear mini-Swedish flags and it is usually these establishments that offer solid favourites guaranteed to stave off tummy bugs but at the same time make you feel as if you never left the aeroplane. This can prove wearing after a time and an air of predictability and safety pervades the beach. Karon's major drawback, physically, is the overly exposed beach despite its cosy curve. Nonetheless, there are good mid-range places to stay on Karon, and the slower pace of life here will appeal to many. Kata consists of two beaches: **Kata Yai** (Big Kata) and **Kata Noi** (Little Kata), divided by a cliff. Both bays are very picturesque with rocks to the edges and sweeping fine pale yellow sands in the centre. Coming down a winding hill, Kata Noi happily surprises, offering an adorable little bay with a small and perfect beach. Although it is dominated somewhat by the **Amari Kata Thani Hotel**, on the whole, this feels very much like a hidden seaside harbour and even the tourist infrastructure of souvenir shops, guesthouses, laundries and restaurants pose a pleasant jumble of locally owned businesses. There are also cheapish bungalows here. The snorkelling is good around Koh Pu, the island in the middle of the bay which looks like a squashed bowler hat, and at the south end of Kata Noi. Kata Yai, just the other side, is a sprawling mass of development: hotels, souvenir shops and roadside restaurants abound. It provides excellent facilities for the holidaymaker including numerous options for watersports and a lot of choices for nightlife down the rambling streets running inland from the coast. Despite this, the huge hotels on the beach overwhelm the bay with umbrellas and sunbeds spread across almost the entire beach area. The beautifully painted and cared-for tour boats replete with smart wooden benches and umbrellas are a far cry from the traditional longboats of the local fishermen, obviously modelled on these boats. Nor are these tour boats owned by local fishermen; instead fleets are owned and rented out by local (and not so local) businessmen.

Nai Harn and Promthep Cape

Nai Harn is a small, gently sloping beach – home to the prestigious Phuket Yacht Club – and one of the island's most beautiful locations with spectacular sunsets. The

slopes of the bay are very steep so most accommodation in this area requires walking up and down numerous steps. From Nai Harn it is possible to walk to **Promthep Cape,** the best place to view the sunset. Near the highest point there is a shrine covered in gold leaf and surrounded by wooden elephants.

Rawai and Koh Kaew Pisadarn → *14 km from Phuket Town.*

To the north of Promthep Cape, up the eastern side of the island, the first beach is Rawai, which was first 'discovered' by King Rama VII in the 1920s. This crescent-shaped beach is now relatively developed although not to the same degree, nor in the same style, as Patong or Karon being more popular with Thai and Southeast Asian tourists, particularly during Chinese New Year and Songkarn. Many locals go to Rawai for the cheap Thai restaurants although this is starting to change as prices go up. The bay is sheltered from the monsoon and it is safe to swim throughout the year. But the beach, though long and relatively peaceful, is rather dirty and rocky. Rawai is more of a jumping-off point for offshore trips to Koh Hae (Coral Island), Koh Bon and Koh Lone. At Rawai's northern end there is also a 'sea gypsy' tribal village, **Chao Le**.

Koh Kaew Pisadarn ① *take a long-tailed boat from Rawai Beach; negotiate with one of the boat-owners, take a picnic and arrange to be picked up at a convenient time,* can be seen from Promthep Cape and is a short 15-minute ride by boat from Rawai Beach. The island is the site of not one, not two, but an amazing three footprints of the Buddha. Two of the footprints are located among the boulders and stone on the upper shore; the third is situated just below the low watermark. For many years important Buddhist festivals were celebrated here because of the island's supposed spiritual power and significance; then, about 40 years ago, these religious pilgrimages stopped. Sam Fang, who researched a story on the island for the *Bangkok Post*, discovered a tragedy had occurred about this time. A storm had sunk some rowing boats en route to the island, which locals blamed on a resident sea serpent that had become enraged by continual trespassing. When attempts were made to construct images of the Buddha on the island between 1952 and 1967, these were continually thwarted by bad weather and high seas. The island quickly gained the reputation of being cursed. Only in 1994 were attempts at erecting a Buddha image renewed. Defying superstition, is a 1½-m-high standing image cast in concrete on the northeastern side of the island, overlooking Promthep Cape, and about a 10-minute walk along a laid path from the boat landing. The image is surrounded by two protective nagas that slither over the top of the encircling balustrade. The footprints themselves are located on the shore beneath the Buddha; steps lead down to them. In 1995 the celebration of Loi Krathong at Koh Kaew Pisadarn was reintroduced.

Laem Ka, Chalong beaches and Wat Chalong

The next beaches up the east coast are Laem Ka Beach and Chalong. Ao Chalong is 1 km off the main road. There is not much here for the sun-and-sea worshipper and the beach is filthy. Offshore tin-dredging is said to have ruined it. Boats can be caught to the offshore islands for game fishing, snorkelling and scuba-diving from Chalong's long pier. There is also a small collection of reasonable seafood restaurants from which you can watch the dozens of working boats and pleasure boats gather off the pier in the harbour. The rest of the east coast is limited for tourists because of a rocky coast.

About 6 km south of Phuket Town, just north of Chalong Junction, is the ostentatious Wat Chalong, best known for its gold-leaf encrusted statues of the previous abbots, Luang Pho Chaem and Luang Pho Chuang. The former was highly respected for his medical skills, which proved to be particularly valuable when Phuket's Chinese miners revolted in 1876. The halving of the international price of tin coupled with Bangkok's attempt to extract excessive taxes from the province inflamed the Chinese. Some 2,000 converged on the governor's house and when they failed to take the building, they rampaged through the less well-defended

Shark's fin

Throughout Asia, wherever there are large populations of Chinese, shark's fin soup is on the menu of the more expensive or traditional restaurants.

For those tempted to partake, be aware, that the shark is a little understood animal with important and complex interactions with key marine systems such as coral reefs. Sharks are critical to maintaining a natural balance in reef systems. Take away the sharks and parrot fish and other species which graze on coral increase leading to excessive grazing and later destruction of the reef system.

Shark fisheries have been increasing dramatically as demand not only for shark fins, but also for other shark products, rises year by year. In 1994, 182,000 million tonnes of sharks were brought to shore by the fisheries sector. This does not include the millions of sharks thrown away into the sea after being caught accidentally during fishing for more lucrative commercial species such as blue tuna. The real total catch is estimated to be as much as twice as great as the statistics show.

Nowadays, sharks are stripped of their fins before being discarded in the oceans. The biology of the shark, unlike other fish, does not lend itself to large-range exploitation. Sharks are at the very top of the food chain. They live for a long time and produce few young, most of which will survive to adulthood, in direct contrast to most commercially fished species. Little is known about many shark species which are highly migratory. Therefore, the impact of this increase in fishing of sharks for products such as the fins is not known. It's also not possible to say whether any species of shark is currently threatened by this fishing activity, but past experience in shark fisheries does not bode well. To date every fishery directed at sharks has collapsed as the shark populations have been decimated.

Until we know more about shark fisheries and understand the impact of our desires for shark products, please take the precautionary approach and stay clear of shark's fin soup. In June 2000, responding to passenger concern, THAI Airways took shark's fin soup off its in-flight menu.

(Statistics taken from the TRAFFIC South East Asia report on species in danger: *Managing Shark Fisheries: Opportunities for International Conservation*, by Michael L Weber and Sonja V Fordham)

villages. The spree of killing and looting was only finally brought to an end at Wat Chalong where the two well-respected monks talked the mob out of their fury.

Cape Panwa

South of Phuket Town, down Sakdidej Road which becomes Route 4023, in the grounds of the **Cape Panwa Hotel**, is **Panwa House**, one of Phuket's finest examples of Sino-Portuguese architecture. Panwa House was formerly inhabited by a fishing family from Phuket and later, by the hotel ground's offical coconut catcher. The catcher's job was to remove coconuts from the trees so that that guests would not be concussed. However, he was under strict order not to take even one coconut from the trees on the beach. In all his years as official coconut catcher, he never disobeyed. The house is now filled with curious artefacts, like the coconut scraper in the shape of an otter-like animal. There are two floors and you are well advised to wander to the top and take in the view of the guests below at their meal, framed by swaying palms and beach and being serenaded by performers – very Fantasy Island. At the tip of Panwa Cape is the **Marine Biological Research Centre and Aquarium** ⓣ *T076-391126*,

1000-1600, ฿20, there are regular public songthaews every hour (฿10) from the market area on Ranong Rd to the Aquarium. The air-conditioned aquarium is well laid out with a moderate collection of salt and fresh water fish, lobsters, molluscs and turtles and promises some really wierdie species. This centre has only recently re-opened thanks to funding from the Danish Government. After a visit to the centre, you could do worse than take in the sunset along the paved seafront. It is sublimely free of tourists and there are a limited number of café/restaurants, all open to a view which always seems to include imposing Thai Navy boats in the distance. It is possible to charter **long-tailed boats** from Cape Panwa to **Koh Hii** (฿600), and **Koh Mai Ton** (฿1200), or to go fishing (฿1200). See below.

Koh Lone, Koh Mai Ton and other southern islands

There are places to stay on several of the islands off the east and southeast coasts of Phuket. All the resorts here play on the desert island getaway theme. These places are hard to reach in the monsoon season and often shut for up to three months. Koh Mai Ton, for instance, is a private island 9 km southeast of Phuket with very little on it except the **Mai Ton Resort**. This fits the bill for those truly 'deserted tropical island' holidays, except the resort seems rather out of place with mock-classical pillars by the pool and rooms that could be on any tropical island.

Kamala Beach

Kamala Beach was laid low by the tsunami and its Muslim population left reeling, with a flattened school, roads wiped out and bungalows crushed. It remains to be seen just how this beach will be re-developed but there is talk of transforming the area into a cultural centre although it lacks the heritage qualities of Phuket's Old Town.

Surin Beach and Pansea Beach

Surin Beach is quite dirty, perhaps because no one is concerned about the cleanliness of the beach. It is lined with casuarina trees and open-air restaurants, patronized mostly by Thais. The seabed shelves away steeply from the shoreline and swimming can be dangerous. There is a short golf course here and no hotels on the beach. Pansea Beach is a tiny soft-sand beach in a steeply sloping bay just north of Surin with two exclusive hotels on it.

Bang Tao Beach

The southern part of the beach sadly caught the brunt of the wave and, though steadily rebuilding, it is not up to its former stylishness. However, to the north is the **Laguna Phuket** which miraculously escaped the waves. This complex consists of four expensive hotels built around a lagoon. Free tuk-tuks and boats link the hotels and guests are able to use all the facilities. There is a great range of watersports and good provision for children – all facilities free. The Canal Village offers 40 or so shops and a lagoon-side café serving satay. The adjoining bakery serves good pastries and cakes. To the south of the **Laguna Phuket** there is a smattering of other places to stay. The most recent additions to this southern section of the beach are all fairly small, stylish and intimate in design. This southern part of the beach is also one of the few areas where you will still see traditional boat builders and, for that matter, traditional fishing boats (instead of the tourist variety used to take people on island tours).

Nai Thon and Layan

Between Bang Tao and Nai Yang are the isolated beaches of Nai Thon and Layan. These beaches have recently been developed with a luxury resort and spa at Layan occupying the whole bay and similarly expensive developments are moving into Nai Thon which only has a 400-m-long beach. South of Nai Thon is an exquisite cove, most easily accessible by boat.

Nai Yang and Nai Yang National Park

Nai Yang is close to the airport and 37 km from Phuket City (entrance ฿5 for car). Nai Yang is the northernmost beach and part of the Nai Yang National Park. The visitor centre is open Monday-Saturday 0830-1630. Further south, there is more activity, with a range of luxury hotels and bungalows. The park encompasses Nai Yang and Mai Khao beaches, which together form the longest stretch of beach on the island (13 km). The area was declared a national park in 1981 to protect the turtles which lay their eggs here from November to March. Eggs are collected by the Fisheries Department and young turtles are released into the sea around the second week of April (check on the date as it changes from year to year), on 'Turtle Release Festival Day'. The north end of the beach (where there is good snorkelling on the reef) is peaceful and secluded, with the only accommodation being in the national park bungalows, see below.

Mai Khao

This is Phuket's mortherntmost and largest beach – still with no proper development. Instead there is the village of Had Mai Khao and the Sirinath National Park. The village is dominated by shrimp nurseries which sell the grown shrimp on to numerous shrimp farms throughout the south of Thailand. These do discharge some waste to the sea off the Mai Khao beach, but not to the same levels as shrimp farms. Again, sea turtles nest on this beach, including the huge **leatherbacks** with the turtle releasing festival in mid-April. The local community effort to conserve the turtles involves collecting the eggs and keeping a hatchery. Details of this work can be found at the one low-budget bungalow resort on the beach – the **Mai Khao Bungalows**. The beach is very steeply shelved so swimming isn't recommended and it isn't really suitable for children. The length of the beach is lined with beach forest and casuarina trees.

Heroines' Monument, Thalang National Museum and Wat Phranang Sang

About 12 km north from Phuket Town on Route 402, towards the airport, is the village of **Tha Rua**. At the crossroads there is a statue of two female warriors: **Muk** and **Chan**. These are the sisters who repelled an army of Burmese invaders in 1785 by dressing up all the women of the town as men, so fooling the Burmese. Rama I awarded them titles for their deeds and they are celebrated in bronze, swords drawn. The statue was erected in 1966 and Thais rub goldleaf on its base as a sign of respect and to gain merit. The **Thalang National Museum** ⓘ *0900-1600, except national holidays, ฿30*, is just east of this crossroads on Route 4027. It has a well-presented collection, displaying various facets of Phuket's history and culture.

Khao Phra Thaeo Wildlife Park

ⓘ *0600-1800*. This wildlife park lies 20 km from Phuket Town. Turn east off the main road in Thalang and follow signs for Ton Sai Waterfall. The beautiful, peaceful road winds through stands of rubber trees and degraded forest. The park supports wild boar and monkeys and represents the last of the island's natural forest ecosystem. The **Ton Sai Waterfall** is in the park, but is really only worth a visit during the rainy season; even then the falls are a bit of a disappointment. There are bungalows and a lakeside restaurant here, and a number of hiking routes. Visitors can paddle in the upper pool.

Bang Pae Waterfall and Gibbon Rehabilitation Project

The road east from Ton Sai Waterfall becomes rough and can only be negotiated on foot or by motorbike. This track leads to **Bang Pae Waterfall**. Alternatively, the falls can be approached from the other direction, by turning off Route 4027 and driving 1 km along a

 dirt track. There is a beautiful lake, refreshment stands, forest trails, and bathing pools ⓘ *0600-1800*. Just south of the waterfall is a **Gibbon centre** ⓘ *follow signs off Route 4027, T076-260491, gibbon@poboxes.com, 1000-1600, free, but donations are welcome as are volunteers*; a rehabilitation centre for these endangered animals funded from the US and apparently the only such initiative in Southeast Asia.

Naka Noi Pearl Farm

ⓘ *T076-219870, 0900-1530, the demo takes around 1½ hrs, A500. Long-tailed boats can be chartered at any time, A700, and the driver will wait for you. Ensure your visit is to Naka Noi, rather than Naka Yai, where the 'Pearl Farm' seems to be a fake.*
Also off Route 4027, at Ao Po, there is a long wooden jetty where boat tours leave for Naka Noi Island and Pearl Farm – Thailand's largest. At the farm, the owner asks you to wait half an hour while they prepare the oysters for the demonstration.

Sleeping

Phuket has literally hundreds of places to stay, largely at the upper price end. During the low season (Jun-Oct) room rates may be as little as half the high season price. All rates quoted are high season. It is recommended visitors book hotel rooms during high season (particulary at Christmas and New Year).

Phuket City *p423, map p424*
The hotels in town are rather uninspired; most people avoid staying here and head straight for the beaches, however there are nicer guesthouses in the old part of town.
AL Novotel Royal Phuket City Hotel, T076-233333, opposite the main bus station in town. Swimming pool, business centre, gym. Expensive but up to 50% discount in the wet season. Hints of Las Vegas with shimmering water fountain out front. Should really be surrounded by skyscrapers in a different city entirely as on its own it dominates the street.
A Phuket Island Pavilion, 133 Satool Rd, T076-210445, www.islandpavilion.com. Almost groovy, circular, high-rise. Nice rooms with a different layout to most places. Pool and all facilities.
B-C Imperial, 51 Phuket Rd, T076-212311, www.imperialphuket.com. Cooperative staff, good clean rooms, appropriately priced. Low-key corporate look – dreary front. Restaurant.
C-D Crystal Guest House, 41/16 Montri Rd, T076-222774-5. Does daily or monthly rent for decently sized a/c and fan rooms. Not much in the way of views. Glum staff. Rooms are clean though dispiriting.
C-D Raya Thai Cuisine, 48 Deebuk Rd, T076-218155. 5 simple rooms in a 70-year-old Macao-style house set in from the road. Part of the **Raya Thai Cuisine** restaurant (see Eating). Quirky in the nicest possible way. The rooms themselves are simply furnished and decorated, but this is a terribly romantic setting with an adjoining bridge leading to the rooms from the restaurant. Very friendly owners full of tales about old Phuket, if you can catch them. The food is also good here. Recommended.
C-D Thalang Guesthouse, Krabi Rd, T076-215892. A pleasant house with an old-world charm, large windows, wood floors, double-panelled doors and ceiling fans. 13 rooms on 3 floors. Varying prices and standards. Do check rooms as some of the rooms 'with windows' do indeed have windows but they look onto a brick wall. These rooms, unsurprisingly, are airless basic set-ups, suitable for overnight kips. Room numbers 21 and 3 are best, though a little pricier – they have balconies overlooking the street. If you get the nicer rooms, stay longer as this is an excellent base from which to explore the old town. The owner Mr Tee is a hands-on operator and has a very good reputation with the guests who are encouraged to leave notes and drawings on the landing so there is a real sense of care here. Attracts earnest studenty types, Japanese, backpackers and divers. Recommended.
D Nana Chart Mansion, 41/34 Montri Rd, T076-230041-2/230050, ext.3. Spotless, characterless and cheerless a/c and fan rooms. Also slightly airless as the building is

slam-bang against the one next door. However, this is perfectly acceptable for brief stays and okay for the price. Staff do try to be helpful in this uninspiring place.

D Nara Mansion, 15/1 Soi Mongkon, Yaowarat Rd, T076-259238. Cheap and reasonable rooms but a little rundown on the whole. Fan and a/c.

D-E On On, 19 Phangnga Rd, T076-211154. Riding on its reputation as Phuket City's first hotel, this establishment, dating from 1929, is situated in the heart of the Old Town. It has a curious Wild-West/Old Savannah colonial feel with far too many sub-divided a/c and fan rooms (a total of 49) and walls that shudder when you sneeze. Cold-water showers, strip-lighting, and at times, dark, forbidding wardrobes, make for a somewhat intimidating overnight as you wonder who really is next door and what are they doing. It doesn't help that the staff at the front desk are more interested in watching the telly than attending to guests. A pity because there are hints, in the lovely worn staircase, that this was once a dignified establishment that practised the old adage 'less is more.' Attached a/c coffee shop and good restaurant plus tour desk.

Patong Beach *p426, map p434*

L Holiday Inn, 52 Thaweewong Rd, T076-340608-9, www.holiday.phuket.com. This mega-hotel which takes up a huge chunk of Patong Beach and was heavily occupied at the time of the tsunami, suffered severe damage and has since been busy with repairs. We have had positive reports from guests staying in the Busakorn Wing, especially on the service front. For pool access rooms you do need to reserve in advance. Regarding clientele, this is not a hotel for single men and their 'lady-friends' and is more suited to couples, mature 25 year olds plus and families. All the comforts you would expect from the Holiday Inn plus surf and turf for the homesick.

L Sunset Beach Resort, 316/2 Phrabarame Rd, T076-0342482, www.sunsetphuket.com. Want to feel safe? – what better place than a hotel with the Early Disaster Warning Tower located on the roof. This is another mega-hotel with a double kidney-shaped pool snaking its refreshing way between terraced, balconied wings. From the upper floor rooms you can see the Andaman Sea. There is also a decent spa here and good-ish though predicatable nosh. The hotel is a 5-min tuk-tuk ride to Bangla Rd. Recommended.

AL Club Andaman, 2 Hadpalong Rd, T076-340530, www.clubandaman.com. A/c, restaurant, pool, large new block and some older thatched cottages, set in large spacious grounds. Fitness centre, tennis courts, watersports, children's games room.

AL Merlin, 44 Moo 4, Thaveewong Rd, T076-340037-9, www.merlinphuket.com/patong. A/c, restaurant, 3 sculptured pools and a children's pool, large 4-storey hotel, quite attractively laid out with well-designed, spacious rooms that would benefit from a brave splash of tropical colour instead of beige. Watersports, fitness club and disabled facilities. The seaside restaurant, beauty salon, kids' corner and playground have all undergone 'renovation', following the tsunami. Recommended for families.

A Thavorn Beach Village, 6/2 Moo 6, Nakalay-Patong Beach (between Kamala and Patong beaches, on the Kao Phanthurat Pass, 5 km from Patong), T076-340436, www.thavornbeachvillage.com. Attractively designed Thai-style villas, with 4 rooms each (2 ground floor, 2 first) many with poolside verandas, large lagoon-like pool. A secluded spot on a sparsely populated beach – Nakalay Bay (rocky at low tide). It also offers extras like Thai Cooking courses and scuba diving. The restaurant overlooks the sea. The gardens need a bit of work.

B Patong Villa, 85/3 Patong Beach Rd, T056-340132, www.patongvilla.com. minimalist decor in these rooms can be soothing after all the neon of Patong. Centre of beach, restaurant, pool.

B Safari Beach, 83/12 Patong Beach Rd, T056-340230, www.safaribeachhotel.com. A/c rooms only, restaurant attached, small pool, small 2- and 3-storey hotel set around pool in leafy compound just north of Soi Bangla. On higher ground than the majority along this strip which perished in the tsunami. The location remains sought after as it is on the beach and the standard rooms are spacious and of a decent standard. Recommended.

B Smile Inn, 108/9 Thaweewong Rd, T076-776240/5. This is a small hotel in the

centre of the Patong Beach with rooms painted bright enough to warrant dim light. However, it is only 2 mins from the beach and well-maintained for the price.

C-D Beau Rivage, 77/15-17 Rat Uthit Rd, T076-340725. Some a/c, large rooms – some suites – with clean bathrooms, spacious and good value although like the other hotels on Rat Uthit Rd, it is some way from the beach.

D White, 81/4 Rat Uthit Rd. Quiet guesthouse down a narrow lane running off Rat Uthit Rd, attractive garden, clean rooms. Recommended.

Patong Beach

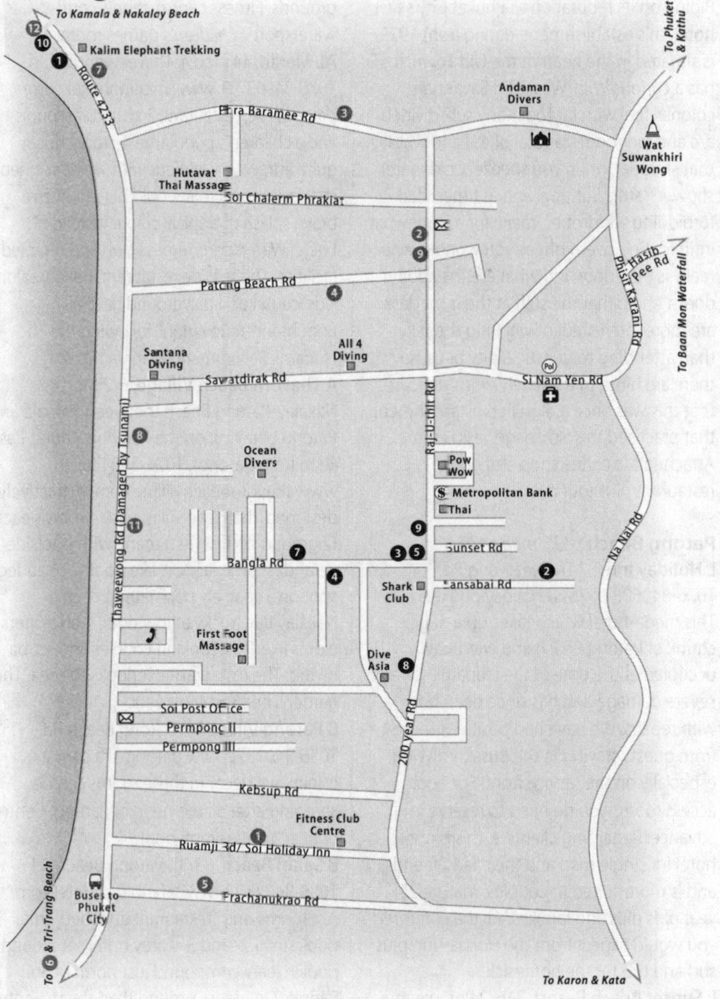

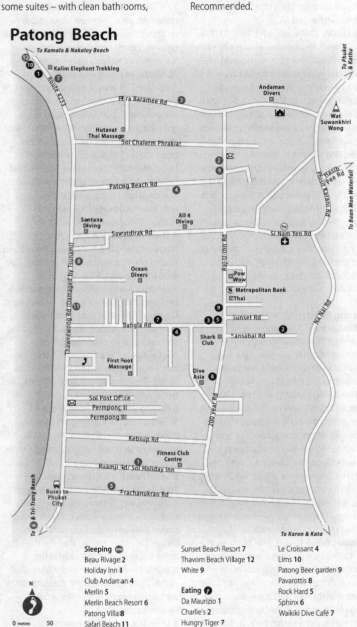

Sleeping
Beau Rivage 2
Holiday Inn 1
Club Andaman 4
Merlin 5
Merlin Beach Resort 6
Patong Villa 8
Safari Beach 11
Smile Inn 3
Sunset Beach Resort 7
Thavorn Beach Village 12
White 9

Eating
Da Maurizio 1
Charlie's 2
Hungry Tiger 7
Lai Mai 3
Le Croissant 4
Lims 10
Patong Beer garden 9
Pavarottis 8
Rock Hard 5
Sphinx 6
Waikiki Dive Café 7

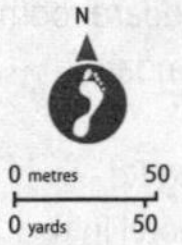

Karon and Kata Beaches *p426, map p435*

L Katathani Resort and Spa, 14 Kata Noi Rd, T076-330124-26, www.katathani.com. Stunning location in this quiet cove. All rooms have sea-front balcony and there are even louvered panels in the bathroom that can be opened if you want to gaze at the sea as you're having a bath. Rather nice understated furniture in the rooms though it is teakwood. Also wooden panels behind the beds. For even greater luxury (and a costlier stay), there is a natural rain shower and soaking tub in the Grand Suite while the Royal Thani Suite has floor-to-ceiling windows. Recommended.

L Merlin Beach Resort, Tri-Trang Beach, T076-294300, www.merlinphuket.com/merlinbeach/. A resort and spa set in a private bay that lies between Karon and the southern end of Patong Beach. Some 60 rooms on the ground floor were damaged, as well as the swimming pool and bars, in the tsunami. This still overly large hotel is in a lovely setting but a hodge-podge of styles makes for an unintentional pompous and comical effect. The rooms are, however, nicely done and not too over the top.

L-AL Boathouse Inn, T076-330015, www.boathouse.net. Southern end of beach, a/c, pool. The ground floor restaurant and lobby was washed away by the tsunami, however, the well-loved beachfront hotel should be completely renovated by now. This establishment, also known as Mom Tri's Boathouse, is clearly a labour of love by its creator – Mom Tri Devakul – who is an architect and an artist. It is a sympathetic outfit from top to bottom with local art shows and art gallery. The villa also has its own salt-water pool and a professional health spa. When it comes to learning how to cook Thai style, there is even a customized cookery book. The wine cellar is one of the nicest surprises, however, with over 400 different wines – an absolute rarity in the land of whiskey and beer. Recommended.

AL Central Karon Village, T076-286300-9, www.centralhotelsresorts.com. This luxury resort and spa is perched almost on the highest point overlooking Karon Bay (between Karon and Patong). The **Centara Spas** are featured in several **Central** hotels around Thailand and are professionally operated with a good range of services. The 72 villas are set in a hilltop steep enough to merit the converted tuk-tuks which transport guests wherever they need to go within the resort. But, while all villas are ocean-facing, not all have a good view of the beach. There are 2 swimming pools (that can be a bit crowded as they are smallish), a spa, a garden area and a walkway over to the beach proper. The resort itself lies on a rocky part of the headland. The garden and spa are both right on the cliff edge – which makes

Karon & Kata Beaches

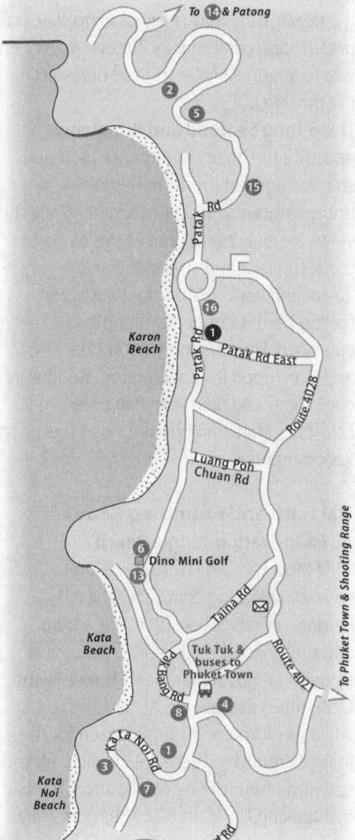

N

Not to scale

Sleeping

Boathouse Inn **1**
Central Karon Village **2**
Felix Karon View Point **5**
Jao Jong Seafood & Bungalows **7**
Karon Beach Resort **6**
Kata Beach Resort **8**
Kata Minta Resort **4**
Katathani Resort & Spa **3**
Marina Phuket **13**
Merlin Beach Resort **14**
Phuket Ocean Resort **15**
South Sea Resort **16**

Eating

Al Dente **1**

for great views. The bungalows are nicely decorated and offer the option of sleeping without a/c (mosquito nets are provided). Bathrooms are spacious and airy – some with glass roofs. You can sunbathe on the room balconies – always a plus. Friendly service and fairly good value.

AL Kata Beach Resort, 5/2 Mue 2 Patak Rd, T076-330530, katagrp@loxinfo.co.th. Southern end, 262 rooms in L-shaped block set around a freeform pool. Run by an English lady married to a Thai, this is a smoothly operated hotel, paired with **Karon Beach Resort** and **Kharon Inn**.

AL Kata Minta Resort, 156 Khok-Thanod Rd, T076-333283. A/c rooms, close proximity to Kata Yai Beach and Kata Noi Beach. Typical Thai luxury look with pointed roof and stone Buddhas in the typically named Elephant restaurant. Predictable and pleasant enough.

AL South Sea Resort, 36/12 Moo 1, Patak Rd, T076-396611, www.phuket-southsea.com. A/c, restaurant, pool, nearly 100 rooms in this low-rise, intimate boutique resort. Rooms feature teakwood and Thai silks and are cool and minimalist. Some bathrooms need renovation. Attractive central pool, gym could be better equipped. Located across from the beach but you have to negotiate a busy street. With nanny-ish concern, the resort has thoughtfully provided a security guard to aid any lemmings amongst us across the road.

A Felix Karon View Point (Swissôtel), 4/8 Patak Rd, T076-396666, www.felixhotels.com/karonphuket. A/c, restaurant, low-rise hotel with 125 rooms at the northern end of Karon Beach, the style of the place is more Spanish than Thai, but nonetheless it is more attractive than most, small pool, away from the beach, inland from the road which saved it from the tsunami.

A Karon Beach Resort, 5/2 Moo 3 Patak Rd, T076-330006, katagrp@loxinfo.co.th. A/c, restaurant, simple laps pool, right on the beach at the southern end of the bay. All rooms with balconies overlooking beach but not all have full on views. Lower floor rooms will have undergone extensive 'renovation' due to tsunami. Owned by the **Kata Group**, the managing director is an English woman.

A Marina Phuket (formerly known as Marina Cottage), 47 Karon Rd, southern end of beach, T076-330625, www.marinaphuket.com. A/c, 2 good restaurants, beautiful secluded pool, individual cottages in lush grounds set in a hilltop. **Marina Divers** here, tours and boat trips organized. Recommended.

B-C Best Western Phuket Ocean Resort, 9/1 Moo 1, T076-396176. A/c, restaurant, pool, on a hillside, this establishment overlooks the Andaman Sea and Karon Lagoon. There are lots of stairs here so it is not good for the elderly, disabled or just plain tired. Looking a little careworn too; the bungalows and rooms in tiered blocks on the hillside could do with a look-in. At the quieter, northern end of the bay, away from the beach, okay mid-range place to stay, no pretensions, comfortable. But one guest's tip was to get up early for the free breakfast or risk missing out.

D Jao Jong Seafood and Bunglaows, opposite the luxury Katathani Resort and spa. A/c and fan rooms behind this unpretentious seaside restaurant. While the views are only partial and of the backs of the restaurant and street, it is only a 30-second walk to Kata Noi beach. The feeling here is rather like being in a courtyard. Upstairs rooms numbers 3, 4, 5 and 6 are good for a sea breeze. Rooms are cool, clean and tiled with balconies. Laid-back staff. Can't go wrong at this price. Recommended.

Nai Harn and Promthep Cape *p427*

AL Baan Krating Jungle Beach, 11/3 Moo 1, Wiset Rd, T076-288264, www.baankrating.com/junglebeach. Remote, attractive position, has a long and pretty good track record. Accessible through **Le Royal Meridien Phuket Yacht Club**, this is actually on Ao Sane beach, which is nicknamed Jungle Beach for the foliage around it. There are 30 villas, all with sea views from the balconies and a pool overlooking Nai Harn Bay. The rooms have a slightly rustic Western feel to them, picked up again by the presence of a pool table and big screens in the relaxation area. If you like to explore, your own transport is a good idea here as it is an isolated spot. The beach is rocky.

D Ao Sane, T076-288306. Also accessible through the yacht club's car park. Bungalows again on a small rocky bay with coral. But this is a refreshingly secluded part of Phuket.

Laem Ka, Chalong beaches and Wat Chalong *p428*

L-AL Evason Phuket Resort and Spa, formerly Phuket Island Resort, 100 Vised Rd, Rawai Beach, T076-38010-7, www.six-senses.com/evason-phuket/. The resort is right on the tip of Laem Ka and has stunning views across to the nearby islands and over Chalong Bay. While the buildings are quite large, the rooms are exquisite with an exceptional cool and airy feel. Equipped with all the facilities you'd expect for the price including tennis courts and a very refined spa. To make up for the poor quality of the beaches on the main island, the resort has its own island in the bay – Bon Island. Set in 64 acres of garden facing the Andaman Sea, this is definitely intended to be a place of escapism as the resort, though large – 285 rooms – is flanked by 2 inland lagoons and surrounded by extensive foliage. What is also nice is the resort comprises low-rise buildings.

Cape Panwa *p429*

L-AL Cape Panwa, T076-391123. Beautifully secluded, good variety of accommodation including bungalows for families or friends, tennis courts, fitness centre, beauty salon, flower arranging and Thai cookery courses. For a touch of silly exclusivity take the Mercedes electric tram down to the beach which can only be accessed through the hotel. There is also a coral reef 40 m offshore. Leonardo Di Caprio stayed here in Room E301 which has a double balcony and the best view of the sea and the bay. Other famous guests include Catherine Zeta Jones, Pierce Brosnan (who was a perfect gentleman apparently) and Elizabeth Taylor who thanked the waiter at Panwa House Restaurant for "bringing her the moon". The choice of restaurants include Italian to Thai fusion and an excellent cocktail bar. Good breakfast buffet though get there in time for the bread selection. While you may never wish to leave the hotel, there is also a shuttle service into Phuket Old Town but be firm if you wish to be collected in the evening rather than at school end. Recommended.

L-A The Bay Hotel, 31/11 Moo 8, Sakdidej Rd, T07-6391514, www.thebay-phuket.com. A pleasant seafront hotel which is just a 10-15 min drive from Phuket.

Koh Tapao Yai

Koh Tapao Yai is a small island off the cape, is home to a few hotels and around 200 hornbills: **A Phuket Paradise Resort**, T076-354712, pprh@phuketweb.com. The idiosyncratic ambience of this resort on Koh Tapao Yai island is largely due to the presence of Bucerotes hornbills who can be seen between 0600-1800 as they fly around and make appearances on the hotel premises (dawn is the best time to catch the shy hornbill). While in 1986 there were a mere handful of these colourful heavy-beaked birds, hornbill fan and hotel manager of the Phuket Paradise Resort - Khun Aroon, insisted that everyone take care of the birds. There are now over 200 on Koh Tapao Yai. Aside from the hornbills, these resort houses set in the hill sides, some with a seaview, are nicely situated. The establishment offers free daily boat trips and car service to town and will also arrange golf trips.

Koh Lone, Koh Mai Ton and other southern islands *p430*

L Mai Ton Island Resort, Koh Mai Ton, T076-214954, maiton@ksc.th.com. A/c, restaurants, pools, 75 individual Thai pavilions with wooden floors and separate sitting rooms, good sports facilities and beautiful white-sand beaches with a decent coral reef in the front of the beach.

AL Ban Mai Cottages, 35/1 Moo 3, Koh Lone, T02-6730966, bannmai@tahi-tour.com. Bungalow/houses decorated with faux 19th-century Burmese furniture and Balinese style bathrooms. This establishment offers both Thai and French cuisine. Pool.

A Coral Island Resort, Koh Hi, T076-281060, www.coralislandresort.com. Around 70 snazzy a/c bungalows - poolside and beachfront. This place is named after Koh Hii's nickname - Coral Island. The resort is situated right near perfect white-sand beaches with coral reefs fit for snorkelling. The tusnami flooded a few rooms but the hotel is already repaired. Plus the marine life was not damaged by the waves. On the other side of the island, you can also visit pleasant secluded bays.

Surin Beach and Pansea Beach *p430*

L Amanpuri Resort, 118/1 Pansea Beach, T076-324333, www.amanpuri.com. A/c, restaurant, pool, the more expensive rooms are beautifully designed Thai pavilions, with attention to every detail. Superb facilities include private yacht, watersports, tennis and squash courts, fitness centre, private beach, library, undoubtedly the best on Phuket. Guests include international potentates from the political arena so expect motorcades from time to time, entering and exiting the hotel. Surroundings, style and service incomparable.

L-AL Chedi Phuket (formerly **Pansea Resort**), T076-324017, www.phuket.com/chedi. South of **Amanpuri**. Exclusive resort set into the hillside above a perfectly secluded sandy white beach. There is a range of beautifully designed traditional thatched Thai cottages to sleep 2-10 people, superb facilities, including all watersports, cinema, library, games room, a/c, restaurant, pool. Rooms can be somewhat small and monastic – would not suit those who feel that Corbusier-inspired furnishings are a little stern. Pool appears almost black in appearance due to stone used but the real concern here is that it is rather small and could easily get crowded with a full-house. Terrifyingly chic and the sound of silence is formidable at times. Staff are professional.

A Pen Villa Hotel, 9/1 Moo 3 Surin Beach, Srisootorn Rd, T076-271100. Bland red-roofed hotel complex with decent enough pool and big clean rooms. Offers good Thai cookery course apparently. Suitable for families. Free transfers to two local beaches - Surin and Laem Sing. The hotel also arranges daytrips, fishing and golf.

Bang Tao Beach *p430*

L Banyan Tree, T076-324374, www.banyantree.com. The Banyan doesn't beat about the bush when it comes to trendy marketing. Not only does the 'unity wedding' package include 'one monk's blessing but there's also the "'Intimate Moments' villa decoration which creates the perfect ambience for you and your partner to massage each other with essential oils. Voted the 'World's Best Spa Resort' by Conde Nast Traveller and 'Best Resort Hotel in Asia' by Asian Wall Street Journal, this is luxury indeed and with lagoon villas replete with jet pool, outdoor shower and sunken bath, happy sybarites never get out of the water.

L-AL Bangtao Beach Cottage, T076-325418, www.phuket.com/bangtaobeach/index.htm. Just before the entrance to the **Bangtao Lagoon Bungalow** and next to one of the main boat-building areas. This was the first of the smaller, more intimate resorts and remains the smallest. Right on the beach, there is no pool. Rooms are stylish and use traditional materials – the only criticism being the lack of mosquito screening for natural ventilation instead of a/c, the garden is quite limited but well designed. Frequently full, and best to book in advance. Recommended.

L-AL Dusit Laguna, T076-324320, www.lagunaphuket.com. The tsunami tore into the beachfront rooms as well as the kids club, fitness centre and restaurants – including the beachfront. So don't be surprised if these areas look entirely revamped. A/c, restaurants, attractive pool, the quietest and most refined of the **Laguna Phuket** complex. Excellent service, beautifully laid-out unimposing hotel, tennis courts, watersports. Rooms can a be a mite small.

L-AL Sheraton Grande Laguna, T076-324101, www.lagunaphuket.com. A/c, 5 restaurants (with a good choice of cuisine), the Thai restaurant has been redone following the tsunami, interesting design in the **Chess Bar**, large pool with interlinked sections, including a sandy 'beach' and a sunken bar, some of the accommodation is on stilts on the lagoon. There are also tennis courts, a health centre, massage and children's corner.

B-C Bangtao Lagoon Bungalow, 72/3 Moo 3, Tambon Cherng Talay, T076-324260. Some a/c, small pool, a bungalow development in a comparatively isolated position. Range of chalets from simple fan bungalows to 'de luxe' a/c affairs, the latter are small and featureless, but very clean, family cottages also available. The tsunami gave this place a fair wallop.

Nai Ton and Layan *p430*

AL-A Layan Resort and Spa, T076-313412, www.layanresort.com/. Set back from the beachfront at some distance, this resort was spared any damage to its rooms, despite the seawater surging back some 400 metres. Low-rise, open design with pleasant rooms and lush gardens. Well-equipped spa with lots of open-air areas.

Nai Yang and Nai Yang National Park *p431*

AL Pearl Village, T076-327006, www.pearlvillage.co.th. A/c, restaurant, attractive pool, well run, friendly management, beautiful gardens, facilities include tennis courts, horse riding, elephant riding, good for families.

A-C Nai Yang Beach Resort, T076-328300, www.phuket.com/naiyangbeach. Well-built bungalows with good facilities and simple decor. Some a/c. Set in large grounds with plenty of trees for shade. Friendly staff. A bit pricey at the upper end but excellent value at the lower end. Right next to the **Pearl Village** and a hop over the road to the beach.

B-D National Park bungalows, T076-327047.

C-E Garden Cottage, T076-327293. 2 mins from the airport, cottage-style guesthouse, friendly owner, willing to show you the island.

Camping In the national park, ฿60.

Mai Khao *p431*

L JW Marriott Phuket Resort and Spa T076-348300, www.marriott.com. A huge resort of over 200 rooms and 2 swimming pools, spa, fitness centre, tennis courts, shops and gallery, and children's activity centre. Throughout the resort brightly painted traditional boats (*korlae*) are dotted, Service is impeccable, as you would expect from a **Marriott**. The rooms are elegant and spacious. Sea turtle nesting grounds feature prominently in **Marriott** publicity materials. Apparently, the hotel developer has donated a large sum of money to the WWF Thailand to start up a turtle conservation fund. Watersports are banned, and guests are asked to use the pools rather than swim in the sea to avoid disturbing sea turtles.

C-E Mai Khao Beach Bungalows, T01-8951233, bmaikhao_beach@hotmail.com. This and the neighbouring campground (run by the same family) has been in operation for 3 years and is quite a find for Phuket. The site is down a dirt track off a side road past Mai Khao village (see Transport for details), tucked away in a grassy clearing shaded by large casuarina trees and shrubs right on the beach. For the DIY set. There are 2 ranges of bungalows, smaller bamboo and palm roof bungalows with shared bathroom facilities and larger concrete and wood bungalows with bathrooms en suite. It is also possible to

pitch a tent in the grounds. The owners really seem to enjoy getting to know their guests and set up a regular campfire to sit and chat during the night. Recommended.

Eating

Phuket City *p423, map p424*

There are quite a few reasonably priced Thai restaurants in the Old Town. The food in Phuket is highly rated throughout Thailand and rightly so for the range of dishes and for the invigorating and sophisticated spices and herbs used in Southern Thai cuisine.

Asian

TTT Lai-An Lao, 58 Rasada Rd. Chinese restaurant with seafood specialities.

TTT Venus Chinese Restaurant, 34-38 Phangnga Rd, classy establishment serving a variety of Chinese and Thai dishes.

T Kow-Tom-Hua-Pla (Boiled Fish Rice) opposite **Caramba Bar and Restaurant** on Phuket Rd past Thalang Rd. Popular with locals, this simple noodle café is open 1700-2400 and is run by Chinese-Thai Mr Pinit. It serves an eclectic mix of local noodles – including Yen-ta-Foa seafood noodles coloured a disturbing blood-red by a sweetish slightly hot sauce. Other noodle soups include fish skin and fish stomach noodles. Then there are the trusty pork and chicken standbys though the chicken might just be offal. Recommended.

T Vegetarian Restaurant, corner of Tilik Uthit 1 Rd and Chanacharoen Rd, near **Crystal Hotel**. Don't be fooled by the hemp leaf decorations everywhere. This place is filled with wholesome Scandinavian families eating wholesome and somewhat bland food. Good for those with allergies.

International

TTT Bondeli Café, Thanon Rat Sada corner by the bridge and Thanon Phuket – now an internet café with pastries and savouries including pizzas.

TTT Kanda Bakery, 31-33 Rasada Rd. Spotlessly clean a/c restaurant with art deco undertones, serves breakfast, Thai and international dishes and good cakes like cinnamon rolls, croissant and chocolate brownies.

TTT Le Café, Rasada Centre. Elegant café serving burgers, steaks, sandwiches, cappuccinos and milkshakes.

TTT Santana Coffee, 54/8-9 Montri Rd. A nicely decorated European-style café that serves Thai food, steaks and European food as well as an excellent selection of coffees. Brews range from Jamaica Pea to Kilananjaro.

TTT Shelter down from the **On-On Hotel** on Phangnga Rd. Burgers, breakfast and Thai food, greasy café, popular with surfers.

TTT Pun Pun. Central Festival mall. Tiny and quirky with chairs and tables shaped like fruit. Don't be put off by the nursery school whimsy. The juices, shakes, smoothies and salads are all rather good and very very fresh. White sugar is not used in this shop – owner CJ Prieur and his wife Jirapa believe it is unhealthy. Instead wildflower honey from Chiang Mai is used. This eeny-weeny establishment also does shakes based on your blood type and for specific body parts like the Stomach Soother which contains pineapple, papaya, mint, ginger, aloe vera and lemon grass. Recommended.

Thai

TTT Baan Talang Restaurant, 65 Talang Rd. Tasty Thai and Islamic food (the lamb curry is excellent but very spicy). As with most places in this part of town, the walls are lined with photographs of old Phuket and there is an old world feel.

TTT Ka Jok See, 26 Takua Pa Rd, T076-217903. Excellent Thai restaurant. The success of the restaurant is leading to some pretty sharp pricing policies, but we have had comments from customers who believe the atmosphere, character, style and first-rate cuisine make it worth paying extra. Booking is essential.

TTT Raya Thai Cuisine, Dibuk Rd. This restaurant is in a 70-year-old Macao-style house with a garden and 3 interconnecting housing units. It has opened 1 section as a guesthouse (see Sleeping, above). It is well preserved with original tiling, windows, lighting and ceiling fans, and with a good selection of photographs of Phuket in years gone by. The room upstairs is a very airy and pleasant place to eat. It serves most Thai dishes and several local specialities; try the *nam bu bai cha plu* if you like spicy food. This is a crab curry with local herbs served with Chinese rice noodles.

TT Nong Jote Café, 16 Yaowarat Rd. This 100-plus-year-old building looks like a café in Lisbon with high ceilings, and, along one

side, ceiling-to-floor antique glassed cabinets in teak. Then, there are the banners for Liverpool, Man U and Tottenham on the other side. Tables are large enough to read a newspaper on and the service is admirably unrushed. Here you can find some of the best southern Thai food, certainly in Phuket. Try the Yum Tour Plu but remember it is unadulterated and spicy. Other dishes have a Chinese edge but the menu on the whole sticks to Southern Thai. The elderly owner Mr Tanaboom was born in this house and came from a wealthy tin-mining family. For stories about Old Phuket Town when it really was old, snare him over a beer. Recommended.

ŸŸ Roak Ros, opposite Fresh Mart on Phuket Rd and Soi Talang Chan. Popular with locals. Spartan interior with stainless steel tabletops and cutlery and plates in plastic tray screwed into the wall above your table. Casually dressed staff in ponytails serve a diverse range of customers from tattooed local lads with their girls to elderly couples. The favourite here is clams in chilli paste. Watch out for the crab – they can be hasty cooking it. Shellfish can also be small.

Foodstalls

The best place to browse on the street is around the market on Ranong Rd. A good and cheap restaurant close by is **Koh Lao Luat Mu** (name only in Thai), on the circle linking Ranong and Rasada roads, which serves tasty noodle and rice dishes. Alternatively, **Khai Muk**, Rasada Rd (opposite the **Thavorn Hotel**) serves superb *kwaytio* (noodle soup).

Patong Beach *p426, map p434*

Thai

ŸŸŸ Hungry Tiger, intersection of Bangla and Second roads. Thai as well as western dishes, one visitor reported with relish that "they have the guts to serve [the food] unmoderated... hot really means hot".

International

Many of the sois off Patong Beach Rd sell a good range of international food.

ŸŸŸ Da Maurizio, Kalim Beach, north of Patong, opposite **Diamond Cliff Hotel**, T076-344079. Italian food in attractive setting.

ŸŸŸ Patong Beer Garden, by K Hotel, 82/47 Rat Uthit Rd. Attractive garden setting, Viennese food cooked by Austrian chef.

ŸŸŸ Pavarotti's, Patong Resort Hotel, Rat-Uthit Rd, good seafood BBQ with set price eat-as-much-as-you-like option.

ŸŸ Charlie's Restaurant, Soi Sansabai. Thai and Tex-Mex. BBQ every Fri from 2100. Good bar.

ŸŸ Rock Hard Café, 82/51 Bangla Rd. Garden, steaks, pizzas.

ŸŸ-Ÿ Le Croissant, Soi Bangla. Thai/European restaurant/bakery. Good selection.

Ÿ Lai Mai, 86/15 Patong Beach Rd. Great Western breakfasts.

Ÿ Waikiki Dive Café, Soi Patong Resort. Food and pool and internet. A cool place to chill out, open until 0200, more a bar than a restaurant.

Karon and Kata Beaches *p426, map p435*

ŸŸ JaoJong Seafood, 4/2 Patak Rd, Katanoi Beach, T076-330136. Unpretentious sea shanty feel to this spacious open-fronted seafood restaurant. Good selection of freshly caught seafood and well-executed. The menu is illustrated with pictures – very useful. Low-key atmosphere. Reasonably priced. Recommended.

ŸŸ Al Dente, Beach Road close to Karon Circle, T076-396569. You can't miss it, this is the traffic island decorated with mythical creatures. Try their fondues (a brave choice for the tropics) of meat and cheese and made-to-order Italian while listening to classical music.

ŸŸ Swiss Bakery, Kata beach, Bougainvillea Terrace House, 117.1 Patak Road, T076-33139. 0800-2400. Open-air terrace, Swiss delicacies here include Bouguionne and Tartaren Hut. Also do burgers, sandwiches from A120 upward.

Laem Ka, Chalong beaches and Wat Chalong *p428*

ŸŸŸ Kan Eang Seafood, on the beach, good choice of seafood. Recommended.

Cape Panwa *p429*

ŸŸŸ-ŸŸ Panwa House, Cape Panwa. On the beach. Everything is in place here for the perfect meal – the Sino-Portugese gem of a 2-story house perched on the very edge of a beach with indoor and outdoor dining, the serenading guitarist and singer, excellent service which is not too attentive and deliciously executed individual dishes. The

spicy beef salad in lime juice is light while the lobster with shavings of caramelized shallot, palm sugar and tamarind is harmonious. Even the desserts are superb with a hint of English nursery yumminess – try the stuffed rambutan with vanilla custard. Finally, if you don't like the sound of the music, you can always listen to the haunting melody of nocturnal birds. Recommended.

Yaun Yen (200 m from the aquarium), reasonable food, seafood is best.

Sawasdee Restaurant, 31/4 Sakdidej Rd. The food here is average and caters too much to a perceived Western taste which is bland, slightly sugary and somewhat slippery with oil. However, the set-up is fun. You sit at old Singer sewing tables in a brick rustic Thai style bungalow with an open front and a great view of the ocean. The 80-plus-year-old bricks were actually taken from the owner's home on the Malaysian border. A good place to snack.

Surin Beach and Pansea Beach *p430*

Amanpuri, see Sleeping, has a Thai restaurant considered one of the best on the island (and the setting is sensational). At least 48 hrs advanced booking needed during peak season, T076-324394. It is very expensive.

Nai Yang and Nai Yang National Park *p431*

Several seafood places, for example Nai Yang Seafood.

Mai Khao *p431*

A full range of restaurants in the Marriott and a simple in-house restaurant at the Mai Khao Beach Bungalows.

Bars and clubs

Patong Beach *p426, map p434*

Bars in Patong are concentrated along Rat Uthit Rd and Bangla Rd. The latter is throbbing with activity in the evening as bars cater with gusto for all nationalities, persuasions and perversions.

Cape Panwa *p429*

The Top of the Reef Bar, Cape Panwa. Excellent house cocktails and a view of the sea on a wicker-chaired veranda. Even if you are not staying here, it is worth a drop-in for a feeling of tropical indulgence and glamour. It is a proper set-up, however, with a jazz singer that takes requests so you will feel somewhat out of place in a sweaty singlet.

Entertainment

Patong Beach *p426, map p434*

Crocodile Pub, (formerly Le Crocodile), located at the back of Soi Crocodile which is jam packed with bars down from Soi Bangla. 2200-0200. You can't miss this place with its fun-fair sign festooned with crocodile figures jamming in a rock band. It's a small disco, with ฿70 cover charge open late Mon, Wed and Sat with cabaret shows from Tiffany's Tiara. Show time is at 0130. For discount cocktails not such a bad place. Also do theme nights including Latino Party Time.

Lim's, Soi 7, Kalim Bay. This opened in a small house in 1999 and now has a vast dining room with high ceilings and outdoor courtyard. Also features bold abstract paintings by one of the owners – 'Gop'. All over has a New York, *Sex in the City* feel. The food concentrates more on the quality of the base ingredients rather than overwhelming (or thrilling) with spices. Suits an exhausted palate. Choices of dishes range from grilled pork ribs to Vietnamese spring rolls with, among other things, capsicum.

Tin Mine 21, in the Paradise Complex, 135/23 Rat-U-thit Rd, T076-340666. 1900- 0200. From here you can go up to the Sky Lounge for cocktails which is 24 floors above Patong. Tin Mine has 300 seats. Yummy neon entrance.

Sphinx Restaurant and Theatre, Rat-u-thit Rd. Gaining popularity among the gay scene, this upmarket set-up offers Thai classical performances as well as Broadway hits and comedy. The food isn't bad – a mix of Thai cuisine and the lighter chicer end of European.

Karon and Kata Beaches *p426, map p435*

Deep Sea Video Theque on the ground floor of the Phuket Arcadia Hotel. The DJ here does a cabaret show with a different theme every night. Semi-Butlins feel in this 700 capacity venue.

Festivals and events

Phuket Island *p419*

The Chao Le Boat Floating Festival falls between the 6th and 11th lunar month.

The villages involved are the Rawai, Sapan, Ko Sire and Laem Ka. This festival is held at night as small boats are set adrift to ward off evil.

Once a year, for the past 2 years, the **L.O.V.E. Foreign Film Festival** has taken place; the brainchild of Marut Lekpetch who runs **Raan (Nang) Sue 252 Bookshop** and operates the Andaman Writers Network. This is a good place to meet the artists and writers of Phuket. For up to date information try the *Phuket Gazette*.

Feb **Phuket Gay Festival**, Patong Beach. 3rd-6th. Katoeys, floats and plain old fun. **Chinese New Year**, 9th-10th.

Mar **Thao Thep Kasattri and Thao Sisunthon Fair** on the 13th. Celebrates the Two Heroines who saved Phuket from the Burmese.

Apr **Fish Releasing Festival** timed to coincide with Songkran or Thai new year. Baby turtles are released at several of Phuket's beaches.

Apr **Bike Week** at Patong Beach – during Songkran in Apr. Get your kicks with Harley and co.

May **Seafood Festival**. Done in conjunction with the Marine Tourism Resources and Phuket Tourism. There is a parade, seafood stalls displaying regional cuisines, and demonstrations as well as cultural shows. For keen foodies anxious to improve their repetoire. **Rugby Tournament**, end of May. Held at Karon Beach and Karon Municipal Stadium.

Jul **Marathon** (2nd week).

Aug-Sep **Por Tor Festival**. Phuket City. 22nd-3rd. This means 'hungry ghosts' and is a time when ancestors are honoured. It is similar to the Roman Catholic month of all souls in that ghosts are supposedly released into the world for the whole month. To keep them quiet and reasonable, they are given food, flowers and candles at family altars. Bribes include cakes in the shape of turtles – the Chinese symbol of longevity.

Oct **Chinese Vegetarian Festival** or *Ngan Kin Jeh* (movable), lasts 9 days and marks the beginning of Taoist lent. No meat is eaten, alcohol consumed nor sex indulged in (in order to cleanse the soul) and men pierce their cheeks or tongues with long spears and other sharp objects and walk over hot coals and (supposedly) feel no pain. The festival is celebrated elsewhere, but most enthusiastically in Phuket, and especially at Wat Jui Tui on Ranong Rd in Phuket Town (see box page 422). This must be one of the star attractions of a visit to Phuket. Visitors are made to feel welcome and encouraged to take part in the event.

Nov **Patong Carnival** welcomes in the tourist season.

Dec **King's Cup Regatta** (5th). Yachting competition in the Andaman Sea, timed to coincide with the King's birthday (the King is a yachtsman of international repute). The event attracts competitors from across the globe. **Laguna Phuket Triathlon**: 1,000-metre swim, 5-km bicycle race, 12-km run. For international athletes.

Shopping

Phuket City *p423, map p424*
Most souvenirs found here can be bought more cheaply elsewhere in Thailand, and if travelling back to Bangkok, it is best to wait. Best buys are pearls and gold jewellery.

Antiques

Antiques House, Rasada Centre, central location, limited stock of Thai and other Asian antiques.

Ban Boran Antiques, 39 Yaowarat Rd (near the circle), recently moved from old shop on Rasada Rd, this is arguably the best antique shop on Phuket; interesting pieces from Thailand and Burma especially, well priced.

Chan's Antiques, Thepkrasatri Rd, just south of the Heroines Monument, not many 'antiques', but a selection of Thai artefacts.

Food

Foodies should get stocked up on a weird and wonderful range of cashew nuts at the **Methee Cashew Nut Factory**, 9/1-2 Tilok Uthit Rd, T076-219622/3. The factory also offers tours so you learn just why cashew nuts are so damned expensive with the Methee experts who have been around for over 40 yrs. Experience garlic, chilli and palm sugar cashews.

Handicrafts

Dam Dam, Rasada Rd (near the fountain circle), interesting selection. Numerous stalls at the **Rasada Centre**, Rasada Rd. There is

also a row of shops in Prachanukhao Road in Patong leading to Karon which sell handpainted copies of the greats – including Gauguin and Van Gogh. Stun families and neighbours with your very own Da Vinci 'Praying Hands.'

Activities and tours

Phuket Island *p419, map p421*
Information on sporting activities on Phuket is provided in the free tourist magazines available from hotels, restaurants and tour companies. In addition to those listed in more detail below, activities include golf, paintball, horse riding and sailing.

Boating

Tour by glass-bottomed boat. Two-hour cruises in the Andaman Sea, ฿300 (or on a chartered basis for ฿5,000 per 2 hrs). Yacht charter. From Nov-May, boats can be chartered to sail around Phuket.
Seal Superyachts, 225 Rat-U-Thi 200 Year Rd, T076-340406. This well-established outfit goes to Similan and Surin Islands, offers PADI courses. Contact Gordon Fernandes. Professional crews, fishing and snorkelling equipment.

Canoeing

Andaman Sea Kayak, T076-235353, www.andamanseakayak.com. Hires out 2-man canoes to explore the grottoes, capes and bays that line Phuket's coast, but which are often not accessible by road. Day trips cost about ฿2,800-3,300; 4-day expeditions, all inclusive, ฿22,000.
John Gray's Sea Canoe Thailand Co Ltd, 124 Soi 1 Yaowarat Rd, Phuket 83000, T076-254- 505/6, www.johngray-seacanoe.net. Many people swear by the John Gray experience, often in gushing tones, as a 'life-changing spiritual event.' While this is debatable, John Gray has had over 20 years experience and is the man for day trips and overnights with the advantage being limited guests in the combo longtail and kayak expeditions.
Santana, 222 Thaweewong Rd, Patong Beach, T076-294220, www.santana phuket.com. River canoeing through the jungle as well as sea canoeing.

Diving

The greatest concentration of diving companies is to be found along Patong Beach Rd, on Kata and Karon beaches, at Ao Chalong and in Phuket Town. Dive centres – over 25 of them – offer the full range of introductory courses for those who have not dived before through to advance courses, day trips and liveaboard – leading to one of the internationally recognized certificates such as PADI and NAUI. For an open water course the cost is about ฿7,200-11,500. The course stretches over 4 days, beginning in a hotel pool and ending on a reef. An advance open water diver course costs around ฿9,500. A simple introductory dive, fully supervized, will cost ฿1,500-2,000 (1 dive) to ฿2,000-2,500 (2 dives). For those with diving experience there are a range of tours from single day, 2-dive outings to dive spots like Koh Raja Yai and Koh Raja Noi (both due south of Phuket and also called Koh Racha) and Shark Point (off to the east of Phuket) which cost ฿2,500-3,000 depending on the location; to 1-week expeditions to offshore islands such as the Similan and Surin Islands. Five days and 4 nights to the Similans costs around ฿20,000-25,000. Other liveaboards, depending on location and length of trip, vary from ฿18,000-30,000. Snorkelling is good on the outer islands; the waters around Phuket Island itself are mediocre. For the best snorkelling and diving it is necessary to go to the Similan Islands.

Game fishing

Dorado Big Game Fishing, 73/37 Praphuket Rd, T076-202679, dorado@phket.loxinfo.co. Dorado offers Phuket's largest deep sea fishing boat - a 60 ft hardwood timber cruiser with shaded deck, sundeck and lounge that is big enough for 12 passengers. Does day trips and sleeps 6-8 passengers for liveaboard safaris. The English owner is an ex-oilman with plenty of juice. The company specialises in long range liveaboard safaris to the Similan Islands.
Phuket Tourist Centre, 125/7 Phangnga Rd, T076-211849.
Wahoo Big Game Fishing, the Sea Center, 48/20, Moo 9, Soi Ao Chalong, T076-281 510, www.wahoo.ws, has been in the biz for over 18 years and knows the area inside-out, from reports. Apparently, the Japanese clients here are content to merely sit on the boat

and eat sashimi (raw) tuna as it is caught. So tours can be tailored for plain epicureans.

Motorbike and jeep tours
In order to explore some of the sights mentioned in the sights section, it is best to hire a motorbike or jeep for the day. A suggested route might run north from Phuket Town or east from Patong to Tha Rua, the Heroines' Monument and the National Museum at Thalang. Take a side trip to Ton Sai Waterfall and the national park, then continue north on Route 402, before turning left for Nai Yang Beach and the national park. Crossing Route 402, drive east through rubber plantations, taking in Bang Pae Waterfall, before returning to the main road at the Heroines' Monument. A ½- to 1- day trip.

Nature tours
There is not much 'nature' left on Phuket but nonetheless **Phuket Nature Tours,** 5/15 Chao Fah Rd, T076-225522, has managed to climb on board the eco-tourism bandwagon and offers tours to forests, rice fields, villages, plantations, secluded beaches and so on.
Siam Safari, 45 Chao Fah Rd, Chalong, T076-280116, www.siam-safari.com. Offers eco nature tours, a similar set-up to the above.

Tours and tour operators
Full-day tours usually cost between ฿700-2,000. To the **Similan Islands** (see page 413), **Phangnga Bay** and **Coral Island** (Koh Hii) including swimming, snorkelling and fishing.

Phuket City *p423, map p424*
Bowling
Ocean Plaza, Bangla Rd. Bowling shoes, ฿30, game ฿75.
Pearl, behind Pearl Theatre, Phangnga Rd.

Shooting range
Indoor and outdoor, snooker club and restaurant, at 82/2 Patak Rd (west of Chalong 5-way intersection). Open daily 0900-1800.

Thai boxing
Every Fri at 2000 (tickets available from 1600), unfriendly place. The stadium is on South Phuket Rd (Saphan Hin), T076-258393, ฿350 (overpriced).

Patong Beach *p426, map p434*
Bungee jumping
Phuket Waterski Cableways, 86/3 Moo 6, Soi Nam Tok Kathu, near Kathu Waterfall, T076-202525-7. Inland waterskiing course on a manmade lake. Skiers are pulled around an oval track at up to 30 kph by giant overhead cables.
Tarzan's Bungee Jump, on road to Phuket Town, 61/3 Moo 6, T076-321351.
Tarzan's Catapult, near **Expat Hotel** on Soi Sunset, T014-641581.

Diving
Trips range from 1-day tours to week-long expeditions to the Similan and Surin islands. See also Diving, Essentials.
All 4 Diving, 5.4 Sawatdirak Rd, Patong, T076-344 611. It does a diving service with other dive operators ans sells equipment.
Andaman Divers, 62 Prabaramee Rd, T076-341126, www.andamandivers.com. Seventeen years in the business, this operation does liveaboards to the Similan Islands and PADI courses. Japanese, English and French speaking instructors. Lays claim to offering the best rates.
Dive Asia, 121/10 Moo 4, Patak Rd, Kata Beach, T076-330598/284117. Established 18 years.
Fantasea Divers, T076-340088 (instruction in English, French, German and Japanese).
Ocean Divers, T076-341273/4.
Phuket Scuba Club, Kata Noi Rd, T076-284026, www.phuket-scuba-club.com. South-African owned. We have had good reports of a Similans liveaboard with this outfit which offers instructors of varying nationalities including Thai and English- speaking. Single dives available from ฿1750.
Santana, 222 Thanon Sawatdirak Rd, T076-294220, www.santanaphuket.com. A prestigious Five-star Padi Instructor Development Centre. This operation is the most experienced, having been 25 years in the business. It does liveaboards to the Similan Islands, Surin and Hin Daeng. Courses in English, German and Thai. It has even named dive sties such as Elephant Head.
Scuba Cats, 94 Thaweewong Road, T076-293120, www.scubacats.com. Also a Five-star Padi Instructor Development

Centre offering liveaboards to the Similan Islands, Koh Bon, Koh Tachai and Richelieu Rock as well as fun dives around Phuket. Phuket's first National Geograhic Dive Centre, it is also a Go-Eco operator and involved in marine clean-up. Finalist in Diver Training Award too.
Seal Asia, 225 Rat-U-Thit Road, Patong Beach, T076-340406, www.seal-asia.com.

Elephant trekking
Kalim Elephant Trekking, Kalim Beach, T076-290056. 0800-1000.

Fitness
Fitness Club Centre, T076-340608, with aerobics, sauna and body building is in the Holiday Inn on Patong Beach. Mon-Sat 0900-2100, Sun 1200-2100. Daily, weekly and monthly membership is available.

Game fishing
Quite a few operators in Patong Beach. Expect to pay about ฿1,500-2,000 per day.

Go-kart racing
Track on left, at the bottom of the hill leading to Patong (Route 4029), T076-321949. Daily 1000-2200.

Golf
Phuket Country Club, on main road between Phuket Town and Patong, T076-213383, 18 holes. ฿150. 0800-1800. Caddy ฿100.

Therapies
Traditional Thai massage is available from countless (usually untrained) women and men on the beach or from more permanent places. Check for a certificate from Wat Po.

Karon and Kata beaches *p426, map p435*
Thai cookery courses
Many luxury spa resorts and 4-star hotels are now offering Thai cookery courses. Check out what dishes you want to learn and find out if they can teach them. You will find these courses can often be tailored to your needs.
Boathouse Inn Cookery School, Kata Beach, T076-3300157, see Kata Beach sleeping section for full address.

Diving
Kon Tiki, T076-396312. Marina Cottage, Kata Beach, T076-381625.
Marina Divers, southern end of Karon Beach, T076-330272. PADI certified courses, very professional set-up. Recommended.
Phuket International Diving Centre (PIDC), Le Meridien, Karon Noi Beach, T076-321480.
Seafarer Divers at Le Meridien Hotel, T076-321479, www.seafarer-divers.com.
Siam Diving Centre, 121/9 Patak Rd, southern end of Karon Beach, T076-330936. Organizes diving expeditions to the Similan Islands (instruction in English and Swedish).

Horse riding
Next to shooting range, T076-381667. ฿600 per hr. 0700-1200, 1300-1830.

Mini golf
Dino Mini Golf Park, between the beaches. 18 holes, ฿250 for 36 holes. Dino Golf, apparently, also does excellent burgers brought from an intriguing fake cave that looks like it's made out of grey styrofoam filled with glum staff in novelty chef outfits.

Shooting
Phuket Shooting Range, 82/2 Patak Rd, T076-381667. Off Route 4028 between Kata and Chalong. Daily 1000-1800.

Nai Harn and Promthep Cape *p427*
Other activities include waterskiing, windsurfing, mini golf and herbal sauna.

Riding
Phuket Riding Club, T076-288213. South of Chalong traffic circle. ฿500 per hr.
Crazy Horse Club, rides on Laem Ka beach or along mountain trails (฿300 per hr). Good for families as it also offers ponies.

Rawai and Koh Kaew Pisadarn *p428*
Herbal sauna, sailing centre and dive shop also available.

Paintball
Top Gun, 82/2 Patak Rd, T076-381667.

Laem Ka, Chalong beaches and Wat Chalong *p428*
Diving
Sea Bees Diving, Chalong, T076-381765.

Golf
18-hole mini-golf course (open daily 1000-2300) left of the narrow road to Ao Chalong from the main road.

Bang Tao Beach *p430*
Golf
The 18-hole **Banyan Tree Golf Club** is situated here, with driving range attached. On Wed nights a 9-hole tournament takes place, T076-324350.

Transport

Phuket Island *p419, map p421*
Air
The airport is to the north of the island, 30 km from Phuket Town. For flight reservations call T076-327230-7. Regular domestic connections on THAI with **Bangkok**, **Chiang Mai**, **Hat Yai**, **Nakhon Si Thammarat**, **Surat Thani** and **Trang**. Bangkok Airways also runs daily connections with **Koh Samui**. **International connections** with **Hong Kong**, **Penang** and **KL** (Malaysia), **Singapore**, **Taipei**, **Tokyo**, **Munich** and **Dusseldorf**. The airport has a café, left luggage (0700-2030, ฿25 per day), *THAI* reconfirmation desk, *Hertz* car rental, tourist information counter, currency exchange, and hotel information.

Transport to town: THAI appears to have a virtual monopoly on transport from the airport and prices are not cheap (unless being picked up by your hotel). There are 2 ways to avoid the ฿80 fare into Phuket Town. One is to walk the 3 km to the main north-south road, Route 402, and pick up a public bus or songthaew there. Alternatively, walk out of the airport gate and wait for a motorcycle taxi dropping someone off (฿30). (They cannot pick up fares at the airport itself). Motorcycle taxis wait at the intersection with Route 402 to ferry people to the terminal (฿30); it's getting from the airport to Route 402 which is more difficult. THAI runs a minibus service into Phuket Town for ฿80 (from Phuket Town to the airport, the minibus leaves from the THAI office, 78 Ranong Rd). It also has a taxi and limousine service to town. Buses take passengers to **Patong**, **Kata** and **Karon beaches** for ฿100, or by private taxi for ฿400.

Airline offices Bangkok Airways, 158/2-3 Yaowarat Rd, T076-225033. **Dragonair**, 156/14 Phang Nga Rd, T076-215734, (from Hong Kong). **Malaysia Airlines**, Merlin Hotel, T076-216675. **SilkAir**, 183/103 Phangnga Rd, T076-213891. **THAI**, 78/1 Ranong Rd, T076-211195. **Tradewinds**, 95/20 Phuket Rd, T076-213891 (from Singapore).

Boat
During the high season (Nov-May) there are four ferries a day to and from **Koh Phi Phi**. However, these services have been disrupted post-tsunami and need to be checked in light of the dented tourist demand. The journey takes an hour and a half and leaves from Rassada Pier on Phuket's east coast. Depending on the speed of the boat and whether it is a/c tickets range from ฿250 - 750. The *King Cruiser*, run by **Ferryline** and **Songserm**, 51-53 Satool Rd, Phuket City, T075-222570, from Makham Bay, 1½ hrs. They also run the a/c jet cruises, ฿660, 50 mins.

Boats from Phuket to **Koh Yao Yai**, ฿50, leave from Laem Hin Pier at 1400, 1hr 20 mins. From Tien Sin Pier at 1000 and 1400. From Rassada Port on Thu and Sun only at 1400 and Sat at 0600. Boats from the village of Bang Rong leave at 1230. Boats from Phuket to **Koh Yao Noi** leave Bang Rong Pier at 1100, 1230 and 1430, 1 hr, ฿50.

Services to **Koh Lanta** are only available during the high season and ferries are limited to one trip. The journey takes four and a half hours. The ferry may also make a pit stop at Ao Nang for more passengers or to change boats. There is a minibus service in Phuket to and from the ferries for around ฿100 although this rate is expected to change slightly. If ferry prices are higher then it could also be because transport to the pier is included.

Long-tailed boats can be hired to visit reefs and the more isolated coves, A600-1200 per day.

Bus
Note that buses leave for the beaches from the market area from around 0600 although the taxi drivers may try to convince you otherwise! The station (*bor ko sor* – BKS) is on Phangnga Rd in Phuket Town, T076-211480. Tickets bought here are

cheaper than through travel agents. The information desk usually stocks a timetable and fare list produced by the TAT detailing all departures as well as local transport. Regular a/c and non-a/c connections with Bangkok's Southern bus terminal (14 hrs). A/c tour buses also ply this route. In Bangkok many depart from Khaosan Rd. Be careful with these and don't economize as thieves have been known to board the Khaosan buses which have a suspicious habit of 'breaking down'. See Krabi, for more details. Regular morning connections with **Hat Yai** (8 hrs), **Trang** (6 hrs), **Surat Thani** (6 hrs) and **Satun** (7 hrs). Regular connections with **Phangnga** (2 hrs), **Takua Pa** (3 hrs), **Ranong** (6 hrs) and **Krabi** (4 hrs). Journey times for these buses will vary between ½ hr and an hr.

Car

Small outfits along most beaches, expect to pay ฿900-1,200 per day, depending on the age of car, etc. It is worth picking up an updated map of the island from the TAT office in Phuket Town as the roads in the north can be confusing. **Avis** has an office opposite Phuket airport, T076-311358, and desks at, the **Holiday Inn**, the **Dusit Laguna** (on Bang Tao Beach) and the **Metropole** (in Phuket Town), ฿1,200 per day, ฿7,200 per week. **Hertz**, at the airport, T076-311162, and at the **Patong Merlin** and **Tara Patong**; prices are similar to **Avis**. There are other local companies down Rasada Rd in Phuket Town (see Phuket Town).

Motorbike

As for car hire above. ฿150-350 per day. There are also several places on Rasada Rd in Phuket Town. Note that not all places insist on taking your passport as a deposit/collateral but it is best not to let it out of your hands if you can help it. In Kata Noi Beach, a reliable agent is **Boy's Shop Travel and Tour**, 4/12 Moo2, T076-284062/ 01-8911910. Does tours, car rental, international tickets, hotels and tours. Contact – Kunakron Suthiprapa (nickname – 'Boy').

Motorbike taxi

Men (and a few women) with red vests will whisk passengers almost anywhere for a minimum of ฿10. They congregate at intersections.

Songthaew

For Patong, Kamala, Surin, Makham Bay, Nai Yang, Kata, Karon, Nai Harn, Rawai, Thalang and Chalong buses leave every 30 mins between 0600-1800 from the market on Ranong Rd in Phuket Town. Fares range from ฿15-25 to whatever the ticket collector thinks he can get away with.

Taxi

Taxis will leave when they are full (usually with 5 passengers). For **Surat Thani**, they leave from the coffee shop opposite the Pearl Cinema on Phangnga Rd (฿150 per person).

Train

There is no rail service to Phuket. However, some visitors take the train to **Phun Phin**, outside Surat Thani, where buses wait to take passengers on to Phuket (6 hrs).

Tuk-tuk

Avoid these unless you can't resist the exotic factor. They are far too overpriced and as comfortable as a rickshaw with one wheel.

Phuket City *p423, map p424*

Car

Avis, Metropole Hotel, 1 Montri Rd, T076-215050, A950 per day. **Phuket Horizon** Car Rent, 235/4 Yaowarat Rd, T076-215200. Pure Car Rent, 75 Rasada Rd, T076-211002, ฿1000 per day.

Motorbike

From the same places as car hire and many others, from A150 per day.

Tuk-tuk

A7 within town, ฿10 from town to suburbs.

Patong Beach *p426, map p434*

Jeep and motorbike

From outlets along Patong Beach Rd. Motorbikes on Rat Uthit Rd. Avis has desks at the *Holiday Inn* (T076-340608) and *Phuket Cabana Hotel* (T076-340138), Hertz is at the *Merlin*, T076-340037.

Songthaew/minibus
Regular departures from Ranong Rd, by the market in Phuket Town, A10.

Tuk-tuk
Charterted tuk-tuk ฿130 one way, from Patong to town or vice versa.

Karon and Kata Beaches *p426, map p435*
Car
Avis has a desk at the Phuket Arcadia (T076-381038), Le Meridien (T076-340480) and Kata Beach Resort (T076-381530). Hertz has a desk at the Thavorn Palm Beach (T076-381034).

Minibus
Chartered minibus to/from town, ฿130.

Songthaew
To both Karon and Kata leave regularly from the Ranong Rd Market, Phuket Town, A15.

Nai Yang and Nai Yang National Park *p431*
Bus
From the market on Ranong Rd in Phuket Town, 30 km away.

Mai Khao *p431*
Take the turn-off to the Marriott at the sign on the main road (402) travelling north from the airport. There are also airport pick-up services for the hotel. The Mai Khao Beach Bungalows are a little trickier to find, though well signposted. Take the 3rd turn-off heading north towards Phangnga to Mai Khao Beach (this should take you past fields of watermelons and head south), the sign and dirt track are on the right-hand side. Alternatively, take an earlier turn off and go right through the village and head back towards the main road, and the sign will be on your left once you start seeing the watermelon fields. It's also a good idea to contact the bungalow in advance to organize transport with their help.

Directory

Phuket City *p423, map p424*
Banks Along Rasada, Phuket, Phangnga and Thepkrasatri roads there are branches of all the major banks, all with ATMs and currency exchange. **American Express agent** Sea Tour, 95/4 Phuket Rd, T076-218417. **Internet** Many hotels and guesthouses now offer internet services – check out the varying prices per hour and whether they are on Broadband. **Post office** Montri Rd (at the corner of Thalang Rd). **Telephone** 122/2 Phangnga Rd, open 24 hrs. Overseas telephone and fax also available from the post office in town. **Useful addresses** Immigration office South Phuket Rd (close to Saphan Hin). Ask for the boxing stadium; the office is next door, T076-212108. Police On corner of Phuket and Phangnga roads. Tourist Police Emergency call, T076-219878 (until 1630), then Police on T076-212046.

Patong Beach *p426, map p434*
Banks Banks and currency exchange booths are concentrated on Patong Beach Rd (Thaweewong Rd) but may have set up offices further away in the wake of the tsunami. **Medical services** Kathu Hospital on Rat Uthit Rd. **Post office** Patong Beach Rd (the beachfront road), near Soi Permpong Pattana (aka Soi Post Office). **Telephone** International service next door to the post office on Patong Beach Rd. 0800-2300. **Useful addresses** Tourist Police On Patong Beach Rd.

Nai Yang and Nai Yang National Park *p431*
Banks Mobile exchange van.

Mai Khao *p431*
Banks Exchange possible in the Marriott or at banks in Thalang.

Phangnga Bay

→ Colour map 4, grid C1.

Phangnga Bay is best known as the location for the James Bond movie The Man with the Golden Gun. *Limestone rocks tower out of the sea (some as high as 100 m); boats can be hired to tour the area from Tha Don, the Phangnga customs pier.*

Travelling from Phuket to Phangnga the road passes through limestone scenery. Much of the land looks scrubby and dry, punctuated here and there by shrimp farms and scrappy farms. But en route, it is possible to watch rubber being processed by smallholders. Not long ago, over-mature rubber trees (those more than 25 years old) were cut down and processed into charcoal. Today, due to the efforts of an enterprising Taiwanese businessman, a rubber-wood furniture industry has developed. ▸▸ *For Sleeping, Eating and other listings, see pages 454-458.*

Ins and outs

Getting there and around

Phangnga has no train station or airport – the only way here is by bus (or private transport). Buses leave through the day from Bangkok's Southern bus terminal, including overnight VIP coaches (15 hours). There are also regular connections with Phuket, Krabi and towns south to the Malaysian border and north to Bangkok. Songthaews are the main form of transport around town (which can be walked through in around an hour anyway) and to surrounding villages. ▸▸ *See Transport, page 457, for further information.*

Best time to visit

The best time to visit the bay is between November and April.

Tourist information

See Activities and tours, page 457, for further information.

Phangnga Bay

The standard tour of Phangnga Bay ⓘ *park entrance fee, ฿200; see Transport, on options to get there*, winds through mangrove swamps, which act as a buffer between land and sea and nipa palm, and past striking limestone cliffs before arriving at **Tham Lod Cave**. This is not really a cave at all, but a tunnel cut into the limestone and dripping with stalagmites that look like petrified chickens hanging upside down. From Tham Lod, the route skirts past **Koh Panyi** – a Muslim fishing village built on stilts which extends out into the bay; its most striking feature being a fairy-tale golden mosque. Through the narrow laneways, the main transport is bicycles giving it an oddly Holland-esque feel. There are also seafood restaurants in this village but sadly, far too overpriced.

Other optional sights include **Khao Mah Ju**, a small mountain located between Tha Dan and Koh Pnay which resembles a dog. There is also **Khao Khian** or 'Mountain of Writings' with ancient depictions of animals and sea life dating back more than 3000 years ago. These drawings include a cartoon-like dolphin which looks suspiciously contemporary. It is believed that seamen who used the place to escape from the monsoon, painted these vivid images. While all of these sights may seem highlights in themselves, it is the 'James Bond' island that is touted as the raison d'etre for these tours. **James Bond Island** or **Koh Tapu** lies in the little bay of Koh Phing Kan or 'Leaning Mountain' which is a huge rock split into two parts with the smaller part having slid

down so that the taller section appears to be leaning. The limestone karst stack that sticks up out from the sea just off this island is called **Koh Tapu** (Nail Island). Somewhat overrated, the 'famous' rock, like a chisel, seems much smaller than it should be, and the tiny beach and cave are littered with trinket-stalls (refreshments available) and other tourists. To get to the beach, you go across a ropey bridge and scramble around some rocks which provides limited excitement. Recently, erosion of Koh Tapu caused by the wash from the hundreds of boats visiting the island has led to a declared intent to limit the numbers of visitors. However, the tsunami has shifted the goalposts on this and there was no indication of a limit when Footprint investigated. For details on the two large islands in the bay, **Koh Yao Yai** and **Koh Yao Noi**, see page 452.

Phangnga town and around

If you liked Larry McMurty's *The Last Picture Show in Town*, then you should get the point of Phangnga. While it has been disparaged as a mere pit-stop in the middle of nowhere, it has everything that a small town needs to keep ticking over without too much outside interference. That is: a really good hardware/general store, a cheap eaterie that doubles as a cinema, a pool-hall (or rather a pool-room) and a wonderful early morning market. There is only one main road that goes straight through the centre of this gun-shaped town which nestles narrowly between dramatic limestone crags. If you are seeking a non-tourist Thai experience, then Phangnga is one place that is still thoroughly itself so you may find what you're looking for. If, however, you want urban sophistication then a town where sleeping dogs lie in the middle of the

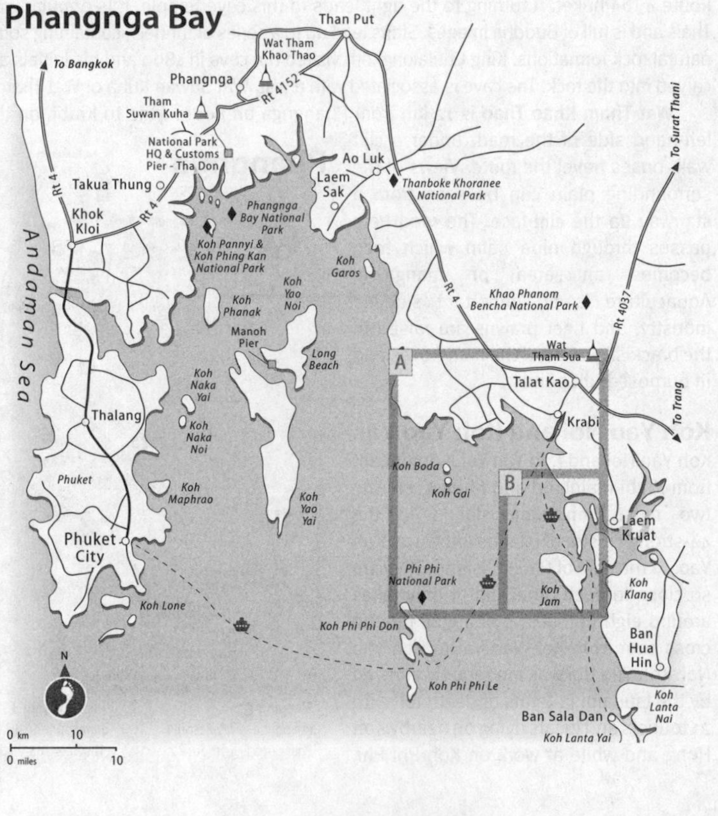

main drag at midday, is sure to disappoint. The drawback is that accommodation, though perfectly acceptable, is uninspired while nosh varies from standard noodles to good Thai standards. As far as the people go, the Phangnga folk come across as somewhat garrulous with an almost grumpy attitude to tourists – a real relief after the feigned jollity of so many of the resorts in more tourist-drenched spots of Thailand.

Due to the limestone geology, there are a number of caves in the vicinity. Just at the outskirts of town on Route 4 towards Phuket, on the left-hand side, is the **Somdet Phra Sinakharin Park**, surrounded by limestone mountains; this is visible from the road and opposite the former City Hall. Within this park is **Tham Luk Sua and Tham Ruesi Sawan**, two adjoining caves with streams, stalactites and stalagmites. These watery, sun-filled caves would be beautiful if it were not for the concrete pathways. At the entrance to the cave sits Luu Sii, the cave guardian, under an umbrella. **Tham Phung Chang** is a little closer into town on the other side of the road, within the precincts of **Wat Phraphat Phrachim Khet** ⓘ *take a songthaew, about 300 m past the traffic lights (themselves past the New Lak Muang Hotel) is the arched entrance to the wat.* The cave is actually located inside the symbol of Phangnga – a huge mountain that looks like a crouched elephant called Khao Chang (or so they say). It can be found behind Phangnga's former City Hall. In this long dark cave, again dripping with stalactites and stalagmites, there is a spring, Buddha images and a small pool where local boys swim. The wat is more visually interesting though not as quirky. It enjoys a fine position against the limestone cliff and set within a large compound.

In the centre of town, behind the **Rattanapong Hotel** is the fresh produce **market and early morning market** while along the main street near the **Thaweesuk Hotel** are some remaining examples of the **Chinese shophouses** that used to line the street.

Tham Suwan Kuha ⓘ *฿10, southwest bound bus*, is 12 km from Phangnga on Route 4 to Phuket. A turning to the right leads to this cave temple. It is popular with Thais and is full of Buddha images. Stairs lead up to a series of tunnels, containing some natural rock formations. King Chulalongkorn visited the cave in 1890 and his initials are carved into the rock. The cave is associated with a wat, Wat Suwan Kuha or Wat Tham.

Wat Tham Khao Thao is 12 km from Phangnga on Route 4152 to Krabi, on the left-hand side of the road, under a cliff wall; buses travel the route. Views of the surrounding plain can be seen from a stairway up the cliff-face. The road here passes through nipa palm which then becomes an area of mangrove. Aquaculture is an important sideline industry, and tiger prawns are raised in the brackish waters of the mangroves and in purpose-built ponds.

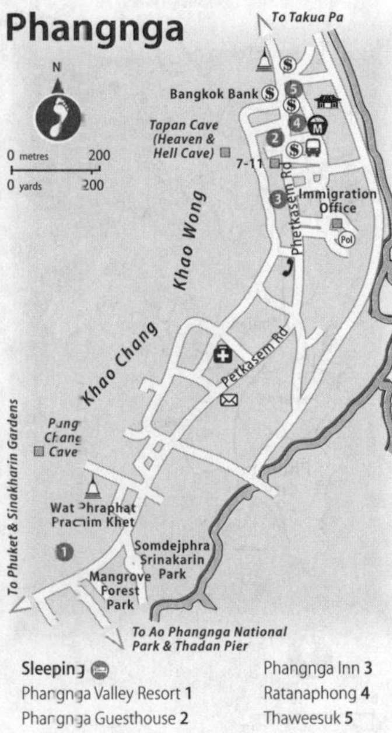

Phangnga
To Takua Pa
N
0 metres 200
0 yards 200
Bangkok Bank
Tapan Cave (Heaven & Hell Cave)
7-11
Immigration Office
Pol
Phetkasem Rd
Khao Wong
Khao Chang
Petkasem Rd
Pung Chang Cave
Wat Phraphat Prachim Khet
Somdejphra Srinakarin Park
Mangrove Forest Park
To Phuket & Sinakharin Gardens
To Ao Phangnga National Park & Thadan Pier
Sleeping
Phangnga Valley Resort 1
Phangnga Guesthouse 2
Phangnga Inn 3
Ratanaphong 4
Thaweesuk 5

Koh Yao Noi and Koh Yao Yai

Koh Yao Noi and Koh Yao Yai, equidistant from Krabi mainland and Phuket, are the two most important islands in the 44-strong cluster of islands known as Koh Yao, to the east of Phuket Island. They are so close to each other that it only takes around eight minutes by longtail ferry to cross over from Koh Yao Yai to Koh Yao Noi. Koh Yao Noi was moderately affected by the tsunami in terms of death toll with 21 tourists and locals dying on nearby Koh Hong and while at work on Koh Phi Phi.

But the fishing village Laem Sai on the southeast end of the island and to the coastline was seriously ravaged. There are now rocks where there were none before and around 40 fishing boats were smashed. Fish and shrimp farms, houses that hung over the water and nets were all lost to the waves while all the small businesses on the east side sea front were demolished. As far as the resorts went, they are back in business – even **Island Resort** which was the worst hit.

Consistently untouched by tourism – due to a strong Muslim and Chao Le community who wanted to retain control over what could have become a rampaging beast – these islands do not have banking, and Koh Noi has only minimal restaurants and shops. Indeed, in 2002, Koh Yao Noi gained world recognition (from eco-tourists anyway) when it received the World Legacy Award for Destination Stewardship from Conservation International and *National Geographic Traveler* magazine jointly for their eco-friendly homestays. Eco-activities include rubber plantation and fishing demonstrations, kayaking, hiking and snorkelling. In keeping with the eco-theme, there are a few sensitively designed resorts on Koh Yao Noi, a project by the responsible tourism company REST, while most other operations are basic bungalows. Visitors to these islands need to remember that the locals prefer outsiders to dress modestly and not to drink alcohol outside their resorts or restaurants.

Traditional ways and handicrafts still persist, as with the inventive 'fish-scale flowers' by the housewives of Koh Yao. These flowers – usually roses, geraniums and bougainvillea – are created from dried fish scales. The uniquely rural heritage is seen in other ways too. On Koh Yao Yai – which means 'long Island' – although expensive resorts are appearing there are still wooden houses, rubber plantations and wandering buffalos. On Koh Yao Noi, with its village in the middle and scattered huts throughout the remainder, road which circles the island but remains only partially paved. For little trips there are beautiful beaches (especially on Koh Nok) and an utterly dreamy lagoon (Koh Hong).

Koh Yao Yai is the larger of the two islands and has better beaches for swimming but has fewer places to stay, most of which tend to be overpriced. There's a spectacular view where the road ends on the west side of the island, overlooking Klong Son Bay. Koh Yao Noi is considerably more advanced than its bigger sister, with better facilities, including a hospital and even internet shops. Cell-phones operate throughout both the islands. On the most northerly tip of this island and best reached by boat, is the most enormous tree, the trunk of which takes 23 men to span. Hiring a bike can make for a delightful few hours taking in the beauty of the island while negotiating the (sometimes difficult) roads. Other than that, the main attraction is the peace and quiet. It has become a bit of a hotspot for alternative traveller groups, who have bagged the place as good for retreats ranging from yoga to healing crystal workshops.

Phangnga to Krabi

From Phangnga to Krabi, the road passes mangrove swamps and nipa palm, more dramatic karst formations and impressive stands of tropical forest. For those travelling independently by car or motorbike, there is a lovely detour worth taking for about half an hour to an hour. Look out for signs to Tham Raird or Ban Bang Toei, and turn left down towards the towering karst formations. The road leads through a pass into a valley in the heart of the karst. It is a little like stepping back in time, and several Thai television commercials idealizing rural life have been filmed here. The backdrop of lush forest on towering karst, with a foreground of rice fields and small villages, is wonderful. Rainy season visitors will be particularly well rewarded with mist and cloud on the peaks and a golden light on the wet paddy. Sadly, behind these wonderful, almost circular limestone crags there are several large limestone concessions blasting the mountains away. To the front there are similar scenes of rice farming against a backdrop of towering mountains, interspersed with the occasional village or temple.

Sleeping

Phangnga *p451, map p452*

C Phangnga Valley Resort, 5/5 Petkasem Rd, T076-412201. Restaurant, just before the turn-off for Phangnga from Route 4, about 6 km or so from the town centre, lovely setting, 15 bungalows, rather basic though, with no hot water.

C-E Rattanapong, 111 Petkasem Rd, T076-411247. In town centre, apparently this 5-story building is a converted hospital. This is a friendly establishment with large, cleanish a/c and fan rooms though there are also large, clean cockroaches. The carpet in some of the rooms really needs to be burned. Rooms are variable and good rooms with wooden floors are Number 11 and 25 which overlook the market and the street.

D Phangnga Guest House, next to Rattanapong at 99/1 Petkasem Rd, T076-411358. Excellent value for money, fan and a/c, fastidiously clean small rooms, tiny sparkling café downstairs. Cantankerous staff that grow on you. Recommended.

D Phangnga Inn, 2/2 Soi Lohakit, Petkasem Rd, T076-411963. Fan rooms before Rattanapong on Petkasem Rd – dingy, needs to be kept cleaner. Just about okay for this bracket and standard for Phangnga.

D-E Thaweesuk, 79 Petkasem Rd, T076-411686. Clean rooms, thin walls, very basic, run by an eccentric family who are forever lingering at the entrance, sunning themselves or engaging in ablutions. Mr Thaweesuk, if that's who he is, is an amiable giggling character with a sharp eye for anyone who's not a guest. So the security is excellent, despite having to walk through what feels like a open garage space to get to the rooms. There is a marvellous unexpected plus to the Thaweesuk though – a narrow stone staircase up to a roof-top terrace at the back of the building where you can view the surrounding limestone mountains at night and hang your wash over a Singha and a fag. Recommended.

Koh Yao Noi and Koh Yao Yai *p452*

The choice on Koh Yao Yai isn't as great, and much of it is overpriced, although the lack of visitors does make a small degree of bargaining possible.

L-AL Koyao Island Resort, 24/2 Moo 5, Koh Yao Noi, T076-597476, www.koyao.com. Operated by a Frenchman. 15 villas incorporating traditional thatched Thai architecture mixed with the latest in French modernity – four of these were damaged by the tsunami so should be looking brand spanking new following renovation. All villas are set around a garden in the middle of a coconut plantation and looking out directly onto an island-spotted stretch of the Andaman Sea – and the only non-rocky stretch of beach on the island. Villas come equipped with small private gardens, satellite TV, phone and fax, minibar etc. A newly opened, largely outdoor spa offers sauna, jaccuzi and traditional Thai massage in a relaxed and airy setting.

L-AL The Paradise Koh Yao Boutique Beach Resort and Spa, 24 Moo 4, T01-8924878-9, www.theparadise.biz. 48 superior studios, 16 deluxe studios and 6 pool villas on the beachfront in the north of Koh Yao Noi Island. It is the newest accommodation on the island with its own passenger transfer boats.

A-B Yao Yai Island Resort, Koh Yao Yai, T076-238265/01-535687, right next to **Tipaza Bungalows**. A/c or fan bungalows with king, twin or small sized beds dictating the price. Pleasantly appointed attached restaurant (mid-range, and therefore expensive for the area) looks out onto a nice stretch of soft sandy beach. Swimming is quite good, even at low tide when there are (easily navigable) rocks. However the 30 thatched roofed bungalows themselves are relatively small, offer a minimum of hanging space and are built on top of each other around a communal central garden. Nothing to write home about and overpriced. The quantity is seriously hindering the quality and making guests feel like commodities.

B-C Ban Tha Khao Bungalows, Koh Yao Noi, T/F076-212172, around half a dozen decently sized bamboo and wooden structures that boast chairs, table, wardrobes, western toilets and mini balconies. No a/c. Located on a near deserted cove up a rough road in the centre of the island so a bit of a hike. But, this is a picturesque choice and the family who runs

it can arrange for a pick up by motorcycle taxi. Run by the Mut family who manage the local Sea Canoe company.

B-C Tipazza Bunglaows and Tour, Koh Yao Yai, T076-215030. Beautifully clean fan bungalows on Loh Pa Reb beach, all with verandas and hanging flower boxes. For rent on a daily basis are canoes (฿300) and snorkelling equipment (฿100). Overpriced.

B-D Sabai Corner Bungalows, Koh Yao Noi, T01-8921827/01-8927827. Run by an Italian woman and her Thai husband. 10 romantic bungalows set among cashew and coconut trees with magnificent views over Pasai Beach. Attached toilets. Motorbikes, mountain bikes and canoes for rent, and the restaurant serves up tasty fare. Between them, the management can speak Italian, Spanish, French, English, German and Thai. A popular option often full so ring ahead.

C Eden Resort, Koh Yao Yai. Owned by a Thai-English couple, the original idea was to build a resort in a tropical garden. However, the garden looks unfinished, and these 2 bungalows are rather arbitrarily situated up a hill (although only a 5-min walk to the beach). Cheap restaurant attached.

C Loh Jaak Resort, Koh Yao Yai, right by the Loh Jaak beach pier where ferries depart for Phuket. Basic, not entirely clean or ant-free bungalows. Attached western toilets. Access is via a rickety old bridge made of old wooden planks that wouldn't look out of place in an Indiana Jones movie, and the suggestion of water below suggests mozzies may be a permanent fixture. Attached (mid-range) restaurant serves Thai food.

C Long Beach Village Bungalows, Koh Yao Noi, T01-6077921. Not much to look at from the outside, but some of these 40 rooms are bigger than most alternative options though all really need repairs of a sort. Clean and airy on the inside, all with attached western toilet and nice views. Some a/c. Long-time manager Suthup is friendly enough as well.

C-D Coconut Corner Bungalows, Koh Yao Noi, T076-597134. A handful of bungalows, all basic but charming, with attached toilets, presided over by the enormously friendly and very knowledgeable Mr Bean, whose tree-climbing abilities are a much-admired form of entertainment. The attached restaurant serves excellent food, and eating with the family is often the norm for those who prefer. Attracts returnees for the hospitality and Mr Bean's sheer verve. Recommended.

C-D Long Island Family Resort, Koh Yao Yai, T01-9792273, a few hundred metres further along the beach from **Loh Jaak Resort**. Operated by a very friendly family, these 5 basic but worthwhile little bungalows contain a big bed and a table, with attached squat toilets, balconies and chairs. The cheap to mid-range attached restaurant serves up astoundingly good food. This stretch of beach is good for both snoozing (in the hammocks provided) or swimming, and although there are rocks at low-tide, they're easy to avoid. Price includes breakfast. Recommended.

C-D Thiwson Bungalows, Koh Yao Yai, T01-9567582/01-7374420. Sweet, very clean little rooms in the usual bamboo and wooden style, with individual bedside lights, western toilets, with deck chairs on the verandas and a pleasant garden overlooking one of the nicest stretches of beach on the whole island, with Koh Yao Noi clearly visible in the distance. Attached restaurant. Recommended.

Eating

Phangnga *p451, map p452*

Cafés on Petkasem Rd, near the market, sell the usual array of Thai dishes, including excellent *khaaw man kai* (chicken and rice) and *khaaw mu daeng* (red pork and rice). There is also a good shop selling all manner of rice crackers, nuts and Thai biscuits on Petakasem Road past **Thaweesuk Hotel**. Try the popular **Kha Muu Restaurant** opposite the **Thaweesuk Hotel**.

TT Duang Seafood, 122 Petkasem Rd (opposite **Bank of Ayudhya**). Mediocre seafood restaurant if you go for the farang menu and Chinese specialities. A tip – the Thai menu really is completely different to the farang menu here so the best move is to be emphatic and point to what the locals are eating if you don't want a Chinese takeaway which tastes like it is from Manchester.

TT-T Khru Thai (Thai Teacher), Petkasem Rd (opposite the post office). Clean and cheap place, where the dishes are openly displayed making selection easy.

ΨΨ-Ψ **Ivy's House**, 38 Petkasem Rd, next door to a dental clinic. A tiny European-style café with a gas-fired oven for pizza, Italian wines and liquors and decent pastries. A little pricey but then the owner has to get all her imports from Phuket – including cheese from Italy. All her food is to a high standard. The owner 'Ivy' lived in Switzerland for many years and used to have a business in Koh Phi Phi but got tired of 'smiling all the time,' so came to Phangnga. Good source of information. Recommended.

Ψ **Open Air Cinema Eaterie**, Petkasem Rd and around Soi Bamrungrat – this no-name eaterie (the sign in Thai script simply describes what it sells) is unmissable for a couple reasons. There is a 100-year-old-plus tree that grows through part of it and a gigantic screen that can be heard along Petkasem Rd as it blares Southeast Asian martial arts flicks and straight-to-video western horror movies. Outside this open-restaurant and cinema, nocturnal stalls also sell sweet pastries, much like the standard ice-cream concession in cinemas of the past. The food here is mainly Thai standards – noodles, soups, fried pork, etc but of good quality and the young female staff are amazingly proficient given the high turnover of customers. While you can get cheap Singha here, most of the customers stick to fizzy drinks over their flick. Very popular with the locals, this Cinema Paradiso is a magical treat. Recommended.

Ψ **Ran Ja Jang**, down Soi Bamrungrat on a corner opposite another café. Superb seafood soup with egg and Tom Yee sauce swimming in tiger prawns and squid. This operation is run by 2 ladies wearing reassuring hair-nets as they bustle over an open kitchen. They also do homemade ices. Recommended.

There is an early morning market behind **Rattanapong Hotel**. This begins as early as 0500 but there is no need to kill yourself to get up that early. There are a couple very good cafés here that do traditional morning rice soup to perfection until around about 0900. This soup is a rice porridge with coriander, basil, ginger, spices, onion, lemon grass, pepper and minced pork. You can also get a fix of sweet tea. The market itself, though small, sells an astonishing array of foodstuffs, fish, meat, flowers for making garlands and lots of sarongs. Recommended.

Koh Yao Noi and Koh Yao Yai *p452*

As far as restaurants go on Koh Yao Noi, most people eat at the restaurant attached to their bungalows, although there is **Tha Khao Seafood** right next to the pier – a misleading name as there are only 7 seafood dishes. Otherwise a good option is to pick your choice of fish from the fishermen's huts on Tha Tondo Pier to the northwest of the island, and take it to the local restaurant just by the pier for cooking while watching arguably the best sunset the island can offer. For a local delicacy on Koh Yao Yai, it is worth trying/buying the dried anchovy paste – pla ching chang which is used with rices and noodles to liven things up.

Bars and clubs

Koh Yao Noi and Koh Yao Yai *p452*

The bar scene is limited to just one. **Reggae Bar**, Koh Yao Noi, which offers beer and cocktails and consists of merely a few tables set out on the non-beach side of the road between **Sabai Corner** and **Long Beach Village Bungalows**. There is also the beachfront **Pyramid Bar**, that narrowly escaped being hit by the wave which turned back on itself millimetres before it reached the bar. Locals now use the bar as a community centre to discuss future developments for the community following the disaster.

Festivals and events

Phangnga *p451, map p452*

There is an annual festival at the Chinese temple dedicated to Machobo on the road parallel to Petkasem Rd by the Krisana-Utit end. This road does not have a name but the next parallel road is Thetsabanbumrung Rd. The temple itself is filled with fantastical art depicting tigers and goddesses and is around 100 years old. Coming on the heels of Chinese New Year, this festival really extends the revelries when an open-air cinema is set up in the space opposite the temple which plays Chinese movies at decibel pitch until past midnight. There are nocturnal stalls selling food and running games of chance so that the whole atmosphere is one of a carnival. Around the same time, during the day, Chinese priestess bless all the shops and the market area.

Activities and tours

Phangnga *p451, map p452*

Tour operators

There are 3 main tour companies in town: **Sayan**, **Kean** and **M.T. Tours**. All three advertise widely, run very similar tours and charge the same – ฿300 for half day, ฿750 for full day. The tours are worthwhile and good value – and for an extra ฿250 the affable and endearing Mr Hassim who grew up in Koh Panyi and came from a long line of fishermen, will put you up in his stilted Muslim village for the night and provide a seafood dinner. Mr Hassim also speaks relatively good English and is a very accommodating host who has quite a loyal following. He operates out of the **Muang Tong Hotel** at 128 Petkasem Rd.

Koh Yao Noi and Koh Yao Yai *p452*

Reggae Tour, next to **Reggae Bar**, Koh Yao Noi, rents a long-tailed boat (฿800 for half a day, or ฿1200 for a full day), kayaks (฿250 half a day, ฿500, full day.)

Transport

Phangnga Bay *p450, map p451*

To get there take a songthaew to the pier, ฿10, from Phangnga town. 7 km along Route 4 there is a turning to the left (Route 4144 – signposted Phangnga Bay and the Ao Phangnga National Park Headquarters) and the pier is another 3 km down this road. Long-tailed boats can also be chartered from the pier for a trip around the sights of Phangnga Bay for about ฿350-450 although it is cheaper for 1 person to take a tour with **Sayan, Kean** or Mr Hussein at **M.T. Tours** (see Tour operators above).

There are also other ways of getting down to the bay and taking tours: as the road nears Phangnga, there are a number of roads down to the coast, from where tours to Phangnga Bay depart. Look out for signs and the next U-turn on this widened and rather fast road. The first of these leads down a long winding road through rubber plantations and over hills to **Khlong Khian pier**. Although there are several tour operators here these are very local small-scale efforts. Most of the boatmen speak little English, but can take you to caves and islands you will never see on larger tours. They are also more flexible in terms of timing, and take no more than 8 people per boat.

Further down the road there are two more routes to the Phangnga Bay tours. The first is in **Takua Thung town** which has been partially bypassed by the main road to Krabi. Once in the town there is a well-marked narrow soi leading to a pier. At the pier, there are several restaurants and souvenir shops, and parking for tour buses. Independent travellers will find plenty of tour operators willing to book you a trip on a boat. The boats here are large, taking up to 20 passengers, and more reminiscent of Bangkok long-tailed boats than local fishing boats. A similar scene is to be found on the last main turn-off to Phangnga Bay near the national park offices, but the national park offices do contain some interesting information on the bay, and feature a mangrove interpretive walk, and some accommodation. Also, this last bay attracts smaller independent tour operators so it is possible to get away from the crowds in this location too.

Phangnga *p451, map p452*

Bus

The bus station is on Petkasem Rd, near the centre of town and a short walk from the **Thaweesuk** and **Lak Muang 1** hotels. T076-434119 for a/c bus information and T076-4345557 for non-a/c bus information. Buses from **Bangkok**'s Southern bus terminal, 15 hrs. 3 VIP buses leave in the evenings for Bangkok. Regular connections with **Phuket**'s bus terminal on Phangnga Rd, 2 hrs and with **Krabi**, 2 hrs. Also buses to **Ranong**, **Takua Pa**, **Hat Yai** and **Trang**. You can wave down these buses if you catch them coming out of the station and pay on board. Motorcycle taxis wait to take passengers further afield, ฿5.

Motorbike

Hire from the **Thaweesuk Hotel** and **M.T. Hotel** for ฿200 daily.

Songthaew

Cramped but rather extraordinary teak wood songthaews constantly ply the main road – slowly and giving some anguish on those unpadded seats, ฿5.

Koh Yao Noi and Koh Yao Yai *p452*
From Koh Yao Yai to **Laem Hin Pier, Phuket**, 0800. To **Tien Sin Pier**, **Phuket** at 0800 and 1500). To **Rassada Port**, **Phuket**, 0830 Thu and Sun and 1430 on Sat. Boats to the village of **Bang Rong** return at 0700, 1300 and 1500.

Boats from both Koh Yao Yai and Koh Yao Noi to **Krabi** and **Phangnga** are for early birds and usually depart from 0700 or thereabouts. You need to check with your bungalow or resort to get the times and it can vary.

Directory

Phangnga *p451, map p452*
Banks ATMs on Petkasem Rd. **Internet** In Kean tour company (at the bus station) and further along Petkasem Road toward Thung Jadee School. **Post office** On Petkasem Rd, 2 km from centre on main road entering town from Phuket. Overseas phone service.

Krabi and around

Colour map 4, grid C2.

Krabi is a small provincial capital, situated on the banks of the Krabi River. It is fairly touristy and a jumping off point for Koh Phi Phi (see page 485), Koh Lanta (see page 494), Ao Nang and Rai Leh and smaller islands like Koh Jum, Koh Bubu and Koh Siboya (see page 472). Krabi town itself is a shambling and amiable waterfront port with easily accessible and excellent tourist sites like the Tham Lod cave and Tiger Temple.

In the past, the town acquired the unfortunate reputation of being a haven for junkies and a place where you really shouldn't leave anything in your hotel room. But, in recent years, Krabi has attempted to cash in on its heritage in an entirely idiosyncratic Krabi-esque way. Hence, the kitsch iron statues on Muharat Road of four bearded prehistoric men carrying the traffic signals. This vision, best viewed at twilight with the jungle foliage behind, is meant to remind visitors that big human skulls were found in Tham Phi Hua To Cave which means Big-headed Ghost cave. Aside from anthropological joys, Krabi town is a perfect place to either prepare for, or recuperate from, island-hopping, especially for those who have been on islands with limited electricity and luxuries. Here, you can stock up on bread – Krabi has excellent bakeries – fetch your newspapers and get a decent café latte before heading back to the nature reserve for some more hammock-swinging.

Rock-climbing, river trips, birdwatching, hiking at national parks and reserves, motorcycle treks and sea canoeing are all available and most tour companies also operate daily and overnight tours around Phangnga Bay (see page 457) often incorporating a visit to Wat Tham Suwan Kuha and other local sights. ▸▸ *For Sleeping, Eating and other listings, see pages 463-470.*

Ins and outs

Getting there and around

Krabi is well connected. From October this year, the new Krabi International Airport, 15 km from town, is offering seven daily flights from Bangkok. The taxi to town from the airport is around ฿400 and to Ao Nang ฿500. There are also songthaews. There are also boats to Koh Phi Phi – still worth a day-trip – and Koh Lanta from the new pier on the outskirts of Krabi Town. Free courtesy tuk-tuk drives from the old pier at Chao Fah to the new one may also still be offered so don't be too keen to flag down a taxi. Meanwhile, Chao Fah Pier continues to operate services to Rai Ley beach and there is a white minibus for ฿30 to Ao Nang from there as well.

There is no train station in Krabi but Phun Phin (the stop for Surat Thani) is a three-hour bus ride away. The overnight sleeper is met by buses for those going on

to Krabi. From the bus station, around 5 km from the centre, there are regular connections with Bangkok's Southern bus terminal (16 hours) as well as with all major towns in the south. The VIP bus from Bangkok is a 12-hour overnight journey. However, do your homework and don't economize – Krabi hoteliers are now warning tourists of a rogue bus service (see box page 154) with contraband 'passengers'. For Koh Samui, companies offer combination bus/boat tickets. Songthaews are the main form of local transport, and motorbikes are widely available for hire. A standard sample rate is the red songthaew from Krabi town to the bus station at ฿10. ➤➤ *See Transport, page 469, for further information.*

Tourist information

Small **TAT** office ⓘ *Uttarakit Rd, across from Kasikorn Bank, 0830-1630*. For more information on Krabi, Ao Nang, Phra Nang, Rai Leh, Koh Phi Phi and Koh Lanta and some good little articles, pick up the free guide, *Flyer*, from various bars and guesthouses (www.yourkrabi.com/flyer). Many other places offer 'tourist information', usually to sell tours, tickets and rooms, which can either be offensive or convenient. In the latter case, **Ibris Travel Tour and Internet Service Group** ⓘ *23 Isara Rd, T075-630276*, do give rather good practical advice and are not at all pushy. The operation is run by an Aussie and his Thai wife. Good maps of Krabi and the surrounding area can be obtained from numerous shops, tour agents and guesthouses around town. A popular map is the *Frank Tour* one whereas tourists have criticized *Prannok Witthaya Maps* as overly complicated.

Background

Krabi's economy used to be based squarely on agriculture and fishing but since the mid to late-1980s tourism has grown by leaps and bounds although rubber and palm-oil plantations are still a mainstay. The tourism takeover in Krabi is all down to the growth in the late 1970s and 1980s of surfaced roads in Ao Nang, Ao Luk, Klong Tom and Panom Bencha areas. Indeed, in the early 1970s either Communist bandits or merely bandits operated the roadblocks at night, along the only surfaced road in Krabi – Highway 4 – which linked the township with Phangnga to the south. Only those motorists who knew an ever-changing password would be allowed to travel while Krabi locals swiftly learned not to venture out after dusk. What scant tourists there were clung to their guesthouses and warm Singhas, not that maps were even available for the more adventurous among them. Ever mindful of the possible spread of Communism, a watchful Royal Thai Survey Department along with the US Defence Mapping Agency in Washington, had published a secret map of the area that no civilian was permitted to see. Then, as the Communism threat receded, Ao Nang, which persisted with a dirt track to Krabi until the mid-1970s, got in on a budding asphalted network. This resulted in a bungalow and bar boom that transformed what was once an isolated beachside village into a Costa Del Sol Bournemouth with a twist of Patong. Meanwhile, Krabi town, on the beach route, steadily grew as a tourist layby and is, today, exceptionally well served with well-priced cafés and restaurants, catering for both tourists and locals and good quirky bars. There is even talk of an annual Thai reggae and Moken 'Sea Gypsy' summer music festival as more musicians are attracted to the area's laid-back nightlife. Over the past five years the demographics of Krabi have also shifted and the present burgeoning Muslim population – well over half – has clearly influenced the food front. Along with spicy Thai salads, halal meat, roti and Malaysian-Thai fusion cuisine are commonplace.

Krabi town

There is a **general market** on Srisawat and Sukhon roads, and a **night market** close to the Chao Fah Pier. Chao Fah Pier at night is flooded with food stalls frequented mainly by locals. The food is highly varied and cheap though, at that volume, the cooking is quick-fire so you need to make sure everything is actually cooked. However, for a nocturnal nibble al fresco and a promenade walk, the pier is ideal, especially as the streets are thronged with people around twilight. Depending on how you feel about young elephants performing tricks for a bag of cucumbers, visitors might also opt to

Krabi

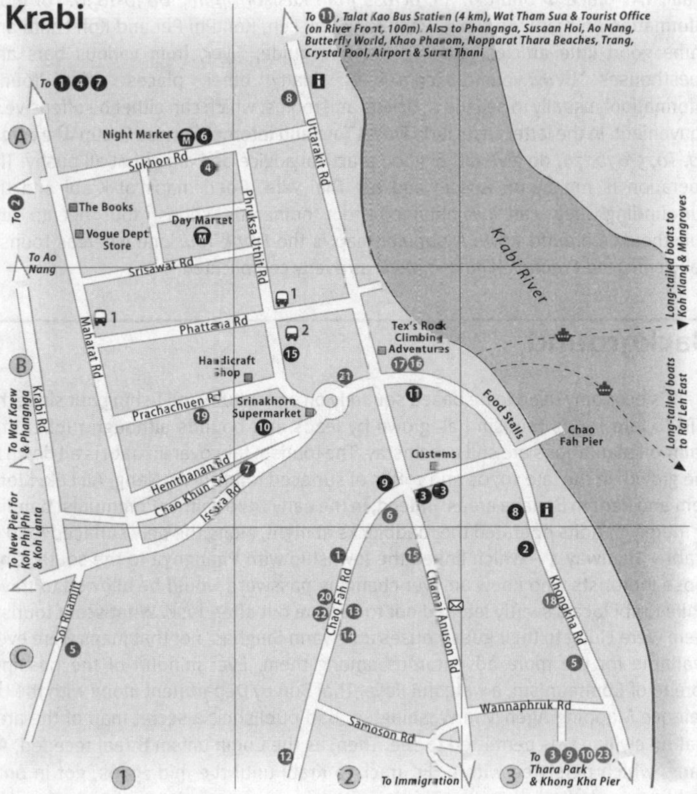
To 11, Talat Kao Bus Station (4 km), Wat Tham Sua & Tourist Office (on River Front, 100m). Also to Phangnga, Susaan Hoi, Ao Nang, Butterfly World, Khao Phanom, Nopparat Thara Beaches, Trang, Crystal Pool, Airport & Surat Thani
To 1 4 7
Night Market
Suknon Rd
Uttarakit Rd
To 2
The Books
Day Market
Phruksa Uthit Rd
Vogue Dept Store
To Ao Nang
Srisawat Rd
Krabi River
Long-tailed boats to Koh Klang & Mangroves
Maharat Rd
Phattana Rd
Tex's Rock Climbing Adventures
Handicraft Shop
Krabi Rd
To Wat Kaew & Phangnga
Prachachuen Rd
Srinakhorn Supermarket
Food Stalls
Chao Fah Pier
Long-tailed boats to Rai Leh East
Customs
Hemthanan Rd
Chao Khun Rd
Issara Rd
To New Pier for Koh Phi Phi & Koh Lanta
Chao Fah Rd
Chamai Anuson Rd
Khongkha Rd
Soi Ruamjit
Wannaphruk Rd
Samoson Rd
To Immigration
To 3 9 10 23, Thara Park & Khong Kha Pier
A
B
C
1
2
3

0 metres 50
0 yards 50

Sleeping
A Mansion 1 *C2*
Bai Fern Guesthouse 22 *C2*
Ban Choafa 20 *C2*
Boon Siam 2 *A1*
City 4 *A1*
Europa Café & Guesthouse 5 *C1*
Grand Tower 6 *B2*
Hollywood 7 *B2*
Jungle Tours & Guesthouse 8 *A2*
Khong Kha Guesthouse 9 *C3*
Krabi City Sea View 10 *C3*
Krabi Meritime 11 *A2*
Krabi River 3 *C3*
KR Mansion 12 *C2*
K Guest House 13 *C2*
New Wave Guesthouse & Bar 14 *C2*
PS Guest House 15 *C2*
River View Guesthouse 16 *B2*
SR Guesthouse 17 *B2*
Star Guest House 18 *C3*
Swallow Guesthouse 19 *B1*
Thai 21 *B2*
Thara Guesthouse 23 *C3*

Eating
Boathouse 7 *A1*
Chawan 2 *C3*
Chok Dee 3 *B2*
Chao Sua 4 *A1*
I-Oon 9 *B2*
Kwan Coffee Corner 8 *B3*
May & Mark's 10 *B2*
Pizzeria Firenze 11 *B2*
Ruen Mai 1 *A1*
Seafood Restaurant 6 *A1*
Sea House 13 *B2*
Viva 15 *B2*

Bars & clubs
Juke Box Pub 5 *C3*

Transport
White Songthaews to Ao Nang & Nopparat Thara 1 *B1, B2*
Minibus to Talat Kao 2 *B2*

feed the performing elephant, then watch as he snatches the carrier bag in his trunk and touches his forehead in a cap-doffing 'thanks 'guv' gesture. There is also a handful of guesthouses, some shabby but intriguing, along the river and opposite the market if you crave to be close to the action.

Around Krabi

Wat Tham Sua (Tiger Cave Temple)

ⓘ *Wat Tham Sua is east along Route 4. Take a red songthaew from Phattana Rd in town for ฿15 to Route 4 (the songthaew is marked 'Airport/Fossil Beach'). From here either walk along Route 4 to the Cave Temple or take a motorcycle taxi (about ฿15). Walk to the cave from the main road.*

Wat Tham Sua is 8 km northeast of town just past Talat Kao down a track on the left and has dozens of kutis (monastic cells) set into the limestone cliff. Here, the monks do still meditate in the forest. Tiger Cave is so called because once, a very long time ago, a large tiger lived there and left his pawprints behind as proof although some visitors have found this a dubious claim and grumble that the pawprints are not at all paw-like. Real wild creatures can be found in the surrounding area of rocky hillsides and mangrove forest. Here, trees that are hundreds of years old ensconce garrulous macaque monkeys. Walk behind the ridge where the bot is situated to find a network of limestone caves, which eventually lead back to the entrance. There is also a staircase on the left; 1,237 steps leading to the top of a 600-metre-high karst peak with fantastic views of the area and meditation areas for the monks which are often occupied. This is a demanding climb as it is steep; it is best reserved for cool weather and early morning. Take water and a sunhat as the walk affords scant protection at times.

Tham Phi Hua To and Tham Lod

ⓘ *The caves of Tham Phi Hua To and Tham Lod can be reached by boat from a pier just down the road from Hat Nopparat Thara (take the first left as you exit towards Khlong Muang), or you can take one of many tours by boat or canoe to the same caves. It is also possible to visit these areas with companies offering sea canoeing. While generally more expensive than the trips via long-tailed boat (bear in mind that sea canoes cost upwards of US$350 each in Thailand), a more private trip is worth it, particularly when passing through the lush and mysterious limestone canyons. Then you can be assured that the main sounds will be eerie watery echos and the dipping of oars rather than 'incredibles' in varying accents.*

Phi Hua To Cave or Big-Headed Ghost Cave is famous for the discovery there of ancient and unusually large human skulls as well as 70 paintings in red and black of people and animals, all of which upholds Krabi Province's claim to having hosted the oldest human settlements in all of Thailand. A large pile of shells was also discovered in the cave. There are two paths in the cave. Take the left for a cathedral-like cavern illuminated by a shaft of light and the right for a hall reputed to have been a shelter for prehistoric people.

Tham Lod Tai is a cavern in the limestone karst through which you can travel by boat along narrow passages filled with stalactites and stalagmites. Tham Lod Nua is a longer and larger cavern with more meandering passages. Both are passable only at low-tide. The boat ride to these caves passes mangroves and limestone karst outcrops – a good day or half-day trip.

Mangrove trips

ⓘ *Long-tailed boats can be hired for a trip into the mangroves at the Chao Fah pier (rates are negotiable and depend on the time of year, length of time and number of people in the boat). It may also be possible to get a rua jaew for this trip – this is the*

traditional boat used in the Krabi area (including Koh Lanta). Paddles are used instead of a motor (though most now use both), with the boatman standing on the bows to paddle. At least you may be able to persuade your boatman to stick to the oars only through the mangroves.

Mangroves line the river opposite Krabi. This is a protected area although heavy logging in the past has left most of the forest quite immature. It is worth visiting for the birds and other wildlife including several families of macaques, but ask the boatman to go slowly when in the mangroves so as not to startle the animals and birds.

Thanboke Khoranee National Park

ⓘ *Entry is ฿200 (the same as for Phanom Bencha National Park and Khao Nor Chu Chi). Take Route 4 towards Phangnga; turn left down Route 4039 for Ao Luk after 45 km. About 2 km down this road there is a sign for the gardens, to the left. By public transport, take a songthaew from Krabi to Ao Luk, and then walk or catch a local songthaew.*

Thanboke Khoranee National Park is a beautiful, cool and peaceful forest grove with emerald rock pools, streams and walkways. In the park, swimming is permitted in the upper pool which is near a small nature trail leading up into the limestone cliffs (sturdy shoes are advised).

Laem Sak

ⓘ *Turn left as you come out of Thanboke Khoranee National Park and continue on Route 4039 into the town of Ao Luk and beyond down a small road to the end of the peninsula.*

Laem Sak juts out from the mainland just north of Ao Luk and makes a good trip before or after a visit to the Thanboke Khoranee National Park. Views back towards the mainland are impressive with a wall of limestone karst in the distance fringed by mangroves. Out to sea and to the west are a group of rocky islands. The fishing pier is a working one with plenty of activity and there are restaurants serving fresh seafood. This is a good place to watch the fishing boats pass by and eat reasonably priced fish. See also Sleeping.

Garos Island

ⓘ *A local tour leaves from a pier down a rough dirt track which can be reached from Ban Thung. (Turn left at Ban Thung, drive about 500 m and take a right turn down the dirt track. There are signs to the pier after about 5 km, and the pier is about 12 km in total from the main road). Pre-arrange a tour by calling T076-649149. Mr Mos speaks reasonably good English. His partner, (Mr Mudura), can also take the tour but speaks much less English, although he knows more about the general area having lived there for most of his 60 years.*

Garos Island lies off the coast of mainland Krabi near Ban Thung (before Ao Luk). A day trip in a small long-tailed fishing boat will take you past mangroves and limestone karst islands to Garos Island, where you can see somewhat sinister prehistoric wall paintings and several caves used as traditional burial grounds for 'sea gypsies' (Chao Le). Good for birdwatching and for seeing the traditional lifestyles of local fishing communities. The tour provides a fantastic lunch cooked on a small island beach where you can also enjoy a swim. Operated by members of the local community. Recommended.

Khao Phanom Bencha National Park

ⓘ *Take a motorcycle or other transport out on the main road going towards Trang (past Talat Kao). The turn-off comes before the exit for Wat Tham Sua. Motorcycle theft from the car park at Kho Panom Bencha happens regularly so be forewarned.*

Khao Phanom Bencha National Park provides a magnificent backdrop to the town with a peak rising more than 600 m above the surrounding land. Near the park entrance is the lovely **Huai To Waterfall** best seen between September and December after the monsoon. The drive to the waterfall is very pleasant with a distinctly rural feel

and the area around the park entrance has some lovely trees and open grassland, good for picnics. Park rangers can take people on treks up to the peak and to a waterfall on the other side. The level of English spoken by park rangers can vary – check that you feel comfortable with any potential guide before setting out. The trek takes more than one day as the climb is quite steep.

Khao Nor Chu Chi forest, Crystal Pool and hot springs

ⓘ *Tours can be arranged from most tour offices in town. For self-drive, the turn-off to Khao Nor Chu Chi is just after the major intersection in Khlong Thom town. It is marked. Once you get on to the road to the Crystal Pool and Hot Springs, you will find clear signposting.*

These sights are all located in Khlong Thom district to the south of Krabi province. Khao Nor Chu Chi, which is in the middle of nowhere, is a mere parcel of rainforest surrounded by plantations. It has a forest trail and bungalow-style accommodation (**Morakot Resort**) that was initiated as part of an ecotourism project aimed at conserving the seriously endangered **Gurney's Pitta**, a bird believed to be extinct; it was re-discovered by the ornithologists Philip Round and Uthai Treesucon. Interestingly, Prince Charles, a keen ornithologist, has also endorsed the fight to save the comically named bird with its flashes of turquoise, red and brown. Gurney's Pitta, which favours heavy forest, can be almost impossible to find and visitors have spent two days looking for a glimpse of this jewel-winged bird, which is listed as one of the top 50 endangered birds in the world. The ongoing fear now is that Gurney's Pitta will become extinct in the next 10 years as deforestation due to rubber and palm-oil plantations continues to dominate over ecological concerns. Ironically, tourism could save the day as the Tourist Authority of Thailand gets increasingly involved in the plight of Gurney's Pitta.

The Crystal Pool, which is visited by the Queen and other members of the Royal Family annually, is so called because of the exceptional clarity of the water and its emerald colour. In fact the colour derives from mineral deposits that are visible through the water. The pool is quite shallow and the water very buoyant. However while the pool may look attractive enough, the deposits feel rather crunchy and not particularly pleasant under foot and the slopes leading into the pool are very slippery.

A visit to hot springs on a hot day may seem rather odd, but the temperature of the water is quite comfortable and it's a relaxing place to spend some time. The springs have been developed into a Thai-style mineral baths with changing facilities, walkway to the original springs, and landscaped gardens for the walk through to the river. There are actually eight of these springs, all with enticing names. They are Nam Lod (Water Passing through), Cheng Kao (Valley), Jorakeh Kao (White Crocodile), Nam Tip (Heavenly Waters) Nam Krahm (Indigo Water), Morakot (Emerald Water), Hun Kaeo (Barking Deer) and Noy (Small).

Sleeping

Krabi and around *p458, maps p460 and p462*

With the rising cost of accommodation at nearby beach resorts and the spectre of burgeoning 4-star complexes on Koh Lanta, Krabi has found a niche in providing low cost but often very friendly and even imaginative accommodation for the lower-budget crowd. This has also meant a lot more guesthouses are cropping up, which has forced some of the original dross out. The fear, however, is that Krabi will go the Phuket-route, pushing prices beyond what many travellers are willing to pay for accommodation in a waterfront-town without a beach on the doorstep.

Generally speaking, the older guesthouses on Ruen-Ruedee Rd are cramped and stuffy; those up the hill and elsewhere in the town are more spacious, better maintained and often cheaper. Note that prices during the high season can be double the rates for the low season. Another good reason to give the nearby beach areas a miss for overnight

stays is the food. Krabi town boasts 2 night markets, a morning market, excellent restaurants offering an eclectic range of cuisines, and fine cafés with good coffee, tea and pastries. Food in Ao Nang and Rai Leh remains dominated by sloppy Western and tourist Thai with a silly number of pizzerias.

A **Krabi Meritime Hotel**, T075-620028-46. Krabi town's first luxury hotel, about 2 km from town, is off the road towards the bus station. Rooms are large and clean with balconies overlooking huge twin limestone outcrops. Situated on the river overlooking the mangroves and limestone karst, they run a ferry service to a private beach and club and have a pool. Mixed reports of staff who have been known to be lax. Somewhat overpriced.

A **Theparat Travel Lodge and Restaurant**, 151-155 Maharaj Rd, T075-622048. This white 4-storey offers a/c and fan rooms with satellite TV and mini-bar. It does a fairly extensive range of tours, including one to a King Cobra Show and even has a bakery/patisserie. Not bad service and clean rooms. Worth checking out but you may find it lacking in atmosphere.

A-B **Krabi River Hotel**, 73/1 Khongkha Rd, T075-612321. Fairly new, 5-storey white-fronted hotel with splendid view of the river, particularly during the day as then you can see the mangrove area and the hustle and bustle of the boats. Rooms are bright and simply decorated if uninspiring and not terribly brave with the colour scheme. Concrete and tiles throughout. Spotless. Has all facilities and restaurant with gorgeous view that is ideal for breakfast. There is also a rooftop terrace. Good value for the money, especially if you can get a room with a small veranda overlooking the river. Also suitable for families. Recommended.

B-C **A Mansion**, 12/6 Chao Fah Rd, T075-630511-3. Hotel-style facilities and prices. The rooms are all a/c and should have hot water though there have been reports of only cold. TV may also be too snowy to watch. Rooms, though box-like, are clean and smell fresh. This is centrally located which is a strong plus. However, it is not unreasonable to ask for a discount for the top-end price and staff can be swayed.

B-C **Boon Siam Hotel**, 27 Chao Khul Rd, T075-632511-5. Prides itself on being deluxe. This 5-storey hotel has a blocky concrete exterior. Rooms are all a/c with hot water, spacious and comfortable. Satellite TV. A bit far out of the town, but still within walking distance of the centre. Does a brisk trade around Chinese New Year. Good value.

B-C **Krabi City Sea View Hotel**, 77/1 Khongkha Rd, T075-622885-8, krabicity seaview@hotmail.com. Hotel block right on the promenade, just down from the road up to the Immigration Department. Great views from the top storey, but the lower floor rooms have no view at all. This hotel offers the good, the bad and the mediocre. While a few of the top rooms have pretty views and are pleasantly sized, other rooms are cramped and need new beds. The restaurant at the top is a fine place to breakfast if you do not mind the intermittent sound of motorized long-tailed boats that are initially part of the local charm and soon become piercing. Be warned – the staff are inclined to push customers into taking rooms on the lower floors so firmness is needed when asking to have a look.

C **Ban Chaofa**, 20/1 Chaofa Rd, T075-630359. Mix of a/c and fan, 2-storey hotel edging to 2-star. Japanese/Ikea feel – clean, chic and minimalist. Rooms overlooking street also have small balconies. The owner is a former surveyor who speaks fairly good English and has put some care and thought into his venture. Internet and all facilities, including laundry. Restaurant on ground floor. Reccommended.

C **Thai**, 7 Issara Rd, T075-6111474. Some a/c, large hotel with 150 rooms, grotty corridors and the rooms are somewhat rundown though large and clean with reasonable bathrooms. The most expensive rooms are much better maintained than the cheaper rooms. Hauntingly, there is a pervasive smell of mildew in this somewhat dimly-lit hotel. It all makes for a borderline acceptable mid-range establishment in immediate need of renovations. Discounts available in the low season.

C-D **Bai Fern Guesthouse**, 24/2 Chaofa Rd, T075-630339. Variable rooms, some airy ones overlooking the street with small verandas while others lack decent windows and are awkwardly proportioned. The hot water also has a knack of coming out cold. Some attempt has been made at personalizing the main entrance with a

large aquarium by the stairs but overall the establishment craves a more intimate lively touch. However, it is safe, secure and clean with trustworthy family staff who do try their best to help and, if you choose your room carefully, it is decent value.

C-D City Hotel, 15/2-3 Sukhon Rd, T075-621280. Some a/c, 3-storey hotel for which we have received mixed reports, rooms are clean with attached bathrooms, faces onto one of the quieter streets in town. Having said that, rooms can be hot and airless and staff unfriendly. Still, better value than the **Thai**.

C-D Grand Tower Hotel, 9 Chao Fah Rd, T075-621456-7. A long-standing average hotel, neither towering nor grand. The rooms are bare but clean, some with attached showers and a tendency to smell musty. Nonetheless, there is a very popular bar out front.

D Chan Chalay, 55 Uttarakit Rd, T075-620952/01-9788081, chanchalay@hotmail.com. Pleasant white and blue building on Uttarakit Rd up near the post office. Very reasonably priced, clean and airy rooms set back a little from the road. The best rooms are out back. This guesthouse also has a breezy café that is highly popular. Recommended.

D Europa Café and Guesthouse, 1/9 Soi Ruamjit Rd, T075-620407. Under Thai and Danish management, the **Europa Café** has 5 rooms above the restaurant. All rooms are nicely decorated, and clean, but the smallest rooms lack windows. Shared bathroom – which is kept spotless – with hot water. The restaurant is cozy and inviting rather like a Danish café/bar and serves good-quality northern European food (imported meats and cheeses). Henrich, his wife Tip and the affable Finn are entertaining sources of local information – all speak excellent English, German and Danish. A good selection of up to date newspapers and magazines.

The **Café Europa** team also offer helpful suggestions for families. A bonus is lovely Molly the dog who is somewhat of a local celebrity. Molly's kitsch birthday party with specially made chocolate cake is now well-known locally and a day-long event, open to guests and friends which occurs at the end of Feb. A final note – the guesthouse closes up at 2300 so guests have to be back by that time. Security is excellent because no strangers are allowed in the guest-room area. Overall, this small but delightful guesthouse comes recommended although some travellers may prefer a more laissez-faire approach.

D Hollywood, 26 Issara Rd, T075-620508. 10 rooms above a restaurant, all with shared bathrooms (separate male and female). Rooms are large, well furnished, cool and very clean with ceiling fans, some rooms have a nice view. Largish restaurant and log cabin bar that resembles a redneck honky-tonk joint off a lost highway, lending a vague feeling of despair and alienation over one's noodles. Serves western and Thai food. Friendly staff but service can be slow and grudging.

D Khong Kha Guest House. Small guest-house with great views over the mangroves, looking across to Koh Klang. To reach it, walk along the promenade past the pier to Phi Phi and away from the town. A converted house rather than shophouse, all rooms have windows. Clean and simply furnished, most rooms are spacious with views over the water. This has to be one of the better locations in Krabi. Easy access to the night market and tour agency facilities. Friendly, helpful owner. The only downside is the noise of long-tailed boats during peak season.

D KR Mansion, 52/1 Chao Fah Rd, T075-612761. Some a/c, well-priced restaurant, clean, bright and airy rooms, rooftop balcony for an evening beer and good views. This place is at the quieter top end of town, a 10-min walk from most of the bars and restaurants. On the surface, it all looks good but we have heard that the staff are overworked and that management can be rather pushy with their overpriced tours and tickets. More worryingly, there have been consistent reports of thefts from the rooms. Visitors have also complained of dud cocktails in the rooftop bar.

D Star Guest House, Chao Fah Rd (opposite the market), T075-611721. A charming wooden guesthouse over the top of a small convenience store and tour office, the 7 rooms are tiny, leaving little space for more than a bed, but there is a pleasant balcony with tables and chairs overlooking the night market and the river. Separate bathrooms are downstairs near a small bar area in a garden at the back. Recommended.

D Thara Guesthouse, 79/3 Kongkha Rd, T075-630499. Not the best location

convenience-wise as it is a little far from the bars and restaurants of Krabi Town. But the rooms are bright and airy with some overlooking the river. The staff are also considerate and everything is well-maintained. In this price range – recommended.

E Jungle Tours & Guesthouse, Uttarakit Rd. Restaurant serving basic meals, shared bathroom facilities, tiny, dark rooms but very friendly family owners, tickets and tours sold.

E Siboya, T075-611258. Brightly painted wooden building with a small café downstairs, souvenir shop and agent for the **Siboya Island Bungalow Resort** on Siboya Island. Rooms are priced according to whether they have a window. Shared bathroom. Clean and simple with friendly, kind owners. Though basic, this set-up receives consistently good reports. Recommended.

E SR Guesthouse, Khong Kha Rd (next to **River View Guesthouse**). Big, clean rooms with shared bathroom, hospitable owners, great value. Downstairs there is a large second-hand bookstore.

E-F K Guest House, 15-25 Chao Fah Rd, T075-623166. Next door to **New Wave**. Mainly fan rooms with mosquito nets. Two-storey building with a long New Orleans-style veranda balcony along the first floor. Moody, secluded atmosphere with partial views over town and of the sunset. Wonderful potted foliage all along the front intensifies the feeling of being in a hideaway. Inside boasts wood flooring and ambient lighting. Do get the rooms in the wooden part though and not the ones with shared bathroom out back which are airless. Restaurant, laundry service and internet. This is a good bargain. Recommended.

E-F New Wave Bar and Guest House, 25-1/2 Chao Fah Rd. Simple accommodation in 3 rooms of a wooden house with a common area and a west-facing balcony overlooking one of the greener parts of town. The **New Wave Bar** is in the adjacent garden. Run by an English woman, Emma, and her Thai boyfriend, both very friendly.

E-F PS Guest House, 71/1 Uttarakit Rd, T075-620480. Small guesthouse with just 4 rooms. Clean with shared bathroom. Quite dark and very simple, but friendly and helpful owners. Rates depend on the room size.

E-F River View Guesthouse, Khong Kha Rd. Only 4 rooms with views of the river, above the **Thammachart Tour Company and Restaurant**, but clean, decent and good value – and with an owner (Acharn Lek), who speaks excellent English and will (for a fee) act as translator should anyone need assistance in legal affairs. The **Thammachart Restaurant** specializes in vegetarian food, although it also serves non-vegetarian dishes.

E-F Swallow Guesthouse, Prachachuen Rd. Depressing boxy exterior and plain but clean rooms, shared bathrooms.

Laem Sak *p462*

C Bulan Anda Eco-Resort, T075-631111. These simple palm bungalows are comfortably equipped and set in a palm plantation by the coast. Far from any other resorts and with access to the limestone features and islands of the area, they make a good base for those who enjoy kayaking, snorkelling etc, but who want to stay away from the crowds. Unfortunately, they are quite difficult to find and really do demand that you have your own transport. Take Route 4 back towards Phangnga; turn left down Route 4039 and continue on through the town and along the winding road along the peninsula.

Eating

Krabi and around *p458, maps p460 and p462*

TTT Ruen Mai, on Maharaj Rd well beyond the **Vogue Department Store** up the hill on the left-hand side as you leave the town. Excellent Thai food in a quiet garden setting. Popular with locals, with good English-language menu and helpful staff. Has a number of southern specialities. Fish dishes are particularly good, as are the salads (yam).

TTT-TT Chao Sua, on Maharaj Rd, along the road from the **Ruen Mai** (the sign, with a leopard on it, is in Thai). Considered by many locals to be one of the best restaurants in Krabi. The restaurant itself has a rambling slightly chaotic feel and service is sometimes a little haphazard. Serves excellent Thai food. Barbecued seafood, crispy duck salad and virtually anything that is fried are especially good (the *pad pak pung* is delicious). A very original menu with lots of house specialities, for example, the *chao sua* eggs are well

worth trying – a bit like a Thai Scotch egg although the appearance may put one off. Also has an English-language menu.

ΨΨΨ-ΨΨ Europa Café, 1/9 Soi Ruamjit Rd, T075-620407. A favourite with locals and expats. Serves tasty Northern European food – including pickled fish and Danish pork. Excellent helpings and always fresh. Quite possibly the best western/European style breakfast in town. Leonardo Di Caprio eat here while filming *The Beach*. Japanese tourists are particularly keen on sitting in the Leonardo seat and scoffing the Leonardo Special which is Banana Milkshake, Meatballs with mashed potatoes, mixed salad and bread and finally – a pancake with strawberry ice cream. Surprised?

ΨΨΨ-ΨΨ May and Mark's Restaurant, Ruen-Ruedee Rd. Good information, friendly atmosphere and attracts old-time ex-pats so the conversation does go beyond predictable backpacker chat. However, this tiny and well-loved hang-out does seem rather to be resting on its laurels and could get out the cleaning products more often, especially as grubby loos do not go hand-in-hand with homemade bread. The much-touted bread also needs to appear more often as stocks are disappointedly low. There is a tendency to overbrew the coffee as well. Italian dishes, Thai food, fresh coffee, breakfasts and all the usual from banana porridge to pizza.

ΨΨΨ-ΨΨ Pizzeria Firenze, Khong Kha Rd. Simple no-nonsense decor though not much atmosphere. Usual mix of Thai and Italian dishes. Perfectly acceptable when the taste buds have reached overload with one too many papaya salads. Unobtrusive staff.

ΨΨΨ-ΨΨ The Seafood Restaurant, Sukhorn Rd, in front of the night market, offers excellent cheap food but do get there early for the best selection.

ΨΨΨ-ΨΨ Viva, Phruksa-Uthit Rd, between Pattana and Issara roads. Serves a range of European, Italian and Thai food and good fresh coffee (Lavazza). This is a hang-out for hard-core travellers having a sneaky break from the rigours of no frills bungalow huts and unfortunately also the British lager lout and his Thai bargirl travelling companion. Along with the customers, the music is often overly loud. However, reassuring Italian favourites like bruschetta and pizza are good and the place has proper olive oil, grappa and other Italian liquors. Reasonable prices and portions.

ΨΨ-Ψ The Boathouse, Soi Hutangkonn. A restaurant in a real wooden boat that looks suspiciously like teak and is set in a garden with a fake moat around it. Even more bizarre –the street appears largely residential. What keeps the whole affair from looking like a theme restaurant nightmare is the skewered romantic glory of the gleaming golden boat with its chandeliers and perfectly executed main courses like steamed bass and plum sauce. However, the staff will hover in this gastronomic Noah's Ark and could go leeward more often. This is the perfect place for couples though it also attracts wheeler-dealers for intimate business meetings. Recommended.

ΨΨ-Ψ Chawan, 38 Khongkha Rd, serves Thai food and the usual western dishes (sandwiches, spaghetti, etc). The Thai food comes in generous portions but can be bland in its eagerness to cater to a western palate.

ΨΨ-Ψ Chok Dee, Chao Fah Rd. Reasonable prices, some dishes are really delicious, and very good value for the quality and quantity of food. The owner has TVs with cable and video – good selection of movies. Friendly management and staff.

ΨΨ-Ψ I-Oon, 7/3 Chao Fah Rd, near the **Grand Tower Hotel**, excellent little café, with good breakfasts and special deals for dinners.

ΨΨ-Ψ Kanchanee Bakery, 12-14 Maharaj Soi 6, T075-630501. Spacious, bright and airy café, maybe a little too bright if you have a hangover but the pastries are good and the coffee is superb. Also has newspapers.

ΨΨ-Ψ Kwan Coffee Corner, 75 Uttarakit Rd, T075-611706, kwan_café_kbi@hotmail.com. Delicious fresh coffee, sandwiches, milkshakes, ice creams, cheap and tasty Thai food, good breakfasts of fruit and muesli, almost everything even if, as they put it, "coffee is not your cup of tea". A good place to acclimatize to Krabi with chatty owners. Kwan has become so much of an institution that they even have their own T-shirts for sale. Recommended.

ΨΨ-Ψ Sea House, Chao Fah Rd. Reasonable prices, menu includes freshly ground coffee.

Foodstalls

A **night market** sets up in the early evening on Khlong Kha Rd, along the Krabi River, good seafood dishes. Halal and Chinese dishes can be found here. Instead of opting

for *banana roti* it's worth trying the *mataba* as a savoury dish. This is made in the area near the town – slightly spicy, slightly sweet and with a pleasant taste of curry and vegetables. Tasty ice cream from the ice-cream stall and good Thai desserts from the dessert stall further up the hill. There should also be a stall selling *khao man kai* (Hainanese chicken with rice), red pork and soups with real ginger and soy sauce to go with the chicken. Stall food is also available from the **fresh market** between Srisawat and Sukhon roads, and from scattered places along Uttarakit Rd, facing onto the Krabi River. For a really marvellous morning treat, try the **Morning Market** on Soi 7 off Maharat Rd. In the middle aisles, are stalls selling extraordinarily complex salads that cannot be found elsewhere for little more than ฿25. Order noodle soup and the stall-owner will set before you a series of tiny dishes that are variously pickled, shredded and dry, prawn-festooned plus baby aubergine salads. There will also be a plate of fresh herbs including mint, coriander, basil and lemon grass. The salads are eaten separately and the herbs added to your noodle soup. All the produce is fresh daily and there is constant dicing, chopping, washing and peeling – all very reassuring. The market is packed with other vendors and the only place to eat is at long tables where elbows jostle for space so it is well worth getting up early for this. The fresh fish stalls are also damned impressive – if you are going back to a smaller island, you can purchase things like shellfish here and have it cooked back at your bungalow.

The **Vogue Department Store** on Maharaj Rd also has an a/c food court on the 3rd floor. A second **night market** is based in the parking lot near the Provincial Electricity Authority office on the road running between Uttarakit Rd and Maharaj Rd. This market sells fruit at night, at much cheaper prices than the market by the pier. Keep your eyes peeled for mango and sticky rice – in season – which is late Feb-Mar. It also has an excellent selection of Halal stalls, *phat thai*, noodle soups, *khanom jeen* (noodles with sauces and vegetables) and desserts. There is a beer garden in the grounds plus clothes and cheap goods stalls. The hum begins in the early evening, continuing until 2200.

Bars and clubs

Krabi and around *p458, maps p460 and p462*

Juke Box Pub, Khong Kha Rd.

Kwan Fang Live Music, next to **Mixer Pub**, on Sudmongkol Rd. For a sense of weirdness and longing, there is always Kwan Fang with its staple of Country and Western bands. This out-of-place haunt looks a little like a western saloon with some of the space out in the wide open air. The crowd includes John Wayne types (though shorter), Hank Snows and sad-eyed long-distance truck drivers. An older crowd than Mixer and a more thoughtful one.

Mixer Pub, 100 Sudmongkol Rd. Plain old wasted in classic farang style although it also pulls in a solid local crowd. At Mixer you take in your own poison that they mix for you all night along with your choice of mixer. Mischievous staff will also videotape you as the evening wears catching those progressive stages of drunkenness, table-top dancing and singing. Doubling the fun (or horror), this is played it on a screen for the amusement of your fellow fall-abouts. So not a place for shrinking violets but then you do only live once. Suits a younger crowd though you will see ex-pats on the tiles here past their sell-by date. For wallflowers this is great for anthropological viewing and for the brave – unparalleled for shameless exhibitionism.

Toyaiman, 228 Uttarakit Rd (on the hill).

Nyvhavn, across from Europa, Soi Ruamjit. Based on Nyhavn in Denmark. They only play jazz and sometimes have live performances. You also get sandwiches and baguettes with roast beef, imported cheese, salami etc. It has a small garden too.

Festivals and events

Krabi and around *p458, maps p460 and p462*

Boat races on the river can be thrilling particularly when the Samsong is flowing.

Nov Berg Fa Andaman Festival in the gardens beyond the pier (coinciding with *Loi Krathong*) – a showcase for traditional dancing and singing from around Thailand. Also features local handicrafts from the Andaman region.

Shopping

Krabi and around *p458, maps p460 and p462*

Books

Many of the guesthouses and tour companies also run book exchanges. **The Books**, 78-80 Maharat Rd (next to Vogue Department Store).

Clothes and tailoring

There is a tailor on the corner of Issara and Khong Kha roads. Lots of clothes stores on Phattana, Prachachuen and Uttarakit roads mostly selling beachwear.

Department stores and supermarkets

Vogue Department Store, Maharat Rd. **Sri Nakhorn**, opposite the Thai Hotel.

Souvenirs

Khun B Souvenir, and other souvenir shops on Khong Kha and Uttarakit Rd, sell a range of souvenirs from all over Thailand and Southeast Asia. **Thai Silver**, opposite Thai Hotel, sells silverware mostly from Nakhon Sri Thammarat.

Activities and tours

Krabi and around *p458, maps p460 and p462*

Canoeing tours

Europa Café, T075-620407, see Eating, offers a mangrove/canoeing tour but with an English- speaking guide which is necessary if you wish to learn a little en route about local history and just why mangroves are so important. The tour, which goes near Bor Thor Village close to Ao Luk, takes in caves and allows for swimming – always exhilarating in the open space.

Game fishing

Phi Phi Marine Travel Co, 201 Uttarakit Rd, Krabi, T075-621297. It can arrange expeditions to catch marlin, sailfish, barracuda and tuna.

Golf

Krabi Golf, 12 Kongka Rd, T09-8711997, www.krabigolftours.com. Golf tours to courses in Krabi, Surat Thani and Phuket. Run by a very knowledgable Aussie named Diane.

Rock climbing

Tex's Rock Climbing Adventure, http://texrockclimbing.com, has moved to Rai Leh Beach. Mr 'Tex' is a bit of a local hero who also runs a children's overnight adventure camp just outside town for orphans and street children. Called Tex's Child Development Camp, it includes rock and rope climbing lessons, fire shows, first aid/rescue on the mountain and in the jungle, and weekend schooling. The education side covers manners, how to observe the law and environmental consciousness along with English lessons.

Tour operators

Concentrated on Uttarakit and Ruen-Ruedee roads and close to the Chao Fah Pier. There are so many tour and travel companies/ agents, and information is so freely and widely available, that it is not necessary to list numerous outfits here. Prices and schedules are all openly posted and a 30-min walk around town will reveal all. **Krabi Somporn Travel and Service**, 72 Khongkha Rd, opposite the old pier, T01-8957873. This is run by Mrs Tree or Tri. She is very friendly and doesn't overcharge.

Transport

Krabi and around *p458, maps p460 and p462*

Air

The new international airport is at 133 Phetkasem Rd, Moo 5, T075-636546.

Boat

The monsoon season affects timetables as does the low season. There is a new pier outside of Krabi Town called Chao Fah Pier which services Koh Lanta and Koh Phi Phi. To **Koh Phi Phi**, 0900, 1030 and 1430, 1½ hrs, ฿300. There is also an additional 0900 boat going via Rai Leh Beach to Phi Phi, ฿300.

Boats leave daily from Klong Chi Lard Pier, Krabi, at 1030 and 1330, 2 hrs, ฿300 with **Family and Co. Ferry Services**, T075-630165.

There is still a boat from Krabi to Koh Lanta via Koh Jum - 1 ½ hrs. This runs from mid-October to mid-May, departing at 1030 and 1330 for around ฿150 - 200. In the wet season, a minibus runs from Klong Chi Lard Pier and via 2 short car ferries across Lanta Noi and to Ban Sala Dan, 2 hrs, ฿150.

There are boat connections with **Ban Hua Hin**, on the southern tip of Koh Klang. Songthaews also go to Ban Hua Hin (฿25).

To **Phuket**, the boat leaves at 1300 on Tue and Thu. There is one direct boat leaving at 1530 from Ao Nang Hat Naopparat Thara Pier, ฿400, 2 hrs.

There are also boats from Krabi to **Koh Yao Yai** and **Koh Yao Noi**, ฿50, 1 hr, leaving Thalane Pier at 1200. Long-tailed boats leave through the day from the pier to **Rai Leh**, 45 mins, ฿70 (if there are enough passengers at any one time, otherwise you can wait for more passengers or take the whole boat for an agreed sum. Often you'll find you have to sit in the boat for a while as the boatman goes to get more passengers – it's his way of cramming them in for the most profit and applies to locals as much as to tourists).

Bus

The station is 5 km out of town, in Talat Kao (Old Market), close to the intersection of Uttarakit Rd and Route 4. Red songthaews regularly run between the bus station and town, ฿5. Motorcycle taxis also wait to ferry bus passengers into town. Numerous evening a/c, VIP and non-a/c connections with **Bangkok**'s Southern bus terminal, 16 hrs. Regular a/c and non-a/c connections with **Phuket**, 3 hrs via **Phangnga**, 1½ hrs. Morning buses to **Koh Samui**, via Surat Thani with ferry connection, 6-7 hrs by Songserm Travel's express boat. Regular connections with **Surat Thani**, 3 hrs and **Trang**, a/c minibuses to **Hat Yai**. Tickets and information about bus connection (both public buses and private tour buses) available from countless travel agents.

International connections with Malaysia and Singapore By a/c minibus to **Singapore**, **Kuala Lumpur** and **Penang** (departs 0700 and 1200, 7-1? hrs, ฿300). Buses stop in **Hat Yai**, for passports to be checked. Some travel agents charge ฿10 'border service' – avoid paying if possible.

Motorbike

Hire guesthouses and tour companies. Scooters and motorbikes, ฿150-200 per day.

Songthaew

Songthaews drive through town, stopping at various places such as Phattana Rd, in front of **Travel & Tour**, for Ao Phra Nang and in front of the foodstalls on Uttarakit Rd for Noppharat Thara Beach. They also run regularly to the bus station at Talaat Kao, 5 km from town. White songthaews leave regularly 0600-1800 from Maharat Rd next to 7-11 and from Phattana Rd stopping at both **Nopparat Thara** and **Ao Nang**, ฿30, ฿50, 0800-2200.

Taxi

To **Trang**, 2 hrs, ฿150).

Train

Some people take the train (usually the over-night sleeper) to **Phun Phin** (Surat Thani) where the train is met by buses for the 3-hr journey to Krabi. Buses drop travellers at the tourist office in Krabi, where bookings for the islands can be made. Alternatively travel to Trang or Nakhon Si Thammarat and take buses from there. Combination tickets from Bangkok via Surat Thani. Travel agencies book tickets.

❶ Directory

Krabi and around *p458, maps p460 and p462*

Banks Branches of all major banks with ATMs. **Internet** Lots of services available around the town, especially on Uttarakit Rd, Chao Fah Rd (towards the pier) and around Hollywood. Connections are still quite slow in Krabi. **API Internet**, excellent internet on Maharat Rd. Rd between Ruen-Rudee Rd and Prachachuen Rd before **Vogue Department Store**. Broadband and only ฿25 per hr. Knowledgable staff. **Post office** Uttarakit Rd (halfway up the hill, not far from the Customs Pier). It has a Poste Restante counter. **Telephone** Quite a way out of the town on the way to the **Krabi Meritime Hotel**. Alternatively, look for services in some tour offices on Uttarakit Rd. **Useful addresses Immigration office** Uttarakit Rd, a little way up from the post office on the same side of the road. The office will extend visas for an extra 30 days (฿500) and provide 14-day visas (free) for people arriving by sailing boat. It will also provide re-entry permits for those travelling on longer-stay visas. Open Mon-Fri 0830-1200, 1300-1630. Photocopies can be made at a couple of shops just across the road from the Immigration office in the row of wooden shophouses.

West of Krabi

The road to the coast from Krabi winds for 15 km past limestone cliffs, a large reclining Buddha, rubber stands and verdant forest. Arriving at the coast in the evening, with the setting sun turning the limestone cliffs of Ao Nang a rich orange and the sea interspersed with precipitous limestone crags, is a beautiful first impression.

The coast west of Krabi consists of the beach areas of Ao Nang and Hat Nopparat Thara, which lie 18 km and 22 km respectively to the west of Krabi town, see below, Ao Phra Nang, page 475, Ao Rai Leh East, page 481, Ao Rai Leh West, page 481 and Ao Ton Sai, page 481. *» For Sleeping, Eating and other listings, see pages 476-484.*

Ins and outs

Tourist information

More than half the native population are now Muslim Thais, discreetly signalled by the absence of pork on restaurant menus even though you will not hear the call of the muzzein at prayer times. Buying alcohol in public at a beach bar should be disallowed, but in typical Thai-style, bar staff are Buddhist in Muslim-run and owned operations which nicely gets around that dilemma. It should be remembered that topless sunbathing is very definitely frowned upon. It is rare to see Thai women even

West of Krabi

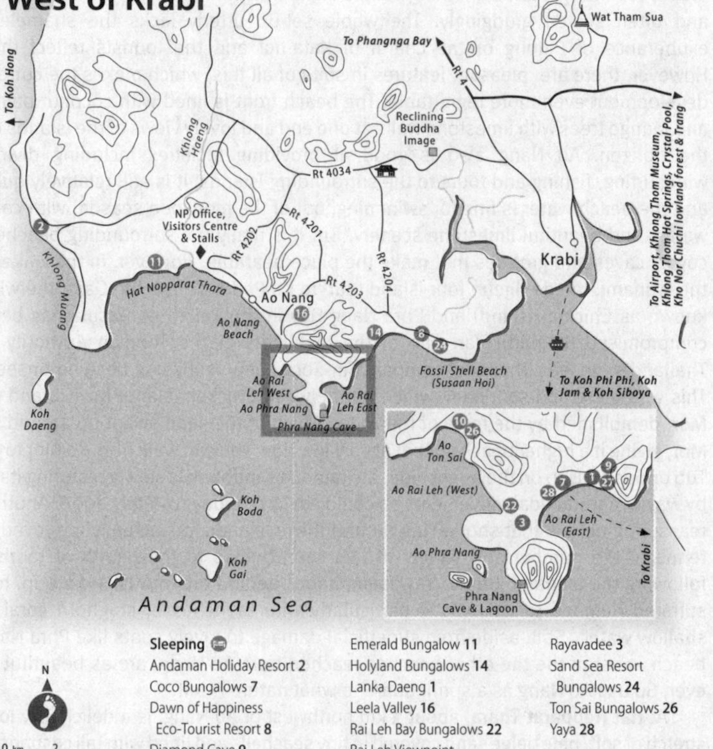

Sleeping
Andaman Holiday Resort 2
Coco Bungalows 7
Dawn of Happiness Eco-Tourist Resort 8
Diamond Cave 9
Dream Valley 10
Emerald Bungalow 11
Holyland Bungalows 14
Lanka Daeng 1
Leela Valley 16
Rai Leh Bay Bungalows 22
Rai Leh Viewpoint Resort & Spa 27
Rayavadee 3
Sand Sea Resort Bungalows 24
Ton Sai Bungalows 26
Yaya 28

N
0 km 2
0 miles 2

 in bikinis at the beach – due to modesty and also an abhorrence of tanning. But, while most sun-starved Westerners come to Thailand to do just that and indeed are encouraged to sunbathe with ever-present deckchairs, cold towels and beach masseurs, it is still a good idea to cover up when you leave the beach for restaurants. These establishments will often be staffed by Thai-Muslims even if the bars aren't. If you get too hot and bothered by this option, there's always takeaway.

Ao Nang, Nopparat Thara and Khlong Muang

Ao Nang beach is neither sweeping nor glorious and has coarse dirty yellow sand intermingled with millions of broken shells that are unpleasant to walk on. One end of the beach is filled with kayaks and long-tail boats for transporting tourists to nearby islands and it is these motorized long-tail boats that punctuate the quiet with ferocious regularity. The concrete wall behind the beach front, the construction of which initially excited much antagonism, saved Ao Nang from the greater force of the tsunami and is being rebuilt in parts. Behind this is the commercial outcrop of Ao Nang itself which has taken up the whole of the beach road and swarmed inland. Curiously reminiscent of Clacton-On-Sea in its dreariness with hints of Bournemouth in its loutish edge come evening, it is mind-boggling to think that just 15 years ago, Ao Nang was a sleepy fishing hamlet. This still exists in part around a kilometre inland from the beach. On the whole, there is little to do in today's Ao Nang including eating. The food is dreadful; if you don't count the gas-oven pizzerias of which there are far too many, even something simple like a fruit salad or toast is substandard and often served grudgingly. The whole set-up utterly lacks the shameless exuberance of Patong or the charm of Kata-noi and the tourists reflect this. However, there are pleasant features in spite of all this, which makes the current development even more regrettable. The beach front is lined with coconut palms and mango trees with limestone walls at one end and lovely views of the islands on the horizon. Ao Nang also is good at providing facilities including diving, windsurfing, fishing and tours to the surrounding islands. It is still relatively quiet and the beach water is fine for swimming, out of the monsoon season, with calm waters and beautiful limestone scenery. But it is really the surrounding beaches, coves, caves and grottoes that make the place bearable. However, in the wake of the tsunami, the de rigeur 'four-island tour' to Ko Poda, Ko Tub, Ko Gai (otherwise known as Chicken Island) and Phra Nang Bay in the Raileh peninsula has been compromised. In particular, one of the highlights of the Tourism Authority of Thailand's 'unseen Thailand' campaign in 2004, now really has become unseen. This was the grand sandbank which ran between Chicken Island, Ko Tub and Ko Mor; demolished by the force of the water. Much of the sand swept up around Ko Mor, giving it a higher beach so that at very low tide, you can walk from Ko Mor to Ko Tub opposite. But, on the bright side, the famous sandbank is slowly restoring itself by way of natural tidal movements so could easily reappear by early 2006. Another reassuring note is that snorkelling around these islands has actually improved in terms of the number and variety of fish seen thanks to the dearth of tourists following the tsunami. But Ko Yawasam, a rock behind the four island group, has suffered damage to its reefs – particularly with branches of staghorn coral in shallow water. Still, aside from superficial damage to lovely spots like Phra Nang beach, most of the the other beaches reached from Ao Nang, are as beautiful as ever. So use Ao Nang as a springboard to what nature is left.

Between June and October swimming is risky.

At **Hat Nopparat Thara**, about 3 km northwest of Ao Nang, is a deliciously long stretch of soft, pale beige sand covered in tiny seashells and lined with tall casuarinas at the beachside. To the back are paperbark forests. Locals used to call this place 'Hat

Ao Nang

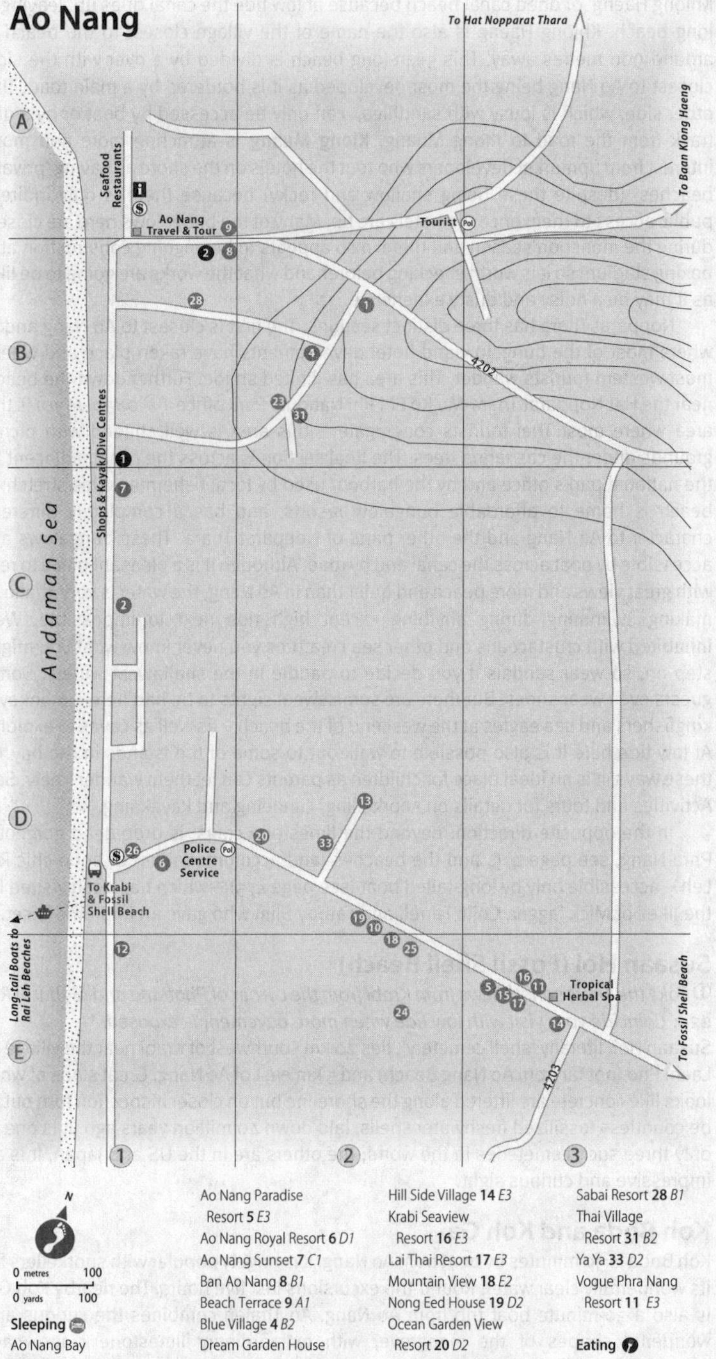
To Hat Nopparat Thara
To Baan Klong Haeng
Seafood Restaurants
Ao Nang Travel & Tour
Tourist
4202
Shops & Kayak/Dive Centres
Andaman Sea
Police Centre Service
To Krabi & Fossil Shell Beach
Long-tail Boats to Rai Leh Beaches
Tropical Herbal Spa
To Fossil Shell Beach
4203
A
B
C
D
E
1
2
3

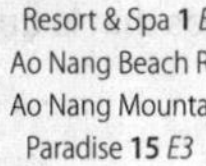
N
0 metres 100
0 yards 100

Sleeping

Ao Nang Bay Resort & Spa **1** *B2*
Ao Nang Beach Resort **2** *C1*
Ao Nang Mountain Paradise **15** *E3*
Ao Nang Paradise Resort **5** *E3*
Ao Nang Royal Resort **6** *D1*
Ao Nang Sunset **7** *C1*
Ban Ao Nang **8** *B1*
Beach Terrace **9** *A1*
Blue Village **4** *B2*
Dream Garden House & Tour **10** *D2*
Golden Beach Resort **12** *E1*
Green Park **13** *D2*
Hill Side Village **14** *E3*
Krabi Seaview Resort **16** *E3*
Lai Thai Resort **17** *E3*
Mountain View **18** *E2*
Nong Eed House **19** *D2*
Ocean Garden View Resort **20** *D2*
Pavillon Queen's Bay **23** *B2*
Peace Laguna Resort **24** *E2*
Penny's **25** *E2*
Phra Nang Inn **26** *D1*
Sabai Resort **28** *B1*
Thai Village Resort **31** *B2*
Ya Ya **33** *D2*
Vogue Phra Nang Resort **11** *E3*

Eating

Azurra **1** *B1*
La Luna **2** *B1*

 Khlong Haeng' or dried canal beach because at low tide the canal dries up, leaving a long beach. Khlong Haeng is also the name of the village closest to the beach – around 900 metres away. This 5-km-long beach is divided by a river with the side closest to Ao Nang being the most developed as it is bordered by a main road. The other side, which is lousy with sandflies, can only be accessed by boat or by a dirt track from the road to Klong Muang. **Klong Muang** is attracting more and more interest from upmarket developers who tout the hotels on the shore as having 'private beaches' (despite these being shallow and rocky) because there is only indirect public access to them once the hotels are up. Many of the bungalows here are closed during the monsoon season and there also appears to be ongoing construction at a boxing stadium so it is worth checking beforehand what the works are going to be like as it may be a noisy and dusty experience.

Nopparat Thara has three distinct sections. The first is closest to Ao Nang and is where most of the bungalow and hotel developments have taken place and where most western tourists wander. This area has limited shade. Further down the beach near the Hat Nopparat Thara-Mu Ko Phi Phi National Park office (ⓘ *0830-1630*) is the area where most Thai tourists congregate – this area is well shaded with picnic grounds under the casuarina trees. The final section is across the canal, adjacent to the national parks office and by the harbour used by local fishermen. This stretch of beach is home to affordable bungalow resorts, and has a completely different character to Ao Nang and the other parts of Nopparat Thara. These bungalows are accessible by boat across the canal and by road. Although it is a pleasant place to rest with great views and more peace and quiet than in Ao Nang, the water is very shallow, making swimming during anything except high tide next to impossible. Well inhabited with crustaceans and other sea creatures you never know what you might step on, so wear sandals if you decide to paddle in the shallowest waters. Some guests even wear shoes. But there are some sweet sights to be had here – monkeys, kingfishers and sea eagles at the west end of the beach – as well as caves to explore. At low tide here it is also possible to walk out to some of the islands in the bay. In these ways, it is an ideal place for children as parents can let them wander freely. See Activities and tours for details on snorkelling, canoeing and kayakaing.

In the opposite direction, beyond the limestone crags, is drop-dead gorgeous Phra Nang, see page 475, and the beaches (and accommodation) of boho-chic Rai Leh – accessible only by long-tailed boat (see page 475) – which has been visited by the likes of Mick Jagger, Colin Farrel, and Fatboy Slim who gave an impromptu set.

Susaan Hoi (Fossil Shell Beach)

ⓘ *Take the white songthaews from Krabi from the corner of Phattana and Maharat Rd. ฿20. Coincide your visit with low tide when more pavement is exposed.*

Susaan Hoi, literally 'shell cemetery', lies 20 km southwest of Krabi near the village of Laem Pho (not far from Ao Nang Beach) and 5 km east of Ao Nang. Great slabs of what looks like concrete are littered along the shoreline but on closer inspection turn out to be countless fossilized freshwater shells, laid down 40 million years ago. It is one of only three such cemeteries in the world; the others are in the US and Japan. It is an impressive and curious sight.

Koh Boda and Koh Gai

Koh Boda is 30 minutes by boat from Ao Nang. It is hugely popular with snorkellers for its wonderfully clear water. Round-trip excursions last five hours. The nearby Koh Gai is also a 30-minute boat trip from Ao Nang. Ao Thalen combines the curious and wonderful shapes of the mangrove, with extraordinary limestone crags, cave paintings, monkey troupes, and an overall sense of mystery in the gorges that is quite magical. ▸▸ *See Sleeping, page 480, and Activities and tours, page 483.*

Phra Nang and Rai Leh

Phra Nang is the peninsula to the south of Ao Nang. There are no roads on Phra Nang, which lends it a secret hideaway ambience – albeit an exclusive one as all the land behind the beach is occupied by the **Rayavadee** resort. The point consists of **Rai Leh West** and **Ao Phra Nang** on the west side and **Rai Leh East** on the east. Further west from Rai Leh West is **Ao Ton Sai**. Over the last few years Rai Leh has become something of a mecca for rock climbers. This is partly because limestone is porous so that the water cuts into it and makes the natural grips ideal for climbers. But, equally alluring, say climbers, is the combination of landscape, climate and rock, which rarely come together in such harmonious splendour.

The best beach is on the west side – a truly picture-postcard affair. However, the east coast beach is still amazing at low tide in a sci-fi end of the world way as the landscape transforms into a 300-metre stretch of sinister shining mud. When Rai Leh East is not a mudbath, there are still the mangroves lining the beach so that it is fairly impossible to get any swimming in here. Rai Leh East also acts as a pier for taxi boats to and from Krabi and you will often spy tourists slogging across the mud with luggage over their heads. At pretty but small Rai Leh West, also knows as 'Sunset Beach', it takes 10 minutes to traverse – this means there is no escaping the daytime noises of the long-tail boats although the evenings are delightful. There is also good snorkelling and swimming in archetypal crystal-clear water. The limestone rock formations are spectacular, and there are interesting caves with stalagmites and stalactites to explore though they require patience and fortitude as the paths are not always straightforward nor easygoing. At the southern extremity of the bay is a mountain cave (**Outer Princess Cave**) on Phra Nang Beach that is dedicated to the goddess of the area and considered 'her summer palace'. Here, you may be delighted to find an abundance of wooden and stone penises, many in yummy colours of candy pink, lime green and pillar box red. It is believed local fishermen put the penises there to bribe the goddess into granting them plenty of fish on the sea. Be that as it may, many non-sailors also like to drop by a penis or two and the cave is suitably endowed. Near the penis cave are lots of monkeys that are rather friendly and several beachside stalls selling trinkets, clothes, beer and snacks like barbecued corn on the cob. There is also one outrageously priced bar that looks totally out of place. If you feel you must make an effort, there is Sa Phra Nang (Princess Pool) to explore. This is a pond inside the cliff that can be accessed along a cave trail at the side of the mountain. You can get to the top of the mountain if you keep climbing. There's a walkway to Rai Leh east from Ao Phra Nang if you care to visit yet another Princess cave called the Inner Princess cave which is three caverns, one of which has a waterfall of quartz like frozen amber.

Take along a beach mat or towel as it is very pleasant to spend a few hours on this dainty fantasy of a beach.

There are several **climbing** schools (see Activities and tours for details) as the tower karst formations offer some truly outstanding climbing opportunities along with spectacular views.

Rai Leh is suffering from being too popular. The area available for development is small, sandwiched between limestone cliffs and crags, and already the bungalows are cheek-by-jowl in places. It is also going upscale with the recent appearances of superstars so prices are starting to soar. On the whole, the entertainment here remains coffee houses/bars/bookshops during the day and low-key parties on the east side at night – still more reggae than rave. Everything on Rai Leh continues to be run by generators as there are no mains currents and there are still no banks. Foodies will be seriously disappointed as the closest and most patronized outpost for food is Ao Nang.

Ao Ton Sai, north of Ao Rai Leh West, largely appeals to climbers who can manage far more than five-minute walks. Climbing is the main activity here, followed by frisbee, volleyball and assorted refreshments a la *The Big Lebowski*.

Sleeping

Ao Nang, Nopparat Thara and Khlong Muang *p472, map p473*
High-season (Nov-May) room rates may be as much as double (or more) the low-season (Jun-Oct) rates.

Accommodation in Ao Nang seems to have settled down into 2 broad groups. Some guesthouses and bungalows are appearing much further inland, while very expensive hotels have swamped the beach. Some of the old favourites in the centre of the beach area had to move on as the owners of the land have terminated contracts and this central area is now dominated by shops, restaurants and bars. Behind these developments there are very few rooms available, but it's crowded and most of it dull. Hotels that have developed in the hills overlooking Hat Nopparat Thara are fairly pricey, and this is the location of Ao Nang's main luxury resorts (the **Ao Nang Pakasai Resort**, the **Thai Village Resort** and the **Queen's Pavilion Resort**). Barefaced in its flouting of Thailand's conservation legislation and land-zoning rules is the **National Park Success Resort**. This 4-storey hotel, with odd hints of a Japanese temple in a corporate layout, is set in among paperbark trees which surely must once have been zoned as belonging in reserve forest. Basically, there are 2 choices at Ao Nang now – a fairly faceless 4-5-star hotel with a pool or a fairly faceless 2-3-star hotel without a pool. Since the difference is negligible and no one is there for the museums, the pool question does need to be considered.

Ao Nang

L Thai Village Resort, 260 Moo 2, T075-6377109. This huge red-winged traditional Thai roofed hotel shoots out of the forest in a rather predatorial way. Three large swimming pools, pool bar and children's pool. Large dull buffets and unadventurous food otherwise. But at night you can hear the crickets.

L Vogue Pranang Bay Resort and Spa, 244 Moo 2, T075-637635, www.vogue resort.com. One of the more appealing of the luxury hotels. Nestled into mountain foliage, this red-roofed complex sprawls beautifully through landscaped gardens and has a very nice pool indeed. It is especially good for honeymooners who like to go from the bath to the poolside. The bath in the de luxe honeymoon suite is big enough for two while the pool is large enough to accommodate a sizeable group without encroaching on anyone's intimacy. The breakfast is also tipped to be top-notch. Recommended.

L-AL Pavilion Queen's Bay, 56 Moo 3, T075-637612, http://krabi.pavilionhotels. com/index.htm. This huge hotel of more than 100 rooms is certainly luxurious and has very friendly staff, but is hampered with some silly design flaws, and lack of attention to detail. International, Thai and Japanese restaurants (the last highly exclusive with top-class sushi on offer), very large spacious rooms but somewhat cramped bathrooms. Very luxurious spa – one of the best features of the hotel and open to non-residents too. All the other facilities expected from a hotel like this – eg, 3-layered swimming pool. Plus good views.

AL Best Western Ao Nang Bay Resort & Spa, 211 Moo 2, T075-637071-4, www.ao-nang-resort-group.com. One of the newest hotels built on the small road leading from Ao Nang up into the hills behind Nopparat Thara beach. This is an odd assortment of Thai-style terraces, pools and gardens. No lifts and lots of stairs. With a simple spa, swimming pool and exercise room, and a rather public sala for massage, the best feature in this hotel has to be the amazing big bathrooms in the cottages; complete with pebbled walls and bath, and a window on to a private garden, they are like the Zen Flintstones. The bedrooms are spacious and well equipped, but like many hotels in Ao Nang the prices are steep, especially as the food is not up to par. 10 mins to beach.

AL-A Golden Beach Resort, 254 Moo 2, T075-637870-4, www.krabi-hotels.com/ goldenbeach. The last hotel on the left-hand side of the beach (looking out to sea), this has one of the best locations on the beach with good views across to the islands and to the west, and relative quiet. Rooms are in cute green-roofed white bungalow style and low-rise hotel blocks. The swimming pool has some rather fantastic ornamentation.

Well-tended gardens. The Thai restaurant (**Thai Thai**) is probably the best in Ao Nang serving flavoursome food at reasonable prices. Recommended in this price range.

AL-A Lai Thai Resort, 25/1 Moo 2, T075-637281, www.laithai-resort.com. About 1 km from the beach, but with a free shuttle service. Family-run resort with great views of the mountains at the back of Ao Nang. The swimming pool is black-tiled. Rooms are spacious and very comfortable. Restaurant has a range of food including Mexican. Consistently good reports aobut service.

AL-A Ocean Garden View Resort, 121/1 Moo 2, T075-637527-31. Large development with several 2-storey blocks of 73 rooms on the hillside back from the main road. Located next to the **Ocean Mart**, just up from the **Phranang Inn**. Rooms are well equipped and comfortable with balconies. All have views of the sea, though the rooms at the back, higher up the hill, have the best views. Pool, children's playground, music corner and reading corner. Not a bad choice for the price and good for families.

AL-B Best Western Ban Ao Nang Resort, 31/3 Moo 2, T075-637071-4. Not really Best Western, just a B W theme with the same snacks sold as in other pseudo-B W hotels. A/c, 3-storey modern block with small balconies overlooking the sea. Rooms have satellite TV and fridge, solid wooden floors, large bathrooms with hot-water showers. This place is competitively priced and the rooms are better than those at most of the more expensive resorts. Pool and tour counter. Breakfast very disappointing for prices here.

AL-B Krabi Seaview Resort, 143 Moo 2, T075-637242-5. Some a/c, solidly built brick A-frame bungalows with zinc roofs, looking almost alpine, set around a rather unattractive pool, attached bathrooms. There are also some much cheaper cottages set back further away from the road, with good views over the tree tops and out to sea. But not all have sea view. Diving Station meant to be good but was changing management. Bland food.

AL-B Sabai Resort, 79/2 Moo 2, T075-637791, www.sabairesort.com. Fan and a/c available. Set back from Nopparat Thara beach down the road which leads to the latest boxing stadium. White concrete bungalows – well equipped but nothing special. Feels strangely like a motel as regards aesthetics though they are anxious to give it a personal feeling. Owned by the Scarpella family who do keep the place spotless. Also has an Italian restaurant – **Da Carla e Poan**. A bit pricey for what it is.

A Andaman Sunset Resort, also known as Wanna's Place, 32/1 Moo 2, T075-637322, www.wannasplace.com. Swiss-Thai owned. Small hotel block and bungalows with American army barracks look, crowded around a small pool. All with a/c. Hotel rooms are ordinary. Service is good but this is nothing special. Bit noisy as it faces main road and beach strip.

A Blue Village, 105 Moo 3, T075-637887. Ignore the goofy name, this is a fantastic lay-out: part *Blue Lagoon*/cool surfer/timeless getaway. Very sympathetic to the environment and away from the beach. Bali-style huts with palm trees growing through the roofs – beds on floor futon-style, sunken bathrooms. Views of the gardens with palm oil trees. Run by a Canadian fellow – Richard – a former diving instructor who has lived in Thailand for 19 years. As regards food, his attitude is that 'the customers are going to want to eat out anyway as part of the holiday schtick so might as well keep the prices low'. Richard will also get you fresh fish or meat at the markets if you prefer to do your own barbecue. Impossible not to chill here. Recommended.

A Emerald Garden Beach Resort (formerly Frito Misto Villa), 90 Moo 3, T075-637692, frittomisto1@hotmail.com. Italian-owned timeshare property that rents out 20 villa cottages. Up on the hill away from the beach in a quiet location with 2 pools, a gym and bar plus good facilities (excellent bathrooms with bidets!). Variable decorations. A bit far from everything, but represents pretty good value for the facilities.

A Peace Laguna Resort, 193 Moo 2, T75-637344-7. Damaged during tsunami but back on its feet now. Some a/c, this is one of the more attractive and better designed of the mid-range places, perched under the limestone crag that dominates the southeastern end of Ao Nang. However, it is too large. 83 solid brick and tile-roofed bungalows. Three pools as well. Off the road, it is so much quieter than many other places,

all bungalows with hot water in bathrooms, cheaper cottages with fan, a path leads down to Ao Nang beach. It is also trying to attract more families and offers a 'kids' school', 'nanny service' and 'playground.' But bungalows need repairs and guests have complained about grubby walls and filthy bathrooms.

A-B Ao Nang Beach Resort, 142 Moo 2, T075-637766-9. Hotel-style accommodation in a white Costa del Sol block along the seafront. The entrance is set back from the front but the hotel lives up to its claim that many of the rooms have excellent sea views. Clean, standard type of rooms central location. Try to get a balcony though.

A-B Ao Nang Sunset Hotel Resort, 268 Moo 2, T075-637441-2. 4-storey building, locally owned, built around a fairly large pool just opposite the entrance to **Krabi Resort**. Rooms are comfortable and clean but there isn't much room for a view or much character in this rather over-crowded stretch of Ao Nang. Breakfast also needs improvement. Friendly and helpful management but not for single men on the razz – you face an additional charge of ฿500 if you decide to linger with a lady in your abode. You get the impression it prefers families.

A-B Beach Terrace, 154 Moo 2, T075-637180-2. There are really 2 hotels here: one is a 6-storey bat-winged block rather incongruously sited on a beach where most places are just a single storey tall; the second 'hotel' is a series of large, solidly made concrete bungalows. At these prices you don't really get very much: a/c comfortable-enough rooms with superb views from the upper floors of the block, but a down-at-heel coffee shop that would look average in a hotel charging half these rates. Pool on the 2nd floor is nice but doesn't make up for disparity in pricing and quality.

A-B Nong Eed House, 126 Moo 2, T075-637237. Looks like a North American subdivision. 7 spartan characterless rooms. A/c and fan. The restaurant seems cosier but you can't sleep there.

A-B Phra Nang Inn, PO Box 25, T075-637130. A/c, restaurant, small pool in the older wing of hotel is on one side of the road, a newer 3-storey concrete structure faced in wood to try and make it more 'natural' on the other – it's an interesting semi-circular shape anyway so departs from the barracks bungalow/boxy Costa del Sol look. There are no lifts here – wearing in the midday heat. A large pool is in the newer wing. Rooms are mediocre at this price, although the views in the evening from the top floor of the new wing are spectacular. Tour desk.

A-D Ao Nang Paradise Resort, 25/18 Moo 2, T075-637650-1, aonangparadise@hotmail.com. Continuing down the road from the **Lai Thai Resort** and near the original boxing stadium, this is a bungalow resort with a very welcoming reception area and good lighting throughout. Good views of the mountains with coconut palms in the foreground. 10 mins to the beach. Bungalows are well designed and the owners/managers/designers live on site and obviously care about the quality of experience they offer (including maintenance of the bungalows). They offer fans and a/c for every bungalow and provide mosquito nets (of variable quality) for those who prefer fans. Hot shower. Good value during the low season, rather overpriced during the high. Unfortunately, the resort is now hemmed in on both sides with a rather tasteless shopping plaza and other resorts. Tour counter. No pool.

A-D Penny's, T075-637295, www.phket.loxinfo.co.th/~johneyre. **Penny's** has made some changes and upgraded its accommodation. It now has a/c and mod cons like satellite TV in rooms and hot showers.

B Dream Garden House, 86/2 Moo 2, T075-637338. Some of the 16 rooms here have balconies which look onto walls so don't believe the advertorials. A/c also quite noisy but the service is good. However, it is rather telling that guests here are thrilled that it is opposite a MacDonalds so that 'they can eat.' A little overpriced.

B-C Ao Nang Mountain Paradise, 26/11 Moo 2, T075-637659. 12 rooms in bungalow-style accommodation (identical to **Ao Nang Garden Home Resort** in style). Ceiling fan with some a/c, hot water. Simply furnished but clean, in a quiet location down a dirt road near the **Lai Thai Resort** with good views of the limestone mountains. Friendly management. Well-priced basic breakfasts are available at the tiny restaurant/office at the front.

B-C Hill Side Village, 168/10 Moo 2, T075-637604, Leem@loxinfo.co.th. Opposite the **Lai Thai Resort**. Converted concrete row of a/c rooms. 19 rooms come in sets of 2 (double at back, twin at front) and would make good family rooms. Rooms to the back are smaller and cheaper, with shower only and no hot water. Rooms at the front are twin beds with a bath and hot water. All rooms come with TV (satellite) and a fridge. Friendly staff also provide information on tours at the front desk, and will take guests to and from the beach.

C Ao Nang Royal Resort, T075-7231071. Group of 15-odd a/c bungalows built in a circle around a concrete pond. Rooms are functional and they have no view (the hotel is set back from the beach). A/c rooms available (especially good rates in the low season). Bathrooms with hot-water showers. A good place to stay if intending to remain out during the day and just want somewhere cool to sleep at night.

C Dutch Mansion, 249/2 Moo 2, T01-3968152. Large renovated rooms in a shophouse, all with a/c, warm water, TV and fridge. Very clean. Simply furnished. Rooms vary so ask to see a few if you can. Some rooms at the back have little natural light, but these are probably quieter as they are away from the road. Good-ish value.

C Sea of Love, 111/1 Moo 2, T01-7880414. Behind the trendy bar and restaurant are 4 rooms in rustic style. If you can get over the embarrassment of staying somewhere called the 'Sea of Love', this is a good choice – rooms are all different, nicely designed with a bit of style. But the back area is too closely packed for comfort or privacy, especially now that Ao Nang has become so overdeveloped. Still a good price though.

C-D Leela Valley, 262/1 Ao Nang, T075-635673. Some simple bamboo bungalows on the ground needing repairs and some smarter fan and a/c houses on stilts with balconies, set in spacious grounds rather lacking in shade. Good views of the mountains. Rooms are clean. Discounts for long lets. Quite a distance from the sea, but excellent value.

D-E Ya Ya, 92 Moo 2, T075-637176. 10 pleasant and simple bungalows in a garden setting up a small road off the main highway into Ao Nang. Reasonable price for the proximity to the beach and still maintaining something of the backpacker feel. That said, not much of a view, fairly cramped and pricey when compared with similar places on Hat Nopparat Thara (over the canal) or nearby islands (eg Koh Jum).

Nopparat Thara

A Srikusant Resort, 145 Moo 3, T075-638002. White 4-storey hotel with 2 pools, children's pool, bar and restaurant. 40 rooms – standard ones on ground floor don't have much of a view. Superior rooms have limited sea views. While the rooms are not particularly riveting, natural textiles and materials have been used to up the comfort level – like cotton sheets and canopies although the ceilings are a little low for canopies. Limited English spoken here. Closer to Ao Nang end. Okay for the price.

A-B Emerald Bungalow, T01-8921072. Catch a boat from Nopparat Thara pier across the estuary, westwards. This place is very peaceful with around 40 large, fan bungalows and some a/c rooms. Restaurant too. Location is the high point; it is south facing the beach so you get a good sunset and there is also a river to swim in at the end of the beach.

B-C Nopparat Thara and Phi Phi Islands National Park Headquarters has some bungalows and camping facilities, PO Box 23, Muang District, Krabi 8100, T075-637436 or make reservations at the Royal Forestry Department in Bangkok, T02-5790529. You have to make reservations ahead of time.

C Na-Thai Resort, near Nopparat Thara and Phi Phi Island National Park Headquarters and the Montessori School, T075-637752. 5-10 mins by motorbike/car from Hat Phra Ao Nang and Hat Nopparat Thara. Free pick up. Surrounded by oil palms and rubber trees, this is a husband and wife set-up – Gerard and Walee who have more of an eco-friendly approach to running things. There are 5 evenly-spaced red-roofed bungalows set around a small pool that you can swim in at night and a restaurant where they promise to cook Thai food as Thai as you like. If that's not to your taste, they can trot out western favourites and are good with Northern European specialities. German, Spanish and English spoken here. Not the most imaginative bungalows but

great attitude and good for a more isolated getaway although your own transport might be best for exploring. Offers diving courses, handicraft workshops. Has internet. Recommended.

Khlong Muang

L-AL Andaman Holiday Resort, 98 Moo 3, T075-644321/02-7111942 (Bangkok). Large (too large really at 116 rooms) resort on a former rubber plantation which extends right down to the beach in a peaceful and semi-isolated spot. Pool is a bit undersized for the number of rooms. Rooms vary, with the more expensive thatched roof villas representing better value. Fitness centre, convention centre, tour counter. Overpriced for what it is and the food lets it down. The beach is also not good for swimming.

C Green Earth Botanical Garden Co. Ltd, Rooms are nicely, if simply, furnished with twin beds and a fan, and the setting is delightful in tropical gardens. This is operated by Mr Gift of **Gift's Restaurant and Bakery**. Also operates various tours (see Activities and tours), teaches Thai cookery, and runs this nursery/botanical garden. Mr Gift has strong environmental principles, and keeps things very low impact and peaceful. Recommended. Both Klai Wang below and Mr Gift's place are for those looking for something very peaceful and off the beaten track.

D Klai Wang. Thai house with 2 simply decorated rooms and a bathroom set in a shady botanical garden near a waterfall and a couple of fish ponds. A couple of kilometres from the sea, the house is right by the stream running down from the waterfall. This is an owner who has his fingers in many pies and also operates a tour service that takes visitors on a trek up past fields and mountain forest to a cave (for a fair price). Vegetables served at the restaurant are organic, grown in a small plot opposite the accommodation. In addition, there is the **Klai Wang Restaurant** with its now famous fried catfish. Here you can lunch in a shambolic wooden pavilion near a river open for bathing in. He rents the whole house for ฿500 a night. The only drawback is the presence of mosquitos and that is easily solved. Do remember repellent. Recommended.

Susaan Hoi *p474*

A-C KT Bay Cottage Resort. A small bungalow style operation which backs on to the road, and shares this beach with **Dawn of Happiness Resort**, numerous shrimp nurseries and farms, and the **Sand Sea Resort and Bungalows**, the resort is very plain, rather rundown and does not have much to commend it.

A-C Sand Sea Resort Bungalows, up the road from the **Dawn of Happiness Resort** down a small dirt road. Set back from the beach, about a 2-min walk past a shrimp nursery and through another resort. Bunglaows a/c and fan.

C Dawn of Happiness Eco-Tourist Resort, PO Box 35 Krabi 81000, T01-4644362, dawnofhappiness@hotmail.com. A guesthouse with a difference, 15 good traditional bungalows, basic but clean, environmentally and culturally sensitive, library, hammocks, trips to local monasteries. The owners try to educate their guests but not in an overbearing way; isolated position in Ao Nam Mao, close to Susaan Hoi. Good for families as the kiddies can trot up and down the beach.

C-D Holyland Bungalows, between Ao Nang and the Fossil Shell Beach down a dirt road through rubber plantations, in a stunning location at the far end of Ao Nam Mao next to the limestone crags that fringe Rai Leh. The cramped layout of the bungalows, sadly, makes little use of its wonderful location. There are some bamboo bungalows with better views and location overlooking the bay, but most are concrete and set back in sparse gardens. A couple of motorbikes can be rented at ฿200 per day.

Koh Boda and Koh Gai *p474*

There are bungalows available on the island for ฿350. Book through the **Krabi Resort**, T075-611389/02-2518094 (Bangkok). The bungalows are a good size, restaurant, western toilets, not particularly friendly staff. **Camping** is possible on the island (฿50).

Phra Nang and Rai Leh *p475*

There is not much to distinguish between the various lower-end bungalow operations at Rai Leh. Most offer a range of bungalows from older, smaller, more rundown and cheaper cottages to larger and more

sophisticated places. Unfortunately, many of the owners have crammed too many structures onto too small an area, and others have grown too large (with 40 or more cottages) and service has consequently suffered. All have their own restaurants, bars and often minimarts, tour desks and international phone facilities. Many also have exchange services often offering poor rates.

Phra Nang headland

L Rayavadee, T075-620740, www.rayavadee.com. 98 two-storey pavilions and 5 villas set amid luscious grounds studded with coconut palms in this luxurious, isolated getaway. Every facility imaginable is provided in the beautifully furnished pavilions including lovely, exclusive bathroom amenities and bedtime chocolates. Some of the pavilions and villas have private pools. The strikingly large main pool faces Rai Leh beach. Restaurants include the **Krua Phranang**, on the renowned Phra Nang beach, where the Mieng Kana, small parcels of kale leaves filled with lime, chilli, shallots, ginger, cashew and shrimp, are to be especially savoured. Unwind and indulge in the magnificent spa building - the Rayavadee Signature Massage which includes a hot herb compress is particularly recommended. Excursions are offered too. Due to its location, bordering three beaches and caves, it feels more like an adventure than just a hotel stay. Room price includes the transfer to and from Krabi airport. Highly recommended.

Rai Leh West

A beautiful beach, but huts have been built too closely together, making for overcrowded conditions and very basic (but not cheap) accommodation. To get there, take a boat from Ao Nang.

AL-B Lanka Daeng, T01-4644338, rbclub@phuket.ksc.co.th. On its own section of beach (at the opposite end to the **Premier Rayavadee**), this has to be one of the most stylish places to stay at Rai Leh. Traditional Thai-style houses have been built and sold on as holiday homes. Their owners now let them out whenever they are not in residence. Fully equipped with kitchens and bathrooms but no a/c. Electricity goes off after 2400. Prices vary depending on the size. Houses are available for 2 people or more. Maid service can be provided.

A-C Rai Leh Bay Bungalows Resort and Spa, 64 Moo 2, T075-622330. Upgraded and far too many bamboo thatched bungalows in either garden at the back/beachfront. Big rooms. Cheaper ones are hot, dark and dreary, but a/c ones are better. Fairly unpleasant staff. Too expensive.

Rai Leh East

B-D Diamond Cave, 36 Moo 1, T01-4770933. Next to a huge limestone outcrop. Almost monstrous number (for the space) of solidly built and clean concrete a/c bungalows set on a hill. Located on sunrise side of Railey peninsula. Pool and mini-mart. Good reports from climbers though as clean and secure. Recommended for price and as most likely place to find a bungalow at short notice.

C Rai Leh Viewpoint Resort and Spa, T075-621686-7. Large upgraded resort. Friendly, well run, and clean and well-maintained rooms. Good restaurant. Mini-mart and internet centre, pool. The least accessible of all the places to stay at the far end of Rai Leh East, but some of the best bungalows available, especially given the rates. Cheaper ones are very far from the water though.

C-D Yaya, T075-611585. Long-running and well-loved by rock climbers. Variable rooms set in 2-storey (some higher) groups. Wooden constructions, different and aesthetically pleasing, varying sizes and views! Friendly place to stay, but if you're the shy retiring and non-athletic type this may not be for you as it is quite loud with well-muscled types strutting about, gazing at their well-sculpted navels and comparing climbs. Also consistent reports of rats (little palm rats more mouse-sized) in the ceilings and sometimes in the rooms. Still well-priced for size and views. Also offers camping but at ฿200 a night per person this is fairly pricey. One of the few places that offers fresh coffee in the morning.

D-E Coco Bungalows, T075-612915. Very basic and natural bungalows made of split bamboo and roofed with thatch, medium operation. Good-ish food.

Ao Ton Sai

Ao Ton Sai has a few bungalow operations accessible after a walk across to the beach.

The restaurants here are generally poor, even for the overall area, and most of the accommodation is a 5-min walk uphill behind the sand.

C Dream Valley, T01-4646479. Simple bamboo bungalows with fans and en suite bathrooms. Poor security.

D Tonsai Bungalows, close end of beach, T075-622584. Bungalows and longhouse. Clean, cramped but cheap.

Eating

Ao Nang, Nopparat Thara and Khlong Muang *p472, map p473*

As one would expect, the best food available at Ao Nang is fresh seafood. Almost all the restaurants along the beachfront road, and then lining the path northwest towards the **Krabi Resort**, serve BBQ fish, chilli crab, steamed crab, prawns and so on. There is little to choose between these restaurants – they tend to serve the same dishes, prepared in the same way, in rather lacklustre sauces: food does not come close to the standards set by the better restaurants in Krabi. Most lay their catches out on ice for customers to peruse – snapper, shark, pomfret, tiger prawns and glistening crabs. For those concerned about conserving the marine environment, avoid the shark and coral fish which usually come at a much higher price than the tag you see on the fish. Evening is certainly the best time to eat, drink and relax, with the sun illuminating the cliffs and a breeze taking the heat off the day.

TTT The Roof Restaurant, attractive building with a flower-filled dining room and setting although not on the beach. Good extensive menu which offers organic steak and Swiss-German specialities as well as Thai dishes. Expensive, but worth it.

TTT Wanna's Place, Beach Front Rd. Produces Swiss cuisine – veal escalopes, rösti and chicken and also serves wine, but the service is terrible or rather up to Ao Nang standards – unfriendly and slow – and the prices are steep for what's on offer.

TTT TT Lavinia restaurant, on the Beach front rd, next to **Encore Café** and **Kodak Shop**. Great view of beach, good selection of bread but London prices for a sandwich. Service slow and scatty.

TTT TT Sushi Hut and Grill, Ao Nang Beach Rd, See if you can get (uni) sea urchin or (toro) tuna belly. It also does tempura, miso soups, tofu steak in mirin, edamame and all the standards. Steak and thai food also available.

TT Azzurra On the beachfront road and can become rather dusty during the drier months of Jan-Mar. Good unpredictable Italian fare with decent ingredients.

Bars and clubs

Ao Nang, Nopparat Thara and Khlong Muang *p472, map p473*

Plenty to choose from but they tend to open and close with great frequency. A 'bar-beer' scene has opened up off the beachfront in Hat Nopparat Thara behind the front row of dive and souvenir shops and is complete with massage services, pink lights, cocktails etc.

For a drink on the beach, there's **The Fisherman Bar**, Ao Nang, which is more flexible about closing hours.

The Full Moon Bar, formerly The Full Moon House, is a tried and trusty and right in the centre of Ao Nang.

The Irish Rover and Grill , 247/8 Moo 2, Ao Nang. Theme pub but still, sometimes Guiness is good for you. Good selection of draughts and have cider too. Fairly high standard of bar food here too including chilli concarne, toasties, pies and chops. Does roast dinner but can be heavy for a tropical climate. Well-run. Live sports. Recommended.

The Luna Beach Bar, Hat Nopparat Thara, has fantastic cocktail prices (for Ao Nang anyway), and a very loose interpretation of closing hours. Can get raucous with Happy Hour becoming Unhappy hours.

The Lost Pirate Bar, Beachfront Rd, down from La Luna. Slightly more adventurous crowd – good information about parties and alternative scenes.

Shopping

Ao Nang, Nopparat Thara and Khlong Muang *p472, map p473*

Shops open on the beachfront during the evening selling garments, leather goods and other products made specifically for the tourist market. There

isn't much unusual on sale – except for batik 'paintings', usually illustrating marine scenes, which are produced from small workshops here. Some jewellery as well.

Activities and tours

Ao Nang, Nopparat Thara and Khlong Muang *p472, map p473*

Canoeing

Sea Canoe, next to the Phra Nang Inn, T075-212252, www.seacanoe.com. Provides small-scale sea canoeing trips (self-paddle), exploring the overhanging cliffs and caves, and the rocky coastline of Phra Nang, Rai Leh and nearby islands.

Sea World Kayaking, T075-637334; **Mr Kayak**, T075-637165, www.krabidir.com/mrkayak; **New Star Kayaking** and **Sea Kayak Krabi**, T075-630270, on the front. It is fairly difficult to choose between these companies. **Sea Canoe** boasts about its strong environmental policies, including restrictions on the number of people per trip, and no foam or plastic-packaged lunches. Some of the other operators such as **Mr Kayak** have adopted these policies too, particularly in the Ao Thalen area where there is a small group of companies operating in amicable fashion. The best thing is probably to spend some time chatting to your prospective guide to see if you like the way they operate and whether you are happy with the level of English they speak. You should also try to get some guarantees on the number of people on the tour. In this regard **Mr Kayak** has been very good about taking very small groups and **Sea Kayak Krabi** has been known to promise no more than 10 participants but then to take up to 30. Remember too that sea canoes in Thailand are open, so you should either wear a strong waterproof sun block or go for long trousers/sleeves and a hat.

Diving

Ao Nang Divers (PADI certification) at Krabi Seaview Resort. Try Andre Gysin. **Aqua Vision Diving** next to Beach Bungalows. **Calypso** (PADI certification), near the Phra Nang Inn. **Phra Nang Divers**, near the new guesthouses. On the beachfront road by La Luna and the Lost Pirate Bar. Old-time ex-pat Kyle Seymour is recommended. **Seafan Divers** (NAUI and PADI certification) by the Phra Nang Inn.

Muay Thai

There is a well-supported stadium for Thai boxing in the Ao Nang area. The old one was next to Ao Nang Paradise. This much larger stadium which attracts national standard boxers is set back from Hat Nopparat Thara beach by about 300 m.

Rock climbing

King Climbers has an office down towards Phra Nang Inn.

Therapies

Most luxury hotels are now offering spa facilities and there is a glorious day spa, **Tropical Herbal Spa**, www.tropicalherbalspa.com, a little away from the beach but set in beautiful gardens and mostly open to the air.

Pavilion Queen's Bay, offers the best in-hotel spa. Others offer the services one might expect, but don't have that aura of peace and tranquillity that leads to a truly pampering experience.

Tour operators

Ao Nang Ban Lae Travel, close to Krabi Resort. **AP Travel**, very helpful and friendly. **Green Earth Botanical Garden Co Ltd**, T075-637190, run by Mr Gift (of Gift's Bungalows), operates tours between Hat Nopparat Thara via boat and land ending up with a tour of the botanical gardens and including lunch. He also operates small group mountain-bike tours of the province and walking tours up the highest peak in Krabi province. Equipment is well maintained, and staff are friendly and helpful. Prices range from ฿950-1,200 per person, usually including a meal. See also Sleeping.

Koh Boda and Koh Gai *p474*

Canoeing and sea kayaking

Although the trips to areas like Koh Hong with its coral reefs are appealing, in some ways the trips to the limestone karst and mangroves along the mainland are more exotic and interesting. It's also worth remembering that coral reefs are only really wonderful when you snorkel and are thus able to catch the Disney World sea-life just inches below the water.

Phra Nang and Rai Leh *p475*

Canoeing

Kayaks are available to explore the limestone grottoes off the Phra Nang headland.

Diving and snorkelling

Most guesthouses hire out masks and fins and many places now have their own dive operations.

Rock climbing

Professional farang and Thai climbers will instruct novices on Phra Nang's limestone cliff faces and their equipment and safety record are both said to be excellent. Most operations are based on Rai Leh East. These include **Tex Rock Climbing**, www.thaibiz.com/texsrockclimbing/, **Phra Nang Rock Climbers** and **King Climbers**. There are several other places operating out of resorts. See www.simonfoley.com/climbing/krabi.htm, for a personal take on climbing in Rai Leh and lots of travel information. Half-day introductory climbing courses should cost ฿500, ฿1,000 for a full-day course and ฿3,000 for a 3-day course. All prices are per person.

Transport

Ao Nang, Nopparat Thara, Khlong Muang *p472, map p473*

Boat

Regular long-tailed boats to **Rai Leh** during the high season (Oct-May), from the beach opposite Sea Canoe, 15 mins, ฿50. The *Ao Nang Princess* links Ao Nang with Rai Leh and **Koh Phi Phi** daily during the high season 2 hrs, ฿150. Arrange a ticket for the boat trip through your guesthouse. The boat departs from Ao Nang at 0900 returning at 1630. This is subject to change post-tsunami and depends on the number of travellers.

The boats to **Krabi** leave with the same regularity as those leaving Krabi. Prices vary. You can also go with Ao Nang Travel Tour, T075-637730, 1030, ฿280.

Jeep and motorbike hire

Jeep hire (฿800-1,200 per day) and motorbike hire (฿250 per day) from travel agents and guesthouses.

Songthaew

Regular white songthaew connections with **Krabi** (30 mins, ฿20). For Krabi, songthaews leave from the eastern end of the beach road, opposite Sea Canoe. The service runs regularly 0600-1800.

Phra Nang and Rai Leh *p475*

Boat

The *Ao Nang Princess* links **Phi Phi**, **Ao Nang** and **Rai Leh** during the high season (2 hrs, ฿150). Note that the sea can be rough between Jun and Oct which is one reason why there are no boats between Ao Nang and Rai Leh at this time.

Directory

Ao Nang, Nopparat Thara and Khlong Muang *p472, map p473*

Banks Mobile exchange booths along Ao Nang beachfront and a more permanent place opposite the Phra Nang Inn, run by the Siam City Bank. Also a bank and exchange along from Vogue Phranang Bay Resort. **Thai Military Bank** booth next to AP Resort, 1000-1730. During low season (Jun-Oct) exchange booths may not open. **Internet** Now available at most guesthouses, hotels and resorts. **Telephone** Overseas telephone facilities available from numerous tour and travel**Best time to visit** It is possible to travel to Koh Phi Phi all year round but during the rainy season (May-October),

the boat trip can be very rough and not for the faint-hearted. The driest months are between June and September. There is no official tourist information service.

agents along the beachfront road. **Useful addresses** Police The station is halfway along the beach road; it is really just a police booth. **Tourist police** near the Ao Nang Bay Resort and Spa and another general police box near the Phra Nang Inn.

Phra Nang and Rai Leh *p475*

Banks It is possible to change money at Rai Leh but rates are poor. Better to change money in Krabi before arriving.

Islands south of Krabi

Anvil-shaped and fringed by sheer limestone cliffs and golden beaches, Koh Phi Phi's reputation as the setting for the Leonardo Di Caprio film – The Beach, *changed for good on 26 December 2004 when one of the most devastating natural catastrophes in recent human history happened – the Andaman Sea tsunami. Ask locals for information about boat services and accommodation. Some luxury accommodation, mainly in the northeast, remained unaffected by the tsunami.* ▸▸ *For Sleeping, Eating and other listings, see pages 489-494.*

Koh Phi Phi ➔ *Colour map 4, grid C2.*

Along with Khao Lak, Kho Phi Phi was one of the worst-hit sites and with particularly cruel effect on Koh Phi Phi's Don's Ton Sai Village and Loh Dalem Bay where more than 70 per cent of the island's accommodation was situated. This thin finger-nail shaped strip where the half-moon bays of Ao Ton Sai and Ao Lo Dalam lay back-to-back was home to family-owned and squatted bungalows, restaurants and bars – all stacked up against each other only yards from the water's edge. Flush with visitors, it received not just one blow from the treacherous waters but a far more lethal dose as the killer waves overlapped simultaneously on either side. Visitors are slowly returning and dive shops, hotels, restaurants, shops and bars are up and running along the Ton Sai strip running from the pier. There is still much clearing work to be done though.

Phi Phi Le is a national park, entirely girdled by sheer cliffs, where swiftlets nest (see box, page 488). It found fame as the location for the film *The Beach* starring Leonardo Di Caprio and Tilda Swinton (see box, page 490). It is not possible to stay on Phi Phi Le but it can be visited by boat. The best snorkelling off Phi Phi is at **Hat Yao** (Long Beach) or nearby Bamboo Island and most boat excursions include a visit to the **Viking Cave**, which contains prehistoric paintings of what look like Viking longboats, and the cliffs where birds' nests are harvested for bird's nest soup.

Getting there The only way to get to Phi Phi is by boat. There are daily connections with Krabi, taking one hour on an express boat and 1½ hours on the normal service. Boats also run from the beaches of Ao Nang and Rai Leh close to Krabi (two hours). There are daily boats from Koh Lanta (one hour) and from various spots on Phuket (one-1½ hours). The quickest way of getting to Phi Phi from Bangkok is to fly to Phuket and catch a boat from there. ▸▸ *See Transport, page 493, for further information.*

Koh Phi Phi's beaches include **Loh Dalam** which faces north and is on the opposite side to Ton Sai Bay so is still under recovery. **Laem Hin**, another, has beautiful fine sand. **Ton Dao** beach is a small and relatively peaceful stretch to the east of Laem Hin, hemmed in with the usual craggy rocks and vegetation.

Hat Yao (Long Beach), post-tsunami, has become a day-trippers destination as curious folk from the mainland resorts hit Koh Phi Phi to see where everything happened and sometimes, to help out. However, it is gradually starting to attract overnighters. There are other reasons to stay here; the beach has excellent snorkelling offshore. Even before the tsunami, it was touted as having the cleanest water in Koh Phi Phi. Early in the morning (the best time being before 0930) Black Tip Sharks are a regular fixture here, before they swim further out to sea as the temperature rises. A walk to Hat Yao along the beach from the former Ton Sai Village takes about 30 minutes. You can also get a boat for around ฿40.

Loh Bakao is one of the larger of the minor beaches dotted around this island. **Phi Phi Island Village** is the only resort on this stretch of wide golden sand and is now fully operational. **Laem Tong (Cape of God)** boasts a wonderful sweep of white

Koh Phi Phi

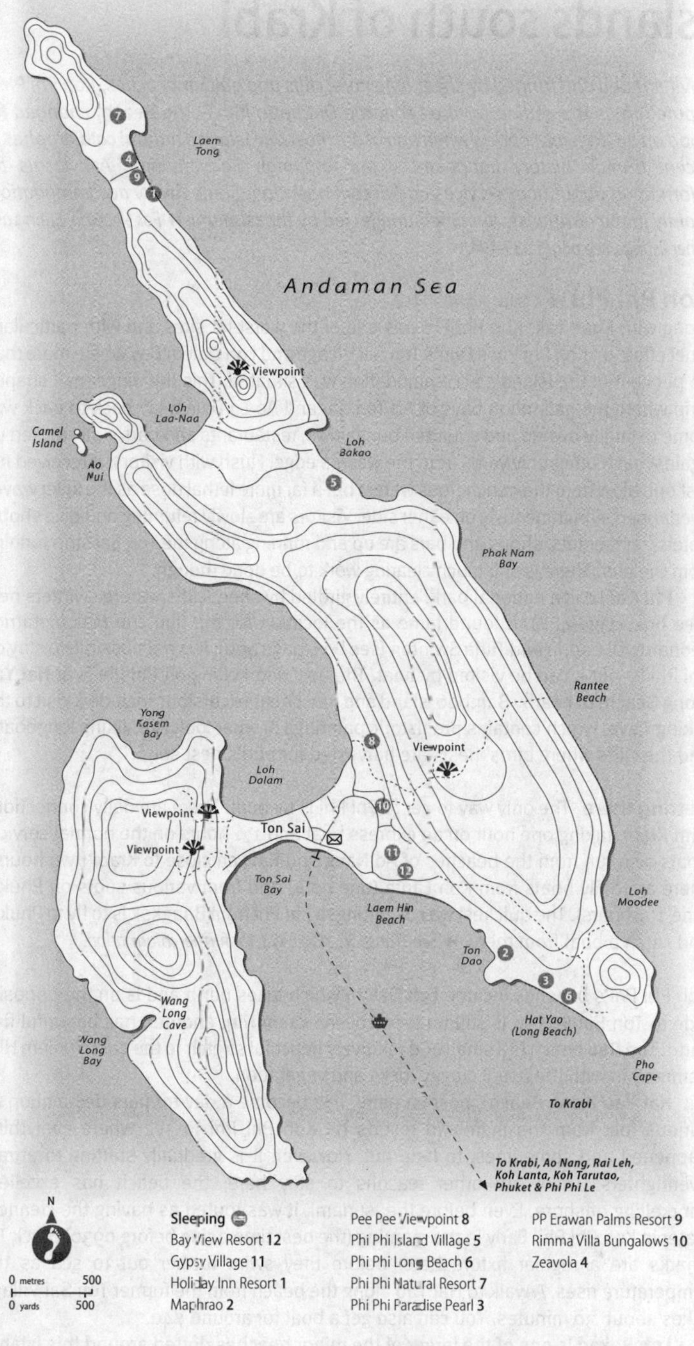
Laem Tong
Andaman Sea
Viewpoint
Loh Laa-Naa
Camel Island
Ao Nui
Loh Bakao
Phak Nam Bay
Rantee Beach
Yong Kasem Bay
Viewpoint
Loh Dalam
Viewpoint
Viewpoint
Ton Sai
Ton Sai Bay
Laem Hin Beach
Loh Moodee
Ton Dao
Wang Long Cave
Wang Long Bay
Hat Yao (Long Beach)
Pho Cape
To Krabi
To Krabi, Ao Nang, Rai Leh, Koh Lanta, Koh Tarutao, Phuket & Phi Phi Le
N
0 metres 500
0 yards 500
Sleeping
Bay View Resort 12
Gypsy Village 11
Holiday Inn Resort 1
Maphrao 2
Pee Pee Viewpoint 8
Phi Phi Island Village 5
Phi Phi Long Beach 6
Phi Phi Natural Resort 7
Phi Phi Paradise Pearl 3
PP Erawan Palms Resort 9
Rimma Villa Bungalows 10
Zeavola 4

sandy beach that's relatively quiet and empty. There are only a few upper range resorts here, where many guests prefer poolside sunbathing, or the privacy of their own verandas, to the beach. The resorts also offer day trips, diving, snorkelling and cave-exploring expeditions. Increasingly, resorts are also conducting cultural workshops in skills such as Thai cookery, batik-painting and language courses.

Around the islands

Hire a long-tailed boat to take a trip around the island. Boats seat eight people, ฿200 per boat. A day trip **snorkelling** is well worthwhile (฿300 per person, including lunch, snorkels and fins), with Bamboo Island, Hat Yao and, on Phi Phi Le, Loh Samah and Maya Bay, being particularly good spots. **Diving** is also possible with a chance of seeing White Tip sharks. Areas of interest include the Bida Islands, south of Phi Phi Le, where the variety of coral is impressive. There is a 50-m underwater tunnel here for more experienced divers. Wrecks can be found behind Mosquito Island – so-named for its mosquitos so do take repellent. The best visibility (25-40 m) is from December to April.

Trips can be taken to see the cliff formations at **Phi Phi Le**, the **Viking Cave, Lo Samah Bay** and **Maya Bay** (about ฿300 per person). Maya Bay was used in the filming of *The Beach* starring Leonardo Di Caprio (see box, page 490).

Koh Jum, Koh Bubu and Koh Siboya

These islands, south of Krabi, are places to escape the crowd. The beaches are not as divine as other Andaman Sea spots but they are quiet and somewhat away from the farang trail.

Koh Jum & Koh Siboya

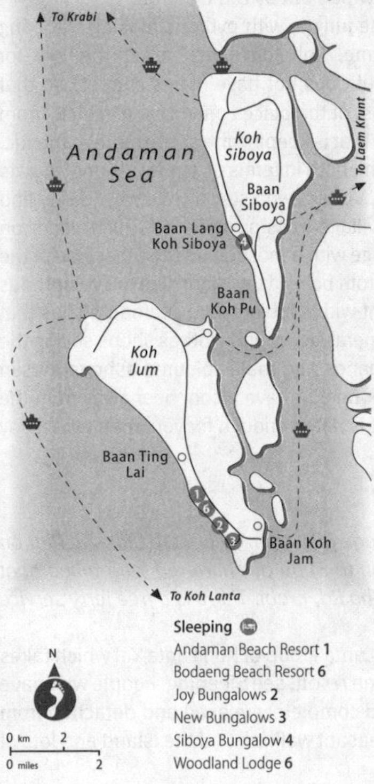
To Krabi
Andaman Sea
Koh Siboya
To Laem Krunt
Baan Siboya
Baan Lang Koh Siboya
Baan Koh Pu
Koh Jum
Baan Ting Lai
Baan Koh Jam
To Koh Lanta
Sleeping
Andaman Beach Resort 1
Bodaeng Beach Resort 6
Joy Bungalows 2
New Bungalows 3
Siboya Bungalow 4
Woodland Lodge 6
N
0 km 2
0 miles 2

Koh Jum (Jam)

ⓘ *The boat from Krabi to Koh Lanta goes via Koh Jum, 1½ hours, ฿150. There are also connections with Koh Phi Phi and with Laem Kruat, on the mainland.*

The island itself, with its beige-yellow beach and shallow waters, is not one of the most beautiful in the Andaman Sea although it does have a magnificent pair of sea eagles who make regular appearances on the village side. Its main attraction is as an escape from the crowds on other islands, a slightly rough-hewn edge and enough variety in accommodation and restaurants that means you are not in Pad Thai Bunglaow Hell day-in day-out. Recently, the island, which only has around a couple of hundred residents – mostly Chao Le and Muslim fishing families – has seen a flourishing of cheap bungalows and there are now over 20 places to choose from although it is often much of a muchness. There is a fear that the resort side of the island is quickly running out of space, thus seriously hampering the privacy and quiet that travellers find here currently. Additionally, there are

Bird's nest soup

The tiny nests of the brown-rumped swift (*Collocalia esculenta*), also known as the edible-nest swiftlet or sea swallow, are collected for bird's nest soup, a Chinese delicacy, throughout Southeast Asia.

The semi-oval nests are made of silk-like strands of saliva secreted by the birds which, when cooked in broth, softens and becomes a little like noodles. Like so many Chinese delicacies, the nests are believed to have aphrodisiac qualities, and the soup has even been suggested as a cure for AIDS.

The red nests are the most highly valued and the Vietnamese Emperor Minh Mang (1820-1840) is said to have owed his extraordinary vitality to his inordinate consumption of bird's nest soup. This may explain why restaurants serving it in Southern Thailand are usually also associated with massage parlours.

Collecting the nests is a precarious business and is only officially allowed twice a year – between February and April and in September. The collectors climb flimsy bamboo poles into total darkness, with candles strapped to their heads. In Hong Kong a kilo of nests may sell for US$2,000 and nest-concessions in Thailand are vigorously protected.

concerns that high-level developers will step in to create hermetically sealed resorts with pools and drive out the smaller set-ups. But this still seems unlikely as the beach is not particularly attractive and there are no sites of note on the island to visit. So far, the operations on Koh Jum do not have pools – the only one that did had its opening day on Boxing Day 2004 and was promptly wiped out by the tsunami.

There is also still a sense of being in the jungle, with pythons making slithering debuts in resort kitchens from time to time. Koh Jum's real ace-in-the-hole for independent travellers continues to be that it does not have mains currents so that resorts depend on individual generators. Most of the places only have electricity from 1800-2200/2300 and it is this inconvenience that is keeping the scene more authentic. The island also has a undeniable quirky charm, both in terms of the locals and ex-pats who have set up semi-permanent base here. Visitors who stay awhile will quickly find themselves craving daily updates on the village gossip, some of which veers on medieval. There is also a working fishing village with a mosque on the other side of the island to the resorts which protects Koh Jum from being a toy island like the voluptuous Koh Ngai. The village has a superb restaurant with sophisticated seafood dishes that would not be out of place in a metropolis, general stores and clothes shops selling the ubiquitous fishermen trousers, hippy Alice-bands and multi-coloured ashram muslin shirts. You can also watch fishermen at work here or have a cool beer away from the resorts. Finally, if you find that Koh Jum is not isolated enough for you, then take a day trip to Koh Bubu or Koh Siboya (see below).

Koh Bubu

ⓘ *Regular vans from Krabi to Bo Muang village pier, then by boat to Samsan Pier on east coast of Lanta Yai (฿100), and finally on to Bubu by chartered long-tailed boat (฿150-200), contact Thammachart, Khong Kha Rd, Krabi. There is a free ferry service from Lanta Pier to Bubu (1 a day).*

Koh Bubu is a tiny uninhabited island in the Lanta group of Koh Lanta Yai which takes a mere 15 minutes to walk around. There is one resort, see Sleeping. People who have stayed here report returning to the mainland completely relaxed and detached from the world they left behind. There is a very pleasant walk around the island and lots of birdwatching opportunities.

Koh Phi Phi's future

Following extensive consultations on what could have been done to limit the damage of the 2004 tsunami, it is clear that the area had been seriously over-developed over the last 15 years, with far too much of the accommodation lying dangerously close to the water and a complete disregard for zoning laws.

At the time of the tsunami there were no proper roads or public spaces for people to run to for safety. Ton Sai, it is now agreed, had become a 'tourist dump' with sewage, rubbish disposal, drought, overfishing and reef problems, and even human faeces regularly turning up in the water supply.

So what does the future now hold for this former jewel of the Andaman Sea? As environmentalists, big business and government continue to tussle, it remains a mystery what will happen to the former backpacker haven. However, it is looking increasingly likely that the island will not be returned to national park area because it is quite simply too lucrative.

Amid tales of buy-outs to locals to leave, the few landowning families on the island are in long-running negotiations with the government and community groups over re-zoning and it is expected that a few luxury resorts will be slotted in to replace the former bungalows.

Meanwhile, as the future of Ton Sai continues to hang in the air, the northernmost tip of the island is anxious to confirm its status as 'open for business.' **Hat Laem Tong** near Tong Cape and Loh Ba Kao Bay further down, while offering far less accommodation at far higher prices, businesses are in full operation and have consistently offered cut-rate prices for luxury suites. **Hat Yao (Long Beach)** is also open to tourists. However, these lower prices should not last beyond mid-2006 as the island banks on the notoriously short memories of tourists and the fact that Koh Phi Phi is emptier and parts of it far lovelier than it has been for years, making it an ideal time to visit. For these reasons, Footprint has decided to list mainly those resorts on the relatively untouched areas of Koh Phi Phi Don, which still have much to commend, in terms of natural sights, both on the island, the smaller, unihabited Koh Phi Phi Leh and offshore.

Koh Siboya

Koh Siboya is a speck of an island with a population of about 1,000 people, most of whom are Muslim and involved in rubber or fisheries. The beach is really just mud-flats that stretch for an astonishing length and bake and crack in the midday heat. However, it is the isolation of Koh Siboya that attracts returnee visitors – a mixture of hardcore travellers and middle-aged zippies. You will also find ex-pats here that came for a couple weeks years ago and who have stayed on living in idiosyncratic and charming bungalows. There is not a lot to do and from our reports, the main attraction/activity for visitors remains watching monkeys catch crabs on the beach and freeform meditation.

Sleeping

Koh Phi Phi *p485, map p486*

L **Holiday Inn Resort**, Laem Tong, T01-4763787, www.phiphi-palmbeach.com. 80 mostly low-rise bungalow style buildings in 20 acres of garden setting right on the beach. Rooms are somewhat antiseptic and frumpy in the Holiday Inn way though they do have wooden floors. Two restaurants, two

Life's a Beach

During 1998 and early 1999 actor Leonardo Di Caprio came head-to-head with environmental correctness on Koh Phi Phi.

Towards the end of the year, 20th Century Fox began filming The Beach, based on Alex Garland's novel, having selected Di Caprio as the bankable heart-throb and Phi Phi as a suitably sun-drenched island. (In fact Phi Phi Le, just to the south of the main island, Phi Phi Don.) But there were three problems – not enough atmospheric palm trees, too much scrubby grass, and lumpy sand dunes. Easy: ship in 92 trees, turf out the grass and bulldoze the dunes. But Phi Phi is also part of a National Park, so when Thailand's environmental movement got wind of what was going on they realized they were onto an environmental winner. Environmental lawyers, local people and activists joined forces to bring the devastation to the wider world.

"In a society which shuns confrontation except in the heat of the moment", opponents said as they took the film company to court to prevent filming, "this is an unprecedented step taken in desperation". In response to an increasingly hysterical and effective anti-Leo campaign, producer Andrew McDonald said that he had sought and received permission from the National Parks' office and had made a payment of US$100,000. He also made a commitment to return everything to its natural state on completion of filming. "We are being picked on", he complained to *The Nation*, "because we are a big studio name and because Leonardo Di Caprio is involved." He said that before filming could begin the crew had to remove six tons of rubbish from Maya Beach.

bars. Lots of activities on offer such as learning Thai cookery, batik painting etc. Swimming pool, Jacuzzi, tennis courts. Even provides picnic hampers for guests who wish to explore. One of the better equipped resorts on Phi Phi. Lovely stretch of turquoise sea, very quiet beaches.

L Zeavola, Laem Tong, T075-627000, www.zeavola.com. This delightful boutique resort is the most perfect and inviting place to relax and unwind. 52 beautifully furnished wooden suites with attractive bright fabrics are set on the beach front, close to the swimming pool or on the hillside among gardens of the half flower tree after which the resort is named (Scaevola Taccada, in Thai the flower's name means Love the Sea). Some have outside showers and bathrooms with beautiful coloured ceramic sinks. Outside living areas with chairs and minibars are also a feature. Dine on the beach by candelight or under the fabulous striped awning at the **Tacada** restaurant or enjoy Italian cuisine at **Baxil**, the covered restaurant. The spa is heavenly. The coffee and spice scrub and aromatherapy massage are particularly recommended. There's a PADI dive centre and excursions are arranged. Staff are friendly, helpful and courteous. Transfers from Phuket and Krabi are ฿1,500 per person. Highly recommended.

L-AL Phi Phi Island Village, Loh Bakao, T075-215014, www.ppisland.com. Set alone to the north of the island this is the only resort on this stretch of beach. It relies on an individual generator for water and electricity. Nearby diving centre, pool, 84 traditional Thai bungalows set in immaculately tended gardens. View of beach. The rooms themselves, are extremely pleasant, a/c, satellite TV, minibar, wooden flooring set off by bamboo and whitewashed walls and muted colours used for en suite bathrooms. Decent sized verandas. There is also a resort speed-boat for quick journeys. Attached spa.

AL P.P. Erawan Palms Resort, Moo 8, T075-613010, www.pperawanpalms.com. Decent-sized wooden bungalows with fresh water

swimming pool on the northern tip. Set in well-manicured paths. Beachside Restaurant. Nightly performances of Thai Classical Music although not necessarily very good ones. Still entertaining and at times, edifying.

A Phi Phi Natural Resort, T075-613010, www.phiphinatural.com. Suffered minor damage from the tsunami. To the north of the island, good diving and snorkelling. Around 70 bungalows with the de luxe options being built right on the hill overlooking the sea and Bamboo Island and incorporating a large area of decking from which to drink in the view. Beachside bar, Coffee house and diving center. Although looking like a stable block, the rooms are simply decorated and offering good views.

A-B Bay View Resort, 43/19 Moo 5, Laem Hin, T075-261360/4, www.phiphibay view.com. Split level bungalows on hill with views of Tonsai Cliffs and Phi Phi Ley. Pool. It suffered extensive damage to the lobby, restaurant, office, kitchen and generators.

A-B Pee Pee Viewpoint, 107 Moo 7, T075-622351. Reopened. Around 60 a/c airy bungalows on stilts in hill, surrounded by coconut trees. Big verandas. View of Loh Dalum Bay. Not all bungalows have good views and they are rather too close together.

B Maphrao, Ton Dao Beach, 3 grades of accommodation, the most expensive have own bathrooms. Restaurant, quiet, private beach, bungalows set on hill. Recent re-opening following tsunami – June-end 2005.

B Phi Phi Paradise Pearl, Hat Yao (Long Beach) T075-622100/618050, info@ ppparadise.com. Big overpriced restaurant, quiet, 80 a/c bungalows with a range of rooms. Some have sea view. All clean. The cheaper ones have limited electricity and no fan, the more expensive ones are spacious, tours organized to Phi Phi Le etc, kayaking, snorkels and fins for hire, videos.

B-C Rimma Villa Bunglows, T075-618086, rimna vila@hotmail.com. Recently re-opened bungalows located up a hill. Inland from Loh Dalum.

C-D Gypsy Village, Ton Sai Bay. Big stone bungalows on southeast side of island inland from former Phi Phi Resort. Bunglaows are spaced around nice open area. Big verandas. Quiet.

D Phi Phi Long Beach, Hat Yao, T075-612217. Very basic huts good food, some private bathrooms, salt water showers in dry season.

Koh Jum (Jam) *p487*

There are around 20 bungalow operations on the tiny island of Koh Jum. Prices vary from low to high season but Koh Jum is generally very reasonably priced compared with some other island destinations although many of the bungalows shut down for six months of the year so you do need to check. Accommodation is simple bamboo bungalows or other basic A-frame bungalows although more upmarket regimental set-ups are appearing. They are evenly spread along the beach.

C Andaman Beach Resort, T075-7241544/01-6931346. Around 20 modern A-frame chalets that look like pathological Wendy Houses in mauve. They even have a fake balcony and second floor. All are set facing each other in a square U-shaped plan on a rather bare site. These are different in ambience and style from other resorts and, one hopes, not a precursor to the homogenized bungalow barracks set-up seen on islands like Koh Lanta. Chalets have attached bathrooms with cold and hot-water showers and electricity from 1800-0500 (fans in rooms), which is a little more upmarket although some guests boasted of having electricity 24 hours. This set-up is usually patronized by members of the Thai military or police when they need to stay on Koh Jum.

C-D Joy Bungalows, T01-7230502. Best known and most established resort; still the most imaginative in terms of variety. There are over 30 wooden family chalets with balconies on the beachfront, bamboo huts on stilts at back and wooden bungalows throughout, and treehouses - some of these set-ups even come with attached bathrooms (hot and cold water) and mosquito nets; tour counter and an average restaurant. The bungalows at the back are not particularly well-kept and are too close together but the deluxe wooden chalet ones at the front are usually taken by families. Joy Bungalows also has hammocks slung along the beach front which become more essential as the days wear on. There is a path behind Joy Bungalows which will take you to the Muslim and Chao Le village. Recommended.

C-D Woodland Lodge, next to Boedeng Bunglaows, T01-8935330, rayandsao@ hotmail.com. Run by Englishman Ray and his

Thai wife Sao, this reliable concrete bungalow set-up was hit by the tsunami and saw its gardens and 'Fighting Fish' Restaurant and Bar decimated. However, the gardens should be on the road to recovery and the bar, last seen, was getting back on its feet. Some of the bungalows, which are nicely spaced from each other, can be too hot as they lack the necessary electricity for day-time fans. But they are kept clean and staff are very helpful, especially the exceptionally considerate and sensitive lady-boy – 'Lek'. What makes this place stand out is a marooned Gilligan's Island feel as it acts as a meeting spot for ex-pats on the island like the marvellous raconteur Scottish Phil. If you want to hear good tales told well, this is the place. The food is generally buffet but if you want anything special, Ray can fetch it at the markets in Krabi. Do be firm about how you want it cooked – in fact hover. One other thing, the establishment is next door to the Chao Le graveyard, apparently anathema to thieves. Recommended.

C-E New Bungalows, T01-4644230. Simple wooden bungalows and a restaurant. Neither are particularly impressive.

D-E Bodaeng Beach Resort. Between Woodland Lodge and the Andaman Beach Resort. These are basic bamboo huts on stilts with shared bathroom. Some bungalows are on a terrifying tilt and really need to be taken down. Most are either on the beach or only a minute away. Attracts hardcore travellers and those seeking spiritual solace in physical discomfort. Excellent restaurant however – the best of all the resorts. Entertaining owner with a roguish tinkle in her eyes and an outrageously contagious giggle. Do check the bills, however, as her maths needs a bit of work.

Koh Bubu *p488*

There is one bungalow establishment here, with 13 concrete bungalows.

C-D Boo Boo Island Resort, T075-612536. Restaurant and little else except sea and solitude. The electricity goes off after 2200 and you are left to the sound of the waves and the moonlight. That said, the beds are rather uncomfortable and the beach is difficult to swim off during low tide because of the sea urchins.

Koh Siboya *p489*

There is only one resort on the island.

C-E Siboya Bungalow, around 500 m south of Lang Koh Village on the west coast of Koh Siboya, T075-612192/01-2291415, www.andaman-island-hopping.com/islands/jum.htm. So if you do plan on staying it is best to make arrangements for transportation after contacting their office in Krabi town or on the island. Bungalows are simple bamboo affairs set in spacious gardens near the sea and vary in size and price.

Private houses can also be rented (**B-C**) but it seems that most people who build them are so attached to them that they stay for months and months and so these are not always available. Excellent reports of friendly staff, good food and interesting residents.

Eating

Koh Phi Phi *p485, map p486*

For the time being, most of the restaurants remain closed but the resorts do offer reasonable fare with many doing BBQ seafood on the beach as well as offering international cuisine in their restaurants.

Koh Jum *p487*

TT Koh Jum Seafood. On a mini pier next to the actual working pier. Choose fine fresh seafood directly from traps. Cooked to perfection with a sophisticated range of ingredients – do not be surprised to find them cooking the shellfish in a broth of around 15 different ingredients. Having anything simply steamed would be a waste of their talents. Sweet views too – you can watch the birds following the boats for fish and all the activities of a working pier while taking in the islands opposite. It may seem expensive after the resorts but it is worth it.

T Boedeng Bungalows. Excellent fare from the owner here, especially the salads and soups. But do take along a mosquito coil or repellent as the restaurant is open and set in a little from the beach. The best you will find among the resorts and the best price too. Recommended.

You can also get simple noodle, chicken and rice dishes in the village street – particularly at **Mamas**. There is only one tiny street – the prices are slightly cheaper than the resorts with little difference in preparation or taste although more atmosphere.

Bars and clubs

Koh Phi Phi *p485, map p486*

Carlito's Bar, east from Ton Sai Bay, became a hub for volunteer clean-up crews and humanitarian aid groups as well as residents following the tsunami. One of the first businesses to be up and running following the disaster, it is well worth visiting just to get the real atmosphere of the island and its people. Did cater to largely Swedish clientele but has since become more international.

Activities and tours

Koh Phi Phi *p485, map p486*

Diving

There are currently around 15 dive shops operating on Koh Phi Phi now. Most of the dive shops charge the same with two local fun dives coming in at around ฿1800. Open Water courses start from ฿9900.

Phi Phi Scuba Diving, T075-612665, www.phiphi-scuba.com. This is located on the main street in Ton Sai.

Visa Diving, also on the main street, T076-618106, www.visadiving.com.

SSI (Scuba School International), which offers a 5-day certificate course, has been recommended. Alternatively, book up with one of the many dive centres on Phuket.

Fishing

Dang Dang Tour, T01-8942708. A full day is ฿3000 with gear for two people.

Kayaking

Kayaking can be arranged through resorts or tour operators for ฿3-400 per day.

Paddle boats

Rent at ฿100 per hr from the northern shore.

Paragliding

A500 a time.

Rock climbing

The limestone cliffs here are known internationally. There are 3 companies operating: Phi Phi Climbers, Cat Climbers and K.E. Hang Out Rock Climbing.

K.E. Hang Out, main street down from the pier at Ton Sai Bay, T01-9581820, www.kehangout.com, is probably the best, the most informative and the friendliest. They are experienced climbers who have been there for 7 years. The funny and pleasant Mr Suthida is the owner. A half day is ฿1000 for 4-5 hours, ฿1500 bhat for 8-9 hours. Includes lunch, water, fruit. A three-day course is ฿5000.

Snorkelling

Snorkels and fins can be hired from most resorts and bungalows, ฿50 per day.

Therapies

Zeavola Spa, Zeavola, T075-627000. 0900-2100. It is definitely worth stopping by here for some wonderful treatments. The signature massage is the Zeavola Body Brush Massage - a full body brushing followed by a head massage then a full body massage with rice oil and lemongrass, kaffir lime and essential oils. Highly recommended.

Waterskiing

Off the north shore.

Koh Jum *p487*

Tour operators

Koh Jum Center Tour. Native Koh Jumian Wasana Laemkoh does tickets for planes, trains, buses and boats. She will also change money, make overseas calls, and arrange one day boat trips. Her husband is a local fisherman so you may end up going with him. You can also rent motorbikes here. Her shop is located on the opposite side of **Koh Jum Seafood** and the pier at 161 Moo 3. Honest and reliable.

Wildside Tours. This set-up, operated by a German lady, offers kayaking and snorkelling expeditions, and some trekking. It is located along the road opposite Koh Jum Village School. It is signposted.

Transport

Koh Siboya *p489*

During the high season (Nov-April), you can get a boat opposite Kasikorn Bank, Uttarakit Road in Krabi where there is a small 'local pier', ฿150, leaving at 0800. Or you can take the hard way which is negligibly cheaper: you need the local bus from Krabi to Nua Klong for ฿30; then change the bus and get one for Ban Lam Kruad for ฿40. From here there are 3 boats daily, 1230, 1400 and 1630, ฿30 to Koh Siboya. Or take a private longtail from Koh Jum.

Koh Phi Phi *p485, map p486*
Phi Phi lies between Krabi and Phuket and can be reached from both.

Boat
To **Krabi** , 4 services a day. These services are subject to change and may well have been extended following the return of tourists to the island. For up to date information contact the resorts. Some of the resorts also offer private boat connections with Krabi. Daily connections with **Ao Nang** and **Rai Leh** on the *Ao Nang Princess* (2 hrs). There are also boat connections with **Koh Lanta** (1 hr). Connections with **Phuket**, 50 mins-2 hrs, ฿300-450. **Ferryline** and **Songserm** run the a/c *Jet Cruise*, 1320 , 50 mins, ฿660. Although there is no service at the moment to **Koh Lanta**, one is expected twice a day from the end of Oct, ฿300.

Directory

Koh Phi Phi *p485, map p486*
Banks Money may be exchanged at the resorts but for very poor rates indeed. It is best to change money in Ao Nang first. There are ATMs up and running on the island now. **Post office** Stamps can be bought and letters posted in the village.

Koh Lanta

→ *Colour map 4, grid C2.*

Until quite recently Koh Lanta lacked telephones, electricity or even a road to the mainland. Only in 2001 were telephone lines installed while back in 1993, this yam-shaped island boasted a mere 14 resorts along the west coast strip of beaches. But step off the boat at Sala Dan Pier and into the rigorous grip of the resort ambushers with their private van service to one of more than 100 resorts and you would have to be Pollyanna not to see that the island is in the grips of real estate mania. Yes, Koh Lanta is headed for the Koh Phi Phi set without so much as a spare breath between mono-bungalows and resorts that shoot beyond ฿4500 a night.

But while three to five-stars are pushing out bargain shoppers, ฿300 backpacker bungalows remain towards the national park end of the island where the road is locally dubbed car killer strip for its elephant foot-sized potholes. However, Koh Lanta, with its 85 per cent Muslim population increasingly attracts families and pensioners, stoutly there for R&R although superb diving, including the world-famous Hin Daeng (Red Rock) and Hin Muong (Purple Rock) also pulls in swashbuckling hardcore divers.

Beach over-development aside, Koh Lanta's east coast teeters on the edge of the Third World with villagers dependent on wells and young people rejecting the traditional economy of rubber, cashew and fishing for the tourist industry. And, while it is worth a motorbike ride to see the east coast's rough and tumble hills with giant umbrella trees and the rare python sunning themselves in the middle of the unfinished road, there are scant architectural gems apart from the Old Town, site of trade routes for China in the early 1900s and home to a sea gypsy village. ▸▸ *For Sleeping, Eating and other listings, see pages 500-506.*

Ins and outs

Getting there

The main access point to Koh Lanta is from Klong Chi Lard Pier, around 5 km out of Krabi Town to Sala Dan, via Koh Jum (two hours). The island largely shuts its tourist season down during the wet season when unpredictable large waves make it too dangerous to cross (May-October). A minibus then takes visitors via two short car ferry crossings from Lanta Noi to Sala Dan (two hours). There are boat connections with Ban Hua Hin at the southern end of Koh Klang, and songthaews from Krabi to Ban Hua Hin. ▸▸ *See Transport, page 506, for further information.*

Getting around

Not one bay area accessible from the road has not been developed. To get to the resorts and bungalows, there is a road which stretches the length of the island from Sala Dan Pier to the national park end. Before you get too excited, it looks as if chunks have been chewed out of red clay earth by an exceptionally greedy giant. Not only is the road poorly lit, paved only for short distances and pocked with lethal holes, it is also filled with chronic thick red dust clouds, making it foolhardy not to take sunglasses or goggles, a scarf for your head and to wear second-best clothing – including longer trousers and proper shoes as accidents on this road are very common, the further down you go. Along this wretched road at regular intervals are dubious lanes, equally pot-holed and dusty that lead to resort-land.

Songthaews are the main form of public transport around the island, though these are few and far between. Motorbikes and mountain bikes are available for hire from guesthouses and some shops and tour companies. It is advisable to check the wheels for softness, the brakes and the tank before you set off as many of the rental places do not offer road-worthy vehicles yet you are expected to sign a contract to pay for any damages entailed before you set off. A more reliable solution is to rent a jeep but these are considerably more expensive unless you find other people to share the costs. Long-tailed boats can be chartered for coastal trips.

Background

Koh Lanta is packed with bungalows and resorts. Some of these set-ups are replete with internet, mini-marts, souvenir shops, spas, restaurants, pools and bars so that guests need never leave. Meanwhile, on the main road, there is almost a total absence of cultural outposts like libraries, bookshops or music stores. Instead, the road is dominated by restaurants in shacks, garages, the occasional massage and tattoo parlour and general crisp and beer grocery shops along with farang-tailored bars that promise the latest football results and pub dinners. Still, in the evening when the fairy lights are switched on and the dust clouds expand with Saharan girth, it is bearable – briefly.

There is a sizeable sea gypsy village to the southeast of the island, where the inhabitants continue with a lifestyle they have maintained for generations. The village comprises shacks – some awash with the flotsam and jetsam of a fishing life – from broken equipment to torn nets mixed in with today's ecologically nightmarish household rubbish. From the lack of any businesses set up to lure in tourists – even the most basic cafés – it is clear they have no wish to become yet another 'tourist attraction.' Walking through the chaotic lay-out of their living space, it is impossible not to intrude and, while the Chao Le are remarkably patient and gracious, it is perhaps better to resist curiosity about the 'indigenous lifestyle' unless invited. Yet local tour operators on the island and further afield are now including this village in their itineraries. If you have a concern about infringing on the rights of these communities, you should check with tour operators about the extent to which their wishes are respected, and the extent to which they receive benefits from the visits.

The island

Ban Koh Lanta Yai

Blink and you miss it; Ban Koh Lanta Yai, the old administrative centre and port on Koh Lanta, now known as 'Ban Koh Lanta' or simply as 'nai talad' (in the market), is developing its own tourism niche. With stunning views across to the islands of Koh Bubu, Koh Po, Ko Kum and Koh Tala Beng, and most of its original old wooden

Koh Lanta

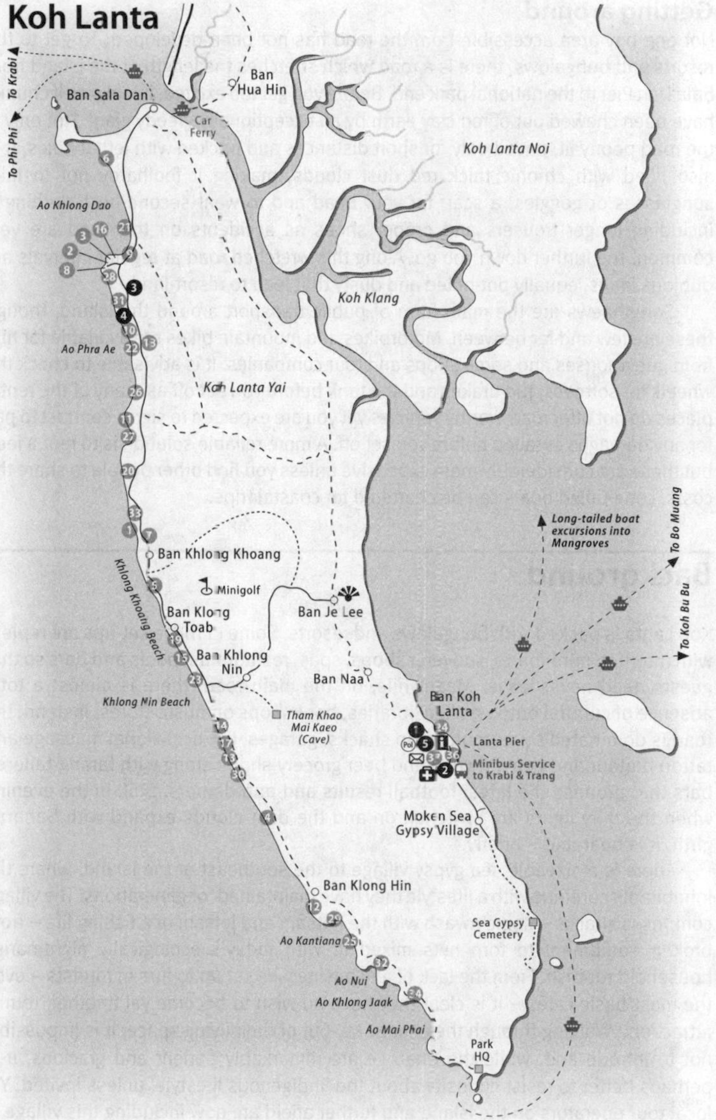
To Krabi
To Phi Phi
Ban Sala Dan
Car Ferry
Ban Hua Hin
Koh Lanta Noi
Ao Khlong Dao
Koh Klang
Ao Phra Ae
Koh Lanta Yai
Long-tailed boat excursions into Mangroves
To Bo Muang
To Koh Bu Bu
Ban Khlong Khoang
Khlong Khoang Beach
Minigolf
Ban Klong Toab
Ban Je Lee
Ban Khlong Nin
Ban Naa
Khlong Nin Beach
Ban Koh Lanta
Tham Khao Mai Kaeo (Cave)
Lanta Pier
Minibus Service to Krabi & Trang
Moken Sea Gypsy Village
Ban Klong Hin
Sea Gypsy Cemetery
Ao Kantiang
Ao Nui
Ao Khlong Jaak
Ao Mai Phai
Park HQ

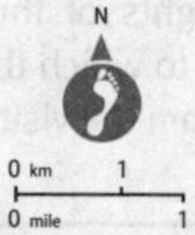
N
0 km 1
0 mile 1

Sleeping
Andaman Lanta Resort 3
Bee Bee 1
Bubu House 36
Dream Team 4
Fisherman's Cottage 5
Freedom Estate 18
Golden Bay 6
Holiday Villa 8
Khlong Jaak Bungalows 34
Lanta Coconut Green Field 7
Lanta Garden Home 9
Lanta Long Beach 10
Lanta Marina Resort & Blue Marlin Resort 11
Lanta Marine Park Resort 12
Lanta Miami 13
Lanta Nature Beach Resort 14
Lanta Palace 15
Lanta Paradise 17
Lanta River Sand 19
Lanta Riviera Bungalow 20
Lanta Sand Resort & Spa 2
Lanta Sea House 21
Lanta Sunny House 22
Narima Bungalows 23
Old Fish Merchant's House B&B 24
Opal 37
Pimalai Resort 25
Rapala Long Beach 26
Relax Bay 27
Royal Lanta 16
Sayang Beach 28
Seasun 29
Sri Lanta 30
Wang Thong Resort 31
Waterfall Bay Resort 32
Where Else 33

Eating
Danny's 3
Fresh 2
Krue Lanta Yai 1
Mr Wee Pizzeria 4
Rom Thai 5

shophouse/fishing houses still standing, this micro-town which is actually only a couple streets has buckets of charm. Here, local entrepreneurs have opened galleries and souvenir shops, there are bed and breakfasts and the closest thing to family stays available on the island, see Sleeping. Ban Koh Lanta really comprises one main street that doesn't even go on for that long. The end of this road is indicated by an extraordinary ancient tree rather like a banyan and a tiny canal rivulet. All along the road in the shophouses are hung exotically coloured birds in wooden cages, lending a distinctly Thai-Chinese ambience. There is also a festival every year that inspires the most intense house pride as everyone joins in to make banners that swoop across the road, costumes for the three-day entertainments and cloth lanterns that swing overhead in the evening and for the parade. Trade on this main street is largely fishing tackle shops and general goods stores, indicating the locals' overruling occupations. Here, you will find, as with small towns of the past, that the shopkeepers' roles often overlap with overtures of familial cooperation between the other tradespeople. The music store owner, for example, also sells fresh orange juice and can get you a papaya salad from the roaming papaya salad maker. There are excellent restaurants offering either good working man's fare or more sophisticated seafood dishes.

This town was the centre of celebrations of the centenary of the island's status as a full administrative district four years ago. This involved the construction of a small park and land reclamation to create a false beach with a stage in the form of a large sailing junk. This could have been horribly tacky, but instead it has added a new feature to the old town reminiscent of the days when the Arab argosy and the Chinese sampon boat regularly docked here on their way down to Penang and Singapore. For their festival, which has now become an annual event, the sea gypsy people played their unique music – Rong-Ngeng – songs in the Malay language played with a violin, Arabian drum and Chinese gongs as well as the Ramana – the Raman Drum.

Ao Khlong Dao

Ao Khlong Dao was the first bay to open to tourism in Koh Lanta and as little as eight years ago had only about six small bungalow resorts and a couple of independent restaurants, not to mention the occasional buffalo family going for a paddle in the sea. While it is a lovely bay with soft sand and pleasant views over to Deer Neck Cape, development here has been rapid and unplanned. The bay is now heavily developed with air-conditioning in most resorts and high walls between them. Khlong Dao itself is a relatively safe place to swim and good for families and with the number of 'proper' hotels, it is often booked via travel agencies offering package tours to Lanta.

Ao Phra-Ae (Long Beach)

Ao Phra-Ae, also known as Long Beach, is a lovely beach to stroll on with soft white sand and a very long stretch of gently sloping beach that allows for safe swimming at both low and high tides. In the late evening, as you splash your feet in the waves close to the shore, a magical phospheresence appears as if you are walking on a thin surface of stars. This beach is catering increasingly to well-healed retirees and families, particularly the Scandinavians although there are still remnants of its earlier days as a backpacker haven with restaurants and bars like the **Ozone**. In its central area, near the **Opium Restaurant and Bar**, Ao Phra-Ae has several bars including the well-established, very popular and predictable **Reggae Bar**. While great for those who like to party all night and sleep all day, the newer lot of tourists have complained about the noise although everyone seems to like the by-now standard fire shows. The area around *Lanta Sandy Beach* has a slightly more laid-back character with late-night pizzerias and fairy-light festooned beach bars. The resorts here are no longer owned by local families and the bungalow resorts make their most lucrative profits through restaurant and bar sales. To encourage their guests to 'stay at home', many of the resorts have created barriers that extend

Koh Lanta's future

The tsunami left the Koh Lanta island group (Koh Lanta Yai, Koh Lanta Noi and Koh Klang) fairly unscathed, as it ploughed first into the unintentional buffer zone of Koh Phi Phi before wiping out Koh Lanta Yai's beaches on the west and destroying most of the fishermen's trawlers and equipment.

Even the death toll on this resort island was minimal as locals and tourists fled into the mountains to stay out the night, returning to the island's town – Saladan – only to stock up on essential supplies. All in all, the main tourist places to bear the brunt on this flourishing hotspot were the flimsy bungalows, beach bars and restaurants sprawling the 30 km length of its nine beaches. The famous dive sites remained virtually untouched while the bungalows were rebuilt and the beaches cleared of debris.

Now, the focus has turned to the beaches which have international consortiums and Bangkok interests salivating in the wake of Koh Phi Phi's uncertain future. The latest attempt to sell Koh Lanta Yai as a new Koh Phi Phi was presaged by the post-tsunami 'Koh Lanta OK' campaign aimed at reassuring tourists and led, in conjunction with local government, by nine spa resorts including the four-star resorts of Pimalai, Sri Lanta, Twin Lotus and Layana.

Only weeks before the tsunami it was revealed that investors showing interest in the island included the Dusit Thani Group, Central Grand Hotel and Thai Nakonn Pattana Co. Ltd – all big players in the resort industry. Certainly, Koh Lanta's mercurial expansion appears to back up predictions of a luxury resort boom. Resorts have gone from 10 to more than 100 in the space of just seven years on this largely Muslim island, with fewer and fewer owned by local families. More than 90 per cent of the resorts are concentrated on the west sunset side, leaving the other half of this long lean island more or less untouched but also underdeveloped with chronic tones of economic apartheid as fresh water supplies, shops and luxuries are maintained for Koh Lanta's guests.

Currently, there are beaches that are relatively undeveloped due to poor transport links; they are closer to the national park end and are occupied largely by basic bungalow set-ups. However, this looks unlikely to remain the case, particularly when the main road from Saladan Pier to the National Park Office is paved in its entirety.

right down to the beach and may use barbed wire or natural borders to keep the tourists in like strategically planted palms. This has resulted in more independently minded travellers feeling trapped and resentful and an atmosphere of comically poisonous competition between the resorts. Perhaps the only delightful upshot of the tsunami was that the waves destroyed many of these barriers, allowing 'rival' guests to almost forget they were actually still in a compound comprised of an endless number or resorts staggered to only one side of the island.

Hat Khlong Khoang

Hat Khlong Khoang beach is advertised by some as the 'most beautiful beach on Lanta'. But the beach is fairly steep down to the sea and the sand not as fine as that at Long Beach. The views along the bay are pleasant, but not spectacular. Behind many bungalow resorts is a canal which is treated as a dump for all sorts of waste from construction debris to coconut husks. In many parts of the beach it smells and is a

mosquito trap and consequently is best avoided if you are offered a room anywhere near. That said, there are a handful of establishments with real character and charm and offshore, there are coral reefs that are increasingly attracting snorkellers and divers.

Khlong Toab

Khlong Toab, just beyond the Fisherman's Cottage and close to Khlong Toab village, supports two resorts in marked contrast to each other. It is a quiet area and the beach shelves gently and the swimming is safe, so is particularly suitable for families.

Ao Khlong Nin

Ao Khlong Nin is a bit of a mixed bag in terms of accommodation ranging from basic backpacker places through to the top-of-the-range resorts. There is, as they say, just about something for everyone. The beach itself is picturesque with rocks dotted about and not just a single sweep of sand; the sand is white and fine. The downside is that this means that swimming, in places, can be tricky. Usually, though, it is possible to find a safe place to swim.

Ao Kantiang

Ao Kantiang was once the cheap and secluded hideaway for many Europeans and Scandinavians who spent months resting in bungalows overlooking the bay. With golden sand, steeply sloping hillsides and only a small village, the only accommodation was locally owned and operated and set well back from the local community. All that has changed with the arrival of the **Pimalai Resort**. This luxury resort has completely changed the feel of this bay. Speedboats send off guests to a floating jetty (thus avoiding putting any money into local coffers through the ferry and avoiding the road which was substantially torn up by the construction vehicles building the resort). The Scandinvians still frequent this beach, as do wealthy European retirees.

Ao Khlong Jaak

Ao Khlong Jaak used to be one of the most peaceful bays on Koh Lanta, a relatively small bay with sloping hills to the north and south and coconut plantations and grassland in the middle. However, there is rampant land speculation in this area now, as with all the beaches. In the bay area there is an elephant trekking station (up to the waterfall), and the barbed wire marking off land plots that was washed away by the waves will no doubt return. It is important to remember that during the dry season the waterfall turns to a trickle as this is one of the main selling points of Klong Jark. However, it is still possible to find cheap accommodation and more independently minded tourists here.

Ao Mai Phai

Ao Mai Phai is the last bay before the national park and one of the few on the west coast of Lanta with good snorkelling opportunities. Again, it is a relatively small bay with steeply sloping hills leading down to the bay on the north and south and with a more extensive area of flatter land in the middle.

Moo Koh Lanta Marine National Park

ⓘ *฿200.*

The park covers much of the southern part of the island and extends over numerous islands in the area including Koh Rok, Hin Muang and Hin Daeng. The national park headquarters is at Laem Tanod and involves either a boat trip or a long and painful

One of the translations for Koh Lanta is 'Lantus' from the Javanese language meaning 'sieve for drying fish' – the method used by the sea gypsies to preserve fish during the monsoon.

drive. The road to the park is in very bad condition and practically impassable during the rainy season. The peninsula is named after the tanod trees (a type of sugar palm) that grow throughout the area and give it an almost prehistoric atmosphere. There are two bays and in the middle is the lighthouse (navy controlled but the peninsula is accessible to the public). One bay has fine soft sand and is great for swimming. The other, which faces west, bears the full brunt of the monsoons and is rocky and a good place to explore if you like rock pools. Beyond the visitor centre and the toilet and shower block, is a lily pond and the park headquarters. Just beyond this, is a nature trail which takes you up a fairly precipitous path into the forest and then along a contour around the back of the offices in a half loop ending at the road entering the park. It's a well-designed trail though not suitable for children or the elderly because the path is very steep in the early parts and can be slippery. Take plenty of water and some snacks with you. The bay is surrounded by forested hills and filled with forest sounds and the gentle or not so gentle sound of waves crashing on to the rocks or beach (depending on the season). It is a beautiful spot to spend a day swimming and walking, and then watching the sunset from the viewpoint on Laem Tanod.

Koh Lanta Noi

If you take the car ferry route to Lanta Yai, Lanta Noi is the island you cross between the two ferry crossings. Undeveloped for tourism, this island is dominated by mangrove forest and paperbark forest. Few tourists visit the island, but it is worth making a quick visit from Sala Dan using the small long-tailed boats. This will take you to the pier used for the district office (now located on Lanta Noi but once based in Ban Koh Lanta Yai). From here you can walk for at least a couple of hours along a stretch of beach complete with casuarina trees and paperbark forest. With good views to the coast and across to islands, this is a pleasant place from which to escape the noise and dust of the main island. Also on Lanta Noi, but on the main road and in the only village passed en route to Koh Lanta, is a women's group shop that sells the woven matting bags, mats etc that you may see in souvenir shops on Lanta Yai. Prices here are not much lower than what you'd pay in the shops, but at least all of the price goes to the makers. The quality of the weaving here is very high.

Had Thung Thale Non-Hunting Area, Koh Klang

ⓘ *There are few organized tours to this area, but you can self-drive. Signs are reasonably well-marked – it's about 17 km off the main road down a couple of turns off and through some small villages and plantations.*

Had Thung Thale Non-Hunting Area is on Koh Klang, but you'll have a hard time spotting that fact even if you do drive over to Lanta Yai and take the car ferries. Koh Klang is joined to the mainland with a bridge. The non-hunting area comprises several hundred hectares of beautiful paperbark forest (*pa samet*), coastal grasslands and casuarina forest, and is bordered with some beautiful long stretches of grey/white beaches. Rarely visited, occasionally it is taken over completely with local school trips for their scouting activities and government groups on corporate bonding sessions – the same sort that go to Tarutao. There are several conservation projects sponsored by the King. The paperbark forests have a bleak but beautiful aspect, are fragrant and present relatively easy walking opportunities.

Sleeping

Koh Lanta *p494, map p496*

Most bungalow operations are scattered down the west coast of Koh Lanta Yai and usually offer free pick-ups from the pier at Sala Dan. Even if you do not have a place sorted out, you will be inundated with reps on the boats traversing between the various islands, most with photo albums showing pics – though not very reliable ones – of their resorts and promising discounts

Black Magic

In a macabre take on disgruntled staff spitting in your food, one traveller in Koh Lanta reported being the target of a Thai black magic curse.

The woman recalled waking up to discover tiny triangles had been cut out of her sandals while her partner had had miniature squares cut out of a shirt. While they had no idea why they were being selected, it isn't the first time that black magic has dogged foreigners.

Jonathon Staples, who has travelled on and around Krabi and Koh Lanta for years, says that staff have been known to seek pay-back from customers they don't like by snipping bits of material and using it in the same way as a voodoo doll and then placing it in a vessel and throwing it in the sea or burying it.

Black magic in Thailand – linked to animism - is remarkably varied and detailed. One such example is the *Kuman Thong* which means 'baby spirit'. For this, you need to obtain a foetus and burn it. You can then cast dark incantations inside the remains. The 'baby spirit' will warn and protect the owner but only if the owner remembers, rather like a Furby, to feed and protect it in return. Nowadays, these protectors tend to be made of wood and resemble a little child with a topcut hairstyle and a beaming smile.

Following the tsunami, there were also several sightings of *'phi tai hong'* or fearful ghosts along the Andaman coast beaches. These are the spirits of people who have passed away violently.

On a more comical note, in 2003, villagers in Northwestern Thailand placed President Bush's spirit in a jar and threw it in the river to protect their natural resources.

As regards the traveller who had her sandals re-designed, not much happened except that later on in her travels, she had her sandals stolen.

because they like you. You might find the hail fellow well met routine unravels once they hand over the key to your room but it is still best to stay on good terms, as there is considerable communication between the various touts. Travel agents and tour companies in Krabi and Ao Nang advertise accommodation on Koh Lanta so it is possible to get a pretty good idea of the various places before arriving. The choice is basically between simple concrete bungalows (some with a/c), bamboo or wood bungalows (usually fan), luxury resorts one step away from a theme song and chic spa boutique resorts that offer total comfort and brand T-shirts. Some resorts have been nicknamed 'chicken farms' for their unimaginative and overcrowded layout and there are more and more of these turning up, erected in cleared land that has been scraped clean of trees and foliage. Further along the coast, there are some new and more interesting resorts and the whole area is much less crowded and has a peaceful atmosphere (although there are regular parties during the high season). There is considerable variation between high-season (roughly, Nov-May) and low-season (Jun-Oct) rates, with a low season rate being roughly half that of the high season rate.

Ban Koh Lanta Yai

The old town of Lanta is tiny and perfect and keenly displays the charm of a non-segregated version of tourism as opposed to the Thai-corp style where tourists stay in one place and residents stay in another. Here tourists can stay in bed and breakfast set-ups along the main street. This is a good stop for those who like to chat and have a love of very small places.

C-D **The Old Fish Merchant's House Bed & Breakfast**, 77 Sri Raya Rd, T075-697242/ 01-8467603, fishmerchant2001@ yahoo.co.uk. Renovated and converted wooden shophouse. No en suite bathrooms

and no rooms with real views of the sea. This is something completely different from most accommodation on Koh Lanta, a real chance to experience more traditional rural life on an island.

C-D Opal, T075-697018/09-8754938 or failing that, go to the Tourist Infromation and Souvenir shop at 44/1 Moo 2 Seraya Rd. Ask the boat maker Viroj Boonloung for help. You will see this as you enter the 'town.' This new 2-storey white building is opposite the homage to the King and offers speed boat rental, bus, train and plane tickets. Also the base for a *rong ngeng* centre (the traditional music of the area) set up by one of the managers.

D Tourist Information and Souvenir, 44/1 Moo 2 Seraya Rd, T075-697198/09-9705248. Contact Viroj Boonloung. Offers a couple rooms in the upper floor of this old Chinese shophouse. Basic – shared bathroom. Recommended.

D-E Bubu House. Offers simple beds and good connections to Bubu Island in a converted wooden shophouse with sea views to the east. The house is managed by artists and decorated with all manner of flotsam and jetsam found in the area.

Ao Khlong Dao

AL Lanta Sand Resort and Spa, Ao Klong Dao edging to Ao Phra-Ae, T075-684833. Excellent reports from this luxury resort next to **Sayang Resort**. Spacious rooms plus amazing bathroom with glass wall so that the monkeys can peer in while you are taking a bath. The tubs are also a good size. Good service, fine food. Recommended.

AL-A Andaman Lanta Resort, 142 Moo 3, Khlong Dao Beach, T075-684200-2, andamanlanta@hotmail.com. Towards the south, this was the first real hotel on Koh Lanta, which is used as a selling point. The 2-storey building of 69 rooms is not very pretty, and although there is a pool, these rooms are overpriced for what they are. The blue-roofed bungalow rooms are better value and nicer. Note also that prices rise by a third during the high season and during peak months another ฿600 is added to the bill. Games room, snooker, restaurant. You could be anywhere. There have also been concerns that Thai guests are given better service than non-Thai guests but this could be because they seem more likely to complain. Closed – re-opening perhaps next season.

AL-A Holiday Villa, 220 Moo 3, Sala Dan, T01-8933737. This is a large 42-room hotel at the southern end of Ao Khlong Dao. Big concrete suite bungalows and a pool. Rooms are spacious but rather dark, and the furniture and decorations look somewhat out of place in this seaside setting. Tiled floors make for a clean, cool surface.

AL-A Royal Lanta, 222 Moo 3, Klong Dao Beach, Saladan, T076–236550. Aiming for the family market with children's pool and playground now. Also offers spa, mini-mart, internet, PADI dive facility. Impersonal large restaurant, rather bare rooms. Over 50 cottages with shiny red steeply pitched roofs.

A-C Lanta Sea House, 15 Moo 3, Sala Dan, T075-684073-4, lantaseahouse@hotmail.com. Bungalows near beach and pool both up for renovation following tsunami so should be sparkling at this consistently well-kept establishement. 2 grades of room, both are clean and well supplied, the more expensive have spacious balconies and their own bathroom. Very good value in the low season.

B-C Sayang Beach, situated just south of the **Lanta Villa** between Klong Dao and Ao Phra-Ae, T01-4766357. This operation is run by a local family that took care to protect the environment while constructing their bungalows (unlike many), leaving trees to provide necessary shade and ambience. Much of the garden was hit hard by the tsunami and the restaurant filled with sand but both are well on the road to recovery. Excellent food cooked by one of the daughters with fresh fish nightly. Large bungalows though the ones towards the beach front are better quality while the others at back are rather too close together. Variable service – staff can be either ingratiating or downright sullen and have been found to give misleading advice on travel arrangements. In fact the service is a weak point for the price of these bungalows.

B-E Lanta Garden Home Resort, T075-684084. 7 A-frame basic huts. Suffered badly in tsunami with the restaurant and 2 rooms destroyed but these are expected to be replaced.

D-E Golden Bay, clean, own bathroom, electricity, some simple wood and bamboo huts, some concrete. Very good value (especially in the low season when it is down to F for a good room). Friendly, helpful owners and an easy place to get to.

Ao Phra-Ae

A Lanta Long Beach, 172 Moo 3. A/c or fan thatched bamboo huts with mosquito nets provided. Also family bungalows with Bali-style bathrooms. Nice feature of sliding doors. Verandas too and new bar.
A-D Wang Thong Resort, 178 Moo 3, T075-684205. Lies about 250 m from the beach amongst trees and along the banks of a canal. The 40 odd thatched bamboo and wood bungalows on high stilts on the left-hand side (looking towards the beach) are lovely. Also amongst the trees, the 2-bedroom affairs are ideal for families. There are also intrusive blocks of a/c rooms at the front on the right-hand side.
B-C Freedom Estate, 157 Moo 2, www.sawadee.com/krabi/freedomestate/details/. At the back of Ao Phra-Ae and up Lanta hill, overlooking the beach. 6 self-contained and serviced fan units with gas-oven kitchens, good for families who tire of eating out all the time, but they would necessitate access to transport into the markets in Sala Dan or the old town. You could also try buying fish directly off the Chao Le fishermen in the Old Town. Balcony. Excellent value in the low season. Recommended.
C-E Relax Bay, 111 Moo 2, T075-684194, www.relaxbay.com. 48 large wooden bungalows raised high off the ground and scattered through a beachside grove, au naturel, unusual angles to the roofs and tremendously comfortable verandas. Very quiet, all rooms have glass and/or mosquito panels in the windows, fans and shower rooms in the open air adjoining. Spartan decor – airy. Two beach bars and café, French owned and managed. Excellent reports of service and lay-out. Recommended.
D Lanta Sunny House, 42 Moo 2, Ao Phra-Ae, T075-684347/01-9786613. Poor old **Sunny House**. In a run of bad luck it had to replace a number of fan bungalows when a guest forgot to blow out the tea candles in his room. Once those were repaired, the tsunami hit. Still returnees to this friendly little place say it's the service that keeps them coming back and the fact that they have the time to remember your face. Restaurant and internet. Recommended.
D Last Horizon Resort, 175 Moo 2, Baan Phu Klom Beach, T01-2283625, last_horizon@hotmail.com. 25 nicely designed stone bungalows in a coconut grove with attached showers, 24-hr electricity, restaurant and beach bar. Friendly management, motorbikes for hire, tours arranged. The beach here is only suitable for swimming at high tide. Recommended.
D-E Lanta Marina Resort, 147 Moo 2, www.msnhomepages.talkcity.com/ResortRd/lantamarina/welcome.html. Bamboo bungalows on stilts which look a bit like haystacks but are comfortably, if basically, furnished with mattresses on the floor and mosquito nets, some with bathrooms attached. Good access to swimmable parts of the beach.
E Blue Marlin Resort, next to Lanta Marina. Simple bamboo huts. Friendly staff, nice rustic feel to this whole area, given the absence of concrete bungalows, and the simple design of bungalows and restaurants.

Hat Khlong Khoang

C-E Fisherman's Cottage, 190 Moo 2, Klong Khong Beach, T01-4761529, www.lanta-th.com. Tiny collection of moody, atmospheric bungalows on a steep bend of the main island road before the turn off to the national park. All 9 have sea view. Decorated with quite a bit of style; most of the many owners and staff appear to be artists. Though trendy, there is nonetheless a family cottage and the staff are a very family friendly – so is the beach area which is gently shelving and a safe place to swim. Good ambient music at the bar – also deep house and hip hop. Recommended.
C-E Lanta Coconut Green Field, 78 Moo 2, Tambon Sala Dan, T075-684284/01-2284602, pleasant bamboo bungalows in a coconut plantation by a rocky shore. Friendly staff and peaceful setting. Restaurant and bar (**Robinhood Bar**) with movie showings.
D-E Bee Bee, a village-like set-up of unusual-looking bamboo bungalows set just back from the beach in a coconut plantation.

Some with 2 levels and all with bamboo bathrooms! Charming and different. Closed during the low season. Recommended.

E Lanta Riviera Bungalow, 121 Moo 1, Sala Dan. Bungalows with fan and attached shower, quiet and relaxed atmosphere. Bar, restaurant, internet. Expected renovation. Recommended.

Khlong Toab

B-C Lanta Palace, T075-697123-4, www.lantapalace.com. Looks like something straight out of a European seaside resort, with white concrete cottages in a small garden. The bungalows are a bit too close together, but this is a quiet part of the coastline, comfortable and popular with families.

D-F Lanta River Sand. This is actually between Klong Toab and Klong Nin beaches. Touted as being made from 'ecological materials grown locally' or trees, these 15 simple bamboo bungalows are set around a brackish water lagoon and in amongst trees with lots of mosquitos. It is also the sister resort of Lanta Marina. Interesting and in a more secluded location, even if a little dark. Also a reasonable-ish price for these parts.

Ao Khlong Nin

L-AL Sri Lanta, T075-697288, www.srilanta.com. Spacious, well-designed bamboo and wood bungalows with a/c (but sadly no mosquito screening or ceiling fans) and hot showers. The bathrooms are semi-outdoors. Beautiful black-tiled pool right on the beach. Fan-cooled restaurant in similar style and a spa in garden area adjacent to the pool and other facilities. Beautiful spot on the bay with rocks adding character to the area, but still with access to a sandy beach for swimming. Attracts prosperous Scandinavians. Recommended.

AL Dream Team, upgraded to 3-star, aiming for family market with big slide at pool. Good restaurant using their own home-grown produce. Wooden houses with fans and a/c and night time electricity, steps leading up, gardens but facing a rocky beach.

AL Narima Bunglaow Resort, 98 Moo 5, Klong Nin, T075-618081. Large bungalows with wooden floors overlooking a quiet part of beach. Wall of sliding glass doors. Doctors own this place. The restaurant here also serves a greater variety of Thai dishes than most places. Pool. Other perks include exercise bicycle, DVDs, CDs and a mini-library. Recommended.

A-E Lanta Miami, T075-697081. A/c and fan available. Family-run, all rooms come with attached bathrooms. Rooms are quite closely packed with vertigo-inducing pseudo marquetry stripes across floor and ceiling and shiny walls. Looks far more peaceful from outside with wide verandas and rustic wooden clapboard fronts. Service meant to be good though. Snorkelling organized from here.

B-D Lanta Paradise, T01-6075114. Not such a pleasant beach, all beds have mosquito nets and fans. Some bungalows are behind the road away from the beach. But atmosphere more hippy-trippy here even if it does have a pool. Tour desk. Motorbike rental available.

C-E Lanta Nature Beach Resort, good bungalows. friendly and helpful owners. Again more of a traveller feel to this place. Good discounts in the off season, reflected in the price range quoted.

Ao Kantiang

L-AL Pimalai Resort, 99 Moo 5, Ba Kan Tiang Beach, T075-607999 . Yet another resort to make big claims about the pristine nature of its setting with the implication that staying here will not be causing damage to the environment or local culture. Huge resort, beautifully designed rooms, although parts of the garden look very sparse and there's an awful lot of concrete used in creating terraces, steps and roads. All facilities are on offer as one would expect for a resort of this type. More of the same to come.

B-E Lanta Marine Park Resort, T075-3970793. Resort set up high on the hill overlooking Ao Kantiang with great views of the bay from the bungalows in the front. Several styles of bungalows: the small bamboo bungalows set back from the view are the cheapest and the larger concrete bungalows with views from the balconies are the most expensive. Rooms are spacious and comfortable. The walk up to the bungalows will keep you fit! Free pick-up service from Sala Dan and taxi service for ฿35-40.

E Seasun, T075-7230497. Rather grotty concrete and some bamboo huts, 1 wooden bungalow up a long staircase with great

views, very pretty and remote cove, not such good snorkelling, friendly Muslim owners.

Ao Khlong Jaak

A-C Waterfall Bay Resort, T075-612084/01-8364877, www.lanta.de/waterfallbay. The owners sold to Anda Lanta resort shortly before the tsunami which caused considerable damage. It is not known yet whether this resort will return to its former conservation ethic, especially with a huge road ploughing through to the resort or whether it will continue with its most recent trend of 'upgrading'. Boat trips are organized to nearby islands and other places of interest.

D-E Khlong Jaak Bungalows, Simple bamboo bungalow resort. Prone to frogs in the room which can be very pleasant to hear late at night. Good slapdash atmosphere. Closed in the low season.

Ao Mai Phai

There are several new bungalow resorts in this bay from Bamboo Bay Resort to Last Resort. All offer roughly the same style accommodation in **C-F** range – simple bamboo bungalows with varying degrees of access to the sea/views etc. All seem friendly. Difficult to get to in the rainy season given the bad state of the road, but a good escape from the more built-up resort areas on Koh Lanta and within easy reach of the national park.

Eating

Koh Lanta *p494, map p496*

All the guesthouses provide restaurants with similar menus; Thai and European food with lots of seafood and fruit.

In Sala Dan there are some small cafés, Swiss Bakery and Santos, good pastries and coffee. Three restaurants overlook the bay between Lanta Yai and Lanta Noi (rather windy): Seaview 1 (aka 'Monkey in the Back'), slow service, good seafood, no electricity, cheap. Seaview 2, larger menu, Thai and seafood, friendly, cheap. The enormous scones are tasty and filling. On the main road nearer Sala Dan Pier up from Royal Lanta Resort and along from the Lanta Tourist Center is Mr Bean's. This café/bar does excellent coffee, roast dinners, breakfast and also offers one-day visa runs. Partly English-run.

Ban Koh Lanta Yai

ΨΨ **Krue Lanta Yai Restaurant**, at end of 'town', T075-697062. Hours variable. A restaurant on the pier along a walkway filled with plants. Good selection of fresh seafood nicely prepared. Recommended.

Ψ **Fresh Restaurant**, in old fishermen's cottage. One half of this place is a grocery store. Standard Thai fare.

Ψ **Rom Thai**, next to Krue Lanta Yai. Downmarket – also sells seafood but not as sophisticated a menu. Again set up on pier .

Ao Khlong Dao

ΨΨΨ **Sayang Beach Resort Restaurant**, Klong Dao Beach by **Lanta Sand Resort and Spa**. Excellent Malay-Thai fusion cuisine here – easily among the best along the West coast cooked with real flair and precision. Recommended.

ΨΨ **Danny's**, southern end of Khlong Dao beach. Huge menu of seafood, Thai and international, Sun evening Thai buffets are very popular.

Ao Phra-Ae

ΨΨ-Ψ **Mr Wee Pizzeria**. This unfortunately named place does rather good oven pizza in an open-air beachfront restaurant on Ao Phra-Ae. Near the **Ozone bar**. Fire shows and cheap drinks too. Hip hop and soul – thumpy and predictable but the pizza hits the spot.

Shopping

Koh Lanta *p494, map p496*

Only basic supplies available in Sala Dan and Ban Koh Lanta Yai. **Minimart** on Khlong Dao beach open in high season.

Activities and tours

Koh Lanta *p494, map p496*

Cookery classes

Time for Lime, T075-684590/09-4745171, www.timeforlime.net. Contact Junie Kovacs. Learn Thai cookery on the beach.

Diving

Several schools in Sala Dan (some with German spoken); check equipment before signing on. Snorkelling is known locally as 'snorking'. Most guesthouses hire out equipment for about ฿30

per day, although the quality varies. **Blue Planet Divers**, 3 Moo 1, T075-684165. **Lanta Discovery Divers**, Long Beach Resort, T075-684035/01-7972703. **Scool Divers**, T075-684654.

Horse riding

Mr Yat Riding School, Long Beach (Ao Phra-Ae), T09-0211924/07-2646368. Riding along the beach and in the forest, 1½ hrs, ฿650.

Island and snorkelling trips

All bungalows offer day trips to Trang's Andaman Islands (see page 509), ฿350 per person or ฿600 per boat including lunch and snorkelling gear. (Note that it is a long trip – 3 hrs each way – and some people find the noise unbearable for just an hour or two's snorkelling.) You can also organize trips from Ban Koh Lanta Yai. For long-tail boat trips contact **Sun Fishing and Island Tours**, 1/4 Sreraya Rd, Moo 1, T09-0760251. Boats leaving from this side of the island can save a couple of hours from the return trip to Koh Ngai and will take you to explore some of the islands on the east side. There are a couple of small tour shops running these businesses in the old town, and **Khrua Lanta Yai** also runs boat trips. A ferry leaves Sala Dan at 0830 for the day trip to Phi Phi, ฿240 per person. Fishing trips are organized by **La Creperie**, ฿450 per day, ฿1,200 for 2 days (which includes camping on a deserted island with food provided). Encourage your boatman to buoy, rather than use an anchor which damages the coral. Comprehensive island tours are offered by a number of tour agencies based in Sala Dan. **Opal** has reasonably priced tours and excellent service. **South Nature Travel** offers a full tour of the island including sea canoes, see also Tour operators below.

Tour operators

Makaira Tour Centre, 18 Moo 1 Sala Dan. **Sala Dan Travel Centre**, **O & M Travel**, **IC Travel**, are all in Sala Dan. **South Nature Travel**, T075-623164. Most bungalows can also make travel arrangements.

Transport

Koh Lanta *p494, map p496*

The laterite roads are rough.

Boat

Boats leave from Sala Dan on the northern tip of the island and from Lanta Pier on the southeast coast. Connections with Klong Chi Lard Pier in **Krabi**, 2 hrs via Koh Jum, ฿150. Departures 0900 and 1300 Lanta to Krabi. There is no ferry from Krabi to Lanta (and vice versa) in the wet season. During the high season there are daily boats between Lanta and **Phi Phi**. In the wake of the 'economic tsunami', it is best to check these services as many were curtailed due to lack of passengers.

Hire long-tailed boats from bungalows for ฿800 per day or from Ban Koh Lanta Yai.

Mountain bike

Hire from bungalows for A130 per day.

Motorbike

Hire from bungalows for ฿250 per day or ฿40 per hr, or in Sala Dan.

Pick-up trucks

Some ply the island, ฿100 to end of the island, others serve individual bungalows only.

Directory

Koh Lanta *p494, map p496*

Banks Siam City Bank Exchange in Sala Dan. **Medical services** Health centre, Sala Dan. Hospital, Lanta Pier. **Post office** Lanta Pier. **Useful addresses** Police Sala Dan.

Trang and its islands

→ Colour map 4, grid C3.

On first sight, Trang looks like a somewhat drab but industrious Chinese-Thai town, filled with temples and decent schools – in other words – a good place to raise your children. Everything shuts down at around 2230 in the evening and even the traffic signals seem to go to sleep while early morning is filled with bustling tradespeople, eager to make their fortunes and provide for their families. But there is an underlying cranky charm and no-nonsense energy to this port town which is famous for its char-grilled pork, sweet cakes and as the birthplace of former Prime Minister Chuan Leekpai. Its unique entertainments include bull-fights (bull to bull) and bird-singing competitions (bird to bird) while the people are hugely friendly and exceptionally helpful the minute they realize that you like Trang too. Curiously, Trang also seems to have the highest concentration of 1970s Starksy and Hutch *Datsuns of anywhere in the world, with everyone from taxi drivers to Chinese matriarchs favouring this make.*

Finally, Trang has a nine-day Vegetarian festival in October, similar to that celebrated in Phuket, where vegetarian patriots dressed all in white parade the street with spikes in their cheeks. If, however, you can't bear the idea of staying in Trang too long, it is an excellent jumping-off point for the exotic coral islands just off the coast.

▸▸ *For Sleeping, Eating and other activities see pages 512-517.*

Ins and outs

Getting there and around

Trang has an airport, 20 mins from town, and an a/c minibus costs ฿50 and drops you outside the train station. Buses arrive at the Thanon Huay Yod terminal but buses from Satun arive at Thanon Ratsada which is further out. To visit the islands you need to arrange minibuses to Pak Bara in the high season (May-Nov). There are also two overnight trains from Bangkok which stop at the station on the western end of Thanon Rama VI. ▸▸ *See Transport, page 516, for further information.*

Best time to visit

The best time to visit is between January and April, out of the monsoon season. In the low season, some of the islands close down except for one or two bungalow set-ups so you do need to check availability. If you have found a place during the low season then you need a bus to Langu and from there a tuk-tuk, songthaew or cab (if you can find one).

Tourist information

There is a temporary tourist office at the railway station.

Background

The town was established as a trading centre in the first century AD and flourished between the seventh and 12th centuries. Its importance rested on its role as a relay point for communications between the east coast of Thailand and Palembang (Srivijaya) in Sumatra. It was then known as Krung Thani and later as Trangkhapura, the 'City of Waves'. The name was shortened in the 19th century to Trang. During the Ayutthaya period, the town was located at the mouth of the river and was a popular port of entry for western visitors continuing north to Ayutthaya. Later, during King Mongkut's reign, the town was moved inland because of frequent flooding.

The arrival of the Teochew (Chinese) community in the latter half of the 19th century was a boon to the local economy which, until the introduction of rubber from Malaysia, was reliant on tin mining. Trang's rubber plantations were the first in

Thailand (the first tree was planted just south of the city) and its former ruler, Phraya Rasdanupradit Mahitsara Phakdi, is credited with encouraging the spread of its cultivation. He also built the twisting road from Trang across the Banthat Range to Phattalung. There is a statue of him 1 km out of town on the Phattalung road.

Trang

Trang has retained the atmosphere of a Chinese immigrant community, many of whom would be descendents of those who fled the corrupt and oppressive Manchu government. There are good Chinese restaurants and several Chinese shrines dotted throughout the town that hold individual festivals. The **Kwan Tee Hun shrine**, dedicated to a bearded war god, is in Ban Bang Rok, 3 km north of Trang on Route 4. The Vegetarian Festival centres around the **Kiw Ong Eia Chinese Temple** and **Muean Ram.** There is also the **Rajamangkala Aquarium** ⓘ *T075-248201-5, open daily during 'official hours'*, which lies 30 km from the city on the road to Pakmeng and is housed in the Fishery Faculty of the Rajamangkala Institute of Technology. The aquarium has 61 tanks of freshwater and marine life. Former **Prime Minister Chuan Leekpai's house** (ask locally for directions) has also become a pilgrimage spot of sorts and is open to visitors.

Beaches around Trang

Trang's embryonic tourism industry has so far escaped the hard sell of Phuket and Pattaya – excellent news for nature lovers, reef divers and explorers. The strip of coast

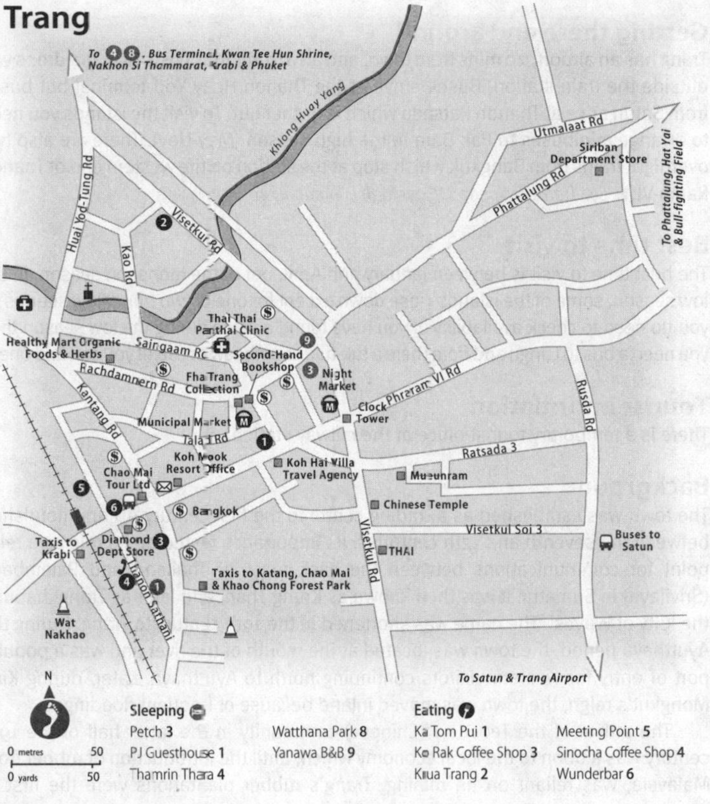
Trang
To 4 8. Bus Terminal, Kwan Tee Hun Shrine, Nakhon Si Thammarat, Krabi & Phuket
Khlong Huay Yang
Utmalaat Rd
Siriban Department Store
Phattalung Rd
To Phattalung, Hat Yai & Bull-fighting Field
Huai Yod-Tung Rd
Visetkul Rd
Kao Rd
Thai Thai
Panthai Clinic
Healthy Mart Organic Foods & Herbs
Saingaam Rd
Second-Hand Bookshop
Rachdamnern Rd
Fha Trang Collection
Night Market
Phraram VI Rd
Kentang Rd
Clock Tower
Municipal Market
Rusda Rd
Tala 1 Rd
Koh Mook Resort Office
Koh Hai Villa Travel Agency
Ratsada 3
Chao Mai Tour Ltd
Muaunram
Bangkok
Chinese Temple
Visetkul Soi 3
Taxis to Krabi
Diamond Dept Store
THAI
Buses to Satun
Thanon Sathani
Taxis to Katang, Chao Mai & Khao Chong Forest Park
Wat Nakhao
To Satun & Trang Airport
N
0 metres 50
0 yards 50
Sleeping
Petch 3
PJ Guesthouse 1
Thamrin Thara 4
Watthana Park 8
Yanawa B&B 9
Eating
Ka Tom Pui 1
Ko Rak Coffee Shop 3
Kua Trang 2
Meeting Point 5
Sinocha Coffee Shop 4
Wunderbar 6

running south from Pakmeng (38 km west from Trang) round to Kantang, boasts some of the south's best beaches. Unfortunately, it is also a relatively expensive place to stay with frankly exorbitant rates charged at some of the more popular beaches and islands and very ordinary food. **Pakmeng and Chang Lang** beaches are the most accessible – 40 km west of Trang town. The sea is poor here for swimming but it's a nice place to walk, although scarcely as scenic as the beaches of Koh Lanta or Krabi.

To the north, down the road from Sikao, is **Hua Hin** which has a good beach and is famed for its *hoi tapao* – sweet-fleshed oysters. Unfortunately the oyster season climaxes in November – the peak of the wet season. Hua Hin Bay is dotted with limestone outcrop islets. Other beaches to the south include **Hat San, Hat Yong Ling, Hat Yao** and **Hat Chao Mai**; private ventures are not permitted at any of the beaches within the national park (ie Hat Chao Mai, Hat Yong Ling and Hat San).

Parks

Hat Chao Mai National Park ⓘ *taxis to Pakmeng, Chao Mai, Katang and Palien leave from outside Trang's Diamond Department Store, near the railway station*, **Hat Yao** has some impressive caves near the village, known for their layered curtain stalactites. The beaches and many of the offshore islands fall under the jurisdiction of the 230 sq km Hat Chao Mai National Park. Accommodation is available at park headquarters (6 km outside Chao Mai). See Sleeping.

Khao Chong Forest Park ⓘ *20 km from town, off the Trang-Phattalung rd, taxis leave from outside the Diamond Department Store, near the railway station, ฿100, or get a local bus (from the bus station on Huay Yod Rd), bound for Phattalung or Hat Yai, ฿10*, supports one of the few remaining areas of tropical forest in the area and has two waterfalls, Nam Tok Ton Yai and Nam Tok Ton Noi). Government resthouses are available here.

Trang's Andaman Islands → *Colour map 4, grid C2.*

Trang's Andaman Islands number 47 in total and spread out to the south of Koh Lanta. More tourists are visiting the islands and their beauty, rich birdlife, and the clear waters that surround them make upmarket future development highly likely. The best time to visit the area is between January-April. The weather is unsuitable for island-hopping from May-December and although it is sometimes still possible to charter boats out of season, it can be expensive and risky: the seas are rough, the water is cloudy and you may be stranded by a squall or equally by the boatmen's incompetency and a vessel which was never seaworthy in the first place. There is a also a tendency to overbook these boats and consequent delays as the operators wait for further customers. See Sleeping for accommodation on the islands.

Check the weather forecast service, T02-3994012/3 (nationwide) if you plan to charter a boat out of season.

Koh Ngai (Hai)

This 5-sq-km island is cloaked in jungle and fringed with glorious beaches. It also enjoys fabulous views of the **limestone stacks** that pepper the sea around it. A coral reef sweeps down the eastern side, ending in two big rocks, between which rips a strong current – but the **coral** around these rocks is magnificent. Koh Ngai is the clichéd resort island retreat where you wake up, eat and sleep at the same place. There are only three resorts on this island and no local community. If you like this sort of intense group intimacy, Koh Ngai is perfect but guests have complained of cabin fever setting in after a week. It is more suited to honeymooners or those who will stay here as a base and do day trips to other islands. Although Koh Ngai forms the southernmost part of Krabi province and is most easily reached from Pakmeng in

Trang province, 16 km away, it is also possible to get there from Koh Phi Phi and Koh Lanta. Tourists also stop here on island-hopping day trips to eat at one of the three resorts and to snorkel in the magnificently clear waters which are rich with marine life.

Koh Chuak and **Koh Waen** (between Koh Hai and Koh Muk) are also snorkellers' havens – the latter is the best reef for **seafan corals.**

Koh Muk (Mook)

On the western side of Koh Muk is the **Emerald Cave** (Tham Morakot) – known locally as Tham Nam – which can only be entered by boat (or fearless swimmers) at low tide, through a narrow opening. After the blackness of the 80-m-long passage it opens into daylight again at an inland beach straight out of Jurassic Park – emerald water ringed with powdery white sand and a backdrop of precipitous cliffs that look as if they are made of black lava frozen over the centuries. This is a tiny beach, however, which could accommodate up to 20 people at a time and that would feel crowded. The cave was only discovered during a helicopter survey not very long ago and is thought to have been a pirates' lair. **Be warned**, you can only leave the pool at low tide. Unfortunately this is being oversold and there have been groups of Southeast Asian tourists who combine the swimming into the cave with positive reinforcement songs that can be heard up to a mile away as everyone shouts in

Trang's Andaman Islands

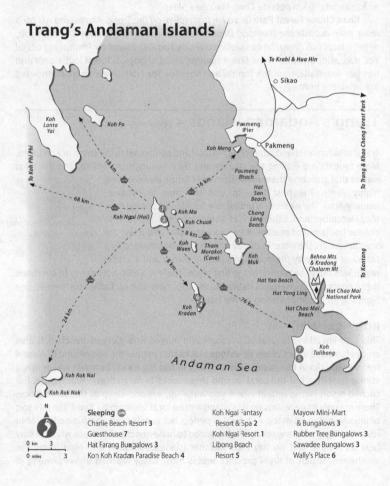

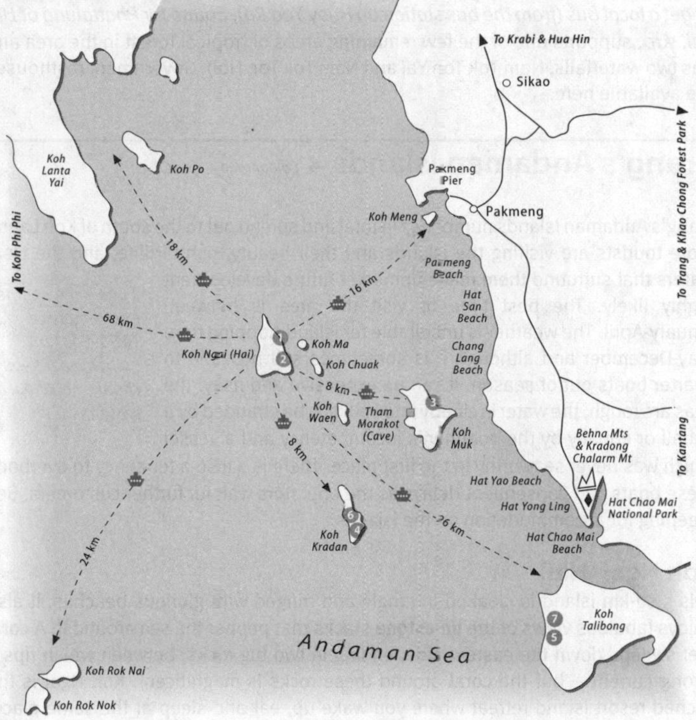

unison – 'we can do this' and 'we will succeed, onward, onward'. Unless you are in with the crowd, this is unfailingly depressing and totally destroys the mystique of this one-off place. The only way around the group scene is to hire a long-tail boat privately and try to go at an early hour although the tide does dictate when it is safe to swim in. The death of some tourists in the Emerald Cave at the peak of the tsunami may have dampened people's urge to visit, particularly as it is a daunting swim. If you hire a private boatmen, he can swim in with you and hold your hand which helps immensely. A torch is also a good idea as is snorkelling gear, which you may just be brave enough to try on the way out. If you do snorkel, you will be rewarded with schools of hundreds of parrot-coloured tropical fish swimming around you. The trick in getting through the cave psychologically intact is to look backwards as you swim so that you can always see a little light reflected on the cave walls. However, unless you are with a boatman who knows the way, this is impossible as you do need to turn left at some point. The entire swim only takes about 15-20 minutes. The island's west coast has white beaches backed by high cliffs where swallows nest. There are also beautiful beaches on the east coast facing the craggy mainland.

Koh Kradan

Koh Kradan, most of which falls within the bounds of the Chao Mai National Park, is regarded as the most beautiful of Trang's islands, with splendid **beaches** and **fine coral**, on the east side. Two **Japanese warships** sunk during the Second World War lie off the shore and are popular dive spots. The area not encompassed by the national park is a mixture of rubber smallholdings and coconut groves. The island – bar the park area – is privately owned, having been bought by tycoon Mon Sakunmethanon in 1985 for ฿5 million. It only has two places to stay, see Sleeping. There has been talk of a day centre set up by one of the major resort groups which would have a restaurant, bar and boutique but nothing has been finalized yet.

Koh Talibong (Libong)

Koh Talibong (Libong), which is part of the Petra Islands group to the south, is renowned for its **oysters** and **birdlife**. The Juhoi Cape and the eastern third of the island is a major stopping-off point for migratory birds, and in March and April the island is an ornithologist's El Dorado. Typical visitors, on their way back to northern latitudes, include brown-headed gulls, crab plovers, four species of terns, waders, curlews, godwits, redshanks, greenshanks, reef egrets and black-necked storks. From October to March the island is famed for its unique Hoi Chakteen oysters. The rare **manatee** (*Manatus senegalensis*) and the **green turtle** also inhabit the waters off the island. The best coral reef is off the southwest coast, directly opposite the **Libong Beach Resort**. Snorkelling equipment is available from the resort which also provides fishing gear. Libong's main town is Ban Hin Kao, where the daily ferry from Kantang docks. Motorcycle taxis take visitors along rough trails to the island's beaches and villages. There is one hotel on the island and no nightlife. The population is almost exclusively Muslim, and alcohol is not widely available so you would need to stock up in Trang.

Koh Sukorn (Muu), Koh Petra, Koh Lao Lieng (Nua and Tai)

Koh Sukorn, Koh Petra, Koh Lao Lieng (Nua and Tai) are also part of the Petra Islands group, off Palien, 47 km south of Trang, and can be reached from there or Kantang. Koh Sukorn (locally known as Koh Muu – or Pig Island) is inhabited by Muslims, who do not seem to mind the name. Apart from its golden powdery beaches, its main claim to fame are the mouth-watering watermelons that are grown here (March/April).

Koh Petra and **Koh Lao Lieng** have sheer cliffs which are the domain of the birds' nest collectors who risk life and limb for swiftlet saliva (see box, page 488). The islands have excellent sandy beaches on their east coasts and impressive reefs which are exposed at low tide. Dolphins can often be seen offshore.

Sleeping

Trang *p508, map p508*

Most of Trang's hotels are on Phraram VI Rd, between the clock tower and the railway station. More recently a number of high-rise luxury hotels have sprung up slightly further out of town, although these are mainly patronized by visiting business men in town on conferences.

A Thamrin Thara, 69/8 Huay Yod Rd, T075-223223. Considered to be the No 1 hotel in town with 285 rooms. The double rooms are more expensive than twins. Dominating, dreary and corporate. Not particularly good service. Plumbing is fine although the water pressure isn't up to much.

B Wattana Park, 315/7 Huayyod Rd, T075-216216/217217, www.wattanaparkhotel.com. Very central on the road in from Krabi. A modern hotel with good rooms and friendly service. Suites are good value for families intending to spend a while in Trang. There's little to choose between the standard and de luxe rooms, but in any case this is probably the best value business-class hotel in Trang. Does not have a pool. Recommended.

D Yannawa Bed and Breakfast, Visetkul Rd. Clean, comfortable rooms in a shophouse. Good price and helpful staff. But slightly crammed with furniture and dark. Recommended at this price.

E Petch, T075-218002. Good value, large, cheap rooms, some have attached bathroom with squat toilet, restaurant, friendly.

E PJ Guesthouse, 25/12 Sathani, down from Diamond Department Store. Home-like set-up with traveller ambience and attention to detail. In fact, for once the catch-line "Your home, second home" really does ring true. Café downstairs serves reasonably priced Western food. 8 fan rooms over 2 floors, some with balconies and window. Small but not too dark and very clean. Shared shower and toilet per floor. Tour service downstairs. Motorbike rental. Joy and Pong are helpful owners and both speak good English. Intriguing and sometimes seedy guests but a good bargain. Recommended.

Beaches around Trang *p508*

AL-A Amari Trang Beach Resort, 199 Moo 5, Had Pak Meng, Changlang Beach, T075-205888, www.amari.com. Newly opened spa and 138 sea front rooms in a contemporary, minimalist low-rise. The Amari also has a speedboat shuttle to the exclusive private day resort of Koh Kradan which you may need as the beach here is poor and not particualarly clean. For entertainment in this isolated spot the Amari offers five restaurants and a pool.

B Lay Trang Resort, Pakmeng, T075-274027-8/9. A bungalow resort just up from the pier. Good seafood restaurant, well built and well equipped resort. Sea canoes and guides for hire. The resort will also arrange camping on the nearby islands, complete with picnic and mobile phone.

B-C Pakmeng Resort, Pakmeng, T075-218940. Turn left after reaching the main seafront and continue on towards the national park. The resort is on the left and is well-marked. Wooden bungalows with attached bathroom and fan and some a/c. The resort backs onto the main khlong leading to the river. Good restaurant. Television in rooms may not always work but staff will change it. Motorbikes (฿250 per day) and bicycles (฿70 per day) for rent.

C-E Barn Chom Talay – Seaview Guest House, Hat Yao. Dormitory room and bungalows all clean and well-furnished. The daughter of the owners speaks excellent English. Also offers every type of tour including kayak rental, trips to the nearby caves, and boat tours to the islands. A pleasant out-of-the-way place to stay. Recommended.

Parks *p509*

D Hat Chao Mai National Park Bungalows. There is no restaurant here – you can buy food from a very small shop in Chao Mai village.

Koh Ngai (Hai) *p509, map p510*

L Koh Ngai Resort, book through the Trang office, 205 Sam-Yaek Mohwith, T075-210317 or on the island T075-211045, see www.asiatravel.com/thailand/prepaidhotels/kohngairesort/. Southeastern corner of the island, with its own magnificent private beach. Completely chi-chi, massive development, around 60 suites, cottages, villas and bungalows all a/c with private

balconies, overpriced, but the service is friendly and the food has improved. Dominates the beachfront.

A-AL Koh Ngai Fantasy Resort and Spa, next door to **Koh Ngai Villa**, T075-211045. A/c bungalows and family suites. Obscured in the foliage of this idyllic island. Pool. Stately rooms. Has been upgraded since its early days and now has decent food.

A-C Koh Ngai Villa, halfway up the eastern side of the island, facing the reef, contact **Koh Koh Ngai Villa Travel Agency** in Trang, T075-210496. A range of new and old chalets some with a/c, others with mosquito nets, restaurant, tents also available (฿150). The food is awful, service unfriendly, and the rooms overpriced but the beach is gorgeous.

Koh Muk *p510, map p510*

The majority of the accommodation here shuts 6 months of the year due to navigational difficulties and drought. Koh Muk has seen a bit of a boom accommodation-wise for an island with this size of a beach – under a 1 km with rocks both ends. There are now around 20 resorts up from only one not so very long ago. The beach side of the island where the resorts are, is dominated by **Charlie Beach Resort** that has a pay toilet while there are scrappier, more individual set-ups behind the beach – including one with tents that have proper spring mattresses inside. The other side of the island also has accommodation, none of which is recommended as the village is fairly unsightly, the beach filthy and the still pools of stagnant water likely to encourage dengue fever. It is improbable that this side of the island will be developed as the beach offers so little in the way of natural beauty. However, it is worth a walk over as there is both a Muslim fishing village and a sea gypsy hamlet side by side. The sea gypsy village was completely demolished by the tsunami, along with all their equipment. However, it is in the process of being rebuilt although it is unclear along what lines and timescale. For the present, Koh Muk attracts an independent traveller still as there is limited electricity and water supplies with the exception of **Charlie Beach Resort**. Entertainment here is rough and ready as you make it – there is a new nightclub set up in a colourfully painted concrete bungalow in the bush and you can always drink with the local characters who are still curious about visitors.

AL-B Charlie Beach Resort, T075-203281-3. Smack dab in the centre of the beach. This is for the Ikea and home entertainment set. The bungalows are faultlessly clean and the restaurant and bar serve decent food including a selection of bread although the pizza is substandard. But there are no surprises here and the pay toilet with attendants outside on an island this size and of this character is unforgiveable, particularly when you have just come off a rough boat journey across the Andaman. With the exception of the manager, the staff are too conspicuously concerned with whether you will stay there, running to the boat the minute it arrives with great cheers of welcome and sidling off grumpily when you go elsewhere despite the fact that it is only yards away and you will no doubt bump into them again. **Charlie**'s offers a souvenir shop selling standard batik skirts and fishermen's trousers plus it operates the only boat service on the island.

D Hat Farang Bunglaows, near **Mayow** on the hilly part, with 13 bamboo bungalows with attached bathroom and toilet. It doesn't get much light as it's in the foliage but it is closer to the beach.

D Mayow Mini-Mart and Bungalows, over a little wooden walkway to the right of **Sawadee**. 5 bungalows with showers and toilet outside. Mayow is the name of the female owner and she also has a café/kitchen which does good fried fish and banana fritters along with Thai curries. It also operates **Dugong Dugong Travel** which arranges snorkelling and diving.

D Rubber Tree Bungalows. T075-203284/01-2704148. Across from **Mayow**, up a long wooden staircase cut into the hill are these marvellous family-run bungalows. Attached toilet and bathroom. These are set in a working rubber tree plantation so that you may be woken early in the morning by the lanterns of the rubber tree tappers. You are welcome to join them in their work as an observer. The attached restaurant has easily the best food on the island – cooked by a Northern Thai native. Let her choose what to cook if you can't

decide. She is good at whatever she does. This is a magical place to have an evening drink too – the twinkling lights up the staircase are strangely reminiscent of a Southern plantation. Recommended.

D Sawadee Bungalows, T075-207964-5, sawadeeresort64@yahoo.com. Next to **Charlie's**. Basic wooden bungalows on stilts set into hill. Own bathroom. Romantic spot as it is at the end of the beach where it is rather rocky and private. Good view of sunset. The owners also employ a wonderful old man from the village who goes about sweeping up the fallen leaves from underneath the bungalows. Attached restaurant does mean and bland portions of Thai food but is okay for morning coffee and fruit salad. Attracts divers, surfers, travellers. Electricity only 4 hrs a day. Recommended.

E Mookies. Down the lane/dirt path towards the sea gypsy village (there is only one path on from Rubber Tree). Cross over a wooden bridge and follow the disco music to **Mookie's Bar** where you are likely to find Aussie expat non pareil Russell Manton a.k.a Mookie reading pulp fiction and drinking in the mid-afternoon. This is a completely eccentric set-up – Russell has large tents set up with spring mattresses and 24-hr electricity with light and fan inside. While the toilet and shower is shared, they are kept clean to military standards. Open all year round. The shower outside also has hot water. The only drawback to **Mookies** are Russell's seriously pongy dogs. Highly recommended. See also Eating.

Koh Kradan *p511, map p510*

B-C Koh Kradan Paradise Beach. Book through Trang office, 25/36 Sathani Rd, T075-211367/02-3920635 (Bangkok). The Trang office also runs a daily boat service to the island, A240 return. Expensive for the quality of accommodation. Concrete bungalows that have been painted to look like wooden bungalows, failing miserably. Recent visitors have been disappointed as the resort is rundown with poor rooms at this price. Visitors regularly complain that the restaurant is one of the poorest in Thailand. However, the staff are friendly and the island is wonderful. Tents are available for ฿150.

D Wally's Place. The only other accommodation on this island. 3 wooden bungalows with outside toilet and shower on southwest side of the island. Does Western and Thai food. Wally, an American ex-sailor, also tells good stories.

Koh Talibong (Libong) *p511, map p510*

A-C Libong Beach Resort, Ban Lan Khao, T075-210013, or in Trang, T075-214676. Large open-fronted restaurant with about 15 basic bungalows set in a coconut grove facing onto a sandy beach. Overpriced, as is most of Trang's island accommodation.

Guesthouse, 5 km from the main town Ban Hin Khao, run by the **Conservation of Wildlife Committee** at Laem Juhol on the east coast. The guesthouse must be booked in advance, and food is not available; letters to the secretary at the Libong Regional Department, PO Box 5, Kantang, Trang 92110, T075-251932.

Koh Sukhorn *p511, map p510*

A-D Sukorn Cabana Resort, T075-207707. Has bungalows and tents so suitable for families and backpackers. Bunglaows are set in coconut trees with attached bathrooms.

C-D Sukhorn Beach Bungalows, T075-211457, www.sukorn-island-trang.com. Owned by a Dutchman, some individual bungalows, some attached. Excellent restaurant, private beach frontage, bikes for rent, tours arranged.

D The Small Sea, Sukorn Island via Ta Sae Pier, T09-7277761/01-5358283. 5 simple bamboo bungalows with fan and attached bathroom on beach corner so that you can see the sun rise and the sun set. Restaurant with Thai food. Arranges fishing trips, snorkelling and motorbikes. Contact Pu who is bald and who offers a 20% discount for 'skinheads'. We believe he means bald people. Recommended.

Eating

Trang *p508, map p508*

Trang's BBQ pork is delicious and one of the town's few claims to national fame. It is made from a traditional recipe brought here by the town's immigrant Chinese community and is usually served with dim sum. It's the speciality of several Chinese restaurants and can also be bought from street vendors. Only available in the morning. The best place to get this is **Trang**

Moo Yang on Huay Yod Rd. This local restaurant is a morning establishment only and is open from 0500-1100/1200. It caters to everyone and you will see the broadest cross-section of people here. About 10 mins by tuk-tuk from the centre of town.

Chinese

¶¶¶-¶¶ **Ko Lan**, Huai Yod Rd. Trang-style BBQ pork.

International

¶ **Meeting Point Restaurant and Internet Café**. Right along from the railway station, this does a good breakfast, decent coffees in an airy café with tiled ceramic floor and wooden benches. For some reason there are pictures of North American Indians on the wall. Also has a little bar. Recommended.

Opposite the Meeting Point are stalls and a Roti Bread Place as well as M & P Bakery.

Thai

There are several restaurants on Visetkul Rd offering excellent Thai food, and a couple of coffee shops catering to more western tastes. This area appears to be a hub for tourism development with souvenir shops on the corner opposite the clock tower and on the road itself.

¶¶ **Krua Trang**, Visetkul Rd. Excellent food and draft Carlsberg beer. The stuffed steamed seabass is a specialty and delicious (filleted, stuffed with shrimp and vegetables and then steamed) but we were very impressed with the entire range of food served on our last visit. Staff were friendly and helpful at recommending dishes.

¶ **Kao Tom Pui Restaurant**, 111 Praram Rd, T075-210127. Since 1967. Family restaurant, very popular with the locals, an unpretentious café setting with Sino-Portugese feel. Does cauldrons of seafood soup, excellent seafood dishes, including steamed bass. Good vegetables – morning glory with garlic especially nice. Regulars include local gangsters and their girls and large families. Recommended.

¶ **Ko Rak Coffee Shop,** also called Somrak, 158-160 Kantang Rd. Superb café in dilapidated old building with wooden shutter doors that are forever open to a street filled with stalls. Sells tender duck and pork rice as well as sticky mango. The family who runs this packed café is originally from Shanghai and first came to Trang over 70 years ago. The elderly owner is exceptionally proud of his marble tables which have never been changed. Full of bustle and good grub. Recommended.

¶ **Sinocha Coffee Shop**. Next to train station on the left, opposite Diamond Department Store. Interesting art deco touches in this café with lovely marquetry though it is rundown and rather dirty. Does a good selection of coffees and decent pastries though the omelettes are too greasy and not very nice at all. Service variable. Popular hang-out with tuk-tuk drivers and locals.

¶ **Wunderbar**, 24 Sathani Rd. Western cuisine in small dark wooden café. Good selection of magazines and papers. Decent breakfast and excellent place to pick up information. Also does cheeses if you have a hankering for dairy products. Comforting drinking hole in the evening. Recommended.

Foodstalls

2 night markets offer good food, one is on Visetkul Rd, north of clock tower, the other is in the square in front of the railway station.

Hat Yao *p508*

$ **Hat Yao Seafood** is a very good restaurant which is open-fronted and looks out onto the beach.

Koh Muk *p510, map p510*

$ **Mookies Bar** does spare ribs, hamburgers, grilled chicken but you need to order ahead of time so he can get the supplies from the mainland. The entertainment here is provided through the colourful tales of Russell who first came to Thailand in 1969.

Festivals and events

Trang *p508*

Oct Vegetarian Festival (movable). 9-day festival in which a strict vegetarian diet is observed to purify the body. Mediums pierce their cheeks and tongues with spears and walk on hot coals. On the 6th day a procession makes its way around town, in which everyone dresses in traditional costumes. The same event occurs in Phuket.

Shopping

Trang *p508, map p508*

Best buys in Trang include locally woven cotton and wickerwork and sponge cake! Thaklang and Municipal markets are next door to each other in the centre of town, off Rachdamnern Rd.

For a good selection of whiskies and liquors visit **Trang Sura Thip Whiskey Shop** which looks like a log cabin on the inside. This tobacco and whiskey shop is on 69/1 Praram 6 near the clocktower.

For English magazines and language books try **Charonemwit Bookstore** at 88-88/1 Praram 6 Rd and Kantang Rd. Family-run and very helpful staff.

Fha Trang Collection, 283 Radchadamneon Rd, T075-217004. Posh and pretty souvenirs reasonably priced. Embroidered shoes, scarves, artistic mobiles and folk craft. There is also a second-hand bookshop next door.

Activities and tours

Trang *p508, map p508*

Bull fighting

Fights between bulls take place at random, depending on whether the farmers have a suitable bull. The only way to find out about whether they are taking place is to ask around. But be warned – this is a very much a local entertainment and you might get some curious looks when you ask, particularly if you are a woman. The fights are usually held during the week and only in the mornings and afternoons. They occur in a field off Trang-Pattalung Rd near the MP Resort Hotel and Praya Ratsadanupradit Monument. The best way to get there is by tuk-tuk which takes about 20 mns from the railway station. Scarcely any women attend these events. They are always packed by an excitable betting crowd yelping with dismay or joy and there are plenty of stalls about selling drinks and foods including noodles and fruit. Dusty and hot but exciting.

Snorkelling

Trang Travel, Thumrin Sq, see below. Equipment for hire.

Therapies

Ministry of Health Spa, Panthai Clinic, 32-34-36 Saingam Rd. This superb spa does everything from ear candles – to remove wax – to moxibusiton (Gwyneth Paltrow is a great fan of this detoxification process which involves hot suction caps) You can also get acupuncture here and Chinese remedies as well as Thai massage. Reasonable prices in beautiful surroundings. Highly professional.

Underwater weddings

Trang Underwater Weddings. These occur in Feb. For information contact the Trang Chamber of Commerce, T075-225353.

Tour operators

Choa Mai Tour Ltd, 15 Satanee Rd, contact Jongkoolnee Usaha, T075-216380. Reliable and trustworthy, go out of their way to help. Does hotel and resort reservation, tourist information, airport reservations and a/c bus/van and tours. Nearly everyone here speaks a decent level of English. Recommended.

Trang Travel, Thumrin Sq, T075-219598/9. Runs a boat and offers day-long excursions for a minimum of 4, visiting islands and reefs on request, for ฿500-600 (including lunch and snorkelling equipment) in high season only (Oct-Apr).

Koh Ngai (Hai) *p509, map p510*

Diving

Rainbow Divers, in *Koh Ngai Resort*, T075-211045. Run by a German couple, they offer PAD courses and excursions, open from mid-Nov until the end of Apr.

Transport

Trang *p508, map p508*

Air

The airport is 7 km from town. Daily connections on THAI with **Bangkok**, 2 hrs 10 mins.

Airline offices **Thai**, 199 Visetkul Rd (not in the centre of town), T075-218066.

Boat

For boats to Trang's Andaman Islands, see below. International connections with **Langkawi, Malaysia**: 4 ferries daily from Satun and Langkawi Island (at 0845, 1200,

1530 and 1700). Get a bus to Satun (1 hr 10 mins, ฿200).

Bus
To most places buses leave from the bus terminal 1 km out of town on the Huay Yat road – the exception are the buses to **Satun** which leave from the terminal on Rusda Rd. Overnight connections with **Bangkok**, 12 hrs, and regular connections with **Satun**, 2 hrs, **Hat Yai**, 2 hrs, **Phuket**, every 30 mins, 5-6 hrs, ฿175, **Krabi**, ฿30, **Phattalung**, ฿15 and **Nakhon Si Thammarat,** ฿30. There are regular buses to **Ban Pak Bara**, for **Tarutao**, (1½ hrs), 100 km north. There are also taxis to Ban Pak Bara.

Motorbike
Hire from the corner of Municipal market, Rachdamnern Rd, ฿200 per day.

Taxi
Shared taxi to **Nakhon Si Thammarat**, A60 and **Surat Thani** leave from Huai Yod Rd (near junction with Rachdamnern Rd) to **Krabi** leave from the railway station, ฿50; to **Phattalung**, ฿30 and **Hat Yai**, ฿50, leave from Phattalung Rd (opposite the police station) and to **Satun**, ฿50, they leave from Jermpanya Rd. Phuket (฿150).

Train
The station is at the end of Phraram VI Rd. 2 daily connections with **Bangkok**, 15½ hrs. You can arrange for van buses to collect you from outside the train station or along Praman 6 and Satanee Rd through your travel agent. This may cost more but if you have a lot of luggage it is worth it. You might also see if they can collect you nearer you hotel, depending on where that is. If it is along Praman 6 or one of the larger hotels they will arrange this for you.

Trang's Andaman Islands *p509, map p510*
The islands can be reached from several small ports and fishing villages along the Trang coast, the main ones being Pakmeng and Kantang, 24 km from Trang. Both are a ฿10 taxi ride from Trang. It is also possible to charter boats with the Muslim fishermen who live on the islands.

Boat
Boats leave from **Pakmeng**, about 25 km west of Trang. Minibuses leave from the junction of Huay Yod and Kantang roads in Trang, ฿30 one way. Boats from Pakmeng to **Koh Hai**, 45 mins, **Koh Muk**, 1 hr, **Koh Kradan**, 1½ hrs, same price ฿150 one way, ฿1,000-1,500 day charter for all destinations.
Kradan Island Resort operates a hovercraft which takes a maximum of 5 people, ฿600 return. For **Koh Talibong** (Libong) it is cheaper and faster to take a taxi the 24 km from Trang to Kantang, ฿10-15. From there a ferry leaves daily at 1200 for Koh Talibong's 'capital' of Ban Hin Khao and motorcycles take visitors the 5 km to the only hotel, the Libong Beach Resort. Trang Travel, opposite the Thumrin Hotel in Trang, also operates a boat which can be chartered to any of the islands. For those with less time on their hands, they offer day excursions, see Activities and tours, Trang.

Directory

Trang *p508, map p508*
Banks Banks are clustered along Phraram VI Rd. **Internet** Plenty of internet locations in town. **Post office** Jermpanya Rd.

Tarutao National Park and the far south

→ *Colour map 5, grid C4.*

While some say that Tarutao is merely a mispronunciation of the Malay word 'Ta Lo Trao' meaning 'plenty of bay', when first spying this ominous humped island rising out of the sea, it is far easier to believe a second interpretation. That is, that Tarutao comes from the Malay word for – old, mysterious and primitive. Resonating with a murky history of pirates, prisoners and ancient curses, it is no wonder the island was picked for the hit reality television series **Survivors** ***in 2002. Despite dynamite-fishing***

in some areas, the island waters still have reasonable coral, and provide some of the best dive sites in Thailand – particularly around the stone arch on Koh Khai. Adang Island has magnificent coral reefs. These are part of Thailand's best preserved and first marine park where turtles, leopard sharks, whales and dolphins can be spotted.

Inland, however, is a different story. Over half of Koh Tarutao is dense dark rainforest with only a single 12 km road cutting through the length of the island and scant paths into a potentially lethal jungle filled with poisonous snakes and volatile beasts like the wild boar. Created in 1974, the total marine national park area comprises 51 islands – the main ones being Tarutao, Adang, Rawi, Lipe, Klang, Dong and Lek. Tarutao Park itself is divided into two main sections– the Tarutao archipelago and the Adang-Rawi Archipelago.

In the far south, there is the Muslim town of Satun with its preserved shophouses and the Thale Ban National Park. ▸▸ *For Sleeping, Eating and other activities, see pages 526-532.*

Ins and outs

Getting there and around

Getting to Tarutao National Park requires some planning. For much of the year, it is not advisable to take a boat to these beautiful islands. Ferries run from November to May, but speed-boats or privately hired long-tail boats can be chartered at other times of year. If you are based on the island of Koh Lipe or Koh Bulon-Leh then private long-tail boats are advised as you will be facing a roundabout route from Satun or Ban Pak Bara otherwise and adding hours to your journey. The ferries depart from Ban Pak Bara and also from Satun's Thammalang Pier. Unless you get the first boat from Tarutao (currently departing at 1200) you can't get to Koh Lipe in one day. See Transport, page 531, for further details.

For getting around Tarutao, there is a clear market for renting bicycles to travel down the main road which, in typical Tarutao fashion, is a gruelling route of steep curves and hills occupied at times by cobras and pythons sunning themselves. The only other road on the island which is around 6 km, was built by the prisoners and links up the two prisons. ▸▸ *See Transport, page 532, for further information.*

Best time to visit

November to April are the best months. The coolest months are November and December. The park is officially closed May to October, but it is still possible to get there. Services run providing the weather is OK. Bulon Leh island is accessible year round although the vast majority of accommodation is closed six months of the year so it is wise to ring ahead.

Tourist information

There is limited eating areas, basic accommodation and scarcely any concessions to mainstream tourist activities. Most accommodation is concentrated on Koh Lipe. Bring plenty of money, as there are no bank facilities on the island, and only the dive centres accept Visa or MasterCards. Bring food as well as the general park shop has very little choice so you might want to stock up on the basics – including alcohol – and even fruit. The entrance fee for an adult is ฿200, children under 14, ฿100. In the high season, visit the national park headquarters, close to the ferry port at Pak Bara, to book accommodation on Tarutao as there can be a shortage (from here messages are radioed to the islands). Tents are bookable when accommodation is in short supply. On Koh Tarutao and Koh Adang the accommodation is Forestry Department (ie government) run; Koh Lipe and Koh Bulon-Leh are the only islands where the private sector has a presence. As a result it is on Koh Lipe and Koh Bulon-Leh where resorts are best and activites are most varied.

Background

Koh Tarutao boasts the remains of the prison that held a total of 10,000 hardened criminals and political prisoners, some of whom became pirates during the Second World War to stave off starvation. Local island rumour also has it that somewhere on Koh Tarutao 1000 kilos of gold dust looted from a French ship still remain buried along with the murdered pirates that attacked the unfortunate vessel. Not all of the prisoners on this enigmatic island were, however, pirates. Indeed the translator of the English/Thai dictionary – Sor Settabut – completed the T section of the book at Tarutao prison. Yet another scholar – staunch Royalist Prince Sithiporn Kridaka – continued his study of crop diversification that helped modernize Thailand's agricultural methods. The prince, who was educated largely in England and was a lifelong Anglophile, had been interned for his involvement in sending railway cars to jam tracks on which tanks were being brought to defend Bangkok during widespread insurrections in 1932. This Prince was also known for having invented Thailand's first shorthand – still used today – and for forming a Boy Scout troop among the youths at the government Opium Factory that he was sent to manage. Imprisoned for 11 years, the prince suffered his worst trials at Koh Tarutao where he fell prey to life-threatening dysentery. Yet, it is now believed that the political prisoners received the best of the treatment on Koh Tarutao where they may even have been served by the general criminal population. Certainly the two groups did not mix socially, with the criminals held in the eastern part at the present-day Taloh Wow Cove and the politicos detained at Udang Cove in the southern tip. Be that as it may, all suffered during the Second World War when the island was completely cut off from the outside world – along with essential food supplies. In cahoots with the guards, prisoners took to ambushing passing ships, originally for food and then, in traditional pirate fashion, for anything of value. This only came to a halt when the British, who were governing Malaysia at the time, went in with the navy to quell the pirates in 1947. Afterwards, the island was left in total isolation with the prison gradually reduced to the remains of the Prison Director's house on top of a dune along with a sawmill below and a mysterious hole indicating a torture cellar underground. Was this all perhaps a fulfilment of an ancient curse? Legend has it that centuries ago, a princess of Langkawi who had been accused of misdeeds declared that the island would never be discovered. Certainly, even today, much of Koh Tarutao holds on to its mystery with its brooding interior and inaccessibility six months of the year.

Tarutao National Park

Ban Pak Bara

The ferries to islands depart from Ban Pak Bara where there is the national park headquarters ⓘ *T074-781285/729002-3*, accommodation and services. See Sleeping.

Koh Tarutao

The mountainous island of Tarutao is the largest of the islands, 26 km long and 11 km wide and covering an area of 151 sq km. A mountainous spine runs north-south down the centre of the island, with its highest point reaching 708 m. The interior remains largely forested, cloaked in dense semi-evergreen rainforest. The main beaches are **Ao Moh Lai, Hin Ngam, Ao Phante, Ao Chak** and **Ao Sone**, mostly on the west of the island which has long sweeps of sandy beach punctuated by headlands and areas of mangrove. Ao Sone, for example, is a 3-km-long stretch of sand fringed with

Like the nearby Malaysian island Langkawi, which was also traditionally a pirates' lair, Tarutao was believed to be cursed and hidden from the outside world for seven generations.

casuarina trees. (Much of the mangrove was cut for charcoal during the early 1960s before the national park was finally gazetted in 1974.) Notorious as the beach where a tourist camping was killed by a lone pirate in the 1980s, this eerie strip has quite a physical presence, unlike any of the other beaches along the west coast. The water is aggressive and choppy while if you face towards Tarutao when you are swimming, the densely forested cliffs quite simply loom. This haunting beach, while it does have a refreshment area to one end, is not as frequented as the other beaches so that you are guaranteed some privacy (though you may not want it). Well worth the visit to Tarutao for the feeling that not everything has been tamed. You can also spot the delightfully electric Kingfisher bird here.

Tae Bu cliff, just behind the park headquarters on Ao Phante, has good views and is the spot for sunset romantics. You climb up an imaginative route which includes a path cut into the hill, wibbly-wobbley Never-Neverland wooden plank steps and around extraordinary rock formations, all the while hearing the sound of monkeys, mouse deer, hornbills and perhaps wild boar. Finally you reach the top and a look-out point over the beach and surrounding forest which in fact, is not as satisfying as the walk itself. You may also find it taken over by groups of young park staff – especially in the early morning.

The **prison** at Ao Talo U-Dang, in the south, was established in 1939 and was once used as a concentration camp for Thailand's political prisoners (see Background); the graveyard, charcoal furnaces and a fish fermentation plant are still there. The other main camp was at Ao Talo Wao on the east side of the island and was used for high-security criminals. During the Second World War, when communications were slow and difficult, the remoteness of the island meant it was cut off from supplies of food. After 700 out of the prison population of 3,000 died, the desperate prisoners and some of the guards too, became pirates in order to stay alive. The prisons have been partially restored as historical monuments but there are no plans to reactivate them – today the only people living on the island are the park wardens and related staff.

Coconut plantations still exist on Tarutao but the forests have barely been touched, providing a natural habitat for flying lizards, wild cats, lemur, wild boar, macaques, mouse deer and feral cows, believed to have bred when the prisoners were taken from

Tarutao National Park

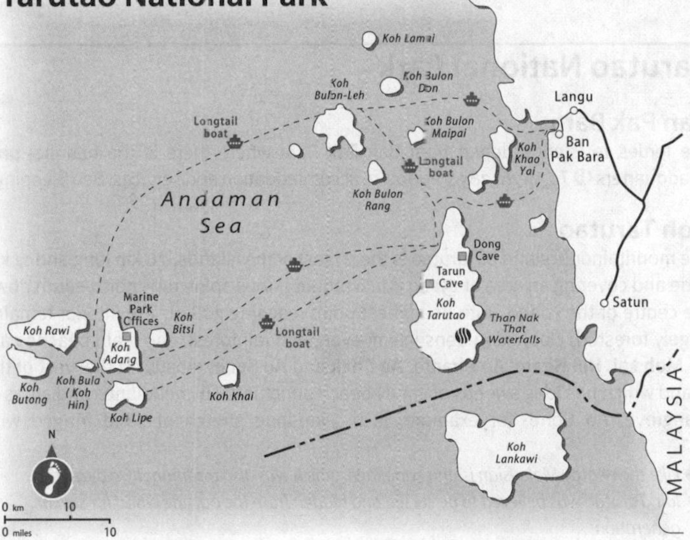

Koh Lamai
Koh Bulon Don
Koh Bulon-Leh
Langu
Longtail boat
Koh Bulon Maipai
Ban Pak Bara
Koh Khao Yai
Longtail boat
Koh Bulon Rang
Andaman Sea
Dong Cave
Tarun Cave
Koh Tarutao
Than Nak That Waterfalls
Satun
Marine Park Offices
Koh Bitsi
Longtail boat
Koh Rawi
Koh Adang
Koh Butong
Koh Bula (Koh Hin)
Koh Khai
Koh Lipe
MALAYSIA
Koh Lankawi
N
0 km 10
0 miles 10

the island. Crocodiles once inhabited Khlong Phante and there is a large cave on the Choraka (crocodile) water system known as Crocodile Cave (bring a flashlight). The best way to see wildlife on Koh Tarutao is to walk down the 12-km stretch during the dry season when animals come out in search of water. There are also many species of birds on the islands including colonies of swiftlets found in the numerous limestone caves – mainly on Koh Lo Tong (to the south of Tarutao) and Koh Ta Kieng (to the northeast). Large tracts of mangrove forest are found here, especially along Khlong Phante Malacca on Tarutao. The islands are also known for their trilobite fossils, 400 to 500 million years old, found not just on Tarutao but all over the national park.

While the waters around Tarutao are home to four species of turtle – the **Pacific Ridleys, green, hawksbill** and **leatherback** – and **dugongs, whales** and **dolphins** are also occasionally seen, the sea is clearer further west in the waters of the Adang-Rawi archipelago (see below).

Adang-Rawi archipelago

Adang and Rawi lie 43 km west of Tarutao and are the main islands in the archipelago of the same name. They offer a stark contrast to Tarutao. While Tarutao is composed of limestone and sandstone, the rugged hills of Adang and Rawi are granite. Adang's highest mountain rises to 703 m while Rawi's is 463 m in height. Koh Adang is almost entirely forested and there is a trail that leads up to the summit, Chado Cliff, for good views over Koh Lipe and the Andaman Sea. There are also a handful of trails through the dense vegetation, and spotting the shy inhabitants of the area – including a variety of squirrels, mouse deer and wild pigs – is best achieved by setting up your hammock and waiting half an hour or so in silence. The main beaches on Adang are Khai, Laem Son, Ao Lo Lae Lae and Lo Lipa, and Sai Khao on Rawi.

Koh Hin Ngam (Koh Bula) is southwest of Adang. The name means 'Beautiful Rocks' and this striking beach is covered in smooth oval stones that appear to have been polished by hand and that twinkle as the waves wash over them. According to legend, these stones should never be removed or you will be cursed with bad luck by the ghost of Hin Ngami. There is excellent snorkelling to be had in the waters nearby. **Koh Khai** has the famous stone arch depicted on many postcards of the area, white powdery sand beaches and some excellent diving. '*Khai*' means 'egg' in Thai, as this island was a popular turtle nesting site in the past. **Chabang**'s sunken reef is home to hundreds of soft corals of many different colours that make for wonderfully rewarding snorkelling.

Koh Tarutao

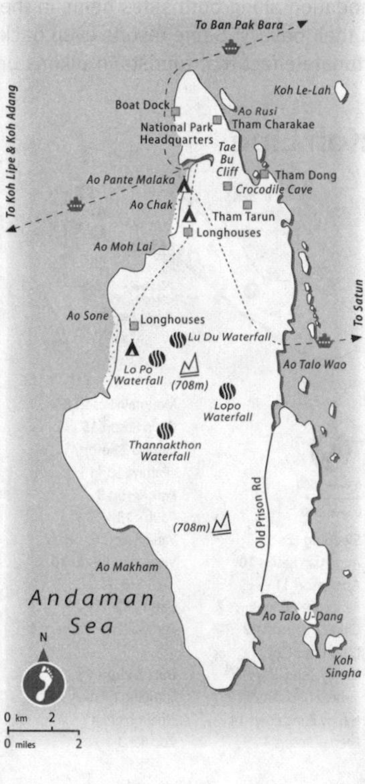

Koh Lipe

Once a tropical idyll of an island, occupied by Chao Le fisherpeople, the main beach here – Pattaya – is now absolutely crammed end to end with bungalows and resorts though thankfully no multi-story pool complexes yet.

Despite clear conundrums (see below), Koh Lipe is a likeable island that attracts many returnees, mainly because of the laid-back and gentle populace, excellent snorkelling in some of the clearest waters in the Andaman Sea and terrific seafood. While much of the accommodation is cack-handed and poorly thought out, the island is still a getaway with a stray dog charm. Plus even for total novices, snorkelling here is unbelievably rewarding. Among the marine life that can be spotted in coral reefs only 60 metres out are trumpet fish, sergeant majors, blue spotted ribbontail rays, angel fish and anemones. There are also fishing and diving expeditions and an excellent massage operation on Pattaya Beach, set up by staff trained by Wat Po – especially Mr Chai (nickname) Bovornpar and Mrs Thanaporn Chimmalee who also offers reflexology and other body treatments. The Chao Le have also managed to hold onto their culture and language and hold a traditional ceremony called *pla juk* twice a year. For this, a miniature boat is built out of *rakam* and *teenped* wood by the villagers. Once the boat is completed, offerings are placed in it, and the Chao Le dance until dawn and then launch the boat out to sea, loaded with the village's communal bad luck. One sincerely hopes that Bangkok interests which are casting their eye Lipe-way, will not take away what little control the Chao Le still have here and bring them bad luck in the long run.

The island has recently acquired a bad reputation for the intrusive racket of motorbikes along the beach, despite a lack of a paved boardwalk or indeed, a paved path anywhere on the island. The bikes are bad news in other ways too as the majority of the owners are Chao Le youth who acquire them on hire purchase. However, the engines quickly fill up with sand rendering them useless when they are not even fully paid off. Current proposals include building a paved path behind the beach resorts to alleviate this problem but Koh Lipe is far too tiny for this to be an ideal solution. Now, only paths criss-cross the island. The combination of a Liliputian-sized island and rampant tourist bungalow expansion creates yet another awkward dilemma as the accommodation along both sides hems in the resident Chao Le and seriously intrudes on their privacy. Some resorts even back directly onto resident areas with the unfortunate effect that tourists in bikinis or singlets can too easily stroll into a communal shower area occupied by the modest Chao Le as so few of their homes have running water and private bathrooms. It is also true that while certain resorts have a surface aura of cleanliness and order, this is quickly dispelled by the smell of burning plastic around the resident areas as rubbish disposal here is largely accomplished on a chaotic and sporadic basis.

The Chao Le areas are quite clearly at shanty town level or barely above, which makes one wonder what benefits they are receiving from unchecked tourism. Indeed, it was only in 1940 that Koh Lipe officially became Thai territory – up to then it was none too clear whether the Chao Le here were putative Malaysians or Thais. Locals maintain the opinion that the Thai authorities encouraged them to plant coconut trees to show that they had settled, presumably on the basis that occupation is as good as ownership.

Koh Lipe

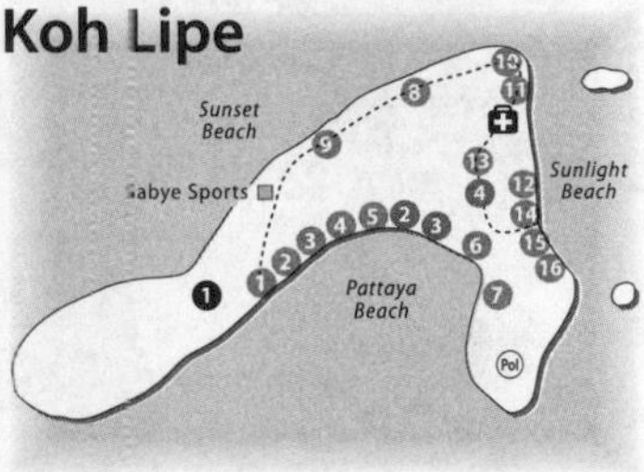

Sleeping
Andaman Resort **10**
Asia Resort **11**
Barracuda Bungalows **7**
Chao Ley Resort **12**
Daya Resort **2**
Family Bungalows **5**
Fishery Department **9**
Happy Bungalows **14**
Leepay Resort **4**
Mountain Resort **8**
Ossin Resort **15**
Pattaya 2 Resort/ Pattaya Song **1**
Pink Resort **3**
Pooh's **13**
Varin Resort **6**
Viewpoint Resort **16**

Eating
Pattaya (Five Brothers) **1**

Bars & clubs
Jumping Monkey **2**
No Problem **4**
Zoo Bar **3**

ⓘ Numerous resorts and fishermen operate boat tours around the area, costing about ฿800 for half a day of swimming, snorkelling and sometimes fishing. Whales, dolphins and turtles are common here.

These two islands have both developed into beach resorts fairly recently. But while Koh Lipe has had Chao Le for perhaps centuries, only in the past 50 years or so has Koh Bulon-Leh had year-round residents – a tiny Muslim population of around 50. The reason for this is down to the superstition of the Moken fisherpeople who believed the island was cursed and that everyone who lived there died. This kept the island unihabited until after the Second World War and since then, it was discovered that the high mortality rate was due to raging tuberculosis.

The lifestyle here is exceedingly laid-back and in the more expensive resorts – boho-chic. One of the perks to having had few tourists and a rather isolated position is that visitors will often join in on simple pleasures like the evening rugby games by the school or go on fishing trips with the locals. Until now, the island has largely attracted returnee visitors – many from Italy and France – and of a wide age range from pensioners to twenty-somethings. More upmarket than Koh Lipe, it does offer greater comfort to the well-heeled who will stay for months at a time.

Development here is still relatively low-key but land speculation has been going on since the 1990s and investors are no doubt hoping that Koh Bulon-Leh will develop, especially as it is relatively near the pier at Pak Bara and offers tourist sites. Koh Bulon-Leh is less than 20 km north of Koh Tarutao and about the same distance west of Ban Pak Bara. While it is part of the same archipelago as Tarutao, the island is outside the boundaries of the Tarutao National Park. Furthermore, Koh Bulon-Leh has two caves of interest: **Bat Cave**, which houses a small colony of fruit bats, and **Nose Cave**, into which it's possible to dive from one side and swim under the rocks and amongst the thousands of little fish (beware the moray eel, though!) to come up on the other.

The far south

Approached through towering karsts and bordered by limstone hills, Satun town is a somnolent sort of place, alleviated only a little by the Kuden Mansion - a good example of British Colonial style architecture (by Penang builders) - which can be seen in a day. Most people use the town as a stopover en route to boat services for Ko Tarutao, Koh Lipe and Malaysia. The majority of the people here are Muslim so there is not a huge boozy nightlife. Thale Ban National Park, filled with birds and animals and forest trails is 37 km from Satun.

Satun province, which borders Malayasia and is situated on the west coast near the Straits of Malacca in the Indian Ocean, now falls within the danger zones for terrorist activity, particularly following the bombing at Hat Yai airport in 2005. (see box, page 525.)

Koh Bulon-Leh

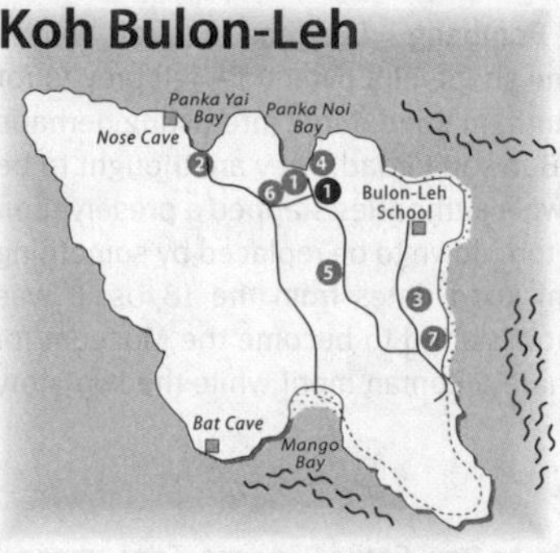

Sleeping
Ban Sulaida Bungalows 1
Bulon Le Resort 3
Bulon View Point Resort & Tours 4
Choolae Food & Bungalows 6
Marina Bungalows 5
Panka Bay Resort 2
Pansand Resort 7

Eating
Orchid 1

N
Not to scale

Satun → *Colour map 5, grid C4.*

Surrounded by mountains, Satun is cut off from the Malaysian Peninsula and the eastern side of the Kra Isthmus. Few towns in Thailand, particularly provincial capitals, have escaped thoughtless

Red Zone, Yellow Zone, Green Zone

For the first time since the violent communist insurgency of the 1970s, the infamous red zone coding has been brought back, this time in the deep south against villages believed to be sympathetic to Islamic militants.

Critics of the contentious coding tactic say that the zoning, which is directly linked to funding for villages, will exacerbate tensions and help breed future militants.

Red Zones, which are to have all funds cut, are villages where the military and militants are infighting. Yellow Zones, which will have their funding slashed, are villages where locals offer aid and shelter to militants. Green Zones, which will receive the most funds, are villages that do not engage in any terrorist activity and which could provide moles for information about militant activities.

The latest draconian measures come in the wake of more than 800 fatalities in 2004 which were blamed on Islamic militants. While the majority of victims in the past have been police and soldiers, increasingly Buddhist monks, teachers and also tourists are being targeted. The most far-reaching incident thus far has been the simultaneous bombings in 2005 of Hat Yai Airport in which foreigners died, part-French owned Carrefcru Department Store In Songkhla and a hotel, also in Songkhla.

redevelopment. Satun, though, has done better than most. It has an attractive, low-key centre with preserved shophouses and is very Malay in feel; 85 per cent of the population are thought to be Muslim. Few tourists include Satun on their itinerary. Instead they make a beeline for Ban Pak Bara 60 km or so north of town and catch a boat to the Tarutao Islands (see page 517). But perhaps Satun deserves a few more visitors.

The province seems to have spent the last century searching for an identity separate from that of its neighbours. In the early years of this century it was administered as part of Kedah in Malaysia. In 1909, following a treaty between Thailand and Britain, it came under the authority of Phuket. Fifteen years later it found itself being administered from Nakhon Si Thammarat and it was not until 1932 that it managed to carve out an independent niche for itself when it was awarded provincial status by Bangkok.

The town's main mosque – the **Mesjid Bombang** – is a modern affair built in 1979 after the previous mosque – also in the shape of a pyramid – fell prey to rot and was torn down. The mosque is on Satunthani Road. More interesting perhaps are the preserved **Chinese shophouses** on Buriwanit Road. They are thought to be around 150 years old and fortunately the town's authorities slapped a preservation order on the buildings before they could be torn down to be replaced by something hideous. **Ku Den's Mansion** on Satunthani Road dates from the 1870s. It was originally the governor's residence but is now slotted to become the Museum for Islamic Studies. The windows and doors share a Roman motif while the two story roof is in Thai Panyi style.

Thale Ban National Park

ⓘ *Thale Ban National Park Office, Amphoe Khuan Don, Satun Province, T074-797073. Open daily during daylight hours. 37 km from Satun, 90 km from Hat Yai. Take Highway 4, 406 and 4184 to the park. By public transport catch a songthaew from Samantha Prasit Road (by the pier) to Wang Prajan. From here there are occasional songthaews the last few kilometres, or take a motorcycle taxi. Best time to visit: Dec-Apr when rainfall in this wet area (2,662 mm per year) is at its least.*

Terrorism in the deep south

Along with Narathiwat, Songkhla, Pattani and Yala, Satun province was a hotbed for Islamic insurgents during the 1970s and 1980s until a government amensty saw 20,000 hardcore Islamic fighters handing in their arms in 1987. Then, in December 2001, it all began again with hit-and-run attacks on police, military outposts, schools and commercial sites.

Now the Australian government, following on the tragedy of the Bali bombing, is warning its citizens to 'exercise particular vigilance in the Satun province, including overland travel to and from the Malaysian border. The UK Foreign and Commonwealth office advises against all but essential travel to these four southern provinces. Among the risks are kidnapping from resorts and piracy in the Straits of Malacca.

Much of the tension in Satun province and throughout the deep south is traced back to the late 1890s when these provinces – once part of Muslim and animist Malaysia - were Siamised, their names changed to Siam words and the people reclassified as Malay-Thais. Satun itself was formerly called Setol. But the deep South also claims that, because it is not fully Thai-Thai, it is punished by a lack of funding, poor education facilities and also that the deep south has become a dumping ground for corrupt and inept military and government officials. Certainly, banditry is rife throughout the provinces, with many of the criminals using the same tactics as Muslim insurgents, making it almost impossible to distinguish between the two. On the street front, crime in the form of snatch and grabs is also becoming more popular.

What is increasingly clear is that the long-standing inhabitants of the deep south still see themselves as more Malaysian and less Thai, speaking Malaysian and maintaining a Muslim majority as opposed to a Thai Buddhist majority. This can also be noticed on a parochial level by the concerted effort to buy only Malay products - the excuse being that they are superior quality and can't be found anywhere but Malaysia and pertains to everything from cleaning products to chilis.

What Satun and the deep South do have to offer – other than the frisson of political intrigue - is excellent cooking and gorgeous national parks – inlcuding Tarutao with its tremendous marine life. You will find the scenery stupendous – even unbeatable - and the cooking less hot than Thai but spicier with quieter, more layered curries and a subtler sweetness. Again, the restaurant owners may often tell you that the ingredients are Malaysian only.

The park lies bordering Malaysia was gazetted in 1980 after four years of wrangling and threats from local so-called *ithiphon muut*, or 'dark influences'. It is a comparatively small park, covering just over 100 sq km. How it got its name is the source of some dispute. Some people believe it is derived from the Malay words *loet roe ban*, meaning sinking ground; others that it is derived from the Thai word *thale*, meaning sea.

At the core of the park is a lake that covers some 30 ha, between the mountains Khao Chin to the east at 720 m and Khao Wangpra to the west. The park has a large bird population: hawks, hornbills, falcons and many migratory birds. Animals include dusky leaf monkeys, white-handed gibbon, lesser mousedeer, wild boar and, it is said, the Sumatran rhinoceros. Forest trails lead from the headquarters and it is not unusual to see hornbills, langurs, macaques, even wild pigs. The round trip takes about four hours.

A hiking trail leads from the park headquarters to the summit of Khao Chin where it is possible to camp. There are also **waterfalls and caves**; the most frequently visited waterfall is Ya Roi, situated 5 km north of the park headquarters and accessible by vehicles. The falls here plunge through nine levels; at the fifth is a good pool for swimming. En route to Ya Roi is a modest cave: Ton Din.

Sleeping

Ban Pak Bara *p519*

C **Bara Resort** has a/c bungalows with hot water, also right on the beach. Nice view but noisy and dusty from traffic.

C-D **Best House Resort**, T074-783058/783568. 10 a/c and very clean bungalows with extremely comfortable beds, friendly owners and a good restaurant attached.

C-E **Pak Nam Resort**, T074-781129/781109, Koh Kebang, a 15-min long-tailed taxi ride from Ban Pak Bara pier. A much more salubrious alternative than the country club is this resort. The accommodation ranges from 17 bungalows to A-frame huts, all with fan and attached bathroom. Excellent restaurant but the water here is dirty.

D **Panyong Country Club Resort**, 20-30 mins' drive from Pak Bara Pier, near Langu town (free transportation is provided), T074-781230, a grand name for quite a simple set-up – a development with simple a/c and fan wooden bungalows and a restaurant in a garden overlooking nipa palms, mangroves and some marshland. It's about a 200-m walk to a beach on a shallow bay. The beach is nothing special although the views are nice, and the resort is quiet.

D-E **Diamond Beach,** T074-783138. Offers bungalows with sea views.

Koh Tarutao *p519, map p521*

Book through the National Park office in Bangkok T02-579052, or the Pak Bara office, T074-781285/729002-3. Accommodation is in the north and west of Tarutao. There are 3 choices: multi-occupancy bunglows which can accommodate families or groups, longhouses and tents. The 3 main beaches – Ao Pante, Ao Molae and Ao Sone all offer some or all of these types, with Ao Pante, the one closest to the pier and where the park warden offices are, offering the most selection. The accommodation may also have shared outside toilets. The bungalows are sparsely furnished wooden structures, set along the side of the road against the cliffs. In the morning, the monkeys raiding the bins can be terrifically noisy but then there are the marvellous hornbills to offset that. Tents are on the beach with a public shower and toilet. Do check your tent for both size and condition. When Footprint visited Tarutao, the tent given for 2 people was a tent for one. Furthermore, it was riddled with holes, some of which were repaired with sticking plasters and was filled with sand. The treatment given to tent visitors also varies. The staff may offer you a site that is already prepared with a tent in place or they may simply hand you a tent. When leaving, they might or might not ask you to take the tent down. The staff were also incredibly unhelpful when asked how to erect the tent. The idea is really to bring your own or find a sympathetic fellow traveller who knows his tent from his elbow. If you take your own tent the space to rent on the beach is ฿30 per night.

Ao Pante

Ban Taboon, ฿1,000. 4-person bungalow. 2 rooms and 1 toilet.

Ban Tabang, ฿1,200. 4-person bungalow with 2 rooms and 2 toilets.

Ban Salika, ฿750. 4-person bungalow. 2 rooms, 2 toilets.

Ban Nangnoi, ฿650. 6-person bungalow. 2 rooms and 2 toilets.

Samed Kaw Long House, ฿500. 4 people per room. Toilet outside.

Samed Dang Long House, ฿500. 4 people per room. Toilet outside.

Ao Molae

Ban Molae, ฿2,000. 4-person bunglows that are more upmarket and look rather like Wendy Houses. 2 rooms and 2 toilets. Damaged by the tsunami but should be up and running now.

Adang-Rawi archipelago *p521*
Accommodation is all on the southern swathe of Adang island, with longhouses offering **B-D** rates, where some rooms accommodate sometimes up to 10 people.

Camping
Tents are available on Adang: big ฿200, small ฿100, own tent ฿60 at Laem Son. There is also a simple restaurant. The island essentially closes down during the rainy season.
The bungalows here differ in terms of the perks offered ie hot showers.
Ban Pakarang, ฿1,500. Bungalows.
Ban Kanlapangha, ฿300. Bungalows.
Ban Kanlangha, ฿900. Bunglows.
Adang Long House, ฿400. 4 people per room. Toilet outside.
Rawi Long House, ฿400. 4 people per room. Toilet outside.
Big tents (8-10 people), ฿300.
Medium/Middle tents (3-5 people), ฿300.
Small tents (2 people), ฿150.

Camping
Hired tent. Big, ฿200, ฿100; own tent ฿60. Best spots for camping are on Ao Jak and Ao Sone. You can also camp on the beach close to the national park bungalows.

Koh Lipe *p521, map p522*
In recent years, accommodation on Lipe has expanded rapidly. A few years ago the guesthouses were mainly operated by the Chao Le, but more commercially astute outsiders have muscled in on the tourism industry. Electricity is only available from dusk onwards, mosquito nets are provided, but not all places have fans or a/c that works. Where there is hot water it is more like warm water with poor pressure. The bungalows are either concrete or bamboo and fall within the **AL-E** price range although most are within the **C-D** range. Pattaya Beach has ideal swimming. On the opposite side of the island is Sunset Beach which does not have much of a shore so is poor for swimming. Sunlight Beach is in from the dusty path that leads to the village. The beach is beautiful with water clear and blue enough to hurt your eyes but it is not good for swimming.
AL-C Leepay Resort, Pattaya Beach. 70ish bungalows of varying sizes, set in part among the pine trees, and all fairly clean with lino/tile floors and attached toilets. The more expensive options are better value and have large verandas while others look over a semi-ravine area filled with rubbish and are dark and far too close together. The lay-out is a hodge-podge mix of tumbledown bungalows and crisp new ones with faux French doors. Electricity is available from 1800-0600, and when the internet works, it costs ฿5 per min. While some of the bungalows are truly attractive here, the owner is a major detraction with guests complaining of intimidation. However, the ground-level staff do go out of their way even if there is high staff turnover. There's also a large, airy restaurant on the beach, open to the sea breezes and serving mid-range fare done very badly in mean portions.
B-C Mountain Resort, Sunset Beach, T074-72813, 47 fan and a/c green corrugated roofed bamboo bunglows. Rather hot.
B-C Varin Resort, Pattaya Beach, T01-5404557. These 81 exceptionally clean bungalows set in a regimental lay-out facing each other, are nonetheless good value for money. There are nice personal touches such as the giant ceramic pots by the porches that are filled with water and a scoop so that you can wash your feet before you go in. The operation is run by a Muslim-Thai Malay family and is the most upmarket spot on this beach. The service is also excellent and attentive. Recommended.
B-D Pattaya 2 Resort/Pattaya Song, Pattaya Beach, T074-728034. Run by the man from Bologna – Stefano – a larger than life character and avid fisherman who set up base in Koh Lipe many years ago. These 39 fan bunglows are set in the hillside overlooking the water which makes for an ideal view. Unfortunately, you have to navigate a seriously rickety wooden staircase with steps hanging off just above the rocks. The rooms themselves are only partly clean with low ceilings and a combination of clashing coloured tiles that make you feel as if you're losing your mind very very quickly. The curtains are also filthy. and the whole set-up feels a bit like a squat. Too bad because the adjoining restaurant does good Italian fare and the views are marvellous. Stefano is also a superb rogue raconteur.

C Andaman resort, Sunlight Beach, T074-728017/729200. A mix of 60 concrete, log and bamboo bungalows. The best are on the beach and are white and blue, reminiscent of Cape Cod, New England. Good reports of clean, bright rooms. Very quiet. Owned by half-Chao Le and half Chinese-Thai. Recommended if you can get blue and white ones.

C Asia Resort, Sunlight Beach, T074-728117. About 20 thatched bungalows on stilts set along a dusty path. Overpriced.

C Family Bungalows, Pattaya Beach, T9590243. Only 3 bungalows run by a Chao Le family. Thatched roof and bamboo toward the scrappier and less developed end of the beach by the dirt path leading to the village. Okay.

C Pooh's, Sunlight Beach, T074-722220. 8 new, very clean bungalows set in Pooh's family-run complex of bar, internet, restaurant travel agency and dive shop. Nice enough bungalows and not too many either though it should stop here. However, there is no view and they are not near the beach. Still very convenient for early morning coffee and everything else at this one-stop operation run by the affable Mr Pooh (his name means crab in English). Funky ambience plus you don't need to toddle home at night with a torch. Also you get a discount at the dive shop if you stay there. Recommended.

C-D Barracuda Bunglaows, Pattaya Beach, T09-6544720. Totally basic bamboo huts with scary shared toilets in a Cool Hand Luke corrugated shack.

C-D Daya Resort, Pattaya Beach, T074-728030. Offers 48 bungalows with attached western toilets and some individual rooms, set in gardens and boasting a very popular restaurant that does a particularly strong line in seafood. However, the bungalows are rather dirty and run-down in concrete and bamboo – also far too many.

C-D Fishery department, Sunset Beach Accommodation. 10 concrete bungalows with wide verandas set amid trees. Clean and reasonable though not the best location as is is in from the beach.

D Happy Bungalows, Sunlight Beach, T09-636915. Perhaps too happy-go-lucky. 7 bungalows at a slapdash angle that need immediate attention before they fall over.

D Ossin Resort, Sunlight Beach, T09-65090333. 15 bungalows – some on the beach and the majority a few mins walk inland, all clean with fans and mattresses on the hard wooden floors. Breezy because it is inland but rather dark. A couple of family-run restaurants at both very peaceful locations.

D Pink Resort, Pattaya Beach, T06-920306. A cute name for a rather cute set-up squeezed between **Leepay** or **Lipe Resort** and **Daya**. There is not much light here but these 12 bungalows are still fairly nice, clean and newish. Recommended.

D Viewpoint Resort, Sunlight Beach, T09-7320724. 15 bungalows on a pretty but very small swatch of beach, studded with boulders and overlooking the nearby islands. Built on the hill, plenty of step-climbing is needed to get to each bungalow which are too close together now that there are more than twice as many. Quiet and very secluded. Attached restaurant.

D-E Chao Ley Resort, Sunlight Beach, T074-728111/728112. 50 characterless white bungalows, all with attached toilets, laid out in orderly lines. Good sea breezes and surrounding pine trees help combat the often stifling heat on Lipe. A friendly, family-run concern with cheap restaurant attached.

Koh Bulon-Leh *p523, map p523*

A-B Bulon Viewpoint Resort and Tours. Variable proportioned bungalows and decent restaurant. Some bungalows get very little light have poor views and beds on raised platforms that look utterly uncomfortable. Others have great views, spotless bathrooms and plenty of sunshine. However, these are some of the the most secure bungalows in Bulon-Ley. Good landscaping too as the manager dearly loves the bird and insect life of Bulon-Lei with contagious enthusiasm. From the drop-off point on the beach, you also have to go on a 15-20-min walk up a dirt hill that becomes a paved path. Offers internet and has a good bar on the beach though.

A-B Pansand Resort, T01-3970802, or **First Andaman Travel**, in Trang, T075-218035. For the upmarket set. A range of bungalow accommodation, all well-maintained and welcoming with attached bathrooms along with dormitories. The views are good, and

the garden extremely pleasant – it even has English-style park benches. Good watersports. It also organizes camping, snorkelling and boat trips and an evening internet service. Set in from main beach but this is actually a plus as it makes it feel more exclusive. Recommended. Closed Jul-Sep.

B-D Bulon Le Resort, T01-8979084. Well-positioned just where the boats dock, overlooking this beautiful stretch of beach. Offers another wide range of bungalows from the rather nice, spacious, almost colonial options to the more basic, single room structures with shared bathrooms. Shared toilets though are kept spotless. All in good shape, and run by friendly and helpful management. Electricity 1800-0200. Good restaurant. Best breakfast is here. Recommended.

B-D Panka Bay Resort, T074-728007/ 728005. Contact Kanneka. Up the hill and down on the Panga Bay side of the island, this is the only resort here. There are 21 bungalows at this Muslim Malay-Thai family-run establishment, all with varying advantages. Some have better views and bigger porches or are sheltered by trees. The bungalows are arranged along the beachfront and in tiers up a hill with handmade stone and sand steps built by the family. The beach is not great here as it has a rocky shore and goes out too far at low tide but you can walk in 20 mins to the other beach and catch some amazing bird and lizard life on the way. Excellent service – they offer a free pick up from the **Bulon-Le Resort** drop-off. Another perk is full electricity to 0500. Huge restaurant with superb food – Thai-Malay fusion. Offers Thai cookery. Recommended.

C Marina Bungalows. These wooden log fan bungalows set into the hill going up towards Panka Bay are utterly charming and romantic but far too overpriced. They are more treehouse than bungalow – you can see the ground through the spaces in the log floor and there is no glass in the windows, simply crossed wooden bars. Consequently security is nil. But, even if snakes and palm rats can clamber through the logs at night, there are perks like wonderfully comfortable double beds, clean linen, large verandas big enough for hammocks and a Castaway ambience. For those who don't mind roughing it.

C-D Ban Sulaida Bungalows, near Panka Noi Bay. Pleasant, clean rooms set in carefully tended gardens, with extremely friendly owner who's delighted to give discounts for longer stays. 5 mins from the beach, but this is not the white sand idyll of the eastern coast, although it's good for snorkelling. Small, airy restaurant is decorated with shells, hanging birds' nests and plants, serving good seafood.

D Chaolae Food and Bungalows. Run by a Chao Le family of 2 brothers, 2 sisters and parents. Contact Watana Benma. 8 raised brick and bamboo bungalows – all adorable – set up hill further on from **Bulon Viewpoint Resort and Tours**. It has sunken bathrooms with squat toilet and shower but no fans. However, the surrounding trees provide considerable respite from the heat. This place is tucked in a little so you might miss it but it is well worth the hunt. Plenty of lovely personal touches – real care has been taken. Even the communal outside toilet has been filled with shells and rocks. Sweet restaurant too with shell mobiles and lined with cacti and brightly hued flowers in pots. You can choose your fish from the daily catch stored in a cooler – one of the brothers is a fisherman. Beautifully cooked with herbs and spices. Excellent reports from guests who are mainly backpackers, divers and independent travellers. Though this is away from the beach – yet only a couple mins to Panka Bay down a slope – it really works as a retreat. Recommended.

Camping

Charan Tours can organize tent hire (see Satun tour operators, page 531).

Satun *p523*

A-C Wangmai, 43 Satunthani Rd, T074-711607. A/c, restaurant, white 5-storey well-run place with good facilities and clean rooms, quite acceptable and well priced.

B-C Sinkiat Thani, 50 Buri Wanit Rd, T074-721055. A hotel with a modicum of style. 108 large, well-kept rooms and great views from the upper floors, Satun's No 1 hotel. Low-season discounts. Also lays claim to having the first 'Disco Club' in Satun.

E Rain Tong, Samantha Prasit Rd (at the western end, by the river). Simple but clean rooms with attached bathrooms and cold-water showers.

Thale Ban National Park *p524*
There are 10 bungalows for rent around the lake, sleeping between 8 and 15. There is also a Thai restaurant and an information centre at the park headquarters. Tents are also available for hire from the park headquarters.

Eating

Koh Tarutao *p519, map p521*
There is a rather irritating system of coupons for paying for food at the restaurants. There's a table next to the restaurants, where you purchase your coupons, once establishing the cost. The food is also appalling although the service and portions magically improve for the government tour groups that regularly do trips here.

Koh Lipe *p521, map p522*
Seafood dishes are divine. Good seafood is served by restaurants along the main Pattaya Beach when tables and chairs are laid out at night. You can choose the cut and fish yourself. **Varin Resort** also does marvellous salads and baked potatoes along with the fish.
ΨΨΨ **Pooh's**, T074-722220, on the path between **Chao Le Resort** and **Pattaya Beach** is usually the busiest place, offering good music, a good bar and tasty food in a well-decorated, seriously chilled out, airy setting.
ΨΨ **Daya**, near the far end of Pattaya Beach, this is one of many eateries that offer cheap, inoffensive food. The fresh fish is excellent.
ΨΨ **Pattaya 2 Restaurant**, right next to Daya, with practically identical buildings and menus. Good, cheap fare.
Ψ **Pattaya Restaurant**, also known as **Five Brothers Restaurant**, and run by Stephano at the monkey-laden, rocky end of Pattaya Beach, has a cool, dark setting amongst the trees offering welcome relief from the glaring sun, and excellent value for money. Italian stand-bys like bruschetta are excellent and his pastas are good for this isolated position. Also absolutely filthy toilets which really need a good scrub.

Bakeries
There are two bakeries of note on the island, the ever-popular **Pooh's** and the one behind **Sabye Sports**, both of which do great chocolate cakes, brownies, fresh bread and cinnamon rolls.

Koh Bulon-Leh *p523, map p523*
Ψ **Orchid**, near **Ban Sulaida Bungalows**, is a good restaurant, not attached to any resort, which offers good, cheap food.

Satun *p523*
Pretty much opposite the **Sinkiat Thani** are several small restaurants serving Malay food and a *roti* shop selling banana, egg and plain *roti* in the mornings.
ΨΨ-Ψ **Banburee**, Buriwanit Rd. One of 2 places with English signs. Modern establishment situated behind the **Sinkiat Thani**. Thai food.
ΨΨ-Ψ **Kualuang**, Satuntanee Phiman. Best in a group of small Thai restaurants.
Ψ **The Baker's**, on Satuntanee Phiman, the main street into town, pastries, ice cream and soft drinks.
Ψ **Smile**, round the corner from **Wangmai Hotel** on Satuntanee Phiman Rd. Fast food, budget prices.
Ψ **Suhana**, 16/7 Buriniwet Rd. The other English-signed place on this road behind the mosque. Muslim food.

Foodstalls
Night market with stalls serving Thai and Malay dishes on Satun Thani Soi 3. There is a plentiful supply of roadside food joints – particularly on Samantha Prasit Rd. All serve cheap rice and noodle dishes.

Bars and clubs

Koh Lipe *p521, map p522*
As the volume of tourist trade picks up, more of these are springing up.
Pooh's remains a favourite watering hole and is exceedingly comfortable with an eclectic decor – including a flying ship – and lots of pillows, but on Pattaya Beach there is **Zoo Bar**, **Jumping Monkey Bar** and **No Problem Bar** (although a night of revelry here with their Thai and herbal whiskys can certainly create problems for the avid boozer the morning after!), all of which are impossibly chilled out, with mats and candles on the beach. **Barracuda Bar**, by the dirt path into the village, is also good though it is located near the police box which could be occupied.

Festivals and events

Mar Tarutao-Adang Fishing Cup Festival.

Activities and tours

Ban Pak Bara *p519*
Tarutao Travel, T074-781284/781360, in La-Ngu town (on the way to Pak Bara Pier), and Udom Tour in Pak Bara itself. The office is round the back near the national park's office. See also below under Tarutao.

Tarutao National Park *p517, map p520*
Kayaking
Paddle Asia, 19/3 Rasdanusorn Rd, Phuket, T/F076-240893, www.paddleasia.com. Offers kayaking/snorkelling tours to Tarutao National Park.

Snorkelling and diving
Some of the best areas for coral in the waters are northwest of Koh Rang Nok, northwest of Tarutao, southeast of Koh Rawi, around Koh Klang between Tarutao and Adang, and off Koh Kra off Koh Lipe's east coast. Equipment is for hire on Adang and Lipe.

Tours and tour operators
For tours to Tarutao, see Satun, page 531. See also under Ban Pak Bara, above.
Khun Udom, T01-8974765, is a licensed tour guide, local to the area, and with a good knowledge of the islands.

Koh Lipe *p521, map p522*
Heading further west from Lipe, there are countless islands and coral reefs teeming with a staggering variety of fish – the locals know all the good spots and the best locations only an hour or two away from home include Koh Dong, Koh Pung and Koh Tong, Koh Hin Son, Koh Hin Ngam and Koh Chabang.

Dang's Tours, a stone's throw from Pooh's on the way to Chao Ley Resort is just one of the outfits that arranges all day snorkelling tours for around ฿1000 per boat for 6 people. **Forra Dive Centre**, near Chao Ley Resort. **Jack's Tours**, on the beach at Koh Lipe. **Lotus Dive** (Poohs), **Ocean Pro Divers** near Leepay Resort.
Sabye Sports, T/F074-734104, the island's first scuba diving and sports centre, next to Porn Resort, offers both diving and the rental of canoe (฿500 per day) and snorkelling equipment (฿200 per day).
Starfish Scuba, T074-728089, www.starfishscuba.com, next to the Leepay Resort on Pattaya Beach, also offers all the usual diving courses.

Satun *p523*
Tour operators
Charan Tour, 19/6 Satunthani Rd, T074-711453/01-9573908. Runs boat tours every day to the islands between Oct-May. Lunch and snorkelling equipment are provided. Good reputation.

Transport

Ban Pak Bara *p519*
Boat
Ferries leave and dock at Ban Pak Bara. Departure times and prices from Ban Pak Bara can be obtained by ringing T074-783010. To see all the islands, the ฿800 return ticket is great value, allowing stops at **Tarutao**, **Lipe/Adang** and **Bulon**. Boats to **Koh Tarutao** at 1100 and 1500 from Nov-May (1½ hrs, ฿300 return). They dock at Ao Phante Malaka on the island's west coast.

Boats to **Koh Adang** and **Lipe** run daily during the season at 1100 for these 2 islands. The ferry stops at Tarutao on the way out and then continues on at 1200, total fare to these islands is ฿800 return and in the rare event of a seamless trip with no breakdowns, the journey takes about 5 hrs in total.

Koh Bulon-Leh is visited twice a day by boat from Ban Pak Bara; the boat leaves at 1330 and 1500 (1½ hrs, A150 one way).

It is often too rough between May and Oct for ferries to operate, and the park is officially closed in any case. However boats can be chartered at the discretion of their captains throughout the year (A1500 plus).
Long-tailed boat charters from Ban Pak Bara to **Koh Bulon Leh** cost ฿700-1000 per boat.

Bus
There are regular buses to **Trang**. Also to **Satun**, 60 km south. Also connections to **Hat Yai**, 1 ½ hrs. Hat Yai is 158 km east of Ban Pak Bara (1½ hrs).

Tarutao National Park *p517, map p520*

Boat

Koh Tarutao lies off the coast 30 km south of Ban Pak Bara; Koh Adang, Raw and Lipe are another 40 km out into the Andaman Sea, while Koh Bulon-Leh is 20 km due west of Ban Pak Bara.

Beware of travelling to any of these islands during bad weather; it is dangerous and a number of boats have foundered.

The boat from Tarutao to **Ban Pak Bara** departs at 0900 and 1300. To **Koh Lipe**, 2½-3½ hrs. Transfer from ferry to long-tailed boat into Koh Lipe and Koh Adang, ฿30. Boats can also be chartered from Tarutao. To **Satun** from Tarutao at 1700.

Koh Lipe *p521, map p522*

There's a return ferry at 0900 from Lipe to **Koh Tarutao**.

Koh Bulon-Leh *p523, map p523*

From Bulon-Leh to **Koh Tarutao** and **Ban Pak Bara**, the boats leave at 0900 and 1200. Boats travel on from Koh Bulon-Leh to **Koh Adang** and **Koh Lipe** at 1430.

Satun *p523*

Boat

It is possible to charter a boat from Satun to **Koh Tarutao**, but it is a lot cheaper to bus it up to Ban Pak Bara and take one of the regular boats from there (see page 531). There are daily connections between these islands and Tammalang Pier in Satun. The boat to Tarutao leaves at 1100. There are several boats that are whimsically described as slow, not so slow, fast, very fast. The faster boats cost more than the slower boats. But it is debatable whether they live up to their description as the boats often break down mid-water. Timing is also spurious in these unpredicatable waters, ฿900 return.

Bus

Overnight connections with **Bangkok** (15 hrs). Buses for Bangkok leave from Sarit Phuminaraot Rd. Regular connections with **Hat Yai** and **Trang** from opposite the wat on Buriwanit Rd. To **Ban Pak Bara**, buses leave from front of Plaza Market. The buses connect with ferries.

Motorbike taxis

For hire from outside Thai Farmers Bank, near the market and from outside Satunthani Hotel on Satunthani Rd.

Taxi

To **Hat Yai** from Bureevanith Rd; to **Trang**, from taxi rank next to Chinese temple.

International connections with Malaysia Ferries leave from Satun and dock at one of 2 places, depending on the tide. If the tide is sufficiently high, boats arrive/leave from the jetty at the end of Samanta Prasit Rd. At low water boats dock at Tammalang Pier, south of Satun. Songthaews run to the pier from Buriwanit Rd. There are connections with Langkawi and Kuala Perlis. Daily ferries to Langkawi. Tickets can be purchased in advance from Charan Tour.

Directory

Satun *p523*

Banks On Buriwanit and SatunThani Rd. Thai Military, Buriwanit Rd (across from Hat Yai taxi rank on Buriwanit Rd). Thai Farmers, opposite the market. **Internet** Near the Sinkiat Hotel on Satunthani Rd is an internet café Satun Cybernet which offers connections for ฿30 per hr. **Post office** Samantha Prasit Rd (near Intersection with Satun Thani Rd). **Telephone** Attached to the GPO. **Useful addresses** Immigration Office at the end of Buriwanit Rd.

Gulf of Thailand

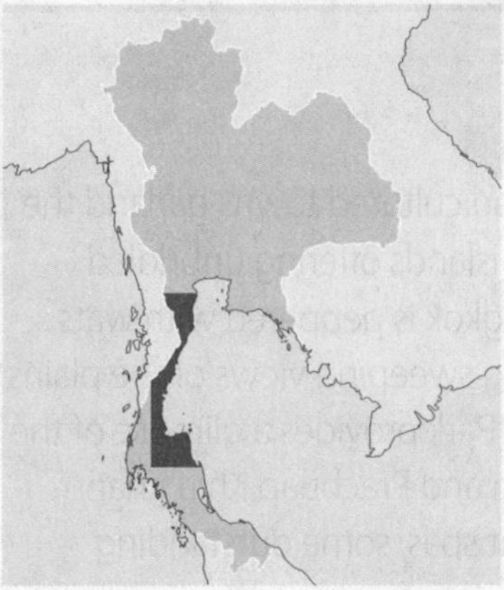

Footprint features

Introduction

Beaches, resorts, national parks and cultured towns garland the length of the Gulf Coast, with the islands offering unbridled hedonism. Phetburi, south of Bangkok is peppered with wats and a hilltop royal palace affording sweeping views of the plains while Khao Sam Roi Yod National Park provides a glimpse of the rare dusky langur. Ch-am, Hua Hin and Prachuap Khiri Khan offer olde-worlde charm, excellent spas, some outstanding resorts and fewer tourists.

However, the appeal of the northern Gulf Coast towns is eclipsed by the delights of Koh Samui, Koh Phangan and Koh Tao. These islands have it all: from the pampering palaces, appealing resorts, fine-dining experiences, streets of thumping bars, action-packed beaches and quiet bays on Koh Samui to the smaller Koh Phangan, where once a month the world's largest outdoor party spins on the sands at Hat Rin when 10,000 people flock to dance and drink in the glow of the full moon. Around the rest of the island, particularly the east coast, the perfect getaways are waiting in cove after cove with sapphire seas tainted only by a glint of granite.

Further north at Koh Tao, the underwater world is an attraction with so many shallow reefs offshore. Around the island remote bays are guarded by huge granite boulder formations and surrounded by perfect tropical seas. At night Hat Sai Ri is enlivened by funky bars and beachfront dining.

The thriving town of Nakhon Si Thammarat, unmuddied by full-scale tourism, offers an opportunity to see the unusual art of shadow puppetry and savour confectioners' delicate pastries.

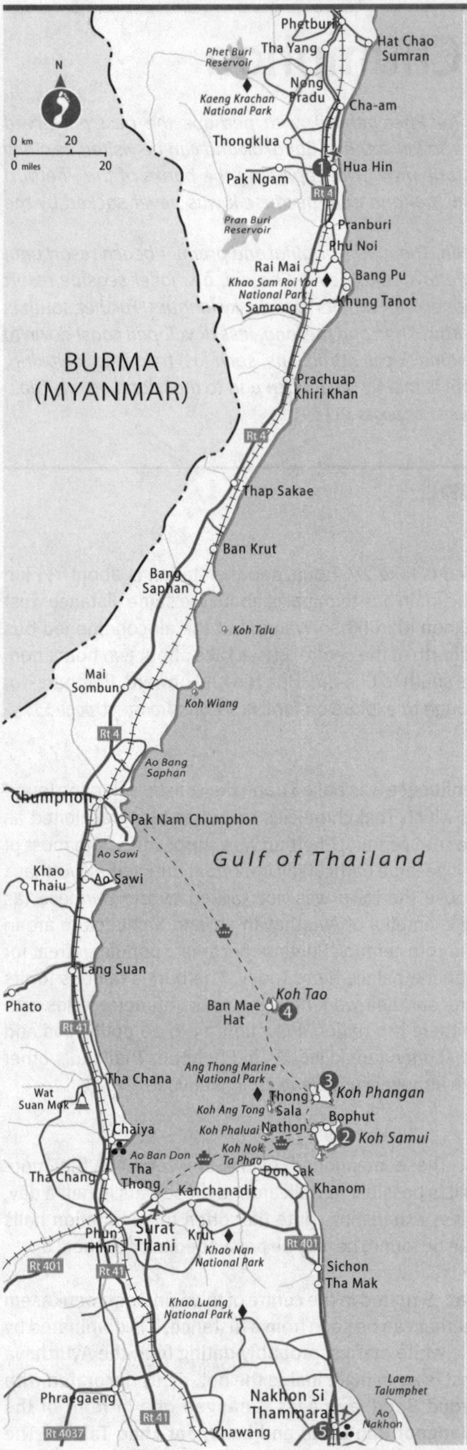

★ Don't miss...

1 **Hua Hin** Take afternoon tea on the terrace at the magnificent, colonial, railway hotel, now the Sofitel Central Hua Hin Resort, pages 541 and 547.

2 **Koh Samui** Indulge the senses with a massage at one of the island's finest spas followed by dinner on the beach at one of the many excellent restaurants, pages 579 and 580.

3 **Koh Phangan** Snorkel by day off one of the secluded east coast shores, watch sunset from the Lighthouse Bungalows, Hat Rin, and party all night at the Full Moon, Black Moon or Half Moon nights, pages 588 and 590.

4 **Koh Tao** After diving the waters, take a spa package at the Jamahkiri Spa & Resort and then dine or drink overlooking the stunning bay of Ao Thian Ok, page 602.

5 **Nakhon Si Thammarat** Sample southern culture, shadow puppetry, food and fairs, page 607.

Phetburi to Chumphon

The historic town of Phetburi (or Phetchaburi), with perhaps the best preserved Ayutthayan wats in Thailand, is 160 km south of Bangkok and can be visited as a day trip from the capital. It is a historic provincial capital on the banks of the Phetburi River and is one of the oldest in Thailand and, because it was never sacked by the Burmese, is unusually intact.

Another 70 km south is Hua Hin, Thailand's original and premier beach resort until it was eclipsed by Phuket and Pattaya. Close by is Cha-am, a smaller seaside resort and the Khao Sam Roi Yod National Park with its rare dusky langurs. Further south is the pleasant resort of Prachuap Khiri Khan and the long, less developed coast down to Chumphon. Chumpon offers some local attractions such as trekking, kayaking, whitewater rafting and diving but is mainly the launch pad to the island of Koh Tao.

▸▸ *For Sleeping, Eating and other listings, see pages 545-555.*

Phetburi and around

Ins and outs

Getting there and around Trains take 2½ hours and the station is about 1½ km northwest of the town centre. The main bus terminal is about the same distance west of town, at the foot of Phra Nakhon Khiri (Khao Wang), but the air-conditioned bus terminal is more central, 500 m north of the centre. Buses take about two hours from Bangkok. There are connections south to Cha-am, Hua Hin and onward. Phetburi – or at least its centre – is small enough to explore on foot. ▸▸ *See also Transport, page 553.*

Background

Initially, Phetburi's wealth and influence was based upon the coastal salt pans found in the vicinity of the town, and which Thai chronicles record as being exploited as early as the 12th century. By the 16th century, Phetburi was supplying salt to most of Siam and the Malay Peninsula. It became particularly important during the Ayutthaya period (14th century) and because the town was not sacked by the Burmese (as Ayutthaya was in 1767) its fine examples of Ayutthayan art and architecture are in good condition. Later, during the 19th century, Phetburi became a popular retreat for the Thai royal family and they built a palace here. Today, Phetburi is famous for its paid assassins who usually carry out their work from the backs of motorcycles with large-calibre pistols. Each time there is a national election, 15 to 20 politicians and their canvassers (so-called *hua khanen*) are killed. As in Chonburi, Thailand's other capital of crime, the police seem strangely unable to charge anyone.

Sights

Phetburi has numerous wats. Those mentioned below are some of the more interesting examples. Although it is possible to walk around these wats in half a day, travelling by saamlor is much less exhausting. Note that often the ordination halls (bots) are locked; if the abbot can be found, he may be persuaded to open them up.

Wat Phra Sri Ratana Mahathat Situated in the centre of town on Damnoenkasem Road, Wat Phra Sri Ratana Mahathat can be seen from a distance. It is dominated by five much-restored, Khmer-style white prangs, probably dating from the Ayutthaya period (14th century); the largest is 42 m high. Inside the bot, richly decorated with murals, are three highly regarded Buddha images, arranged one in front of the other: **Luangpor Mahathat**, **Luangpor Ban Laem** and **Luangpor Lhao Takrao**. The

principal image depicts the crowned Buddha. The complex makes an attractive cluster of buildings. Musicians and dancers are paid by those who want to give thanks for wishes granted.

Wat Yai Suwannaram, Wat Boromvihan and Wat Trailok Across Chomrut Bridge and east along Pongsuriya Road is Wat Yai Suwannaram; it's on the right-hand side, within a spacious compound and a large pond. The wat was built during the Ayutthaya period and then extensively restored during the reign of Rama V. The bot contains some particularly fine Ayutthayan murals showing celestial beings and, facing the principal Buddha image, Mara tempting the Buddha. Note the six-toed bronze Buddha image on the rear wall which is thought to be pre-Ayutthayan in date. Behind the bot is a large teak pavilion (*sala kan parian*) with three doorways at the front and two at the back. The front door panels have fine coloured-glass insets, while the mark on the right-hand panel is said to have been made by a Burmese warrior en route to attack Ayutthaya. The wat also houses an elegant, old wooden library. Wat Boromvihan and Wat Trailok are next to one another on the opposite side of the road and are being restored. They are distinctive only for their wooden dormitories (*kuti*) on stilts.

Wat Kamphaeng Laeng South down Phokarong Road and west a short distance along Phrasong Road, is Wat Kamphaeng Laeng. The five Khmer laterite prangs (one in very poor condition) have been dated to the 12th century and are reminiscent of those in the northeast of the country. Little of the original stucco work remains, but they are nonetheless rather pleasing. Surrounded by thick laterite walls, the wat may have originally been a Hindu temple – a statue of a Hindu goddess was found here in 1956.

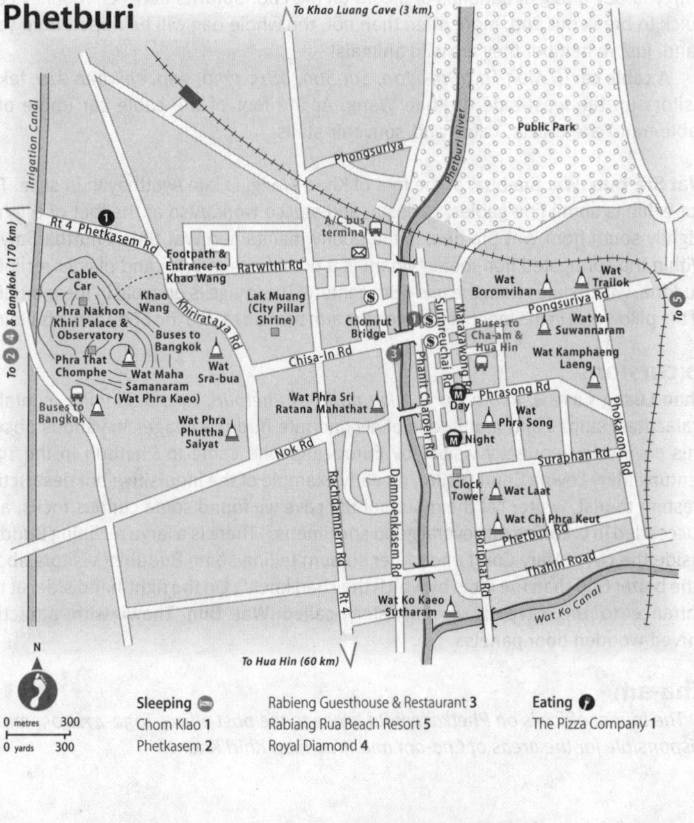

Other wats West back towards the centre of town and south down Matayawong Road, are, in turn, **Wat Phra Song**, **Wat Laat** and **Wat Chi Phra Keut**, all on the left-hand side of the road. Just before reaching a bridge over Wat Ko Canal, is **Wat Ko Kaeo Sutharam**. The bot contains early 18th-century murals showing scenes from the Buddha's life and from Buddhist cosmology. The fact that the mural of the Buddha subduing Mara is on the rear wall, behind the principal Buddha image, has led to speculation that the entrance to the building was relocated at some time, possibly to gain access to a newly constructed road. The wat also houses interesting quarters for monks – long wooden buildings on stilts, similar to those at Wat Boromvihan.

Phra Nakhon Khiri (Khao Wang) At the western edge of the city is Phra Nakhon Khiri, popularly known as Khao Wang (Palace on the Mountain), built in 1858 during the reign of Rama IV. Perched on the top of a 95-m hill, the palace represents an amalgam of Thai, Western and Chinese artistic styles. The hill complex is dotted with frangipani trees and there are areas of architectural interest on the three peaks. On the west rise is the **royal palace** ⓘ *daily 0900-1600, ฿40*, which has recently been restored and is now a well-maintained museum. It contains an eclectic mixture of artefacts (including bed pans) collected by Ramas IV and V who regularly stayed here. The building is airy with a Mediterranean feel and has good views over the surrounding plain.

Also on this peak is the **Hor Chatchavan Viangchai**, an observatory tower which Rama IV used to further his astronomical studies. On the central rise of the hill is the **Phra That Chomphet**, a white stupa erected by Rama IV. On the east rise sits **Wat Maha Samanaram** (also known as Wat Phra Kaeo), which dates from the Ayutthayan period. Within the bot are mural paintings by Khrua In Khong, quite a well-known Thai painter. Watch out for the monkeys here; they seem innocent and friendly enough until you buy a bag of bananas or a corn on the cob. Sprawls between monkeys are quick to break out and, more often than not, the whole bag will be ripped from your hand. Just remember they are wild animals!

A **cable car** ⓘ *Mon-Fri 0815-1700, Sat-Sun, 0815-1730, ฿30, children ฿10*, takes visitors up the west side of Khao Wang. At the foot of the cable car (more of a cable-tram) are toilets, cafés and souvenir stalls.

Wat Sra-bua Wat Sra-bua, at the foot of Khao Wang, is late Ayutthayan in style. The bot exhibits some fine gables, pedestal and stucco work. Also at the foot of the hill, slightly south from Wat Sra-bua, is the poorly maintained **Wat Phra Phuttha Saiyat**. Within the corrugated iron-roofed viharn is a notable 43-m brick and plaster reclining Buddha, which dates from the mid-18th century. The image is unusual in the moulding of the pillow and in the manner in which the arm protrudes into the body of the building.

Excursions

Khao Luang Cave ⓘ *Route 3173, 3 km north of Phetburi, take a saamlor*, contains stalactites, stupas and multitudes of second-rate Buddha images in various poses. This cave was frequently visited by Europeans who came to Phetburi in the 19th century. Mary Lovina Court (1886), an early example of the inquisitive but destructive western tourist, wrote: "At the mouth of the cave we found some curious rocks, and succeeded in breaking off several good specimens." There is a large reclining Buddha inside the cave. Mary Court ended her sojourn telling some Buddhist visitors about "the better God than the idols by which they had knelt". On the right-hand side, at the entrance to the cave, is a monastery called **Wat Bun Thawi** with attractive carved-wooden door panels.

Cha-am

ⓘ *The tourist office is on Phetkasem Rd, close to the post office, T032-471005, and is responsible for the areas of Cha-am and Prachuap Khiri Khan.*

Cha-am is reputed to have been a stopping place for King Naresuan's troops when they were travelling south. The name Cha-am may have derived from the Thai word *cha-an*, meaning to clean the saddle. Cha-am is a beach resort with some excellent hotels and a sizeable building programme of new hotels and condominiums for wealthy Bangkokians. The beach is a classic stretch of golden sand, though rather featureless. The town also has a good reputation for the quality of its seafood. It has become a popular weekend spot, so sizeable discounts are available during the week when most hotels are close to empty. At the weekend something of a transformation occurs and it buzzes with life for 48 hours before returning to its comatose state.

Maruekkhathayawan Palace ⓘ *between Cha-am and Hua Hin, daily 0800-1600, entry by donation, take a saamlor or catch a bus heading for Hua Hin and walk 2 km from the turn-off*, was designed by an Italian and built by Rama VI in 1924; the king is reputed to have had a major influence in its design. The palace is made of teak and the name means 'Place of love and hope', which is rather charming. It consists of 16 pavilions in a very peaceful setting.

Hua Hin and around

Thailand's first beach resort, Hua Hin, has had an almost continuous royal connection since the late 19th century. In 1868, King Mongkut journeyed to Hua Hin to observe a total eclipse of the sun. In 1910, Prince Chakrabongse, brother of Rama VI, visited Hua Hin on a hunting trip and was so enchanted by the area he built himself a villa. Sadly, today, central Hua Hin has become a rather tawdry beach resort. However, there are still some beautiful and attractive places to stay and the white-sand beach is pleasant in front of some of the hotels.

Ins and outs

Getting there There are daily flights with **SGA** to Bangkok. A taxi from the airport costs ฿40-50, a local bus costs ฿10. The train station is on the western edge of town, within walking distance of the centre. The journey from Bangkok takes three hours and there are onward connections to all points south. The bus terminal is quite central and provides regular connections with Bangkok and many southern towns.

Getting around Hua Hin is an increasingly compact beach resort and many of the hotels and restaurants are within walking distance of one another. There is also a good network of public transport: songthaews run along fixed routes, there are taxis and saamlors, and bicycles, motorbikes and cars are all available for hire.

Tourist information Tourist Office ⓘ *114 Phetkasem Rd, T032-511047, Mon-Fri 0800-1630. Also useful is www.huahin-tourist-information.com.*

Background

The first of the royal palaces, **Saen Samran House**, was built by Prince Naris, son of Rama V. In the early 1920s, King Vajiravudh (Rama VI) – no doubt influenced by his brother Chakrabongse – began work on a teakwood palace, **'Deer Park'**. The final stamp of royal approval came in the late 1920s, when King Phrajadipok (Rama VII) built another palace, which he named **Klai Kangwon**, literally 'Far From Worries'. It was designed by one of Prince Naris' sons. The name could not have been more inappropriate: the king was staying at Klai Kangwon in 1932 when he was dislodged from the throne by a coup d'état.

Early guidebooks, nostalgic for English seaside towns, named the resort Hua Hin-on-Sea. *Hua* (head) *Hin* (rock) refers to a stone outcrop at the end of the fine white-sand beach. The resort used to promote itself as the 'Queen of Tranquillity'; until

 the 1980s, it was a forgotten backwater of an earlier, and less frenetic, tourist era. However, in the last few years the constant influx of tourists has livened up the atmosphere considerably; with massage parlours, tourist shops and numerous western restaurants and bars lining the streets, it's hard to get a moment's peace. And just when you think the town is as chock-a-block as possible, the sound of drills and construction work reminds you otherwise. Concominiums are springing up all along the coast to cater for wealthy holidaymakers from Bangkok; high-rise buildings scar the horizon and vehicles clog the streets. New golf courses are being constructed to serve Thailand's growing army of golfers – as well as avid Japanese players – and the olde-worlde charm that was once Hua Hin's great selling point has been lost.

Hua Hin

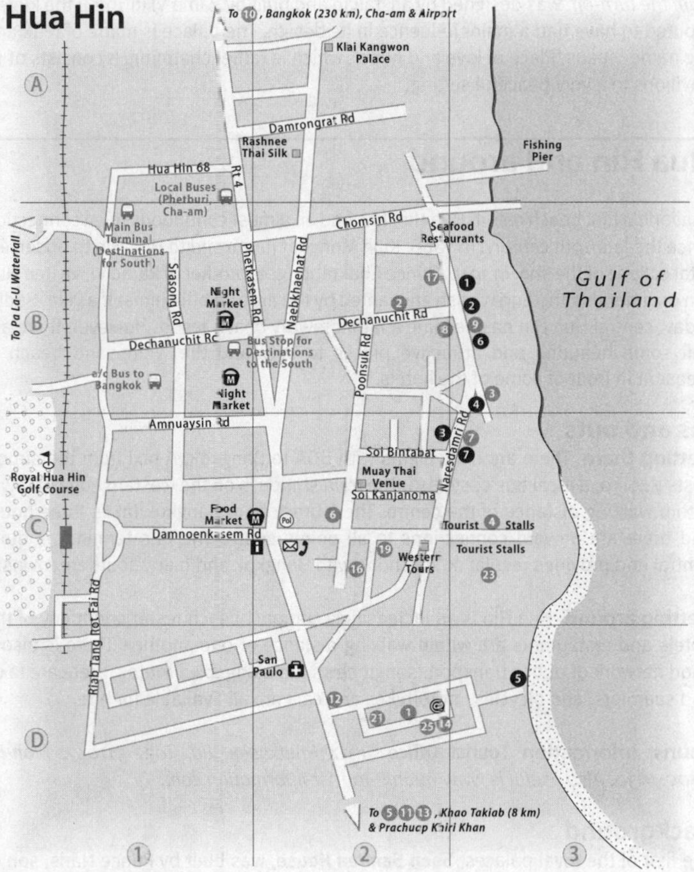

0 metres 100
0 yards 100

Sleeping
A & B Guesthouse 1 *D2*
All Nations Guesthouse 2 *B2*
Anantara Resort & Spa 10 *A2*
Bird Guesthouse 3 *B3*
Central Hua Hin Village 4 *C2*
Chiva Som International Health Resort 5 *D2*
City Beach Resort 6 *C2*
Evason Hua Hin Resort & Spa 13 *D2*
Fu-Lay 8 *B3*
Fu-Lay II 9 *B3*
Hilton Hua Hin Resort & Spa 7 *C3*
Hyatt Regency Hua Hin 11 *D2*
Hua Hin Marriott Resort & Spa 12 *D2*
Jinning Beach 14 *D2*
Patchara House 16 *C2*
Pattana Guesthouse 17 *B2*
PP Villa & Pulang Pen 19 *C2*
Royal Beach 21 *D2*
Sofitel Central (Railway Hotel) 23 *C3*
Sunshine Guesthouse 25 *D2*

Eating
Brasserie de Paris 1 *B3*
Chao Ley 2 *B3*
Hua Hin Brewing Co 7 *C3*
Lo Stivale 3 *C2*
Maharaja 6 *B3*
Veranda Grill 5 *D3*
World News Coffee 4 *B3*

Sights

Beach As Hua Hin is billed as a beach resort people come here expecting a beautiful tropical beach but that isn't quite the case. Many of the nicest stretches of sand are in front of hotels – the **Hilton, Marriott** and **Sofitel** in particular.

Railway Hotel This famous hotel was built in 1923 by a Thai prince, Purachatra, who headed the State Railways of Thailand. It became Thailand's premier seaside hotel, but by the 1960s had fallen into rather glorious disrepair. It experienced a short burst of stardom when the building played the role of the Phnom Penh Hotel in the film the *Killing Fields*, but it still seemed destined to rot into oblivion. Saved by privatization, it was renovated and substantially expanded in 1986 and is now an excellent five-star hotel. Unfortunately, it has been renamed, and goes under the unromantic name of the **Sofitel Central Hua Hin Resort** (see Sleeping). At the other end of Damnoenkasem Road from the hotel is the railway station itself. The station has a rather quaint Royal Waiting Room on the platform.

Khao Takiab Khao Takiab (Chopstick Hill), south of town, is a dirty, unremarkable hill with a large standing Buddha facing the sea. Nearby is **Khao Krilat**, a rock covered in assorted shrines, stupas, ponds, salas and Buddha images. To get there, take a local bus from Dechanuchit Road.

Kaeng Krachan National Park and caves

ⓘ *For the park, take a minibus from the station on Srasong Rd to the village of Fa Prathan, 53 km (฿15). For the caves, take the same bus but get off at Nongphlab village (฿10) and ask at the police station for directions. The caves are a 45-min to 1-hr walk.*

The park, 63 km northwest of Hua Hin, is Thailand's largest protected area covering 2,915 sq km. It was gazetted in 1981 and is said to support significant populations of large mammal species (elephant, tiger, leopard, gibbon, the Malayan pangolin) and birds (hornbills, minivets, pheasants and bee-eaters). Endangered species include the woolly-necked stork and the plain-pouched hornbill. Few visitors see many of these animals though. Extensive trails lead through undisturbed forest and past a succession of waterfalls (the best being **Pa La-U**, which has 11 tiers and is renowned for its butterflies) to hot springs and a Karen village. Guides are advisable and cost ฿500 per day, but many of them don't speak English, so make sure you meet the guide before paying your money. The Tenasserim mountain range cuts through the park; the highest peak stands at 1,207 m. **Phanoen Thung Mountain** offers superb views of the surrounding countryside. It's a six-hour hike to the summit; warm clothes are needed for the chilly mornings.

Companies run tours to Kaeng Krachan National Park (around ฿1,000, with lunch) and to the Pa La-U waterfall, see Tour operators.

En route to Pa La-U, 27 km from Hua Hin and close to Nongphlab village, are three caves: **Dao**, **Lablae** and **Kailon**, which contain the usual array of stalactites and stalagmites. Guides with lanterns will take visitors through the caves for ฿30 and boat trips can be made on the reservoir. Until recently, entrance to the park was only ฿20, but was suddenly increased to ฿200 with another charge of ฿200 for the Pa La-U waterfalls. Due to this dramatic increase, a number of tour operators have decided to boycott the park, in the hope the price will drop. Accommodation is available at the park HQ, see Sleeping.

Khao Sam Roi Yod National Park

ⓘ *Park HQ, T032-619078, ฿200, children ฿100. Take a bus from Hua Hin to Pranburi (there are also trains to Pranburi, as well as trains and buses from Bangkok). From*

The plains of Sam Roi Yod were used as the location for Pol Pot's killing fields in the film of the same name.

Pranburi it is necessary to charter a songthaew (฿250) or take a motorcycle taxi (฿150) to the park HQ. Be sure you are taken to Khao Sam Roi Yod National Park, and not Khao Sam Roi Yod village. For Laem Sala Beach (located within the park), there are regular songthaews from Pranburi market to Bang Pu village from 0800-1600, ฿20. Or take a tour with one of the many tour operators in town, ฿900.

Khao Sam Roi Yod National Park ('Mountain of Three Hundred Peaks') occupies an area of limestone hills surrounded by saltwater flats and borders the Gulf of Thailand. It lies about 45 km south of Hua Hin, east off Route 4. Its freshwater marshes provide 11 different categories of wetland habitat – as much as the Red River Delta in Vietnam which covers an area nearly 200 times greater. The area is a haven for waterbirds and has been extensively developed (and exploited) as a centre for prawn and fish farming, limiting the marshland available to the waterbirds who breed here. The park has the advantage of being relatively small (98 sq km) with readily accessible sights: **wildlife** (including the rare and shy serow), **forest walks** and **quiet beaches**. The main beach is Laem Sala where a campsite, bungalows and a restaurant are located. Search the beach here for sand dollars and mother of pearl.

There are also some caves. **Phraya Nakhon**, close to Ban Bang Pu beach, has two large sinkholes where the roof collapsed a century ago, and a pavilion which was built in 1896 for the visit of King Rama V and is currently being restored. The climb to the cave takes one hour and can be slippery. If you are lucky you may spot some rare dusky langurs with their babies. **Sai Cave** contains impressive stalactites and stalagmites and a 'petrified waterfall' created from dripping water. At least 237 species of land and

Khao Sam Roi Yod National Park

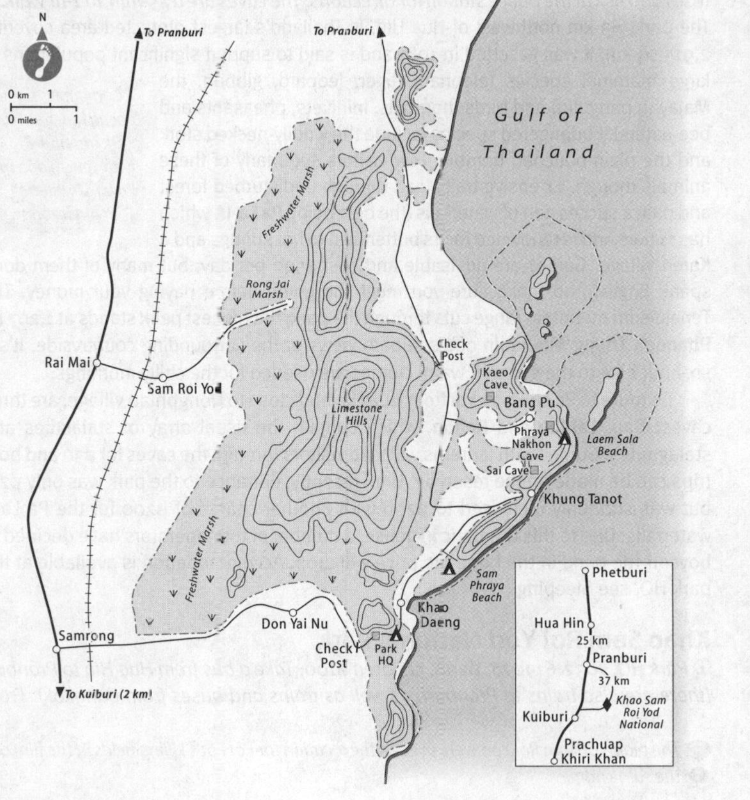

waterbirds have been recorded including painted storks, herons, egrets and many different waders. To visit the caves and beaches, boats can be hired from local fishermen at the park HQ (฿200-700). Schools of dolphins are often sighted on the way.

The biggest challenge facing the park – which supports a remarkable range of habitats for such a small area – is encroachment by private shrimp ponds. More than a third of the park area was cleared for fish and shrimp farming in 1992. Ironically, most of the prawn farms are now deserted, due to prawn disease. Available at the park HQ is a very useful guide with comprehensive details on fauna, flora and other natural sights in the park.

Prachuap Khiri Khan

Prachuap Khiri Khan is a small and peaceful resort with a long, crescent-shaped beach. At either end of the crescent, vegetation-draped limestone towers rear up from the sea creating beautiful symmetry and stunning views. The town is more popular with Thais than with farangs and has a reputation for good seafood. Bob, who runs the internet office and tourist information in the **Hadthong Hotel**, speaks good English and is helpful.

At the northern end of town, at the end of Salashiep/Sarathip Road, is **Khao Chong Krachok**. An exhausting 15- to 20-minute climb up the 'Mountain with the Mirror' (past armies of preening monkeys) is rewarded with fine views of the surrounding countryside and bay. At the summit there is an unremarkable shrine built in 1922 containing a footprint of the Buddha.

There is a good **night market** at the corner of Phitakchat and Kong Kiat roads and a daily market with stacks of fruit along Maitri Ngam (the road south of the post office, opposite the **Hadthong Hotel**). The daily market which runs along Salashiep/Sarathip Road has stalls of orchids, fruit and metal sculptures. South of the **Hadthong Hotel** on Susuek Road are a couple of Chinese shophouses.

Ao Manao ⓘ *take a motorbike taxi or tuk-tuk* (*฿30*), is an attractive bay 5 km south of town and is popular with day trippers. There are restaurants, toilets, deckchairs and umbrellas to hire. Ao Manao is on a military base and you must sign in and out at the entrance.

Bang Saphan to Chumphon

South of Prachuap Khiri Khan, the coastline to Chumphon is dotted with hotels and resorts; all are signposted in English off the main Route 4. At **Bang Saphan**, 60 km south of Prachuap Khiri Khan, several small beach resorts are developing, geared as much to Thais as to foreigners. **Hat Somboon** is the nearest beach to Bang Saphan, just 1 km away. The position is attractive enough although the sand soon degenerates into mud below the low-water mark. Continuing south from Bang Saphan are a series of other small groups of resorts and guesthouses – all still very low key.

Around 5 km further south is a ferry link to the offshore island of **Koh Talu** ⓘ *15 mins from the mainland by boat from Bang Saphan Noi*. It is an excellent dive site with particularly good deep water diving and turtles. The name of the island is derived from its extraordinary 45-m hill which is shot through with a 30-m hole – '*talu*' means to pass through. For land lubbers there are rare bats and an abundance of swiftlets. The nests of the latter are harvested for bird's nest soup (see page 488).

North of Bang Saphan is the village of **Ban Krut** ⓘ *it is on the north-south railway line and can be reached by slow train. Tourist information at Ban Krut, T032-695337.* The village and beach area are particularly appealing. The drive from the main road through to the beach passes a charming town with mostly wooden buildings, and then winds past a lovely rural scene of large raintrees and lily ponds. The beach area is lined with casuarina trees and coconut palms. The northern end leads past the usual line of small beachside restaurants, through a fishing community and then up to a large Buddha image on the northern hillside overlooking the bay. It is at the southern end of the bay where most of the accommodation is concentrated.

Chumphon

Chumphon is considered the 'gateway to the south' and is where the southern highway divides, one route running west and then south on Route 4 to Ranong, Phuket and the Andaman Sea; the other, south on Route 41 to Surat Thani, Koh Samui, Nakhon Si Thammarat and the waters of the Gulf of Thailand.

There is not much to see in Chumphon town itself. There are, however, some good beaches nearby and some islands offshore (see below) and it is used as an access point for Koh Tao (see page 597).

The waters off the coast provide excellent diving opportunities. There are dive sites around the islands of **Koh Ngam Noi** (parcelled out to birds' nest concessionaires) and **Koh Ngam Yai**. Rock outcrops like **Hin Lak Ngam** and **Hin Pae**, are also becoming increasingly popular with dive companies for their coral gardens, caves and rock piles. Of particular note are the 500 varieties of rare black corals found in the vicinity of Hin Lak Ngam. The sea here is plankton-rich, which means an abundance of sea life including whale shark, several other species of shark, and sea turtles, as well as coral gardens. Visibility, though, is variable and certainly not as crystalline as on the Andaman Sea side of the Isthmus. On a good day it may be more than 20 m, but at low tide less than half of this.

In his book *Surveying and exploring in Siam*, published in 1900, James McCarthy writes of 'Champawn' marking the beginning of the Malay Peninsula. A group of

Chumphon

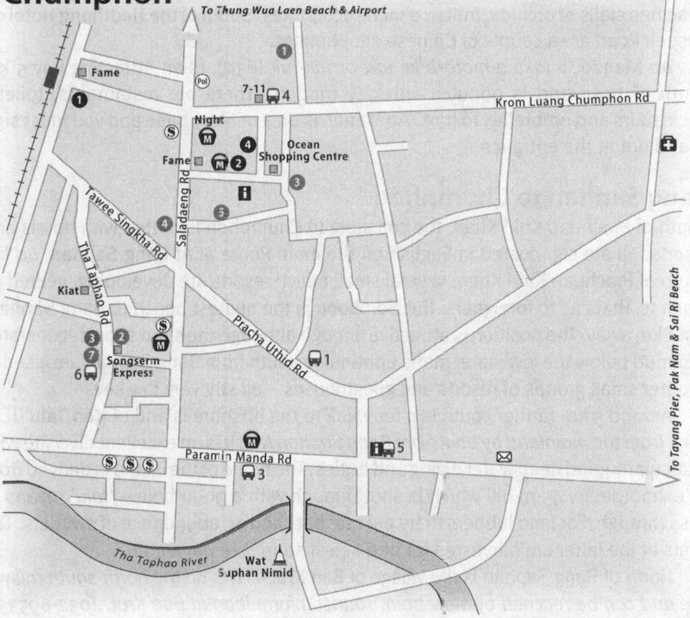

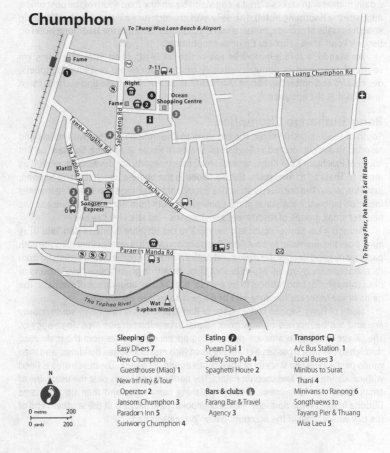

Sleeping
Easy Divers 7
New Chumphon Guesthouse (Miao) 1
New Infinity & Tour Operator 2
Jansom Chumphon 3
Paradorn Inn 5
Suriwong Chumphon 4

Eating
Puean Djai 1
Safety Stop Pub 4
Spaghetti House 2

Bars & clubs
Farang Bar & Travel Agency 3

Transport
A/c Bus Station 1
Local Buses 3
Minibus to Surat Thani 4
Minivans to Ranong 6
Songthaews to Tayang Pier & Thuang Wua Laeu 5

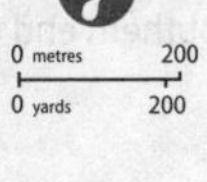

French engineers had already visited the area with a view to digging a canal through the Kra Isthmus and it was clearly a little place at that time: the "harbour was full of rocks covered with oysters. The usual cocoa-nut palms and grass shanties marked the position of the village".

Beaches

Hat Thung Wua Laen ⓘ *take a bus from the market in Chumphon (฿30)*, 18 km north of Chumphon, is a beautiful beach. It's probably the best beach in the area with a broad curving bay and a long stretch of white sand which slopes gently towards the sea, though this also means it's a long walk out to the water at low tide. There are a number of hotels and bungalow operations here but the beach is still mercifully free of the paraphernalia of tourism and even when most accommodation is fully occupied the area is large enough to maintain a sense of peace and seclusion. In March the waters become inundated with plankton, which locals harvest using nets. It is considered a delicacy and is known as *kuey*.

Hat Sai Ri ⓘ *take a songthaew (฿20) from opposite the New Infinity Travel Agency in Chumpon, or from the post office*, is 3 km south of Hat Pharadon and close to Koh Thong Luang. There is good snorkelling in the area. There is also a shrine to His Royal Highness Prince Chumphon, the self-styled father of the Royal Thai Navy.

Amphoe Lang Suan ⓘ *take a bus from the bus station in Chumphon*, is 62 km south of Chumphon. There are two beautiful caves in the area – **Tham Khao Ngoen** and **Tham Khao Kriep**. There are 370 steps leading to the latter which is studded with stalagmites and stalactites. The district is also locally renowned for the quality of its fruit.

Excursions

Pak Nam Chumphon ⓘ *11 km southeast of Chumphon on Route 4901, take a songthaew from opposite the morning market on the southern side of town*, lies on the coast, at the mouth of the Chumphon River. It's a big fishing village with boats for hire to the nearby islands where swiftlets build their nests. The swiftlets are used to make the Chinese speciality of bird's nest soup – *yanwo*, in Chinese (see box, page 488). Many concessionaires are accompanied by bodyguards; visitors should seek permission before venturing to the nest sites. Islands include **Koh Phrao, Koh Lanka Chiu** and **Koh Rang Nok**. Other activities such as diving, jungle treks and boat trips to the caves can be organized through a guesthouse or travel agent (see Tour operators).

Much of the coastline and islands off Chumphon form part of the **Chumphon Marine National Park** (Mu Ko Chumphon). The park headquarters, T077-558144, is 8 km from Had Si Ree and can provide details of bungalows and campsites. The park contains mangrove forest, limestone mountain forest as well as marine life offshore.

Sleeping

Phetburi and around *p536, map p537*
Phetburi has limited accommodation in the upper price bracket.

AL-A Rabiang Rua Beach Resort, 80/1-5 Moo 1 Anamai Rd, Chao Samran Beach, T02-9671911, www.rabiangrua.com. Right on the beach, with great views and within easy reach of Phetburi, this is the first really comfortable, intimate and de luxe place to stay. Rooms are in 'boats' (rice-barge style) set around a small pool. Popular with Thai families. Bedrooms are strong on wood features, but light and airy nonetheless. Furnishings are refreshingly simple and although it's an odd-looking place to stay, it is fun and the staff are friendly. Bungalows also available. Recommended.

B Royal Diamond Hotel, 555 Phetkasem Rd, T032-411061, www.royaldiamondhotel.com. Luxurious hotel compared to most others in Phetburi. The 58 rooms have a/c and are adequately furnished. The restaurant does a range of international food. There's a beer garden and pleasant, peaceful atmosphere. Internet access.

C-D Phetkasem, 86/1 Phetkasem Rd, T032-425581. Best value place to stay in this category. 30 clean rooms, some with a/c. Friendly management. There is no restaurant but it is located very close to some of the best eats in Phetburi (see Eating below). Motorcycle rent ฿250 and Thai massage ฿350 offered.

D Rabieng Guesthouse, Damnoenkasem Rd, T032-425707. Wood-panelled rooms with tiled floors on the ground floor. Pokier rooms upstairs but all clean. A good night's sleep is impossible though if your room faces the noisy bridge. Open-air seating area upstairs and cleanish communal facilities. Appealing restaurant overlooking the river serving a very wide range of dishes (see Eating). Motorbikes can be rented out for ฿250 per day; bicycles for ฿120. Laundry service. Trekking and rafting tours in the national parks are available. Good English is spoken.

E Chom Klao, 1 Tewet Rd, on the east bank of the river diagonally opposite the **Rabieng** with duck-blue shutters, T032-425398. Offers clean, quiet and fair-sized rooms, though they are bare and unattractive. The rooms with views over the river are by far the best and have balcony areas. More expensive rooms have shower rooms attached, ones without have basins. Friendly, helpful and informative management.

Cha-am *p538*

A number of new hotels have opened on the seafront offering more bungalows and simple rooms in the **B-C** price range, with a few in the **D** range. Unless you speak Thai, it will be difficult to make a phone booking, but it is highly likely that you'll find available rooms on arrival.

L-AL Dusit Resort, 1349 Phetkasem Rd, T032-520009, www.dusit.com. Large, stylish hotel block (300 rooms), with polo 'motifs' throughout. Superb facilities including range of watersports, fitness centre, spa, tennis courts, horse riding and an enormous swimming pool, Thai arts and crafts demonstrations.

L-AL Regent, 849/21 Phetkasem Rd, south of the main beach area, T032-451240, www.regent-chaam.com. A/c, restaurants, pools, hotel and cottage accommodation on a 120-ha site, and every conceivable facility including squash and tennis courts, and a fitness centre.

L-A Methavalai, 220 Ruamchit Rd, T032-433250, www.methavalai.com. A/c bungalows, some with several bedrooms – ideal for families – and a small area of private beach, pool, good seafood and Thai restaurant

B-C Santisuk, 263/3 Ruamchit Rd, south of the main stretch, T032-471212. Range of accommodation – some with a/c – including wooden cottages or a hotel block. Both are good.

B-D Jitravee, 241/20 Ruamchit Rd, T032-471382. Clean rooms, friendly. More expensive rooms have a/c, TV, fridge, room service, bathroom. Cheaper rooms have clean, shared bathroom, some English spoken.

C Viwathana, 263/21 Ruamchit Rd, T032-471289. One of the longer established with some simple, fan-cooled wooden bungalows as well as a new brick-built block. All are set in a garden of sorts. The more expensive bungalows have 2 or 3 rooms and a/c. Good value for families.

C-D Pratarnchoke House, 240/3 Ruamchit Rd, T032-471215. Range of rooms available here from simple fan-cooled through to more luxurious a/c rooms with bathrooms. Some English spoken.

D-E Som's Guesthouse, 234/30 Ruamchit Rd, T032-433753. Nice clean rooms and one of the cheapest places to stay in Cha-am.

Hua Hin and around *p539, map p540*

Many hotels reduce prices in the low season. Rack rates are extortionate. For better deals check the internet or go through a tour operator. Prices quoted here are for high season.

Soi Thipurai

Slightly more expensive guesthouses are to be found just south of the town in an area called Soi Thipurai (named after the first guesthouse opened there, and all tuk-tuk drivers know it as such). They are just southeast of the **Marriott**. It's very much its own little community with internet facilities, restaurants in all the guesthouses, motorbike and bicycle rental, tours available, and even a fashion house for tailor-made clothes. Everyone speaks good English and the people are very hospitable and friendly. The beach here is much

quieter and cleaner than the main beach in Hua Hin. A highly recommended area for a quiet retreat. All the guesthouses have similar spacious rooms with a/c, hot water, satellite TV, and access to a swimming pool.

L Anantara Resort and Spa, 43/1 Phetkasem Rd, T032-520260, www.anantara.com. 187 rooms in teak pavilions set around a gorgeous pool. There's an Italian, Thai and international restaurant and good sports facilities but no beach to speak of. The spa is run by **Mandara Spa**, www.mandaraspa-asia.com. Recommended.

L Chiva Som International Health Resort, 73/4 Phetkasem Rd, T032-536536, www.chivasom.com. This is a luxury health resort (*Chiva-Som* means 'Haven of Life) set in 3 ha of luxury grounds which ooze calm and peace. It has a large spa building housing a spacious gym, Roman bath, enormous jacuzzi, circular steam room and dance studio. There is also an outdoor freshwater pool close to the sea. With health consultants, hydrotherapy and lots of herbal tea and healthy food, this is the place to come to lose weight or firm up those buttocks without feeling that life is too miserable. There are numerous treatment and accommodation packages on offer.

L Hilton Hua Hin Resort and Spa, 33 Naresdamri Rd, T032-522235, www.hilton.com. This rather unappealing white tower block dominates the town centre. However, it is a very pleasant and comfortable hotel offering a luscious spa, lovely pool, restaurants and a nice stretch of beach. The 296 rooms are attractively decorated although the bathrooms are lacking in grandeur in comparison. Views from the rooms are superb. Staff are helpful and friendly.

L Hua Hin Marriott Resort and Spa, 107/1 Phetkasem Rd, T032-511881, www.marriotthotels.com. A large resort with a very attractive lobby. The **Mandara Spa** architecture and ambience is beautiful with a blend of Thai and Balinese style and large stepping stones to cross ponds. The 216 rooms enjoy top facilities. The beach in front of the hotel is white, clean and pleasant. The pool gets extremely busy and there are 4 restaurants and 2 bars. Good sports facilities including tennis, fitness centre, watersports and a kids' club. Recommended.

L Hyatt Regency Hua Hin, 99 Hua Hin-Khao Takiap Rd, T032-521234, www.huahin.regency.hyatt.com. All the facilities you'd expect from a top-class hotel including an extensive range of watersports and cyber games centre. It is a lovely low-rise luxurious resort of 204 rooms set in an expanse of well-maintained gardens. A spa is due to open in 2006.

L Sofitel Central Hua Hin Resort, 1 Damnoenkasem Rd, T032-512021, www.sofitel.com. Hua Hin's original premier hotel, formerly the **Railway Hotel**. A beautiful place set in luscious gardens with some very creative topiary. It maintains excellent levels of service and enjoys a very good position on the beach, and while the new rooms are small they are well appointed. Rooms are beautifully decorated and bathrooms are finished with marble. Lovely grounds with pools right near the beach and frangipani trees, and an interesting small museum. In addition the seafood restaurant here – with a French chef – is truly worth seeking out. Colonial tea on the steps of the tea room and museum should not be missed. The hotel also boasts the **Centara Spa**. Recommended.

L-AL Evason Hua Hin Resort and Spa, 9 Paknampran Beach, Prachuap Khiri Khan, T032-618200, www.six-senses.com. About 20 km south of Hua Hin (not far from Pranburi) is this stylish resort, set in spacious grounds with a beautiful pool. It is hard to beat for anyone wanting to 'get away from it all'. The owners have created a unique environment, with light and airy rooms, furnished with contemporary, locally produced furniture. Some of the more expensive villas have private plunge pools. The spa provides the last word in pampering and there are plenty of other (complimentary) facilities including watersports (sailing, kayaking), tennis courts, a gym, archery. The kids' club has a separate pool and playground plus daily activities. Low-season prices are good value.

AL Central Hua Hin Village, 1 Damnoenkasem Rd, T032-512021, www.centralhotelresorts.com. 41 Thai village bungalows in a garden setting with direct access to the beach. Has all facilities: sauna, pool, spa, tennis courts etc. The bungalows are designed totally in keeping with the traditional local style and are really charming.

The whole resort is attractively petite compared to the towering **Hilton** which dwarfs it. Surprisingly spacious on the inside and again decorated in keeping with Hua Hin's tradition (albeit one which is being lost in most parts) of an elegant beach resort of a bygone era. The **Centara Spa**, 0900-2100, offers massage pavillions in the hotel grounds as well as massage rooms and sauna in the main spa buildings.

A City Beach Resort, 16 Damnoenkasem Rd, T032-512870, www.citybeach.co.th. 162 very outdated and overpriced rooms. Restaurant, strange pool, pub with live music and karaoke. A good central location though. Staff are helpful and there is an excellent breakfast included in the price.

A-D Fu Lay II, Naresdamri Rd, T032-513145, www.fulayhuahin.com. A delightful little place with olde worlde look with teak frontage and white carved wooden railings and splashes of pastel green. Only a/c rooms have hot water. Fan rooms have shared bathrooms. Good restaurant. The Thai house is a cute little getaway on the top deck with ocean views.

B A&B, 113/16-17 Phetkasem Rd, T032-532340, www.abguesthouse.com. Friendly Swedish management at this guesthouse with 12 ultra-clean rooms and bathrooms. TV, a/c and fridge.

B Fu Lay, 110/1 Naresdamri Rd, T032-513610, www.huahinguide.com/guesthouses/fulay. 11 a/c rooms with TV in this small modern hotel.

B PP Villa and Puang Pen Hotel, 11 Damnoenkasem Rd, T032-533785, ppvillahotel@hotmail.com. 40 a/c plainly decorated rooms, pool. Recommended for excellent value and its central location, but some reception staff are very rude.

B-C Jinning Beach,113/25-26 Phetkasem Rd, T032-513950, www.jinningbeachguesthouse.com. 15 a/c rooms with minibar and TV. Not as friendly as the others in this street.

B-C Patchara House, Naresdamri Rd, T032-511787. Some rooms with a/c, clean, friendly, room service, hot water, TV, pleasant restaurant. Recommended.

B-C Royal Beach, 113/13 Phetkasem Rd, T032-532210, royalbeach@hotmail.com. 12 rooms with minibar and TV available.

B-C Sunshine Guesthouse, T032-515309, 113/30 Soi Hua Hin, Phetkasem Rd, sunshineguesthouse@yahoo.com. Super-friendly management at this guesthouse which is slightly cheaper than the others. Rooms have minibars, a/c and TVs. Internet café in the lobby.

C-D Bird Guesthouse, T032-511630, birdguesthousehuahin@hotmail.com. 10 rooms on a wooden platform on stilts above the beach. Sweet little atmospheric place with a pastel green theme and friendly management. There is no restaurant but you can get breakfast here, sitting area with views over the sea, more ambience and character than most. Rooms with a/c cost more.

D All Nations Guesthouse, 10 Dechanuchit Rd, T032-512747, cybercafehuahin@hotmail.com. Rooms with fan or a/c with your own balcony, clean. One of the cheapest in Hua Hin.

D Pattana Guesthouse, 52 Naresdamri Rd, T032-513393, huahinpattana@hotmail.com. Attractive location down a small alley. 13 twin-bedded rooms with fans in 2 original Thai teakwood buildings set around a flower-filled compound, some rooms with own bathrooms. 50 m from the beach, breakfast available.

Kaeng Krachan National Park *p541*

B Bungalows sleeping 5-6 are available at the park HQ but you must bring all necessities with you (eg blankets, food and water) as nothing is provided.

Khao Sam Roi Yod National Park *p541, map p542*

B-C Bungalows either for hire in their entirety or per couple and a camping ground, with tents for hire, ฿100. You can also pitch your own tent here for around ฿20. Bungalows are available at both the park HQ and at Laem Sala Beach. Take mosquito repellent.

Prachuap Khiri Khan *p543*

With the influx of Thais at weekends, accommodation is hard to find. During the week, room rates can be negotiated down.

B-C Hadthong, 21 Susuek Rd, T032-601050, www.hadthong.com. Comfortable rooms (but small bathrooms in the standard rooms) overlooking the sea with great views. The pool also enjoys views of the

bay. It is good value and the best hotel in town. The restaurant serves good Thai food. The breakfast is reasonable.

C Golden Beach Hotel, 113-115 Suanson Rd, north of town past Khao Chong Krachock, 600 m north of the river, south of Happy Inn, T032-601626, goldenbeachhostel@hotmail.com. Basic clean rooms with a/c but rooms are smaller than at Happy Inn.

C Happy Inn, 600 m north of Khao Chong Krachok, T032-602082. Quite nice a/c bungalows with TV and bathroom attached. Just across the road from the beach, beside the river.

D-E Yuttichai, 115 Kong Kiat Rd, T032-611055. This is a large, characterful family-run place. The vast front living area is like a little museum. Clean rooms with own bathroom and fans have oriental toilets and shared bathrooms have western toilets.

Bang Saphan to Chumphon *p543*

The southern end of the bay near Ban Krut village has quite a variety of accommodation from large wood and bamboo bungalows to colourful concrete houses reminiscent of some European seaside resorts. Many of the latter are let in a timeshare style or are owned by Bangkokians looking for a quieter (and cheaper) place to stay than Hua Hin or Cha-am. The area tends to attract families rather than individuals or couples and consequently has excellent accommodation for larger groups, such as 2- or 3-bedroom bungalow houses. Most resorts have ample and landscaped grounds. Resorts do tend to be a little pricey for couples or individual travellers but are good value for larger groups. Accommodation tends to be quite simple but is clean and comfortable. A problem with the area is that there are very few restaurants at the resorts and it's quite a walk to the main restaurant area.

C Nipa Beach Bungalows, Hat Somboon. A/c, hot water, telephone and TV. Good value and comfortable.

Chumphon *p544, map p544*

A-C Jansom Chumphon, 188/138 Saladaeng Rd, T077-502502, jansombeach@yahoo.com. Clean rooms with a/c and spacious bathrooms, but the place is quite run down and the curtains need replacing. Restaurant serves a wide range of Thai food. The breakfast is measly. Disco attached.

B-D Paradorn Inn, 180/12 Saladang Rd, T077-511500, www.chumphon-paradorn.com. A/c rooms with TV that are brighter, whiter and nicer than anything the competition offers. The restaurant is furnished with bamboo furniture and offers a wide range of reasonably priced food (0800-2200).

D-E Suriwong Chumphon Hotel, 125/30 Saladang Rd, T077-511203. Basically furnished rooms which are a little dark. Some bathrooms have damp ceilings but are OK. Reception is not too friendly. Better value can be found elsewhere.

E Farang Bar and Travel Agency, Tha Tapao Rd, T077-501003. 9 dark, airless rooms with fan next to the restaurant with very clean toilets and showers out the back. However, Easy Divers up the road is nicer and cheaper. Half-day rent and showers, ฿20.

E New Infinity, 68/2 Tha Taphao Rd, T077-570176. 6 rooms, 1 is larger with balcony, some smaller ones with no windows – all have fans, very basic but clean, shared bathrooms. Very friendly and helpful management. Good travel service offered here, see Tour operators, below.

E-F Easy Divers, Tha Taphao Rd, T077-570085, chumphon@dive.com. 6 twin or triple rooms that are decent sized and clean but windowless. Clean and pleasant shared bathrooms. The place is open from 0300-2100.

E-F New Chumphon Guesthouse (otherwise known as Maio Guesthouse), close to the Krong Luam Chumphon Rd on soi 1, T01-0792856. Clean, cosy rooms with wood-panelled floors upstairs and darker, cheaper rooms downstairs. Shared bathrooms. Homely atmosphere, friendly and helpful with management who speak good English. Tours to caves and waterfalls also arranged. Motorbike rental ฿200.

Beaches *p545*

There are a number of hotels and bungalow operations at Hat Thung Wua Lean. In terms of accommodation, the Chumpon Cabana is the most upmarket and right on the

beach. Bungalow resorts are mostly separated from the beach by the road (but this is narrow and not busy), and usually set in smallish gardens.

A-D Clean Wave, T077-560151. Some rooms with a/c. Cheaper fan-cooled bungalows.

B Chumphon Sunny Beach Resort, Amphoe Thung Tako, T077-579182. Fan-cooled and a/c bungalows.

B-C Chumphon Cabana Resort, T077-560245-7, www.cabana.co.th. Some nicely decorated a/c bungalows set in attractive gardens and 2 hotel blocks all with a/c and hot water. The newer buildings have all been designed on energy-saving principles in keeping with the owner's environmental concerns. The resort has all the usual facilities including a pool, good watersports (including a PADI dive centre), a very peaceful location and a great view of the beach from the restaurant and some of the bungalows.

C-E Tawat Hotel, Amphoe Lang Suan, T077-541341. 100 rooms, some with fan and some a/c.

D Maio House, 600 m from the beach, T0792856/01-691226. Run by the same lady who runs the **New Chumphon Guesthouse** in town. 6 rooms with fridge and fan. Some rooms have cooker. Price is negotiable for longer stays.

Eating

Phetburi and around *p536, map p537*

Phetburi is well known for its desserts including *khanom mo kaeng* (a hard custard made of mung bean, egg, coconut and sugar, baked over an open fire), *khao kriap* (a pastry with sesame, coconut and sugar) and excellent *kluai khai* (sweet bananas). There are several restaurants along Phetkasem Rd selling Phetburi desserts.

The Pizza Company, on Phetkasem Rd, T1112 (free delivery). Will satisfy pizza cravings.

Rabieng Restaurant Guesthouse, Damnoenkasem Rd, 0830-0100. Attractively furnished riverside restaurant, serving a good range of Thai and western food. The spicy squid salad is particularly good. Breakfasts are small and overpriced. Recommended.

There is a small but excellent **night market** at the southern end of Surinreuchai Rd underneath the clock tower – you can get a range of delicious snacks here and may want to try the local *patai* (omelette/pancake fried with mussels and served with bamboo shoots).

Cha-am *p538*

There are plenty of seafood restaurants along Ruamchit Rd, mostly serving the same dishes, including chilli crab and barbecued snapper with garlic.

Hua Hin and around *p539, map p540*

Try the central market for breakfast. Good seafood is widely available particularly at the northern end of Naresdamri Rd. Most of the fish comes straight from the boats which land their catch at the pier at the northern end of the bay. There is also a concentration of restaurants and bars geared to farang visitors along Naresdamri Rd and surrounding lanes.

International

Brasserie de Paris, 3 Naresdamri Rd, T032-530637. A French restaurant with a great position on the seafront sandwiched between the squid piers. Attentive and prompt service. The specialty of Hua Hin crab is absolutely delicious.

Lo Stivale, 132 Naresdamri Rd, T032-513800, 1030-2230. The best Italian restaurant in town although the pizzas are pretty standard. The house specialty of short pasta with crabmeat and tomato sauce is recommended. Terrace and indoor seating available. Good and prompt service. Popular with foreign families. Recommended.

Maharaja, 25 Naresdamri Rd, T032-530347. Reasonable prices at this highly a/c Indian which is all peach decor, flower fabrics and fake chandeliers. Great naan bread and curries. Attentive service.

Seafood

Palm Pavillion, Sofitel Central, 1 Damnoenkasem Rd, 1900-2300. This seafood restaurant is probably the best in Hua Hin. Don't expect the usual range of Thai dishes; the chef is French.

¥¥¥-¥¥ Hua Hin Brewing Co, 33 Naresdamri Rd, T032-512888, 0900-0200. A partly open-air chaotic restaurant serving good barbecued food. Also serves 3 home brews. Under-staffed during busy periods.

¥¥ Chao Lay, 15 Naresdamri Rd, T032-513436, 1000-2200 daily. This place with its blue and white checked cloths on a stilted building jutting out into the sea is hugely popular with Thais. It has 2 decks and is a great place from where to watch the sunset. Fruits of the sea including steamed squid, huge seabass, rock lobster and prawns, are served up with military precision.

¥¥-¥ Veranda Grill, **Veranda Lodge**, 113 Hua Hin 67, Phetkasem Rd, T032-533678, www.verandalodge.com, 0700-2300. Enjoy terraced dining on lapis lazuli blue tiles overlooking the beach. The basil air-dried squid is worth savouring.

Cafés and bakeries

World News Coffee, Naresdamri Rd, next to the **Hilton**, 0800-2230 daily. Bagels, cakes, coffee and newspapers – at a price. Internet access too.

Museum and tea shop, **Sofitel Central**. Take colonial tea here for a taste of olde-worlde charm. Earl Grey followed by ham buns, scones, jam and cream, biscuits and peach tarts is a treat for ฿315.

Foodstalls

There is an excellent **food market** opposite the Town Hall on Damnoenkasem Rd. The night market just off Phetkasem Rd does the usual selection of cheap Thai food as well as seafood that is so fresh that they have to tie the crabs' and lobsters' pincers shut.

Prachuap Khiri Khan *p543*

Prachuap is famous for its seafood and there are a number of excellent restaurants (as well as some more average ones) in the centre of town and along the seafront.

¥¥¥-¥¥ Laplom Seafood, north of the river. Offers an extensive range of seafood, probably the best selection in town (with a few meat dishes too), reasonably priced and friendly.

¥¥¥-¥¥ Shiew Ocha II, on the seafront towards the north of the town. Good range of seafood and meat dishes.

¥¥-¥ Mong Lai, 2½ km north of Laplom on the north end of the bay below the mountain. Country-style restaurant that is well known for its spicy dishes.

¥¥-¥ Panphochana, in the centre of town, 2 doors down from the **Hadthong Hotel**, T032-611195, 1000-2200. Welcoming, English-speaking owner, offers a vast range of seafood, pork and chicken. Breakfasts also served. Interior and outdoor dining possible with great views of the bay.

¥¥-¥ Plern Smud, on the seafront next to the **Hadthong Hotel**, T03-611115. Serves a large range of seafood and other meat dishes. As well as a full English breakfast you can try fried pig's stomach here. Super-friendly service.

Chumphon *p544, map p544*

There are 2 **night markets** on Krom Luang Chumphon Rd and on Tha Taphao Rd.

¥¥-¥ Farang Bar and Travel Agency, Tha Tapao Rd, T077-501003, 0430-0100. Thai-style soups and salads, noodles, spaghetti dishes and baguettes. Porridge for breakfast too. Cocktails are served at ฿100. Drink and eat while watching a movie. The night staff here are a lot friendlier than the day staff.

¥¥-¥ Puean Djai Restaurant, opposite the railway station, 1000-0200. This restaurant is in an attractive garden setting. Very tasty pizzas using cheese from an Italian cheese factory in Prachuap Khiri Khan. Pasta, crêpes and Thai cuisine also concocted.

¥¥-¥ Safety Stop Pub, next to **Ocean Department Store**, T077-571907, 1200-2400. Pleasant, leafy ranch-style pub with live sports and imported and draught beer. Has a full international menu of breakfasts, baguettes, burgers, pizzas, leg of lamb and salads with some Thai food. Shoot some pool while enjoying the full range of cocktails. *Bangkok Post* also available to read.

¥ Spaghetti House, 188/132 Saladaeng Rd, T077-507320, 0900-2200. A comfortable a/c restaurant serving tasty and filling spaghetti at reasonable prices. Also delicious smoothies and ice creams with some unusual offerings: Japanese cucumber and the famous durian ice creams. There's also a coffee house inside. Staff are really friendly here. Recommended.

Entertainment

Hua Hin and around *p539, map p540*
The sois between Poonsuk and Naresdamri roads are stuffed, cheek by jowl, with bars catering to most tastes. The Hua Hin Brewing Company (see Eating), has a vast cavern-like pub with a giant screen for sports, open until 0200.

Festivals and events

Phetburi and around *p536*
Feb Phra Nakhon Khiri Fair (movable) *son et lumière* show.

Hua Hin and around *p539*
Jun Hua Hin Jazz Festival, www.huahinjazzfestival.com. Organized by the Hilton. Stages are set up in front of the Sofitel Central and railway station.
Sep The King's Cup Elephant Polo tournament, www.thaielepolo.com. Takes place at the Som Dej Phra Suriyothai military ground, south of Hua Hin. It is organized by the Anantara Hotel and has become quite an attraction in recent years.

Shopping

Hua Hin and around *p539, map p540*
The most distinctive buy is a locally produced printed cotton called *pha khommaphat*. The usual tourist shops and stalls can be found lining most streets in the town.

Night market Dechanuchit Rd, close to the bus station, dusk-2200. Sells a range of goods including Tibetan jewellery, paper dragons, T-shirts, cassettes, watches and silk scarves.

Books
Bookazine, 116 Naresdamri Rd, T032-532071, 0900-2200. English language books, magazines and stationery.

Silk
Jim Thompson shop in the Sofitel Central or the Hilton.
Rashnee Thai Silk Village, 18/1 Naebkhehehars Rd, T032-531155, 0900- 2100. Allows visitors to see the full silk making process from worm to finished product.

Activities and tours

Hua Hin and around *p539, map p540*
There are watersports and horse riding along the beach.

Golf
There are 5 championship golf courses close to Hua Hin including the **Royal Hua Hin**, the **Springfield Royal Country Club**, the **Palm Hills Golf Resort and Country Club**, **Lake View** and **Majestic Creek Country Club**.
Royal Hua Hin Golf Course, behind the railway station, T032-512475, royal_golf@hotmail.com, designed in 1924 by a Scottish engineer working on the Royal Siamese Railway. It is the oldest in Thailand. Open to the public daily 0530-1930. Green fees ฿1500 at the weekend and ฿1200 during the week.

Thai boxing
Muay Thai Boxing Garden, 8/1 Th Phunsuk, T032-515259. Every Tue and Sat, 2100, ฿300 plus free drink.

Therapies
Anantara Spa, attached to the resort of the same name. Set in a quiet area with 6 suites in individual courtyards with baths filled with frangipani. Offers spa indulgence packages which are reduced during the low season of Apr-Oct. These include accommodation and meals. The signature treatment is a 3-hr warm sesame compress.
Mandara Spa, T032-511881, ext 1810, www.mandaraspa.com, 0800-2000, at the Marriott. A heavenly experience. Its signature treatment is a red mud body detox (฿3100). Aroma-stone therapy (฿5520). Thai massage (฿2400) and body scrubs (exotic lime and ginger salt glow, ฿3300) are also offered.
The Spa at the Hilton, 1000-2100. Has a large menu of different massages, facials using Guinot products, Thai fruit wrap (฿1850) and ancient Thai massage (฿1090). Twin share packages enjoy a 20% discount.

Tour operators
Concentrated on Damnoenkasem and Phetkasem rds.
Western Tours, 1 Damnoenkasem Rd, T032-533303, www.westerntours

huahin.com. Daily tours, THAI agent, transport tickets. Its trip to Khao Sam Roi Yod (฿900) is recommended. Kayaking, elephant riding and golf tours organized.

Chumphon *p544, map p544*

Diving

Easy Divers, Ta Taphao Rd, T077-570085, www.chumphoneasydivers.com. Takes divers to sites around the 41 islands off Chumphon. Also has bungalows and a restaurant at Thung Makham Noi and a guesthouse in Chumphon, see under Sleeping.

Tour operators

Fame Tour and Service, 118/20-21 Saladang Rd, T077-571077, www.chumphon-kohtao.com, 0430-2400. Tours, boat tickets (taxi to pier included), visa extension, internet, motorbike and car rental, restaurant, taxi, shower service (free, but ฿20 if towel required) and guesthouse. Internet ฿1 per min. 2-day/1-night trekking excursions to Pak Lake where you may see wild buffaloes, elephants and monkeys come to drink at its shores, ฿1900 per person including all meals and transport, minimum 4 people. Long tail boat cruises on the Lang Suan River, ฿2900 per person, minimum 4. Whitewater rafting on the Luang Suan River and Bout Fai River, ฿900 per person, minimum 4. Kayaking, night safaris and trips to Haew Lom waterfall also organized.

Farang Bar and Travel Agency, Tha Tapao Rd, T077-501003, farangbar@yahoo.com. Friendly staff offering lots of information and selling all tickets. Free taxi to train station offered. Also restaurant and rooms to rent.

Kiat travel, 115 Thatapao Rd, T077-502127, www.chumphonguide.com.

New Infinity Travel Agency, 68/2 Tha Taphao Rd, T077-570176, To1-6871825, new_infinity@hotmail.com, 0600-2400. Offers all tourist services including a guesthouse, run by the very helpful manager. Internet ฿1 per min. Free transfer to the **Lomprayah** and **Songserm** boats, ฿50 for transfer to night boat. Free transfers for guests to train or bus station. Motorbike rental ฿200 per day. Whitewater rafting, ฿550 per person. 1-day snorkelling trip to a choice of 3 islands, ฿700. Agent for **Chumphon Cabana**. It also does a visa run from Chumpon to Ranong and the border. Leave at 0545 return 1145. Burmese immigration, ฿300. Motorbike hire ฿200 per day, 4WD ฿1500 per day.

Songserm, Tha Tapao Rd, next to New Infinity Travel, T077-506205.

Transport

Phetburi and around *p536, map p537*

Bus

Regular a/c connections with **Bangkok**'s Southern bus terminal near the Thonburi train station (2 hrs); non-a/c buses from the terminal near Khao Wang (2 hrs). Songthaews meet the buses and take passengers into the town centre. Also connections with **Cha-am** (1½ hrs), **Hua Hin** (2¼ hrs, ฿35) and other southern destinations, between 0600-1800. These buses leave from the centre of town (see map). Buses from Phetburi run past the turn-off for Kaeng Krachan Dam (Route 3175). From here, there are occasional minibuses which take visitors to the dam and the national park headquarters (another 8 km), or hitch a lift.

Motorbike

These can be rented from **Rabieng** Guesthouse for ฿250 per day.

Saamlor

These can be hired for about ฿100 per hr.

Train

The station is 1½ km northwest of town, T032-425211. Regular connections with **Bangkok**'s Hualamphong station (2½ hrs). Trains to Bangkok mostly leave Phetburi in the morning. Trains to **Hua Hin**, **Surat Thani** and southern destinations.

Cha-am *p538*

Bus

Cha-am is 25 km north of Hua Hin. There are regular connections with **Bangkok**'s Southern bus terminal (2½ hrs), **Phetburi**, **Hua Hin** and south destinations. A/c buses from Bangkok drop you right on the beach but other buses from Phetburi or Hua Hin stop on the Phetkasem Highway at its junction with Narathip Rd. Motorbike taxis from here to the beach cost ฿20. To get to

other southern destinations catch a bus to Hua Hin and change there.

Hua Hin and around *p539, map p540*

Air

Hua Hin's **Bofai Airport**, T032-520343. SGA, T032-522300, www.sga.aero, operates the Hua Hin Air Shuttle 4 times a day to **Bangkok**, 45 mins, ฿3100 one way, ฿5200 return.

Bicycle

Can be hired for ฿100 per day on Damnoenkasem and Phetkasem rds.

Bus

There are 3 bus stations. The a/c bus station to BKK is on Srasong Rd, next to the Chatchai market, T032-511654. Regular a/c connections with **Bangkok**'s Southern bus terminal near the Thonburi train station, 3½ hrs, ฿128, every 40 mins from 0300-2100. A/c buses to the south leave from the main terminal and from opposite the Bangkok bus terminal on Srasong Rd, T01-7085319. Departures between 2100-2330. To **Prachuap Khiri Khan**, ฿40-50, **Chumphon**, ฿80-120, **Surat Thani**, ฿180-200. Local buses to **Phetburi**, ฿30, **Cha-am**, ฿20 leave from Srasong Rd between streets 70 and 72 off Phetkasem Rd.

Car

It is presently a 3-hr drive to **Bangkok**, along a hazardous 2-lane highway (particularly bad over the first 80 km to Phetburi), jammed with *siplors* (10-wheel trucks).

Jeeps can be hired for ฿1,000-1500 per day on Damnoenkasem and Phetkasem rds. Avis, www.avisthailand.com has offices at the **Hyatt, Sofitel Central** and **Hilton**. Prices from ฿1350 per day. One-way rentals are possible.

Motorbike

Can be hired for ฿1200 per day upwards, on Damnoenkasem and Phetkasem rds.

Saamlor

Can be hired for ฿20-30 around town, ฿150 for a sightseeing tour.

Songthaew

There are set routes around town and out to Khao Takiab, ฿10.

Taxis

Run along prescribed routes for set fares. There's a taxi stand on Phetkasem Rd, opposite **Chatchai Hotel**. Taxis can be hired for the day for ฿400 plus petrol.

Baipoo Service, Baipoo shop, Dechanuchit Rd, T01-3072352, baipoo_shop4@hotmail.com. A reliable taxi service, about ฿1000 per 100 km. Also rents motorbikes and cars.

Motorcycle taxis (identified by 'taxi' sign) will take you wherever you want to go. A taxi to **Bangkok** is 3 hrs (฿1,600-1,800).

Train

The station is on Damnoenkasem Rd, T032-511073/1690. Regular connections with **Bangkok**'s Hualamphong station, same train as to Phetburi (3½-4 hrs). Regular connections with **Phetburi** (1 hr).

Lomprayah, Soi Kanjanomai, T032-533738, runs bus and boat transport to **Koh Tao**, ฿850, **Phangan**, ฿1200 and **Samui**, ฿1400, with its own bus and catamaran.

Prachuap Khiri Khan *p543*

Bus

Buses no longer come into town. They pull over on the highway where you will need to get a motorbike or tuk-tuk into town. To **Bangkok**'s Southern bus terminal, 5 hrs; also destinations south including **Chumphon**.

Saamlor

Prachuap has its own distinctive form of tuk-tuk – motorcycles with sidecars and bench seats.

Train

The station, T032-611175, is on the west side of town, regular connections with **Bangkok** 5 hrs, **Hua Hin** and destinations south.

Chumphon *p544, map p544*

Boat

Koh Tao (see page 597) can be reached by boat from 2 piers, one 10 km southeast of the town, the other 30 km away at Thung Makham Noi. Tickets for these boats can be bought at all the travel agents in town.

Lomprayah speed ferry uses the Thung Makham Noi Pier. Leaving at 0700 and 1300, 1½ hrs, ฿550. **Songserm** leaves Chumphon at 0700, ฿400. Arrives **Koh Tao** 0945, leaves

at 1030 arriving at **Koh Phangan** at 1200, leaving at 1230 arriving **Koh Samui** at 1330. The return boat leaves Koh Samui at 1100, arriving Koh Phangan at 1200, leaving at 1230 arriving Koh Tao at 1430, leaving at 1500 arriving in Chumphon at 1730.

The night boat, ฿300 leaves at 2300 (you get a blanket and pillow on this one), 6 hrs on Mon, Wed and Fri returning Tue, Thu and Sat and daily at 2400, 6 hrs, ฿250.

Bus
The terminal is 15 km outside of town, ฿200 per person in taxi to get there. There are regular a/c connections with Chokeanan Tour off Pracha Uthid Rd, T077-511480, office hours 0430-2130. To **Bangkok**, 1030, 1400, 2130, 7 hrs, ฿322; to **Phuket** ฿300, and **Ranong** at 0800, 1000 and 1200. To **Hat Yai**, 0830, 0930, 1130, 2130, ฿320. Minivans to **Surat Thani** leave from Krom Louang Rd, next to the *7-11* shop; depart when full (2½ hrs, ฿150). Minivans to **Ranong** depart every 40 mins from 0600-1700, ฿90, from in front of the closed Tha Taphao hotel.

Bus or train and boat
Songserm, Ta Thao Rd, next to New Infinity Travel Agency, sells a combination ticket to and from **Bangkok** to **Koh Tao**, ฿550. Leaves Bangkok at 1800 arrives Chumphon at 0200. Passengers kip on the office floor before getting the 0700 boat to Koh Tao. The return journey leaves Chumphon at 2030 to Bangkok.

The train connection leaves Bangkok at 2250 arriving Chumphon at 0552. Ticket price depends on class.

Taxi
To **Hat Thung Wua Laen**, ฿250, one way; **Hat Sai Ree** ฿200, one way; **Thung Makam** (for the Lomprayah catamaran) ฿250; **Tha Yang** pier ฿50; to **Muang Mai**, the new out of town bus station, 15 km away, ฿200.

Train
Station at west end of Krom Luang Chumphon Rd. Regular connections with **Bangkok**'s Hualamphong station, (7½-9 hrs) and all stops south.

Directory

Phetburi and around *p536, map p537*
Banks Siam Commercial Bank, on Damnoenkasem Rd changes cash and TCs, and has an ATM. There are also several banks on Pongsuriya Rd. **Telephone** Overseas calls can be made from the post office on Ratwithi Rd.

Cha-am *p538*
Banks There are several banks either side of Phetkasem Rd where the buses pull up. **Post office** The main post office is on the Narathip Rd, close to the bus station and Phetkasem Highway. Overseas calls can be made from here. There is also a small post office on Ruamchit Rd.

Hua Hin and around *p539, map p540*
Banks There are dozens of banks, ATMs and currency exchange booths all over town. **Internet** A number of small internet cafés have opened up around town. Also at CAT office, see Telephone, below ฿100 for 3hrs. **Medical services** San Paulo Hospital, Phetkasem Rd, opposite the Marriott, T032-532581. Medihouse Pharmacy, Naresdamri Rd, daily 0930-2300. **Post office** 21 Damnoenkasem Rd. **Telephone** CAT, Damnoenkasem Rd, www.cattelecom.co.th. Next to the post office, 0830-2300. **Useful addresses** Police station, Damnoenkasem Rd, T032-515995.

Prachuap Khiri Khan *p543*
Banks Bangkok Bank, corner of Sarathip/ Salashiep and Maitri Ngam rds, one block west of the Hadthong Hotel, has an ATM. **Internet** In the CAT phone office attached to the post office. Also inside the Hadthong Hotel, ฿30/hr. **Post office** Opposite the Hadthong Hotel.

Chumphon *p544, map p544*
Banks Thai Farmers' Bank, Saladaeng Rd. **Post office** On the Paramin Manda Rd about 1 km out of town on the left-hand side. **Telephone** For overseas calls slightly further on the right.

Surat Thani and around

The riverside town of Surat Thani is the main launch pad for transport to the gulf islands of Samui, Phangan and Tao. North of the town is the ancient settlement of Chaiya, once an important outpost of the Srivijayan Empire that was based in Sumatra. Also north is Wat Suan Mok, a Buddhist retreat, known for its meditation courses which are open to foreigners. The pig-tailed macaque has been trained to collect the millions of coconuts that grow in the region and on the islands. Just outside Surat Thani is a macaque training centre that can be visited. *» For Sleeping, Eating and other listings, see pages 558-560.*

Surat Thani

Surat Thani or 'City of the Good People' is a provincial capital and although the town has an interesting riverfront worth a visit and some fabulously stocked markets, its main purpose is as a transportation hub to the gulf islands or south to Krabi. About 50 km north of Surat Thani is the important historic town of Chaiya.

Ins and outs

The tourist office, **TAT** ⓘ *5 Talat Mai Rd, T077-281828, tatsurat@samart.co.th*, near **Wang Tai Hotel**, southwest of the town, is a good source of information for less-frequented sights in the province.

Sights

Boats can be hired for trips on the river (฿200 for up to six people). The better journey is upstream. There is a big **Chinese temple** and an attractive old viharn in the compound of **Wat Sai**, both on Thi Lek Road. The town brightens up considerably during the **Chak Phra Festival** in September or October (see Festivals, below).

Chaiya and around

ⓘ *Northbound trains from Surat Thani's Phun Phin station stop at Chaiya (40 mins). There are regular buses from Surat Thani to Chaiya from Talat Kaset Nung (1). Regular songthaews from close to Talat Kaset Song (2) (฿30).*

This city, lying 50 km north of Surat Thani on Route 41, was an important outpost of the Sumatra-based Srivijayan Empire and dates from the late seventh century making it one of the most ancient settlements in Thailand. Given the quantity of antiquities found in the area, some scholars have suggested that Chaiya may have been the capital of Srivijaya, rather than Palembang (Sumatra) as is usually thought. Recent excavations in Sumatra, however, seem to have confirmed Palembang as the capital. The Mahayana Buddhist empire of Srivijaya dominated Sumatra, the Malay Peninsula, and parts of Thailand and Java between the seventh and 13th centuries. It had cultural and commercial links with Dvaravati, Cambodia, north and south India and particularly Java. The syncretic art of this civilization clearly reveals these links. Many of the artefacts found in the area are now exhibited in the National Museum in Bangkok. Chaiya today is a pleasant, clean town with many old wooden houses.

About 2 km outside Chaiya, 1 km from the Chaiya railway station, stands **Wat Phra Boromthat Chaiya**, one of the most revered temples in Thailand. Within the wat compound, the central chedi is strongly reminiscent of the eighth-century *candis* of central Java, square in plan with four porches and rising in tiers topped with miniature chedis. The chedi is constructed of brick and vegetable mortar and is thought to be 1,200 years old. Even though it was extensively restored in 1901 and again in 1930, its

Srivijayan origins are still evident. A **museum** ⓘ *Wed-Sun, 0900-1600, ฿30*, nearby, exhibits relics found in the vicinity which have not been 'acquired' by the National Museum in Bangkok. Another architectural link with Srivijaya can be seen at **Wat Kaeo**, which contains a restored sanctuary reminiscent of Cham structures of the ninth century (Hoa-lai type, South Vietnam), but again with Javanese overtones (with links to Candi Kalasan on the Prambanan Plain). Just outside Chaiya is the village of Poomriang, where visitors can watch silk being woven.

Wat Suan Mok

ⓘ *50 km north of Surat Thani on Route 41, T077-431597, www.suanmokkh.org. Take a bus from Talat Kaset Nung (1); the road passes the wat (1 hr). The town of Chaiya is closer to the monastery, so if arriving by train direct from Bangkok alight here and catch a songthaew to Wat Suan Mok.*

Wat Suan Mok, or **Wat Suan Mokkhabalarama** in full, is a popular forest wat (*wat pa*), which has become an international Buddhist retreat. Courses for westerners are run with the assistance of a number of foreign monks and novices. The monastery was founded by one of Thailand's most revered monks, the late Buddhadasa Bhikkhu, on a peaceful plot of land covering around 50 ha of fields and forest. Since he died in 1993, the monastery has been run by monks who have continued to teach his reformist philosophy of eschewing consumerism and promoting simplicity and purity. (Buddhadasa Bhikku developed and refined the study of Buddhist economics and he follows a long tradition in Thailand of scholar-monks.)

Ten-day *anapanasati* meditation courses are held here, beginning on the first day of each month. Enrolment onto the course takes place on the last day of the previous month, on a first-come first-served basis. Courses are ฿1,500, which covers the cost of the meals (rice and vegetable dishes at 0800 and 1300). For those considering taking the course, bear in mind that students sleep on straw mats, are woken by animal noises at 0400, bathe in a communal pool, and are expected to help with chores around the monastery. No alcohol, drugs or tobacco are permitted and the sexes tend to be segregated. If intending to visit the monastery or enrol on a course, it is worth bringing a torch and mosquito repellent (or buy these at the shop by the entrance).

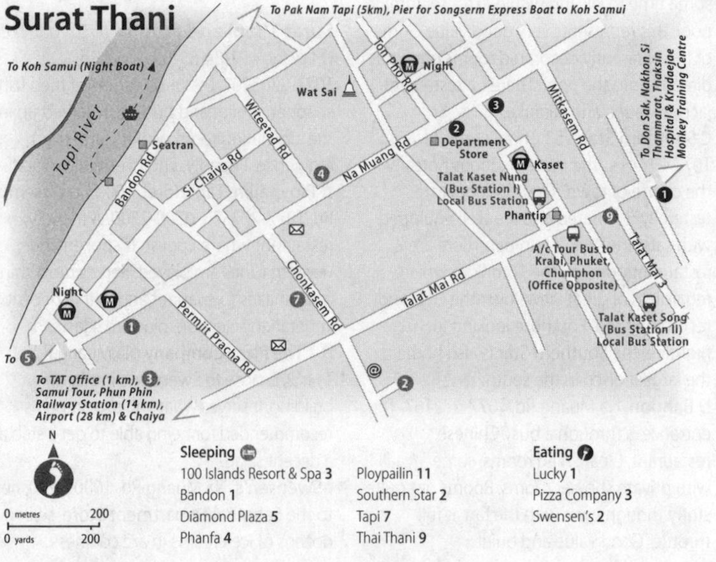

Kradaejae Monkey Training Centre

ⓘ T09-8718017, call to make a reservation. The centre is south of Surat Thani on Route 401, towards Nakhon Si Thammarat, 2 km off the main road. Take a songthaew or bus from Surat Thani heading towards Nakhon Si Thammarat, on Talat Mai Rd, which becomes Route 401. The turning to the centre is on the right-hand side, just over the Thathong Bridge, past a wat and a school. The centre is 2 km down this road.

The only monkey capable of being trained to pick coconuts is the pig-tailed macaque (*ling kung* in Thai). The female is not usually trained as it is smaller and not as strong as the male; strength is needed to break off the stem of the coconut. The training can start when the animals are eight months old. The course lasts three to five months, and when fully trained, the monkeys can pick as many as 800 coconuts in a day and will work for 12 to 15 years. "Working monkeys are very cheap – they cost no more than ฿10 a day but make millions of baht a year", according to Somphon Saekhow, founder of a coconut-collecting school.

Sleeping

Surat Thani and around *p556, map p557*

L-A Diamond Plaza, 83/27 Srivichai Rd, T077-205333, www.diamondplazahotels.com. Slightly further out of town than the **Wang Tai** as you approach from Phun Phin, and also just on the other side of a bridge. A luxury hotel with 400 rooms and good facilities, including a fitness centre and swimming pool on the 4th floor with almost no shade at all. Comfortable rooms and friendly staff.

B-C 100 Islands Resort and Spa, 19/6, Moo 3, T077-201150-8, www.roikoh.com. This is an attractive hotel in a very strange location. It is right on the highway diagonally opposite the Tesco Lotus and Boots, right out of town. However, should you have some time to kill and would like a swimming pool, this represents very good value. Some of the pleasantly decorated rooms open out directly onto the pool. There's a restaurant, jacuzzi, sauna and karaoke.

C Southern Star, 253 Chonkasem Rd, T077-216414. The most luxurious hotel in the centre of town. The 150 rooms are tastefully decorated and are well equipped with satellite TV and minibar. There are 2 restaurants, one on the 16th floor which regardless of great views over the city is not recommended. For those looking for nightlife, the **Southern Star** is also home to the largest disco in the south.

D Bandon, Na Muang Rd, T077-272167. The entrance is through a busy Chinese restaurant. Clean, tiled rooms, some a/c, all with private shower rooms. Rooms get quite stuffy though even with the fan at full throttle. Good value and quiet.

D Tapi, 100 Chonkasem Rd, T077-272575. Large, nice, clean rooms, some a/c, with large shower rooms and TV.

D Thai Thani, 442/306-8 Talat Mai Rd, T077-272977. Large, cleanish rooms with attached shower rooms. More expensive rooms have a/c and TV. Bleak corridors and a bit rough around the edges but conveniently positioned for an early bus.

F Phanfa, 247/2-5 Namuang Rd, T077-272288. These large, cleanish rooms with attached shower rooms are the cheapest in town but the place is dour and the corridors bleak.

Eating

Surat Thani and around *p556, map p557*

ΨΨ Lucky, 452/84-85 Talat Mai Rd, T077-273267, 0900-2200. Lots of fried fish – snapper, mullet and butterfish served up in the airy dining room with its faux-ranch ambience. Friendly, English-speaking staff.

ΨΨ Ploypailin, Tapi Hotel, 100 Chonkasem Rd, T077-272575, 0700-2300. A friendly restaurant where English is spoken and western tunes are played. Serves most things from shakes to snapper and with a decent vegetarian selection, plus breakfasts.

ΨΨ-Ψ The Pizza Company, Na Muang Rd, T1112, is close to **Swensen's** in a large building. It serves what you expect but is recommended for being able to get a stab at a decent salad.

Ψ Swensen's, Na Muang Rd, 1000-2200, next to the **Sahathai Department Store**, selling dozens of ice creams in a/c coolness.

Foodstalls
Foodstalls on Ton Pho Rd, near to the intersection with Na Muang Rd, sell delicious mussel omelettes. There's a good **night market** on Na Muang Rd, and on Ton Pho Rd and vicinity. There's a plentiful supply of fruit and *khanom* stalls along the waterfront. Market next to the local bus terminal (Talat Kaset 1).

Festivals and events

Surat Thani and around *p556, map p557*
Aug Rambutan Fair (movable).
Oct-Nov Chak Phra Festival (movable) marks the end of the 3-month Buddhist Rains Retreat and the return to earth of the Buddha. Processions of Buddha images and boat races on the Tapi River, in longboats manned by up to 50 oarsmen. Gifts are offered to monks as this is also *krathin*, celebrated across Buddhist Thailand, see also Essentials, page 59.

Shopping

Surat Thani and around *p556, map p557*
Department stores
Sahathai Department Store, Na Muang Rd.

Jewellery
Can be found in shops near the corner of Chonkasem and Na Muang rds.

Activities and tours

Surat Thani and around *p556, map p557*
Swimming
Non-residents can use the pools at the Diamond Plaza Hotel for ฿50.

Tour operators
Phantip Travel, 293/6-8 Talat Mai Rd, T077-272230. A well-regarded and helpful agency dealing with boats, buses, trains and planes. Recommended.
Samui Tour, 346/36 Talat Mai Rd, T077-282352. Deals with Raja ferries to Samui and Phangan, see Transport, as well as other travel services.
Songserm Travel Centre Co Ltd, 297/4 Mitkasem Rd or at the port although very unhelpful at the port. May be best to deal with them through other agents.

Transport

Surat Thani and around *p556, map p557*
Songthaew
Known as 'taxis'. These are ubiquitous and cost ฿10 a ride.

Air
The airport is 28 km south of town on Phetkasem Rd, T077-253500.
Airline offices One-two-go, T1126, www.fly12go.com, has daily to **Bangkok**. THAI, offices at 3/27-28 Karunrat Rd, T075-273710, has twice daily connections with **Bangkok**.

Boat
Seatran Ferry, Bandon Rd, T077-275060/ 251555, www.seatranferry.com. Office hours 0500-1800. There's a coffee bar, toilets and bag-guarding service at the office. Buses leave Surat Thani for Don Sak every hour 0530-1730. Boats leave Don Sak hourly 0600-1900 for **Koh Samui**. The return times are the same from Nathon but the first return ferry is at 0500 and the last at 1800, ฿180, children ฿130, including bus transfer from Surat Thani with Phantip Travel, see Tour operators, above. Just ferry ticket, ฿100 (2½ hrs). Combination tickets with trains and buses are available. The train from Bangkok that arrives at Phun Phin is met by Phantip Travel for the 0900 ferry. The return through journey to Bangkok leaves Nathon at 1430 for the 1300 ferry back to Surat Thani. Airport transfer with Samui boat ticket, ฿280. Just downtown transfer, ฿70. Seatran ferries go to **Koh Phangan** 3 times daily, ฿280, children ฿180, for the bus and boat. The 0730, 1230, 1530 (direct), 3½ from Surat Thani, returning 0600 (direct), 0700, 1300. Seatran also plans to start direct services to **Koh Tao**.

Songserm, 29/47 M Mitkasem Rd, 077-205418-9, Surat Thani pier, T077-289894, advtour_bangkok@ yahoo.com. To **Koh Samui**, 0800, 2 hrs, ฿150; to **Koh Phangan**, 0800, 3 hrs 40 mins, ฿290; through to **Koh Tao**, ฿580. The bus from Surat Thani is included in the price.

Samui Tour, T077-282352, office hours 0600-1700, deals with Raja ferries and provides the bus transfer to Don Sak. Raja ferries depart Don Sak for **Koh Samui** hourly

0800-1800 returning 0730-1900, 1½ hrs on the boat. Bus transfers to the ferry arranged from 0650-1630. Pick ups from the station at 0600 and 0800.

Phangan Tour, 2000, 402/2 Talat Mai Rd, T077-205799, office hours 0530-2200. Buses for the ferries leave Surat Thani at 0530, 0830, 1230, 1600 arriving at **Koh Phangan** 4 hrs later, ฿270. The return ferries depart Koh Phangan at 0700, 1000, 1300, 1700, 4 hrs.

Night boats leave from the pier behind the Seatran office. To **Koh Tao**, 2300, 8 hrs, ฿500. To **Koh Samui**, 2300, 6 hrs, ฿150. To **Koh Phangan**, ฿250. See also transport to and from Koh Samui, page581 .

Bus

The 2 central stations in Surat Thani are within easy walking distance of one another – Talat Kaset Nung (1) is for local buses and buses to Phun Phin (train station) and Talat Kaset Song (2) for longer-distance journeys. To **Trang**, (minibus) 3 hrs, 0700-1730, ฿130; **Phuket**, 4-6 hrs, 0640-1800, ฿113-203. The Phuket buses stop at **Khao Sok National Park**, 2½ hrs, ฿80-100; **Nakhon Si Thammarat**, 2½ hrs, 0630-1800, ฿60; **Krabi**, 3-4 hrs, 0630-1710, ฿80-130 (bus and minibus) and **Hat Yai** 5 hrs, 0600-1730, ฿126-227 (minibus and bus); to **Ranong**, 3½-5 hrs, 0600-1630, ฿80-130 (bus and minibus); to **Chumphon**, 2½-3½ hrs, 030-1730, ฿80-130 bus and minibus); to **Khanom**, 19 hrs, 0700-1800, ฿70. Regular a/c connections with **Bangkok**'s southern bus terminal in Thonburi (10 hrs), 0730-2100, from the out of town terminal, T077-200031.

Private tour companies

These run bus services to/from **Bangkok** (10 hrs, ฿285-440) and **Krabi** (3-4 hrs, ฿80), see Tour operators above for listings. The advantage of taking a tour bus from here to Krabi is that they go all the way into Krabi town, to the Chao Fah Pier, rather than stopping at the bus station, out of town.

A/c minibus For some destinations there are few buses but minibuses leave for most places regularly from the bus terminal, Talat Kaset II, and cost 50% more than the a/c bus. To **Nakhon Si Thammarat**, from 442/347 Talat Mai 33, every ½ hr, 0600-1800, 2 hrs, ฿110.

Taxi

The taxi terminal is next to the bus terminal. To **Trang** (3 hrs, ฿110), **Nakhon** (2 hrs, ฿60), **Krabi** (2 hrs, ฿150), **Hat Yai** (3½ hrs, ฿150), **Phuket** (4 hrs, ฿150), **Phangnga** (4 hrs, ฿150).

International connections There are a/c buses to **Kuala Lumpur** (Malaysia) and **Singapore**. Note that the border at Sungei Golok closes at 1700; not all buses make it there before then so be prepared to spend a night in Sungei Golok.

Train

The station is at Phun Phin, T077-311213, 14 km west of Surat Thani. Local buses go to town stopping at the **Talat Kaset Nung** (1) terminal, ฿12, 0500-1900, every 5 mins, 40 mins. Connections with Hualamphong station, **Bangkok**, 11-13 hrs. Trains out of Phun Phin are often full; advance booking can be made at **Phantip Travel**, see tour operators above. **Songserm Travel Service** also arranges reservations. There are connections with **Hua Hin**, **Trang**, **Yala**, **Hat Yai** and **Sungei Golok**. Buses meet the train for the transfer to the ferry terminals for **Koh Samui**, **Koh Phangan** and **Koh Tao** (see page 559).

International connections An international express leaves for **Butterworth** (Malaysia) at 0131 (11 hrs) where it continues on to **Kuala Lumpur** and **Singapore**.

Directory

Surat Thani and around *p556, map p557*
Banks Several banks with ATMs on Na Muang and Chonkasem rds. **Internet** There are about 4 internet shops on Chonkasem Rd between Talat Mai Rd and the Southern Star, all charging ฿20/hr. There is also internet in a café at the front of the Thai Thani hotel. **Medical services** Taksin Hospital, Talat Mai Rd, heading south towards Nakhon, T077-273239. **Post office** Near the corner of Talat Mai and Chonkasem rds and on the corner of Na Muang and Chonkasem rds.

Koh Samui

Koh Samui is the third largest of Thailand's islands, after Phuket and Koh Chang. Over the last decade tourism has exploded and now that it is accessible by air, the palm-studded tropical island is making the transition from a backpackers' haven to a sophisticated beach resort. Unlike Phuket, it does still cater for the budget traveller with a variety of bungalows scattered around its shores. Its popularity is deserved as it boasts some beautiful bays with sandy beaches hemmed in by coconut palms, seducing many a traveller in search of a tropical paradise beach. However, Koh Samui is slowly disappearing under concrete and billboards as the tourism bandwagon continues to gather speed. There are approaching 500 registered bungalows and hotels providing well over 610,000 rooms which means the choice of accommodation is overwhelming. For nightlife, the two most popular beaches are still Lamai and Chaweng, both on the east side of the island. They also have the longest stretches of uninterrupted beach, with good swimming and watersports. Mae Nam and Bophut, on the north shore, are also becoming popular and are a little more laid-back with more backpacker options although more expensive resorts are beginning to dot the north coast.

There are still isolated spots, mainly in the south and west. For a much quieter scene, head for the remote bungalows down the west shore, although it is best to hire a vehicle as many of them are off the main road. The advantage of staying on this side of the island is to watch the spectacular sunsets.

Close to Koh Samui are the beautiful islands of the Ang Thong Marine National Park, see page 564. The following sections have been organized by beach, beginning at Nathon (Samui's 'capital') and working clockwise around the island. ▸▸ *For Sleeping, Eating and other listings, see pages 568-584.*

Ins and outs

Getting there

Flying is the easiest and quickest option. It is relatively inexpensive and hassle free. The airport, in the northeast, is privately owned by **Bangkok Airways**. There are multiple daily connections with Bangkok, connections with Phuket and Pattaya, and international connections with Singapore and Hong Kong. The alternative to flying is to take a ferry. Most leave from one of Surat Thani's piers and the journey takes about two hours. Or catch a boat from Chumphon to Koh Tao and from there to Koh Samui via Koh Phangan. But this is a much longer sea journey and only really makes sense if intending to stop off on Koh Tao. It is possible to buy 'combination' bus or train and ferry tickets from any travel agent in Bangkok. ▸▸ *See Transport, page 581, for further details.*

Getting around

Koh Samui is a large island – well over 20 km both long and wide. Beaches, hotels and guesthouses can be found on just about every stretch of coastline although the two most popular and developed beaches are both on the east coast, Chaweng and Lamai. The main town of Nathon, where most of the ferries dock, is on the west side of the island. A ring road follows the coast along the north, east and south sides of the island, but runs inland cutting off the southwestern corner. Many resorts are on small tracks off this main circuit road running down to the beach. Songthaews run around the island during daylight hours and can be flagged down anywhere. The destination is displayed on the front. From dusk the service becomes increasingly intermittent. There are scores of places renting out motorbikes and jeeps but note that the accident rate on Koh Samui is horrendously high (see box, page 582).

Best time to visit

March to June is hot and fine with a good breeze and only the occasional thunderstorm. At this time of year good discounts can be had on accommodation. June to October is also sunny and hot, with short showers. The 'worst' time of year is October to February, when the monsoon breaks and rain is more frequent. However, even during this period daily hours of sunshine average five to seven hours.

Tourist information

TAT ⓘ *370 Moo 3, T077-420720, tatsamui@tat.or.th, daily 0830-1630*, is helpful. Several tourist magazines and maps are distributed free of charge. Be aware that there are several agencies advertising themselves as TAT booking offices in Bangkok. Customers book accommodation through them and then on arrival, if they don't like the sleeping choice they have no means to redress it. The official TAT is not a booking office. Companies using its acronym write it as follows: t.a.t. The official **Tourism Authority of Thailand** is just TAT.

Numbers dialled on the island require the area code as well.

Background

Koh Samui is the largest in an archipelago of 80 islands, six of which are inhabited. Many of Koh Samui's inhabitants are not Thai, but Chinese from Hainan who settled on the island between 150 and 200 years ago. So far as most visitors are concerned, this little nugget of history is not apparent; the Chinese across Thailand have assimilated to such a degree that they are almost invisible. A number of traditional homes can still be seen.

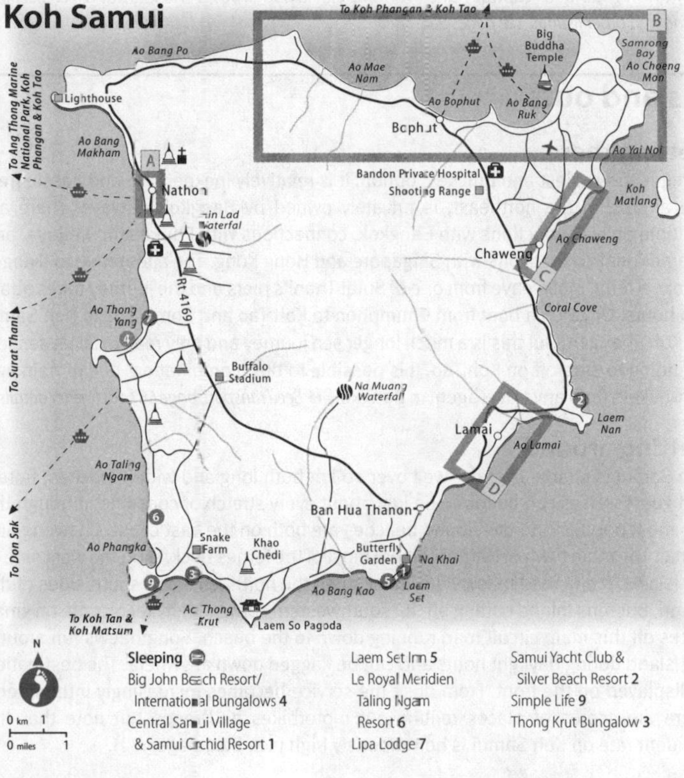

Sea, water and weather conditions on Koh Samui

March-October Light winds (averaging 5 knots), calm seas, the driest period of the year but downpours can still occur. Water visibility is good. This is the period of the southwest monsoon and though generally calm, Bophut and Mae Nam beaches can be windy, with choppy conditions offshore. Chaweng is normally calm even when Bophut and Mae Nam are rough.

October-February The northeast monsoon brings rain and stronger winds, averaging 10-15 knots but with gusts of 30 knots on some days. Sea conditions are sometimes rough and water visibility is generally poor although Koh Tao, see page 597, offers good year-round diving.

About 60,000 people live on Koh Samui, many of whom are fishermen-turned hoteliers. The number of annual visitors is many times this figure: 820,000 in 2000 and close to a million in 2002. The first foreign tourists began stepping ashore on Samui in the mid-1960s. At that time there were no hotels, no electricity (except generator-supplied), no telephones, no surfaced roads – nothing, it seems, but an over-abundance of coconuts. This is still evident because, apart from tourism, the mainstay of the economy is coconuts; two million are exported to Bangkok each month. Monkeys are taught to scale the trees and pluck down the ripe nuts; even this traditional industry has cashed in on tourism – visitors can watch the monkeys at work. A monkey training centre has been established outside Surat Thani, see page 558.

For the moment at least, Koh Samui – *in toto* – has managed to absorb a massive increase in tourist numbers without eroding the island's qualities that brought people here in the first place (although some long-term fans of the island would dispute that). Currently much of the island looks like a construction site as every available piece of land is built on. Against the odds many of the island's beautiful spots remain unaffected by the excessive development.

Sights

The island's main attractions are its wonderful **beaches**; most people head straight to one, where they remain until they leave. However, there are motorbikes or jeeps for hire to explore inland and there are a multitude of activities on offer, see Activities and tours. Evidence of the immigration of Hainanese can be seen reflected in the **traditional architecture** of the island. Houses, though they may also incorporate Indian, Thai and Khmer elements, are based on Hainanese prototypes. The use of fretwork to decorate balconies and windows; the tiled, pitched roofs; the decoration of the eaves make the older houses of Samui distinctive in Thai terms. Sadly, it is unlikely that many will survive the next decade or two. They are being torn down to make way for more modern structures, or renovated and extended in such a way that their origins are obscured.

Two-thirds of the island is forested and hilly with some impressive (in the wet season) **waterfalls**. Hin Lad Waterfall and wat are 3 km south of Nathon and can be reached from the town on foot, or by road 1 km off Route 4169. It's a 45-minute walk from the vehicle parking area. Na Muang Waterfall, in the centre of the island, has a 30-m drop and a good pool for swimming. The fact that it's the only waterfall on the island which is accessible by paved road makes it very busy at weekends and during holidays.

Nathon → *Colour map 4, grid B3.*

Nathon is Koh Samui's capital and is where the ferry docks. It is a town geared to tourists with travel agents, exchange booths, clothes stalls, bars and restaurants supplying travellers' food. Nathon consists of three roads running parallel to the seafront, with two main roads at either end linking them together. Although it is used mainly as a transit point, it still has a friendly feel to it.

Ang Thong ('Golden Basin') Marine National Park

ⓘ *Daily tours leave from piers around the island. There are no public boats but you can leave the tour, stay on Koh Wua Talap and rejoin it several days later at no extra charge (make sure you tell the ferry driver which day you want to be picked up).*

The park is made up of 40 islands lying northwest of Koh Samui, featuring limestone massifs, tropical rainforests and beaches. Particular features are **Mae Koh** (a beautiful beach) and **Thale Nai** (an emerald saltwater lake), both on **Koh Mae Koh** and **Koh Sam Sao**; the latter??WHICH?? has a coral reef and a huge rock arch as well as a hill providing good views of the surrounding slands. The area is the major spawning ground of the short-bodied mackerel, a popular edible fish in Thailand. There is also good snorkelling (the main attraction), swimming and walking. The park's headquarters are on **Koh Wua Talap**. It is best to visit between late March and October, when visibility is at its best.

North coast

Bang Po (Ban Poh) A quiet, secluded and clean beach which is very good for swimming. One of the better options for those wanting to escape the constant buzz of Chaweng and Lamai.

Mae Nam A clean, beautiful, serene beach with lots of coconut palms and fringed with coral reefs to tempt swimmers and snorkellers. It is a popular spot and a number of new beautifully designed resorts have opened here.

Bophut Bophut is one of the few places on the island where there are still traditional wooden Samui houses with Chinese lettering above the doors side by side with modern tourist accommodation. Unsurprisingly, it has grown increasingly popular in the last few years and there are now currency exchanges, bookshops, restaurants and good watersports facilities, yet these haven't really spoilt the ambience. The beach itself is straight and narrow and lacks the sweeping expanse of Chaweng, or the quiet intimacy of Laem Set, yet the place maintains a refined and friendly village atmosphere with the string of restaurants popping up making the beachfront a popular evening location. Most accommodation providers offer fishing, snorkelling and sightseeing charters, although there are plenty of individual outfits competing for business.

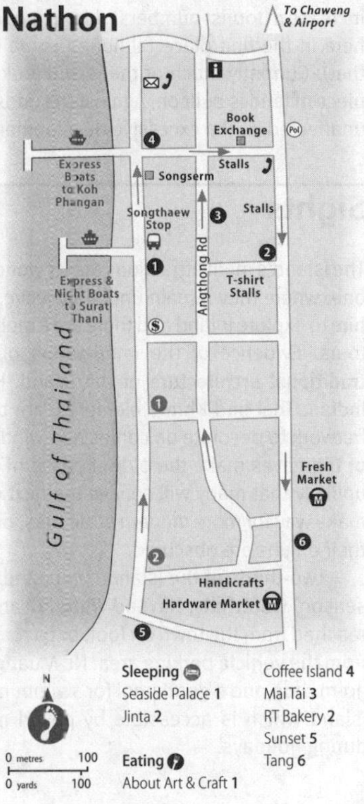

Nathon
To Chaweng & Airport
Book Exchange
Express Boats to Koh Phangan
Stalls
Songserm
Songthaew Stop
Stalls
Angthong Rd
T-shirt Stalls
Express & Night Boats to Surat Thani
Gulf of Thailand
Fresh Market
Handicrafts
Hardware Market
Sleeping
Seaside Palace 1
Jinta 2
Eating
About Art & Craft 1
Coffee Island 4
Mai Tai 3
RT Bakery 2
Sunset 5
Tang 6
0 metres 100
0 yards 100
N

Big Buddha (Bang Ruk) This small bay has typically been a favourite stomping ground with ex-pats although in recent years it has become increasingly popular with travellers. Accommodation is rather cramped and it also tends to be rather noisy as the bungalows are squashed between the beach and the road. However, the beach is quiet and palm-fringed and the water is always good. During the choppier weather from October to February, this sheltered cove is a popular haven with fishing boats.

The **Temple of the Big Buddha** sits on an island linked to the mainland by a short causeway, near Bophut Beach. This unremarkable, rather featureless, modern seated image is 12 m high. In recent years, the site has been smartened up and made into a 'proper' tourist attraction; there are now 50 or so trinket stalls at the entrance and several foodstalls. It has become a popular spot on the motorbike touring trail.

Samrong Bay Set at the far northeastern corner of the island, this spot is also known as 'Secret Beach'. But it is not a secret any longer, as there are two resorts here. The scenery is more wild and raw up here.

Choeng Mon At the northeasternmost part of the island is arguably the prettiest bay on Samui. The crescent of extremely fine white sand has an island at its eastern end, attached to the mainland by a sandbar, traversable at low tide. While in places it is rocky underfoot in the centre of the bay, the sand continues well out to sea. The restaurant scene is pretty lively, particularly in the centre of the beach where bamboo tables with oil lamps reach right down to the water's edge and there are a couple of beach bars at the far eastern end. The beach is most popular with couples and families.

Chaweng This is the biggest beach on the island, split into three areas – north, central and Chaweng Noi. **Chaweng Noi** is to the south, round a headland, and has three of the most expensive hotels on the island. **Central Chaweng** is a vast, attractive sweep of sand with lovely water for swimming and is lined with resorts, bungalows, restaurants and bars. The town that has grown up here is entirely geared towards tourists and in recent years it has become swamped. Along the road behind the beach there is a further proliferation of bars, clubs, tourist agencies, restaurants, fast-food chains, stalls and watersports facilities. However, the infrastructure has not kept pace with the concrete expansion and the drains stink in the searing heat. In comparison to the other beaches on the island it is very crowded

North coast

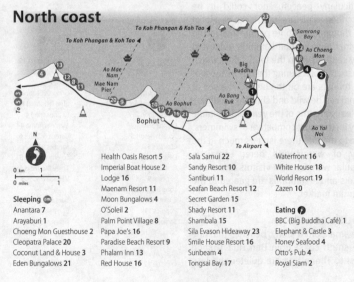

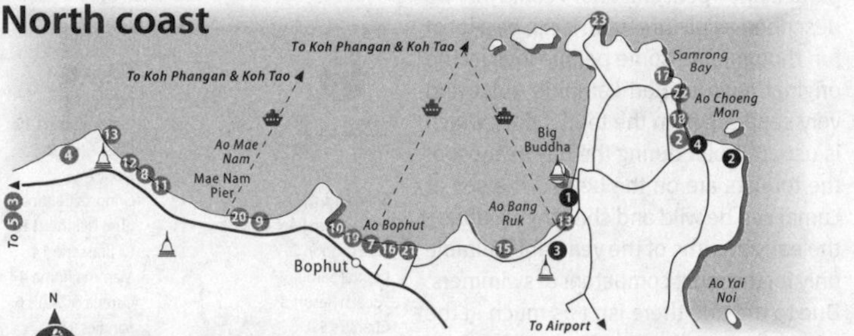
To Koh Phangan & Koh Tao
To Koh Phangan & Koh Tao
Samrong Bay
Ao Choeng Mon
Big Buddha
Ao Mae Nam
Mae Nam Pier
Ao Bophut
Bophut
Ao Bang Ruk
Ao Yai Noi
To Airport
To 5 3
N

0 km 1
0 miles 1

Sleeping
Anantara 7
Arayaburi 1
Choeng Mon Guesthouse 2
Cleopatra Palace 20
Coconut Land & House 3
Eden Bungalows 21
Health Oasis Resort 5
Imperial Boat House 2
Lodge 16
Maenam Resort 11
Moon Bungalows 4
O'Soleil 2
Palm Point Village 8
Papa Joe's 16
Paradise Beach Resort 9
Phalarn Inn 13
Red House 16
Sala Samui 22
Sandy Resort 10
Santiburi 11
Seafan Beach Resort 12
Secret Garden 15
Shady Resort 11
Shambala 15
Sila Evason Hideaway 23
Smile House Resort 16
Sunbeam 4
Tongsai Bay 17
Waterfront 16
White House 18
World Resort 19
Zazen 10

Eating
BBC (Big Buddha Café) 1
Elephant & Castle 3
Honey Seafood 4
Otto's Pub 4
Royal Siam 2

and it's getting more resort-ridden by the year, but it's still Samui's most popular beach. Despite the facilities, most visitors seem to eschew energetic activities in favour of that alternative high-octane occupation: sunbathing.

Chaweng to Lamai There is not much beach along this stretch of coast but there is some snorkelling off the rocky shore. Snorkelling is best at Coral Cove, between Chaweng and Lamai or at Yai Noi, north of Chaweng.

Lamai Koh Samui's 'second' beach is 5 km long and has a large assortment of accommodation. The beach is nice but not as attractive as Chaweng and the sea is rocky underfoot in many places. Rates are similar to Chaweng, but the supporting 'tourist village' has developed rapidly and cheaper accommodation can be found there. Just south of Lamai, there is a Cultural Hall and a group of phallic rock formations known as **Grandmother** and **Grandfather rocks** (*Hinyai* and *Hinta*). There's an array of touristy shops leading up to it. Companies along the main road parallel to the beach offer fishing and snorkelling trips around the islands.

Depending on who you talk to, or who you are, this is either a rather tawdry, downmarket Pattaya, or an idiosyncratic, slightly hip and colourful Hua Hin. It is not particularly peaceful nor could it be described as picturesque. It can be a lot of fun though, and some people love it. The original town of Ban Lamai is quiet and very separate from the tourist part, which is usually quiet during the day as most of the tourists are on the beach. The sea at Lamai can be wild and challenging during the early months of the year, and suitable only for the most competent of swimmers. Due to the tide there isn't as much in the way of watersports here. Lamai is popular with German visitors and many hotels and restaurants are geared to the German market.

South coast

The small, often stony, beaches that line the south coast from Ban Hua Thanon west to Thong Krut are quieter and less

Chaweng Beach

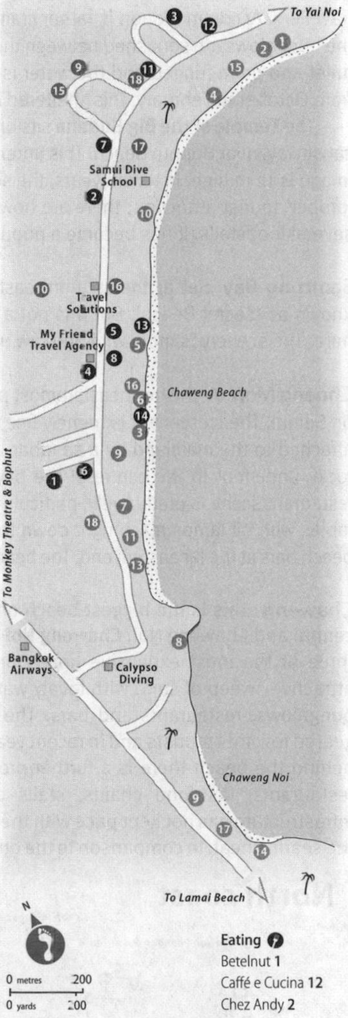
To Yai Noi
Samui Dive School
Travel Solutions
My Friend Travel Agency
Chaweng Beach
To Monkey Theatre & Bophut
Bangkok Airways
Calypso Diving
Chaweng Noi
To Lamai Beach
N
0 metres 200
0 yards 200

Sleeping
Amari Palm Reef 1
Blue Lagoon 2
Central Samui Beach Resort 3
Charlie's 5
Dew Drop Hut 6
First Bungalow Beach Resort 8
Imperial 9
Long Beach Lodge 10
Lucky Mother 4
Poppies 11
Samui Resotel 13
Samui Yacht Club 14
The Island 15
Tradewinds 16
Impiana 17

Eating
Betelnut 1
Caffé e Cucina 12
Chez Andy 2
Deck 7
Gringo's Cantina & The Islander 11
La Brasserie 14
Mamma Roma 4
Osteria & Zico's 6
Sandies 13
Sojeng Kitchen 8
Three Monkeys 5
Vecchia Napoli 3

Bars & clubs
Christy's 18
Green Mango 9
Reggae Pub 10
Sound Pub 15
Star Club 17
Tropical Murphy's 16

developed with only a handful of hotels and bungalows although more construction continues at a breathless pace. While most tourists head for the white sands and sweeping shores of other parts of the island, there are some staggeringly beautiful little coves peppered along this more southerly stretch.

Ban Hua Thanon Ban Hua Thanon is an attractive rambling village with wooden shophouses and *kwaytio* stalls – and the only Muslim community on Koh Samui. The forebears of the inhabitants come from Pattani in Thailand's far south. With its stony beach being the biggest anchorage for fishing boats on the island, this village is quiet and rarely visited by tourists. North of the village are a couple of restaurants, well situated and benefiting from the cooling sea breezes, see Eating.

Lamai Beach

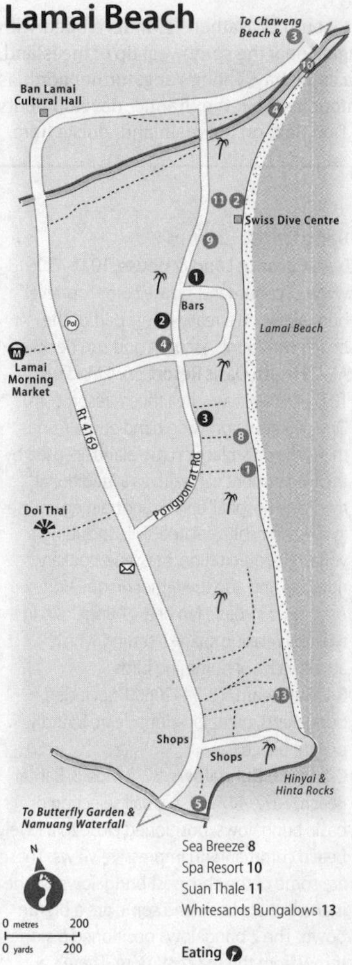

Sleeping
Aloha **1**
Lamai Coconut Resort **2**
Long Island Resort **3**
Rocky Resort **5**
Sand Sea Resort & Spa **4**
Sea Breeze **8**
Spa Resort **10**
Suan Thale **11**
Whitesands Bungalows **13**

Eating
Il Tempio **1**
Sala Thai **2**
Will Wait Bakery **3**

Bars & clubs
Bauhaus **4**

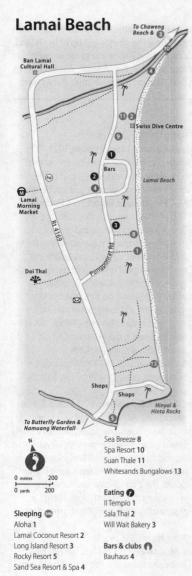

Na Khai Na Khai is a small beach with just a handful of resorts. The swimming can be rocky, but if you are looking for a quiet place to stay and don't require a classic sweep of golden sand extending into the distance then this is an option.

Laem Set This is not really much of a beach at all – at least compared with the long stretches of Chaweng and Lamai. However, it is quiet, clean and palm fringed and there is some reasonable snorkelling close by. There is also a narrow ribbon of sand to keep the beach-wallahs happy.

Samui Butterfly Garden ⓘ *T077-424020, csv@chr.co.th, 0830-1730, ฿170,* is set on the side of the hill behind **Laem Set Inn** opposite **Central Samui Village**. It features a screened butterfly garden with a limited collection of butterflies, a display of (dead) insects, moths and butterflies, a few beehives, a hillside observatory, observation platforms for views of the coast, a glass-bottomed boat for viewing a coral reef and a restaurant.

Thong Krut Thong Krut Bay and the hamlet of Ban Thong Krut are at the southern extremity of the island. The stony beach is around a kilometre long and the swimming is average but there are excellent views from here and it is peaceful and undeveloped with just a handful of shops including a little supermarket and **The Beach**, **Java** and **Green Ta'Lay** restaurants. The upgrading of the road, however, is likely to lead to further expansion and development. Boat trips can be made to Koh Tan and Koh Matsum and there are several tour companies that will organize fishing and snorkelling trips.

Nearby, is the **Samui Snake Farm** ⓘ *88/2 Moo 4, T077-423247*. Shows are held at 1100 and 1400. The commentary, apparently, is hilarious. Not for the squeamish.

Koh Tan and Koh Matsum **Koh Tan** lies due south of Thong Krut and is about 3 km long and 2 km wide. It was first colonized by Hainanese; there is a Chinese cemetery with those first colonizers' graves on the island. There are three small villages and a few bungalow developments on the island which, though undeveloped, are not blessed with spotless beaches and crystal-clear waters as one might suppose. Still, it is quiet and just about away from it all.

Koh Matsum is a sorry sight – all the coconut trees have been stripped by beetles, leaving a desolate landscape.

West coast

Like the south coast, the western coastline south of Nathon is undeveloped with secluded coves and beautiful sunsets. Phangka, near the southwest tip of the island, has good snorkelling in the quiet waters of a small bay; Thong Yang, further north, is an isolated strip of beach, relatively untouched by the frantic developments underway elsewhere. The vehicle ferry from Don Sak, on the mainland, docks here.

Sleeping

Accommodation prices tend to soar during the peak months but are a bargain during the off-season. See each area for details. Prices on Koh Samui have doubled in the past few years and it's rare to find fan bungalows under ฿400-500 in the high season. Backpacker havens are being forced out to make way for high-end establishments. Even world-famous Charlie's Huts, stalwart of backpackers for a generation, is due to close at the end of 2006 to make way for an expensive resort. High season roughly runs from 1 Jul-30 Aug, 1 Dec-30 Apr.

Nathon *p564, map p564*
Few people stay in Nathon for obvious reasons.

C **Jinta Hotel**, 310 Moo 3, T077-236369, www.tapee.com. Small, attractive hotel on the seafront with a/c and fan rooms.

C **Seaside Palace Hotel**, on the seafront road, T077-421079. A/c, clean, adequate and well-maintained rooms, hot water.

Ang Thong Marine National Park *p564*
Accommodation is available on Koh Wua Talap, T077-280222, 5 guesthouses sleep 10-20 people each, ฿800-2000 per guesthouse, tents available for rent (฿200), ฿100 if you bring your own tent. There are showers and a small restaurant.

Bang Po *p564, map p565*
L-AL **Coconut Land & House**, T077-420613, www.coconut-land-house.com. Top-level bungalows on a really lovely part of the beach with pools, jacuzzis and sun decks.

AL-C **Health Oasis Resort**, 26/4 Moo 6, T077-420124, www.healthoasisresort.com. One of Samui's growing band of spa resorts, this is the only place on the island licensed by the Department of Health as a 'traditional medicine hospital' and it runs training courses in spa and health-related skills, including yoga, reiki, meditation, massage, cookery, nutrition and also the rather unique Vortex Astrology. 31 basic fan or a/c bungalows in a typically relaxing spa-like setting which attracts a lot of humming birds.

B-C **Sunbeam**, T077-420600. Secluded bungalows, quiet location, clean, friendly, private beach.

C-E **Moon Bungalows**, 32/2 Moo 5, Bantai Beach, T077-447129. A small selection of basic bungalows, positioned close to a lovely beach commanding impressive views. These are some of the cheapest bungalows on the island but are basic and some are a bit run down. The 2 bungalows positioned a stone's throw from the sea cost more. There's a restaurant, communal TV and games room.

Mae Nam *p564, map p565*
L **Anantara**, 101/3 Bophut, T077-428300, www.anantara.com. This is a most elegantly

designed resort. Utterly chic but comfortable and personal. The striking lobby is dominated by a cluster of lanterns and doors imprinted with golden stencilling. This opens out onto a stunning long, rectangular lotus pond. The infinity pool overlooks a nice stretch of sand. The spa (1000-2200) is a cool oasis in the grounds. The Italian full-moon restaurant occupies a stylish raised platform with superb views.

L Paradise Beach Resort, T077-247227, www.samuiparadisebeach.com. Now a **Best Western** with 95 bungalows on the beach and in a main building. Attractive touches in rooms include brightly coloured silk cushions and drapes on the beds. Each room has a double and single bed. There's a large secluded and nicely shaded pool, a kids' paddling pool, slides, dive shop, canoeing, windsurfing, massage and a growing number of fabulous restaurants – Thai and seafood. There's only a very small bit of beach but sunbeds are perched on a sandy terrace with great views of Koh Phangan. Popular with families.

L Santiburi, 12/12 Moo 1, T077-425031, www.santiburi.com. A superb and incredibly large resort of 91 beautifully furnished Thai-style villas and suites with a massive pool, watersports, sauna, tennis and squash courts, situated on a quiet stretch of beach. There is also a spa (open 1100-2300) with a full range of massage, reflexology and facials. There's also a **Hertz** desk. The golf resort opened 2 years ago. See Activities and tours, below.

L-AL Zazen, near where Mae Nam and Bophut merge, T077-425085, www.samuizazen.com. This is an utterly gorgeous compact resort of 27 rooms stuffed full of attractive design features on a large stretch of beach framed by a headland to the west. Cabins nestle amid the vegetation as do massage cabins. There is a lovely beach bar and the restaurant is recommended.

AL-A Seafan Beach Resort, T077-425204, www.seafanresort.com. Overpriced but lovely a/c wooden bungalows on stilts, whirlpools, attractive gardens, a pool and restaurant.

A Maenam Resort, 1/3 Moo 4, Maenam Beach, T077-247286, www.maenam resort.com. Alpinesque bungalows with little balconies, wicker furniture, wardrobes, desk and a/c closely situated in luscious gardens. Some have wonderful positions set on the lovely, gently sloping beach with shallow waters. Popular with young families. Friendly management. Recommended.

A-C Shady Resort, T077-425392, 20 bungalows on a lovely stretch of yellow-sand beach bordered by bowing coconut palms. The restaurant looks right out onto the beach. Rooms are nice, white and bright with desks and fridges. A/c bungalows with gardens are the most expensive. Very friendly people, good value. Recommended.

B-C Cleopatra Palace, 44/1 Maenam, T077-425486, orasa75@hotmail.com. Nice, small bungalows with big balconies with a/c or fan. Sea view bungalows cost a little more. Cute little blue wooden bar on the beach and chess tables too. The beach here isn't as nice as it is a bit further west. Its outstanding Thai food is its major attraction. Very friendly owner who speaks excellent English.

B-C Palm Point Village, T077-425095. 15 mins' walk from Mae Nam village, this place has good-value cute wooden and concrete bungalows on a lovely stretch of steep sloping beach (quiet and peaceful here). The more expensive rooms have a/c and balcony. Cheaper fan rooms available. Good food and motorbikes for hire. Recommended.

B-C Phalarn Inn 33, T077-247111, phalarn_inn@hotmail.com. Set back some way from the beach and so not the most ideal of locations. Concrete bungalows with big balconies, TV and a/c have a garish colour scheme. Cheaper fan rooms are available. Not the best deals considering the location but pleasant grounds, friendly staff and a good selection of facilities: restaurant, motorbike rental, package tours and ticket reservations.

Bophut *p564, map p565*

L-A Smile House Resort, T077-425361, www.smilehouse-samui.com. Choice of either a/c, or fan bungalows in a pleasant layout. Both are kept meticulously clean and have unusual Chinese lampstands but small bathrooms. There is a large pool on the roadside, so it is a little public. The fan accommodation is very good value considering the access to the pool. There's a beachside restaurant over the road (see Eating).

L-A The Waterfront, 71/2 Moo 1, T077-425438, www.thewaterfrontbophut.com. Modern and attractive bungalows set around a small pool very close to the beach. A cosy atmosphere and popular with families. A well as the usual facilities, rooms have tea and coffee making facilities and a DVD player. Free childminding is offered. The low season prices are a bargain.

AL-B World Resort, 175/Moo 1, T077-425355, www.samuiworldresort.com. Fan and a/c bungalows. The a/c accommodation is particularly appealing, as the rooms are spacious and wood panelled. There is a large pool and a beach restaurant that serves Thai and western food.

A Eden Bungalows, T077-427645, www.edenbungalows.com. This French-owned oasis is delightful. 15 tiled double and family fan or a/c rooms with large bathrooms and romantically dim lighting. They are cleverly arranged around a small pool, and plenty of vegetation, giving the impression of much greater space than there actually is. Fairly pricey, but the ambience is worth it.

A The Lodge, 91/1 Moo 1, T077-425337, www.apartmentsamui.com/lodge. This small, appealing hotel has 10 well-decorated a/c rooms, all of which have satellite TV, a minibar, and en suite bathroom. While there is no restaurant, there is a bar that serves basic western food.

A The Red House, T077-245238, www.design-visio.com. This delightful place has 4 boudoirs with balconies which are elegantly furnished with Chinese textiles in deep reds and attractive furniture. The 4- poster beds look right out over the sea. The downstairs is a shoe emporium. Friendly and recommended.

A-B Sandy Resort and Spa, 177/1 Bophut Beach, T077-425353, sandy@sawadee.com. Accommodation ranges from fan-cooled bungalows to a/c rooms in a somewhat ugly 2-storey building. There are 2 restaurants, one of which is on the beach.

E Papa Joe's, 34/7 Moo 1, T077-427697, www.rhinos63.com/samui. Located close to the entrance to the **Fisherman's Village** on the left-hand side. Probably the cheapest sleeping spot on Koh Samui. Beds in a dorm with outside cold shower, fan, locker and good-value twin-bedded rooms with fan and hot shower room attached. Handmade leather shoes and crafts are sold next door.

Big Buddha *p565, map p565*

A-B Secret Garden, T077-245255, www.secretgarden.co.th. This very small, private bungalow complex, arranged around the beach-fronted open-air restaurant (serving extremely tasty Thai, Chinese and western food), has become a favourite haunt with many ex-pats and a good mix of tourists, on Sun in particular, when live bands are shipped in to promote the weekly beach party that kicks off at 1830. The bungalows are a little stuffy but have separate sitting areas and TV. Some are close to the main road.

C Shambala, 23/2 Moo 4, T077-425330, www.samui-shambala.com. 14 cute, bright, blue-painted, fan bungalows amid a sweet little garden with flourishing bougainvillea. They are a good choice for those looking for a serene beach atmosphere. There's a great chill out area with books and games. Run by Brits Julz and Jessica.

Samrong Bay *p565, map p565*

L Sila Evason Hideaway, T077-245678, www.sixsenses.com. This is an ultra-chic resort with cool, calm and minimalist lines. The piece de resistance is the infinity pool struck by jagged bamboo poles, from where you can watch the sunset. There are 66 hideaway villas, pool villas, pool villa suites and a presidential suite. The villas are 2-storey with rectangular private pools or sundecks on the lower floor while hugely comfortable white beds on platforms overlook the sea. From these beds, the seascape and the view of Koh Phangan appear like a watercolour painting, framed by the large glass windows. Sunken baths, cow hide lamp shades and coconut sinks in the bathroom complete the luxury. There are 2 restaurants (see Eating), a gym, a shop and a **Six Senses Spa** (1000-2200). Here, the massage rooms overlook rocks and the sea. The **Drinks on the Hill** bar has cracking cocktails – especially the Bellinis. Recommended.

AL-A Arayaburi, formerly **Bay View Village**, 6/14 Moo 5, T077-427500, www.samuibayviewvillage.com. 65 individual villas, with small private terraces that are fairly closely packed together. Superior rooms are nice and light and there are flowers on all beds. Garden view bungalows do not get much of a view. All bathroom sky lights need cleaning and some bath tubs need updating.

Beachside pool, bike, motorbike and canoe hire available. It shares a private beach with the Silva Evason Hideaway.

Choeng Mon *p565, map p565*

L Imperial Boat House, 83 Moo 5, Choeng Mon, T077-425041, www.imperialhotels.com. 34 converted teak rice barges make for unusual suites, 182 other rooms in 3-storey ranch-style blocks, with limited views and rather disappointing compared to the boats. Watersports are available and a boat-shaped pool adds to the theme-park feel of the place. The garden pool is more secluded. The buffet breakfast is extensive. It seems very outdated now compared to its elegant neighbours.

L Sala Samui, www.salasamui.com. This is a seriously gorgeous hotel. It has a winning design with an appealing beachside pool surrounded by decking and hidden private villas with pools, raised relaxing platforms and outdoor bathtubs. There's a Mediterranean feel to the place in terms of design and the all-white buildings. The Mandara Spa is open 1000-2200.

L Tongsai Bay, T077-245480, www.tongsaibay.co.th. Attractive bungalows, painted in all colours from aquamarine to seaweed green, scattered across a hillside coconut plantation, overlooking their own private bay. Watersports, tennis courts, gym and 2 pools (one seawater) close to the sea. The best bungalows are the newer ones which are very appealing and well designed with outdoor bathtubs and 4-poster beds. Food in the main restaurant is excellent, particularly the buffet breakfast. There are 2 further restaurants, one a beachside bar and café and a rather more sophisticated place for dinner. Overall an excellent place with friendly and professional management and staff and a winning location. Buggies are used to get around the resort but there are considerable flights of stairs to access some rooms so you will need to make enquiries if this presents any problems for you. Recommended.

L The White House, centre of the beach, 59/3 Moo 5, T077-245315, www.samuidreamholiday.com. Set in a delightful shady tropical garden, this is a small collection of large white houses with Thai-style architectural detailing. The hotel also has a medium-sized pool in a cosy position just behind the beach and restaurants. Overall, a highly refined place. Recommended.

B Choeng Mon Guesthouse, centre of the beach, T077-448007, www.choengmonburi.com. 20 rooms right on the beach which offer a cheap alternative on this very attractive bay. No pool.

C O Soleil, T077-425232. Some a/c rooms with hot water. Even the cheapest rooms here are solidly built and bamboo lined with mosi-screens on the windows and attached (and clean) private shower rooms. Single rooms are available even more cheaply for solo travellers. Good restaurant. Recommended.

Chaweng *p565, maps p562 and p566*

Chaweng contains a rather jarring combination of international hotels and basic bungalows. This gives it an unusual feel and enables visitors staying in US$150-a-night hotels to cross the road and have a full American breakfast for under US$2. Compared with Lamai, Chaweng is more upmarket.

L Blue Lagoon, northern end, T077-422037, www.bluelagoonhotel.com. Well-designed accommodation with 60 rooms in 2-storey Thai-style blocks. The resort also features an international restaurant and a large and attractive pool.

L Poppies, T077-422419, www.poppiessamui.com. Beautifully designed to maximize space, these a/c Thai-style houses have open-air bathrooms and are set in a tropical garden with water running through it. An excellent and very popular open-air restaurant (see Eating) is on the premises. There's a small pool. Exceptionally refined, its Swiss hotel management offers outstanding service and one of its marketing gimmicks has been to set up a live video cam overlooking Chaweng beach 24 hrs a day.

L-AL Amari Palm Reef, northern end, T077-422015, www.amari.com. The hotel is built on 2 sides of the main road. The original part is on the seaward side of the road. Rooms here are in blocks in a garden compound. There is also a rather public swimming pool, right next to the beach. It is all slightly cramped. On the other side of the road are the newer Thai-style bungalows and duplexes. There is a quieter, more secluded pool here. Facilities include

a tennis court, dive centre, the new Sivara Spa and restaurant, which is average.

L-AL Central Samui Beach Resort, T077-230500, www.centralhotelsresorts.com. Accommodation comprises an elegant, if expensive, low-rise 'Greek temple comes to the Orient'-style resort. Wood panelled blocks with good facilities set in a palm grove. There's a large pool, health centre and 4 very good restaurants. It is extremely popular.

L-AL Imperial, southern end, T02-2619000, www.imperialsamui.com. The first 5-star hotel on the island has rooms in a large 5-storey Tuscan-style block. The hotel also has saltwater and freshwater pools.

L-AL Impiana, T077-422011, www.impiana.com. A brand new modernized block with pool and 2 good restaurants. The downstairs Thai operation boasts a nice beach setting, while upstairs is Tamarind's Restaurant (1800-2230) offering very well-received Pacific-rim with Asian influence fusion cuisine.

AL First Bungalow Beach Resort, T077-422327, www.firstbungalowsamui.com. As implied by its name, this was the first resort to appear on Chaweng Beach and the a/c bungalows are spacious and nicely laid out.

AL-A Samui Resotel (previously Munchies), T077-422374, www.samuiresotel.com. A wide range of well-decorated accommodation from fan rooms to luxurious suites. They are, predictably, too close to one another, but this place emerges as being better than most as it has a pleasant beachside restaurant and live music.

AL-A Tradewinds, 17/14 Moo 3, T077-230602, www.tradewinds-samui.com. A very appealing resort as the excellent bungalows are set out in an attractive part of the beach. As a result of its size, it is an intimate place and is peaceful at night. There is a beachside bar and restaurant.

A-B The Island, northern end, T077-424202. Individual huts right on the beach with an attractive garden and run by farang. There's a pool and the bar is open after 2200.

B-D Charlie's Huts, T077-422343. The original backpackers' haunt. Very simple accommodation. The cheapest huts are clean and fan-cooled wooden affairs with thatched roofs. The most expensive have a/c and/or are on the beach. The shared washing facilities, however, are of variable cleanliness. A ฿500 deposit is required. If you can, avoid getting a hut towards the road: the huts aren't soundproof and you are unlikely to get a good night's sleep. The restaurant is open 0600-2100. **Charlie's Huts** will close at the end of 2006.

B-D Long Beach Lodge, 14 Chaweng Beach, Moo 2, T077-422372, longbeach_samui@hotmail.com. Some a/c, very large coconut-studded plot for so few bungalows, laid back and peaceful, bungalows are a reasonable size, a/c rooms are good value.

C Lucky Mother, northern end, T077-230931. Friendly, clean, excellent food, some private bathrooms. Recommended.

D Dew Drop Hut, T07-2636381. Standard, small, darkish bungalows right on Chaweng Beach. Many are not on the beach and the ones that are are usually constantly occupied.

Chaweng to Lamai *p566, map p562*

AL Coral Cove Chalet, T077-422260, www.coralcovechalet.com. Lovely chalets on a hillside linked by decking walkways with steps down to very small private beach with little sand but some snorkelling offshore. It is a well run with a tropical ambience. There's a small pool. Reception staff could be friendlier.

AL-A Samui Yacht Club, T077-422225, www.samuiyachtclub.com, south end of Chaweng, just before the headland in a peaceful bay. Traditional-style thatched bungalows which are attractive and well-sized, set in coconut plantation, with pool, restaurant, fitness centre, children's room and private beach.

B-D Silver Beach Resort, 124/4, Moo 4, T077-422478, silverbeach_@hotmail.com. 20 clean but quite basic rooms with 2 or 3 beds in each. The bungalows are a bit run down and rather close together but are on a lovely little bay with an interesting beach featuring large boulders. Quiet, relaxing atmosphere with friendly management.

Lamai *p566, map p567*

L-A Aloha, T077-424418, www.alohasamui.com. Well-designed a/c rooms in this relaxing resort. There is a good pool and the restaurant offers a wide range of good seafood, though it is not locally caught. Tours can be booked here.

L-A Rocky Resort, T077-418367, www.rockyresort.com. This has had a major revamp. Each of the artistically decorated bungalows, with furnishings from Chiang Mai, has a veranda. The well-placed restaurant commands beautiful views.

L-C Spa Resort, T077-230976, www.spasamui.com. As far as health resorts go, this is excellent: the services provided are very good value and the staff are very welcoming. Run by an American and his Thai wife, it has a sauna, steam room and excellent bungalows with attached bathrooms. Great veggie food and it's worth booking early as this place fills up quickly. There's a small pool. See also under Therapies, below.

AL-B Long Island Resort,146/24 Moo 4, T077-418456, www.longislandresort.com, offers a good variety of quality accommodation including cheaper rooms. All are charming and artistically decorated with bamboo furniture and balconies but bungalows are dark and bathrooms are small. The most expensive bungalows have multiple windows and are right on the beach with decking jutting out onto the sand. There's a cracking spa.

AL-B Sand Sea Resort & Spa, northern end of Lamai beach, T077-424026, www.samuisandsea.com. A mixture of concrete and wooden bungalows. All have tiled bathrooms and are mosquito proof. The gardens are nice and there are good views of the sea. The resort has a restaurant and a 20-m swimming pool. During the low season room rates are cut by up to a third.

A-C Lamai Coconut Resort, 124/4 Moo 3, next to the Weekender Resort, T077-232169. The a/c bungalows are basic, but nevertheless attractively decorated and the management are friendly. Fan rooms are also available. The restaurant serves a range of Thai food.

A-C Sea Breeze, 124/3 Moo 3, T077-424258. One of the oldest places on the island. The accommodation ranges from basic fan rooms to comfortable a/c bungalows with hot water. The restaurant serves Thai and western food at reasonable prices and the staff are very friendly.

B-D Suan Thale, T077-424230. A/c and fan rooms in bungalow 'blocks' on a largish plot. The rooms are reasonable with a bit more character than most.

D-F Whitesands Bungalow, T077-424298. Some of the cheapest rooms on the island. 40 clean bungalows on quite a nice beachfront with attached bathrooms. Some come with communal toilets and no fans. Some are very dark but have mosi-screened windows. Run by a friendly woman who speaks very good English. There's an on-site restaurant in the large compound.

Na Khai *p567*

A-B Samui Orchid Resort, 33/2 Moo 2, T077-424017, www.samuiorchid.com. Rooms are cheap looking with old carpeting, old-fashioned accessories and clashing colours. Beds are small. The pool is nice though. However, the on-site zoo with tigers and birds is a sorry site. Sealion training is available, T077-418987, www.sealionsearch-rescue.com.

Laem Set *p567*

L-B Laem Set Inn, 110 Moo 2, Hua Thanon, T077-424393, www.laemset.com. This is an exclusive, secluded resort in an attractive compound, with a range of accommodation. The 50 rooms are prettily decorated in reds with bathrooms featuring hand-stencilled decoration. The cheapest fan rooms represent excellent value for money considering the surroundings. Several private a/c suites with small pools attached and beautiful views of the sea. Many of the buildings are reconstructed wooden Samui houses. There is a restaurant (0600-2200), pool, children's playground and spa (1000-1900). The room rate includes use of mountain bikes, kayaks, pedal boats, masks and snorkels. Ideal for families with a day nursery and babysitting facilities, children's and toddler's playground. Cookery courses are held. Recommended.

AL-A Central Samui Village, T077-424020, www.centralhotelsresorts.com/samuivillage. An unfortunate addition to this once peaceful stretch of beach, situated opposite the butterfly garden (see Sights). The emphasis is on 'rustic' living, with 100 villas, set rather too close together in the tropical garden setting. 3 pools, spa, bikes for hire and beachside sports on offer. Well equipped.

Thong Krut *p567, map p30*

B-C Thong Krut Bungalow, 30/5 Moo 5, T077-334052, tktour@thaimail.com. Rather close to the road but very quiet, friendly

and unspoilt. Fan rooms are stuffy with 2 beds and are a little run down. The beach in front of these huts needs a good tidy. A/c rooms are a better option. Also runs TK Tour – snorkelling, kayaking and big game fishing trips.

Koh Tan and Koh Matsum *p568*
You cannot stay on Koh Matsum. Charter a boat for ฿400.
D-E Tan Village Bungalow, Koh Tan, T077-9684131. Rather bare compound studded with bungalows within a stone's throw of the sea.
D-E Coral Beach Bungalow, Koh Tan, T09-8665106.

West coast *p568, map p562*
L Le Royal Meridien Ban Taling Ngam Resort, www.lemeridien.com. In an isolated position, on the side of the hill, Thai-style houses spill down to the shore, very plush but somehow rather out of place here, the suites, tennis courts and one of the pools and restaurant are down by the beach. The beach is disappointing with dirty water because of the nearby ferry lanes and the pool is small for the size of the resort.
AL-B International Bungalows/Big John Beach Resort, 912 Moo 2, Lipanoi, T077-415537, www.bigjohnsamui.com. The garden bungalows, which are light and bright with wall hangings, are very good value. Each bungalow has a TV, DVD player, kitchen sink and fridge. They are set around a pool. The beach is not as attractive as that at Lipa Lodge up the coast. Part of this set up is Big John Seafood, near the old car ferry. Away from the frenetic buzzing of Chaweng and Lamai, this is a great place for both food and ambience. The sunsets are arguably the best on the island and you can choose to eat out under the stars or inside listening to the gentle sounds of the live music bar. The lobsters are simply enormous. There's a free pick up service to and from your hotel within a 10 km range.
AL Lipa Lodge, T077-423028, lipalodge@hotmail.com. These lovely white, thatched bungalows with modern fittings are scattered around a lawn plot on a gorgeous stretch of beach. The restaurant (0800-2300) serves international cuisine.
C-D Simple Life Bungalow, Tong Ta Node Beach, T077-334191. Around 10 very basic bunglows, typically packed together, but commanding a lovely view of the small sweeping beach. A/c bungalows also available but it's the same basic room. It's an outstanding spot and Koh Matsum and Koh Tan can be seen from the shore. Impossibly rustic beach restaurant with bamboo furniture and simple fare. There are plans to upgrade. A one-day boat charter to Koh Tan is ฿1000.

Eating

Nathon *p564, map p564*
There are plenty of places to eat here, particularly good are the 'coffee shop' patisseries – there are a couple off the main road and some on the seafront. Seafood restaurants are also found on the seafront.
Mai-Tai, 259/8 Moo 3, T077-236488, 0900-2100. German restaurant serving fantastic meats, sausages and cheeses, can also be bought by weight. The Hungarian Goulash is admired by locals throughout the island.
Sunset, 175/3 Moo3, T077-421244, 1000-2200, south end of town overlooking the sea. Great Thai food, especially the fish dishes.
Coffee Island, T077-423153, 0600-2400. Open-fronted café right opposite the pier with good Colombian, Brazilian and Ethiopian coffee and a full range of cakes as well as steaks, shakes, curry and seafood. Pity the poor pug dressed in baby clothes though.
About Art and Craft, 90/3 Moo 3, T01-4959354, Mon-Sat 0900-1700. Lovely veggie dishes, sandwiches, breakfasts, fresh juices and shakes plus great hot muffins and sauce. Sit amid the pottery and art work created by the owners. The Thai salad with glass noodles makes a great lunch.
RT Bakery, wide range of international dishes. Excellent breakfasts, rolls and croissants.
Tang, near the market at the south end of main road. Serves up pizza, pasta, sandwiches and pastries.

Mae Nam *p564, map p565*
Angela's Bakery, 64/29 Moo 1, opposite the police station on the main road, T077-

427396, 0800-1800. Sells sandwiches, bagels, cakes and pretzels, and also has a deli offering cheeses and cold meat. Popular with foreigners.

Bophut *p564, map p565*

Unlike Chaweng and Lamai, Bophut is small enough to cater for the demand for seafood without having to import produce from elsewhere. There are, therefore, a number of restaurants that set up elaborate seafood displays. Naturally, the choice on offer varies from day to day. The choice has expanded astronomically over recent years, with a string of new eateries popping up, so below is just a selection.

ΨΨΨ-ΨΨ Happy Elephant, 79/1 Moo 1, T077-245347, 1230-2200, on the beachfront. A popular stop with travellers, doing a particularly good line in Thai seafood. The fish steaks and ginger and mushroom sauce are delicious. The barracuda steak is a bit tasteless though. Shark steaks and fondues also available. Staff cook on the streets. Its specialty is hot stone steaks. There's decent wine cellar too.

ΨΨΨ-ΨΨ La Sirene, 65/1 Moo 1, T077-425301, 1000-2300. A delightful little restaurant run by a friendly Frenchman. The seafood is fresh and locally caught and displayed outside the restaurant, the coffee excellent. French and Thai food offered. Recommended.

ΨΨΨ-ΨΨ Smile House Restaurant, Smile House Resort, T077-425361. Offers a wide variety of seafood and serves good pepper steaks.

ΨΨΨ-ΨΨ Villa Bianca, 79/3 Moo 1, T077-245041, 1200-1500, 1800-2400. A very good Italian-run restaurant located in a typically lovely, romantic Bophut setting. Everything, even the ice cream, is made on the premises.

ΨΨ Alla Baia, 49/1 Moo 1, T077-245566, 1100-2300. Right on the seafront, this affordable Italian boasts impressive views of Koh Phangan in a delightful Mediterranean-like setting. Veteran chef Mario prepares his own pasta and pizzas, and pulls in a good proportion of Bophut's hungry population.

ΨΨ Starfish & Coffee,51/7, Moo 1, T077-427201, 1100-0100. Another lovely setting for a meal or a quick drink on the outside terrace in this big airy building. Plenty of seafood and international cuisine in the maroon-themed restaurant with wrought-iron and leopard print decor.

ΨΨ-Ψ Chandra, east of the pier. A tiny teashop overlooking the sea along with a shop selling clothes, jewellery and little decorated paperweights.

ΨΨ-Ψ Yoga Café, T077-245046, www.healthyandfun.net, to the right of the pier. Wholefood café with movie screenings, naturopathy, astrology, reiki, palmistry, tarot, numerology consultations, dance classes and a kids' zone.

Ψ Coffee Junction, 37 Moo 1, T09-8661085, 0800-2200. A good spot to watch the comings and goings from the pier or to wait for your boat. Good coffee but tasteless brownies. Other cakes and a food menu available. Smoothies with energy-boosting spirulina, ฿160.

Big Buddha *p565, map p565*

ΨΨΨ-Ψ BBC (Big Budda Café), 202 Moo 5, T077-425089, right next to the wat, 0900-2300. High quality Thai and international food, reasonably priced in this island-style open-plan layout – an enjoyable place to sit and watch the sunset. BBC offers all-you-can eat BBQs a full English Sun lunch, lobster thermidor as a special and live sporting events. There's an ATM on site.

Ψ Elephant & Castle. Upholds the English tradition. Excellent choice of food.

Samrong Bay *p565, map p565*

ΨΨΨ Dining on the Rocks, Sila Evason Hideaway. Eating here on a large wooden platformed area is a true fine dining experience with some of the most delicious and tantalizingly presented food on the island. The 'Experiences' menu allows you to sample a number of different creations, such as reduction of coconut and truffle with rosemary roasted chicken. From the à la carte menu start with oysters in gazpacho or tuna carpaccio with red pepper salsa, wasabi drizzle, truffle oil and caramelized mango, followed by the chermoulah spiced tiger prawns with mango-chilli salad and an avocado-coriander mash drizzled with curried oil, or the tower of duck-rolled goat's cheese with rocket and a citrus-duck jus. This is a wonderful gourmet experience with plenty of wines to choose from to accompany your meal.

Choeng Mon *p565, map p565*
Choeng Mon is blessed with a number of excellent eateries. This is a selection of the best.

ƚƚƚ Royal Siam Restaurant, Samui Peninsula Spa & Resort, T077-428100. 1100-2300. Dine in style at this superb location overlooking the infinity pool and the sea. The *gaeng poo* – blue crab curry with vermicelli – is absolutely delicious. Service is attentive but not intrusive.

ƚƚƚ Tongsai Bay. This luxury hotel offers 3 restaurants, all of which are top notch. The decking – or 'Plaza' as they call it – of Chef Chom's restaurant commands a marvellous view of the entire bay and although there's room for oodles of people, they seat only 50 outside, and 80 inside. There's a wide range of Thai dishes, all of which are outstanding. It's less expensive than it has been, but it's still top end.

ƚƚ Honey Seafood Restaurant and Bar, at the most easterly tip of the beach. Great seafood. Recommended.

ƚƚ-ƚ Otto's Pub and Restaurant, centre of the beach. Thai food and a Thai interpretation of pizza and pasta dishes.

ƚ O Soleil, towards the western end. Best value for money, particularly good fried rice. Recommended.

Chaweng *p565, map p566*
Chaweng offers a range of international restaurants as well as plenty of seafood. It also features the majority of international food chains.

ƚƚƚ Betelnut Restaurant, 43/04 Moo 3, T077-413370, 1800-2300, just over the road from **Central Samui Beach Resort**. This small, extremely exclusive restaurant serves trendy Californian/Thai fusion cuisine and is going down a storm.

ƚƚƚ Chez Andy, 164/2 Chaweng Beach Rd, T077-422593, 1600-2300. A popular Swiss grill house with roof-garden dining. It also provides Thai food and the beer garden serves beer from a microbrewery and BBQ food.

ƚƚƚ Hagi, Central Samui Beach Resort, 1800-2230. Japanese restaurant in sophisticated surroundings.

ƚƚƚ La Brasserie, **Beachcomber Hotel**, 3/5 Moo 2, T077-422041, 0700-2230. This is a very pleasant beachfront dining experience where Italian and Thai are served. White- clothed tables are softened by night lanterns. The Sat night European set menu at ฿495 is a giveaway with 3 courses and a glass of red wine. The coconut pannacotta with grilled mango and orange sesame tuile is divine.

ƚƚƚ Poppies, T077-422419. An excellent Thai and international restaurant, one of the best on the beach. Live classical guitar accompaniment on Tue, Thu and Fri and a Thai night on Sat. Booking recommended.

ƚƚƚ Spice Island, 1800- 2230. Part of the **Central Samui Beach Resort**. Sit either in the a/c or the relaxing beachside part of the restaurant and try a wide range of excellent, and sophisticated Thai dishes.

ƚƚƚ Vecchia Napoli, T077-231229, on the soi behind **Starbucks**. Beautifully decorated with a few tables spilling out from the airy inside onto the street. Friendly Italian owner who moves from table to table to ensure his guests are having the best possible time. This place is always buzzing with Italians, which can only be a huge thumbs up.

ƚƚƚ Zico's, 38/2 Moo 3, T077-231560, 1800-2230, opposite **Central Samui Beach Resort**. This 150-seater, predominantly BBQ, Brazilian restaurant is one of a wave of seriously upmarket eateries. Contemporary Brazilian decor, roving musicians and waiters bring the action to the tables. Recommended but be prepared to spend!

ƚƚƚ-ƚƚ Sandies, **Silver Sand Resort**, T077-422777, 0630-2400. Dine at candlelit tables on the beach accompanied by live music at this lovely spot. The shark steak in garlic butter is particularly recommended. The service is excellent but check your bill on paying.

ƚƚƚ-ƚƚ The Three Monkeys, 13/11 Moo 2, Chaweng Beach Rd, 1030-0200. Great grub including chicken, salmon and beef dishes. The 'mango monkey' – marinated king prawns with a mango sauce – is filling and delicious. Canned Guinness, TV and a pool table available. Happy hour is 1430-1630 and there's free internet access for customers.

ƚƚ Caffe e Cucina, T01-8942576. A pizzeria run by Angelo from Rome. Good Italian food, friendly and excellent value. Recommended.

ƚƚ The Deck, Beach Rd, 0800-0200. Great location in the centre of the action and noise. Enjoy or tolerate the Fri night Elvis impersonator strutting his stuff in the

Quarterdeck pub opposite. Upstairs there's a great chilled out drinking deck overlooking the main road with triangle cushions and floor cushions to relax on. It serves Thai, western and fusion dishes. Avoid the Thai fish-cake starter.

ƬƬ **Gringos Cantina**, behind The Islander Restaurant, T077-413267. For authentic Tex Mex.

ƬƬ **The Islander**, near soi Green Mango, T077-230836. For anyone missing true English fare, this place provides 'full monty' breakfasts, Sun roast with all the trimmings, as well as pizzas, curry and lasagne.

ƬƬ **Mamma Roma**, 155/30 Moo 2, T077-230649, 1100-2300. Notable for its pizza. The signature pizza of tomato, cheese, ham, salami, olives and capers is very tasty although they're a bit stingy with the capers, but not the meat. There's also home-made pasta here and seafood dishes but these latter are expensive.

ƬƬ **Osteria**, T077-422530, 0900-0100, along from the Chaweng Resort. A good Italian, pizza/pasta place.

Ƭ **Sojeng Kitchen**, 155/9 Chaweng Beach, T01-8922841, 1000-2200, opposite My Friend Travel Agency, offering a good variety of very tasty food at excellent prices.

ƬƬ **Will Wait Bakery**, T077-230093, 0700-0100. For excellent pastries and breakfast or late night snacks.

Lamai *p566, map p567*

There are several seafood restaurants along the Lamai beach road offering a wide choice. Prices vary enormously and there is nowhere particularly good and cheap. International cuisine is widely available along the road parallel to the beach in restaurants such as Il Tempio.

ƬƬƬ **Sala Thai**, T077-233180. Serves good Thai food, seafood, steaks and Italian. It is, however, far too expensive.

ƬƬ **Will Wait Bakery**, T077-0424263. Delicious pastries and croissants, a popular breakfast joint.

ƬƬ-Ƭ **The Spa**, Spa Resort. Serves a wide range of vegetarian and Thai food.

Ban Hua Thanon *p567*

There are 2 restaurants here. Try Hua Thanan for seafood or Aow Thai, T077-418348, for northeastern Thai food.

Bars and clubs

Bophut *p564, map p565*

Billabong Surf Club, 79/2 Moo 1, T077-430144. A full-on sports bar with TVs and sports pictures plastering the wall with a small balcony for drinking.

Frog and Gecko, 91/2 Moo 1, T077-425248, 1200-0200. The first of several English pubs/sports bars on the beachfront run by Graham and Raphaela. The music is extremely good and surprisingly, so is their Thai food. They show all major sporting events on a big projector screen, as well as recent movies. It has just acquired a pool table, ฿20 a game. Pub quiz Wed nights at 2000. Very popular.

The Tropicana, T077-425304. With large fish tanks built into the walls, The Tropicana offers a unique venue for an evening drink and can make for a refreshing change from the increasingly popular sports bars. It's run by the extremely friendly Paul and Lek.

Chaweng *p565, map p566*

Most of the bars are at the northern end of the strip. The strip where Green Mango is located is also home to a variety of go-go bars mixed in with the occasional European-style pubs. The girls who work at the go-go bars outnumber patrons by about 4 to 1.

Dew Drop Huts. Tends to draw a young crowd and puts on beach parties during high season.

Green Mango, on the main road. A rather jaunty venue with farang DJs playing garage and house music. Also host to live Thai bands performing western pop and rock, and they do actually sound like the real thing.

The Reggae Pub, Chaweng lagoon. Popular, but pick your night, as sometimes it's more techno than reggae.

Sound Pub, close to Green Mango. Classier than the rest of the bars on this street, which are mainly girly joints. There's a DJ, tables and a long bar.

Tropical Murphys, 14/40 Chaweng Rd, T077-413614, 0900-0200, opposite McDonald's in Central Chaweng. An Irish pub and the only place on the island serving draught Guinness and Kilkenny beers. Live music most nights and Tue night pub quizzes.

Lamai *p566, map p567*
Most are located down the sois which link the main road and the beach.
Bauhaus is a large, popular venue consisting of a pub, restaurant and discotheque. Shows mainstream western movies during the day and early evening and also, hosts live bands.

Entertainment

Big Buddha *p565, map p565*
Thai cookery
Classes with 'Toy' at the Blue Banana, 2 Moo 4, Big Budda Beach, T077-245380.

Chaweng *p565, map p566*
Christy's. If you fancy sampling some of Thailand's drag cabaret acts then is the place to go. Performances start around 2300 and last about an hour.
Star Club, 200/11 Chaweng Rd, T077-414218. A rival to **Christy's**. Puts on a pretty hilarious show with audience participation, a lot of feathers and make-up at 2230 nightly. Beers are ฿100. No admission charge, customers must buy drinks. Recommended.

Lamai *p566, map p567*
Buffalo fighting
In the stadium at the north end (ask at your hotel for date of the next fight).

Thai boxing
At Lamai's new stadium. Fights 2-3 times weekly during high season, well advertised around the island (฿500). Also at Chaweng Stadium, T077-413504, free transfers. 8 fights from 2100.

Shopping

Nathon *p564, map p564*
Nathon is a good centre for shopping on the island. It is worth a visit to browse through the stalls and take a walk down the main road, past the fresh market on the left and on down to the 'hardware' market on the right. The stalls provide the usual array of T-shirts, CDs/DVDs, watches and handicrafts. As usual, remember to bargain hard. The inner road – Angthong Rd – is worth walking down too.

Bophut *p564, map p565*
There are a number of shops along the main road of Bophut. There is a good bookshop selling books in German, English and French, and shops selling gifts, clothes and produce from around Thailand, Laos and Cambodia.

Chaweng *p565, map p566*
There is a plethora of tailors scattered throughout Chaweng, including **Armani International Suits, Joop! and Baron Fashion**.

Lamai *p566, map p567*
Jewellery, beachwear and clothing boutiques along the main road.

Activities and tours

Jet skis are available on Chaweng Beach. There are now numerous activities on Samui: horse riding, elephant trekking, jungle canopy rides, training to be a sealion trainer, sail boat tours, snorkelling, kayaking and cooking classes. You will find flyers and information everywhere.

Diving
The best time for diving is Apr and the best water is to be found around Koh Tao, Tan, Matsum and the Marine Park. Visibility is obviously variable, depending on the weather. Most of the schools dotted around the island organize all dive courses. PADI Open Water courses cost around ฿8650. There is a hyperbaric chamber at Big Buddha.

Therapies
Spas and massage places have mushroomed on Samui in the last few years. There are some seriously gorgeous spas attached to hotels as well as day spas. Treatments vary in prices as do the incredible range of packages on offer. See under each area for details.

Nathon *p564, map p564*
There are many travel agents cluttered along the seafront (particularly around the pier) and main roads, providing ticketing and tours.
Samui Dharma Healing Centre, 63 Moo Tee 1, Ao Santi Beach, near Nathon, T077-234170, www.dharmahealing.com, runs alternative health programmes to

inspire and rejuvenate. 7- to 21-day fasting courses are directed according to Dharma Buddhist principles in alternative health: fasting, colonic irrigation, yoga, reflexology, iridology and many other therapies. Accommodation is available.

Ang Thong Marine National Park *p564*
Marine park tax (฿200) is included in all tour prices. Operators include **Big John**, T077-421744; **Caveman**, T06-2822983, www.samuireef.com; and **Seatran**, T077-426000. Prices, for the time being, have been set island-wide at ฿2800.

Mae Nam *p564, map p565*
Diving is offered by many resorts, including Paradise Beach Resort.

Golf
Santiburi Golf, T077-425031, www.santiburi.com. An 18-hole course that opened in 2003. Designed by Pirapon Namatra and Edward Thiele. Green fees, ฿3350. Hotel guests enjoy a 20% discount.

Bophut *p564, map p565*
Diving
Aquademia, T077-427203, www.aquademiadive.com.
Bo Phut Diving School, next to Eden Bungalows, T077-425496, www.bophutdiving.com. Also offers snorkelling.
Easy Divers, T077-245026, www.easydivers-thailand.com.

Fishing and Snorkelling
Organized by most accommodation providers as well as individual tour operators scattered throughout the village.

Big Buddha *p565, map p565*
Charter trips
One Hundred Degrees East, 23/2 Moo 4, T06-2822983, www.100degreeseast.com. Run by Ivan Douglas who runs Captain Caveman. Private charters. A direct charter from Samui to Tao is ฿15,000.

Diving
Captain Caveman, at the Shambala Resort, and on Chaweng Beach Rd, T06-2822983, www.samuireef.com. Office hours 1000-2100, closed Sun am. A 5-star PADI dive centre. Prides itself on small classes. Snorkelling trips to Ang Thong Marine National Park, ฿2200, to Koh Tao and Nangyuan and Mango Bay, ฿2100.
Easy Divers, T077-448129, www.easydivers-thailand.com.
Samui International Diving School, 30/1 Moo 4, T09-7724002, www.dial-samui.com.

Sailing, fishing and snorkelling
Organized by **Pra-Yai Fishing and Tours**, T077-427155, 0800-2200, offering both day and night fishing tours, as well as private speed boat chartering.

Choeng Mon *p565, map p565*
Minigolf
Minigolf International, T01-7879148, yogibearhaha@hotmail.com, 0900-1830. 18 tracks near Choeng Mon.

Therapies
Thalasso Spa, Samui Peninsula Spa & Resort, T077-428100, www.samuipeninsula.com. Very professional treatments in attractive rooms. It specializes in mud treatments.

Chaweng *p565, map p566*
There is a wide range of shops along the beach road, where most things can be bought. Many places remain open until late. There is the usual array of tourist shops selling beachwear, T-shirts, jewellery and handicrafts. A number of minimarts are scattered along the main road and the British-owned pharmacy chain, **Boots**. **Bookazine**, which sells newspapers, magazines and books, is next to **Tropical Murphy's**. For genuine branded surfwear, including Quiksilver and Roxy, try the shops next to McDonald's in the centre of town.

Bowling
Living Bowl, 2nd floor, Living Square Shopping Centre, above McDonald's, T077-413258.

Bungee jumping
Sami Bungy Jump and Entertainment Complex, Reggae Pub Rd, T01-8913314, daily from 1000. Offers hourly jumps (50 m), huge pool and sun lounge area.

Diving

Big Blue Diving, South Chaweng Beach Rd, T077-422617, www.bigbluediving samui.com. A well thought of Swedish dive centre.

Calypso Diving, southern end of beach, T077-422437, www.calypso-diving.com.

Discovery Dive Centre, Amari Palm Reef Resort, T 077-413196, www.discoverydivers.com.

The Dive Shop, central Chaweng Beach Rd, T077-230232, www.thediveshop.net.

Easy Divers, head office in Chaweng, T077-413373, www.easydivers-thailand.com.

Samui International Diving School, Chaweng Beach Rd, T077-422386, www.planet-scuba.net.

Jet skiing

Jet Dolphins, on the beach near the lifeguard tower, ฿800/20 mins.

Tan Speed Project, in front of Banana fan. Same prices. Also offers banana boat, ฿400 per person/15 mins.

Kayaking

Blue Stars Sea Kayaking, Chaweng Beach Rd, T077-413231, www.bluestars.info.

Treasure Island, behind the Islander Restaurant, T077-413267, 1100-2400.

Mountain biking

Red Bicycle, T077-232136, www.red bicycle.org. Has bikes for hire and offers guided trips.

Snorkelling

Masks and fins can be hired from most bungalows.

Thai cooking courses

Samui Institute of Thai Culinary Arts, T077-413172, www.sitca.net. Thai cooking and fruit and vegetable carving courses. All equipment is provided, and you can keep the recipes. The lunchtime cooking class costs ฿1200 per person, the evening class ฿1600 per person. Carving courses (6 hrs of lessons over 3 days) are ฿3500 per person. To get there, get dropped off at (or walk to) the **Central Samui Beach Resort** on Chaweng Beach. Walk up the side street for about 150 m across from the **Central** with **Classic Gems** jewellery store at the corner. The Institute is on the right side.

Therapies

It's boom time for any kind of healing/ wellbeing/treatment centre and Chaweng has not missed a trick here. As well as several spas within hotels, there are some independent establishments in town.

Four Seasons Tropical Spa, next to the Baan Samui Resort, close to McDonald's, T077-414141, www.spafourseasons.com. A recommended relaxing experience.

Tour operators

There are dozens along Chaweng Beach Rd.

My Friend Travel Agency, 14/62-64 Mo 2, Chaweng Beach Rd, T077-413364, 1000-2300. Run by a very friendly and helpful lady called Amporn who speaks English.

Travel Solutions, T077-239007, chongkon@ hotmail.com. Down the side of **The Pizza Company** opposite the **Baan Samui Resort**. Particularly recommended as it has 12 years of experience in the industry and can arrange all travel-related matters.

Watersports

Samui Ocean Sports, on the beach at Chaweng Regent Hotel, T01-9401999, www.samui.sawadee.com/oceansports. Offers a wide range of activities and lessons: kayaking, snorkelling, windsurfing, catsailing and yachting.

Lamai *p566, map p567*

Diving

Easy Divers, near Lamai Resort (north end of beach), T077-231990, www.easydivers-thailand.com. German, English and Swedish spoken.

Pro Divers, T077-233399, www,prodivers.nu.

Therapies

The Spa Resort, T077-230855, www.spasamui.com, next to the **Weekender Villa** at the north end of the beach. Offers 'exotic rejuvenation', anything from a herbal steam room to a 'liver flush fast'. A 7-day programme costs around US$260. Accommodation (**A-D** with fan or a/c suite) is in an attractive chalet set around a pool. The beach here is not great at all.

Tamarind Springs, 205/7 Thong Takian, T077-230571, www.tamarindretreat.com, 1000-2000. Upmarket spa set in a peaceful

compound. Offers range of treatments: body scrubs, herbal sauna and a variety of massages. Has adopted quite a strong alternative or complementary health philosophy and makes much of its environmental consciousness. Accommodation is also available at the spa in some beautifully designed and imaginative villas – but these are quite pricey (**L-AL**) and focused on longer term stays.

Tour operators
Several companies along the main road. **G.U.P Travel**, 109 Moo 2, T077-232021, www.guptravel.com. This is a particularly good company, whose English, Swedish and Thai speaking staff offer a very professional service.

Watersports
Jet skis, windsurfing and snorkelling equipment is available for hire at the southern end of the beach.

Transport

Air
The airport is in the northeast of the island, T077-425029-30. **Bangkok Airways** is a private airline, which accounts for the grossly inflated airport international departure tax (฿500 from Koh Samui, ฿300 for domestic departure tax). There are multiple daily connections with **Bangkok** and regular connections with **Phuket**, **U-Tapao** (Pattaya), **Krabi**, **Trat** (in the pipeline), **Hong Kong** and **Singapore**. Berjaya Air, T077-414302, flies twice a week to **Kuala Lumpur**.

Airport facilities An information desk deals with hotel reservations (note that this is owned by Bangkok Airways and attempts are made to divert clients to Samui Palm Beach – owned by the airline), reconfirmation of flights. Restaurant, free left luggage and through check-in for international flights for a large number of airlines. Hertz and Budget car rental, currency exchange and ATM. Transport to town or the beach is by a/c minibus to Bophut, Mae Nam, Chaweng, Choeng Mon, Lamai and Big Buddha. Prices are enormously inflated.

There's a Limousine service at domestic arrivals, T077-245598, samuiaccom@hotmail.com. Cars and a/c minibuses cost the same as the taxis (฿150 to Chaweng, ฿300 to Lamai, ฿150-300 to the north coast). The alternative is to walk out onto the road but it is a 1-km walk and tricky with luggage.

Boat
There are numerous boat options to and from Koh Samui. See transport sections for **Surat Thani**, **Koh Phangan** and **Koh Tao** for boat services to Samui. See also, Bophut and Big Buddha, pages 583 and 583 for services from the north coast to Koh Phangan and Koh Tao.

Songserm Travel, seafront road, Nathon, T077-420157, office hours 0800-1800, runs express passenger boats daily. These boats leave from the southerly pier in Nathon. To **Surat Thani**, 1330, 2½ hrs, ฿150; to **Koh Tao**, 1100, 2½ hrs, ฿345, to **Koh Phangan** 1100, 40 mins, ฿95.

Seatran (office on pier, 0500-1700 daily, T077-426001-2) operates boats to **Surat Thani** from the main northerly pier in Nathon hourly from 0500-1800 with the bus arriving in Surat Thani 2½ hrs later, ฿220. Boats leave for **Koh Phangan** at 1100, 1600 (30 mins) and 1830 (1 hr).

The slow overnight boat leaves from the pier in Nathon at 2100 to **Don Sak**, ฿150.

The Raja ferry leaves from the Tong Yang pier, south of Nathon, to **Don Sak**. To get to Tong Yang, take a songthaew from Nathon or the beaches.

Cattcorp, T077-414215, www.cattcorp.com, from Coral Grand Pier to **Koh Phangan**, 0750, 30 mins, ฿250; to **Koh Tao**, 0750, 1½ hrs, ฿550.

Haad Rin Queen, T077-375113, from Big Buddha Pier to Hat Rin on **Koh Phangan**, 1030, 1300, 1600, 1830, 50 mins, ฿120.

Speed Boat Line from Bo Phut to Thong Sala on **Koh Phangan**, 0430, 0900, 1200, 1430, 20 mins.

Bus
There are several buses that leave Surat Thani for the overnight trip to **Bangkok**. Ask at one of the tour operators or an agency on the island who will furnish you with details of a connecting boat too.

To **Surat Thani**, from Bangkok's Southern bus terminal, a/c buses leave 2000-2200 (12

Road madness on Samui, Phagnan and Tao

By some measures, Thailand has the world's highest death rate on the roads. Koh Samui has the highest rate in Thailand and accidents, fatal and otherwise, are certainly horrifyingly common. (The islands are full of walking wounded wearing bandages on their arms legs and faces). There are several reasons for this state of affairs:

- narrow and impossibly steep roads
- poorly maintained vehicles and machines
- visitors unused to driving on the left
- visitors unused to driving in Thailand. First time riders can be absolutely fine when bowling along most of the time, however should something happen ahead that makes an emergency stop necessary, they simply don't have the natural reflexes to handle their bikes appropriately
- locals driving without lights
- visitors drink driving or on drugs

This means that visitors should be careful when driving on the islands and make sure that they test their motorbike or car before completing a rental agreement. It is also advised that people **do not leave their passports** as collateral. Should there be an accident, it leaves the renter of the vehicle at the mercy of its owner.

For more details on driving in Thailand see Essentials, page 45.

hrs). See page 560 for further details. A popular option is also to catch the 1800-ish bus from Khaosan Rd in Bangkok, also 12 hrs.

Motorbike and jeep/car hire

This is cheaper from the town of Nathon than on the beaches. Motorbikes cost ฿150-200 per day, and around ฿300 for an automatic not including insurance although the price is negotiable if you rent for several days. Helmets must be provided. The fine for not wearing one is ฿200-500. Jeep/car hire is ฿800-1000 per day including insurance or ฿1000-1800 if you hire from an international company such as **Budget** (see box, p582 for cautions about driving).

Motorbike taxi

Available all over the island. They wait in clusters wearing coloured cloth jackets. **Nathon-Chaweng**, ฿150-180. **Bophut-Chaweng**, ฿100. **Nathon-Maenam**, ฿100.

Songthaew

The most common form of transport, songthaews visit all of the island's beaches during daylight hours. Their final destination is usually written on the front of the vehicle and they stop anywhere (prices start at ฿50 per person). Night-time songthaew run from 1830 and charge double. From Nathon, songthaews travel in a clockwise direction to Chaweng and anti-clockwise to Lamai. After 2100 songthaews are thin on the ground and expensive.

Taxi

Yellow meter taxis cruise the island all day. They are few and far between after 0100 but any bar or hotel owner will know one so you will not get stuck. As yet there is no central number to call. The taxis do not use their meters but will if requested. The minimum fare is ฿50. Fares do vary according to the time of day. On average a fare from **Nathon- Chaweng** and from **Bophut-Chaweng** is ฿280-350. The majority of taxis are to be found in Chaweng. A taxi can be chartered for ฿400 per hr.

Train

There are 11 trains a day from Phun Phin to **Bangkok**. The most comfortable times for overnight journeys are the 1950, 2108, 2123, 2246 and 2306. They take around 11-12 hrs. Travel agencies in town can

provide details and tickets that combine the boat from Samui, bus from Don Sak to the railway station and then the train ticket, or some of these combinations.

From Bangkok's Hualamphong station to **Phun Phin**, outside Surat Thani, (10-12 hrs). There are about 5 trains a night, with the 1820 departure being the most highly sought after, arriving at a convenient time to catch an early morning ferry to Koh Samui the next morning. The State Railway runs a rail/bus/ferry service from Bangkok to Koh Samui (18 hrs). This needs to be booked 2-3 days in advance. It is not necessary, however, to buy a combination ticket; buses from all the ferry companies meet trains to transfer passengers to the various ferry terminals.

Nathon *p564, map p564*
Motorbikes and jeeps can be hired in Nathon and songthaews travel from here to all the beaches. Motorbikes wait at the end of the pier. Songthaew wait next to the second southernmost pier.

Mae Nam *p564, map p565*
Boat
Lomprayah, main road, Mae Nam, on the corner of the road to the Baan Fah Resort, office Mon-Sat 0800-1700, telephone lines open daily. Boats to **Koh Phangan** from Wat Na Phra Lam pier,. Transfer from hotels, ฿50.

Motorbike
Hire is available on the beach or at the resorts.

Bophut *p564, map p565*
As with most of the more remote beaches on Samui, the songthaews that are allotted for the beach run rather infrequently. It is possible to charter them, and there are always motorcycle taxis around.

Boat
Samui Island Tour boat from Bophut Pier, T09-5900969. To Thong Sala on **Koh Phangan**, 0930, 50 mins, 1100, 20 mins, 1700, 20 mins, ฿150. The 0930 departure goes onto Ban Mae Hat on **Koh Tao**, arriving 1345, ฿200. Returning from Thong Sala at 1130, 20 mins and 1600, 50 mins.

Big Buddha *p565, map p565*
Boat
Big Buddha Pier, next to 7/11. To Haad Rin on **Koh Phangan**, 1030, 1300, 1600, 1830, 50 mins, ฿120.

Petcherat Marina, 82/1 Moo 4, Bophut, T077-425262, www.samuispeedboat.com. Boats go to Haad Rin on **Koh Phangan**, every full moon, from Petcherat Marina, 1700-2400 hourly, 30 mins, ฿600 return. Return 0100-0800. Boats leave when full. Recommended. Note that in Jan 2005 an overloaded boat capsized with the loss of more than a dozen lives. Make sure the boat you board there and back does not exceed capacity and has lifejackets.

Choeng Mon *p565, map p565*
Car hire
Avis, T077-425454. TA Car Rental, T077-245129, opposite The White House and The Boathouse.

Songthaew
Choeng Mon is off the main Samui road. There is a songthaew station at the far eastern side of the area, behind the beach.

Lamai *p566, map p567*
Jeeps and motorbikes are widely available for hire.

Directory

Banks While only 3 years ago Nathon was the only place boasting a bank, there are now countless exchanges and ATMs scattered all over the island. **Internet** There are internet cafés in all the beach resort areas, ฿1/min. **Medical services** All offer a 24-hr emergency clinic and the Samui International Hospital also has a dental clinic. Note that if someone is involved in a serious accident it is best to take the injured person to the hospital; the ambulance service can be very slow. A reasonable level of English is spoken. **Telephone** Calls are much cheaper if made at the post office. High-street 'booths' are 3-4 times more expensive. International calls can also be made from many hotels and travel agents. **Useful addresses** Tourist police, T077-421281 or T1699 for emergency.

Nathon *p564, map p564*
Banks Exchange booths and banks along the seafront and main roads. **Post office** To the north of the pier, international telephone and poste restante service and CAT internet, Mon-Fri 0830-1630, Sat-Sun 0830-1200. Internet in most travel agencies. **Useful addresses** Immigration office, on main road next to the police station, T077-421069, Mon-Fri 0830-1630. Visas can be extended here. Tourist police, 3 km south of town, T077-4212815, open 24 hrs, just past turning to Hin Lad Waterfall. T1169 emergency, T191 local police.

Bophut *p564, map p565*
Banks Several bank booths as well as tour agencies change money. **Medical services** Bandon International Hospital, T077-245236, www.bandonhospital.com.

Chaweng *p565, map p566*
Airline offices Bangkok Airways, at southern end of Chaweng, T077-422513. **Banks** Money-changing facilities and ATMs are strung out all along Chaweng Beach Rd. **Medical services** Samui International Hospital, T077- 422272, www.sih.co.th.

Lamai *p566, map p567*
Banks Currency exchanges along the main road parallel to the beach. ATMs in town. **Post office** South end of the main road.

Big Buddha *p565, map p565*
Medical services Hyperbaric Services, 34/8 Moo 4, at Big Buddha, T077427427, T01-0848485 www.ssnsnetwork.com.

Koh Phangan

→ *Colour map 4, grid B3.*

Koh Phangan (pronounced Pa-ngan) is the Gulf's party island. World renowned for the Full Moon Party, it attracts thousands of young people looking for the night of their life on the sands at Hat Rin, the most developed part of the island. The pace of development on the island has been rapid. Though still unspoilt, in the main it is not as beautiful as parts of Koh Samui and Koh Tao although the beaches at Hat Rin and some along the east coast are very attractive and – except for Hat Rin – they are uncrowded. The water is good for snorkelling, particularly during the dry season when clarity is at its best. Boats leave from Thong Sala, the island's main town, for nearby Ang Thong Marine National Park (see page 564). Between May and September the tide is out all day between Mae Hat and Hat Rin. Fishing and coconut production remain mainstays of the economy, and villages still have a traditional air – although tourism is now by far the largest single industry. ▸▸ *For Sleeping, Eating and other listings, see pages 588-597.*

Ins and outs

Getting there There is no airport on the island so everyone arrives by boat. There are daily ferries from Don Sak Pier and Bandon near Surat Thani on the mainland and also from the larger, neighbouring island of Koh Samui and its northerly neighbour, Koh Tao. The quickest way to Koh Phangan is to fly from Bangkok to Koh Samui (see and then to catch an express boat from Samui to Koh Phangan. Alternatively, it is possible to fly to Surat Thani and take a boat from there. ▸▸ *See Transport, page 596, for further details.*

Numbers dialled on the island require the area code as well.

Getting around Koh Phangan stretches 15 km north to south and 10 km east to west. The main settlement is Thong Sala. Thong Sala and Hat Rin are connected by a paved road. Two roads run between Thong Sala and Ao Chaloklum: the west coast route and the one through the centre of the island. Around the remainder of the island there is a limited network of poor roads and tracks. For off-the-road beaches it is often easiest to travel by long-tailed boat. Motorbikes and mountain bikes are available for hire. In many instances walking is the best option. See also box on road madness, page 582.

Tourist information There is no official tourist information on the island. The TAT on Koh Samui, see page 562, is responsible for the island. See www.kohphangan.com and www.phangan.info, for information.

Sights

Koh Phangan offers natural sights such as waterfalls, forests, coral and viewpoints but little of historical or cultural interest. The best way to explore the island is on foot, following one of the many tracks that link the various villages and beaches, which cannot be negotiated by songthaew or (sometimes) by motorbike. Even the longest hike is an easy day's walk. It is possible to walk on a trail from Hat Rin up the east coast to Hat Sadet and then on to Thong Nai Pan, where four-wheel-drive vehicles offer a daily service to Thong Sala, depending on the weather.

Although it's possible to navigate the roads by motorbike, first-timers should think seriously before heading southeast to Hat Rin, as the roads are often at a 40° slant which makes them treacherous at best and a death trap when wet. The high number of walking wounded is testimony to the danger of these mountainous roads.

Phaeng Waterfall is to be found in the interior of the island, about 4½ km from Thong Sala and 2 km from the village of Maduawan. The walk east to Hat Sadet runs parallel to a river along which are three waterfalls and the carved initials of several Thai kings who visited here, including King Chulalongkorn (Rama V) who was so enamoured

Koh Phangan

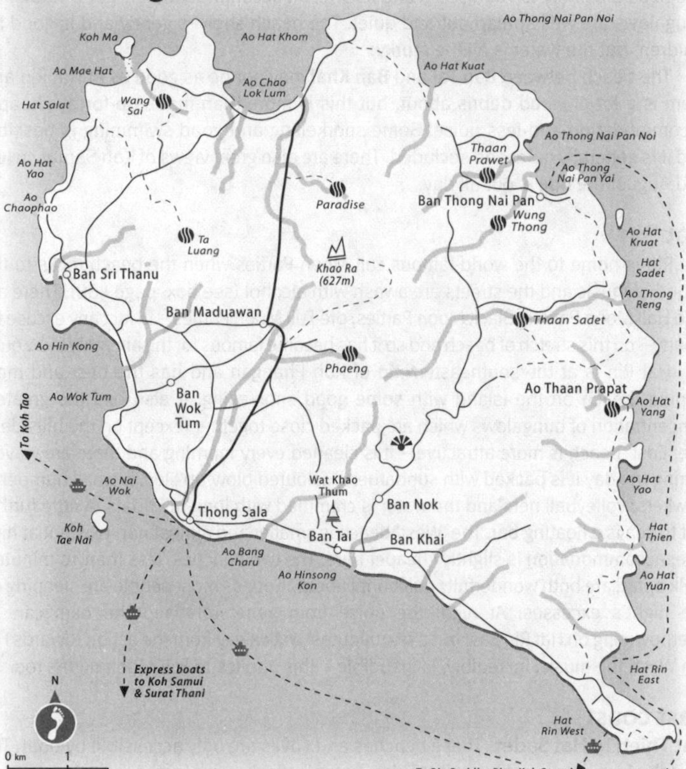

 that he reportedly came here on 10 occasions between 1888 and 1909, and the present King Bhumibol (Rama IX) in 1962. The waterfalls can be reached on foot or on mountain bikes. Other waterfalls include **Ta Luang** and **Wang Sai** in the northwest corner, **Paradise** in the north (near the **Paradise Resort**), and **Thaan Prawet** and **Wung Thong** in the northeast corner. The highest point is **Khao Ra** (627 m). A path runs to the summit although visitors have reported that the trail is indistinct and a guide is necessary.

Thong Sala and around

The main town of Koh Phangan is the port of Thong Sala (pronounced Tong-sala) where most boats from Koh Samui, Surat Thani and Koh Tao dock. Thong Sala has banks, ATMs, telephone, internet access, travel and tour agents, a small supermarket, dive shops, motorbike hire and a second-hand bookstore. Humming during the day with all the departures and arrivals, this can be a bit of a ghost town during the evenings.

On the coast to the east of Thong Sala, outside Ban Tai, is **Wat Khao Tum** and the **Vipassana Meditation Centre** ① *all-inclusive fees are ฿4000 for 10 days, contact Wat Khao Tum, Koh Phangan, Surat Thani, for more information, or www.watkowtahm.org, where they provide a contact and booking facility*. There are views from the hilltop wat to Samui and the Ang Thong Islands. Ten-day meditation courses are held every month with 20-day courses and three-month retreats also available. All the courses are conducted in English and taught by Australian-US couple Rosemary and Steve Weissman who have been here since 1988.

South coast

The stretch of beach from **Ao Bang Charu** to **Ao Hinsong Kon** is unpopular with visitors due to its proximity to Thong Sala and as a result accommodation is good value and bungalows are well spread out and quiet. The beach shelves gently and is good for children, but the water is a little murky.

The beach between **Ban Tai** and **Ban Khai** may not be as good as at Hat Rin and there is a lot of wood debris about, but this is more than made up for by cheaper accommodation and less noise. Some snorkelling and good swimming is possible and it is generally quiet and secluded. There are also great views of Koh Samui. In July and August the tide is out all day.

Hat Rin

Hat Rin is home to the world-famous Full Moon Parties when the beach rocks to the sound of music and the streets are awash with alcohol (see box, page 588). There are also Half Moon Parties, Black Moon Parties, pre-Full Moon Parties – in fact any excuse for a party – on this stretch of beach and so it has become famous for the almighty blow outs.

Hat Rin is at the southeastern tip of Koh Phangan and has the best and most popular beach on the island with some good snorkelling. It also has the greatest concentration of bungalows which are packed close together (except on the hillsides). The 'East' beach is more attractive – it is cleaned every morning and there are waves. During the day it is packed with sunbathers, coloured blow-up lilos, a small number of hawkers, volleyball nets and the water is crammed with long-tail boats. A little further out to sea is a floating bar. The 'West' beach is smaller and almost non-existent at high tide; accommodation is slightly cheaper here. The two beaches, less than 10 minutes' walk apart, are both wonderfully quiet until about 1300, as most people are sleeping off the night's excesses. At night the noise from generators and the bars can be overpowering on Hat Rin East but a few minutes' walk away from the action towards Hat Rin West, the music, incredibly, is inaudible – this applies to Full Moon nights too.

East coast

Hat Thien to Hat Sadet These beaches and coves are only accessible by boat. The stretch of gravelly coastline at Hat Thien doesn't afford much for those seeking a good

spot to lie and fry, but its rocky, tree-lined character makes it an attractive and rugged area. In fact, it's not a bad option at all: there are cheap guesthouses and it's possible to walk over the headland to Hat Yuan where the beautiful and very popular white-sand beach is much more palatable to sun worshippers and swimmers alike. Further up **Hat Yao East** is a good family spot, utterly dreamy, with rocks framing either end, and a small reef a short swim away makes it good for snorkelling. There's currently only one bungalow operation there.

Ao Thong Nai Pan Noi and Ao Thong Nai Pan Yai The double bay of Ao Thong Nai Pan Noi and Ao Thong Nai Pan Yai boasts some of the most beautiful, quiet, white-sand beaches on the island, romantically hemmed in by the mountains, with among the highest recurring visitor rates. The very attractive beach is topped by boulders at its northern end but there is an unsightly unfinished concrete construction on the hill above. The appealing Panviman dominates the headland which separates Ao Thong Nai Pan Noi and Ao Thong Nai Pan Yai. Yai has more palms leaning over the beach and so is slightly more picturesque than Noi, but Noi has a wider stretch of sand. There's a minimart on the beach and bikes can be rented from here. There's also internet, snorkel gear and kayaks for hire on the beach. It is said to have been Rama V's favourite beach on the island, and it's not hard to see why – plenty of people come here for a short holiday and end up staying for months. There's still only a dirt track leading to it so it remains fairly off the beaten tourist track and is more a place to relax for those whose main aim is not to party. The journey by truck from Thong Sala takes almost an hour and the road is very muddy in the rainy season, but it does take you through untouched jungle and so is quite an experience. It is also possible to get a boat from Hat Rin here which is much more comfortable.

North coast

About 5 km northwest of Thong Nai Pan, **Ao Hat Kuat** is even more isolated, with a beautiful beach. Staff at the bungalows here are not as friendly as they could be. Some say it has developed a reputation for being a bit of an English ghetto.

Along a rutted track, **Ao Hat Khom** is another very relaxed place to be based and many people stay here for long stretches of time. The bay is fringed by a reef offering some of the best snorkelling on Phangan, however, because the seabed shelves very gently swimming is sometimes only really possible at high tide and getting out to the reef can be tricky. Bear in mind that the bay faces north, so don't expect romantic sunsets or sunrises.

Ao Chao Lok Lum is a deep, sheltered bay on Koh Phangan's north coast. There is now an excellent road from Thong Sala to here. This fishing village is gradually developing into a quiet, comparatively refined, beach resort area, with the best part of the beach being to the east. In the village of Ban Chao Lok Lum, there are bikes and diving equipment for rent. There's also a **7-11** shop and an ATM.

Hat Salat is one of the most peaceful parts of the island and is a lovely bay. **Ao Mae Hat** has a super beach with a sandy bank extending outwards and along which it is possible to walk to Koh Ma when it hasn't rained for some time. There are palm trees, a small number of bungalows and good snorkelling.

West coast

Ao Hat Yao is an attractive curved, clean beach on the west coast with good swimming and snorkelling, 20 minutes by songthaew from Thong Sala. Bungalows are spread out and quiet.

To the south of Ao Hat Yao, **Ao Chaophao** is a relatively quiet and undeveloped bay with just a handful of places to stay. The perfect crescent of sand and sunsets make the bay particularly attractive. There is also good swimming because the seabed shelves steeply before reaching the reef around 100 m off shore where there

Full Moon Parties

The Full Moon Parties which have been going since 1989, are now accompanied by Half and Black Moon Parties, Saturday Night Parties and Pre-Full Moon parties.

On Full Moon night, if you are not planning to party till dawn, it is advisable to stay on Hat Rin West or elsewhere on the island, unless you feel you can sleep to the boom of the bass from the beach. Up to 10,000 people turn up on Hat Rin East every month to dance to the excellent music, watch the jugglers, fire eaters and fireworks displays and drink themselves into oblivion. Even the dogs take part as partygoers paint their pooches in psychedelic paint!

Tips for the party

⊗ Don't bring valuables with you; if a safety deposit box is an option at your bungalow, leave everything there. Don't leave anything of value in bungalows that are easily broken into. Reportedly it's a big night for burglars.

⊗ Do not eat or drink anything that is offered by strangers.

✔ Wear shoes. The beach gets littered with broken glass and some people suffer serious injury from this.

✔ If you lose your brain and your way (and a lot of people do) carry the business (name) card of your bungalow to show sober folk once you've left the party.

⊗ Don't take drugs. It's not worth the risk. At almost every party plainclothes policemen take a number of westerners down to the jail from where they will only be released on bail if they can pay the fine. Otherwise they will be held for five to six weeks prior to trial.

Further information can be found on the following websites: www.fullmoon.phangan.info; www.halfmoonfestival.com; and www.kohphangan.com.

is good snorkelling. At the southern end is an attractive lagoon and the coast here also has some remnant mangroves.

Ao Sri Thanu is a long but rather narrow strip of sand, 15 minutes by songthaew from Thong Sala. It is a peaceful spot to spend a few days and is sparsely settled but is not very attractive. Behind the beach is a freshwater lake fringed by pine trees which is ideal for swimming.

North of Thong Sala and south of Ban Sri Thanu, the beaches at **Ao Wok Tum** are average and the swimming is poor. Accommodation is good value though.

North of Thong Sala and south of Ban Sri Thanu, the beaches between **Ao Hin Kong** and **Ao Nai Wok** aren't particularly striking and swimming is difficult as the seabed shelves so gently. However, it is quite attractive with shallow boulders near **Cookies** and it is not rocky underfoot for the first 10 m or so. Accommodation is correspondingly good value.

Sleeping

There are no big hotels in Thong Sala. Hat Rin is more expensive than other beaches and some accommodation is very overpriced. During the high season (Dec-Feb and Jul-Sep), prices are 50% higher than in the low season: bargain if bungalows seem empty. Over full moon most places insist on a 7-night stay at inflated prices. Don't just turn up 2, 3 or even 4 days beforehand expecting any availability in Hat Rin. There really won't be any and tramping around with luggage in the heat is no fun whatsoever. At super-peak times accommodation runs out and visitors have to sleep in the temples.

Thong Sala *p586*

C Phangan Chai Hotel, 45/65 Mu 1, T077-377068. Price varies with the view – the more expensive look out to the sea, the others to the garden. All are a/c, with fridge, shower and a western toilet. The choice of decor, however, leaves something to be desired.

South coast *p586*

Bang Charu and Hinsong Kon

AL-A First Villa, T077-377225, www.firstvilla.com. Garishly decorated but clean a/c and fan rooms along the beachfront in a pleasant tropical garden.

A-D Charm Beach Resort, T077-377165, www.charmbeachresort.com. The bungalows are well laid out and the most expensive are a/c. The cheap rooms, which are bamboo and thatch huts, are particularly good value but often full. The restaurant serves Thai and European food.

D-E Liberty Bungalows, T077-238171, libertybantai@hotmail.com. This is a nice compound of 10 bungalows with bamboo furnishings and hammocks set amid bougainvillea and cactus. Rooms are clean and comfortable with attached shower rooms. The more expensive ones are on the beach. Music and movies shown in the chilled out restaurant area. There's volleyball on the beach too.

Ban Tai to Ban Khai

B-D Chokana Resort, T077-238085. A huge choice of rooms ranging from basic huts to very smart, round a/c bungalows. There's a pool table and motorbike rental.

B-D Triangle Lodge, T077-377432. Some rooms beginning to look slightly dilapidated but they all have hammocks and private bathrooms. The more expensive bungalows on the beach sport nicely carved wooden balcony decoration. The restaurant is appealing as it has a wide and imaginative menu with tasty interpretations of western dishes and the staff are friendly. Bikes for rent.

C-D Lee's Garden Resort, no signpost so you'll need to ask, T077-238150, lees_garden@yahoo.com. 5 bungalows set in a garden next to the beach with balconies and hammocks in a quiet part of the beach. There are funky tunes, a giant tree swing, good food and great views, well run. Recommended.

C-D Mac's Bay Resort, T077-238443, www.macbayresort.com. A very popular spot, especially with Israelis, with basic huts and smart white concrete bungalows, lined up attractively on the beach, which all enjoy great views. Slightly better than most, well run and clean. The more expensive rooms are large and have attached shower rooms and a/c. There is a restaurant with a wide menu and nightly videos plus table tennis. Money exchange and an international collect-call service.

Hat Rin *p586*

Hat Rin East

Bear in mind that accommodation on this little slice of the island gets extremely booked up around the full moon, so it's worth arriving a week in advance, or booking ahead.

A-C Palita Lodge, T01-375170, palitas9@hotmail.com. Fan-cooled and a/c rooms at this very popular resort with 35 bungalows. The restaurant is given over to a food festival every Full Moon when a wide range of Thai food is available.

A-C Sun Cliff, just behind the 7/11 shop in the centre of Hat Rin, T077-375134. Built around the mountain and incorporating many of the rock features in its rooms, so don't be surprised if a giant rock divides your bathroom in 2! Minibars, a/c and French doors conspire to make this a very appealing choice. Recommended.

A-D Tommy Resort, T077-375215, tommyresort@hotmail.com. Tommy's is building some very pleasant traditional style bungalows near the beach. Further back are older bungalows with attached shower rooms. Those without shower rooms are tatty board constructions crammed in behind the others.

B Delight Resort, 140 Hat Rin, T077-375527, www.delightresort.com. Situated a street back from the beach, this brand new place offers 40 comfortable a/c rooms. There's a restaurant and a large clothes store next to it.

B-C Sea Bungalow, blue and brown bungalows on the rocks at the northern end of the beach. Some have a/c. Fantastic location with great views. Some are more secluded than others.

B-D Paradise, T077-375245. The originators of the Full Moon Party, the management of this set-up run around 50 bungalows, some of which are slightly tatty, some significantly bigger and better with hot water and a/c and all with attached shower rooms. A big plus point is the pleasant garden and prime beach position around which everything is situated. Most importantly, some bungalows can accommodate up to 4 people in 2 double beds, which makes it the best-value option in the area. The owners also run a restaurant, The Rock (see Eating). Recommended.

C Phangan Bay Shore Resort, T077-375224. Nice bungalows set in rows leading down to the beach. The most expensive are a/c and kept very clean. There are hammocks on the verandas of some rooms. However, the management here are astoundingly rude and surly to the point of it being farcical.

Hat Rin West

The advantage of staying on Hat Rin West is that it is quieter whatever the night and on full moon nights the party cannot be heard if you do slope back earlier than dawn. It's only a few mins walk to the centre of Hat Rin and Hat Rin East beach.

AL-A Phangan Buri Resort & Spa, T077-375481, www.phanganburiresort.net. A more expensive resort away from the crowds with a lovely beachfront pool and a secondary one further back. Bungalows are attractively furnished and are nicely spaced in rows leading down to the beach. Non-guests can use the pool for ฿100.

AL-B Neptune's Villa, T077-375251, neptune1@thaimail.com. The accommodation ranges from very nice a/c concrete bungalows to huts with thatched roofs. The second floor rooms have great views of the sea and there is a fairly pleasant stretch of beach immediately in front. However, some of the rooms are hideously overpriced in peak season and lack shower curtain, TV and in-room safe. However, it is a nice, quiet and pleasant place to stay.

AL-C Sarikantang, Hat Sikantang, towards the headland, T077-375055, www.sarikantang.com. Gorgeous rooms with large windows at this luscious resort with a beach-front pool. The cheaper, wooden rooms are very good value. A spa is due to open. It's a 10-15 min walk to the centre of Hat Rin.

B-E Charung Bungalow, T077-375168. Simple bungalows with attached shower room and fan. Hammocks in front of every room. Restaurant has Thai cushions and mats on the floor.

C-D Lighthouse Bungalows, T077-375075, www.lighthousebungalows.com. This great little place is a 20- to 30-min walk from the centre of action in Hat Rin on the western side of the headland beyond the 2 beaches. It is reached by a long wooden bridge that winds its way around the rocks to the bungalows of various sizes and prices. The staff are friendly and helpful, there's a great restaurant and the sunsets are fantastic.

C-D Palm Beach Bungalows, T077-375508. A range of bungalows – some with communal bathrooms, others with attached shower rooms, and some with a/c – on the side of the small headland which is less affected by litter.

D-E Tiara Palace, right at the very west tip of this stretch. This family-run place encapsulates a truly local feel, with the proprietors offering these extremely basic bungalows with outside toilets right in the middle of going about their everyday lives. Some private bathrooms too.

East coast *p586*

Hat Thien to Hat Sadet

AL-F Sanctuary, Hat Yuan, www.thesanctuarythailand.com. A very well-run set-up, managed by westerners. A quiet and appealing little place, only accessible by boat. The resort accommodation offers everything from the seriously lovely to dorms for under ฿100, a great vegetarian restaurant where the food is quite pricey but top quality, and courses in yoga, meditation and massage.

C-D Mai Pen Rai, Hat Sadet, T077- 377413. 40 basic bungalows, with attached bathrooms, right on the beach (which isn't particularly attractive) with newer ones on the hillside. Well situated near the biggest waterfall on the island and of course the beach. Many of Thailand's kings have been here, and the present king owns the land.

D Ploy Resort, Ao Hat Yao East, T01-9686001. Currently the sole bungalow operation in Ao Hat Yao East, boasting about 20 no-frills wooden rooms, all with attached toilets. Electricity is from a generator and kicks off at

1800 ending whenever the restaurant shuts. Kayaks for hire. Friendly staff.

D-E Haad Tien Resort, T01-2293919. There is no road access to this peaceful resort which is 15 mins from Hat Rin by boat. The wood and bamboo bungalows all have attached shower rooms and veranda areas.

E Horizon Bungalows, between Ao Hat Yuan and Ao Hat Thien, T01-2293919, these very basic, thatched huts with outside toilets are on the left-hand side up the hill, overlooking the beach.

Ao Thong Nai Pan Noi

L-A Panviman Resort, T077-445101, www.panviman.com. Mediterranean-style villas with large glass windows or large, airy rooms in the hotel block, which is set high on the cliffs, commanding impressive views and access to good beach frontage. Its taxi service will collect you from the pier at Thong Sala. Huge thatched restaurant.

B-D Nice Beach Resort, T077-238547, nice_beach@hotmail.com. Cheap rooms with fan and a shower room and expensive a/c rooms in large, concrete, tiled bungalows with western toilets, but they are rather unappealing. Motorbikes and jeeps are available for rent and fishing and snorkelling equipment are available. Management could be friendlier.

Ao Thong Nai Pan Yai

AL-D Baan Pranburi, T077-238599, www.baanpanburivillage.com. This place has gorgeous red, teal and mustard yellow Chinese brollies fronting its entrance. The outdoor tables made from bamboo from the large restaurant are set amid frangipani trees. The thatched roofed bungalows are set back a little off the beach facing the sea. They are cute with wooden shutters, bamboo chairs and balconies with hammocks.

A-C Dreamland, T077-238539, www.dreamlandresort.net. Cheap wooden bungalows and very nice a/c bungalows in a manicured, low-level garden.

A-C Tong Ta Pan, T077-238538, www.thongtapan.com. 34 wooden bungalows set either on a hillside, or on the beach. The restaurant has an almost Mediterranean feel with its terracotta floor tiles and mosaics. The food is also good and very reasonably priced.

A-D Central Cottage, T077-445128, http://go.to/central_cottage. Attractive bamboo huts with wooden shutters and thatched roofs. They have a tiled shower room and a veranda. The restaurant offers cheap Thai food.

A-D Star Hut, T077-445085, star_hut@hotmail.com. By far the largest, and certainly the most popular, place on the beach. The 40 bamboo huts with thatched roofs are attractive, though built too close together. Some are without shower and others have a/c. There are cute paths made from paving stones. The good restaurant serves cheap Thai and western food. It is well managed and efforts are made to keep the beach clean. Good information about the island is available. A boat runs 3 times daily to Thong Sala. Recommended.

C-E White Sand, T077-445123. Offers a range of accommodation, but the cheapest huts are particularly good value. The food is tasty and very reasonably priced, and the staff are friendly. Recommended.

D Pingjun, T077-299004. A friendly resort with large bungalows all of which have verandas, hammocks, fans and en suite bathrooms.

North coast *p587*

Ao Hat Kuat

B-C Bottle Beach Bungalow 3, T077-445127. 17 fan bungalows that are more expensive the closer they are to the beach. The concrete bungalows are very nice and come with roof annexes. It also has an attractive beach restaurant which is very popular and comes with a chill-out zone for laid-back eating and drinking.

C Bottle Beach Bungalow No 1, T077-445152, bottlebeach@hotmail.com. This is the smartest of the Bottle Beaches and features wooden bungalows under coconut palms and is very peaceful. The bungalows are set in a nice garden with little platform verandas right on the beach. The wooden ones have a Swiss feel. All have shower and fan. More expensive rooms have 4 beds for groups. There's a small chill-out zone behind the restaurant area.

C Smile, T01-9563133. 28 bungalows of varying prices according to the size. The blue-roofed bungalows are set up amongst the boulders reached by little stone paths

that twist and turn. It has an attractive restaurant with hanging shell mobiles, newspapers to read, and a pleasant chilling out area. There's a tree swing and sofa swings on the beach. The resort runs a boat 4 times a day to Thong Sala.

D-E Bottle Beach 2 Bungalow, T077-445156, kadbottlebeach@hotmail.com. 45 cheap blue bungalows that are right on the beach at the southern end of the bay which vary in price according to size. All have fan and bathroom. There's a nice restaurant on the beach too. Boat 4 times a day arranged to Thong Sala.

Ao Hat Khom

D-E Coral Bay, T077-374245. Bungalows from the very basic with shared bathrooms to posh ones with interesting bathrooms built into the rock. All have mosquito nets. The resort also rents out snorkelling equipment.

D-E Oceanview Resort, T077-377231, ocean_view@hotmail.com. A relative newcomer with 13 rooms. Mosquito nets provided. Restaurant on the beach opens 0700-2200, taxi from Thong Sala to resort every day. Limited electricity.

Ao Chao Lok Lum

D-E Try Thong. Attached shower, friendly management, good food, quiet.

E Wattana Resort, T077-374022. The larger rooms have balconies on 2 sides with hammocks and mosquito screens. The cheaper rooms are large, but very basic, though they do have mosquito nets.

Hat Salat and Ao Mae Hat

AL-B Salad Beach Resort, T077-349149. Bungalows and 2-storey rooms set around a lovely pool. There's a pool table and jacuzzi too.

B-D Salad Hut, T077-349246, salad_hut@hotmail.com. 10 bungalows including 4 family rooms. The bungalows facing the beach have nice big rooms with carved balconies complete with a rest bed and 2 hammocks. There's a restaurant, and snorkelling and boat trips. Friendly management.

C-D Wang Sai Resort, T077-374238. In a beautiful setting behind a stream close to the sandbar, the 18 attractive bungalows, some perched on boulders, are clean and well maintained, though few have sea views. It is quiet and secluded but the sea is not such a pretty colour here. Snorkelling equipment for hire, book exchange and volleyball net. Restaurant serves cheap Thai and western food.

D-F Island View Cabana, T077-374172. One of the oldest places on the island, set in a wide part of the beach where a sandbar stretches out to Koh Ma which provides good snorkelling. Fairly simple huts, some have attached shower rooms with western toilets. The restaurant has a wide menu and serves good, cheap food, pool table. This is a popular, well-organized place.

E-F My Way Bungalows, T077-349267. Bamboo bungalows with thatched roofs and hammocks, no fan. Electricity stops at 2300. Clean, tiled communal shower room. The restaurant serves good, cheap Thai cuisine.

West coast *p587*

Ao Hat Yao

AL-B Long Bay, T077-349057. A classy option – they've flattened and cleared a big area to build pleasant, a/c and some cheaper rooms with relative luxuries such as dressing tables and wardrobes. Swimming pool.

A-D Sandy Bay, T077-349119. Some a/c rooms and some traditional fan bungalows. All are kept clean and all have veranda areas with hammocks. This is a popular place with tables and chairs on the sand and the best restaurant on the beach which mainly serves cheap Thai food. Kayaking and island trips offered. Movies shown. **Haad Yao Divers** attached. Recommended.

C-D Sea Board Bungalows, T077-349157. Accommodation is board-lined and has mosquito screens, with attached tiled shower rooms and western toilets. Travel agent with overseas call facility. Good snorkelling equipment for hire. Restaurant.

C-E Hat Yao Bungalows, T077-349152-3. An extremely popular place with 40 basic huts and a/c bungalows with tiled shower rooms that are very tightly packed together in rows. Hammocks in front of every room and a tidily kept garden. 4WD and motorbike rental.

E-F Blue Coral, T077-349131. Very basic bungalows without fans, though some have a shower. Restaurant serves cheap Thai and western food.

Ao Chaophao

B-E Jungle Huts, T077-349088. 2 rows of large and airy huts made of board, timber and thatch with attached shower rooms ranging from the cheapest with just fans to those with a/c. On the large verandas there are hammocks. Restaurant specializes in cocktails, of which they have 38 varieties plus Thai and Western dishes. Motorbike rental available.
D Great Bay Resort. Rather characterless bungalows with attached shower rooms. Restaurant offering Thai and western food.
D-E Haad Chaophao Resort. Bungalows set in pleasant garden. All have verandas, attached shower rooms and mosquito nets. Restaurant offers Thai and farang food.
D-E Seaflower, T077-349090. Prices vary with distance from the beach. Run by a Canadian-Thai couple, well-laid out wooden bungalows, with high peaked thatched roofs set in a mature, shady garden. Camping expeditions, snorkelling (their equipment is free for guests), fishing, cliff diving and caving trips. Restaurant has an interesting menu. Recommended.

Ao Sri Thanu

C-D Laem Son, T077-349032. Family-run pretty blue bungalows close to a pine tree plantation and set back a bit off the beach. There's a volleyball net and beach bar. There are no rocks and so the sea is sandy underfoot here. It's one of the nicest places on this stretch and is popular.
C-D Loyfa Bungalows, T077-377319, loyfa@hotmail.com. A range of bungalows on the sunset side of the hillside overlooking Ao Sri Thanu. Some are very worn out and new sheets are needed and curtains need cleaning. Most rooms have hammocks. A/c rooms are under construction. There's bar football, a restaurant, and bike and snorkel hire. There is a small beach is which is not so pretty but it is solitary.

Ao Ban Wok Tum

A-C Siripun, south of Wok Tum, T077-377140. Popular bungalows with fans or a/c.

Ao Hin Kong to Ao Nai Wok

B-D Cookies, Ao Plailaem, T077-377499, cookies_bungalow@hotmail.com. 18 very attractive bamboo bungalows, set in a pleasant garden. Some have shared bathroom, some have a/c. The restaurant has a nice seating area on a raised platform. The helpings are slightly thin (cheap). Staff could be friendlier. Windsurfing (฿250 per hr), kayaking (฿100 per hr) and laser boats (฿300 per hr) offered.
B-D Sea Scene, Ao Plaay Leam, T077-377516, www.seascene.com. The more expensive rooms are characterless concrete bungalows. However the cheapest rooms are charming, solidly built wood and bamboo constructions with thatched roofs, a veranda and hammocks. Fan and a/c available in the 19 rooms. Motorbikes can be rented and snorkelling and fishing tours organized.
C Lipstick, north of Wok Tum, T077-349252. Family-run establishment with 7 rooms set in a shady garden with views in a quiet location, rocky swimming.
D-E Bounty Bungalows, Ao Plaay Laem, T077-377517. 15 clean and attractive board huts with tiled shower rooms and fans run by very friendly staff. Snorkelling gear available. There's also a restaurant. There are lovely granite boulders in front of this property.
E Darin, Ao Plaay Laem, T077-238551. Fairly large bungalows lined up along the seafront. Bamboo weave walls and thatched roofs, roomy verandas, and tiled shower rooms are attached to some of them.

Eating

Most visitors eat at their bungalows and some serve excellent, cheap seafood. There are also increasing numbers of restaurants and cafés in virtually every village and hamlet. Word-of-mouth recommendations are the best guide; new ones are opening all the time. See each area for details.

Thong Sala *p586*

Klad Klow, T077-238384. Thai food only, always full of locals, which is testimony to the quality of the food.
Yellow Café, T077-238615. A very popular, breezy stop, painted an appealing yellow, and looking out onto the pier, well situated for post-arrival and pre-departure trade.

Hat Rin *p586*

Bamboozle, Hat Rin West, T09-5293997. Open till late. This is run by an English chap and his Thai wife who serve Mexican food. There's covered seating or a little garden with tables and umbrellas and a cute row of terracotta lamps marking the boundaries of the restaurant.

Lazy House, on the road to Hat Rin West. Run by an Englishman and offering full English breakfast and movies all day. Wooden and cosy, it's popular with ex-pats and those who happen to come across it.

Lucky Crab, T077-375124. The original seafood place in Hat Rin, on the main road between East and West. Full of 'unlucky' crabs, since the popularity of this outfit and its extensive menu means they're eaten at the rate of knots. However, it has become too popular for its own good. It is absolutely packed every night but is severely under-staffed leading to excruciatingly slow and unacceptable service. Punters eating at long tables à la school dining room are treated to Christmas decs, tinsel and 1980s love tunes. The seafood is good but the soups and salads are better.

Outback Bar and Restaurant. Big, big TV screen and multiple others make this a popular place with the sports mad crowd. Big cushions and comfy seating areas add to its pull. Its full monty breakfast is mighty fine. Self-service menu ordering seems to be the order of the day though.

The Rock, run by **Paradise Bungalows**, dishes out unbeatable views of the beach, truly exquisite seafood, a unique range of bar snacks including the ever-popular garlic bread and salads, imported organic coffee, super cocktails and higher quality wine than you'll find anywhere else. Relaxing music makes for a welcome break from the booming tunes elsewhere. Recommended.

Hiatus, Hat Rin West, T077-375233, 0800-0100. A reasonably good full monty comes in at ฿100 but the sausage isn't the real deal. This is a cosy little joint on the road leading to the bungalows of sunset beach where you can eat lying down at tables leaning against triangle cushions.

Nira's Bakery, T077-375109, 24 hrs. A bakery selling a gorgeous range of cakes, pastries, brownies and bread. The spinach and feta pastries and spinach muffins are highly recommended. The next door café (0800-2400) does great coffee, spirulina shakes and breakfasts. Sit back and watch *BBC World* out the back or sit roadside on wooden picnic tables and chairs.

North coast *p587*

Sheesha, Chao Lok Lum, T077-374161. A funky addition to the north coast catering for this craze that has seized Phangan and Koh Tao. Food and cocktails served.

Bars and clubs

Hat Rin *p586*

At full moon, every store, bar and restaurant turns itself into a bar selling plastic buckets stuffed with spirits and mixers. The 3 best and loudest clubs on Hat Rin Beach East are **Vinyl**, **Zoom** and the **Drop in Club**, www.dropinclub.com, which play excellent dance music – and not just on full moon nights. The **Cactus Club**, a little further down the beach with a great bar on the beach, plays hip hop and R'n'B.

Esco Bar, 1200-2400. Fabulous position on some rocks overlooking the sea at Hat Rin West between the **Siam Healing Centre** and the **Phangan Buri Resort**. Reggae tunes seem the order of the day at this great little wooden bar.

Nargile House, close to the **Drop in Bar** on Hat Rin East, open till late. Smoke the sheesha at tables, costs ฿300 for a wadge of tobacco at this roadside bar (various flavours available). Full alcoholic works available.

East coast *p586*

In Thong Nai Pan Yai there's the wooden **Jungle Bar**, featuring images of Che Guevara, **Rasta Baby**, **Que Pasa** and the **Hideaway Bar**, decorated in bunting.

West coast *p*

The Eagle, Ao Hat Yao, T04-8397143. A good option for a bit of house.

The Pirate's Bar, Ao Chaophao, accessed through the Seatanu Bungalows, hosts the Moon Set Party, 3 days before full moon. The bar in the shape of a ship is set in the tiniest of coves accessed by a wooden bridge that winds around boulders.

Entertainment

Hat Rin *p586*

Cabaret
Cabaret is sometimes held at Coral Bungalows on Hat Rin West. See flyers for details.

Movies
At some of the restaurants with screenings all day.

Muay Thai
Matches are held at Hat Rin Stadium at 2100. Look out for flyers for fight days.

Shopping

Hat Rin *p586*
Shops selling leather goods, funky clothes and books are flourishing in Hat Rin. JD Exotic sells truly funky shirts for men and Napo-po sells lovely Indian skirts, accessories and photographs. Fusion also sells clothes.

Therapies
Chakra, off the main drag leading up from the pier, T077-375401, chakramassage@hotmail.com, closes 2400. This is undoubtedly the most reputable place on the island and is run by a real master, Yan, and his English wife Ella. Whether you're looking for simple relaxation, or you've a specific complaint that needs working on, the staff here dish out any number of extremely good traditional body, face and foot Thai massages, and reiki, reflexology and acupressure treatments. For those looking to learn the art themselves, they also run certificated courses: traditional Thai massage (30 hrs), reiki, levels 1-4; oil massage (30 hrs), foot and head massage (15 hrs), and massage therapy course – similar to acupuncture, but with thumbs instead of needles (30 hrs).

Activities and tours

Diving
For the trained diver, the west coast offers the best diving with hard coral reefs at depths up to about 20 m. There are also some islets which offer small walls, soft coral and filter corals. Dive trips are also available to further sites such as Koh Wao Yai in the north of the Ang Thong Marine National Park or Hin Bai (Sail Rock). Here the dives are deeper.
Chaloklum Diving, T077-374025, www.chaloklum-diving.com, based in Chao Lok Lum Village. Open Water courses are ฿10,500. Other dive prices varies. Sail Rock dive, ฿400.
Lotus Diving, Ao Chao Lok Lum, T077-374097, www.lotusdiving.com. Offers PADI courses and dive trips.
Phangan Divers, based in Hat Rin, near the pier on the west side, Ao Hat Yao, Ao Thong Nai Pan and Koh Ma, T077-375117, www.phangandivers.com.
Tropical Divers, Thong Noi Pan, T077-445081, www.tropicaldiveclub.com.

Fishing and sailing
Castaway Cats,T09-2893355, www.castawaycats.net. Private charters on the catamaran *Nok Talay*.

Gym and Thai boxing
At Thong Sala, boxers from Bangkok and elsewhere fight every 2-3 weeks, especially on holidays.
Jungle Gym, www.junglegym.co.th. Offers Thai boxing courses as well as aerobics, yoga and other training and courses.

Snorkelling
Coral is to be found off most beaches, except for those on the east coast. Particularly good are those in Mae Hat where corals are just a few metres below the surface.

Boat tours
Numerous operators run trips around the island to several beaches and waterfalls and the price includes food and drink on the tour.
Lomprayah, T077-427765, www.lomprayah.com. Daily trips to Koh Tao and Koh Nangyuan, ฿1600.
Phangan Adventure, Ao Chao Lok Lum, T077-374142, www.phanganadventure.com. Boat trips, snorkelling, fishing trips, wakeboarding, kayaking trips and rental, and mountain bike tours and rental.
Wicked Boat Trip, Chicken Corner, T06-2688973, ฿500.

Thong Sala *p586*
Asia Travel Co, opposite Krung Thai Bank, and part of **Asia Hotel,** Thong Sala, T077-238607.
Songserm Travel Co, 35/1 Talat, T077-377045.

Hat Rin *p586*
My Travel, main road, T077-375093, myhut13@hotmail.com. The full travel service operation run by a woman and her family. Recommended.

Transport

The roads remain poor on Phangan. There is a concrete road from Thong Sala to Hat Rin but the stretch from Ban Khai to Hat Rin is ridiculously steep and treacherous and inadvisable for anything but a 4WD during the rainy season. The number of accidents is huge. Also, it's advisable not to keep anything of any value in the front basket as it's not uncommon for locals on zippier bikes to zip past and snatch whatever's is in there.

Boat

Long-tailed boats take passengers from Hat Rin, Ao Thong Nai Pan, Ao Hat Yao and Ao Hat Kuat to Thong Sala (the island's capital) and Ban Khai piers. Most boats dock at the pier at Thong Sala, although there's a ferry, the *Haad Rin Queen*, T077-375113, from **Big Buddha pier** on **Samui** that leaves 3 times a day, 50 mins, 1030, 1300, 1600 and 1830 going straight to Hat Rin (฿120). It returns at 0930, 1140, 1430, 1730.

From Thong Sala to **Koh Samui**: with CattCorp, T077-377716, www.cattcorp.com, 1600, 30 mins, ฿250. With **Phangan Cruise**, T077-377274, 1100, 25 mins.

Speed Boat Line to **Bo Phut**, **Koh Samui**, 0600, 0930, 1300, 1530, 20 mins. With **Lomprayah**, T077-238412, to **Mae Nam**, 1100, 1600, 30-45 mins, ฿250. With **Songserm Express**, T077-377704, to **Nathon**, 1200, ฿95. With Seatran at 0600, 0700, 1300, ฿130.

To **Koh Tao** with Lomprayah at 0730 and 1230, 1 hr, ฿400. With **Songserm Express**, at 1000 and 1200, 1 hr 45 mins, ฿300. With **Phangan Cruises** at 1230, 1½ hrs, ฿300. With **CattCorp**, 0820, 1 hr, ฿350.

To **Surat Thani** from Thong Sala with **Songserm Express** at 1200, ฿290. With **Seatran** at 0600, 3½ hrs, 0700, 2½ hrs and 1230, 2½ hrs. With **Raja Ferries** at 0700, 1000, 1300, 1700, 2½ hrs. The night boat leaves Koh Phangan for Surat Thani at 2200 (although times can vary, so it's worth checking in good time), 6 hrs, ฿200.

To **Chumphon** with **Lomprayah** at 0830, 3¼ hrs, and 1240, 3 hrs 50 mins, ฿900.

Motorcycle hire

Available in Thong Sala and from the more popular beaches. Some of the guesthouses also hire out motorbikes. Expect to pay from ฿150 per day.

Mountain bike hire

The most appealing area in which to ride bikes is in the north and west of the island, which are fairly flat areas. Bikes can be hired from agencies around the island.

Songthaew

Songthaews run from the pier to any of the bays served by road. A trip to **Hat Rin** from Thong Sala is ฿50-100. The cost to the other bays depends on how many people are going with you.

Taxi

Minibus taxis meet the boats and take people from Thong Sala pier to **Hat Rin** for ฿100.

Train

The **State Railways of Thailand** runs a train/bus/ferry service between Koh Phangan and **Bangkok**'s Hualamphong Station.

Hat Rin *p586*
Hat Rin is reached from Thong Sala on a hair-raising, twisting, winding road. The more restful alternative is to catch a boat here – boats run from both Thong Sala and Ban Khai to Hat Rin.

Songthaew

Songthaew wait close to the **Drop in Club Resort** between Hat Rin East and West. Prices start at ฿50 per person minimum but if you are on your own the fare could be ฿100 to Thong Sala, for example.

Directory

Internet There are now plenty of internet cafés, all vying for business and charging ฿2 per min. **Telephone** Virtually every agency and internet café offer this service, ฿25 per min for international calls.

Thong Sala *p586*
Banks There are banks with ATMs on the main road in Thong Sala. International money transfer facility – Moneygram – is available at the Siam Bank. **Useful addresses** Police, 2 km down the road from Thong Sala towards Chao Lok Lum.

Hat Rin *p586*
Banks There are 5 or 6 ATMs in Hat Rin and plenty of foreign exchange outlets. **Medical services** Clinic Bandon International, Hat Rin, T077-375471. A 24-hr private clinic with English-speaking staff. **Post office** In Hat Rin close to pier. **Telephone** IDD telephone facilities at nearly all internet places. Around ฿25/min.

Koh Tao

→ *Colour map 4, grid B3.*

Koh Tao, the smallest of the three famous islands in the Gulf of Thailand, is a big dive and snorkelling centre with plenty of shallow coral beds and tropical fish. The waters – especially in the south and east – are stunning, a marbling of turquoise blue, sapphire, emerald and seaweed green. The name Koh Tao, literally translated as turtle island, relates to the shape of the island. ▸▸ *For Sleeping, Eating and other listings, see pages 599-606.*

Ins and outs

Getting there Several companies operate regular express boats from Chumphon, Surat Thani, Koh Samui and Koh Phangan as well as a slow, night ferry direct from Surat Thani.

Numbers dialled on the island require the area code as well.

Getting around There is just one surfaced road on Koh Tao, which runs from the north end of Sai Ri to Chalok Ban Kao, passing through Ban Mae Hat. Motorbike taxis and pickups are the main form of local transport. These can be found just north of the dock next to the exchange booth. They operate from dawn to 2300; rates tend to double after dark. Motorbikes, jeeps and bicycles are available for hire. Long-tailed boats can be chartered to reach more out-of-the-way beaches and coves, either by the trip, hour or day. ▸▸ *See Transport, page 606.*

Koh Tao
Ao Mamuang (Mango Bay)
Koh Nang Yuan
Ao Kluai Tuen
Khao Hat Sai Re
Ao Hinwong
To Chumphon
Hat Sai Ri
Ao Mao
Laem Thian
Ban Mae Hat
Jansom Bay
Ao Ta Not
Hat Sai Nuan
Lang Khaai Bay
To Thong Sala (Koh Phangan) & Koh Samui
Ao Leuk
Ao Chun Chua
Ao Chalok Ban Kao
Ao Thian Ok
Hat Sai Daeng
Hat Taa Toh Yai
Laem Tato
N
0 km 1
0 miles 1

Tourist information The TAT office on Koh Samui, see page 562, is responsible for Koh Tao but there is no official office on the island. The website www.koh tao.com provides lots of information.

Background

Avoid bringing any plastic bottles or tin cans to the island as these are very difficult to dispose of. In addition, due to reduced rainfall in recent years, water is now a great problem on the island, and much of it is imported from the mainland. Islanders ask visitors to use it sparingly.

The easy accessibility of interesting **marine life** at depths available to beginners, the fairly gentle currents and the relatively low costs all contribute to making Koh Tao a particularly good place to learn to dive. The presence of **giant manta rays** and **whale sharks** (plankton feeders which can reach 6 m in length) means that more experienced divers will also find something of interest here. With these attractions in its favour, Koh Tao's reputation as a good, low-cost dive centre has grown rapidly, and in the space of just 10 years the island has made the transition from out-of-the-way backwater to mainstream destination. See Diving, page 605 and 60, for more details. Improved transport links with the mainland have also made the island more accessible to the short-stay tourist, and so it is no surprise that the former economic mainstay of coconuts has now been eclipsed by the still-expanding tourist trade. Already, the number of rooms for tourists outnumbers the Thai residents on the island. Sensibly, though, as on Koh Samui, there are height restrictions on new buildings and this, in conjunction with the poor infrastructure, means the 'palm tree horizon' has not yet been blotted by multi-storey monstrosities. While most people come here for the swimming, snorkelling and diving – as well as beach life in general – the fact that most paths are not vehicle friendly makes the island walker-friendly and there are some good trails to explore. Land-based wildlife includes monitor lizards, fruit bats and various non-venomous snakes. If planning to go on walks it is worth purchasing V Honsombud's *Guide Map of Koh Phangan & Koh Tao*.

Ban Mae Hat and the west coast

The harbour is at the island's main village of **Ban Mae Hat**. On both sides of the harbour there are small beach areas with a few resorts. These areas have easy access to all the facilities in town. There are good and numerous shops and some of the best restaurants as well as a developing nightlife, post office, money exchange facilities, dive shops, tour operators and more.

To the north of Ban Mae Hat on the west coast, is the white-sand curved beach of **Hat Sai Ri**. Stretching to around 2 km, it is the longest beach on the island, the sweep of sand only interrupted by the occasional large boulder. It has the widest range of accommodation, and many restaurants, shops, dive centres, bars and other facilities. Although it is a great beach with some great bars, the debris – plastic bottles, rotting wood and the like – left by the retreating tide is really unsightly.

North coast

The little cove of **Ao Mamuang** is only accessible by boat so it remains quiet and unfrequented. It is a great place to come to for solitude and there is some good snorkelling.

Off the northwest coast of Koh Tao is **Koh Nang Yuan**. Once a detention centre for political prisoners, this privately owned island consists of three peaks and three connecting sandbars, making it a mini-archipelago. It's surrounded by crystal-clear water and some wonderful coral. **Lomprayah** runs boats to the island at 1030, 1500 and 1800, returning 0830, 1330, 1630.

East coast

Ao Hin Wong is a very peaceful bay with fantastic views but no beach to speak of. However, you can swim off the rocks and boulders and there is some great snorkelling – turtles have been spotted here. The accommodation consists of very simple huts.

South of Ao Hin Wong, the bay of **Ao Mao** has just one resort and some great snorkelling opportunities, particularly at the **Laem Thian** pinnacle. It is among the more remote and secluded places to stay on Koh Tao.

Continuing south, the bay of **Ao Ta Not** is served by a poor road but vehicles brave the conditions to ferry guests to and fro. This is one of the more remote bays and has a

good stretch of beach. Although it is not as pretty as Hin Wong, it is wider, has boulders, and more facilities, more expensive accommodation, restaurants, watersports and scuba diving (see Diving, page 60).

Lang Khaai Bay is mostly littered with dozens of boulders which are reached from a steep slope. The bay is good for snorkelling. There is a tiny slither of beach.

The beach at **Ao Leuk** shelves more steeply than most of the others around Koh Tao and so is good for swimming and has some of the best snorkelling on the island. Although groups visit from elsewhere, on the whole this is a very quiet beach.

South coast

Next to Ao Chalok Ban Kao, **Ao Thian Ok** is a privately owned and very beautiful bay with the **Jamahkiri Spa and Resort** set on one hillside. The sea is a stunning mix of blues and greens while the beach is lined with a strip of coconut palms and is very attractive. The bay is known for the black tip reef sharks that congregate here.

The area of **Taa Toh** 'lagoon' is on the south coast and consists of three beaches, the largest of which is **Hat Taa Toh Yai**. There is good snorkelling on the far side of the lagoon from Hat Taa Toh Yai with reef sharks and more. There is easy access from here to Chalok Ban Kao.

Ao Chalok Ban Kao is a gently shelving beach, enclosed within a horseshoe bay on the south coast capped with weirdly-shaped giant boulders. It has a good range of accommodation, restaurants and nightlife. This large bay also has the highest concentration of diving resorts.

Hat Sai Nuan is a quiet, isolated bay, only accessible by long-tail boat or by foot. There are just a handful of places to stay and a very relaxed atmosphere.

Sleeping

The densest areas of accommodation are Hat Sai Ri and Ao Chalok Ban Kao. These offer restaurants, bars and easy access to the dive schools. If you are looking for a greater sense of remoteness, the other bays are more secluded. This has largely been due to the poor quality of the roads which makes them considerably more difficult to reach without a bit of a trek or the use of taxi boats.

Despite the rapid rate of bungalow construction it remains difficult for non-divers to find empty, cheap accommodation unassisted during the high season. If you don't want to risk having to hike around with a heavy backpack for several hours in search of free rooms, the simplest option is to follow a tout from the pier. You can always move out the following day, but try and book the next place in advance.

Alternatively, make your way straight to one of the more remote bays where places are often less booked out, but be warned that if they are full you may have to walk some way to locate a final resting place. If diving, you should head straight for the dive shops where they will find you a place to stay in affiliated accommodation – often at a subsidized rate on the days when you are diving.

The other unusual point about accommodation in Koh Tao is the early check-out times. These reflect the need to free up rooms for those arriving on the early boats from the mainland. Finally, it is not unknown for guests to be evicted from their bungalows if they have not been spending enough in the restaurant so it is worth enquiring if there is a minimum expenditure before checking in. Most guesthouses have restaurants attached to them.

West coast *p598, map p600*

Ban Mae Hat

L-A Charm Churee Villa, Jansom Bay, T077-456393, www.charmchureevilla.com. The most expensive resort on the island, situated in an exquisite little cove, just south of Mae Hat. Bungalows on stilts are perched on the hillside, amongst coconut trees, with wonderful sea views from the balconies. Seafood restaurant. Tranquility guaranteed.

L-B Sensi Paradise, T077-456244, www.kohtaoparadise.com. A great range of rooms. At the top of the price range the

buildings are sensitively designed wooden affairs with traditional Thai architectural features. The garden in which it is set is also richly planted and the small bay behind the resort is truly idyllic. The beach in front is tiny but adorned with higgledy piggledy boulders.

AL-B Koh Tao Royal Resort, T077-456156. Smart, well-maintained wood and bamboo bungalows. Cheaper rooms climb the hill behind the beach. Friendly staff and a lively restaurant with a great location. It has a reasonable stretch of secluded beach.

A Beach Club T077-456222, www.kohtaobeachclub.com. Very attractive, airy rooms with high bamboo-lined ceilings, some with a/c. Discounts for divers available.

Hat Sai Ri

L-AL Koh Tao Cabana, T077-456505, www.kohtaocabana.com. 33 villas built into the headland at the northern end of Sai Ri Beach including 10 very attractive white circular villas climbing up the hillside which have a Mediterranean feel to them. Bathrooms are open-air and built into rock faces. It has pleasant gardens and attractive solid wood sun loungers.

L-A Koh Tao Coral Grand Resort, T077-456431, www.kohtaocoral.com. Large, dusty pink cabins with wooden floors, TVs, fridges, coffee making facilities and shower rooms dot the landscape of this quiet resort popular with older and younger couples and families. The pool is close to the beach with the resorts own sun loungers and the restaurant is right on the beach. The breakfast is good and filling. The sea is really beautiful at this far northern end of the beach. Dive centre attached, www.coralgranddivers.com. Recommended.

AL-A Thipwimarn Resort, T077-456409, www.thipwimarnresort.com. Beyond the northern end of the beach on the northwest headland, this beautiful new place has 11 bungalows perched on the rocks. Its infinity pool enjoys spectacular views. The restaurant (0730-2200) overlooks Sai Ri Bay and the sea. There is a free pick-up for the restaurant before 1800 only.

A-C Bow Thong Beach, T077-456351. 30 well-spaced white board bungalows with a very attractive restaurant (0500-1900), quite private and quieter than most. Pleasant and good value.

A-C Sai Ree Huts, T077-456000, saireehutresort@hotmail.com. Bamboo weave and timber bungalows with hammocks and a swing on the beach. A/c and fan rooms available.

A-C Seashell Resort, T077-456299, www.kohtaoseashell.com. Attractive wood and bamboo huts with spacious verandas in well-manicured grounds. Some a/c rooms and family bungalows available. Divers get cheaper rates. Roasted rice with shrimp and pineapple is among the best dishes at the restaurant. Movies shown. Massage available and courses in massage too. PADI dive centre attached, T077-456300, seashelldivers@hotmail.com.

A-D Ban's Diving Resort, T077-456466, www.amazingkohtao.com. Set on the other side of the road this resort offers everything from a/c luxury rooms with silk furnishings and large balconies to plain fan rooms around the pool for divers. Partial views of the sea only. As well as diving, wake-boarding, water skiing and kayaking is offered. ฿200/hr.

Ban Mae Hat

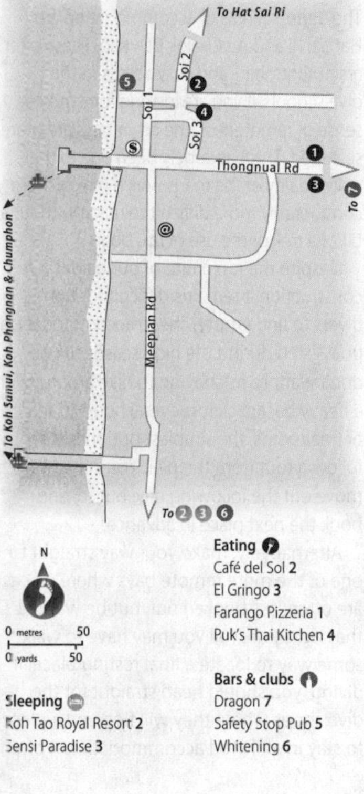
To Hat Sai Ri
Soi 2
Soi 1
Soi 3
Thongnual Rd
To 7
To Koh Samui, Koh Phangnan & Chumphon
Meepian Rd
To 2 3 6
N
0 metres 50
0 yards 50
Sleeping
Koh Tao Royal Resort 2
Sensi Paradise 3
Eating
Café del Sol 2
El Gringo 3
Farango Pizzeria 1
Puk's Thai Kitchen 4
Bars & clubs
Dragon 7
Safety Stop Pub 5
Whitening 6

A-D View Cliff, T077-456353, viewclifftao@hotmail.com. A mixture of concrete, wood and bamboo huts mostly with twin beds, some a/c, all clean.

A-E AC Resort, T077-456197, www.acresort.com. Well-maintained bungalows in a pleasing resort on the 'wrong' side of the road with mosquito screens on the windows and nets over the beds. Tiled shower rooms, fan and verandas. The resort has a nice pool. **Phoenix Divers**, www.phoenix-divers.com, is attached. Divers using the school get cheaper accommodation.

B-D Blue Wind, T077-456116, bluewind_wa@yahoo.com. Small and friendly set-up. A range of cheap rooms and some a/c rooms. Basic wood bungalows nestled in a beautiful mature garden. Restaurant serves pastries, pasta and ice cream. Recommended.

B-D Silver Cliff, north of Sai Ri Beach on the northwest headland, T09-2907546. 10 rooms in wooden or concrete bungalows which are on stilts in a boulder-strewn garden and enjoy fabulous views out to the sea which looks incredible on this part of the island. Mind your step at night. Hammocks on all verandas, but no beach.

B-D Tommy's Dive Resort, T077-456039, www.tommyresort.sytes.net. Large a/c rooms with large bathrooms in concrete bungalows close to the beach or smaller rooms above the office with or without a/c. All rooms are ultra clean and spacious.

C-D Queen Resort, T077-456002, moo_mmm@hotmail.com. Rooms with fan, a/c and rooms with shared bathroom available. Some blocks look right out over the sea. ฿20 to use the shower for beach users if you are not a hotel guest. There's a friendly lady running this place.

C-D Sairee Cottage, T077-456374, nitsairee@hotmail.com. A well-established resort with the more expensive rooms situated on the beachfront in a grassy compound with the remainder across the road. Relaxed and friendly. The restaurant serves reasonably priced food and does cheap cocktails. There's a volleyball net in the garden.

C-E Here & Now, Sai Ri Beach, T077-456730, www.hereandnow.be. Rooms with shared showers and private showers. This is the last establishment on the northwest headland of the island, north of Sai Ri Beach, see also Therapies, below. You can swim off the rocks here into the sea. The restaurant has a great view of Nang Yuan Island. Some of the staff are very unfriendly though.

D AC Two Resort, T077-456195. On the landward side of the road, this small, older resort has large rooms with small bathrooms, fan and veranda. They are a little dark but set in a slightly ramshackle garden which is appealing. The restaurant is opposite, overlooking the sea. See Eating.

D Sun Lord, T077-456139. This guesthouse is only accessible by an unconvincing track through the jungle on the northwest headland of the island, north of Sai Ri Beach. Nevertheless, it commands fantastic views and the cheapest rooms made of bamboo and without shower room are perched precariously on huge granite boulders. Beneath them there is good coral, perfect for snorkelling.

E Scuba Junction, T077-456164, www.scuba-junction.com. Has just 6 bungalows, exclusively for the use of divers. Shared shower room.

E Sun Sea, on the northwest headland, north of Sai Ri Beach. 10 bungalows with fans and shower rooms amid boulder-strewn land that attracts dozens of butterflies. Rooms are also available to rent by the month. Most rooms have great views out to sea. The place needs a tidy up though as it's looking a little ramshackle. There is no restaurant or access to the beach. The owners chew betel-nut and have a coconut business so life is pretty authentic here.

North coast *p598*

A-B Mango Bay Grand Resort, Ao Mamuang, T077-456097, www.mangobaygrandresortkohtaothailand.com. 15 bungalows of various prices on stilts overlooking the bay in this secluded spot. This bay is popular for snorkelling.

Koh Nang Yuan

L-B Nangyuan Island Dive Resort, T077-456088, www.nangyuan.com. The only bungalow complex on the island offering a range of accommodation, some with a/c. PADI dive courses and organized diving trips arranged. Water and electricity is only

available 1700-1000. Environmental awareness is encouraged. Resort guests enjoy a free transfer to/from Koh Samui.

East coast *p598*

Ao Hin Wong

C Hin Wong Bungalows, T077-456006. 9 well-spaced and clean wooden huts with verandas overlooking the sea. Plenty of windows to let in the sea breeze, reasonably priced restaurant, snorkelling equipment and canoes for hire. Discounts available after 3 nights' stay. Electricity available 1800-0600. Mol, the friendly owner, used to have a gallery in town and can paint to order.

D Green Tree Resort, T077-456742. 5 rooms at this place with a restaurant. Snorkelling equipment available for free. Welcoming owners.

Ao Mao and Laem Thian

C-D Laem Thian, T077-456477, pingpong_laemthian@hotmail.com. Range of rooms and bungalows with attached showers and fans in this very secluded bay. Free pick-up service from ferry. Electricity 1800-0700.

Ao Ta Not

A-C Tanote Family Bay Dive Resort, T077-456757, www.familytanotebay.com. At the northern end of the bay, spread out amid the rocks, this resort offers cheap, very dark fan rooms or more expensive nicer and brighter rooms with balconies. Some rooms have dressing tables. The 30 rooms all have tables and chairs which are welcome. No special rates for divers; (www.calypso-diving-kohtao.de), taxi to main island pier twice a day. Restaurant open 0700-2200.

C-D Mountain Reef Resort, T077-456697-9. At the southern end of the bay. A family-run resort which will take guests out fishing for their dinner. There are 16 bungalows. Larger rooms are more expensive – go for the ones overlooking the beach so you get the great sunrises. There's a daily taxi to the island pier. Friendly and welcoming staff. Sells ice cream too.

C-D Poseidon, T077-456735, poseidonkohtao@hotmail.com. Cheaper rooms are small, stuffy and dark but with balconies and some are set right back from the beach. It's a small set up with only 14 bungalows and a restaurant, see Eating. A taxi leaves the resort daily at 1300 for the island pier.

Lang Khaai Bay

A-D Nok's Garden Resort, T077-456770, isara_k5@hotmail.com. 7, small, green-roofed bungalows with balconies perched amid boulders. The more expensive ones are close to the sea. Bright rooms with big beds and hammocks on the balconies. Although there is no beach here there are flat rocks on which to sunbathe. Snorkelling and taxi service. Run by the friendly Taew and David. The restaurant serves lots of coconut dishes, porridge and deep-fried Thai flowers among other things.

Ao Leuk

Both the establishments here are very small and simple and neither have fans in the rooms.

A-D Aow Leuk Bungalows, T077-456692. 13 bungalows, with the more expensive ones being closer to the beach. Restaurant, snorkel hire and taxi service available.

D Nice Moon Bungalows, T077-456737, nicemoon43@hotmail.com. Just a couple of hundred metres south of the beach itself on cliffs overlooking the bay. Free snorkelling equipment, friendly and informative. Restaurant serves delicious Thai food. Recommended.

South coast *p599*

Ao Thian Ok

L Jamahkiri Spa & Resort, T077-456400, www.jamahkiri.com. A well-designed resort which incorporates large boulders into the fabric of the buildings. Just 5 rooms with luscious furnishings but there are plans for an expansion to 12. The restaurant enjoys an incredible view over the bay and sea and the set dinner menu of 7 courses costing between ฿450-650 is very good value. The spa (1000-2200) uses fresh aloe vera in its treatments. Free pick-up for the resort, restaurant and spa. There's car, kayak and snorkel hire. See also under Therapies, below.

B-D Rocky Resort, T077-456035. 25 bungalows in a great location in this beautiful bay – definitely one of the most stunning on the island. Bungalows with nice

high ceilings and bathrooms have both toilets and urinals. Rooms have dressing tables, and balconies have tables and chairs. Basic, but well spaced out, and friendly with reasonably priced food.

Hat Taa Toh Yai

B-D Taa Toh Lagoon Dive Resort, T077-456503, www.taatohdivers.com. Very good deals available for divers. The cheapest rooms for non-divers are those above the office. All have fans, mosquito nets and balconies and are positioned looking out over the bay.

Ao Chalok Ban Kao

A-D View Point Resort, T077-456444, www.viewpoint.com. The large bamboo and thatch rooms in Balinese-style are clean and pleasant with great views. The cheapest have shared shower rooms. Particularly good bargains available for those diving with the school. Recommended.

B-C Bhora Bhora, formerly Porn Resort, T077-456044, www.bhorabhora.com. 21 spacious rooms in either wood or concrete with nice bamboo beds and mosquito netting on the windows. Both are rather unusual, with the concrete rooms including sections of massive granite boulders as part of the walls and the wooden rooms having bathroom walls made of glass bottles set in concrete giving a rather quaint stained-glass effect. Restaurant on site, 1800-2400. 2 private villas are being built next to the sea with jacuzzis for ฿10,000. Recommended.

B-C Buddha View Dive Resort, 45 Moo 3, T077-456074, www.buddhaview-diving.com. Clean, well-maintained painted timber, bamboo or thatch bungalows with mosquito screens on the windows and verandas, or rooms in a rather characterless hotel block. Friendly, very welcoming and helpful. Also has the Buddha on the Beach bar at the front with different music and attractions every night. There's a pool too.

B-D Laemklong, T077-456333. A white concrete 2-storey affair that looks very out of place. More attractive, low slung bungalows are close to the beach. Travel agency attached.

B-D Sunshine 2, T077-456154. 62 attractive blue-roofed wooden bungalows lined with bamboo weave with tiled bathrooms. Set a little back from the beach in nicely manicured gardens. The more expensive ones have a/c.

Hat Sai Nuan

C Siam Cookies, T077-456301. Attractive bamboo huts. The cheaper rooms share very clean and well-maintained shower rooms.

C-F Tao Thong Villa, T077-456078. On the headland so seaviews on both sides. Simple wood and bamboo huts with large verandas, well placed to make the most of sea breezes. Recommended. Cheapest rooms have shared bathroom.

Eating

West coast *p598, map p600*

Ban Mae Hat

¶¶ Café del Sol, Mae Hat Sq, T077-456578, 0800-2300. Great place for breakfast. It also serves sandwiches, bruschetta and coffee, and for dinner, salmon or steak and other world cuisine.

¶¶ El Gringo, Pier Rd, T077-456323, 0900-2330. The full Mexican works with fajitas, nachos, steaks and burgers served on tables overlooking the main road. Takeaways and deliveries possible.

¶¶ Farango Pizzeria, Pier Rd, T077-456205, 1200-1500, 1800-2200. Italian restaurant which serves excellent pizzas and has a delivery and takeaway service.

¶ Puk's Thai Kitchen, Mae Hat Sq, T077-456685, 0800 till late. Serves Thai but also does a full English breakfast.

Hat Sai Ri

¶¶¶ Papa's Tapas, opposite Siam Scuba Dive Center, Sai Ri village, T077-456298, 1900-late. A fine addition to the Koh Tao dining scene. Sample wonderfully concocted Asian and Asian fusion tapas with amazing attention to detail – the tandoori prawn and the panacotta are particularly delicious. The chorizo is not the real deal though. Before, during and after your meal indulge in the alcoholic creations created by Jesper, the mixologist, who was once asked to shake up Absolut Vodka's cocktail list. The mojitos are wicked, also try the passionfruit vodka, and for a bittersweet killer the chilli-lemongrass (lemongrass, chilli, coconut liqueur, vodka

and gin). You'll be crawling back for more. If you're still on your toes, retire to the sheesha lounge or smoke one at your table. A great gourmet extravaganza. Recommended.

ŸŸ **AC Seafood**, centre of the beach. Large complex with impressive fresh seafood displays. Dine on the tables lying down on the triangle cushions out on the deck or inside with giant TV screens showing sport. Portions are overwhelming large; the barbecued tuna is quite tasty. Service is annoyingly slack even with a few customers.

ŸŸ **White Elephant**, main road, Sai Ri Village, T09-2928249. A sweet little restaurant in a little garden with a pond serving up delicious seafood and succulent duck dishes.

ŸŸ-Ÿ **Blue Wind Bakery**, towards the northern end of the beach, T077-456116. Specializes in breads and desserts and serves reasonable sandwiches. Also offers fresh pasta including speciality fillings.

ŸŸ-Ÿ **Intouch Restaurant and Bar**, T077-456514. Breakfasts, including porridge, burgers, sandwiches, soups, salads and noodles form part of a vast menu at this place which has decking right out on the beach. Chill in a hammock, play pool or eat sat on the floor looking out over the sea.

ŸŸ-Ÿ **Suthep Restaurant**, centre of the beach. Thai food, lasagne, fish cakes, fish pie, burgers, great mashed potato, toad in the hole and Marmite sandwiches. The Bailey's cheesecake is an indulgence. Popular with long-term western residents on the island. Good value. Stops serving at 2200.

Ÿ **Coffee Boat**, on the main road just before the main drag down to the beach in Sai Ri Village. A cheap and cheerful authentic Thai diner. Ample proportions of tasty, very spicy Thai food.

Ÿ **Pon Bakery**, close to Sai Ree Cottage, T077-456655. Rye, granary and sour dough bread sold.

East coast *p598*

Ao Ta Not

ŸŸ **Poseidon**, T077-456735, 0730-2200. A popular restaurant serving fried fish, a good range of vegetarian dishes and unusual milkshakes – cookie vanilla flavour and prune lassies.

Ÿ **Mountain Reef**, T077-456697-9. A breakfast of hash browns and peanut butter bagels is sometimes what's required.

Ao Chalok Ban Kao

ŸŸ **New Heaven**, rather a climb, at the top of the hill, T077-456462. Only open in the evenings. A bit pricey but very good food and fantastic views over the gorgeous Thian Og Bay.

ŸŸ **Sunshine Dive School**. Has a BBQ evening buffet every night with baked potatoes, garlic bread, calamari, kebabs, salad and some rice dishes.

ŸŸ **Taraporn Bar & Restaurant**, across the slatted walkway at the most westerly end of the beach. Seating on hammocks, cushions and mats on the floor. The restaurant itself is on stilts above the sea. A great venue.

Ÿ **Viewpoint Restaurant**, beyond the Bubble Dive Resort at the eastern end of the beach, T077-456777, 0700-2200. Wide menu of Thai and some western food that is very filling and tasty served in this very laid-back restaurant. Also perched just above the sea it enjoys great views of the horse-shoe shaped Chalok Ban Kao Bay.

Bars and clubs

Koh Tao, once a quiet neighbour of Koh Phangan, is now well provided with night spots. The best way to discover what is happening is to look out for flyers and advertisements in shop windows.

West coast *p598, map p600*

Ban Mae Hat

Dragon Bar, Pier Rd. Wooden tables spill onto the street from this new bar playing different music every night: indy, 1980s, hip hop, jazz and alternative rock. Look out for flyers.

Safety Stop Pub, Mae Hat Sq, close to the pier. Popular with tourists and locals alike, with a late night disco on Sat nights and sports coverage throughout the week.

The Whitening, on the road to the Sensi Paradise Resort. A pleasant bar and some food too. Party night here is Fri.

Hat Sai Ri

Choppers, Sai Ri Village, T077-456641, 0800-late. A hugely popular large, western style pub which knows how to please the punters by screening all the major sporting events on large screens. It pastes timetables for all events outside the pub on a weekly basis. Friendly staff.

Dry Bar. A very popular place amongst the trees on the beach and is decked out with Chinese lanterns, fairly lights and candles in the sand.

Lotus Beach Bar, close to **Papa's Tapas**. This is where it's at on Mon nights. Fancy dress parties are popular. Free drinks and buckets for punters. Loud tunes until the early hours and flame throwers until the fires completely die.

South coast *p599*

Babaloo, Ao Chalok Ban Kao. Excellent bar set in the rocks and decorated with sculptures, open from 2100. Party night is Mon.

Shopping

There are numerous shops at Ban Mae Hat and Sai Ri village selling beach wear. Both places also feature minimarts/7-11 shops.

Ban Mae Hut *p598, map p600*

Zunami, Mae Hat Sq. For the latest brand of surf clothes.

Activities and tours

Diving

Diving is popular all year round on Koh Tao and there are well over 20 dive shops. It is said to be the cheapest place in Thailand to learn to dive, and the shallow waters and plenty of underwater life, make it an easy and interesting place to do so. See also Essentials, page 60. There's also now a recompression chamber in Ban Mae Hat. (**Badalveda**, opposite the main petrol station on the island, north up the main road and turn right, T077-456664, vedainfo@badalveda.com.)

Dive schools have an arrangement where they charge exactly the same for an Open Water course (฿9000). Fixed prices also apply to other courses: ฿7800 for Advanced, and ฿8800 for rescue. What varies are the sizes of the groups and the additional perks such as a free dive or free/subsidized accommodation. A discover scuba dive is around ฿2000, and a fun dive for qualified divers is around ฿1000, although the more dives you do the cheaper each dive becomes. All schools will accept credit cards. If you are considering diving but want to watch the divers in action before making the investment, many of the dive schools are prepared to take you out to dive sites with their groups. You only pay for the snorkelling equipment.

Asia Divers, Ban Mae Hat, T077-456054, www.asia-divers.com.

Big Blue, Ban Mae Hat, T077-456050, or Hat Sai Ri, T077-456179, www.bigbluediving.com.

Big Bubble, Chalok Ban Kao, T077-456669, www.tauchen-diving.de, European management.

Black Tip Diving and Watersports, at Ban Mae Hat, T077-456204, and at Ao Ta Not, T077-456488, blacktipdiving@yahoo.com.

Buddha View Dive Resort, Chalok Ban Kao, T077-456074, www.buddhaview-diving.com.

Calypso Diving, Ao Ta Not , T077-456745, eugentao@yahoo.de.

Crystal Dive Resort, Ban Mae Hat and Sai Ri, T077-456107, www.crystaldive.com.

Easy Divers, Ban Mae Hat, T077-456010, www.thaidive.com.

Kho Tao Divers, Hat Sai Ri, T06-0699244, kohtaodivers@hotmail.com.

Planet Scuba, Ban Mae Hat, T077-456110, www.planet-scuba.net.

Scuba Junction, Sai Ri Beach, T077-456164, www.scuba-junction.com.

Siam Scuba Dive Center, Sai Ri village, T077-456628, www.scubadive.com.

Snorkelling

Many of the guesthouses hire out their own equipment, but this can be of low quality. The most reliable gear is that hired from the dive shops. You generally pay ฿50 for the mask and snorkel and a further ฿50 for fins. Boats around the island cost around ฿500 per person for a day trip with stops for snorkelling.

Kayak hire

Available from hotels and guesthouses, including **Ban's Diving Resort**, page 600.

Muay Thai

Sai Ri Stadium, near **Asia Divers**. ฿500. Look out for flyers for dates.

Hat Sai Ri *p598*

Therapies

Here & Now, Sai Ri Beach, T077-456730, www.hereandnow.be. T'ai chi courses (10 sessions, ฿3100) and 12-day traditional Thai massage courses, ฿12,400 are held here at

this remote spot. The restaurant overlooks the famous Nangyuan Island. Reception staff are the most unfriendly and dour on Koh Tao.

South coast *p599*

Therapies

Jamahkiri Spa & Resort, Ao Thian Ok, T077-456400, 1000-2200. Free pick ups available. Indulge in one of the reasonably priced packages available at this spa in grounds overlooking the sea. The aloe vera body wrap is the signature experience and produces quite a strange sensation. There's a steam sauna and facials and a variety of massages are available. After your massage have a drink overlooking the sea. Recommended.

Transport

Bicycle hire

Mountain bikes are available for hire from guesthouses and travel agencies throughout the island.

Boat

There are boats of various speeds and sizes going to and from Koh Tao. Connections are with Chumphon (see page 554), and Koh Samui, via Koh Phangan

To **Chumphon** with Koh Tao Cruiser, T077-456064, 1030, 2½ hrs; with Lomprayah, T077-456176, office hours 0830-1900, 1000, 1¾ hrs, and 1500, 1½ hrs, ฿550; with Songserm, T077-456274, 1430, 3 hrs; with Ko Jaroen, T01-7970276, the nightboat at 2200, 5 hrs.

To **Koh Samui**, Lomprayah is the most comfortable, with a/c and TV and shortest journey time, ฿550, 0930, 1 hr 50 mins and 1500, ฿450, 1½ hrs; with Phangan Cruise, T077- 377274, ฿400, 0930, 2 hrs 20 mins; with Songserm, T077-456274, ฿350, 1000, 2½ hrs; with Pra Yai, T077-456263, ฿450, 1430, 2 hrs.

To **Koh Phangan** with Lomprayah, ฿350, 0930 and 1500, 1 hr; with Phangan Cruise, ฿300, 0930, 1 hr 20 mins; with Songserm, T077-456274, ฿250 1000, 1½ hrs; with Pra Yai, ฿300, 1430, 1½ hrs; with CattCorp, T077-456728, www.cattcorp.com, ฿350, 1445, 1 hr with Koh Tao Express, T077-456012, ฿180, 1530, 2 hrs.

To **Surat Thani** with Songserm, ฿550, 1000, 6½ hrs; with the nightboat, ฿550, 2030, 8½ hrs.

To **Hua Hin** with Lomprayah, 1000, 7 hrs, ฿850, 1430, 6 hrs, ฿650.

To **Bangkok** with Lomprayah, with boat and VIP bus, 1000, 10½ hrs, ฿850, 1430, 9 hrs 45 mins, ฿650.

Jeep and motorbike hire

Unless you are a very experienced dirt bike rider this is not really an advisable form of transport as reaching any of the isolated bays involves going along very narrow, twisting bumpy, severely potholed and carved-up tracks.

Lederhosenbikes, Ban Mae Hat, T01-7528994, www.cycling-koh-tao.com. Rents bikes from ฿200/day.

Long-tailed boat

A trip around the island would start from about ฿1500 for up to 4 people.

Taxi

Taxis and motorbike taxis wait at the end of Mae Hat pier. Sharing taxis makes sense as the cost is per journey, not per person. From Mae Hat to Ao Ta Not costs ฿200-300 with a minimum of 4 in the car. To Sai Ri or Chalok, ฿150-200.

Directory

Banks There is an exchange office just east of the pier in Ban Mae Hat, run by the **Krung Thai Bank**, 0900-1600. **Siam City Bank**, Pier Rd. Ban Mae Hat, east of the pier on the left with ATM, exchange and TCs changed, Mon-Fri 0830-1630. There are also a couple of ATMs between Ban Mae Hat and Sai Ri and in Chalok. **Internet** There are numerous email centres in Ban Mae Hat and Sai Ri and Chalok, ฿2/min everywhere. **Medical services** Thai International Clinic, T077-456358, 0800-1900. **Post office** Thongnual Rd, Ban Mae Hut, straight up from the pier and turn left, Mon-Fri 0830-1630. **Telephone** Facilities are easily available on Sai Ri Beach, Ao Chalok Ban Kao and Ban Mae Hat.

Nakhon Si Thammarat and around

→ *Colour map 4, grid C3.*

Nakhon Si Thammarat ('the Glorious city of the Dead') or Nagara Sri Dhammaraja ('the city of the Sacred Dharma Kings') has masqueraded under many different aliases: Marco Polo referred to it as Lo-Kag, the Portuguese called it Ligor – thought to have been its original name – while to the Chinese it was Tung Ma-ling. Today, it is the second biggest city in the south and most people know it simply as Nakhon or Nakhon Si.

It is not a very popular tourist destination and it has a rather unsavoury reputation as one of the centres of mafia activity in Thailand, but otherwise it is busy but manageable with a wide range of hotels, some excellent restaurants, a good museum and a fine monastery in Wat Phra Mahathat. It is also famed for its shadow puppetry.

Around Nakhon are the quiet beaches of Khanom and Nai Phlao. The Khao Luang and Khao Nan national parks offer waterfalls, caves, whitewater rafting and homestays. ▸▸ *For Sleeping, Eating and other listings, see pages 612-616.*

Nakhon

Ins and outs

Getting there Nakhon is a provincial capital and therefore well connected. There is an airport north of town with daily flights to Bangkok. Nakhon lies on the main north-south railway line linking Bangkok with points south and the station is within easy walking distance of the town centre. The main bus station is about 1 km west of town, with connections to Bangkok and most destinations in the south. There are also minibus and share taxi services to many destinations in the south. ▸▸ *See Transport, page 615.*

Getting around The centre is comparatively compact and navigable on foot. But for sights on the edge of town – like Wat Phra Mahathat – it is necessary to catch a public songthaew, saamlor or motorcycle taxi. The songthaew is the cheapest option.

Tourist information TAT ⓘ *Sanam Na Muang, Rachdamnern Rd, T075-346515-6, daily 0830-1630*, is situated in an old, attractive club building. The staff here produce a helpful pamphlet and hand-out sheets of information on latest bus and taxi prices. It is a useful first stop.

Background

Nakhon is surrounded by rich agricultural land and has been a rice exporter for centuries. The city has links with both the Dvaravati and Srivijayan empires. Buddhist monks from Nakhon are thought to have propagated religion throughout the country perhaps even influencing the development of Buddhism in Sukhothai, Thailand's former great kingdom.

Nakhon was at its most powerful and important during King Thammasokarat's reign in the 13th century, when it was busily trading with south India and Ceylon. But as Sukhothai and then Ayutthaya grew in influence, the city went into a gradual decline. During the 17th century, King Narai's principal concubine banished the bright young poet Si Phrat to Nakhon. Here he continued to compose risqué rhymes about the women of the governor's court. His youthful impertinence lost him his head.

Nakhon used to have the dubious honour of being regarded as one of the crime capitals of Thailand – a position it had held, apparently, since the 13th century. Locals maintain that the city has now cleaned up its act and Nakhon is probably best known today for its prawn farms (see box, page 614) and nielloware industry (see page 696). The shop where the industry started some 50 years ago still stands on Sitama Road and production techniques are demonstrated on Si Thammasok I Road. Elsewhere, other than in a few handicraft shops on Tha Chang Road, nielloware is an elusive commodity, although the National Museum has some examples on display. The art and craft and performance of shadow puppetry is also being kept alive in Nakhon, see page 614 and Background, page 693.

Wat Phra Mahathat

ⓘ *Cloisters open daily 0830-1200, 1300-1630.*

A 2-km long wall formerly enclosed the old city and its wats – only a couple of fragments of this remain (the most impressive section is opposite the town jail on Rachdamnern Road). Wat Phra Mahathat, 2 km south of town on Rachdamnern Road, is the oldest temple in town and the biggest in South Thailand – as well as being one of the region's most important. The wat dates from AD 757 and was originally a Srivijayan Mahayana Buddhist shrine. The 77-m high stupa, *Phra Boromathat* – a copy of the Mahathupa in Ceylon – was built early in the 13th century to hold relics of the Buddha from Ceylon. The wat underwent extensive restoration in the Ayutthayan period and endured further alterations in 1990. The chedi's square base, its voluptuous body and towering spire are all Ceylonese-inspired. Below the spire is a small square platform decorated with bas-reliefs in gold of monks circumambulating (*pradaksina*) the monument. The spire itself is said to be topped with 962 kg of gold, while the base is surrounded by small stupas. The covered cloisters at its base contain many beautiful, recently restored Buddha images all in the image of subduing Mara. The base is dotted with attractive elephant heads. Also here is **Vihara Bodhi Langka** ⓘ *0800-1600, entry by donation*, a jumbled treasure trove of a museum. It contains a large collection of archaeological artefacts, donated jewellery, bodhi trees, Buddhas and a collection of sixth to 13th-century Dvaravati sculpture – some of the latter are particularly fine. The mural at the bottom of the stairs tells the story of the early life of the Buddha, while the doorway at the top is decorated with figures of Vishnu and Phrom dating from the Sukhothai period.

Phra Viharn Luang

The nearby Phra Viharn Luang (to the left of the main entrance to the stupa) is an impressive building with an intricately painted and decorated ceiling, dating from the 18th century. The best time to visit the monastery is in October during the Tenth Lunar Month Festival when Wat Mahathat becomes a hive of activity. Foodstalls, travelling cinemas, shadow-puppet masters, the local mafia, businessmen in their Mercedes, monks and handicraft sellers all set up shop – making the wat endlessly interesting.

Puppet workshop and museum

ⓘ *110/18 Si Thammasok, Soi 3, T075-346394. daily 0900-1800, 20-min performance, ฿100 for 2; 3 or more ฿50 each.*

Not far from Wat Mahathat is the puppet workshop of Nakhon's most famous *nang thalung* master – Khun Suchart Subsin. His workshop is signposted off the main road near the Chinese temple (hard to miss). As well as giving shows (see Entertainment) and selling examples of his work starting at ฿200 or so for a simple elephant, the compound itself is interesting and peaceful with craftsmen hammering out puppets under thatched awnings and dozens of buffalo skulls hung everywhere. There is also a small museum exhibiting puppet characters from as far back as the 18th century.

Saan Chao Mae Thap Thim Chinese Pagoda

ⓘ *It's a 2-km hike out to the monastery; blue songthaews constantly ply the road to the monastery and back (฿6).*

Returning to the main road, this Chinese pagoda offers a respite from Theravada Buddhist Thailand. Magnificent dragons claw their way up the pillars and inside, wafted by incense, are various Chinese gods, Bodhisattvas and demons.

Nakhon Si Thammarat National Museum

ⓘ *Rachdamnern Rd, about 700 m beyond Wat Mahathat, Tue-Sun 0800- 1630. ฿50. The museum is a 2-km walk from most of the hotels; catch one of the numerous blue songthaews running along Rachdamnern Rd and ask for 'Pipitipan Nakhon Si Thammarat' (฿6).*

The Nakhon branch of the National Museum is one of the town's most worthwhile sights. The impressive collection includes many interesting Indian-influenced pieces as well as rare pieces from the Dvaravati and later Ayutthaya periods. Some exhibits are labelled in English. The section on art in South Thailand explains and charts the development of the unusual local Phra Phutthasihing (or Buddha Sihing) style of Buddha image, which was popular locally in the 16th century. Also in this section is the oldest Vishnu statue in Southeast Asian art (holding a conch shell on his hip) dating from the fifth century. The museum has sections on folk arts and crafts and local everyday implements. To the right of the entrance hall, in the prehistory section, stand two large Dongson bronze kettle drums – two of only 12 found in the country. The one decorated with four ornamental frogs is the biggest ever found in Thailand.

Chapel of Phra Buddha Sihing

The Chapel of Phra Buddha Sihing, sandwiched between two large provincial office buildings just before Rachdamnern Road splits in two, may contain one of Thailand's most important Buddha images. During the 13th century an image, magically created, was shipped to Thailand from Ceylon (hence the name – Sihing for the Sinhalese people). The Nakhon statue, like the other two images that claim to be the Phra Buddha Sihing (one in Bangkok, see page 93, and one in Chiang Mai, Northern Thailand, see page 226), is not Ceylonese in style at all; it conforms with the Thai style of the peninsula.

Wat Wang Tawan Tok

Back in the centre of town is Wat Wang Tawan Tok, across Rachdamnern Road from the bookshop. It has, at the far side of its sprawling compound, a southern Thai-style wooden house built between 1888 and 1901. Originally the house (which is really three houses in one) was constructed without nails – it has since been poorly repaired using them. The door panels, window frames and gables, all rather weather-beaten now, were once intricately carved but it is still infinitely more appealing than the concrete shophouses going up all over Thailand.

Hindu temples

There are two 13th- to 14th-century Hindu temples in the city, along Rachdamnern Road. **Hor Phra Isuan,** next to the Semamuang Temple, houses an image of Siva, the destroyer. Opposite is **Hor Phra Narai** which once contained images of Vishnu, now in the city museum.

Morning market

A worthwhile early morning walk is west across the bridge along Karom Road to the morning market (about 1 km), which sells fresh food. This gets going early and is feverish with activity from around 0630.

Thai Traditional Medicine Centre

ⓘ *Take a local bus, ฿8.*

On the outskirts of the city, after Wat Mahathat is the small **Wat Sa-la Mechai**. While the temple is fairly ordinary, at one end of the temple grounds is a recently established centre for traditional medicine, including massage. If you want a traditional massage, it costs about ฿100 per hour. You can also take a course in massage, paying by the hour, and learn more about traditional herbal medicine (there is a small garden of medicinal plants at the front).

Around Nakhon

Khanom and Nai Phlao beaches

ⓘ *Regular buses from Nakhon (฿20), a/c micro buses (฿60) leave from Wat Kit Rd and also from Surat Thani. The beaches are about 8 km off the main road; turn at the Km 80 marker.*

Eighty kilometres north of Nakhon, near Khanom district, there are some secluded stretches of shoreline: Khanom beach (2 km from the village), Nai Phlao beach to the south, and a couple of other bays are opening up to development. This area is predominantly visited by Thai tourists. Newer operations seem to be targeting western tourists who are beginning to look towards the mainland in this area for reasonably priced peace and quiet, and convenience they have failed to find on Samui.

Khao Luang National Park

ⓘ *To get to Karom Waterfall take a bus to Lan Saka (then walk 3 km to falls) or charter a minibus direct. To get to Phrom Lok Waterfall take a minibus from Nakhon then hire a motorbike taxi for the last very pleasant 8 km. The villagers at Khiriwong village can organize trips up Khao Luang mountain but do not speak English. See Activities and tours for further options, homestays and guides. Songthaews leave Nakhon for Khiriwong every 15 mins or so (฿15).*

The Khao Luang National Park is named after Khao Luang, a peak of 1835 m – the highest in the south – which lies less than 10 km west of Nakhon. Within the boundaries of the mountainous, 570-sq-km national park are three waterfalls. **Karom Waterfall** lies 30 km from Nakhon, off Route 4015, and has a great location with views over the lowlands. Also here are cool forest trails and fast-flowing streams. The park is said to support small populations of **tiger**, **leopard** and **elephant**, although many naturalists believe they are on the verge of extinction here. **Phrom Lok Waterfall** is about 25 km from Nakhon, off Route 4132. However, the most spectacular of the waterfalls is **Krung Ching** – 'waterfall of a hundred thousand raindrops' – 70 km out of town, and a 4-km walk from the park's accommodation. The 1835-m climb up **Khao Luang** starts from Khiriwong village, 23 km from Nakhon, off Route 4015. The mountain is part of the Nakhon Si Thammarat range, running from Koh Samui south through Surat Thani to Satun. The scenic village, surrounded by forest, was partially destroyed by mudslides in 1988 – an event which led to the introduction of a nationwide logging ban at the beginning of 1989. The climb takes three days and is very steep in parts, with over 60° slopes. If you plan to do this walk on your own, there is no accommodation so it is necessary to carry your own equipment and food. See also Sleeping, below.

Khao Wang Thong Cave

ⓘ *Charter a songthaew for around ฿800 per day. The entrance is past the cave keeper's house, 15 mins' walk uphill from the village.*

One of the less-publicized sights in the Nakhon area is Khao Wang Thong Cave. The cave is on the south side of the middle peak of three limestone mountains near Ban

Nakhon Si Thammarat

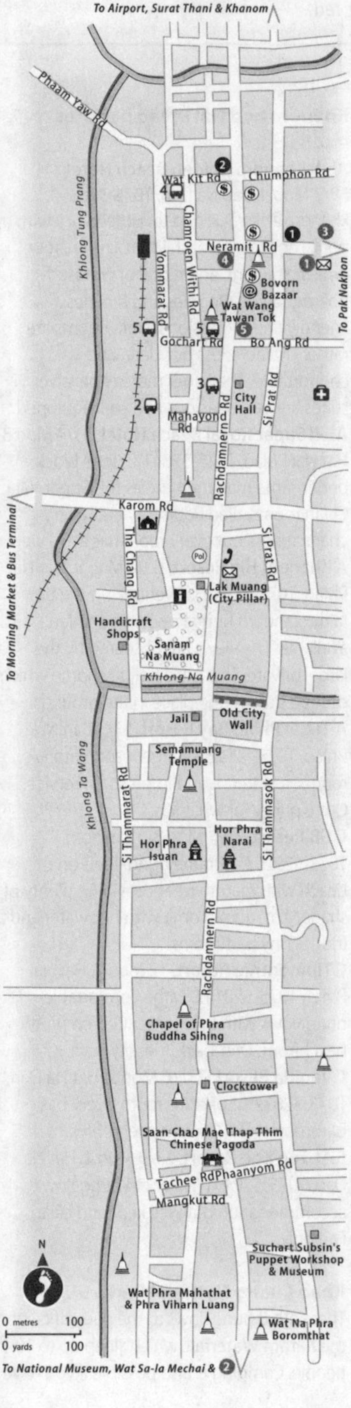
To Airport, Surat Thani & Khanom
Phaam Yaw Rd
Khlong Tung Prang
Wat Kit Rd
Chumphon Rd
Chamroen Withi Rd
Yommarat Rd
Neramit Rd
Bovorn Bazaar
Wat Wang Tawan Tok
To Pak Nakhon
Gochart Rd
Bo Ang Rd
City Hall
Si Prat Rd
Mahayond Rd
Rachdamnern Rd
Karom Rd
To Morning Market & Bus Terminal
Tha Chang Rd
Pol
Lak Muang (City Pillar)
Handicraft Shops
Sanam Na Muang
Khlong Na Muang
Jail
Old City Wall
Semamuang Temple
Khlong Ta Wang
Si Thammarat Rd
Si Thammasok Rd
Hor Phra Narai
Hor Phra Isuan
Chapel of Phra Buddha Sihing
Clocktower
Saan Chao Mae Thap Thim Chinese Pagoda
Tachee Rd
Phaanyom Rd
Mangkut Rd
Suchart Subsin's Puppet Workshop & Museum
Wat Phra Mahathat & Phra Viharn Luang
Wat Na Phra Boromthat
N
0 metres 100
0 yards 100
To National Museum, Wat Sa-la Mechai & 2

Khao Wang Thong in Khanom district. It lies 100 km north of Nakhon, 11 km off Route 4142. Villagers and a group of Nakhon conservationists saved the cave from a dolomite mining company in 1990. A few tight squeezes and a short ladder climb are rewarded by some of Thailand's most spectacular cave formations. Its four spacious chambers – one of which has been dubbed 'the throne hall' – are decorated with gleaming white curtain stalactites. It is presently maintained by groups of local villagers and plans are afoot to install a lighting system. Until then, it is advisable that you bring your own flashlight.

Khao Nan National Park

ⓘ *Take the main route up to Khanom beyond Ta Sala and turn left down the road from where there are signposts to the park.*

Just north of Khao Luang National Park is the new Khao Nan National Park. At 1,430 m, Khao Nan Yai is not as high as Khao Luang, but is still tall enough to support cloud forest on its summit. The national park has a beautiful waterfall near its entrance, lush forests, waterfalls and caves. One cave, **Tham Hong**, has a waterfall inside it and is well worth visiting, and fairly easily accessible but you'll need a flashlight. Treks to the top of Khao Nan Yai taking three to four days are organized by the Forestry Department staff. You should call the Forestry Department in Bangkok at least a couple of days in advance to arrange a guide. The treks go to the top of Khao Nan where you can camp out in cloud forest. Temperatures at the top are always cool and there is a wide variety of ferns and mosses in the

Sleeping
Grand Park 1
Nakhon Garden Inn 3
Thai 4
Thai Lee 5
Twin Lotus 2

Eating
A&A 1
Dam Kan Eng 2
Hao Coffee Shop & Krour Nakorn 3

Minibuses
Minivan to Hat Yai 5
Minivan to Surat Thani & Khanom 4
Share taxi terminal to Airport, Trang & Songkhla 2
To Phuket 3

understorey of the forest. Khao Nan and Khao Luang are also known for *pa pra* – a deciduous tree which loses its leaves during the dry season (February to April) with the leaves first changing colour to a brilliant red.

Sleeping

Nakhon *p607, map p611*
At the top level of accommodation, Nakhon is well served with a decent 5-star hotel, and the middle range now has a couple of hotels worthy of a mention, but as for the rest, there is little to choose between them.

AL Twin Lotus Hotel, 97/8 Hatankarnkhukwag Rd, on the outskirts of the town centre, T075-323777. Nearly 400 a/c rooms with TV and minibars, and a reasonably sized swimming pool and fitness centre. The usual services expected for a 5-star hotel. The reasonable tariff includes a good buffet-style breakfast. A well-run and well-maintained hotel, and the staff are friendly but the hotel is too large to offer a personal service.

C Grand Park Hotel, 1204/79 Pak Nakhon Rd, T075-317666-73. Opposite the **Nakhon Garden Inn**, this is a bit of a block architecturally and doesn't really live up to its grand name, but it has adequate rooms and is centrally located with lots of parking. A/c, hot water, bathtubs, TV, minibar. One of the better hotels in this category.

C Nakhon Garden Inn, 1/4 Pak Nakhon Rd, T075-313333. One of the nicest mid-range places to stay – a rustic feel for Nakhon, with 2 brick buildings on either side of a large garden compound with clean a/c rooms and hot water. The rooms have been nicely decorated in keeping with the rustic feel – rather dark, but good value and a bit different from most of the places in the city centre. Recommended. Better value than the **Grand Park**.

D Thai, 1375 Rachdamnern Rd, T075-341509. Some a/c in newer rooms away from the noise of the street with beds large enough to sleep 4. Restaurant and internet access too. Over the **Twin Lotus Hotel**, it has the advantage of a central location.

E Thai Lee, 1130 Rachdamnern Rd, T075-356948. Large, bright, clean rooms with fan and attached bathroom (western toilet), best-value accommodation in the lower end of the market.

Khanom and Nai Phlao beaches *p610, map p613*

AL-B Khanom Golden Beach Hotel, 59/3 Moo 4, Ban Na Dan, T075-326690, khanom@nksrat.ksc.co.th. Hotel block with pool, snooker room, children's room, tour desk, restaurant, and rental of windsurf boards, sailing dinghies and bicycles. Friendly and professional staff. Rooms are rather characterless but clean and comfortable. The larger more expensive suites are very spacious and well equipped.

AL-B Supar Royal Beach Hotel, 51/4 Moo 8, Hat Nai Phlao, T075-528417. Hotel block under same management as the **Supar Villa**. Clean rooms, tiled floors, generally very characterless but every room has a sea view.

A Khanom Hill Resort, 60/1 Moo 8, Hat Nai Phlao, T075-529403. Overlooking the bay, fairly standard bungalows. A/c and fan available. The views are obscured by the large, private, Thai-style holiday home which occupies the prime place in the grounds.

A-D Nai Phlao Bay Resort, 51/3 Ban Nai Phlao, T075-529039. Large resort with a/c rooms, restaurant and impersonal service. Quite pricey for what it is.

C GB Resort, 30/1 Moo 8, T Khanom, T075-529253. A-frame bungalows on the beach with mature trees providing plenty of shade. A/c rooms come with hot water and a fridge. Tiny bathrooms.

C Tipmontree Resort, 12 Moo 7, Hat Nai Phret, T075-528147. Large comfortable bungalows with basic amenities on pretty beachfront. Laid-back, friendly staff.

C Vanida Resort, 23/10 Moo 2, Hat Na Dan, T075-326329. Spacious rooms, very basic bathrooms, TV (Thai channels only).

C-D Tan Koo Resort, 23/9 Moo 2, Hat Na Dan, T075-529491. Fairly old bungalow accommodation but well kept and clean. Fan only.

Khao Luang National Park *p610*
There are **B** bungalows at the park office of the **Karom Waterfall**, which sleep up to 10 people. Camping is also possible if you have

your own gear. The second park office at **Krung Ching Waterfall**, T075-309644-5, has 2 guesthouses **AL-C**. There is also a campsite. For homestay accommodation, see Activities and tours, below.

Eating

Nakhon *p607, map p611*
Prawns are Nakhon's speciality and farms abound in the area. Good seafood (including saltwater prawns) is available at reasonable prices in most of the town's restaurants. Roadside stalls sometimes sell a Nakhon speciality: small prawns in their shells, deep fried in a spicy batter and served as a sort of prawn pattie. The **Bovorn Bazaar**, in the centre of town off Rachdamnern Rd, is a good place to start in any hunt for food. It has restaurants, a bakery, a bar and a coffee shop.

A & A Restaurant, T075-311047, 0700-2400. A/c restaurant just down the road from the **Nakhorn Garden Inn** and marked with flags boasting fresh coffee. Serves Thai-style toasted bread with jam, marmalade, condensed milk and sugar, excellent fresh coffee, and very tasty Thai food. It also does western breakfasts for a very reasonable price. Try the pork rib noodle soup and the fried minced chicken noodles. It also offers a line in delicious brownies and sticky cakes, puddings and jellies. There is a menu in English.

Dam Kan Eng, intersection of Wat Kit and Rachdamnern rds. Very good Sino-Thai restaurant which locals believe serves some of the best food in town, seafood is especially good.

Hao Coffee Shop, Bovorn Bazaar, off Rachdamnern Rd. It is charmingly decorated

Beaches north of Nakhon Si Thammarat

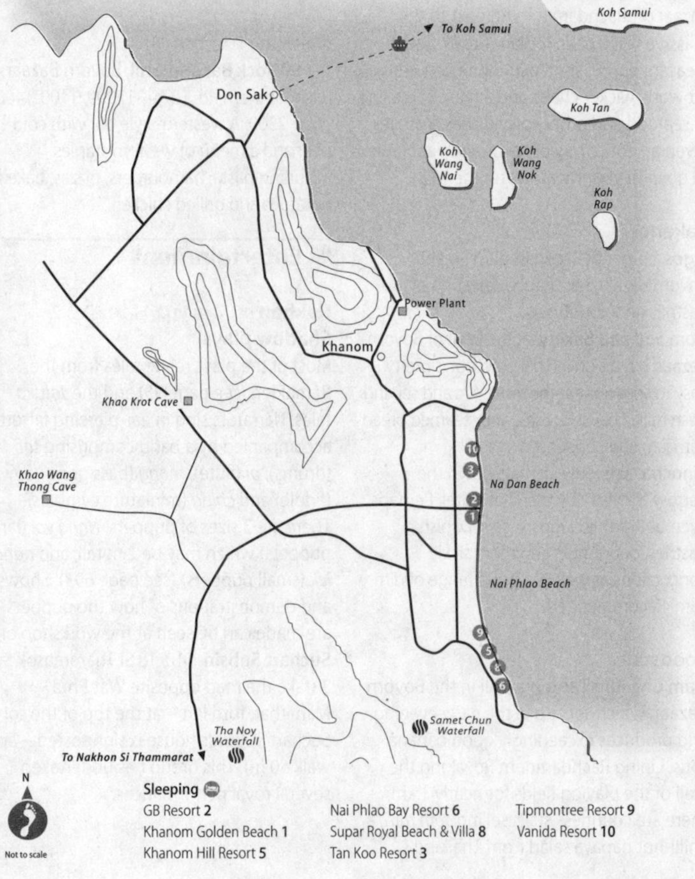
Koh Samui
To Koh Samui
Don Sak
Koh Tan
Koh Wang Nai
Koh Wang Nok
Koh Rap
Power Plant
Khanom
Khao Krot Cave
Khao Wang Thong Cave
Na Dan Beach
Nai Phlao Beach
Samet Chun Waterfall
Tha Noy Waterfall
To Nakhon Si Thammarat
N
Not to scale
Sleeping
GB Resort 2
Khanom Golden Beach 1
Khanom Hill Resort 5
Nai Phlao Bay Resort 6
Supar Royal Beach & Villa 8
Tan Koo Resort 3
Tipmontree Resort 9
Vanida Resort 10

Making a killing from the tiger prawn

The coastline north from Sating Phra and Ranot is one of Thailand's major prawn farming areas. The paddy fields have been dug out, aerators have been installed and since the early 1980s the farmers of the area have taken out large loans to get into the lucrative business of farming tiger prawns. Environmentally the effects have sometimes been disastrous. The protective mangroves and nipa palms were uprooted to make more space for prawns and in so doing destroyed the breeding grounds for many fish and crustacea as well as promoting erosion along the exposed shoreline. The water from the ponds polluted nearby ricelands and viral infections often killed the prawns that farmers had invested so much money in raising. In recent years the government has been researching and promoting more sustainable prawn aquaculture.

with antiques and assorted oddities and is like a museum piece with glass display cabinets everywhere. Recommended.

¥ **Krour Nakorn**, at the back of Bovorn Bazaar off Rachdamnern Rd next to the massive trunk of an Indian rubber tree. Pleasant eating spot, with open verandas, art work, wicker chairs and a reasonable line in seafood and other spicy dishes. You get given an entire tray of herbs and vegetables to go with your meal. Recommended.

Bakeries

Ligos, corner of Rachdamnern Rd and Bovorn Bazaar, has a good selection of pastries and doughnuts.

Nom Sod and Bakery, at the front of Bovorn Bazaar, has a sign in Thai only, but is pretty easy to spot right at the front. A/c and serving fresh milk, Thai-style toast and steamed bread with jam and condensed milk.

Sinocha (sign only in Thai), down the narrow alleyway by the **Thai Hotel**. Perhaps even better than **Ligos**, it sells Danish pastries, doughnuts and more sickly concoctions as well as a good range of dim sum. Recommended.

Foodstalls

Nam Cha Rim Tang is a stall in the **Bovorn Bazaar**, which sets up in the early evening and produces exceedingly good banana rotis. Lining Rachdamnern Rd, along the wall of the playing fields for nearly 1 km, there are countless stalls selling *som tam*, a chilli-hot papaya salad from Thailand's northeastern region usually served with grilled chicken (*kai yaang*).

Bars and clubs

Nakhon *p607, map p611*

¥¥-¥ **99 Rock Bar and Grill**, Bovorn Bazaar, Rachdamnern Rd, T075-317999, 1100-1400, 1600-2300. A western-style bar with cold beer and a menu of western staples including pasta, hamburgers, pizzas, baked potatoes and grilled chicken.

Entertainment

Nakhon *p607, map p611*

Shadow plays

Most of the plays relate tales from the Ramakien (see page 95) and the *Jataka* tales. Narrators sing in ear-piercing falsetto accompanied by a band comprising *tab* (drums), *pi* (flute), *mong* (bass gong), *saw* (fiddle) and *ching* (miniature cymbals). There are 2 sizes of puppets. *Nang yai* (large puppets) which may be 2 m tall, and *nang lek* (small puppets) (see page 693). Shows and demonstrations of how the puppets are made can be seen at the workshop of **Suchart Subsin**, 110/18 Si Thammasok Soi 3 (take the road opposite Wat Phra Mahathat, turn left – at the top of the soi Suchart Subsin's house is signposted – and walk 50 m). This group has undertaken several royal performances.

Festivals and events

Nakhon *p607, map p611*

Feb Hae Pha Khun That (20-29) 3-day event when homage is paid to locally enshrined relics of the Buddha.

Sep-Oct Tenth Lunar Month Festival (movable) A 10-day celebration, the climax of which is the colourful procession down Rachdamnern Rd to Wat Phra Mahathat.

Chak Phra Pak Tai (movable) Centred around Wat Phra Mahathat, includes performances of *nang thalung* (shadow plays) and *lakhon* (classical dance). This is a southern Thai festival also held in Songkhla and Surat Thani.

Shopping

Nakhon *p607, map p611*

Nakhon is the centre of the South Thai handicrafts industry. Nielloware, *yan liphao* basketry (woven from strands of vine of the same name), shadow puppets, Thai silk brocades and *pak yok* weaving are local specialities.

Handicrafts

Shops on Tha Chang Rd, notably the **Thai Handicraft Centre** (in the lime green traditional wooden house on the far side of the road behind the tourist office), **Nabin House** and **Manat Shop**. With the exception of the **Thai Handicraft Centre**, silverware predominates.

Nielloware

Original shop on Chakrapetch Rd. A few handicraft shops on Tha Chang Rd also sell it.

Shadow puppets

From the craftsmen at **Suchart Subsin's House**, Si Thammasok Rd, Soi 3 (see Sights and Entertainment above) and stalls around Wat Phra Mahathat.

Activities and tours

Nakhon *p607, map p611*

Thai boxing

Every Sun 2100 in the stadium, Rachdamnern Rd.

Khao Luang National Park *p610*

Tours in the province can be also organized through tour companies in Nakhon Sri Thammarat or at the park office.

Khiriwong Agro Tourism Promotion Center, Moo 5, Tambon Kam Lon, Amphoe Lan Saka (near the park office), T075-309010/ T01-2290829. Offers tours to Krung Ching Waterfall, including whitewater rafting. Can organize homestays and guides.

TVS-REST, T02-6910437-9, www.ecotour.in.th/indexen.html. A Thai not-for-profit organization involved in community development, offers tours and visits to Khiriwong village, with activities and accommodation at the village and with treks into the forest. The tour leaves from Bangkok and costs ฿3600.

Transport

Nakhon *p607, map p611*

A **songthaew** across town costs ฿10. The old pedal **saamlor** is still in evidence though it is gradually being pushed out by the noisier and more frightening **motorcycle taxi** of which there seem to be hundreds. For **shared taxis**, the terminal is on Yommarat Rd. Prices are fixed (they are listed on a board at the terminal) and most large centres in the south are served from here including Hat Yai, Phuket, Krabi, Trang, Surat Thani, Phattalung and Songkhla.

Air

The airport lies north of town. There are daily connections with **Bangkok** with THAI, T075-342491, 1612 Rachdamnern Rd.

Bus

The bus station (*bor kor sor*) for non-a/c connections is 1 km out of town over the bridge on Karom Rd, west of the mosque. Most people pick up a bus as it works its way through town though.

Overnight connections with **Bangkok**'s Southern bus terminal, 12 hrs, ฿350. Regular non a/c and a/c connections with **Krabi**, 3 hrs, ฿65; **Surat Thani**, 2½-3 hrs, ฿55; **Hat Yai**, 3 hrs, ฿73; **Phuket**, 8 hrs, ฿125; **Trang**, 2 hrs, ฿65; **Songkhla**, 3 hrs, ฿70; and with other southern towns.

A number of **minibus** services also operate to destinations in the south including **Hat Yai**, ฿90; **Phuket**, ฿500; **Krabi**, ฿120; **Trang** ฿80; and **Surat Thani**, ฿110. They tend to be marginally quicker and slightly more expensive than a/c coaches. See map for locations but check beforehand as their 'patches' seem to change from time to time.

Khao Luang National Park *p610*

Train

The station is on Yommarat Rd. There are overnight connections with **Bangkok**. Most southbound trains stop at the junction of Khao Chum Thong, 30 km west of Nakhon, from where you must take a bus or taxi. Only 2 trains go into Nakhon itself.

Directory

Nakhon *p607, map p611*

Banks Bangkok, 1747 Rachdamnern Rd. There are numerous other banks in the centre. **Internet** Inside the Bovorn Bazaar. **Post office** Rachdamnern Rd (opposite the police station). There is also a small post office opposite the **Nakhon Garden Inn** on Pak Nakhon Rd. **Telephone** Attached to the post office on Rachdamnern Rd, overseas calls available.

Note **This guide does not cover the provinces of Narathiwat, Songkhla, Pattani and Yala, which extend to the Malaysian border, as the UK Foreign office and US State Department currently ban travel to this area, see page 40 and page 525.**

Background

Footprint features

History

Prehistory

Research since the end of the Second World War has shown Thailand to be a 'hearth' – or core area – in Southeast Asian prehistory. Discoveries at archaeological sites such as Ban Chiang (see page 349) and Non Nok Tha in the northeast, Spirit Cave in the north, and Ban Kao in the west have revealed evidence of early agriculture (possibly, 7000 BC) – particularly rice cultivation – pottery (3500 BC) and metallurgy (2500 BC). Although heated arguments over the significance and the dating of the finds continue, there is no doubt that important technologies were being developed and disseminated from an early date. These finds have altered the view of this part of the world from being a 'receptacle' for outside influences to being an area of innovation in its own right.

Today, the population of Thailand is made up of Tai-speaking peoples. For long it has been thought that the Tai migrated from southern China about 2,000 years ago, filtering down the valleys and along the river courses that cut north-south down the country. These migrants settled in the valleys of North Thailand, on the Khorat Plateau, and in parts of the lower Chao Phraya basin. Even at this early date there was a clear division between hill and lowland people. The lowland Tai mastered the art of wet rice cultivation (see page 707), supporting large populations and enabling powerful states and impressive civilizations to evolve. In the highlands, people worked with the forest, living in small itinerant groups, eking out a living through shifting cultivation or hunting and gathering. In exchange for metal implements, salt and pottery, the hill peoples would trade natural forest products: honey, resins such as lac, wild animal skins, ivory and herbs. Even today, lowland 'civilized' Thais view the forest (*pa*) as a wild place (*thuan*), inhabited by spirits and hill peoples. This is reflected in the words used to denote 'civilized' lowland Thais – *Khon Muang*, People of the Town – and 'barbaric' upland people – *Khon Pa*, People of the Forest.

Mon, Srivijayan and Khmer influences

Before the Tais emerged as the dominant force in the 13th century, Thailand was dominated by **Mon** and **Khmer** peoples. The Mon were a people and a civilisation centred on the western edge of the Central Plains. They established the enigmatic kingdom of Dvaravati, see below, of which very little is known even to the extent that the location of its capital is far from certain. From the small collection of inscriptions and statues scholars do know, however, that the kingdom was Buddhist and extended eastwards towards Cambodia, northwards towards Chiang Mai, and westwards into Burma.The Khmer were the people, and (usually) a kingdom, centred on present day Cambodia with their capital at Angkor. They controlled large areas of Thailand (particularly the northeast) and Laos (the south) as well as Cambodia.

Prior to the 13th century the people of the **Srivijayan kingdom** also extended their influence across Thailand. This was a Hindu-Buddhist kingdom that had its capital near present day Palembang (Sumatra) and which built its wealth on controlling the trade through the Straits of Melaka between China and India/Middle East. Because of the monsoon winds (northeast/southwest) boats powered by sail had to 'winter' in island Southeast Asia, waiting for the winds to change before they could continue their journeys. Srivijaya, for which we have little solid evidence, is thought to have been one of the most – if not the most – powerful maritime kingdom in the region.

Thailand's Prehistory (11,000 BP-1,500 BP)

11,000 BP	Evidence of hunter-gatherers (Spirit Cave, Northern Thailand)
8,000 BP	Earliest excavated pottery in Thailand (Spirit Cave)
5,500 BP	Rice chaff associated with human habitation, probably wild (Banyan Valley Cave, Northern Thailand)
5,000 BP	Evidence from Northeast Thailand of the origins of agriculture and domestication of animals (pig, dog, chicken, cattle)
5,000 BP	Beautiful, cord-marked pottery excavated (Ban Chiang, Northeast Thailand)
4,000-3,500 BP	Early evidence of bronze metallurgy (Ban Chiang)
3,000 BP	Cave and cliff paintings (Pha Taem, Northeast Thailand)
2,500 BP	Silk impressions in bronzeware (Ban Na Di)
2,300 BP	Ironware (Ban Na Di)
2,000 BP	Red-on-buff pottery (Ban Chiang)
1,500 BP	Moated settlements (Northeast Thailand)

Note Some of the dates above are contested, especially for such things as the origins of agriculture and the domestication of animals. BP = Before the Present.

Dvaravati

The Mon kingdom of Dvaravati was centred close to Bangkok, with cities at modern day Uthong and Nakhon Pathom and was an artistic and political outlier of the Mon Empire of Burma. Dvaravati relics have also been found in the north and northeast, along what are presumed to have been the trade routes between Burma east to Cambodia, north to Chiang Mai and northeast to the Khorat Plateau and Laos. The Dvaravati Kingdom lasted from the sixth to the 11th centuries; only the tiny Mon kingdom of Haripunjaya, with its capital at Lamphun in the north, managed to survive annexation by the powerful Khmer Empire and remained independent until the 13th century. Unfortunately, virtually nothing of the architecture of the Dvaravati period remains. Buildings were constructed of laterite blocks, faced with stucco (a mixture of sand and lime) and, apparently, bound together with vegetable glue. In Thailand, only the stupa of Wat Kukut outside Lamphun shows Dvaravati architecture (it was last rebuilt in 1218, see 683). Dvaravati sculpture is much better represented and the National Gallery in Bangkok has some fine examples. The sculptors of the period drew their inspiration from India's late-Gupta cave temples, rendering human form almost supernaturally.

Srivijaya

The powerful Srivijayan Empire, with its capital at Palembang in Sumatra, extended its control over south Thailand from the seventh to the 13th centuries. Inscriptions and sculptures dating from the Srivijayan period have been found near the modern Thai towns of Chaiya and Sating Phra in Surat Thani, and Songkhla provinces. They reveal an eclectic mixture of Indian, Javanese, Mon and Khmer artistic influences, and incorporate both Hindu and Mahayana Buddhist iconography. Probably the best examples of what little remains of Srivijayan architecture in Thailand are Phra Boromthat and a sanctuary at Wat Kaeo, both in Chaiya (see page 556).

The Khmer

Of all the external empires to impinge on Thailand before the rise of the Tai, the most influential was the Khmer. Thailand lay on the fringes of the Angkorian Kingdom, but nonetheless many Thai towns are Khmer in origin: That Phanom, Sakhon Nakhon and

The Dvaravati, Srivijaya and Khmer empires in Thailand (6th-14th centuries)

Dvaravati — **6th-11th centuries (west, central and northern Thailand)**

AD 661 (19 February): Haripunchaya reputed to have been founded at Lamphun in Northern Thailand by a group of Buddhist holy men.

late 7th century: Queen Chamadevi, a daughter of the ruler of Lopburi, becomes queen of the Mon (Dvaravati) kingdom of Haripunchaya.

Srivijaya — **7th-13th centuries (Southern Thailand)**

7th century: evidence of a thriving Buddhist entrepôt based at Palembang in Sumatra, with a presence in southern Thailand.

13th-14th centuries: Srivijaya loses its control of the Malay peninsula and southern Thailand to the young and vigorous Tai states of Sukhothai and, later, Ayutthaya.

Khmer — **9th-13th centuries (Northeast and central Thailand)**

AD 889-900: reign of Yasovarman I. He expands the Khmer empire onto the Khorat Plateau of Northeast Thailand.

1001-1002: reign of Udayadityavarman, who mounts an invasion of Haripunjaya following an attack by Haripunjaya on the Khmer town of Lopburi.

12th century: Lopburi is regarded by Angkor as Syam – ie Siam.

1113-1150: reign of Suryavarman II.

1181-1219?: reign of the great Jayavarman VII, who develops the Angkorian communications system, helping to hold together his vast empire. Lopburi is firmly incorporated into the Khmer Empire.

1220-1243: reign of Indravarman II.

Phimai in the northeast; Lopburi, Suphanburi and Ratburi in the lower central plain; and Phitsanulok, Sawankhalok and Sukhothai in the upper central plain.

The peak of the Khmer period in Thailand lasted from the 11th to the 13th centuries, corresponding with the flowering of the Angkorian period in Cambodia. However, antiquities have been found that date back as far as the seventh and eighth century AD. The period of Khmer inspiration is referred to as 'Lopburi', after the Central Thai town of the same name which was a Khmer stronghold. The most impressive architectural remains are to be found in the Northeastern region: Phimai, not far from Nakhon Ratchasima (Korat) (see page 312), Muang Tham (page 319) and Phnom Rung (page 317), both south of Buriram. As Cambodia's treasures are still relatively expensive and hard to get to, these 'temple cities' are a substitute, giving some idea of the economic power and artistic brilliance of the Khmer period. There are also many lesser Khmer ruins scattered over the Northeastern region, many barely researched, and these offer worthwhile forays for those with a real interest in Thailand's historical and archaeological past.

The Tai

The Tai did not begin to exert their dominance over modern Thailand until the 12th-13th centuries when the Khmer empire had begun to decline. By then they had taken control

Lanna Thai (1239-1660)

1239	King Mengrai, the founder of the Lanna Kingdom, is born in Chiang Saen
1259	Mengrai becomes ruler of Chiang Saen, succeeding his father
1262	Mengrai founds Chiang Rai
1281	After years of preparation, Mengrai takes the Haripunchaya kingdom based at Lamphun
1289	Mengrai takes Pegu (Burma) and extends his empire into Burma
1292	Mengrai establishes Chiang Mai as his new capital
1317	Mengrai dies and the Lanna kingdom enters a period of instability
1355	King Ku Na of Lanna brings some stability and direction back to the kingdom; he is a fine scholar and a cultured man
1369	King Ku Na invites a monk from Sukhothai to establish a monastery in Chiang Mai
1404-5	Lanna is invaded by a large Chinese army from Yunnan; they are repulsed after the king raises an army said to be 300,000-strong
1442-43	Ayutthaya sends an army against Lanna and the principality of Nan revolts against Lanna domination. In time, Lanna defeats both
1456-57	The beginning of a long period of conflict between Lanna and Ayutthaya over control of the upper Central Plains and lower North, which continues until about 1486
1478-79	A Vietnamese army from Luang Prabang (Laos) tries to take Nan, and is repulsed
1526	The death of King Muang Kaeo marks the beginning of the decline of Lanna
1546	Lanna comes under the suzerainty of Lane Xang (Laos)
1564-1660	Lanna is controlled over much of the period by Burma, whose king puts a series of puppet rulers on the throne of Lanna
1595	Kings of Lane Xang and Nan try to oust the Burmese from Lanna, but fail
1660	King Narai takes Chiang Mai and Lampang, but is eventually repulsed by a Burmese army

of Lamphun in the north, founded Chiang Mai, established the Sukhothai Kingdom in the Yom River valley, and gained control of the southern peninsula. From the 13th century onwards, the history of Thailand becomes a history of the Tai people.

An important unit of organization among the Tai was the *muang*. Today, muang is usually translated as 'town'. But it means much more than this, and to an extent defies translation. The muang was a unit of control, and denoted those people who came under the sway of a *chao* or lord. In a region where people were scarce but land was abundant, the key to power was to control manpower, and thereby to turn forest into riceland. At the beginning of the 13th century, some Tai lords began to extend their control over neighbouring muang, forging kingdoms of considerable power. In this way, the Tai began to make a history of their own, rather than merely to be a part of history.

Chiang Maior Lanna Thai

In Northern Thailand, various Tai chiefs began to expand at the expense of the Mon. The most powerful of these men was **King Mengrai**, born in October 1239 at Chiang Saen, a

 fortified town on the Mekong. It is said that Mengrai, concerned that the constant warring and squabbling between the lords of the north was harming the population, took it upon himself to unite the region under one king That, inevitably, was himself. Entranced by the legendary wealth of Haripunjaya, Mengrai spent almost a decade hatching a plot to capture this powerful prize. He sent one of his scribes – Ai Fa – to ingratiate himself with the King of Haripunjaya, and having done this encouraged the scribe to sow seeds of discontent. By 1280, the king of Haripunjaya was alienated from his court and people, and in 1281, Mengrai attacked with a huge army and took the city without great trouble. Mengrai then set about uniting his expansive, new kingdom. This was helped to a significant degree by the propagation of Ceylonese Theravada Buddhism, which transcended tribal affiliations and helped to create a new identity of Northern Thai. The Lanna (literally, 'Million rice fields') Thai Kingdom created by Mengrai was to remain the dominant power in the north until the mid-16th century, and was not truly incorporated into the Thai state until the 19th century.

In 1296, Mengrai built a new capital which he named Chiang Mai – or 'New Town' (see page 223). The art of this era is called Chiang Saen and dates from the 11th century. It is still in evidence throughout the north – in Chiang Saen, Chiang Mai, Lamphun and Lampang – and shows strong stylistic links with Indian schools of art (see page 684).

Sukhothai

South of Chiang Mai, at the point where the rivers of the north spill out onto the wide and fertile Central Plains, a second Thai kingdom was evolving during the 13th century: the Sukhothai Kingdom. Sri Indraditya was the first known king of Sukhothai, in the 1240s when it was a small kingdom, and it remained a weak local power until the reign of its most famous king, **Ramkhamhaeng** (?1279-98) or 'Rama the Brave', who gained his name – so it is said – after defeating an enemy general in single-handed elephant combat at the age of 19. When Ramkhamhaeng ascended to the throne in 1275, Sukhothai was a relatively small kingdom occupying part of the upper Central Plain. When he died in 1298, extensive swathes of land came under the King of Sukhothai's control, and only King Mengrai of Lanna and King Ngam Muang of Phayao could be regarded as his equals. In his first few years as king, Ramkhamhaeng had incorporated the area around Sukhothai into his mandala alongside Sawankhalok, Uttaradit, Kamphaeng Phet and Tak. But King Ramkhamhaeng is remembered as much for his artistic achievements as for his raw power. Under Khmer tutelage, he is said to have devised the Thai writing system and also made a number of administrative reforms. The inscription No 1 from his reign, composed in 1292, is regarded as the first work of Thai literature, and contains the famous lines:

'In the time of King Ramkhamhaeng, this land of Sukhothai is thriving. In the water there is fish, in the fields there is rice. The lord of the realm does not levy toll on his subjects for travelling the roads; they lead their cattle to trade or ride their horses to sell; whoever wants to trade in elephants does so; whoever wants to trade in horses, does so; whoever wants to trade in silver and gold, does so. When any commoner or man of rank dies, his estate – his elephants, wives, children, granaries, rice, retainers and groves of areca and betel – is left in its entirety to his son. ... When [the King] sees someone's rice he does not covet it, when he sees someone's wealth he does not get angry ... He has hung a bell in the opening of the gate over there: if any commoner in the land has a grievance which sickens his belly and gripes his heart, and which he wants to make known to his ruler and lord, it is easy; he goes and strikes the bell which the King has hung there; King Ramkhamhaeng, the ruler of the kingdom, hears the call; he goes and questions the man, examines the case, and decides it justly for him. So the people of this *muang* [city/state] of Sukhotai praise him.'

Every Thai schoolchild is taught to memorize the opening lines of the inscription, ones which seemingly just about every book on Thailand also repeats: *Nai naam mii plaa, nai naa mii khao*: 'in the water there are fish, in the fields there is rice'.

Although the kingdom of Sukhothai owed a significant cultural and artistic debt to the Khmers, by the 13th century the Tais of Sukhothai were beginning to explore and develop their own interpretations of politics, art and life. The kingdom promoted Theravada Buddhism (see page 697), sponsoring missionary monks to spread the word. In 1298, Ramkhamhaeng died and was succeeded by his son Lo Thai. His father's empire began to wane and by 1321 Sukhothai had declined in influence and become a small principality among many competing states. For many Thais today, the Sukhothai period – which lasted a mere 200 years – represents the apogee, the finest flowering of Thai brilliance. A visit to the ruins of Sukhothai or its sister city of Si Satchanalai reinforces this (see pages 189-210).

Ayutthaya

From the mid-14th century

In the middle of the 14th century, Sukhothai's influence began to be challenged by another Thai kingdom, Ayutthaya. Located over 300 km south on the Chao Phraya River, Ayutthaya was the successor to the Mon kingdom of Lavo (Lopburi). It seems that from the 11th century, Tais began to settle in the area and were peacefully incorporated into the Mon state, where they gradually gained influence. Finally, in 1351, a Tai lord took control of the area and founded a new capital at the confluence of the Pa Sak, Lopburi and Chao Phraya rivers. He called the city Ayutthaya – after the sacred town of Ayodhya in the Hindu epic, the Ramayana (see page 95). This kingdom would subsequently be known as Siam. From 1351, Ayutthaya began to extend its power south as far as Nakhon Si Thammarat, and east to Cambodia, raiding Angkor in the late 14th century and taking the city in 1432. The palace at Angkor was looted by the Thai forces and the Khmers abandoned their capital, fleeing eastwards towards present-day Phnom Penh. Although Sukhothai and Ayutthaya initially vied with one another for supremacy, Ayutthaya proved the more powerful. In 1438, King Boromraja II placed his seven-year-old son, Ramesuan (later to become King Boromtrailokant), on the throne, signalling the end of Sukhothai as an independent power.

During the Ayutthayan period, the basis of Thai common law was introduced by King Ramathibodi (1351-69), who drew upon the Indian legal Code of Manu, while the powerful King Boromtrailokant (1448-88) centralized the administration of his huge kingdom and introduced various other civil, economic and military reforms. Perhaps the most important was the *sakdi naa* system, in which an individual's social position was related to the size of his landholdings. The heir apparent controlled 16,000 ha, the highest official 1,600 ha, and the lowest commoner 4 ha. A code of conduct for royalty was also introduced, with punishments again linked to position: princes of high rank who had violated the law were to be bound by gold fetters, those of lower rank by silver. The execution of a member of the royal family was, it has been said, carried out by placing them in a sack and either beating them to death with scented sandalwood clubs or having them trampled by white elephants. Even kicking a palace door would, in theory, lead to the amputation of the offending foot.

By King Boromtrailokant's reign, Ayutthaya had extended its control over 500,000 sq km, and the capital had a population of 150,000. Although the art of Ayutthaya is not as 'pure' as that of Sukhothai, the city impressed 16th and 17th century European visitors. The German surgeon Christopher Fryke remarked that 'there is not a finer City in all India'. Perhaps it was the tiger and elephant fights which excited the Europeans so much. The elephants (regarded as noble and representing the state) were expected to win by tossing the tiger (regarded as wild and

Ayutthaya (1314-1767)

1314	Birth of Uthong, reputed to have been the founder of Ayutthaya
1351	Ayutthaya is established and Uthong – renamed King Ramathibodi – ascends to the throne
1390	King Ramesuan captures Chiang Mai
1409-24	Reign of King Intharacha
1424	Following King Intharacha's death, his two elder sons contest a duel on elephant back for the throne – both die from their injuries, allowing a third son to accede
1431-32	King Borommaracha II takes and then sacks Angkor in Cambodia
1448-88	Reign of King Boromtrailokant, best known for his administrative and legal reforms
1507-15	Drawn out war between Ayutthaya and Lanna
1549	Burmese invade and are repulsed
1555	Naresuan, later to free Ayutthaya from the yoke of the Burmese, is born
1558	Burmese take Chiang Mai
1564	Burmese invade Ayutthaya
1569	Burmese take the city of Ayutthaya and put their own puppet ruler, Maha Thammaracha, on the throne. The Burmese period lasts until 1593
1570-87	Cambodians forces invade Ayutthaya on six occasions in 18 years
1585-87	Naresuan defies and defeats the Burmese occupiers on two occasions
1593	The Burmese send a massive army to defeat Naresuan, and are vanquished at Nong Sarai. Ayutthaya is restored as an independent kingdom
1608	Siam sends its first diplomatic mission to Europe and trade relations, especially with the Dutch, grow
1662	King Narai mounts an invasion of Burma
1664	Trading treaty concluded with the Dutch
1687	A large French diplomatic mission arrives in Ayutthaya
1688	Narai's death leads to the Ayutthaya 'Revolution' and the execution of Constantine Phaulcon. Links with Europe and Western traders and emissaries are cut
1733-58	Reign of King Boromtrailokant, marking the apogee of Ayutthaya's power
1760	Burmese forces beseige Ayutthaya, but retreat
1766-67	Burmese forces, after defeating Chiang Mai and other northern towns, beseige, capture and sack Ayutthaya, marking the end of the Ayutthaya period

representing disorder) repeatedly into the air. The fact that the tigers were often tied to a stake or attacked by several elephants at once must have lengthened the odds against them. (In Vietnam it was reported that tigers sometimes had their claws removed and jaws sewn together.) Despite the undoubted might of Ayutthaya and the absolute power that lay within each monarch's grasp, kings were not, in the main,

able to name their successors. Blood was not an effective guarantee to kingship and a strong competitor could easily usurp a rival, even though he might – on paper – have a better claim to the throne. As a result, the history of Ayutthaya is peppered with court intrigues, bloody succession struggles and rival claims.

16th-18th centuries (Burmese invasion)

During this period, the fortunes of the Ayutthayan Kingdom were bound up with those of Burma. Over a 220-year period, the Burmese invaded on no less than six occasions. The first time was in 1548 when the Burmese king of Pegu, Tabengshweti, encircled the capital. King Mahachakrapat only survived the ensuing battle when one of his wives drove her elephant in front of an approaching warrior. Elephants figured heavily in war and diplomacy during the Ayutthayan period: Tabengshweti justified his invasion by pointing out that he had no white elephants, the holiest of beasts (the Buddha's last reincarnation before his enlightenment was as a white elephant). The Ayutthayan king meanwhile had a whole stable of them, and was not willing to part with even one. Although this attack failed, in 1569, King Bayinnaung mounted another invasion and plundered the city, making Ayutthaya a vassal state. When the Burmese withdrew to Pegu, they left a ravaged countryside devoid of people, and large areas of riceland returned to scrub and forest. But a mere 15 years later, Prince Naresuan re-established Thai sovereignty, and began to lay the foundations for a new golden age in which Ayutthaya would be more powerful and prosperous than ever before (see page 163).

17th century (commercial and diplomatic expansion)

The 17th century saw a period of intense commercial contact with the Dutch, English and French. In 1608, Ayutthaya sent a diplomatic mission to the Netherlands and in 1664 a trading treaty was concluded with the Dutch. Even as early as the 17th century, Thailand had a flourishing prostitution industry. In the 1680s an official was given a monopoly of prostitution in the capital; he used 600 women to generate considerable state revenues. The kings of Ayutthaya also made considerable use of foreigners as advisers and ministers at the court. The most influential such family was founded by two Persian brothers, who arrived at the beginning of the 17th century. However, the best known was the Greek adventurer Constantine Phaulcon, who began his life in the East as a mere cabin boy with the East India Company and rose to become one of King Narai's (1656-88) closest advisers and one of the kingdom's most influential officials before being executed in 1688 (see page 169). He was implicated in a plot with the French against King Narai and his execution heralded 100 years of relative isolation as the Thais became wary of, and avoided close relations with, the West.

18th century (Ayutthaya's zenith)

The height of Ayutthaya's power and glory is often associated with the reign of King Boromkot (literally, 'the King in the urn [awaiting cremation]', as he was the last sovereign to be honoured in this way). Boromkot ruled from 1733 to 1758 and he fulfilled many of the imagined pre-requisites of a great king: he promoted Buddhism and ruled effectively over a vast territory. But, in retrospect, signs of imperial senility were beginning to materialize even as Ayutthaya's glory was approaching its zenith. In particular, King Boromkot's sons began to exert their ambitions. Prince Senaphithak, the eldest, went so far as to have some of the king's officials flogged; in retaliation, one of the officials revealed that the prince had been having an affair with one of Boromkot's three queens. He admitted to the liaison and was flogged to death, along with his lover.

The feud with Burma was renewed in 1760 when the Burmese King Alaungpaya invaded Thailand. His attack was repulsed after one of the seige guns exploded, seriously injuring the Burmese king. He died soon afterwards during the arduous

The early Chakri period (1767-1855)

1767	Ayutthaya sacked and capital moves to Thonburi
1769-70	Taksin begins to piece Siam back together when he takes control of Cambodia, Phitsanulok, Nakhon Si Thammarat and Fang
1782	Rama I relocates capital from Thonburi to Bangkok
1785	Burmese mount a huge invasion force, which is eventually repulsed
1787	Burmese invade Lanna; also repulsed
1788-89	The Pali-language Buddhist Tripitaka is re-written in definitive style
1800	Threat from Burma is ended and Siam becomes the leading power in the area
1805	As part of his modernization programme, Rama I gives a committee of judges the job of reforming the Siamese legal code. They produce the Three Seals Laws
1812	Growing friction between Siam and Vietnam
1813	Siamese suzerainty of Cambodia ends, with Vietnam filling the void
1821	John Crawfurd visits Siam on behalf of the governor-general of British India
1825	John Burney is sent as British emissary to Siam
1826	The commercial and diplomatic Burney Treaty is signed
1827	King Anou of Laos invades Northeastern Siam; his forces are eventually decimated and Vientiane is sacked by the Siamese army
1829	Anou is captured and dies in captivity in Bangkok
1833-34	A Siamese and Lao army invades Cambodia; it is defeated by Vietnamese forces and Cambodia falls within the Vietnamese sphere of influence
1855	Signing of the Bowring Treaty

march back to Pegu. Three years later his successor, King Hsinbyushin, raised a vast army and took Chiang Mai, Lamphun and Luang Prabang (Laos). By 1765, the Burmese were ready to mount a second assault on Ayutthaya. Armies approached from the north and west and at the beginning of 1766 met up outside the city, from where they laid siege to the capital. King Suriyamarin offered to surrender, but King Hsinbyushin would hear nothing of it. The city fell after a year, in 1767. David Wyatt, in *Thailand: A short history*, wrote: 'The Burmese wrought awful desolation. They raped, pillaged and plundered and led tens of thousands of captives away to Burma. They put the torch to everything flammable and even hacked at images of the Buddha for the gold with which they were coated. King Suriyamarin is said to have fled the city in a small boat and starved to death 10 days later.'

The city was too damaged to be renovated for a second time, and the focus of the Thai state moved southwards once again – to Thonburi, and from there to Bangkok.

Bangkok and the Rattanakosin period

After the sacking of Ayutthaya in 1766-67, **General Taksin** moved the capital 74 km south to Thonburi, on the other bank of the Chao Pharaya River from modern day Bangkok. Taksin's original name was Sin. Proving himself an adept administrator, he was appointed Lord of Tak (a city in the upper Central Plain), or Phraya Tak. Hence his

History matters

In July 2001 the Lao ambassador to Thailand threatened unspecified retaliation if a planned film depicting a Thai heroine's glorious struggle against the invading army of King Chao Anou offended the Lao people. He didn't specify what might happen but there was talk in Vientiane of a boycott of Thai goods. The Lao ambassador said he would have to see if the king, revered in Laos as someone who stood up to the Thais, 'is depicted in a disgraceful way'. The planned film was to be a historical drama retelling the story of how Khunying Mo, the wife of the deputy governor of Korat in Northeast Thailand, organised the population of the city to thwart the invading army of Chao Anou in 1827. Chao Anou was later defeated by the Siamese army who raced north from Bangkok. He escaped to Hué in Vietnam but was later sent back to Bangkok a prisoner, where he died in 1829. Historians continue to argue whether there is any veracity in this account of Khunying Mo's exploits, but that would seem to be beyond the point. It is part-and-parcel of school history lessons.

While it might seem odd for a Communist government to get hot under the collar about a king who lived and died more than a century and a half ago, when it comes to Lao-Thai relations the merest hint of a slight can cause great offence. The Thais, too, can be very sensitive when it comes to film producers playing around with their history. It is still not possible to see Yul Brunner as King Mongkut cavorting with Anna Leonowens in *The King and I*. When 20th Century Fox released a remake of the film, *Anna and the King* with Jodi Foster as Anna it was banned as well.

As if to make the point that history really does matter in mainland Southeast Asia, at the end of February 2003 a mob of disgruntled Cambodians burnt down the Thai embassy in Phnom Penh. The reason? A two-bit, Thai soap star was reported as saying she thought the ruins of Angkor Wat should be returned to Thailand.

name Tak-sin. From Thonburi, Taksin successfully fought Burmese invasions, until the stress caused his mental health to deteriorate to the extent that he was forced to abdicate in 1782. A European visitor wrote in a letter that 'He [Taksin] passed all his time in prayer, fasting, and meditation, in order by these means to be able to fly through the air'. He became madder by the month and on 6 April 1782 a group of rebels marched on Thonburi, captured the king and asked one of Taksin's generals, Chao Phya Chakri, to assume the throne. The day that Chao Phya Chakri became King Ramathobodi, 6 April, remains a public holiday in Thailand – Chakri Day – and marks the beginning of the current Chakri Dynasty. Worried about the continuing Burmese threat, Rama I (as Chao Phya Chakri is known) moved his capital to the opposite, and safer, bank of the Chao Phraya River, founded Bangkok and began the process of consolidating his kingdom. By the end of the century, the Burmese threat had dissipated, and the Siamese were once again in a position to lead the Tai world.

19th century (Rama II's reign)

During Rama II's reign (1809-24), a new threat emerged to replace the Burmese: that of the Europeans. In 1821, the English *East India Company* sent John Crawfurd as an envoy to Siam to open up trading relations. Although the king and his court remained unreservedly opposed to unfettered trade, Crawfurd's visit served to impress upon those more prescient Siamese where the challenges of the 19th century would lie.

Rama II's death and succession illustrates the dangers inherent in having a claim to the throne of Siam, even in the 19th century. The court chronicles record that in 1824 Prince Mongkut (the second son of Rama II) was ordained as a monk because the death of a royal elephant indicated it was an 'ill-omened time'. Historians believe that Rama II, realizing his death was imminent, wished to protect the young prince by bundling him off to a monastery, where the robes of a monk might protect him from court intrigues.

Rama III was the son of Rama II by a junior wife. When King Rama II died he was chosen by the accession council over Mongkut because the latter was in the monkhood. Rama III's reign (1824-51) saw an invasion by an army led by the Lao King Anou. In 1827, Anou took Nakhon Ratchasima on the edge of the Central Plain and was within striking distance of Bangkok before being defeated. After their victory, the Siamese marched on Vientiane, plundering the city and subjugating the surrounding countryside. In 1829, King Anou himself was captured and transported to Bangkok, where he was displayed to the public in a cage. Anou died shortly after this humiliation – some say of shame, others say of self-administered poison. Before he died he is said to have laid a curse on the Chakri dynasty, swearing that never again would a Chakri king set foot on Lao soil. None has, and when the present king Bhumibol attended the opening of the Thai-Lao Friendship bridge over the Mekong in 1994, he did so from a sand bar in the middle of the river.

There were also ructions at the court in Bangkok: in 1848 Prince Rakrannaret (a distant relative of Rama III's) was found guilty of bribery and corruption and, just for good measure, homosexuality and treason as well. Rama III had him beaten to death with sandalwood clubs, in time-honoured Thai fashion.

The 19th century was a dangerous time for Siam. Southeast Asia was being methodically divided between Britain, France and Holland as they scrambled for colonial territories. The same fate might have befallen Siam, had it not been blessed with two brilliant kings: **King Mongkut (Rama IV – 1851-68)** and **King Chulalongkorn (Rama V – 1868-1910)**.

Mongkut (the second son of Rama II) was a brilliant scholar. He learnt English and Latin and when he sat his oral Pali examination, performed brilliantly. Indeed, his 27 years in a monastery allowed him to study the religious texts to such depth that he concluded that all Siamese ordinations were invalid. He established a new sect based upon the stricter Mon teachings, an order which became known as the *Thammayutika* or 'Ordering Adhering to the Dharma'. To distinguish themselves from those 'fallen' monks who made up most of the Sangha, they wore their robes with both shoulders covered. Mongkut derisively called the main Thai order – the *Mahanikai* – the 'Order of Long-standing Habit'.

But Mongkut was not an other-wordly monk with scholarly inclinations. He was a rational, pragmatic man who well appreciated the economic and military might of the Europeans. He recognized that if his kingdom was to survive he would have to accept and acquiesce to the colonial powers, rather than try to resist them. He did not accede to the throne until he was 47, and it is said that during his monastic studies he came to realize that if China, the Middle Kingdom, had to bow to Western pressure, then he would have to do the same.

He set about modernizing his country, along with the support of other modern-thinking princes. He established a modern ship-building industry, trained his troops in European methods and studied Western medicine. Most importantly, in 1855, he signed the **Bowring Treaty** with Britain, giving British merchants access to the Siamese market, and setting in train a process of agricultural commercialization and the clearing of the vast Central Plains for rice cultivation. As David Wyatt wrote: 'At the stroke of a pen, old Siam faced the thrust of a surging economic and political power with which they were unprepared to contend or compete'. Mongkut's meeting with Sir John Bowring illustrates the lengths to which

Penis balls and sexual roles in historical southeast Asia

One notable feature of Thai – and more widely, Southeast Asian – society is the relative autonomy of women. This is most clearly illustrated in sexual relations. As the historian Anthony Reid wrote in his book *Southeast Asia in the Age of Commerce 1450-1680*: "Southeast Asian literature of the period leaves us in little doubt that women took a very active part in courtship and lovemaking, and demanded as much as they gave by way of sexual and emotional gratification". He then went on to describe the various ways – often involving painful surgery – that men would try to satisfy their partners. Metal pins, for example, were inserted into the penis, and wheels, studs and spurs attached as accessories to increase the female's pleasure. Alternatively, metal balls or bells, sometimes made of gold or ivory, would be inserted beneath the skin of the penis. Numerous early European visitors expressed their astonishment at the practice. Tome Pires, the 16th-century Portuguese apothecary, observed that Pegu lords in Burma 'wear as many as nine gold ones [penis bells], with beautiful treble, contralto and tenor tones, the size of the Alvares plums in our country; and those who are too poor...have them in lead...Malay women rejoice greatly when the Pegu men come to their country... [because of] their sweet harmony'. Whereas, in Africa, genital surgery was, and is, often intended to suppress pleasure for women or increase it for men, in Southeast Asia the reverse was the case. The surgery described above was also widely practised in Burma, Siam, Makassar, among the Torajans of Sulawesi, and Java.

he went to meet the West on its own terms: he received the British envoy and offered him port and cigars from his own hand, an unheard of action in Thai circles.

It would seem that King Mongkut and **Sir John Bowring** were men of like mind. Both were scholars who believed in the power of rational argument. Bowring was a close friend of the philosophers Jeremy Bentham and John Stuart Mill, and he wrote a number of articles for the *Westminster Review*. He was a radical reformer, in favour of free trade and prison reform and bitterly opposed to slavery. He was a member of the House of Commons for six years, governor of Hong Kong, and Her Majesty's Consul in Canton (China). He was a remarkable man, just as Mongkut was a remarkable man, and his achievements during a long 80-year life were enough to satisfy a dozen ambitious men. It seems that Bowring used a mixture of veiled military force and rational argument to encourage Mongkut to sign the Bowring Treaty, perhaps the single most important treaty in Thailand's history. Bowring's account of his visit, the two volume *The kingdom and people of Siam*, published in 1857, is a remarkably perceptive work, especially given the brevity of Bowring's visit to Siam. As David Wyatt wrote in a reprint of the work (Oxford University Press, 1977), the book is undoubtedly 'the finest account of Thailand at the middle of the 19th century, when it stood on the threshold of revolutionary change'.

Unfortunately, in the West, Mongkut is not known for the skilful diplomacy which kept at bay expansionist nations considerably more powerful than his own, but for his characterization in the film *The King and I* (in which he is played by Yul Brynner). Poorly adapted from Anna Leonowens' own distorted accounts of her period as governess in the Siamese court, both the book and the film offend the Thai people. According to contemporary accounts, Mrs Leonowens was a bad

tempered lady obviously given to flights of fantasy. She never became a trusted confidant of King Mongkut, who scarcely needed her limited skills, and there is certainly no evidence to indicate that he was attracted to her sexually. It appears that she was plain in appearance.

King Mongkut died on 1 October 1868 and was succeeded by his 15-year-old son **Chulalongkorn**. However, for the next decade a regent controlled affairs of state, and it was not until 1873, when Chulalongkorn was crowned for a second time, that he could begin to mould the country according to his own vision. The young king quickly showed himself to be a reformer like his father – for in essence Mongkut had only just begun the process of modernization. Chulalongkorn set about updating the monarchy by establishing ministries and ending the practice of prostration. He also accelerated the process of economic development by constructing roads, railways, schools and hospitals. The opium trade was regulated, court procedures streamlined and slavery finally completely abolished in 1905. Although a number of princes were sent abroad to study – Prince Rajebuidirekrit went to Oxford – Chulalongkorn had to also rely on foreign advisors to help him undertake these reforms. In total he employed 549 foreigners – the largest number being British, but also Dutch, Germans, French and Belgians. Chulalongkorn even held fancy dress parties at New Year and visited Europe twice. These visits included trips to the poor East End of London and showed Chulalongkorn that for all the power of Britain and France, they were still unable to raise the living standards of a large part of the population much above subsistence levels.

These reforms were not introduced without difficulty. The *Hua Boran* – or 'The Ancients' – as the King derogatorily called them, strongly resisted the changes and in late December 1874 Prince Wichaichan attempted to take the royal palace and usurp the king. The plot was thwarted at the last possible moment, but it impressed upon Chulalongkorn that reform could only come slowly. Realizing he had run ahead of many of his subjects in his zeal for change, he reversed some of his earlier reforms, and toned-down others. Nevertheless, Siam remained on the path of modernization – albeit progressing at a rather slower pace. As during Mongkut's reign, Chulalongkorn also managed to keep the colonial powers at bay. Although the king himself played a large part in placating the Europeans by skilful diplomacy and by presenting an image of urbane sophistication, he was helped in this respect by a brilliant minister of foreign affairs, his son, Prince Devawongse (1858-1923), who controlled Siam's foreign relations for 38 years. Devawongse looked into European systems of government with the aim of reforming Siam's administration and even attended the celebrations marking Queen Victoria's 50 years on the throne of Great Britain in 1887. During his time controlling Siam's foreign affairs, a new administrative system and a new system of ministries was introduced to extend Bangkok's power to the outer provinces.

The fundamental weakness of the Siamese state, in the face of the European powers, was illustrated in the **dispute with France over Laos**. Despite attempts by Prince Devawongse to manufacture a compromise, the French forced Siam to cede Laos to France in 1893 and to pay compensation – even though they had little claim to the territory. (The land on the far banks of the Mekong came under Thai suzerainty. The French annexed Laos on some rather dubious evidence that Vietnam – which they controlled – claimed suzerainty over Laos.) As it is said, power grows out of the barrel of a gun, and Chulalongkorn could not compete with France in military might. After this humiliating climbdown, the king essentially retired from public life, broken in spirit and health. In 1909, the British chipped away at more of Siam's territory, gaining rights of suzerainty over the Malay states of Kelantan, Terengganu, Kedah and Perlis. In total, Siam relinquished nearly 500,000 sq km of territory to maintain the integrity of the core of the kingdom. King Chulalongkorn died on 24 October 1910, sending the whole nation into deep and genuine mourning.

20th century

The kings that were to follow Mongkut and Chulalongkorn could not have been expected to have had such illustrious, brilliant reigns. Absolute kingship was becoming increasingly incompatible with the demands of the modern world, and the kings of Thailand were resisting the inevitable. Rama VI, **King Vajiravudh** (1910-25), second son of Chulalongkorn, was educated at Oxford and Sandhurst Military Academy and seemed well prepared for kingship. However, he squandered much of the wealth built up by Chulalongkorn and ruled in a rather heavy-handed, uncoordinated style. He did try to inculcate a sense of 'nation' with his slogan 'nation, religion, king', but seemed more interested in Western theatre and literature than in guiding Siam through a difficult period in its history. He died at the age of only 44, leaving an empty treasury.

Like his older brother, **King Prajadhipok** (Rama VII – 1925-35), was educated in Europe: at Eton, the Woolwich Military Academy and at the Ecole Superieure de Guerre in France. But he never expected to become king and was thrust onto the throne at a time of great strain. Certainly, he was more careful with the resources that his treasury had to offer, but could do little to prevent the country being seriously affected by the Great Depression of the 1930s. The price of rice, the country's principal export, declined by two-thirds and over the same two-year period (1930-32) land values in Bangkok fell by 80%. The economy was in crisis and the government appeared to have no idea how to cope. In February 1932, King Prajadhipok told a group of military officers:

"The financial war is a very hard one indeed. Even experts contradict one another until they become hoarse. Each offers a different suggestion. I myself know nothing at all about finances, and all I can do is listen to the opinions of others and choose the best. I have never experienced such a hardship; therefore if I have made a mistake I really deserve to be excused by the officials and people of Siam".

The people, both the peasantry and the middle class, were dissatisfied by the course of events and with their declining economic position. But neither group was sufficiently united to mount a threat to the King and his government. Nevertheless, Prajadhipok was worried: there was a prophesy linked to Rama I's younger sister Princess Narinthewi, which predicted that the Chakri Dynasty would survive for 150 years and end on 6 April 1932.

The Revolution of 1932

The date itself passed without incident, but just 12 weeks later on 24 June a clique of soldiers and civilians staged a **coup d'état**, while the king was holidaying at the seaside resort of Hua Hin. This episode is often called the Revolution of 1932, but it was not in any sense a revolution involving a large rump of the people. It was orchestrated by a small èlite, essentially for the èlite. The king accepted the terms offered to him, and wrote:

'I have received the letter in which you invite me to return to Bangkok as a constitutional monarch. For the sake of peace; and in order to save useless bloodshed; to avoid confusion and loss to the country; and, more, because I have already considered making this change myself, I am willing to co-operate in the establishment of a constitution under which I am willing to serve.'

Reign of Prince Ananda Mahidol

However, King Prajadhipok had great difficulty adapting to his lesser role and, falling out with the military, he abdicated in favour of his young nephew, Prince Ananda Mahidol, in 1935. The prince at the time was only 10 years old, and at school in Switzerland, so the newly created National Assembly appointed two princes to act as

Thai, Siamese or Tai?

Is a Thai a Tai? And is this the same as a Siamese? Sometimes. Thai here is used to mean a national of Thailand. Prior to the Second World War, Thailand was known as Siam, a name by which Europeans had referred to the kingdom from the 16th century. However, in 1939 Prime Minister Phibun Songkhram decided a change was in order, largely because he wished to disassociate his country from the past, but also because of his xenophobia towards the Chinese. The name he chose is a more direct translation of the Thai term prathet Thai, and firmly established Thailand as the 'country of the Tais'. Nonetheless, because the change is associated with the right-wing Phibun government, some academics still refuse to use the name and talk, rather pointlessly, of Siam.

Tai here is used to refer to the Tai-speaking peoples who are found not just in Thailand, but also in Burma, Laos and southern China. Some Thais are not Tai (for example, the Malay-speaking Thais of the south), while many Tais are not Thais. As David Wyatt wrote in his Thailand: A Short History:

'The modern Thai may or may not be descended by blood from the late-arriving Tai. He or she may instead be the descendant of still earlier Mon or Khmer inhabitants of the region, or of much later Chinese or Indian immigrants. Only over many centuries has a 'Thai' culture, a civilization and identity emerged as the product of interaction between Tai and indigenous and immigrant cultures.'

A slightly different issue is the question of what makes a Thai a Thai. In other words, what are the defining characteristics of Thai-ness. This is shaky ground, dotted with metaphorical minefields. Ethnicity is noted on every Thai's identity card, but there is no system governing the categories applied. A person with 'Chinese' parents is counted a 'Thai', yet a Muslim Thai from the south is counted a 'Muslim', not a Thai. Some would say that there is method in this muddle, and that being a Theravada Buddhist is a critical component of being counted a true 'Thai'. Rather less contentious is an uncritical love of the King. All schoolchildren are taught that Thai-ness is encapsulated in three symbols, 'King, Nation, Religion', and this goes much of the way to explaining what the average Thai views as representative of being a Thai.

regents. From this point, until after the Second World War, the monarchy was only partially operative. Ananda was out of the country for most of the time, and the civilian government took centre stage. Ananda was not to physically reoccupy the throne until December 1945 and just six months later he was found dead in bed, a bullet through his head. The circumstances behind his death have never been satisfactorily explained and it remains a subject on which Thais are not openly permitted to speculate. Books investigating the death are still banned in Thailand.

Phibun Songkhram and Pridi Panomyong

While the monarchy receded from view, the civilian government was going through the intrigues and power struggles which were to become such a feature of the future politics of the country. The two key men at this time were the army officer Phibun Songkhram and the left-wing idealist lawyer Pridi Panomyong. Between them they managed to dominate Thai politics until 1957.

When **Prime Minister Pridi Panomyong** tried to introduce a socialist economic programme in 1933, pushing for the state control of the means of production, he was forced into exile in Europe. This is often seen as the beginning of the tradition of authoritarian, right-wing rule in Thailand, although to be fair, Pridi's vision of economic and political reform was poorly thought through and rather romantic. Nonetheless, with Pridi in Paris – at least for a while – it gave the more conservative elements in the government the chance to promulgate an anti-communist law, and thereby to usher in a period of ultra-nationalism. Anti-Chinese propaganda became more shrill, with some government positions being reserved for ethnic Tais. In 1938 the populist writer Luang Wichit compared the Chinese in Siam with the Jews in Germany, and thought that Hitler's policies might be worth considering for his own country.

This shift in policy can be linked to the influence of one man: Luang Phibun Songkhram. Born of humble parents in 1897, he worked his way up through the army ranks and then into politics. He became Prime Minister in 1938 and his enduring influence makes him the most significant figure in 20th century Thai politics. Under his direction, Siam became more militaristic, xenophobic, as well as 'religiously' nationalistic, avidly pursuing the reconversion of Siamese Christians back to Buddhism. As if to underline these developments, in 1939 Siam adopted a new name: Thailand. Phibun justified this change on the grounds that it would indicate that the country was controlled by Thais and not by the Chinese or any other group.

Second World War

During the Second World War, Phibun Songkhram sided with the Japanese who he felt sure would win. He saw the war as an opportunity to take back some of the territories lost to the French (particularly) and the British. In 1940, Thai forces invaded Laos and Western Cambodia. A year later, the Japanese used the kingdom as a launching pad for their assaults on the British in Malaya and Burma. Thailand had little choice but to declare war on the Allies and to agree a military alliance with Japan in December 1941. As allies of the Japanese, Phibun's ambassadors were instructed to declare war on Britain and the United States. However, the ambassador in Washington, Seni Pramoj, refused to deliver the declaration (he considered it illegal) and Thailand never formally declared war on the USA. In Thailand itself, Pridi, who had returned as regent to the young monarch King Ananda, helped to organize the Thai resistance – the Free Thai Movement. They received help from the US Office of Strategic Services (OSS) and the British Force 136, and also from many Thais. As the tide of the war turned in favour of the Allies, so Prime Minister Phibun was forced to resign. He spent a short time in gaol in Japan, but was allowed to return to Thailand in 1947.

Post-war Thailand

After the war, Seni Pramoj, Thailand's ambassador in the USA, became Prime Minister. He was soon followed by Pridi Panomyong as Prime Minister, who had gathered a good deal of support due to the role he played during the conflict. However, in 1946 King Ananda was mysteriously found shot dead in his royal apartments and Pridi was implicated in a plot. He was forced to resign, so enabling Phibun to become Prime Minister once again – a post he kept until 1957. Phibun's fervent anti-Communism quickly gained support in the USA, who contributed generous amounts of aid as the country became a front-line state in the battle against the 'red tide' that seemed to be engulfing Asia. Phibun's closest brush with death occurred in June 1951. He was leading a ceremony on board a dredge, the *Manhattan*, when he was taken prisoner during a military coup and transferred to the Thai navy flagship *Sri Ayutthaya*. The airforce and army stayed loyal to Phibun, and planes bombed the ship. As it sank, the Prime Minister was able to swim to safety. The attempted coup resulted in 1,200 dead – mostly civilians. For the navy, it has meant that ever since it has been treated as the junior member of the armed forces, receiving far less resources than the army and airforce.

Thailand enters the modern period (1911-46)

1910	King Chulalongkorn dies, his second son Vajiravudh accedes to the throne
1911	Wild Tiger Corp established - an adult unit and a youth unit, is formed which became Thailand's scout movement. They also became ultra-nationalist and ultra-monarchist and were implicated, for example, in the massacre of students outside Thammasat University in 1976
1912	Attempted coup against the king is thwarted
1917	A small force of Siamese soldiers is sent to Europe to fight with the Allies in the First World War
1919-20	Appalling rice harvest and other economic problems lead to severe economic difficulties
1925	King Vajiravudh dies at the age of only 44 on 26 November
1927	King Prajadhipok (educated at Eton and the Woolwich Military Academy) writes a paper on 'Democracy in Siam', and also appoints an advisory council to deliberate on government reform
1930-32	Great Depression hits Siam
1932	The Revolution of 24 June, and Siam becomes a constitutional monarchy. Phraya Mano becomes the first Prime Minister
1935	King Prajadiphok abdicates on 2 March. King Ananda Mahidol comes to the throne aged just 10. Two princes rule while he is finishing his schooling in Switzerland.
1938	Phibun Songkram becomes PM and introduces nationalistic and anti-Chinese policies
1939	Phibun changes the country's name from Siam to Thailand
1940	Thai forces invade Laos and Cambodia following the German defeat of France
1941	Japanese forces invade Thailand, and Bangkok is forced to agree a military alliance with Japan in December
1944	Phibun is forced to resign with the Japanese on the verge of defeat
1945	King Ananda Mahidol returns to Thailand to take his throne
1946	King Ananda Mahidol is killed in mysterious circumstances. His brother King Bhumibol Adulyadej comes to the throne

Prime Minister Phibun Songkhram was deposed following a coup d'état in 1957, and was replaced by **General Sarit Thanarat**. General Sarit established the National Economic Development Board (now the National Economic and Social Development Board) and introduced Thailand's first five-year national development plan in 1961. He was a tough, uncompromising leader, and following his death in 1963 was replaced by another General – **Thanom Kitticachorn**. With the war in Indochina escalating, Thanom allowed US planes to be based in Thailand, from where they flew bombing sorties over the Lao panhandle and Vietnam. In 1969 a general election was held, which Thanom won, but as the political situation in Thailand deteriorated, so Prime Minister Thanom declared martial law. However, unlike his predecessors Sarit and Phibun, Thanom could not count on the loyalty of all elements within the armed forces, and although he tried to take the strongman – or *nak laeng* – approach, his

administration always had a frailty about it. In addition, historian David Wyatt argues that developments in Thai society – particularly an emergent middle-class and an increasingly combative body of students – made controlling the country from the centre rather harder than it had been over the previous decades.

The October Revolution

It was Thailand's students who precipitated probably the single most tumultuous event since the Revolution of 1932. The student body felt that Thanom had back-tracked and restricted the evolution of a more open political system in the country. In June 1973 they began to demonstrate against the government, printing highly critical pamphlets and calling for the resignation of Thanom. A series of demonstrations, often centred on Sanaam Luang near the radical Thammasat University and the Grand Palace, brought crowds of up to 500,000 onto the streets. During the demonstrations, Thanom lost the support of the army: the Commander-in-Chief, General Krit Sivara, was unwilling to send his troops out to quell the disturbances, while Thanom, apparently, was quite willing to kill thousands if necessary. With the army unwilling to confront the students, and with the King – crucially – also apparently siding with Thanom's army opponents, he was forced to resign from the premiership and fled the country.

David Wyatt wrote of the **October revolution**: 'In many important respects, the events of October 1973 deserved far more the name *revolution* than either the events of 1932 or the authoritarian program of Sarit. They brought about an end to one-man, authoritarian rule; and if they did not bring an end to the military role in politics, then they at least signaled a new consciousness of the necessity of sharing political power more widely than had ever been the case in the past.'

The October revolution ushered in a period of **turbulent democratic government** in Thailand, the first such period in the country's history. It was an exciting time: radical scholars could openly speak and publish, students could challenge the establishment, labour unions could organize and demonstrate, and leftist politicians could make their views known. But it was also a period of political instability. While there had been just five prime ministers between 1948 and 1973, the three years following 1973 saw the rapid coming and going of another four: Sanya Dharmasakti (October 1973-February 1975), Seni Pramoj (February-March 1975), Kukrit Pramoj (March 1975-January 1976) and Seni Pramoj (April-October 1976). This instability was reinforced by the feeling among the middle classes that the students were pushing things too far. The fall of Vietnam, Cambodia and Laos to Communism left many Thais wondering whether they would be the next 'domino' to topple. This gave an opening for rightist groups to garner support, and anti-Communist organizations like the Red Gaurs and the Village Scouts gained in influence and began, with the support and connivance of the police, to harrass and sometimes to murder left-wingers. 'Violence, vituperation, and incivility', as Wyatt wrote, 'were now a part of public life as they never had been before in Thailand'.

Thammaset University Massacre

This was the background that led the army to feel impelled to step in once again. However, the trigger for the **appalling events of October 1976** was the return of former Prime Minister Thanom from exile, who joined the sangha and became a monk. Installed in a Bangkok monastery, Thanom was visited by members of the royal family. The students took this as royal recognition of a man who had led the country into violence and to the edge of civil war. Demonstrations broke out in Bangkok, again centred on Sanaam Luang and the nearby Democracy Monument. This time, though, the students were not able to face down the forces of the Right. Newspapers printed pictures apparently showing the Crown Prince being burnt in effigy by students at Thammasat, and right wing groups, along with the police and the army, advanced on

 the university on 6 October. Details of the hours that followed are hazy. However, it seems clear that an orgy of killing ensued. With the situation rapidly deteriorating, the army stepped in and imposed martial law. Tanin Kraivixien was installed as Prime Minister, to be replaced the following year by Kriangsak Chomanan.

In 1996, on the **20th anniversary** of the massacre, newspapers in Thailand were filled with the reminiscences of those from both sides who were involved. The bones of the tragic episode were picked over exhaustively and the still grieving parents of some of those who were murdered or 'disappeared' were interviewed. Such was the coverage of the event – far more detailed and honest than anything at the time – that it was almost as if the Thai nation were engaged in a collective catharsis, cauterizing the wounds of 20 years earlier. Yet in a way the debate over the massacre said as much about the present as the past. Kasian Tejapira, one of the student leaders involved, and by 1996 a university lecturer, suggested that the anniversary was an opportunity "to redefine the meaning of Thai identity – one that is anti-elitist and not conservative; one that was put down at Thammasat 20 years ago". The former student activists are now in positions of power and influence. Some are wealthy businessmen, others university lecturers, while more still are involved in politics. Most seem to have retained their commitment to building a more just society. It must be somewhat depressing for them to find the students of today more interested in fashions and consumer goods than in social justice. In a way that – in microcosm – is the problem with Thailand's political culture: too much money and too few ethics.

The 1976 massacre was a shot in the arm for the **Communist Party of Thailand (CPT)**. Left-wing intellectuals and many students, feeling that they could no longer influence events through the political system, fled to the jungle and joined the CPT. The victories of the Communists in neighbouring Indochina also reinforced the sense that ultimately the CPT would emerge victorious. By the late 1970s the ranks of the party had swelled to around 14,000 armed guerrillas, who controlled large areas of the northeast, north and south. However, with the ascendancy of Prem Tinsulanond to the premiership in 1980 and a rapidly changing global political environment, the CPT fragmented and quickly lost support. Its leaders were divided between support for China and the Cambodian Khmer Rouge on the one hand, and the Soviet Union and Vietnam on the other. When the government announced an amnesty in 1980, many of the students who had fled into the forests and hills following the riots of 1973 returned to mainstream politics, exhausted and disenchanted with revolutionary life. In true Thai style, they were largely forgiven and re-integrated into society. But those who died on Sanaam Luang and in the streets leading off it have never been acknowledged, and in many cases their parents were never informed that they had been killed. Nor were they allowed to collect their children's bodies. As the Thai historian Thongchai Winichakul lamented on the 20th anniversary of the massacre in 1996, this showed the extent to which Thai society still valued national stability over individual rights: "Life is more significant than the nation."

Prem Tinsulanond presided over the most stable period in Thai politics since the end of the Second World War. He finally resigned in 1988, and by then Thailand – or so most people thought – was beginning to outgrow the habit of military intervention in civilian politics. Chatichai Choonhaven replaced Prem after general elections in 1988, by which time the country was felt to be more stable and economically prosperous than at any time in recent memory. During his reign, the present King Bhumibol has played a crucial role in maintaining social stability, while the political system has been in turmoil. He is highly revered by his subjects, and has considerable power to change the course of events. There are essentially two views on the role of the king in contemporary Thailand. The general view is that he has influence far beyond that which his constitutional position strictly permits, but that he is careful not to overexercise that power and only intervenes at times of crisis. The king, in short, is his own man and acts in the best interests of the Thai people. The

alternative view is that after his coronation, influential courtiers and generals tried to diminish the power of the king by making him a semi-divine figurehead and surrounding him in protocol. The king became a tool used by right-wing dictators and the army to justify their authoritarian ways. (For further background on the King, see the box on page 644.)

From massacre to crisis: 1991-97

The widely held belief that the Thai political system had come of age proved ill-founded. In February 1991, with the Prime Minister daring to challenge the armed forces, **General Suchinda Kraprayoon staged a bloodless coup d'état** and ousted the democratically elected government of Chatichai Choonhavan. The last decade of the 20th century was a pretty eventful one for Thailand. At the end of the year, egged on by two generals-turned-politicians – Chamlong Srimuang and Chaovalit Yongchaiyut – 100,000 people gathered in Bangkok to protest against a Suchinda and military-imposed constitution. Elections in March 1992 produced no clear winner and General Suchinda tearfully agreed to become premier – something he had previously promised he would not do. Chamlong Srimuang took this as his cue to call his supporters onto the streets and announced he was going on hunger strike. Tens of thousands of people gathered around the Parliament buildings and Sanaam Luang, near the Grand Palace. Suchinda buckled under this weight of public outrage and appeared to agree to their demands. But Suchinda went back on his word, and in response tens of thousands of demonstrators returned to the streets. Suchinda called in the army and scores of people were killed.

Three days after the confrontation between the army and the demonstrators, **King Bhumibol** ordered both Suchinda and opposition leader Chamlong – who had to be released from gaol for the meeting – to his palace. There, television cameras were waiting to witness Suchinda's global, public humiliation. He and Chamlong prostrated themselves on the floor while the king lectured them, asking rhetorically: "What is the use of victory when the winner stands on wreckage?" Immediately afterwards, the army and the demonstrators withdrew from the streets. On Friday, Suchinda offered his resignation to the King, and on Saturday, less than one week after the killing began, Suchinda Kraprayoon fled the country. In a televised address, Suchinda accepted responsibility for the deaths.

After the riots of May 1992, and General Suchinda's humiliating climbdown, Anand Panyarachun was appointed interim prime minister. New elections were set for September, which the Democrat Party won. **Chuan Leekpai** was appointed 1992's fourth prime minister. Chuan, a mild-mannered Southerner from a poor background – his father was a fish vendor in Trang – gained his law degree while living as a novice monk in a monastery. Never one for flashiness and quick fixes, Chuan became known as Chuan Chuengcha – or Chuan the slowmover. He may have been slow but his government lasted more than 2½ years, making it the longest serving elected government in Thai history, before he was forced to resign over a land scandal.

The Chart Thai Party, led by 62-year-old **Banharn Silpa-Archa**, won the election – or at least the largest number of seats – and formed a coalition government of seven parties. Bangkok's intelligentsia were horrified. Like Chuan, Banharn came from a poor background and was very much a self-made man. But in almost all other respects, Banharn and Chuan could not have been more different. Banharn's Chart Thai was closely associated with the military junta and was viewed as incorrigibly corrupt. As British political scientist Duncan McCargo explained: 'there's no movement for [true] democracy. There's nothing but the money, and the results [of the election] bear that out'. Two Chart Thai candidates in the elections were even accused of involvement in the narcotics trade. Thanong Wongwan was indicted in California with drug trafficking, where he was reportedly known as 'Thai Tony', and the party's deputy leader Vatana Asavahame had a visa request turned down by the US

Jit Poumisak's radical history

Most histories of Thailand tell a conservative tale: of peasants working in the fields, protected by the merit of a benevolent king. Indeed, many Thai historians seem to go out of their way to paint a picture of Thailand's history, which is notable for its conservativism. It is no accident that perhaps the greatest early Thai historian, Damrong Rajanubhab, was himself a Chakri prince. Throughout the 19th century and the first half of the 20th century, Thai scholars eschewed radicalism and perpetuated a conservative view of Thai history.

In 1957 this cosy world was disrupted by the publication (in Thai) of Jit Poumisak's *The real face of Thai feudalism today*. The book turned Thai history on its head. For the first time, it presented a picture of Thailand where feudalism, and not just benevolent monarchs, reigned; where the masses were engaged in a struggle against oppressive rulers; where history was interpreted through economics; and where the social system governed relations between classes. It was Thailand's history with a Marxist visage.

Jit's reinterpretation of Thai history was, at least in the Thai context, astounding for its daring. Religion and culture were recast as the agents through which kings maintained their positions of power. Peasants – the great mass of the population – became pawns manipulated in the interests of the ruling classes, their impoverished position both maintained and justified in terms of religion and culture.

Jit's work was not received particularly warmly by Thailand's elite. In 1958 the book was banned and Jit was imprisoned for sedition. In 1973 it was republished during Thailand's experiment in democracy, only to be banned again in 1977, as the forces of dictatorship gained the upper hand. In 1979 it was reprinted for a third time as the threat of Communism receded and

authorities on similar grounds. Banharn was even accused of plagiarism in his Masters thesis, which is said to bear a striking similarity to a paper by his academic advisor – who Banharn appointed to his cabinet.

While the press may have hated Banharn – *The Nation* stated that 'the only way for 1996 to be a good year is for the Banharn government to go' – he survived because he was an arch populist politician. He used to step from his limousine and order local officials to mend roads, provide electricity, or improve health services. Here was a man getting things done, sweeping away red tape, and putting the interests of ordinary people first. But while Banharn might have been able to ignore the press, he couldn't ignore the King. In late summer 1995, Banharn's government found itself explicitly criticized by the palace when the King highlighted government failures to address Bangkok's infrastructural mess and its shortcomings in dealing with serious flooding. Ministers, the King said, only "talk, talk, talk and argue, argue, argue". Taking the King's cue, the great and the good including businessmen, influential civil servants, four former Bank of Thailand governors, opposition politicians (of course), even his own daughter, demanded that he step down. On 21 September 1996 Banharn announced his resignation. The King dissolved parliament.

The **elections of 17 November 1996** were close, with **Chaovalit Yongchaiyudh's** New Aspirations Party (NAP) just managing to win the largest number of seats, and after the usual bickering and horse-trading he managed to stitch together a six-party coalition controlling 221 seats in the 393-seat House of Representatives. Chaovalit, a canny 64-year-old former army commander-in-chief, never completely managed to hide his ambition to become premier. He was an old-style patronage

remains in print, required reading by every student of Thai history.

During the brief phase of democratic politics between 1973 and 1976, Jit became a central figure in the Left's struggle against the Right. Students read his works and seminars were arranged to discuss his life and thoughts. Jit became an emblem of – and an emblem for – the Left. By all accounts he was a brilliant scholar with a highly original mind.

His radical inclinations first became evident in 1953 when he was appointed editor of the Chulalongkorn University Yearbook. But just before the book went to press, the university authorities tried to halt its publication, claiming it was seditious. A university assembly was called to discuss the affair and some 3,000 students attended. Jit made an impassioned and eloquent speech defending his editorial role, but just as the audience seemed to be swinging in his favour a group of engineering students rushed the stage and knocked Jit unconscious.

From that moment on, Jit was on the outside. He continued to enrage the authorities with his radical writings. He was arrested and interrogated by the police. He moved closer to the Communist Party of Thailand – although he was not made a member until after his death. The final break with the establishment came in 1965, when he left Bangkok and fled to the jungle to join in the Communist Party of Thailand's struggle against the government. Less than a year later, in May 1966, he was shot and killed in Sakhon Nakhon province in the Northeastern region. Accounts differ on who shot him. However, it seems that a local headman killed him, possibly as he and a fellow insurgent stopped to barter for supplies. According to one source, a hand was cut from the corpse and sent to Bangkok for identification.

politician who depended on his links with the army and on handing out lucrative concessions to his supporters. "Transparency", as Democrat MP Surin Pitsuwan was quoted as saying in August 1996, "is not in his dictionary".

In retrospect, the mid-1990s were a watershed in contemporary Thailand's history. On 18 July 1995 the Princess Mother (the King's mother) died. After the King she was probably the most revered person in the country. Born a commoner and trained as a nurse, she married a prince. Their two sons, Mahidol and Bhumipol, unexpectedly became kings (Mahidol for only a short time before his tragic death). Her funeral in 1996 was a grandiose affair and her death has been likened to that of Britain's Princess Diana. Even Bangkok's massage parlours closed as a mark of respect. 1996 also saw the 50th anniversary of King Bhumibol's accession to the throne and the country threw a massive party to celebrate the event. The celebrations were as much a mark of Thailand's coming of age as of the King's golden jubilee. No expense was spared by the newly self-confident Tiger Thailand. Both events – the Princess Mother's funeral and the King's jubilee – were, for those so inclined, omens. The night before the funeral there was an unseasonable rainstorm; and during the procession of royal boats on the Chao Phraya it also poured. The King's boat was washed off course and had to be rescued by the navy. As it turned out, 1996 was the last year when money was no object.

Today Thailand is stable and although there is no way to predict what might happen tomorrow or next year there is little sense that army generals are plotting in smoke-filled rooms. That said, it is worth reflecting on the raw political data of the 71 years since the abolition of the absolute monarchy in 1932: 17 coups, 53 governments and 16 constitutions. Moreover, army strongmen have been in power for 49 of those 71 years. Quite a record.

Modern Thailand (1997-)

Constitutional and political makeup

Thailand is a constitutional monarchy. The head of state is King Bhumibol Adulyadej (Rama IX). The head of government is the Prime Minister, currently Taksin Shinawatra who leads a coalition headed by his own Thai Rak Thai Party. A new constitution was introduced in March 2000 reforming the legislative system. The legislature comprises a 500-member House of Representatives (the Lower House) which consists of 400 constituency MPs and 100 MPs drawn from party lists. The maximum term of a government is four years, but the PM can dissolve parliament earlier. There is also a 200-member Senate (the Upper House), also democratically elected but for a period of six years. Senators cannot stand for re-election. The next election for the Lower House must be held before 2005, and for the Upper House by March 2006. The new constitution, as well as reforming the political system, also established a National Counter Corruption Commission, a Constitutional Court, a national Human Rights Commission, and a new national Election Commission.

Bust, boom and bust

As Thailand entered the 21st century and the third millennium, the country was also, rather shakily, recovering from the deepest contraction of the economy since the 1930s. Until July 1997, everything was hunkydory in Thailand. Or that, at least, is what the World Bank and most business people and pundits thought. The Kingdom's economy was expanding at close to double-digit rates and the country was being showered with strings of congratulatory epithets. It was a 'miracle' economy, an Asian 'tiger' or 'dragon' ready to pounce on an unsuspecting world. Thailand has become the 'Cinderella' of Southeast Asia – a beautiful woman long disguised beneath shabby clothes – and academics and journalists were turning out books with glowing titles like *Thailand's Boom* (1996), *Thailand's Turn: Profile of a New Dragon* (1992) and *Thailand's Macro-economic Miracle* (1996). Wealth was growing, poverty falling and Bangkok was chock-full of designer shops, meeting the consumer needs of a growing – and increasingly hedonistic – middle-class.

Of course even in the heady days of double digit economic growth there were those who questioned the direction and rapidity of the country's development, and the social, economic and environmental tensions and conflicts that arose. By the mid-1990s Bangkok was overstretched, its transport system on the verge of collapse and the air barely fit to breath. While a few breezed from boutique to club in their air-conditioned Mercedes, around one million people were living in slum conditions in the capital. Deforestation had become so rampant, and so uncontrolled, that the government felt impelled to impose a nationwide logging ban in 1989. Even the Kingdom's national parks were being systematically poached and encroached. In the poor Northeastern region, incomes had stagnated, causing social tensions to become more acute and millions to migrate to the capital each dry season in a desperate search for work. In some villages in the North, meanwhile, AIDS had already spread to the extent that scarcely a household was not touched by the epidemic.

Most of these problems, though, were viewed by many analysts as side effects of healthy economic growth – problems to be managed through prudent planning and not reasons to doubt the wisdom of the country's broader development strategy.

Economic crisis

Then everything went horribly wrong. The local currency, the baht, went into freefall, the stockmarket crashed, unemployment more than doubled, and the economy contracted. Bankrupt business people, the *nouveau pauvre*, cashed in their

Post-war Thailand (1946-present)

1946	King Bhumibol accedes to the throne
1951	Attempted coup by the Navy against PM Phibun Songkhram (he became PM again) is thwarted by the army and airforce
1957	Sarit Thanarat become PM; he ushers in the era of modern development, known as samai pattana
1961	Publication of the first of Thailand's Five Year Development Plans
1963	Thanom Kitticachorn replaces Sarit as PM following Sarit's death
1964	US military aircraft are based on Thai soil. Operations increase as the Vietnam War escalates
1967	Thailand becomes a founder member of the Association of Southeast Asian Nations (ASEAN), following the signing of the Bangkok Treaty in the Thai capital
1967	Bangkok agrees to send a ground combat unit to support the USA in South Vietnam
1968	45,000 US personnel in Thailand and 600+ aircraft
1973	Massive demonstrations at Thammasat University in support of democracy leads to the resignation of Thanom
1973-76	Period of turbulent democratic government
1976	Massacre of students at Thammasat University in Bangkok as the military step in again. A shot in the arm for the CPT
late 1970s	CPT has 14,000 men and women under arms
1980	Prem Tinsulanond becomes PM
mid-1980s	CPT a spent force. Thailand enters its period of rapid economic growth
1988	Democratic elections, Chatichai Choonhaven becomes PM
1991	Suchinda Kraprayoon leads a succesful coup against Chatichai's administration
1992	Massacre of anti-dictatorship demonstrators in Sanaam Luang
1992	Democratic elections
1995	The King of Thailand celebrates 50 years on the throne
1997	Baht is devalued and Thailand's economic crisis begins
2000	Thaksin Shinawatra becomes prime minister after landslide election victory

Mercedes, and wives were put on strict spending diets. Almost overnight, apparently prescient commentators, who had remained strangely silent during the years of growth, were offering their own interpretations of Thailand's fall from economic grace. A distinct whiff of schadenfreude filled the air. Epithet writers went back to their computers and came up with titles like the 'Asian contagion', the 'Asian mirage', 'Frozen miracles' and 'Tigers lose their grip'. In Thailand itself, locals began to talk of the *Thaitanic* as it sank faster than the doomed liner.

The financial crisis of July 1997 quickly became a much wider economic crisis. The failure of the economy was, in turn, interpreted as a failure of government. Prime Minister Chaovalit Yongchaiyut tried to sound convincing in the face of a collapsing currency and a contracting economy, but he resigned before the year was out. Chuan Leekpai, his successor, manfully struggled to put things to rights but after little more than two years at the helm was trounced in a general election in early 2001 by

 telecoms billionaire Thaksin Shinawatra. Perhaps most importantly in the long term, while Thailand was on the economic ropes, Parliament approved a radically new constitution aimed at cleaning up Thailand's notoriously corrupt political system.

In the 1970s some scholars suggested that the country could be encapsulated by reference to the 'four Rs': rice, rivers, religion and royalty. Today, computer parts, jewellery and garments all exceed rice in terms of export value. Highways have replaced rivers as arteries of communication and religion has become so commercialized that Thais have coined a word to describe it: *Buddhapanich*. Only the King has stood head and shoulders above the fray, the one thread of continuity in a country changing and re-inventing itself with bewildering speed.

'Traditional' Thai life is becoming the stuff of history as modernity engulfs people and places. But just as the recent past becomes sepia-tinted, so the future becomes less compelling. The country's green movement has long lamented the environmental costs of economic growth, and sociologists have highlighted the wasted youth, the drug culture and the underclass as evidence of the corrosive social effects of modernization. Tourism has brought its own problems as popular islands creak under the pressure of growing numbers of visitors. Some educated Thais blame tourists for the explosion of the sex industry and the proliferation of AIDS (see page 661). Where Thailand is headed as it continues its roller coaster ride is as much a mystery as a challenge.

Politics

Politics during an economic crisis: 1997-2000

Chaovalit was, in a sense, unlucky to take over the reins of government when he did. Economic conditions were a cause for concern in the country in late 1996, but no one – scholar or pundit – predicted the economic meltdown that was just a few months away. He appointed the well-respected Amnuay Virawan as Finance Minister. But the collapse of the baht, the Bangkok stock market, the property and finance sectors, and a haemorrhaging loss of domestic and international confidence created conditions that were impossible to manage. Even so, his performance was hardly memorable. As *The Economist* tartly put it, 'he dithered when decisions were needed, bumbled when clear words might have helped, and smiled benignly while the economy got worse'. The central bank spent a staggering US$10bn trying to defend the baht's peg to the US dollar, and interest rates were raised to 1,300% for offshore borrowers in an ultimately futile attempt to keep the speculators at bay. The baht was allowed to float on 2 July, ending 13 years during which it had been pegged to the US dollar. Two cabinet reshuffles during August did little to stem the criticism of Chaovalit and his administration, and there was talk of military intervention – though the army commander-in-chief quickly distanced himself from any such suggestion. In September, Chaovalit used his promised support for a vote on a new constitution (see below) to defeat a no-confidence motion. Even so, the end of Chaovalit's administration was in sight. On 7 November, Chaovalit resigned as Prime Minister after less than a year in power.

Following Chaovalit's resignation, **Chuan Leekpai**, leader of the Democrat Party, stitched together a new seven-party, 208-person coalition and became Prime Minister for the second time. Given talk of military intervention a few months earlier, it was a relief to many that Thailand had achieved a peaceful change of government. The key question, however, was whether Chuan could do any better than Chaovalit, particularly given the mixed make-up of his coalition government. Chuan and his finance minister, Tarrin Nimmanahaeminda – the year's fourth – vigorously implemented the International Monetary Fund's rescue package and even managed to negotiate a slight loosening of the terms of the package.

The economic crisis enabled a coterie of young, reform-minded politicians to gain high office – like urbane, US-educated foreign minister Surin Pitsuwan. Fed up with coups and corruption, and backed by an increasingly assertive middle-class, these politicians were committed to change. As Chuan's special assistant, Bunaraj Smutharaks, explained to journalist Michael Vatikiotis, "If we don't seize this opportunity to instigate change, the future generations will see this [economic] crisis as a lost opportunity". (Far Eastern Economic Review, 30.6.98)

Under Chuan's leadership, Thailand became a role model for the IMF and foreign investors applauded the government's attempts to put things in order. The difficulty that Chuan faced throughout his second stint as premier was that the economy didn't bounce back after Thailand Inc had taken the IMF's unpalatable medicine. Many foreign commentators praised Chuan's efforts seeing him as honest and pragmatic. But domestic commentators tended to depict him as bumbling and ineffectual, toadying to the IMF while Thailand's poor were squeezed by multilateral organisations and Thai companies were sold to foreign interests at 'fire sale' prices

Thaksin Shinawatra takes over, 2001-

The beginning of January 2001 saw the election of Thaksin Shinawatra and the Thai Rak Thai party, in a landslide victory over Chuan Leekpai and the Democrats. Thaksin won for two reasons: first, he made grand promises and second, his opponent, Chuan, was stuck with the charge that he had sold the country out to the IMF and foreign business interests. A good dose of populism won the day. But his victory was remarkable in one telling respect: for the first time in Thai political history a party won (almost) a majority of seats in the lower House of Representatives. While Thaksin decided to form a coalition he had no need to do this. And a few months after the election a minor party – Seritham – with 14 MPs merged with Thai Rak Thai to give Thaksin an absolute majority. Here was a man with an unprecedented mandate to rule.

Thaksin won the election by promising the world – or at least rather more than the dour Chuan could manage. Fed up with three-and-a-half years of belt tightening, the electorate grabbed at Thaksin's pledges of grants of one million baht (US$23,200) to each of Thailand's 70,000 villages, a debt moratorium for poorer farmers, cheap medical care, and more. But Thaksin is more than a populist prime minister; he has brought to Thai politics a business sense honed whilst managing one of the country's most successful companies. Rather than handing out bottles of fish sauce and 100 baht notes to poor farmers in a crass attempt to buy their support he employs pollsters and consultants to judge the mood of the electorate. Moreover, he has delivered on his promises: the debt moratorium was introduced in July 2001 and in October 2001 health care became available to all Thais at a standard rate of 30 baht per visit.

There are those, however, who fear that Thaksin is too powerful. Like Italian Prime Minister Silvio Berlusconi, he not only heads the country, but also the country's largest and most influential media group. He has little time for the checks and balances of the new constitution – designed to prevent Thailand reverting to its old political ways – and when his family's company purchased the only remaining private television station, iTV, journalists and commentators critical of his ways were promptly sacked.

Liberal authoritarian

As his first term progressed Thaksin revealed an authoritarian side that was increasingly alarming. With an economic boom slowly re-establishing itself, a whole set of social problems had to be evaporated. To this end, in 2003, a war against drugs was declared. This wasn't a poster campaign nor an attempt to stop smuggling. It involved the wholesale extra-judicial murder of thousands of suspected drug dealers, drug addicts and anyone else the police didn't really like that much. Some commentators felt that the notoriously corrupt Thai police were just getting rid of their competition,

King Bhumibol and the Monarchy

Although Thailand has been a constitutional monarchy since the Revolution of 1932, King Bhumibol Adulyadej and the Royal Family have an influence that far exceeds their formal constitutional powers. It seems that the leaders of the Revolution shied away from emasculating the monarchy, and decided to keep the king at the centre of the Thai social and political universe. Nonetheless, the only truly active king since 1932 has been the present one, King Bhumibol, who acceded to the throne in 1945 and in 1995 celebrated 50 years as Sovereign.

King Bhumibol Adulyadej – the name means Strength of the Land, Incomparable Power – has virtually single-handedly resurrected the Thai monarchy. The King was born in the USA, where his father was a doctor in Boston. He graduated in engineering from Lausanne, Switzerland and speaks English and French. He is a skilled jazz saxophonist (he has played with Benny Goodman) and an accomplished yachtsman (he won a gold medal at the Asian Games).

After returning from his studies abroad to become King he entered the monkhood, and since then has continuously demonstrated his concern for the welfare of his people. The King and his Queen, Sirikit, travel the country overseeing development projects which they finance, visiting remote villages and taking a keen interest in the poor. The King has largely managed to maintain his independence from the hurly-burly of Thai politics. When he has intervened, he has done so with great effect. In October 1973, after the riots at Thammasat University, he requested that Prime Minister Thanom, along with his henchmen Praphat and Narong, leave the country to stem the tide of civil disorder. They obeyed. In a repeat of the events of 1973, in May 1992 the King called Prime Minister General Suchinda Kraprayoon to his palace where, recorded on television, he was publicly – though not overtly – humiliated for ordering the army to quell demonstrations against his premiership. Three days later, Suchinda had resigned and left the country. Most recently, at the end of January 2003, he requested that Thais rallying outside the Cambodian embassy in Bangkok

others that this form of social cleansing was the only way to control the nefarious criminals who ran the illegal drug trade. Organisations such as Amnesty condemned the deaths – many victims were shot in the back or executed with a single headshot while restrained - though the international community, to its shame, was largely silent.

2003 also marked the invasion of Iraq with Thailand taking its place as the tenth largest member in the coalition of the willing. This was a bold step for a country not known for foriegn adventure. The troops, all of whom were used in civil activities, left in 2004, just in time for the beginning of an **insurgency in the south of Thailand** that is slowly coming to dominate the nation's politics.

The Muslim south has long felt apart from the mainstream of Thai society. With another period of economic prosperity in place – something which hardly touched the Muslims of the south – a series of demonstrations, killings and bombings took place. However, it wasn't until October 2004 that an event occurred that gave this insurrection a sense of legitimacy and urgency.

After a violent demonstration outside a government building in the small town of Tak Bai, hundreds of Muslim demonstrators were arrested. Beaten and shackled, they were then loaded into army trucks like human logs, stacked one on top of another, four or five deep. More than 80 died of suffocation. A wave of violence followed with Buddhist monks and teachers becoming targets and explosions a regular occurrence.

intent on responding to the torching of Thailand's embassy in Phnom Penh calm down and go home. So they did.

The undoubted love and respect that virtually all Thais hold for their King raises the question of the future and whether the monarchy can remain a stabilizing force. The suitability of his eldest son Crown Prince Vajiralongkorn has been questioned, while his eldest daughter Crown Princess Sirindhorn is respected and loved almost as much as the King himself. In January 1993, Vajiralongkorn – in an unprecedented move – lashed out at his critics. He was quoted in the Bangkok Post as saying: "[They say] I act as a powerful chao poh [Godfather] providing protection for sleazy business ... Do I look like a chao poh type? The money I spend is earned honestly. I do not want to touch money earned illegally or through the suffering of others."Thais worried about the succession are comforted by a legend that the Chakri Dynasty would only have nine monarchs: King Bhumibol is the ninth.

Visitors should avoid any open criticism of the Royal Family: lèse majesté is still an offence in Thailand, punishable by up to 15 years in prison. In early 1995 Frenchman Lech Tomacz Kisielwicz uttered an expletive on a THAI flight, apparently directed at fellow passenger Thai Princess Soamswali and her daughter. On arrival at Don Muang Airport he found himself arrested and then incarcerated, before being released on bail. When the Far Eastern Economic Review commented on the King's allegedly less than positive views of Prime Minister Thaksin and the latter's business links with the Crown Prince in a short piece in January 2002, the Prime Minister became so worried that the two journalists involved had their visas revoked, only to be reinstated after they had apologised. In cinemas, the national anthem is played before the film and the audience – including foreigners – are expected to stand. In towns in the countryside, at 0800 every morning, the national anthem is relayed over PA systems, and pedestrians are again expected to stop what they are doing and stand to attention. It is in ways like this that the continuing influential role of the monarchy becomes clear.

Thaksin's response to the situation was surreal. He ordered school children around Thailand to make origami cranes – the bird is a symbol of peace and goodwill in Asian cultures. Millions were loaded onto planes and dropped onto the Islamic communities of the south. The bizarre rationale was that the tiny paper birds would show the Muslims that the rest of the country cared about them. The insurgency gathered pace, draconian emergency rule was declared – suspending many judicial and constitutional rights – and by September 2005 the death toll had reached 1000.

Second term

The December 2004 tsunami came to overshadow many of the events in the south. Thaksin's handling of this disaster was seen by most – at least initially – to be efficient and statesmanlike. An election was called soon after in February 2005 and with the economy in a full-scale boom and free face whitening cream for female voters, Thaksin's TRT won a landslide.

In many ways it will be this second-term that will create Thaksin's legacy. By late-2005 the Thai economy was in danger of overheating – it is now impossible to move for luxury flats in central Bangkok. There are still enormous disparities between rich and poor with the vast slums of the capital providing a pool of virtual

 slave labour for the wealthy. Everyone is also waiting for the south's problems – and bombings - to visit Bangkok and Thaksin's government has been widely criticised in the press for ignoring the tsunami-hit poor while helping the tourist industry.

It is clear, that by the end of 2005, Thailand and Thaksin had reached a pivotal and defining point. How both deal with the country's present problems will shape Thailand for a generation.

Getting to grips with the Thai political system: the traditional way of doing things

Thai politics has traditionally been a game of money, not of ideas. In rural and provincial constituencies – and that means over 90% of constituencies – candidates were expected to buy their votes. It was estimated that between ฿20bn and ฿30bn, or a staggering US$800m-US$1.2 bn, was spent on the November 1996 elections – widely thought to have been the dirtiest in Thai election history (quite a claim). *Bank of Thailand* figures show that an unusually high sum of money was transferred out of commercial banks during the election period – the assumption being that a significant slice was withdrawn for vote buying.

Until the electoral reforms of 1997, it was common for whole villages to be bought. In the 1995 elections villages cost ฿30,000 to ฿50,000 and up-country bank branches ran out of ฿100 notes as they were pressed into hundreds of thousands of eager hands. No wonder Banharn, the leader of the Chart Thai Party which won the largest number of seats in the 1995 election, earned himself the nickname 'Mr ATM' (Mr Automatic Teller Machine): all one had to do was key in the right series of digits and out would spew ฿100 notes. In 1996, Gordon Fairclough of the *Far Eastern Economic Review* accompanied the Northeast MP Newin Chidchob while he pressed the flesh in Buriram. Fairclough wrote that the MP 'paused to talk to a young girl' and then 'handed her a crisp ฿20 note, and she got her first lesson in what politics is all about'. Boonyok Hankla, an elder in a village in Lampang province in the north, explained the farmers' electoral logic to Gordon Fairclough in simple terms: "The MP gets what he wants, and we get what we want." Another farmer in Lampang, 59-year-old Jai Manefan, added: "They're generous with us, so we have to give something in return. I don't think that's really vote buying, do you?"

In Bangkok, ideas and integrity have always counted for much more. It is this divide in the electoral environment which accounts for the fact that few parties – until Thaksin's victory – managed to bridge the gap between the rural and urban electorates (or rather between Bangkok and the rest of the country). The tale of Thailand's electoral history has been a tale of two constituencies: a comparatively sophisticated urban (capital city) electorate, and the rest. Nor has it just been a case of the votes of constituents being bought; candidates have also traditionally put themselves up for sale. The notion of being a committed party animal was rare. ฿10m or US$400,000 was said to have been the going rate to encourage a politician to switch allegiances in 1995, and it was probably rather more in the 1996 contest. And as up-country voters tend to vote for characters, not for parties or policies, candidates usually took their supporters with them when they indulged in a spot of party-hopping. (The new constitution introduced in 1997 prevents such party hot-footing – see below.)

The Thai political system, then, has always been something of an anomaly. It was widely thought to be 'fair', even before the reforms: *PollWatch*, an independent organization with around 50,000 workers, watched out for fraud and intimidation during the vote itself; newspapers have been notably free and free-wheeling compared with those in some neighbouring countries; and the army, at least over the last decade, has kept well out of the way. Yet elections in Thailand are still about power, wealth and muscle. The association of truly vast sums of money with the democratic process traditionally meant that so-called *ithiphon muut* or 'dark

influences' were always close at hand. Godfathers after lavishing millions on a candidate or party expected their reward after their chosen ones had won. Money politics ruled and violence was not far from the surface.

But while this approach to politics may have been acceptable from the 1950s until the 1970s, by the 1980s there were calls for greater accountability and transparency, and an end to money politics. By the 1990s these had become more insistent still and in late 1997 a new constitution was passed with the single but monumental purpose of cleaning up Thailand's political system.

Parliamentary and political reform

On 27 September 1997 parliament approved a **new constitution** – the country's 16th since 1932 – by a massive margin. Two weeks later the King signed the 171-page constitution, with its 336 articles, into law. The constitution, which was months in the drafting, had its origins in the widespread belief that the only way to change Thai politics was to radically reform the political system. The new constitution, it was hoped, would set the Kingdom off on a new democratic path where money politics might be replaced by debate. It has three key objectives: to stamp out electoral corruption; to end short-lived coalition governments; and to decentralise power from the centre to local people.

The constitution contains various innovations which, on paper at least, should clean up the country's sordid political system: there is a constitutional court, a parliamentary ombudsman and a National Counter Corruption Commission, for example. It has also effectively ended party-hopping. Sitting MPs who switch parties lose their seats and are barred from standing in the subsequent by-election. If they party-hop after an election is called then they cannot stand in that poll either. In addition, the constitution recognizes citizens' rights, strengthens civil liberties, allows for greater political participation, includes a provision encouraging greater freedom of information, and guarantees the freedom of the press. The constitution is the first really concerted attempt to address the issue of money politics (which explains why so many MPs initially resisted it). It also established a new national election commission as well as a directly elected upper house. Under the new constitution, some MPs are elected to single-member constituencies, while others are drawn from party slates and elected by proportional representation. All MPs need to have, at a minimum, a university degree. Another new step is that all Cabinet ministers have to make public financial statements listing their assets.

The opening test of the new constitution came in the elections to Thailand's new 200-seat Senate in March 2000. This was the first time the Upper House had been elected since 1932. There were reports of widespread vote buying (the *Bank of Thailand* revealed that 20 billion baht was withdrawn from banks in the days leading up to the election). Many commentators expected the new Election Commission to allow tainted victories to go through on the nod, particularly if those standing had links with powerful and well-established political dynasties. As it turned out, the watchdog proved itself to have teeth: the victories of 78 senatorial candidates were annulled on the basis of fraud or suspected fraud and re-elections called. In one constituency the Electoral Commission demanded no fewer than five re-runs!

Former Prime Minister, privy councillor and Thai worthy, Anand Panyarachun, said in an interview in the *Far Eastern Economic Review* in April 2000: It's the beginning of the end of Thailand's old political culture. The checks and balances enshrined in the new constitution are no longer just concepts on paper – they are coming to life in implementation. (*Far Eastern Economic Review*, 13.4.00)

So, does this mean Thailand – in terms of its political system – has been reborn? Yes, and no. There is little question that the constitution has changed things, in some respects profoundly. But the patterns of old are still there, too. In the March 2000 elections for the Senate, for example, the Election Commission disqualified just two of the 18 victors in Bangkok, but 76 out of 182 in the provinces. The rural/urban divide

lives on, it would seem. When a police sergeant-major was allegedly shot dead by the son of a local political godfather in October 2001 in front of scores of clubbers in a well-known Bangkok nightspot he managed to slip through the police and army net – simply because of his connections.

Commentators read these sorts of events in two opposing ways. Detractors of the new constitution say that they show that Thailand has not, fundamentally, changed: raw power and influence affords protection, even when it comes to murder. *ithiphon muut* or 'dark influences' are still at work beneath the façade of normal politics. Supporters – and optimists – point out that the simple fact that fraudulent elections are spotlighted in this way, and that the actions of criminals, however powerful, are debated openly in the media is a very significant advance on the past.

Getting to grips with corruption

A question much debated in the bars of Bangkok is why is Thailand so corrupt? Putting aside for one moment the fact that Thailand is clearly not unique in being corrupt, there are various arguments that do the rounds. Some people point to the fact that Thailand is a 'soft' state without the rigid rules that apply in countries like Singapore. Being soft and fuzzy means that people can argue that corruption is really not that bad – just part of the cultural landscape. Polls reveal, for example, that most Thais do not regard giving a few hundred baht to a public servant to ensure speedy service as wrong. Others highlight the low salaries paid to civil servants and others in public service. Civil servants' salaries are pitched low because everyone knows that they benefit from corruption. The logic becomes circular: civil servants are paid little because they are corrupt/they are corrupt because their salaries are so low. Suthichai Yoon, a commentator for *The Nation*, described in 1998 how senior officers in the Police Department set targets for the number of motorists who have to be fined. For each fine, the policeman on the beat receives 20%, the rest being passed up the ladder to line the pockets of more senior officers. To meet the targets, innocent motorists are framed.

There is now a more concerted effort to educate people regarding the corrosive effects of corruption: the misallocation of resources, the lower economic growth rate, the loss of competitiveness – and the fact that it is the poor who are hurt most by corruption. All-in-all, corruption is far from being just a harmless part of the cultural landscape. Interior Minister Purachai Piumsomboon has made dealing with corruption in the police force one of his prime objectives. In April 2002 police spokesman Major-General Pongsapat Pongcharoen told reporter Shawn Crispin, "Many Thai people are sick and tired of police corruption. Thai society is changing – the police must change too."

Foreign relations

Thailand is a founder member of Asean – the Association of Southeast Asian Nations. This was created in 1967 as a bulwark against communism but now comprises all ten countries of the region, including the communist countries of Vietnam and the Lao People's Democratic Republic. In general terms the country is Western-leaning and has conducted, over the years, joint exercises with the United States armed forces, for example. It is also a keen supporter of the war against terrorism.

Thailand's most delicate relations are with its neighbours, and particularly Cambodia, Laos and Burma (Myanmar). The former two countries are small, poor and economically weak and there lurks the constant fear of economic domination by Big Brother Thailand. Indeed, this is more than just a fear. Thailand is the largest foreign investor and controls much of each country's economy.

The bureaucracy

Thai bureaucracy, like that in the other countries of Southeast Asia, is a many-headed hydra. Becoming a civil servant, or in Thai *kharatchakan* ('servant of the crown'),

Tsunami

Obliterating miles of picture perfect coastline and killing thousands, the tsunami of Boxing Day, 2004, left the world reeling in shock. Among the dead were countless Burmese, Mon and Karen intinerant workers without papers, while those who escaped the tsunami fled into the dense hills and rubber plantations of Phangnga or to Phuket or Ranong to evade repatriation. While the full impact of the wave devastated the burgeoning holiday destination of Khao Lak, where many of the workers were based, the waves cruel effects were also felt as far south as Tarutao National Park, with smashed bungalows and giant upended palms. The main coastal victims, however, after Khao Lak were Kamala, Bang Tao and Patong beaches in Phuket, Ton Sai Bay in Koh Phi Phi, and in Ranong, the Laem Son National Park and Prathong Island, home to a well-loved and internationally respected turtle conservation project. But many of the smaller islands, including Koh Jum and Koh Muk also suffered from the brutal triple waves, with their Muslim fishing villages left decimated.

In the wake of the disaster, the dearth of tourists compounded the horrors as small businesses suffered bankruptcy while traditional sea gypsies remained in limbo, unable to return to their former coastal homes because they lacked property deeds and also because they feared another wave. Since those early days, the tourist industry has been rebuilt, most famously Patong Beach which now boasts the cleanest sands in years.

However, the future of Koh Phi Phi remains in limbo while Khao Lak, where the soil was seriously compromised by saline deposits, has become more of a destination for aid workers than for travellers.

Increasingly tourists are flocking to Koh Lanta and many of the smaller islands in the deep south like Koh Lipe as well as tackling the still unsaturated national parks with their gruelling treks.

Fortunately, many of the dive sites, including the Similan Islands, Ko Bon, Ko Tachai, Surin and Richelieu Rock received only superficial damage. And, while it will be some time before Khao Lak returns to a lucrative holiday strip, much of the Andaman remains gloriously lush with an abundance of accommodation and rare sights.

For many locals, however, the nightmare is not yet over. Along with the tsunami came the hired hench men of the *nai toons* or money barons who descended on villages that had been devastated by the waves, demanding property deeds from impoverished and often illiterate villagers. All up and down the coast from Laem Pon in Ban Nem Khem to Ban Sangka-oo on Koh Lanta and Kamala in Ranong, the same story was told of villagers who had been evicted and even barred from searching for the bodies of their loved ones in their former villages, following the tsunami. However, while many were loath to speak out for fear of losing compensation administered by corrupt local administrators, others fought back by refusing to move into new homes far from their original coastal sites. The oft-disparaged sea gypsies, in particular the Moken at Ban Tung Wa and Ban Tap Tawan in Phangnga, turned out to be the most united in their fight and successful, returning to their homes to rebuild rather than move into the small concrete bungalows far from the sea. At the time, Hon Klatalay, leader of the Ban Tung Wa community said: "We are one big family and we speak and move as one."

The Saudi Gem Scam: Thailand in the dock

More foreign visitors are duped by buying fake or undervalued gems than in any other way in Thailand (see page 145). The Kingdom's embassies have even taken to inserting a leaflet into every visa applicant's passport, warning them of the dangers. Still it continues. But no tourist has been tricked like the Saudi Prince Faisal Fahd Abdulaziz. The Saudi Gem Affair is simply astounding.

This long and very, very drawn out story begins in 1989 when a Thai contract worker, employed as a cleaner by the Saudi Prince Faisal Fahd Abdulaziz in Riyadh, stole 90 kg of jewellery – valued at US$20 mn – from his employer. Among the gems was the priceless 70-carat Blue Diamond. Kriangkrai Techamong fled the country and buried the gems in his back garden. A year later the police tracked down Kriangkrai and unearthed the stolen gems. It is at this point that the story changes from one of simple thieving – albeit on a monumental scale – to duplicity, intrigue and corruption at the highest level, and murder. The gems were displayed by the proud and successful policemen, filmed for television, and photographed for the newspapers. They were then flown back to Saudi Arabia. Unfortunately, when the Prince looked through the cache he realized that over half the pieces were missing. Later, others were confirmed as poor fakes.

As some of the missing gems were identified in the newspaper and television coverage of the haul, and as others had reportedly been seen adorning the necks and wrists of police generals' wives, the Saudis reacted with fury. They withdrew their ambassador and halted the issuing of all new visas for Thai contract labourers. As there were an estimated 250,000 such workers in Saudi Arabia in 1989, sending back US$340 mn in remittances, this was a huge blow not just to Thailand's international image, but also to the country's foreign exchange earnings. The Saudis also stopped their nationals travelling to Thailand as tourists. In 1988 nearly 55,000 Saudi Arabian tourists arrived in the Kingdom. In 1992 this had dropped precipitously to under 3,000. Just to make absolutely sure that the Thai authorities knew that they meant business, the Saudis also appointed Mohammed Said Khoja as special envoy, charged with the sole task of untangling the mess. He began his work in March 1990, initially for a period of just three years. In 2002 he was still trying to untangle the mess and, by then, had had dealings with nine prime ministers.

It was not until August 1994 that the debacle turned really nasty. A Thai gems dealer and jeweller, Santi Srithanakhan, was said to have knowledge of the whereabouts of the missing gems. A short time later his wife and son were found battered to death on the

brings with it considerable prestige, a certain amount of power, a great deal of job security and a small salary. One way that bureaucrats have overcome the last of these is by *kin muang* – literally 'eating the country' – extracting from the land and its people far more than their own meagre salaries. There are also many committed government officials who act in what they perceive to be the best interests of the people they (in theory) serve.

In spite of King Chulalongkorn's reforms of the civil service at the turn of the century, and the more recent decentralisation connected with the 1997 constitution, the relationship between bureaucrats and the people is still a 'top-down' one in which the official talks and the people listen. To a large extent, this is just a reflection of Thai social relations, and the pervasive superior-inferior/patron-client ties. In general, petty officials are recruited locally. They will

unfortunately named 'Friendship' Highway, north of Bangkok. To begin with, the police said it was murder; then it became an accident; then, when the impossibility of such injuries being sustained in an accident became clear, the police reverted to their original murder supposition. A witness is said to have turned up the radio of his pick-up to drown the screams of the woman and her child as they were battered to death with a steel pipe.

Most commentators always suspected that the police were closely involved in the crime, but thought that those at the top were simply too powerful to be caught. The world of the rich and powerful in Thailand, as British journalist Terry McCarthy explained, "is a world of cynical, grasping people whose money can paper over any crime and whose connections and influence make them virtually untouchable". However, they did not count on the relentless Said Khoja nor on the willingness of the Saudi government to put the immense resources of that Kingdom behind the case. To speed up the process, Said Khoja threatened to reveal the names of the 'top' people he thinks are involved. He was protected by four bodyguards and always carried a gun. It seems that everyone except some sections of the police – and perhaps some sections of the government – wanted the truth revealed. The Thai public, in particular, had become sick of the corruption that pervades their police and worry about the battered reputation of their country. The Nation newspaper called the affair 'delayed and twisted justice' and worried that it 'would expose Thailand's law-enforcement and political institutions to almost unendurable embarrassment'. Every Thai knew that the police were corrupt; few thought their law enforcement officers would stoop this deep in the filth – 'Staggering greed', as Terry McCarthy put it.

Gradually the truth – or parts of it – came out. In early 2002 two senior police officers, a major and a Lieutenant-General, were jailed for 7 years for corruption and kidnapping. One, Lieutenant-General Chalor Kerdthes, also faces murder charges.

Whatever the outcome, this case has done nothing but harm. Said Koja said that whoever touched the gems would be cursed, and Thais seem to believe him.To date, six people have been murdered as a result of the affair: three Saudi diplomats (in February 1990), a Saudi businessman (later in February 1990), and Santi's wife and son (in 1995). Some people have put the number of deaths linked with the case as high as 17. The case has been so protracted that the poor migrant labourer who originally spirited the gems out of Saudi Arabia, Kriangkrai Techamong has been released from jail having served 2 years and 7 months: he received a royal pardon.

usually have been educated to secondary school level and have little chance of advancing to the higher echelons of the civil service. More senior officials are university-educated and often have their roots (and hearts) in Bangkok. A challenge for the bureaucracy today is that Thailand's rapid economic growth during the 1980s and much of the 1990s dramatically widened wage differentials between the public and private sectors. With a decline in the prestige associated with joining the civil service and becoming a *kharatchakan*, fewer talented young Thais are being enticed into the bureaucracy. This is leading to a gradual erosion in the quality of the intake into the civil service.

Education

Traditionally, young men gained a limited education when they entered the monkhood. A system of secular education was not introduced until the reign of King Chulalongkorn, who called on the expertise of many monks and employed them as teachers. Compulsory, universal primary school education was inaugurated in 1921 and was for a period of four years (to *bor sii*). Since 1978, all children have had to undergo six years of primary education (to *bor hok*). In 1996 the government extended the period of compulsory education by another three years to nine years. Primary school education is free, but school uniforms and stationery must be paid for, which can make the cost quite onerous for a poor family. In the past farmers would complain that schooling meant their children were not around to look after the buffalo and undertake other farm chores and questioned the utility of a conservative, urban-orientated and Western-based curriculum to children who would spend their lives in agriculture. No longer. Even poor farmers realise that for their children to make progress in the modern world they need an education and the more, the better.

Secondary school education is divided into two periods of three years each: lower and upper secondary school. At both levels fees are levied. Most secondary school students live in urban areas, but the former stark rural/urban divide is beginning to narrow. Even so, it is comparatively rare for a rural Thai to progress to upper secondary level and even rarer for them to gain entrance to higher education. In 2000 309,000 students enrolled on courses in public universities and another 50,000 in private institutions. (Note that far fewer than this actually graduated.) Of Thailand's institutes of higher education, more than half are located in Bangkok and they graduate 70% of students. The most prestigious is Chulalongkorn University, followed by the more radical Thammasat University. Businessmen complain that the country trains too many students in the arts, and not enough in the sciences and engineering. In 1999 of the 94,000 students who graduated from public institutions, two-thirds were in the arts, humanities and social sciences. Many Thais feel that a humanities degree is superior to one in the sciences or engineering (see page 656 for further discussion of Thailand's educational deficiencies).

The press and media

The first newspapers to appear in Thailand were published by American missionaries. The *Bangkok Recorder* (in Thai) appeared each month between 1844 and 1845, while the *Bangkok Daily Advertiser* (in English) appeared between 1868 and 1878. Today there are numerous daily and weekly publications, serving a variety of markets. The widest-selling Thai language newspapers are *Sayam Rat* and *Thai Rat*, the latter with a circulation of around 750,000 and a readership of as much as 10 times that. *Matichon* with a far smaller circulation, is regarded as the leading 'serious' Thai language newspaper. Of the English language press, the two most respected newspapers are the Bangkok Post and *The Nation*, both enjoying a high reputation for their reporting.

Thailand's press has traditionally been one of the least controlled in Southeast Asia. While this free-wheeling approach has all too often been used to expose sexual and other scandals (Thai newspapers can make the British tabloids appear tame), there is also an honourable campaigning tradition. Over the years this has encompassed, for example, encroachment and logging of national parks, corruption in the police and judiciary, the interests of slum and squatter residents in Bangkok, and the environmental effects of dam construction. The only area where no hint of controversy is permitted is concerning the monarchy. However some see in the

actions of the current Prime Minister a return to the old days when authoritarian governments tried to control the press. Thaksin not only controls the country's only independent TV station (see below) but also blocked the distribution and sale of *The Economist* and the *Far Eastern Economic Review* in February and March 2002 for comments that were deemed to be too politically sensitive. The former publication remarked in an editorial: "Until recently, the press has been delightfully free in Thailand. Now the trend is towards the authoritarianism of Malaysia." (9.3.2002)

While radio may have broken out, television remains relatively tightly controlled. Up to July 1996, of the country's five television networks, two were owned by a state-run corporation, two by the military, and one by the government's Public Relations Department. In view of this, it is hardly surprising that Thai television tends to broadcast a judicious mix of government propaganda, crass comedies and dubbed martial arts films. Recognizing that there was ample room for a good independent station, on 1 July 1996 Thailand's first independent TV channel, iTV, began transmitting. In 2001, however, this station was purchased by Prime Minister Thaksin's media group. When journalists critical of the prime minister and his government were sacked commentators and opposition MPs suggested that Thaksin was trying to control public debate.

Economy

The end of a miracle

Thailand has had a helter-skelter economic ride over the last decade. At the beginning of the 1990s it was the fastest growing economy in the world. In 1998 the economy contracted by almost 10%. And in the first few years of the 21st century it has been staggering – none too confidently – to its feet again.

The final years of the 20th century are ones that most Thais would choose to forget. The death of the Asian Miracle, and of the Asian century, can be dated from the collapse of the Thai baht in mid-1997. This volte-face in Thailand's economic fortunes is reflected in two books written by a pair of the country's most influential academics. In 1996, at the height of the miracle, Chris Baker and Pasuk Phongpaichit published a book with the title *Thailand's Boom!* Two years later they released a new edition. They called it *Thailand's Boom ... and Bust!* Their latest volume is just entitled *Thailand's Crisis*.

What happened to Thailand is clear: currency speculators attacked the baht, forcing the central *Bank of Thailand* to spend some US$10bn trying to defend – unsuccessfully – the stricken currency. On 2 July the Bank threw in the towel and allowed the baht to float. The revelation that Thailand's banks and finance companies were shouldering massive bad debts (perhaps 10-20% of total debt, against 1% in the US) led to a haemorrhaging of domestic and international confidence. Because businesses had grown used to stable exchange rates (the baht had been pegged to the US dollar for 13 years), many had not hedged their currencies and became insolvent as they saw their US dollar debts more than double in local currency terms. With scores of businesses going under (and workers being made redundant in droves) so the finances of many smaller local banks became more rickety still. To prevent a complete loss of confidence, the IMF agreed to extend US$17bn in emergency loans to Thailand in August 1997. The IMF's rescue package demanded wide-ranging reforms of the financial sector, with a view to making it both more transparent and more accountable.

Explaining the crisis

While what happened is clear enough, why it happened remains a source of contention. As with so many things, it was probably a coincidence of factors. For some, it can be linked to the operation of the global economy. Amnuay Virawan, the first of 1997's four finance ministers, blamed the crisis on 'very greedy people' – or

 rather, currency speculators – who initiated the run on the Thai baht that marked the beginning of the Asian economic crisis. The date: 2 July. There is some credence in this claim. In 1996, the year before the Asian crisis, the flow of private capital into Indonesia, Malaysia, the Philippines, South Korea and Thailand amounted to US$93bn. In 1997 there was an outflow of US$12bn. Many people in Thailand – including the King – called for a partial de-linking from the global economy as a way of insulating the country from such machinations. In this explanatory schema, Thailand's economic problems lie in the dependency and vulnerability that has arisen because of the process of global economic integration reflected in the country's strategy of export-oriented, foreign investment-driven industrialization.

But not everyone sees Thailand's problems generated only – or mostly – in the international arena. Some look back to the late 1980s and early 1990s, when the government of Chatichai Choonhaven was corrupt and venal, even by Thai standards. 'In country after country', Nayan Chanda wrote at the beginning of 1998, 'corruption and crony capitalism had weakened solid economies built on years of hard work and prudent investment'. But the country's domestic shortcomings extend beyond crony capitalism – a tempting catch-all for those searching for an answer to the *fin de siecle* difficulties. There was also an institutional vacuum: Thailand lacked the institutions to manage global integration (and financial liberalisation) of the type that was being pursued from the mid-1990s.

Dealing with the crisis

In dealing with the crisis the Thai government made – some would say, was forced to make – some profound changes to the operation of the Thai economy and the wider Thai political economy. These were part of the deal that secured the emergency IMF loan of US$17 bn. Most focused on reforms to the finance and banking sectors. In March 1999 the Senate approved a Corporatization Bill to smooth the privatization of state owned businesses. The following month a bankruptcy bill was also approved by the Senate. For the first time in Thai history, a swathe of domestic banks are majority foreign owned –the *Thai Danu Bank*, *Nakornthon Bank*, *Radanasin Bank* and the *Bank of Asia*, for example. This would have been unthinkable before the crisis. The presence of foreign companies in the domestic banking scene has shaken up the hide-bound and rather stuffy atmosphere that existed pre-crisis. Even family-owned banks realize that they now have to compete against international players, even in their (previously) protected domestic market.

"It was the rich who benefited from the boom ... but we, the poor, pay the price of the crisis. Even our limited access to schools and health is now beginning to disappear. We fear for our children's future. What is the justice in having to send our children to the garbage site every day to support the family?", said Khun Bunjan, a community leader from the slums of Khon Kaen, North East Thailand.

The human impact

With the focus on the massive loan package from the IMF, failing companies and plunging exchange rates, there was a tendency in the international press to ignore the human costs of Thailand's economic crisis that, in some ways, are still being felt.

Migrants from rural areas who found work in Bangkok and other towns drifted back to their villages as employment opportunities dried up. International migrants in their hundreds of thousands faced the prospect of expulsion, including over 600,000 Burmese along with 300-400,000 assorted migrants from Laos, Cambodia, Vietnam and China. For Thais who had lost their jobs, the effects of the crisis were just as great. Urban work financed the rising expectations of rural households, buying consumer goods, paying for school fees, and subsidizing agricultural modernization. This source of funds, on which many households had become dependent, evaporated as the crisis bit.

The effects of the economic crisis were visible in numerous small and large ways. Taxi drivers in Bangkok found their regular customers switching to public transport. In provincial towns people began to walk to work and the shops, rather than take a *saamlor*. Travelling salesmen found that with less disposable income there was no market for their wares. The turnover of small village shopkeepers tumbled as fellow villagers cut back on their outlays. Factory workers returning to their farms displaced landless wage labourers, who hitherto had filled the labour void. Without a social security system to speak of, and with the 'moral' community economy of old fractured by years of modernization, there were few places for these people to turn. Households whose regular incomes had disappeared were forced to pawn their motorbikes, bicycles and televisions to meet their immediate, essential needs.

Humans are, of course, cunning creatures, and this particularly applies to the poor and the near poor. Pushed out of formal work, many found opportunities in the informal sector. For example, in 1998, to the casual observer at least, there seemed to be more noodle carts and hawkers on the streets of Bangkok. The rural, agricultural sector also absorbed many of those displaced from urban areas. In his 70th birthday speech, the King suggested that returning to a self-sufficient, subsistence-oriented, farm-based economy might be the answer to the crisis. "Whether or not we are a tiger is unimportant", he said. "The important thing is for the economy to be able to support our people", adding "We need to go back so that we can go forward." (*Thai Development Newsletter* 33, July-December 1997) But not everyone hit by the economic retrenchment was able – or willing – to go 'back to the farm'. Many younger workers, particularly, are not enamoured with the agricultural way of life. Others found that their bolt-holes in the countryside had been undermined by years of neglect.

Perhaps the most remarkable aspect of the crisis was the degree to which people hunkered down and got by. The more cataclysmic predictions did not materialise. There was not a marked drop in school enrolments or a noticeable rise in mortality rates. Incomes did decline, and poverty levels did rise – but not to the extent that most commentators expected.

The economy today

The aftershocks of the crisis are still evident some 6 years after the event. There are half-built high-rise buildings across the country. Thailand's banks are still saddled with bad loans which amount to 10% of the total. And a large slice of the country's manufacturing capacity remains idle. In a report in the *Economist* in March 2002, Thailand analyst Edward McBride explained the stubborn refusal of the Thai economy to recover in the following terms: "...analysts have long complained that Thailand is neither fish nor fowl: not as cheap a place to do business as poor countries such as Vietnam and Indonesia, but not as well provided with skilled workers and infrastructure as more affluent places such as Malaysia and Singapore".

This might sound rather depressing. But growth is gradually returning. In 2001 the economy expanded by a measly 1.8%; the figure for 2002 was 5.2 %. In 2003, it is projected to be 3.5-4.5%. Foreign reserves are healthy and the country's foreign debt is on a downward trend. Foreign analysts – so crucial for the restoration of confidence – are beginning to suggest that Thailand has, at last, addressed its deep-seated structural problems. However there remain questions about the long term costs of Thaksin's populist expansionist policies.

Growth, modernization and inequality

Between the late 1980s and 1997, Thailand's economy grew faster than almost any other country. This rapid growth was accompanied by a huge inflow of foreign investment, the rapid expansion of the industrial sector and fundamental structural change – and a boom in the sale of such luxury items as Mercedes' cars, mobile phones and golf clubs.

In 1993 the World Bank published a study which tried to make sense of the Asian economic success story, with the snappy title *The East Asian Miracle:* Economic Growth and Public Policy. The report was commissioned because Asia's – including Thailand's – unprecedented rate of economic growth demanded an explanation so that other, less fortunate, regions of the world might also embark on this road to fortune. Although the World Bank study began by pointing out that there is no 'recipe' for success, it did highlight a number of critical elements which countries and governments needed, in their view, to get right. As the World Bank put it, the so-called High Performing Asian Economies, or HPAEs, 'achieved high growth by getting the basics right'. These basics included: investment in physical and human capital; allowing the market to determine prices; and creating a business-friendly environment. In retrospect, the report was notable more for what it didn't say than what it did. Even critics of the report never envisaged an economic meltdown. Their concern was with the negative side-effects of the type of fast-track industrialization that Thailand was 'enjoying'. In their view – and they were just a minority and of more radical persuasion – Thailand was an example of 'mal-development'. Or, as some put it at the time, of 'modernization without development'.

Most glaring of all has been the **unequal distribution** of the country's breakneck economic growth. In 1981 Thailand was already an unequal society: the richest 10% of the population earned 17 times more than the poorest 10%. By 1992 they earned 38 times more. The figures are just as startling in terms of quintiles: in 1975 the richest 20% grabbed 49% of the income cake; in 1995 they absorbed 63%. Over the same period the poorest 20% saw their share of income halve from a paltry 6% to a derisory 3%. This has narrowed slightly with the respective figures for the richest and poorest quintiles in 1999 being 58% and 4%. Nonetheless, Thailand remains a very unequal society.

At the beginning of 1997 the Assembly of the Poor, a congregation of over 10,000 villagers with a range of grievances, descended on Bangkok and began a drawn-out sit-in outside Government House. Initially the government tried to ignore the demonstration. But as the months ticked by and the make-shift shelters took on the air of a permanent camp, so more senior ministers tried to settle the affair. Bangkokians with a social conscience began to make donations of cash and food. The demonstrators vowed to remain until their demands had been met. The main issue concerned land, and in particular those villagers alienated from their land due to dam construction or because they were designated as living on protected forest land. However, the demonstration also highlighted a new concern for 'social justice', a concept which hitherto had never courted much attention in Thailand. The Assembly of the Poor has continued to be a thorn in the side of Thai governments. Thaksin Shinawatra, like his predecessor, has found himself embarrassed by the presence of a make shift 'village' in the heart of the city. He, though, has vowed not to be bowed by a handful of activists. Moreover he can claim to have an unprecedented mandate to govern.

Although it is the inequity of Thailand's growth which grabbed the headlines before the crisis, there were some economists – even then – who pointed to what they regarded as more fundamental weaknesses in the Kingdom's economic development. Thailand's growth has been based upon foreign technology and capital. Thailand is not a Taiwan or South Korea, with a creative, innovative, class of industrialists. Indeed, education – or rather the lack of it – is highlighted by most economists as one of the major constraints facing the Kingdom. Only one in five workers has anything more than primary level education, and a mere fraction enter higher education. Periodically commentators lament the absence of inventors in the Kingdom, noting the small number of copyright applications lodged each year. And it's not just the lack of Nobel prizewinners. Thailand's growth is also retarded by such basic shortcomings as a woefully poor facility with foreign languages, especially English. A 2003 study of 377,947 TEFL students who had taken the test between 1995

and 1998 found that Thailand ranked ninth out of ten Southeast Asian countries – only Laos scored lower. Another recent report from Hong Kong-based Political and Economic Risk Consultancy observed that Thailand's facility with the English language is 'among the very worst in East Asia'.

One of Thailand's key challenges is how to boost and improve education. More children enter secondary school in Indonesia and the Philippines than they do in Thailand, despite the fact that Thailand is considerably wealthier on a per capita income basis. While close to 100% of Thais of the relevant age group attend primary school, the figure for upper secondary school is 35% and for higher education, 20%. In the countryside, just a fifth of primary school leavers continue with their education. On average, a Thai completes 5.3 years of education – hardly the foundations for building a modern, 'thinking' economy. Part of the reason may be cultural, but probably more important is the money that the government allots to education – just 4% of GDP, the lowest in the region. Without the skills that come from education, some commentators find it hard to see how the country can continue to entice foreign companies to invest.

The rich express their dissatisfaction with Thailand's public education system by sending their children to private schools. In the heady years before the crisis this sometimes meant abroad, to English 'public' schools. Now with money a little tighter, sister schools have set up in Thailand itself. Schools modelled on Dulwich and Harrow set up in Phuket and Bangkok in 1996 and 1998 respectively, and in 2003 a Thai Shrewsbury opened. Fees at these schools are around one-half of those at their English counterparts. This is fine for the well-heeled, of course. But the poor don't have the choice of opting out.

Planning Thailand's miracle

Thailand embarked on its current path to development in the late 1950s, when General Sarit Thanarat became Prime Minister after a coup d'état and decided to abandon the preceding policy of economic nationalism. Government intervention in the economy was reduced, foreign investment welcomed, and a national development plan drawn up. Even the Thai term for 'development' – *kanpattana* – only came into widespread use at this time and Thais talk of *samay pattana* – the 'development era' – following Sarit's change of economic tack more than four decades ago.

Since 1961 the National Economic and Social Development Board (NESDB) has published a series of Five-Year Economic and Social Development Plans. Most commentators, however, see these as little more than paper plans – wish lists that reflect the concerns of the day. Governments appear to rarely take any notice of them in formulating their economic policies and it would seem that the economy succeeded in the 1980s and 1990s not so much because of the government, but in spite of it. It is also true – and this has been particularly true recently – that plans have often been overtaken by events. The crisis, for example, made the targets and assumptions of the Eighth Plan (1997-2001) redundant within months of the document being released.

Since the 1950s, there has seen a rapid expansion of the industrial and service sectors, and a relative decline of agriculture. Today, agriculture contributes just 9% of GDP (2000), while manufacturing alone contributes more than 33%. Rice, the main export for hundreds of years, is exceeded in value terms by textiles, electronics and tourism. In 2000 Thailand sold more frozen shrimps than it did rice. Even so, the country remains the world's largest exporter of rice. Although the economy has diversified significantly, government statistics still show that marginally more than 50% of the labour force are employed in agriculture. (This figure is slightly dubious because many Thais work in both agriculture and non-agriculture, keeping one metaphorical foot on the factory floor and the other in the paddy field.) The slow growth of the agricultural sector compared with industry has meant that inequalities between town and country have widened.

Discrepancies between rural and urban areas

The yawning expectation gap between what rural areas have to offer and what young Thais (especially) want has led to a massive migration of men and women from the countryside to the towns and cities, and especially to Bangkok. Young men and women, enticed by the culture of consumerism which has infiltrated the most remote villages and frustrated by the lack of opportunities at home, have, to coin a phrase, got on their bikes. They work as tuk-tuk and saamlor drivers, labourers on building sites and in textile mills, domestic servants, and as prostitutes. Each month they remit money back to their families, saving up so they can afford to send their children to secondary school, buy a television, or extend their house.

Even before the crisis, whether the Thai economy could continue to absorb this army of 'surplus' labour – somewhere between one and two million temporary migrants flood into the capital each dry season – was a key challenge. Rural industrialization is one solution that is being tried. In effect, this means relocating industries such as textiles, shoemaking and gem cutting to rural areas, thereby employing people in the countryside and stemming the flow of migrants to Bangkok. There have been some notable successes: North East Textile in Nakhon Ratchasima, for example. On the face of it, it appears that everyone 'wins': rural people can live cheaply at home and benefit from wages that are not too much lower than in Bangkok; Bangkok does not suffer from the added congestion and infrastructural strain that each migrant creates; companies can save in lower wages, land and overhead costs; and the government can feel smug that it is helping to reduce poverty and under-production in the countryside. As Banjob Kaewsra, a 23-year-old worker at North East Textile, was quoted as saying in an article in the *Far Eastern Economic Review*: "Working here is better [than in Bangkok]. Wages aren't much lower and the cost of living is far less. Besides, it's home." The trouble is that this all sounds rather familiar. Successive Thai governments have been trying to decentralize economic activity since the first Five-Year Development Plan was introduced in 1961, and the gap between Bangkok and the rest of the kingdom has yawned wider ever since.

Although Thailand's townspeople lead more comfortable lives than their country cousins, Thai farmers are relatively well-off, indeed rich, compared with those in India, Bangladesh or on Java, Indonesia. Thai farmers usually own their land – although tenancy is a problem in some areas, especially in the Central region and parts of the North – nutrition is reasonable, and agricultural surpluses are the norm rather than the exception. Some farmers and intellectuals complain that the incorporation of rural Thailand into the national and international cash economies has meant that they have become vulnerable to fluctuations in the global market – and they plead for a return to 'traditional' life. Most farmers, however, have embraced the cash economy with alacrity and seem unimpressed by such protestations.

Tourism in Thailand

Looking at the experience of the 1990s emphasizes the fickleness of the tourist industry. In 1990, Thailand was the place where everyone wanted to go and where every tour operator and hotel owner was making money. On the basis of the growth in the number of arrivals from the late 1980s, analysts and the *Tourist Authority of Thailand* (TAT) projected that arrivals would just keep on growing. Instead, arrivals stagnated. This was a shock for those who saw investing in tourist facilities as a sure thing. Hotel occupancy rates dropped to 50% or lower, and hoteliers resorted to slashing their room rates to encourage custom. The problem was that over-optimism fuelled over-construction, which led, in turn, to over-capacity.

Why this should happen to a country with so much to offer is a lesson in the uncertainties of the tourist industry. But to understand what happened, one has to look back to the early 1990s. First of all there were the domestic political problems that sullied the smiling face of Thailand, the coup d'état of 1991 and the widely

reported massacre of demonstrators in 1992. Rather harder to pin down is Thailand's poor PR. By the mid-1980s, the Kingdom was perceived to be yesterday's destination. People had moved on to Indonesia, Vietnam and elsewhere. Among 'travellers' or 'backpackers', Thailand had become spoilt. Among family holidaymakers, Thailand's AIDS crisis (see page 661) had become a cause for concern and among those looking for pristine beaches and a clean environment, overdevelopment in places like Pattaya and Phuket had turned them away. All in all, the Tourist Authority of Thailand had an image problem. It invented a new word – *wattanathammachaat* or 'culture and nature' – to try and cash in on the eco-tourism bandwagon, but it took, nonetheless, almost a decade for Thailand's tourist industry to recover a semblance of vitality.

Rather ironically it was Thailand's economic crisis which really put some fizz back into the tourist industry. Even before the economic crisis, the growth in the number of foreign tourists appeared to have picked up. In 1995, an encouraging 6.95m tourists visited the country and in 1996, coinciding with the Tourist Authority of Thailand's PR effort connected with the 50th anniversary of King Bhumibol's accession to the throne, 7.2m. But with the collapse in the value of the Thai baht, so the country became – overnight – incredibly good value for money. 1998 saw a record 7.8m tourists visit the country, coinciding with the new 'Amazing Thailand' campaign . The campaign saw a number of particularly tacky attempts to entice visitors to different corners of the country: the world's biggest ever omelette, largest plate of fried rice, longest beach party, and such like. In Nakhon Pathom the world's tallest joss stick collapsed in November 1998, tragically killing five people. In 2002 10.8 million tourists visited Thailand, with 6.5 million arriving from East Asia, 2.5 million from Europe and 0.6 million from the Americas.

Prostitution

Embarrassingly for many Thais, their country is synonymous in many foreigners' minds with prostitution and sex tourism, and now with AIDS. That prostitution is big business cannot be denied: various estimates put the numbers of women employed in the industry at between 120,000 and two million, in some 60,000 brothels.

Despite the ubiquitousness of the prostitute in Thai life, the government has often appeared blind to the scale of the industry. This is clear in one official estimate of the numbers of prostitutes and brothels in the Kingdom: 67,067 and 5,754 respectively. Part of the problem is admitting to the problem in a society where these things are usually left unsaid. As US-based Thai author Somtow Sucharitkul explained: "The main difference between American and Thai sexuality is that in America you can only talk about it but can't do it, but in Thailand you can't talk about it, you can only do it."

Although the growth of prostitution is usually associated with the arrival of large numbers of GIs on 'Rest & Recreation' during the Vietnam War, and after that with the growth of sex tourism, it is an ancient industry here, just as it is in most countries. In the 1680s, for example, an official was granted a licence to run the prostitution monopoly in Ayutthaya, using 600 women who had been captured and enslaved.

Prostitution has been illegal since 1960. Until the introduction of a new legal code in 1996, only the pimp and the prostitute were liable for prosecution. The act made it a crime to 'promiscuously [render] sexual services for renumeration', and police interpreted this as applying only to the provider of such services, not the recipient. With the 1996 Act, customers are now also liable for prosecution if the prostitute is under 18 years of age.

The scale of the prostitution industry in Thailand indicates that the police turn a blind eye and at the same time no doubt gain financial reward. There is a brothel or 'tea house' in every town, no matter how small. Farmers are trucked in from the countryside, and it has been the norm in many universities for male 'freshers' (first year

 undergraduates) to be taken to a brothel by the older students as part of their initiation into university life. One survey recorded that 95% of all men over 21 had slept with a prostitute; another put the figure at 75%. Girls in these 'tea houses' are paid ฿30-50 per customer, and Pamela DaGrossa wrote: 'The women I interviewed told me that prostitutes in these brothels [for Thais] are not required to participate in the actual sex act in any way except for lying on their backs. The men expect and receive no more. It is even rumoured that some more experienced prostitutes read newspapers while they 'work''.

In the North and Northeast, families have been known to 'sell' their daughters (and occasionally their sons) for between ฿10,000 and ฿30,000. But for families mired in poverty, and for daughters who are expected to help their parents, this is not seen as reprehensible. One father, in Phayao Province in the north, explained to Thai journalist Sanitsuda Ekachai: "I didn't sell my daughter ... she saw me suffer, she saw the family suffer, and she wanted to help". Some people maintain that the subordinate role of women in Buddhism means that there is less stigma attached to becoming a prostitute. In some villages, having a daughter who has 'gone South', as it is euphemistically termed, is viewed as a good thing. The benefits are clear. Sanitsuda Ekachai continues: "Riam has given her father more than a house, a television set, a refrigerator and a stereo. She has made him someone in the village. He was once a landless peasant, one of those who sat in the back row at village meetings. Now he sits at the front ..."

During the 1990s, with the wide availability of alternative employment in garment and electronics factories for girls with nimble fingers, and the heightened awareness of the dangers of prostitution following successive public health campaigns, the flow of girls from rural Thailand began to diminish. To fill the void, the flesh trade looked to Thailand's 800,000-strong hilltribe population and to neighbouring countries for women. It has been estimated that there are 30,000 Burmese women in Thai brothels, with 10,000 new recruits joining their ranks each year. Asia Watch believes there is "clear evidence of direct official involvement in every stage of the trafficking process". There are also women working in the trade from Yunnan (South China), Laos and Cambodia.

A disturbing development in the 1980s and 1990s was the apparent spread of **child prostitution** and the attraction of paedophiles to Thailand, where under-age girls and boys are more available than in Western countries – and where the risks of getting caught are perceived to be less. (Foreign paedophiles also seem to think that having sex with children is safe in terms of the HIV risk. The medical evidence does not bear this out.) There was a spate of 'outings' of foreign paedophiles in the late 1990s. The police have also become more assiduous in tracking down paedophiles and bringing them to court. In the last decade there has been an increase in co-operation between the Thai police and overseas forces, especially in Europe. Under Thai law, sex with a child under 15 is illegal and penalties for the sexual abuse of children range from four to 20 years. If the child is under 13, the sentence can be extended to life.

As with adult prostitutes, how many children are involved in the commercial sex industry is a source of considerable dispute. The police estimated in 1990 there were 100,000 under-age prostitutes in the Kingdom. The Ministry of Public Health in 1993 put the figure at 13,000-15,000; while Sanphasit Koompraphant, the director of the Centre for the Protection of Children's Rights, quoted a figure of 800,000. This latter estimate seems to be grossly inflated, and designed more to impress on people the seriousness of the issue than to be based on any accurate survey. It would mean that nearly one in five girls aged seven to 15 are engaged in prostitution, or one in 10 boys and girls.

The difficulty of dealing effectively with the problem is that the police are, in some cases, in league with those who traffic in under-age prostitutes. Their modest salaries make them easy targets for corruption, and they are paid to overlook brothels where child sex occurs. In addition, as Thailand develops and local children become less available (Thailand's generally improving standard of living means that fewer parents have to resort to such drastic action), so under-age prostitutes from neighbouring

countries, especially Burma, are filling the void. Some are little more than sex slaves; sold into prostitution and living illegally in Thailand, they have little choice but to do exactly as the brothel owner or pimp requires until they have worked off their indemnity. Pressured by poverty at home and living outside the law, it is these children who are most at risk. There is also the question of where the main problem lies. Much of the media attention has been on foreign paedophiles. But the police are the first to admit that, in terms of numbers, Thai men and their activities are more of a problem.

The following NGOs are working to minimize child prostitution in Thailand: Centre for the Protection of Chidren's Rights (CPCR), T02-4121196/4120739; Friends of Women Foundation, T02-2797158; Task Force to Fight Against Child Exploitation (FACE), T02-5095782.

Prime Minister Chuan Leekpai, during his first shot at the premiership, tried to clean up the prostitution business. There has been discussion of legalizing the industry so that it can be more effectively regulated, and the police have been entrusted with a crackdown on establishments. In places like the southern Thai town of Hat Yai, where the tourist industry is largely based on prostitution (there isn't much else in the place to attract the discerning visitor), this has brought wails of anguish from local businessmen. There are also some new laws on the books: it is now, for example, illegal for men to have sex with women and girls aged under 18 years old, and parents selling their children will also face prosecution. Fines and terms of imprisonment have also been increased substantially. The problem for the government is that prostitution is so widely accepted and so ingrained into the Thai way of life that combating commercial sex work requires a national change of attitude. The Thai government is pressing hard for tour operators and foreign governments to take action. In particular, the government has been hoping that more Western countries will introduce legislation that will make it a crime in their own countries for tourists to commit child sex offences in Thailand (or anywhere else). Such legislation is already on the statute books in Australia, Britain, Germany and Sweden. However, the increasing role of women from neighbouring countries in Thailand's commercial sex industry makes the problem yet more intractable. These women are 'doubly illegal': they are working in an outlawed industry, and are illegal immigrants to boot. In addition, the police are often involved in the industry in one way or another.

The modern scourge: AIDS

Thailand's AIDS crisis is the worst in Asia. The first person to be tested HIV positive in Thailand was in 1984; by the end of the century this had risen to close to one million, with a cumulative total of more than 400,000 people dying of the disease.

The spread of HIV in Thailand has been explosive. It seems, as Tim Brown and Peter Xenos of the East-West Population Institute in Hawaii describe, to have gone through five overlapping phases. To begin with, in the mid-1980s, it afflicted homosexual and bisexual men; by the end of the 1980s it had spread to the intravenous drug-using population; in the early 1990s high levels of infection were being reported among female sex workers; shortly afterwards, there was a marked increase in infection among the wives and girlfriends of men who frequented brothels; and, most recently of all, babies born to women with HIV have been identified as carrying the virus.

Thailand's first AIDS case, reported in 1984, was a homosexual student who had returned from study in the USA. For the next two years, almost all cases in Thailand involved either homosexual or bisexual men. But between November 1987 and August 1988, methodone treatment centres for drug addicts in Bangkok found, to their horror, that the presence of the HIV virus in blood samples rose from 0% to 30% – this constituted the second 'wave' in Thailand's AIDS crisis. Partly in

 response, a nationwide system for ascertaining levels of HIV infection by province was introduced in 1989 – known as Sentinel Surveillance. The data from this study shed light on the third wave: they indicate that by December 1993, levels of infection among sex workers had reached 30%. More recent still, HIV infection levels among wives and girlfriends have risen and this is feeding into the fifth and most recent phase: the infection of babies. In June 1993, 1.8% of women visiting pre-natal clinics tested HIV positive and by 1995, 5,000 HIV-infected children were being born each year.

What makes the pattern of spread of HIV in Thailand so worrying is that it has not been confined largely to the homosexual and drug-using populations, as HIV has in Europe and North America. By the early 1990s, 2% of the reproductive-age population in Thailand were infected – a catastrophic rate of spread. Also extraordinary was the geographical dispersal of the disease. Some 15% of army conscripts from the North – mostly country people – tested HIV positive in the mid-1990s. This reflects the prevalence of prostitution, and the mobility of Thais. Now that girls from neighbouring countries – Burma, Laos, Cambodia and southern China – are being attracted or forced into the industry, the disease is being spread across international borders. (More recent figures on HIV-infection rates among army conscripts have shown a steady fall, reflecting the success of the country's AIDS-awareness campaign.)

The cause of Thailand's HIV epidemic does not lie with the tourist industry, but with the culture of prostitution in the country. It is a way of life. It seems that the pattern of sexuality in the Kingdom has also contributed to the tragedy. Thai women are still expected to be virgins on marriage; at the same time, most Thai men expect, and are expected, to have had sexual relations. Nick Ford and Sirinan Kittisuksathit surveyed 1,469 young women in Bangkok and found that 91% had never had sexual relations. By contrast, only 37% of the 564 young men interviewed remained virgins. This means that very large numbers of men are looking for sex from comparatively small numbers of women – a scenario in which the spread of AIDS is likely to be rampant. It has been estimated that some 80% of Thai men have paid for sex with a prostitute by the time they reach their mid-20s. Compounding this, studies have further shown that a high proportion of prostitutes have other sexually transmitted diseases (which dramatically increases the likelihood of HIV infection), while men also like to change prostitutes regularly.

Initially, the Thai government played down the problem, fearing that it would harm the tourist industry – the country's largest foreign exchange earner. But soon it was realized that the problem was of crisis proportions. This heralded the introduction of perhaps the largest and most innovative anti-AIDS programme in Southeast Asia. The charismatic Mechai Viravaidhya, the former head of Thailand's family planning programme was put in charge of the anti-AIDS campaign and the Prime Minister himself chaired the National AIDS Committee. (Mechai's success in promoting birth control is reflected in the fact that condoms in Thailand are known as 'mechais'.) The National AIDS committee launched a '100% condom campaign' in April 1991, threatening to shut down brothels that did not comply. The government assisted this effort by providing 60 million free condoms a year. Experts claim Mechai's success in raising AIDS consciousness in Thailand is unparalleled in the developing world. As Sidney Westley wrote in a paper published in July 1999: 'Between 1990 and 1993, the proportion of men reporting any pre-marital or extra-marital sex in the previous year fell from 28% to 15%. The proportion reporting a visit to a sex worker fell from 22% to 10%, and the proportion reporting condom use in commercial sex increased from 36% to 71%.' That's some success rate.

As a result of Mechai's efforts, condom use has changed from being very rare to being the norm. Close to 90% of prostitutes now use condoms and one side-effect has been that the prevalence of male sexually-transmitted diseases has slumped

from over 200,000 per year at the end of the 1980s to around 20,000 by the mid-1990s. Even so, the future cost to Thai society of treating large numbers of terminally ill AIDS patients is huge. In addition, HIV is unusual in that it characteristically strikes the young, decimating the population of producers of the future. It also leave thousands of orphans, who either need to be cared for by their grandparents, or the state.

Drugs, youth and social malaise

The modernisation of Thailand has brought with it just the sort of social problems that the West has had to deal with for decades. This, though, doesn't make them any easier to handle. A crack down on anti-social elements and activities is being pursued more vigorously than ever before. Interior Minister Purachai Piumsomboon has made cleaning up the country – and by this he doesn't mean of rubbish (although that would be a good start) – one of his key objectives. He talks of a 'new social order', one that harks back to the golden years before Westernisation undermined traditional mores. Bangkok's nightclubs are raided, curfews imposed, traffic laws enforced – and he is even trying to tackle corruption in the 240,000-strong police force.

Thailand's big problem, though, is drugs. Traditionally seen as a producer and then as a transit point for drugs destined for the West, the country itself has become a prime target market for drug traffickers. The drug of choice among Thailand's youth isn't coke or crack but *yaa baa*, methamphetamine, akin to speed. It is said that close to 10% of adult Thais have tried the drug and it is easily obtained in schools across the country. There is little doubt that Thailand has a serious – and escalating – drug problem.

The government is now playing hard ball. Prime Minister Thaksin made the war against drugs one of the pillars of his election campaign and from the beginning of his administration he upped the ante as he sought to meet his election promise. Small time dealers are jailed for long periods, and the number of drug offenders in prison has increased nearly ten fold over the last decade, from a little more than 10,000 in 1991 to approaching 100,000 in 2001. Some very tough targets have been set by politicians and the police are cracking down as never before, sending scores of officers to root out dealers and users in areas like Bangkok's Khlong Toey. The campaign was ratcheted up another notch at the beginning of 2003 when Thaksin and his interior minister, Wan Muhamad Nor Matha, said that they would reduce the number of drug dealers by a quarter in a single month and eradicate the scourge of drugs in Thailand within three months. The police, critics say, went beserk seeing the politicians' target as an excuse to shoot on sight. In February alone, the first month of the campaign, 1,000 'drug dealers' were killed, and by the end of the first ten days of March had reached 1,500. Amnesty International criticised the government for sanctioning extra-judicial killings while Thai-based groups saw Thaksin's blunt approach as worryingly similar to dictator Field Marshall Sarit Thanarat's own brutal and rather ill-thought war against drugs in the 1950s. In response to the criticisms of foreign groups Thaksin retorted 'We are an independent country [and] do not need to give away our independence to others'. For Thais worried about the sheer mayhem he said that 'In this war, drug dealers must die' and explained that 'we do not kill them...it is a matter of the bad guys killing the bad guys'. Reform groups say that this is the wrong approach and call for education and rehabilitation. Sounds familiar?

Culture

Lao

The largest, and least visible, 'minority' group in Thailand are the Lao of the Northeastern region, who constitute nearly a third of the total population of the country. The region and its people are also referred to as 'Isan' (meaning northeastern) and they are often regarded by Central Thais as being the equivalent of country bumpkins. Their linguistic and cultural distinctiveness, and the patronizing attitude of the central authorities, led considerable numbers of the population in the Northeast, as in the South, to support the CPT during the 1960s and 1970s. The murder, by the police, of prominent Northeastern politicians during this period also did little to help integrate Northeasterners into the fabric of Thailand. Although the situation has since stabilized, and separatist sentiments are much reduced, the Northeast is still the poorest and least developed part of the country, with the highest incidence of poverty, malnutrition and child mortality. As a result, the government invests considerable resources trying to develop the area.

Sino-Thais (Chinese)

Anything between 9% and 15% of the population of Thailand is thought to be Sino-Thai (depending on how 'Chinese' is defined). Hundreds of thousands emigrated from China during the 19th and early 20th centuries, escaping the poverty and lack of opportunity in their homeland. In Thailand they found a society and a religion which was inclusive rather than exclusive. Forced to learn Thai to communicate with the ruling classes (rather than English, French or Dutch, as in neighbouring colonial countries), they were relatively quickly and easily assimilated into Thai society. They took Thai names, married Thai women, converted to Buddhism – although they were not required to renounce ancestor worship – and learnt Thai: in short, they became Thai. As elsewhere in the region, these Chinese immigrants proved to be remarkably adept at moneymaking and today control a disproportionate slice of businesses.

While the Chinese are well integrated into Thai society, compared with other countries in the region like Malaysia and Indonesia, there have been times when the Chinese have felt the hot breath of Tai nationalism. In 1914 King Rama VI wrote an essay under the *nom de plume* Atsawaphaahu, entitled *The Jews of the East*, blaming many of his country's problems on the Chinese. During Phibun Songkram's premiership between 1938 and 1944, anti-Chinese xenophobia was also pronounced and was a major reason why, in 1939, the country's name was changed from Siam to Thailand. This was to be a country of the Tais, and not any other ethnic group . Even today, it is common for government documents to maintain that the plight of the farmer is due to the unscrupulous practices of Chinese traders and moneylenders.

Although the Chinese have been well assimilated into the fabric of the nation, Bangkok still supports a large Chinatown. Here, the Chinese language can be heard spoken, shop signs are in Chinese, and Chinese cultural and religious traits are clearly in evidence.

Some commentators report a resurgence of pride in being Chinese. While from the 1930s through to the 1980s the Chinese wished in the most part to be invisible, wealth has brought confidence and Sino-Thais are once more learning the 'mother' tongue (Mandarin), praying to Mahayanist and Taoist deities like Kuan Im (Kuan Yin), and travelling to China to discover their roots. Partly, this makes good economic sense. Trade with China is booming and China is the great emerging economic (and military) powerhouse in the Asia-Pacific. To be able to converse in Mandarin and draw on family links with the homeland is perceived to be good for business. There are

dangers in this rediscovered love of China, however: Thailand's past shows periods of xenophobia when Sino-Thais have been persecuted and their businesses burnt, and most are quick to add that their allegiances are to Thailand.

Thai Malays

Of the various minority ethnic and religious groups in Thailand, the Thai Malays and Thai Muslims have often felt most alienated from the Thai nation. Not only do many in the southern four provinces of the country – Yala, Narathiwat, Pattani and Satun – speak Malay rather than Thai, but the great majority (about 80%) are also Muslim rather than Buddhist. The fact that the government has sometimes been rather heavy-handed in its approach to their welfare and citizenship gave great impetus to the growth of the Communist Party of Thailand (CPT) in the South, during the 1960s and 1970s. Pattani was only incorporated into the Thai state at the beginning of the 20th century, and even then just loosely. It was not until the 1930s that the government in Bangkok began to try and Thai-ify the far south, and many of the problems that remain evident today in relations between Tai-Thais and Thai-Malays can be dated from that period.

Relations are far better today, but it is still true that few Thai Muslims have been recruited into the civil service or army, and schools in the south still give lessons in Thai and present an essentially 'Tai' view of the country. (It is for this reason that the majority of Muslim parents still choose to send their children to private Islamic *pondok* schools, even though it means paying fees.) The Islamic revival in Southeast Asia has brought the issue of Muslim disaffection in the south to the fore once again.

King Bhumibol has done more than most to incorporate the Thai Malays into the fabric of the nation. He presents awards for Koranic study and regularly visits the region, staying in his newly-built palace at Narathiwat. Certainly things seemed to have cooled down a little since the 1980s, and today most Thai Muslims, rather than calling for a separate state, are using the political system to raise their profile and make their voices heard. The difficulty is that the acceptance that they should work within the system to achieve change has been accompanied by the spread of orthodox, conservative Islam. Unlike the Chinese, Thai Muslims are unwilling to compromise over matters of faith and simply blend in with the mass.

In April 1997 the Thai army clashed with armed separatists linked with the Barisan Revolusi Nasional (BRN), in Narathiwat province. While few people believe that the BRN, or other similar groups, represent a threat to the integrity of the Thai state, clashes like this demonstrate that the task of integrating the far south into the mainstream of Thai political life is still to be completed.

Hilltribes

Thailand's assorted hilltribes, concentrated in the North and West, number over 800,000 people. For more background information, see page 36, Chiang Mai and Sport and special interest travel. See also www.chmai.com/tribal/content.html. Much of the information contained here has been sourced from the Chiang Mai Tribal Research Institute's website and other publications.

Hilltribe economy and culture

Traditionally, most of the hilltribes in Thailand practised slash and burn agriculture , also known as swiddening or shifting cultivation. They would burn a small area of forest, cultivate it for a few years by planting rice, corn and other crops, and then, when the soil was exhausted, abandon the land until the vegetation had regenerated to replenish the soil. Some groups merely shifted fields in a 10-15 year rotation; others

Women in Thai society

Although the logic of Buddhism relegates women to a subordinate position, women in Thailand have considerable influence. In the rural North and Northeast, land was traditionally inherited by the female members of a household (usually the youngest daughter), and husbands reside with their wives. It is common to find the wife controlling the finances in a family, determining where and how much fertilizer to buy, and even giving her husband an 'allowance'. This has been noted for centuries: in 1433 the Chinese Muslim traveller Ma Huan recorded: 'It is their [Siamese] custom that all affairs are managed by their wives ... all trading transactions great and small'. Although in public the role of the man is accentuated, in private, equality of the sexes or the reverse is more usually the case. In the fields, ploughing is usually done by men, but other tasks are equally shared – and often women do more than their fair share.

The relative strength of the woman's role even extends to sexual relations. Ma Huan's 15th-century account of Siam noted how men would have penis balls inserted under their foreskin to increase their partner's pleasure: 'If it is the king ... or a great chief or a wealthy man, they use gold to make hollow beads, inside which a grain of sand is placed ... They make a tinkling sound, and this is regarded as beautiful'.

The contrast between the subordinate position of women in Thai society and their much more influential underlying role is a recurring theme. This would seem to lend credence to the old Thai adage that the two front legs of an elephant are male and the two rear legs, female – the implication being that men lead the way and women follow. Female traders and businesswomen, for instance, are well represented – indeed, there are thought to be more female than male traders. But at the same time, their influential role in private enterprise arises partly because they are largely excluded from high office in the public sector. As a result, ambitious women are forced to enter the private sector. Politics is an almost exclusively male domain. It took 17 years from when women were granted equal political rights to men in 1932 for the first female MP to enter Parliament. But even today women are grossly under-represented. In the elections of 2000 just 21 of the 200 seats in the Senate were filled by women.

The few women who do become MPs, Juree Vichit-Vadakan wrote, 'are perceived to be mere decorative flowers to brighten and lighten the atmosphere' (Bangkok Post, 25.3.97). They are not expected to contribute much to the political process and are not taken seriously by their male counterparts. Thai law also reveals a streak of discrimination: Thai men are permitted to demand a divorce if their wives have just one affair; Thai women can only request a divorce if their husband honours another woman as his wife – he can have as many affairs as he likes.

In previously booming Thailand, mia noi (minor wife) became de rigeur, and having a mistress was rather like having a limited edition Mercedes with a badge showing membership of the Royal Bangkok Sports Club. When it comes to mia noi, there is an unwritten set of rules over how they are to be treated, rules

not only shifted fields but also their villages, relocating in a fresh area of forest when the land had become depleted of nutrients. To obtain salt, metal implements and other goods which could not be made or found in the hills, the tribal peoples would trade forest products such as resins and animal skins with the settled lowland Thais.

that are accepted by both errant husbands and their (first) wives. It is only when these rules are transgressed that all hell breaks loose. Mia noi get BMWs; first wives get rather staider Mercedes, probably with a chauffeur thrown in for good measure. The mia noi will drive herself, wearing Armani sunglasses and perhaps a Versace suit. Mia noi are to be enjoyed in (semi) private. They can be taken for discreet weekends, or out to dinner, but they must not attend official functions and should not grace society pages arm-in-arm with their men. As long as the men and their mia noi stick to the rules, things seem to work just fine.

The collapse in the Thai economy changed things. For most men, there was simply not as much money to throw around on luxuries like minor wives. However, the mia noi of senior politicians may have benefited from the rules introduced in late 1997 that require cabinet ministers to declare their assets (see page 647). Apparently, some politicians, rather than have their improbably extensive holdings exposed to the glare of publicity, transferred cars, houses and other baubles to their minor wives. Even first wives have got something out of the new asset-revealing measures. Former Prime Minister Chaovalit Yongchaiyut, who resigned in 1997, valued his own assets at ฿17m; his wife's amounted to ฿124m.

Not every woman in Thailand becomes a mia noi, of course. In fact it has been argued that education and a career have put many middle-class Thai women off marriage of any sort, whether as first or second wives. They are reluctant to 'marry down' to secure a partner and instead develop their careers and gain social status in that way. While women do face discrimination, Thai society does give them the social space to acquire status on their own, independent of a husband. Some Thai women sense a change in the role and position of women in Thailand, especially in politics. In the 1998 local government elections, nearly 1,500 women were voted in as village heads. This may be just 2½% of the total, but to have a women as a village head was hitherto almost unheard of. Moreover, in the municipal and provincial council elections of early 2000, the proportion of women winning seats reached 10% of the total, double the figure for the previous elections. Perhaps things are changing; but there's still some way to go before Thailand metamorphoses into a tropical Sweden. Maybe it will only be when Buddhism becomes more amenable to the idea that men and women are equal that really profound change will occur.

The Buddha, so far as we know, did not make the road to enlightenment gender specific. Yet women cannot be ordained in Thailand, and religious schools are male-only establishments. There are nuns – mae chi – but they are not generally held in high regard. Thai feminists are trying to break down these religious barriers. In 2001, the (female) Buddhist scholar Chatsumarn Kabilsingh went to Sri Lanka (where these things are possible) to be ordained. She returned to Bangkok to try and establish a 'monastery' for women. The conservative clergy reacted with anger and incomprehension. How could a woman possibly imagine that she was equal to a man in these matters?

This simplified picture of the hilltribe economy is being gradually eroded for a variety of reasons, the most significant being that today there is simply not enough land available in most areas to practise such an extensive system of agriculture.

The Lady Boys

Katoeys, transvestites or, as they tend to be known by farang in Thailand, 'Lady Boys', are larger in number than one might expect. They are also part of a long tradition of transvestites in Southeast Asia. Many bars and clubs will have katoeys working for them, whether as bar 'girls' or in shows of one sort or another. They are often very beautiful and extraordinarily difficult, if not impossible, to tell apart from the real thing. In Bangkok there are also groups of katoeys who have been known to surround and pick-pocket farang men on the street – particularly on the Landmark side of Sukhumvit Road and along sois 5-11.

The Karen (Kariang, Yang)

Origins

The Karen, also known as the Kariang or Yang, are found along the Thai-Burmese border, concentrated in the Mae Hong Son region. They are the largest tribal group in Thailand, numbering about 270,000. Their origins are in Burma, where today many more are fighting a long-term and low-intensity war against the Burmese authorities for greater autonomy. The Karen started to infiltrate into Thailand in the 18th century and moved into areas occupied by the Lawa, possibly the oldest established tribe in Thailand. The evidence of this contact between the two groups can still be seen in the dress, ornamentation and implements of the Karen.

Economy and society

The Karen are divided into two main sub-groups, the Sgaw and the Pwo and these are divided into two sub-groups, the Pa-O and Bwe. The Sgaw and the Pwo are also known as the White Karen. The differences between the two principal groups are in language and dress. The Pwo make up about 20% of the total population and the Sgaw the remaining 80%. Most Karen live in mountain villages and practise shifting cultivation of the rotating field type (that is they move their fields, but not their villages). They prevent soil erosion on the steep slopes by taking care to maintain belts of forest growth between 'swiddens' or fields, by leaving saplings and tree roots to help bind the soil, and by not turning the soil before planting. When a community grows so large that the distance to the outer fields becomes excessive, a group of villagers establish a satellite village beyond the boundaries of the mother village. However, with the pressure on land and the incentive to commercialize production, this traditional pioneering strategy is often no longer possible. Karen are being forced to try and increase yields by developing irrigation, and some Karen have moved down into the valleys and taken-up settled agriculture, imitating the methods of the lowland Thais.

Karen houses are built on stilts out of bamboo, with thatched roofs. Animals are kept under the house at night for protection against wild animals and rustlers. Most houses have only one room and a spacious verandah. A household usually consists of a husband and wife plus their unmarried children. Should a man's wife die, he is not permitted to remarry until his children have left the home, as this would cause conflict with the spirits. Indeed, much of Karen life is dictated by the spirits. The most important is the 'Lord of Land and Water', who controls the productivity of the land and calls upon the rice spirit to grow. Also important is the matrilineal ancestor guardian spirit (*bga*).

The priest is the most revered individual in the village: he is the ritual leader and it is he who sets dates for the annual ceremonies. The post is an ancestral one and

only changes when the priest dies – at which time the village must change location as well (although the distance may only be nominal). As the Karen have been incorporated into the Thai state, so increasing numbers have turned to Buddhism. The role of European missionaries in the highland areas also means that there are significant numbers of Christian Karen. A central Karen myth tells of a younger 'white brother' from across the water, who would arrive with the skills of writing given to him by God. This no doubt helped the missionaries enormously when they arrived, pasty-faced and clutching bibles. In most cases, however, while converting to Buddhism or Christianity, the Karen have at the same time maintained a healthy belief in their traditional spirits.

Material culture

The Karen are prolific weavers. Weaving is done on simple backstrap looms and many Karen still spin their own thread. The upper garments worn by men, women and children are all made in the same way: two strips of material are folded in half, the fold running along the shoulder. They are then sewn together along the centre of the garment and down the sides, leaving holes for the head and arms. The stitching is not merely functional, it is an integral part of the design. Until girls marry, they wear only this garment, full length to just below their knees and made of white cotton. The Sgaw embroider a band of red or pink around their waists, the Pwo embroider red diamond patterns along the lower edge. Married women wear this garment as an over-blouse and they also wear a sarong. The over-blouse is considerably more elaborate than that of the girls: Job's-tear seeds (seeds from a grass) are woven into the design, or a pattern is woven around the border. Pwo women tend to embroider all over the blouse.

The sarong is made up of two strips of material, sewn horizontally and stitched together to make a tubular skirt. They are held up with a cord or metal belt and are worn knee or ankle-length, longer for formal occasions. The colour is predominantly red. The men's shirts are usually hip length, with elaborate embroidery. They wear sarongs or Thai peasant-style pants.

The Sgaw women and girls wear strands of small beads, which hang from mid-chest to waist length, normally red, white or yellow. The Pwo wear them around their neck and to mid-chest length and they are mostly black. Their necklaces are made from old 'bullet coins', strung on braided red thread. Pwo women wear lots of bracelets of silver, copper, brass or aluminium. Sgaw are more moderate in their use of jewellery. All Karen wear silver cup-shaped earrings, which often have coloured tufts of wool attached.

The Hmong (or Meo)

Origins

The Hmong, also known as the Meo, are the second largest tribal group in Thailand, numbering about 82,000. Although their origins are rather hazy, the Hmong themselves claim that they have their roots in the icy north. They had arrived in Laos by 1850 and by the end of the 19th century had migrated into the provinces of Chiang Rai and Nan. Today they are scattered right across the Northern region and have spread over a larger area than any other tribe, apart from the Karen.

Economy and society

There are two sub-groups of the Hmong, the Blue and the White Hmong. (Blue Hmong, aka Black Meo, Flowery Meo or Striped Meo, women wear the distinctive indigo-dyed pleated skirt with a batik design which you often see in northern Thailand. During ceremonial occasions White Hmong women wear white pleated skirts. Day-to-day they wear indigo-dyed trousers. See below). The Hmong value

The hilltribes of Thailand

Tribe	Population	Origins	Date of arrival in Thailand	Location (province)
Karen (Yang/Kariang)	402,095	Burma	C18th	Mae Hong Son
Hmong (Meo)	126,147	China	late C19th	Chiang Rai, Nan
Lahu (Mussur)	78,842	Yunnan (China)	late C19th	Chiang Mai Chiang Rai
Akha (Kaw)	48,468	Yunnan (China)	early C20th	Chiang Rai
Mien (Yao)	47,305	southern China	mid C19th	Chiang Rai, Nan
Htin & Kha Haw	32,755	Laos	—	Nan
Lisu (Lisaw)	31,536	southern China	early C20th	Chiang Mai
Lawa	15,711	—	C7th-8th	Chiang Mai, Mae Hong Son
Khamu	10,153	Laos	—	—
Mlabri	227	—	—	Nan and Phrae
Total hill people population	793,012	—	—	

Sources: http://www.chmai.com/tribal/content.html and others.

their independence, and tend to live at high altitudes, away from other tribes. This independence, and their association with poppy cultivation, has meant that of all the hilltribes it is the Hmong who have been most severely persecuted by the Thai authorities. They are persecuted by the Thai government for three main reasons: because they were thought (less so now) to be a security risk, prone to banditry and so on; because they cultivate the higher lands and clear primary forest on watersheds, and are therefore seen as environmentally destructive; and because they were the main cultivators of opium in the north (again, less so now). Finally, and in general, they are seen as the 'hardest' of the hill peoples, commercially savvy. Like most hilltribes, they practise shifting cultivation, moving their villages when the surrounding land has been exhausted. The process of moving is stretched out over two seasons: an advance party finds a suitable site, builds temporary shelters, clears the land and plants rice, and only after the harvest do the rest of the inhabitants follow on.

Hmong villages tend not to be fenced, while their houses are built of wood or bamboo at ground level. Each house has a main living area and two or three sleeping rooms. The extended family is headed by the oldest male: he settles family disputes and has supreme authority over family affairs. Like the Karen, the Hmong too are spirit worshippers and believe in household spirits. Every house has an altar, where protection for the household is sought. Despite 21st-century pressures (particularly scarcity of land), they maintain a strong sense of identity. The children may be educated in Thai schools, but they invariably return to farming alongside their parents.

Material culture

The Hmong are the only tribe in Thailand who make batik: indigo-dyed batik makes up the main panel of their skirts, with appliqué and embroidery added to it. The women also wear black leggings from their knees to their ankles, black jackets (with embroidery), and a black panel or 'apron', held in place with a cummerbund. Even the smallest children wear clothes of intricate design with exquisite needlework. Today much of the cloth is purchased from the market or from traders; traditionally it would have been woven by hand on a foot-treddle/back-strap loom.

The White Hmong tend to wear less elaborate clothing from day to day, saving it for special occasions only. Hmong men wear loose-fitting black trousers, black jackets (sometimes embroidered) and coloured or embroidered sashes.

The Hmong particularly value silver jewellery: it signifies wealth and a good life. Men, women and children wear silver: tiers of neck rings, heavy silver chains with lock-shaped pendants, earrings and pointed rings on every finger. All the family jewellery is brought out at New Year and is an impressive sight, symbolizing the wealth of the family.

Hilltribes

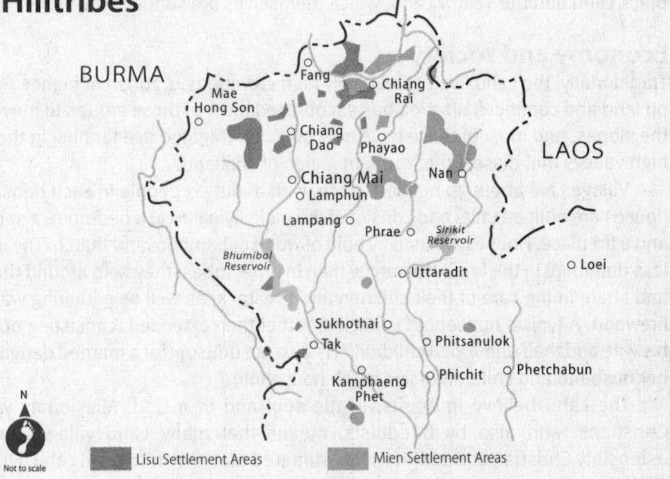

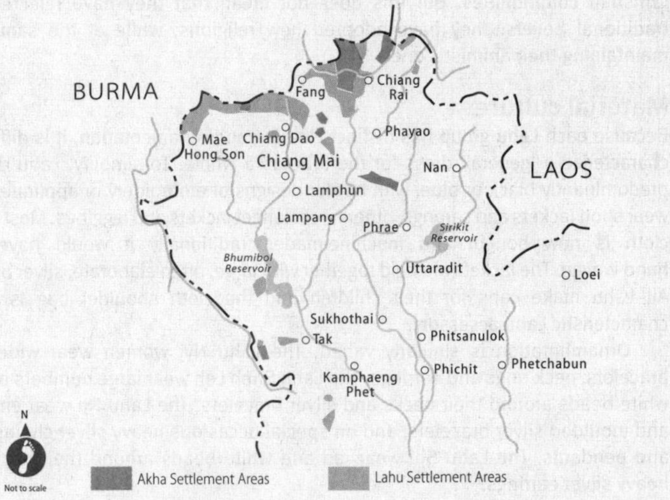

Even though the Hmong are perhaps the most independent of all the hilltribes, they too are being drawn into the 'modern' world. Some still grow the poppy at higher elevations, but the general shortage of land is forcing them to descend to lower altitudes, to take up irrigated rice farming, to grow cash crops, and to mix with the lowland Thais. This has led to conflicts between the Hmong and the lowlanders as they compete for the same resources – previously they would have been occupying quite different ecological niches.

The Lahu (or Mussur)

Origins

The Lahu in Thailand are found along the Burmese border and number about 60,000. They originated in Yunnan (South China) and migrated from Burma into Thailand at the end of the 19th century. Today, the majority of Thai Lahu are found in the provinces of Chiang Mai and Chiang Rai. There are a number of Lahu sub-groups, each with slightly different traditions and clothing. The two dominant groups are the Black Lahu and the Yellow Lahu, which themselves are subdivided.

Economy and society

Traditionally, the Lahu lived at relatively high elevations, 1,200 m or higher. Pressure on land and commercialization has encouraged most of these groups to move down the slopes, and most of these have now taken up irrigated rice farming in the small, high valleys that dissect the Northern region of Thailand.

Villages are about 30 houses strong, with about six people in each house. Their houses are built on stilts and consist of the main living area, a bedroom, a spirit altar and a fireplace. Houses are usually built of wood or bamboo, and thatch. The men are less dominant in the family hierarchy than in other tribes: they help around the home and share in the care of their children and livestock, as well as gathering water and firewood. A typical household is nuclear rather than extended, consisting of a man, his wife and their unmarried children. It is also not unusual for a married daughter and her husband and children to live in the household.

The Lahu believe in spirits, in the soul and in a God. Missionary work by Christians, and also by Buddhists, means that many Lahu villages are now ostensibly Christian or Buddhist. It is estimated that one-third of all Lahu live within Christian communities. But this does not mean that they have rejected their traditional beliefs: they have adopted new religions, while at the same time maintaining their animistic ones.

Material culture

Because each Lahu group has distinct clothing and ornamentation, it is difficult to characterize a 'general' dress for the tribe as a whole. To simplify, Lahu dress is predominantly black or blue, with border designs of embroidery or appliqué. Some wear short jackets and sarongs, others wear longer jackets and leggings. Most of their cloth is now bought and machine-made; traditionally it would have been hand-woven. The jackets are held together with large, often elaborate, silver buckles. All Lahu make caps for their children and the cloth shoulder bag is also a characteristic Lahu accessory.

Ornamentation is similarly varied. The Lahu Nyi women wear wide silver bracelets, neck rings and earrings. The Lahu Sheh Leh wear large numbers of small white beads around their necks and silver bracelets. The Lahu Na wear engraved and moulded silver bracelets, and on special occasions heavy silver chains, bells and pendants. The Lahu Shi wear red and white beads around their necks and heavy silver earrings.

The Akha (or Kaw)

Origins

The Akha, or Kaw, number about 33,000 in Thailand and are found in a relatively small area of the North, near Chiang Rai. They have their origins in Yunnan, southern China, and from there spread into Burma (where there are nearly 200,000) and rather later into Thailand. The first Akha village was not established in Thailand until the very beginning of the 20th century. They prefer to live along ridges, at about 1,000 m.

Economy and society

The Akha are shifting cultivators, growing primarily dry rice on mountainsides but also a wide variety of vegetables. The cultivation of rice is bound up with myths and rituals: the rice plant is regarded as a sentient being, and the selection of the swidden, its clearance, the planting of the rice seed, the care of the growing plants, and finally the harvest of the rice, must all be done according to the Akha Way. Any offence to the rice soul must be rectified by ceremonies.

Hilltribes

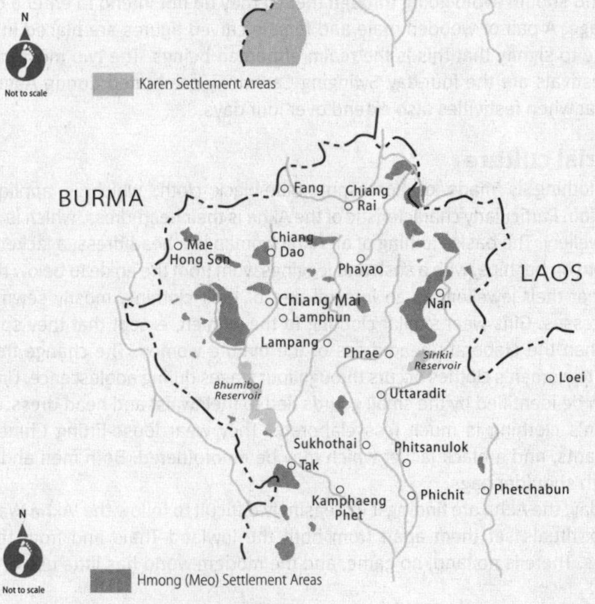

The hilltribe calendar

	Karen	Hmong	Mien (Yao)
January	village ceremony	New Year festival	embroidering
February	site selection	scoring poppies	scoring poppies
March	clearing field	clearing field	clearing field
April	burning field	burning field	burning field
May	rice planting	rice planting	rice and maize planting
June	field spirit offering	weeding	weeding
July	field spirit offering	weeding	weeding
August	weeding	weeding	harvesting
September	rat trapping	poppy seeding	poppy seeding
October	rice harvest	thinning poppy field	rice harvest
November	rice harvest	rice harvest	rice harvest
December	rice threshing	New Year festival	rice threshing

Source: Tribal Research Institute, Chiang Mai University.

Akha villages are identified by their gates, a village swing and high-roofed houses on posts. They have no word for religion, but believe in the 'Akha Way'. They are able to recite the names of all their male ancestors (60 names or more) and they keep an ancestral altar in their homes, at which food is offered up at important times in the year such as New Year, during the village swing ceremony, and after the rice harvest.

At the upper and lower ends of the village are gates which are renewed every year. Visitors should walk through them in order to rid themselves of the spirit of the jungle. The gates are sacred and must not be defiled. Visitors must not touch the gates and should avoid going through them if they do not intend to enter a house in the village. A pair of wooden male and female carved figures are placed inside the entrance to signify that this is the realm of human beings. The two most important Akha festivals are the four-day Swinging Ceremony celebrated during August, and New Year when festivities also extend over four days.

Material culture

Akha clothing is made of homespun blue-black cloth, which is appliquéd for decoration. Particularly characteristic of the Akha is their head-dress, which is adorned with jewellery. The basic clothing of an Akha woman is a head-dress, a jacket, a short skirt worn on her hips, with a sash and leggings worn from the ankle to below the knee. They wear their jewellery as an integral part of their clothing, mostly sewn to their head-dresses. Girls wear similar clothing to the women, except that they sport caps rather than the elaborate head-dress of the mature women. The change from girl's clothes to women's clothes occurs through four stages during adolescence. Unmarried girls can be identified by the small gourds tied to their waist and head-dress.

Men's clothing is much less elaborate. They wear loose-fitting Chinese-style black pants, and a black jacket which may be embroidered. Both men and women use cloth shoulder bags.

Today, the Akha are finding it increasingly difficult to follow the 'Akha Way'. Their complex rituals set them apart from both the lowland Thais and from the other hilltribes. There is no land, no game, and the modern world has little use or time for

Akha	Lisu	Lahu
weaving	New Year Festival	scoring poppies
clearing fields	Second New Year festival	New Year Festival
burning field	clearing field	burning field
rice spirit ceremony	burning field	field spirit house
rice planting	rice dibbling	rice planting
weeding	weeding	weeding
weeding	weeding	weeding
swinging ceremony	soul calling ceremony	weeding
poppy seeding	maize harvest	maize harvest
rice harvest	poppy seeding	field spirit offering
rice harvest	rice harvest	rice harvest
New Year festival	rice threshing	field spirit offering

their ways. The conflicts and pressures which the Akha currently face, and their inability to reconcile the old with the new, is claimed by some to explain why the incidence of opium addiction among the Akha is so high.

The Mien (or Yao)

Origins

The Mien, or Yao, are unique among the hilltribes in that they have a tradition of writing based on Chinese characters. Mien legend has it that they came from 'across the sea' during the 14th century, although it is generally thought that their roots are in South China where they originated about 2,000 years ago. They first migrated into Thailand from Laos in the mid-19th century and they currently number about 36,000, mostly in the provinces of Chiang Rai and Nan, close to the Laotian border.

Economy and society

The Mien village is not enclosed and is usually found on sloping ground. The houses are large, wooden affairs, as they need to accommodate an extended family of sometimes 20 or more members. They are built on the ground, not on stilts, and have one large living area and four or more bedrooms. As with other tribes, the construction of the house must be undertaken carefully. The house needs to be orientated appropriately, so that the spirits are not disturbed, and the ancestral altar installed on an auspicious day.

The Mien combine two religious beliefs: on the one hand they recognize and pay their dues to spirits and ancestors (informing them of family developments); on the other, they follow Taoism as it was practised in China in the 13th and 14th centuries. The Taoist rituals are expensive, and the Mien appear to spend a great deal of their lives struggling to save enough money to afford the various ceremonies, such as weddings, merit-making and death ceremonies. The Mien economy is based upon the shifting cultivation of dry rice, corn and small quantities of opium poppy.

Material culture

The Mien women dress distinctively, with black turbans and red-ruffed tunics, making them easy to distinguish from the other hilltribes. All their clothes are made of black or indigo-dyed homespun cotton, which is then embroidered using distinctive cross-stitching. Their trousers are the most elaborate garments. Unusually, they sew from the back of the cloth and cannot see the pattern they are making. The children wear embroidered caps, with red pompoms on the top and by the ears. The men's dress is a simple indigo-dyed jacket and trousers, with little embroidery.

The Htin

Origins

The Htin go by a number of other names: Tin, Thin or Kha T'in in Thailand, and Phai or Kha Phai in Laos. They are said to prefer Mal or Prai. The Htin have probably been living in Thailand for a considerable time, although their arrival in the country and their origins are not well documented. In total there were 32,755 Htin living in Thailand in 1995.

Economy and society

The Htin are concentrated in Nan province along the border with Laos and, traditionally, were migratory shifting cultivators growing glutinous (sticky) dry rice and a range of other dryland crops. Some continue to cultivate opium, although these are very small in number. Today, because of land shortages, few can continue to cultivate land in their traditional, extensive manner. The emphasis of the Htin economy may remain on farming but few are food secure and they need to engage in other activities to meet their needs. The general view, however, is that the Htin have found it difficult to adapt to modern, commercial life and have been marginalised by the process of modernisation, unable to compete effectively with other groups.

The Htin are monogamous and matrilocal (ie the husband lives with his wife), like many other people in Northern and Northeastern Thailand. There has been some conversion of Htin to Buddhism, mostly among those living on lower slopes where they have come into contact with lowland Tai settlements. The majority, though, are still animist. While their religious beliefs may have shown some resilience, the same is not true of their material culture. Very few Htin wear their traditional clothes, except for a handful of older women.

The Kha Haw

The Kha Haw are one of the smallest - in terms of number - groups of hill people living in Thailand. When they were last surveyed in the mid-1990s there was just a single Kha Haw village of 28 houses and 196 individuals. This village is situated in Nan province's district of Rae. They are also one of the most recent to have settled in the country, arriving not more than 50 years ago. Like the Htin, the Kah Haw were traditionally migratory shifting cultivators growing glutinous dry rice.

The Lisu (or Lisaw)

Origins

The Lisu number some 25,000 in Thailand, and live in the mountainous region northwest of Chiang Mai. They probably originated in China, at the headwaters of the Salween River, and did not begin to settle in Thailand until the early 20th century.

Economy and society

The Lisu grow rice and vegetables for subsistence and opium for sale. Rice is grown at lower altitudes and the opium poppy at over 1,500 m. Villages are located so that the inhabitants can maintain some independence from the Thai authorities. At the same time they need to be relatively close to a market so that they can trade.

Lisu houses may be built either on the ground or raised above it: the former are more popular at higher altitudes as they are said to be warmer. The floors and walls are made from wood and bamboo, and the roof is thatched. The house is divided into a bedroom, a large living area, and also contains a guest platform. Within each house there will also be a fireplace and an ancestral altar.

Each village has a 'village guardian spirit shrine' which is located above the village, in a roofed pavilion that women are forbidden to enter. Local disputes are settled by a headman, and kinship is based upon patrilineal clans. As well as the village guardian, the Lisu worship Wu Sa – the creator – and a multitude of spirits of the forest, ancestors, trees, the sun, moon and everyday objects. Coupled with this, the Lisu fear possession by weretigers (*phi pheu*) and vampires (*phu seu*).

Material culture

Lisu clothing is some of the most brightly coloured, and most distinctive, of all the hilltribes. They make up their clothes from machine-made cloth. The women wear long tunics – often bright blue, with red sleeves and pattern-work around the yoke – black knee-length pants and red leggings. A wide black sash is wound tightly round the waist. Looped around this at the back is a pair of tassels consisting of many tightly woven threads, with pompoms attached to the ends (sometimes as many as 500 strands in a pair of tassels). Turbans, again with coloured tassels attached, are worn for special occasions. The man's attire is simpler: a black jacket, blue or green trousers and black leggings.

The most important ceremony is New Year (celebrated on the same day as the Chinese), when the villagers dress up in all their finery and partake in a series of rituals. At this time, the women wear copious amounts of silver jewellery: tunics with rows of silver buttons sewn onto them, and abundant heavy necklaces.

The Lawa (or Lua)

Origins

The Lawa, known as the Lua by the Thai, are only to be found in northern Thailand. They are thought to have migrated into the valley of the Mae Ping in the 7th century and were among the very first hill tribe settlers in present day Thailand. In the 1995 census they numbered 15,711 individuals, mostly concentrated to the southeast of Mae Hong Son, to the southwest of Chiang Mai and in the upland areas around Umpai. However a significant number have probably assimilated into mainstream Thai society and, as a tribal minority, have effectively disappeared from view.

Economy and society

Those who maintain their traditional ways practice rotational shifting cultivation. They are regarded as among the most environmentally-aware of swidden cultivators. A fair number have embraced wet rice culture, although whether they are hill or padi farmers they tend to be subsistence oriented in terms of production. In addition to farming, the Lawa have a long tradition of working as iron smiths and most have also taken on supplementary non-farm income earning activities. Due to limited land and environmental degradation few can survive adequately from agriculture alone.

In terms of social structure, the Lawa are monogamous and patrilineal. While many have converted to Buddhism, this is creatively combined with ancestor

A Thai hilltribe clothing primer

Karen are among the best and most prolific of hilltribe weavers. Their traditional striped warp ikat, dyed in soft hues, is characteristically inter-sewn with job's seeds. Girls wear creamy white smocks with red stitching, whilst women wear coloured smocks and strings of beads. Their tunics are made up of two lengths of cloth, worn vertically, sewn together down the centre and sides, leaving a hole for the neck and the arms.

Hmong (Meo) produce exquisite embroidery made up of appliquéd layers of fabric of geometric shapes, worn by men, women and children. Some of the patternwork on their pleated skirts is achieved by batik (the only hilltribe to do this). Jackets are of black velvet or satinized cotton, with embroidered lapels. They wear black or white leggings and sashes to hold up their skirts. Hand weaving is a dying art among the Hmong.

Lahu (Mussur) groups traditionally wore a diverse array of clothing. All embroider, but many have now abandoned the use of traditional dress. Another common feature is the shoulder bag – primarily red in the case of the Lahu Nyi (the 'Red' Lahu), black among the Lahu Sheh Leh (and often tasselled), black with patchwork for the Lahu Na, and often striped in the case of the Lahu Shi.

Mien (Yao) embroidery is distinguished by cross-stitching on indigo fabric, worn as baggy trousers and turbans. They are one of the easiest of the hilltribes to identify because of their distinctive red-collared jackets. Virtually none of the cloth is hand woven – it is bought and then sometimes re-dyed before being decorated.

Akha are most easily distinguished by their elaborate head-dresses, made up of silver beads, coins and buttons. Akha cloth is limited to plain weave, dyed with indigo (after weaving) – and still often made from home-grown cotton. This is then decorated with embroidery, shells, buttons, silver and seeds. Akha patchwork is highly intricate work, involving the assembly of tiny pieces of cloth.

Lisu wear very brightly coloured clothing and (at festivals) lots of jewellery. Particularly notable are the green and blue kaftans with red sleeves, worn with baggy Chinese trousers and black turbans. Lisu weaving has virtually died out.

worship and their former animist belief system. The Lawa have wavy hair and the men, often, quite thick beards. Unfortunately very few wear their traditional clothes, most having adopted Thai/Western dress. But among those who do, the women wear plain cotton clothes: off-white (girls) or blue blouses (married women), which are sometimes embroidered on the sleeves. Leggings are also worn by women, although jewellery and silver bracelets are rarely displayed. Men have given up their traditional dress almost entirely.

The Khamu

The Khamu are mainly concentrated in neighbouring Laos and there are few living in Thailand - in 1995, just 10,153 concentrated in Nan province close to the border with Laos. There are also, however, settlements in Lampang, Chiang Rai and as far away as Kanchanaburi in the west of Thailand. They are thought to have settled here from Luang Prabang, Xieng Khouang and Vientiane in Laos, arriving first of all as

labourers. Most have assimilated to varying degrees into mainstream Thai society although some have established themselves as swidden farmers and maintained their ethnic distinctiveness.

Their dress is similar to that of the Lawa but, for the women, with more embroidery, jewellery and beads. During festivals men wear distinctive embroidered long-sleeved jackets fastened at the side at the neck. Day-to-day however the men wear lowland Thai clothes. There are also strong linguistic similarities between the Khamu and Lawa.

The Khamu are patrilineal and patrilocal and many continue with their animist beliefs. They construct spirit gates on the approach to the village and make offerings of food and sacrifice chickens to the spirits. To varying degrees elements of Buddhism have been incorporated into their traditional belief system and some have also converted to Christianity. The Khamu practice shifting cultivation in addition to hunting, fishing and the collection of non-timber forest products. Like other groups, because of the falling productivity of agriculture they also engage in various non-farm occupations, working as labourers on construction sites, for example.

Phu Thai

The Phu Thai are a sub-group of the Thai. There are over 150,000 Phu Thai speakers in Thailand, and close to this number also in Laos and Vietnam. They wear distinctive *pha sin* tube skirts and also have their own dances and ceremonies similar to those of the Lao of Northeastern Thailand and Laos. Perhaps the most familiar custom is the *ba sii* ceremony when sacred thread, *sai sin*, is tied around a person's wrists.

Mlabri

The elusive Mlabri 'tribe' of Eastern Thailand represent one of the few remaining groups of hunter-gatherers in Southeast Asia. They are also known as the Phi Tong Luang or 'Spirits of the Yellow Leaves', because when their shelters of rattan and banana leaves turn yellow, they take this as a sign from the spirits that it is time to move on.

Padaung

The Padaung are a Burmese people from the state of Kayah who were forced out of Burma during their long struggle for autonomy. They have become refugees in Northern Thailand and objects of tourist fascination, also known as the 'Long-Necked Karen' or, derogatorily, as the 'giraffe people' because of the wearing of neck coils. See also box on page 264.

Suay

The Suay are a 'tribe' of elephant catchers speaking their own dialect of Thai and with their own customs. They are thought to have come from Cambodia and settled in Thailand where they honed their skills of catching, taming and training elephants. Unfortunately, with the end of logging in Thailand the work of elephants – and therefore of the Suay – has dried up. They have become a people without a purpose.

Refugees

Thailand's relative economic prosperity, coupled with the wars that have afflicted neighbouring countries, have brought in waves of refugees to the Kingdom in recent years. Following the victory of Communist forces in Cambodia and Laos in the mid-1970s, many thousands fled to the safety of Thailand. Those escaping the atrocities of the Khmer Rouge – over 300,000 – settled in refugee camps along the southern rim of the Northeastern region and have since been repatriated. The several hundred thousand Lao who crossed the Mekong River as the Pathet Lao took control of Laos took shelter in refugee camps along the northern sweep of the Northeast. These camps too have been closed and their inmates largely resettled in the USA, Australia, France and Canada.

More recently, the crushing of the democracy movement in Burma in 1988 caused several tens of thousands of Burmese to flee to Thailand. More than 100,000 continue to live in camps along the Thai-Burmese border, from Prachuap Khiri Khan in the south to Mae Hong Son in the North. Guesthouses in Mae Sot, and also in Sangkhlaburi, often collect clothes and medicines for distribution to the refugee camps. These political refugees, fleeing persecution – or the fear of persecution – in their own countries, have been joined since the late 1980s by a new army of economic refugees. In 1997 there were an estimated one million illegal migrant workers in Thailand, most of them (around 75%) from Burma, but with large numbers also from China, Laos, Cambodia and Vietnam, and smaller populations from India, Bangladesh and Pakistan. There are probably more illegal labour migrants and refugees in Thailand than there are hill peoples, making them the largest 'minority' group in the country.

In mid-1996 the government announced it would permit illegal migrants already in the country (but not new arrivals) to work for two years before their repatriation. At the end of the three-month amnesty that was granted to allow illegal immigrants to register, the Immigration Department had compiled a list 342,000 names long. The reason for this strange policy decision was that Thailand, at that time, was woefully short of cheap labour: rapid economic growth had priced many Thai workers out of the lower paid, unskilled manual jobs, and illegal labour migrants from neighbouring Burma, Cambodia and Laos were seen as a neat (and cheap) way to fill the gap. Jobs in road maintenance, sugar cane cutting, construction, food packing and freezing, for example, were characteristically filled by immigrants willing to take so-called 3-D jobs (dangerous, dirty and demeaning – sometimes, for good measure, difficult, too).

With the economic crisis, the logic of the government's decision was, seemingly, undermined. In 1997 and 1998, Thais were being laid off as factories shut down. Immigrant workers, in their turn, were displaced as the sensibilities of Thais over what they did eased in the face of economic necessity. The result was that tens of thousands of Burmese found themselves living in camps on the Thai-Burmese border, waiting for repatriation. But while the crisis certainly made life hard for Thailand's economic migrants, many continued to fill the least attractive jobs. There is little doubt that many thousands of Burmese, Cambodian and Lao workers remain in Thailand, many illegally, often taking on the jobs which are too dirty, dangerous and poorly paid to attract the average Thai.

Language

According to the Thai census, 97% of the population of Thailand speak Thai – the national language. However, it would be more accurate to say that 97% of the population speak one of several related 'Tai' dialects.

The Thai language is an amalgam of Mon and Khmer, and the ancient Indian languages, Pali and Sanskrit. It has also been influenced by Chinese dialects and by Malay. There remains strong academic disagreement as to whether it should be seen as primarily a language of the Sino-Tibetan group, or more closely linked to Austronesian languages. It is usually accepted that the Thai writing system was devised by King Ramkhamhaeng in 1283, who modelled it on an Indian system using Khmer characters (although see page 193). The modern Thai alphabet contains 44 consonants, 24 vowels and four diacritical tone marks. Words often link with other languages, particularly technical words. For example, *praisani*/post office (Sanskrit), *khipanawut*/guided missile (Pali) and *supermarket*/supermarket (English). There is also a royal court language (*rachasap*) with a specialized vocabulary, as well as a vocabularly to be used when talking to monks.

See also words & phrases, page 720.

The usual view of Thailand is one of homogeneity in language terms. Even long-term residents and those who speak Thai will observe that the Kingdom is almost mono-lingual. But, as William Smalley – a linguistics professor at Bethel College and a former missionary linguist in Vietnam, Laos and Thailand – explained in his book *Linguistic Diversity and National Unity: Language Ecology in Thailand* (University of Chicago Press: Chicago, 1994), there are over 80 languages spoken in Thailand and great diversity in linguistic terms. What is interesting is that despite this great diversity, language has not become a divisive and politicized issue. There are those in the Northeast and the South who argue the case for a greater recognition of regional languages – Lao (or Isan) and Pak Tai respectively – but so-called Standard Thai is still perceived to be the language of *all* Thais. Thus, the view of Thailand being a country of 'one' language, though it may in academic terms be incorrect, in functional and political terms is broadly accurate. Thailand is a country with a united sense of itself, yet with a fragmented linguistic pattern. Successive governments have contributed to this by portraying the country as culturally homogenous and assuming that everyone who speaks one of a number of Tai dialects speaks Thai. William Smalley illustrates this diversity by giving the example of a teacher from the Northeast: 'A high school teacher in the provincial capital of Surin in Northeast Thailand speaks the Northern Khmer language of the area to her neighbors and in many other informal situations around town. She learned it by living and working in the city for several years. On the other hand, she speaks Lao with her husband, a government official, because that is his mother tongue. She learned it (and met him) when she was in training as a teacher in the Lao-speaking area of the Northeast. She teaches in Standard Thai, which she herself learned in school. She talks to her children in Lao or Northern Khmer or Standard Thai, as seems appropriate at the time. When she returns to her home village, an hour's ride by bus to the east of Surin, she speaks Kuy, her own native language, the language of her parents, the language in which she grew up.' (Smalley 1994:1)

Thailand's four main regional languages are Lao (spoken in the Northeast), Kham Muang ('language of the principalities', spoken in the North), Thai Klang (spoken in the Central region) and Pak Tai ('southern tongue', spoken in the South). These four languages, and Standard Thai, are spoken by the following proportions of the total population: Thai Klang (27%), Lao (23%), Standard Thai (20%), Kam Muang (9%), Pak Tai (8%). **Note** Thai Klang (Central Thai) is not the same as Standard Thai.

Thai, like many languages, has borrowed extensively from the English language. However, Thai has always pillaged other languages – particularly Chinese, Khmer, Pali and Sanskrit. Sometimes there are different words for pieces of modern technology which span this divide. For example, anyone being taught formal Thai will learn that the word for television is *thoorathat*. This is constructed from two classical words meaning 'far away' and 'view'. However, saying *thoorathat* is a little like saying gramophone in English, and may elicit a giggle. Most Thais now talk about the *thii wii*, clearly borrowed from the English. There are many other Thai words with English borrowings: *thek* from discotheque, *piknik* from picnic, *chut* from suit (for a set of something), and so on.

Literature

The first piece of Thai literature is recognized as being King Ramkhamhaeng's inscription No 1 of 1292 (see page 622). The *Suphasit Phra Ruang* ('The maxims of King Ruang'), perhaps written by King Ramkhamhaeng himself, is regarded as the first piece of Thai poetry of the genre, known as *suphasit*. It shows clear links with earlier Pali works and with Indian-Buddhist religious texts, and an adaptation of the original can be seen carved in marble at Wat Pho in Bangkok (see page 91).

Another important early piece of prose is the *Traiphum Phra Ruang* or the 'Three worlds of Phra Ruang', probably written by King Lithai in the mid-14th century. The work investigates the Three Buddhist realms – earth, heaven and hell – and also offers advice on how a *cakravartin* – a Universal Monarch – should govern. According to Phra Ruang, or the *Traibhumikata*, it is regarded as the masterpiece of Tai Buddhist cosmology. Authorship is usually attributed to King Lithai of Sukhothai, although this is far from conclusively settled. He is thought to have written the book while heir apparent, in 1345. The book sets out the desired relationship of a ruler to his subjects and the characteristics of a righteous monarch. The merit of the ruler spreads out like an umbrella to touch and shield all those who come within its protecting and civilizing powers. In this way the *Three Worlds* is seen to describe the form and function of the Tai city state or *müang*, most clearly reflected in Sukhothai and Si Satchanalai.

The literary arts flourished during the Ayutthayan period, particular poetry. Five forms of verse evolved during this period, and they are still in use today – *chan*, *kap*, *khlong*, *klon* and *rai*. The first two are Indian in origin, the last three are Thai. Each has strict rules of rhyme and structure.

The genre of poetry known as *nirat* reached its height during the reign of King Narai (1656-88). These are long narrative poems, written in *khlong* form, usually describing a journey. They have proved useful to historians and other scholars in their attempts to reconstruct Thai life. The poem *Khlong Kamsuan Siprat* is regarded as the masterpiece of this genre. Unfortunately, many of the manuscripts of these Ayutthayan works were lost when the Burmese sacked the city in 1767.

During the Rattanakosin period, focused on Bangkok/Thonburi, the first piece of Thai prose fiction was written – a historical romance written by Chao Phraya Phra Khlang. The first full version of the Ramakien was also produced in *klon* verse form (see page 95). The acknowledged poetic genius of the period was Sunthorn Phu (1786-1855) – who the Thais think of as their Shakespeare – whose masterpiece is the 30,000 line romance *Phra Aphaimani* (see page 384).

The Revolution of 1932 led to a transformation in Thai literature. The first novel to be received with acclaim was Prince Arkartdamkeung Rapheephat's *Lakhon haeng chiwit* ('The circus of life'), published in 1929 (which has been translated into English – see below). Sadly, this gifted novelist died at the age of 27. Two other talented novelists were the commoner Si Burapha, whose masterpiece is *Songkhram chiwit* ('War of life') (1932), and the female writer Dokmai Sot, whose publications include *Phu dii* ('The good person') (1937). The works of Dokmai Sot, like those of Prince Akat, deal with the theme of the clash of Thai and Western cultures. Their works are particularly pertinent today, when many educated Thais are re-examining their cultural roots.

Since the Second World War, second rate love/romance writing has flourished. The plots vary only marginally from book to book: love triangles, jealousy, macho men, faithful women... This dismal outpouring is partly balanced by a handful of quality works. Notable are those of Kukrit Pramoj, a journalist and former Prime Minister, whose most famous and best work is *Si phaen din* ('The four reigns') (1953). This traces the history of a noble family from the late-19th century to the end of the Second World War – a sort of Barbara Cartland à la Thailand.

During the political turmoil from the 1950s through to the present day, but particularly from 1973 to 1976, literature began to be used more explicitly as a tool of political commentary and criticism. *Phai daeng* ('Red Bamboo') (1954) is a carefully constructed anti-communist novel by Kukrit Pramoj, while the poems of Angkhan Kanlayanaphong became favourites of the radical student movement of the 1970s. Many of the more radical novelists were gaoled during the 1950s, of whom the most talented was probably Si Burapha He, and the other radical novelists' and poets' work, represent a genre of socialist realism in which the country's afflictions are put down to capitalism and right-wing politics. But perhaps the most successful of Thai novels are

those that deal with the trials and tribulations of rural life: Kamphoon Boontawee's *Luuk Isan* ('Child of the Northeast') (1976) and Khammaan Khonkai's *Khru ban nok* ('The Rural Teacher'), later made into the film *The Teacher of Mad Dog Swamp*. See Books, page 716.

Art and architecture

The various periods of Thai art and architecture were characterized by their own distinctive styles. For illustrations, see the Buddha images on page 691.

One of the problems with reconstructing the artistic heritage of any Southeast Asian civilization is that most buildings were built of wood. Wood was abundant, but it also rotted quickly in the warm and humid climate. Although there can be no doubt that fine buildings made of wood were constructed by the various kingdoms of Thailand, much of the art that remains – and on which our appreciation is built – is made of stone, brick or bronze. There are few wooden buildings more than a century or so old.

Dvaravati style (c6th-11th centuries)

The Dvaravati Kingdom is rather an enigma to art historians. Theravada Buddhist objects have been unearthed in various parts of the Central Plains which date from the sixth century onwards, among them coins with the inscription 'the merit of the king of Dvaravati'. The capital of this kingdom was probably Nakhon Pathom, west of Bangkok, and it is thought that the inhabitants were Mon in origin. The kingdom covered much of Lower Burma and Central Thailand, and may have been influential from as early as the third century to as late as the 13th.

Dvaravati Buddha images show stylistic similarities with Indian Gupta and post-Gupta images (4th-8th centuries), and with pre-Pala (also Indian) images (8th- 11th centuries). Most are carved in stone, with only small images cast in bronze. Standing images tend to be presented in the attitude of vitarkamudra (see page 691), and later carvings show more strongly indigenous facial features: a flatter face, prominent eyes, and thick nose and lips. Fragments of red paint have been discovered on some images, leading art historians to believe that the carvings would originally have been painted.

Also characteristic of Dvaravati art are terracotta sculptures – some intricately carved (such as those found at Nakhon Pathom and exhibited in the museum there) – carved bas-reliefs and stone Wheels of Law. As well as Nakhon Pathom, Dvaravati art has also been discovered at Uthong in Suphanburi province, and Muang Fa Daed in Kalasin (Northeastern region). But perhaps the finest and most complete remnants of the Dvaravati tradition are in the town of Lamphun, formerly Haripunjaya (see below).

Haripunjaya style (7th-13th centuries)

It seems that during the seventh century the Dvaravati-influenced inhabitants of Lopburi (Lavo) migrated north to found a new city: Haripunjaya, now called Lamphun (see page 235). Although the art of this Mon outlier was influenced by the Indian Pala tradition, as well as by Khmer styles, it maintained its independence long after the rest of the Dvaravati Kingdom had been subsumed by the stronger Tai kingdoms. Indeed, it was not until the late-13th century that Haripunjaya was conquered by the Tais, and as a result is probably the oldest preserved city in Thailand.

Srivijaya (8th-13th centuries)

The Srivijayan Empire was a powerful maritime empire which extended from Java northwards into Thailand, and had its capital at Palembang in Sumatra. Like Dvaravati art, Srivijayan art was also heavily influenced by Indian traditions. It seems likely that this part of Thailand was on the trade route between India and China, and as a result local artists were well aware of Indian styles. A problem with characterizing the art of this period – which spanned five centuries – is that it is very varied.

 Srivijaya was a Mahayana Buddhist Empire, and numerous Avalokitesvara Bodhisattvas have been found, in both stone and bronze, at Chaiya (see page 556). Some of these are wonderfully carved, and particularly notable is the supremely modelled bronze Avalokitesvara (eighth century, 63 cm high), unearthed at Chaiya and now housed in the National Museum in Bangkok. In fact, so much Srivijayan art has been discovered around this town that some experts went so far as to argue that Chaiya, and not Palembang, was the capital of Srivijaya. Unfortunately, however, there are few architectural remnants from the period. Two exceptions are Wat Phra Boromthat and Wat Kaeo, both at Chaiya (see page 556).

Khmer or Lopburi style (7th-14th centuries)

Khmer art has been found in the Eastern, Central and Northeastern regions of the country, and is closely linked to the art and architecture of Cambodia. It is usually referred to as Lopburi style because the town of Lopburi in the Central Plains is assumed to have been a centre of the Khmer Empire in Thailand (see page 168). The art is Mahayana Buddhist in inspiration and stylistic changes mirror those in Cambodia. In Thailand, the period of Khmer artistic influence begins with the reign of Suryavarman I (1002-50) and includes Muang Tham, Prasat Phranomwan and the beginnings of Phanom Rung; Phimai, the most visited of the Khmer Shrines, was built during the reign of the great King Jayavarman VII (1181-1217).

Lopburi Buddhas are authoritative, with flat, square faces and a protuberance on the crown of the head signifying enlightenment. They are the first Buddhas to be portrayed in regal attire, as the Khmers believed that the king, as a *deva raja* (god king), was himself divine. They were carved in stone or cast in bronze. Sadly, many of the finer Khmer pieces have been smuggled abroad. Khmer temples in Thailand are among the most magnificent structures in Southeast Asia. The biggest are those of the Northeastern region, including Phimai, Muang Tham and Phanom Rung, although Khmer architecture is also to be found as far afield as Lopburi and at Muang Kao outside Kanchanaburi.

Chiang Saen or Chiang Mai style (c11th-18th centuries)

This period marks the beginning of Tai art. Earlier works were derivative, being essentially the art of empires and kingdoms whose centres of power lay beyond the country – like Cambodia (Khmer), Sumatra (Srivijaya) and Burma (Mon/ Dvaravati).There are two styles within this Northern tradition: the Chiang Saen and Chiang Mai (or Later Chiang Saen) schools. The Chiang Saen style, in which the Buddha is portrayed with a round face, arched eyebrows and prominent chin, is stylistically linked to Pala art of India. Nevertheless, local artists incorporated their own vision and produced unique and beautiful images. The earliest date from around the 11th century and their classification refers to the ancient town of Chiang Saen,

Khmer style Prang

situated on the Mekong in Northern Thailand, where many of the finest pieces have been found. The second style is known as Later Chiang Saen or, less confusingly, Chiang Mai. The influence of Sukhothai can be seen in the works from this period: oval face, more slender body and with the robe over the left shoulder. Images date from the mid-14th century.

Buddha images from both of the Northern periods were carved in stone or semi-precious stone, and cast in bronze. The most famous Buddha of all, the Emerald Buddha housed in Wat Phra Kaeo, Bangkok, may have been carved in Northern Thailand during the Late Chiang Saen/Chiang Mai period, although this is not certain.

Architecturally, the Northern school began to make a pronounced contribution from the time of the founding of the city of Chiang Mai in 1296. Perhaps the finest example from this period – indeed, some people regard the buildings that make up the complex as the finest in all Thailand – is the incomparable Wat Lampang Luang, outside the town of Lampang in the North (see page 236).

Sukhothai style (late 13th-early 15th centuries)

The Sukhothai Buddha is one of the first representations of the Ceylonese Buddha in Siam, the prototypes being from Anuradhapura, Sri Lanka (Ceylon). The Buddha is usually represented in the round, either seated cross-legged in the attitude of subduing Mara; or the languid, one-foot forward standing position, with one hand raised, in the attitude of giving protection as the enlightened one descends from the Tavatimsa Heaven. Most were cast in bronze, as Thailand is noticeably lacking in good stone. Some art historians have also argued that Sukhothai artists disliked the violence of chiselling stone, maintaining that as peaceful Thais and good Buddhists they would have preferred the art of modelling bronze. This is fanciful in the extreme.

For the seated Buddha, the surfaces are smooth and curved, with an oval head and elongated features, small hair curls, arched eyebrows and a hooked nose. The classic, enigmatic Sukhothai smile is often said to convey inner contentment. The head is topped by a tall flame-like motif or *ketumula*. The shoulders are broad and the waist is narrow. The length of cloth hanging over the left shoulder drops quite a long way down to the navel, and terminates in a notched design.

The graceful walking Buddha – perhaps the greatest single artistic innovation of the Sukhothai period – features rather strange projecting heels (which follows the ancient writings describing the Buddha's physical appearance). The figure is almost androgynous – this was Buddha depicted having achieved enlightenment, which meant that sexual characteristics no longer existed. The finest examples were produced in the decades immediately prior to Ayutthaya conquering the city in 1438.

Steve van Beek and Luca Tettoni wrote in *The Arts of Thailand*: 'Sukhothai sculpture suggests a figure in the process of dematerializing, half way between solid and vapour. He doesn't walk so much as float. He doesn't sit, he levitates, and belies his masculine nature which should be inflexible. Even his diaphanous robes portray a Buddha which has already shed the trappings of this world.'

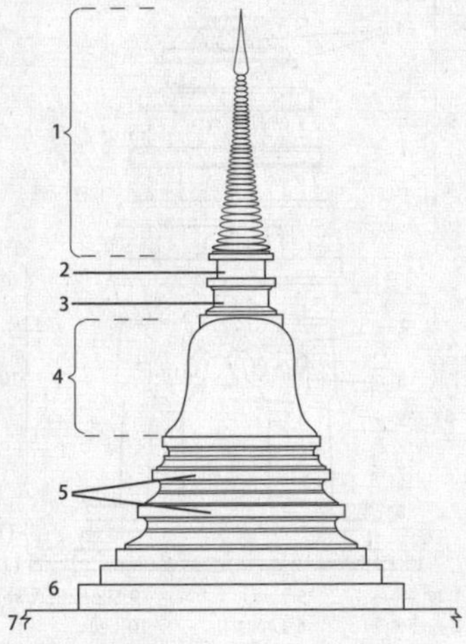

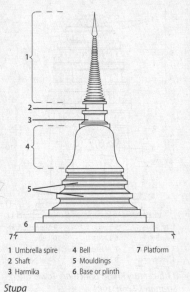

1 Umbrella spire
2 Shaft
3 Harmika
4 Bell
5 Mouldings
6 Base or plinth
7 Platform

Stupa

The initial influence upon Sukhothai art and architecture was from Cambodia. Khmer influence can be seen reflected, for example, in the distinctive 'prang' towers of the period (see illustration). Subsequent stupas can be classified into three styles. First, there is the Ceylonese bell-shaped stupa (see illustration, page 685). This is characterized by a square base surrounded by caryatids, above which is another base with niches containing Buddha images. Wat Chang Lom, in Si Satchanalai, is a good example. The second style of stupa is the lotus bud chedi, examples of which can be found at Wat Mahathat and Wat Trapang Ngoen in Sukhothai, Wat Chedi Jet Thaew in Si Satchanalai, and also in Kamphaeng Phet, Tak, Phitsanulok and Chiang Mai. The third style of stupa constructed during this period is believed to be derived from Srivijayan prototypes, although the links are not well established. It is, however, very distinctive, consisting of a square base, above which is a square main body, superimposed with pedestals, containing niches within which are standing Buddha images. Above the main body are bell-shaped *andas* of reducing size.

Examples of this style can be found on the corner stupas at Wat Mahathat and some subsiduary stupas at Wat Chedi Jet Thaew (Si Satchanalai). Mention should be made of the mondop, built in place of the stupa on a square plan and always containing a large Buddha image. A good example is Wat Sri Chum (Sukhothai). It is said that the stupa 'evolved' as the Buddha lay dying. One of the disciples, Ananda, asked how they might remember the Enlightened One after his death, to which the Buddha replied it was the doctrine, not himself, that should be remembered. As this reply was clearly unsatisfactory to his distraught followers, the Buddha added that after cremation a relic of his body might be placed within a mound of earth – which, over time, became the stupa.

Ayutthayan style (mid 14th-mid 18th centuries)

Both the art and architecture of this period can be split into four sub-periods spanning the years from 1351 to 1767, when Ayutthaya was sacked by the Burmese.

As far as Ayutthayan Buddha images are concerned, for much of the time the artists of the city drew upon the works of other kingdoms for inspiration. To begin with, Uthong Buddhas were popular (themselves drawing upon Khmer prototypes). Then, from the mid-15th century, Sukhothai styles became highly influential – although the images produced looked rather lifeless and are hardly comparable with the originals. In the mid-16th century, when Cambodia came under Thai control, Ayutthayan artists looked to, and imitated, Khmer sculpture (identifiable by the double lips and indistinct moustache). Finally, in the Late Ayutthayan period, a home-grown but rather fussy style arose, with the Buddha often portrayed crowned.

The first of the four sub-periods of Ayutthayan architecture commenced in 1351 and may have been influenced by the prang of Wat Phra Sri Ratana Mahathat in Lopburi, though prangs at Ayutthaya are slightly taller. The second period (1488-1629) is dominated by the round Ceylonese-style stupa, the major example of this being Wat Phra Sri Samphet. During the third period (the

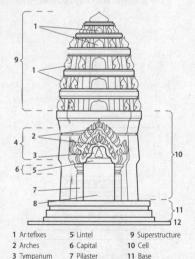

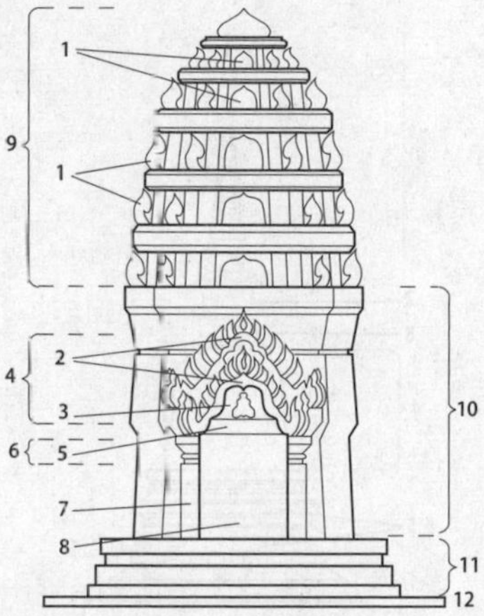

1 Artefixes · 5 Lintel · 9 Superstructure
2 Arches · 6 Capital · 10 Cell
3 Tympanum · 7 Pilaster · 11 Base
4 Pediment · 8 Niche or door · 12 Platform

13th-century Khmer Sanctuary Tower after Stratton & Scott, 1981

first half of the 17th century), the King sent architects to Cambodia to study the architectural characteristics of the Khmer monuments. As a result, the prang became fashionable again – Wat Watthanaram and Wat Chumphon (Bang Pa-In) were built at this time. The final period was from 1732 until the sacking of Ayutthaya by the Burmese in 1767. The many-rabbeted chedis were popular during this period, although fewer new buildings were constructed as King Boromkot was more interested in restoring existing buildings. Most of the viharns and ubosoths have long since perished. What remains dates mainly from the Late Ayutthayan period.

Bangkok style (late 18th-20th centuries)

The Bangkok or Rattanakosin period dates from the founding of the Chakri Dynasty in 1782. But, initially at least, the need for Buddha images was met not by making new ones, but by recovering old ones. King Rama I ordered that images be collected from around his devastated kingdom and brought to Bangkok. About 1,200 in all were recovered in this way, and they were then distributed to the various wats (see, for example, the fine array at Wat Pho, page 91).

It is generally accepted that the Buddhas produced during the Bangkok era are, in the main, inferior compared with the images of earlier periods. In particular, art historians characterize them as 'lifeless'. Initially, they followed the Uthong and Ayutthayan traditions. King Mongkut (1851-68) did 'commission' a new style: these Buddhas are more lively in style, with carefully carved robes. But Mongkut's new-style Buddha did not catch on, and more often than not old images were merely copied.

Architecturally, there is a similar aping of the past rather than the development of any new styles. During the first three reigns (1782-1851), the prang (eg Wat Rakhang, see page 106; and Wat Arun, page 106) and redented (angular) chedi (eg Wat Pho, see page 91) were popular, as were Ayutthayan-style viharns and ubosoths. There are one or two new developments, but these were peripheral to the mainstream. During the third reign, for example, the influence of Chinese art becomes quite pronounced. Other 'oddities' include the early 20th-century Wat Nivet Thamaprawat at Bang Pa-in, which is Gothic in inspiration (see page 119), and Wat Benchamabophit in Bangkok, which is a fusion of Eastern and Western styles (see page 108). In general, Rattanakosin wat buildings are airier and less ornate than those of Ayutthaya.

Wat Suwannaram (Bangkok)

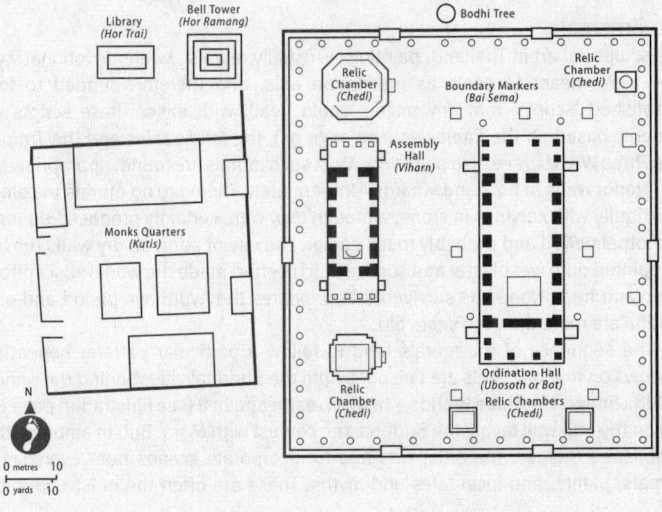
Library
(Hor Trai)
Bell Tower
(Hor Ramang)
Bodhi Tree
Relic Chamber (Chedi)
Boundary Markers
(Bai Sema)
Relic Chamber (Chedi)
Assembly Hall
(Viharn)
Monks Quarters
(Kutis)
Relic Chamber
(Chedi)
Ordination Hall
(Ubosoth or Bot)
Relic Chambers
(Chedi)
N
0 metres 10
0 yards 10

The Thai Wat

Wats are usually separated from the secular world by **two walls**. Between these outer and inner walls are found the **monks quarters** or dormitories (*kutis*), perhaps a **bell tower** (*hor rakang*) that is used to toll the hours and to warn of danger and, in larger complexes, schools and other administrative buildings. Traditionally, the kutis were placed on the south side of the wat. It was believed that if the monks slept directly in front of the principal Buddha image, they would die young; if they slept to the left, they would become ill; and if they slept behind it, there would be discord in the community of monks. This section of the compound is known as the sanghavasa, or sanghawat (ie for the Sangha – the monkhood).

The inner wall, which in bigger wats often takes the form of a **gallery** or cloister (*phra rabieng*) lined with Buddha images, represents the division between the worldly and the holy, the sacred and the profane. It is used as a quiet place for meditation. This part of the wat compound is known as the buddhavasa, or phutthawat (ie for the Buddha). Within the inner courtyard, the holiest building is the **ordination hall**, or ubosoth, often shortened to just **bot**. This building is reserved for monks only. It is built on consecrated ground, and has a ring of eight stone tablets or boundary markers (*bai sema*), sometimes contained in mini-pavilions, arranged around it at the cardinal and subcardinal points. These bai sema are shaped like stylized leaves of the bodhi tree, and often carved with representations of Vishnu, Siva, Brahma or Indra, or of nagas. Buried in the ground beneath the bai sema are luuk nimit – stone spheres – and sometimes gold and jewellery. The bai sema mark the limit of earthly power – within the stones, not even a king can issue orders.

The bot is characteristically a large, rectangular building with high walls and multiple sloping roofs, covered in glazed clay tiles (or wood tiles, in the North). At each end of the roof are chofaa, or 'bunches of sky', which represent garuda grasping two nagas in its talons. Inside, often through elaborately carved and inlaid doors, is a Buddha image. There may also be numerous subsidiary images. The inside walls of the bot may be

Thai murals

Like sculptural art in Thailand, paintings – usually murals – were devotional works. They were meant to serve as meditation aids, and therefore tended to follow established 'scripts' that any pilgrim could 'read' with ease. These scripts were primarily based on the *Ramakien* (see page 95), the *Jataka* tales and the *Traiphum* (*The Three Worlds*), see also page 682. Most such murals are found, appropriately, on the interior walls of bots and viharns. Unfortunately, there are no murals to compete in antiquity with carvings in stone, although they were certainly produced during the Sukhothai period and probably much earlier. The use of paint on dry walls (frescoes are painted onto wet plaster and survive much better) made the works susceptible to damp and heat. None has survived that pre-dates the Ayutthaya period and only a handful are more than 150 years old.

The sequence of the murals tend to follow a particular pattern: beneath the windows on the long walls are episodes from the Buddha's life; behind the principal Buddha image, the Three Worlds – heaven, earth and hell (see illustration page 691); and on the end wall facing the Buddha, the contest with Mara. But, in amongst these established themes, the artist was free to incorporate scenes from everyday life, animals, plants, and local tales and myths. These are often the most entertaining

decorated with murals depicting the Jataka tales, or scenes from Buddhist and Hindu cosmology. Like the Buddha image, these murals are meant to serve as meditation aids. It is customary for pilgrims to remove their shoes on entering any Buddhist building (or private house for that matter), although in state ceremonies, officials in uniform are not required to do so.

The other main building within the inner courtyard is the **assembly hall**, or **viharn**, but not all wats have one, and some may have more than one. Architecturally, this is often indistinguishable from the bot. It contains the wat's principal Buddha images. The main difference between the bot and viharn is that the latter does not stand on consecrated ground, and can be identified by the absence of any bai sema – stone tablets – set around it. The viharn is for general use and, unlike the bot, is rarely locked. Both bot and viharn are supposed to face water, because the Buddha himself was facing a river when he achieved enlightenment under the bodhi tree. If there is no natural body of water, the monks may dig a pond. In the late Ayutthayan period, the curved lines of the bot and viharn were designed to symbolize a boat.

Also found in the inner courtyard may be a number of other structures. Among the more common are **chedis**, bell-shaped **relic chambers** with tapering spires. In larger wats these can be built on a massive scale (such as the one at Nakhon Pathom, see page), and contain holy relics of the Buddha himself. More often, chedis are smaller affairs containing the ashes of royalty, monks or pious lay people. A rarer Khmer architectural feature sometimes found in Thai wats is the **prang**, also a relic chamber. The best known of these angular corn-cob-shaped towers is the one at Wat Arun in Bangkok (see page 105).

Another rarer feature is the **library** or scripture repository (hor trai), usually a small, tall-sided building where the Buddhist scriptures can be stored safely, high off the ground.

Salas are open-sided **rest pavilions**, which can be found anywhere in the wat compound; the sala kan parian or **study hall** is the largest and most impressive of these and is almost like a bot or viharn without walls. Here the monks say their prayers at noon.

sections. All were portrayed without perspective using simple lines and blocks of uniform colour, with no use of shadow and shading.

Modern Thai architecture

Few visitors – or residents for that matter – see much but crudity in modern Thai buildings: elegant wooden shophouses are torn down to make way for the worst in concrete crassness; office buildings are erected with apparently not a shred of thought as to their effects on the surrounding environment; multi-storeyed condominiums are built with abandon and bad taste. This is tragic, given the beauty and environmental common sense that informed traditional designs; much like Singapore, in a few years' time the Thais may be frantically putting back what they have so recently pulled down. But there are Thai architects who are attempting to develop a modern Thai architecture that does not merely ape the worst in Western designs, and there are some notable new buildings.

In wat architecture, there is a move away from the gaudy, rather over-worked (to Western eyes) traditions of the Bangkok period, towards a sparer, almost ascetic vision. Bright colours have been replaced by expanses of white and subdued hues; the hectic angles of tradition, with simpler geometric shapes. Monasteries like Wat Sala

Mudras and the Buddha image

An artist producing an image of the Buddha does not try to create an original piece of art: he or she is trying to be faithful to a tradition which can be traced back over centuries. It is important to appreciate that the Buddha image is not merely a work of art, but an object of – and for – worship. Sanskrit poetry even sets down the characteristics of the Buddha – albeit in rather unlikely terms: legs like a deer, arms like an elephant's trunk, a chin like a mango stone and hair like the stings of scorpions. The Pali texts of Theravada Buddhism add the 108 auspicious signs, long toes and fingers of equal length, body like a banyan tree and eyelashes like a cow's. The Buddha can be represented either sitting, lying (indicating paranirvana) or standing, and (in Thailand) occasionally walking. He is often represented standing on an open lotus flower: the Buddha was born into an impure world, and likewise the lotus germinates in mud, but rises above the filth to flower. Each image will be represented in a particular mudra or 'attitude', of which there are 40. The most common are:

Abhayamudra
Dispelling fear or giving protection; right hand (sometimes both hands) raised, palm outwards, usually with the Buddha in a standing position.

Varamudra
Giving blessing or charity; the right hand pointing downwards, the palm facing outwards, with the Buddha either seated or standing.

Vitarkamudra
Preaching mudra; the ends of the thumb and index finger of the right hand touch to form a circle, symbolizing the Wheel of Law. The Buddha can be seated or standing.

Dharmacakramudra
'Spinning the Wheel of Law'; a preaching mudra symbolizing the teaching of the first sermon. The hands are held in front of the chest, thumbs and index fingers of both joined, one facing inwards and one outwards.

Bhumisparcamudra
'Calling the earth goddess to witness' or 'touching the earth'; the right hand rests on the right knee, with the tips of the fingers 'touching ground', thus calling the earth goddess Thoranee to witness his enlightenment and victory over Mara, the king of demons. The Buddha is always seated.

Dhyanamudra
Meditation; both hands open, palms upwards, in the lap, right over left.

Other points of note:

Vajrasana
Yogic posture of meditation; cross-legged, both soles of the feet visible.

Virasana
Yogic posture of meditation; cross-legged, but with the right leg on top of the left, covering the left foot (also known as paryankasana).

Buddha under Naga
A common image in Khmer art; the Buddha is shown seated in an attitude of meditation, with a cobra rearing up over his head. This refers to an episode in the Buddha's life when he was meditating: a rain storm broke and Nagaraja, the king of the nagas (snakes), curled up under the Buddha (seven coils) and then used his seven-headed hood to protect the Holy One from the falling rain.

Buddha calling for rain
A common image in Laos; the Buddha is standing, both arms held at the side of the body, fingers pointing down.

Bhumisparcamudra – calling the earth goddess to witness. Sukhothai period, 13th-14th century.

Dhyanamudra – meditation. Sukhothai period, 13th-14th century.

Abhayamudra – dispelling fear or giving protection. Lopburi Buddha, Khmer style, 12th century.

Vitarkamudra – preaching, 'spinning the Wheel of Law'. Dvaravati Buddha, 7th-8th century, seated in the 'European' manner.

Abhayamudra – dispelling fear or giving protection; subduing Mara position. Lopburi Buddha, Khmer style, 13th century.

The Buddha – 'Calling for rain'.

Loi, in Nakhon Ratchasima (Korat) in the Northeast, and Wat Dhammakaya in Pathum Thani province, keep decoration to a minimum. Wirot Srisuro, of Khon Kaen University and the architect of Wat Sala Loi, explained to the *Bangkok Post*: "Buddhism teaches us to follow the middle path, to avoid extravagance. Our buildings should reflect this thinking by staying simple." Although Ajaan Wirot's work and that of other modernists has attracted great attention – much of it negative – far more monasteries are being built in traditional style, but with cement and concrete blocks replacing brick and stucco.

Cinema

Thailand has a suddenly resurgent domestic film industry, so much so that some critics are writing of a 'New Thai Cinema'. Certainly something new is stirring, but it must be remembered that this comes after years of dross when Thai cinema was notable only for poor quality and crass story lines. In 1997, the year of the economic crisis in Thailand, it seemed that Thai cinema was in terminal decline. Just 17 films were made that year, as against around 100 in the 1970s. But 1997 was also the year when a generation of new directors began to make a difference. Penek Rattanaruang made *Fun Bar Karaoke* which was screened to some critical acclaim at the Berlin International Film Festival. A year later, Nonzee Nimibutr made *Dang Bireley's and Young Gangster* a film which, importantly, was not only critically acclaimed but also commercially successful. Other notable directors include Oxide Pang who made *Who is running?* and Wisit Sasanatieng who directed *Tear of the Black Tiger*. But the biggest film of many years – indeed of all time – is the historical epic *Suriyothai* released in 2002. This was not only hugely expensive for a Thai film but has also proved to be well received by the public and pundits alike. And just to emphasise the point that 1997 marks – possibly – a turning point in Thai cinema, it was also the inaugural year of the Bangkok International Art Film Festival.

It is not just Thai cinema which has seen a resurgence over the last few years. So too has Thailand as a production centre for overseas films. Excellent locations, value for money, and an increasingly professional support network have all raised the profile of the country. Best known among films made in Thailand is *The Beach* (see page 490). But there have been many others and in 2003 the industry expects to make US$35m from some 25 films, 200 documentaries and 200 commercials all made in the country.

Dance, drama and music

The great Indian epic, the Ramayana (in Thai known as the Ramakien, see page 95), has been an important influence on all Thai arts, but most clearly in dance and drama such as *nang* and *nang thalung* (shadow plays, see page 693), *khon* (masked dramas) and *lakhon* (classical dance dramas). Also important is the likay (folk drama).

Dance

Lakhon These dance dramas are known to have been performed in the 17th century, and probably evolved from Javanese prototypes. They became very popular not just in the court, but also in the countryside and among the common people. Consisting of three main forms, they draw upon the Jatakas (tales of the former lives of the historic Buddha), the Ramakien, and upon local fables, legends and myths, for their subject matter. Performers wear intricate costumes based on ancient dress, and character parts – such as demons and yogis – wear masks. In genuine lakhon, all performers – bar clowns – are played by women. A chorus sing the parts, not the actors.

Drama

Khon masked drama evolved in the royal court of Siam, although its roots lie in folk dances of the countryside. Performers don elaborate jewelled costumes, men wearing masks and women crowns or gilded head-dresses. Music accompanies the dance, and words and songs are performed by an off-stage chorus. Many of the dances are interpretations of traditional myths, and performers begin their training at an early age.

Muay Thai: kick boxing

Along with Siamese cats and inaccurate films, Thailand is known in the West for muay Thai – literally Thai boxing – or 'kick boxing'. This art of self-defence is first mentioned in the Burmese chronicles of 1411. King Naresuan (1590-1605), one of Thailand's greatest monarchs, made muay Thai a compulsory element of military training and gradually it developed into a sport. Today it is Thailand's most popular sport and is one of the few ways that a poor country boy can turn his rags into riches. It is no coincidence that most of Thailand's best boxers have come from the harsh and impoverished Northeastern region, which seems to turn out a never-ending stream of tough, determined young men.

A boy will begin training at the age of six or seven; he will be fighting by the age of 10, and competing in professional bouts at 16. Few boxers continue beyond the age of 25. In the countryside, boys herding buffalo will kick trees to hone their skills and learn to transcend pain, all with the intention of using their strength and agility to fight their way out of poverty. Trainers from Bangkok send scouts up-country to tour the provinces, in search of boys with potential.

In muay Thai, any part of the body can be used to strike an opponent, except the head. Gloves were only introduced in the 1930s; before then, fists were wrapped in horse hide and studded with shell or glass fragments set in glue. Fatalities were common, and for a time in the 1920s muay Thai was officially banned. Today, fights are staged much like boxing in the West: they are held in a ring, with gloves, and consist of five three-minute rounds, with two-minute rest periods between each round. Before beginning, the boxers prostrate themselves on the canvas while an orchestra of drums and symbols raises the tension. The opponents *wai* to each corner before the music stops, and the fight begins. Punching is rare – far more effective are the kicks and vicious elbow stabs. The intensity of many contests make Western heavyweight boxing seem slow and ponderous. As Doug Lansky, who sent us an amusing email, commented:

"These kickboxers may have been small, but I wouldn't want to step into a ring with any of them. They are kicking machines. Apparently, defense has not been introduced in this sport. It was like watching a battery commercial where two robots go at it until the cheaper battery runs out of power, or in this case, one of the fighters runs out of blood."

The **ramwong** is a dance often performed at ceremonies and originates from the central region. The **fawn** is a similar Northern dance. Slow, graceful, synchronized dancing, accompanied by drums and symbols – in which hand movements are used to evoke meaning – characterize the dance. Ungainly Westerners are often encouraged to perform these dances, to the obvious amusement of Thais.

It is thought that **likay** evolved from Muslim Malay religious performances. It was adopted by the Thais and in time became primarily a comedy folk art enjoyed by common people, with singing and dancing. In recent years, likay artists have begun to incorporate political jibes into their repertoires. Cultured people in Bangkok used to look upon likay as rough and unsophisticated, although in recent years it has gained greater recognition as an art form.

Nang shadow plays, with characters beautifully engraved on leather, are frequently performed at cremation ceremonies, particularly in the South (see page

 614). There are usually 10 puppeteers in a nang troupe, who wear traditional costume and are often made-up. The narrator (usually the oldest member of the troupe) offers some help with the story line, while a traditional phipat band provides musical accompaniment. (The classical phipat orchestra consists of gongs and cymbals (*ching*), a xylophone (*ranat ek*), drums and a traditional wind instrument – rather like an oboe – called a *phi nai*). Nang was probably introduced into Thailand from Java during the early Ayutthaya period. *Nang thalung* puppets are smaller, more finely carved, and usually have articulated arms (see page 697). In both cases, the figures 'perform' in front of – or behind – a screen, usually enacting stories from the Ramakien. Like likay, nang and nang thalung have, in the past, been looked down upon as rather crude, unsophisticated arts.

Unfortunately for those who are trying to preserve traditional Thai arts – among them the Thai Royal Family – they are gradually, but steadily, losing their popular appeal. Although tourists may expect and hope to witness a performance, most Thais, both urban and rural, would rather watch the TV or go to the movies.

Music

Thai traditional music is a blending of musical elements from a number of cultures, namely Chinese, Indian and Khmer. This applies not just to the instruments, but also to the melodies. Although Thai music can therefore be seen to be derivative, it nonetheless developed into a distinctive form that is regarded as belonging to the 'high' musical cultures of Southeast Asia. In the past, talented young musicians would become attached to the king's court or that of a nobleman, and would there receive training from established musicians. Musicians and composers independent of such patronage were rare, and public guilds seldom lasted very long.

With the ending of the absolute monarchy in 1932, the role of the nobility in supporting musicians began to die. Traditional music became viewed as 'un-modern' and performances were actively discouraged by the authorities. It has only been in about the last 25 years that an interest in traditional Thai music has re-emerged. But because of the years of neglect, the pool of talented musicians is very small.

Although court music may have withered, folk music remained popular and vibrant throughout this period – and perhaps nowhere more so than in the Northeastern region of the country. Here *mor lam* singers are renowned, and in some cases they have become national celebrities. Accompanied by the haunting sound of the *khaen* (bamboo pipes) and singing 'songs from the rice fields' about rural poverty and unrequited love, they are among the most traditional of performers.

While non-Thai music (both Western and Eastern) is popular in Thailand there is also a booming local **popular music** industry. Some of this draws on local musical traditions. For example, a band called *Fong Nam* plays traditional phipat music using modern instruments such as electric keyboards. More popular still are re-workings of traditional folk music traditions to serve a population – particularly in rural areas – who are struggling with the pressures of modernisation. So *luk thung* and the accompanying likay theatre are played and sung using electric guitars and keyboards. The themes, though, generally remain the same: lost love and the hard life of the farmer. That said, in the 1960s and particularly during the 1970s a new genre of *luk thung* appeared in Thailand: the protest song. Foremost among the bands to politicise music in this manner was the band Caravan, one of Thailand's most successful groups. Songwriters began to struggle with issues of poverty, democracy and the environment. Caravan split up in the 1980s and perhaps Thailand's biggest rock band now (although they play only very occasionally) is Carabao. Like Caravan, Carabao is a band with a social conscience writing and playing songs that dwell on the destructiveness of consumerism and the tragedy of AIDS in Thailand. More popular among younger Thais is the more sugary band Bird who have embraced rap and disco and given them a Thai flavour.

Textiles

Thai traditional textiles have experienced something of a rebirth since the end of the Second World War, with the support of the Royal Family, NGOs and the *Jim Thompson Thai Silk Company*. In 1947, Jim Thompson – an American resident in Bangkok – sent a sample of Thai silk to the editor of *Vogue* in New York. Then a near moribund industry, today it produces over 10,000,000 m of silk a year. In the past, cloth was made from silk, cotton or hemp. Because of a shortage of such natural yarns, it is common today to find cloth being woven from synthetic yarn. Likewise, chemical aniline dyes are used in place of natural animal and vegetable dyes although there has been a revival of interest in vegetable dyes, (particularly on cotton) in recent years. Among the most distinctive of Thai textiles is *matmii* cloth, produced using the ikat dyeing technique (see below). The dyed yarn is then woven into cloth using plain weave, float weave, supplementary weft and tapestry weave techniques. In the North, hill peoples also produce appliqué cloth.

Silk weaving appears to be of considerable antiquity in Thailand. Excavations at Ban Chiang in the Northeast (see page 349) have revealed silk threads, in association with artifacts dated to 1,000-2,000 BC. If this is corroborated by other evidence (it remains contested), then the accepted view that the technology of sericulture filtered south from China will have to be revised. According to legend, the origins of sericulture date back to 4,000 BC, when China's first emperor noticed that the leaves of the mulberry trees in his garden were being eaten at a prodigious rate by a small grub. Having eaten their fill, the voracious grubs spun cocoons of fine thread. Lei Zu, a concubine, collected the cocoons and dropped some into boiling water, whereupon they unravelled into long lengths of fine, but strong, thread.

The silk 'worm' lives for just 20 days, and 35,000 hatch from 30 g of eggs. In their short lives, this number of worms consume mulberry leaves (fresh, preferably young) three times a day, or 680 kg in under three weeks. Laid out on circular bamboo trays, the noise of 35,000 tiny jaws chomping their way through barrow-loads of leaves is like a gentle rustling sound. Susceptible to cold, disease, pest attack and all manner of other threats, the worms must be lovingly cultivated if they are to live long enough to weave their cocoons of silk. After they have formed cocoons – a process which takes around 36 hours – the worm metamorphoses into the silk moth. This gives the silk reelers just 10 days before the moth chews its way out of the cocoon, destroying the silk thread in the process. The cocoons are dropped into boiling water, killing the forming moth, and then unreeled, often by hand. A single cocoon can yield a thread between 200 and 1,500 m long, and about 12,500 cocoons are needed to produce 1 kg of silk yarn.

Clothing

The *pha sin* is an ankle length tubular piece of cloth, made up of three pieces and worn by women. The waistband (*hua sin*) is usually plain, the main body of the skirt (known as the *pha sin*) plain or decorated, while the lower hem (*dtin sin*) may be intricately woven. Traditionally, the pha sin was worn with a blouse or shawl (*pha sabai*), although it is common today to see women wearing T-shirts with the pha sin.

The *pha sarong* is the male equivalent of the pha sin and is now a rare sight. As the name suggests, it is a tubular piece of cloth which is folded at the front and secured with a belt. It is worn with either a Western-style shirt or a *prarachatan* (a tight-collared long-sleeved shirt).

Cloth

Matmii ikat – woven cotton cloth – is characteristic of the Northeastern region. Designs are invariably geometric and it is very unusual to find a piece which has not

been dyed using chemicals. Designs are handed down by mothers to their daughters and encompass a broad range from simple *sai fon* ('falling rain') designs, where random sections of weft are tied, to the more complex *mee gung* and *poom som*. The less common *pha kit* is a supplementary weft ikat, although the designs are similar to those found in matmii. The characteristic 'axe cushions' – or *mawn kwan* – of the Northeast are usually made from this cloth, which is thick and loosely woven. These cushions are traditionally given to monks (usually at the end of the Buddhist Rains Retreat) to rest upon. *Pha fai* is a simple cotton cloth, in blue or white and sometimes simply decorated, made for everyday use and also as part of the burial ceremony, when a white length of *pha fai* is draped over the coffin. Centres of weaving in the Northeast include: Khon Kaen, Udon Thani, Renu Nakhon (outside That Phanom), Surin, and Pak Thong Chai (outside Korat).

Except for the hilltribe textiles (see page 678), weaving in the North and Central regions is far less diverse than that of the Northeast. Indeed, most of the cloth that is handwoven is produced in Lao (ie Northeastern) villages that have been relocated to this part of the country. Distinctive *pha sin* are woven by the Thai Lu of Phrae and Nan, featuring brightly coloured horizontal stripes interspersed with triangular designs. Centres of weaving in the North include: Pasang and San Kamphaeng (both outside Chiang Mai), and Nan and Phrae.

The textiles of the South exhibit links with those of Malaysia and Sumatra. In general, the handwoven textile tradition is weak in this part of the country. *Pha yok* is similar to *songket* (a Malay cloth), consisting of cotton or silk interwoven with gold or silver yarns. *Han karok* is a technique in which two-coloured twisted thread is woven. Centres of production in the South include villages around Trang and in the Songkhla Lake area.

Crafts

Mother-of-pearl

The method used to produce mother-of-pearl in Thailand differs from that in China and Vietnam. The 'pearl' is from the turban shell, from which pieces are cut and sanded to a thickness of 1 mm. These are then glued to a wooden panel and the gaps between the design filled with layers of lac (a resin), before being highly polished. This art form reached its peak during the 17th and 18th centuries. Masterpieces include the doors at Wat Pho, Wat Phra Kaeo and Wat Benchamabophit (all in Bangkok), and the footprint of the Buddha at Wat Phra Singh in Chiang Mai. In Vietnam and China, the wood is chiselled-out and the mother-of-pearl cut to fit the incisions.

Nielloware

To produce nielloware, a dark amalgam of lead, copper and silver metals is rubbed into etched silver. The craft was introduced to Nakhon Si Thammarat (see page 607) from India and then spread north. It is used to decorate trays, betel boxes, vases, cigarette cases and other small objects.

Khon masks

Khon masks depict characters from the Ramakien (the Thai Ramayana) and are made from plaster moulds. Layers of paper are pasted over the mould, glued, and then coated in lac. The masks are then painted and decorated.

Lacquerware

In the production of lacquerware, three layers of lacquer from the sumac tree (*Gluta usitata*) are brushed onto a wood or wicker base, and each layer polished with charcoal. Then a fourth layer of lac is added, and once more highly polished with

charcoal. After drying, the piece is inscribed with a sharp instrument and then soaked in a red dye for two to three days. The polished black part of the surface resists the dye, while the inscribed areas take it. Because this traditional method is so time-consuming, artists today tend to paint the design on to the lacquer. The art dates from the mid-Ayutthaya period and was possibly introduced by visiting Japanese artists. Some of the finest examples of lacquerware are to be found at Bangkok's Suan Pakkard Palace (see page 108).

Kites

Kite-flying has been a popular pastime in Thailand, certainly from the Sukhothai period (where it is described in the chronicles). During the Ayutthaya period, an imperial edict forbade kite-flying over the Royal Palace, while La Loubère's journal (1688) records that it was a favourite sport of noblemen. Today it is most common to see competitions between 'chula' (formerly 'kula') and 'pukpao', at Sanaam Luang in Bangkok. The chula kite is large – over 2 m in length – while the diamond-shaped pukpao is far smaller and more agile. The frame is made from bamboo (*sisuk* variety), cut before the onset of the rains and, preferably, left to mature. The bamboo is then split and the paper skin attached, according to a long-established system.

Puppets

Nang yai puppets, literally 'large skin', are carved from buffalo or cow hide and may be over 2 m in height. Though they can be skilfully decorated, nang yai are mechanically simple: there are no moving parts. Interestingly, some characters require particular types of hide. For example, a Rishi must be cut from the skin of a cow or bull that has been struck by lightning or died after a snakebite, or from a cow that has died calving. After curing and stretching the hide on a frame, the figure is carved out and then painted (if it is to be used for night performances, it is painted black).

Nang thalung are smaller than nang yai and are related to Javanese prototypes. They are more complex and have even stranger hide requirements than the nang yai: traditionally, key characters such as Rishi and Isavara need to be made from the soles of a dead (luckily) nang thalung puppet master. If master puppeteers are thin on the ground, then an animal which has died a violent death is acceptable. For the clown character, a small piece of skin from the sexual organ of a master puppeteer (again dead) should be attached to the lower lip of the puppet. One arm of the figure is usually articulated by a rod, enabling the puppet master to provide some additional expression to the character.

Religion

For a general account of Buddhism see box, page 702.

The Thai census records that 94% of the population is Buddhist. In Thailand's case, this means Theravada Buddhism, also known as Hinayana Buddhism. Of the other 6% of the population, 3.9% are Muslim (living predominantly in the south of the country), 1.7% Confucianist (mostly Sino-Thais living in Bangkok) and 0.6% Christian (mostly hilltribe people living in the north). Though the king is designated the protector of all religions, the constitution stipulates that he must be a Buddhist.

Theravada Buddhism

Theravada Buddhism was introduced into Southeast Asia in the 13th century, when monks trained in Ceylon (Sri Lanka) returned actively to spread the word. As a universal and a popular religion, it quickly gained converts and spread rapidly amongst the Tai. Theravada Buddhism, from the Pali word *thera* ('elders'), means the

 'way of the elders' and is distinct from the dominant Buddhism practised in India, Mahayana Buddhism or the 'Greater Vehicle'. The sacred language of Theravada Buddhism is Pali rather than Sanskrit, Bodhisattvas (future Buddhas) are not given much attention, and emphasis is placed upon a precise and 'fundamental' interpretation of the Buddha's teachings, as they were originally recorded.

Buddhism, as it is practised in Thailand, is not the 'other-worldly' religion of Western conception. Ultimate salvation – enlightenment, or *nirvana* – is a distant goal for most people. Thai Buddhists pursue the Law of Karma, the reduction of suffering. Meritorious acts are undertaken and demeritorious ones avoided so that life, and more particularly future life, might be improved. Outside many wats it is common to see caged birds or turtles being sold: these are purchased and set free, and in this way the liberator gains merit. 'Karma' (act or deed, from Pali – *kamma*) is often thought in the West to mean 'fate'. It does not. It is true that previous karma determines a person's position in society, but there is still room for individual action – and a person is ultimately responsible for that action. It is the law of cause and effect.

It is important to draw a distinction between 'academic' Buddhism, as it tends to be understood in the West, and 'popular' Buddhism, as it is practised in Thailand. In Thailand, Buddhism is a syncretic religion: it incorporates elements of Brahmanism, animism and ancestor worship. Amulets are worn to protect against harm and are often sold in temple compounds (see page 100). Brahmanistic 'spirit' houses can be found outside most buildings (see box, above). In the countryside, farmers have what they consider to be a healthy regard for the spirits (*phi*) and demons that inhabit the rivers, trees and forests. Astrologers are widely consulted by urban and rural dwellers alike. Even former prime minister, Chaovalit Yongchaiyudh, employed a monk to knock his head with a wooden mallet for good luck. It is these aspects of Thai Buddhism which help to provide worldly assurance, and they are perceived to be complementary, not in contradiction, with Buddhist teachings. But Thai Buddhism is not homogeneous. There are deep scriptural and practical divisions between 'progressive' monks and the *sangha* (the monkhood) hierarchy, for example.

The wat and the life of a monk

Virtually every village in Thailand has its wat. There is no English equivalent of the Thai word. It is usually translated as either monastery or temple, although neither is correct. It is easiest to get around this problem by simply calling them wats.

While secularization has undoubtedly undermined the role of Buddhism to some extent (see below), and therefore the place of the wat, they still remain the focus of any community. The wat serves as a place of worship, education, meeting and healing. Without a wat, a village cannot be viewed as a 'complete' community, there are some 30,000 scattered across the country, supporting a population of around 300,000 monks and novices. During Lent the population of monks and novices swells by some 100,000 as people are ordained for the Buddhist Rains Retreat that runs from July to October. Large wats may have up to 600 monks and novices, but most in the countryside will have less than 10, many only one or two.

The wat represents the mental heart of each community, and most young men at some point in their lives will become ordained as monks, usually during the Buddhist Rains Retreat. Previously, this period represented the only opportunity for a young man to gain an education and to learn how to read. The surprisingly high literacy rate in Thailand before universal education was introduced (although some would maintain that this was hardly *functional* literacy) is explained by the presence of temple education.

The wat does not date as far back as one might imagine. Originally, there were no wats, as monks were wandering ascetics. It seems that although the word 'wat' was in use in the 14th century, these were probably just shrines, and were not

monasteries. By the late 18th century, the wat had certainly metamorphosed into a monastery, so sometime in the intervening four centuries, shrine and monastery had united into a whole.

Royal wats, or *wat luang* – of which there are only 186 in the country – can usually be identified by the use of the prefixes *Rat*, *Raja* or *Racha* in their names. (Different ways of transliterating Thai into English arrive at slightly different spellings of the prefix.) This indicates royal patronage. Wats that contain important relics also have the prefix *Maha* or Great – as in Wat Mahathat. Community wats make up the rest and number about 30,000. Although wats vary a great deal in size and complexity, there is a traditional layout to which most conform (see box, page 688).

It seems that wats are often short-lived. Even great wats, if they lose their patronage, are deserted by their monks and fall into ruin. Unlike Christian churches, they depend on constant support from the laity; the wat owns no land or wealth, and must depend on gifts of food to feed the monks and money to repair and expand the fabric of its buildings.

Ordination

Today, ordination into the monkhood is seen as an opportunity to study the Buddhist scriptures, to prepare for a responsible moral life – to become 'ripe'. Farmers sometimes still say that just as a girl who cannot weave is 'raw' (*dip*) and not yet 'ripe' (*suk*) for marriage, so the same is true of a man who has not entered the monkhood. An equally important reason for a man to become ordained is so that he can accumulate merit for his family, particularly for his mother, who as a woman cannot become ordained. The government still allows civil servants to take leave, on full pay, to enter the monkhood for three months. Women gain merit by making offerings of food each morning to the monks and by performing other meritorious deeds. They can also become nuns. In 1399, the Queen of Sukhothai prayed that through such actions she might be fortunate enough to be 'reborn as a male'. Lectures on Buddhism and meditation classes are held at the World Fellowship of Buddhists in Bangkok (see page 149).

For male Thais from poor backgrounds the monkhood may be the only way that they can continue their education beyond primary level. In 1995 there were almost 87,000 novice monks in monasteries in Thailand; many come from poor, rural families. In light of this, there is clearly an incentive for youngsters to join the monkhood not for spiritual reasons, but for pecuniary and educational ones. This is beginning to worry some in the Buddhist hierarchy who would like to think that novices join primarily to become monks, not to become educated. It is a drain on their resources – the government only pays 20% of the costs of educating these novices – and in some instances may pollute the atmosphere of the *wat*. In addition, it means that the quality of monks is probably lower than many in the Buddhist hierarchy would wish. The Venerable Phra Dhammakittiwong, the abbot of Wat Rachaorot and a member of the Supreme Sangha Council, was quoted in 1997 saying, quite plainly, that the problem with Thai Buddhism is that "people who are considered bright and smart do not want to become monks" (*The Nation*, 20.7.97). Nonetheless, there have been some notable successes of this form of education: former Prime Minister Chuan Leekpai, who comes from a poor southern family, studied law for six years while a novice.

Another problem which has emerged in recent years is that of empty wats. Of the country's 30,000 wats, around 5,000 are thought to stand empty. Often people give alms to build new monasteries, as this is the main means of gaining merit. But Thailand is not producing enough monks to man these new monasteries. There is, simply, over-building and under-manning. This has led some Buddhist scholars to question the assumption that building more wats is good for Thai society. In mid-1998 the Sangha Supreme Council took the unprecedented step of ordering monasteries to stop all new, non-essential construction work. The overt reason was to

 pare down costs in the face of the economic crisis; an additional reason was probably the belief that construction had got out of hand as monasteries vied with each other in the size and opulence of their buildings.

The Thammakai movement and Santi Asoke

As Thailand has modernized, so there have appeared new Buddhist 'sects' designed to appeal to the middle-class, sophisticated, urban Thai. The Thammakai movement, for example, counts among its supporters large numbers of students, businessmen, politicians and members of the military. Juliane Schober maintains that the movement has garnered support from these groups because it has managed to appeal to those people who are experiencing 'disenchantment with modern Thai society, but [are] reluctant to forego the benefits of modernization'. 'Through effective use of modern media, marketing, fund raising strategies, and mass appeal of religious consumerism', the author suggests, 'it offers its followers concrete methods for attaining spiritual enlightenment in this life and membership in a pristine Buddhist community that promises to restore the nation's moral life, individual peace, and material success.' During 1998 the Thammakai movement was criticized for its unorthodox money-raising activities – getting supporters to solicit door-to-door – and in November the Education Ministry ordered an investigation of its activities by the Supreme Sangha Council. The movement is trying to raise US$360m to build a massive chedi, but claims of miracles are raising suspicions that the hard sell has gone too far. The movement has even won a business management prize. But as defenders point out, miracles and claims that generous donors will be rewarded in heaven is common to many Thai monasteries. What really bugs the opposition is that the Thammakai movement is so successful.

Another movement with a rather different philosophy is Santi Asoke. This movement rejects consumerism and materialism in all its guises, and enjoins its members to 'eat less, use little, work a lot, and save the rest for society'. Both Santi Asoke and Thammakai have come in for a great deal of scrutiny and have been criticized for their recruiting methods and their fundamentalist positions. They are indicative, in the eyes of some Thais, of a crisis in Thai Buddhism.

A crisis in Thai Buddhism?

The intrusion of modern life and mores into the wat has created considerable tensions for the sangha in Thailand, reflected in a growing number of scandals. At the beginning of 1995 a monk, Phra Sayan, took the law into his own hands when he beheaded his abbot, Chamnong, for having sexual relations with a woman. He explained his actions in the context of a very popular Chinese television series about the legendary Song Dynasty magistrate Judge Pao, who rights wrongs and fights for the little person, by explaining: "Judge Pao used to say, 'Even if the emperor commits crimes, he should be punished just like ordinary people.' So there was no excuse for the abbot."

More recently, in late December 2000, Abbot Wanchai Oonsap was captured on camera dressed as an army colonel, disguised behind dark glasses and underneath a wig, with a bevvy of girls in tow and an assortment of pornographic videos and empty bottles of spirits in the house where he was living it up. Earlier, Phra Pativetviset was found at a karaoke bar where the girls pronounced him a real 'party animal'. Of the last few years numerous other monks have been implicated in drug dealing, rape and murder – one was even caught having sex under a crematorium.

The wider problem concerns how monk superstars deal with their fame and fortune. While monks are technically prohibited from handling money, the exigencies of modern life mean that most cannot avoid it. This, in turn, opens monks up to a whole series of temptations that their predecessors, living in rural monasteries and supported by poor rural communities, never faced.

In short, keeping the Buddhist precepts is far harder in modern than in traditional Thailand. Many Thais lament the visible signs of worldly wealth that monks display. It is

House of spirits

It does not take long for a first-time visitor to Thailand to notice the miniature houses, often elaborately decorated, that sit in the corner of most house compounds. Private homes, luxury hotels and international banks do not seem to be without them; the more grandiose the building, the more luxurious their miniature alter ego. The house outside the World Trade Centre is one of the most ostentatious. Some look like gaudy miniature Thai wats made from cement and gilded; other, more traditional examples are attractively-weathered wooden houses. *Phi* – spirits – are also apparently not adverse to living in Corbusier-eque modern affairs, like the angular house outside the Pan Pacific Hotel at the end of Silom and Surawong roads.

These san phra phum or 'spirit houses' are home to the resident spirit or phra phum of the compound, who has the power to help in emergencies but also to wreak havoc should the spirit not be contented. Small models of the guardian spirit and his retainers, moulded from plaster, usually occupy the building. The spirit occupies the inner room of the abode, and is usually represented as a figure holding a sword or fly whisk in the right hand and a book in the left. The book is a death register. Around the house on the raised platform (the spirit house should be at or above eye level) are arranged the retainers: servants, animals and entertainers. Sunday is traditionally designated house cleaning day.

Usually the spirit house will occupy one corner of the house compound – the shadow of the main house should never fall on the spirit house. This would court disaster and entice the spirit to move from its residence into the main house. But the art of placing the spirit house goes much further than just keeping it out of the shadow of the main house and is akin to the Chinese art of geomancy or feng shui. Often, when misfortune strikes a family, one of their first actions is to refurbish and move the spirit house. In the normal run of events though, the spirit merely needs placating with food, incense, flowers, candles and other offerings. Each has its own character and tastes: one family, facing serious difficulties, employed a mor du ('seeing doctor', a medium) to be told that, as their spirit was a Muslim, he had been offended by being offered pork. The family changed the spirit's diet and the difficulties melted away. Guests who stay the night should ideally ask the spirit for permission and then visit the shrine again before leaving.

this gradual erosion of the ideals that monks should embrace, rather than the odd lurid scandal, which is the more important. Many monks come from poor backgrounds and few are well educated. The temptations are all too clear in a society where a newly wealthy laity see the lavish support of individual monks and their monasteries as a means to accumulate merit. Thais talk with distaste of *Buddhapanich* – commercialized Buddhism – where amulets are sold for US$20,000 and monks attain the status and trappings of rock stars. It was reported in 1995 that one wat had earned a business school marketing award. The abbot of Wat Bon Rai in Northern Thailand, Luang Poh Koon, gave away nearly ฿64 mn in 1994. The reason why he managed to generate such staggering sums is because people believe he can bring wealth and health. Each morning his monastery throngs with people, itching to hand over cash in the hope that it will be a wise investment. It is thought that he takes

In Siddhartha's footsteps: a short history of Buddhism

Buddhism was founded by Siddhartha Gautama, a prince of the Sakya tribe of Nepal, who probably lived between 563 and 483 BC. He achieved enlightenment and buddha means 'fully enlightened one' or 'one who has woken up'. He is known by a number of titles. In the west, he is usually referred to as *The Buddha*, ie the historic Buddha (but not just Buddha); more common in Southeast Asia is the title *Sakyamuni*, or Sage of the Sakyas (referring to his tribal origins).

Over the centuries, the life of the Buddha has become part legend, and the Jataka tales are colourful and convoluted. (These are tales of the former lives of the historic Buddha as he passed through a series of births and re-births on the way to nirvana. There are 547 in total. Some of the tales are more popular than others although this varies between countries and cultures.) But central to any Buddhist's belief is that he was born under a sal tree, he achieved enlightenment under a bodhi tree in the Bodh Gaya Gardens (India), he preached the First Sermon at Sarnath and that he died at Kusinagara (all in India or Nepal).

The Buddha was born at Lumbini (in present-day Nepal), as Queen Maya was on her way to her parents' home. She had had a very auspicious dream before the child's birth of being impregnated by an elephant, whereupon a sage prophesied Siddhartha would become either a great king or a great spiritual leader. His father, being keen that the first option of the prophesy be fulfilled, brought him up in all the princely skills – at which Siddhartha excelled – and ensured that he only saw beautiful things, not the harsher elements of life.

Despite his father's efforts, Siddhartha saw four things while travelling between palaces: a helpless old man, a very sick man, a corpse being carried by relatives, and an ascetic, calm and serene man as he begged for food. The young prince renounced his princely origins and left home to study under a series of spiritual teachers. He finally discovered the path to enlightenment at the Bodh

US$1,000 a day in this manner. Taken together, Thailand's monasteries have a turnover of billions of baht; individual monks have personal bank accounts running into millions. It is this concern for money, in a religion where monks take a vow of poverty, which critics find particularly worrying.

Most of these stories of greed, commercialism and sexual peccadillos rarely make the leap from the Thai to the international media. However, the murder in January 1996 of Johanne Masheder, a British tourist, by a monk at Wat Tham Kao Poon (a cave wat), outside the town of Kanchanaburi in western Thailand, led Western journalists to look more closely at Buddhism in Thailand. In court it was revealed that the monk, Yodchart Suaphoo, was a former member of the Thai underworld and had already served time for rape. How could he have possibly been allowed to join the monkhood, many foreigners wondered. Yet taking the saffron robes of the monk has been a traditional way for men to make up for past crimes. Dictators, hit-and-run drivers, drug addicts hoping to dry out, even murderers, have all found sanctuary in Thailand's monasteries. As Police Colonel Vorathep Mathwaj, head of the Investigation Division of the Immigration police, put it: "This does not look good for Thailand and our monkhood'. A month after his arrest, Yodchart was sentenced to death by firing squad after a one-day trial. He pleaded to be taken to the mouth of the cave and shot right away, but his wish was not granted. His death sentence was later commuted to life – as is usual in Thailand.

Gaya Gardens. He then proclaimed his thoughts to a small group of disciples at Sarnath, near Benares, and continued to preach and attract followers until he died at the age of 81 at Kusinagara.

In the First Sermon at the deer park in Sarnath, the Buddha preached the Four Truths – still considered the root of Buddhist belief and practical experience: suffering exists; there is a cause of suffering; suffering can be ended; and to end suffering it is necessary to follow the 'Noble Eightfold Path' – namely, right speech, livelihood, action, effort, mindfulness, concentration, opinion and intention.

Soon after the Buddha began preaching, a monastic order – the Sangha – was established. As the monkhood evolved in India, it also began to fragment into different sects. An important change was the belief the Buddha was transcendent: he had never been born, nor had he died; he had always existed and his life on earth had been mere illusion. The emergence of these new concepts helped to turn what up until then was an ethical code of conduct into a religion. It eventually led to the appearance of Mahayana Buddhism, which split from the more traditional Theravada 'sect'.

Despite the division of Buddhism into two sects, the central tenets of the religion are common to both. Specifically, the principles pertaining to the Four Noble Truths, the Noble Eightfold Path, the Dependent Origination, the Law of Karma, and nirvana. In addition, the principles of non-violence and tolerance are also embraced by both. In essence, the differences between the two are of emphasis and interpretation. Theravada Buddhism is strictly based on the original Pali Canon, while the Mahayana tradition stems from later Sanskrit texts. Mahayana Buddhism also allows a broader and more varied interpretation of the doctrine. Other important differences are that while the Theravada tradition is more 'intellectual' and self-obsessed, with an emphasis upon the attaining of wisdom and insight for oneself, Mahayana Buddhism stresses devotion and compassion towards others.

The Sangha Council, which is supposed to police the monkhood, has, at times, seemed perplexed as to what to do. In July 1998, for example, they found Phra Khru Sopitsutkhun, the abbot of Wat Sanam Chang in Chachoengsao, not guilty of bringing Buddhism into bad repute with his murals of naked men and women, his image of the Buddha in the so-called Superman mudra – arms outstretched and foot planted firmly on a globe – and his sale of lustral water. The *Bangkok Post* deplored the Council's unwillingness to confront unsavoury commercialism within the sangha, and viewed the case of Wat Sanam Chang as an example of "Buddhism gone horribly wrong" (*Bangkok Post*, 22.7.98).

Sulak Sivaraksa, one of Thailand's most respected scholars and critics, has suggested that there is a "crisis at the core of organized Thai Buddhism". In his view, Buddhism has simply failed to adapt in line with wider changes in economy and society. It evolved as a religion suited to a country where there was a feudal court system and where most people were subsistence farmers. Now most people live in the cash economy and work in modern sectors of the economy. These views are not restricted to those outside the monkhood. Prayudh Payutto, perhaps Thailand's greatest living monk-scholar, was quoted in 1996 as saying "More and more monks are living luxurious lives", adding that they "are no longer keeping to the letter or to the spirit of the rules [the 227 precepts]". Even more dramatically, Sompong Rachano, the director of the Religious Affairs' Buddhist Monastery

The practice of Islam: living by the Prophet

Islam is an Arabic word meaning 'submission to God'. As Muslims often point out, it is not just a religion but a total way of life. The main Islamic scripture is the Koran or Quran, the name being taken from the Arabic al-qur'an or 'the recitation'. The Koran is divided into 114 sura, or 'units'. Most scholars are agreed that the Koran was partially written by the Prophet Mohammad. In addition to the Koran there are the hadiths, from the Arabic word hadith meaning 'story', which tell of the Prophet's life and works. These represent the second most important body of scriptures.

The practice of Islam is based upon five central tenets, known as the Pillars of Islam: *Shahada* (profession of faith), *Salat* (worship), Zakat (charity), *saum* (fasting) and *Haj* (pilgrimage). The mosque is the centre of religious activity. The two most important mosque officials are the *imam* – (leader) – and the *khatib* (preacher) – who delivers the Friday sermon.

The **Shahada** is the confession, and lies at the core of any Muslim's faith. It involves reciting, sincerely, two statements: 'There is no god, but God', and 'Mohammad is the Messenger [Prophet] of God'. A Muslim will do this at every **Salat**. This is the daily prayer ritual which is performed five times a day, at sunrise, midday, mid-afternoon, sunset and at night. There is also the important Friday noon worship. The Salat is performed by a Muslim bowing and then prostrating himself in the direction of Mecca (in Malaysian kiblat, in Arabic qibla). In hotel rooms throughout there is nearly always a little arrow, painted on the ceiling – or sometimes inside a wardrobe – indicating the direction of Mecca and labelled kiblat. The faithful are called to worship by a mosque official. Beforehand, a worshipper must wash to ensure ritual purity. The Friday midday service is performed in the mosque and includes a sermon given by the khatib.

A third essential element of Islam is **Zakat** – charity or alms-giving. A Muslim is supposed to give up his

Division, stated in 1997 that "Not many Buddhist monks can adhere to the 227 Buddhist precepts, few can discuss the teachings of the Buddha with lay people and fewer still – perhaps one in a thousand – have the ability to deliver a sermon before a congregation" (*The Nation*, 20.7.97).

Islam

While Thailand is often portrayed as a 'Buddhist Kingdom', the provinces of the far south are majority Muslim. This is because these provinces have, historically, come under the cultural influence of the former sultanates of the Malay peninsula. See box, The practice of Islam: living by the prophet.

Christianity

When Europeans first made trading contact with the Kingdom of Ayutthaya some of these early visitors also aimed to convert Siam to Christianity. This reached a peak when the Greek adventurer Constantine Phaulcon inveigled his way to becoming Mahatthai or chief minister to King Narai and, it is said, held the ambition of converting the King to Roman Catholicism. This came to nothing, and Phaulcon lost his life. Since then missionaries have had the odd success in the Buddhist heartland of Thailand but it still remains a solidly Buddhist nation. Missionaries, though, have had far more success among the formerly largely animist hill peoples. Here significant numbers of Karen and Lahu, and other minority groups, have converted to Christianity.

'surplus' (according to the Koran); through time this took on the form of a tax levied according to the wealth of the family. In Malaysia there is no official Zakat as there is in Saudi Arabia, but good Muslims are expected to contribute a tithe to the Muslim community.

The fourth pillar of Islam is **saum** or fasting. The daytime month-long fast of Ramadan is a time of contemplation, worship and piety – the Islamic equivalent of Lent. Muslims are expected to read one-thirtieth of the Koran each night. Muslims who are ill or on a journey have dispensation from fasting, but otherwise they are only permitted to eat during the night until "so much of the dawn appears that a white thread can be distinguished from a black one".

The **Haj** or Pilgrimmage to the holy city of Mecca in Saudi Arabia is required of all Muslims once in their lifetime if they can afford to make the journey and are physically able to. It is restricted to a certain time of the year, beginning on the eighth day of the Muslim month of Dhu-l-Hijja. Men who have been on the Haj are given the title Haji, and women hajjah.

The Koran also advises on a number of other practices and customs, in particular the prohibitions on usury, the eating of pork, the taking of alcohol, and gambling.

While the provinces of the far South of Thailand support a majority Muslim population, Islam has not – in general – been radicalised to the extent it has in some other countries and regions. The veil, for example, is not widely worn while the consumption of alcohol is fairly widespread. There has been an Islamic revival of sorts, and an increased interest in Islamic scholarship, but this has been restricted to a small segment of the population. There may have been considerable disquiet at the US-led invasion of Iraq and calls for boycotts of US products and companies but this should not been interpreted as a sea-change in attitudes. Indeed, many Thai Buddhists share these concerns.

Land and environment

Geography

Thailand covers an area of 500,000 sq km (about the size of France) and had a population in 2001 of 62.3 million, which is growing at 1½% per year. It shares its borders with Burma, Laos, Cambodia and Malaysia. Administratively, the country is divided into five main regions: the North, Northeast, Central Plains, South and the Bangkok Metropolitan Region. Two smaller, additional regions are also sometimes identified: the East and West. Each of these seven regions has its own distinctive geographical character.

The **Central region** is Thailand's 'rice bowl', encompassing the wide and fertile Central Plains: this is the economic and cultural heartland of the Thai (or Tai) nation. The construction of dams, and the spread of irrigation in the region, has enabled Thailand to become, and remain, the world's largest rice exporter. Yet most farms remain small, family-owned affairs. Towards the southern extremity of the Central Plains lies the **Bangkok Metropolitan Region**. With an official population of 5.7 million (2001), it is many times larger than Thailand's second city and is the country's economic and political hub. Indeed, it has outgrown its administrative

 borders and the population of the entire urban agglomeration is nearer to 10 million. Bangkok supports both the greatest density of businesses, as well as the key institutions of government.

The **North** is Thailand's largest region, and includes the Kingdom's second city of Chiang Mai. It is a mountainous region with narrow river valleys, and supports most of the minority hilltribes. The area was not incorporated fully into the Thai state until the 19th century. Doi Pha Hom Pok, the country's highest peak at 2,300 m, is located in Chiang Mai Province.

The **Northeast** or **'Isan'** is the second largest, and poorest, region of Thailand. It is also known as the Khorat Plateau and is environmentally harsh. The people of the Northeast speak a dialect of Thai – Lao – and they are culturally distinct in terms of food, dress and ritual. Most are rice farmers living in approaching 29,000 villages.

Just south of the Northeast, sandwiched between the sea and the Damrek range of hills, is the **Eastern region**. This has become an overspill area for Bangkok, with businesses moving to take advantage of cheaper land and less congested infrastructure. The Eastern region also contains the renowned seaside resort of Pattaya.

To the west of the Central Plains and Bangkok is the **Western region**. Until recently this was a relatively undeveloped, mountainous and largely forested area. But over the past 10-20 years, pioneer agriculturalists and logging companies have moved into the West, clearing large tracts of forest, and planting the land with cash crops such as sugar-cane and cassava. Despite these developments, the beautiful mountains which rise up towards the border with Burma remain relatively unspoilt. Towns here have a 'frontier' atmosphere.

Thailand's seventh region is the **South**, which stretches 1,150 km south to the border with Malaysia. The far south has more in common with island Southeast Asia than mainland Southeast Asia; the climate is tropical, many of the inhabitants are Malay, Islam is the main religion and rubber is the dominant crop. Most visitors visit the beach resorts of Koh Samui, Phuket, Koh Phi Phi, Hua Hin and Koh Phangan.

Below the region, there are a series of further administrative subdivisions. First, the changwat, or province, of which there are 75 (Bangkok is a separate administrative division), each with a governor at its head. Below the province is the *amphoe*, or district, numbering 811 in all, each headed by a *nai amphoe*, or district officer. Then comes the *tambon*, a 'commune' of villages, of which there are 7,409, each with a *kamnan* in charge. And finally, the lowest level of administration is the *mubaan* – the village – of which there are 67,581, each headed by a democratically elected *phuuyaibaan*, or village head.

Climate

Thailand lies within the humid tropics and remains hot throughout the year. Mean temperatures vary between 24°C in the far north to 29°C in the Central region, while rainfall ranges from 1,200 mm in parts of the Northeast to over 4,000 mm in some parts of the South (eg Ranong) and East (eg Khlong Yai, Chantaburi). Far more important than these mean annual figures are seasonal fluctuations in rainfall and, to a lesser extent, temperature. With the exception of the southern isthmus, which receives rainfall throughout the year, Thailand has a dry season which stretches from November to April, corresponding with the period of the northeast monsoon, and a wet season from May to October, corresponding with the southwest monsoon.

For best time to visit, see page 20.

The distinction between the dry and the rainy seasons is most pronounced in the Northeast, where as much as 98% of rain falls between April and October. Nonetheless, like the English, Thai's talk endlessly about the weather. The seasons – and this means rain – determine the very pattern of life in the region. Rice cultivation,

Temperature and rainfall: selected towns

Town	Region	Height Above sea level	Annual Temp, °C Max	Min	Av	Average Rainfall, mm	% rain falling, May-Oct
Bangkok	C	3m	39.9	9.9	28.1	1418	86%
Lopburi	C	14m	41.8	8.4	28.1	1239	87%
Chiang Mai	N	314m	41.5	6.0	25.8	1268	89%
Mae Hong Son	N	417m	42.0	6.0	26.2	1256	92%
Korat	NE	189m	43.4	4.9	27.1	1197	82%
Udon Thani	NE	181m	43.9	2.5	26.8	1367	88%
Kanchanaburi	W	29m	43.5	5.5	27.8	984	81%
Chantaburi	E	5m	40.8	8.9	27.2	3164	89%
Sattahip	E	56m	40.5	12.3	29.0	1366	65%
Nakhon Si Thammarat	S	7m	37.7	17.1	27.4	2491	39%
Narathiwat	S	4m	36.4	17.1	27.0	2644	41%

and its associated festivals, is dependent in most areas on the arrival of the rains, and religious ceremonies are timed to coincide with the seasons.

The dry season can be divided into two: cool and hot. During the cool season in the North, (December to February), it can become distinctly chilly, with temperatures falling to as low as 7°C at night. The hot season runs between March and May and temperatures may exceed 40°C, before the cooling rains arrive towards the end of the period. But for much of the time, and in most places, it is hot whatever the month.

Seasons

Hot season March-May, dry with temperatures 27°C-35°C, but sometimes in the 40s for extended periods.

Wet or rainy season June-October, wet with lower temperatures (due to the cooling effect of the rain and increased cloud cover) 24°C-32°C, but higher humidity.

Cool season December-February, when conditions are at their most pleasant, with little rain and temperatures ranging from 18°C to 32°C.

Seasons in the South Similar weather to that of the Malay peninsula, with hot, humid and sunny weather most of the year. Chance of rain at any time, although more likely during the period of the two monsoons, May-October (particularly on west side of the peninsula) and November-April (particularly on east coast).

Wet rice cultivation

Rice probably spread into Southeast Asia from a core area, which spanned the highlands from Assam (India) to north Vietnam. Some of the earliest evidence of agriculture in the world has been uncovered in and around the village of Ban Chiang in Northeastern Thailand, and also from Bac-son in north Vietnam. However, archaeologists are far from agreed about the dating and significance of the evidence. Some believe that rice may have been cultivated as early as 7,000 BC; others say it dates back no further than 3,000-2,000 BC.

By the time the first Europeans arrived in the 15th century, the crop was well-established as the staple for the region. Today, other staples are frowned upon, being widely regarded as 'poor man's food'. The importance of rice can be seen reflected in the degree to which culture and crop have become intermeshed, and in the mythology and ceremony associated with its cultivation. The American anthropologist DeYoung, who worked in a village in Central Thailand in the late 1950s, wrote that the farmer: 'reverences the crop he grows as a sentient being; he marks its stages of growth by ceremonies; and he propitiates the spirit of the soil in which it grows and the good or evil spirits that may help or harm it. He considers rice to possess a life spirit (kwan) and to grow much as a human being grows; when it bears grain, it has become 'pregnant' like a mother, and the rice is the seed or child of the Rice Goddess.'

Wet rice, more than any other staple crop, is dependent on an ample and constant supply of water. The links between rice and water, wealth and poverty, and abundance and famine are clear. Throughout the region, there are numerous rituals and songs which honour the 'gift of water' and dwell upon the vagaries of the monsoon. Water-throwing festivals, designed to induce abundant rainfall, are widespread, and if they do not have the desired effect villagers will often resort to magic. The struggle to ensure a constant supply of water can also be seen reflected in the sophisticated *müang fai*, traditional irrigation systems of Northern Thailand. Less obvious, but no less ingenious and complex, is that farmers without the benefits of irrigation have also developed sophisticated cultivation strategies designed to maintain production through flood and drought.

While rice remains Thailand's key crop and a marker of Thai-ness, it does not occupy the central position in life and livelihood that it once did. Young people, increasingly, wish to avoid the drudgery of farming which has become, through the twin effects of education and the media, a low status occupation. Anyone spending time in the Northern region or the Central Plains may notice uncultivated land, effectively abandoned because there is no one to farm it. (An alternative explanation is that it has been purchased for speculative reasons.) Many farmers have sold their buffalo and bought rotavators – known as *kwai lek* or iron buffalo – because they plough the land more quickly and don't have to be fed, grazed and bedded. Broadcasting has replaced transplanting in some areas because it saves time. There are even cases of weekend farmers who travel up from Bangkok on Saturdays to keep their farms ticking over. Today, it is not uncommon for rural households to earn 50% or more of their income from non-farm sources. In the countryside, older Thais sometimes lament this loss of subsistence innocence, but the young, of course, will have nothing of it. The future, so far as they are concerned, does not lie in farming.

Flora and fauna

It has been estimated that Thailand supports 18,000 species of plant, 6,000 insect species, 1,000 kinds of bird, and 300 species of mammal. Even so, it is difficult not to escape the conclusion that the Kingdom's flora and fauna are woefully depleted. As recently as 1950, over half the country's land area was forested. Today, barely a day goes by before yet another scandal with an environmental tinge is revealed in the newspapers. This concern for the environment, though, is comparatively recent, dating only from 1973. In that year, an army helicopter crashed, and as investigators picked over the wreckage they discovered not just the bodies of the crew and passengers, but also the corpses of several protected wild animals. It became clear that the human victims – prominent army officers – had been illegally hunting in the Thung Yai Naresuan Wildlife Sanctuary. A public scandal ensued and the environmental movement in Thailand was born.

From the mid-1980s, the environment became an issue of considerable political importance and public concern in Thailand. In no small way this was linked to the environmental destruction that had accompanied the country's rush to development: the stripping of much of the forest resource, the devastation of coastal mangroves, the decimation of many large mammals, the pollution of rivers, the denudation of watersheds, widespread soil erosion, rampant over-fishing, and more. Newspapers increasingly began to highlight abuses of power and environmental pressure groups such as the Project for Ecological Recovery (PER) enjoyed growing public support. To begin with the government and business saw such environmental movements as 'the enemy', to be vanquished. Today – however grudgingly – the government and most major players have come to realize that the environment cannot be ignored, and nor can public concerns. Agencies and research outfits such as the Thailand Environment Institute (TEI) work with the mainstream and plans formulated by the National Economic and Social Development Board are thoroughly 'green'. Of course cynics and critics see this as largely window dressing and that beneath the sheen of greenery are groups and individuals who have changed barely at all.

Flora

Thailand's dominant natural vegetation is **tropical forest**. In the south, parts of the west, and in pockets such as Chanthaburi province in the east, this means 'jungle' or tropical rain forest. Tigers, elephants, banteng (wild ox), sambar (deer) and tapirs still roam the lowland forests, although not in great numbers. Thailand's forests have been depleted to a greater extent than in any other country in Southeast Asia (with the one exception of Singapore, which doesn't really count). In 1938, 70% of Thailand's land area was forested; by 1961 this had been reduced to just over 50%. Today, natural forest cover accounts for only a little more than 15% of the land area and projections indicate that by 2010 this will have declined to less than 10%. The Royal Forestry Department still insists on a figure of over 20% and puts the area of National Reserve Forest at 40% – despite the fact that over large areas not a single tree remains standing, a glance at satellite images will show both figures to be palpably fraudulent.

The causes of this spectacular, and depressing, **destruction of Thailand's forests** are numerous: simple population growth, commercial logging, commercialization and the spread of cash cropping, and dam construction. Cronyism and corruption, which is part and parcel of logging across the region, has also marred the management of Thailand's forests. In late 1988, such was the public outcry after floods in the South killed 300 people – and whose severity was linked in the public imagination to deforestation – that a nationwide logging ban was introduced in January 1989. Few doubt, though, that deforestation continues. 'The Forestry Department', as Nok Nguak (a pseudonym) argued, "can be described at best as ineffective and at worst as one of the main culprits in the destruction of our forests". (*Bangkok Post*, 24.3.98) In February 1998 it was revealed that a logging mafia, in league with the Royal Forestry Department (RFD), had been instrumental in the logging of protected forest in the Salween area near Mae Hong Son, in Northern Thailand. After the revelation of a ฿5 mn bribe, *The Nation* opined that the RFD was 'hopelessly corrupt'.

The tropical rain forests of Thailand, although not comparable with those of Malaysia and Indonesia, have a high diversity of species, exceeding 100 per hectare in some areas. In total, it is estimated that Thailand supports 20,000-25,000 species of plant.

In the North and the Northeast the vegetation adapts to a climate, with a dry season that stretch over months. For this reason, the forests here support fewer species than in the south. In many cases they are also highly degraded due to logging and farming. Other sub-types of tropical forest in Thailand include semi-evergreen forest (in the Peninsula and North, along the border with Burma), dry evergreen forest (in the wetter parts of the Northeast and the North), *ixed deciduous* and dry dipterocarp savanna forest (mostly in the Northeast and parts of the northern Central Plains).

Elephants have nowhere to go

According to the local office of the World Wide Fund for Nature, there are 2,705 domesticated elephants in Thailand and 1,975 wild animals. In 1782 there were around 200,000; by 1900 this had declined to less than 100,000. But the trained elephants and their mahouts are out of a job and out of luck. With the imposition of a logging ban in 1989, their traditional work in the forests of the country all but dried up. Some took the rather degrading alternative option of working in tourist-oriented elephant 'camps', where the stately pachyderms are forced to play football and harmonicas. But there is a limit to the tourist potential of the elephant, and many of these down-on-their-luck animals and mahouts took to begging for food. As it is Bangkok where most of the money is to be found, it was Bangkok where elephants gravitated. Because the elephant is the holiest of beasts, Buddhists can make merit by buying sugar cane and bananas for the animals. It was in this way that the mahouts managed to feed their mounts – at an estimated cost of ฿2-3,000 a month.

But in 2000 the governor of Bangkok banned elephants from the city. The mahouts saw the hands of environmentalists in this ban - and in particular, foreign environmentalists. It was suggested that Roger Lohanan, of the Thai Society for the Prevention of Cruelty to Animals, and Solaida Salwala, of the Asian Elephant Lovers Foundation, had been instrumental in convincing the governor that elephants are not designed for city life. There were reports of elephants being hit by cars, having their feet lacerated by nails and broken glass, and going beserk in the heat and fumes. Mahouts were accused of cruelty, and of furthering their own interests at the expense of the elephants. The mahouts reacted

Fauna

Thailand's fauna is even more threatened than its forests. Of the Kingdom's 282 species of mammal, 40 are endangered and 14 are critically endangered. For its birds, the picture is equally gloomy: 190 endangered species out of 928, with 38 critically endangered. While for the country's reptiles and amphibians, there are 37 endangered species out of 405, of which seven are on the critical list. A century ago, wild elephants and tigers roamed the Bang Kapi area east of Bangkok – now it is overrun with shopping malls. It was only in 1960 that a law was enacted protecting wild animals, and even today it doesn't take an investigative journalist to find endangered – and protected – animals for sale, whether whole (and alive) or in bits.

Thailand supports a rich and varied fauna, partly because it lies on the boundary between several zoogeographic regions: the Indochinese, Indian and Sundaic (Malesia). It also lies on a crossroads between North and South, acting as a waystation for animals dispersing north from the Sundaic islands, and south from the Asian mainland. The problem in trying to maintain the country's biodiversity is that most of its national parks and wildlife sanctuaries are thought to be too small to be sustainable. A single male tiger, for example, needs about 50 sq km of forest to survive; some of Thailand's parks cover less than 100 sq km.

Mammals During the 1980s, some of Thailand's endangered species of mammal disappeared entirely. The Javan and Sumatran rhinoceros, the kouprey (*Bos sauveli*, the largest cattle in the world), the wild water buffalo and Eld's deer (*Cervus eldi*) are probably all extinct in Thailand, or on the verge of extinction. The world's last Schomburgk's deer (*Cervus schomburgki*) was kept as a pet in the grounds of a

furiously, accusing the elephant lovers of ignorance. One mahout, 60-year-old Ta Jongjaingam, even asked "Why do they let the Burmese and Khmers stay [in Bangkok]– but not our elephants?". As is usual with these things in Thailand, lots of slightly crazed people (and some sensible ones) wrote letters to the newspapers, arguing one way or the other.

In 2002 the US-based People for the Ethical Treatment of Animals (PETA) publicised a film showing young elephants being tortured in northern Thailand. Again Thailand found itself in the dock. Thai officials and experts claimed that the film has been doctored and was not representative of the animals' treatment in the Kingdom; PETA, meanwhile, called for a tourist ban of Thailand and proposed a law for elephant welfare. This, for most Thais, was going too far: foreigners interfering in the sovereign affairs of a country and suggesting to Thais how they should look after their national symbol. It does seem a rather heavy-handed way of dealing with the issue and while publicity might have been gained rather more would have been achieved with a subtler approach.

Some people have pointed out that even before the logging ban, life was not always a bed of bananas for the elephants. There have been reports that they were fed on amphetamines to keep them working, and when they became too ill or exhausted they were simply sold – often to be slaughtered. An elephant trunk is said to be worth ฿40,000 and the genitals ฿15-20,000; a good pair of tusks considerably more than this. Unfortunately, Thailand is really not in a position to support a large number of elephants any longer. There is neither the work, the space, nor the interest. Even wild elephants are becoming a pest in some areas, as they venture out of national park areas and destroy crops.

Buddhist monastery in Samut Sakhon province before, reputedly, being clubbed to death by a drunk in 1938.

The reasons for this pattern of extermination are not difficult to fathom: destruction of habitat and over-hunting (see below). Thailand does have national legislation protecting rare species from hunting, capturing and trade, but too often the legislation is ignored and even officials have actively flouted the law, sometimes hunting in national parks. Of Thailand's 282 species of mammal, 40 are listed in the International Union for the Conservation of Nature and Natural Resources' (IUCNs) Red List of Endangered Species. These include the pileated gibbon (*Hylobates pileatus*), the clouded leopard (*Neofelis nebulosa*), the Malayan tapir (*Tapirus indicus*) and the tiger (*Panthera tigris*). Indeed, almost all Thailand's large mammals are in danger of extinction in the country.

Birds Birdlife in Thailand is also under pressure. Birds' habitats are being destroyed, pollution is increasing, and hunting is barely controlled. Even in Thailand's national parks, a lack of resources and widespread corruption mean that bird populations are under threat.

Over the last three decades or so, 80% of Thailand's forests have disappeared – and with them, many bird habitats. Birds are also hunted by farmers for food and virtually any size and shape of bird is considered fair game. The rarer and more colourful species are hunted by collectors for the bird trade – for which Thailand is a centre. It is not unusual to walk in the countryside and neither see nor hear a bird of any type. Three of Thailand's birds are listed by the IUCN as threatened with extinction: the giant ibis (*Pseudibis gigantea*), the Chinese egret (*Egretta*

The 'Siamese' Cat

There were, originally, 23 breeds of cat that came from Thailand. Of these, only one is regarded by cat fanciers as the Siamese Cat – the Korat or Si Sawat. The original 23 breeds are described in the Cat Book Poems, a 14th-century manuscript including paintings and verse now housed in Bangkok's National Library. Of the 23, 17 were regarded as good luck cats, and the remaining six as cats of ill fortune. Today, however, only six of the original 23 breeds remain and, fortunately, all are good luck cats.

Korat (officially, Nakhon Ratchasima) is a large town in Thailand's Northeastern region, and the original name of the Siamese cat is said to have arisen when King Rama V (1868-1910) asked a court official where a particularly beautiful cat came from, to be told 'Korat'. Certainly, Western visitors to this part of the Northeast remarked on the breed's existence at the beginning of the 20th century.

It was not, however, until 1959 that the first confirmed pair of Korats were imported into the US. Today the Korat is more usually called Si Sawat, a reference to the cat's colour (silver-blue). The sawat is a grey-green non-edible fruit; sawat also happens to mean good fortune. Why the Si Sawat is associated with good luck is not clear. It has been said that its colour is symbolic of silver, signifying good fortune. Others have argued that the colour is akin to rain clouds, indicating a bountiful rice crop. Even the colour of the cat's eyes have been likened to the colour of ripening rice. A pair of Si Sawats given to a bride before marriage is said to bring good fortune to the partnership. Other than the Korat's distinctive colour, it is also unique in that its hair does not float off when it is stroked, making the animal particularly suitable for those with a cat allergy.

For further information, contact: Rose Meldrum, President, Korat Cat Fanciers' Association Inc, 6408 Shinnwood Road, Wilmington, NC 28409, USA; or The Cat Fanciers' Association Inc, PO Box 1005, Manasquan NJ 08736-1005, USA.

eulophotes), and the white-winged wood duck (*Cairina scutulata*); many others have had their populations decimated.

In total, Thailand has 928 species of bird – more than double the number found in Europe – which account for a tenth of the world's species. This richness of birdlife is due to the varied nature of Thailand's habitats and the country's position at the junction of three zoological realms. The country is also an important wintering area for migrant birds from the northern latitudes.

Reptiles & amphibians Thailand supports an impressive and varied population of snakes, lizards and other assorted cold-blooded creatures. In total there are 298 reptile and 107 amphibian species, of which 37 are regarded as endangered. The closest most people come to a snake (at least knowingly) is at Bangkok's Red Cross Snake Farm, or at the snake farm near the floating market in Thonburi.

The large **non-venomous** pythons are active around dusk and kill their prey by constriction. The reticulated python (*Python reticulatus*) can grow to a length of 15 m and, although non-venomous, their bite is powerful. Other smaller pythons include the blood python (*Python curtus*) and rock python (*Python molurus bivittatus*).

Some of the most beautiful non-venomous snakes in Thailand are the racers (genus Elaphe and Gonyosoma). They live in a variety of habitats, and because they are diurnal are often seen. The visually striking, gold-coloured copperhead racer

(*Elephe radiata*) can grow to a length of 2 m and lives in open grasslands; the bright green, red-tailed racer (*Gonyosoma oxycephalum*) lives in trees. It can also grow to 2 m and is easily identified by its brown tail. Other snakes found in Thailand include the rat snakes (genus Zaocys and Ptyas), the beautiful whip-like bronzebacks (genus Dendrelaphis), and the keelbacks (sub-family Natricinae).

But it is the dread – often misplaced – of the **venomous species** which make them the most fascinating of snakes. There are two types: the front-fanged (more venomous) and back-fanged (mildly venomous) snakes. The latter include whip snakes (genus Ahaetulla and Dryophiops), water snakes (sub-family Homalopsinae) and cat snakes (genus Boiga). The former include cobras, the best known of which is the king cobra (*Ophiophagus hannah*), common Chinese cobra (*Naja naja atra*) and the monocled cobra (*Naja naja kaouthia*). The king cobra is said to be the longest venomous snake in the world; it has been known to reach lengths of up to 6 m. It is also among the most dangerous due to its aggressive nature. One specimen shot in the mountains of Nakhon Si Thammarat in 1924 measured 5.6 m. Their venom is a very powerful neurotoxin, and victims can be dead within half an hour. It has even been claimed that elephants have died after being bitten, the snake puncturing the soft skin at the tip of the trunk. King cobras are found throughout the country, in most habitats. It should be emphasized that despite their aggressiveness, few people die from cobra bites in Thailand.

The venom of **sea snakes** (family *Hydrophiidae*) is even more powerful than that of cobras, and the common sea snake's (*Enhydrina schistosa*) is said to be the most toxic of any snake. Fortunately, sea snakes are not particularly aggressive, and it is rare for swimmers to be bitten. Twenty-two species have been found in the waters of Southeast Asia, and all bar one (*Laticauda colubrina*, which lays its eggs in rock crevices) produce their young live. They grow to a length of 2 m and feed on fish.

Snakes of the viper family (*Viperidae*) grow to a length of 1 m, and the kraits (genus Bungarus) to 2 m. Vipers are easily identifiable by their arrow-shaped heads. The vipers' long fangs, their position at the front of the mouth, and their aggressiveness, makes them more dangerous than other more poisonous species. The Malayan pit viper (*Agkistrodon rhodostoma*) and Pope's pit viper (*Trimeresurus popeiorum*) are both highly irritable. Kraits, though possessing a toxic venom which has been known to kill, are of sleepy temperament and rarely attack unless provoked. The banded krait (*Bungarus fasciatus*), with its black and yellow striped body, is very distinctive.

A rather different, and less dangerous – at least in its current form – reptile is *Siamotyrannus isanensis*, a tyrannosaur beloved of school children around the world. On 19 June 1996, Thai and French palaeontologists announced the discovery of a 7 m-long tyrannosaur. This may not be the largest member of the family – 'rex' is twice the size – but it is the oldest, predating the next most senior by 20 million years. It is also Thailand's very own dinosaur (see page 341).

Insects Insects are not usually at the top of a visitor's agenda to Thailand. But, as with the Kingdom's birds and flora, the country also has a particularly rich insect population due to its position at a crossroads between different, and varied, zoogeographic zones. There are over 1,400 species of butterfly and moth (*Lepidoptera*), including one of the world's largest moths, the giant atlas (*Attacus atlas*) which has a wing span of up to 28 cm. Beetles are even more numerous, although how numerous is not known: one single sq km of the Thung Yai-Huai Kha Khaeng area was found to support 10,000 species alone.

Marine life Thailand's coastline abuts onto both the Indian Ocean (Andaman Sea) and the South China Sea (Gulf of Thailand), and therefore has marine flora and fauna characteristic of both regions. In the Gulf, 850 species of open-water fish have been

identified including tuna, of which Thailand is the world's largest exporter (although most are now caught outside Thailand's waters). In the Andaman Sea, game fish such as blue and black marlin, barracuda, sailfish and various sharks are all present.

Among sea mammals, Thailand's shores provide nesting sites for four species of **sea turtle**: the huge leatherback, green, Ridley's and the hawksbill turtle. The latter is now very rare, while a fifth species, the loggerhead turtle, has disappeared from Thailand's shores and waters. Other marine mammals include several species of sea snake (see above), the saltwater crocodile (which may now be extinct), three species of dolphin, and the dugong or sea cow.

Coral reefs probably contain a richer profusion of life than any other ecosystem – even exceeding the tropical rainforest in terms of species diversity. Those in Thailand's Andaman Sea are among the finest in the region – and maritime parks like the Surin and Similan islands have been gazetted to help protect these delicate habitats. Although the country's reefs remain under-researched, 210 species of hard coral and 108 coral reef fish have so far been identified in the Andaman Sea. Literally tens of thousands of other marine organisms, including soft corals, crustacea, echinoderms and worms, would have to be added to this list to build up a true picture of the ecosystem's diversity.

But like the rest of Thailand's natural heritage, life under the sea is also threatened. Collin Piprell and Ashley J Boyd vividly recount this story in their book *Thailand's Coral Reefs: Nature under Threat* (see Books, page 716). Some reefs have been virtually wiped out by human depredations – for example, that off Koh Larn near Pattaya. Fish stocks in the Gulf of Thailand are seriously depleted and the destruction of mangroves along both the eastern and western seaboards has seriously eroded the main breeding grounds for many fish. Untreated effluent and raw sewage are dumped into the Gulf and, because it is an almost enclosed body of water, this tends to become concentrated. Marine biologists have identified some instances of sex-changes in shellfish communities – apparently because of the build-up of toxic compounds.

It has to be acknowledged that although tourism in some areas of Thailand has an interest in maintaining the sanctity of the marine environment, it has also been a major cause of destruction. Anchors, rubbish and sewerage, the thrashing fins of novice divers, and the selfish grabbing hands of collectors of shells, all contribute to the gradual erosion of the habitat that tourists come to experience. Other sources of destruction have less or nothing to do with tourism: the accumulation of toxic chemicals, Thailand's voracious fishermen, cyanide and dynamite fishing, the trade in aquarium fish, and collection and sale of certain species for their use in traditional Chinese medicines. The Kingdom is, for example, the world's largest exporter of seahorses. Around 15 tonnes of the dried creatures are exported each year, mostly to Taiwan and Hong Kong, where their crushed bodies are believed to be an aphrodisiac and a cure for certain respiratory ailments. Like the Kingdom's forests, there are fears that within a decade there might be little left for the discerning diver to enjoy.

National parks

In 1961 Khao Yai became Thailand's first national park – although King Ramkhamhaeng of Sukhothai created a royal reserve in the 13th century, and the grounds of Buddhist wats have always provided havens for wildlife. By late 1995 there were 81 parks covering over 41,000 sq km spread throughout the kingdom, encompassing all the principal ecological zones – and more have been gazetted since. Including Thailand's 35 wildlife sanctuaries (which cover another 29,000 sq km), and 48 non-hunting areas, nearly 15% of Thailand's land area is protected in some way. Though impressive on paper, this does not mean that there are some 70,000 sq km of protected forest, grassland, swamp and sea. Settled and shifting

Thailand's blooming business

Thailand's forests, wetlands and grasslands support over 1,000 varieties of orchid and the country has become Southeast Asia's largest exporter of the blooms. In 1991, flower exports – mostly orchids – earned US$80m. The industry began in the 1950s, but only really expanded in the mid-1980s as orchid farms were established around Bangkok. Of the various genuses, the most popular is Dendrobium, which is particularly suited to Thailand's seasonal climate and has the added attraction of blooming throughout the year.

Over half of Thailand's orchid exports go to Japan – where customers have a particular predilection for pink and purple blooms. Despite such healthy growth, there are fears that a change of fashion in Japan might undermine the market. The price of the pink Sonia dendrobium has declined from ฿5-6 to ฿2-3 per bloom. An area of the economy which has bloomed even faster than orchids is that of artificial flower production. In 1996, exports of plastic and silk flowers and foliage totalled nearly US$70 mn.

agriculturalists live in many parks, illegal logging is widespread (though better controlled today than in the 1980s), and poaching continues to be a problem. Poor pay, lack of manpower and corruption, all contribute to the difficulties of maintaining the integrity of these 'protected' areas. Even so, 40 park wardens have been murdered doing their job.

There has been an increase of late in public awareness towards wildlife and the environment. Certainly, there have been some notable successes: the logging ban of 1989, the shelving of the plan to build the Nam Choan dam in the contiguous Huai Kha Khaeng and Tha Thungna Wildlife Sanctuaries (see page 180), and – without being patronizing – a far wider concern for the environment amongst average Thais. But the battle is far from won. Loggers, poachers and tree plantation companies wield enormous financial and political power. In 1990, such was the exasperation of Sueb Makasathien, the highly regarded director of the incomparable Huai Kha Khaeng Wildlife Sanctuary, that he committed suicide. It is generally agreed that Sueb killed himself because he was unable to prevent corrupt officials, loggers and poachers from degrading his park – 2,400 sq km of the finest forest in all Southeast Asia. (Sueb was hoping to get the sanctuary accepted as a World Heritage area by UNESCO.) Tourism has also left its mark on the parks. Khao Yai is now so popular as a weekend trip from Bangkok that its capacity has been exceeded, while coastal and island marine parks suffer from refuse-littered beaches and campsites. The National Parks Division's management of the country's protected areas has been woefully inadequate. Koh Samet and Koh Phi Phi, both national parks, are – illegally – covered with accommodation developments. Khao Yai, Thailand's first park, has hotels and golf courses within its area. The Thaplan National Park in the Northeast is extensively logged by army-backed interests. The national parks, as they stand, are being ruined by poor management.

Central region **Phu Hin Rongkla National Park**: As much of historical as natural interest, this park was a centre for Communist Party activities during the 1970s. The park rises to nearly 2,000 m and has a good range of wildlife including small populations of bear and tiger. **Thung Salaeng National Park**: best known for its birdlife which is easy to view in the park's characteristic open meadows. Species include hornbills, pheasants and eagles. **Khlong Lan National Park**: one of Thailand's most pristine – and rugged – protected areas; good for trekking.

Northern region Doi Inthanon National Park: a very popular national park within easy reach of Chiang Mai. Named after Thailand's highest peak, which climbs to more than 2,500m. Wide range of flora, waterfalls, hiking trails and good facilities.

Northeastern region Khao Yai National Park: Thailand's first park and one of the most popular. Gets particularly crowded at weekends; good facilities, trails, waterfalls – but wildlife tends to keep out of the way of all the people. **Kaeng Tana National Park**: on the Mun River; it is possible to swim here in the dry season. **Phu Wiang National Park**: best known as the site of numerous dinosaur bone 'quarries'. It is possible to explore these. **Phu Kradung National Park**: a popular place for student groups who climb the 1,500m-high mountain after which this park is named. Particularly known for its wild flowers, range of vegetation types, and 130 species of bird. Good trekking.

Eastern region Khao Laem Ya National Park: the island resort of Koh Samet comes within the boundaries of this marine park; very popular but not the best protected marine area. **Koh Chang National Park**: this is focused on the large island of Koh Chang. Good diving and snorkelling as well as waterfalls and trekking trails on the island.

Western region Erawan National Park: a very popular park with waterfalls, some stunning landscapes, caves, trails and good facilities. **Tham Than Lot National Park**: this small park has a rich diversity of fauna and the cave of Than Lot, after which it is named.

Southern region Kaeng Krachan National Park: a large park covering almost 2,000 sq km. Extensive trails, mountain hikes and waterfalls. **Khao Sam Roi Yod National Park**: the best place in Thailand to see water birds; good facilities. **Khao Sok National Park**: one of Thailand's finest protected areas with a wide range of forest types and good trails. **Similan Islands National Park**: arguably Thailand's best marine park; excellent diving opportunities. **Koh Surin National Park**: another fine marine park in the Andaman Sea; the reefs here are said to be the most diverse in Thailand. **Tarutao National Park**: Thailand's first protected marine area and one of the best; closed between May and October. **Ang Thong National Park**: a protected marine area close to the resort island of Koh Samui, so the dive sites are much frequented. **Khao Luang National Park**: this encompasses the southern region's highest peak, Khao Luang (1,835 m). Mountain trails and waterfalls.

Books

Hilltribes

Boyes, Jon and **Piraban S**, *A life apart: viewed from the hills* (1992) Silkworm Books: Bangkok. This has been written with the trekker intentionally in mind. It is a series of hilltribe vignettes, written from the tribal people's perspective. In this respect the book is fine; where it fails is in providing a context for these vignettes. Here the authors over-generalize and sometimes provide misleading information. Take the book for the thumbnail sketches of life, not for background accuracy.

Guntamala, Ada and **Kornvika, Puapratum**, *Trekking through Northern Thailand* (1992) Silkworm Books: Chiang Mai.

Lewis, Paul and **Lewis, Elaine**, *Peoples of the Golden Triangle: six tribes in Thailand* (1984)Thames and Hudson: London. Glossy coffee table book with a good supporting text. Too heavy to take on the road, but a good book for before or after.

McKinnon, John and **Vienne, Bernard**, *Hill tribes today: problems in change* (1989) White-Lotus/Orstom: Bangkok. This volume, though beginning to become rather dated in some respects, is accurate and informative. It

also suffers from being a fairly hefty tome to lug around the hills.

Tapp, Nicholas, *The Hmong of Thailand: opium people of the Golden Triangle* (1986) report No 4, Anti-slavery Society: London.

Tapp, Nicholas, *Sovereignty and rebellion: the White Hmong of Northern Thailand* (1989) Oxford University Press: Singapore. Nick Tapp is an anthropologist at the University of Edinburgh. This book is intended mostly for an academic audience; it is interesting because it tries to challenge the established wisdom that the Hmong are a 'bad' tribe.

Living in Thailand

A useful book delving deeper into the do's and don'ts of living in Thailand is Robert and Nanthapa Cooper's *Culture shock: Thailand*, Time Books International: Singapore (1990). It is available from most bookshops.

Thai literature available in English

Increasing numbers of Thai novels and short stories are being translated into English. In particular, TMC (Thai Modern Classics) are publishing a number of what their editorial team regard as the best works of Thai literature. (Some Thai literature scholars have been offended that a farang was chosen to head the editorial board and to play a leading role in identifying those novels and short stories worthy of the 'classic' label.) By mid-1995 three volumes had come out: Arkartdamkeung Rapheephat's *The Circus of Life*, Sila Khoamchai's *The Path of the Tiger*, and an anthology of pieces from 20 Thai novels. All are very competitively priced and more have been published since then.

Boontawee, Kampoon, *A Child of the Northeast* [*Luuk Isan*] (1988) Duang Kamol: Bangkok. This novel covers a year in the life of a village in the Northeast in the 1930s. It centres on the experiences of an eight-year-old boy, Koon, and concentrates on the sheer struggle to make ends meet in a capricious land. The image here of traditional life could be usefully set against Pira Sudham's more golden view of the past. The original Thai version of the book won the 1976 Best Novel of the Year award and is highly recommended.

Botan, *Letters from Thailand* (1991) Duang Kamol Books: Bangkok.

Ekachai, Sanitsuda, *Behind the Smile: Voices of Thailand* (1990)Thai Development Support Committee: Bangkok. This is not a novel, but a series of vignettes of contemporary Thai life, written in English by a Bangkok Post reporter. They are well-written, perceptive and stimulating, providing a realistic view of the pressures, aspirations and opportunities facing ordinary people in Thailand. A more recent, more expensive and considerably glossier book, by the same author, is *Seeds of Hope*: *Local Initiatives in Thailand* (1994) which also focuses on the theme of development, but with an emphasis on self-help and the work of NGOs.

Khonkhai, Khammaan, *The Teacher of Mad Dog Swamp* (1992) Silkworm Books: Bangkok. Another book about life in the Northeast, this centres upon the experiences of a diligent young teacher who, on graduation, is sent to an up-country primary school. Almost inevitably, his concern for the people of the area results in him being labelled a communist. The book provides an excellent insight into the concerns of villagers and also incorporates a political plot. It was originally published in Thai as Khru Ban Nok – or Rural Teacher – in 1978; the author was brought up in the Northeast and also trained as a teacher, and is semi-autobiographical.

Pramoj, Kukrit, *The Four Reigns* [*Si phaen din*] (1953) DK Books: Bangkok. This novel, one of the most famous written in Thai, is a historical saga recounting the experiences of a nobel Thai family through the reign of four kings from the late-19th century. Written by a former prime minister of the country, some view it as a masterpiece of Thai literature; others may simply see it as a historical novel in the Cartland/Cookson mould. Entertaining, but hardly high art.

Rayawa, Nikorn, *High Banks, Heavy Logs* (1992) Penguin. Story of a woodcarver in Northern Thailand and his struggle against change, and the declining moral and artistic standards that are seen to accompany that change.

Siburapha, *Behind the painting and other stories* (1990)OUP: Singapore. These short stories, only recently translated into English by David Smyth – who teaches Thai at the School of Oriental and African Studies in London – are written by an author who is regarded as one of the 'greats' of modern Thai literature. He was at the forefront of the transformation of Thai literature into a

modern genre, and was also an influential social and political activist.

Srinawk, Khamsing, *The Politician and Other Stories* (1991) OUP: Singapore. This volume consists of 12 short stories. The author comes from a farming background and the stories largely describe the difficulties that rural households are facing in coming to terms with modernization.

Sudham, Pira, *Monsoon Country* (1988) Shire Books: Bangkok, *People of Esarn* (1987) Shire Books: Bangkok, *Siamese Drama* (1983) Shire Books: Bangkok, *Pira Sudham's Best* (1993) Shire Books: Bangkok. All four of these books are widely available in Bangkok and essentially have the same tale to tell: one of country life in the poor Northeastern region. Pira comes from a rural background and won a scholarship to study English in New Zealand; he has since become a bit of a gadfly in farang circles. However, it is intriguing that his books have not been translated into Thai and his main admirers remain farangs and not Thais; indeed, many Thais find his rather romantic view of rural life somewhat unconvincing. His books are all rather similar in style and content; there is little here to identify Pira as one of the greats of Thai literature, but they are worth reading nonetheless – although some of his views should be viewed with scepticism. *Monsoon Country* has also been translated into French.

Textiles

Conway, Susan, *Thai Textiles* (1992) British Museum Press: London. A richly illustrated book with informative text, placing Thai textiles in the context of Thai society and history.

Wildlife

Lekagul, Boonsong and **McNeely, JA**, *Mammals of Thailand* (1988) Association for the Conservation of Wildlife.

Lekagul, Boonsong and **Cronin, Edward**, *Bird guide of Thailand* (1974) Association for the Conservation of Wildlife: Bangkok. For keen ornithologists.

Lekagul, Boonsong and **Round, Philip**, *The Birds of Thailand* (1991) Sahakarn Bhaet: Bangkok.

Lekagul, Boonsong, et al, *Fieldguide to the Butterflies of Thailand* (1977) Association for the Conservation of Wildlife: Bangkok. Available from most large bookshops in Bangkok.

Piprell, Collin and **Boyd, Ashley J**, *Thailand's Coral Reefs: Nature under Threat* (1995) Bangkok: White Lotus. A well-illustrated plea for the conservation of the Kingdom's reefs.

Footnotes

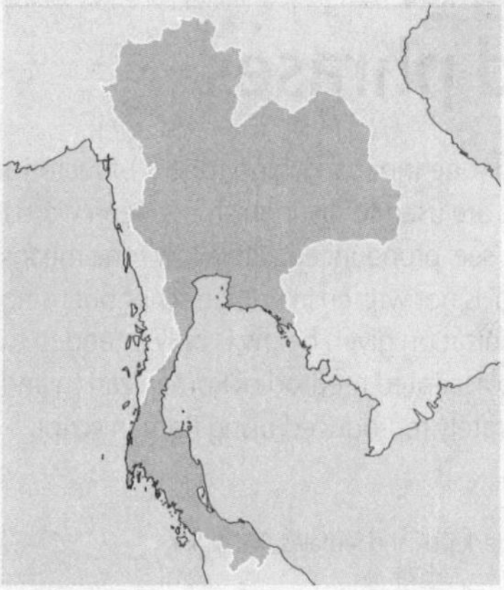

Footprint features

Useful words and phrases

Thai is a tonal language with five tones: mid tone (no mark), high tone (´), low tone (`), falling tone (^), and rising tone (ˇ). Tones are used to distinguish between words which are otherwise the same. For example, 'see' pronounced with a low tone means 'four'; with a rising tone, it means 'colour'. Thai is not written in Roman script but using an alphabet derived from Khmer. The Romanization given below is only intended to help in pronouncing Thai words. There is no accepted method of Romanization and some of the sounds in Thai cannot be accurately reproduced using Roman script.

Polite particles

At the end of sentences males use the polite particle 'krúp', and females, 'kâ' or 'ká'.

Learning Thai

The list of words and phrases below is only very rudimentary. For anyone serious about learning Thai it is best to buy a dedicated Thai language text book or to enrol on a Thai course. Recommended among the various 'teach yourself Thai' books is Somsong Buasai and David Smyth's *Thai in a Week*, Hodder & Stoughton: London (1990). A useful mini-dictionary is the Hugo *Thai phrase book* (1990). For those interested in learning to read and write Thai, the best 'teach yourself' course is the *Linguaphone* course.

General words and phrases

Yes/no	*chái/mâi chái, or krúp (kâ)/mâi krúp (kâ)*
Thank you/no thank you	*kòrp-kOOn/mâi ao kòrp-kOOn*
Hello, good morning, goodbye	*sa-wùt dee krúp(kâ)*
What is your name? My name is...	*Koon chêu a-rai krúp (kâ)? Pom chêu...*
Excuse me, sorry!	*kor-tôht krúp(kâ)*
Can/do you speak English?	*KOON pôot pah-sah ung-grìt*
a little, a bit	*nít-nòy*
Where's the...?	*yòo têe-nai...*
How much is...?	*tâo-rài...*
Pardon?	*a-rai ná?*
I don't understand	*pom (chún) mâi kao jái*
How are you?	*Mâi sa-bai*
Not very well	*sa-bai dee mái?*

At hotels

What is the charge each night?	*kâh hôrng wun la tâo-rài?*
Is the room air conditioned?	*hôrng dtìt air reu bplào?*
Can I see the room first please?	*kor doo hôrng gòrn dâi mái?*
Does the room have hot water?	*hôrng mii náhm rórn mái?*
Does the room have a bathroom?	*hôrng mii hôrng náhm mái?*
Can I have the bill please?	*kor bin nòy dâi mái?*

Travelling

Where is the train station?	*sa-tahn-nee rót fai yòo têe-nai?*
Where is the bus station?	*sa-tahn-nee rót may yòo têe-nai?*
How much to go to...?	*bpai...tâo-rài?*
That's expensive	*pairng bpai nòy*
What time does the bus/ train leave for...?	*rót may/rót fai bpai...òrk gèe mohng?*

Is it far?	*glai mái?*
Turn left/turn right	*lée-o sái / lée-o kwah*
Go straight on	*ler-ee bpai èek*
It's straight ahead	*yòo dtrong nâh*

At restaurants

Can I see a menu?	*kor doo may-noo nòy?*
Can I have...?/ I would like...?	*Kor...*
Is it very (hot) spicy?	*pèt mâhk mái?*
I am hungry	*pom (chún) hew*
Breakfast	*ah-hahn cháo*
Lunch	*ah-hahn glanhg wun*

Time and days

in the morning	*dtorn cháo*	Monday	*wun jun*
in the afternoon	*dtorn bài*	Tuesday	*wun ung-kahn*
in the evening	*dtorn yen*	Wednesday	*wun pÔOt*
Today	*wun née*	Thursday	*wun pá-réu-hùt*
Tomorrow	*prÔOng née*	Friday	*wun sÒOk*
Yesterday	*mêu-a wahn née*	Saturday	*wun sao*
		Sunday	*wun ah-tít*

Numbers

1	*nèung*	20	*yêe-sìp*
2	*sorng*	21	*yêe-sìp-et*
3	*sahm*	22	*yêe-sìp-sorng...etc*
4	*sèe*	30	*sahm-sìp*
5	*hâa*	100	*(nèung) róy*
6	*hòk*	101	*(nèung) róy-nèung*
7	*jèt*	150	*(nèung) róy-hâh-sìp*
8	*bpàirt*	200	*sorng róy...etc*
9	*gâo*	1,000	*(nèung) pun*
10	*sìp*	10,000	*mèun*
11	*sìp-et*	100,000	*sairn*
12	*sìp-sorng...etc*	1,000,000	*láhn*

Basic vocabulary

airport	*a-nahm bin*	cold	*yen*
bank	*ta-nah-kahn*	day	*wun*
bathroom	*hôrng náhm*	delicious	*a-ròy*
beach	*hàht*	dirty	*sòk-ga-bpròk*
beautiful	*oo-ay*	doctor	*mor*
big	*yài*	eat	*gin (kâo)*
boat	*reu-a*	embassy	*sa-tahn tôot*
bus	*ót may*	excellent	*yêe-um*
bus station	*sa-tah-nee rót may*	expensive	*pairng*
buy	*séu*	food	*ah-hahn*
chemist	*ráhn kai yah*	fruit	*pon-la-mái*
clean	*sa-àht*	hospital	*rohng pa-yah-bahn*
closed	*bpìt*	hot (temp)	*rórn*

hot (spicy)	*pèt*	sick (ill)	*mâi sa-bai*
hotel	*rôhng rairm*	silk	*mai*
island	*gòr*	small	*lék*
market	*dta-làht*	stop	*yÒOt*
medicine	*yah*	taxi	*táirk-sêe*
open	*bpèrt*	that	*nún*
police	*dtum-ròo-ut*	this	*née*
police station	*sa-tah-nee,*	ticket	*dtoo-a*
	dtum-ròo-ut	toilet	*hôrng náhm*
post office	*bprai-sa-nee*	town	*meu-ung*
restaurant	*ráhn ah-hahn*	train station	*sa-tah-nee rót fai*
road	*thanon*	very	*mâhk*
room	*hôrng*	water	*náhm*
shop	*ráhn*	what	*a-rai*

Glossary

A

Amitabha the Buddha of the Past (see Avalokitsvara)
Amphoe district; administrative division below the province
Amulet protective medallion
Ao bay
Arhat a person who has perfected himself; images of former monks are sometimes carved into arhat
Avadana Buddhist narrative, telling of the deeds of saintly souls
Avalokitsvara also known as Amitabha and Lokeshvara, the name literally means 'World Lord'; he is the compassionate male Bodhisattva, the saviour of Mahayana Buddhism, and represents the central force of creation in the universe; usually portrayed with a lotus and water flask

B

Bai sema boundary stones marking consecrated ground around a Buddhist bot
Ban village; shortened from muban
Baray man-made lake or reservoir
Batik a form of resist dyeing
Bhikku Buddhist monk
Bodhi the tree under which the Buddha achieved enlightenment (*Ficus religiosa*)
Bodhisattva a future Buddha. In Mahayana Buddhism, someone who has attained enlightenment, but who postpones nirvana to help others reach it.
Bor Kor Sor (BKS) Government bus terminal
Bot Buddhist ordination hall, of rectangular plan, identifiable by the boundary stones placed around it; an abbreviation of ubosoth
Brahma the Creator, one of the gods of the Hindu trinity, usually represented with four faces, and often mounted on a hamsa
Brahmin a Hindu priest
Bun to make merit

C

Caryatid elephants, often used as buttressing decorations
Celadon pottery ware with blue/green to grey glaze
Chakri the current royal dynasty in Thailand. They have reigned since 1782
Champa rival empire of the Khmers, of Hindu culture, based in present-day Vietnam
Changwat province
Chao title for Lao and Thai kings
Chat honorific umbrella or royal multi-tiered parasol
Chedi from the Sanskrit *cetiya* (Pali, *caitya*), meaning memorial. Usually a religious monument (often bell-shaped), containing relics of the Buddha or other holy remains.

Used interchangeably with stupa
Chofa 'sky tassel' on the roof of wat buildings
CPT Communist Party of Thailand

D

Deva a Hindu-derived male god
Devata a Hindu-derived goddess
Dharma the Buddhist law
Dipterocarp family of trees (*Dipterocarpaceae*), characteristic of Southeast Asia's forests
Dvarapala guardian figure, usually placed at the entrance to a temple

F

Farang westerner

G

Ganesh elephant-headed son of Siva
Garuda mythical divine bird, with predatory beak and claws, and human body; the king of birds, enemy of naga and mount of Vishnu
Gautama the historic Buddha
Geomancy the art of divination by lines and figures
Gopura crowned or covered gate, entrance to a religious area

H

Hamsa sacred goose, Brahma's mount; in Buddhism it represents the flight of the doctrine
Hang yaaw long-tailed boat, used on canals
Harmika box-like part of a Burmese stupa that often acts as a reliquary casket
Hat beach
Hinayana 'Lesser Vehicle', major Buddhist sect in Southeast Asia, usually termed Theravada Buddhism
Hong swan
Hor kong a pavilion built on stilts, where the monastery drum is kept
Hor takang bell tower
Hor tray/trai library where manuscripts are stored in a Thai monastery
Hti 'umbrella' surmounting Burmese temples, often encrusted with jewels

I

Ikat tie-dyeing method of patterning cloth
Indra the Vedic god of the heavens, weather and war; usually mounted on a three-headed elephant

J

Jataka(s) the birth stories of the Buddha; they normally number 547, although an additional three were added in Burma for reasons of symmetry in mural painting and sculpture. The last 10 are the most important

K

Kala (makara) literally 'death' or 'black'; a demon ordered to consume itself, often sculpted with grinning face and bulging eyes over entranceway to act as a door guardian; also known as kirtamukha
Kathin/krathin a one-month period during the eighth lunar month, when lay people present new robes and other gifts to monks
Ketumula flame-like motif above the Buddha head
Khao mountain
Khlong Canal
Khruang Amulet
Kinaree half-human, half-bird, usually depicted as a heavenly musician
Kirtamukha see kala
Koh island
Koutdi see kuti
Krating wild bull, most commonly seen on bottles of *Red Bull* (Krating Daeng) drink
Krishna incarnation of Vishnu
Kuti living quarters of Buddhist monks in a monastery complex

L

Laem cape (as in bay)
Lakhon traditional Thai classical music
Lak muang city pillar
Laterite bright red tropical soil/stone, commonly used in construction of Khmer monuments
Linga phallic symbol and one of the forms of Siva. Embedded in a pedestal, shaped to

Thai dishes

It is impossible to provide a comprehensive list of Thai dishes. However (and at the risk of offending connoisseurs by omitting their favourites) popular dishes include:

Soups (*gaeng chud*)
Tom yam kung – hot and sour prawn soup spiced with lemon grass, coriander and chillies
Tom ka kai – chicken in coconut milk with laos (loas, or ka, is an exotic spice)
Khaaw tom – rice soup with egg and pork (a breakfast dish) or chicken, fish or prawn. It is said that it can cure fevers and other illnesses. Probably best for a hangover.
Kwaytio – Chinese noodle soup served with a variety of additional ingredients, often available from roadside stalls and from smaller restaurants – mostly served up until lunchtime.
Kaeng juut – bean curd and vegetable soup, non-spicy

Rice-based dishes
Single-dish meals served at roadside stalls and in many restaurants (especially cheaper ones).
Khaaw phat kai/mu/kung – fried rice with chicken/pork/prawn
Khaaw naa pet – rice with duck
Khaaw gaeng – curry and rice
Khaaw man kai – rice with chicken
Khaaw mu daeng – rice with red pork

Noodle-based dishes
Khaaw soi – a form of *Kwaytio* with egg noodles in a curry broth
Phak si-u – noodles fried with egg, vegetables and meat/prawns
Kwaytio haeng – wide noodles served with pork and vegetables
Ba-mii haeng – wheat noodles served with pork and vegetables
Phat thai – Thai fried noodles
Mee krop – Thai crisp-fried noodles

Curries (*gaeng*)
Gaeng phet kai/nua – hot chicken/beef curry
Gaeng khiaw waan kai/nua/phet/pla – green chicken/beef/duck/fish curry (the colour is due to the large number of whole green chillies pounded to make the paste that forms the base of this very hot curry)
Gaeng phanaeng – chicken/beef curry
Gaeng plaa duk – catfish curry
Gaeng mussaman – Muslim beef curry served with potatoes

Meat dishes
Laap – chopped (once raw, now more frequently cooked) meat with herbs and spices
Kai/nua phat prik – fried chicken/beef with chillies
Nua priaw waan – sweet and sour beef
Mu waan – sweet pork
Kai/mu/nua phat kapow – fried meat with basil and chillies

allow drainage of lustral water poured over it; the linga typically has a succession of cross sections: from square at the base, through octagonal, to round. These symbolize, in order, the trinity of Brahma, Vishnu and Siva
Lintel a load-bearing stone spanning a doorway; often heavily carved
Lokeshvara see Avalokitsvara

M

Mahabharata a Hindu epic text, written about 2,000 years ago
Mahayana 'Greater Vehicle', Buddhist sect
Maitreya the future Buddha
Makara a mythological aquatic reptile, somewhat like a crocodile and sometimes with an elephant's trunk; often found along with the kala framing doorways
Mandala a focus for meditation; a representation of the cosmos
Mara personification of evil and tempter of the Buddha
Matmii Northeastern Thai cotton ikat
Meru sacred or cosmic mountain at the centre of the world in Hindu-Buddhist

Kai tort – Thai fried chicken
Kai tua – chicken in peanut sauce
Kai yang – garlic chicken
Priao wan – sweet and sour pork with vegetables

Seafood
Plaa priaw waan – whole fried fish with ginger sauce
Plaa too tort – Thai fried fish
Haw mok – steamed fish curry
Plaa nerng – steamed fish
Plaa pao – grilled fish
Thotman plaa – fried curried fish cakes
Luuk ciin – fishballs

Salads (*yam*)
Yam nua – Thai beef salad
Som tam – green papaya salad with tomatoes, chillies, garlic, chopped dried shrimps and lemon (can be extremely hot)

Vegetables
Phak phat ruam mit – mixed fried vegetables

Sweets (*kanom*)
Khaaw niaw sankhayaa – sticky rice and custard
Khaaw niaw mamuang – sticky rice and mango (a seasonal favourite)
Kluay buat chee – bananas in coconut milk
Kanom mo kaeng – baked custard squares
Kluay tort – Thai fried bananas
Leenchee loi mek – chilled lychees in custard

Fruits (see page 726)
Chomphu – rose apple
Khanun – jackfruit. Season: January-June
Kluay – banana. Season: year round
Lamyai – longan; thin brown shell with translucent fruit similar to lychee. Season: June-August
Linchi – lychee. Season: April-June
Lamut – sapodilla
Makham wan – tamarind. Season: December-February
Malakho – papaya. Season: year round
Manaaw – lime. Season: year round
Mang khud – mangosteen. Season: April-September
Maprao – coconut. Season: year round
Majeung – star apple
Mamuang – mango. Season: March-June
Ngo – rambutan. Season: May-September
Noi na – custard (or sugar) apple. Season: June-September
Sapparot – pineapple. Season: April-June, December-January
Som – orange. Season: year round
Som o – pomelo. Season: August-November
Taeng mo – watermelon. Season: October-March
Thurian – durian. Season: May-August.

cosmology; home of the gods.
Mon race and kingdom of southern Burma and central Thailand, from 7th-11th century
Mondop from the sanskrit, *mandapa*. A cube-shaped building, often topped with a cone-like structure, used to contain an object of worship like a footprint of the Buddha
Muang 'town' in Thai, but also sometimes 'municipality' or 'district'
Muban village, usually shortened to ban
Mudra symbolic gesture of the hands of the Buddha

N

Naga benevolent mythical water serpent, enemy of Garuda
Naga makara fusion of naga and makara
Nalagiri the elephant let loose to attack the Buddha, who calmed him
Namtok Waterfall
Nandi/nandin bull, mount of Siva
Nang thalung shadow play/puppets
Nikhom resettlement village
Nirvana release from the cycle of suffering in Buddhist belief; 'enlightenment'

Distinctive fruits

Custard apple (*Annona cherimola* Mill) Scaly green skin, squeeze the skin to open the fruit and scoop out the flesh with a spoon. Season: June-September.
Durian (*Durio zibethinus*) A large prickly fruit, with yellow flesh, about the size of a football. Infamous for its pungent smell. While it is today regarded by many visitors as simply revolting, early Europeans (16th-18th centuries) raved about it, possibly because it was similar in taste to western delicacies of the period. Borri (1744) thought it was "God himself, who had produc'd that fruit". But by 1880 Burbridge was writing: "Its odour – one scarcely feels justified in using the word 'perfume' – is so potent, so vague, but withal so insinuating, that it can scarcely be tolerated inside the house". Banned from hotel rooms throughout the region, and beloved by most Southeast Asians, it has an alluring taste. Durian-flavoured chewing gum, ice cream and jams are all available. Season: May-August.
Jackfruit, *(Artocarpus heteropyllus)* Similar in appearance to durian but not so spiky. Yellow flesh, tasting slightly like custard. Season: January-June.
Mango (*Mangifera indica*) A rainforest fruit which is now cultivated. Widely available in the West; there are hundreds of different varieties with subtle variations in flavour. Delicious eaten with sticky rice and a sweet sauce. The best mangoes in the region are considered to be those from South Thailand. Season: March-June.
Mangosteen (*Garcinia mangostana*) An aubergine-coloured hard shell covers this small fruit which is about the size of a tennis ball. Cut or squeeze the purple shell to reach its sweet white flesh which is prized by many visitors above all others. In 1898, an American resident of Java wrote, erotically and in obvious ecstasy: "The five white segments separate easily, and they melt on the tongue with a touch of tart and a touch of sweet; one moment a memory of the juiciest, most fragrant apple, at another a remembrance of the

P

Pa kama Lao men's all-purpose cloth, usually woven with checked pattern
paddy/padi unhulled rice
Pali the sacred language of Theravada Buddhism
Parvati consort of Siva
Pha sin tubular bit of cloth, similar to sarong
Phi spirit
Phnom/phanom Khmer for hill/mountain
Phra sinh see pha sin
Pradaksina pilgrims' clockwise circumambulation of holy structure
Prah sacred
Prang form of stupa built in Khmer style, shaped like a corncob
Prasada stepped pyramid (see prasat)
Prasat residence of a king or of the gods (sanctuary tower), from the Indian prasada

Q

Quan Am Chinese goddess (Kuan-yin) of mercy

R

Rai unit of measurement, 1 ha = 6.25 rai
Rama incarnation of Vishnu, hero of the Indian epic, the *Ramayana*
Ramakien Thai version of the *Ramayana*
Ramayana Hindu romantic epic, known as *Ramakien* in Thailand

S

Saamlor three-wheeled bicycle taxi
Sakyamuni the historic Buddha
Sal the Indian sal tree (*Shorea robusta*), under which the historic Buddha was born
Sala open pavilion
Sangha the Buddhist order of monks

smoothest cream ice, the most exquisite and delicately flavoured fruit-acid known – all of the delights of nature's laboratory condensed in that ball of neige parfumée". Southeast Asians believe it should be eaten as a chaser to durian.
Season: April-September.

Papaya (*Carica papaya*) A New-World fruit that was not introduced into Southeast Asia until the 16th century. Large, round or oval in shape, yellow or green-skinned, with bright orange flesh and a mass of round, black seeds in the middle. The flesh, in texture and taste, is somewhere between a mango and a melon. Some maintain that it tastes 'soapy'. Season: Year round.

Pomelo (*Citrus Grande*) A large round fruit the size of anything from an ostrich egg to a football, with thick, green skin and pith, and flesh similar to a grapefruit's, but less acidic.
Season: August-November.

Rambutan (*Nephelium lappaceum*) The bright red and hairy rambutan – *rambut* is the Malay word for 'hair' – with its slightly rubbery but sweet flesh is a close relative of the lychee of southern China. The Thai word for rambutan is *ngoh*, which is the nickname given by Thais to the fuzzy-haired Negrito aboriginals In the southern jungles.
Season: May-September.

Salak (*Salacca edulis*) A small pear-shaped fruit about the size of a large plum with a rough, brown, scaly skin (somewhat like a miniature pangolin) and yellow-white, crisp flesh. It is related to the sago and rattan trees.

Tamarind (*Tamarindus indicus*) Brown seedpods with dry brittle skins and a brown tart-sweet fruit which grow on a tree introduced into Southeast Asia from India. The name is Arabic for 'Indian date'. The flesh has a high tartaric acid content and is used to flavour curries, jams, jellies and chutneys as well as for cleaning brass and copper. Elephants have a predilection for tamarind balls.
Season: December-February.

Sawankhalok type of ceramic
Singha mythical guardian lion
Siva the Destroyer, one of the three gods of the Hindu trinity; the sacred linga was worshipped as a symbol of Siva
Sofa see dok sofa
Songthaew 'two rows': pick-up truck with benches along either side
Sravasti the miracle at Sravasti, when the Buddha subdues the heretics in front of a mango tree
Stele inscribed stone panel
Stucco plaster, often heavily moulded
Stupa Chedi

T

Talaat market
Tambon a commune of villages
Tam bun see bun
Tavatimsa heaven of the 33 gods, at the summit of Mount Meru
Tazaungs small pavilions, found within Burmese temple complexes
Tham cave
Thanon street in Thai
That shrine housing Buddhist relics, a spire or dome-like edifice commemorating the Buddha's life or the funerary temple for royalty; peculiar to parts of Northeastern Thailand, as well as Laos
Thein Burmese ordination hall
Theravada 'Way of the Elders'; major Buddhist sect, also known as Hinayana Buddhism ('Lesser Vehicle')
Traiphum the three worlds of Buddhist cosmology – heaven, hell and earth
Trimurti the Hindu trinity of gods: Brahma, the Creator, Vishnu the Preserver and Siva the Destroyer
Tripitaka Theravada Buddhism's Pali canon
Tuk-tuk motorized three-wheeled taxi
Tukata doll

U

Ubosoth see bot
Urna the dot or curl on the Buddha's forehead, one of the distinctive physical marks of the Enlightened One
Usnisa the Buddha's top knot or 'wisdom bump', one of the physical marks of the Enlightened One

V

Vahana 'vehicle', a mythical beast, upon which a deva or god rides
Viharn from Sanskrit *vihara*, an assembly hall in a Buddhist monastery; may hold Buddha images and is similar in style to the bot
Vishnu the Protector, one of the gods of the Hindu trinity, generally with four arms holding a disc, conch shell, ball and club

W

Wai Thai greeting, with hands held together at chin height as if in prayer
Wat Buddhist 'monastery', with religious and other buildings

Z

Zayat prayer pavilion found in Burmese temple complexes
Zedi Burmese term for a stupa

Food glossary

A-haan food
Ba-mii egg noodles
Bia beer
Chaa tea
check bin/bill cheque
Chorn spoon
Gaeng curry
gaeng chud soup
Jaan plate
kaafae (ron) coffee (hot)
Kaew glass
Kai chicken
kap klaem snacks to be eaten when drinking
Khaaw/khao rice
khaaw niaw sticky rice
khaaw tom rice gruel
Khai egg
khai dao fried egg
Khanom sweet, dessert or cake
khanom cake cake
khanom pang bread
khanom pang ping toast
Khing ginger
Khuan scramble
Khuat bottle
Kin to eat
Kleua salt
krueng kieng side dishes
Kung crab
Kwaytio noodle soup, white noodles
laap pa raw fish crushed into a paste, marinated in lemon juice and mixed with chopped mint, chilli and rice grains
laap sin raw meat dish, prepared the same way as the above
Lao liquor
Man root vegetable
man farang potatoes
Manaaw lemon
Mekong Thai whisky
Mit knife
Muu pork
nam chaa tea
nam kheng ice
nam kuat bottled water
nam manaaw soda lime soda
nam plaa fish sauce
nam plaa prik fish sauce with chilli
nam plaaw plain water
nam som orange juice
nam taan sugar
nam tom boiled water
Nom milk
Nua meat (usually beef)
Phak vegetables
Phat to stir fry
Phet hot (chilli)
phon lamai fruit
Pla fish

Priaw sour
priaw waan sweet and sour
Prik hot chilli
raan a-haan restaurant
Ratnaa in gravy
Rawn hot (temperature)
Sa-te satay
Sorm fork
Talaat market
thao mai luai morning glory
Thua nut/bean
Tom to boil
Tort to deep fry
Waan sweet
Yam salad
Yen cold

Acknowledgements

Andrew Spooner would like to thank Claire Boobbyer, Alan Murphy, Daemienne Sheehan, Chris Lee and all at Travelmood, Phil Cornwel-Smith, Richard and Romana Chapman, Jade Tustin, Ruengsang Sripaoraya, Pop Ruttanaporn, Piyachat "Tum" Katanyuta, Vicky and all the staff at Asia World, Richard Hume and staff of TAT London, Usa Boonkosol, Mark from Gecko, Debbie from Capehouse, Kevin Gould, Max Wooldridge, Yves Marie, Tolis Marinos, Tina and Heiko, Khun Lek and my mum.

Claire Boobbyer would like to thank Chris Lee and Jessica Rowles at Travelmood, Nat Frogley at Bacall Associates, staff at the Sila Evason, Zeavola and Rayavadee, Richard Hume at TAT London, Mont at TAT Surat Thani, staff at TAT Koh Samui and in Nakhon Si Thammarat, Phantip Travel, Seatran, staff at Fame Tour & Service and R at New Infinity both in Chumphon. Also a big thanks to Sam and Simon for the James Bond and lady boy adventures on Koh Samui!

Daemienne Sheehan would like to thank Poomiphat Navakroh, Claude Sauter, Kannika and Richard from TAT London, Ray Iveson, the staff of Chao Mai Tour, Trang, Aussie Adam Revil, Henrick Enevoldsen, Tip, Finn, Molly, Charles Henn, Lek the Lady Boy of Koh Jum and the girls of Nana House and finally Raffy for staying put and Wilde for sticking with me.

Andrew, Claire and Daemienne would like to thank the previous authors and contributors: Joshua Eliot, Jane Bickersteth, Sophia Buranakul, Natapon Buranakul and Zee Gilmore.

The health section was written by Dr Charlie Easmon MBBS MRCP MSc Public Health DTM&H DOccMed, Director of Travel Screening Services.

The diving section was written by Master Scuba Diver, Beth Tierney who contributes to several international magazines. Her editorial work covers both land and dive travel, marine biology and conservation. Beth and her husband Shaun, an underwater photographer, are co-authors for Footprint's forthcoming publication, *Diving the World*.

Index

Advertisers' index

Map index

Credits

Footprint credits

Text editors: Claire Boobbyer, Nicola Jones
Map editor: Sarah Sorensen
Picture editor: Rob Lunn
Proofreader: Stephanie Lambe

Publisher: Patrick Dawson
Editorial: Alan Murphy, Sophie Blacksell, Sarah Thorowgood, Felicity Laughton, Angus Dawson
Cartography: Robert Lunn, Claire Benison, Kevin Feeney
Series development: Rachel Fielding
Design: Mytton Williams and Rosemary Dawson (brand)
Sales and marketing: Andy Riddle
Advertising: Debbie Wylde
Finance and administration: Sharon Hughes, Elizabeth Taylor

Photography credits

Front cover: Jon Arnold (Photolibrary)
Back cover: SuperStock
Inside colour section: Claire Boobbyer, Steve Davey, SuperStock, Wilde Fry, Henry Westheim (Alamy), Terry Whittaker (Alamy)

Print

Manufactured in Italy by LegoPrint
Pulp from sustainable forests

Footprint feedback

We try as hard as we can to make each Footprint guide as up to date as possible but, of course, things always change. If you want to let us know about your experiences – good, bad or ugly – then don't delay, go to **www.footprintbooks.com** and send in your comments.

Publishing information

Footprint Thailand
5th edition

November 2005

ISBN 1 904 777 44 9
CIP DATA: A catalogue record for this book is available from the British Library

Published by Footprint

6 Riverside Court
Lower Bristol Road
Bath BA2 3DZ UK
T +44 (0)1225 469141
F +44 (0)1225 469461
discover@footprintbooks.com
www.footprintbooks.com

Distributed in the USA by

Publishers Group West

Neither the black and white nor colour maps are intended to have any political significance.

Every effort has been made to ensure that the facts in this guidebook are accurate. However, travellers should still obtain advice from consulates, airlines etc about travel and visa requirements before travelling. The authors and publishers cannot accept responsibility for any loss, injury or inconvenience however caused.

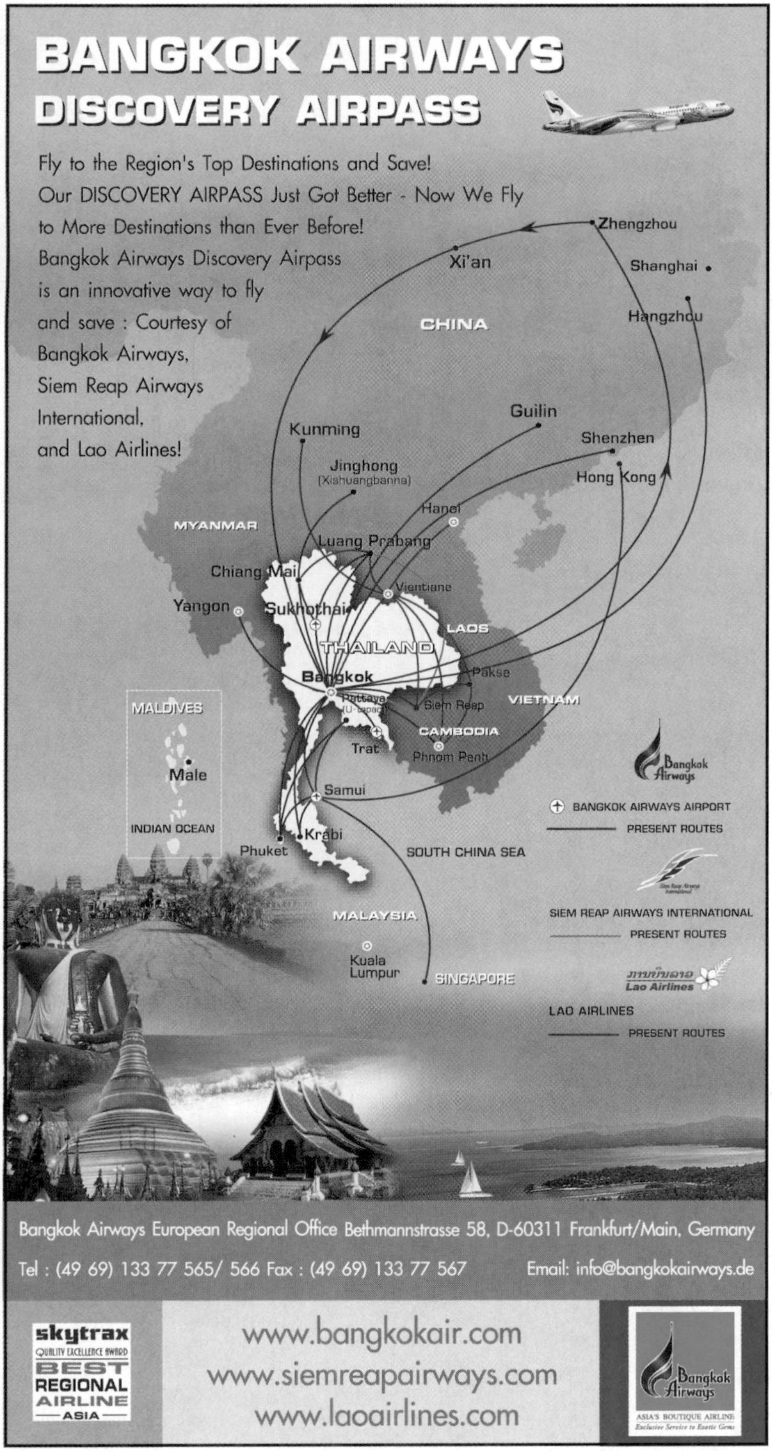
BANGKOK AIRWAYS
DISCOVERY AIRPASS
Fly to the Region's Top Destinations and Save!
Our DISCOVERY AIRPASS Just Got Better - Now We Fly to More Destinations than Ever Before!
Bangkok Airways Discovery Airpass is an innovative way to fly and save : Courtesy of Bangkok Airways, Siem Reap Airways International, and Lao Airlines!
Zhengzhou
Xi'an
Shanghai
Hangzhou
CHINA
Guilin
Kunming
Shenzhen
Jinghong
(Xishuangbanna)
Hong Kong
Hanoi
MYANMAR
Luang Prabang
Chiang Mai
Vientiane
Yangon
Sukhothai
LAOS
THAILAND
Bangkok
Pakse
MALDIVES
Pattaya
(U-tapao)
Siem Reap
VIETNAM
CAMBODIA
Trat
Phnom Penh
Male
Samui
INDIAN OCEAN
Krabi
Phuket
SOUTH CHINA SEA
MALAYSIA
Kuala
Lumpur
SINGAPORE
Bangkok Airways
BANGKOK AIRWAYS AIRPORT
PRESENT ROUTES
SIEM REAP AIRWAYS INTERNATIONAL
PRESENT ROUTES
Lao Airlines
LAO AIRLINES
PRESENT ROUTES
Bangkok Airways European Regional Office Bethmannstrasse 58, D-60311 Frankfurt/Main, Germany
Tel : (49 69) 133 77 565/ 566 Fax : (49 69) 133 77 567
Email: info@bangkokairways.de
skytrax
QUALITY EXCELLENCE AWARD
BEST
REGIONAL
AIRLINE
ASIA
www.bangkokair.com
www.siemreapairways.com
www.laoairlines.com
Bangkok Airways
ASIA'S BOUTIQUE AIRLINE
Exclusive Service to Exotic Gems

Thailand

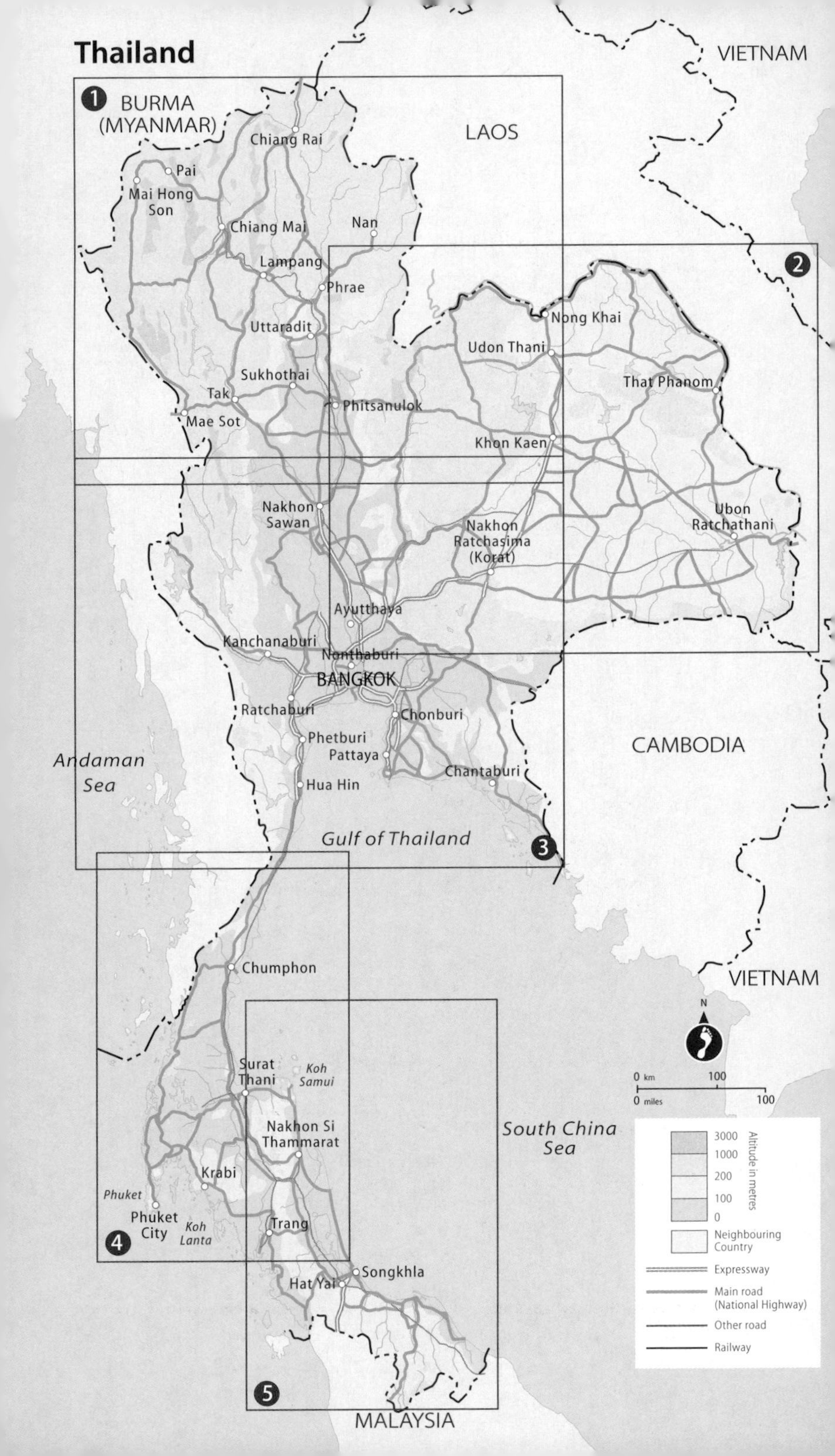
VIETNAM
BURMA (MYANMAR)
LAOS
Chiang Rai
Pai
Mai Hong Son
Chiang Mai
Nan
Lampang
Phrae
Uttaradit
Sukhothai
Tak
Mae Sot
Phitsanulok
Nong Khai
Udon Thani
That Phanom
Khon Kaen
Nakhon Sawan
Nakhon Ratchasima (Korat)
Ubon Ratchathani
Ayutthaya
Kanchanaburi
Nonthaburi
BANGKOK
Ratchaburi
Chonburi
Phetburi
Pattaya
Hua Hin
Chantaburi
CAMBODIA
Andaman Sea
Gulf of Thailand
Chumphon
VIETNAM
Surat Thani
Koh Samui
Nakhon Si Thammarat
South China Sea
Krabi
Phuket
Phuket City
Koh Lanta
Trang
Songkhla
Hat Yai
MALAYSIA
N
0 km 100
0 miles 100
3000
1000
200
100
0
Altitude in metres
Neighbouring Country
Expressway
Main road (National Highway)
Other road
Railway

Map 1

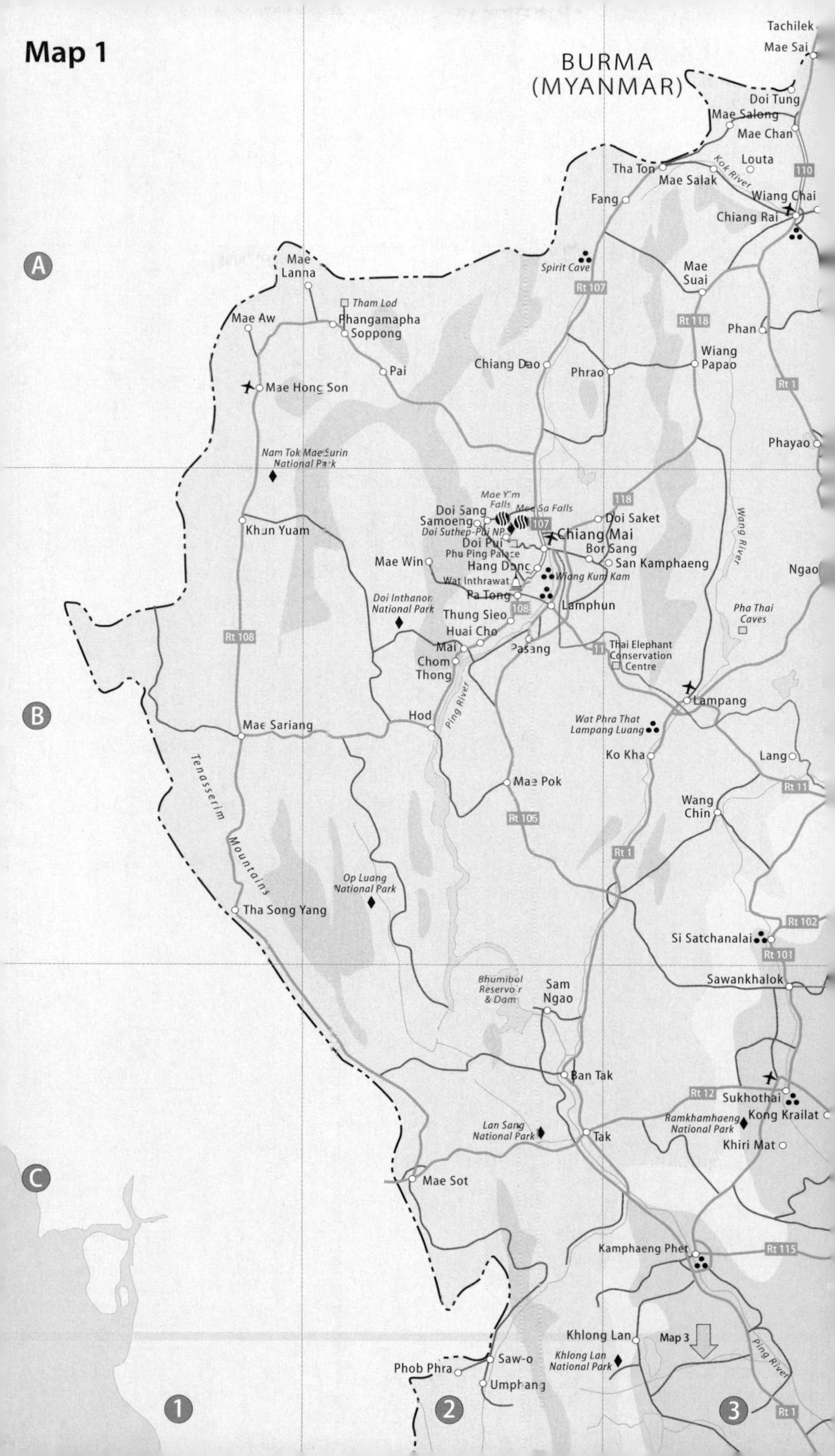

BURMA (MYANMAR)
Tachilek
Mae Sai
Doi Tung
Mae Salong
Mae Chan
Louta
Tha Ton
Kok River
Mae Salak
110
Wiang Chai
Fang
Chiang Rai
Spirit Cave
Rt 107
Mae Suai
Mae Lanna
Tham Lod
Phangamapha
Soppong
Mae Aw
Rt 118
Phan
Wiang Papao
Chiang Dao
Phrao
Pai
Mae Hong Son
Rt 1
Phayao
Nam Tok Mae Surin National Park
Mae Yim Falls
Mae Sa Falls
118
Doi Sang
Samoeng
Doi Suthep-Pui NP
107
Doi Saket
Chiang Mai
Khun Yuam
Doi Pui
Bor Sang
Phu Ping Palace
San Kamphaeng
Mae Win
Hang Dong
Wiang Kum Kam
Wang River
Ngao
Wat Inthrawat
Pa Tong
Doi Inthanon National Park
Lamphun
108
Thung Sieo
Pha Thai Caves
Rt 108
Huai Cho
Mai
Pasang
11
Thai Elephant Conservation Centre
Chom Thong
Ping River
Lampang
Hod
Wat Phra That Lampang Luang
Mae Sariang
Tenasserim Mountains
Ko Kha
Lang
Mae Pok
Rt 11
Wang Chin
Rt 105
Rt 1
Op Luang National Park
Tha Song Yang
Rt 102
Si Satchanalai
Rt 101
Bhumibol Reservoir & Dam
Sam Ngao
Sawankhalok
Ban Tak
Rt 12
Sukhothai
Kong Krailat
Lan Sang National Park
Tak
Ramkhamhaeng National Park
Khiri Mat
Mae Sot
Kamphaeng Phet
Rt 115
Khlong Lan
Map 3
Saw-o
Khlong Lan National Park
Phob Phra
Umphang
Ping River
Rt 1
A
B
C
1
2
3

LAOS
Golden Triangle
Sop Ruak
Chiang Saen
Chiang Khong
Mekong River
Chiang Kham
Pua
Tha Wang Pha
Doi Phu Kha National Park
Nan
Ban Nong Bua
Nan River
Amphoe Na Noi
Sao Din
Rt 103
Map 2
Phrae
Sung Men
Den Chai
Sirikit Reservoir
Uttaradit
Mekong River
Sangkhom
Pak Chom
VIENTIANE
Friendship Bridge
Si Chiangmai
Chiang Khan
Tha Bo
Rt 211
Rt 2
Phu Phra Bat Historical Park
Ban Phu
Ngoi
Phu Rua National Park
Loei
Rt 2020
Udon Thani
Rt 210
Nong Bua Lamphu
Erawan Cave
Non Cha
Rt 11
Rt 203
Phu Kradung National Park
Phu Hin Rongkla National Park
Rt 201
Yaeng
Phitsanulok
Thung Salaeng Luang National Park
Rt 12
Lom Sak
Nam Nao National Park
Phu Kradung
Phetchabun Hills
Phu Wiang National Park
Ubon Rat Reservoir
Phu Wiang
Yom River
Phra Cave
Chumphae
Khon Kaen
Phichit
Phetchabun
Rt 201
Rt 2057
Taphan Hin
Mancha Kiri
Rt 113
Rt 21
Chonnabot
Pa Sak River
Samran
Ban Phai
Bang Mun Nak
4
5
6
Chumsaeng
Nong Bua
Chaiyaphum
Phon
A
B
C
N
0 km 20
0 miles 20

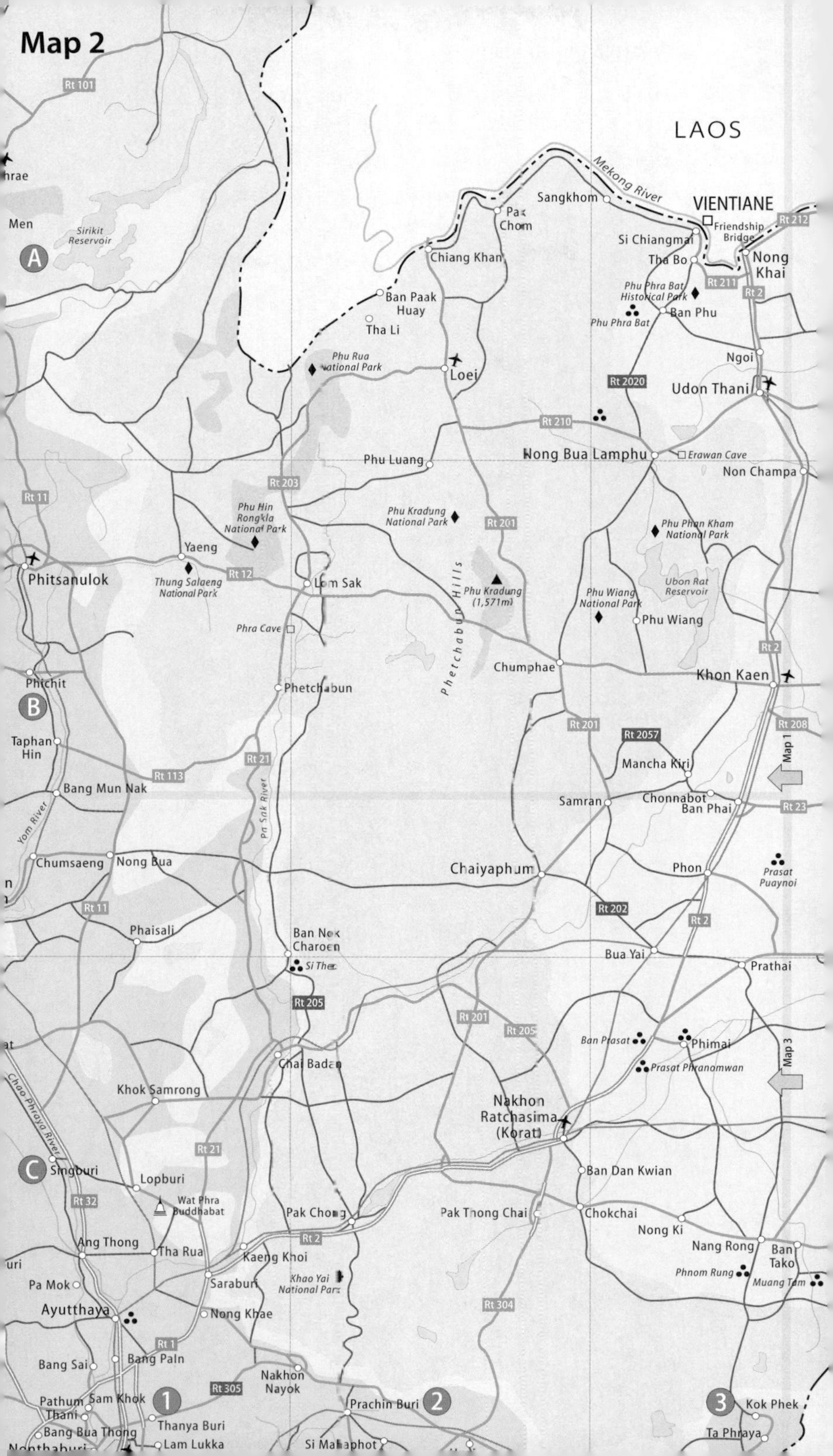

Map 2
LAOS
VIENTIANE
Mekong River
Sangkhom
Pak Chom
Chiang Khan
Si Chiangmai
Friendship Bridge
Tha Bo
Nong Khai
Phu Phra Bat Historical Park
Ban Phu
Phu Phra Bat
Ban Paak Huay
Tha Li
Phu Rua National Park
Loei
Ngoi
Udon Thani
Phrae
Men
Sirikit Reservoir
Nong Bua Lamphu
Erawan Cave
Non Champa
Phu Luang
Phu Hin Rongkla National Park
Phu Kradung National Park
Phu Phan Kham National Park
Yaeng
Phitsanulok
Thung Salaeng National Park
Lom Sak
Phu Kradung (1,571m)
Phetchabun Hills
Ubon Rat Reservoir
Phu Wiang National Park
Phu Wiang
Phra Cave
Chumphae
Khon Kaen
Phichit
Phetchabun
Taphan Hin
Mancha Kiri
Bang Mun Nak
Yom River
Pa Sak River
Chonnabot
Ban Phai
Samran
Chumsaeng
Nong Bua
Chaiyaphum
Phon
Prasat Puaynoi
Phaisali
Ban Nok Charoen
Si Thep
Bua Yai
Prathai
Ban Prasat
Phimai
Prasat Phanomwan
Chai Badan
Khok Samrong
Nakhon Ratchasima (Korat)
Chao Phraya River
Singburi
Lopburi
Wat Phra Buddhabat
Ban Dan Kwian
Pak Chong
Pak Thong Chai
Chokchai
Nong Ki
Ang Thong
Tha Rua
Kaeng Khoi
Nang Rong
Ban Tako
Pa Mok
Saraburi
Khao Yai National Park
Phnom Rung
Muang Tam
Ayutthaya
Nong Khae
Bang Sai
Bang Paln
Nakhon Nayok
Pathum Thani
Sam Khok
Prachin Buri
Kok Phek
Thanya Buri
Bang Bua Thong
Lam Lukka
Si Mahaphot
Ta Phraya
Rt 101
Rt 212
Rt 211
Rt 2
Rt 2020
Rt 210
Rt 203
Rt 201
Rt 11
Rt 12
Rt 208
Rt 2057
Rt 21
Rt 113
Rt 23
Rt 202
Rt 205
Rt 32
Rt 304
Rt 1
Rt 305
Map 1
Map 3
A
B
C
1
2
3

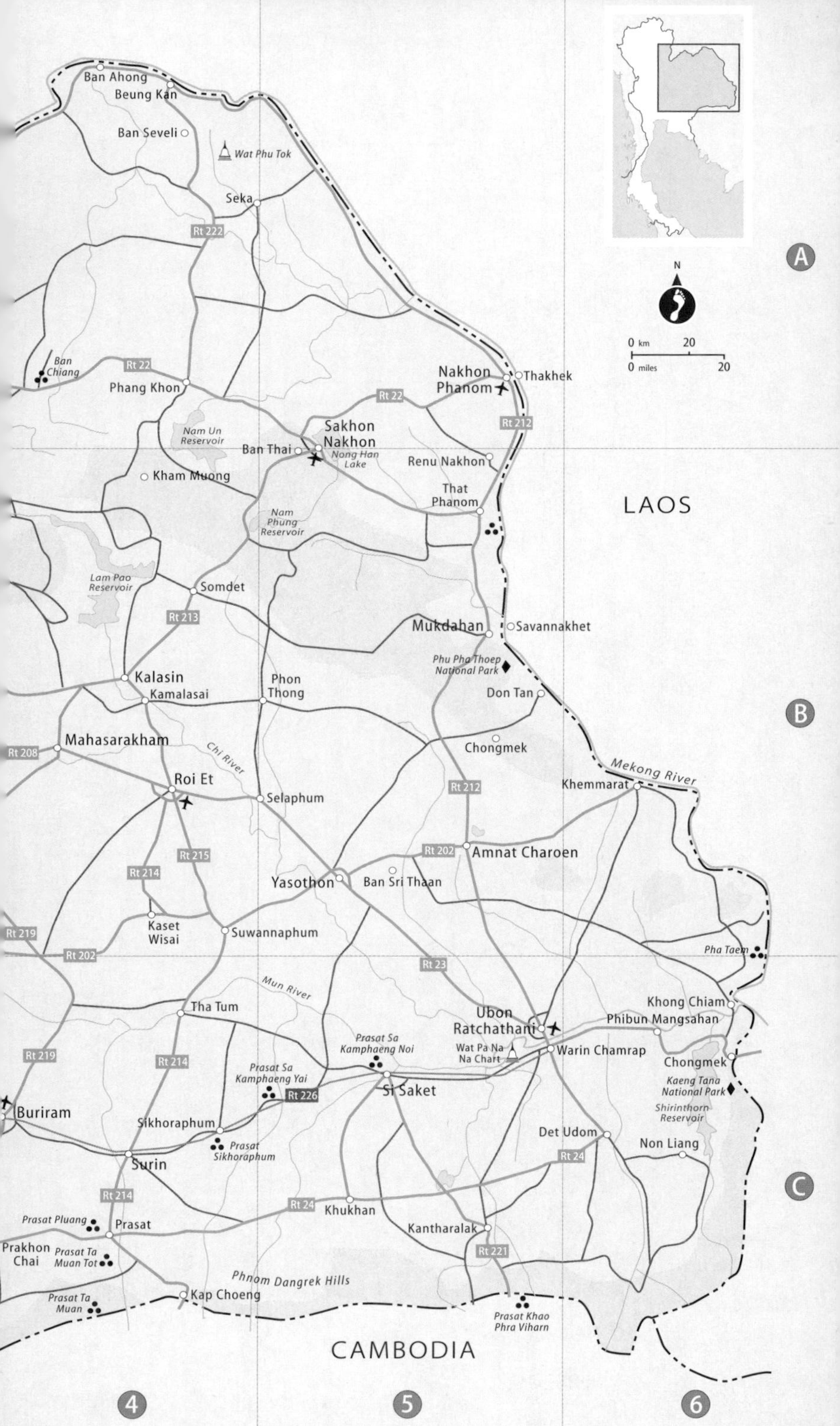

Ban Ahong
Beung Kan
Ban Seveli
Wat Phu Tok
Seka
Rt 222
Ban Chiang
Rt 22
Phang Khon
Nakhon Phanom
Thakhek
Rt 22
Rt 212
Sakhon Nakhon
Nong Han Lake
Ban Thai
Nam Un Reservoir
Renu Nakhon
Kham Muong
That Phanom
LAOS
Nam Phung Reservoir
Lam Pao Reservoir
Somdet
Rt 213
Mukdahan
Savannakhet
Phu Pha Thoep National Park
Kalasin
Kamalasai
Phon Thong
Don Tan
Mahasarakham
Rt 208
Chi River
Chongmek
Roi Et
Mekong River
Rt 212
Khemmarat
Selaphum
Rt 215
Rt 214
Rt 202
Amnat Charoen
Yasothon
Ban Sri Thaan
Kaset Wisai
Suwannaphum
Rt 219
Rt 202
Rt 23
Pha Taem
Mun River
Tha Tum
Ubon Ratchathani
Khong Chiam
Phibun Mangsahan
Rt 219
Rt 214
Prasat Sa Kamphaeng Noi
Wat Pa Na Na Chart
Warin Chamrap
Prasat Sa Kamphaeng Yai
Rt 226
Si Saket
Chongmek
Kaeng Tana National Park
Buriram
Shirinthorn Reservoir
Sikhoraphum
Prasat Sikhoraphum
Det Udom
Surin
Rt 24
Non Liang
Rt 214
Rt 24
Khukhan
Prasat Pluang
Prasat
Kantharalak
Prakhon Chai
Prasat Ta Muan Tot
Rt 221
Phnom Dangrek Hills
Kap Choeng
Prasat Ta Muan
Prasat Khao Phra Viharn
CAMBODIA
N
0 km 20
0 miles 20
A
B
C
4
5
6

Map 3

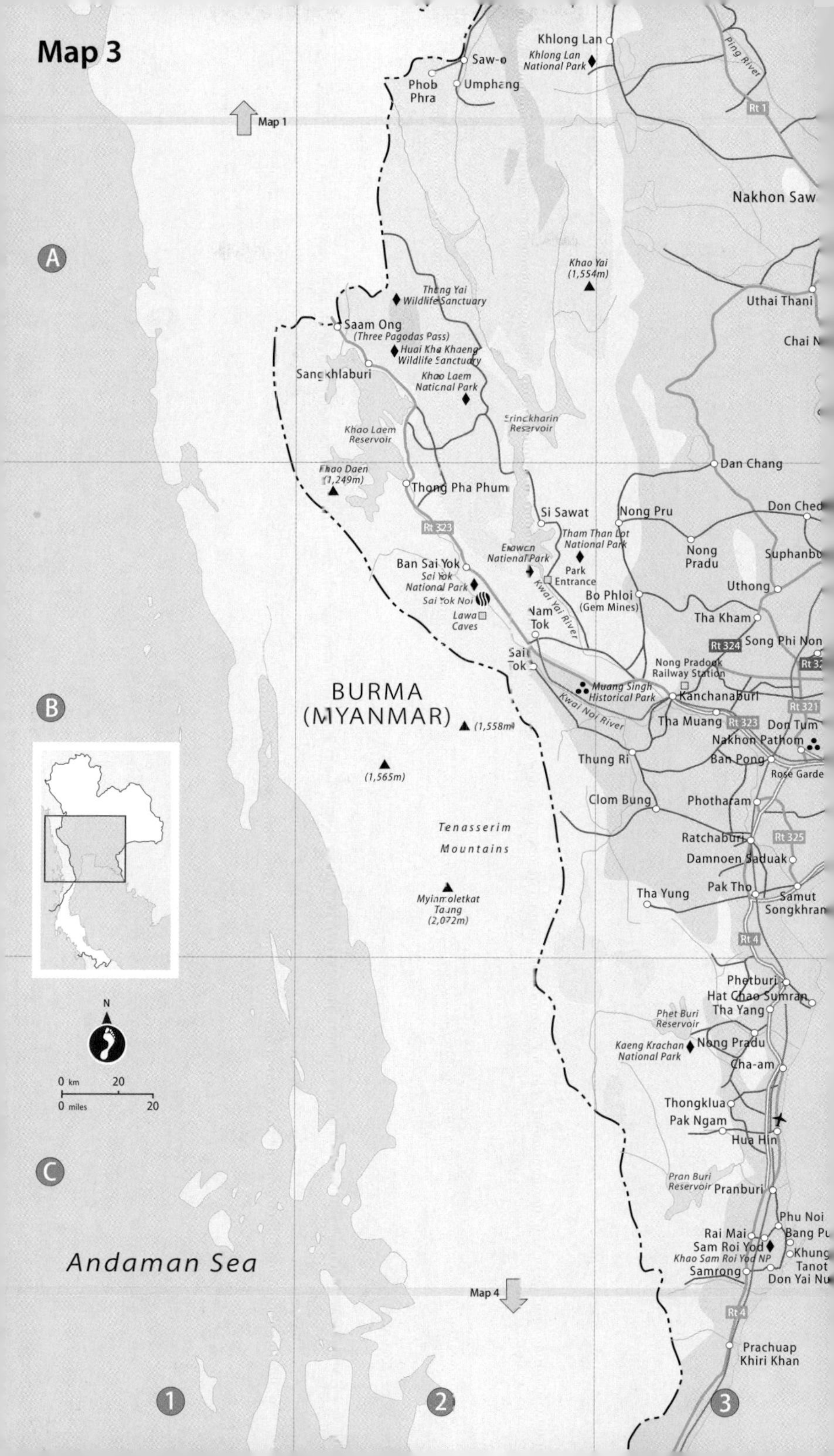
Khlong Lan
Khlong Lan National Park
Saw-o
Phob Phra
Umphang
Ping River
Rt 1
Map 1
Nakhon Saw
A
Khao Yai (1,554m)
Thung Yai Wildlife Sanctuary
Uthai Thani
Saam Ong (Three Pagodas Pass)
Huai Kha Khaeng Wildlife Sanctuary
Chai N
Sangkhlaburi
Khao Laem National Park
Srinakharin Reservoir
Khao Laem Reservoir
Dan Chang
Khao Daen (1,249m)
Thong Pha Phum
Si Sawat
Nong Pru
Don Ched
Rt 323
Tham Than Lot National Park
Erawan National Park
Nong Pradu
Suphanbu
Ban Sai Yok
Sai Yok National Park
Park Entrance
Bo Phloi (Gem Mines)
Uthong
Sai Yok Noi
Lawa Caves
Nam Tok
Kwai Yai River
Tha Kham
Rt 324
Song Phi Non
Sai Tok
Nong Pradok Railway Station
Rt 32
Muang Singh Historical Park
Kanchanaburi
B
BURMA (MYANMAR)
Kwai Noi River
Rt 321
Tha Muang
Rt 323
Don Tum
(1,558m)
Nakhon Pathom
Thung Ri
Ban Pong
(1,565m)
Rose Garde
Clom Bung
Photharam
Tenasserim Mountains
Ratchaburi
Rt 325
Damnoen Saduak
Pak Tho
Tha Yung
Samut Songkhran
Myinmoletkat Taung (2,072m)
Rt 4
Phetburi
Hat Chao Sumran
N
Tha Yang
Phet Buri Reservoir
Kaeng Krachan National Park
Nong Pradu
0 km 20
0 miles 20
Cha-am
Thongklua
Pak Ngam
Hua Hin
C
Pran Buri Reservoir
Pranburi
Phu Noi
Rai Mai
Bang Pu
Sam Roi Yod
Khung Tanot
Andaman Sea
Khao Sam Roi Yod NP
Samrong
Don Yai Nu
Map 4
Rt 4
Prachuap Khiri Khan
1
2
3

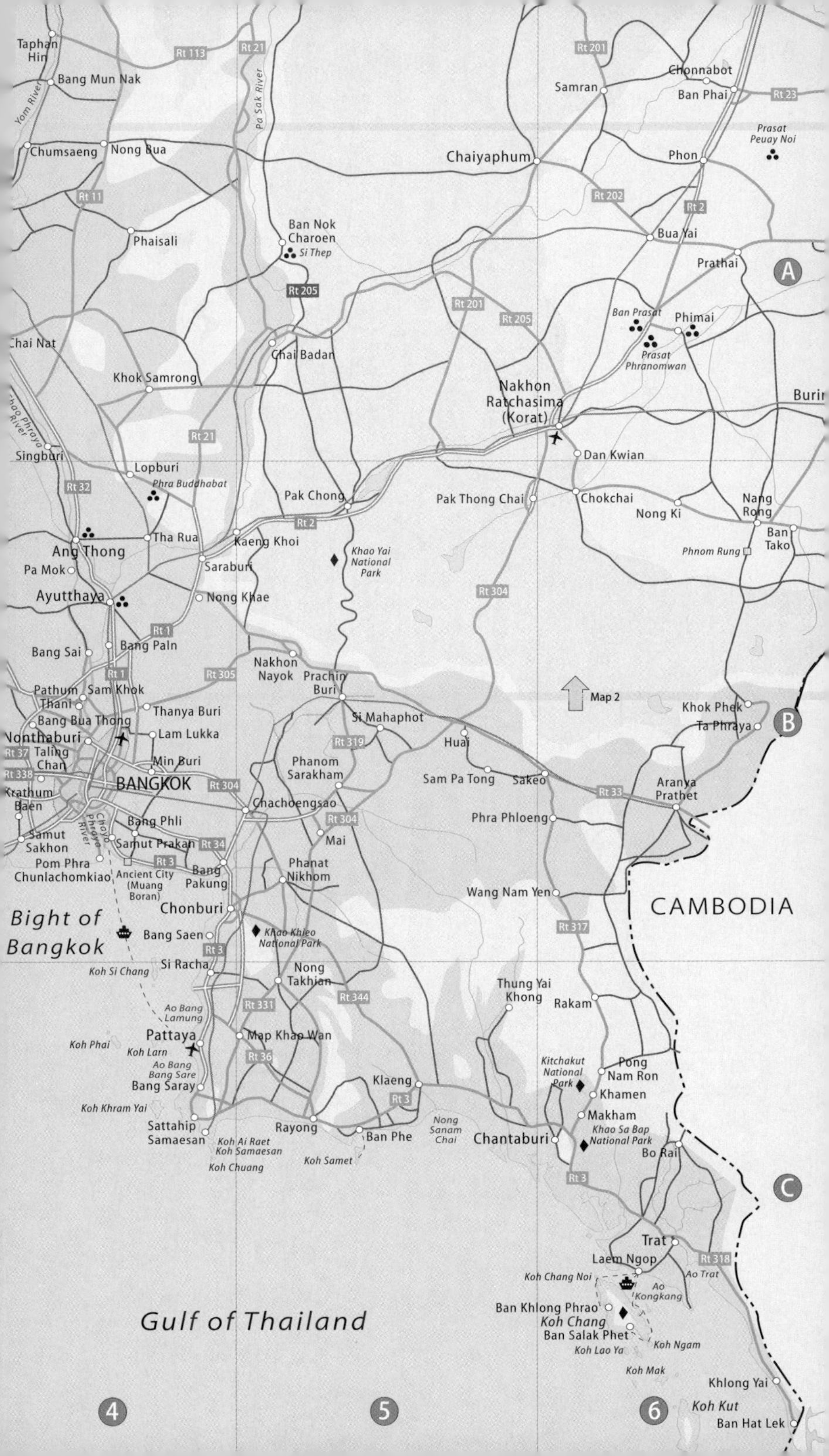

Taphan Hin
Bang Mun Nak
Yom River
Chumsaeng
Nong Bua
Rt 113
Rt 21
Pa Sak River
Rt 11
Phaisali
Ban Nok Charoen
Si Thep
Rt 205
Chai Nat
Chai Badan
Khok Samrong
Chao Phraya River
Singburi
Rt 21
Lopburi
Phra Buddhabat
Rt 32
Ang Thong
Tha Rua
Pa Mok
Saraburi
Kaeng Khoi
Pak Chong
Rt 2
Khao Yai National Park
Ayutthaya
Nong Khae
Rt 1
Bang Sai
Bang Paln
Nakhon Nayok
Prachin Buri
Rt 305
Pathum Thani
Sam Khok
Thanya Buri
Bang Bua Thong
Nonthaburi
Lam Lukka
Rt 37
Taling Chan
Rt 338
Min Buri
BANGKOK
Rt 304
Krathum Baen
Chachoengsao
Bang Phli
Samut Sakhon
Chao Phraya River
Samut Prakan
Rt 34
Pom Phra Chunlachomkiao
Rt 3
Ancient City (Muang Boran)
Bang Pakung
Phanat Nikhom
Chonburi
Bight of Bangkok
Bang Saen
Khao Khieo National Park
Rt 3
Si Racha
Koh Si Chang
Nong Takhian
Rt 331
Rt 344
Ao Bang Lamung
Pattaya
Koh Phai
Koh Larn
Map Khao Wan
Rt 36
Ao Bang Bang Sare
Bang Saray
Koh Khram Yai
Sattahip
Samaesan
Koh Ai Raet
Koh Samaesan
Koh Chuang
Rayong
Koh Samet
Klaeng
Rt 3
Ban Phe
Nong Sanam Chai
Si Mahaphot
Rt 319
Phanom Sarakham
Rt 304
Mai
Rt 201
Samran
Chonnabot
Ban Phai
Rt 23
Prasat Peuay Noi
Chaiyaphum
Phon
Rt 202
Rt 2
Bua Yai
Prathai
A
Rt 201
Rt 205
Ban Prasat
Phimai
Prasat Phranomwan
Nakhon Ratchasima (Korat)
Burir
Dan Kwian
Pak Thong Chai
Chokchai
Nong Ki
Nang Rong
Ban Tako
Phnom Rung
Rt 304
Map 2
Khok Phek
Ta Phraya
B
Huai
Sam Pa Tong
Sakeo
Rt 33
Aranya Prathet
Phra Phloeng
Wang Nam Yen
CAMBODIA
Rt 317
Thung Yai Khong
Rakam
Kitchakut National Park
Pong Nam Ron
Khamen
Makham
Khao Sa Bap National Park
Chantaburi
Bo Rai
Rt 3
C
Trat
Rt 318
Laem Ngop
Ao Trat
Koh Chang Noi
Ao Kongkang
Ban Khlong Phrao
Koh Chang
Ban Salak Phet
Koh Ngam
Koh Lao Ya
Koh Mak
Khlong Yai
Koh Kut
Ban Hat Lek
Gulf of Thailand
4
5
6

Map 4

Prachuap Khiri Khan
Map 3
Thap Sakae
BURMA (MYANMAR)
Ban Krut
Bang Saphan
Koh Talu
Mai Sombun
Koh Wiang
Rt 4
Ao Bang Saphan
Chumphon
Fak Nam Chumphon
N
0 km 20
0 miles 20
A
Similan Islands
Koh Bon
Koh Ba Ngu (9)
Koh Similan (8)
Hin Luk Chang
Koh Pa Yu (7)
Koh Miang (4)
Koh Pa Yan (3)
Koh Pa Yang (2)
Koh Hu Yong (1)
To Takua Pa (3hrs)
To Phuket (5hrs)
Similan Islands
Boat to Koh Similan, 110km from Patong, Koh Phuket
Phuket
Kra Buri
Ao Sawi
Khao Thaiu
Ao Sawi
Gulf of Thailand
Kawthoung
Ranong
Lang Suan
Phato
Rt 41
Map 5
Ban Mae Hat
Koh Tao
Koh Chang
Khuan
Isthmus of Kra
Koh Phayam
Nam Sai
B
Hat Bang Baen
Tha Chana
Ang Thong Marine National Park
Koh Kam Yai
Laem Son National Park
Koh Kam Noi
Wat Suan Mok
Thong Sala
Koh Phangan
Koh Surin Nua
Koh Surin Tai
Koh Ang Tong
Bophut
Koh Phaluai
Nathon
Koh Samui
Chaiya
Koh Nok Ta Phao
Tong Yang
Andaman Sea
Ao Ban Don
Chong Samui
Koh Ra
Kuraburi
Tha Chang
Tha Thong
Don Sak
Kanchanadit
Khanom
Krut
Koh Prathong
Chieo Lar Reservoir
Phun Phin
Surat Thani
Khao Nan National Park
Rt 401
Sichon
Tha Mak
Takua Pa
Kwang
Khao Wong
Khao Luang National Park
Laem Pakarang
Khao Sok National Park
Bang Sak
To Koh Similan
Khao Lak
Kapong
Rt 415
Khao Lak Lam Ru National Park
Khao Lampee-Had Thai Muang National Park
Khao To
Thap Lamu
Than Phet
Phraegaeng
Laem Talumphet
Thai Muang National Park
Phangnga
Wat Tham Khao Thao
Rt 4037
Ao Nakhon
Chawang
Khiriwong
Wat Suwan Kuha
Rt 4152
Ao Luk Nua
Lan Saka
Nakhon Si Thammarat
To Koh Similan
Thai Muang
Ao Luk
Dong Tau
Khok Kloi
Phangnga Bay National Park
Ko Wa Yai
Chong Lom
Ron Phibun
Rt 403
Sarasin Bridge
Koh Yao Noi
Rt 408
C
Nai Yang National Park
Khao Phrao Thaeo Wildlife Park
Wat Tham Sua
Chong Phli
Talat Kao
Chai Mai
Bo Lo
Thalang
Ao Nang
Krabi
Phuket
Koh Naka Yai
Koh Yao Yai
Hua Sai
Cherng Talay
Tha Rua
Koh Boda
Kamala
Rt 402
Phuket City
Laem Kruat
Patong Beach
Koh Siray
Koh Kai
Koh Siboya
Karon Beach
Kata Beach
Nai Harn
Makham Bay
Phi Phi National Park
Koh Klang
Khlong Phon
Tha Pradu
Huai Yot
Thale Noi Bird Sanctuary
Koh Jum
Thale Noi
Ranot
Promthep Cape
Koh Hii (Coral Island)
Koh Phi Phi
Ban Hua Hin
Hat Noppharat Thara
Chai Khlong
Koh Lanta Noi
Koh Phi Phi Le
Bo Muang
Phattalung
Thale Luang
Ban Sala Dan
Ton Chot
Trang
Di Luang
Koh Lanta Yai
Koh Po
Na Wong
Sating Phra
Ban Koh Lanta Yai
Koh Meng
Pakmeng
Rt 404
Koh Ma
Koh Ngai (Hai)
Kantang
Koh Chuak
Koh Kradan
Koh Muk
Hat Chao Mai National Park
1
2
3
Hin Muang & Hin Daeng

Map 5

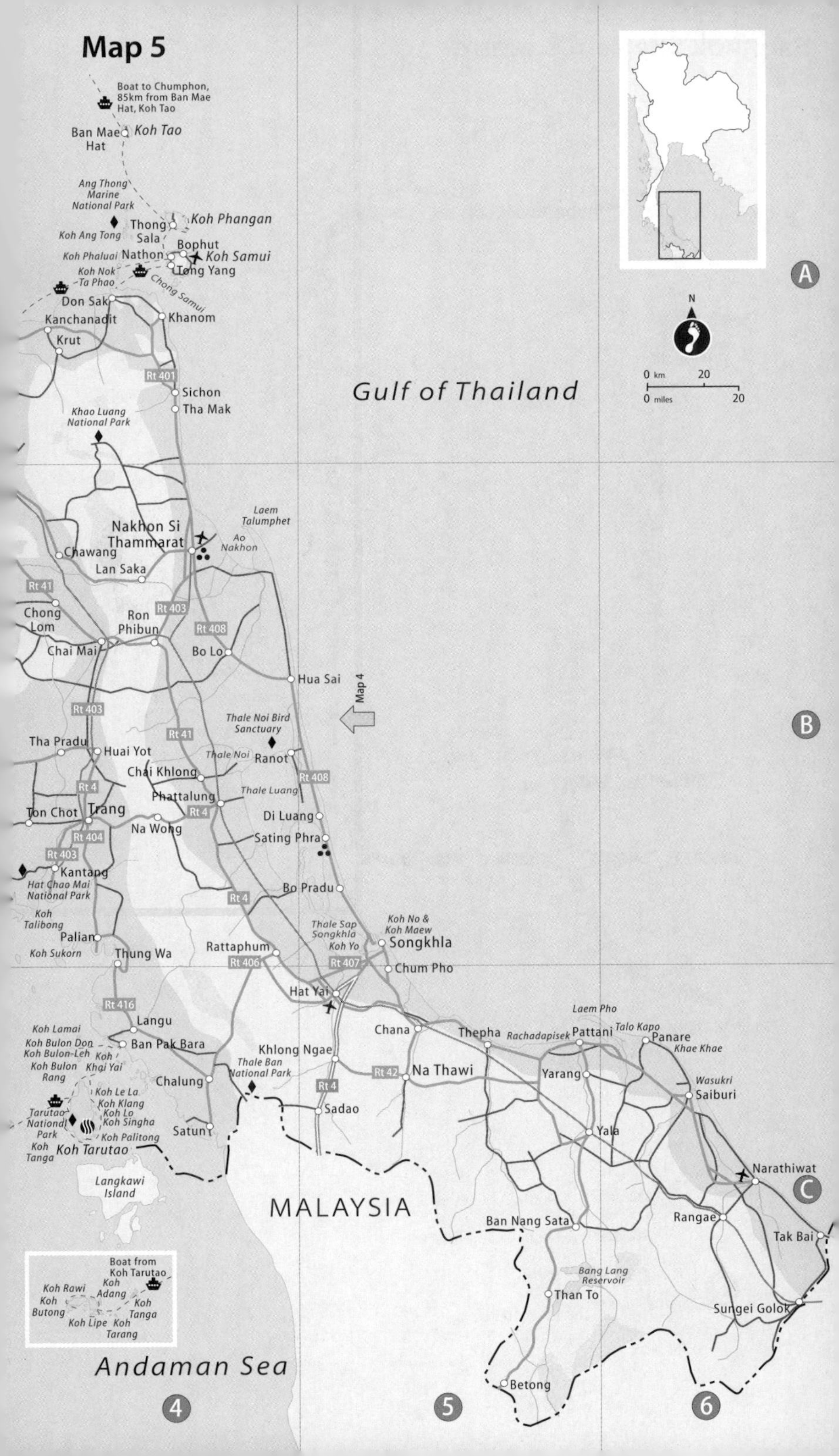

Boat to Chumphon, 85km from Ban Mae Hat, Koh Tao
Ban Mae Hat
Koh Tao
Ang Thong Marine National Park
Koh Ang Tong
Thong Sala
Koh Phangan
Bophut
Koh Samui
Koh Phaluai
Nathon
Koh Nok
Ta Phao
Tong Yang
Chong Samui
Don Sak
Khanom
Kanchanadit
Krut
Rt 401
Sichon
Tha Mak
Khao Luang National Park
Gulf of Thailand
0 km 20
0 miles 20
N
A
Laem Talumphet
Nakhon Si Thammarat
Ao Nakhon
Chawang
Lan Saka
Rt 41
Chong Lom
Rt 403
Ron Phibun
Rt 408
Chai Mai
Bo Lo
Hua Sai
Map 4
Rt 403
Thale Noi Bird Sanctuary
B
Rt 41
Tha Pradu
Huai Yot
Thale Noi
Ranot
Chai Khlong
Rt 408
Rt 4
Thale Luang
Phattalung
Ton Chot
Trang
Rt 4
Na Wong
Di Luang
Rt 404
Sating Phra
Rt 403
Kantang
Hat Chao Mai National Park
Bo Pradu
Rt 4
Koh Talibong
Thale Sap Songkhla
Koh No & Koh Maew
Palian
Koh Yo
Songkhla
Koh Sukorn
Thung Wa
Rattaphum
Rt 406
Rt 407
Chum Pho
Hat Yai
Rt 416
Laem Pho
Langu
Chana
Thepha
Rachadapisek
Pattani
Talo Kapo
Panare
Koh Lamai
Khae Khae
Koh Bulon Don
Ban Pak Bara
Koh Bulon-Leh
Koh Khai Yai
Khlong Ngae
Koh Bulon Rang
Thale Ban National Park
Rt 42
Na Thawi
Wasukri
Chalung
Yarang
Saiburi
Koh Le La
Rt 4
Koh Klang
Tarutao National Park
Koh Lo
Sadao
Koh Singha
Satun
Yala
Koh Palitong
Koh Tanga
Koh Tarutao
Narathiwat
Langkawi Island
C
MALAYSIA
Rangae
Ban Nang Sata
Tak Bai
Bang Lang Reservoir
Boat from Koh Tarutao
Koh Rawi
Koh Adang
Koh Butong
Koh Tanga
Than To
Sungei Golok
Koh Lipe
Koh Tarang
Andaman Sea
Betong
4
5
6

Bangkok Skytrain & Metro

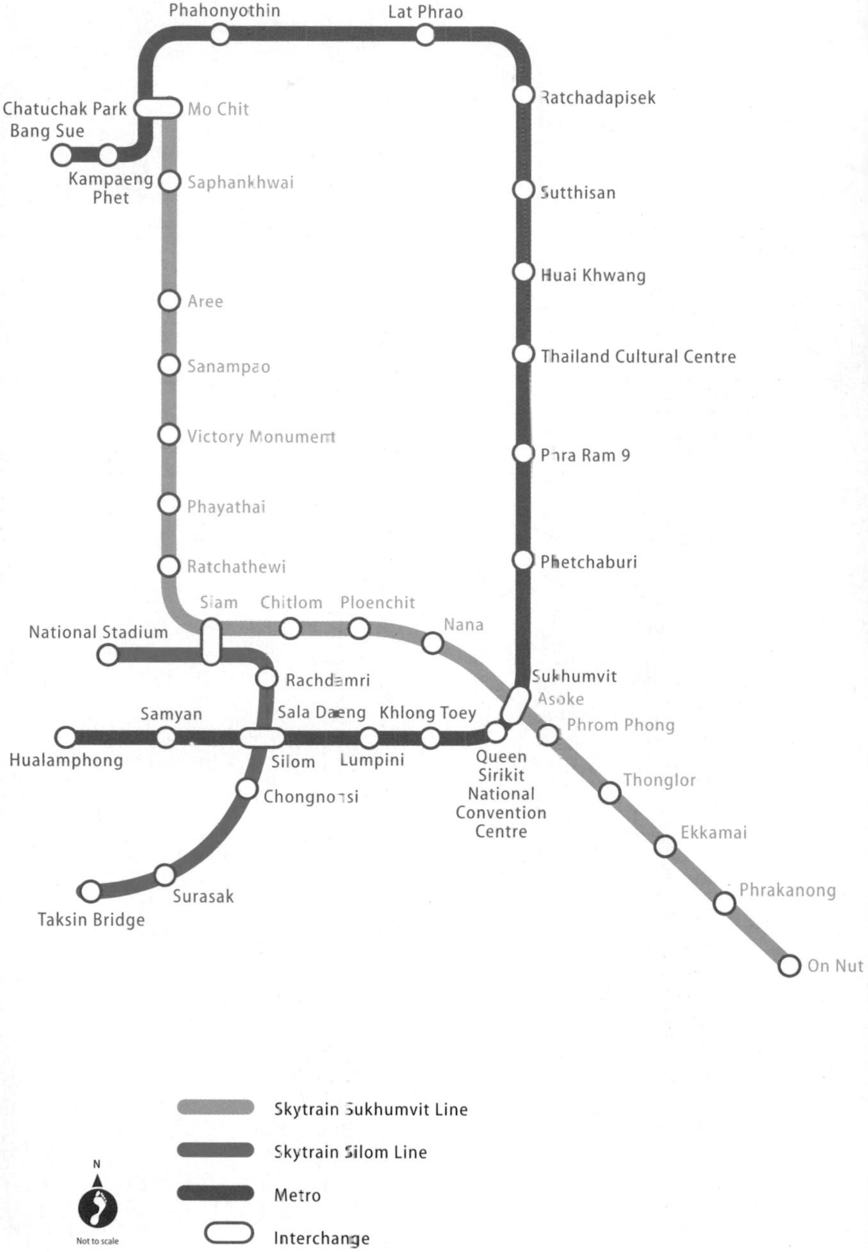